Praise for *Visual Studio Tools for Office*

"Visual Studio Tools for Office has always been one of my favorite technologies to come out of Microsoft. There are millions of people who use Office applications all day, every day; with VSTO, you can create applications for them. Eric Carter and Eric Lippert helped create VSTO, so they know as much about it as anybody, making this book a must-have. After reading it, you'll know everything needed to begin building solutions that take advantage of the .NET Framework features, in the UI your users are familiar with."

—Robert Green, senior consultant, MCW Technologies

"With the application development community so focused on the Smart Client revolution, a book that covers VSTO from A to Z is both important and necessary. This book lives up to big expectations. It is thorough, has tons of example code, and covers Office programming in general terms—topics that can be foreign to the seasoned .NET developer who has focused on ASP.NET applications for years. Congratulations to Eric Lippert and Eric Carter for such a valuable work!"

—Tim Huckaby, CEO, InterKnowlogy; Microsoft Regional Director

"Eric Carter and Eric Lippert really get it. Professional programmers will love the rich power of Visual Studio and .NET, along with the ability to tap into Office programmability. This book walks you through programming Excel, Word, and Outlook solutions."

—Vernon W. Hui, test lead, Microsoft Corporation

"This book is both a learning tool and a reference book, with a richness of tables containing object model objects and their properties, methods, and events. I would recommend it to anyone considering doing Office development using the .NET Framework; especially people interested in VSTO programming."

—Rufus Littlefield, software design engineer/tester, Microsoft Corporation

"This book will help Office .NET Developers optimize their work. It goes beyond providing an introduction to VSTO and the object models of Word, Excel, and Outlook. The overview of other technologies available for interacting with Office assist in analyzing how to best approach any Office project. In addition, the authors' insights into the design of this RAD tool make it possible to get the most out of VSTO applications."

—Cindy Meister, Microsoft MVP for VSTO,
author of Word Programmierung, *Das Handbuch*

"This book is an in-depth, expert, and definitive guide to programming using Visual Studio Tools for Office 2007. It is a must-have book for anyone doing Office development."

—Siew Moi Khor, programmer/writer, Microsoft Corporation

"We don't buy technical books for light reading, we buy them as a resource for developing a solution. This book is an excellent resource for someone getting started with Smart Client development. For example, it is common to hear a comment along the lines of, 'It is easy to manipulate the Task Pane in Office 2007 using VSTO 2008,' but until you see something like the example at the start of Chapter 14, it is hard to put 'easy' into perspective."

"This is a thorough book that covers everything from calling Office applications from your application, to building applications that are Smart Documents. It allows the traditional Windows developer to really leverage the power of Office 2007."

—Bill Sheldon, principal engineer, InterKnowlogy; MVP

"Eric Carter and Eric Lippert have been the driving force behind Office development and Visual Studio Tools for Office. The depth of their knowledge and understanding of VSTO and Office is evident in this book. Professional developers architecting enterprise solutions using VSTO 2008 and Office system 2007 now have a new weapon in their technical arsenal."

—Paul Stubbs, program manager, Microsoft Corporation

"This book, also known as 'The Bible of VSTO,' has been rewritten for Office 2007 and I was delighted to read the sections on new VSTO features that were added in Visual Studio 2008. It explains how the VSTO team hid the plumbing and cumbersome coding tasks to allow you to be more productive and to just create excellent business applications. New or experienced in Office development, you will want to add this book to your library!"

—Maarten van Stam, Microsoft MVP, Visual Developer, VSTO,
http://blogs.officezealot.com/maarten

"This book covers all of the ins and outs of programming with Visual Studio Tools for Office in a clear and concise way. Given the authors' exhaustive experiences with this subject, you can't get a more authoritative description of VSTO than this book!"

—Paul Vick, principal architect, Microsoft Corporation

Visual Studio Tools for Office 2007

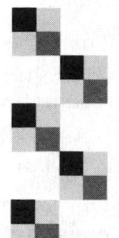

Visual Studio Tools for Office 2007

VSTO for Excel, Word, and Outlook

- **Eric Carter**
- **Eric Lippert**

✦Addison-Wesley

Upper Saddle River, NJ • Boston • Indianapolis • San Francisco
New York • Toronto • Montreal • London • Munich • Paris • Madrid
Capetown • Sydney • Tokyo • Singapore • Mexico City

Library of Congress Cataloging-in-Publication Data

Carter, Eric.
    Visual Studio tools for Office 2007 : VSTO for Excel, Word, and
Outlook / Eric Carter, Eric Lippert. — 2nd ed.
        p.   cm.
    Includes bibliographical references and index.
    ISBN 978-0-321-53321-0 (pbk. : alk. paper)
    1. Microsoft Visual BASIC. 2. BASIC (Computer program language) 3.
Microsoft Visual studio. 4. Microsoft Office. I. Lippert, Eric. II. Title.

    QA76.73.B3C3452 2009
    005.13'3—dc22   2009000638

ISBN-13: 978-0-321-53321-0
ISBN-10:   0-321-53321-6
Text printed in the United States on recycled paper at Courier Stoughton in Stoughton, Massachusetts.
Second printing, December 2009

To my wife, Tamsyn, and our children Jason, Hayley,
Camilla, Rand, Elizabeth, and Miles.
—Eric Carter

To Leah Lippert, for embarking with me
on a fabulous adventure. And to David Lippert,
who taught me to expect the unexpected along the way.
—Eric Lippert

Contents at a Glance

Contents

Figures

Tables

Foreword

I FACE THE CHALLENGE of composing a foreword to this particular book with some amount of trepidation. Let's face it: The names on the cover of this book inspire some amount of awe. It is humbling to know that one's words will introduce what one believes is to be the seminal work on a given topic, and believe me, I'm relatively sure that this one will meet those lofty goals. When approached with the invitation to grace the front matter of the book, my first response was to wonder what I could possibly add; couldn't they find some luminary at Microsoft to preface the book? It seems, however, that an outside voice adds some credence to the proceedings, so, dear reader, I speak meekly in the presence of greatness.

First, a little about me (it's the last chance I'm going to get in this short piece): I've been lurking about, programming Office in its various guises, for upward of 10 years. I've written a lot about the wonders, and gotchas, of Office development, and survived the glory years surrounding Office 2000, when it looked like Office might finally make a successful integrated development platform. Around 2001, it became clear that no matter how hard I and like-minded folks wanted Office to become a respected development standard, it just wasn't going to make it with VBA as the programming language.

With the release of Visual Studio Tools for Office 2003, it finally looked like we had made some progress. No longer relegated to the 1990s, Office developers could embrace .NET and all its goodness, taking advantage of managed code, code-access security, xcopy deployment, and all the rest that .NET supplied. I loved this product, but it never really reached critical mass with the developer community. Most likely, the fact that you could only use COM-based controls on documents, and the fact that the product supplied no design-time experience at all, made it a slow starter.

Around that time, I remember very clearly sitting down at some Microsoft event and meeting Eric Carter. I didn't really know who he was at the time (and he certainly didn't know anything about me), but he seemed nice enough, and we chatted for several hours about Office development in general and about VSTO in specific. Only later did I learn that he was high up in the development side of the product. (I spent hours worrying that I had said something really stupid while we were chatting. Hope not.) We began a long correspondence, in which I've more often than not made it clear that I've got a lot to learn about how .NET and Office interact. I've spent many hours learning from Eric's blog, and Eric Lippert's blog is just as meaty. If you are spending time doing Office development, make sure you drop by both:

http://blogs.msdn.com/ericlippert/
http://blogs.msdn.com/eric_carter/

I spent some measurable hours perusing the draft copy of this book and in each chapter attempted to find some trick, some little nugget, that I had figured out on my own that didn't appear in the book. I figured that if I was going to review the book, I should add something. The result: I was simply unable to find anything missing. Oh, I'm sure you'll find some little tidbit that you've figured out that won't appear here, but in my quick pass, I wasn't able to. I thought for sure I would catch them on something. Alas, I failed. And, I suppose, that's a good thing, right? Every time I thought I had them in a missing trick, there it was, right there in print. What that means is that you'll have the best possible reference book at your fingertips. Of course, you need to get your expectations set correctly; it's simply not possible, even in a 60-page chapter, to describe the entirety of the Excel or Word object model. But E&E have done an excellent job of pointing out the bits that make the biggest impact on .NET development.

If you're reading this foreword before purchasing the book, just do it. Buy the thing. If you've already bought it, why are you reading this? Get to the heart of the matter—skip ahead, and get going. You can always read this stuff later. There's a considerable hill ahead of you, and it's worth the climb. Office development using managed code has hit new strides with the release of Visual Studio 2008, and personally, I can't wait to take advantage of the answers I find in this book to build great applications.

—*Ken Getz, senior consultant for MCW Technologies*

Preface

I N 2002 THE first release of Visual Studio .NET and the .NET Framework was nearing completion. A few of us at Microsoft realized that Office programming was going to miss the .NET wave unless we did something about it.

What had come before was Visual Basic for Applications (VBA), a simple development environment integrated into all the Office applications. Each Office application had a rich object model that was accessed via a technology known as COM. Millions of developers identified themselves as "Office developers" and used VBA and the Office COM object models to do everything from automating repetitive tasks to creating complete business solutions that leveraged the rich features and user interface of Office. These developers realized that their users were spending their days in Office. By building solutions that ran inside Office, they not only made their users happy, but also were able to create solutions that did more and cost less by reusing functionality already available in the Office applications.

Unfortunately, because of some limitations of VBA, Office programming was starting to get a bad rap. Solutions developed in VBA by small workgroups or individuals would gain momentum, and a professional developer would have to take them over and start supporting them. To a professional developer, the VBA environment felt simple and limited, and of course, it enforced a single language: Visual Basic. VBA embedded code in every customized document, which made it hard to fix bugs and update solutions because a bug would get replicated in documents across the enterprise. Security weaknesses in the VBA model led to a rash of worms and macro viruses that made enterprises turn VBA off.

Visual Studio .NET and the .NET Framework provided a way to address all these problems. A huge opportunity existed not only to combine the richness of the new .NET Framework and developer tools with the powerful platform that Office has always provided for developers, but also to solve the problems that were plaguing VBA. The result of this realization was Visual Studio Tools for Office (VSTO).

The first version of VSTO was simple, but it accomplished the key goal of letting professional developers use the full power of Visual Studio .NET and the .NET Framework to put code behind Excel 2003 and Word 2003 documents and templates. It let professional developers develop Office solutions in Visual Basic and C#. It solved the problem of embedded code by linking a document to a .NET assembly instead of embedding it in the document. It also introduced a new security model that used .NET code-access security to prevent worms and macro viruses.

The second version of VSTO, known as VSTO 2005, was even more ambitious. It brought with it functionality never available to the Office developer before, such as data binding and data/view separation, design-time views of Excel and Word documents inside Visual Studio, rich support for Windows Forms controls in the document, the ability to create custom Office task panes, server-side programming support against Office—and that's just scratching the surface. Although the primary target of VSTO is the professional developer, that does not mean that building an Office solution with VSTO is rocket science. VSTO makes it possible to create very rich applications with just a few lines of code.

The third version of VSTO, which this book focuses on, shipped as a core feature of Visual Studio 2008. It is sometimes said that it takes Microsoft three versions to get something right, and we truly feel that this version of VSTO has the most amazing support for Office programming that Microsoft has ever built. In VSTO, you can now build add-ins for all the major Office applications; you can build application-level custom task panes; you can customize the new Office Ribbon; you can modify Outlook's UI using Forms Regions, and you can easily deploy everything you build using ClickOnce. The Office 2007 applications themselves are more extensible and provide many new programmability features.

If you've been reluctant to use VSTO because of the issues in previous versions—such as the difficulty of deployment, the nonsupport of VSTO in the Visual Studio Professional SKU, and the limited support for add-ins—we're happy to tell you that these issues have been fixed in the third version of VSTO.

This book tries to put in one place all the information you need to succeed using VSTO to program against Word 2007, Excel 2007, and Outlook 2007. It introduces the Office 2007 object models and covers the most commonly used objects in those object models. In addition, this book helps you avoid some pitfalls that result from the COM origins of the Office object models. This book also provides necessary backround for developers using VSTO to customize Visio 2007, Publisher 2007, PowerPoint 2007, and InfoPath 2007. Although it doesn't specifically focus on these applications, it teaches how to use the VSTO add-in model, how to create custom task panes and ribbons, and how to code against Office object models using C#.

This book also provides an insider view of all the rich features of VSTO. We participated in the design and implementation of many of these features; therefore, we can speak from the unique perspective of living and breathing VSTO for the past six years. Programming Office using VSTO is powerful and fun. We hope you enjoy using VSTO as much as we enjoyed writing about it and creating it.

—Eric Carter
—Eric Lippert
January 2009

Acknowledgments

THOUGH ONLY TWO names are on the cover, no book of this magnitude gets written without the efforts of many dedicated individuals.

Eric Carter would like to thank his entire family for the patience they showed while "Dad" was working on his book: Jason, Hayley, Camilla, Rand, Elizabeth, and Miles. Extreme thanks are due to his wife, Tamsyn, who was ever supportive and kept everything together somehow during this effort.

Eric Lippert would like to thank his excellent wife, Leah, for her support and tremendous patience over the many months that it took to put this book together.

Many thanks to everyone at Addison-Wesley who made this book possible. Joan Murray and Olivia Basegio provided expertise, guidance, encouragement, and feedback through every step of the process. Thanks are also due to the production and marketing teams at Addison-Wesley, especially Curt Johnson, Brendan Prebynski, and Julie Nahil.

A huge thank-you to everyone at Microsoft who over the past five years contributed to Visual Studio Tools for Office. Many people from different disciplines—design, development, education, evangelism, management, marketing, and testing—dedicated their passion and energy to bringing Office development into the managed code world. We could not have written this book without the efforts of all of them. One could not ask for a better group of people to have as colleagues.

A considerable number of industry experts gave the VSTO team valuable feedback over the years. Many thanks to everyone who came so far to give so much of their time and expertise by participating in Software Design Reviews and using early versions of the product. Their suggestions made VSTO a better product than the one we originally envisioned.

Many thanks to our technical reviewers, whose always-constructive criticism was a huge help. They helped us remove a huge number of errors in the text; those that remain are our own. For this new edition of the book, we thank Cindy Meister, Maarten van Stam, Robert Green, Randy Byrne, and Ryan Gregg. For their previous contributions to this book, we thank Andrew Clinick, Rufus Littlefield, Siew Moi Khor, Stephen Styrchak, Paul Vick, Paul Stubbs, Kathleen McGrath, Misha Shneerson, Mohit Gupta, and Vernon Hui. Finally, we'd like to thank K. D. Hallman, Ken Getz, Mike Hernandez, B. J. Holtgrewe, and Martin Heller for their ongoing insight and support.

About the Authors

Eric Carter is a development manager on the Visual Studio team at Microsoft. He helped invent, design, and implement many of the features that are in VSTO today. Previously at Microsoft he worked on Visual Studio for Applications, the Visual Studio Macros IDE, and Visual Basic for Applications for Office 2000 and Office 2003.

Eric Lippert's primary focus during his twelve years at Microsoft has been improving the lives of developers by designing and implementing useful programming languages and development tools. He has worked on the Windows Scripting family of technologies, on Visual Studio Tools for Office, and most recently on the C# compiler team.

PART I
An Introduction to VSTO

The first part of this book introduces the Office object models and the Office primary interop assemblies (PIAs). You also learn how to use Visual Studio to build automation executables, add-ins, and code behind the document by using features of Visual Studio 2008 Tools for Office 2007 (VSTO 3.0).

- Chapter 1, "An Introduction to Office Programming," introduces the Office object models and examines their basic structure. The chapter describes how to work with objects, collections, and enumerations— the basic types used in all Office object models. You learn how to use properties, methods, and events exposed by objects and collections in the Office object models. Chapter 1 also introduces the PIAs, which expose the Office object models to .NET code, and describes how to use and reference Office PIAs in a VSTO project.

- Chapter 2, "Introduction to Office Solutions," covers the main ways Office applications are customized and extended. The chapter describes the various kinds of Office solutions you can create using VSTO.

The Other Parts of This Book

Part II: Office Programming in .NET

Part II of this book covers the Office object models in more depth. Chapters 3 through 5 cover Excel, Chapters 6 through 8 cover Word, and Chapters 9 through 11 cover Outlook. These chapters also include some discussion of application-specific features and issues. Chapter 3, for example, talks about how to build custom formulas in .NET for Excel, and Chapter 5 discusses the Excel-specific locale issue in some detail. You can select which chapters of Part II to read; if you are interested only in Excel development, you can read Chapters 3 through 5 and then skip to Part III of this book.

Part III: Office Programming in VSTO

Part III of this book, comprised of Chapters 12 through 21, describes the features that Visual Studio 2008 Tools for Office 2007 brings to Office development. This part describes all the features of VSTO, including using Windows Forms and Windows Presentation Foundation controls in Excel and Word documents, using data binding against Office objects, building Smart Tags, and adding Windows Forms and Windows Presentation Foundation controls to Office's task pane.

■ 1 ■
An Introduction to Office Programming

Why Office Programming?

The family of Office 2007 applications covered by this book (Excel 2007, Word 2007, and Outlook 2007) represents an attractive platform on which to build solutions. You can customize and extend Office applications by developing solutions against their object models. By building a solution using the Office system, you can reuse some of the most feature-rich and popular applications available. A solution that analyzes or displays data can take advantage of the formatting, charting, calculation, and analysis features of Excel. A solution that creates documents can use the capability of Word to generate, format, and print documents. A solution that manipulates business information can present it in an Outlook folder or in an Info-Path form. It is far better to reuse the applications that you already know than to build these features from scratch.

Office Business Applications

Information workers use the Office environment on a daily basis. A solution built using Office can become a seamless part of that environment. Too frequently, users must go to a Web page or some other corporate application to get data that they want to cut and paste into an Excel workbook or a Word document anyway. Many users want to use Outlook as their business information portal. By integrating a solution with Office, you enable users to get the information they need without having to switch to another application.

Custom applications that bring business data into Office and SharePoint are called Office Business Applications or OBAs. Microsoft continues to make it easier to integrate line of business data into the Office system through advances in the Office platform. The most recent example of this is the new Business Data Catalog (BDC) in SharePoint that can be extended to bring custom business data into SharePoint. Within Office client applications like Excel and Word, you can use data binding to bring line of business data into Excel and Word documents.

Office Programming and the Professional Developer

Historically, most Office programming has been done via Visual Basic for Applications (VBA) and the macro recording features built in to some Office applications. Users would record a macro to automate a repetitive task within an Office application. Sometimes the code created by recording a macro would be further modified using VBA and turned into more complicated departmental solutions—often by users who were not trained as programmers and whose primary job was not programming. These solutions would sometimes make their way up the corporate food chain and get taken over by professional developers and turned into business solutions.

Professional developers had a different set of needs from VBA developers—they wanted the ability to scale an Office solution to an entire enterprise. They wanted better support for updating Office solutions once they were deployed. They wanted to use languages like C# and even have solutions that mixed several languages. They also wanted features that supported team development, like source code control.

Why .NET for Office?

The .NET Framework and its associated class libraries, technologies, and languages address many of the concerns that professional developers had with Office development. Today's Office development can be done using Visual Studio 2008, which is a rich programming environment for professional developers. Developers can use .NET languages such as Visual Basic or C#. The Office PIAs (Primary Interop Assemblies) allow .NET code to call the unmanaged object models that Office applications expose. The rich .NET class libraries enable developers to build Office solutions using technologies such as the Windows Presentation Foundation (WPF) to show user interface (UI) and the Windows Communication Foundation (WCF) to connect to corporate data servers.

Why Visual Studio Tools for Office?

Visual Studio 2008 Tools for Office 2007 (VSTO 3.0) provides .NET programming support for Word, Excel, Outlook, PowerPoint, Project, Visio, and InfoPath in Visual Studio. VSTO turns the Word or Excel document being programmed against into a .NET class, replete with data binding support, controls that can be coded against much like a Windows Forms control, and other .NET features. It makes it easy to integrate .NET code into Outlook. It enables developers to put .NET code behind InfoPath forms. Developers can program against key Office objects without having to traverse the entire Office object model.

Table 1-1 shows the Office applications that are supported by VSTO 3.0 and the various VSTO features that are enabled for each Office application. In general, VSTO has the most features and support for Word, Excel, and Outlook. This book only covers these three applications, although much of what you learn in this book about add-ins, custom task panes, the visual Ribbon designer, and ClickOnce can be applied to PowerPoint, Visio, InfoPath, and Project development.

VSTO 3.0 has now been integrated directly into Visual Studio Professional and higher level SKUs where in the past it was only available as a standalone product or with Visual Studio Team System. Office programming is now available to more developers than ever before. VSTO 3.0 also supports Office 2003—in particular it supports the same set of Document Level projects and Application Level Add-in Projects shown in Table 1-1 (except for Application Level Add-ins for InfoPath 2003). For more on Office 2003 support in VSTO, consult the first edition of this book.

TABLE 1-1: VSTO Features That Are Enabled for Each Office Application

Office Application	Document-Level Projects	Application-Level Add-In Projects	Data Binding Support	.NET Controls in the Document	Document-Level Task Panes	Application-Level Task Panes	Visual Ribbon Designer	ClickOnce Deployment
Word 2007	X	X	X	X	X	X	X	X
Excel 2007	X	X	X	X	X	X	X	X
Outlook 2007		X				X	X	X
PowerPoint 2007		X				X	X	X
Visio 2007		X						X
InfoPath 2007	X	X				X		X
Project 2007		X						X

How .NET Is It?

This book discusses many new .NET ways of programming against Office applications. However, some aspects of Office programming remain awkward using .NET. Most of these awkward areas are attributable to the fact that the Office object models were designed to work with a technology called COM. Although .NET code can talk to the Office object models via PIAs, the object models sometimes do not feel very .NET-friendly. Furthermore, the Office object models do not always follow the naming conventions or design patterns of classes that were designed for .NET.

In the future, many of the Office object models will likely be redesigned for .NET, and the object models will feel friendlier to a .NET developer. For now, developers must live in a transitional period in which some aspects of Office programming feel like they were designed for .NET and other aspects do not. This book discusses some of the most difficult problems developers encounter when using .NET with Office and how to work around these problems.

One recent advance that makes programming against Office object models more palatable to the .NET developer are the Office Interop API extensions (part of the VSTO Power Tools available here: http://www .microsoft.com/downloads/details.aspx?FamilyId=46B6BF86-E35D-4870-B214-4D7B72B02BF9&displaylang=en). These are a set of classes that help the C# developer write more elegant code when using parameterized properties and optional or named parameters. Because these extensions aren't in wide use yet, this book will show coding directly against the PIAs. But the Office Interop API extensions are an attractive option for the developer looking for more .NET-friendly APIs.

Office Object Models

Almost all Office programming involves writing code that uses the object model of an Office application. The object model is the set of objects provided by the Office application that running code can use to control the Office application. The object model of each Office application is organized hierarchically with the object called Application forming the root of the hierarchy. From the Application object, other objects that make up the object model of the Office application can be accessed.

As an example of how object model objects are related in the object model hierarchy, Figure 1-1 shows some of the most important objects in the Word object model. The root object is the Application object. Also shown in this diagram are some other objects, including Documents, Document, Paragraphs, and Paragraph. The Application object and Documents

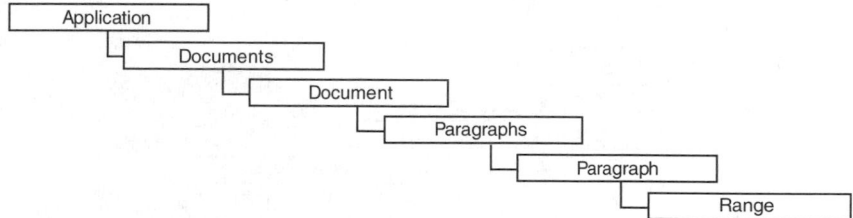

Figure 1-1: Hierarchy in the Word object model.

object are related because the Documents object is returned via a property on the Application object. Other objects are not directly accessible from the root Application object, but are accessible by traversing a path. For example, the Paragraphs object is accessed by traversing the path from Application to Documents to Document to Paragraphs. Figure 1-2 shows a similar diagram for some major objects in the Excel object model hierarchy.

Objects

Each Office application's object model consists of many objects that you can use to control the Office application. Word has 294 distinct objects, Excel has 243, and Outlook has 139. Objects tend to correspond to features and concepts in the application itself. For example, Word has objects such as Document, Bookmark, and Paragraph—all of which correspond to features of Word. Excel has objects such as Workbook, Worksheet, Chart, and Series—all of which correspond to features of Excel. As you might suppose, the most important and most used objects in the object models are the ones that correspond to the application itself, the document, and key elements in a document such as a range of text in Word. Most solutions use these key objects and only a small number of other objects in the object models. Table 1-2 lists some of the key objects in Word, Excel, and Outlook along with brief descriptions of what these objects do.

Where objects in an Office object model start to differ from typical .NET classes is that the vast majority of object model objects are not creatable or "new-able." In most Office object models, the number of objects that can be created by using the new keyword is on the order of one to five objects. In most Office solutions, new will never be used to create an Office object— instead, an already created Office object, typically the root Application object, is passed to the solution.

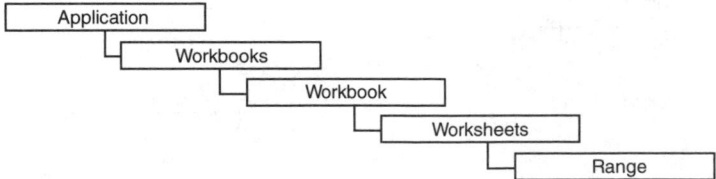

Figure 1-2: Hierarchy in the Excel object model.

New in Office 2007

Many new objects have been added in Office 2007. Word 2007 now has 54 more objects than it did in Word 2003, for example. Many of those new objects allow programmatic access to the new equation-editing features in Word 2007. Also added in Word are object model objects for the new Building Blocks and content controls features. Excel 2007 has 51 new objects. Some of the objects that were added support the new conditional formatting rules in Excel 2007, as well as work with page layout and pivot tables.

TABLE 1-2: Key Office Object Model Objects

Object Name	What It Does
All Office Applications	
Application	The root object of the object model. Provides properties that return other objects in the object model. Provides methods and properties to set application-wide settings. Raises application-level events.
Window	Enables the developer to position windows and modify window-specific settings. In Outlook, the objects that perform this function are the Explorer and Inspector objects.
Word Objects	
Document	Represents the Word document. Is the root object of the content-specific part of the Word object model. Raises document-level events.
Paragraph	Enables the developer to access a paragraph in a Word document.
Range	Enables the developer to access and modify a range of text in a Word document. Provides methods and properties to set the text, set the formatting of the text, and perform other operations on the range of text.

Continues

TABLE 1-2:　**Key Office Object Model Objects** *(Continued)*

Object Name	What It Does
Excel Objects	
Workbook	Represents the Excel workbook. Is the root object of the content-specific part of the Excel object model. Raises workbook-level events.
Worksheet	Enables the developer to work with a worksheet within an Excel workbook.
Range	Enables the developer to access and modify a cell or range of cells in an Excel workbook. Provides methods and properties to set the cell value, change the formatting, and perform other operations on the range of cells.
Outlook Objects	
MAPIFolder	Represents a folder within Outlook that can contain various Outlook items such as MailItem, ContactItem, and so on as well as other folders. Raises events at the folder level for selected actions that occur to the folder or items in the folder.
MailItem	Represents a mail item within Outlook. Provides methods and properties to access the subject and message body of the mail along with recipient and other information. Raises events when selected actions occur that involve the mail item.
ContactItem	Represents a contact within Outlook. Provides methods and properties to access the information in the contact. Raises events when selected actions occur that involve the contact.
AppointmentItem	Represents an appointment within Outlook. Provides methods and properties to access the information in the appointment. Raises events when selected actions occur that involve the appointment.

Because most Office object model objects cannot be created directly, they are instead accessed via the object model hierarchy. For example, Listing 1-1 shows how to get a Worksheet object in Excel starting from the Application object. This code is a bit of a long-winded way to navigate the hierarchy because it declares a variable to store each object as it traverses the hierarchy. The code assumes that the root Excel Application object has been passed to the code and assigned to a variable named app. It also uses C#'s as operator to cast the object returned from the Worksheets collection as a Worksheet, which is necessary because the Worksheet collection is a collection of object for reasons described in Chapter 3, "Programming Excel."

Listing 1-1: Navigating from the Application Object to a Worksheet in Excel

```
Excel.Workbooks myWorkbooks = app.Workbooks;
Excel.Workbook myWorkbook = myWorkbooks.get_Item(1);
Excel.Sheets myWorksheets = myWorkbook.Worksheets;
Excel.Worksheet myWorksheet = myWorksheets.get_Item(1) as
  Excel.Worksheet;
```

If the code does not need to cache each object model object in a variable as it goes but only needs to get a Worksheet object, a more efficient way to write this code is as follows:

```
Excel.Worksheet myWorksheet2 = app.Workbooks.get_Item(1).
Worksheets.get_Item(1) as Excel.Worksheet;
```

Collections

Paragraphs and Documents are examples of a type of object called a collection. A collection is a specialized object that represents a group of objects. Typically, a collection is named so that its name is the plural of the type of the object it contains. For example, the Documents collection object is a collection of Document objects. Some collection objects may be collections of a value type such as a string.

Collections typically have a standard set of properties and methods. A collection has a Count property, which returns the number of objects in the collection. A collection also has an Item method, which takes a parameter, typically a number, to specify the index of the desired object in the collection. A collection may have other properties and methods in addition to these standard properties and methods.

Listing 1-2 shows iteration over a collection using the Count property of the collection and the Item method of the collection. Although this is not the preferred way of iterating over a collection (you typically use foreach instead), it does illustrate two key points. First, collections in Office object models are almost always 1-based, meaning they start at index 1 rather than index 0. Second, the parameter passed to the get_Item method is often passed as an object so you can either specify a numeric index as an int or the name of the object within the collection as a string.

Why get_Item?

If you are new to Office development in C#, you may be surprised to see Listing 1-2 use a strange method called get_Item rather than just a property called Item. This is a result of C#'s lack of support for properties that take parameters (like the Item property on Excel's Workbooks collection)—C# must convert the parameterized property to a method which it prefixes with get_ or set_. For more information on parameterized properties, see the section "Parameterized Properties" later in this chapter.

Listing 1-2: Iterating Over a Collection Using the Count Property and the get_Item Method with Either an int or a string Index

```
Excel.Workbooks myWorkbooks = app.Workbooks;
int workbookCount = myWorkbooks.Count;

for (int i = 1; i <= workbookCount; i++)
{
  // Get the workbook by its int index
  Excel.Workbook myWorkbook = myWorkbooks.get_Item(i);

  // Get the workbook by its string index
  string workbookName = myWorkbook.Name;

  Excel.Workbook myWorkbook2 = myWorkbooks.get_Item(workbookName);
  MessageBox.Show(String.Format("Workbook {0}", myWorkbook2.Name));
}
```

If you were to look at the definition for the Workbooks collection's get_Item method, you would see that it takes an object parameter. Even though the get_Item method takes an object parameter, we pass an int value and a string value to it in Listing 1-2. This works because C# can automatically convert a value type such as an int or a string to an object when you pass the value type to a method that takes an object. This automatic conversion is called boxing. C# automatically creates an `object` instance known as a box to put the value type into when passing it to the method.

The preferred way of iterating over a collection is using the `foreach` syntax of C#, as shown in Listing 1-3.

Listing 1-3: Iterating over a Collection Using foreach

```
Excel.Workbooks myWorkbooks = app.Workbooks;

foreach (Excel.Workbook workbook in myWorkbooks)
{
  MessageBox.Show(String.Format("Workbook {0}", workbook.Name));
}
```

Sometimes you may want to iterate over a collection and delete objects from the collection by calling a Delete method on each object as you go. This is a risky practice because behavior of a collection in the Office object models is sometimes undefined if you are deleting items from it as you iterate over it. Instead, as you iterate over the Office object model collection, add the objects you want to delete to a .NET collection you have created, such as a list or an array. After you have iterated over the Office object model collection and added all the objects you want to delete to your collection, iterate over your collection and call the Delete method on each object.

Enumerations

An enumeration is a type defined in an object model that represents a fixed set of possible values. The Word object model contains 292 enumerations, Excel 230, and Outlook 145.

As an example of an enumeration, Word's object model contains an enumeration called WdWindowState. WdWindowState is an enumeration that has three possible values: `wdWindowStateNormal`, `wdWindowStateMaximize`, and `wdWindowStateMinimize`. These are constants you can use directly in your code when testing for a value. Each value corresponds to an integer value. (For example, `wdWindowStateNormal` is equivalent to 0.) However, it is considered bad programming style to make comparisons to the integer values rather than the constant names themselves because it makes the code less readable.

Properties, Methods, and Events

Objects in an Office application's object model are written in unmanaged code (typically C++ classes which are exposed as COM objects). Your .NET code can access the unmanaged object models of Office through .NET classes defined in a special .NET assembly called a Primary Interop Assembly or PIA. An object in the object model is required to have at least one property, method, or event. Most of the objects in an Office application's object model have several properties, a few methods, and no events. In Office object models, properties predominate, followed by methods, and trailed distantly by events. The most important objects in the object model, such as Application and Document, are typically much more complex and have a much larger number of properties and methods as well as events. For example, Word's Application object has about 114 properties, 65 methods, and 28 events. Table 1-3 lists some of the properties, methods, and events on the Word Application object to give a sense of the types of functionality an object model object provides.

TABLE 1-3: Selected Properties, Methods, and Events from Word's
Application Object

Name	What It Does
Properties	
ActiveDocument	Returns a Document object for the active document—the document that is currently being edited by the user.
ActivePrinter	Gets and sets the default printer.
Caption	Gets and sets the caption text for the application window—typically this is set to "[Active Document Name] - Microsoft Word."
Documents	Returns a Documents collection that represents the collection of open Word documents.
Methods	
Activate	Brings Word to the front of other windows and makes it the active window.

TABLE 1-3:   Selected Properties, Methods, and Events from Word's Application Object *(Continued)*

Name	What It Does
Methods	
NewWindow	Creates a new Word window that shows the same document as the currently active window and returns a Window object model object representing that new window.
Quit	Closes Word.
Events	
DocumentBeforeClose	An event that is raised before a document is closed. The Document object for the document being closed is passed as a parameter to the event along with a `bool cancel` parameter. If the code handling the event sets the `cancel` parameter to `true`, the document will not be closed.
DocumentOpen	An event that is raised when a document is opened. The Document object for the document being opened is passed as a parameter to the event.
WindowActivate	An event that is raised when a Word window is activated by the user, typically by clicking an inactive window thereby making it active. The Document object for the document being activated is passed as a parameter to the event along with a Window object for the window that was activated (because two windows could be showing the same document).

Properties

Properties are simple methods which allow you to read or write particular named values associated with an object. For example, Word's Application object has a property called CapsLock, which returns a `bool` value. If the Caps Lock key is down, it will return `true`; if the Caps Lock key is up, it will return `false`. Listing 1-4 shows some code that examines this property. The code assumes that the root Application object of the Word object model has already been assigned to a variable called app.

Listing 1-4: A Property That Returns a Value Type—the bool CapsLock Property on Word's Application Object

```
if (app.CapsLock == true)
{
  MessageBox.Show("CapsLock key is down");
}
else
{
  MessageBox.Show("CapsLock key is up");
}
```

Another thing to note about the CapsLock property is that it is a read-only property. That is, you cannot write code that sets the CapsLock property to false; you can only get the value of the CapsLock property. If you try to set a read-only property to some value, an error will occur when you compile your code.

The CapsLock property returns a bool value. It is also possible for a property to return an enumeration. Listing 1-5 shows some code that uses the WindowState property to determine whether Word's window is maximized, minimized, or normal. This code uses C#'s switch statement to evaluate the WindowState property and compare its value to the three possible enumerated value constants. Notice that when you specify enumerated values in C#, you must specify both the enumerated type name and the enumerated value—for example, if you just used wdWindowStateNormal rather than WdWindowState.wdWindowStateNormal the code will not compile.

Listing 1-5: A Property That Returns an Enumeration—the WindowState Property on Word's Application Object

```
switch (app.WindowState)
{
  case Word.WdWindowState.wdWindowStateNormal:
    MessageBox.Show("Normal");
    break;

  case Word.WdWindowState.wdWindowStateMaximize:
    MessageBox.Show("Maximized");
    break;

  case Word.WdWindowState.wdWindowStateMinimize:
    MessageBox.Show("Minimized");
    break;
```

```
    default:
      break;
}
```

Properties can also return other object model objects. For example, Word's Application object has a property called ActiveDocument that returns the currently active document—the one the user is currently editing. The ActiveDocument property returns another object in the Word object model called Document. Document in turn also has properties, methods, and events. Listing 1-6 shows code that examines the Active-Document property and then displays the Name property of the Document object.

Listing 1-6: A Property That Returns Another Object Model Object—the ActiveDocument Property on Word's Application Object

```
Word.Document myDocument = app.ActiveDocument;
MessageBox.Show(myDocument.Name);
```

What happens if there is no active document—for example, if Word is running but no documents are opened? In the case of the ActiveDocument property, it throws an exception. So a safer version of the preceding code would catch the exception and report no active document was found. Listing 1-7 shows this safer version. An even better approach is to check the Count property of the Application object's Documents collection to see whether any documents are open before accessing the ActiveDocument property.

Listing 1-7: A Property That Might Throw an Exception—the ActiveDocument Property on Word's Application Object

```
Word.Document myDocument = null;
try
{
    myDocument = app.ActiveDocument;
    MessageBox.Show(myDocument.Name);
}
catch (Exception ex)
{
    MessageBox.Show(
      String.Format("No active document: {0}", ex.Message));
}
```

Object models sometimes behave differently in an error case in which the object you are asking for is not available or does not make sense in a particular context. The property can return a null value. The way to determine whether an object model property will throw an exception or return a null value is by consulting the object model documentation for the property in question. Excel's Application object uses this pattern for its Active-Workbook property. If no Excel workbook is open, it returns null instead of throwing an exception. Listing 1-8 shows how to write code that handles this pattern of behavior.

Listing 1-8: A Property That Might Return null—the ActiveWorkbook Property on Excel's Application Object

```
Excel.Workbook myWorkbook = app.ActiveWorkbook;

if (myWorkbook == null)
{
    MessageBox.Show("No active workbook");
}
else
{
    MessageBox.Show(myWorkbook.Name);
)
```

Parameterized Properties

The properties examined so far in this section are parameterless. However, some properties require parameters. For example, Word's Application object has a property called FileDialog that returns a FileDialog object. The FileDialog object is an object that is shared across all the Office applications. The FileDialog property takes an enumeration parameter of type MsoFileDialogType, which is used to pick which FileDialog is returned. Its possible values are msoFileDialogOpen, msoFileDialogSaveAs, msoFile-DialogFilePicker, and msoFileDialogFolderPicker.

C# does not support calling parameterized properties as properties. When you go to use the Word object model from C# and look for the File-Dialog property on Word's Application object, it is nowhere to be seen. The FileDialog property is callable from C#, but only via a method—the method is named get_FileDialog. So when you are looking for a parameterized property in C#, be sure to look for the get_*Property* method (where

Property is the name of the property you want to access). To set parameterized properties in C# (assuming they are not read-only properties), there is a separate method called set_*Property* (where *Property* is the name of the property you are going to set).

An exception to this is found when using VSTO document-level projects for Word and Excel. A handful of Word and Excel object model objects are extended by VSTO. These objects have been extended to give you a different way of accessing a parameterized property—via an indexer. An indexer enables you to access the property in the same way you would access an array—with the name of the property followed by a parameter list between the delimiters [and]. So for an object model object extended by VSTO, such as Worksheet, a parameterized property such as Range, which takes two parameters, can be called using the indexer syntax: Range[*parameter1*, *parameter2*] instead of get_Range(*parameter1*, *parameter2*).

The code in Listing 1-9 uses the FileDialog property called as a method and passes msoFileDialogFilePicker as a parameter to specify the type of FileDialog object to be returned. It then calls a method on the returned FileDialog object to show the dialog box.

Listing 1-9: A Parameterized Property Called as a Method That Takes an Enumeration Parameter and Returns an Object Model Object—the FileDialog Property on Word's Application Object

```
Office.FileDialog dialog = app.get_FileDialog(
  Office.MsoFileDialogType.msoFileDialogFilePicker);
dialog.Show();
```

The Office object models also have properties that have optional parameters. Optional parameters are parameters that can be omitted and the Office application will fill in a default value for the parameter. Optional parameters are typically of type object because of how optional parameters are passed to the underlying COM API. In C#, you must pass a special value to optional parameters that are of type object if you do not want to specify the parameter. This special value is called System.Type.Missing, and it must be passed for optional parameters that you do not want to specify directly (unlike Visual Basic in which you can omit the parameter entirely). In VSTO projects, a "missing" variable is predeclared for you (that is set to System.Type.Missing). Therefore, in VSTO code, you will often see missing passed rather than System.Type.Missing.

Occasionally, you will find an optional parameter is of some enumeration type rather than of type object. For this kind of optional parameter, you cannot pass System.Type.Missing and must instead pass a specific enumerated type value. You can find out what the default enumerated type value is for the optional parameter by consulting the documentation for the method or by using the object browser in a Visual Basic project—unfortunately, the C# object browser does not show the default value for an optional enumerated type parameter.

Listing 1-10 shows an example of calling a parameterized property called Range, which is found on Excel's Application object. The Range property is accessed via the get_Range method because parameterized properties can only be called via a method in C#. Calling the get_Range method on Excel's Application object returns the Range object in the active workbook as specified by the parameters passed to the method. The get_Range method takes two parameters. The first parameter is required, and the second parameter is optional. If you want to specify a single cell, you just pass the first parameter. If you want to specify multiple cells, you have to specify the top-left cell in the first parameter and the bottom-right cell in the second parameter.

Listing 1-10: A Parameterized Property Called as a Method with Optional Parameters— the Range Property on Excel's Application Object

```
// Calling a parameterized property with a missing optional parameter
Excel.Range myRange = app.get_Range("A1", System.Type.Missing);

// Calling a parameterized property without missing parameters
Excel.Range myRange2 = app.get_Range("A1", "B2");
```

In Word, optional parameters are handled differently than in the other Office applications. Word's object model requires that optional parameters be passed by reference. This means that you cannot pass System.Type.Missing directly as the code in Listing 1-10 did. Instead, you must declare a variable, set it to System.Type.Missing, and pass that variable by reference. You can reuse the same declared variable that has been set to System.Type.Missing if a parameter has multiple parameters you want to omit. In a VSTO project, you can just pass by reference the missing variable that is prede-clared for you. Listing 1-11 shows how to specify optional parameters in Word. In this example, the code uses a parameterized property from Word's Application object called SynonymInfo, which has a required string param-eter to specify a word you want a synonym for and an optional parameter to specify the language ID you want to use. The SynonymInfo property is accessed via the get_SynonymInfo method because parameterized properties can only be called via a method in C#. By omitting the optional language ID parameter and passing by reference a variable set to System.Type.Missing, Word will default to use the current language you have installed.

Listing 1-11: A Parameterized Property Called as a Method with Optional Parameters Passed by Reference—the SynonymInfo Property on Word's Application Object

```
object missing = System.Type.Missing;

// Calling a parameterized property in Word
// with a missing optional parameter
Word.SynonymInfo synonym = app.get_SynonymInfo(
  "happy", ref missing);
```

Properties Common to Most Objects

Because all the object model objects have object as their base class, you will always find the methods GetType, GetHashCode, Equals, and ToString on every object model object. In addition to these methods that are required by .NET, the Office object model follows a pattern that results in the frequent appearance of Application, Creator, and Parent properties. The Application property returns the Application object associated with the Office object model object. This is provided as a quick way to get back to the root of the object model. Many Office object model objects have a property called Creator, which gives you a code indicating which applica-tion the object was created in. Finally, you will often find a Parent property that returns the object that is the parent in the object model hierarchy.

Methods

A method is typically more complex than a property and represents a "verb" on the object that causes something to happen. It may or may not have a return value and is more likely to have parameters than a property.

The simplest form of a method has no return type and no parameters. Listing 1-12 shows the use of the Activate method from Word's Application object. This method activates the Word application, making its window the active window (the equivalent of clicking the Word window in the taskbar to activate it).

Listing 1-12: A Method with No Parameters and No Return Type—the Activate Method on Word's Application Object

```
MessageBox.Show("Activating the Word window.");

app.Activate();
```

Methods may also have parameters and no return type. Listing 1-13 shows an example of this kind of a method. The ChangeFileOpenDirectory method takes a `string` that is the name of the directory you want Word to default to when the Open dialog box is shown. For a method this simple, you might wonder why a property was not used instead—for example, you can imagine Word having a FileOpenDirectory property. In this case, the ChangeFileOpenDirectory only changes the default open directory temporarily—for the lifetime of the current Word session. When you exit Word and then restart Word, the default will no longer be what you set with this method. One reason that object models sometimes use a simple method such as this rather than a property is because some values exposed in an object model are "write-only"; that is, they can only be set but cannot be read. It is common to create a read-only property, but not common to create a write-only property. So when a write-only property is needed, a simple method is often used instead.

Listing 1-13: A Method with Parameters and No Return Type—the ChangeFileOpenDirectory Method on Word's Application Object

```
app.ChangeFileOpenDirectory(@"c:\temp");

MessageBox.Show("Will open out of temp for this session.");
```

Methods can have no parameters and a return type. Listing 1-14 shows an example of this kind of a method. The DefaultWebOptions method returns the DefaultWebOptions object, which is then used to set options for Word's Web features. In this case, DefaultWebOptions really should have been implemented as a read-only property as opposed to a method.

Listing 1-14: A Method with No Parameters and A Return Type—the DefaultWebOptions Method on Word's Application Object

```
Word.DefaultWebOptions options = app.DefaultWebOptions();

MessageBox.Show(String.Format("Pixels per inch is {0}.",
  options.PixelsPerInch));
```

Methods can have parameters and a return type. Listing 1-15 shows an example of this kind of a method. The CentimetersToPoints method takes a centimeter value and converts it to points, which it returns as the return value of the method. Points is a unit often used by Word when specifying spacing in the document.

Listing 1-15: A Method with Parameters and a Return Type—the CentimetersToPoints Method on Word's Application Object

```
float centimeters = 15.0F;

float points = app.CentimetersToPoints(centimeters);

MessageBox.Show(String.Format("{0} centimeters is {1} points.",
  centimeters, points));
```

Methods can also have optional parameters. Optional parameters do not need to be specified directly to call the method. For any parameters you do not want to specify, you pass a special value defined by .NET called `System.Type.Missing`. Listing 1-16 shows a method called CheckSpelling in Excel that has optional parameters. Listing 1-16 illustrates the syntax you use to omit parameters you do not want to specify. The CheckSpelling method takes a required `string`—the word you want to check the spelling of—along with two optional parameters. The first optional parameter enables you to pick a custom dictionary to check the spelling against. The second optional parameter enables you to tell the spell checker to ignore words in all uppercase—such as an acronym. In Listing 1-16, we check a phrase without specifying any of the optional parameters—we pass `System.Type.Missing` to each optional parameter. We also check a second phrase that has an acronym in all uppercase so we pass System.Type .Missing to the first optional parameter because we do not want to use a custom dictionary, but we specify the second optional parameter to be true so the spell checker will ignore the words in all uppercase.

Listing 1-16: A Method with Optional Parameters and a Return Type—the CheckSpelling Method on Excel's Application Object

```
string phrase1 = "Thes is spelled correctly. ";
string phrase2 = "This is spelled correctly AFAIK. ";

bool isCorrect1 = app.CheckSpelling(phrase1,
  System.Type.Missing, System.Type.Missing);

bool isCorrect2 = app.CheckSpelling(phrase2,
  System.Type.Missing, true);
```

Optional Parameters in Word

Optional parameters in Word can produce some strange-looking C# code because the values passed to optional parameters must be passed by reference. For example, Listing 1-17 shows how to spell check a string using the Word object model in C#.

Listing 1-17: A Method with Optional Parameters Passed by Reference—the CheckSpelling Method on Word's Application Object

```
void SpellCheckString()
{
    string phrase1 = "Speling erors here.";
    object ignoreUpperCase = true;
    object missing = System.Type.Missing;

    bool spellingError = !app.CheckSpelling(phrase1,
        ref missing, ref ignoreUpperCase, ref missing,
        ref missing, ref missing, ref missing,
        ref missing, ref missing, ref missing,
        ref missing, ref missing, ref missing);

    if (spellingError)
        MessageBox.Show("Spelling error found");
    else
        MessageBox.Show("No errors");
}
```

The first thing that probably comes to mind if you are a Visual Basic programmer and you have never seen code written against Word in C# is "Why is this so verbose?" Visual Basic does some special things for you when there are optional arguments in a method, so the Visual Basic version of this is much simpler, as shown in Listing 1-18.

Listing 1-18: A Method with Optional Parameters Passed by Reference Using Visual Basic— the CheckSpelling Method on Word's Application Object

```
Public Sub SpellCheckString()
    Dim phrase1 As String = "Speling erors here."
    Dim spellingError As Boolean
    spellingError = Not app.CheckSpelling(myString, , True)

    If spellingError Then
      MsgBox("Spelling error found.")
    Else
      MsgBox("No error found.")
    End If
End Sub
```

In Visual Basic, you do not have to worry about passing a value for each optional argument—the language handles this for you. You can even use commas, as shown in Listing 1-18, to omit one particular variable you do not want to specify. In this case, we did not want to specify a custom dictionary, but we did want to pass a value for the parameter IgnoreUpper-Case, so we omitted the custom dictionary argument by just leaving it out between the commas. It is also possible to use named parameters to specify only the parameters you want to supply. Note that some of this functionality provided natively to Visual Basic is made available when C# programmers use the Office Interop API Extensions.

The first thing that probably comes to mind if you're a C# programmer and you have never seen code written against Word in C#, such as the code shown in Listing 1-17, is "Why is all that stuff passed by reference?" When you are talking to Office object model methods, properties, and events, you are talking to the object model through a .NET technology called COM interop (short for interoperate). The Office object models are all written in unmanaged code (C and C++) that is exposed via COM interfaces. You will read more detail later in this chapter about the technology called interop assemblies that allows managed code to call COM objects.

If you were to examine the COM definition for the CheckSpelling method used in Listing 1-17 as defined by Word's COM type library, you would see something like this:

```
HRESULT CheckSpelling(
    [in] BSTR Word,
    [in, optional] VARIANT* CustomDictionary,
    [in, optional] VARIANT* IgnoreUppercase,
    [in, optional] VARIANT* MainDictionary,
    [in, optional] VARIANT* CustomDictionary2,
    [in, optional] VARIANT* CustomDictionary3,
    [in, optional] VARIANT* CustomDictionary4,
    [in, optional] VARIANT* CustomDictionary5,
    [in, optional] VARIANT* CustomDictionary6,
    [in, optional] VARIANT* CustomDictionary7,
    [in, optional] VARIANT* CustomDictionary8,
    [in, optional] VARIANT* CustomDictionary9,
    [in, optional] VARIANT* CustomDictionary10,
    [out, retval] VARIANT_BOOL* prop);
```

Note that any parameter that is marked as optional is specified as a pointer to a VARIANT in Word (VARIANT*). A VARIANT is a type in COM that is roughly equivalent to object in .NET—it can contain many different types of values. Excel does not typically use a pointer to a VARIANT for optional parameters, so you do not have this by ref issue for most of Excel. When the PIA is generated, the C# IntelliSense looks like this:

```
bool _Application.CheckSpelling(string Word,
    ref object CustomDictionary,
    ref object IgnoreUppercase,
    ref object MainDictionary,
    ref object CustomDictionary2,
    ref object CustomDictionary3,
    ref object CustomDictionary4,
    ref object CustomDictionary5,
    ref object CustomDictionary6,
    ref object CustomDictionary7,
    ref object CustomDictionary8,
    ref object CustomDictionary9,
    ref object CustomDictionary10)
```

Because of how Word defined optional parameters in its COM objects (as pointer to a VARIANT) and because of how that translates into .NET code (an object passed by reference), any optional argument in Word has to be passed by reference from C# and has to be declared as an `object`. Even though you would like to strongly type the `IgnoreUppercase` parameter to be a `bool` in the CheckSpelling example, you cannot. You have to type it as an object or you will get a compile error. This ends up being a little confusing because you can strongly type the first argument—the string you want to check. That's because in the CheckSpelling method, the `Word` argument (the string you are spell checking) is not an optional argument to CheckSpelling. Therefore, it is strongly typed and not passed by reference. Also note that optional arguments are always listed after all required arguments—that is, you will never find a situation where *argument1* is optional and *argument2* is not.

This brings us back to `System.Type.Missing`. In C# to omit an optional argument you pass an object by reference set to `System.Type.Missing`. In our example, we just declared one variable called `missing` and passed it in 11 times.

When you pass objects by reference to most managed functions, you do so because the managed function is telling you that it might change the value of that object you passed into the function. So it might seem bad to you that we are declaring one variable and passing it to all the parameters of CheckSpelling that we do not care about. After all, imagine you have a function that takes two parameters by reference. If you pass in the same variable set to `System.Type.Missing` to both parameters, what if the code evaluating the first parameter changes it from `System.Type.Missing` to some other value such as the `bool` value `true`? This would also affect both the first parameter and the second parameter, and the function might do something different when it looks at the second parameter that was originally set to `System.Type.Missing` because it is now set to `true` as well.

To avoid this, you might think we would have to declare a `missing1` through `missing11` variable because of the possibility that Word might go and change one of the by ref parameters on you and thereby make it so you are no longer passing `System.Type.Missing` but something else such as `true` that might cause unintended side effects.

Fortunately, you do not have to do this when working with Office object models. Remember that the underlying Word Application object is an unmanaged object, and you are talking to it through COM interop. The COM interop layer realizes that you are passing a `System.Type.Missing` to an optional argument on a COM object. So interop obliges, and instead of passing a reference to your `missing` variable in some way, the interop layer passes a special COM value that indicates that the parameter was missing. Your `missing` variable that you passed by reference is safe because it was never really passed directly into Word. It is impossible for Word to mess with your variable, even though when you look at the syntax of the call it looks like it would be possible because it is passed by reference.

Therefore, the CheckSpelling code in Listing 1-17 is completely correct. Your `missing` variable is safe—it will not be changed on you by Word even though you pass it by reference. But remember, this is a special case that only applies when talking through COM interop to an unmanaged object model that has optional arguments. Do not let this special case make you sloppy when calling methods on objects outside the Office object model that require parameters to be passed by reference. When talking to non-Office object model methods, you have to be careful when passing parameters by reference because the managed method can change the variable you pass.

Events

You have now read about the use of properties and methods in some detail—these are both ways that your code controls the Office application. Events are the way the Office application talks back to your code and enables you to run additional code in response to some condition that occurred in the Office application.

In the Office object models, there are far fewer events than there are methods and properties—for example, there are 41 events in Word and 85 in Excel. Some of these events are duplicated on different objects. For example, when the user opens a Word document, both the Application object and the newly created Document object raise Open events. If you wanted to handle all Open events on all documents, you would handle the Open event on the Application object. If you had code associated with a particular document, you would handle the Open event on the corresponding Document object.

In most of the Office object models, events are raised by a handful of objects. The only objects that raise events in the Word object model are Application, Document, and OLEControl. The only objects that raise events in the Excel object model are Application, Workbook, Worksheet, Chart, OLEObject, and QueryTable. Outlook is a bit of an exception: About half of the objects in the Outlook object model raise events. However, most of these objects raise the same set of events, making the total number of unique events small in Outlook as well.

Table 1-4 shows all the events raised by Excel's Application object. This table represents almost all the events raised by Excel because events prefaced

TABLE 1-4: Events Raised by Excel's Application Object

Event Name	When It Is Raised
AfterCalculate*	When a calculation completes
NewWorkbook	When a new workbook is created
SheetActivate	When any worksheet is activated
SheetBeforeDoubleClick	When any worksheet is double-clicked
SheetBeforeRightClick	When any worksheet is right-clicked
SheetCalculate	After any worksheet is recalculated
SheetChange	When cells in any worksheet are changed by the user
SheetDeactivate	When any worksheet is deactivated
SheetFollowHyperlink	When the user clicks a hyperlink in any worksheet
SheetPivotTableUpdate	After the sheet of a PivotTable report has been updated
SheetSelectionChange	When the selection changes on any worksheet
WindowActivate	When any workbook window is activated
WindowDeactivate	When any workbook window is deactivated

* New in Excel 2007

Continues

TABLE 1-4:   Events Raised by Excel's Application Object *(Continued)*

Event Name	When It Is Raised
WindowResize	When any workbook window is resized
WorkbookActivate	When any workbook is activated
WorkbookAddinInstall	When any workbook is installed as an add-in
WorkbookAddinUninstall	When any workbook is uninstalled as an add-in
WorkbookAfterXmlExport	After data in a workbook is exported as an XML data file
WorkbookAfterXmlImport	After data in a workbook is imported from an XML data file
WorkbookBeforeClose	Before any workbook is closed
WorkbookBeforePrint	Before any workbook is printed
WorkbookBeforeSave	Before any workbook is saved
WorkbookBeforeXmlExport	Before data in any workbook is exported as an XML data file
WorkbookBeforeXmlImport	Before data in any workbook is imported from an XML data file
WorkbookDeactivate	When any workbook window is deactivated
WorkbookNewSheet	When a new worksheet is created in any workbook
WorkbookOpen	When any workbook is opened
WorkbookPivotTableClose-Connection	After a PivotTable report connection has been closed
WorkbookPivotTableOpen-Connection	After a PivotTable report connection has been opened
WorkbookRowsetComplete*	When a user drills through a recordset or invokes the rowset action on a PivotTable object
WorkbookSync	When a workbook that is part of a document workspace is synchronized with a copy on the server

* New in Excel 2007

by Sheet are duplicated on Excel's Worksheet object, and events prefaced by Workbook are duplicated on Excel's Workbook object. The only difference in these duplicated events is that the Application-level Sheet and Workbook events pass a parameter of type Sheet or Workbook to indicate which worksheet or workbook raised the event. Events raised by a Workbook object or Sheet object do not have to pass the `Sheet` or `Workbook` parameter because it is implicitly determined from which Workbook or Sheet object you are handling events for.

To handle the events raised by Office object models, you must first declare a handler method in your code that matches the signature expected by the event being raised. For example, the Open event on the Application object in Excel expects a handler method to match the signature of this delegate:

```
public delegate void AppEvents_WorkbookOpenEventHandler(Workbook wb);
```

To handle this event, you must declare a handler method that matches the expected signature. Note that we omit the `delegate` keyword shown in the signature above in our handler method because we are not defining a new delegate type, just implementing an existing one defined by the Office object model.

```
public void MyOpenHandler(Excel.Workbook wb)
{
  MessageBox.Show(wb.Name + " was opened. ");
}
```

Finally, you must connect your handler method , to the Excel Application object that raises this event. We create a new instance of the delegate object defined by the Excel object model called AppEvents_Workbook-OpenEventHandler. We pass to the constructor of this object our handler method. We then add this delegate object to the Excel Application Work-bookOpen event using the += operator.

```
app.WorkbookOpen +=
  new AppEvents_WorkbookOpenEventHandler(MyOpenHandler);
```

Although this seems complex, Visual Studio 2008 helps by auto-generating most of this line of code as well as the corresponding event handler automatically. If you were typing this line of code, after you type += , Visual Studio displays a pop-up tooltip. If you press the Tab key twice, then Visual Studio generates the rest of the line of code and the handler method automatically.

Pascal Casing in Code Generated by Visual Studio

Visual Studio determines how to name the variables by reading information from the PIA definition. The definitions of the event parameters in the PIAs use Pascal casing, wherein the first letter of each word in a parameter is capitalized (CancelDefault, for example). Proper .NET style, however, says that parameters should be Camel cased (cancelDefault, for example). In this book, we've changed the casing from Pascal casing, which Visual Studio generates, to Camel casing to match .NET style guidelines.

Listing 1-19 shows a complete implementation of a handler method and event hookup in a simple class. The handler method is called `MyOpenHandler` and is a member method of the class `SampleListener`. This code assumes that a client creates an instance of this class, passing the Excel Application object to the constructor of the class. The `ConnectEvents` method connects the handler method `MyOpenHandler` to the Excel Application object's WorkbookOpen event. The `DisconnectEvents` method removes the handler method `MyOpenHandler` from the Excel Application object's WorkbookOpen event by using the `-=` operator on the delegate object. It might seem strange that we create a new instance of our delegate object when removing it, but this is the way C# supports removing delegates.

The result of this code is that any time a workbook is opened and `ConnectEvents` has been called, `MyOpenHandler` will handle the WorkbookOpen event raised by Excel's Application object and it will display a message box with the name of the workbook that was opened. `DisconnectEvents` can be called to stop `MyOpenHandler` from handling the WorkbookOpen event raised by Excel's Application object.

Listing 1-19: A Class That Listens to the Excel Application Object's WorkbookOpen Event

```
using Excel = Microsoft.Office.Interop.Excel;

class SampleListener
{
  private Excel.Application app;

  public SampleListener(Excel.Application application)
  {
    app = application;
  }

  public void ConnectEvents()
  {
    app.WorkbookOpen +=
      new AppEvents_WorkbookOpenEventHandler(this.MyOpenHandler);
  }

  public void DisconnectEvents()
  {
    app.WorkbookOpen -=
      new AppEvents_WorkbookOpenEventHandler(this.MyOpenHandler);
  }

  public void MyOpenHandler(Excel.Workbook workbook)
  {
    MessageBox.Show(String.Format("{0} was opened.",
      workbook.Name));
  }
}
```

The "My Button Stopped Working" Issue

One issue commonly encountered when beginning to program against
Office events in .NET is known as the "my button stopped working" issue.
A developer will write some code to handle a Click event raised by a CommandBarButton in the Office toolbar object model. This code will sometimes work temporarily but then stop. The user will click the button, but
the Click event appears to have stopped working.

The cause of this issue is connecting an event handler to an object whose
lifetime does not match the desired lifetime of the event. This typically
occurs when the object to which you are connecting an event handler goes
out of scope or gets set to null so that it gets garbage collected. Listing 1-20

shows an example of code that makes this mistake. In this case, an event handler is connected to a newly created CommandBarButton called `btn`. However, btn is declared as a local variable, so as soon as the Connect-Events function exits and garbage collection occurs, btn gets garbage collected and the event connected to btn is not called.

Listing 1-20: A Class That Fails to Handle the CommandBarButton Click Event

```
using Excel = Microsoft.Office.Interop.Excel;
using Office = Microsoft.Office.Core;

class SampleListener
{
  private Excel.Application app;

  public SampleListener(Excel.Application application)
  {
    app = application;
  }

  // This appears to connect to the Click event but
  // will fail because btn is not put in a more permanent
  // variable.
  public void ConnectEvents()
  {
    Office.CommandBar bar = Application.CommandBars["Standard"];

    Office.CommandBarButton myBtn = bar.Controls.Add(1,
        System.Type.Missing, System.Type.Missing,
        System.Type.Missing, System.Type.Missing) as
        Office.CommandBarButton;

    if (myBtn!= null)
    {
      myBtn.Caption = "My Button";
      myBtn.Tag = "SampleListener.btn";
      myBtn.Click += new  Office.
          _CommandBarButtonEvents_ClickEventHandler(
          myBtn_Click);
    }
  }

  // The Click event will never reach this handler.
  public void myBtn_Click(Office.CommandBarButton ctrl,
      ref bool cancelDefault)
  {
    MessageBox.Show("Button was clicked");
  }
}
```

The complete explanation of this behavior has to do with btn being associated with something called a Runtime Callable Wrapper (RCW). Without going into too much depth, btn holds on to an RCW that is necessary for the event to propagate from the unmanaged Office COM object to the managed event handler. When btn goes out of scope and is garbage collected, the reference count on the RCW goes down and the RCW is disposed—thereby breaking the event connection.

CommandBar Versus Ribbon

CommandBar objects are the way developers would customize Office menus and toolbars up through the Office 2003 release. Office 2007 introduces a new UI model called the Office Fluent Ribbon that is used to add menus and buttons. This new UI model also has a new programming model that is discussed in detail in Chapter 17, "Working with the Ribbon in VSTO." Although most of the time in your Office 2007 development you will want to use the Ribbon programming model, there are still times when you need to fall back to the CommandBar style object model—for example, for customizing context menus in Outlook or for customizing Outlook's Explorer window. Older code that uses CommandBarButtons to create custom menus and toolbars continues to work, but any custom menus or toolbars are displayed in the Add-Ins tab of the Ribbon.

Listing 1-21 shows a second example of a failed event listener class that is attempting to connect to Outlook's NewInspector event, which is raised by Outlook's Inspectors object. This event is raised whenever an inspector window opens (a window where you are viewing or editing an Outlook item). This code will also fail to get any events. In this case, it is more subtle because the event handler is connected to the Inspectors object, which is temporarily created in the line of code that begins with app.Inspectors. Because the Inspectors object returned by app.Inspectors is not stored in a permanent variable, the temporarily created Inspectors object is garbage collected, and the event connected to it will never get called.

Listing 1-21: A Class That Fails to Handle the Outlook Inspectors Object's NewInspector Event

```
using Outlook = Microsoft.Office.Interop.Outlook;

class SampleListener
{
  private Outlook.Application app;

  public SampleListener(Outlook.Application application)
  {
    app = application;
  }

  // This will appear to connect to the NewInspector event, but
  // will fail because Inspectors is not put in a more permanent
  // variable.
  public void ConnectEvents()
  {
    app.Inspectors.NewInspector += new Outlook.
      InspectorsEvents_NewInspectorEventHandler(
      MyNewInspectorHandler);
  }

  // The NewInspector event will never reach this handler.
  public void MyNewInspectorHandler(Outlook.Inspector inspector)
  {
    MessageBox.Show("New inspector.");
  }
}
```

The fix for this issue is to declare a variable whose lifetime matches the lifetime of your event handler and set it to the Office object for which you are handling the event. Listing 1-22 shows a rewritten class that successfully listens to the CommandBarButton Click event. This class works because instead of using the method-scoped variable btn, it uses a class-scoped member variable called myBtn. This ensures that the event handler will be connected for the lifetime of the class when ConnectEvents is called.

Listing 1-22: A Class That Succeeds in Handling the CommandBarButton Click Event Because It Stores the CommandBarButton Object in a Class Member Variable

```
using Excel = Microsoft.Office.Interop.Excel;
using Office = Microsoft.Office.Core;

class SampleListener
{
  private Excel.Application app;
  private Office.CommandBarButton myBtn;

  public SampleListener(Excel.Application application)
  {
    app = application;
  }

  public void ConnectEvents()
  {
    Office.CommandBar bar = Application.CommandBars["Standard"];

    myBtn = bar.Controls.Add(1,  System.Type.Missing,
      System.Type.Missing,  System.Type.Missing,
      System.Type.Missing) as Office.CommandBarButton;

    if (myBtn != null)
    {
      myBtn.Caption = "My Button";
      myBtn.Tag = "SampleListener.btn";
      myBtn.Click += new Office.
        _CommandBarButtonEvents_ClickEventHandler(
        myBtn_Click);
    }
  }

  public void myBtn_Click(Microsoft.Office.Core.CommandBarButton ctrl,
    ref bool cancelDefault)
  {
    MessageBox.Show("Button was clicked");
  }
}
```

Listing 1-23 shows a similar fix for our failed Outlook example. Here we declare a class-level variable called myInspectors that we assign to app.Inspectors. This ensures that our event handler will be connected for the lifetime of the class when ConnectEvents is called because the lifetime of myInspectors now matches the lifetime of the class.

Listing 1-23: A Class That Succeeds in Handling the Outlook Inspectors Object's
NewInspector Event Because It Stores the Inspectors Object in a Class Member Variable

```
using Outlook = Microsoft.Office.Interop.Outlook;

class SampleListener
{
  private Outlook.Application app;
  private Outlook.Inspectors myInspectors;

  public SampleListener(Outlook.Application application)
  {
    app = application;
  }

  public void ConnectEvents()
  {
    this.myInspectors = app.Inspectors;

    myInspectors.NewInspector += new Outlook.
        InspectorsEvents_NewInspectorEventHandler(
        MyNewInspectorHandler);
  }

  public void MyNewInspectorHandler(Outlook.Inspector inspector)
  {
    MessageBox.Show("New inspector.");
  }
}
```

When Method Names and Event Names Collide

In several cases in the Office object models, an object has an event and a
method that have the same name. For example, Excel's Workbook object
has an Activate event and an Activate method. Outlook's Inspector and
Explorer objects have Close events and Close methods.

When using an Office object model object that has events such as Workbook, you are actually using an object that implements several interfaces.
One of those interfaces has the definition of the Close method and a separate interface has the definition of the Close event. To handle an event for
which a method name collides, you must cast your object to the interface
that contains the event definitions. The interface that contains the event
interfaces is named *ObjectName*Events_Event, where *ObjectName* is the
name of the object, such as Workbook or Inspector.

Listing 1-24 casts the Workbook object `myWorkbook` to Excel.Workbook-Events_Event when adding the event handler. By casting `myWorkbook` to the WorkbookEvents_Event interface, we disambiguate between the Close method (which is on the Workbook interface) and the Close event (which is on the WorkbookEvents_Event interface).

Listing 1-24: A Class That Will Listen to the Excel Workbook Object's Activate Event by Casting to WorkbookEvents_Event

```
using Excel = Microsoft.Office.Interop.Excel;

class SampleListener
{
  private Excel.Workbook myWorkbook;

  public SampleListener(Excel.Workbook workbook)
  {
    myWorkbook = workbook;
  }

  public void ConnectEvents()
  {
    ((Excel.WorkbookEvents_Event)myWorkbook).Activate +=
        new Excel.WorkbookEvents_ActivateEventHandler(Activate);
  }

  public void Activate()
  {
    MessageBox.Show("Workbook Activated");
  }
}
```

The Office Primary Interop Assemblies (PIAs)

Before learning any more about how to build Office solutions, you need to understand in more detail the managed assemblies that you use to talk to the Office object model in .NET. The managed assemblies used to talk to Office are called the Office primary interop assemblies (PIAs).

As mentioned previously, when you are talking to an Office object model in .NET, you talk to it through a .NET technology called COM interop. The Office object models are all written in unmanaged code (C and C++) that exposes COM interfaces. To talk to these COM interfaces from managed code (C# or Visual Basic), you talk via a wrapper that allows managed code to interoperate with the unmanaged COM interfaces of Office. This wrapper is a set of .NET classes compiled into an assembly called a PIA.

The word *primary* is used when describing these assemblies because they are the Office-approved wrappers for talking to the Office object models. This designation is needed because you could create your own wrapper for the Office COM object models by using a tool provided with .NET called TLBIMP. A wrapper you create on your own is called an interop assembly (IA) rather than a PIA. Even though you might be tempted to go play with TLBIMP and build your own interop assemblies, you should never use anything other than the Office-provided interop assemblies to do Office development. If every developer created his or her own sets of wrappers for Office development, then no Office solution could interoperate with anyone else's solution; each interop wrapper class of, say, Worksheet created by each developer would be considered a distinct type. Even though the interop assembly I created has a Worksheet object and the interop assembly you created has a Worksheet object, I cannot pass you my Worksheet object and you cannot pass me your Worksheet object. We need to both be using the same interop assembly: the primary interop assembly.

A second reason to not build your own interop assemblies is that Office has made special fixes to the PIAs to make them work better when doing Office development. If you generate your own, then you are likely to run into issues that are fixed in the PIAs.

Installing the PIAs

The Office 2007 PIAs are available through the Office 2007 installer. The Office 2007 PIAs are also available as a Microsoft Windows Installer package that you can redistribute with your application. To install the Office 2007 PIAs through the Office 2007 Installer, when you do a setup, check the Choose advanced customization of applications check box in the first step of the Office 2007 Setup Wizard. Then in the tree control that appears in the next screen of the wizard, you will see a .NET Programmability Support node under each application for which PIAs are available, as shown in Figure 1-3. Click each of these .NET programmability support nodes and make sure that you set Run from my computer. Also, under the Office Tools node

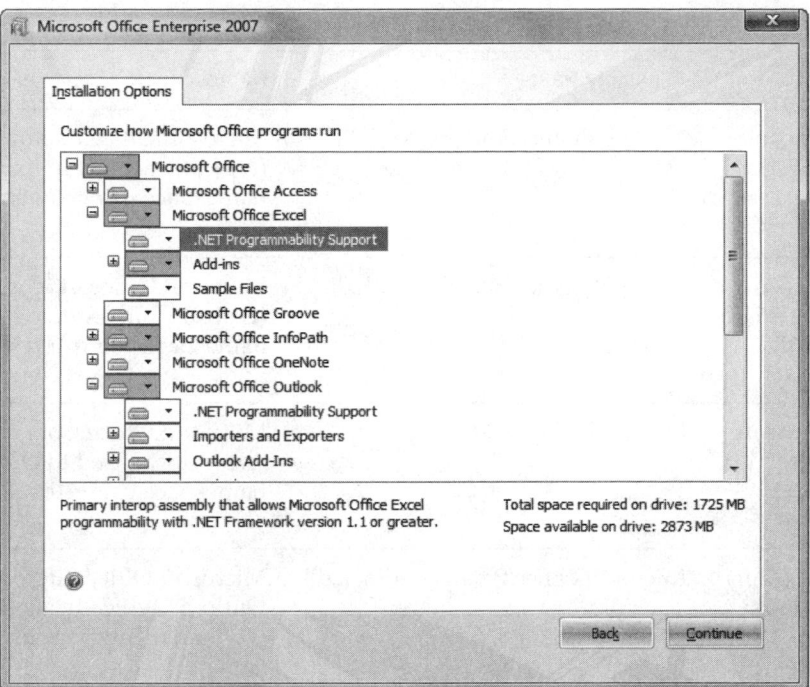

Figure 1-3: Installing the Office 2007 PIAs.

in the tree, you might want to turn on Microsoft Forms 2.0 .NET Programmability Support and Smart Tag .NET Programmability support. A second method to getting the Office 2007 PIAs is to do a complete install of Office 2007—all the .NET programmability support will be turned on for you automatically.

The Office PIAs get installed to the Global Assembly Cache (GAC). The GAC is usually in the Assembly subdirectory of the Windows directory.

A number of Office PIAs are available. Table 1-5 lists some of the most common ones. One PIA listed here of note is the Office.dll PIA, which is where common types that are shared between the Office applications such as CommandBar are found.

Referencing the PIAs

Adding a reference to a PIA is not necessary for most VSTO projects because the reference is automatically added for you. The console application

TABLE 1-5: Common Office PIAs

Description	Assembly Name	Namespace
Microsoft Excel 11.0 Object Library	Microsoft.Office.Interop.Excel.dll	Microsoft.Office.Interop.Excel (typically aliased to Excel namespace using Import)
Microsoft Graph 11.0 Object Library	Microsoft.Office.Interop.Graph.dll	Microsoft.Office.Interop.Graph (typically aliased to Graph namespace using Import)
Microsoft Office 11.0 Object Library	Office.dll	Microsoft.Office.Core (typically aliased to Office namespace using Import)
Microsoft Outlook 11.0 Object Library	Microsoft.Office.Interop.Outlook.dll	Microsoft.Office.Interop. Outlook (typically aliased to Outlook namespace using Import)
Microsoft SmartTags 2.0 Type Library	Microsoft.Office.Interop.SmartTag.dll	Microsoft.Office.Interop.Smart Tag (typically aliased to SmartTag namespace using Import)
Microsoft Word 11.0 Object Library	Microsoft.Office.Interop.Word.dll	Microsoft.Office.Interop.Word (typically aliased to Word namespace using Import)

examples in this book, such as the ones that automate Excel, can be typed into a Visual Studio console project and compiled, but you must first add a reference to the necessary PIA. To add a reference, right-click the References folder under your project in the Visual Studio Solution Explorer, as shown in Figure 1-4. Choose Add Reference from the menu that pops up when you right-click the References folder.

Choose the COM tab of the Add Reference dialog box that appears, as shown in Figure 1-5. The COM references are listed by component name,

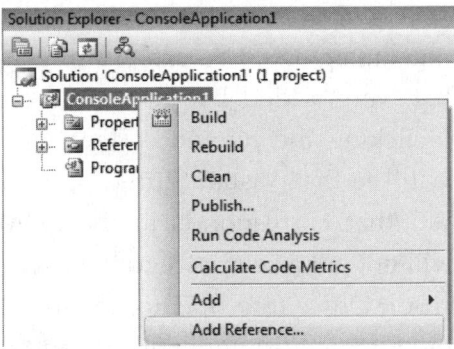

Figure 1-4: Adding a reference to a project.

which matches the description column in Table 1-5. So, to add a reference to the Excel PIA, you choose the Microsoft Excel 12.0 Object Library and click the OK button to add the Excel 2007 PIA reference to your project, as shown in Figure 1-5.

Note in Figure 1-5 that the Path column in the COM tab of the Add References dialog box displays the path to the COM library that the PIA wraps. For example, the Microsoft Excel 12.0 Object Library points to the

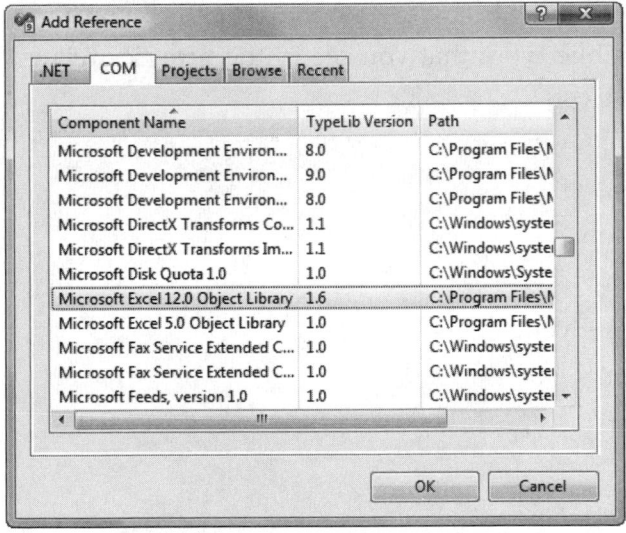

Figure 1-5: The Add Reference dialog box.

location on your machine of the Excel.EXE executable. When you select these references and close the dialog box, you can examine the properties of the actual references that were added by expanding the References folder in the project, right-clicking the references that you added, and choosing Properties. You will see that Visual Studio figures out the PIA managed object in the GAC that corresponds to the COM object you selected. In this case, you will not get a reference to the Excel.EXE executable but instead to the Microsoft.Office.Interop.Excel.dll in the GAC.

Finally, note that even though you did not explicitly add a reference to the Microsoft Office 12.0 Object Library (office.dll), a reference is added for you. This is because the Excel 12.0 Object Library uses types from the Microsoft Office 12.0 Object Library. Visual Studio detects this and adds the required Office PIA to your project references automatically.

Browsing the PIAs

When you look at the PIA you have referenced in the object browser in Visual Studio, you might find yourself very confused. The object browser shows many helper objects that are created as part of the interop wrapper. For example, consider what .NET Interop does to the seemingly simple Excel Application object. It turns it into a multiple-headed (8 heads to be exact, 36 if you count each delegate individually) monster. All of the following are public types that you see in the browser related to the Excel Application object:

Interfaces
_Application
AppEvents
AppEvents_Event
Application
IAppEvents

Delegates
AppEvents_*EventHandler (29 of them)

Classes

AppEvents_SinkHelper (AppEvents)

ApplicationClass (_Application, Application, AppEvents_Event)

This pattern repeats for Chart, OLEObject, QueryTable, Worksheet, and Workbook.

Let's try to untangle this mess by working our way backward from the original COM definition of the Excel Application object. The COM coclass for the Application object looks like this—it has two interfaces, a primary interface called _Application and an event interface called AppEvents. You can think of a coclass as something that defines the interfaces that a COM class implements.

```
coclass Application {
        [default] interface _Application;
        [default, source] dispinterface AppEvents;
    };
```

TLBIMP (which is used to process the COM type library for Excel and make the PIA) directly imports the _Application and AppEvents interfaces, so this explains where two of the eight types come from. But the AppEvents interface is not very useful—it seems like an artifact of the TLBIMP conversion in some ways. It has to be processed further to create another interface described later called AppEvents_Event to be of any use.

When TLBIMP processes the COM coclass, it creates a .NET class called ApplicationClass, which is named by taking the coclass name and appending Class. It also creates a .NET interface with the same name as the coclass called Application for our example. If you look at Application in the browser, it has no properties and methods of its own, but it derives from the other two interfaces associated with the coclass: _Application and AppEvents_Event.

We have not yet explained where the AppEvents_Event interface comes from. When TLBIMP processes the AppEvents event interface on the coclass, it creates several helper types. First it creates AppEvents_Event, which looks like AppEvents but with events and delegate types replacing the methods in AppEvents. It also creates delegates named

AppEvents_*EventHandler, where * is the method name for each method on the original AppEvents interface. Finally, it creates an AppEvents_ SinkHelper, which can be ignored.

That leaves only the IAppEvents interface unexplained. TLBIMP imports this interface directly because it is a public type in the Excel type library. You can ignore this also. This is effectively a duplicate of AppEvents, except AppEvents is declared as a dispinterface in the type library, and IAppEvents is declared as a dual interface type.

So which of these do you really use? Basically, you should only use in your code the Application interface (which derives from _Application and AppEvents_Events) and the delegates. You can usually pretend the others do not exist. The one exception to this rule is when a method and event name collide, as described earlier in this chapter. To disambiguate between a method and an event you must cast to the _Application interface when you want to call the method or the AppEvents_Event interface when you want to connect to the event. Table 1-6 presents a summary.

TABLE 1-6:   Interfaces, Delegates, and Events Associated with the
Application Object in Excel

Name	Description
Interfaces	
_Application	Direct import from type library. (Ignore. Typically you do not use this directly unless a method and event name collide—Application interface derives from this.)
AppEvents	Direct import from type library. (Ignore—artifact that is not used in real coding.)
AppEvents_Event	Created while processing the AppEvents event interface. (Ignore. Typically you do not use this directly unless a method and event name collide—Application interface derives from this.)
Application	Created while processing the Application coclass. (Use this interface.)
IAppEvents	Dual interface version of AppEvents in the type library. (Ignore—artifact that is not use in real coding.)

TABLE 1-6: Interfaces, Delegates, and Events Associated with the
Application Object in Excel *(Continued)*

Name	Description
Delegates	
AppEvents_*EventHandler (29 of them)	Created while processing the AppEvents event interface. (Use these. You use these when declaring delegates to handle events.)
Classes	
AppEvents_SinkHelper	Created while processing the AppEvents event interface. (Ignore.)
ApplicationClass	Created while processing the Application coclass. (Ignore. This is used behind the scenes to make it look like you can "new" an Application interface.)

The Application interface that is created by TLBIMP for the coclass behaves in an interesting way. You can write code in C# that makes it look like you are creating an instance of the Application interface, which we all know is impossible:

```
Excel.Application myApp = new Excel.Application();
```

Really, this is syntactical sugar that is using the ApplicationClass behind the scenes (the Application interface is attributed to associate it with the ApplicationClass) to create an Excel Application object and return the appropriate interface.

Finally, we mentioned earlier that this pattern repeats for Chart, OLE-Object, QueryTable, Worksheet, and Workbook. The mapping to Chart is straightforward—replace Application with Chart and AppEvents with ChartEvents and you'll get the general idea. Worksheet is a bit different. Its coclass looks like this:

```
coclass Worksheet {
    [default] interface _Worksheet;
    [default, source] dispinterface DocEvents;
};
```

So for Worksheet, replace Application with Worksheet, but replace AppEvents with DocEvents—yielding DocEvents_*EventHandler as the delegates for WorkSheet events.

QueryTable is even weirder. Its coclass looks like this:

```
coclass QueryTable {
        [default] dispinterface _QueryTable;
        [default, source] dispinterface RefreshEvents;
    };
```

So for QueryTable, replace Application with QueryTable and replace AppEvents with RefreshEvents—yielding RefreshEvents_*EventHandler as the delegates for QueryTable events.

When you look at the Excel PIA in the object browser in Visual Studio, you might notice a slew of methods with the text *Dummy* in them. There's even an interface called IDummy.

No, this is not Excel's way of insulting your intelligence. Everything with Dummy in it is a test method that actually has a legitimate purpose and more descriptive names in Microsoft's internal "debug" version of Excel. For example, Application.Dummy6 is called Application.DebugMemory in the debug version of Excel. Each method was renamed to Dummy in the retail version of Excel. All 508 of these Dummy methods actually do something in debug Excel, but in the retail version of Excel, they do nothing except raise an error when called.

Excel has marked these as "hidden," but the C# object browser shows hidden methods by default. When you view the PIA in the C# object browser, you will see these Dummy methods. If you create a Visual Basic project, the Visual Basic object browser will hide methods and properties with this attribute.

Conclusion

This chapter introduced the Office object models and examined the basic structure followed by the Office object models. You learned how to work with objects, collections, and enumerations—the basic types found in any object model. You also learned how to use properties, methods, and events exposed by objects and collections in the Office object models.

This chapter introduced the Office primary interop assemblies that expose the Office object models to .NET code. You learned how to use and reference Office PIAs in a Visual Studio project. This chapter also described what you can ignore when viewing the PIA in the object browser.

The next chapter begins examining the basic patterns of development used in Office programming and provides examples of each.

◼2◼
Introduction to Office Solutions

The Three Basic Patterns of Office Solutions

Now that you understand the basic pattern of the Office object models, this chapter explains how developers pattern and build their Office solutions. Most solutions built using Office follow one of three patterns:

- Office automation executable
- Office add-in
- Code behind an Office document

An automation executable is a program separate from Office that controls and automates an Office application. An automation executable can be created with development tools such as Visual Studio. A typical example is a stand-alone console application or Windows Forms application that starts up an Office application and then automates it to perform some task. To start a solution built this way, the user of the solution starts the automation executable, which in turn starts up the Office application. Unlike the other two patterns, the automation code does not run in the Office process but runs in its own process and talks cross process to the Office process being automated.

An add-in is a class in an assembly (DLL) that Office loads and creates when needed. An add-in runs in process with the Office application instead of requiring its own process separate from the Office application process. To start a solution built this way, the user of the solution starts the Office application associated with the add-in. Office detects registered add-ins on startup and loads them. An add-in can customize an Office application in the same ways that code behind a document can. However, code behind a document unloads when the document associated with the code is closed—an add-in can remain loaded throughout the lifetime of the Office application.

The code-behind pattern was popularized by Visual Basic for Applications (VBA)—a simple development environment that is included with Office that enables the developer to write Visual Basic code against the object model of a particular Office application and associate that code with a particular document or template. A document can be associated with C# or Visual Basic code behind using Visual Studio 2008 Tools for Office (VSTO). To start a solution built this way, the user of the solution opens a document that has code behind it or creates a new document from a template that has code behind it. The code behind the document will customize the Office application in some way while the document is open. For example, code behind the document might add Ribbon buttons that are only present when the document is open or associate code with events that occur while the document is open.

We discuss several advanced patterns later in this book. The server document pattern involves running code on a server to manipulate data stored in an Office document without starting the Office application. VSTO makes this scenario possible through a feature called cached data. Chapter 20, "Server Data Scenarios," discusses this pattern. The XML pattern is similar to the server document pattern and involves writing code to generate Word or Excel documents in Open XML formats without starting the Office application.

Hosted Code

The add-in and code-behind patterns are sometimes called hosted code, which means that your code runs in the same process as the Office application.

Discovery of Hosted Code

For code to run in the Office application process, the Office application must be able to discover your code, load the code into its process space, and run your code. Office add-ins are registered in the Windows registry so that Office can find and start them.

The code behind a document pattern does not require a registry entry. Instead, code is associated with a document by adding some special properties to the document file. Office reads these properties when the document opens, and then Office loads the code associated with the document.

Context Provided to Hosted Code

It is critical that your hosted code get context—it needs to get the Application object or Document object for the Office application into which it is loading. Application level add-ins in VSTO are provided with context through a class created in the project that has a member variable representing the application being customized. Code behind a document in VSTO is provided with context through a class created in the project that represents the document being customized.

Entry Points for Hosted Code

At startup, Office calls into an entry point where your code can run for the first time and register for events that might occur later in the session. For both add-ins and code behind a document, this entry point is the Startup event handler.

How Code Gets Run After Startup

After hosted code starts up, code continues to run in one or more of the following ways.

Code Runs in Response to Events Raised by Office

The most common way that code runs after startup is in response to events that occur in the Office application. For example, Office raises events when a document opens or a cell in a spreadsheet changes. Listing 1-24, on page 39, shows a simple class that listens to the Activate event that Excel's Worksheet object raises. Typically, you will hook up event listeners, such as the one shown in Listing 1-24, when the initial entry point of your code is called.

Code Runs in Response to Controls Provided by the Hosted Code

An add-in or code behind a document can create controls that result in hosted code being run after startup. For example, hosted code can create a task pane with controls on it or add controls to the document surface. Hosted code can register Ribbon extensions and Ribbon controls. When the user interacts with these controls, event handlers are raised that can be handled by the hosted code.

How Code Gets Unloaded

Your code gets unloaded in a number of ways, depending on the development pattern you are using. If you are using the automation executable pattern, your code unloads when the automation executable you have written exits. If you are using the add-in pattern, your code unloads when the Office application exits or when the user turns off the add-in via an add-in management dialog box. If you are using the code-behind pattern, your code unloads when the document associated with your code is closed.

In the hosted patterns of running code, there is some method that is called or event that is raised notifying you that you are about to be unloaded. For VSTO code-behind documents and add-ins, Office raises the Shutdown event before your code is unloaded.

Office Automation Executables

We will now consider each of these three patterns of Office solutions in more detail, starting with the office automation executable pattern. Office solutions that use the automation executable pattern start up an Office application in a very straightforward manner—by creating a new instance of the Application object associated with the Office application. Because the automation executable controls the Office application, the automation executable runs code at startup and any time thereafter when executing control returns to the automation executable. In the next section we will also consider how to make an automation executable that attaches to an already running Office application.

When an automation executable uses new to create an Application object, the automation executable controls the lifetime of the application by holding the created Application object in a variable. The Office application determines whether it can shut down by determining the reference count or number of clients that are using its Application object.

In Listing 2-1, as soon as new is used to create the myExcelApp variable, Excel starts and adds one to its count of clients that it knows are holding a reference to Excel's Application object. When you double-click on a worksheet, it sets exit to false causing Main to exit. When the myExcelApp variable goes out of scope (when Main exits), .NET garbage collection releases the object and Excel is notified that the console application no longer needs Excel's Application object. This causes Excel's count of clients holding a reference to Excel's Application object to go to zero, and Excel exits because no clients are using Excel anymore.

When you create an Office application by creating a new instance of the Application object, the application starts up without showing its window, which proves useful because you can automate the application without distracting the user by popping up windows. If you need to show the application window, you can set the Visible property of the Application object to true. If you make the main window visible, the user controls the lifetime of the application. In Excel, the application will not exit until the user quits the application and your variable holding the Excel Application object is garbage collected. Word behaves differently—the application exits when the user quits the application even if a variable is still holding an instance of the Word Application object.

Listing 2-1 sets the status bar of Excel to say "Hello World" and opens a new blank workbook in Excel by calling the Add method of Excel's Workbooks collection. Chapters 3 through 5—"Programming Excel," "Working with Excel Events," and "Working with Excel Objects," respectively—cover the Excel object model in more detail.

Listing 2-1: Automation of Excel via a Console Application

```
using System;
using System.Collections.Generic;
using System.Linq;
using System.Text;
using Excel = Microsoft.Office.Interop.Excel;
using System.Windows.Forms;

namespace ConsoleApplication
{
  class Program
  {
    static bool exit = false;

    static void Main(string[] args)
    {
      Excel.Application myExcelApp = new Excel.Application();
      myExcelApp.Visible = true;
      myExcelApp.StatusBar = "Hello World";
      myExcelApp.Workbooks.Add(System.Type.Missing);

      myExcelApp.SheetBeforeDoubleClick +=
        new Excel.AppEvents_SheetBeforeDoubleClickEventHandler(
          myExcelApp_SheetBeforeDoubleClick);

      while (exit == false)
        System.Windows.Forms.Application.DoEvents();
    }

    static void myExcelApp_SheetBeforeDoubleClick(object sheet,
      Excel.Range target, ref bool cancel)
    {
      exit = true;
    }
  }
}
```

Listing 2-1 also illustrates how an automation executable can yield time back to the Office application. A reference to the System.Windows.Forms assembly must be added to the project. After event handlers are hooked up, System.Windows.Forms.Application.DoEvents is called in a loop to allow the Excel application to run normally. If the user double-clicks a cell, Office yields time back to the event handler in the automation executable. In the handler for the DoubleClick event, we set the static variable exit to true, which will cause the loop calling DoEvents to exit and the automation executable to exit.

You can see the lifetime management of Excel in action by running the automation executable in Listing 2-1 and exiting Excel without double-clicking a cell. Excel will continue to run in a hidden state, waiting for the console application to release its reference to Excel's Application object.

Creating a Console Application That Automates an Already Running Office Application

Sometimes you won't want to start a new instance of an Office application but will instead want to attach to an already running instance. To do this, you can use one of two methods provided by .NET. System.Runtime.Interop-Services.Marshal.GetActiveObject allows you to attach to a running instance of an Office application by passing a string identifier for the Office application called a program ID or ProgID. The ProgID for an Office application is in the format [ApplicationName].Application. So for Excel it is Excel .Application, and for Word it is Word.Application. GetActiveObject returns an `object` that must be cast to the correct application object from the application's object model, so for our Excel example it must be cast to Excel's Application object.

The second method is System.Runtime.InteropServices.Marshal.Bind-ToMoniker which allows you to attach to a running instance of an Office document by passing the full path to an Office document that is currently open. BindToMoniker returns an `object` that must be cast to the document object from the application's object model, so for our Excel example it must be cast to Excel's Workbook object.

Listing 2-2 shows a console application that uses both of these methods. It first uses GetActiveObject to get an already running Excel instance. If Excel isn't running, a COMException is thrown, and the code catches that exception and returns. Then, it creates a workbook, saves the workbook, stores the filename in a variable, and disconnects from the running Excel instance. Finally, the code uses BindToMoniker and the stored filename to reconnect to the running Excel instance and get the Workbook object associated with the filename. Once again, if the workbook specified

by the filename is not open, a COMException is thrown, and the code
catches that exception and returns.

Listing 2-2: Automation of Excel via a Console Application

```
using System;
using Excel = Microsoft.Office.Interop.Excel;
using System.Windows.Forms;

namespace ConsoleApplication
{
  class Program
  {
    static void Main(string[] args)
    {
      Excel.Application myExcelApp = null;

      try
      {
        myExcelApp =
          System.Runtime.InteropServices.Marshal.GetActiveObject(
          "Excel.Application") as Excel.Application;
      }
      catch (System.Runtime.InteropServices.COMException e)
      {
        MessageBox.Show(
          String.Format("Excel application was not running: {0}",
          e.Message));
        return;
      }

      if (myExcelApp != null)
      {
        MessageBox.Show(
          "Successfully attached to running instance of Excel.");
        myExcelApp.Visible = true;
        myExcelApp.StatusBar = "Hello World";
        Excel.Workbook myExcelWorkbook =
          myExcelApp.Workbooks.Add(System.Type.Missing);

        // Save the workbook
        myExcelWorkbook.Save();
        string fileName = myExcelWorkbook.FullName;

        // Discard the application object
        myExcelApp = null;
```

```
      // Reconnect using the filename and BindToMoniker
      Excel.Workbook myExcelWorkbook2 = null;
      try
      {
        myExcelWorkbook2 =
          System.Runtime.InteropServices.Marshal.BindToMoniker(
          fileName) as Excel.Workbook;
      }
      catch (System.Runtime.InteropServices.COMException e)
      {
        MessageBox.Show(String.Format(
          "Filename {0} was not found running: {1}",
          fileName, e.Message));
        return;
      }

      if (myExcelWorkbook2 != null)
      {
        MessageBox.Show(String.Format(
          "Successfully bound to moniker {0}.", fileName));
        myExcelWorkbook2 = null;
      }
    }
  }
}
}
```

Creating a Console Application That Automates Word

This section walks you through the creation of a simple console application that automates Word to create a table specified in wiki text format. A wiki is a kind of online encyclopedia that users can contribute to. For an example, see http://www.officewiki.net for a wiki that documents the Office primary interop assemblies (PIAs). Wikis use simple, easy-to-edit text files that any visitor to the wiki can edit without having to know HTML. These text files have simple representations of even complex elements such as tables. Our console application will read a simple text file that specifies a table in wiki text format. It will then automate Word to create a Word table that matches the text file specification.

In the wiki text format, a table that looks like Table 2-1 is specified by the text in Listing 2-3.

TABLE 2-1:   A Simple Table Showing the Properties and Methods of Word's Add-In Object

Property or Method	Name	Return Type
Property	Application	Application
Property	Autoload	Boolean
Property	Compiled	Boolean
Property	Creator	Int32
Method	Delete	Void
Property	Index	Int32
Property	Installed	Boolean
Property	Name	String
Property	Parent	Object
Property	Path	String

Listing 2-3: A Wiki Text Representation of Table 2-1

```
||Property or Method||Name||Return Type||
||Property||Application||Application||
||Property||Autoload||Boolean||
||Property||Compiled||Boolean||
||Property||Creator||Int32||
||Method||Delete||Void||
||Property||Index||Int32||
||Property||Installed||Boolean||
||Property||Name||String||
||Property||Parent||Object||
||Property||Path||String||
```

We will use Visual Studio 2008 to create a console application. After launching Visual Studio, choose New Project from the File menu. The New Project dialog box shows a variety of project types. Choose the Visual C# node from the list of project types, and choose the Windows node under the Visual C# node. This is slightly counterintuitive because there is an Office node available, too, but the Office node shows VSTO code behind only document projects, VSTO add-in projects, and SharePoint workflow projects.

After you choose the Windows node, you will see in the window to the right the available templates. Choose the Console Application template. Name your console application project, and then click the OK button to create your project. In Figure 2-1, we have created a console application called WordWiki. Note that the New Project dialog box can have a different appearance than the one shown in Figure 2-1 depending on the profile you are using. In this book, we assume you are using the Visual C# Development Settings profile. You can change your profile by choosing Import and Export Settings from the Tools menu.

When you click the OK button, Visual Studio creates a console application project for you. Visual Studio displays the contents of the project in the Solution Explorer window, as shown in Figure 2-2.

By default, a newly created console application references the assemblies System, System.Core, System.Data, System.DataSetExtensions, System.Xml,

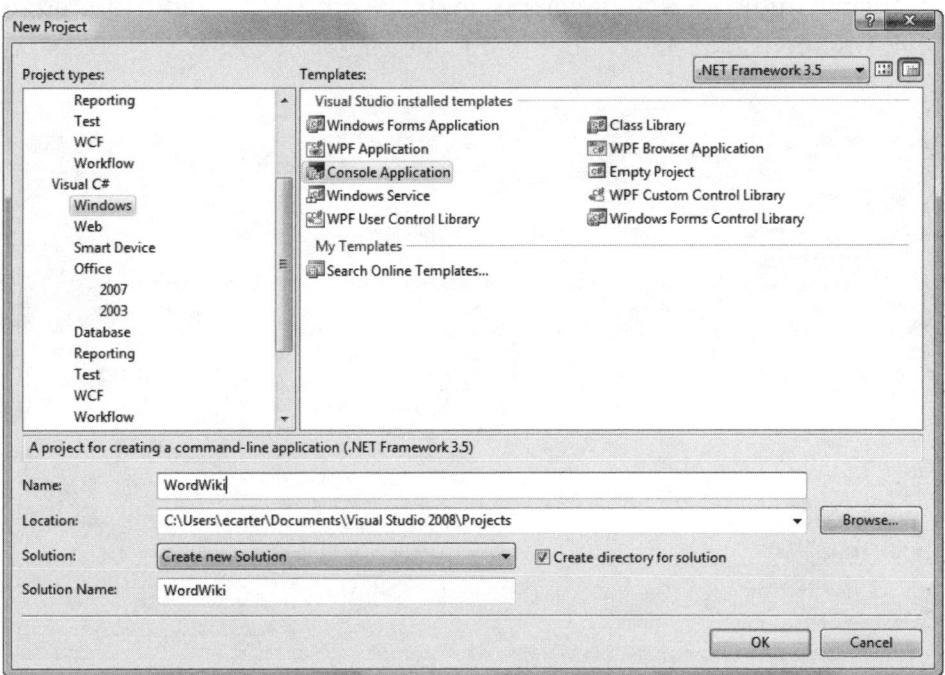

Figure 2-1: Creating a console application from the New Project dialog box.

Figure 2-2: The Console application project
WordWiki shown in Solution Explorer.

and System.Xml.Linq. We also need to add a reference to the Word 2007 PIA. We do this by right-clicking the References folder and choosing Add Reference from the pop-up menu that appears. This shows the Add Reference dialog box in Figure 2-3. Click the COM tab and choose the Microsoft Word 12.0 Object Library to add a reference to the Word 2007 PIA, and then click the OK button.

Visual Studio adds the reference to the Word 2007 PIA and adds additional references to the VBIDE, and the Microsoft.Office.Core PIAs, as

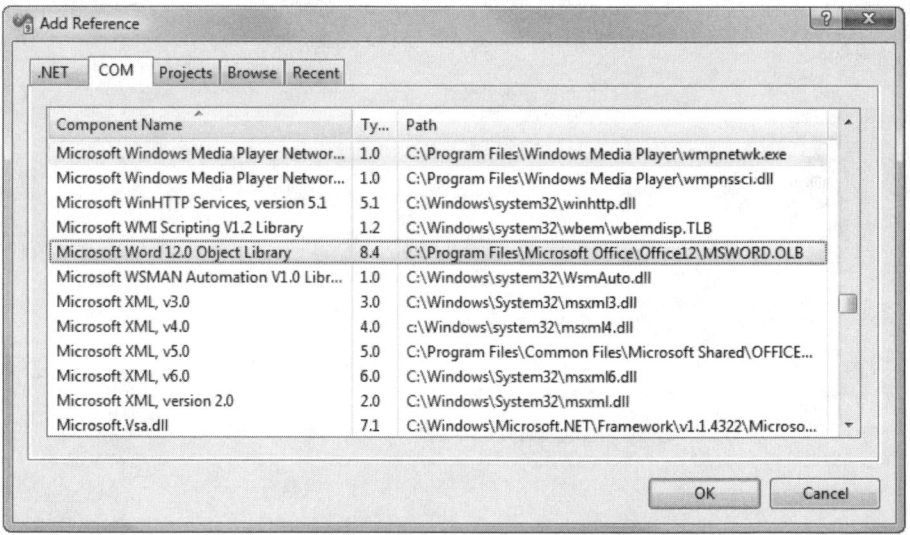

Figure 2-3: Adding a reference to the Microsoft Word 2007 PIA.

shown in Figure 2-4. These additional PIAs are ones that the Word PIA depends on. VBIDE is the PIA for the object model associated with the VBA editor integrated into Office. Microsoft.Office.Core (office.dll) is the PIA for common functionality shared by all the Office applications, such as dialog boxes used by all Office applications.

Now that the proper references have been added to the console application, let's start writing code. Double-click Program.cs in the Solution Explorer window to edit the main source code file for the console application. If you have outlining turned on, you will see the text "using …" at the top of the Program.cs file with a + sign next to it. Click the + sign to expand out the code where the using directives are placed. Add the following three using directives so that you can more easily use objects from the Word PIA and the Microsoft.Office.Core PIA as well as classes in the System.IO namespace.

```
using Office = Microsoft.Office.Core;
using Word = Microsoft.Office.Interop.Word;
using System.IO;
```

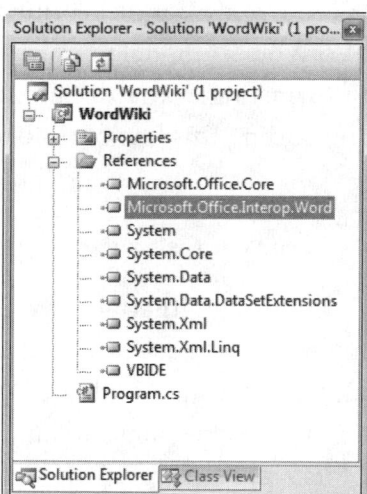

Figure 2-4: When you add the Word 2007 PIA, dependent PIA references are automatically added to the project.

We alias some of these namespaces so we do not have to type out the entire namespace, such as Microsoft.Office.Interop.Word, every time we want to declare a Word object. With the alias in place, we can just type Word to specify the namespace. We keep an alias namespace in place for the Microsoft.Office.Interop.Word and Microsoft.Office.Core namespaces instead of just typing using `Microsoft.Office.Interop.Word` and importing all the types into global scope. This is because Microsoft.Office.Interop.Word and Microsoft.Office.Core namespaces contain hundreds of types, and we do not want all these type names potentially colliding with types we define in our code or with other referenced types. Also for the purpose of this book, the code is clearer when it says Word.Application rather than Application, so you know what namespace the Application type is coming from.

We are now ready to write some code that automates Word to create a table after reading a text input file in the wiki table format. Listing 2-4 shows the entire listing of our program. Rather than explain every line of code in that listing, we focus on the lines of code that automate Word. We assume the reader has some knowledge of how to read a text file in .NET and parse a string via the Split method. We briefly touch on some objects in the Word object model here, but Chapters 6 through 8—"Programming Word," "Working with Word Events," and "Working with Word Objects," respectively—cover the Word object model in much more detail.

The first thing we do in Listing 2-4 is declare a new instance of the Word application object by adding this line of code to the Main method of our program class.

```
Word.Application wordApp = new Word.Application();
```

Although Word.Application is an interface, we are allowed to create a new instance of this interface because the compiler knows that the Word.Application interface is associated with a COM object that it knows how to start. When Word starts in response to an automation executable creating a new instance of its Application object, it starts up without showing any windows. You can automate Word in this invisible state when you want to automate Word without confusing the user by bringing up the Word window. However, know that there are some actions in Word that require the application window to be visible for them to work correctly—

for example, operations relating to word wrap and layout. For this example, we want to make Word show its main window, and we do so by adding this line of code:

```
wordApp.Visible = true;
```

Next, we want to create a new empty Word document into which we will generate our table. We do this by calling the Add method on the Documents collection returned by Word's Application object. The Add method takes four optional parameters that we want to omit. Optional parameters in Word methods are specified as omitted by passing by reference a variable containing the special value System.Type.Missing. We declare a variable called missing that we set to System.Type.Missing and pass it by reference to each parameter we want to omit, as shown here:

```
object missing = Type.Missing;
Word.Document theDocument = wordApp.Documents.Add(
    ref missing, ref missing, ref missing, ref missing);
```

With a document created, we want to read the input text file specified by the command-line argument passed to our console application. We want to parse that text file to calculate the number of columns and rows. When we know the number of columns and rows, we use the following line of code to get a Range object from the Document object.

```
Word.Range range = theDocument.Content;
```

We then use our Range object to add a table by calling the Add method of the Tables collection returned by the Range object. We pass the Range object again as the first parameter to the Add method to specify that we want to replace the entire contents of the document with the table. We also specify the number of rows and columns we want:

```
Word.Table table = range.Tables.Add(range, rowCount,
    columnCount, ref missing, ref missing);
```

The Table object has a Cell method that takes a row and column and returns a Cell object. The Cell object has a Range property that returns a Range object for the cell in question that we can use to set the text and formatting of the cell. The code that sets the cells of the table is shown here. Note that as in most of the Office object models, the indices are 1-based, meaning they start with 1 as the minimum value rather than being 0-based and starting with 0 as the minimum value:

```
for (columnIndex = 1; columnIndex <= columnCount; columnIndex++)
{
  Word.Cell cell = table.Cell(rowIndex, columnIndex);
  cell.Range.Text = splitRow[columnIndex];
}
```

A More Efficient Method of Creating a Table

This example is meant to introduce you to some of the Word object model, and as such it doesn't represent the most efficient way of creating a table. To create a table more efficiently, you should use the Convert-ToTable method of the Range object.

Code to set the formatting of the table by setting the table to size to fit contents and bolding the header row is shown below. We use the Row object returned by `table.Rows[1]`, which also has a Range property that returns a Range object for the row in question. Also, we encounter code that sets the first row of the table to be bolded. One would expect to be able to write the code `table.Rows[1].Range.Bold = true`, but Word's object model expects an `int` value (0 for false and 1 for true) rather than a `bool`. The Bold property doesn't return a `bool` because the range of text could be all bold, all not bold, or partially bold. Word uses the enumerated constant `WdConstants.WdUndefined` to specify the partially bold case.

```
// Format table
table.Rows[1].Range.Bold = 1;
table.AutoFitBehavior(Word.WdAutoFitBehavior.wdAutoFitContent);
```

Finally, some code at the end of the program forces Word to quit without saving changes:

```
// Quit without saving changes
object saveChanges = false;
wordApp.Quit(ref saveChanges, ref missing, ref missing);
```

If you do not write this code, Word will stay running even after the console application exits. When you show the Word window by setting the Application object's Visible property to true, Word puts the lifetime of the application in the hands of the end user rather than the automating program. So even when the automation executable exits, Word continues running. To force Word to exit, you must call the Quit method on Word's Application object. If this program didn't make the Word window visible—say, for example, it created the document with the table and then saved it to a file all without showing the Word window—it would not have to call Quit because Word would exit when the program exited and released all its references to the Word objects.

To run the console application in Listing 2-4, you must create a text file that contains the text in Listing 2-3. Then pass the filename of the text file as a command-line argument to the console application. You can set up the debugger to do this by right-clicking the WordWiki project in Solution Explorer and choosing Properties. Then click the Debug tab and set the Command line arguments field to the name of your text file.

Listing 2-4: The Complete WordWiki Implementation

```
using System;
using System.Collections.Generic;
using System.Linq;
using System.Text;
using Office = Microsoft.Office.Core;
using Word = Microsoft.Office.Interop.Word;
using System.IO;

namespace WordWiki
{
  class Program
  {
    static void Main(string[] args)
    {
      Word.Application wordApp = new Word.Application();
      wordApp.Visible = true;

      object missing = System.Type.Missing;
      Word.Document theDocument = wordApp.Documents.Add(
        ref missing, ref missing, ref missing, ref missing);

      TextReader reader = new System.IO.StreamReader(args[0]);
```

```csharp
string[] separators = new string[1];
separators[0] = "||";
int rowCount = 0;
int columnCount = 0;

// Read rows and calculate number of rows and columns
System.Collections.Generic.List<string> rowList =
  new System.Collections.Generic.List<string>();

string row = reader.ReadLine();

while (row != null)
{
  rowCount++;
  rowList.Add(row);

  // If this is the first row,
  // calculate the number of columns
  if (rowCount == 1)
  {
    string[] splitHeaderRow = row.Split(
      separators, StringSplitOptions.None);

    // Ignore the first and last separator
    columnCount = splitHeaderRow.Length - 2;
  }

  row = reader.ReadLine();
}

// Create a table
Word.Range range = theDocument.Content;
Word.Table table = range.Tables.Add(range, rowCount,
  columnCount, ref missing, ref missing);

// Populate table
int columnIndex = 1;
int rowIndex = 1;

foreach (string r in rowList)
{
  string[] splitRow = r.Split(separators,
    StringSplitOptions.None);

  for (columnIndex = 1; columnIndex <= columnCount;
    columnIndex++)
  {
    Word.Cell cell = table.Cell(rowIndex, columnIndex);
    cell.Range.Text = splitRow[columnIndex];
  }
```

```
      rowIndex++;
   }

   // Format table
   table.Rows[1].Range.Bold = 1;
   table.AutoFitBehavior(Word.WdAutoFitBehavior.
     wdAutoFitContent);

   // Wait for input from the command line before exiting
   System.Console.WriteLine("Table complete.");
   System.Console.ReadLine();

   // Quit without saving changes
   object saveChanges = false;
   wordApp.Quit(ref saveChanges, ref missing,
     ref missing);
  }
 }
}
```

Office Add-Ins

The second pattern used in Office development is the add-in pattern. There are several types of Office add-ins that you can create. These include VSTO add-ins, COM add-ins, and automation add-ins for Excel:

- **VSTO add-ins**—This VSTO feature makes it extremely easy to create an add-in for most of the Office applications. The model is the most ".NET" of all the add-in models and is very similar to the VSTO code behind model for documents. Chapter 12, "The VSTO Programming Model," describes this model in detail.

- **COM add-ins**—A C# class in a class library project can implement the IDTExtensibility2 interface and register in the registry as a COM object and COM add-in. Through COM interop, Office creates the C# class and talks to it. Visual Studio also includes something called a Shared Add-in project that creates this style of COM add-in. However, for Office 2007 and Office 2003, the use of COM add-ins or the Shared Add-in project is not recommended as there are several significant issues with creating COM add-ins in .NET that are solved by the VSTO add-in model. The issues with COM add-ins written in .NET include lifetime issues, which cause the Office application to not shut down, and isolation issues, which can cause one add-in to adversely impact another add-in. For this reason, this book will not cover the COM add-in approach further. If you do use COM add-ins, perhaps because you want to target an older version of Office, be sure to use a COM add-in shim to solve the isolation issues (search the web for COM Shim Wizard to find a Visual Studio tool to help you create a COM add-in shim).

- **Automation add-ins for Excel**—These managed classes expose public functions that Excel can use in formulas. The C# class must register in the registry as a COM object. Through COM interop, Excel can create an automation add-in and use its public methods in formulas. Automation add-ins and their use in Excel formulas are discussed in Chapter 3, "Programming Excel."

Another style of add-in, a Smart Documents add-in, is not discussed because VSTO provides a much easier way of accessing Smart Document functionality. For more information on VSTO's support for Smart Documents, see Chapter 14, "Working with Document-Level Actions Pane."

Creating an Outlook 2007 Add-In in VSTO

To create an Outlook add-in project in VSTO, choose Project from the New menu of the File menu in Visual Studio. Select the Visual C# node from the list of project types, and select the Office node under the Visual C# node. Then select the 2007 node to filter to just the Office 2007 project types. The Outlook 2007 add-in project appears in the list of templates as shown in Figure 2-5. Type a name for your new Outlook add-in project, and pick a location for the project. Then click the OK button.

VSTO creates a project with references to the Outlook 2007 PIA, the core Office PIA, and other needed references, as shown in Figure 2-6. VSTO also adds a project item to the project called ThisAddIn.cs. This project item contains a C# class that you will add to when implementing your Outlook add-in.

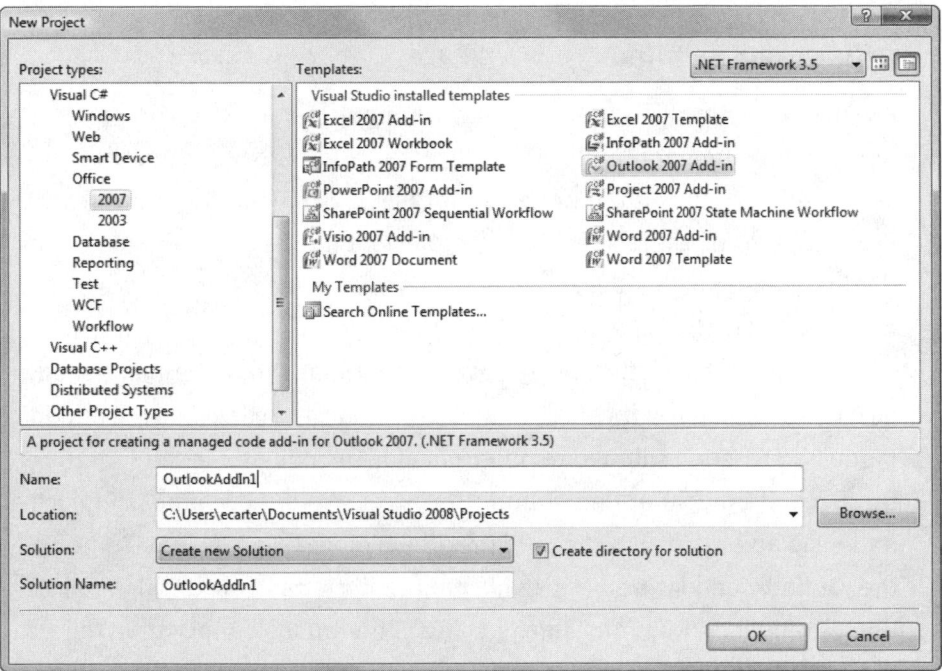

Figure 2-5: Creating a new Outlook add-in project.

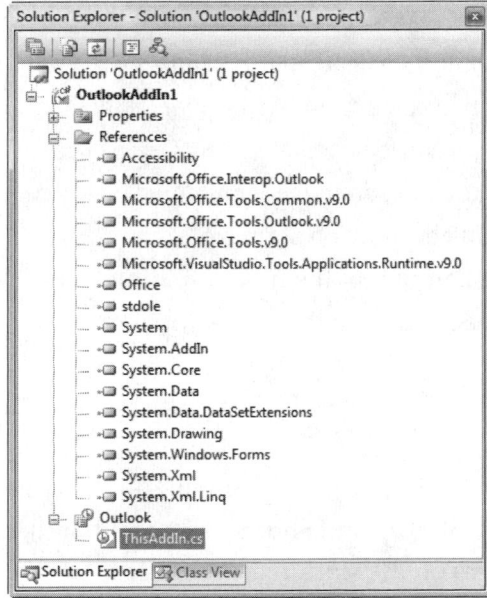

Figure 2-6: The Outlook add-in project in Solution Explorer.

Office 2003 Add-Ins

As you create an add-in project, you will notice several Office 2003 project types below the 2003 node. These types include Excel and Word document projects, and add-in projects for Excel, PowerPoint, Word, Outlook, Project, and Visio. The Office 2003 projects and features are covered in the first edition of this book, whereas this edition focuses on Office 2007 projects and features.

One point about Office 2003 development that should be mentioned, as it wasn't covered in the first edition of the book, is a change to the add-in model. VSTO 2005 shipped support only for Outlook add-ins. VSTO 2005 SE (Second Edition) added support for Excel, Word, PowerPoint, Project, and Visio add-ins. It also changed the add-in model slightly. In VSTO 2005, the Outlook add-in project's main project item was called ThisApplication.cs, and it derived from an aggregate of the Outlook Application object that allowed you to access a property of the Outlook Application object such as the Inspectors property by writing the code `this.Inspectors`.

In VSTO 2005 SE, this model was changed, so the main project item for an add-in is now called ThisAddIn.cs, and the ThisAddIn class no longer derives from an aggregate of the Application object. Instead, the ThisAddIn class has a member variable called Application that contains the Application object. So now to access the Inspectors property, you would write the `this.Application.Inspectors`. This change makes the add-in model more flexible, so your code is less tightly bound to a particular version of Office.

Other than that change and the addition of the new add-in projects, no other significant changes have been made in the Office 2003 projects since the first edition of this book.

If you double-click the ThisAddIn.cs project item, you will see the code shown in Listing 2-5. There is a simple Startup and Shutdown event handler where you can write code that executes on the startup and shutdown of the add-in. The ThisAddIn class also has a member variable called Application that is set to the Outlook Application object. This allows you to access properties and methods of the Outlook Application object by writing code such as this.Application.Inspectors.Count in the ThisAddIn class.

Listing 2-5: The Initial Code in the ThisAddIn Class in an Outlook Add-In Project

```
using System;
using System.Collections.Generic;
using System.Linq;
using System.Text;
using System.Xml.Linq;
using Outlook = Microsoft.Office.Interop.Outlook;
using Office = Microsoft.Office.Core;

namespace OutlookAddIn1
{
  public partial class ThisAddIn
  {
    private void ThisAddIn_Startup(object sender,
      System.EventArgs e)
    {
    }

    private void ThisAddIn_Shutdown(object sender,
      System.EventArgs e)
    {
    }

    #region VSTO generated code

    /// <summary>
    /// Required method for Designer support - do not modify
    /// the contents of this method with the code editor.
    /// </summary>
    private void InternalStartup()
    {
      this.Startup += new System.EventHandler(ThisAddIn_Startup);
      this.Shutdown += new System.EventHandler(ThisAddIn_Shutdown);
    }

    #endregion
  }
}
```

Looking at Listing 2-5, you might wonder about the use of partial in the class definition. VSTO uses partial classes, introduced in the .NET Framework 2.0, that enable you to define part of a class in one file and another part of a class in a second file and then compile them together as one class.

VSTO uses this feature to hide some additional generated code associated with the ThisAddIn class from you to reduce the complexity of the class where you write your code. The final ThisAddIn class will be compiled from the partial class in Listing 2-4 and additional code in a partial class generated by VSTO that is hidden from you.

The InternalStartup method is generated by VSTO and used to hook up any event handlers generated by VSTO. This is where the Startup and Shutdown event handlers are hooked up. You should not edit this section of the code. We may omit this block of code in some of the listings in this book, but the block of code must be in the class—otherwise, the class will fail to compile.

We are going to add to the code in Listing 2-5 to create an add-in that will solve an annoying problem—people replying inadvertently to an e-mail sent out to a mailing alias that contains a large number of people. Unless you have "Vice President" in your title, you probably do not want to be sending e-mail to more than, say, 25 people at any given time. We are going to create an add-in that will warn you if you do this and give you the "This is a potentially career-limiting move. Are you sure you want to send this e-mail to 25,000 people?" message.

Outlook's Application object has an ItemSend event that is raised whenever a user sends an e-mail. We will add additional code to the Startup method of the ThisAddIn class to connect an event handler for the Item-Send event, as shown in Listing 2-6. Because the ThisAddIn class has a member variable called Application that is set to Outlook's Application object, we can write the code this.Application.ItemSend because Item-Send is an event raised by the ThisApplication class. The ItemSend event handler takes an object parameter called item, which is the Outlook item being sent. Because item could be any of a number of things, such as a meeting request or an e-mail message, item is passed as an object rather than as a specific type. The ItemSend event handler also has a bool parameter passed by reference called cancel that can be set to true to prevent the Outlook item from being sent.

In our ItemSend event handler, we need to check to see whether the item parameter which is passed as an object is actually an e-mail. The easiest way to achieve this is to use the as keyword to try to cast the item parameter to an Outlook.MailItem. If the cast succeeds, the resulting value will be non-null, and we will know that the item being sent is an Outlook.MailItem and therefore an e-mail message. We can then iterate through the Recipients collection on the MailItem object and count how many address entries we are sending to. If we find the count to be more than 25, we will show a dialog box and ask the user if she really wants to send the mail. If the user clicks the No button, we will set the `cancel` parameter of the ItemSend event to `true` to cancel the sending of career-limiting e-mail. Note that the algorithm here is slightly naïve in that it doesn't guarantee that the address entries found are all unique—so in the case that you send the mail to a person and a distribution list that includes the same person, that person would be counted twice.

Listing 2-6: A VSTO Outlook Add-In That Handles the ItemSend Event and Checks for More Than 25 Recipients

```csharp
using System;
using System.Collections.Generic;
using System.Linq;
using System.Text;
using System.Xml.Linq;
using Outlook = Microsoft.Office.Interop.Outlook;
using Office = Microsoft.Office.Core;
using System.Windows.Forms;

namespace OutlookAddIn1
{
  public partial class ThisAddIn
  {
    private void ThisAddIn_Startup(object sender,
      System.EventArgs e)
    {
      this.Application.ItemSend += new
        Outlook.ApplicationEvents_11_ItemSendEventHandler(
        Application_ItemSend);
    }

    int CountRecipients(Outlook.AddressEntry entry)
    {
      int count = 1;
      if (entry.Members == null)
        return 1;
      else
      {
```

```
      foreach (Outlook.AddressEntry e in entry.Members)
      {
        count = count + CountRecipients(e);
      }
    }
    return count;
  }

  void Application_ItemSend(object Item, ref bool Cancel)
  {
    Outlook.MailItem myItem = Item as Outlook.MailItem;
    int recipientCount = 0;

    if (myItem != null)
    {
      foreach (Outlook.Recipient recip in myItem.Recipients)
      {
        recipientCount += CountRecipients(recip.AddressEntry);
      }

      if (recipientCount > 25)
      {
          // Ask the user if she really wants to send this e-mail
          string message = "Send mail to {0} people?";
          string caption = "More than 25 recipients";
          MessageBoxButtons buttons = MessageBoxButtons.YesNo;
          DialogResult result;

          result = MessageBox.Show(String.Format(message,
            recipientCount),
            caption, buttons);

          if (result == DialogResult.No)
          {
            Cancel = true;
            return;
          }
        }
      }
    }

  #region VSTO generated code
  private void InternalStartup()
  {
    this.Startup += new System.EventHandler(ThisAddIn_Startup);
  }
  #endregion
  }
}
```

When you run the project with the code shown in Listing 2-6, Outlook launches and the add-in loads. Try sending a mail to an alias that includes more than 25 people. If all works right, the add-in will display a dialog box warning you that you are sending an e-mail to more than 25 people, and you will be able to cancel the send of the e-mail. Exit Outlook to end your debugging session.

Removing an Add-In by Using Clean

When you build and run an add-in project in Visual Studio, the add-in is registered on your system, and if you exit Visual Studio after building or running, the add-in continues to be installed and load into the host application (Outlook, for Listing 2-6). To remove the add-in, choose Build › Clean Solution in Visual Studio. This command unregisters the add-in so that it won't continue to load.

Changes Between Outlook 2003 VSTO Add-Ins and Outlook 2007 VSTO Add-Ins

It's instructive to compare Listing 2-6 in the previous edition of this book to see what changed between Outlook 2003 and Outlook 2007, as well as the changes to the add-in model between VSTO 2.0 and VSTO 3.0.

First, the add-in class is now called ThisAddIn rather than ThisApplication and is located in the file ThisAddIn.cs rather than ThisApplication.cs. Because the Outlook Application object is now provided via a member variable called Application rather than as an aggregate of the base class, the event hookup code that previously started with `this.ItemSend` in the VSTO 2.0 add-in model is now `this.Application.ItemSend`.

Also interesting is one line that did not change between versions: the delegate definition ApplicationEvents_11_ItemSendEventHandler. One would think that this line would have changed to be prefaced with ApplicationEvents_12, as 12 is the internal version number for Outlook 2007.

But the Outlook team decided not to create a new events interface for Outlook 2007; instead, it extended the existing ApplicationEvents_11 interface.

Chapters 9 through 11—"Programming Outlook," "Working with Outlook Events," and "Working with Outlook Objects," respectively—discuss the Outlook object model.

Code Behind a Document

VSTO supports code behind a document by requiring that the developer use classes generated in a VSTO project that have pre-hooked-up context and pre-hooked-up events. These classes are sometimes called "code-behind" classes because they are code associated with a particular document or worksheet. In Word, there is one code-behind class corresponding to the document. In Excel, there are multiple code-behind classes—one for the workbook and one for each worksheet or chart sheet in the workbook.

The first time your code runs in a code-behind-the-document project is when Office raises the Startup event handled by any of the code-behind classes created for you. VSTO provides context via the base class of the code behind class you are writing code in. A VSTO code-behind class customizing an Excel worksheet derives from a base class that contains all the methods, properties, and events of an Excel worksheet. This enables you to write code such as this in the Startup method of a worksheet class.

```
MessageBox.Show(String.Format("{0} is the sheet name", this.Name));
```

By using `this.Name`, you are referring to the Name property of the Excel Worksheet object inherited from the base class. Listing 2-7 shows a VSTO code-behind class for an Excel Worksheet. In addition to the Startup and Shutdown methods in the code-behind class, there is also a generated method called InternalStartup. You should not put any of your code in this InternalStartup method because it is auto-generated by VSTO and modifying it can break Visual Studio's support for code-behind classes. Instead, your startup code should go in the Startup event handler. VSTO code-behind document classes also use partial classes to hide some additional code generated by VSTO.

Listing 2-7: A VSTO Excel Workbook Customization

```csharp
using System;
using System.Collections.Generic;
using System.Data;
using System.Linq;
using System.Text;
using System.Windows.Forms;
using System.Xml.Linq;
using Microsoft.VisualStudio.Tools.Applications.Runtime;
using Excel = Microsoft.Office.Interop.Excel;
using Office = Microsoft.Office.Core;

namespace ExcelWorkbook1
{
  public partial class Sheet1
  {
    private void Sheet1_Startup(object sender, System.EventArgs e)
    {
      // Initial entry point.
      // This code gets run first when the code behind is created
      // The context is implicit in the Sheet1 class
      MessageBox.Show("Code behind the document running.");
      MessageBox.Show(String.Format("{0} is the sheet name",
        this.Name));
    }

    private void Sheet1_Shutdown(object sender, System.EventArgs e)
    {
    }

    #region VSTO Designer generated code

    /// <summary>
    /// Required method for Designer support - do not modify
    /// the contents of this method with the code editor.
    /// </summary>
    private void InternalStartup()
    {
      this.Startup += new System.EventHandler(Sheet1_Startup);
      this.Shutdown += new System.EventHandler(Sheet1_Shutdown);
    }

    #endregion

  }
}
```

In this section, we create some simple code behind a document in Excel using VSTO. First, start up VSTO and choose the File > New > Project menu item. As you have seen previously, navigate to the Office node under the Visual C# root as shown in Figure 2-7.

We will create an Excel workbook project using C#. If you already have a workbook that you want to add VSTO customization code behind, you can specify its location in the dialog box shown in Figure 2-8 that appears after you click OK in the New Project dialog box. This time we will just start from scratch, creating a new, blank workbook.

After we have created the project, the Designer view appears, as shown in Figure 2-9.

Notice a few interesting things in Figure 2-9. First, Excel is running inside Visual Studio 2008 as a designer, just the same as a Windows Forms designer would when developing a Windows Forms project.

Second, because Office 2007 uses the Ribbon for its buttons and menus, VSTO no longer merges the Visual Studio menus with the Excel menus, as

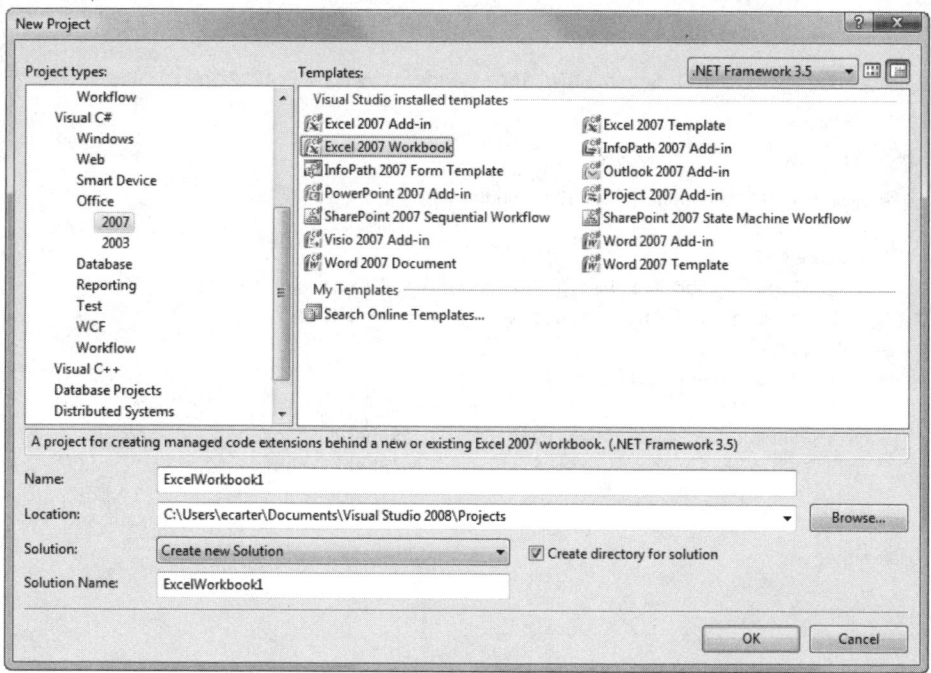

Figure 2-7: Using the New Project dialog box to create an Excel Workbook project.

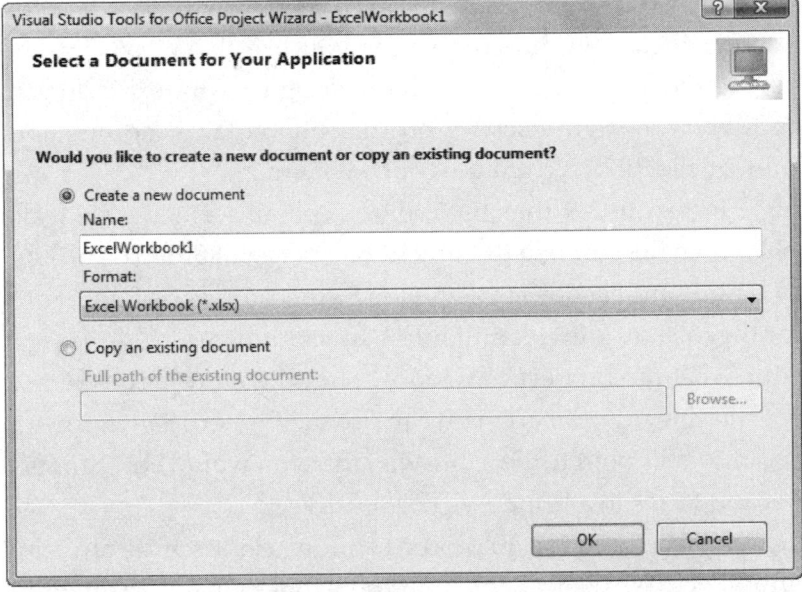

Figure 2-8: Selecting the workbook to associate with your code behind.

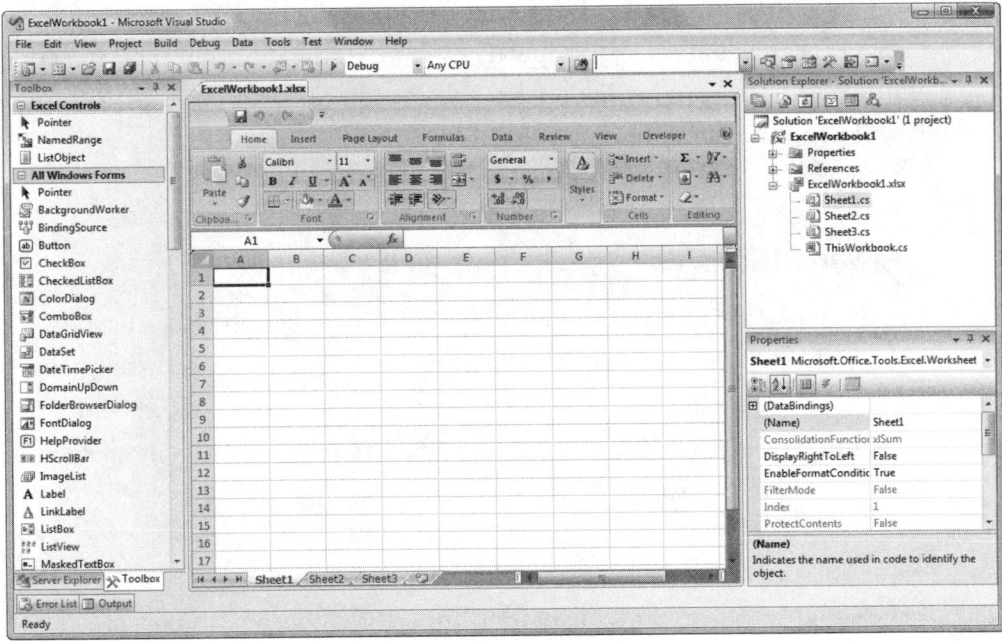

Figure 2-9: The design view for VSTO Excel code behind.

it did for Office 2003. Instead, to access Excel commands you use the Ribbon, and to access Visual Studio commands you use the Visual Studio menus. If you want to make more room in the designer window, you can minimize the Ribbon by right-clicking on the Ribbon tab headings and choosing Minimize the Ribbon from the context menu.

Third, notice in Figure 2-9 that the toolbox contains a new category: Excel Controls. When designing a document using Visual Studio, you can create named ranges and list objects using the Excel commands familiar to Excel users, or the toolbox idiom familiar to Visual Studio users.

Fourth, notice that the Properties window shows the properties of the selected object—in this case, Sheet1. You can use the Properties window to edit properties of Excel's objects the same way that you would edit properties of controls and forms in a Windows Forms project.

Fifth, notice that the Solution Explorer has four classes in it already. Each underlying Excel Worksheet and Workbook object is represented by a .NET class that you can extend and customize. As you make changes to the document in the designer, the code behind updates automatically. For example, drag a list object from the toolbox onto the Sheet1 designer, and draw it to be 10 rows by 4 columns, as shown in Figure 2-10.

As you can see from the Properties window, the designer has chosen a default name for the new list object. We could edit it, but in this example, we will keep the default name `list1`.

New in Office 2007

Office now calls ListObject a table in its UI, although the object model object is still called ListObject. When you create a ListObject using the Visual Studio toolbox, it will be named something like list1, but if you insert a list using the Excel Ribbon it will be named something like Table1. Either way, the type of the object is still Microsoft.Office.Tools.Excel.ListObject.

Let's take a look at the code behind this worksheet and make some simple changes to it. Right-click Sheet1.cs in the Solution Explorer and choose View Code. We are going to briefly illustrate two VSTO features: Actions-

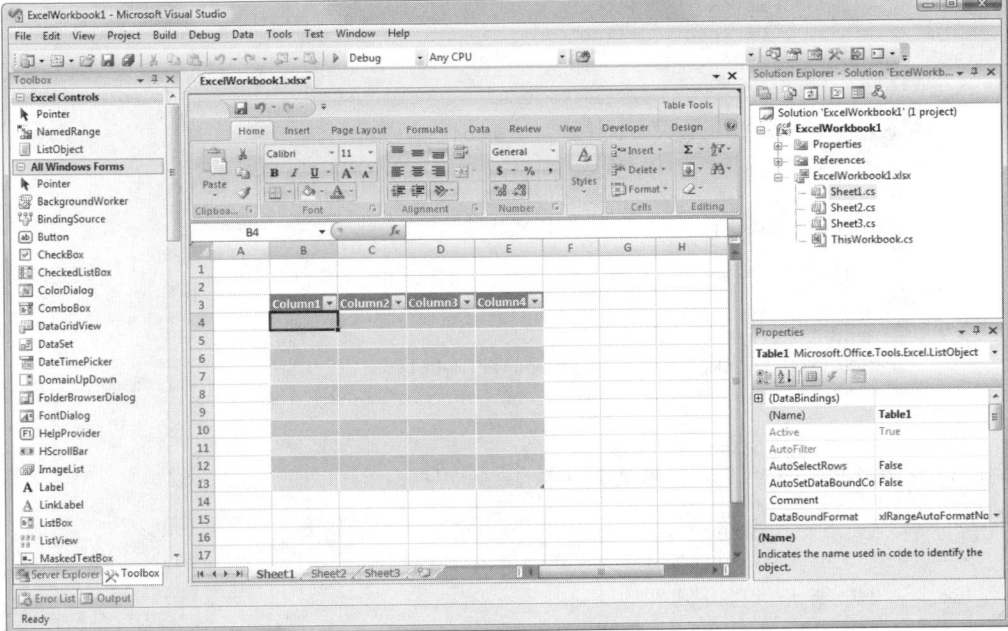

Figure 2-10: Creating a ListObject in the designer.

Pane and list object data binding. We will declare a Windows Forms button as a member variable of the class and call it myButton. In the Startup event, we will show that button in the Document Actions task pane of Excel by adding it to the ActionsPane's Controls collection. Doing so will cause Excel to show the Document Actions task pane and display our button. We will also handle the Click event of the button, and when the button is clicked we will data bind our list object to a randomly generated Data-Table. Listing 2-8 shows this code.

Listing 2-8: A VSTO Customization That Adds a Control to the Document Actions Task Pane and Data Binds a ListObject Control to a DataTable

```
using System;
using System.Collections.Generic;
using System.Data;
using System.Linq;
using System.Text;
using System.Windows.Forms;
using System.Xml.Linq;
using Microsoft.VisualStudio.Tools.Applications.Runtime;
```

```csharp
using Excel = Microsoft.Office.Interop.Excel;
using Office = Microsoft.Office.Core;

namespace ExcelWorkbook1
{
  public partial class Sheet1
  {
    Button myButton = new Button();
    DataTable table;

    private void Sheet1_Startup(object sender, EventArgs e)
    {
      myButton.Text = "Databind!";
      myButton.Click += new EventHandler(myButton_Click);
      Globals.ThisWorkbook.ActionsPane.Controls.Add(myButton);
    }

    void myButton_Click(object sender, EventArgs e)
    {
      list1.DataSource = null;
      table = new DataTable();
      Random r = new Random();

      for (int i = 0; i < 4; i++)
        table.Columns.Add("Col " + i.ToString());

      for (int i = 0; i < 20; i++)
        table.Rows.Add(r.NextDouble(), r.NextDouble(),
          r.NextDouble(), r.NextDouble());

      list1.DataSource = table;
    }

    private void Sheet1_Shutdown(object sender, System.EventArgs e)
    {
    }

    #region VSTO Designer generated code

    /// <summary>
    /// Required method for Designer support - do not modify
    /// the contents of this method with the code editor.
    /// </summary>
    private void InternalStartup()
    {
      this.Startup += new System.EventHandler(Sheet1_Startup);
      this.Shutdown += new System.EventHandler(Sheet1_Shutdown);
    }

    #endregion

  }
}
```

Build and run the code, and, sure enough, Excel starts up, the Startup event is raised for the sheet, and the button is added to the actions pane. Click the button and a random DataTable is generated and bound to the list object, as shown in Figure 2-11. Exit Excel to end your debugging session.

We have briefly illustrated VSTO's support for the Document Actions task pane and the ability to data bind that VSTO adds to Excel's list object. For more information on VSTO's support for the Document Actions task pane, see Chapter 14, "Working with Document-Level Actions Panes." For more information on VSTO's support for data binding, see Chapter 19, "VSTO Data Programming."

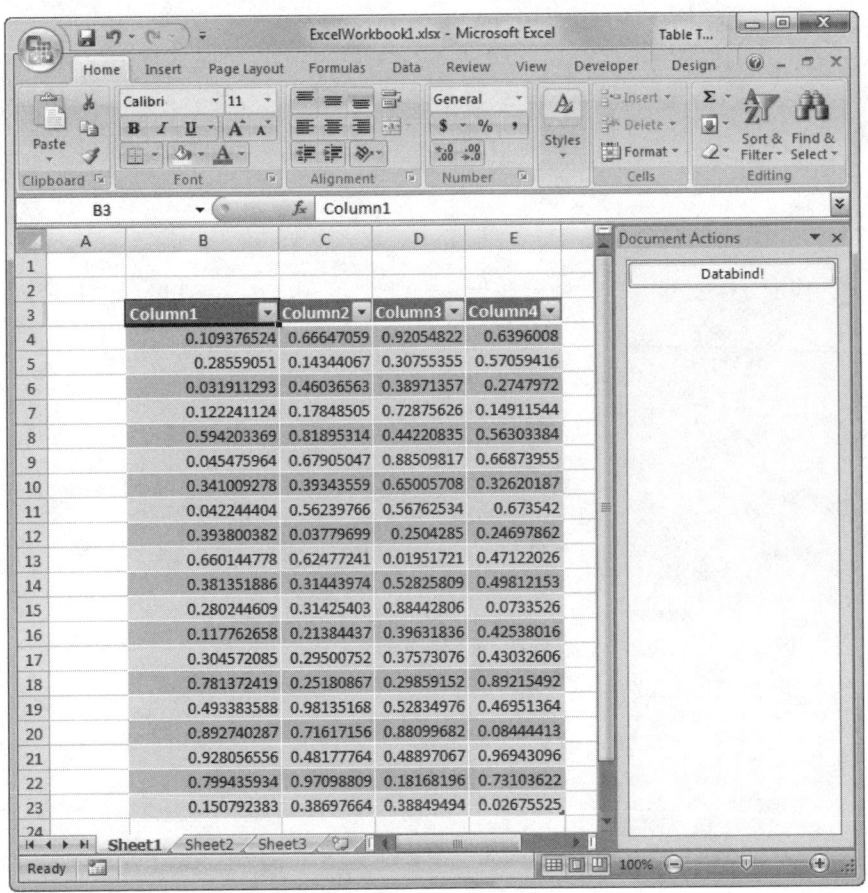

Figure 2-11: The result of running Listing 2-8 and clicking the button we added to the Document Actions task pane.

Conclusion

This chapter introduced the three basic patterns of Office solutions: an automation executable, an add-in, and code behind a document. The chapter also introduced how to build solutions following these three basic patterns using Visual Studio 2008 Tools for Office.

Now that you know how to create a basic automation executable, add-in, and code behind the document solution, you will use these skills in the next chapters as the focus turns to specific functionality of Excel, Word, and Outlook that you can use in your solutions.

This chapter has only served as an introduction to add-ins and code-behind documents. Chapters 12 through 16 cover the code-behind document model of VSTO in detail.

PART II

Office Programming in .NET

The first two chapters of this book introduce Office object models and the Office primary interop assemblies (PIAs). Part I also shows you how to use Visual Studio to build console applications, add-ins, and code behind the document using features of VSTO. The second part of this book covers the Office object models in more depth. If you are interested only in Excel development, read Chapters 3 through 5. If you are interested only in Word development, read Chapters 6 through 8. If you are interested only in Outlook development, read Chapters 9 through 11.

- Chapter 3, "Programming Excel," shows how you can customize Excel and, in particular, how you can create custom formulas for Excel.
- Chapter 4, "Working with Excel Events," covers the events Excel raises that your code can handle.
- Chapter 5, "Working with Excel Objects," covers the object model of Excel in some detail, focusing on the most commonly used objects, properties, and methods.
- Chapter 6, "Programming Word," shows how you can customize Word and, in particular, how you can create research services for Word and other Office applications.

- Chapter 7, "Working with Word Events," covers the events Word raises that your code can handle.
- Chapter 8, "Working with Word Objects," covers the object model of Word in some detail, focusing on the most commonly used objects, properties, and methods.
- Chapter 9, "Programming Outlook," shows how you can customize Outlook and, in particular, how you can create custom property pages for Outlook.
- Chapter 10, "Working with Outlook Events," covers the events Outlook raises that your code can handle.
- Chapter 11, "Working with Outlook Objects," covers the object model of Outlook in some detail, focusing on the most commonly used objects, properties, and methods.

3

Programming Excel

Ways to Customize Excel

Excel is the application most frequently programmed against in the Office family. Excel has a very rich object model with 247 objects that combined have more than 5,000 properties and methods. It supports several models for integrating your code, including add-ins and code behind documents. Most of these models were originally designed to allow the integration of COM components written in Visual Basic 6, VBA, C, or C++. However, through COM interop, managed objects written in C# or Visual Basic can masquerade as COM objects and participate in most of these models. This chapter briefly considers several of the ways that you can integrate your code with Excel and refers you to other chapters that discuss these approaches in more depth. This chapter also explores building user-defined functions for Excel and introduces the Excel object model.

New Objects in Excel 2007

Excel 2007 introduces 51 new objects to the object model. These new objects are, listed alphabetically: AboveAverage, Action, Actions, Chart-Format, ChartView, ColorScale, ColorScaleCriteria, ColorScaleCriterion,

ColorStop, ColorStops, ConditionValue, Connections, Databar, Dialog-SheetView, FormatColor, HeaderFooter, Icon, IconCriteria, IconCriterion, IconSet, IconSetCondition, IconSets, LinearGradient, ModuleView, Multi-ThreadedCalculation, ODBCConnection, OLEDBConnection, Page, Pages, PivotAxis, PivotFilter, PivotFilters, PivotLine, PivotLineCells, PivotLines, Ranges, RectangularGradient, Research, ServerViewableItems, SheetViews, Sort, SortField, SortFields, TableStyle, TableStyleElement, TableStyle-Elements, TableStyles, Top10, UniqueValues, WorkbookConnection, and WorksheetView.

Automation Executable

As mentioned in Chapter 2, "Introduction to Office Solutions," the simplest way to integrate with Excel is to start Excel from a console application or Windows Forms application and automate it from that external program. Chapter 2 provides a sample of an automation executable that automates Word and an automation executable that automates Excel.

VSTO Add-Ins

When building add-ins for Excel, you have two choices: You can build a COM add-in (sometimes called a shared add-in) or a VSTO Excel add-in. A VSTO Excel add-in solves many of the problems associated with COM add-in development and is the preferred model for Excel 2003 and Excel 2007 add-in development. The only time you would want to consider building a COM add-in instead is if you need to target versions of Excel older than Excel 2003.

An add-in is typically written to add application-level functionality—functionality that is available to any workbook opened by Excel. For example, you might write an add-in that adds a Ribbon button to convert a currency in the selected Excel worksheet cell to another currency based on current exchange rates.

Excel has a COM Add-Ins dialog box that enables users to turn COM and VSTO add-ins on and off. To access the COM Add-Ins dialog box, you must perform the following steps:

1. Click the Office menu (the large circle with the Office logo on it in the top-left corner of the Excel window), and choose Excel Options from the bottom of the menu that drops down.

2. Click the Add-Ins tab on the left side of the Excel Options dialog box.

3. Choose COM Add-Ins from the drop-down Manage menu, and click the Go button.

After you complete these steps, the COM Add-Ins dialog box appears. Figure 3-1 shows this dialog box.

The COM Add-ins dialog box shows both older-style COM add-ins and newer-style VSTO add-ins. In Figure 3-1, you can tell that ExcelAddIn1 is a VSTO add-in because of the Location information shown below; rather than showing the path to a DLL, which would indicate a COM add-in, the dialog box shows the path to a .vsto file, which indicates a VSTO add-in.

You can add COM add-ins by using the Add button and remove them by using the Remove button. Typically, you will not have your users use this dialog box to manage COM add-ins. Instead, you will install and remove a COM add-in by manipulating registry settings with the installer you create for your COM add-in. You can't add VSTO add-ins by using the Add button in the COM Add-Ins dialog box; you must install them by double-clicking a .vsto file or a setup.exe file associated with the VSTO add-in.

Excel discovers the installed add-ins by reading from the registry. You can view the registry on your computer by going to the Windows Start

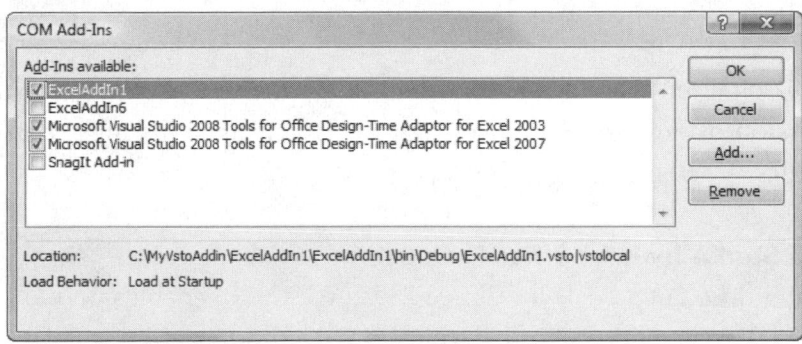

Figure 3-1: The COM Add-Ins dialog box in Excel.

menu and choosing Run. In the Run dialog box, type regedit for the pro-gram to run, and then click the OK button. In Vista, type regedit in the search box that appears at the bottom of the Windows Start menu. Excel looks for VSTO and COM add-ins in the registry keys under HKEY_CURRENT_USER\Software\Microsoft\Office\Excel\Addins. Excel also looks for COM add-ins in the registry keys under HKEY_LOCAL_MACHINE\Software\Microsoft\Office\Excel\Addins. COM add-ins reg-istered under HKEY_LOCAL_MACHINE are not shown in the COM Add-Ins dialog box and cannot be turned on or off by users. It is recommended you do not register your COM add-in under HKEY_LOCAL_MACHINE because it hides the COM add-in from the user.

VSTO add-ins are discussed in detail in Chapter 12, "The VSTO Pro-gramming Model."

Automation Add-Ins

Automation add-ins are classes that are registered in the registry as COM objects that expose public functions that can be used in Excel formulas. Automation add-ins that have been installed are shown in the Add-Ins dialog box, which you can access by following these steps:

1. Click the Office menu (the large circle with the Office logo on it in the top-left corner of the Excel window), and choose Excel Options from the bottom of the menu that drops down.
2. Click the Add-Ins tab on the left side of the Excel Options dialog box.
3. Choose Excel Add-Ins from the drop-down Manage menu, and click the Go button.

This chapter examines automation add-ins in more detail during the discussion of how to create user-defined Excel functions for use in Excel formulas.

Visual Studio Tools for Office Code Behind

Visual Studio 2008 Tools for Office 2007 (VSTO 3.0) enables you to put C# or Visual Basic code behind Excel templates and workbooks. The code-behind model was designed from the ground up for managed code, so this model is the most ".NET" of all the models used to customize Excel. This model is used when you want to customize the behavior of a particular workbook or a particular set of workbooks created from a common template. For example, you might create a template for an expense-reporting workbook that is used whenever anyone in your company creates an expense report. This template can add commands and functionality that are always available when the workbook created with it is opened.

VSTO's support for code behind a workbook is discussed in detail in Part III of this book.

Smart Documents and XML Expansion Packs

Smart documents are another way to associate your code with an Excel template or workbook. Smart documents rely on attaching an XML schema to a workbook or template and associating your code with that schema. The combination of the schema and associated code is called an XML Expansion Pack. An XML Expansion Pack can be associated with an Excel workbook by choosing XML Expansion Packs from the XML menu in the Data menu. Figure 3-2 shows the XML Expansion Packs dialog box.

When an XML Expansion Pack is attached to a workbook, Excel loads the associated code and runs it while that workbook is opened. Smart document solutions can create a custom user interface in the Document Actions task pane. Figure 3-3 shows a custom Document Actions task pane in Excel.

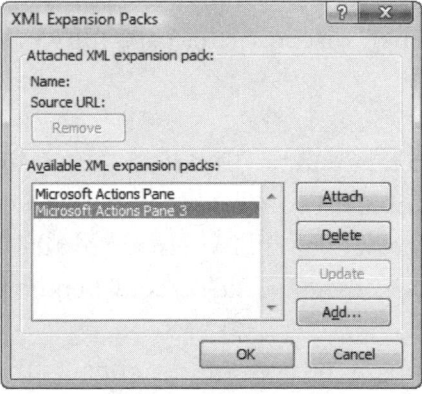

Figure 3-2: The XML Expansion Packs dialog box in Excel.

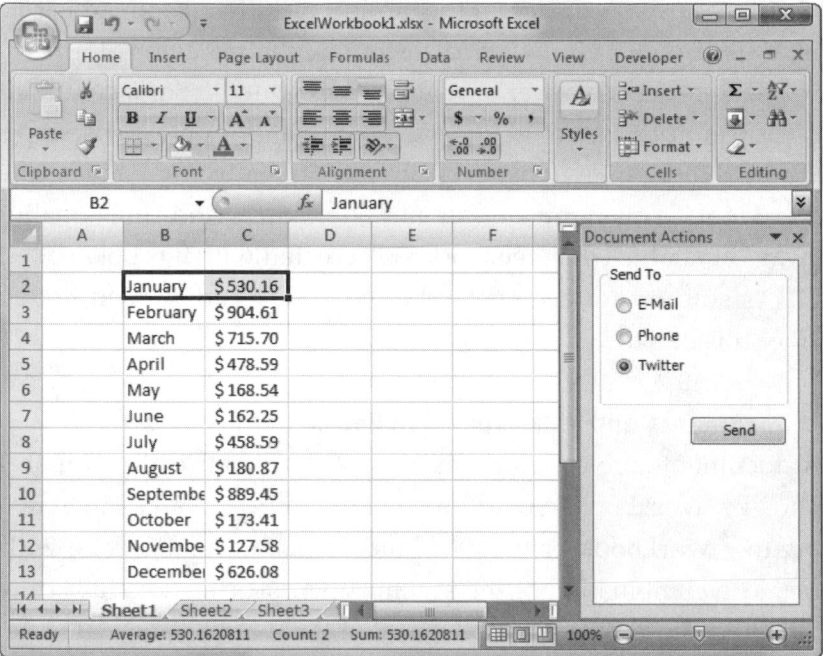

Figure 3-3: A custom Document Actions task pane in Excel.

It is possible to write smart document solutions "from scratch" in C# or Visual Basic. This book does not cover this approach. Instead, this book focuses on the VSTO approach, which was designed to make smart document development much easier and allow you to create a custom Document Actions task pane using Windows Forms. Chapter 14, "Working with Document-Level Actions Pane," discusses this capability in more detail.

Smart Tags

Smart Tags enable a pop-up menu to be displayed containing actions relevant for a recognized piece of text in a workbook. You can control the text that Excel recognizes and the actions that are made available for that text by creating a Smart Tag DLL or by using VSTO code behind a document or a VSTO add-in.

A Smart Tag DLL contains two types of components that are used by Excel: a recognizer and associated actions. A recognizer determines what text in the workbook is recognized as a Smart Tag. An action corresponds to a menu command displayed in the pop-up menu.

A recognizer could be created that tells Excel to recognize stock-ticker symbols (such as the MSFT stock symbol) and display a set of actions that can be taken for that symbol: buy, sell, get the latest price, get history, and so on. A "get history" action, for instance, could launch a Web browser to show a stock history Web page for the stock symbol that was recognized.

When a recognizer recognizes some text, Excel displays a little triangle in the lower-right corner of the associated cell. If the user hovers over the cell, a pop-up menu icon appears next to the cell that the user can click to drop down a menu of actions for the recognized piece of text. Figure 3-4 shows an example menu. When an action is selected, Excel calls back into the associated action to execute your code.

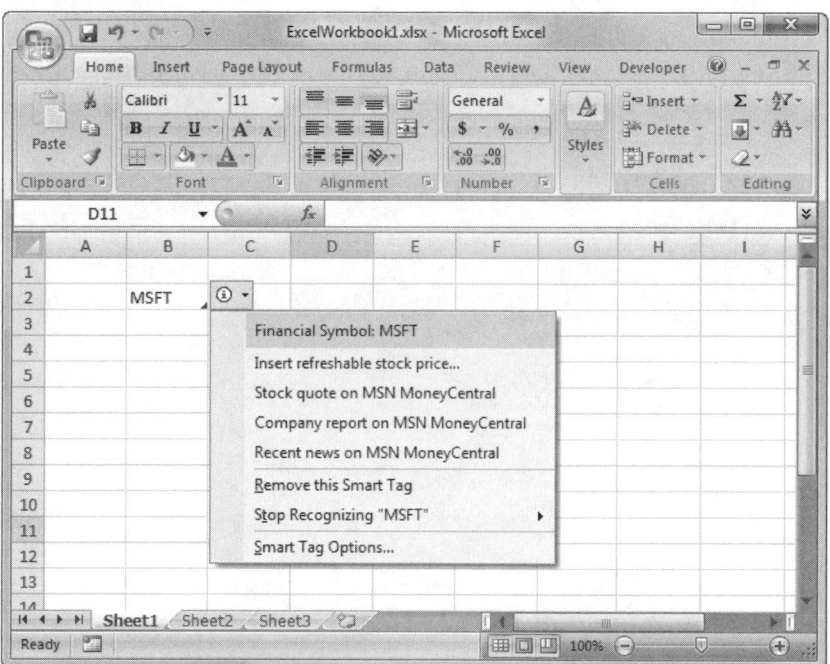

Figure 3-4: Smart Tags in Excel.

Smart Tags are managed from the Smart Tags page of the AutoCorrect dialog box, as shown in Figure 3-5. You can display the Smart Tags page by following these steps:

1. Click the Office button (the large circle with the Office logo on it in the top-left corner of the Excel window), and choose Excel Options from the bottom of the menu that drops down.
2. Click the Proofing tab on the left side of the Excel Options dialog box.
3. Click the AutoCorrect Options button.
4. Click the Smart Tags page.

On the Smart Tags page of the AutoCorrect dialog box, the user can turn on and off individual recognizers as well as control other options relating to how Smart Tags display in the workbook.

It is possible to write Smart Tags from scratch in C# or Visual Basic, and the first edition of this book covers this approach. VSTO provides a simpler model for creating a Smart Tag that works at the workbook, template, and (new in VSTO 2008 SP1) add-in levels. Chapter 18, "Working with

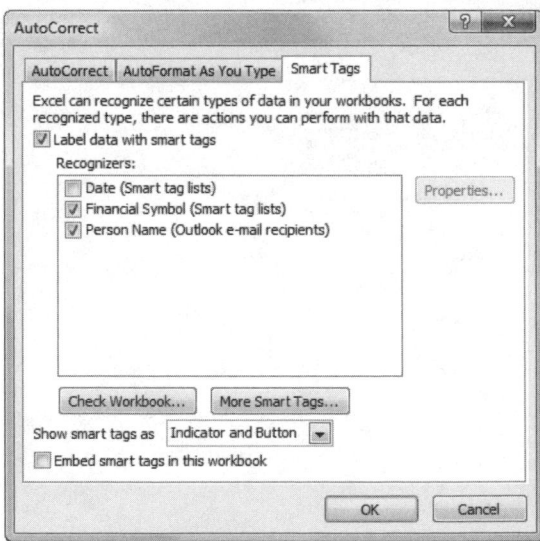

Figure 3-5: The Smart Tags page in the AutoCorrect dialog box.

Smart Tags in VSTO," describes the VSTO model for working with Smart Tags in more detail.

XLA Add-Ins

Also listed in the Excel Add-Ins dialog box (follow the steps for showing the dialog box for Automation add-ins, described earlier in this chapter) are XLA add-ins. An XLA add-in starts life as a workbook that has VBA code behind it. The developer can then save the workbook as an XLA or Excel add-in file by using Save As from the File menu and selecting XLA as the file format. An XLA file acts as an application-level add-in in the form of an invisible workbook that stays open for the lifetime of Excel. Although it is possible to save a workbook customized with VSTO as an XLA file, many of the features of VSTO do not work when the workbook is converted to an XLA file. Some of the features that do not work include VSTO's support for the Document Actions task pane and for Smart Tags. For this reason, Microsoft does not support or recommend saving a workbook customized with VSTO as an XLA file. Therefore, this book does not cover it further.

Server-Generated Documents

VSTO enables you to write code on the server that populates an Excel workbook with data without starting Excel on the server. You might create an ASP.NET page that reads some data out of a database and then puts it in an Excel workbook and returns that workbook to the client of the Web page. VSTO provides a class called ServerDocument that makes this process easy. Chapter 20, "Server Data Scenarios," describes generating documents on the server using the ServerDocument class.

You can also use the XML features and file formats of Office to generate Excel workbooks on the server—an approach that is more complex but that allows you to generate more complex documents.

Research Services

Excel has a task pane, called the Research task pane, that enables you to enter a search term and search various sources for that search term. To show the Research task pane, click the Research button in the Review tab. Figure 3-6 shows the Research task pane.

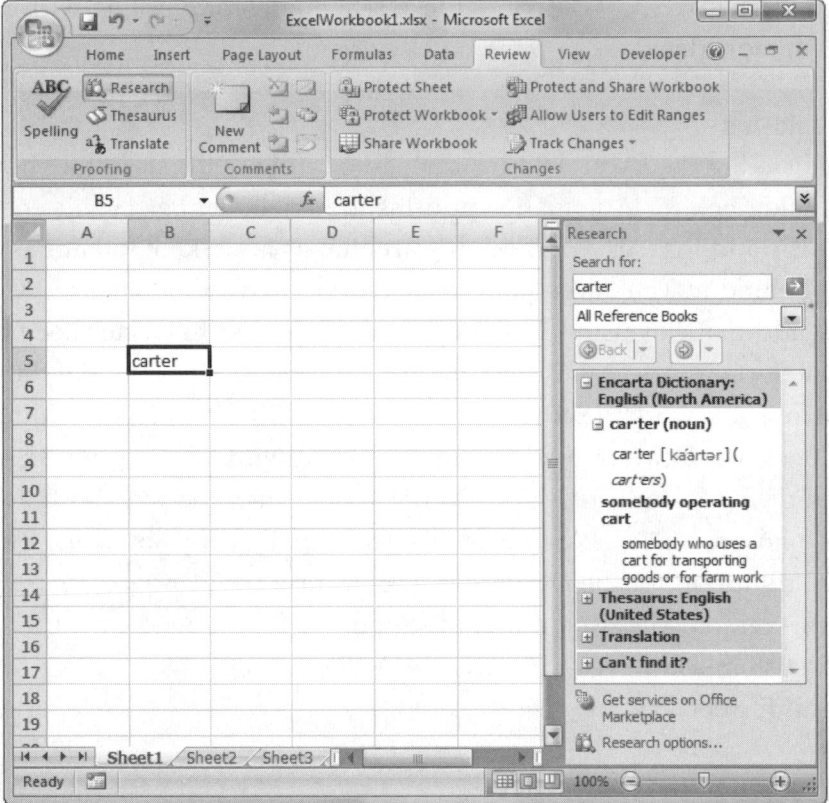

Figure 3-6: The Research task pane.

Excel enables developers to write a special Web service, called a research service, that implements a set of Web methods defined by Excel. A research service can be registered with Excel and used in Office's Research task pane. For example, you might write a research service that searches for a search term in a company database. Chapter 6, "Programming Word," discusses creating a research service in more detail.

Programming User-Defined Functions

Excel enables the creation of user-defined functions that can be used in Excel formulas. A developer must create a special kind of DLL called an XLL. Excel also allows you to write custom functions in VBA that can be used in Excel formulas. Unfortunately, Excel does not support writing an XLL that uses managed code.

Building a Managed Automation Add-In That Provides User-Defined Functions

Fortunately, there is an easier way to create a user-defined function that does not require you to create an XLL. Excel 2007 supports a customization technology called an automation add-in that can easily be created in C# or Visual Basic.

First, launch Visual Studio and create a new C# class library project. Name the project AutomationAddin. In your Class1.cs file created for you in the new project, replace Class1 with the code shown in Listing 3-1. Replace the GUID string in the listing with your own GUID by choosing Tools > Generate GUID. In the Generate GUID dialog box, pick option 4, Registry Format. Click the Copy button to put the new GUID string on the clipboard. Click Exit to exit the Generate GUID tool. Finally, select the GUID string in the listing ("5268ABE2-9B09-439d-BE97-2EA60E103EF6"), and replace it with your new GUID string. You'll also have to remove the { } brackets that get copied as part of the GUID.

Listing 3-1 defines a class called MyFunctions that implements a function called MultiplyNTimes. We will use this function as a custom formula. Our class also implements RegisterFunction and UnregisterFunction, which are attributed with the ComRegisterFunction attribute and ComUnregisterFunction attribute respectively. The RegisterFunction will be called when the assembly is registered for COM interop. The UnregisterFunction will be called when the assembly is unregistered for COM interop. These functions put a necessary key in the registry (the Programmable key) that allows Excel to know that this class can be used as an automation add-in. RegisterFunction also works around another issue that occurs when registering the class. Excel needs a full path to the .NET component that loads the automation add-in—a component called mscoree.dll. So RegisterFunction contains some code to put the full path to mscoree.dll in the registry.

Listing 3-1: A C# Class Called MyFunctions That Exposes a User-Defined
Function MultiplyNTimes

```
using System;
using System.Collections.Generic;
```

```csharp
using System.Linq;
using System.Text;
using System.Runtime.InteropServices;
using Microsoft.Win32;

namespace AutomationAddin
{
  // Replace the GUID below with your own GUID that
  // you generate using Create GUID from the Tools menu
  [Guid("5268ABE2-9B09-439d-BE97-2EA60E103EF6")]
  [ClassInterface(ClassInterfaceType.AutoDual)]
  [ComVisible(true)]
  public class MyFunctions
  {
    public MyFunctions()
    {
    }

    public double MultiplyNTimes(double number1,
      double number2, double timesToMultiply)
    {
      double result = number1;
      for (double i = 0; i < timesToMultiply; i++)
      {
        result = result * number2;
      }
      return result;
    }

    [ComRegisterFunctionAttribute]
    public static void RegisterFunction(Type type)
    {
      Registry.ClassesRoot.CreateSubKey(
        GetSubKeyName(type, "Programmable"));
      RegistryKey key = Registry.ClassesRoot.OpenSubKey(
        GetSubKeyName(type, "InprocServer32"), true);
      key.SetValue("",
        System.Environment.SystemDirectory + @"\mscoree.dll",
        RegistryValueKind.String);
    }

    [ComUnregisterFunctionAttribute]
    public static void UnregisterFunction(Type type)
    {
      Registry.ClassesRoot.DeleteSubKey(
        GetSubKeyName(type, "Programmable"), false);
    }

    private static string GetSubKeyName(Type type,
      string subKeyName)
    {
```

```
      System.Text.StringBuilder s =
        new System.Text.StringBuilder();
      s.Append(@"CLSID\{");
      s.Append(type.GUID.ToString().ToUpper());
      s.Append(@"}\");
      s.Append(subKeyName);
      return s.ToString();
    }
  }
}
```

With this code written (remember to replace the GUID in the listing with your own GUID that you generate by choosing Tools > Generate GUID), you need to configure the project to be registered for COM interop so that Excel can see it. Go to the properties for the project by double-clicking the Properties node in Solution Explorer. In the properties designer that appears, click the Build tab, and check the check box labeled Register for COM Interop, as shown in Figure 3-7. This step causes Visual Studio to register the assembly for COM interop when the project is built.

If you are running under Vista or later, you need to run Visual Studio as administrator, because registering for COM interop requires administrative privileges. If you aren't already running Visual Studio as administrator, save your project and exit Visual Studio. Then find the Visual Studio 2008 icon in the Start menu, right-click it, and choose Run as Administrator (see Figure 3-8). When you're running Visual Studio as administrator, reopen your project and choose Build > Rebuild Solution. Visual Studio will do the necessary registration to make your class visible to Excel.

Using Your Managed Automation Add-In in Excel

Now that the add-in is built and registered, to load the managed automation add-in into Excel, follow these steps:

1. Launch Excel, and click the Microsoft Office button in the top-left corner of the window.
2. Choose Excel Options.
3. Click the Add-Ins tab in the Excel Options dialog box.
4. Choose Excel Add-Ins from the combo box labeled Manage, and click the Go button.

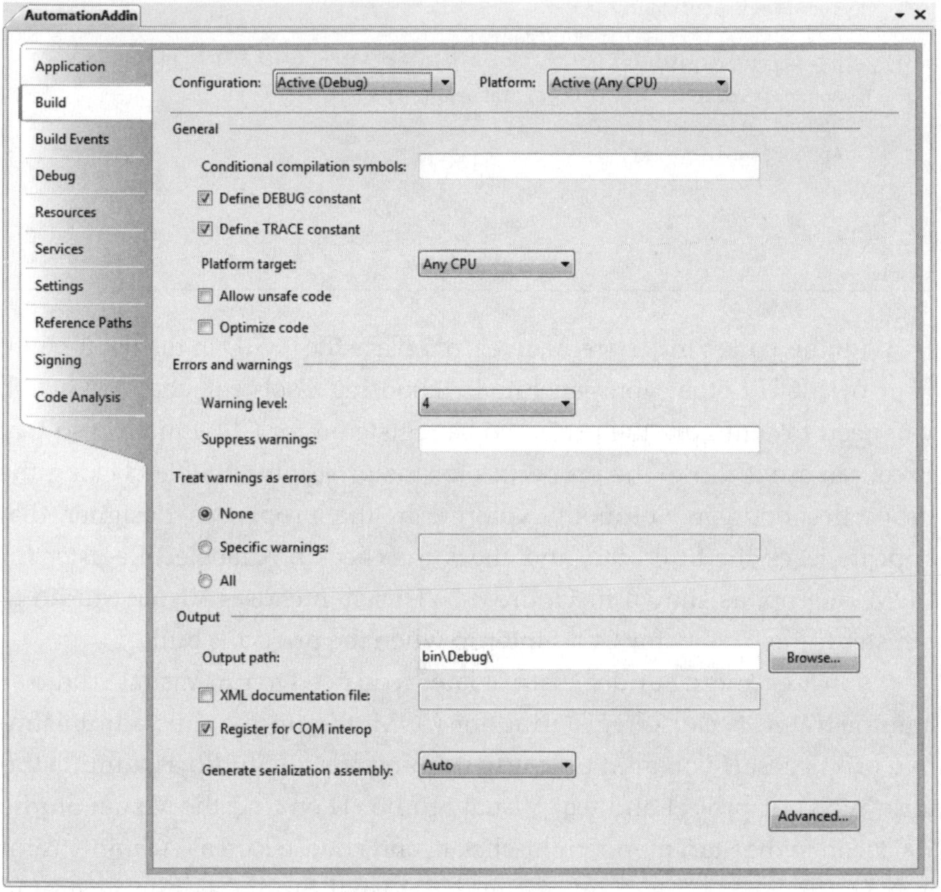

AutomationAddin　　　　　　　　　　　　　　　　　　　　　　　　▾ ✕

| Application |
| Build |
| Build Events |
| Debug |
| Resources |
| Services |
| Settings |
| Reference Paths |
| Signing |
| Code Analysis |

Configuration: [Active (Debug) ▾]　　Platform: [Active (Any CPU) ▾]

General

Conditional compilation symbols: [＿＿＿＿＿＿＿＿＿＿＿＿＿]

☑ Define DEBUG constant

☑ Define TRACE constant

Platform target:　　　　[Any CPU　　▾]

☐ Allow unsafe code

☐ Optimize code

Errors and warnings

Warning level:　　　　　[4　　　　　▾]

Suppress warnings:　　　[＿＿＿＿＿＿＿＿＿＿＿＿]

Treat warnings as errors

◉ None

○ Specific warnings:　　[＿＿＿＿＿＿＿＿＿＿＿＿]

○ All

Output

Output path:　　　　　　bin\Debug\　　　　　　　　[Browse...]

☐ XML documentation file:　[＿＿＿＿＿＿＿＿＿＿＿＿]

☑ Register for COM interop

Generate serialization assembly:　[Auto　　▾]

　　　　　　　　　　　　　　　　　　　　　　[Advanced...]

Figure 3-7:　Checking the Register for COM Interop check box in the project properties designer.

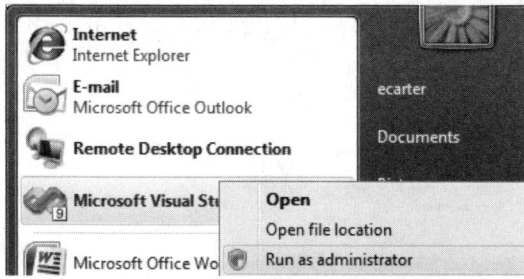

Figure 3-8:　Launching Visual Studio 2008 as administrator under Vista.

5. Click the Automation button in the Add-Ins dialog box.

6. Look through the list of Automation Servers, and find the class you created; it will be listed as AutomationAddin.MyFunctions, as shown in Figure 3-9.

By clicking OK in this dialog box, you have added the `Automation-Addin.MyFunctions` class to the list of installed automation add-ins, as shown in Figure 3-10.

Now, try to use the function `MultiplyNTimes` in an Excel formula. First create a simple spreadsheet that has a number, a second number to multiply the first by, and a third number for how many times you want to multiply the first number by the second number. Figure 3-11 shows the spreadsheet.

Click an empty cell in the workbook below the numbers, and then click the Insert Function button (the button with the "fx" label) in the formula bar. From the dialog box of available formulas, drop down the "Or select a category" drop-down box and choose `AutomationAddin.MyFunctions`. Then click the `MultiplyNTimes` function, as shown in Figure 3-12.

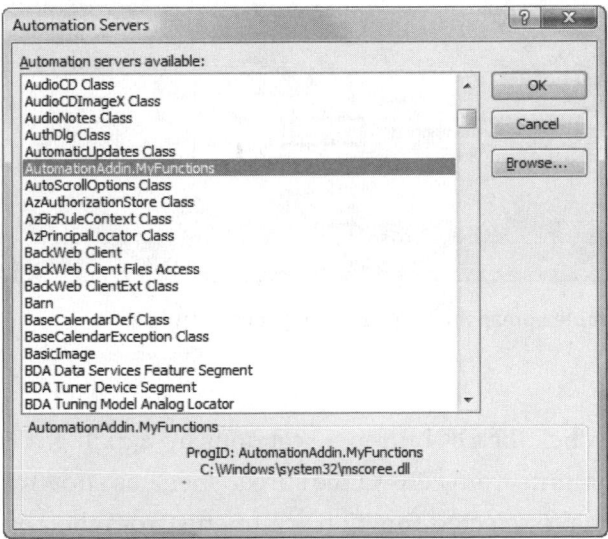

Figure 3-9: Selecting AutomationAddin.MyFunctions from the Automation Servers dialog box.

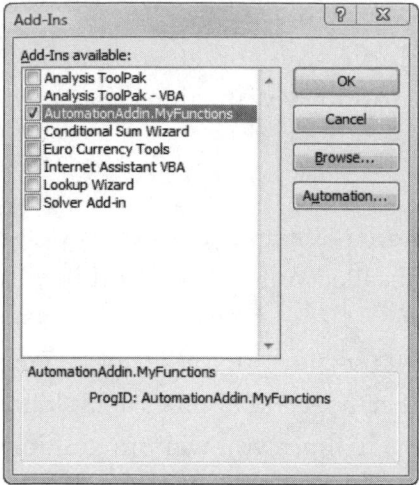

Figure 3-10: AutomationAddin.MyFunctions is now installed.

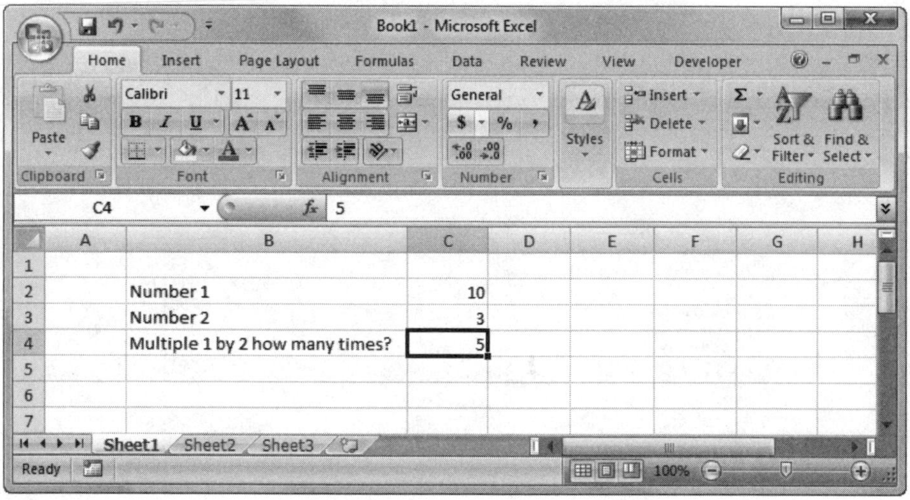

Figure 3-11: A simple spreadsheet to test the custom formula in.

When you click the OK button, Excel pops up a dialog box to help select function arguments from cells in the spreadsheet, as shown in Figure 3-13.

After you have selected function arguments from the appropriate cells, click OK to create the final spreadsheet, as shown in Figure 3-14, with the custom formula in cell C5.

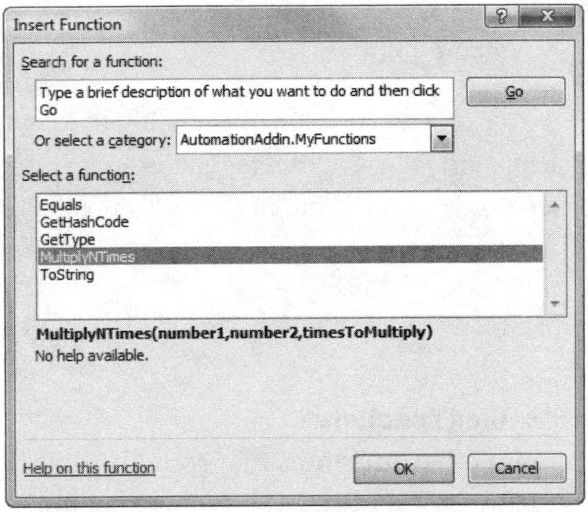

Figure 3-12: Picking MultiplyNTimes from the Insert Function dialog box.

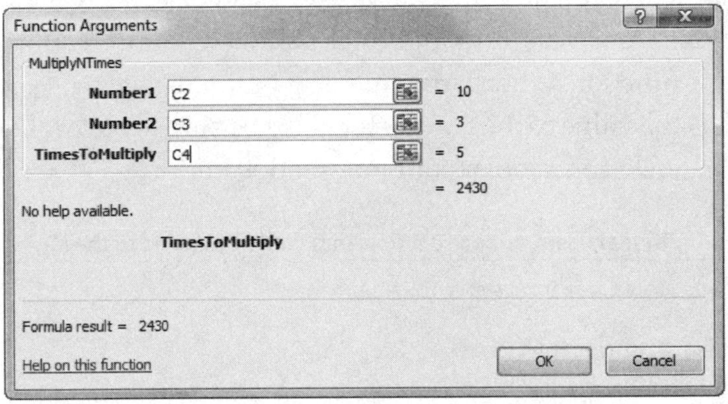

Figure 3-13: Setting arguments using the Function Arguments dialog box.

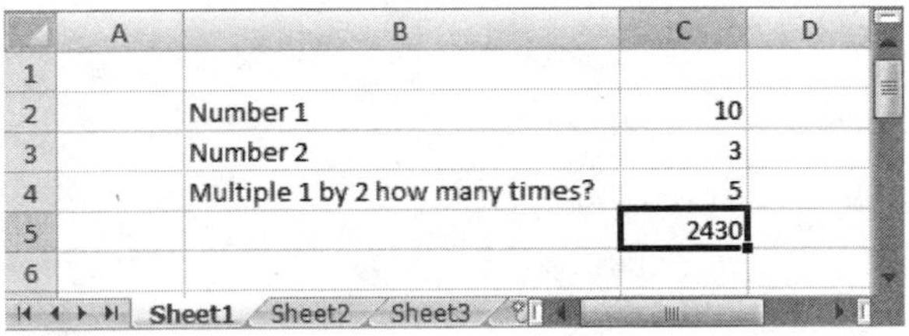

Figure 3-14: The final spreadsheet.

Non-English Locales and Excel

Excel and .NET have some special issues when running in a non-English locale that may cause an automation add-in to fail. For more information, see the section "Special Excel Issues" in Chapter 5, "Working with Excel Objects." VSTO add-ins have some additional features that protect you from these issues.

Some Additional User-Defined Functions

You might experiment with other functions that could be used in an Excel formula. For example, Listing 3-2 shows several other functions you could add to your MyFunctions class. To use Listing 3-2, you must add a reference to the Excel 12.0 Object Library and add the code using Excel = Microsoft.Office.Interop.Excel to the top of your class file. Note in particular that when you declare a parameter as an object, Excel passes you a Range object. Also note how optional parameters are supported by the AddNumbers function. When a parameter is omitted, System.Type.Missing is passed as the value of the parameter. Also be sure to restart Excel so that it loads the newest version of your automation add-in.

Listing 3-2: Additional User-Defined Function That Could Be Added to the MyFunctions Class

```
public string GetStars(int number)
{
  System.Text.StringBuilder s =
    new System.Text.StringBuilder();
  s.Append('*', number);
  return s.ToString();
}

public double AddNumbers(double number1,
  [Optional] object number2, [Optional] object number3)
{
  double result = number1;

  if (number2 != System.Type.Missing)
  {
    Excel.Range r2 = number2 as Excel.Range;
    double d2 = Convert.ToDouble(r2.Value2);
    result += d2;
  }
```

```csharp
  if (number3 != System.Type.Missing)
  {
    Excel.Range r3 = number3 as Excel.Range;
    double d3 = Convert.ToDouble(r3.Value2);
    result += d3;
  }

  return result;
}

public double CalculateArea(object range)
{
  Excel.Range r = range as Excel.Range;
  return Convert.ToDouble(r.Width) *
    Convert.ToDouble(r.Height);
}

public double NumberOfCells(object range)
{
  Excel.Range r = range as Excel.Range;
  return r.Cells.Count;
}

public string ToUpperCase(string input)
{
  return input.ToUpper();
}
```

Debugging User-Defined Functions in Managed Automation Add-Ins

You can debug a C# class library project that is acting as an automation add-in by setting Excel to be the program your class library project starts when you debug. Show the properties for the project by double-clicking the Properties node under the project node in Solution Explorer. In the properties designer that appears, click the Debug tab, and in the Start external program text box, type the full path to Excel.exe, as shown in Figure 3-15. Now, set a breakpoint on one of your user functions, press F5, and use the function in the spreadsheet. The debugger will stop in the implementation of your user function where the breakpoint was set.

Deploying Managed Automation Add-Ins

To deploy an automation add-in, right-click your solution in Solution Explorer and choose New Project from the Add menu. From the Add New Project dialog box, choose Setup Project from Other Project Types\Setup and Deployment in the Project Types tree.

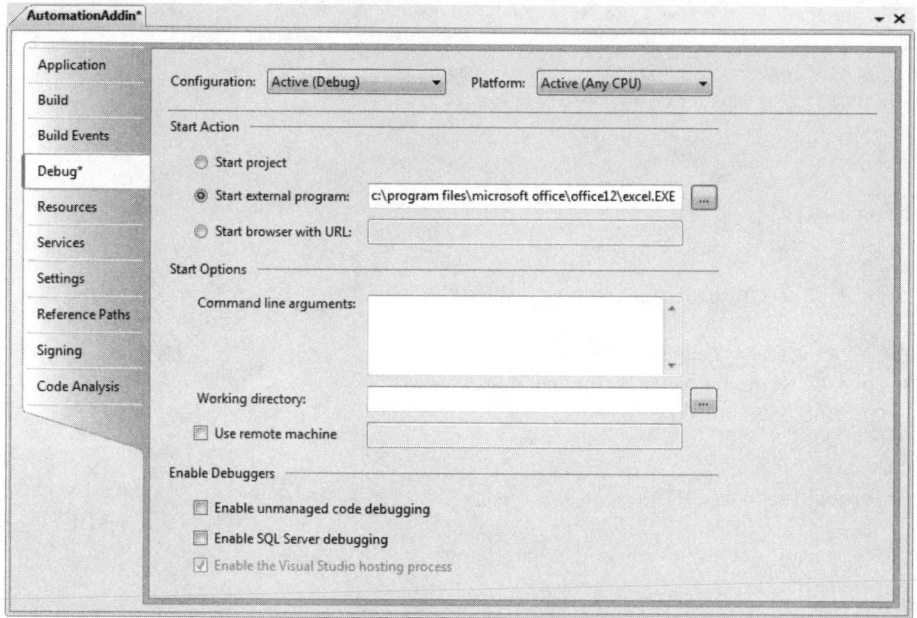

Figure 3-15: Setting Debug options to start Excel.

Right-click the newly added setup project in Solution Explorer and choose Project Output from the Add menu. From the Add Project Output Group dialog box, choose the AutomationAddin project and select Primary Output, as shown in Figure 3-16.

You must also configure the install project to register the managed object for COM interop at install time. To do this, click the Primary output from AutomationAddin node in the setup project. In the Properties window for the primary output (our C# DLL), make sure that Register is set to vsdrpCOM.

Introduction to the Excel Object Model

Regardless of the approach you choose to integrate your code with Excel, you will eventually need to talk to the Excel object model to get things done. It is impossible to completely describe the Excel object model in this book, but we try to make you familiar with the most important objects in the Excel object model and show some of the most frequently used methods, properties, and events on these objects.

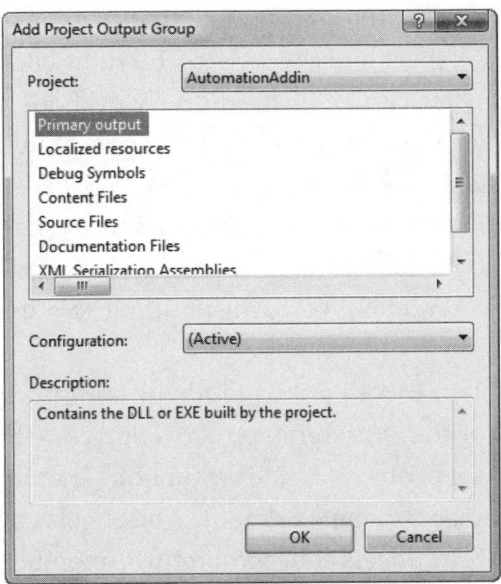

Figure 3-16: Adding the Primary Output of the AutomationAddin project to the setup project.

The first step in learning the Excel object model is getting an idea for the basic structure of the object model hierarchy. Figure 3-17 shows the most critical objects in the Excel object model and their hierarchical relationship.

A Workbook object has a collection called Sheets. The Sheets collection can contain objects of type Worksheet or Chart. A Chart is sometimes

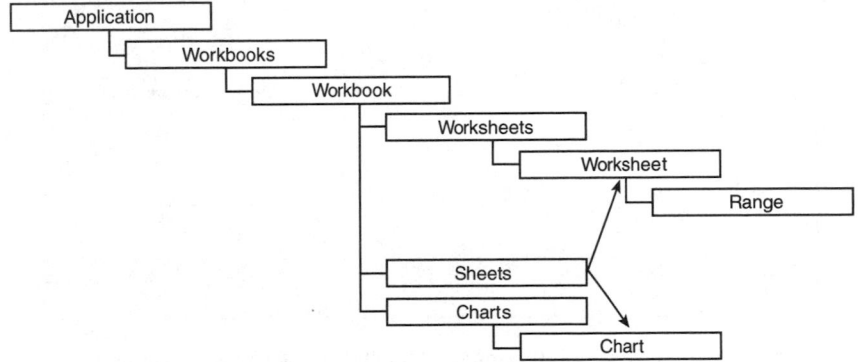

Figure 3-17: The basic hierarchy of the Excel object model.

called a chart sheet because it covers the entire area that a worksheet would cover. You can insert a chart sheet into a workbook by right-clicking the worksheet tabs in the lower-left corner of the Excel workbook and choosing Insert. Figure 3-18 shows the dialog box that appears. Note that two additional objects are found in the Sheets collection: MS Excel 4.0 macro sheets and MS Excel 5.0 dialog sheets. If you insert a macro sheet or dialog sheet into an Excel workbook, it is treated as a special kind of worksheet—there is not a special object model type corresponding to a macro sheet or a dialog sheet.

Because a workbook can contain these various kinds of objects, Excel provides several collections off of the Workbook object. The Worksheets collection contains just the Worksheet objects in the workbook. The Charts collection contains just the chart sheets in the workbook. The Sheets collection is a mixed collection of both. The Sheets collection returns members of the collection as type object—you must cast the returned object to a Worksheet or Chart. In this book, when we talk about an object that could be either a Worksheet or a Chart, we refer to it as a sheet.

Figure 3-19 shows a more complete hierarchy tree with the major objects associated with the objects in Figure 3-17. This starts to give you an

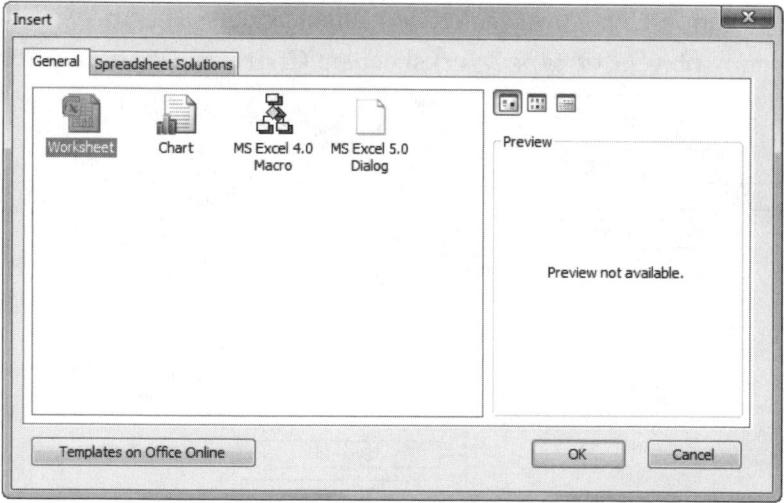

Figure 3-18: Inserting various kinds of "sheets" into an Excel Workbook.

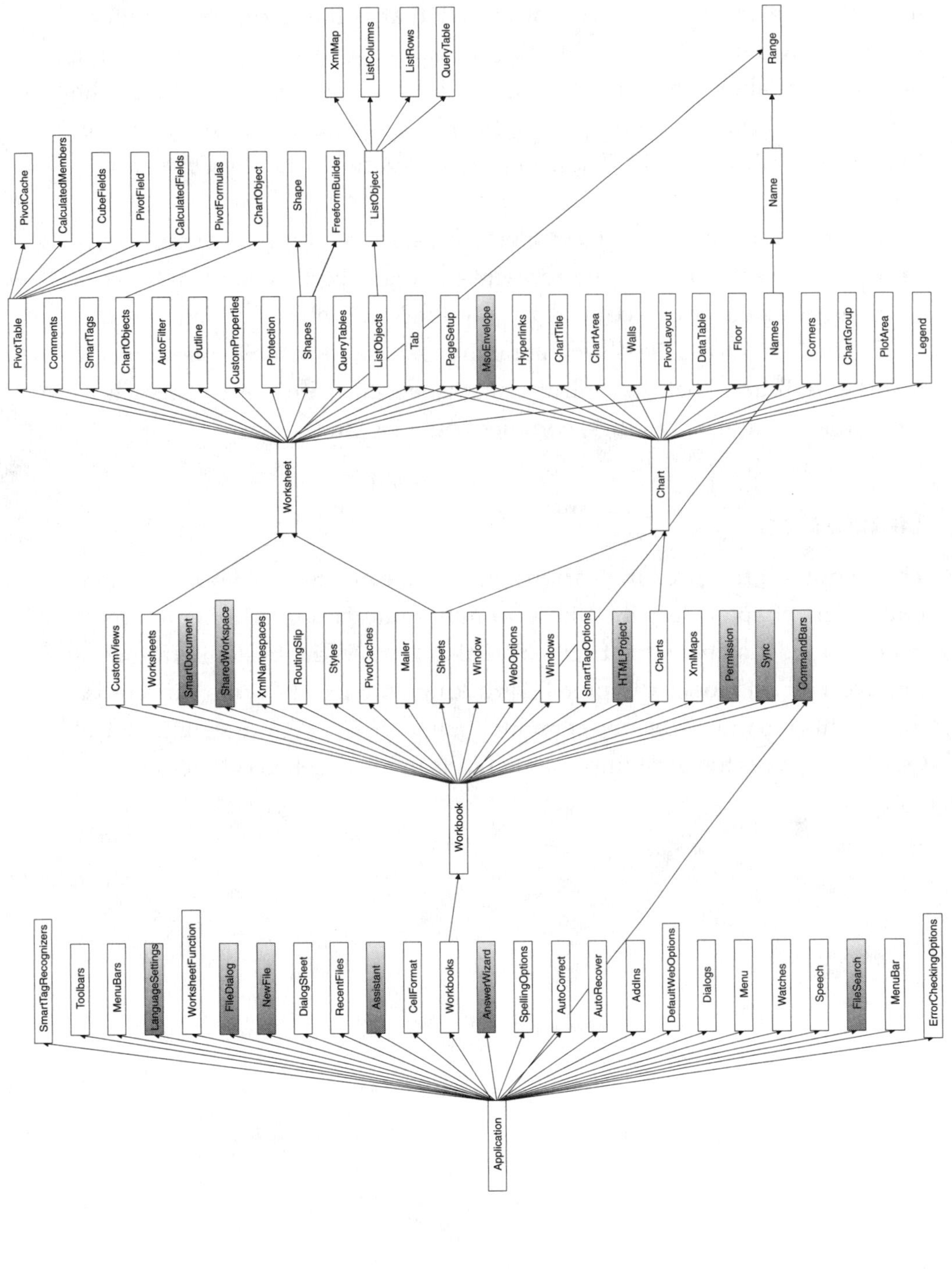

Figure 3-19: A more detailed hierarchy of some major objects in the Excel object model.

idea of the extensive hierarchy of objects that is the Excel object model, especially when you realize that this diagram shows less than half of the objects available. The objects shown in gray are coming from the Microsoft.Office.Core namespace, which is associated with the Microsoft Office 12.0 PIA (office.dll). These objects are shared by all the Office applications.

Figure 3-20 shows the object hierarchy associated with Range, a very important object in Excel that represents a range of cells you want to work with in your code. We have already used the Range object in Listing 3-2.

Figure 3-21 shows the object hierarchy associated with Shape—a Shape represents things that float on the worksheet that are not cells, such as embedded buttons, drawings, comment bubbles, and so on.

Conclusion

This chapter introduced the various ways you can integrate your code into Excel. The chapter described how to build automation add-ins to create user-defined functions for Excel. You also learned the basic hierarchy of the Excel object model. Chapter 4, "Working with Excel Events," discusses the events in the Excel object model. Chapter 5, "Working with Excel Objects," covers the most important objects in the Excel object model.

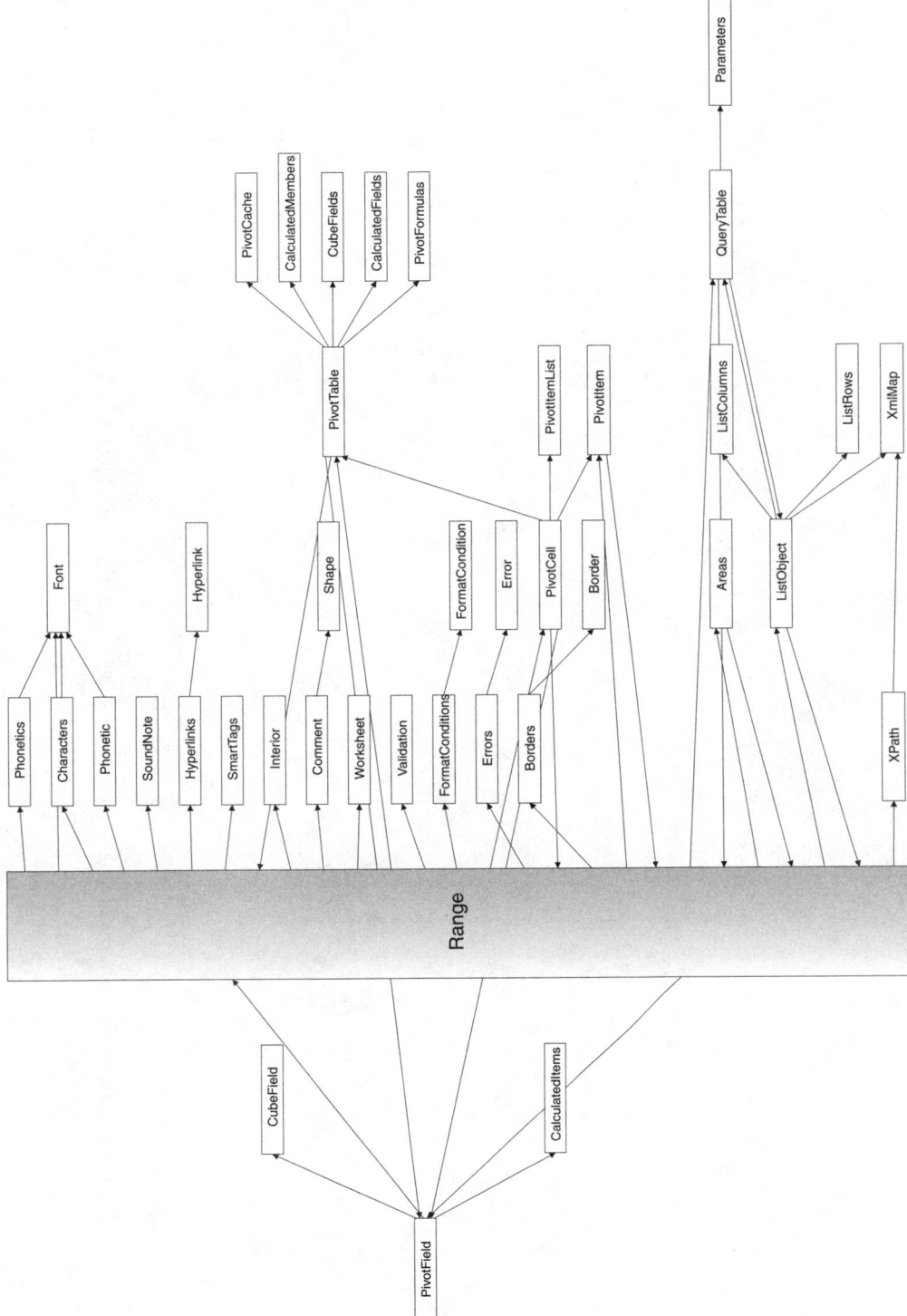

Figure 3-20: A more detailed hierarchy of objects associated with Range in the Excel object model.

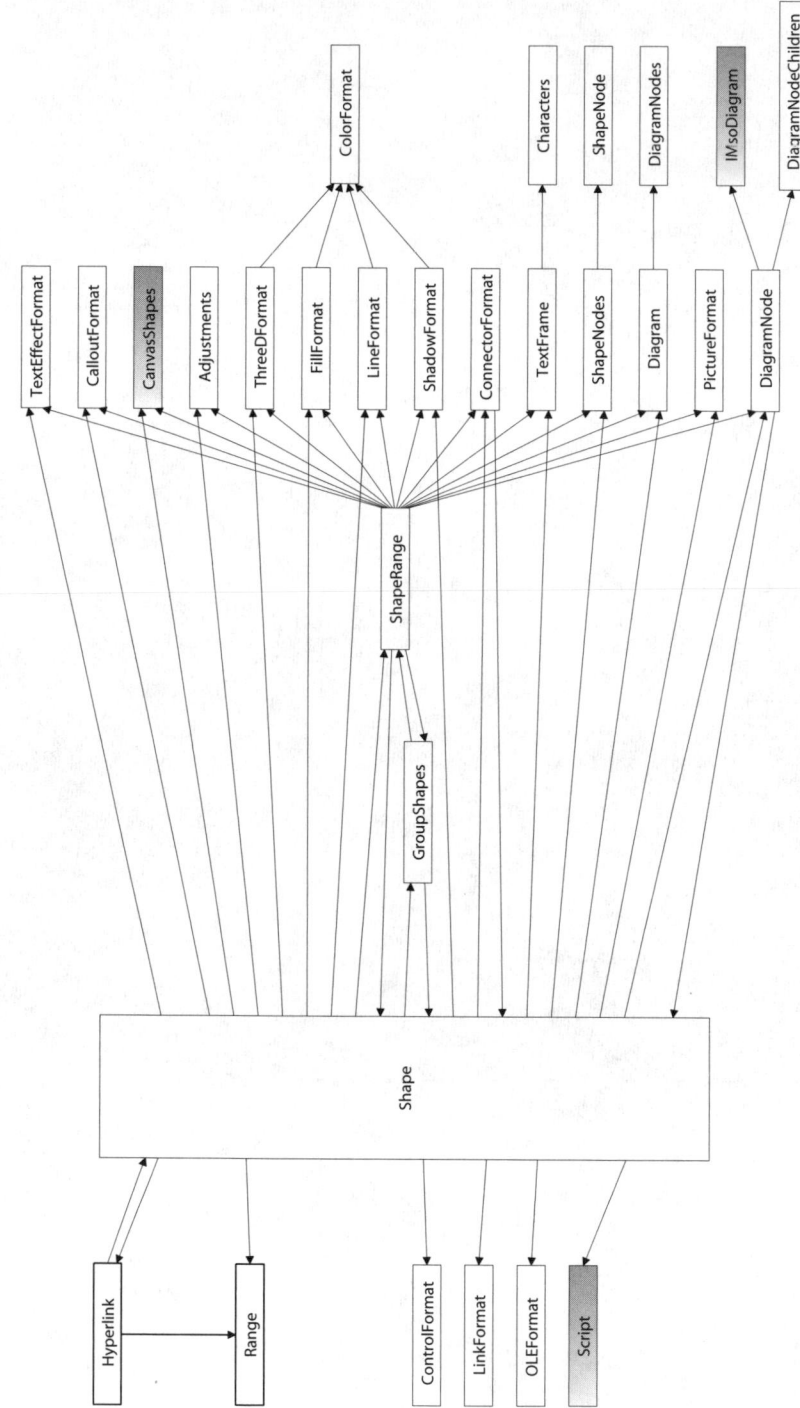

Figure 3-21: A more detailed hierarchy of objects associated with Shape in the Excel object model.

■ 4 ■
Working with Excel Events

Events in the Excel Object Model

Understanding the events in the Excel object model is critical because this is often the primary way that your code is run. This chapter examines all the events in the Excel object model, when they are raised, and the type of code you might associate with these events.

Many of the events in the Excel object model are repeated on the Application, Workbook, and Worksheet objects. This repetition allows you to decide whether you want to handle the event for all workbooks, for a particular workbook, or for a particular worksheet. For example, if you want to know when any worksheet in any open workbook is double-clicked, you would handle the Application object's SheetBeforeDoubleClick event. If you want to know when any worksheet in a particular workbook is double-clicked, you would handle the SheetBeforeDoubleClick event on that Workbook object. If you want to know when one particular sheet is double-clicked, you would handle the BeforeDoubleClick event on that Worksheet object. When an event is repeated on the Application, Workbook, and Worksheet object, it typically is raised first on Worksheet, then Workbook, and finally Application.

New Workbook and Worksheet Events

Excel's Application object raises a NewWorkbook event when a new blank workbook is created. This event is not raised when a new workbook is created from a template or an existing document. Excel also raises events when new worksheets are created in a particular workbook. Similarly, these events are only raised when a user first creates a new worksheet. They are never raised again on subsequent opens of the workbook.

This discussion now focuses on the various ways in which new workbook and worksheet events are raised:

- **Application.NewWorkbook** is raised when a new blank workbook is created. Excel passes the new Workbook object as a parameter to this event.

> **NOTE**
>
> NewWorkbook is the name of both a property and an event on the Application object. Because of this collision, you will not see the NewWorkbook event in Visual Studio's pop-up menu of properties, events, and methods associated with the Application object. Furthermore, a warning displays at compile time when you try to handle this event. To get Visual Studio's pop-up menus to work and the warning to go away, you can cast the Application object to the AppEvents_Event interface, as shown in Listing 4-1.

- **Application.WorkbookNewSheet** is raised when a new sheet is created in any open workbook. Excel passes the Workbook object that the new sheet was created in as a parameter to this event. It also passes the new sheet object. Because a workbook can contain both worksheets and chart sheets, the new sheet object is passed as an `object`. You can then cast it to either a Worksheet or a Chart.
- **Workbook.NewSheet** is raised on a workbook that has a new sheet created in it. Excel passes the new sheet object as a parameter to this event. The new sheet object is passed as an `object` that you can cast to either a Worksheet or a Chart.

Listing 4-1 shows a console application that handles the Application object's NewWorkbook and WorkbookNewSheet events. It also creates a new workbook and handles the NewSheet event for that newly created workbook. The console application handles the Close event for the workbook, so when you close the workbook the console application will exit and Excel will quit. Listing 4-1 shows several other common techniques. For the sheets passed as object, we use the as operator to cast the object to a Worksheet or a Chart. We then will check the result to verify it is not null to ascertain whether the cast succeeded. This method proves more efficient than using the is operator followed by the as operator, because the latter method requires two casts. Remember to add a reference to the Excel PIA and to System.Windows.Forms to get Listing 4-1 to compile.

Listing 4-1: A Console Application That Handles New Workbook and Worksheet Events

```
using System;
using System.Collections.Generic;
using System.Linq;
using System.Text;
using Excel = Microsoft.Office.Interop.Excel;
using System.Windows.Forms;

namespace ConsoleApplication
{
  class Program
  {
    static private Excel.Application app;
    static private Excel.Workbook workbook;
    static bool exit = false;

    static void Main(string[] args)
    {
      app = new Excel.Application();
      app.Visible = true;

      // We cast to AppEvents_Event because NewWorkbook
      // is the name of both a property and an event.
      ((Excel.AppEvents_Event)app).NewWorkbook +=
        new Excel.AppEvents_NewWorkbookEventHandler(
        App_NewWorkbook);

      app.WorkbookNewSheet +=
        new Excel.AppEvents_WorkbookNewSheetEventHandler(
        App_WorkbookNewSheet);
```

```csharp
      workbook = app.Workbooks.Add(Type.Missing);
      workbook.NewSheet +=
        new Excel.WorkbookEvents_NewSheetEventHandler(
        Workbook_NewSheet);

      workbook.BeforeClose +=
        new Excel.WorkbookEvents_BeforeCloseEventHandler(
        Workbook_BeforeClose);

      while (exit == false)
        System.Windows.Forms.Application.DoEvents();

      app.Quit();
    }

    static void App_NewWorkbook(Excel.Workbook workbook)
    {
      Console.WriteLine(String.Format(
        "Application.NewWorkbook({0})", workbook.Name));
    }

    static void App_WorkbookNewSheet(Excel.Workbook workbook,
      object sheet)
    {
      Excel.Worksheet worksheet = sheet as Excel.Worksheet;

      if (worksheet != null)
      {
        Console.WriteLine(String.Format(
          "Application.WorkbookNewSheet({0},{1})",
          workbook.Name, worksheet.Name));
      }

      Excel.Chart chart = sheet as Excel.Chart;

      if (chart != null)
      {
        Console.WriteLine(String.Format(
          "Application.WorkbookNewSheet({0},{1})",
          workbook.Name, chart.Name));
      }
    }

    static void Workbook_NewSheet(object sheet)
    {
      Excel.Worksheet worksheet = sheet as Excel.Worksheet;

      if (worksheet != null)
      {
```

```
      Console.WriteLine(String.Format(
        "Workbook.NewSheet({0})", worksheet.Name));
    }

    Excel.Chart chart = sheet as Excel.Chart;

    if (chart != null)
    {
      Console.WriteLine(String.Format(
        "Workbook.NewSheet({0})", chart.Name));
    }
  }

  static void Workbook_BeforeClose(ref bool cancel)
  {
    exit = true;
  }
 }
}
```

As you consider the code in Listing 4-1, you might wonder how you will ever remember the syntax of complicated lines of code such as this one:

```
app.WorkbookNewSheet +=
  new Excel.AppEvents_WorkbookNewSheetEventHandler(
  App_WorkbookNewSheet);
```

Fortunately, Visual Studio 2008 helps by generating most of this line of code as well as the corresponding event handler automatically. If you were typing this line of code, after you type +=, Visual Studio displays a pop-up tooltip (see Figure 4-1). If you press the Tab key twice, Visual Studio generates the rest of the line of code and the event handler method automatically.

If you are using Visual Studio Tools for Office (VSTO), you can also use the Properties window to add event handlers to your workbook or worksheet classes. Double-click the project item for your workbook class (typically called ThisWorkbook.cs) or one of your worksheet classes (typically

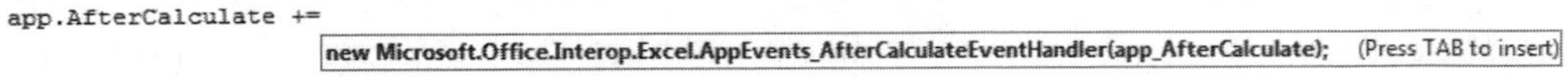

```
app.AfterCalculate +=
```
| new Microsoft.Office.Interop.Excel.AppEvents_AfterCalculateEventHandler(app_AfterCalculate); | (Press TAB to insert) |

Figure 4-1: Pop-up tooltip for generating event handlers.

called Sheet1.cs, Sheet2.cs, and so on). Make sure the Properties window is visible. If it is not, choose Properties Window from the View menu to show the Properties window. Make sure that the workbook class (typically called ThisWorkbook) or a worksheet class (typically called Sheet1, Sheet2, and so on) is selected in the combo box at the top of the Properties window. Then click the lightning bolt icon to show events associated with the workbook or worksheet. Type the name of the method you want to use as an event handler in the edit box to the right of the event you want to handle.

Activation and Deactivation Events

Sixteen events in the Excel object model are raised when various objects are activated or deactivated. An object is considered activated when its window receives focus, or when it is made the selected or active object. For example, worksheets are activated and deactivated when you switch from one worksheet to another within a workbook. Clicking the tab for Sheet3 in a workbook that currently has Sheet1 selected raises a Deactivate event for Sheet1 (it is losing focus) and an Activate event for Sheet3 (it is getting focus). You can activate/deactive chart sheets in the same manner. Doing so raises Activate and Deactivate events on the Chart object corresponding to the chart sheet that was activated or deactivated.

You can also activate/deactivate workbooks. Consider the case where you have the workbooks Book1 and Book2 open at the same time. If you are currently editing Book1 and you switch from Book1 to Book2 by choosing Book2 from the Window menu, the Deactivate event for Book1 is raised and the Activate event for Book2 is raised.

Windows are another example of objects that are activated and deactivated. A workbook can have more than one window open that is showing the workbook. Consider the case where you have the workbook Book1 opened. If you choose New Window from the Window menu, two windows will open in Excel viewing Book1. One window has the caption Book1:1, and the other window has the caption Book1:2. As you switch between Book1:1 and Book1:2, the WindowActivate event is raised for the workbook. Switching between Book1:1 and Book1:2 does not raise the Workbook Activate or Deactivate events because Book1 remains the active workbook.

Note that Activate and Deactivate events are not raised when you switch to an application other than Excel and then switch back to Excel. You might expect that if you had Excel and Word open side by side on your monitor that switching focus by clicking from Excel to Word would raise Deactivate events inside Excel. This is not the case—Excel does not consider switching to another application a deactivation of any of its workbooks, sheets, or windows.

The discussion now turns to the various ways in which Activate and Deactivate events are raised:

- **Application.WorkbookActivate** is raised whenever a workbook is activated within Excel. Excel passes the Workbook object that was activated as a parameter to this event.
- **Workbook.Activate** is raised on a particular workbook that is activated. No parameter is passed to this event because the activated workbook is the Workbook object raising the event.

> **▪ NOTE**
>
> Activate is the name of both a method and an event on the Workbook object. Because of this collision, you will not see the Activate event in Visual Studio's pop-up menu of properties, events, and methods associated with the Application object. Furthermore, a warning displays at compile time when you try to handle this event.
>
> To get Visual Studio's pop-up menus to work and to remove the warning, you can cast the Workbook object to the WorkbookEvents_Event interface, as shown in Listing 4-1.

- **Application.WorkbookDeactivate** is raised whenever any workbook is deactivated within Excel. Excel passes the Workbook object that was deactivated as a parameter to this event.
- **Workbook.Deactivate** is raised on a particular workbook that is deactivated. No parameter is passed to this event because the deactivated workbook is the Workbook object raising the event.

- **Application.SheetActivate** is raised whenever a worksheet is activated within Excel. Excel passes the sheet object that was activated as a parameter to this event. Because a workbook can contain both worksheets and chart sheets, the activated sheet is passed as an `object`. You can then cast it to either a Worksheet or a Chart.

- **Workbook.SheetActivate** is raised on a workbook that has a sheet that was activated. Excel passes the sheet object that was activated as a parameter to this event. Because a workbook can contain both worksheets and chart sheets, the activated sheet is passed as an `object`. You can then cast it to either a Worksheet or a Chart.

- **Worksheet.Activate** and **Chart.Activate** are raised on an activated worksheet or chart sheet. No parameter is passed to these events because the activated sheet is the Worksheet or Chart object raising this event.

■ NOTE

Activate is the name of both a method and an event on the Worksheet and the Chart object. Because of this collision, you will not see the Activate event in Visual Studio's pop-up menu of properties, events, and methods associated with the Worksheet or Chart object. Furthermore, a warning displays at compile time when you try to handle this event. To get Visual Studio's pop-up menus to work and the warning to go away, you can cast the Worksheet object to the DocEvents_Event interface and cast the Chart object to the ChartEvents_Events interface, as shown in Listing 4-2.

It is strange that the interface you cast the Worksheet object to is called DocEvents_Event. This is due to the way the PIAs are generated—the event interface on the COM object Worksheet was called DocEvents rather than WorksheetEvents. The same inconsistency occurs with the Application object; it has an event interface called AppEvents rather than ApplicationEvents.

- **Application.SheetDeactivate** is raised whenever any worksheet is deactivated within Excel. Excel passes the sheet object that was deactivated as a parameter to this event. Because a workbook can contain both worksheets and chart sheets, the deactivated sheet is passed as an object. You can then cast it to either a Worksheet or a Chart.

- **Workbook.SheetDeactivate** is raised on a workbook that has a sheet that was deactivated. Excel passes the sheet object that was deactivated as a parameter to this event. Because a workbook can contain both worksheets and chart sheets, the deactivated sheet is passed as an object. You can then cast it to either a Worksheet or a Chart.

- **Worksheet.Deactivate** and **Chart.Deactivate** are raised on a deactivated worksheet or chart sheet. No parameters are passed to these events because the deactivated sheet is the Worksheet or Chart object raising this event.

- **Application.WindowActivate** is raised whenever a window is activated within Excel. Excel passes the Workbook object corresponding to the window that was activated as a parameter to this event. Excel also passes the Window object that was activated.

- **Workbook.WindowActivate** is raised on a workbook that has a window that was activated. Excel passes the Window object that was activated as a parameter to this event.

- **Application.WindowDeactivate** is raised whenever a window is deactivated within Excel. Excel passes the Workbook object corresponding to the window that was deactivated as a parameter to this event. Excel also passes the Window object that was deactivated.

- **Workbook.WindowDeactivate** is raised on a workbook that has a window that was deactivated. Excel passes the Window object that was deactivated as a parameter to this event.

Listing 4-2 shows a class that handles all of these events. It is passed an Excel Application object to its constructor. The constructor creates a new workbook and gets the first sheet in the workbook. Then it creates a chart sheet. It handles events raised on the Application object as well as the created workbook, the first worksheet in the workbook, and the chart sheet that it adds to the workbook. Because several events pass as a parameter a sheet as an object, a helper method called ReportEventWithSheetParameter is used to determine the type of sheet passed and display a message to the console. Remember to add a reference to the Excel PIA to make Listing 4-2 compile.

Listing 4-2: A Class That Handles Activation and Deactivation Events

```
using System;
using System.Collections.Generic;
using System.Linq;
using System.Text;
using Excel = Microsoft.Office.Interop.Excel;

namespace ActivationAndDeactivation
{
  public class TestEventHandler
  {
    private Excel.Application app;
    private Excel.Workbook workbook;
    private Excel.Worksheet worksheet;
    private Excel.Chart chart;

    public TestEventHandler(Excel.Application application)
    {
      this.app = application;
      workbook = application.Workbooks.Add(Type.Missing);
      worksheet = workbook.Worksheets.get_Item(1)
        as Excel.Worksheet;

      chart = workbook.Charts.Add(Type.Missing, Type.Missing,
        Type.Missing, Type.Missing) as Excel.Chart;

      app.WorkbookActivate +=
        new Excel.AppEvents_WorkbookActivateEventHandler(
        App_WorkbookActivate);

      ((Excel.WorkbookEvents_Event)workbook).Activate +=
        new Excel.WorkbookEvents_ActivateEventHandler(
        Workbook_Activate);

      app.WorkbookDeactivate +=
        new Excel.AppEvents_WorkbookDeactivateEventHandler(
        App_WorkbookDeactivate);

      workbook.Deactivate +=
        new Excel.WorkbookEvents_DeactivateEventHandler(
        Workbook_Deactivate);

      app.SheetActivate +=
        new Excel.AppEvents_SheetActivateEventHandler(
        App_SheetActivate);

      workbook.SheetActivate +=
        new Excel.WorkbookEvents_SheetActivateEventHandler(
        Workbook_SheetActivate);
```

```csharp
((Excel.DocEvents_Event)worksheet).Activate +=
  new Excel.DocEvents_ActivateEventHandler(
  Worksheet_Activate);

((Excel.ChartEvents_Event)chart).Activate +=
  new Excel.ChartEvents_ActivateEventHandler(
  Chart_Activate);

app.SheetDeactivate +=
  new Excel.AppEvents_SheetDeactivateEventHandler(
  App_SheetDeactivate);

workbook.SheetDeactivate +=
  new Excel.WorkbookEvents_SheetDeactivateEventHandler(
  Workbook_SheetDeactivate);

worksheet.Deactivate +=
  new Excel.DocEvents_DeactivateEventHandler(
  Worksheet_Deactivate);

chart.Deactivate +=
  new Excel.ChartEvents_DeactivateEventHandler(
  Chart_Deactivate);

app.WindowActivate +=
  new Excel.AppEvents_WindowActivateEventHandler(
  App_WindowActivate);

workbook.WindowActivate +=
  new Excel.WorkbookEvents_WindowActivateEventHandler(
  Workbook_WindowActivate);

app.WindowDeactivate +=
  new Excel.AppEvents_WindowDeactivateEventHandler(
  App_WindowDeactivate);

workbook.WindowDeactivate +=
  new Excel.WorkbookEvents_WindowDeactivateEventHandler(
  Workbook_WindowDeactivate);
}

void ReportEventWithSheetParameter(string eventName, object sheet)
{
  Excel.Worksheet worksheet = sheet as Excel.Worksheet;

  if (worksheet != null)
  {
    Console.WriteLine(String.Format("{0} ({1})",
      eventName, worksheet.Name));
  }
```

```
      Excel.Chart chart = sheet as Excel.Chart;

      if (chart != null)
      {
        Console.WriteLine(String.Format("{0} ({1})",
          eventName, chart.Name));
      }
    }

    void App_WorkbookActivate(Excel.Workbook workbook)
    {
      Console.WriteLine(String.Format(
        "Application.WorkbookActivate({0})", workbook.Name));
    }

    void Workbook_Activate()
    {
      Console.WriteLine("Workbook.Activate()");
    }

    void App_WorkbookDeactivate(Excel.Workbook workbook)
    {
      Console.WriteLine(String.Format(
        "Application.WorkbookDeactivate({0})", workbook.Name));
    }

    void Workbook_Deactivate()
    {
      Console.WriteLine("Workbook.Deactivate()");
    }

    void App_SheetActivate(object sheet)
    {
      ReportEventWithSheetParameter(
        "Application.SheetActivate", sheet);
    }

    void Workbook_SheetActivate(object sheet)
    {
      ReportEventWithSheetParameter(
        "Workbook.SheetActivate", sheet);
    }

    void Worksheet_Activate()
    {
      Console.WriteLine("Worksheet.Activate()");
    }

    void Chart_Activate()
    {
```

```csharp
    Console.WriteLine("Chart.Activate()");
}

void App_SheetDeactivate(object sheet)
{
  ReportEventWithSheetParameter(
    "Application.SheetDeactivate", sheet);
}

void Workbook_SheetDeactivate(object sheet)
{
  ReportEventWithSheetParameter(
    "Workbook.SheetDeactivate", sheet);
}

void Worksheet_Deactivate()
{
  Console.WriteLine("Worksheet.Deactivate()");
}

void Chart_Deactivate()
{
  Console.WriteLine("Chart.Deactivate()");
}

void App_WindowActivate(Excel.Workbook workbook,
  Excel.Window window)
{
  Console.WriteLine(String.Format(
    "Application.WindowActivate({0}, {1})",
    workbook.Name, window.Caption));
}

void Workbook_WindowActivate(Excel.Window window)
{
  Console.WriteLine(String.Format(
    "Workbook.WindowActivate({0})", window.Caption));
}

void App_WindowDeactivate(Excel.Workbook workbook,
  Excel.Window window)
{
  Console.WriteLine(String.Format(
    "Application.WindowDeactivate({0}, {1})",
    workbook.Name, window.Caption));
}

void Workbook_WindowDeactivate(Excel.Window window)
{
  Console.WriteLine(String.Format(
```

```
        "Application.WindowActivate({1})",
        window.Caption));
    }
}
```

Double-Click and Right-Click Events

Several events are raised when a worksheet or a chart sheet is double-clicked or right-clicked (clicked with the right mouse button). Double-click events occur when you double-click in the center of a cell in a worksheet or on a chart sheet. If you double-click the border of the cell, no events are raised. If you double-click column headers or row headers, no events are raised. If you double-click objects in a worksheet (Shape objects in the object model), such as an embedded chart, no events are raised. After you double-click a cell in Excel, Excel enters editing mode for that cell—a cursor displays in the cell allowing you to type into the cell. If you double-click a cell in editing mode, no events are raised.

The right-click events occur when you right-click a cell in a worksheet or on a chart sheet. A right-click event is also raised when you right-click column headers or row headers. If you right-click objects in a worksheet, such as an embedded chart, no events are raised.

The right-click and double-click events for a chart sheet do not raise events on the Application and Workbook objects. Instead, BeforeDouble-Click and BeforeRightClick events are raised directly on the Chart object.

All the right-click and double-click events have a "Before" in their names. This is because Excel is raising these events before Excel does its default behaviors for double-click and right-click—for example, displaying a context menu or going into edit mode for the cell you double-clicked. These events all have a bool parameter that is passed by a reference called cancel that allows you to cancel Excel's default behavior for the double-click or right-click that occurred by setting the cancel parameter to true.

Many of the right-click and double-click events pass a Range object as a parameter. A Range object represents a range of cells—it can represent a single cell or multiple cells. For example, if you select several cells and then right-click the selected cells, a Range object is passed to the right-click event that represents the selected cells.

Double-click and right-click events are raised in various ways, as follows:

- **Application.SheetBeforeDoubleClick** is raised whenever any cell in any worksheet within Excel is double-clicked. Excel passes as an `object` the Worksheet that was double-clicked, a Range for the range of cells that was double-clicked, and a `bool` `cancel` parameter passed by reference. The `cancel` parameter can be set to `true` by your event handler to prevent Excel from executing its default double-click behavior. (This is a case where it really does not make sense that Worksheet is passed as `object` because a Chart is never passed. You will always have to cast the `object` to a Worksheet.)

- **Workbook.SheetBeforeDoubleClick** is raised on a workbook that has a cell in a worksheet that was double-clicked. Excel passes the same parameters as the Application-level SheetBeforeDoubleClick.

- **Worksheet.BeforeDoubleClick** is raised on a worksheet that is double-clicked. Excel passes a Range for the range of cells that was double-clicked and a `bool` `cancel` parameter passed by reference. The `cancel` parameter can be set to `true` by your event handler to prevent Excel from executing its default double-click behavior.

- **Chart.BeforeDoubleClick** is raised on a chart sheet that is double-clicked. Excel passes as `int` an `elementID` and two parameters called `arg1` and `arg2`. The combination of these three parameters allows you to determine what element of the chart was double-clicked; consult the Excel object model documentation for more information on the values possible for these parameters. Excel also passes a `bool` `cancel` parameter by reference. The `cancel` parameter can be set to `true` by your event handler to prevent Excel from executing its default double-click behavior.

- **Application.SheetBeforeRightClick** is raised whenever any cell in any worksheet within Excel is right-clicked. Excel passes as an `object` the Worksheet that was right-clicked, a Range for the range of cells that was right-clicked, and a `bool` `cancel` parameter passed by reference. The `cancel` parameter can be set to `true` by your event handler to prevent Excel from executing its default right-click behavior. (This is a case where it really does not make sense that Worksheet is passed as an object because a Chart is never passed. You will always have to cast the object to a Worksheet.)

- **Workbook.SheetBeforeRightClick** is raised on a workbook that has a cell in a worksheet that was right-clicked. Excel passes the same parameters as the Application-level SheetBeforeRightClick.

- **Worksheet.BeforeRightClick** is raised on a worksheet that is right-clicked. Excel passes a Range for the range of cells that was right-clicked and a bool cancel parameter passed by reference. The cancel parameter can be set to true by your event handler to prevent Excel from executing its default right-click behavior.

- **Chart.BeforeRightClick** is raised on a chart sheet that is right-clicked. Strangely enough, Excel does not pass any of the parameters that it passes to the Chart.BeforeDoubleClickEvent. Excel does pass a bool cancel parameter by reference. The cancel parameter can be set to true by your event handler to prevent Excel from executing its default right-click behavior.

Listing 4-3 shows a VSTO Workbook class that handles all of these events. This code assumes that you have added a chart sheet to the workbook and it is called Chart1. The chart sheet must reference some data in another worksheet and display some sort of chart; otherwise, no events will be raised when you click the chart sheet. In VSTO, you do not have to keep a reference to the Workbook object or the Worksheet or Chart objects when handling events raised by these objects because they are already being kept by the project items generated in the VSTO project. You do need to keep a reference to the Application object when handling events raised by the Application object because it is not being kept anywhere in the VSTO project.

The ThisWorkbook class generated by VSTO derives from a class that has all the members of Excel's Workbook object, so we can add workbook event handlers by adding code that refers to this, as shown in Listing 4-3. We can get an Application object by using this.Application because Application is a property of Workbook. Because the returned application object is not being held as a reference by any other code, we must declare a class member variable to hold on to this Application object so that our events handlers will work. Chapter 1, "An Introduction to Office Programming," discusses this issue in more detail.

To get to the chart and the worksheet that are in our VSTO project, we use VSTO's Globals object, which lets us get to the classes Chart1 and Sheet1 that are declared in other project items. We do not have to hold these objects in a class member variable because they have lifetimes that match the lifetime of the VSTO code behind.

We also declare two helper functions in Listing 4-3. One casts the sheet that is passed as an object to a Worksheet and returns the name of the worksheet. The other gets the address of the Range that is passed to many of the events as the target parameter.

The handlers for the right-click events all set the bool cancel parameter that is passed by reference to true. This will make it so that Excel will not do its default behavior on right-click, which is typically to pop up a menu.

Listing 4-3: A VSTO Workbook Customization That Handles Double-Click and Right-Click Events

```csharp
using System;
using System.Collections.Generic;
using System.Data;
using System.Linq;
using System.Text;
using System.Xml.Linq;
using System.Windows.Forms;
using Microsoft.VisualStudio.Tools.Applications.Runtime;
using Excel = Microsoft.Office.Interop.Excel;
using Office = Microsoft.Office.Core;

namespace ExcelWorkbook1
{
  public partial class ThisWorkbook
  {
    private Excel.Application app;

    private void ThisWorkbook_Startup(object sender, EventArgs e)
    {
      app = this.Application;

      app.SheetBeforeDoubleClick +=
        new Excel.AppEvents_SheetBeforeDoubleClickEventHandler(
        App_SheetBeforeDoubleClick);
```

```csharp
    this.SheetBeforeDoubleClick +=
        new Excel.WorkbookEvents_SheetBeforeDoubleClickEventHandler(
        ThisWorkbook_SheetBeforeDoubleClick);

    Globals.Sheet1.BeforeDoubleClick +=
        new Excel.DocEvents_BeforeDoubleClickEventHandler(
        Sheet1_BeforeDoubleClick);

    Globals.Chart1.BeforeDoubleClick +=
        new Excel.ChartEvents_BeforeDoubleClickEventHandler(
        Chart1_BeforeDoubleClick);

    app.SheetBeforeRightClick +=
        new Excel.AppEvents_SheetBeforeRightClickEventHandler(
        App_SheetBeforeRightClick);

    this.SheetBeforeRightClick +=
        new Excel.WorkbookEvents_SheetBeforeRightClickEventHandler(
        ThisWorkbook_SheetBeforeRightClick);

    Globals.Sheet1.BeforeRightClick +=
        new Excel.DocEvents_BeforeRightClickEventHandler(
        Sheet1_BeforeRightClick);

    Globals.Chart1.BeforeRightClick +=
        new Excel.ChartEvents_BeforeRightClickEventHandler(
        Chart1_BeforeRightClick);
}

private void ThisWorkbook_Shutdown(object sender, EventArgs e)
{
}

private string RangeAddress(Excel.Range target)
{
    return target.get_Address(missing, missing,
        Excel.XlReferenceStyle.xlA1, missing, missing);
}

private string SheetName(object sheet)
{
    Excel.Worksheet worksheet = sheet as Excel.Worksheet;
    if (worksheet != null)
        return worksheet.Name;
    else
        return String.Empty;
}

void App_SheetBeforeDoubleClick(object sheet,
    Excel.Range target, ref bool cancel)
```

```
{
  MessageBox.Show(String.Format(
    "Application.SheetBeforeDoubleClick({0},{1})",
    SheetName(sheet), RangeAddress(target)));
}


void ThisWorkbook_SheetBeforeDoubleClick(object sheet,
  Excel.Range target, ref bool cancel)
{
  MessageBox.Show(String.Format(
    "Workbook.SheetBeforeDoubleClick({0}, {1})",
    SheetName(sheet), RangeAddress(target)));
}


void Sheet1_BeforeDoubleClick(Excel.Range target,
  ref bool cancel)
{
  MessageBox.Show(String.Format(
    "Worksheet.SheetBeforeDoubleClick({0})",
    RangeAddress(target)));
}


void Chart1_BeforeDoubleClick(int elementID, int arg1,
  int arg2, ref bool cancel)
{
  MessageBox.Show(String.Format(
    "Chart.SheetBeforeDoubleClick({0}, {1}, {2})",
    elementID, arg1, arg2));
}


void App_SheetBeforeRightClick(object sheet,
  Excel.Range target, ref bool cancel)
{
  MessageBox.Show(String.Format(
    "Application.SheetBeforeRightClick({0},{1})",
    SheetName(sheet), RangeAddress(target)));
  cancel = true;
}


void ThisWorkbook_SheetBeforeRightClick(object sheet,
  Excel.Range target, ref bool cancel)
{
  MessageBox.Show(String.Format(
    "Workbook.SheetBeforeRightClick({0},{1})",
    SheetName(sheet), RangeAddress(target)));
  cancel = true;
}


void Sheet1_BeforeRightClick(Excel.Range target,
  ref bool cancel)
```

```
    {
      MessageBox.Show(String.Format(
        "Worksheet.SheetBeforeRightClick({0})",
        RangeAddress(target)));
      cancel = true;
    }

    void Chart1_BeforeRightClick(ref bool cancel)
    {
      MessageBox.Show("Chart.SheetBeforeRightClick()");
      cancel = true;
    }

    #region VSTO Designer generated code

    /// <summary>
    /// Required method for Designer support - do not modify
    /// the contents of this method with the code editor.
    /// </summary>
    private void InternalStartup()
    {
      this.Startup += new System.EventHandler(ThisWorkbook_Startup);
      this.Shutdown += new System.EventHandler(ThisWorkbook_Shutdown);
    }

    #endregion

  }
}
```

Listing 4-3 raises an interesting question. What happens when multiple objects handle an event such as BeforeRightClick at multiple levels? Listing 4-3 handles the BeforeRightClick event at the Worksheet, Workbook, and Application level. Excel first raises the event at the Worksheet level for all code that has registered for the Worksheet-level event. Remember that other add-ins could be loaded in Excel handling Worksheet-level events as well. Your code might get the Worksheet.BeforeRightClick event first followed by some other add-in that also is handling the Worksheet.Before-RightClick event. When multiple add-ins handle the same event on the same object, you cannot rely on any determinate order for who will get the event first. Therefore, do not write your code to rely on any particular ordering.

After events are raised at the Worksheet level, they are then raised at the Workbook level, and finally at the Application level. For a cancelable event, even if one event handler sets the cancel parameter to true, the events will continue to be raised to other event handlers. So even though the code in Listing 4-3 sets the `cancel` parameter to `true` in `Sheet1_BeforeRightClick`, Excel will continue to raise events on other handlers of the worksheet BeforeRightClick and then handlers of the Workbook.SheetBeforeRight-Click followed by handlers of the Application.SheetBeforeRightClick.

Another thing you should know about cancelable events is that you can check the incoming `cancel` parameter in your event handler to see what the last event handler set it to. So in the `Sheet1_BeforeRightClick` handler, the incoming `cancel` parameter would be `false` assuming no other code is handling the event. In the `ThisWorkbook_SheetBeforeRightClick` handler, the incoming `cancel` parameter would be `true` because the last handler, `Sheet1_BeforeRightClick`, set it to `true`. This means that as an event bubbles through multiple handlers, each subsequent handler can override what the previous handlers did with respect to canceling the default right-click behavior in this example. Application-level handlers get the final say—although if multiple Application-level handlers exist for the same event, whether the event gets cancelled or not is indeterminate because no rules dictate which of multiple Application-level event handlers get an event first or last.

Calculate Events

Five events are raised when formulas in the worksheet are recalculated. The worksheet is recalculated whenever you change a cell that affects a formula referring to that cell or when you add or modify a formula:

- **Application.SheetCalculate** is raised whenever any sheet within Excel is recalculated. Excel passes the sheet as an `object` that was recalculated as a parameter to this event. The sheet object can be cast to a Worksheet or a Chart.
- **Application.AfterCalculate** is raised when all calculations that are pending are complete. This event can be used to determine whether all workbooks have been completely updated by any calculations or queries that are in progress.
- **Workbook.SheetCalculate** is raised on a workbook that has a sheet that was recalculated. Excel passes the sheet as an `object` that was

recalculated as a parameter to this event. The sheet object can be cast to a Worksheet or a Chart.

- **Worksheet.Calculate** is raised on a worksheet that was recalculated.

> **NOTE**
>
> Calculate is the name of both a method and an event on the Worksheet object. Because of this collision, you will not see the Calculate event in Visual Studio's pop-up menu of properties, events, and methods associated with the Worksheet object. Furthermore, a warning displays at compile time when you try to handle this event. To get Visual Studio's pop-up menus to work and the warning to go away, you can cast the Worksheet object to the DocEvents_Event interface, as shown in Listing 4-4.

- **Chart.Calculate** is raised on a chart sheet that was updated because data it referenced changed. This event does not occur until the chart is forced to redraw—so if the chart is not currently visible because it is not selected or displayed in its own window, the event will not be raised until the chart is visible.

Listing 4-4 shows a console application that handles all the calculation events. Note that you must add a reference to System.Windows.Forms and the Excel PIA for this listing to compile. The console application creates a new workbook, gets the first worksheet in the workbook, and creates a chart in the workbook. The console application also handles the Close event for the created workbook to cause the console application to exit when the workbook is closed. To get Excel to raise worksheet and workbook Calculate events, add some values and formulas to the first worksheet in the workbook. To raise the Chart object's Calculate event, you can right-click the chart sheet that you are handling the event for and choose Source Data from the pop-up menu. Then, click the button to the right of the Data Range text box, switch to the first worksheet, and select a range of values for the chart sheet to display. When you change those values and switch back to the chart sheet, the Chart's Calculate event will be raised.

Listing 4-4: A Console Application That Handles Calculate Events

```csharp
using System;
using System.Collections.Generic;
using System.Linq;
using System.Text;
using System.Windows.Forms;
using Excel = Microsoft.Office.Interop.Excel;

namespace ConsoleApplication
{
  class Program
  {
    static private Excel.Application app;
    static private Excel.Workbook workbook;
    static private Excel.Worksheet worksheet;
    static private Excel.Chart chart;
    static bool exit = false;

    static void Main(string[] args)
    {
      app = new Excel.Application();
      app.Visible = true;

      workbook = app.Workbooks.Add(Type.Missing);
      worksheet = workbook.Sheets.get_Item(1) as Excel.Worksheet;
      chart = workbook.Charts.Add(Type.Missing, Type.Missing,
        Type.Missing, Type.Missing) as Excel.Chart;

      app.SheetCalculate +=
        new Excel.AppEvents_SheetCalculateEventHandler(
        App_SheetCalculate);

      app.AfterCalculate +=
        new Excel.AppEvents_AfterCalculateEventHandler(
        App_AfterCalculate);

      workbook.SheetCalculate +=
        new Excel.WorkbookEvents_SheetCalculateEventHandler(
        Workbook_SheetCalculate);

      ((Excel.DocEvents_Event)worksheet).Calculate +=
        new Excel.DocEvents_CalculateEventHandler(
        Worksheet_Calculate);

      chart.Calculate +=
        new Excel.ChartEvents_CalculateEventHandler(
        Chart_Calculate);
```

```csharp
    workbook.BeforeClose +=
      new Excel.WorkbookEvents_BeforeCloseEventHandler(
      Workbook_BeforeClose);

    while (exit == false)
      System.Windows.Forms.Application.DoEvents();

    app.Quit();
}

static void Workbook_BeforeClose(ref bool cancel)
{
  exit = true;
}

static string SheetName(object sheet)
{
  Excel.Worksheet worksheet = sheet as Excel.Worksheet;

  if (worksheet != null)
  {
    return worksheet.Name;
  }

  Excel.Chart chart = sheet as Excel.Chart;
  if (chart != null)
  {
    return chart.Name;
  }

  return String.Empty;
}

static void App_SheetCalculate(object sheet)
{
  Console.WriteLine(String.Format(
    "Application.SheetCalculate({0})",
    SheetName(sheet)));
}

static void App_AfterCalculate()
{
  Console.WriteLine("Application.AfterCalculate()");
}

static void Workbook_SheetCalculate(object sheet)
{
  Console.WriteLine(String.Format(
    "Workbook.SheetCalculate({0})", SheetName(sheet)));
}
```

```
    static void Worksheet_Calculate()
    {
      Console.WriteLine("Worksheet.Calculate()");
    }

    static void Chart_Calculate()
    {
      Console.WriteLine("Chart.Calculate()");
    }
  }
}
```

Change Events

Excel raises several events when a cell or range of cells is changed in a worksheet. The cells must be changed by a user editing the cell for change events to be raised. Change events can also be raised when a cell is linked to external data and is changed as a result of refreshing the cell from the external data. Change events are not raised when a cell is changed because of a recalculation. They are not raised when the user changes formatting of the cell without changing the value of the cell. When a user is editing a cell and is in cell edit mode, the change events are not raised until the user exits cell edit mode by leaving that cell or pressing the Enter key:

- **Application.SheetChange** is raised when a cell or range of cells in any workbook is changed by the user or updated from external data. Excel passes the sheet as an object where the change occurred as a parameter to this event. You can always cast the sheet parameter to a Worksheet because the SheetChange event is not raised for chart sheets. Excel also passes a Range as a parameter for the range of cells that was changed.

- **Workbook.SheetChange** is raised on a workbook when a cell or range of cells in that workbook is changed by the user or updated from external data. Excel passes the sheet as an object where the change occurred as a parameter to this event. You can always cast the sheet parameter to a Worksheet because the SheetChange event is not raised for chart sheets. Excel also passes a Range as a parameter for the range of cells that was changed.

- **Worksheet.Change** is raised on a worksheet when a cell or range of cells in that worksheet is changed by the user or updated from external data. Excel passes a Range as a parameter for the range of cells that was changed.

Listing 4-5 shows a class that handles all the Change events. It is passed an Excel Application object to its constructor. The constructor creates a new workbook and gets the first worksheet in the workbook. It handles events raised on the Application object, the workbook, and the first worksheet in the workbook.

Listing 4-5: A Class That Handles Change Events

```csharp
using System;
using System.Collections.Generic;
using System.Linq;
using System.Text;
using Excel = Microsoft.Office.Interop.Excel;

namespace ChangeEvents
{
  public class ChangeEventHandler
  {
    private Excel.Application app;
    private Excel.Workbook workbook;
    private Excel.Worksheet worksheet;
    object missing = System.Type.Missing;

    public ChangeEventHandler(Excel.Application application)
    {
      this.app = application;
      workbook = app.Workbooks.Add(missing);
      worksheet = workbook.Worksheets.get_Item(1) as Excel.Worksheet;

      app.SheetChange +=
        new Excel.AppEvents_SheetChangeEventHandler(
        App_SheetChange);

      workbook.SheetChange +=
        new Excel.WorkbookEvents_SheetChangeEventHandler(
        Workbook_SheetChange);

      worksheet.Change +=
        new Excel.DocEvents_ChangeEventHandler(
        Worksheet_Change);
    }
```

```csharp
// Change events only pass worksheets, never charts.
private string SheetName(object sheet)
{
  Excel.Worksheet worksheet = sheet as Excel.Worksheet;
  return worksheet.Name;
}

private string RangeAddress(Excel.Range target)
{
  return target.get_Address(missing, missing,
    Excel.XlReferenceStyle.xlA1, missing, missing);
}

void App_SheetChange(object sheet, Excel.Range target)
{
  Console.WriteLine(String.Format(
    "Application.SheetChange({0},{1})",
    SheetName(sheet), RangeAddress(target)));
}

void Workbook_SheetChange(object sheet, Excel.Range target)
{
  Console.WriteLine(String.Format(
    "Workbook.SheetChange({0},{1})",
    SheetName(sheet), RangeAddress(target)));
}

void Worksheet_Change(Excel.Range target)
{
  Console.WriteLine(String.Format(
    "Worksheet.Change({0})",
    RangeAddress(target)));
  }
 }
}
```

Follow Hyperlink Events

Excel raises several events when a hyperlink in a cell is clicked. You might think this event is not very interesting, but you can use it as a simple way to invoke an action in your customization. The trick is to create a hyperlink that does nothing, and then handle the FollowHyperlink event and execute your action in that event handler.

To create a hyperlink that does nothing, right-click the cell where you want to put your hyperlink and choose HyperLink. For our example, we select cell C3. In the dialog box that appears, click the Place in This Document button to the left of the dialog box (see Figure 4-2). In the Type the cell reference text box, type **C3** or the reference of the cell to which you are adding a hyperlink. The logic behind doing this is that Excel will select the cell that C3 is linked to after the hyperlink is clicked and after your event handler runs. If you select a cell other than the cell the user clicked, the selection will move, which is confusing. So we effectively link the cell to itself, creating a do nothing link. In the Text to display text box, type the name of your command—the name you want displayed in the cell. In this example, we name the command Print.

The following events are raised when a hyperlink is clicked:

- **Application.SheetFollowHyperlink** is raised when a hyperlink is clicked in any workbook open in Excel. Excel passes a Hyperlink object as a parameter to this event. The Hyperlink object gives you information about the hyperlink that was clicked.

- **Workbook.SheetFollowHyperlink** is raised on a workbook when a hyperlink is clicked in that workbook. Excel passes a Hyperlink object as a parameter to this event. The Hyperlink object gives you information about the hyperlink that was clicked.

- **Worksheet.FollowHyperlink** is raised on a worksheet when a hyperlink is clicked in that worksheet. Excel passes a Hyperlink object as a parameter to this event. The Hyperlink object gives you information about the hyperlink that was clicked.

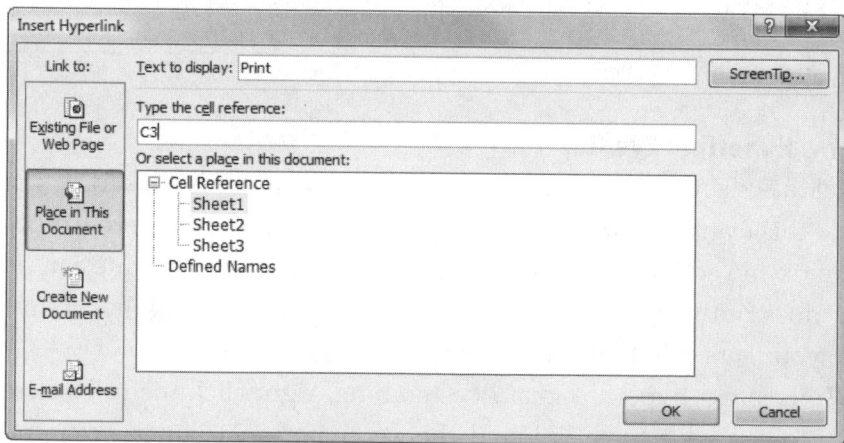

Figure 4-2: The Insert Hyperlink dialog box.

Listing 4-6 shows a VSTO customization class for the workbook project item. This class assumes a workbook that has a Print hyperlink in it, created as shown in Figure 4-2. The customization does nothing in the handlers of the Application or Workbook-level hyperlink events but log to the console window. The Worksheet-level handler detects that a hyperlink named Print was clicked and invokes the PrintOut method on the Workbook object to print the workbook.

Listing 4-6: A VSTO Workbook Customization That Handles Hyperlink Events

```
using System;
using System.Collections.Generic;
using System.Data;
using System.Linq;
using System.Text;
using System.Windows.Forms;
using System.Xml.Linq;
using Microsoft.VisualStudio.Tools.Applications.Runtime;
using Excel = Microsoft.Office.Interop.Excel;
using Office = Microsoft.Office.Core;

namespace ExcelWorkbook1
{
  public partial class ThisWorkbook
  {
    private Excel.Application app;

    private void ThisWorkbook_Startup(object sender, EventArgs e)
    {
      app = this.Application;

      app.SheetFollowHyperlink +=
        new Excel.AppEvents_SheetFollowHyperlinkEventHandler(
        App_SheetFollowHyperlink);

      this.SheetFollowHyperlink +=
        new Excel.WorkbookEvents_SheetFollowHyperlinkEventHandler(
        Workbook_SheetFollowHyperlink);

      Globals.Sheet1.FollowHyperlink +=
        new Excel.DocEvents_FollowHyperlinkEventHandler(
        Sheet_FollowHyperlink);
    }

    private string SheetName(object sheet)
    {
      Excel.Worksheet worksheet = sheet as Excel.Worksheet;
```

```csharp
        if (worksheet != null)
          return worksheet.Name;
        else
          return String.Empty;
    }

    void App_SheetFollowHyperlink(object sheet, Excel.Hyperlink target)
    {
      MessageBox.Show(String.Format(
        "Application.SheetFollowHyperlink({0},{1})",
        SheetName(sheet), target.Name));
    }

    void Workbook_SheetFollowHyperlink(object sheet, Excel.Hyperlink target)
    {
      MessageBox.Show(String.Format(
        "Workbook.SheetFollowHyperlink({0},{1})",
        SheetName(sheet), target.Name));
    }

    void Sheet_FollowHyperlink(Excel.Hyperlink target)
    {
      if (target.Name == "Print")
      {
        this.PrintOut(missing, missing, missing, missing,
          missing, missing, missing, missing);
      }
    }

    private void ThisWorkbook_Shutdown(object sender, EventArgs e)
    {
    }

    #region VSTO Designer generated code

    /// <summary>
    /// Required method for Designer support - do not modify
    /// the contents of this method with the code editor.
    /// </summary>
    private void InternalStartup()
    {
      this.Startup += new System.EventHandler(ThisWorkbook_Startup);
      this.Shutdown += new System.EventHandler(ThisWorkbook_Shutdown);
    }

    #endregion

  }
}
```

Selection Change Events

Selection change events occur when the selected cell or cells change, or in the case of the Chart.Select event, when the selected chart element within a chart sheet changes:

- **Application.SheetSelectionChange** is raised whenever the selected cell or cells in any worksheet within Excel change. Excel passes the sheet upon which the selection changed to the event handler. However, the event handler's parameter is typed as `object`, so it must be cast to a Worksheet if you want to use the properties or methods of the Worksheet. You are guaranteed to always be able to cast the argument to Worksheet because the SheetSelectionChange event is not raised when selection changes on a Chart. Excel also passes the range of cells that is the new selection.

- **Workbook.SheetSelectionChange** is raised on a Workbook whenever the selected cell or cells in that workbook change. Excel passes as an `object` the sheet where the selection changed. You can always cast the sheet object to a Worksheet because this event is not raised for selection changes on a chart sheet. Excel also passes a Range for the range of cells that is the new selection.

- **Worksheet.SelectionChange** is raised on a Worksheet whenever the selected cell or cells in that worksheet change. Excel passes a Range for the range of cells that is the new selection.

- **Chart.Select** is raised on a Chart when the selected element within that chart sheet changes. Excel passes as `int` an `elementID` and two parameters called `arg1` and `arg2`. The combination of these three parameters allows you to determine what element of the chart was selected; consult the Excel object model documentation for more information on the possible values for these parameters.

> **NOTE**
>
> Select is the name of both a method and an event on the Chart object. Because of this collision, you will not see the Select event in Visual Studio's pop-up menu of properties, events, and methods

associated with the Chart object. Furthermore, a warning displays at compile time when you try to handle this event. To get Visual Studio's pop-up menus to work and the warning to go away, you can cast the Chart object to the ChartEvents_Events interface, as shown in Listing 4-2.

WindowResize Events

The WindowResize events are raised when a workbook window is resized. These events are only raised if the workbook window is not maximized to fill Excel's outer application window (see Figure 4-3). Events are raised if you resize a nonmaximized workbook window or minimize the workbook window. No resize events occur when you resize and minimize the outer Excel application window.

- **Application.WindowResize** is raised when any nonmaximized workbook window is resized or minimized. Excel passes the Window

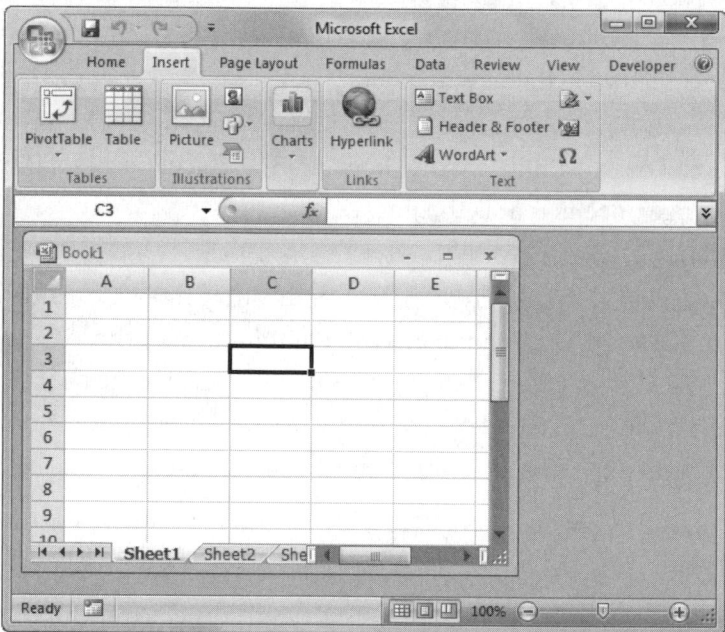

Figure 4-3: Window Resize events are raised only if the workbook window is not maximized to fill the application window.

object corresponding to the window that was resized or minimized as a parameter to this event. Excel also passes the Workbook object that was affected as a parameter to this event.

- **Workbook.WindowResize** is raised on a Workbook when a nonmaximized window associated with that workbook is resized or minimized. Excel passes the Window that was resized or minimized as a parameter to this event.

Add-In Install and Uninstall Events

A workbook can be saved into a special add-in format (XLA file) by choosing Save As from the Office menu and then picking Microsoft Office Excel Add-in as the desired format. The workbook will then be saved to the Application Data\Microsoft\AddIns directory found under the user's document and settings directory or, in Vista, to the AppData\Roaming\ Microsoft\AddIns folder under the user's directory. It will appear in the list of available Excel add-ins that displays when you show the Excel Add-ins dialog box via the Excel Options dialog box's Add-Ins tab. When you click the check box to enable the add-in, the workbook loads in a hidden state, and the Application.AddinInstall event is raised. When the user clicks the check box to disable the add-in, the Application.AddinUninstall event is raised.

Although you can theoretically save a workbook customized by VSTO as an XLA file, Microsoft does not support this scenario, because many VSTO features, such as support for the Document Actions task pane and Smart Tags, do not work when a workbook is saved as an XLA file.

XML Import and Export Events

Excel supports the import and export of custom XML data files by allowing you to take an XML schema and map it to cells in a workbook. It is then possible to export those cells to or import those cells from an XML data file that conforms to the mapped schema. Excel raises events on the Application and Workbook object before and after an XML file is imported or exported, allowing the developer to further customize and control this feature.

Before Close Events

Excel raises events before a workbook is closed. These events are to give your code a chance to prevent the closing of the workbook. Excel passes a bool cancel parameter to the event. If your event handler sets the cancel parameter to true, the pending close of the workbook is cancelled and the workbook remains open.

These events cannot be used to determine whether the workbook is actually going to close. Another event handler might run after your event handler—for example, an event handler in another add-in—and that event handler might set the cancel parameter to true preventing the close of the workbook. Furthermore, if the user has changed the workbook and is prompted to save changes when the workbook is closed, the user can click the Cancel button, causing the workbook to remain open.

If you need to run code only when the workbook is actually going to close, VSTO provides a Shutdown event that is not raised until all other event handlers and the user has allowed the close of the workbook.

- **Application.WorkbookBeforeClose** is raised before any workbook is closed, giving the event handler the chance to prevent the closing of the workbook. Excel passes the Workbook object that is about to be closed. Excel also passes by reference a bool cancel parameter. The cancel parameter can be set to true by your event handler to prevent Excel from closing the workbook.

- **Workbook.BeforeClose** is raised on a workbook that is about to be closed, giving the event handler the chance to prevent the closing of the workbook. Excel passes by reference a bool cancel parameter. The cancel parameter can be set to true by your event handler to prevent Excel from closing the workbook.

Before Print Events

Excel raises events before a workbook is printed. These events are raised when the user chooses Print or Print Preview from the File menu or presses the print toolbar button. Excel passes a bool cancel parameter to the event. If your event handler sets the cancel parameter to true, the pending print of the workbook will be cancelled and the Print dialog box or Print Preview view will not be shown. You might want to do this because you want to replace Excel's default printing behavior with some custom printing behavior of your own.

These events cannot be used to determine whether the workbook is actually going to be printed. Another event handler might run after your event handler and prevent the printing of the workbook. The user can also press the Cancel button in the Print dialog box to stop the printing from occurring. An alternative would be to customize the Ribbon to repurpose the Ribbon's print command to invoke your custom code. This method is discussed in more detail in Chapter 17, "Working with the Ribbon in VSTO."

- **Application.WorkbookBeforePrint** is raised before any workbook is printed or print previewed, giving the event handler a chance to change the workbook before it is printed or change the default print behavior. Excel passes as a parameter the Workbook that is about to be printed. Excel also passes by reference a `bool cancel` parameter. The `cancel` parameter can be set to `true` by your event handler to prevent Excel from performing its default print behavior.

- **Workbook.BeforePrint** is raised on a workbook that is about to be printed or print previewed, giving the event handler a chance to change the workbook before it is printed or change the default print behavior. Excel passes by reference a `bool cancel` parameter. The `cancel` parameter can be set to `true` by your event handler to prevent performing its default print behavior.

Before Save Events

Excel raises cancelable events before a workbook is saved, allowing you to perform some custom action before the document is saved. These events are raised when the user chooses Save, Save As, or Save As Web Page commands. They are also raised when the user closes a workbook that has been modified and chooses to save when prompted. Excel passes a `bool cancel` parameter to the event. If your event handler sets the `cancel` parameter to `true`, the save will be cancelled and the Save dialog box will not be shown. You might want to do this because you want to replace Excel's default saving behavior with some custom saving behavior of your own.

These events cannot be used to determine whether the workbook is actually going to be saved. Another event handler might run after your event handler and prevent the save of the workbook. The user can also press Cancel in the Save dialog box to stop the save of the workbook.

- **Application.WorkbookBeforeSave** is raised before any workbook is saved, giving the event handler a chance to prevent or override the saving of the workbook. Excel passes as a parameter the Workbook that is about to be saved. Excel also passes a `bool` `saveAsUI` parameter that tells the event handler whether Save or Save As was selected. Excel also passes by reference a `bool` `cancel` parameter. The `cancel` parameter can be set to `true` by your event handler to prevent Excel from performing its default save behavior.

- **Workbook.BeforeSave** is raised on a workbook that is about to be saved, giving the event handler a chance to prevent or override the saving of the workbook. Excel passes a `bool` `saveAsUI` parameter that tells the event handler whether Save or Save As was selected. Excel passes by reference a `bool` `cancel` parameter. The `cancel` parameter can be set to `true` by your event handler to prevent Excel from performing its default save behavior.

Open Events

Excel raises events when a workbook is opened or when a new workbook is created from a template or an existing document. If a new blank workbook is created, the Application.WorkbookNew event is raised.

- **Application.WorkbookOpen** is raised when any workbook is opened. Excel passes the Workbook that is opened as a parameter to this event. This event is not raised when a new blank workbook is created. The Application.WorkbookNew event is raised instead.

- **Workbook.Open** is raised on a workbook when it is opened.

Listing 4-7 shows a console application that handles the BeforeClose, BeforePrint, BeforeSave, and Open events. Note that you must add a reference to System.Windows.Forms and the Excel PIA for this listing to compile. It sets the `cancel` parameter to `true` in the BeforeSave and BeforePrint handlers to prevent the saving and printing of the workbook.

Listing 4-7: A Console Application That Handles Close, Print, Save, and Open Events

```
using System;
using System.Collections.Generic;
using System.Linq;
using System.Text;
using System.Windows.Forms;
using Excel = Microsoft.Office.Interop.Excel;

namespace ConsoleApplication
{
  class Program
  {
    static private Excel.Application app;
    static private Excel.Workbook workbook;
    static private bool exit = false;

    static void Main(string[] args)
    {
      app = new Excel.Application();
      app.Visible = true;

      workbook = app.Workbooks.Add(Type.Missing);

      app.WorkbookBeforeClose +=
        new Excel.AppEvents_WorkbookBeforeCloseEventHandler(
        App_WorkbookBeforeClose);

      workbook.BeforeClose +=
        new Excel.WorkbookEvents_BeforeCloseEventHandler
        Workbook_BeforeClose);

      app.WorkbookBeforePrint +=
        new Excel.AppEvents_WorkbookBeforePrintEventHandler(
        App_WorkbookBeforePrint);

      workbook.BeforePrint +=
        new Excel.WorkbookEvents_BeforePrintEventHandler(
        Workbook_BeforePrint);

      app.WorkbookBeforeSave +=
        new Excel.AppEvents_WorkbookBeforeSaveEventHandler(
        App_WorkbookBeforeSave);

      workbook.BeforeSave +=
        new Excel.WorkbookEvents_BeforeSaveEventHandler(
        Workbook_BeforeSave);
```

```csharp
    app.WorkbookOpen +=
      new Excel.AppEvents_WorkbookOpenEventHandler(
      App_WorkbookOpen);

    while (exit == false)
      System.Windows.Forms.Application.DoEvents();

    app.Quit();
  }

  static void App_WorkbookBeforeClose(Excel.Workbook workbook,
    ref bool cancel)
  {
    Console.WriteLine(String.Format(
      "Application.WorkbookBeforeClose({0})",
      workbook.Name));
  }

  static void Workbook_BeforeClose(ref bool cancel)
  {
    Console.WriteLine("Workbook.BeforeClose()");
    exit = true;
  }

  static void App_WorkbookBeforePrint(Excel.Workbook workbook,
    ref bool cancel)
  {
    Console.WriteLine(String.Format(
      "Application.WorkbookBeforePrint({0})",
      workbook.Name));
    cancel = true; // Don't allow printing
  }

  static void Workbook_BeforePrint(ref bool cancel)
  {
    Console.WriteLine("Workbook.BeforePrint()");
    cancel = true; // Don't allow printing
  }

  static void App_WorkbookBeforeSave(Excel.Workbook workbook,
    bool saveAsUI, ref bool cancel)
  {
    Console.WriteLine(String.Format(
      "Application.WorkbookBeforeSave({0},{1})",
      workbook.Name, saveAsUI));
    cancel = true; // Don't allow saving
  }

  static void Workbook_BeforeSave(bool saveAsUI, ref bool cancel)
  {
```

```
        Console.WriteLine(String.Format(
          "Workbook.BeforePrint({0})",
          saveAsUI));
        cancel = true; // Don't allow saving
    }

    static void App_WorkbookOpen(Excel.Workbook workbook)
    {
        Console.WriteLine(String.Format(
          "Appplication.WorkbookOpen({0})",
          workbook.Name));
    }
  }
}
```

Toolbar and Menu Events

A common way to run your code is to add a custom toolbar button or menu item to Excel and handle the click event raised by that button or menu item. Before Office 2007, you would use an object called the CommandBar and a hierarchy of CommandBar-related objects. Although code using CommandBar objects continues to work, Office 2007 introduces a new paradigm for creating custom toolbar buttons and menus: the Ribbon. We discuss working with the Office Ribbon in Chapter 17, "Working with the Ribbon in VSTO." Although you will use the Ribbon predominantly in Office 2007 customizations, at times you need to use the CommandBar object model—to customize the context menu that appears when you right-click a cell in Excel, for example. For this reason, in this section we briefly discuss the CommandBar object model.

Both a toolbar and a menu bar are represented by the same object in the Office object model, an object called CommandBar. Figure 4-4 shows the

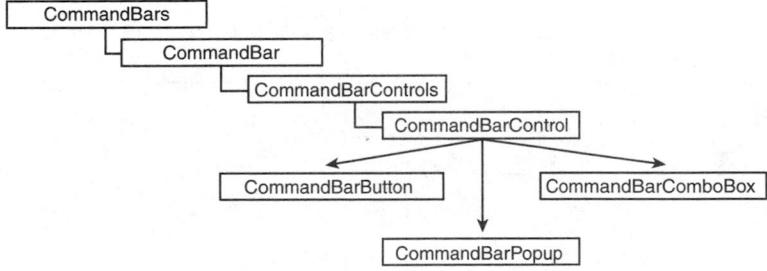

Figure 4-4: The hierarchy of CommandBar objects.

hierarchy of CommandBar-related objects. The Application object has a collection of CommandBars that represent the main menu bar and all the available toolbars in Excel.

The CommandBar objects are made available to your application by adding a reference to the Microsoft Office 12.0 Object Library PIA (office.dll). The CommandBar objects are found in the Microsoft.Office .Core namespace.

A CommandBar has a collection of CommandBarControls that contains objects of type CommandBarControl. A CommandBarControl can often be cast to a CommandBarButton, CommandBarPopup, or CommandBar-ComboBox. It is also possible to have a CommandBarControl that cannot be cast to one of these other types—for example, it is just a CommandBar-Control and cannot be cast to a CommandBarButton, CommandBarPopup, or CommandBarComboBox.

Listing 4-8 shows some code that iterates over all of the CommandBars available in Excel. Even though Excel 2007 uses the Ribbon model to display menus and commands, it represents these menus and commands through the CommandBar object model as well to maintain backward compatibility with older add-ins. The code displays the name or caption of each CommandBar and associated CommandBarControls. When Listing 4-8 gets to a CommandBarControl, it first checks whether it is a Command-BarButton, a CommandBarComboBox, or a CommandBarPopup, and then casts to the corresponding object. If it is not any of these object types, the code uses the CommandBarControl properties. Note that a CommandBar-Popup has a Controls property that returns a CommandBarControls collection. Our code uses recursion to iterate the CommandBarControls collection associated with a CommandBarPopup control.

Listing 4-8: A Console Application That Iterates Over All the CommandBars and CommandBarControls in Excel

```
using System;
using Excel = Microsoft.Office.Interop.Excel;
using Office = Microsoft.Office.Core;
using System.Text;

namespace ConsoleApplication
{
```

```csharp
class Program
{
  static private Excel.Application app;

  static void Main(string[] args)
  {
    app = new Excel.Application();
    Office.CommandBars bars = app.CommandBars;

    foreach (Office.CommandBar bar in bars)
    {
      Console.WriteLine(String.Format(
        "CommandBar: {0}", bar.Name));
      DisplayControls(bar.Controls, 1);
    }

    Console.ReadLine();
  }

  static void DisplayControls(Office.CommandBarControls ctls,
    int indentNumber)
  {
    System.Text.StringBuilder sb = new System.Text.StringBuilder();
    sb.Append(' ', indentNumber);

    foreach (Office.CommandBarControl ctl in ctls)
    {
      Office.CommandBarButton btn = ctl as Office.CommandBarButton;
      Office.CommandBarComboBox box = ctl as Office.CommandBarComboBox;
      Office.CommandBarPopup pop = ctl as Office.CommandBarPopup;

      if (btn != null)
      {
        sb.Append("CommandBarButton: ");
        sb.Append(btn.Caption);
        Console.WriteLine(sb.ToString());
      }
      else if (box != null)
      {
        sb.Append("CommandBarComboBox: ");
        sb.Append(box.Caption);
        Console.WriteLine(sb.ToString());
      }
      else if (pop != null)
      {
        DisplayControls(pop.Controls, indentNumber + 1);
      }
      else
      {
        sb.Append("CommandBarControl: ");
```

```
        sb.Append(ctl.Caption);
        Console.WriteLine(sb.ToString());
      }
    }
  }
 }
}
```

Excel raises several events on CommandBar, CommandBarButton, and CommandBarComboBox objects:

- **CommandBar.OnUpdate** is raised when any change occurs to a CommandBar or associated CommandBarControls. This event is raised frequently and can even raise when selection changes in Excel. Handling this event could slow down Excel, so you should handle this event with caution.

- **CommandBarButton.Click** is raised on a CommandBarButton that is clicked. Excel passes the CommandBarButton that was clicked as a parameter to this event. It also passes by reference a `bool cancel-Default` parameter. The `cancelDefault` parameter can be set to `true` by your event handler to prevent Excel from executing the default action associated with the button. For example, you could handle this event for an existing button such as the Print button. By setting `cancelDefault` to `true`, you can prevent Excel from doing its default print behavior when the user clicks the button and instead replace that behavior with your own.

- **CommandBarComboBox.Change** is raised on a CommandBarComboBox that had its text value changed—either because the user chose an option from the drop-down or because the user typed a new value directly into the combo box. Excel passes the CommandBarComboBox that changed as a parameter to this event.

Listing 4-9 shows a console application that creates a CommandBar, a CommandBarButton, and a CommandBarComboBox. It handles the CommandBarButton.Click event to exit the application. It also displays changes made to the CommandBarComboBox in the console window. The CommandBar, CommandBarButton, and CommandBarComboBox are added temporarily; Excel will delete them automatically when the application exits. This is done by passing true to the last parameter of the Command-BarControls.Add method.

Listing 4-9: A Console Application That Adds a CommandBar and a CommandBarButton

```
using System;
using Office = Microsoft.Office.Core;
using Excel = Microsoft.Office.Interop.Excel;

namespace ConsoleApplication
{
  class Program
  {
    static private Excel.Application app;
    static bool close = false;
    static Office.CommandBarButton btn;
    static Office.CommandBarComboBox box;
    static object missing = Type.Missing;

    static void Main(string[] args)
    {
      app = new Excel.Application();
      app.Visible = true;

      Office.CommandBars bars = app.CommandBars;
      Office.CommandBar bar = bars.Add("My Custom Bar", missing,
        missing, true);
      bar.Visible = true;

      btn = bar.Controls.Add(Office.MsoControlType.msoControlButton,
        missing, missing, missing, true) as Office.CommandBarButton;
      btn.Click +=
        new Office._CommandBarButtonEvents_ClickEventHandler(
        Btn_Click);

      btn.Caption = "Stop Console Application";
      btn.Tag = "ConsoleApplication.btn";
      btn.Style = Office.MsoButtonStyle.msoButtonCaption;

      box = bar.Controls.Add(
        Office.MsoControlType.msoControlComboBox, missing,
        missing, missing, true) as Office.CommandBarComboBox;
      box.AddItem("Choice 1", 1);
      box.AddItem("Choice 2", 2);
      box.AddItem("Choice 3", 3);
      box.Tag = "ConsoleApplication.box";
```

```
    box.Change +=
      new Office._CommandBarComboBoxEvents_ChangeEventHandler(
      Box_Change);

    while (close == false)
      System.Windows.Forms.Application.DoEvents();
  }

  static void Btn_Click(Office.CommandBarButton ctrl,
    ref bool cancelDefault)
  {
    close = true;
  }

  static void Box_Change(Office.CommandBarComboBox ctrl)
  {
    Console.WriteLine("Selected " + ctrl.Text);
  }
 }
}
```

Additional Events

Table 4-1 lists several other, less commonly used events in the Excel object model.

TABLE 4-1:   Additional Excel Events

Events	Description
Application.SheetPivotTableUpdate Workbook.SheetPivotTableUpdate Worksheet.PivotTableUpdate	Raised when a sheet of a PivotTable report is updated.
Application.WorkbookPivotTable-CloseConnection Workbook.PivotTableCloseConnection	Raised when a PivotTable report connection is closed.
Application.WorkbookPivotTable-OpenConnection Workbook.PivotTableOpenConnection	Raised when a PivotTable report connection is opened.
Application.WorkbookSync Workbook.Sync	Raised when a workbook that is part of a document workspace is synchronized with the server.

TABLE 4-1: Additional Excel Events *(Continued)*

Events	Description
Chart.DragOver	Raised when a range of cells is dragged over a chart.
Chart.DragPlot	Raised when a range of cells is dragged and dropped on a chart.
Chart.MouseDown	Raised when the user clicks the mouse button while the cursor is over a chart.
Chart.MouseMove	Raised when the user moves the mouse cursor within the bounds of a chart.
Chart.MouseUp	Raised when the user releases the mouse button while the cursor is over a chart.
Chart.Resize	Raised when the chart is resized.
Chart.SeriesChange	Raised when the user changes the data being displayed by the chart.
OLEObject.GotFocus	Raised when an OLEObject—an embedded ActiveX control or OLE object—gets the focus.
OLEObject.LostFocus	Raised when an OLEObject—an embedded ActiveX control or OLE object—loses focus.
QueryTable.AfterRefresh	Raised after a QueryTable is refreshed.
QueryTable.BeforeRefresh	Raised before a QueryTable is refreshed.

Events in Visual Studio 2008 Tools for Office

Several events are found in Visual Studio 2008 Tools for Office objects that are not found when using the Excel PIA alone. Table 4-2 lists these events. Almost all of these are events from the Excel PIA that are re-raised on different objects. For example, in the Excel PIA, there is no BeforeDoubleClick event on a Range object—in fact, there are no events on the Range object at all. In VSTO, the two objects that VSTO defines that represent a Range (NamedRange and XMLMappedRange) have a BeforeDoubleClick event. VSTO adds the BeforeDoubleClick event to these objects and raises the event whenever the Worksheet.BeforeDoubleClick event is raised and passed a Range object that matches the given NamedRange or XML-MappedRange object.

Another case where VSTO changes events is in the naming of the Activate event and the Select event on the Worksheet object. Both of these event names conflict with method names on Worksheet. To avoid this conflict, VSTO renames these events to ActivateEvent and SelectEvent.

There are also some new events such as the Startup and Shutdown events raised on VSTO project host items such as Workbook, Worksheet, and ChartSheet. ListObject also has several new events that are raised when ListObject is data bound.

TABLE 4-2: Events That Are Added in VSTO

Events	Re-Raised From
NamedRange Object (Aggregates Range)	
BeforeDoubleClick	Worksheet.BeforeDoubleClick
BeforeRightClick	Worksheet.BeforeRightClick
Change	Worksheet.Change
SelectionChange	Worksheet.SelectionChange
Selected	Worksheet.SelectionChange
Deselected	Worksheet.SelectionChange
XmlMappedRange Object (Aggregates Range)	
BeforeDoubleClick	Worksheet.BeforeDoubleClick
BeforeRightClick	Worksheet.BeforeRightClick
Change	Worksheet.Change
SelectionChange	Worksheet.SelectionChange

TABLE 4-2: Events That Are Added in VSTO *(Continued)*

Events	Re-Raised From
XmlMappedRange Object (Aggregates Range)	
Selected	Worksheet.SelectionChange
Deselected	Worksheet.SelectionChange
Workbook	
New	Application.NewWorkbook
Startup	New event
Shutdown	New event
ChartSheet (Aggregates Chart)	
Startup	New event
Shutdown	New event
Worksheet	
Startup	New event
Shutdown	New event
ListObject	
BeforeAddDataBoundRow	New event
BeforeDoubleClick	Worksheet.BeforeDoubleClick
BeforeRightClick	Worksheet.BeforeRightClick
Change	Worksheet.Change
DataBindingFailure	New event
DataMemberChanged	New event
DataSourceChanged	New event
Deselected	Worksheet.SelectionChange

Continues

TABLE 4-2: Events That Are Added in VSTO *(Continued)*

Events	Re-Raised From
ListObject	
ErrorAddDataBoundRow	New event
OriginalDataRestored	New event
Selected	Worksheet.SelectionChange
SelectedIndexChanged	New event
SelectionChange	Worksheet.SelectionChange

Conclusion

This chapter examined the various events raised by objects in the Excel object model. The chapter introduced some of the major objects in the Excel object model, such as Application, Workbook, and Document. You also learned the additional events that are raised by VSTO objects in Excel.

Chapter 5, "Working with Excel Objects," discusses in more detail how to use the major objects in the Excel object model.

■ 5 ■
Working with Excel Objects

Working with the Application Object

This chapter covers some of the major objects in the Excel object model starting with the Application object. The major objects in the Excel object model have many methods and properties, and it is beyond the scope of this book to describe all these objects. Instead, this chapter focuses on the most commonly used methods and properties.

The Application object has the largest number of methods, properties, and events of any object in the Excel object model. The Application object is also the root object in the Excel object model hierarchy. You can access all the other objects in the object model by starting at the Application object and accessing its properties and the properties of objects it returns. The Application object also has a number of useful application-level settings.

Non-English Locales and Excel

A reminder: Excel and .NET have some issues when running in a non-English locale. These issues may cause code in this section to fail if you try to use it in an automation executable or a COM add-in. As long as you use VSTO add-ins, you should not have any problems, as VSTO add-ins have some special features that work around these issues. For more information, see the section "Special Excel Issues" in this chapter.

Controlling Excel's Screen Updating Behavior

When your code is performing a set of changes to a workbook, you may want to set the ScreenUpdating property to `false` to prevent Excel from updating the screen while your code runs. Setting it back to `true` will refresh the screen and allow Excel to continue updating the screen.

Beyond the cosmetic benefit of not forcing the user to watch Excel change cells while your code runs, the ScreenUpdating property proves very useful for speeding up your code. Repainting the screen after each operation can be quite costly. Be sure to set this property back to `true` when your code is finished—otherwise, the user will be left with an Excel that does not paint. As you will see below, a `try-finally` block is a handy way to ensure that the property is reset even if an exception is thrown.

An even better convention to follow than just setting the ScreenUpdating property back to `true` is to save the value of the ScreenUpdating property before you change it and set it back to that value when you are done. An important thing to remember when doing Office development is that your code is not going to be the only code running inside of a particular Office application. Add-ins might be running, as well as other code behind other documents, and so on. You need to think about how your code might affect other code also running inside of Excel.

As an example, another add-in might be running a long operation of its own, and that add-in might have set the ScreenUpdating property to `false` to accelerate that operation. That add-in does an operation that triggers an event that is handled by your code. If your code sets the ScreenUpdating property to `false`, does something, and then sets it to `true` when it is done, you have now defeated the add-in's attempt to accelerate its own long operation because you have now turned screen updating back on. If instead you store the value of ScreenUpdating before you set it to `false` and later set ScreenUpdating back to its original value, you coexist better with the other code running inside of Excel.

Listing 5-1 shows an example of using the ScreenUpdating property with VSTO. Because it is important that you set ScreenUpdating back to its original value after your code runs, you should use C#'s support for exception handling to ensure that even if an exception occurs in your code, ScreenUpdating will be set back to its original value.

> **◾ NOTE**
>
> C# supports try, catch, and finally blocks to deal with exceptions. You should put the code to set ScreenUpdating back to its original value in your finally block because this code will run both when an exception occurs or when no exception occurs.

Listing 5-1: A VSTO Customization That Sets the ScreenUpdating Property

```csharp
private void Sheet1_Startup(object sender, System.EventArgs e)
{
  bool oldScreenUpdatingSetting = this.Application.ScreenUpdating;

  try
  {
    this.Application.ScreenUpdating = false;
    Random r = new Random();

    for (int i = 1; i < 1000; i++)
    {
      string address = String.Format("A{0}", i);
      Excel.Range range = Range[address, missing];
      range.Value2 = r.Next();
    }
  }
  finally
  {
    this.Application.ScreenUpdating = oldScreenUpdatingSetting;
  }
}
```

Controlling the Dialog Boxes and Alerts that Excel Displays

Occasionally the code you write will cause Excel to display dialog boxes prompting the user to make a decision or alerting the user that something is about to occur. If you find this happening while a section of your code runs, you might want to prevent these dialog boxes from being displayed.

You can set the DisplayAlerts property to false to prevent Excel from displaying dialog boxes and messages when your code is running. Setting this property to false causes Excel to choose the default response to any dialog boxes or messages that might be shown. Be sure to get the original value of this property and set the property back to its original value after your code runs. Use try, catch, and finally blocks to ensure that you always set the property back to its original value, as shown in Listing 5-1.

Changing the Mouse Pointer

During a large operation, you might want to change the appearance of Excel's mouse pointer to an hourglass to let users know that they are waiting for something to complete. The Cursor property is a property of type XlMousePointer that allows you to change the appearance of Excel's mouse pointer. It can be set to the following values: xlDefault, xlIBeam, xlNorthwestArrow, and xlWait.

Be sure to get the original value of Cursor before changing it and set it back to its original value using try, catch, and finally blocks. Listing 5-2 shows use of the Cursor property.

Listing 5-2: A VSTO Customization That Sets the Cursor Property

```
private void Sheet1_Startup(object sender, System.EventArgs e)
{
  Excel.XlMousePointer originalCursor = this.Application.Cursor;

  try
  {
    this.Application.Cursor = Excel.XlMousePointer.xlWait;
    Random r = new Random();

    for (int i = 1; i < 2000; i++)
    {
      string address = String.Format("A{0}", i);
      Excel.Range range = this.Range[address, missing];
      range.Value2 = r.Next();
    }
  }
  finally
  {
    this.Application.Cursor = originalCursor;
  }
}
```

Displaying a Message in Excel's Status Bar

StatusBar is a property that allows you to set the message displayed in Excel's status bar, found at the lower-left corner of the Excel window. You can set the StatusBar property to a string representing the message you want to display in the status bar. You can also set StatusBar to `false` to display Excel's default status bar message. If Excel is displaying the default status bar message, the StatusBar property returns a `false` value.

As with the other application properties in this section, you want to save the original value of the StatusBar property before changing it and be sure to set it back to its original value using `try`, `catch`, and `finally` blocks. Remember to save the value of the StatusBar property to an `object` variable because it can return a `string` or a `bool` value. Listing 5-3 shows an example.

Listing 5-3: A VSTO Customization That Uses the StatusBar Property to Show Progress

```
private void Sheet1_Startup(object sender, System.EventArgs e)
{
  object oldValue = this.Application.StatusBar;

  try
  {
    Random r = new Random();

    for (int i = 1; i < 2000; i++)
    {
      string address = String.Format("A{0}", i);
      Excel.Range range = this.Range[address, missing];
      range.Value2 = r.Next();

      string status = String.Format("Updating {0} of 2000...", i);
      this.Application.StatusBar = status;
    }
  }
  finally
  {
    this.Application.StatusBar = oldValue;
  }
}
```

A Property You Should Never Use

Excel provides a property called EnableEvents that can be set to `false` to prevent Excel from raising any of its events. Although you might be tempted to use this property, don't do it. Think again about the fact that your code is almost never going to be running by itself in Excel. Other developers will be creating add-ins and code behind documents that will also be running inside Excel. By setting this property to `false`, you effectively break all the other code that is loaded inside of Excel until you set it back to `true`.

The problem that this property is trying to fix is the problem of your code calling a method that in turn raises an event on your code. You might not want that event to be raised because you called the method and you therefore do not want your code to be notified of something it already knows.

For example, your code might call a method such as the Close method on the Workbook object that will cause Excel to raise the BeforeClose event. If you want to prevent your BeforeClose event handler from running in this case, you have several options that are better than using EnableEvents. The first option is to stop listening to the BeforeClose event before you call the Close method. A second option is to create a guard variable that you can set before you call Close. Your event handler for Before-Close can check that guard variable and return immediately if the guard variable is set.

Controlling the Editing Experience in Excel

Excel provides a number of properties that you can use to control the editing experience in Excel. To understand the part of the Excel editing experience that these properties control, launch an instance of Excel and create a blank worksheet. Click a cell in that worksheet and type in a number. Notice that Excel lets you type in the cell, or it lets you type in the formula bar, which is shown at the top of the window. You can move the insertion point inside of the cell to further edit the contents of the cell. When you press the Enter key after editing the cell, Excel moves to the next cell down. (Your editing settings might differ, but this explanation represents the default behavior of Excel 2007.)

Excel enables you to control whether the contents of the cell can be edited directly inside the cell through the Allow Editing Directly in Cell option in the Advanced tab of Excel's Options dialog box. The EditDirectly-InCell property lets you change this setting in your code. Setting this property to `false` makes it so the user can only edit the contents of a cell using the formula bar.

When you press Enter after editing a cell, Excel typically moves to the cell below the cell you were editing. You can control this behavior in the Advanced tab of Excel's Options dialog box. The MoveAfterReturn property and MoveAfterReturnDirection property enable you to control this behavior in your code. By setting MoveAfterReturn to true, you tell Excel to change the selected cell after the user presses Enter. MoveAfter-ReturnDirection controls the cell Excel moves to after the user presses Enter if MoveAfterReturn is set to true. MoveAfterReturnDirection can be set to a member of the XlDirection enumeration: xlDown, xlToLeft, xlToRight, or xlUp.

Controlling the Look of Excel

You can control the look of Excel through the properties listed in Table 5-1.

TABLE 5-1: Properties That Control Elements of the Excel User Interface

Property Name	Type	What It Does
DisplayFormulaBar	bool	Controls whether Excel displays the formula bar.
DisplayFullScreen	bool	Shows Excel in full-screen mode.
DisplayScrollBars	bool	Controls whether Excel displays the horizontal and vertical scroll bars for workbooks.
DisplayStatusBar	bool	Controls whether Excel displays the status bar in the bottom-left corner of the Excel window.
Height	double	Sets the height, in pixels, of the main Excel window when WindowState is set to XlWindowState.xlNormal.
Left	double	Sets the left position, in pixels, of the main Excel window when WindowState is set to XlWindowState.xlNormal.
ShowToolTips	bool	Controls whether Excel shows tooltips for toolbar buttons.

Continues

TABLE 5-1: Properties That Control Elements of the Excel User Interface *(Continued)*

Property Name	Type	What It Does
ShowWindowsInTaskbar	bool	Controls whether Excel shows open Excel windows with one taskbar button in the Windows taskbar for each open window.
Top	double	Sets the top position, in pixels, of the main Excel window when WindowState is set to XlWindow-State.xlNormal.
Visible	bool	Sets whether the Excel application window is visible.
Width	double	Sets the width, in pixels, of the main Excel window when WindowState is set to XlWindow-State.xlNormal.
WindowState	XlWindowState	Sets whether the main Excel window is minimized (xlMinimized), maximized (xlMaximized), or normal (xlNormal). The Width, Height, Top, and Left settings work only when WindowState is set to XlWindowState.xlNormal.

Controlling File and Printer Settings

You can configure the behavior when a new blank workbook is created through the SheetsInNewWorkbook property. This property takes an int value for the number of blank worksheets that should be created in a new workbook. The default is three blank worksheets. This property can also be set in the Popular page of Excel's Options dialog box.

The DefaultFilePath property corresponds to the default file location setting in the Save tab of Excel's Options dialog box. You can set this to a string representing the file path that you want Excel to use by default when opening and saving files.

You can set the default file format you want Excel to use when saving files by using the DefaultSaveFormat property. This property is of type

XlFileFormat—an enumeration that has values for the various file formats Excel supports. For example, to save Excel files by default in Excel 97-2003 binary format, you set this property to xlExcel8.

Another useful property when dealing with files is the RecentFiles property, which returns a collection of strings containing the names of all the recently opened files.

Properties That Return Active or Selected Objects

The Application object has a number of properties that return active objects—objects representing things that are active or selected within Excel. Table 5-2 shows some of these properties.

TABLE 5-2: Application Properties That Return Active or Selected Objects

Property Name	Type	What It Does
ActiveCell	Range	Returns the top-left cell of the active selection in the active window. If there isn't a worksheet with an active cell, or if no workbooks are open, this property throws an exception.
ActiveChart	Chart	Returns the active chart sheet. If no chart sheet is active, this property returns null.
ActiveSheet	object	Returns the active worksheet or a chart sheet. The object returned can be cast to either a Worksheet or a Chart.
ActiveWindow	Window	Returns the active Window. If no windows are open, this property returns null.
ActiveWorkbook	Workbook	Returns the workbook that is associated with the active window. If no workbooks are open, this property returns null.
Charts	Sheets	Returns all the chart sheets in the active workbook. If no workbooks are open, this property returns null.
Names	Names	Returns all the names associated with the active workbook.

Continues

TABLE 5-2:　Application Properties That Return Active or Selected Objects *(Continued)*

Property Name	Type	What It Does
Selection	object	Returns the current selection in the active window. This property can return a Range when cells are selected. If other elements are selected (such as a chart or an autoshape), it can return other types. You can use the is and as operators in C# to determine the returned type.
Sheets	Sheets	Returns all the sheets in the active workbook. This collection can contain both worksheets and chart sheets. Objects returned from this collection can be cast to either a Worksheet or a Chart.

Properties That Return Important Collections

The Application object is the root object of the object model and has properties that return several important collections. The Workbooks property returns the collection of open workbooks in Excel. The Windows property returns a collection representing the open windows in Excel. Both the Workbooks and Windows collections are discussed in more detail later in this chapter.

Controlling the Calculation of Workbooks

Excel provides a number of settings and methods that correspond to some of the options in the Formulas page of Excel's Options dialog box. The Application object provides a Calculation property of type XlCalculation that you can use to set Excel's calculation behavior. By default, Calculation is set to automatic calculation or xlCalculationAutomatic. You can also set Calculation to xlCalculationSemiautomatic, which means to calculate all dependent formulas except data tables. Finally, Calculation can be set to xlCalculationManual, which means Excel only recalculates the workbook when the user or your code forces a calculation.

If you have set Calculation to xlCalculationManual or xlCalculation-Semiautomatic, you can force a complete recalculation of all open workbooks with the Calculate method. Using manual calculation may be another way to speed up your code if you are updating a large number of cells that are referred to by formulas. As with other application-level properties, you should restore the original value of the property in a `finally` block, as shown earlier in this chapter.

Using Built-In Excel Functions in Your Code

The WorksheetFunction property returns a WorksheetFunction object that enables you to call the built-in Excel formulas from your code. It provides access to more than 270 formulas. Listing 5-4 illustrates three of them.

Listing 5-4: A VSTO Customization That Uses the WorksheetFunction Object

```
private void Sheet1_Startup(object sender, System.EventArgs e)
{
  Excel.WorksheetFunction func = this.Application.WorksheetFunction;
  double result = func.Acos(.1);
  double result2 = func.Atan2(.1, .2);
  double result3 = func.Atanh(.1);
}
```

New Functions in Excel 2007

Excel 2007 has many new functions. Those new functions, in alphabetical order, are AccrInt, AccrIntM, AmorDegrc, AmorLinc, AverageIf, AverageIfs, BesselI, BesselJ, BesselK, BesselY, Bin2Dec, Bin2Hex, Bin2Oct, Complex, Convert, CountIfs, CoupDayBs, CoupDays, CoupDaysNc, CoupNcd, Coup-Num, CoupPcd, CumIPmt, CumPrinc, Dec2Bin, Dec2Hex, Dec2Oct, Delta, Disc, DollarDe, DollarFr, Duration, EDate, Effect, EoMonth, Erf, ErfC, Fact-Double, FVSchedule, Gcd, GeStep, Hex2Bin, Hex2Dec, Hex2Oct, IfError, ImAbs, Imaginary, ImArgument, ImConjugate, ImCos, ImDiv, ImExp, ImLn, ImLog10, ImLog2, ImPower, ImProduct, ImReal, ImSin, ImSqrt, ImSub, ImSum, IntRate, IsEven, IsOdd, Lcm, MDuration, MRound, MultiNomial, NetworkDays, Nominal, Oct2Bin, Oct2Dec, Oct2Hex, OddFPrice, OddFYield, OddLPrice, OddLYield, Price, PriceDisc, PriceMat, Quotient, RandBetween, Received, SeriesSum, SqrtPi, SumIfs, TBillEq, TBillPrice, TBillYield, WeekNum, WorkDay, Xirr, Xnpv, YearFrac, YieldDisc, and YieldMat.

Selecting and Activating a Range of Cells

Goto is a method that causes Excel to select a range of cells and activate the workbook associated with that range of cells. It takes an optional object parameter that can be either a string containing cell reference (in "Sheet1!R1C1" format) or a Range object. We talk more about cell reference formats such as "Sheet1!R1C1" in the section "Working with the Range Object" later in this chapter. It also takes an optional object parameter that can be set to true to tell Excel to scroll the window so that the selection is at the upper-left corner of the window. Listing 5-5 shows some examples of calling the Goto method.

Listing 5-5: A VSTO Customization That Uses the Goto Method

```
private void Sheet1_Startup(object sender, System.EventArgs e)
{
  Excel.Application app = this.Application;

  app.Goto("R3C3", missing);
  app.Goto("Sheet2!R10C5", true);
  app.Goto("[BOOK1.XLSX]Sheet1!R4C4", true);
  app.Goto(this.get_Range("R8C2", missing), true);
  app.Goto(this.get_Range("R1C1", "R20C3"), true);
}
```

Spell Checking

Excel provides a method called CheckSpelling that you can use to check the spelling of a single word. It takes a required string parameter containing the word to check. It also takes an optional object parameter that can be set to a string for the filename of the custom dictionary to use. Finally, it takes an optional object parameter that can be set to true to ignore uppercase words when spell checking. CheckSpelling returns false if the word passed to it is misspelled. Listing 5-6 shows an example of calling the CheckSpelling method.

Listing 5-6: A VSTO Customization That Uses the CheckSpelling Method

```
private void Sheet1_Startup(object sender, System.EventArgs e)
{
  Excel.Application app = this.Application;

  if (!app.CheckSpelling("funtastic", missing, missing))
  {
```

```
    MessageBox.Show("Funtastic was not spelled correctly.");
  }

  if (!app.CheckSpelling("fantastic", missing, missing))
  {
    MessageBox.Show("Fantastic was not spelled correctly.");
  }

  if (!app.CheckSpelling("FUNTASTIC", missing, true))
  {
    MessageBox.Show("FUNTASTIC was not spelled correctly.");
  }
}
```

Sending a Workbook in E-mail

Excel provides a simple way to send a workbook as an e-mail message
using three methods called MailLogon, Workbook.SendMail, and Mail-
Logoff. MailLogon logs on to the mail system and takes the username as a
string, the user's password as a string, and whether to download new
mail immediately as a bool. It is also important to check the MailSession
property to make sure that a mail session is not already established. If
MailSession is not null, you do not need to call the MailLogon method.
Workbook's SendMail method takes the recipients as a required string if
there is only one recipient or as an array of strings if there are multiple
recipients. It also takes a subject for the message as a string and whether
to request a read receipt as a bool. Listing 5-7 shows a simple example that
mails a workbook.

Listing 5-7: A VSTO Customization That Mails a Workbook

```
private void ThisWorkbook_Startup(object sender, EventArgs e)
{
  Excel.Application app = this.Application;

  if (app.MailSession == null)
  {
    app.MailLogon(@"DOMAIN\JOHN", @"JOHN", missing);
  }

  this.SendMail(@"bar@domain.com", "Test message", missing);
  app.MailLogoff();
}
```

Quitting Excel

You can use the Quit method to exit Excel. If any unsaved workbooks are open, Excel prompts the user to save each unsaved workbook. You can suppress the prompts by setting the DisplayAlerts property to `false`, which causes Excel to quit without saving workbooks. You can also check the Workbook.Saved property on each workbook and call Workbook.Save to save each unsaved workbook. Remember that when users are prompted to save, they get a dialog box that looks like the one shown in Figure 5-1. If the user clicks the Cancel button or if any code is running that handles the BeforeClose event and sets the `cancel` parameter to `true`, Excel will not quit.

Undo in Excel

Excel has an Undo method that can be used to undo the last few actions taken by the user. However, Excel does not support undoing actions taken by your code. As soon as your code touches the object model, Excel clears the undo history and it does not add any of the actions your code performs to the undo history.

Sending Keyboard Commands to Excel

Excel provides a method called SendKeys that you can use as a last resort when you cannot find a way to accomplish a command through the object model but you know how to accomplish it through a keyboard command. It takes the keys you want to send to the application as a `string` and a `Wait` parameter that if set to `true` causes Excel to wait for the keystrokes to be processed by Excel before returning control to your code. You can specify modifier keys like Alt, Ctrl, and Shift by prefacing the keystroke you want to send by another character. For example, to send an Alt+T key command,

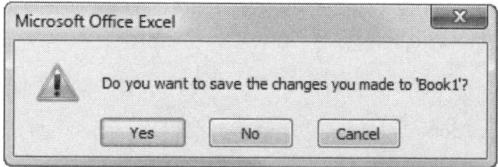

Figure 5-1: Excel prompts when you call Quit
and a workbook needs to be saved.

you call SendKeys("%t", System.Type.Missing), because % is the symbol SendKeys recognizes as Alt. The symbol SendKeys recognizes as Ctrl is ^ and Shift is +. In addition, special strings correspond to keys such as the down arrow. To send a down-arrow keystroke to Excel, you call Send-Keys("{DOWN}", System.Type.Missing). Table 5-3 lists the other special strings that correspond to common keys.

TABLE 5-3: Codes Used by SendKeys

Key	Key Code
Backspace	{BACKSPACE} or {BS}
Break	{BREAK}
Caps Lock	{CAPSLOCK}
Clear	{CLEAR}
Delete or Del	{DELETE} or {DEL}
Down arrow	{DOWN}
End	{END}
Enter	~ (tilde)
Enter (numeric keypad)	{ENTER}
Esc	{ESCAPE} or {ESC}
F1 through F15	{F1} through {F15}
Help	{HELP}
Home	{HOME}
Ins	{INSERT}
Left arrow	{LEFT}
Num Lock	{NUMLOCK}

Continues

TABLE 5-3: Codes Used by SendKeys *(Continued)*

Key	Key Code
Page Down	{PGDN}
Page Up	{PGUP}
Return	{RETURN}
Right arrow	{RIGHT}
Scroll Lock	{SCROLLLOCK}
Tab	{TAB}
Up arrow	{UP}

Working with the Workbooks Collection

The Workbooks collection, available from the Application object's Workbooks property, contains a collection of the Workbook objects currently open in the application. It also has methods used to manage open workbooks, create new workbooks, and open existing workbook files.

Iterating over the Open Workbooks

Collections implement a special method called GetEnumerator that allows them to be iterated over. You do not ever have to call the GetEnumerator method directly because the foreach keyword in C# uses this method to iterate over a collection of Workbooks. See Listing 5-8 for an example of using foreach.

Listing 5-8: A VSTO Customization That Iterates over the Workbooks Collection Using foreach

```csharp
private void Sheet1_Startup(object sender, System.EventArgs e)
{
  Excel.Workbooks workbooks = this.Application.Workbooks;

  foreach (Excel.Workbook workbook in workbooks)
  {
    MessageBox.Show(workbook.Name);
  }
}
```

Accessing a Workbook in the Workbooks Collection

To access a Workbook in the Workbooks collection, you use the get_Item method, which returns a Workbook object. The get_Item method has an Index parameter that is of type `object`. You can pass an `int` representing the one-based index of the Workbook in the collection you want to access. (Almost all collections in the Office object models are one-based.)

Alternatively, you can pass a `string` representing the name of the Workbook you want to access. The name for a workbook is the name of the file if it has been saved (for example, `"Book1.xlsx"`). If the workbook has not yet been saved, it will be the temporary name that Excel creates for a new workbook, typically Book1 with no file extension. Listing 5-9 shows an example of calling get_Item with both kinds of indexing.

Listing 5-9: A VSTO Customization That Gets a Workbook Using get_Item with an int and string Index

```
private void Sheet1_Startup(object sender, System.EventArgs e)
{
  Excel.Workbooks workbooks = this.Application.Workbooks;

  if (workbooks.Count > 0)
  {
    // Get the first workbook in the collection (1-based)
    Excel.Workbook wb = workbooks.get_Item(1);
    MessageBox.Show(wb.Name);

    // Get the same workbook by passing the name of the workbook.
    Excel.Workbook wb2 = workbooks.get_Item(wb.Name);
    MessageBox.Show(wb2.Name);
  }
}
```

You can also use the Workbooks collection's Count property to determine the number of open workbooks. You should check the Count property before accessing a workbook by index to make sure your index is within the bounds of the collection.

Creating a New Workbook

To create a new workbook, you can use the Workbooks collection's Add method. The Add method returns the newly created Workbook object. It takes as an optional parameter an object that can be set to a `string` specifying the filename of an existing workbook to use as a template. Alternatively, you can pass a member of the XlWBATemplate enumeration (xlWBATChart or xlWBATWorksheet) to specify that Excel should create a workbook with a single chart sheet or a single worksheet. If you omit the parameter by passing `System.Type.Missing`, Excel will create a new blank workbook with the number of worksheets specified by Application.SheetsInNewWorkbook property. Listing 5-10 shows several ways to create a new workbook.

Listing 5-10: A VSTO Customization That Creates New Workbooks Using Workbooks.Add

```
private void Sheet1_Startup(object sender, System.EventArgs e)
{
  Excel.Workbooks workbooks = this.Application.Workbooks;

  // Create a new workbook using mytemplate.xls as a template
  Excel.Workbook workbook1 = workbooks.Add(
    @"c:\mytemplate.xlsx");

  // Create a new workbook with one chart sheet
  Excel.Workbook workbook2 = workbooks.Add(
    Excel.XlWBATemplate.xlWBATChart);

  // Set default number of new sheets to create in a
  // new blank workbook to 10
  this.Application.SheetsInNewWorkbook = 10;

  // Create a blank workbook with 10 worksheets
  Excel.Workbook workbook3 = workbooks.Add(missing);
}
```

Opening an Existing Workbook

To open an existing workbook, you can use the Workbooks collection's Open method, which returns the opened Workbook object. Open has one required parameter—a `string` representing the filename of the workbook to open. It also has 14 optional parameters for which you can pass `System .Type.Missing` if you do not want to use any of these parameters. Listing 5-11 shows the simplest possible way of calling the Open method.

Listing 5-11: A VSTO Customization That Opens a Workbook Using the Workbooks.Open Method

```
private void ThisWorkbook_Startup(object sender, EventArgs e)
{
  Excel.Workbook workbook = this.Application.Workbooks.Open(
```

```
    @"c:\myworkbook.xlsx", missing, missing, missing,
    missing, missing, missing, missing, missing,
    missing, missing, missing, missing, missing, missing);

  MessageBox.Show(workbook.Name);
}
```

Closing All the Open Workbooks

Excel provides a Close method on the Workbooks collection to close all the open workbooks. The user is prompted to save any unsaved workbooks unless Application.DisplayAlerts is set to `false`. As with Application.Quit, you cannot be guaranteed that all the workbooks will actually be closed because the user can press the Cancel button when prompted to save a workbook and other event handlers that are loaded in Excel from other add-ins can handle the BeforeClose event and set the cancel parameter to `true`.

Working with the Workbook Object

The Workbook object represents an open workbook in Excel. The workbook has a Name property that returns the name of the workbook as a `string` (for example `"book1.xlsx"`). If the workbook has not yet been saved, this property returns the temporary name of the document, typically Book1. This name can be passed to get_Item on the Workbooks collection to access the workbook by name from that collection. Workbook also has a FullName property that returns the full filename of the workbook if the workbook has been saved (for example, `"c:\temp\book1.xlsx"`). For a new unsaved workbook, it returns the default name Excel gave to the workbook, such as Book1.

Properties That Return Active or Selected Objects

The Workbook object has a number of properties that return active objects—objects representing things that are selected within the Excel workbook. Table 5-4 shows two of these properties.

TABLE 5-4: Workbook Properties That Return Active Objects

Property Name	Type	What It Does
ActiveChart	Chart	Returns the selected chart sheet in the workbook. If the selected sheet is not a chart sheet, this property returns null.
ActiveSheet	object	Returns the selected sheet in the workbook, which can be either a worksheet or a chart sheet. You can cast this property to either a Worksheet or a Chart.

Properties That Return Important Collections

The Workbook object has a number of properties that return collections that you will frequently use. Table 5-5 shows some of these properties.

TABLE 5-5: Workbook Properties That Return Important Collections

Property Name	Type	What It Does
Charts	Charts	Returns the Charts collection, which contains all the chart sheets in the workbook. The Charts collection has methods and properties to access a particular chart sheet or to add a new chart sheet.
Sheets	Sheets	Returns the Sheets collection, which contains all the sheets in the workbook (both worksheets and chart sheets). The Sheets collection has methods and properties to access a particular sheet or to add a new sheet.
Windows	Windows	Returns the Windows collection, which contains all the open windows that are showing the workbook. The Windows collection has methods and properties to arrange and access windows.
Worksheets	Sheets	Returns the Worksheets collection, which contains all the worksheets in the workbook in a Sheets collection. The Worksheets collection has methods and properties to access a particular worksheet or to add a new worksheet.

Accessing Document Properties

Workbook has a BuiltinDocumentProperties property that returns an `object` that can be cast to a Microsoft.Office.Core.DocumentProperties collection representing the built-in document properties associated with the workbook. These are the properties that you see when you choose Prepare from the Office menu and then choose Properties. A task pane appears above the worksheet. At the top of the task pane is a drop-down menu labeled Document Properties. From this drop-down menu, choose Advanced Properties to bring up a Properties dialog box. Click the Summary tab of this dialog box. In the Summary tab you see properties such as Title, Subject, Author, and Company. Table 5-6 shows the names of the built-in document properties associated with a workbook. Some of these properties, such as Number of Slides, look out of place for Excel, but they are all valid built-in document properties that you can set.

TABLE 5-6: Names of the Built-In Document Properties in Excel

Application name	Language*	Number of pages
Author	Last author	Number of paragraphs
Category	Last print date	Number of slides
Comments	Last save time	Number of words
Company	Manager	Revision number
Content status*	Number of bytes	Security
Content type*	Number of characters	Subject
Creation date	Number of characters (with spaces)	Template
Document version*	Number of hidden slides	Title
Format	Number of lines	
Hyperlink base	Number of multimedia clips	
Keywords	Number of notes	

* New in Excel 2007

Workbook also has a CustomDocumentProperties property that returns an object that can be cast to a Microsoft.Office.Core.DocumentProperties collection representing any custom document properties associated with the workbook. These custom properties are the ones you see when you choose Prepare from the Office menu, choose Properties, choose Advanced Properties from the Document Properties drop-down menu, and click the Custom tab. Custom properties can be created by your code and used to store name and value pairs in the workbook. The DocumentProperties collection is discussed in more detail in the section "Working with Document Properties" later in this chapter.

Saving an Excel Workbook

The Workbook object has a number of properties and methods that are used to save a workbook, detect whether a workbook has been saved, and get the path and filename of a workbook.

The Saved property returns a bool value that tells you whether the latest changes to the workbook have been saved. If closing the document will cause Excel to prompt the user to save, the Saved property will return false. If the user creates a blank new workbook and does not modify it, the Saved property will return true until the user or your code makes a change to the document. You can set the Saved property to true to prevent a workbook from being saved, but be careful: Any changes made in that document may be lost because the user will not be prompted to save when the document is closed.

A more common use of the Saved property is to try to keep the state of the Saved property the same as before your code ran. For example, your code might set or create some custom document properties, but if the user does not make any changes to the document while it is open, you might not want the user to be prompted to save. Your code can get the value of the Saved property, make the changes to the document properties, and then set the value of Saved back to the value before your code changed the workbook. This way the changes your code made will only be saved if the user makes an additional change to the document that requires a save. Listing 5-12 shows this approach.

Listing 5-12: A VSTO Customization That Manipulates Document Properties Without Affecting the Saved Property

```
private void ThisWorkbook_Startup(object sender, EventArgs e)
{
  bool oldSaved = this.Saved;

  try
  {
    Office.DocumentProperties props = this.
      BuiltinDocumentProperties as Office.DocumentProperties;

    props["Author"].Value = "Mark Twain";
  }
  finally
  {
    this.Saved = oldSaved;
  }
}
```

To save a workbook, you can use the Save method. If the workbook has already been saved, Excel just overwrites the file from the previous save. If the workbook is newly created and has not been saved yet, Excel tries to create a filename (such as Book2.xlsx if the new workbook was called Book2) and save it to the default file path set by Application.DefaultFilePath.

If you want to specify a filename to save the workbook to, you must use the SaveAs method. SaveAs takes the filename as a `string` parameter. It also takes a number of optional parameters that you can omit by passing `System.Type.Missing`.

If you want to save a copy of the workbook, use the SaveCopyAs method and pass it the copy's filename as a `string` parameter. SaveCopyAs creates a backup copy of the workbook. It does not affect the filename or save location of the Workbook it is called on.

You can also save the workbook while closing it using the Close method. If you omit all the optional parameters, the user will be prompted to save the workbook if it has been changed since it was created or opened. If you pass `false` to the `SaveChanges` parameter, it will close the workbook without saving changes. If you set the `SaveChanges` parameter to `true` and pass a filename as a `string` for the `Filename` parameter, it will save the workbook to the filename you specified.

Several additional properties are used to access the filename and location of the Workbook, as shown in Table 5-7.

Table 5-8 shows a number of other properties related to saving.

Naming Ranges of Cells

Excel enables you to associate a name (a `string` identifier) with any range of cells. You can define a name for a range of cells by writing code or by using the Define Name dialog box that is shown when you right-click some selected cells and choose Name a Range. You can also select a cell or range of cells you want to associate a name with and then type the name into the Name Box to the left of the formula bar, as shown in Figure 5-2. When you type the name into the Name Box, you need to press the Enter key after typing the name to set the name.

TABLE 5-7: Workbook Properties That Return Filename and Path Information

Property Name	Type	What It Does
FullName	string	Returns the full name of the workbook, including the path. For a saved workbook, it returns the full filename of the workbook. For a new, unsaved workbook, it returns the default name Excel gave the workbook, such as Book1.
FullNameURLEncoded	string	Returns as a URL-encoded string the full name of the workbook, including the path.
Path	string	Returns the full path to the workbook (for example, `"C:\temp\book1.xlsx"`). If the workbook has not yet been saved, this property returns an empty string.
Name	string	Returns the name of the workbook (for example, `"book1.xlsx"`). If the workbook has not yet been saved, this property returns the temporary name of the document—typically, Book1. This can be passed to Item on the Workbooks collection to access this workbook.

TABLE 5-8:   Workbook Properties Related to Saving an Excel Workbook

Property Name	Type	What It Does
CreateBackup	bool	Sets whether a backup is created when the workbook is saved.
EnableAutoRecover	bool	Sets whether the autosave feature of Excel is enabled. If that feature is enabled, Excel saves the workbook on a timed interval so that if Excel should crash or the system should fail, a backed-up file is available.
FileFormat	XlFileFormat	Returns the file format this workbook is saved as.
ReadOnly	bool	Returns true if the file was opened as read-only.

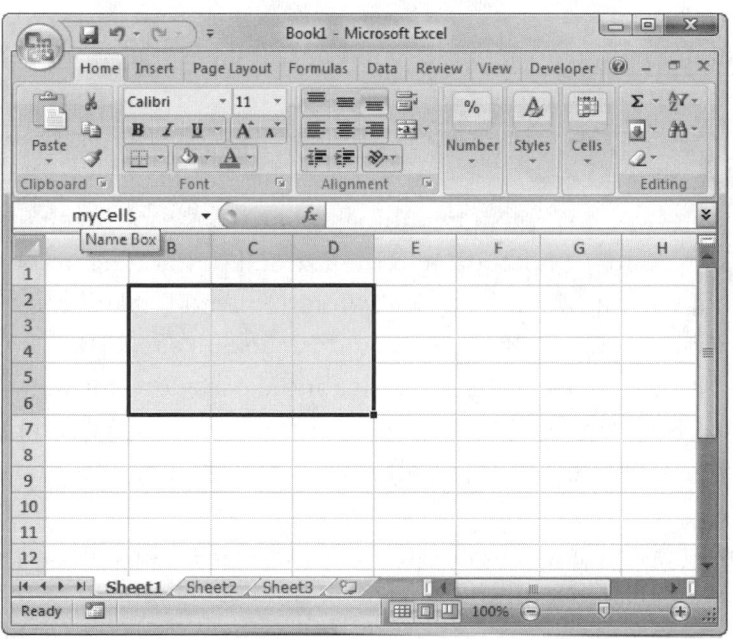

Figure 5-2: Naming a range of cells myCells using the Name Box.

The Names property returns the Names collection that can be used to access any ranges you have named within the workbook. The Names collection also enables you to create new named ranges. The Names collection is discussed in more detail in the section "Working with the Names Collection and Name Object" later in this chapter.

Creating and Activating Windows

The Workbook class has a NewWindow method that you can use to create a new window on the workbook. Although you might expect the way to create new windows would involve calling Add on the Windows collection, it does not. The only way to create a new window is by using this method.

There is also an Activate method that activates the workbook by making the first window associated with the workbook the active window. You can activate a window other than the first window associated with the workbook by using the Windows collection and the Window object. For more information on the Windows and Window objects, see the section "Working with the Window Object" later in this chapter.

Printing a Workbook

The PrintOut method prints the workbook. It takes nine optional parameters, as shown in Table 5-9.

Protecting a Workbook

Excel enables you to protect two things at the workbook level: the order of the worksheets in a workbook, and the size and positioning of the windows associated with a workbook. The Protect method takes three optional parameters: Password, Structure, and Windows. Password is an optional parameter that you can pass a string for the password for the workbook. Structure is an optional parameter that can be set to true to protect the sheet order so that the user cannot rearrange the order of the sheets in the workbook.

Windows is an optional parameter that can be set to true to protect the windows associated with the workbook from being moved or resized. For example, you could have two "tiled" windows showing a workbook; locking them prevents the user from moving them from the tiled positions.

TABLE 5-9: The Optional Parameters of the PrintOut Method

Parameter Name	What It Does
From	Sets the page number at which to start printing.
To	Sets the last page number to print.
Copies	Sets how many copies to print.
Preview	Set to true to show print preview.
ActivePrinter	Set to a string representing the printer to print to.
PrintToFile	Set to true to print to a file.
Collate	Set to true to collate multiple copies.
PrintToFileName	Set to a string representing the filename to print to if PrintToFile is set to true.
IgnorePrintAreas*	Set to true to ignore print areas.

* New in Excel 2007

(See the section "Arranging Windows" later in this chapter for more information about tiling windows.)

Although all these parameters are optional, workbook protection does not really do anything unless you set the Structure or Windows parameter to true. If you want to protect cells in the workbook from being edited, you must use the Worksheet.Protect method.

Working with the Worksheets, Charts, and Sheets Collections

The Worksheets, Charts, and Sheets collections are all very similar, so this section covers them together. They differ mainly in whether they contain worksheets (Worksheets) or chart sheets (Charts) or both (Sheets). In this section, as in the rest of the chapter, we use the word *sheet* to refer to either a chart sheet or a worksheet.

Iterating over the Open Sheets

These collections have a GetEnumerator method that allows them to be iterated over using the foreach keyword in C#, as shown in Listing 5-13.

Listing 5-13: A VSTO Customization That Iterates over the Worksheets, Charts, and Sheets Collections

```
private void ThisWorkbook_Startup(object sender, EventArgs e)
{
  Excel.Application app = this.Application;
  this.Charts.Add(missing, missing, missing, missing);

  foreach (Excel.Worksheet sheet in this.Worksheets)
  {
    MessageBox.Show(String.Format(
      "Worksheet {0}", sheet.Name));
  }

  foreach (Excel.Chart chart in this.Charts)
  {
    MessageBox.Show(String.Format(
      "Chart {0}", chart.Name));
  }

  foreach (object sheet in this.Sheets)
  {
    Excel.Worksheet worksheet = sheet as Excel.Worksheet;

    if (worksheet != null)
    {
      MessageBox.Show(String.Format(
        "Worksheet {0}", worksheet.Name));
    }

    Excel.Chart chart = sheet as Excel.Chart;

    if (chart != null)
    {
      MessageBox.Show(String.Format(
        "Chart {0}", chart.Name));
    }
  }
}
```

Accessing a Sheet in the Collection

To access a sheet in the Worksheets, Charts, and Sheets collections, you use a method called get_Item, which returns an object. You need to cast the returned object to a Worksheet or Chart. Objects returned from the Worksheets collection can always be cast to Worksheet. Objects returned from the Charts collection can always be cast to Chart. Objects returned from the Sheets collection should be tested using the `is` operator to determine whether the object returned is a Worksheet or a Chart. It can then be cast to the appropriate object.

The get_Item method takes an `Index` parameter of type `object`. You can pass a `string` representing the name of the worksheet or chart sheet or you can pass a 1-based index into the collection. You can check how many items are in a given collection by using the Count property.

Adding a Worksheet or Chart Sheet

To add a worksheet or chart sheet to a workbook, you use the Add method. The Add method on the Sheets and Worksheets collection takes four optional parameters of type `object`: `Before`, `After`, `Count`, and `Type`. The Charts collection Add method only takes the first three parameters.

The `Before` parameter can be set to a Worksheet or Chart representing the sheet before which the new sheet is to be added. The `After` parameter can be set to the Worksheet or Chart representing the sheet after which the new sheet is to be added. The `Count` parameter can be set to the number of new sheets you want to add. The `Type` parameter is set to `XlSheet-Type.xlWorksheet` to add a worksheet or `XlSheetType.xlChart` to add a chart sheet. Note that if you try to use `xlChart` as the `Type` parameter when using Worksheets.Add, Excel will throw an exception because Worksheets is a collection of only Worksheet objects. You can specify either `Before` or `After`, but not both parameters. If you omit the `Before` and `After` parameters, Excel adds the new sheet after all the existing sheets.

Listing 5-14 shows several different ways of using the Add method on the various collections.

Listing 5-14: A VSTO Customization That Uses the Add Method on the Charts, Sheets, and Worksheets Collections

```
private void ThisWorkbook_Startup(object sender, EventArgs e)
{
  Excel.Chart chart1 = this.Charts.Add(missing,
    missing, missing, missing) as Excel.Chart;

  Excel.Chart chart2 = this.Sheets.Add(missing,
    missing, missing, Excel.XlSheetType.xlChart) as Excel.Chart;
```

```
Excel.Worksheet sheet1 = this.Sheets.Add(chart1,
    missing, 3, missing) as Excel.Worksheet;

Excel.Worksheet sheet2 = this.Worksheets.Add(missing,
    chart2, missing, missing) as Excel.Worksheet;
}
```

Copying a Sheet

You can make a copy of a sheet by using the Copy method, which takes two optional parameters: `Before` and `After`. You can specify either `Before` or `After`, but not both parameters.

The `Before` parameter can be set to a Worksheet or Chart representing the sheet before which the sheet should be copied to. The `After` parameter can be set to a Worksheet or Chart representing the sheet after which the new sheet should be copied to. If you omit the `Before` and `After` parameters, Excel creates a new workbook and copies the sheet to the new workbook.

Moving a Sheet

The Move method moves the sheet to a different location in the workbook (that is, it moves it to a different tab location in the worksheet tabs) and has two optional parameters: `Before` and `After`. You can specify either `Before` or `After`, but not both parameters. If you omit both parameters, Excel creates a new workbook and moves the sheet to the new workbook.

Working with Document Properties

The DocumentProperties collection and DocumentProperty object are found in the Microsoft Office 12.0 Object Library (office.dll), which contains objects shared by all the Office applications. These objects are in the Microsoft.Office.Core namespace and are typically brought into your code in an Office namespace alias as shown here:

```
using Office = Microsoft.Office.Core;
```

Iterating over the DocumentProperties Collection

Listing 5-15 shows an example of iterating over the DocumentProperties collection returned by Workbook.CustomDocumentProperties and Workbook.BuiltInDocumentProperties. Properties that aren't set throw an exception when you try to access their value, so the code uses try catch blocks to display just the name of the property if it isn't set to anything.

Listing 5-15: A VSTO Customization That Iterates over DocumentProperties Collection

```
private void ThisWorkbook_Startup(object sender, EventArgs e)
{
  Office.DocumentProperties customProps = this.
    CustomDocumentProperties as Office.DocumentProperties;

  Office.DocumentProperties builtinProps = this.
    BuiltinDocumentProperties as Office.DocumentProperties;

  foreach (Office.DocumentProperty builtinProp in builtinProps)
  {
    try
    {
      MessageBox.Show(String.Format(
        "{0} - {1}", builtinProp.Name, builtinProp.Value));
    }
    catch
    {
      MessageBox.Show(String.Format(
        "{0}", builtinProp.Name));
    }
  }

  foreach (Office.DocumentProperty customProp in customProps)
  {
    try
    {
      MessageBox.Show(String.Format(
        "{0} - {1}", customProp.Name, customProp.Value));
    }
    catch
    {
      MessageBox.Show(String.Format(
        "{0}", customProp.Name));
    }
  }
}
```

Accessing a DocumentProperty in the DocumentProperties Collection

To access a DocumentProperty in a DocumentProperties collection, you use the C# indexing syntax docProperty[object], which returns a Document-Property object. The indexer takes an Index parameter of type object. You can pass an int representing the 1-based index of the DocumentProperty in the collection you want to access. Alternatively, you can pass a string representing the name of the DocumentProperty you want to access. As with other collections, the Count property returns how many Document-Property objects are in the collection.

A DocumentProperty object has a Name property that returns a string containing the name of the property. It also has a Value property of type object that returns the value of the property. You can check what the type is of Value by using the Type property that returns a member of the MsoDocProperties enumeration: msoPropertyTypeBoolean, msoPropertyTypeDate, msoProperty-TypeFloat, msoPropertyTypeNumber, or msoPropertyTypeString.

Listing 5-16 shows how a DocumentProperty is accessed.

Listing 5-16: A VSTO Customization That Accesses a DocumentProperty Using an Indexer

```
private void ThisWorkbook_Startup(object sender, EventArgs e)
{
  Office.DocumentProperties builtinProps = this.
    BuiltinDocumentProperties as Office.DocumentProperties;

  Office.DocumentProperty authorProp = builtinProps["Author"];

  MessageBox.Show(String.Format(
    "Property {0} is {1}", authorProp.Name, authorProp.Value));

  Office.DocumentProperty thirdProp = builtinProps[3];

  MessageBox.Show(String.Format(
    "Property {0} is {1}", thirdProp.Name, thirdProp.Value));
}
```

Adding a DocumentProperty

You can add a custom DocumentProperty using the Add method. The Add method takes the parameters shown in Table 5-10.

Listing 5-17 shows an example of adding a custom DocumentProperty of type msoPropertyTypeString. Note that Excel will let you set the value to a long string, but it will truncate it to 255 characters. Fortunately, VSTO provides developers with a way to store larger amounts of data in a document through a feature called cached data. For more information on the cached data feature of VSTO, see Chapter 20, "Server Data Scenarios."

TABLE 5-10: Parameters for the DocumentProperties Collection's Add Method

Parameter Name	Type	What It Does
Name	string	Sets the name of the new DocumentProperty.
LinkTo-Content	bool	Sets whether the property is linked to the contents of the container document.
Type	optional object	Sets the data type of the property. Can be one of the following MsoDoc-Properties enumerated values: msoPropertyTypeBoolean, msoPropertyTypeDate, msoProperty-TypeFloat, msoPropertyTypeNumber, or msoPropertyTypeString.
Value	optional object	Sets the value of the property if Link-ToContent is false.
LinkSource	optional object	Sets the source of the linked property if LinkToContent is true.

Listing 5-17: A VSTO Customization That Adds a Custom DocumentProperty

```
private void ThisWorkbook_Startup(object sender, EventArgs e)
{
  Office.DocumentProperties props = this.
    CustomDocumentProperties as Office.DocumentProperties;

  Office.DocumentProperty prop = props.Add("My Property",
    false, Office.MsoDocProperties.msoPropertyTypeString,
    "My Value", missing);

  MessageBox.Show(String.Format(
    "Property {0} has value {1}.", prop.Name, prop.Value));
}
```

Working with the Windows Collections

The Application.Windows property returns a Windows collection that lets you iterate and access all the windows that are open in Excel. Similarly, the

Workbook.Windows property lets you access windows that are associated with a particular workbook. These collections provide methods to arrange the open windows. Windows collections do not have a method to add a new window. Instead, you must call the Workbook.NewWindow method.

Iterating over the Open Windows

The Windows collection has a GetEnumerator method that allows it to be iterated over using the foreach keyword in C#, as shown in Listing 5-18.

Listing 5-18: A VSTO Customization That Iterates over the Windows Collection

```
private void ThisWorkbook_Startup(object sender, EventArgs e)
{
  Excel.Workbooks workbooks = this.Application.Workbooks;

  Excel.Workbook workbook1 = workbooks.Add(missing);
  Excel.Workbook workbook2 = workbooks.Add(missing);

  for (int i = 0; i < 10; i++)
  {
    workbook1.NewWindow();
    workbook2.NewWindow();
  }

  foreach (Excel.Window window in workbook1.Windows)
  {
    MessageBox.Show(String.Format(
      "Workbook1 Window: {0}", window.Caption));
  }

  foreach (Excel.Window window in this.Application.Windows)
  {
    MessageBox.Show(String.Format(
      "Application Window: {0}", window.Caption));
  }
}
```

Accessing a Window in the Collection

To access a Window in the Windows collection, you use a method called get_Item, which returns a Window. The get_Item method takes an Index parameter that is of type object. You can pass a string representing the caption of the Window or you can pass a 1-based index into the Windows collection. You can check how many items are in a given collection by using the Count property. Listing 5-19 shows both getting a window by a 1-based index and by passing in the caption of the window.

Listing 5-19: A VSTO Customization That Gets a Window from the Windows Collection Using get_Item

```csharp
private void ThisWorkbook_Startup(object sender, EventArgs e)
{
  string caption = "";
  Excel.Windows windows = this.Windows;

  if (windows.Count >= 1)
  {
    Excel.Window window = windows.get_Item(1);
    caption = window.Caption as string;
    MessageBox.Show(caption);
  }

  if (!String.IsNullOrEmpty(caption))
  {
    Excel.Window window2 = windows.get_Item(caption);
    string caption2 = window2.Caption as string;
    MessageBox.Show(caption2);
  }
}
```

Arranging Windows

Excel has various ways of arranging windows and synchronizing those windows so that when one window scrolls, the others scroll as well. The Arrange method lets you arrange a collection of windows as tiled, horizontal, vertical, or cascaded. This method also lets you synchronize two or more windows that are showing the same workbook so that when one window scrolls, the other windows scroll the same amount. Table 5-11 shows the optional parameters passed to the Arrange method.

The CompareSideBySideWith method allows you to synchronize the scrolling of two windows showing the same workbook or two windows showing different workbooks. This method takes a string that represents the caption of the window to compare the currently active window with. The window you want to compare to the currently active window must be a member of the Windows collection you are using—so to be safe, you should use the Application.Windows collection because it contains all open windows.

TABLE 5-11: Optional Parameters for the Arrange Method

Property Name	Type	What It Does
ArrangeStyle	XlArrangeStyle	Sets the style to use when arranging the windows: xlArrangeStyle-Cascade, xlArrangeStyleTiled, xlArrangeStyleHorizontal, or xlArrangeStyleVertical.
ActiveWorkbook	bool	If set to true, arranges the windows only for the active workbook; if set to false, arranges all open windows.
SyncHorizontal	object	If set to true, when one window associated with a workbook scrolls horizontally, the other windows associated with the workbook also scroll.
SyncVertical	object	If set to true, when one window associated with a workbook scrolls vertically, the other windows associated with the workbook also scroll.

As Listing 5-20 shows, it is important to activate the workbook whose windows you want to arrange. If you do not do this, the windows of the active workbook will be arranged rather than the workbook associated with the Windows collection. Listing 5-20 also illustrates the issue where the Activate method and the Activate event collide on the Workbook object. To get the compiler to not complain and IntelliSense to work, we cast the Workbook to an Excel._Workbook interface to let the compiler know we want the method and not the event.

Listing 5-20: A VSTO Customization That Arranges and Synchronizes Windows

```
private void ThisWorkbook_Startup(object sender, EventArgs e)
{
  Excel.Workbooks workbooks = this.Application.Workbooks;

  Excel.Workbook workbook1 = workbooks.Add(missing);
  Excel.Workbook workbook2 = workbooks.Add(missing);
```

```
Excel.Window workbook1Window = workbook1.NewWindow();
workbook2.NewWindow();

((Excel._Workbook)workbook1).Activate();

workbook1.Windows.Arrange(
  Excel.XlArrangeStyle.xlArrangeStyleTiled,
  true, true, true);

MessageBox.Show(String.Format(
  "Workbook {0} has its windows arranged tiled.",
  workbook1.Name));

((Excel._Workbook)workbook2).Activate();

this.Application.Windows.CompareSideBySideWith(
  workbook1Window.Caption);

MessageBox.Show(String.Format(
  "The windows {0} and {1} are synchronized",
  this.Application.ActiveWindow.Caption,
  workbook1Window.Caption));
}
```

Working with the Window Object

The Window object represents an Excel window. You can use the Window object to position a window associated with a workbook. You can also use the Window object to set display settings for a workbook such as whether to display gridlines and headings.

Positioning a Window

The Window object lets you position and change the way Excel displays a workbook within a window. Window has a WindowState property of type XlWindowState that can be used to set the window to xlMaximized, xlMinimized, or xlNormal.

When the WindowState is set to xlNormal, you can position the window using the Left, Top, Width, and Height properties. These properties are double values that represent points, not screen pixels. You can use the Window's PointsToScreenPixelsX and PointsToScreenPixelsY methods to convert points to pixels.

Display Settings Associated with a Window

A number of additional properties allow you to control the display of a window. Table 5-12 lists some of the most commonly used ones.

Listing 5-21 shows an example of using many of these properties. Note that we add a reference to System.Drawing.dll so that we can use the ColorTranslator object to set the GridlineColor property. The ColorTranslator object provides a method called ToOle, which takes a System.Drawing color and converts it to an Ole color format—the kind of color format that Office methods and properties that take colors expect.

TABLE 5-12: Window Properties That Control the Display of a Window

Property Name	Type	What It Does
DisplayGridline	bool	If set to false, Excel won't display gridlines around cells.
DisplayHeadings	bool	If set to false, Excel won't display the row and column headers.
DisplayHorizontalScrollBar	bool	If set to false, Excel won't display the horizontal scroll bar.
DisplayVerticalScrollBar	bool	If set to false, Excel won't display the vertical scroll bar.
DisplayWorkbookTabs	bool	If set to false, Excel won't display the tabs to allow the user to switch to another worksheet.
EnableResize	bool	If set to false, Excel won't let the user resize the window when WindowState is set to xlNormal.
GridlineColor	int	Set to the color of the gridlines. Add a reference to your project to System.Drawing.dll, and use the System.Drawing.ColorTranslator.ToOle method to generate a color Excel understands from a .NET color.
ScrollColumn	int	Sets the left column that the window should scroll to.

TABLE 5-12: Window Properties That Control the Display of a Window *(Continued)*

Property Name	Type	What It Does
ScrollRow	int	Sets the top row that the window should scroll to.
SplitColumn	double	Sets the column number where the window will be split into vertical panes.
SplitRow	double	Sets the row number where the window will be split into horizontal panes.
Visible	bool	Sets whether the window is visible.
Zoom	object	Zooms the window; set to 100 to zoom to 100%, 200 to zoom to 200%, and so on.

Listing 5-21: A VSTO Customization That Controls the Display Options for a Window

```csharp
private void ThisWorkbook_Startup(object sender, EventArgs e)
{
  Excel.Window win = this.NewWindow();

  win.WindowState = Excel.XlWindowState.xlNormal;
  win.Width = 200;
  win.Height = 200;
  win.Top = 8;
  win.Left = 8;
  win.DisplayGridlines = true;
  win.DisplayHeadings = false;
  win.DisplayHorizontalScrollBar = false;
  win.DisplayVerticalScrollBar = false;
  win.DisplayWorkbookTabs = false;
  win.EnableResize = false;

  win.GridlineColor = System.Drawing.ColorTranslator.
    ToOle(System.Drawing.Color.Red);

  win.ScrollColumn = 10;
  win.ScrollRow = 20;
  win.Visible = true;
  win.Zoom = 150;
}
```

Working with the Names Collection and Name Object

The Names collection represents a set of ranges in the workbook that have been given names so that the range can be accessed by a name in a formula or by your code accessing the Names collection. The user can create and edit names using the Name Box, as shown in Figure 5-2, or by right-clicking selected cells and choosing Name a Range from the context menu. Also, names are sometimes automatically created by features of Excel. For example, when the user defines a custom print area, Excel creates a named range with the name Print_Area.

Iterating over the Names Collection

The Names collection has a GetEnumerator method that allows it to be iterated over using the `foreach` keyword in C#. For example, the following snippet iterates the Names collection associated with a workbook and displays the name of each Name object as well as the address of the range it refers to in standard format (for instance, `"=Sheet1!$A$5"`).

```
foreach (Excel.Name name in workbook.Names)
{
  Console.WriteLine(String.Format(
    "{0} refers to {1}", name.Name, name.RefersTo));
}
```

Accessing a Name in the Names Collection

To access a Name in the Names collection, you use a method called Item, which takes three optional parameters, as shown in Table 5-13.

TABLE 5-13:   Optional Parameters for the Item Method

Parameter Name	What It Does
Index	Pass the name of the Name or the index of the Name in the Names collection.
IndexLocal	Pass the localized name of the Name. A localized name typically exists when an Excel feature has created the name.
RefersTo	Pass the standard "RefersTo" format (=Sheet1!$A$5) to get back the Name object that refers to that address.

Listing 5-22 shows some code that creates a Name and then accesses it in several ways. It creates the Name using the Add method that takes the name to be used for the Name object and the standard format address string (such as "=Sheet1!$A$5") that the newly created name will refer to.

Listing 5-22: A VSTO Customization That Creates a Name Object and Accesses It

```
private void ThisWorkbook_Startup(object sender, EventArgs e)
{
  Excel.Names names = this.Names;

  names.Add("MyName", "=Sheet1!$A$5", missing, missing,
    missing, missing, missing, missing, missing,
    missing, missing);

  Excel.Name name1 = names.Item(missing, missing,
    "=Sheet1!$A$5");

  MessageBox.Show(String.Format(
    "Name: {0} RefersTo: {1} RefersToR1C1: {2} Count: {3}",
    name1.Name, name1.RefersTo, name1.RefersToR1C1,
    name1.RefersToRange.Cells.Count));

  Excel.Name name2 = names.Item("MyName", missing, missing);

  MessageBox.Show(String.Format(
    "Name: {0} RefersTo: {1} RefersToR1C1: {2} Count: {3}",
    name2.Name, name2.RefersTo, name2.RefersToR1C1,
    name2.RefersToRange.Cells.Count));
}
```

The Name Object

Given a Name object, you will commonly use several properties. The Name returns the name as a `string`. The RefersTo property returns the standard format address as a `string` that the Name refers to. The RefersToR1C1 returns the "rows and columns" format address as a `string` (such as "=Sheet1!R26C9") that the Name refers to. Most importantly, the RefersToRange property returns an Excel Range object representing the range of cells that the name was assigned to.

To hide the name from the Define Name dialog box and the Name Box drop-down menu, you can set the Visible property to `false`. To delete a Name, use the Delete method.

Working with the Worksheet Object

The Worksheet object represents a worksheet inside an Excel workbook. The Worksheet has a Name property that returns the name of the worksheet (for example "Sheet1").

Worksheet Management

The Worksheet object has an Index property that gives a 1-based tab position for the worksheet in the tabbed worksheet tabs shown at the lower-left corner of a workbook window. You can move a worksheet to a different tab position by using the Move method. The Move method takes two optional parameters: a Before parameter that you can pass the sheet you want to move the worksheet before, and an After parameter that you can pass the sheet that you want to come after the moved worksheet. If you omit both optional parameters, Excel creates a new workbook and moves the worksheet to the new workbook. Note that the Move, Copy, and Delete methods are found on a Worksheet object but also on a Worksheets collection; you can use either to accomplish the same operation.

It is also possible to make a copy of a worksheet using the Copy method. Like the Move method, it takes two optional parameters: a Before and After parameter that specify where the copied worksheet should go relative to other sheets. You can specify either Before or After, but not both parameters. If you omit both optional parameters, Excel creates a new workbook and copies the worksheet to the new workbook.

To activate a particular worksheet, use the Activate method. This method activates the sheet by making the first window associated with the worksheet the active window. It also selects the tab corresponding to the worksheet and displays that worksheet in the active window.

The equivalent of right-clicking a worksheet tab and choosing Delete from the context menu is provided by the Delete method. When you use this method, Excel shows a warning dialog box. You can prevent this warning dialog box from appearing by using the Application object's DisplayAlerts property, which is discussed in the section "Controlling the Dialog Boxes and Alerts that Excel Displays" earlier in this chapter.

You can hide a worksheet so that its tab is not shown at all by using the Visible property. The Visible property is of type XlSheetVisibility and can be set to xlSheetVisible, xlSheetHidden, and the xlSheetVeryHidden. The last value hides the worksheet so that it can only be shown again by setting the Visible property to xlSheetVisible. Setting the Visible property to xlSheetHidden hides the sheet, but the user can still unhide the sheet by right-clicking a visible sheet tab and choosing Unhide from the context menu.

Sometimes a sheet is hidden using the Visible property so that the sheet can be used to store additional data that an application uses in a "scratch" worksheet that the user will not see. A better way to do this is provided by VSTO's cached data feature, described in Chapter 18. It has the added benefit that you can manipulate your hidden data in the Excel spreadsheet without starting up Excel. This lets you prefill an Excel worksheet with custom data on the server.

Note that a workbook must contain at least one visible worksheet. So when using the Delete method and the Visible property, you must keep this restriction in mind. If your code tries to hide or delete the last visible sheet in a workbook, an exception is thrown.

Listing 5-23 illustrates the usage of several of these properties and methods.

Listing 5-23: A VSTO Customization That Works with the Worksheets Collection

```
private void ThisWorkbook_Startup(object sender, EventArgs e)
{
  Excel.Worksheet sheetA = this.Worksheets.Add(
    missing, missing, missing, missing) as Excel.Worksheet;
  sheetA.Name = "SheetA";

  Excel.Worksheet sheetB = this.Worksheets.Add(
    missing, missing, missing, missing) as Excel.Worksheet;
  sheetB.Name = "SheetB";

  Excel.Worksheet sheetC = this.Worksheets.Add(
    missing, missing, missing, missing) as Excel.Worksheet;
  sheetC.Name = "SheetC";

  // Tab indexes
  string msg = "{0} is at tab index {1}";
  MessageBox.Show(String.Format(msg, sheetA.Name, sheetA.Index));
  MessageBox.Show(String.Format(msg, sheetB.Name, sheetB.Index));
  MessageBox.Show(String.Format(msg, sheetC.Name, sheetC.Index));
```

```
sheetC.Move(sheetA, missing);
MessageBox.Show("Moved SheetC in front of SheetA");

// Tab indexes
MessageBox.Show(String.Format(msg, sheetA.Name, sheetA.Index));
MessageBox.Show(String.Format(msg, sheetB.Name, sheetB.Index));
MessageBox.Show(String.Format(msg, sheetC.Name, sheetC.Index));

sheetB.Copy(sheetA, missing);
Excel.Worksheet sheetD = this.Worksheets.get_Item(
  sheetA.Index - 1) as Excel.Worksheet;

((Excel._Worksheet)sheetA).Activate();

MessageBox.Show(String.Format(
  "Copied SheetB to create {0} at tab index {1}",
  sheetD.Name, sheetD.Index));

sheetD.Delete();
sheetA.Visible = Excel.XlSheetVisibility.xlSheetHidden;
MessageBox.Show("Deleted SheetD and hid SheetA.");
}
```

Working with Names

As previously discussed, you can define named ranges at the workbook level by using Workbook.Names. You can also define named ranges that are scoped to a particular worksheet by using the Names property associated with a Worksheet object. The Names property returns a Names collection with only the names that are scoped to the Worksheet. For more information on the Names collection, see the section "Working with the Names Collection and the Name Object" earlier in this chapter.

Working with Worksheet Custom Properties

You can add custom properties that have a name and a value to the worksheet. Custom properties are a convenient way to associate additional hidden information with a worksheet that you do not want to put in a cell. Custom properties are not shown anywhere in the Excel user interface, unlike the document properties associated with a workbook. Custom properties at the worksheet level do not have the 256-character limit that document properties have for their value. You can store much larger chunks of data in a worksheet custom property.

The CustomProperties property returns a collection of custom properties associated with the worksheet. You can add a custom property by using the CustomProperties collection's Add method and passing a string for the name of the custom property you want to create and an object for the value you want to associate with the custom property. To get to a particular custom property, use the CustomProperties.Item method and pass the index of the property you want to get. Unfortunately, the Item method only takes a 1-based index and not the name of a custom property you have added. Therefore, you must iterate over the collection and check each returned CustomProperty object's Name property to determine whether you have found the custom property you want. Listing 5-24 shows an example of creating a custom property, then accessing it again.

Listing 5-24: A VSTO Customization That Accesses Custom DocumentProperty Objects

```
private void ThisWorkbook_Startup(object sender, EventArgs e)
{
  Excel.Worksheet sheet = this.Worksheets.Add(missing,
    missing, missing, missing) as Excel.Worksheet;

  // Add a custom property
  Excel.CustomProperties props = sheet.CustomProperties;

  props.Add("myProperty", "Some random value");
  props.Add("otherProperty", 1);

  // Now, enumerate the collection to find myProperty again.
  foreach (Excel.CustomProperty prop in props)
  {
    if (prop.Name == "myProperty")
    {
      MessageBox.Show(String.Format(
        "{0} property is set to {1}.",
        prop.Name, prop.Value));
      break;
    }
  }
}
```

If you are using VSTO to associate code with a workbook, it is usually better to use cached data rather than custom properties. The cached data feature lets you put data sets and any XML serializable type into a data island in the document. This data island can also be accessed on the server without starting Excel. For more information on the cached data feature of VSTO, see Chapter 18.

Protecting a Worksheet

The Protect method protects the worksheet so that users cannot modify the worksheet. When a worksheet is protected using the Protect method, all the cells in the workbook are automatically locked. The Protect method corresponds to the Protect Sheet dialog box, shown in Figure 5-3. You can access this dialog box by clicking the Protect Sheet button on the Review tab.

A number of optional parameters passed to the Protect method control exactly what can be modified, as shown in Table 5-14. Many of these options correspond to the checked list shown in Figure 5-3.

You have two ways to exclude certain ranges of cells from being locked when the worksheet is protected. The first way is to add exclusions to protection using the AllowEditRanges collection that is returned from Worksheet.Protection.AllowEditRanges. The AllowEditRanges collection corresponds to the Allow Users to Edit Ranges dialog box, shown in Figure 5-4. You can access this dialog box by clicking the Allow Users to Edit Ranges button on the Review tab.

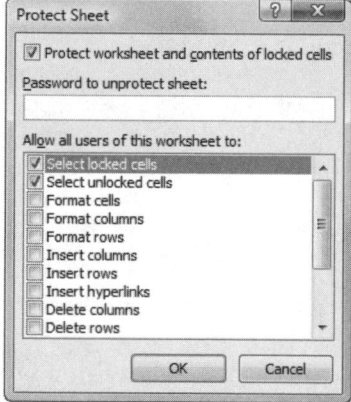

Figure 5-3: The Protect Sheet dialog box.

TABLE 5-14: Optional Parameters for the Protect Method

Parameter Name	What It Does
Password	You can pass the password as a `string` that you want to use to protect the document. You must pass this same password to the Unprotect method when you want to unprotect the document (or type the password when you choose to unprotect the document using Excel's Unprotect Sheet button in the Review tab). If you omit this parameter, the worksheet can be unprotected without requiring a password.
DrawingObjects	Pass `true` to protect any shapes that are in the worksheet. The default value is `false`.
Contents	Pass `true` to protect the values of cells that have been locked (Range.Locked is `true`) and are not in the AllowEditRange collection (Range.AllowEdit is `false`). The default value is `true`.
Scenarios	Pass `true` to prevent scenarios from being edited. The default value is `true`.
UserInterfaceOnly	Pass `true` to apply the protection settings to the actions taken by the user using the user interface. Pass `false` to protect the worksheet from code that tries to modify the worksheet. The default value is `false`. When the workbook is saved and closed, and then reopened later, Excel sets protection back to apply both user interface and code protection. You must run some code each time your workbook opens to set this option back to `true` if you want your code always to be able to modify protected objects.
AllowFormattingCells	Pass `true` to allow the user to format cells in the worksheet. The default value is `false`.
AllowFormattingColumns	Pass `true` to allow the user to format columns in the worksheet. The default value is `false`.
AllowFormatingRows	Pass `true` to allow the user to format rows in the worksheet. The default value is `false`.
AllowInsertingColumns	Pass `true` to allow the user to insert columns into the worksheet. The default value is `false`.

Continues

TABLE 5-14:   Optional Parameters for the Protect Method *(Continued)*

Parameter Name	What It Does
AllowInsertingRows	Pass true to allow the user to insert rows into the worksheet. The default value is false.
AllowInsertingHyperlinks	Pass true to allow the user to insert hyperlinks into the worksheet. The default value is false.
AllowDeletingColumns	Pass true to allow the user to delete columns in the worksheet. The default value is false. If you pass true, the user can delete only a column that has no locked cells (Range.Locked for all the cells in the column is false).
AllowDeletingRows	Pass true to allow the user to delete rows in the worksheet. The default value is false. If you pass true, the user can delete only a row that has no locked cells (Range.Locked for all the cells in the row is false).
AllowSorting	Pass true to allow the user to sort in the worksheet. The default value is false. If you pass true, the user can sort only a range of cells that has no locked cells (Range.Locked is false) or that has cells that have been added to the AllowEditRanges collection (Range.AllowEdit is true).
AllowFiltering	Pass true to allow the user to modify filters in the worksheet. The default value is false.
AllowUsingPivotTables	Pass true to allow the user to use pivot table reports in the worksheet. The default value is false.

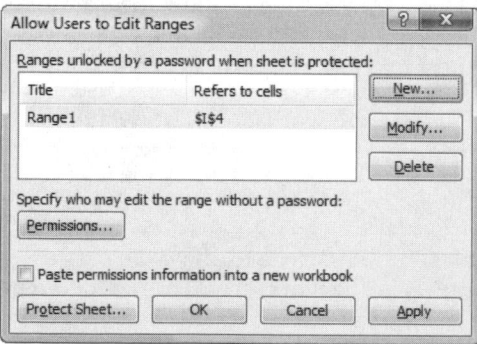

Figure 5-4: The Allow Users to Edit Ranges dialog box.

Exclusions you make using the AllowEditRanges collection must be made before you use the Protect method to protect the worksheet. After you have protected the worksheet, no changes can be made to the AllowEditRanges collection until you unprotect the worksheet again. Exclusions you make in this way can be given a title and will display in the Allow Users to Edit Range dialog box. A Range that is excluded from protection in this way will return true from its Range.AllowEdit property. Listing 5-25 shows a VSTO customization that creates two exclusions to protection using AllowEditRanges and then protects the worksheet using the Protect method.

Listing 5-25: A VSTO Customization That Adds Exclusions to Protection Using AllowEditRanges

```
private void ThisWorkbook_Startup(object sender, EventArgs e)
{
  Excel.Worksheet sheet = this.Worksheets.Add(missing,
    missing, missing, missing) as Excel.Worksheet;

  Excel.AllowEditRanges allowEdits = sheet.Protection.
    AllowEditRanges;

  allowEdits.Add("Editable Cell",
    sheet.get_Range("A1", missing), missing);

  sheet.Protect(missing, missing, missing, missing,
    missing, missing, missing, missing, missing,
    missing, missing, missing, missing, missing,
    missing, missing);

  Excel.Range protectedRange = sheet.get_Range("A2", missing);


  MessageBox.Show(String.Format(
    "A2's Locked is set to {0}", protectedRange.Locked));

  MessageBox.Show(String.Format(
    "A2's AllowEdit is set to {0}", protectedRange.AllowEdit));

  try
  {
    protectedRange.Value2 = "Should fail";
  }
  catch (Exception ex)
  {
    MessageBox.Show(ex.Message);
  }
```

```
  try
  {
    allowEdits.Add("This should fail",
      sheet.get_Range("A2", missing), missing);
  }
  catch (Exception ex)
  {
    // You can't add to the AllowEditRanges collection
    // when the worksheet is protected
    MessageBox.Show(ex.Message);
  }

  Excel.Range allowEditRange = sheet.get_Range("A1", missing);

  MessageBox.Show(String.Format(
    "A1's Locked is set to {0}", allowEditRange.Locked));

  MessageBox.Show(String.Format(
    "A1's AllowEdit is set to {0}", allowEditRange.AllowEdit));

  allowEditRange.Value2 = "Should succeed";
}
```

The second way to exclude certain ranges of cells from being locked when the worksheet is protected is by using the Range.Locked property. Cells you exclude in this way do not show up in the Allow Users to Edit Ranges dialog box. Listing 5-26 shows adding exclusions to protection using the Range.Locked property.

Listing 5-26: A VSTO Customization That Adds Exclusions to Protection Using Range.Locked

```
private void ThisWorkbook_Startup(object sender, EventArgs e)
{
  Excel.Worksheet sheet = this.Worksheets.Add(missing,
    missing, missing, missing) as Excel.Worksheet;

  Excel.Range range1 = sheet.get_Range("A2", missing);
  range1.Locked = false;

  sheet.Protect(missing, missing, missing, missing,
    missing, missing, missing, missing, missing,
    missing, missing, missing, missing, missing,
    missing, missing);

  MessageBox.Show(String.Format(
    "A2's Locked is set to {0}", range1.Locked));
```

```
MessageBox.Show(String.Format(
    "A2's AllowEdit is set to {0}", range1.AllowEdit));

  range1.Value2 = "Should succeed";
}
```

After a worksheet is protected, a number of properties let you examine the protection settings of the document and further modify protection options, as shown in Table 5-15.

TABLE 5-15: Properties That Let You Examine and Further Modify Document Protection

Property Name	Type	What It Does
EnableAutoFilter	bool	If set to false, Excel won't display the AutoFilter arrows when the worksheet is protected.
EnableOutlining	bool	If set to false, Excel won't display outlining symbols when the worksheet is protected.
EnablePivotTable	bool	If set to false, Excel won't display the pivot table controls and commands when the worksheet is protected.
EnableSelection	XlEnableSelection	If set to xlNoSelection, Excel won't allow anything to be selected on a protected worksheet. If set to xlUnlocked, Excel will allow only unlocked cells (Range.Locked is set to false) to be selected. If set to xlNoRestrictions, any cell on a protected worksheet can be selected.

Continues

TABLE 5-15:   Properties That Let You Examine and Further Modify Document Protection *(Continued)*

Property Name	Type	What It Does
ProtectContents	bool	Read-only property that returns false if locked cells can be edited in the worksheet.
ProtectDrawingObjects	bool	Read-only property that returns false if shapes in the worksheet can be edited.
Protection	Protection	Returns a Protection object that has read-only properties corresponding to most of the optional parameters passed to the Protect method.
Protection.AllowEdit-Ranges	AllowEditRanges	Returns an AllowEditRanges collection that lets you work with the ranges that users are allowed to edit.
ProtectionMode	bool	Read-only property that returns true if the worksheet is protected.
ProtectScenarios	bool	Read-only property that returns false if scenarios in the worksheet can be edited.

Working with OLEObjects

In addition to containing cells, a worksheet can contain embedded objects from other programs (such as an embedded Word document) and ActiveX controls. To work with these objects, you can use the OLEObjects method on the Worksheet object. The OLEObjects method takes an optional Index parameter of type object that you can pass the name of the OLEObject or the 1-based index of the OLEObject in the collection. The OLEObjects method also doubles as a way to get to the OLEObjects collection, which can be quite confusing. If you pass it a `string` that represents a name or a 1-based index as an `int`, it returns the specified OLEObject. If you pass it `System.Type.Missing`, it returns the OLEObjects collection.

Any time you add an OLEObject to a worksheet, Excel also includes that object in the Shapes collection that is returned from the Shapes property on the Worksheet object. To get to the properties unique to an OLEObject, you use the Shape.OLEFormat property.

It is possible to write C# code that adds ActiveX controls to a worksheet and talks to them through casting OLEObject.Object or Shape.OLE-Format.Object to the appropriate type. You have to add a reference in your C# project for the COM library associated with the ActiveX control you want to use. Doing so causes Visual Studio to generate an interop assembly and add it to your project. Alternatively, if a primary interop assembly is registered for the COM library, Visual Studio automatically adds a reference to the pre-generated primary interop assembly. You can then cast OLEObject.Object or Shape.OLEFormat.Object to the correct type added by Visual Studio for the COM library object corresponding to the ActiveX control.

VSTO enables you to add Windows Forms controls and Windows Presentation Foundation (WPF) controls to the worksheet—a much more powerful and .NET-centric way of working with controls. For this reason, we do not consider using ActiveX controls in any more detail in this book. For more information on VSTO's support for Windows Forms and WPF controls, see Chapter 13, "Using Windows Forms and WPF in VSTO."

Working with Shapes

The Shapes property returns a Shapes collection—a collection of Shape objects. A Shape object represents various objects that can be inserted into an Excel spreadsheet, including a drawing, an AutoShape, WordArt, an embedded object or ActiveX control, or a picture.

The Shapes collection has a Count property to determine how many shapes are in the Worksheet. It also has an Item method that takes a 1-based index to get a particular Shape out of the collection. You can also enumerate over the Shapes collection using `foreach`.

Several methods on the Shapes collection let you add various objects that can be represented as a Shape. These methods include AddCallout, Add-Connector, AddCurve, AddDiagram, AddLabel, AddLine, AddOLEObject, AddPicture, AddPolyline, AddShape, AddTextbox, and AddTextEffect.

The Shape object has properties and methods to position the Shape on the worksheet. It also has properties and methods that let you format and modify the Shape object. Some of the objects returned by properties on the Shape object were shown in Figure 3-20.

Working with ChartObjects

In this book, we have used the phrase chart sheet when referring to a chart that is a sheet in the workbook. Figure 5-5 shows the dialog box that appears when you right-click a sheet tab in the bottom-left corner of the workbook and choose Insert from the context menu. Excel enables you to insert a chart as a new sheet—what we have called a chart sheet—and it allows you to add a chart as an object in a sheet. The object model calls a chart that is added as an object in a sheet a ChartObject.

What complicates the matter is that the object in the object model for a chart sheet is a Chart, but a ChartObject also has a property that returns a Chart. A ChartObject has its own set of properties that control the place-

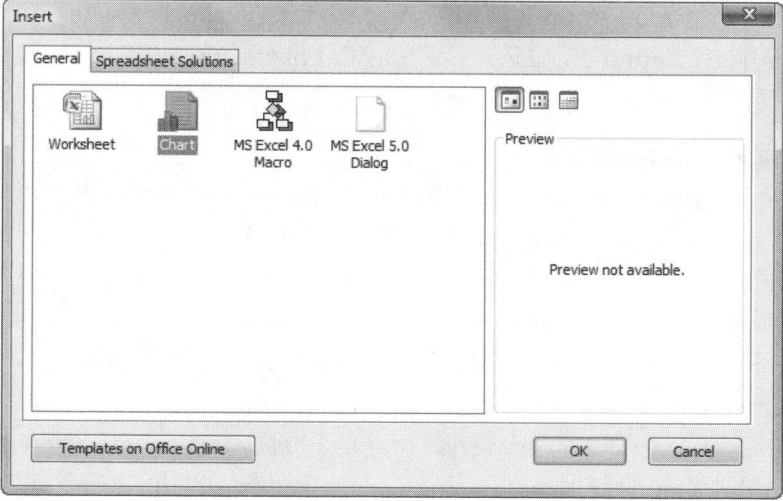

Figure 5-5: Inserting a chart.

ment of the chart in a worksheet. But the properties and methods to actually manipulate the chart contents are found on the Chart object returned by the ChartObject.Chart property.

To work with ChartObjects, you can use the ChartObjects method on the Worksheet object. The ChartObjects method takes an optional `Index` parameter of type `object` that you can pass the name of the ChartObject or the 1-based index of the ChartObject in the collection. The ChartObjects method also doubles as a way to get to the ChartObjects collection, which can be quite confusing. If you pass it a `string` that represents a name or a 1-based index, it returns the specified ChartObject. If you pass it `System`.`Type`.`Missing`, it returns the ChartObjects collection.

To add a ChartObject to a worksheet, you use the ChartObjects.Add method, which takes `Left`, `Top`, `Width`, and `Height` as `double` values in points. Any time you add a ChartObject to a worksheet, Excel also includes that object in the Shapes collection that is returned from the Shapes property on the Worksheet object.

Working with Tables

Excel has the ability to create a table from a range of cells. Just select a range of cells, and choose Table from the Insert tab. A table has column headers with drop-down options that make it easy for the user to sort and apply filters to the data in the table. It has a totals row that can automatically sum and perform other operations on a column of data. It has an insert row marked with an asterisk at the bottom of the table that allows users to add additional rows to the table. Figure 5-6 shows an example of a table in Excel.

You can access the tables in a worksheet by using the ListObjects property. The ListObjects property returns the ListObjects collection. The ListObjects collection has a Count property to determine how many tables are in the Worksheet. It also has an Item method that takes a 1-based index or the name of the table as a `string` to get a ListObject object out of the collection. You can also enumerate over the ListObjects collection using `foreach`.

Table 5-16 shows some of the most commonly used properties for the ListObject object. You will read more about ListObject in the discussion of VSTO's support for data in Chapter 19, "VSTO Data Programming."

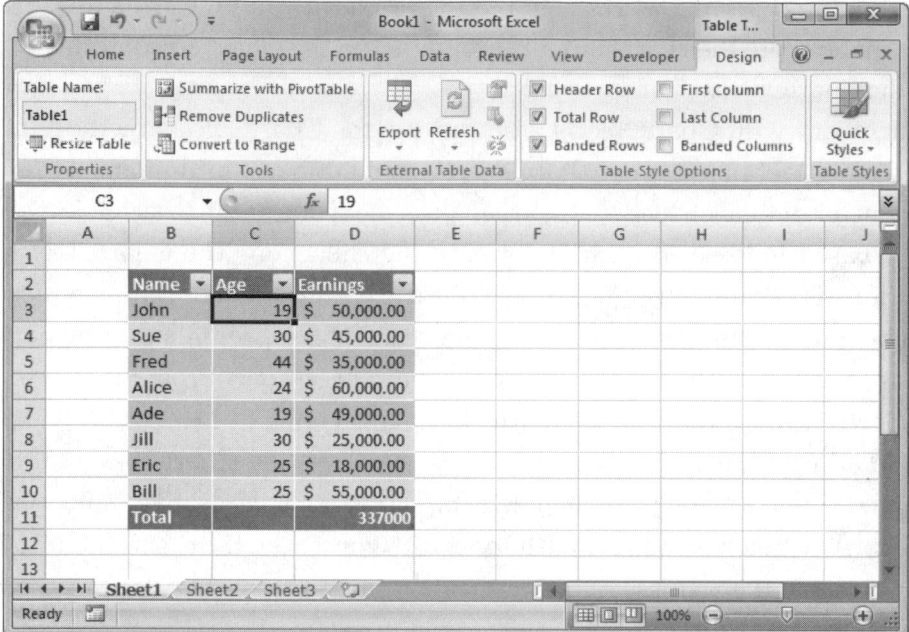

Figure 5-6: A table in Excel.

TABLE 5-16: Key Properties of ListObject

Property Name	Type	What It Does
DataBodyRange	Range	Returns a Range representing the cells containing the data—the cells between the headers and the insert row.
HeaderRowRange	Range	Returns a Range representing the header cells.
InsertRowRange	Range	Returns a Range representing the cells in the insert row.
ShowAutoFilter	bool	If set to `false`, the drop-down filtering and sorting features associated with the column headers won't be shown.
ShowTotals	bool	If set to `false`, the totals row will not be shown.
TotalsRowRange	Range	Returns a Range representing the cells in the totals row.

Table Versus List Versus ListObject

Tables were introduced in Excel 2003, but in that version of Excel they were called lists. In Excel 2007, the naming was changed in the Excel UI to Table. The object model object representing a table, however, is called ListObject, reflecting the earlier naming in Excel 2003. No matter what you call them—Tables, Lists, or ListObjects—they are key features of Excel that are well supported by VSTO. VSTO allows you to do complex data binding to Tables. For more on VSTO's support for tables see Chapter 19, "VSTO Data Programming."

Working with the Range Object

The Range object represents a range of cells in a spreadsheet. A range can contain one cell, multiple contiguous cells, and even multiple noncontiguous cells. You can select multiple noncontiguous cells by holding down the Ctrl key as you select in Excel.

Getting a Range Object for a Particular Cell or Range of Cells

Excel provides a variety of ways to get a Range object. The Range object is the object you use when you want to work with a cell or range of cells in an Excel worksheet. Two ways to get a Range object were mentioned in the description of the Application object. Application.ActiveCell returns the top-left cell of the active selection in the active window. Application.Selection returns an `object` that represents the active selection in the active window. If the active selection is a range of cells, you can cast Application.Selection to a Range object. If something else is selected in the active window, such as a shape or a chart, Application.Selection returns that selected object instead.

Worksheet also provides several ways to get a Range object. The Worksheet.get_Range method is the most common way to get a Range object from a Worksheet. This method takes a required `object` parameter to which you can pass a string. It has a second optional parameter to which you can pass a second string. The strings you pass are in what is called A1-style reference format. The easiest way to explain the A1-style reference format is to give several examples.

The reference A1 specifies the cell at row 1, column A. The reference D22 specifies the cell at row 22, column D. The reference AA11 specifies the cell at row 11, column AA (column 27).

The reference $A$1 also refers to the cell at row 1, column A. If you use $ signs in an A1-style reference, they are ignored.

You can use the range operator (:) to specify a range of cells where the first A1-style reference is the top-left corner of the range followed by a colon operator followed by a second A1-style reference for the bottom-right corner of the range. The reference A1:B1 refers to the two cells at row 1, column A and row 1, column B. The reference A1:AA11 refers to all 297 cells in the block whose top-left corner is at row 1, column A and bottom-right corner is at row 11, column AA (column 27).

You can use the union operator (,) to specify multiple cells that could be noncontiguous. For example, the reference A1,C4 specifies a range of two cells where the first cell is at row 1, column A and the second cell is at row 4, column C. Users can select noncontiguous ranges of cells by holding down the Ctrl key as they select various cells. The reference A1,C4,C8,C10 is another valid A1-style reference that specifies four different cells.

The intersection operator (a space) lets you specify the intersection of cells. For example, the reference A1:A10 A5:A15 resolves to the intersecting six cells starting at row 5, column A and ending at row 10, column A. The reference A1:A10 A5:A15 A5 resolves to the single cell at row 5, column A.

You can also use any names you have defined in the worksheet in your A1-style reference. For example, suppose that you defined a named range called foo that refers to the cell A1. Some valid A1-style references using your name would include foo:A2, which refers to the cells at row 1, column A and row 2, column A. The reference foo,A5:A6 refers to the cells at row 1, column A; row 5, column A; and row 6, column A.

As mentioned earlier, the get_Range method takes a second optional parameter to which you can pass a second A1-style reference string. The first parameter and the second parameter are effectively combined using the range operator (:). So the range that get_Range returns when you call `get_Range("A1", "A2")` is equivalent to the range you get when you call `get_Range("A1:A2", System.Type.Missing)`.

A second way to get a Range object is by using the Worksheet.Cells property, which returns a Range for all the cells in the worksheet. You can then use the same get_Range method on the returned Range object and pass A1-style references to select cells in the same way you do using get_Range from the Worksheet object. So `Cells.get_Range("A1:A2", System.Type.Missing)` is equivalent to `get_Range("A1:A2", System.Type.Missing)`. A more common use of the Cells property is to use it in conjunction with Range's get_Item property, which takes a row index and an optional column index. Using get_Item is a way to get to a particular cell without using the A1-style reference. So `Cells.get_Item(1,1)` is equivalent to `get_Range("A1", System.Type.Missing)`.

Another way to get a Range object is by using the Worksheet.Rows or Worksheet.Columns properties. These return a Range that acts differently than other Range objects. For example, if you take the Range returned by Columns and display the count of cells in the range, it returns 16384—the number of columns. But if you call the Select method on the returned Range, Excel selects all the cells in the worksheet. The easiest way to think of the ranges returned by Rows and Columns is that they behave similarly to how column and row headings behave in Excel.

Finally, other useful properties to mention are the EntireRow and Entire-Column properties of the Range object. These properties are useful for navigating from a particular Range to the entire row or column associated with that range. The singular naming of these properties is actually misleading; if the initial range covers multiple rows or multiple columns, the properties will return ranges spanning multiple rows and multiple columns as well.

Listing 5-27 shows several examples of using the get_Range method and the Cells, Rows, and Columns properties. We use the Value2 property of range to set every cell in the range to the string value specified. Figure 5-7 shows the result of running the program in Listing 5-27.

Listing 5-27: A VSTO Customization That Gets Range Objects

```
private void Sheet1_Startup(object sender, System.EventArgs e)
{
  Excel.Range r1 = this.get_Range("A1", missing);
  r1.Value2 = "r1";

  Excel.Range r2 = this.get_Range("B7:C9", missing);
  r2.Value2 = "r2";

  Excel.Range r3 = this.get_Range("C1,C3,C5", missing);
  r3.Value2 = "r3";

  Excel.Range r4 = this.get_Range("A1:A10 A5:A15", missing);
  r4.Value2 = "r4";

  Excel.Range r5 = this.get_Range("F4", "G8");
  r5.Value2 = "r5";

  Excel.Range r6 = this.Rows.get_Item(12, missing)
    as Excel.Range;

  r6.Value2 = "r6";

  Excel.Range r7 = this.Columns.get_Item(5, missing)
    as Excel.Range;

  r7.Value2 = "r7";
}
```

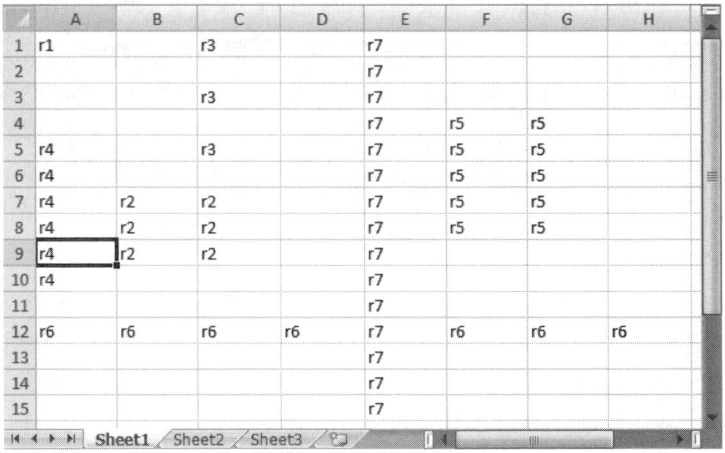

	A	B	C	D	E	F	G	H
1	r1		r3		r7			
2					r7			
3			r3		r7			
4					r7	r5	r5	
5	r4		r3		r7	r5	r5	
6	r4				r7	r5	r5	
7	r4	r2	r2		r7	r5	r5	
8	r4	r2	r2		r7	r5	r5	
9	r4	r2	r2		r7			
10	r4				r7			
11					r7			
12	r6	r6	r6	r6	r7	r6	r6	r6
13					r7			
14					r7			
15					r7			

H ◂ ▸ H   **Sheet1** ╱ Sheet2 ╱ Sheet3 ╱ ⏋

Figure 5-7: Result of running Listing 5-27.

Working with Addresses

Given a Range object, you often need to determine what cells it refers to. The get_Address method returns an address for the range in either A1 style or R1C1 style. You have already learned about A1-style references. R1C1-style references support all the same operators as discussed with A1-style references (colon for range, comma for union, and space for intersection). R1C1-style references have row and column numbers prefaced by R and C respectively. So cell A4 in R1C1 style would be R4C1. Figure 5-8 shows a range that consists of three areas that we consider in this section.

The address for the range in Figure 5-8 is shown here in A1 style and in R1C1 style:

```
$A$15:$F$28,$H$3:$J$9,$L$1
R15C1:R28C6,R3C8:R9C10,R1C12
```

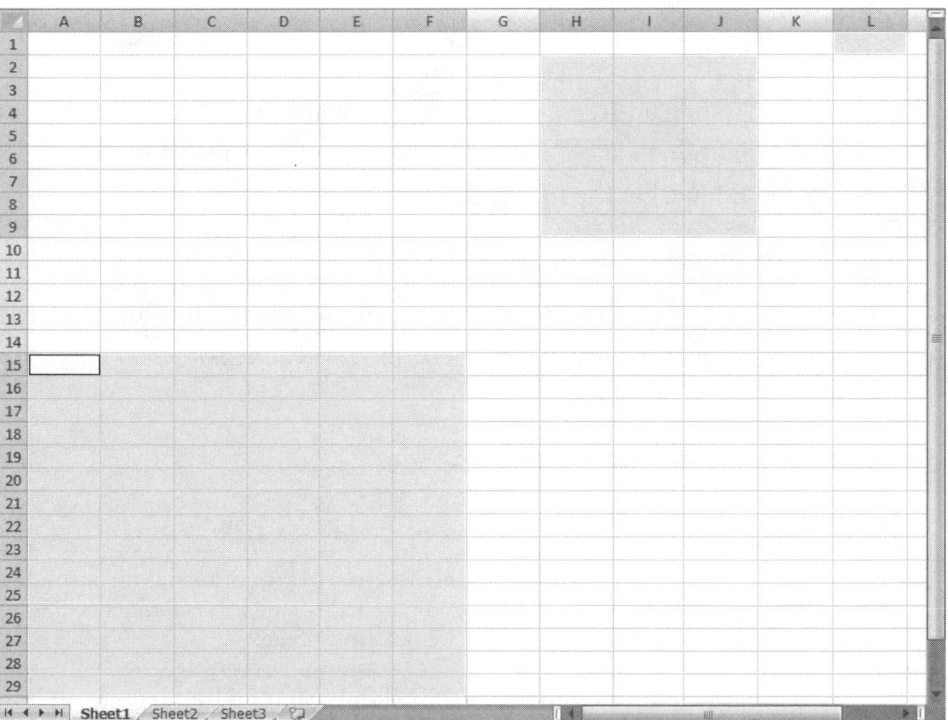

Figure 5-8: A range with three noncontiguous areas.

Another option when getting an address is whether to get an external reference or a local reference. The addresses we have already shown for Figure 5-8 are local references. An external reference includes the name of the workbook and sheet where the range is. Here is the same range in Figure 5-8 expressed as an external reference in A1 style and R1C1 style.

```
[Book1]Sheet1!$A$15:$F$28,$H$3:$J$9,$L$1
[Book1]Sheet1!R15C1:R28C6,R3C8:R9C10,R1C12
```

For our example, the workbook we created the range in was not saved. When we save it as Book1.xls, the addresses look like this:

```
[Book1.xls]Sheet1!$A$15:$F$28,$H$3:$J$9,$L$1
[Book1.xls]Sheet1!R15C1:R28C6,R3C8:R9C10,R1C12
```

Another option when getting an address is whether to use an absolute address or a relative one. The addresses we have already considered have been absolute. The same addresses in relative format (relative to cell A1) look like this:

```
R[14]C:R[27]C[5],R[2]C[7]:R[8]C[9],RC[11]
A15:F28,H3:J9,L1
```

For an R1C1-style address, you can also specify the cell you want your address to be relative to. If we get an R1C1-style for our range in Figure 5-4 relative to cell B2, we get the following result:

```
R[13]C[-1]:R[26]C[4],R[1]C[6]:R[7]C[8],R[-1]C[10]
```

The get_Address method takes five optional parameters that control the way the reference is returned, as described in Table 5-17.

TABLE 5-17: Optional Parameters for Address

Parameter Name	What It Does
RowAbsolute	Pass true to return the row part of the address as an absolute reference ($A$1). If you pass false, the row reference will not be absolute ($A1). The default is true.
ColumnAbsolute	Pass true to return the column part of the address as an absolute reference ($A$1). If you pass false, the column reference will not be absolute (A$1). The default is true.

TABLE 5-17: Optional Parameters for Address *(Continued)*

Parameter Name	What It Does
ReferenceStyle	Pass xlA1 from the XlReferenceStyle enumeration to return an A1-style reference. Pass xlR1C1 to return an R1C1-style reference.
External	Pass true to return an external reference. The default is false.
RelativeTo	Pass a Range object representing the cell that you want an R1C1-style reference to be relative to. Has no effect when used with A1-style references.

Listing 5-28 shows several examples of using get_Address with our example range.

Listing 5-28: A VSTO Customization That Uses get_Address

```
private void Sheet1_Startup(object sender, System.EventArgs e)
{
  Excel.Range range1 = this.get_Range(
    "$A$15:$F$28,$H$3:$J$9,$L$1", missing);

  System.Text.StringBuilder sb = new System.Text.StringBuilder();
  sb.AppendLine("A1-Style Addresses:");
  sb.AppendFormat("Default: {0}\n", range1.get_Address(
    missing, missing, Excel.XlReferenceStyle.xlA1,
    missing, missing));

  sb.AppendFormat("Relative rows: {0}\n",
    range1.get_Address(false, missing,
    Excel.XlReferenceStyle.xlA1, missing, missing));

  sb.AppendFormat("Row & Column Relative: {0}\n",
    range1.get_Address(false, false,
    Excel.XlReferenceStyle.xlA1, missing, missing));

  sb.AppendFormat("External: {0}\n", range1.get_Address(
    missing, missing, Excel.XlReferenceStyle.xlA1,
    true, missing));

  sb.AppendLine();
  sb.AppendLine("R1C1-Style Addresses:");
  sb.AppendFormat("Default: {0}\n", range1.get_Address(
    missing, missing, Excel.XlReferenceStyle.xlR1C1,
    missing, missing));
```

```
sb.AppendFormat("Row & Column Relative to C5: {0}\n",
  range1.get_Address(false, false,
  Excel.XlReferenceStyle.xlR1C1, missing,
  this.get_Range("C5", missing)));

sb.AppendFormat("External: {0}", range1.get_Address(
  missing, missing, Excel.XlReferenceStyle.xlR1C1,
  true, missing));

MessageBox.Show(sb.ToString());
}
```

Creating New Ranges Using Operator Methods

We have discussed several "operators" that can be used in address strings, including the union operator (a comma) and the intersection operator (a space). You can also apply these operators through the Application.Union and Application.Intersection methods.

It is also possible to take a Range and get a new Range that is offset from it by some number of rows and columns by using the get_Offset method. This method takes a row and column value to offset the given range by and returns the newly offset range. So calling get_Offset(5, 5) on the example range in Figure 5-8 returns a range with this A1-style address:

```
"$F$20:$K$33,$M$8:$O$14,$Q$6"
```

Listing 5-29 shows an example of using these operators. Note that Union and Intersection take a lot of optional parameters, allowing you to union or intersect more than just two ranges.

Listing 5-29: A VSTO Customization That Uses Union, Intersection, and get_Offset

```
private void Sheet1_Startup(object sender, System.EventArgs e)
{
  Excel.Application app = this.Application;

  Excel.Range range1 = this.get_Range("$A$15:$F$28", missing);
  Excel.Range range2 = this.get_Range("$H$3:$J$9", missing);
  Excel.Range range3 = this.get_Range("$L$1", missing);
  Excel.Range range4 = this.get_Range("$A$11:$G$30", missing);

  Excel.Range rangeUnion = app.Union(range1, range2,
    range3, missing, missing, missing, missing, missing,
    missing, missing, missing, missing, missing, missing,
    missing, missing, missing, missing, missing, missing,
```

```
    missing, missing, missing, missing, missing, missing,
    missing, missing, missing, missing);

  Excel.Range rangeIntersection = app.Intersect(range1,
    range4, missing, missing, missing, missing, missing,
    missing, missing, missing, missing, missing, missing,
    missing, missing, missing, missing, missing, missing,
    missing, missing, missing, missing, missing, missing,
    missing, missing, missing, missing, missing);

  Excel.Range rangeOffset = rangeUnion.get_Offset(5, 5);

  MessageBox.Show(String.Format("Union: {0}",
    rangeUnion.get_Address(missing, missing,
    Excel.XlReferenceStyle.xlA1, missing, missing)));

  MessageBox.Show(String.Format("Intersection: {0}",
    rangeIntersection.get_Address(missing, missing,
    Excel.XlReferenceStyle.xlA1, missing, missing)));

  MessageBox.Show(String.Format("Offset: {0}",
    rangeOffset.get_Address(missing, missing,
    Excel.XlReferenceStyle.xlA1, missing, missing)));
}
```

Working with Areas

When there are multiple noncontiguous ranges of cells in one Range, each noncontiguous range is called an area. If there are multiple noncontiguous areas in the Range, use the Areas property to access each area (as a Range) via the Areas collection. The Areas collection has an Areas.Count property and an Areas.get_Item method that takes an `int` parameter representing the 1-based index into the array. Listing 5-30 shows an example of iterating over our example range (which has three areas) and printing the address of each area.

Listing 5-30: A VSTO Customization That Works with Areas

```
private void Sheet1_Startup(object sender, System.EventArgs e)
{
  Excel.Range range1 = this.get_Range(
    "$A$15:$F$28,$H$3:$J$9,$L$1", missing);

  MessageBox.Show(String.Format("There are {0} areas",
    range1.Areas.Count));

  foreach (Excel.Range area in range1.Areas)
  {
```

```
      MessageBox.Show(String.Format("Area address is {0}",
        area.get_Address(missing, missing,
          Excel.XlReferenceStyle.xlA1, missing, missing)));
    }
}
```

Working with Cells

The Count property returns the number of cells in a given Range. You can get to a specific single-cell Range within a Range by using the get_Item method. The get_Item method takes a required row index and an optional column index. The column index can be omitted when the range is a one-dimensional array of cells because it only has cells from one column or one row—in this case, the parameter called RowIndex really acts like an array index. If the Range has multiple areas, you must get the area you want to work with first—otherwise, get_Item only returns cells out of the first area in the Range.

Listing 5-31 shows an example of using get_Item.

Listing 5-31: A VSTO Customization That Uses get_Item

```
private void Sheet1_Startup(object sender, System.EventArgs e)
{
  Excel.Range range1 = this.get_Range("$A$15:$F$28", missing);

  int rowCount = range1.Rows.Count;
  int columnCount = range1.Columns.Count;

  for (int i = 1; i <= rowCount; i++)
  {
    for (int j = 1; j <= columnCount; j++)
    {
      Excel.Range cell = range1.get_Item(i, j) as Excel.Range;
      string address = cell.get_Address(missing,
        missing, Excel.XlReferenceStyle.xlA1,
        missing, missing);

      cell.Value2 = String.Format("get_Item({0},{1})", i, j);
    }
  }
}
```

Working with Rows and Columns

Given a Range object, you can determine the row and column number of the top-left corner of its first area using the Row and Column properties. The row and column number are returned as int values.

You can also determine the total number of rows and columns in the first area using the Rows and Columns properties. These properties return special ranges that you can think of as corresponding to the row or column headers associated with the range. When we get Rows.Count from our example range in Figure 5-8, it returns 14, and Columns.Count returns 6. This makes sense because the first area in our selection (A15:F28) spans 6 columns and 14 rows.

To get the row and column position of the bottom-right corner of the first area, you can use the rather awkward expressions shown in Listing 5-32. Listing 5-32 also illustrates the use of get_Item, which takes the row and column index (relative to the top of the given range) and returns the cell (as a Range) at that row and column index. When you get a Rows or a Columns range, these ranges are one-dimensional—hence the parameter called RowIndex acts like an array index in this case.

Listing 5-32: A VSTO Customization That Gets Row and Column Positions

```
private void Sheet1_Startup(object sender, System.EventArgs e)
{
  Excel.Range range1 = this.get_Range(
    "$A$15:$F$28,$H$3:$J$9,$L$1", missing);
  Excel.Range area = range1.Areas.get_Item(1);

  int topLeftColumn = area.Column;
  int topLeftRow = area.Row;
  int bottomRightColumn = ((Excel.Range)area.Columns.
    get_Item(area.Columns.Count, missing)).Column;

  int bottomRightRow = ((Excel.Range)area.Rows.
    get_Item(area.Rows.Count, missing)).Row;

  MessageBox.Show(String.Format(
    "Area Top Left Column {0} and Row {1}",
    topLeftColumn, topLeftRow));
  MessageBox.Show(String.Format(
    "Area Bottom Right Column {0} and Row {1}",
    bottomRightColumn, bottomRightRow));
```

```
  MessageBox.Show(String.Format(
    "Total Rows in Area = {0}", area.Rows.Count));
  MessageBox.Show(String.Format(
    "Total Columns in Area = {0}", area.Columns.Count));
}
```

Working with Regions

The CurrentRegion property returns a Range that is expanded to include all cells up to a blank row and blank column. This expanded Range is called a region. So, for example, you might have a Range that includes several cells in a table—to get a Range that encompasses the entire table (assuming the table is bordered by blank rows and columns) you would use the Current-Region property on the smaller Range to return the entire table.

The get_End method is a method that works against the region associated with a Range. The get_End method takes a member of the XlDirection enumeration: either xlDown, xlUp, xlToLeft, or xlToRight. This method when passed xlUp returns the topmost cell in the region in the same column as the top-left cell of the Range. When passed xlDown, it returns the bottom-most cell in the region in the same column as the top-left cell of the Range. When passed xlToLeft, it returns the leftmost cell in the region in the same row as the top-left cell of the Range. And when passed xlTo-Right, it returns the rightmost cell in the region in the same row as the top-left cell of the Range.

Another useful property for working with regions is the Worksheet object's UsedRange property. This property returns a single Range object that includes all cells that have values in them or are used. So for Figure 5-7, the UsedRange would be A1:H15.

Selecting a Range

You can make a range the current selection using the Select method on a Range. Remember that calling Select changes the user's current selection, which is not a very nice thing to do without good reason. In some cases, however, you want to draw the user's attention to something, and in those cases selecting a Range is reasonable to do.

Editing the Values in a Range

Two methods are typically used to get and set the values in a range. The first way is to use the methods get_Value and set_Value. The second way is to use the property Value2. Value2 and get_Value differ in that the Value2 property returns cells that are currency or dates as a double value. Also, get_Value takes an optional parameter of type XlRangeValueData-Type. If you pass XlRangeValueDataType.xlRangeValueDefault, you will get back an object representing the value of the cell for a single cell Range. For both Value2 and get_Value, if the Range contains multiple cells, you will get back an array of objects corresponding to the cells in the Range.

Listing 5-33 shows several examples of using Value2 including an example of passing an array of values to Value2. Setting the values of the cells in a Range all at once via an array is more efficient than making multiple calls to set each cell individually.

Listing 5-33: A VSTO Customization That Uses Value2

```
private void Sheet1_Startup(object sender, System.EventArgs e)
{
  Excel.Range range1 = this.get_Range("$A$15:$F$28", missing);
  range1.Value2 = "Test";

  int rowCount = range1.Rows.Count;
  int columnCount = range1.Columns.Count;

  object[,] array = new object[rowCount, columnCount];

  for (int i = 0; i < rowCount; i++)
  {
    for (int j = 0; j < columnCount; j++)
    {
      array[i, j] = i * j;
    }
  }

  range1.Value2 = array;
}
```

Copying, Clearing, and Deleting Ranges

Excel provides a number of methods to copy, clear, and delete a Range. The Copy method takes a Destination parameter that you can pass the destination of the copied range. The Clear method clears the content and formatting of the cells in the range. ClearContents clears just the values of the cells in the range, and ClearFormats clears just the formatting. The Delete method deletes the range of cells and takes as a parameter the direction in which to shift cells to replace deleted cells. The direction is passed as a member of the XlDeleteShiftDirection enumeration: xlShiftToLeft or xlShiftUp.

Finding Text in a Range

The Find method allows you to find text in a Range and return the cell within the Range where the text is found. The Find method corresponds to the Find and Replace dialog box, shown in Figure 5-9. If you omit parameters when calling the Find method, it uses whatever settings were set by the user the last time the Find dialog box was used. Furthermore, when you specify the parameters, the settings you specified appear in the Find dialog box the next time the user opens it.

The Find method takes a number of parameters described in Table 5-18. Find returns a Range object if it succeeds and null if it fails to find anything. You can find the next cell that matches your find criteria by using the FindNext method. FindNext takes an optional After parameter to which you need to pass the last found Range to ensure you do not just keep finding the same cell over and over again. You must also save the addresses of the first cell found and subsequent cells found, and compare the addresses to break out of the loop when the search wraps around and finds the first cell address again. Listing 5-34 shows an example of using the Find and FindNext method where we search for any cells containing the character "2" and bold those cells.

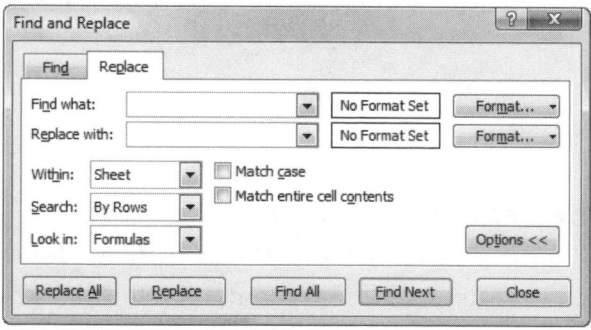

Figure 5-9: The Find and Replace dialog box.

TABLE 5-18: Parameters for the Find Method

Parameter Name	What It Does
What	Pass the data to search for as a required `string`.
After	Pass a single cell after which you want the search to begin as a Range. The default is the top-left cell if this parameter is omitted.
LookIn	Pass a member of the XlFindLookIn enumeration.
LookAt	Pass `xlWhole` from the XlLookAt enumeration to match the whole cell contents, `xlPart` to match parts of the cell contents.
SearchOrder	Pass `xlByRows` from the XlSearchOrder enumeration to search by rows, `xlByColumns` to search by columns.
Search-Direction	Pass `xlNext` from the XlSearchDirection enumeration to search forward, `xlPrevious` to search backward.
MatchCase	Pass `true` to match case.
MatchByte	Pass `true` to have double-byte characters match only double-byte characters.
SearchFormat	Set to `true` if you want the search to respect the FindFormat options. You can change the FindFormat options by using the Application.FindFormat.

Listing 5-34: A VSTO Customization That Uses Find and FindNext

```
private void Sheet1_Startup(object sender, System.EventArgs e)
{
  Excel.Range range1 = this.get_Range("$A$15:$F$28", missing);

  int rowCount = range1.Rows.Count;
  int columnCount = range1.Columns.Count;

  object[,] array = new object[rowCount, columnCount];

  for (int i = 0; i < rowCount; i++)
  {
    for (int j = 0; j < columnCount; j++)
    {
      array[i, j] = i * j;
```

```
      }
    }
    range1.Value2 = array;

    Excel.Range foundRange = range1.Find("2",
      range1.get_Item(1, 1), missing,
      Excel.XlLookAt.xlPart, missing,
      Excel.XlSearchDirection.xlNext,
      missing, missing, missing);

    string firstAddress = foundRange.get_Address(
      missing, missing,
      Microsoft.Office.Interop.Excel.XlReferenceStyle.xlA1,
      missing, missing);

    while (foundRange != null)
    {
      foundRange.Font.Bold = true;
      foundRange = range1.FindNext(foundRange);

      string foundAddress = foundRange.get_Address(
        missing, missing,
        Microsoft.Office.Interop.Excel.XlReferenceStyle.xlA1,
        missing, missing);

      if (foundAddress == firstAddress)
        break;
    }
}
```

Formatting a Range of Cells

Excel provides several methods and properties to format a range of cells.
Among the most useful is the NumberFormat property that you can set to
format strings corresponding to the strings in the Custom category of the
Format Cells dialog box. For example, you can set NumberFormat to General to set no specific number format. Setting NumberFormat to m/d/yyyy
sets a date format, and 0% sets the format to a percentage format. When
using NumberFormat, be sure to consider the locale issue discussed in the
section "Special Excel Issues" later in this chapter if you are building a console application or a COM or automation add-in, because reading and setting this string can cause problems when running in different locales. If
you are using a VSTO code behind a workbook or template project or a
VSTO add-in, you do not have to worry about the locale issue.

The Font property returns a Font object that can be used to set the Font to various sizes and styles. Listing 5-34 showed an example of the Font object used to bold the font of a cell.

Excel also enables you to create styles associated with a Workbook and apply those styles to a Range. You can create styles using Workbook .Styles. Listing 5-35 shows an example of creating a style and applying it to a Range.

Listing 5-35: A VSTO Customization That Creates and Applies Styles

```
private void Sheet1_Startup(object sender, System.EventArgs e)
{
  Excel.Range range1 = this.get_Range("$A$15:$F$28", missing);
  range1.Value2 = "Hello";

  Excel.Style style = Globals.ThisWorkbook.Styles.Add(
    "My Style", missing);

  style.Font.Bold = true;
  style.Borders.LineStyle = Excel.XlLineStyle.xlDash;
  style.Borders.ColorIndex = 3;
  style.NumberFormat = "General";

  range1.Style = "My Style";
}
```

Special Excel Issues

You need to be aware of several special considerations when using the Excel object model with .NET. This section examines two of the most important: working with multiple locales and working with Excel dates.

The Excel Locale Issue for Automation Executables and COM Add-Ins

When you program against the Excel object model using managed code in an automation executable or a COM or automation add-in, Excel methods and properties can behave differently depending on the locale of the current thread. Note that this problem does not occur in code behind the document solutions or add-ins built with VSTO. For example, if you want to set a formula for a Range and you are in the French locale, Excel requires you to use the localized French formula names and formatting:

```
sheet.get_Range("A1", System.Type.Missing).Formula = "=SOMME(3; 4)";
```

This behavior differs from VBA and VSTO solutions that work independent of locale. VBA and VSTO always tell Excel that the locale is US English (locale id 1033). In VBA and VSTO solutions, you do not have to think about locale when talking to Excel. You can write this code and have it work even in a French locale:

```
sheet.get_Range("A1", System.Type.Missing).Formula = "=SUM(3, 4)";
```

When managed code calls into the Excel object model, it tells Excel the locale it is running under (the locale of the current thread), which causes Excel to expect that you will provide formulas and other values in the localized format of that locale. Excel will also return formulas and other values in the localized format of that locale. Excel expects localized strings for such things as date formats, NumberFormat strings associated with a Range, color names associated with NumberFormat strings, and formula names.

Using DateTime for Dates

As an example of the badness that can ensue if you do not think about this issue, consider what the following code does:

```
sheet.get_Range("A1", System.Type.Missing).Value2 = "03/11/02";
```

This value may be interpreted by Excel as March 11, 2002, November 3, 2002, or November 2, 2007 depending on the locale of the current thread.

For dates, you have a clear workaround. Do not pass dates as literal strings to Excel. Instead, construct a date using the System.DateTime object and pass it to Excel using DateTime's ToOADate method, as shown in Listing 5-36. The ToOADate method converts a DateTime to an OLE Automation date, which is the kind of date format that the Excel object model expects.

Listing 5-36: A VSTO Customization That Properly Passes a Date to Excel

```
private void Sheet1_Startup(object sender, System.EventArgs e)
{
  Excel.Range range1 = this.get_Range("$A$1", missing);

  // March 11, 2002
  System.DateTime date = new System.DateTime(2002, 3, 11);
  range1.Value2 = date.ToOADate();
}
```

Switching the Thread Locale to English and Back Is Not Recommended

You might think that a solution to the problems associated with setting or getting Range.NumberFormat and Range.Formula is to save the locale of the thread, temporarily switch the locale of the thread to English (locale id 1033), execute code that sets or gets a locale affected property such as NumberFormat or Formula, and then switch back to the saved locale. This approach is not recommended because it affects other add-ins that will not be expecting the locale switch.

Consider the following example. Your add-in is running on a French machine. Your add-in switches the locale to 1033 and sets a formula value. Another add-in is handling the Change event and displays a dialog box. That dialog box displays in English rather than French. So by changing the thread locale, you have changed the behavior of another add-in and been a bad Office citizen in general.

Using Reflection to Work Around the Locale Issue

The recommended workaround for COM or automation add-ins and automation executables encountering the locale issue (when they access properties affected by the current locale such as the NumberFormat or Formula property) is to access these properties via reflection. Reflection enables you to specify an English locale to Excel and write code that will work regardless of the current thread locale. Listing 5-37 illustrates how to use reflection to set the NumberFormat and Formula properties. Note that to get this code to compile, you must add a reference to the Excel PIA.

Listing 5-37: Using Reflection to Work Around the Locale Issue in Excel

```
static void Main(string[] args)
{
  Excel.Application application = new Excel.Application();
  application.Visible = true;
  object missing = System.Type.Missing;

  Excel.Workbook workbook = application.Workbooks.Add(missing);
  Excel.Worksheet sheet = (Excel.Worksheet)workbook.Worksheets.Add(missing,
    missing, missing, missing);
  Excel.Range range1 = sheet.get_Range("$A$1", missing);

  // Set Formula in English (US) using reflection
  typeof(Excel.Range).InvokeMember("Formula",
```

```
      System.Reflection.BindingFlags.Public |
      System.Reflection.BindingFlags.Instance |
      System.Reflection.BindingFlags.SetProperty,
      null, range1,
      new object[] { "=SUM(12, 34)" },
      System.Globalization.CultureInfo.GetCultureInfo(1033));

  // Set NumberFormat in English (US) using reflection
  typeof(Excel.Range).InvokeMember("NumberFormat",
    System.Reflection.BindingFlags.Public |
    System.Reflection.BindingFlags.Instance |
    System.Reflection.BindingFlags.SetProperty,
    null, range1,
    new object[] { "General" },
    System.Globalization.CultureInfo.GetCultureInfo(1033));
}
```

Old Format or Invalid Type Library Error

A second issue that further complicates the Excel locale issue is that you can get an "Old format or invalid type library" error when using the Excel object model in an English Excel installation on a machine where the locale is set to a non-English locale. Excel is looking for a file called xllex.dll in Program Files\Microsoft Office\OFFICE12\1033 that it cannot find. The solution to this problem is to install the xllex.dll file or install the MUI language packs for Office. You can also make a copy of excel.exe, rename it to xllex.dll, and copy it to the 1033 directory.

VSTO and the Excel Locale Issue

VSTO solutions solve the Excel locale issue by using a transparent proxy object that sits between you and the Excel object model. This proxy always tells Excel that the locale is US English (locale id 1033), which effectively makes VSTO match VBA behavior. If you are using VSTO solutions, the Excel locale issue is solved for you and you do not have to worry about it further. If you are building a managed COM or automation add-in for Excel or an automation executable, the issue still exists.

There are some caveats to VSTO's solution to the Excel locale issue. The VSTO transparent proxy can slow down your code slightly. It also causes Excel objects to display slightly differently when inspected in the debugger. Finally, if you compare a proxied Excel object such as Application to an unproxied Application object using the Equals operator, they will not evaluate to be equal.

If you want to bypass VSTO's transparent proxy for a particular object, you can use the Microsoft.Office.Tools.Excel.ExcelLocale1033Proxy.Unwrap method and pass the Excel object that you want to bypass the proxy for. This method removes the proxy and returns the raw PIA object which exposes you once again to the locale issue. You can also set the assembly level attribute ExcelLocale1033 in a VSTO project's AssemblyInfo.cs file to false to turn the transparent proxy off for the entire Excel solution.

If you navigate to objects from another PIA and then navigate back again to the Excel PIA, you can lose the transparent proxy. For example, if you get a CommandBar object from the Microsoft.Office.Core PIA namespace from the Application.CommandBars collection and then use the CommandBar.Application property to get back to the Excel Application object, you have now lost the proxy and the locale issue will occur again.

Finally, if you create a new instance of Excel from a Word VSTO code-behind solution, you are talking directly to the Excel PIA with no transparent proxy object, and the locale issue will continue to be in effect.

Converting Excel Dates to DateTime

Excel can represent dates in two formats: the 1900 format or the 1904 format. The 1900 format is based on a system where when converted to a number, it represents the number of elapsed days since January 1, 1900. The 1904 format is based on a system where when converted to a number, it represents the number of elapsed days since January 1, 1904. The 1904 format was introduced by early Macintosh computers because of a problem with the 1900 format that we describe later. You can determine which format a workbook is using by checking the Workbook.Date1904 property, which returns true if the workbook is using the 1904 format.

If an Excel workbook is using the 1904 format, and you convert a date from that workbook into a DateTime directly, you will get the wrong value. It will be off by 4 years and 2 leap days because DateTime is expecting the 1900 format where the value of the Excel date represented by a number is the number of elapsed days since January 1, 1900, not January 1, 1904. So this code would give bad date-times if you are using the 1904 format in your workbook.

```
object excelDate = myRange.get_value(System.Type.Missing);
DateTime possiblyBadDateIfExcelIsIn1904Mode = (DateTime)excelDate;
```

To get a 1904 format date into a DateTime format, you must add to the 1904 format date 4 years and 2 leap days (to make up for the fact that the 1904 has its 0 in 1904 rather than 1900). So if you write this code instead and use the function ConvertExcelDateToDate in Listing 5-38, you will get the right result if the 1904 date system is used.

```
object excelDate = myRange.get_value(System.Type.Missing);
DateTime goodDate = ConvertExcelDateToDate(excelDate);
```

Listing 5-38: Converting Excel Dates to DateTime and Back Again

```
static readonly DateTime march1st1900 = new DateTime(1900, 03, 01);
static readonly DateTime december31st1899 = new DateTime(1899, 12, 31);
static readonly DateTime january1st1904 = new DateTime(1904, 01, 01);
static readonly TimeSpan date1904adjustment = new TimeSpan(4 * 365 + 2, 0, 0, 0, 0);
static readonly TimeSpan before1stMarchAdjustment = new TimeSpan(1, 0, 0, 0);
bool date1904 = ActiveWorkbook.Date1904;

object ConvertDateToExcelDate(DateTime date)
{
    LanguageSettings languageSettings = Application.LanguageSettings;
    int lcid = languageSettings.get_LanguageID(
      MsoAppLanguageID.msoLanguageIDUI);
    CultureInfo officeUICulture = new CultureInfo(lcid);
    DateTimeFormatInfo dateFormatProvider = officeUICulture.
      DateTimeFormat;
    string dateFormat = dateFormatProvider.ShortDatePattern;

    if (date1904)
    {
        if (date >= january1st1904)
            return date - date1904adjustment;
        else
            return date.ToString(dateFormat, dateFormatProvider);
    }
    if (date >= march1st1900)
        return date;
    if (date < march1st1900 && date > december31st1899)
        return date - before1stMarchAdjustment;
    return date.ToString(dateFormat, dateFormatProvider);
}
```

```
DateTime ConvertExcelDateToDate(object excelDate)
{
    DateTime date = (DateTime)excelDate;
    if (date1904)
        return date + date1904adjustment;
    if (date < march1st1900)
        return date + before1stMarchAdjustment;
    return date;
}
```

Listing 5-38 also has a correction for 1900 format dates. It turns out that when Lotus 1-2-3 was written, the programmers incorrectly thought that 1900 was a leap year. When Microsoft wrote Excel, they wanted to make sure they kept compatibility with existing Lotus 1-2-3 spreadsheets by making it so that they calculated the number of days elapsed since December 31, 1899, rather than January 1, 1900. When DateTime was written, its creators did not try to back up to December 31, 1899—they calculated from January 1, 1900. So to get an Excel date in 1900 format that is before March 1, 1900 into a DateTime properly, you have to add one day.

Finally, Excel cannot represent days before January 1, 1900 when in 1900 format or days before January 1, 1904 when in 1904 format. Therefore, when you are converting a DateTime to an Excel date, you have to pass a string rather than a number representing the date—because these dates cannot be represented as dates in Excel (only as strings).

Conclusion

This chapter explored some of the most important objects in the Excel object model. We use many of these objects in the Excel examples in subsequent chapters.

This chapter described these objects as defined by the primary interop assemblies for Excel. You should be aware that VSTO extends some of these objects (Workbook, Worksheet, Range, Chart, ChartObject, and List-Object) to add some additional functionality such as data binding support. Part III of this book examines those extensions.

6

Programming Word

Ways to Customize Word

Word has a very rich object model that consists of 294 objects that combined have more than 4,200 properties and methods. Word also supports several models for integrating your code, including add-ins and code-behind documents. Most of these models were originally designed to allow the integration of COM components written in VB 6, VBA, C, or C++. However, through COM interop, managed objects written in C# or Visual Basic can masquerade as COM objects and participate in most of these models. This chapter briefly considers several of the ways that you can integrate your code with Word and refers you to other chapters that discuss these approaches in more depth. This chapter also explores building research services and introduces the Word object model.

Automation Executable

As mentioned in Chapter 2, "Introduction to Office Solutions," the simplest way to integrate with Word is to start Word from a console application or Windows Forms application and automate it from that external program. Chapter 2 provides a sample of an automation executable that automates Word.

VSTO Add-Ins

When building add-ins for Word, you have two choices: You can build a COM add-in (sometimes called a shared add-in) or a VSTO Word add-in. A VSTO Word add-in solves many of the problems associated with COM add-in development and is the preferred model for Word 2003 and Word 2007 add-in development. The only time you would want to consider building a COM add-in instead is when you need to target versions of Word that are older than Word 2003 or when your add-in needs to support more than one Office application.

Word has a COM Add-Ins dialog box that enables users to turn COM and VSTO add-ins on and off. To access the COM Add-Ins dialog box, you must perform the following steps:

1. Click the Office menu (the large circle with the Office logo on it in the top-left corner of the Word window), and choose Word Options from the bottom of the menu that drops down.
2. Click the Add-Ins tab on the left side of the Word Options dialog box.
3. Choose COM Add-Ins from the drop-down Manage menu, Manage, and click the Go button.

Figure 6-1 shows the COM Add-Ins dialog box.

You can add COM add-ins by using the Add button and remove them by using the Remove button. Typically, you won't have your users use this dialog box to manage COM add-ins. Instead, you install and remove a COM add-in by manipulating registry settings with the installer you create

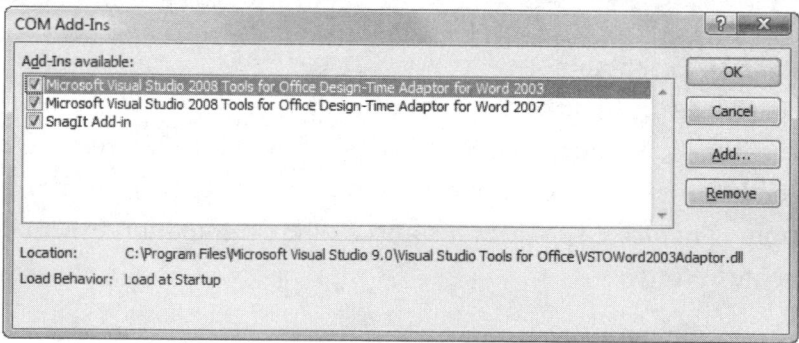

Figure 6-1: The COM Add-Ins dialog box in Word.

for your COM add-in. VSTO add-ins cannot be added via the Add button in the COM Add-Ins dialog box; they must be installed by double-clicking a .vsto file or a setup.exe file associated with the VSTO add-in.

Word discovers the installed add-ins by reading from the registry. You can view the registry on your computer by going to the Windows Start menu and choosing Run. In the Run dialog box, type regedit for the program to run, and click the OK button. Word looks for VSTO and COM add-ins in the registry keys under HKEY_CURRENT_USER\Software\Microsoft\Office\Word\Addins. Word also looks for COM add-ins in the registry keys under HKEY_LOCAL_MACHINE\Software\Microsoft\Office\Word\Addins. COM add-ins registered under HKEY_LOCAL_MACHINE cannot be turned on or off by users without administrative privileges. Therefore, it is recommended you do not register your COM add-ins under HKEY_LOCAL_MACHINE, because they can't be managed by a nonadministrator account.

Visual Studio Tools for Office Code Behind

Visual Studio 2008 Tools for Office (VSTO) enables you to put C# or Visual Basic code behind Word templates and documents. The code-behind model was designed from the ground up for C# and Visual Basic—so this model is the most ".NET" of all the models used to customize Word. This model is used when you want to customize the behavior of a particular document or a particular set of documents created from a common template. For example, you might want to create a template that is used whenever anyone in your company creates an invoice. This template can add commands and functionality that are always available when the document created with it is opened.

Note that Word templates in VSTO do not behave in the same way that templates behave in VBA. In VBA, both the code associated with the template and the code associated with the document run concurrently. In VSTO, the code associated with the template is associated with the document when a new document is created, and only the code associated with the document runs.

VSTO's support for code behind a document is discussed in detail in Part III of this book.

Smart Documents and XML Expansion Packs

Smart documents are another way to associate your code with a Word template or document. Smart documents rely on attaching an XML schema to a document or template and associating your code with that schema. The combination of the schema and associated code is called an XML Expansion Pack. To associate an XML Expansion Pack with a Word document, click the Office menu and choose Word Options, click the Add-Ins tab, choose Templates from the drop-down Manage menu, click the Go button, and then click the XML Expansion Packs tab of the Templates and Add-Ins dialog box. Figure 6-2 shows the Templates and Add-Ins dialog box.

When an XML Expansion Pack is attached to a document, Word loads the associated code and runs it while that document is opened. Smart document solutions can create a custom user interface in the Document Actions task pane that can be brought up in Word by choosing Document Actions from the View tab in the Show/Hide group.

It is possible to write smart document solutions from scratch in C# or Visual Basic. This book does not cover this approach. Instead, this book focuses on the VSTO approach, which was designed to make smart docu-

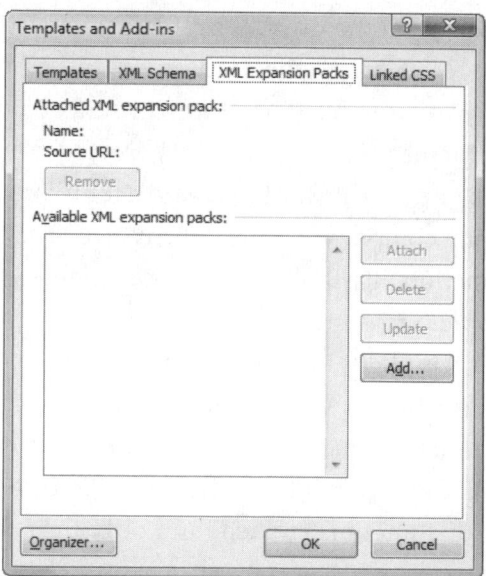

Figure 6-2: The XML Expansion Packs tab of
the Templates and Add-Ins dialog box.

ment development much easier and allow you to create a custom Document Actions task pane using Windows Forms or WPF. Chapter 15, "Working with Document-Level Actions Panes," discusses this capability in more detail.

Smart Tags

Smart Tags enable a pop-up menu to be displayed containing actions relevant for a recognized piece of text in a document. You can control the text that Word recognizes and the actions that are made available for that text by creating a Smart Tag DLL or by using VSTO's Smart Tag Support.

A Smart Tag DLL contains two types of components that are used by Word: a recognizer and associated actions. A recognizer determines what text in the document is recognized as a Smart Tag. An action corresponds to a menu command displayed in the pop-up menu.

A recognizer could be created that tells Word to recognize stock-ticker symbols (such as the MSFT stock symbol) and display a set of actions that can be taken for that symbol: buy, sell, get the latest price, get history, and so on. A "get history" action, for instance, could launch a Web browser to show a stock history Web page for the stock symbol that was recognized.

When a recognizer recognizes some text, Word displays red-dotted underlining under the recognized text, as shown in Figure 6-3. If the user hovers over the text, a pop-up menu icon appears next to the text that the user can click to drop down a menu of actions for the recognized piece of text. Figure 6-4 shows an example menu. When an action is selected, Word calls back into the associated action to execute your code.

Smart Tags are managed from the AutoCorrect dialog box, shown in Figure 6-5. To display the AutoCorrect dialog box, click the Office menu

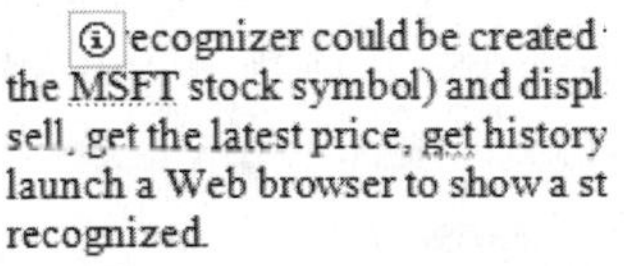

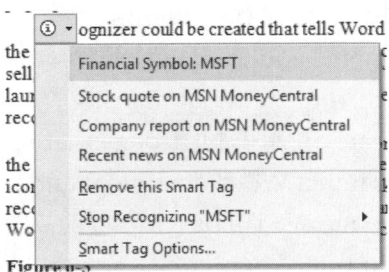

(i) ecognizer could be created the MSFT stock symbol) and displ sell, get the latest price, get history launch a Web browser to show a st recognized.

Figure 6-3: Some recognized text.

Figure 6.4: Dropping down the Smart Tag menu.

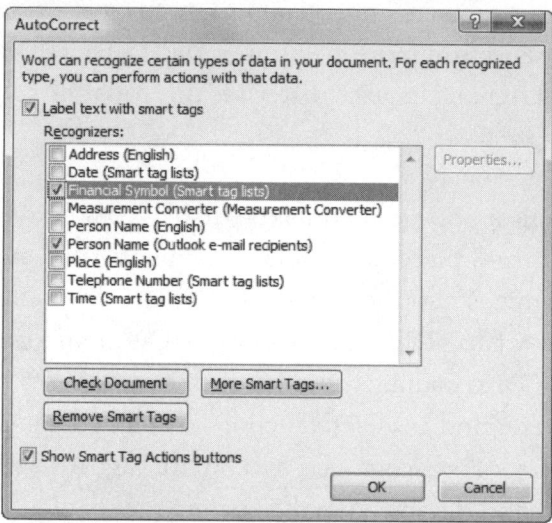

Figure 6.5: The AutoCorrect dialog box.

and choose Word Options, click the Proofing tab, click the AutoCorrect Options button, and click the Smart Tags tab. Here the user can turn on and off individual recognizers as well as control other options relating to how Smart Tags display in the document.

It is possible to write Smart Tags from scratch in C# or Visual Basic; the first edition of this book covers this approach. VSTO provides a simpler model for creating a Smart Tag that works at the document, template, and (new in VSTO 2008 SP1) add-in levels. Chapter 18, "Working with Smart Tags in VSTO," describes the VSTO model for working with Smart Tags in more detail.

Server-Generated Documents

VSTO enables you to write code on the server that populates a Word document with data without starting Word on the server. For example, you might create an ASP.NET page that reads some data out of a database and then puts it in a Word document and returns that document to the client of the Web page. VSTO provides a class called ServerDocument that makes it easy to do this. Chapter 20, "Server Data Scenarios," describes generating documents on the server using the ServerDocument class.

You can also use the XML features and file formats of Office to generate Word documents on the server—an approach that is more complex but that allows you to generate more complex documents.

Programming Research Services

This section examines how to build research services for Word and other Office applications. Word has a task pane called the Research task pane that enables you to enter a search term and search various sources for that search term. To display the Research task pane, click the Research button in the Review tab. Figure 6-6 shows the Research task pane.

Office enables developers to write a special Web service called a research service that implements two Web methods defined by Office: Registration and Query. Both Web methods take a `string` and return a `string`. A research service can be registered with Office and used in Office's Research task pane. For example, you might write a research service that searches for the search term in a corporate database.

Although the signatures of the two Web methods you must declare are simple, the actual implementation of these methods is somewhat complex because Word has four separate XML schemas that must be used for the

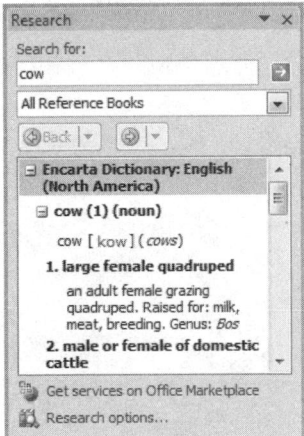

Figure 6-6: The Research task pane.

request passed to Registration, the response returned by Registration, the request passed to Query, and the response returned by Query.

Getting Started with Research Services

To build a research service, launch Visual Studio 2008, and choose File > New Project. Select Web from the Visual C# Projects list in the Project types window, and click ASP.NET Web Service Application in the Templates window, as shown in Figure 6-7.

When you click OK, a Web service project is created for you. Within the project is a file called Service1.asmx.cs. Service1.asmx.cs contains a class called Service1 that contains one Web method called HelloWorld. We are going to delete the HelloWorld Web method and replace it with an implementation of the two Web methods required by Research services: Registration and QueryResponse.

Edit Service1.asmx.cs to produce the result shown in Listing 6-1. If the user searches for the string "Eric", the service will send back information about one of the authors of this book.

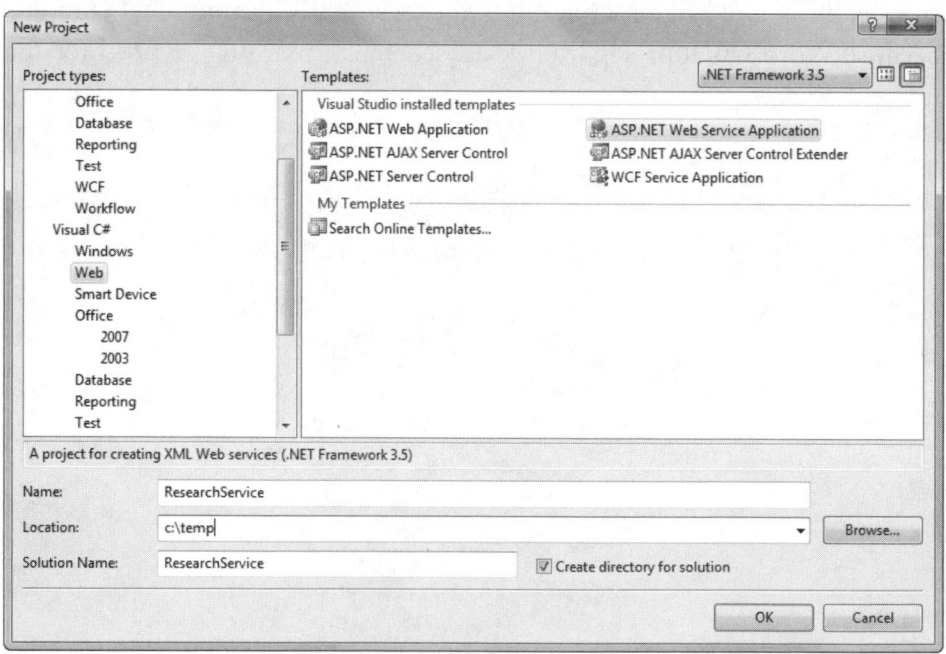

Figure 6-7: Creating a Web Service Application project.

Listing 6-1: The Service1.asmx.cs File

```csharp
using System;
using System.ComponentModel;
using System.Web;
using System.Web.Services;
using System.Web.Services.Protocols;
using System.Xml;
using System.IO;
using System.Web.Util;

namespace ResearchService
{
  [WebService(Namespace = "urn:Microsoft.Search", Description =
    "My First C# Research Service")]
  [WebServiceBinding(ConformsTo = WsiProfiles.BasicProfile1_1)]
  [ToolboxItem(false)]
  public class Service1 : System.Web.Services.WebService
  {
    [WebMethod]
    public string Registration(string registrationXml)
    {
      MemoryStream stream = new MemoryStream();
      XmlTextWriter writer = new XmlTextWriter(
        stream, System.Text.Encoding.UTF8);

      writer.Formatting = Formatting.Indented;
      writer.WriteStartDocument();

      // Registration Response Packet
      writer.WriteStartElement("ProviderUpdate",
        "urn:Microsoft.Search.Registration.Response");
      writer.WriteElementString("Status", "SUCCESS");

      // Provider
      writer.WriteStartElement("Providers");
      writer.WriteStartElement("Provider");
      writer.WriteElementString("Message", "This is an example " +
        "research library written in Visual Studio 2008 with C#.");

      writer.WriteElementString("Id",
        "{C37EE888-D74E-47e5-B113-BA613D87F0B2}");
      writer.WriteElementString("Name",
        "My First Research Service");
      writer.WriteElementString("QueryPath",
        @"http://" + HttpContext.Current.Request.Url.Host + ":" +
        HttpContext.Current.Request.Url.Port.ToString() +
        HttpContext.Current.Request.Url.AbsolutePath);
```

```
      writer.WriteElementString("RegistrationPath",
        @"http://" + HttpContext.Current.Request.Url.Host + ":" +
        HttpContext.Current.Request.Url.Port.ToString() +
        HttpContext.Current.Request.Url.AbsolutePath);

      writer.WriteElementString("Type", "SOAP");

      // Services
      writer.WriteStartElement("Services");
      writer.WriteStartElement("Service");
      writer.WriteElementString("Id",
        "{8DD063CA-94FC-4514-8D83-3B36B12432BE}");

      writer.WriteElementString("Name",
        "My First Research Service in C#");

      writer.WriteElementString("Description",
        "My First Research Service, " +
        "created in C# and Visual Studio 2008.");

      writer.WriteElementString("Copyright", "(C) 2008");
      writer.WriteElementString("Display", "On");
      writer.WriteElementString("Category", "RESEARCH_GENERAL");
      writer.WriteEndElement(); // Service
      writer.WriteEndElement(); // Services
      writer.WriteEndElement(); // Provider
      writer.WriteEndElement(); // Providers
      writer.WriteEndElement(); // ProviderUpdate
      writer.WriteEndDocument();

      writer.Flush();

      stream.Position = 0;
      StreamReader reader = new StreamReader(stream);
      string result = reader.ReadToEnd();
      return result;
    }

    [WebMethod]
    public string Query(string queryXml)
    {
      XmlDocument xmlQuery = new XmlDocument();
      xmlQuery.LoadXml(queryXml);

      XmlNamespaceManager nm1 =
        new XmlNamespaceManager(xmlQuery.NameTable);
      nm1.AddNamespace("ns", "urn:Microsoft.Search.Query");
      nm1.AddNamespace("oc",
        "urn:Microsoft.Search.Query.Office.Context");
      string queryString = xmlQuery.SelectSingleNode(
        "//ns:QueryText", nm1).InnerText;
```

```
XmlNamespaceManager nm2 = new XmlNamespaceManager(
  xmlQuery.NameTable);
nm2.AddNamespace("msq", "urn:Microsoft.Search.Query");
string domain = xmlQuery.SelectSingleNode(
  "/msq:QueryPacket/msq:Query",
  nm2).Attributes.GetNamedItem("domain").Value;
string queryId = xmlQuery.SelectSingleNode(
  "/msq:QueryPacket/msq:Query/msq:QueryId",
  nm2).InnerText;

MemoryStream stream = new MemoryStream();
XmlTextWriter writer = new XmlTextWriter(stream, null);
writer.Formatting = Formatting.Indented;

// Compose the Query Response packet.
writer.WriteStartDocument();
writer.WriteStartElement("ResponsePacket",
  "urn:Microsoft.Search.Response");
// The providerRevision attribute can be used
// to update the service.
writer.WriteAttributeString("providerRevision", "1");
writer.WriteStartElement("Response");
// The domain attribute identifies the service
// that executed the query.
writer.WriteAttributeString("domain", domain);
writer.WriteElementString("QueryID", queryId);

if (String.Compare("Eric", queryString, true) == 0)
{
  writer.WriteStartElement("Range");
  writer.WriteStartElement("Results");

  // Begin Document element
  writer.WriteStartElement("Document",
    "urn:Microsoft.Search.Response.Document");
  writer.WriteElementString("Title", "Eric Carter's Blog");
  writer.WriteStartElement("Action");
  writer.WriteStartElement("LinkUrl");
  writer.WriteAttributeString("fileExt", "htm");
  writer.WriteString("http://blogs.msdn.com/eric_carter");
  writer.WriteEndElement(); //LinkUrl
  writer.WriteEndElement(); //Action
  writer.WriteElementString("DisplayUrl",
    "http://blogs.msdn.com/eric_carter");
  writer.WriteElementString("Description",
    ".NET for Office, the blog of Eric Carter.");
  // Include an image
  writer.WriteStartElement("Media");
  writer.WriteAttributeString("type", "IMAGE");
  writer.WriteElementString("SrcUrl",
```

```
        "http://ericca.members.winisp.net/eric.jpg");
      writer.WriteElementString("AltText", "Eric Carter");
      writer.WriteEndElement(); //Media
      writer.WriteEndElement(); //Document

      // Include additional text
      // End Document element
      // Begin Content element
      writer.WriteStartElement("Content",
        "urn:Microsoft.Search.Response.Content");
      writer.WriteStartElement("HorizontalRule");
      writer.WriteEndElement(); //Horizontal rule
      writer.WriteElementString("P",
        ".NET for Office Highlights");
      writer.WriteStartElement("HorizontalRule");
      writer.WriteEndElement(); //Horizontal rule
      writer.WriteStartElement("Heading");
      writer.WriteElementString("Text", "Top Articles");
      writer.WriteEndElement(); //Heading
      writer.WriteElementString("P", "Excel and UDFs");
      writer.WriteElementString("P", "VSTO 3.0 Features");
      writer.WriteStartElement("P");
      writer.WriteString("Using ");
      writer.WriteStartElement("Char");
      writer.WriteAttributeString("bold", "true");
      writer.WriteString(".NET");
      writer.WriteEndElement(); //Char
      writer.WriteString(" in Office.");
      writer.WriteEndElement(); //P
      writer.WriteElementString("P", "");
      writer.WriteEndElement(); //Content

      // Finish up.
      writer.WriteEndElement(); //Results
      writer.WriteEndElement(); //Range
    }
    writer.WriteElementString("Status", "SUCCESS");
    writer.WriteEndElement(); //Response
    writer.WriteEndElement(); //ResponsePacket
    writer.WriteEndDocument();

    writer.Flush();

    // Move the results into a string.
    stream.Position = 0;
    StreamReader reader = new StreamReader(stream);
    string result = reader.ReadToEnd();
    return result;
  }
 }
}
```

Registering the Research Service with Word

After building the project, press Ctrl+F5 to run the project. A Web browser window appears, with a page you can use to invoke the Web service. Copy the address from the address bar in the Web browser (the address will be something like http://localhost:2139/Service1.asmx), as you will need this address to register the Web service with Word.

Launch Word. Then bring up Word's Research task pane by choosing Research from the Review tab in the Proofing group. At the very bottom of the Research task pane is some text that says *Research options*. Click that text to get the dialog box shown in Figure 6-11 later in this chapter. Then click the Add Services button. The dialog box shown in Figure 6-8 appears. In this dialog box, paste the address to the Web service .asmx file. Then click the Add button.

When you click the Add button, Word calls the research service and invokes the Registration Web method. The implementation of this method returns the block of XML shown in Listing 6-2 to Word.

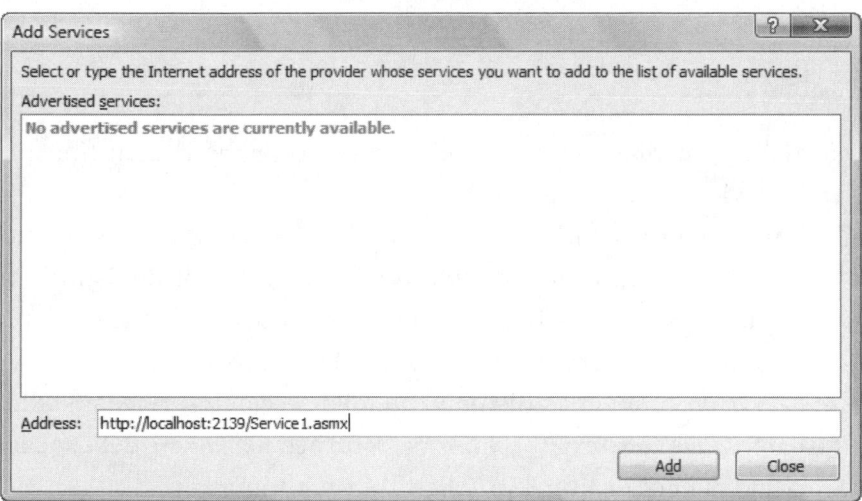

Figure 6-8: Word's Add Services dialog box.

Listing 6-2: The Return Value of the Registration Web Method

```xml
<?xml version="1.0" encoding="utf-8" ?>
<ProviderUpdate xmlns="urn:Microsoft.Search.Registration.Response">
  <Status>SUCCESS</Status>
  <Providers>
    <Provider>
      <Message>This is an example research library written in
        Visual Studio 2008 with C#.</Message>
      <Id>{C37EE888-D74E-47e5-B113-BA613D87F0B2}</Id>
      <Name>My First Research Service</Name>
      <QueryPath>http://localhost:2139/Service1.asmx/
        Registration</QueryPath>
      <RegistrationPath>http://localhost:2139/Service1.asmx/
        Registration</RegistrationPath>
      <Type>SOAP</Type>
      <Services>
        <Service>
          <Id>{8DD063CA-94FC-4514-8D83-3B36B12432BE}</Id>
          <Name>My First Research Service in C#</Name>
          <Description>My First Research Service, created in C#
            and Visual Studio 2008.</Description>
          <Copyright>(C) 2008</Copyright>
          <Display>On</Display>
          <Category>RESEARCH_GENERAL</Category>
        </Service>
      </Services>
    </Provider>
  </Providers>
</ProviderUpdate>
```

Word then displays a dialog box announcing the description of the research service, as shown in Figure 6-9.

Clicking Continue brings up a dialog box showing details about the research service (as determined from the return value of Registration), as shown in Figure 6-10. Click Install to install the research service.

Clicking Install returns to the Research Options dialog box, shown in Figure 6-11, which now has the newly added research service installed in the Research Sites category (because we returned RESEARCH_GENERAL in the Category element of Listing 6-2). Click OK to continue.

Using the Research Service

Now you can type the text **Eric** in the Research task pane search box and drop down the list of sites to search to select My First Research Service in

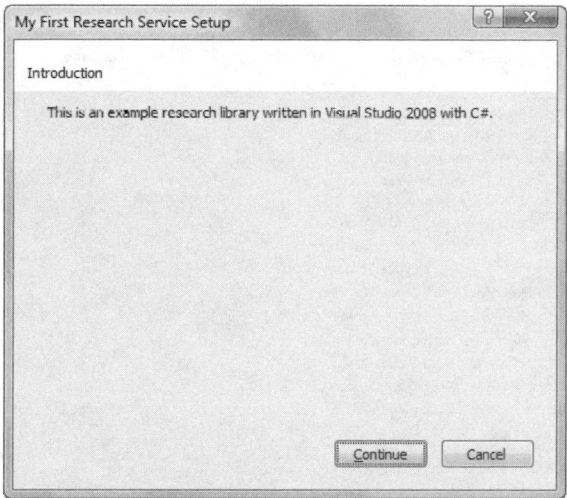

Figure 6-9: Word's Research Service Setup dialog box.

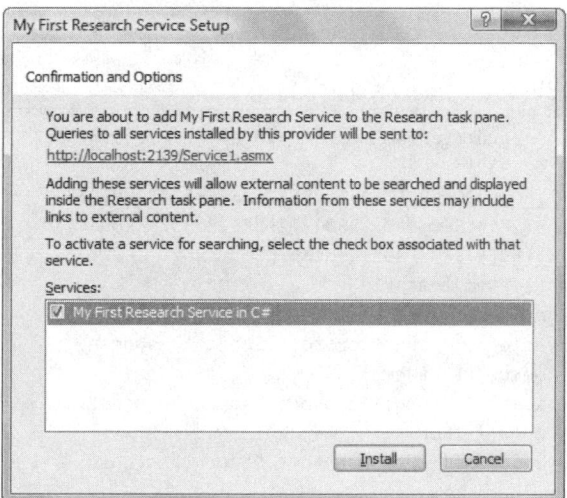

Figure 6-10: Research Service Confirmation and Options dialog box.

C#. Click the green arrow button to search. An alternative way to search for text is to type it in the document, select it, and then click it while holding down the Alt key. The research service is contacted, and the Query Web method is called. The Query Web method is passed XML from Word, as shown in Listing 6-3.

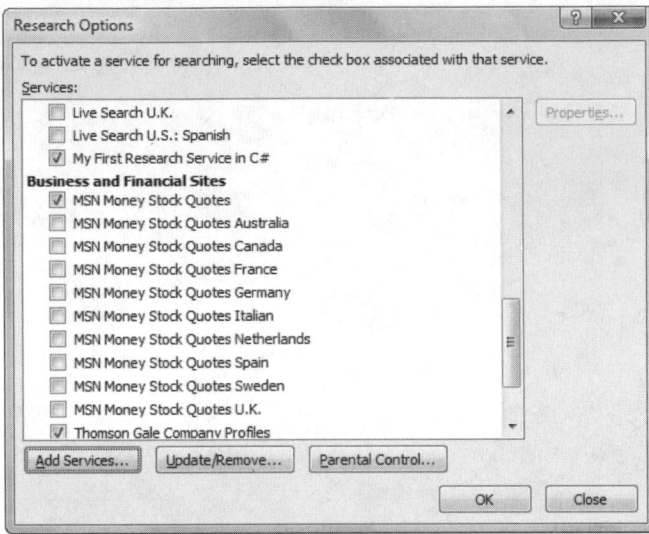

Figure 6-11: Research Options dialog box.

Listing 6-3: The Input to the Query Web Method

```
<QueryPacket xmlns="urn:Microsoft.Search.Query" revision="1"
    build="(12.0.6213)">
  <Query domain="{8DD063CA-94FC-4514-8D83-3B36B12432BE}">
    <QueryId>{98E522B1-5680-4371-8804-72F9FE283807}</QueryId>
    <OriginatorId>{F6FF7BE0-F39C-4ddc-A7D0-
      09A4C6C647A5}</OriginatorId>
    <SupportedFormats>
      <Format revision="1">urn:Microsoft.Search.Response.
        Document:Document</Format>
      <Format revision="1">urn:Microsoft.Search.Response.
        Content:Content</Format>
      <Format revision="1">urn:Microsoft.Search.Response.
        Form:Form</Format>
    </SupportedFormats>
    <Context>
      <QueryText type="STRING" language="en-us">eric</QueryText>
      <LanguagePreference>en-us</LanguagePreference>
      <Requery />
    </Context>
    <Range id="result" />
    <OfficeContext xmlns="urn:Microsoft.Search.Query.
      Office.Context" revision="1">
```

```
  <UserPreferences>
    <ParentalControl>false</ParentalControl>
  </UserPreferences>
  <ServiceData />
  <ApplicationContext>
    <Name>Microsoft Office Word</Name>
    <Version>(12.0.6213)</Version>
    <SystemInformation>
      <SkuLanguage>en-us</SkuLanguage>
      <LanguagePack>en-us</LanguagePack>
      <InterfaceLanguage>en-us</InterfaceLanguage>
      <Location>US</Location>
    </SystemInformation>
  </ApplicationContext>
  <QueryLanguage>en-us</QueryLanguage>
  <KeyboardLanguage>en-us</KeyboardLanguage>
  </OfficeContext>
  <Keywords xmlns="urn:Microsoft.Search.Query.
    Office.Keywords" revision="1">
    <QueryText>eric</QueryText>
    <Keyword>
      <Word>eric</Word>
      <StemWord>eric</StemWord>
    </Keyword>
  </Keywords>
  </Query>
</QueryPacket>
```

The implementation of the Web method Query in Listing 6-1 reads the input XML in Listing 6-3 and extracts from it the query text—the text searched for by the user. It also extracts the query id and domain, which are returned to Office in the response to the Web method call. If the query text matches "Eric", the Query method returns the response shown in Listing 6-4. If the query text does not match "Eric", the Query method returns the response shown in Listing 6-4 but omits everything within the Range element. The response uses a schema defined by Office for returning results. This schema is documented in the Research Service SDK, but you can get an idea of the types of results Office can render by looking at Figure 6-12, which shows what Word renders in the research pane for the XML returned in Listing 6-4.

Listing 6-4: Return Value of the Query Method When "Eric" Is Found

```xml
<?xml version="1.0" ?>
<ResponsePacket providerRevision="1" xmlns="urn:Microsoft.Search.Response">
  <Response domain="{8DD063CA-94FC-4514-8D83-3B36B12432BE}">
    <QueryID>{98E522B1-5680-4371-8804-72F9FE283807}</QueryID>
    <Range>
      <Results>
        <Document xmlns="urn:Microsoft.Search.Response.Document">
          <Title>Eric Carter's Blog</Title>
          <Action>
            <LinkUrl fileExt="htm">http://blogs.msdn.com/
              eric_carter</LinkUrl>
          </Action>
          <DisplayUrl>http://blogs.msdn.com/
              eric_carter</DisplayUrl>
          <Description>.NET for Office, the blog of Eric
              Carter.</Description>
          <Media type="IMAGE">
            <SrcUrl>http://ericca.members.winisp.net/
              eric.jpg</SrcUrl>
            <AltText>Eric Carter</AltText>
          </Media>
        </Document>
        <Content xmlns="urn:Microsoft.Search.Response.Content">
          <HorizontalRule />
          <P>.NET for Office Highlights</P>
          <HorizontalRule />
          <Heading>
            <Text>Top Articles</Text>
          </Heading>
          <P>Excel and UDFs</P>
          <P>VSTO 3.0 Features</P>
          <P>
            Using
            <Char bold="true">.NET</Char>
            in Office.
          </P>
          <P />
        </Content>
      </Results>
    </Range>
    <Status>SUCCESS</Status>
  </Response>
</ResponsePacket>
```

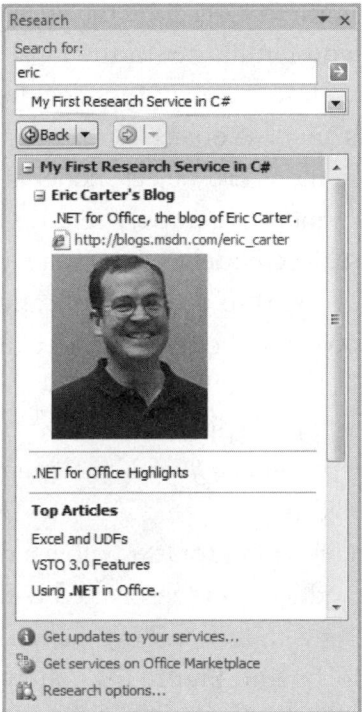

Figure 6-12: The Research task pane shows results from the new research service.

More Research Service Resources

This section has been a brief introduction to creating research service in C# using Visual Studio. For more information about creating research services, search http://msdn.microsoft.com for the phrase *research services*. You will find an SDK (listed under Office 2003) that documents the schemas and provides additional sample research services.

Introduction to the Word Object Model

Regardless of the approach you choose to integrate your code with Word, you will eventually need to talk to the Word object model to get things done. It is impossible to completely describe the Word object model in this book, but we try to make you familiar with the most important objects in the Word object model and show some of the most frequently used methods, properties, and events on these objects.

The first step in learning the Word object model is to get an idea of the basic structure of the object model hierarchy. Figure 6-13 shows the most critical objects in the Word object model and their hierarchical relationship.

The Application object is used to access application-level settings and options. It also is the root object of the object model and provides access to the other objects in the object model. Figure 6-14 shows some of the object model objects associated with the Application object.

The Document object represents a Word document. Figure 6-15 shows some of the object model objects associated with the Document object.

The Range object represents a range of text within a document. Figure 6-16 shows some of the object model objects associated with the Range object.

The Shape object represents a figure, chart, picture, or other object that is embedded in a Word document. Figure 6-17 shows some of the object model objects associated with the Shape object.

Conclusion

The chapter introduced the various ways you can integrate your code into Word. The chapter described how to build research services for Word and for other Office applications. You also learned the basic hierarchy of the Word object model. Chapter 7, "Working with Word Events," discusses the events in the Word object model. Chapter 8, "Working with Word Objects," covers the most important objects in the Word object model.

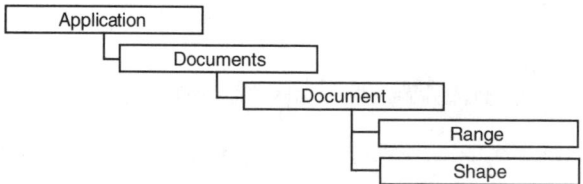

Figure 6-13: The basic hierarchy of the Word object model.

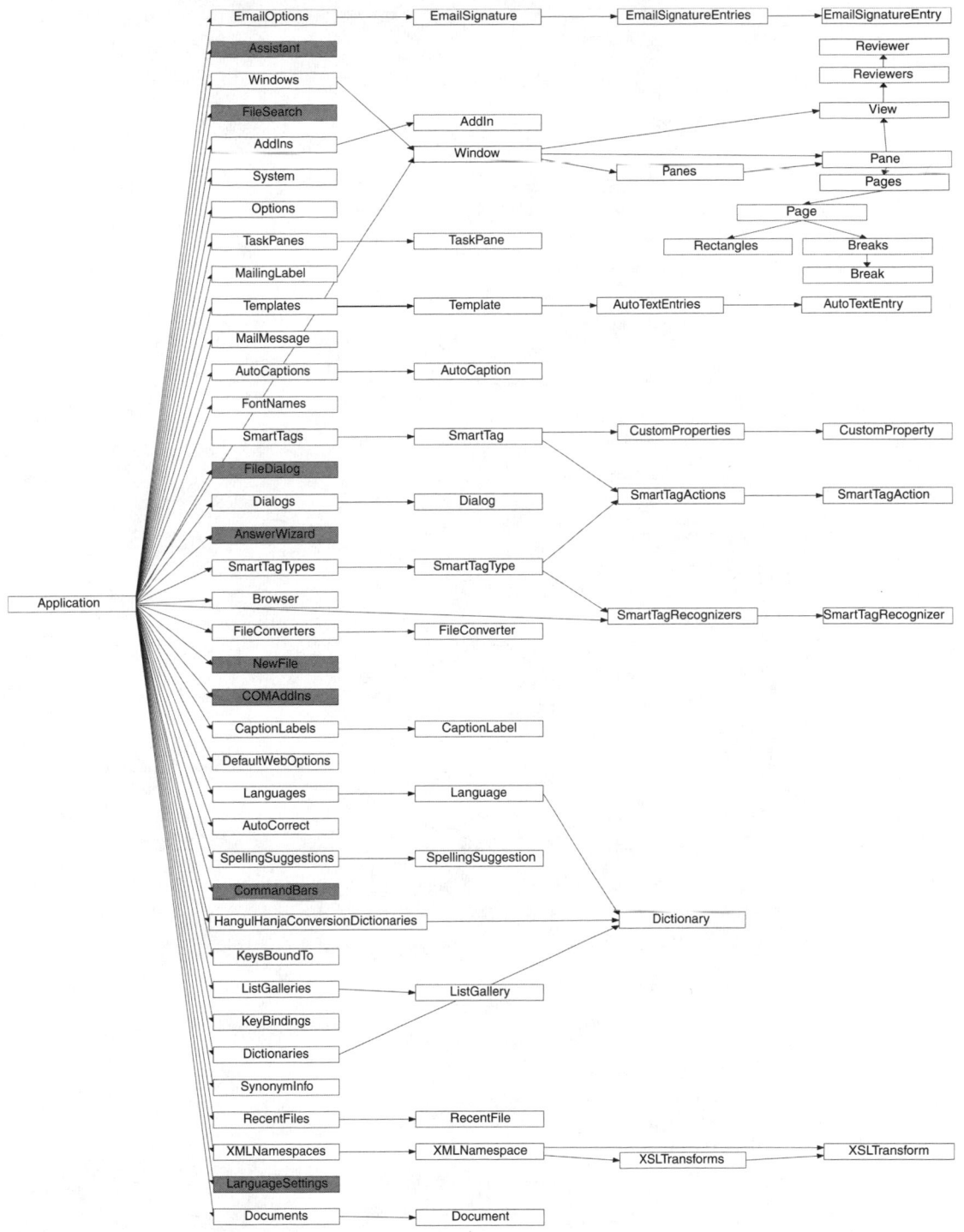

Figure 6-14: Objects associated with Word's Application object.

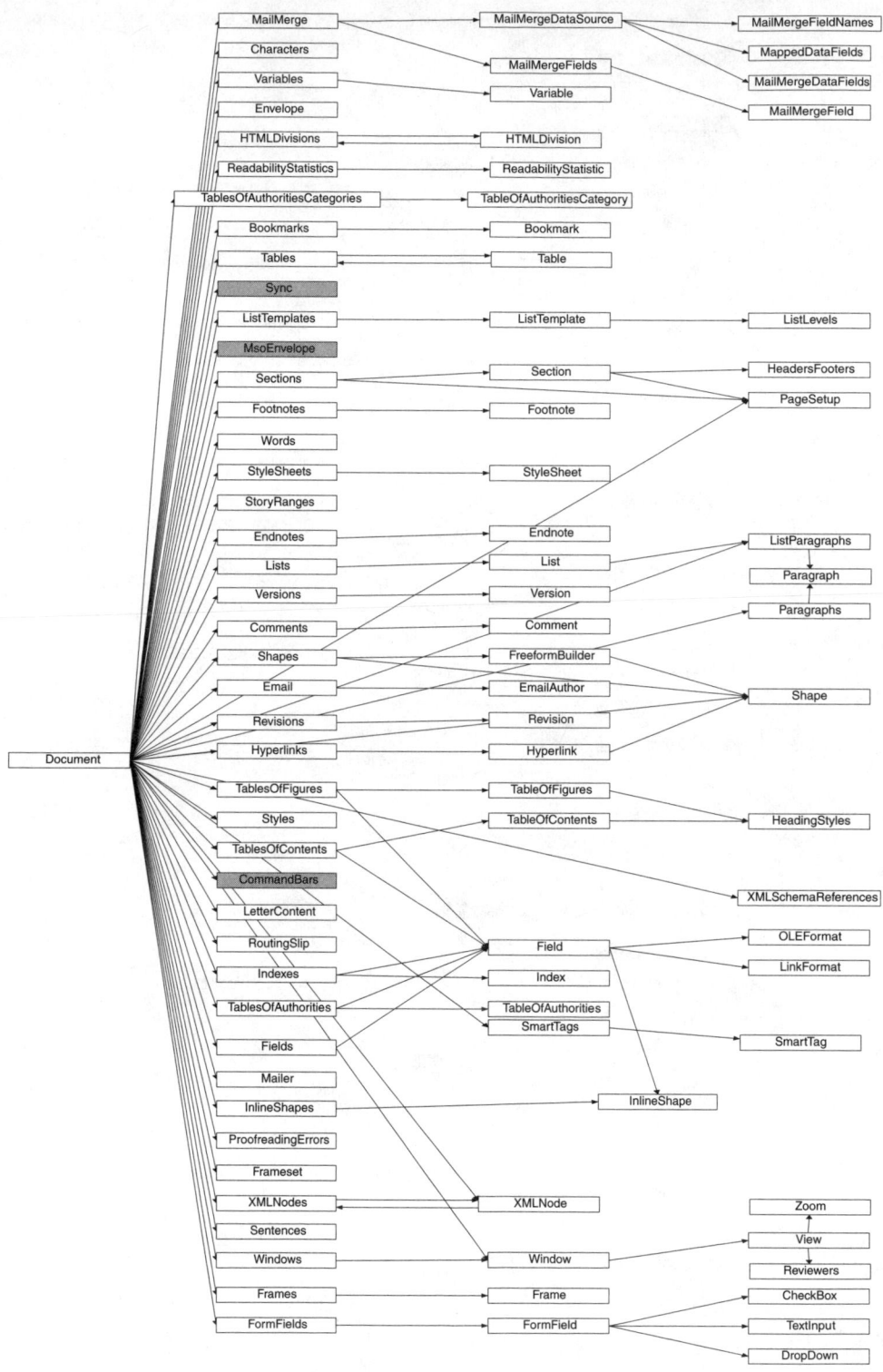

Figure 6-15: Objects associated with Word's Document object.

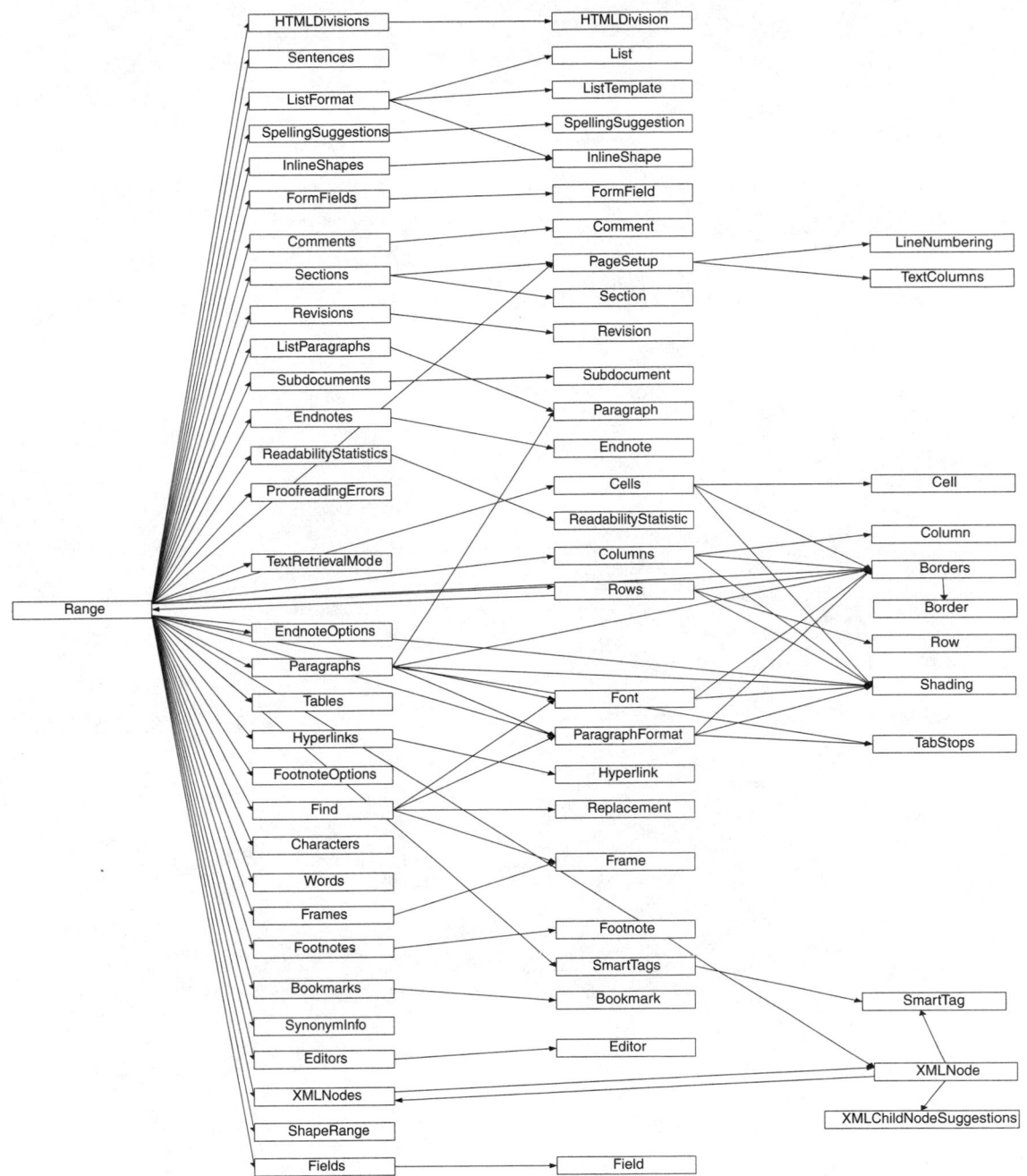

Figure 6-16: Objects associated with Word's Range object.

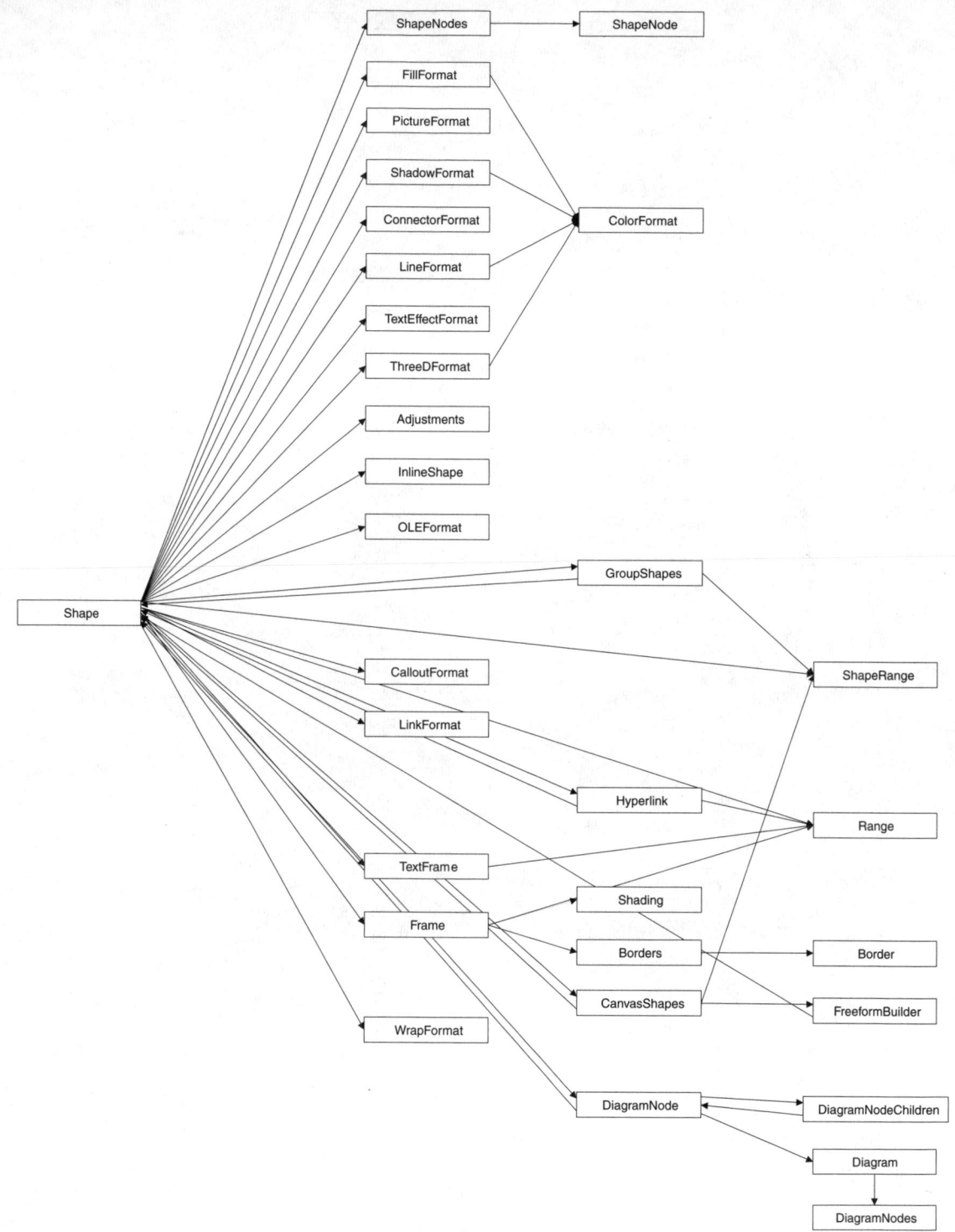

Figure 6-17: Objects associated with Word's Shape object.

◾ 7 ◾
Working with Word Events

Events in the Word Object Model

Understanding the events in the Word object model is critical because this is often the primary way that your code is run. This chapter covers all the events in the Word object model, when they are raised, and the type of code you might associate with these events.

Some of the events in the Word object model are repeated on the Application and Document objects. This repetition allows you to decide whether you want to handle the event for all documents or for a particular document. For example, if you want to know when any document is closed, you would handle the Application object's DocumentBeforeClose event. If you want to know when a particular document is closed, you would handle the Close event on a particular Document object. When an event is repeated on the Application and Document object, it is raised first on the Document object and then the Application object.

Why Are There Multiple Application and Document Event Interfaces?

When you work with the Word Object model, you will quickly notice multiple public interfaces, classes, and delegates that contain the text "ApplicationEvents" and "DocumentEvents":

- ApplicationEvents Interface
- ApplicationEvents_Event Interface

- ApplicationEvents_SinkHelper class
- ApplicationEvents2 Interface
- ApplicationsEvents2_Event Interface
- ApplicationEvents2_* Delegates
- ApplicationEvents2_SinkHelper class
- ApplicationEvents3 Interface
- ApplicationsEvents3_Event Interface
- ApplicationEvents3_* Delegates
- ApplicationEvents3_SinkHelper class
- ApplicationEvents4 Interface
- **ApplicationsEvents4_Event Interface**
- **ApplicationEvents4_* Delegates**
- ApplicationEvents4_SinkHelper class
- DocumentEvents Interface
- DocumentEvents_Event Interface
- DocumentEvents_* Delegates
- DocumentEvents_SinkHelper class
- DocumentEvents2 Interface
- **DocumentEvents2_Event Interface**
- **DocumentEvents2_* Delegates**
- DocumentEvents2_SinkHelper class

The only items from this list that you should ever use in your code are these: ApplicationEvents4_Event interface, the ApplicationEvents4_* delegates, the DocumentEvents2_Event interface, and the DocumentEvents2_* delegates. You should only use the ApplicationEvents4_Event interface and the DocumentEvents2_Event interface when you have to cast an object declared as Application or Document to the corresponding event interface because a method name and event name collide. An example of this is the Document object that has both a Close method and a Close event. To disambiguate between the two, you will have to cast the Document object to the DocumentEvents2_Event interface when you want to handle the Close event.

The reason for the other items in this list is partially explained in Chapter 1, "An Introduction to Office Programming." However, this explanation only covers the existence of the SinkHelper class and why there is both an ApplicationEvents/DocumentEvents interface and an ApplicationEvents_Event/DocumentEvents_Event interface. The reason there are multiple numbered event interfaces goes back to the original COM implementation of the Word object model.

The Word Application and Document COM objects are defined by the IDL definition shown in Listing 7-1. Note that the Application object has four event interfaces, and Document has two. ApplicationEvents4 is the default event interface for Word's Application object, and DocumentEvents2 is the default event interface for Word's Document object. ApplicationEvents, ApplicationEvents2, ApplicationEvents3, and DocumentEvents are supported for legacy purposes. Word had to keep these older interfaces in place for backward-compatibility reasons because older versions of Word used these interfaces.

Listing 7-1: The IDL Definition of Word's Application and Document Objects

```
[
  uuid(000209FF-0000-0000-C000-000000000046),
]
coclass Application {
  [default] interface _Application;
  [source] dispinterface ApplicationEvents;
  [source] dispinterface ApplicationEvents2;
  [source] dispinterface ApplicationEvents3;
  [default, source] dispinterface ApplicationEvents4;
};

[
  uuid(00020906-0000-0000-C000-000000000046),
]
coclass Document {
  [default] interface _Document;
  [source] dispinterface DocumentEvents;
  [default, source] dispinterface DocumentEvents2;
};
```

Visual Studio Generation of Event Handlers

As you consider the code in some of the listings in this chapter, you might wonder how you will ever remember the syntax of complicated lines of code such as this one:

```
application.DocumentBeforeClose +=
    new Word.ApplicationEvents4_DocumentBeforeCloseEventHandler(
    app_DocumentBeforeClose);
```

Fortunately, Visual Studio helps by generating most of this line of code as well as the corresponding event handler automatically. If you were typing this line of code, after you type +=, Visual Studio displays a pop-up tooltip, as shown in Figure 7-1. If you press the Tab key twice, Visual Studio generates the rest of the line of code and the event handler method automatically.

If you are using Visual Studio Tools for Office (VSTO), you can also use the Properties window to add event handlers to your document class. Double-click the project item for your document class. Make sure the Properties window is visible. If it is not, choose Properties Window from the View menu to show the Properties window. Make sure that the document class (typically called ThisDocument) is selected in the combo box at the top of the Properties window. Then click the lightning bolt icon to show events associated with the document. Type the name of the method you want to use as an event handler in the edit box to the right of the event you want to handle.

Figure 7-2 shows the Properties window and an event handler we have added by typing the text "ThisDocument_New" in the edit box next to the New event. This will cause the New event to be handled by a method called ThisDocument_New in the document class. If the method does not already exist, Visual Studio will add the method for you.

```
void ThisDocument_Startup(object sender, EventArgs e)
{
    Application.DocumentBeforeClose +=
        new Microsoft.Office.Interop.Word.ApplicationEvents4_DocumentBeforeCloseEventHandler(Application_DocumentBeforeClose);   (Press TAB to insert)
```

Figure 7-1: Adding an event handler using the pop-up tooltip.

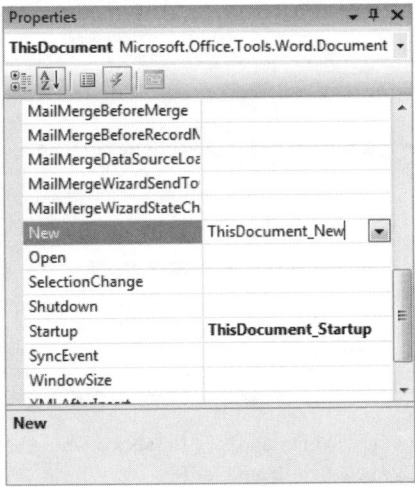

Figure 7-2: Adding a Document event handler
using the Properties window in VSTO.

Startup and Shutdown Events

Several events are raised when the application is started and shut down. The Word Application object has a Startup event that is raised when the application is started up before any documents are loaded. However, this event is marked as "restricted" in the COM object model and probably should not be used at all. The only kind of customization that can handle this event is an add-in. The event is raised before documents are loaded and before an automation executable can establish an event handler. Even add-ins do not need to use this event because they already implement OnConnection, which serves the same purpose. Our recommendation is not to use the Application object's Startup event.

For VSTO customizations, we recommend that you use the Startup and Shutdown events raised by VSTO on a document project item. Startup is raised when the document is opened or created from a template. Shutdown is raised when the document is closed. In the project item created for you by VSTO, these events are already connected for you, as shown in Listing 7-2. The InternalStartup method shown in Listing 7-2 is used by VSTO to connect the Startup and Shutdown event handlers as well as other events you might add using VSTO.

Listing 7-2: A VSTO Word Document Customization That Handles the Startup and Shutdown Events

```
public partial class ThisDocument
{
  private void ThisDocument_Startup(object sender, EventArgs e)
  {
  }

  private void ThisDocument_Shutdown(object sender, EventArgs e)
  {
  }

  private void InternalStartup()
  {
    this.Startup += new System.EventHandler(ThisDocument_Startup);
    this.Shutdown += new System.EventHandler(
      ThisDocument_Shutdown);
  }
}
```

Word raises the Quit event when the application shuts down. Listing 7-3 shows an example of handling the Quit event. Quit is the name of both a method and an event on Word's Application object. Because of this collision, you will not see the Quit event in Visual Studio's pop-up menu of properties, events, and methods associated with the Application object. Furthermore, a warning displays at compile time when you try to handle this event. To get Visual Studio's pop-up menus to work and the warning to go away, you can cast the Application object to the ApplicationEvents4_ Event interface, as shown in Listing 7-3.

Listing 7-3: A VSTO Word Add-In That Handles the Quit Event

```
public partial class ThisAddIn
{
  private void ThisAddIn_Startup(object sender, System.EventArgs e)
  {
    ((Word.ApplicationEvents4_Event)this.Application).Quit += new
      Word.ApplicationEvents4_QuitEventHandler(ThisAddIn_Quit);
  }

  void ThisAddIn_Quit()
  {
    MessageBox.Show("Quit Event Raised");
  }
```

```
#region VSTO generated code
private void InternalStartup()
{
    this.Startup += new System.EventHandler(ThisAddIn_Startup);
}
#endregion
}
```

New and Open Document Events

Word raises a NewDocument event on the Application object and a New event on a Document object when a new document is first created by the user either as a blank document or from a template or existing document. These events are never raised again on subsequent opens of the document. Word also raises a DocumentOpen event on the Application object and an Open event on a Document object when an existing document is opened:

- **Application.NewDocument** is raised whenever a document is created. Word passes the newly created Document as a parameter to this event.

- **Document.New** is raised on a template or a new blank document. So for example, when a document is first created from a template, you can handle the New event to set up the document for the first time. For subsequent opens of the document, you can handle the Open event or the Startup event raised by VSTO.

- **Application.DocumentOpen** is raised whenever an existing document is opened. Word passes the opened Document as a parameter to this event.

- **Document.Open** is raised on an existing document when it is opened.

Listing 7-4 shows a VSTO add-in that handles the Application object's NewDocument event and puts into the footer of every new document created in Word the date the document was created and the name of the user who created the document. It also handles the Application object's DocumentOpen event to put into the header of an existing document that is opened the date the document was opened and the name of the user who opened the document.

Listing 7-4: A VSTO Word Add-In That Handles the Application Object's NewDocument and DocumentOpen Events

```
public partial class ThisAddIn
{
  private void ThisAddIn_Startup(object sender, System.EventArgs e)
  {
    ((Word.ApplicationEvents4_Event)Application).NewDocument +=
      new Word.ApplicationEvents4_NewDocumentEventHandler(
      App_NewDocument);

    Application.DocumentOpen +=
      new Word.ApplicationEvents4_DocumentOpenEventHandler(
      App_DocumentOpen);
  }

  void App_NewDocument(Word.Document document)
  {
    MessageBox.Show(String.Format(
      "NewDocument event on {0}", document.Name));

    Word.Range range = document.Sections[1].Footers[
      Word.WdHeaderFooterIndex.wdHeaderFooterPrimary].Range;

    range.Text = String.Format("Created on {0} by {1}.",
      System.DateTime.Now, Application.UserName);
  }

  void App_DocumentOpen(Word.Document document)
  {
    MessageBox.Show(String.Format(
      "DocumentOpen event on {0}", document.Name));

    Word.Range range = document.Sections[1].Headers[
      Word.WdHeaderFooterIndex.wdHeaderFooterPrimary].Range;

    range.Text = String.Format("Last opened on {0} by {1}.",
      System.DateTime.Now, Application.UserName);
  }

  private void ThisAddIn_Shutdown(object sender,
    System.EventArgs e)
  {
  }

  #region VSTO generated code
  private void InternalStartup()
  {
    this.Startup += new System.EventHandler(ThisAddIn_Startup);
  }
  #endregion
}
```

Listing 7-5 shows VSTO code behind a template that handles the Document object's New event to display the time in the footer when the document is first created from a template. It also handles the Document object's Open event to put into the header the date and user who last opened the document each time the document is opened.

To understand this listing, it is important to understand how Word templates work in VSTO. You should only write handlers for the Document object's New event in a template project. When a user creates a new document from that template, the code associated with the template will be associated with the newly created document, and the New event will be raised on the newly created document.

Listing 7-5: A VSTO Word Template Customization That Handles the Document Object's New and Open Events

```
public partial class ThisDocument
{
  private void ThisDocument_New()
  {
    MessageBox.Show("New event");
    Word.Range range = this.Sections[1].Footers[
      Word.WdHeaderFooterIndex.wdHeaderFooterPrimary].Range;

    range.Text = String.Format("Created on {0} by {1}.",
      System.DateTime.Now, this.Application.UserName);
  }

  private void ThisDocument_Open()
  {
    MessageBox.Show("Open event");
    Word.Range range = this.Sections[1].Headers[
      Word.WdHeaderFooterIndex.wdHeaderFooterPrimary].Range;

    range.Text = String.Format("Opened on {0} by {1}.",
      System.DateTime.Now, this.Application.UserName);
  }

  private void InternalStartup()
  {
    this.New += new Word.DocumentEvents2_NewEventHandler(
      this.ThisDocument_New);
    this.Open += new Word.DocumentEvents2_OpenEventHandler(
      this.ThisDocument_Open);
  }
}
```

Document Close Events

Word raises events when a document is closed. The DocumentBeforeClose event is raised on the Application object before the document closes, which allows the handler to cancel the closing of the document. The Close event raised on the Document object does not allow canceling the closing of the document.

Unfortunately, the Close event is raised even in cases where the document is not really going to close. The event is raised before a dialog box is shown to the user prompting the user to save the document. Users are asked whether they want to save with a Yes, No, and Cancel button. If the user selects Cancel, the document remains open even though a Close event was raised. It is also possible for another add-in to handle the Document-BeforeClose event and cancel the close of the document. For this reason, it is better to use VSTO's Shutdown event on the document, which is not raised until after the user and any handlers of the DocumentBeforeClose event have been given a chance to cancel the closing of the document.

- **Application.DocumentBeforeClose** is raised before a document is closed. Word passes the Document that is about to close as a parameter to this event. It also passes by reference a `bool cancel` parameter. The `cancel` parameter can be set to `true` by your event handler to prevent Word from closing the document.

- **Document.Close** is raised when a document is about to be closed. However, as discussed earlier, the user can still cancel the closing of the document, so you cannot trust this event to tell you whether the document is going to close. Use VSTO's Shutdown event instead.

> **■ NOTE**
>
> Close is the name of both a method and an event on the Document object. Because of this collision, you will not see the Close event in Visual Studio's pop-up menu of properties, events, and methods associated with the Document object. Furthermore, a warning displays at compile time when you try to handle this event. To get Visual Studio's pop-up menus to work and the warning to go away, you can cast the Document object to the DocumentEvents2_Event interface, as shown in Listing 7-6.

Listing 7-6 shows a VSTO customization that handles the Application object's DocumentBeforeClose event and the Document object's Close event. In the handler of the DocumentBeforeClose event, the code checks to see if the document contains any spelling errors. If it does, a dialog box displays with the number of spelling errors, and the user is told to correct them before closing the document. The cancel parameter is set to true to prevent the document from closing. Another thing to try when running this code is to press the Cancel button when you are prompted to save and observe that the Document object's Close event fires in this case.

Listing 7-6: A VSTO Word Document Customization That Handles the Application Object's DocumentBeforeClose Event and the Document Object's Close Event

```
public partial class ThisDocument
{
  Word.Application app;
  Word.Document doc;

  void ThisDocument_Startup(object sender, EventArgs e)
  {
    app = this.Application;
    doc = app.Documents.Add(ref missing, ref missing,
      ref missing, ref missing);

    doc.Range(ref missing, ref missing).Text =
      "Lawts uf spellin errers!";

    app.DocumentBeforeClose += new
      Word.ApplicationEvents4_DocumentBeforeCloseEventHandler(
      App_DocumentBeforeClose);

    ((Word.DocumentEvents2_Event)doc).Close += new
      Word.DocumentEvents2_CloseEventHandler(
      Doc_Close);
  }

  void Doc_Close()
  {
    MessageBox.Show("Thanks for fixing the spelling errors.");
  }

  void App_DocumentBeforeClose(Word.Document document,
    ref bool cancel)
  {
    int spellingErrors = document.SpellingErrors.Count;
    if (spellingErrors > 0)
```

```
    {
      MessageBox.Show(String.Format(
        "There are still {0} spelling errors in this document.",
          spellingErrors));
      cancel = true;
    }
  }

  private void InternalStartup()
  {
    this.Startup += new EventHandler(ThisDocument_Startup);
  }
}
```

Document Save Events

Word raises the DocumentBeforeSave event on the Application object before any document is saved. Word passes the Document that is about to be saved as a parameter to this event. It also passes by reference a `bool` `saveAsUI` parameter and a `bool` `cancel` parameter. If you set `saveAsUI` to `true`, the Save As dialog box displays for the document. If you set the `cancel` parameter to `true`, the save will be canceled. Often this event is handled to implement a custom save routine—for example, you might cancel the DocumentBeforeSave event but call the SaveAs method on Document to enforce a particular file format.

Note that the DocumentBeforeSave event is also raised when Word does an AutoSave on a document. You should be careful that you test your code to make sure that it works properly when AutoSave is triggered.

Listing 7-7 shows a VSTO customization that handles the Document-BeforeSave event. If the document contains any spelling errors, it cancels the save by setting the `cancel` parameter to `true`. It also sets the `saveAsUI` parameter to `true` to force a Save As dialog box to be shown for every save. When the DocumentBeforeSave event is triggered for an AutoSave, the dialog box shown in Figure 7-3 is displayed if the save is canceled by setting the `cancel` parameter to `true`.

Listing 7-7: A VSTO Word Document Customization That Handles the Application Object's DocumentBeforeSave Event

```
public partial class ThisDocument
{
  Word.Application app;
```

```csharp
void ThisDocument_Startup(object sender, EventArgs e)
{
  app = this.Application;

  app.DocumentBeforeSave += new Word.
    ApplicationEvents4_DocumentBeforeSaveEventHandler(
    App_DocumentBeforeSave);
}

void App_DocumentBeforeSave(Word.Document document,
  ref bool saveAsUI, ref bool cancel)
{
  saveAsUI = true;

  if (document.SpellingErrors.Count > 0)
  {
    MessageBox.Show(
      "You shouldn't save a document with spelling errors.");
    cancel = true;
  }
}

private void InternalStartup()
{
  this.Startup += new EventHandler(ThisDocument_Startup);
}
}
```

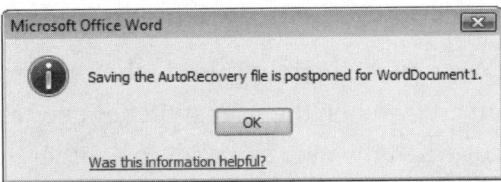

Figure 7-3: The message displayed by Word when an automatic save is canceled.

Document Activation Events

Word raises several events on the Application object when the active document changes. One such event is the DocumentChange event. The name DocumentChange makes you think that maybe this event would tell you when the contents of the document change—unfortunately, Word does not have a general event that tells you this.

The active document changes when you create a new document—the new document becomes the active document. The active document changes when you open an existing document—the document you opened becomes the active document. The active document changes when you switch between open documents by clicking a document that is not currently active or selecting a document using the Window menu or the Windows taskbar.

It is also possible to have multiple windows viewing the same document—for example, because the user chose New Window from the Window menu. Word raises an event called WindowActivate that tells you when a particular window becomes the active window and an event called WindowDeactivate when a particular window is deactivated. Unlike Excel, switching to another application causes Word's WindowDeactivate event to be raised, and switching back to Word causes the WindowActivate event to be raised.

- **Application.DocumentChange** is raised when the active document changes (not when the contents of the document change). Word passes no parameters to this event. To determine the new active document, you must use the Application object's ActiveDocument property.

- **Application.WindowActivate** is raised when a Word window is activated. This can occur when the user switches between windows within Word or when the user switches to another application and then switches back to Word. Word passes the Document associated with the window that was activated as a parameter to this event. Word also passes the Window that was activated as a parameter to this event.

- **Application.WindowDeactivate** is raised when a Word window is deactivated. This can occur when the user switches between windows within Word or when the user switches to another application. Word passes the Document associated with the window that was deactivated as a parameter to this event. Word also passes the Window that was deactivated as a parameter to this event.

Listing 7-8 shows a VSTO customization that handles the Document-Change, WindowActivate, and WindowDeactivate events and displays a message box when these events are raised.

Listing 7-8: A VSTO Word Document Customization That Handles the Application Object's WindowActivate, WindowDeactivate, and DocumentChange Events

```csharp
public partial class ThisDocument
{
  Word.Application app;

  void ThisDocument_Startup(object sender, EventArgs e)
  {
    app = this.Application;

    app.WindowActivate += new Word.
      ApplicationEvents4_WindowActivateEventHandler(
      App_WindowActivate);

    app.WindowDeactivate += new Word.
      ApplicationEvents4_WindowDeactivateEventHandler(
      App_WindowDeactivate);

    app.DocumentChange += new Word.
      ApplicationEvents4_DocumentChangeEventHandler(
      App_DocumentChange);
  }

  void App_WindowActivate(Word.Document document,
    Word.Window window)
  {
    MessageBox.Show(String.Format(
      "Window {0} was activated.", window.Caption));
  }

  void App_WindowDeactivate(Word.Document document,
    Word.Window window)
  {
    MessageBox.Show(String.Format(
      "Window {0} was deactivated.", window.Caption));
  }

  void App_DocumentChange()
  {
    MessageBox.Show(String.Format(
      "The active document is now {0}.",
      app.ActiveDocument.Name));
  }
```

```
    private void InternalStartup()
    {
      this.Startup += new EventHandler(ThisDocument_Startup);
    }
}
```

Document Print Events

Word raises a DocumentBeforePrint event on the Application object before a document is printed. Word passes the Document that is about to be printed as a parameter to this event. It also passes by reference a `bool` `cancel` parameter. If you set the `cancel` parameter to `true`, the default printing of the document will be canceled. Often this event is handled to implement a custom print routine—for example, you might cancel Word's default print behavior and use the PrintOut method on Document to enforce a certain print format.

Listing 7-9 shows a VSTO customization that handles the DocumentBeforePrint event to enforce some custom print settings. It forces two copies to be printed and collation to be turned on when the user prints the document.

Listing 7-9: A VSTO Word Document Customization That Handles the Application Object's DocumentBeforePrint Event

```
public partial class ThisDocument
{
  Word.Application app;

  void ThisDocument_Startup(object sender, EventArgs e)
  {
    app = this.Application;

    app.DocumentBeforePrint += new Word.
      ApplicationEvents4_DocumentBeforePrintEventHandler(
      app_DocumentBeforePrint);
  }

  void app_DocumentBeforePrint(Word.Document document,
    ref bool cancel)
  {
    // Print 2 copies and collate.
    object copies = 2;
    object collate = true;
```

```
    document.PrintOut(ref missing, ref missing, ref missing,
      ref missing, ref missing, ref missing, ref missing,
      ref copies, ref missing, ref missing, ref missing,
      ref collate, ref missing, ref missing, ref missing,
      ref missing, ref missing, ref missing);

    // Cancel because we printed already
    // and don't want Word to print again.
    cancel = true;
  }

  private void InternalStartup()
  {
    this.Startup += new EventHandler(ThisDocument_Startup);
  }
}
```

Mouse Events

Word raises events when the user right-clicks or double-clicks in the document area of a window. If the user right-clicks or double-clicks in an area of the window such as the ruler or the scrollbar, no events are raised.

- **Application.WindowBeforeDoubleClick** is raised when the document area of a window is double-clicked. Word passes the selection that was double-clicked. This can be a range of text or other objects in the document, such as a shape. Word also passes by reference a `bool` `cancel` parameter. The `cancel` parameter can be set to `true` by your event handler to prevent Word from doing the default action associated with a double-click.

- **Application.WindowBeforeRightClick** is raised when the document area of a window is right-clicked. Word passes the selection that was right-clicked. This can be a range of text or other objects in the document, such as a shape. Word also passes by reference a `bool` `cancel` parameter. The `cancel` parameter can be set to `true` by your event handler to prevent Word from doing the default action associated with a right-click.

Listing 7-10 shows a VSTO customization that handles the WindowBefore-DoubleClick and WindowBeforeRightClick events. When the document is double-clicked, this application sets the selected range of text to be all caps. The range of text that is selected depends on where the user double-clicked. If the user double-clicks a word, the selection changes to be the word. If the user triple-clicks, the selection changes to be a paragraph. If the user double-clicks the page margin, the selection changes to be the line next to where the user double-clicked.

When a range of text is right-clicked, this customization sets the range of text to be title case. Finally, if you double-click a shape in the document, the color is set to a dark red. We also set cancel to true to prevent the shape Properties dialog box from being shown when a shape is double-clicked and to prevent the right-click menu from appearing when a range of text is right-clicked.

Listing 7-10: A VSTO Word Document Customization That Handles the Application Object's WindowBeforeDoubleClick and WindowBeforeRightClick Events

```
public partial class ThisDocument
{
  Word.Application app;

  void ThisDocument_Startup(object sender, EventArgs e)
  {
    app = this.Application;

    app.WindowBeforeDoubleClick += new Word.
      ApplicationEvents4_WindowBeforeDoubleClickEventHandler(
      App_WindowBeforeDoubleClick);

    app.WindowBeforeRightClick += new Word.
      ApplicationEvents4_WindowBeforeRightClickEventHandler(
      App_WindowBeforeRightClick);
  }

  void App_WindowBeforeRightClick(Word.Selection selection,
    ref bool cancel)
  {
    if (selection.Type == Word.WdSelectionType.wdSelectionNormal)
    {
      selection.Range.Case = Word.WdCharacterCase.wdTitleWord;
      cancel = true;
    }
  }

  void App_WindowBeforeDoubleClick(Word.Selection selection,
    ref bool cancel)
```

```
{
  if (selection.Type == Word.WdSelectionType.wdSelectionNormal ||
      selection.Type == Word.WdSelectionType.wdSelectionIP ||
      selection.Type == Word.WdSelectionType.wdSelectionBlock)
  {
    selection.Range.Case = Word.WdCharacterCase.wdUpperCase;
  }
  else if (
    selection.Type == Word.WdSelectionType.wdSelectionShape)
  {
    selection.ShapeRange.Fill.ForeColor.RGB = 3000;
    cancel = true;
  }
}

private void InternalStartup()
{
  this.Startup += new EventHandler(ThisDocument_Startup);
}
}
```

Selection Events

Word raises several events when the selection changes in the active document.

- **Application.WindowSelectionChange** is raised when the selection in a document changes. This event is also raised when the location of the insertion point changes within the document because of clicking with the mouse or moving via navigation keys (such as page up and page down). This event is not raised when the insertion point is moved as a result of typing new text into the document. Word passes a Selection object representing the new selection as a parameter to this event. If only the insertion point has moved and no range of text is selected, the Selection object will be passed as a one-character-long Range object containing the character after the current location of the insertion point, and the Type property of the Selection object will return WdSelectionType.wdSelectionIP.

- **Application.XMLSelectionChange** is raised when the selected XML element changes in a document with XML mappings. Word passes the new Selection object as a parameter to this event. It also passes the old XMLNode object that was selected previously and the XMLNode object that is now selected. It also passes a reason for the selection change of type WdXMLSelectionChange, which can be wdXML-SelectionChangeReasonDelete, wdXMLSelectionChangeReason-Insert, or wdXMLSelectionChangeReasonMove.

Listing 7-11 shows a VSTO customization that uses the Range.Start and Range.End properties to display the start and end location of the selection. The code first checks whether the selection type is wdSelectionIP or wdSelectionNormal. It also prints the selection type using a helpful feature of .NET—when you use the ToString() method associated with an enumerated type, it displays the string name of the enumeration instead of just displaying a number.

Listing 7-11: A VSTO Word Document Customization That Handles the Application Object's WindowSelectionChange Event

```
public partial class ThisDocument
{
  Word.Application app;

  void ThisDocument_Startup(object sender, EventArgs e)
  {
    app = this.Application;

    app.WindowSelectionChange += new Word.
      ApplicationEvents4_WindowSelectionChangeEventHandler(
      App_WindowSelectionChange);
  }

  void App_WindowSelectionChange(Word.Selection selection)
  {
    Word.WdSelectionType selType = selection.Type;

    MessageBox.Show(String.Format(
      "Selection type is {0}.", selType.ToString()));

    if (selType == Word.WdSelectionType.wdSelectionIP ||
      selType == Word.WdSelectionType.wdSelectionNormal)
    {
      MessageBox.Show(String.Format(
        "Start is {0} and End is {1}.",
        selection.Range.Start, selection.Range.End));
    }
  }
}
```

```
  private void InternalStartup()
  {
    this.Startup += new EventHandler(ThisDocument_Startup);
  }
}
```

Window Sizing Events

Word raises a WindowSize event on the Application object when a window associated with a document is resized. Once again, the behavior of this event is different than the window sizing event in Excel. The Window-Size event in Word is raised even when the document window is maximized to fill the Word application window and the Word application window is resized. The event is not raised for the Word application window when it is resized and no documents are opened.

Word passes the Document object associated with the window that was resized as a parameter to this event. Word also passes the Window object for the window that was resized.

XML Events

Word raises several events when XML elements have been mapped into the document using the XML Structure feature of Word. You have already learned about the Application object's XMLSelectionChange that is raised when the selection changes from one XML element to another.

- **Application.XMLValidationError** is raised when the XML in the document is not valid when compared to the schema associated with the document. Word passes the XMLNode object corresponding to the invalid element as a parameter to this event.

- **Document.XMLAfterInsert** is raised after the user adds a new XML element to the document. If multiple XML elements are added at the same time, the event will be raised for each element that was added. Word passes the XMLNode object for the newly added element as a parameter to this event. It also passes an `inUndoRedo` `bool` parameter that indicates whether the XML element was added because undo or redo was invoked.

- **Document.XMLBeforeDelete** is raised when the user deletes an XML element from the document. If multiple XML elements are removed at the same time, the event will be raised for each element that was removed. Word passes a Range object representing the range of text that was deleted. If an element was deleted without deleting any text, the Range will be passed as null. Word also passes the XMLNode object that was deleted and a bool inUndoRedo parameter that indicates whether the XML element was deleted because undo or redo was invoked.

Sync Events

Word raises the Document object's Sync event when a local document is synchronized with a copy on the server using Word's document workspace feature. Word passes a parameter of type MsoSyncEventType that gives additional information on the status of the document synchronization.

EPostage Events

Word supports a feature called electronic postage, which enables you to create an envelope or label with printed postage that is printed on an envelope or package along with the address. Figure 7-4 shows the Envelopes and Labels dialog box, which has an Add electronic postage check box and an E-postage Properties button that are used to configure electronic postage. Word provides three events to allow third parties to create an e-postage add-in: EPostageInsert, EPostageInsertEx, and EPostagePropertyDialog. An e-postage add-in is distinguished from other Word add-ins by a special registry key. There can only be one active e-postage add-in installed in Word. This book does not consider these events further because it is unlikely that you will ever need to create your own electronic postage add-in. You can read more about e-postage add-ins by downloading the E-postage SDK at http://support.microsoft.com/?kbid=304095.

Mail Merge Events

Word raises eight events associated with the mail merge feature when you use the Step by Step Mail Merge Wizard. To understand these events, you must first understand how mail merge works, and when and why each of these events is raised.

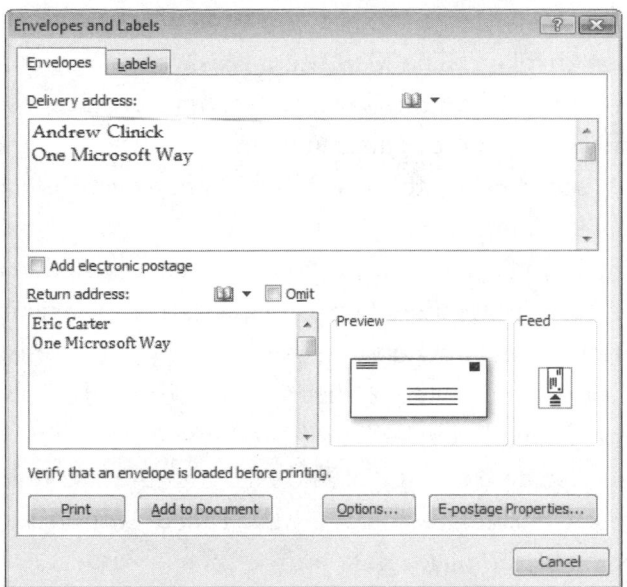

Figure 7-4: The Envelopes and Labels dialog box with electronic postage options.

Step by Step Mail Merge Wizard Versus Mailings Tab

The two approaches to customizing the mail merge experience are handling the mail merge events or customizing the behavior of the Ribbon buttons on the Mailings tab. Handling mail merge events works only if the user invokes the Step by Step Mail Merge Wizard. If the user instead does a mail merge by using the other buttons in the mailings tab, the events described in this section aren't raised. Although this section describes the former approach, the latter approach may be a more practical way to customize mail merge if your users don't want to be forced into always using the Step by Step Mail Merge Wizard.

The user starts a mail merge by going to the Mailings tab and choosing Step by Step Mail Merge Wizard from the Start Mail Merge drop-down menu. This causes the Application object's MailMergeWizardStateChange event to be raised, notifying us that we are moving from Step 0 to Step 1 of the Step by Step Mail Merge Wizard. The Mail Merge task pane shown in Figure 7-5 then displays. The Mail Merge task pane is a wizard that can move back and forth through six steps. Whenever you move from step to step, the MailMergeWizardStateChange event is raised. When you close the document, the MailMergeWizardStateChange event is raised, moving from Step 6 back to Step 0.

Step 2 is not shown here—it prompts you as to whether you want to start from the current document or from a template or existing document on disk. In Step 2, we will choose to use the current document. When we get to Step 3 of the Mail Merge Wizard, the user is prompted to select a data source for the mail merge. Figure 7-6 shows Step 3.

We choose Use an existing list and click the Browse link to locate an Access database we have previously created called Authors.mdb. Figure 7-7 shows the dialog box to pick a data source.

After we select the data source and choose Open, the Application object's MailMergeDataSourceLoad event is raised. This event lets us know that a data source has been chosen and we can now examine the data source through the OM. After the MergeDataSourceLoad event has been raised, the

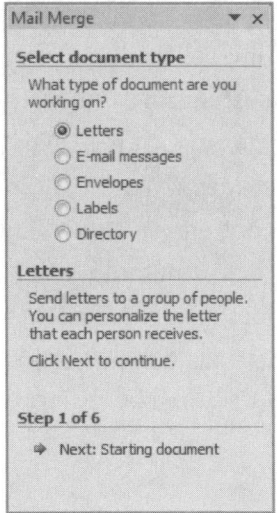

Figure 7-5: Step 1 of the Mail Merge Wizard.

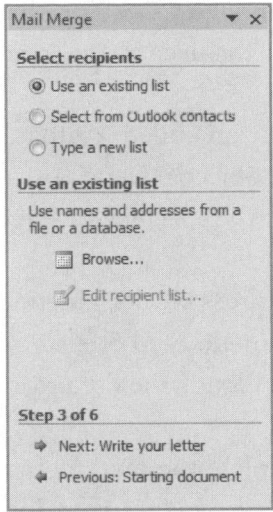

Figure 7-6: Step 3 of the Mail Merge Wizard.

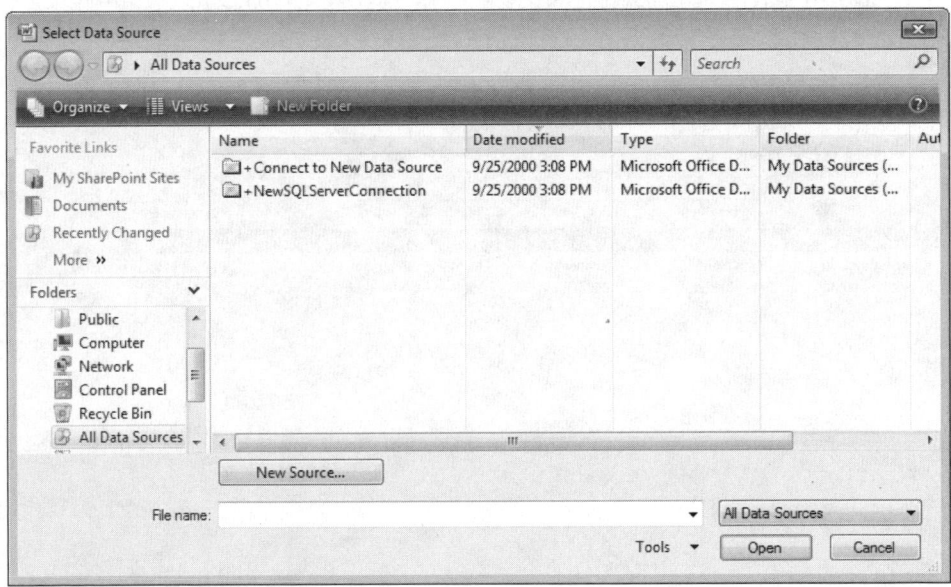

Figure 7-7: Selecting a data source.

Mail Merge Recipients dialog box appears, as shown in Figure 7-8. This dialog box shows each record in the data source and lets the user further control which records you want to use for the mail merge.

The Mail Merge Recipients dialog box has a button called Validate. When clicked, this button raises the Application object's DataSource-Validate2 event. However, it only raises this event for the special e-postage add-in described earlier.

Step 4 of the Mail Merge Wizard lets you insert address blocks, greeting blocks, and other fields into the body of your document. Step 5 lets you preview the final look of your document when Word loads the data from your data source into the blocks you have defined.

Step 6 displays two actions you can take to complete the mail merge. The first is to print the generated letters. The second is to create a new document and insert each letter into the new document. You can also specify a third action by writing a line of code such as the following before Step 6 of the wizard is shown:

```
document.MailMerge.ShowSendToCustom = "My Custom Action...";
```

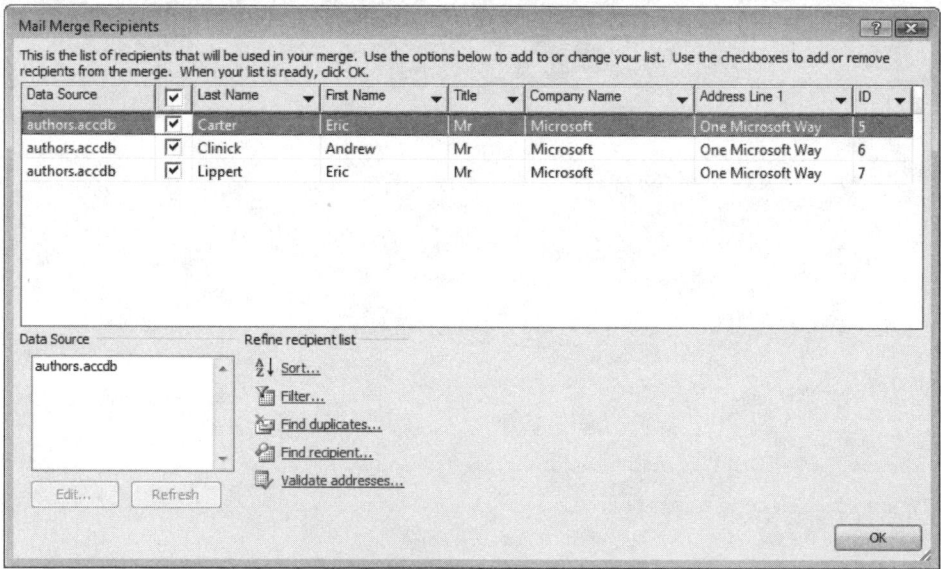

Figure 7-8: The Mail Merge Recipients dialog box.

The MailMerge object's ShowSendToCustom property takes a `string` value and allows you to add a third custom action defined by your code to do at the end of a mail merge. When the user clicks this custom action, the Application object's MailMergeWizardSendToCustom event is raised. Figure 7-9 shows Step 6 of the Mail Merge Wizard with a custom action called My Custom Action.

When the user chooses Print or Edit individual letters, the Application object's MailMergeBeforeMerge event is raised. Word passes the start record and the end record that will be merged as `int` parameters. The default is to merge all the records. When all the records are going to be merged, Word passes `1` for the start record and `–16` for the end record. Word also passes by reference a `bool cancel` parameter. If you set the `cancel` parameter to `true`, the mail merge will be canceled.

After the MailMergeBeforeMerge event is raised, Word shows a dialog box letting the user change the records to merge, as shown in Figure 7-10. Unfortunately, if the user changes the records to be merged, Word does not re-raise the MailMergeBeforeMerge event. To get a more reliable event, you may need to use MailMergeBeforeRecordMerge. The next time the user does a mail merge, the user's last selection in the dialog box will be reflected in the parameters passed to MailMergeBeforeMerge.

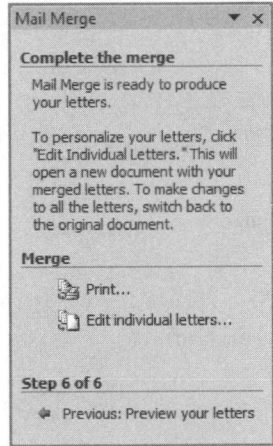

Figure 7-9: Step 6 of the
Mail Merge Wizard.

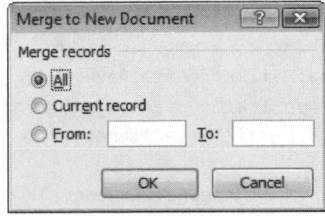

Figure 7-10: Selecting the
records to merge.

When the user clicks the OK button in the dialog box shown in Figure 7-10, the mail merge begins in earnest. Before Word merges a record from the data source to create a letter, it first raises the Application object's Mail-MergeBeforeRecordMerge event. It then creates the letter from the record and raises the Application object's MailMergeAfterRecordMerge event when the letter for the record has been generated. This sequence of Mail-MergeBeforeRecordMerge followed by MailMergeAfterRecordMerge repeats for each record that is going to be merged. When all the records have been merged, Word raises the Application object's MailMergeAfterMerge event and passes the newly created Document object as a parameter if the user chose to Edit individual letters in Figure 7-9. If the user chose Print, null will be passed for the newly created document.

Listing 7-12 shows a VSTO customization that handles all the mail merge events.

Listing 7-12: A VSTO Word Document Customization That Handles Mail Merge Events

```
public partial class ThisDocument
{
  Word.Application app;

  void ThisDocument_Startup(object sender, EventArgs e)
  {
    app = this.Application;

    // Have to set ShowSendToCustom so that there is a custom
    // command that can be clicked to raise the
    // MailMergeWizardSendToCustom event

    this.MailMerge.ShowSendToCustom = "My Custom Command";

    app.MailMergeAfterMerge += new Word.
      ApplicationEvents4_MailMergeAfterMergeEventHandler(
      App_MailMergeAfterMerge);

    app.MailMergeAfterRecordMerge += new Word.
      ApplicationEvents4_MailMergeAfterRecordMergeEventHandler(
      App_MailMergeAfterRecordMerge);

    app.MailMergeBeforeMerge += new Word.
      ApplicationEvents4_MailMergeBeforeMergeEventHandler(
      App_MailMergeBeforeMerge);
```

```csharp
    app.MailMergeBeforeRecordMerge += new Word.
      ApplicationEvents4_MailMergeBeforeRecordMergeEventHandler(
      App_MailMergeBeforeRecordMerge);

    app.MailMergeDataSourceLoad += new Word.
      ApplicationEvents4_MailMergeDataSourceLoadEventHandler(
      App_MailMergeDataSourceLoad);

    app.MailMergeDataSourceValidate2 += new Word.
      ApplicationEvents4_MailMergeDataSourceValidate2EventHandler(
      App_MailMergeDataSourceValidate);

    app.MailMergeWizardSendToCustom += new Word.
      ApplicationEvents4_MailMergeWizardSendToCustomEventHandler(
      App_MailMergeWizardSendToCustom);

    app.MailMergeWizardStateChange += new Word.
      ApplicationEvents4_MailMergeWizardStateChangeEventHandler(
      App_MailMergeWizardStateChange);
}

void App_MailMergeAfterMerge(Word.Document document,
  Word.Document documentResult)
{
  MessageBox.Show(String.Format(
    "MailMergeAfterMerge: Source = {0}, Result = {1}",
    document.Name, documentResult.Name));
}

void App_MailMergeAfterRecordMerge(Word.Document document)
{
  MessageBox.Show(String.Format(
    "MailMergeAfterRecordMerge for {0}",
    document.Name));
}

void App_MailMergeBeforeMerge(Word.Document document,
  int startRecord, int endRecord, ref bool cancel)
{
  MessageBox.Show(String.Format(
    "MailMergeBeforeMerge for {0}", document.Name));

  // Word passes -16 as the EndRecord if the user
  // chose to merge all records.events>
  if (endRecord == -16)
  {
    endRecord = document.MailMerge.DataSource.RecordCount;
  }
```

```csharp
    MessageBox.Show(String.Format(
      "Merging records from record {0} to record {1}."
      , startRecord, endRecord));
  }

  void App_MailMergeBeforeRecordMerge(Word.Document document,
    ref bool cancel)
  {
    MessageBox.Show(String.Format(
      "MailMergeBeforeRecordMerge for {0}.",
      document.Name));
  }

  void App_MailMergeDataSourceLoad(Word.Document document)
  {
    MessageBox.Show(String.Format(
      "MailMergeDataSourceLoad for {0}.",
      document.Name));

    MessageBox.Show(String.Format(
      "The data source is {0}.",
      document.MailMerge.DataSource.Name));
  }

  void App_MailMergeDataSourceValidate(Word.Document document,
    ref bool handled)
  {
    MessageBox.Show(String.Format(
      "MailMergeDataSourceValidate for {0}.",
      document.Name));
  }

  void App_MailMergeWizardSendToCustom(Word.Document document)
  {
    MessageBox.Show(String.Format(
      "MailMergeWizardSendToCustom for {0}.",
      document.Name));
  }

  void App_MailMergeWizardStateChange(Word.Document document,
    ref int fromState, ref int toState, ref bool handled)
  {
    MessageBox.Show(String.Format(
      "MailMergeWizardStateChange for {0}.",
      document.Name));
  }

  private void InternalStartup()
  {
```

```
        this.Startup += new EventHandler(ThisDocument_Startup);
    }
}
```

ContentControl Events

New in Word 2007, content controls can be inserted into a document to provide more structure and control—when you have a section of the document that you want to allow the user to put a picture into or to pick a value from a drop-down list, for example. There are eight content controls: rich text, plain text, picture, combo box, drop-down list, date picker, group, and building block gallery. These controls can be found in the Developer tab of Word's Ribbon. The developer tab isn't displayed by default in Word. To display it, choose Word Options from the Office menu; then select the Show Developer tab in the Ribbon from the Popular tab of the Word Options dialog box. Figure 7-11 shows the Controls group in the Developer tab of the Ribbon.

Figure 7-12 shows the result of inserting a rich text control into a blank document. When the rich text control is selected, as it is in Figure 7-12, the control displays with a border UI to which you can add a title to identify the control. When the control is deselected, it displays without the border

Figure 7-11: Content controls in Word's Developer tab.

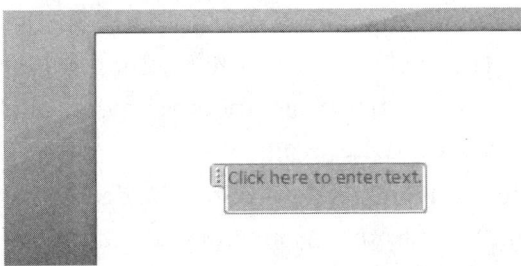

Figure 7-12: A rich text control in a Word document.

UI and optional title, and just looks like any other region of text in the document. This is important, as it allows you to have a control paradigm in the document—but only while the user is editing the contents of the control. When the user reads or prints the document, no control border UI is displayed.

We discuss content controls in more detail in Chapter 8, "Working with Word Objects." For now, we move on to examine the events that can be raised on content controls:

- **Document.ContentControlAfterAdd** is raised after a content control is added to the document. Word passes the ContentControl object for the newly added content control as a parameter to this event. It also passes an `inUndoRedo` `bool` parameter that indicates whether the content control was added because undo or redo was invoked.

- **Document.ContentControlBeforeDelete** is raised before a content control is deleted from the document. Word passes the Content-Control object for the content control that is about to be deleted as a parameter to this event. It also passes an `inUndoRedo` `bool` parameter that indicates whether the content control was deleted because undo or redo was invoked.

- **Document.ContentControlOnExit** is raised when a user leaves a content control that currently has focus and sets the focus to another part of the document. Word passes the ContentControl object for the content control that lost focus as a parameter to this event. It also passes by reference a `bool` `cancel` parameter. The `cancel` parameter can be set to `true` by your event handler to prevent the user from leaving the content control.

- **Document.ContentControlOnEnter** is raised when a user enters a content control by setting the focus to the content control. Word passes the ContentControl object for the content control that gained focus as a parameter to this event.

- **Document.ContentControlBeforeStoreUpdate** is raised when a content control that is bound to a CustomXMLPart in the document (using the XMLMapping property) has an update to pass to the XML data store. Word passes the ContentControl object for the content control that is about to update the CustomXMLPart. It also passes by reference a `string content` parameter. The `content` parameter can be modified by your event handler to change the data before it is put in the CustomXMLPart.

- **Document.ContentControlBeforeContentUpdate** is raised when a content control that is bound to a CustomXMLPart in the document (using the XMLMapping property) is updated from the CustomXML-Part. Word passes the ContentControl object for the content control that is about to be updated from the CustomXMLPart. It also passes by reference a `string content` parameter. The `content` parameter can be modified by your event handler to change the data coming from the CustomXMLPart before it updates the bound content control.

- **Document.BuildingBlockInsert** is raised when a building block (a block of predefined content in a Word template that can include text, images, and so on) is added to the document. Word passes the Range object for where the building block is inserted into the document as a parameter to this event. Word passes the name of the building block in the `string name` parameter, the category of the building block in the `string category` parameter, the type of the building block in the `string type` parameter, and the name of the template that contains the building block in the `string template` parameter.

Listing 7-13 shows a VSTO document customization that handles the events related to content controls. To see all these event handlers work, add the code to a document and, while running the document, add content controls to the document by clicking the control icons in the Controls group of the Developer tab.

To see the ContentControlBeforeStoreUpdate and ContentControlBefore-ContentUpdate events raise, you need to add a content control that is bound to the XML store in the document. The easiest way to add this control is to use the Quick Parts drop-down list in the Insert tab. From the Quick Parts drop-down list, add a document property like Author from the Document Property menu. The content control that is added will be mapped to Author in the document properties in the XML data store. When you edit the content control and then exit the content control, the ContentControl-BeforeStoreUpdate event will be raised as the contents of the content control get written back to the Author property in the XML data store. To see the ContentControlBeforeContentUpdate event raise, use the Office menu; choose Prepare and then choose Properties. The document properties will be shown in the document information pane. Edit the Author field in the document properties pane; then exit the Author field. This step causes the ContentControlBeforeContentUpdate event to be raised, as the change you made in the document information pane is pushed from the XML data store back to the bound content control in the document.

Figure 7-13 shows a Word document with a content control bound to the Author property in the XML data store. It also shows the document information pane where the Author property is displayed directly out of the XML data store.

Finally, to see the BuildingBlockInsert event, use the Quick Parts drop-down list in the Insert tab and choose Building Blocks Organizer. In the Building Block Organizer dialog box, pick a building block to insert, and click the Insert button.

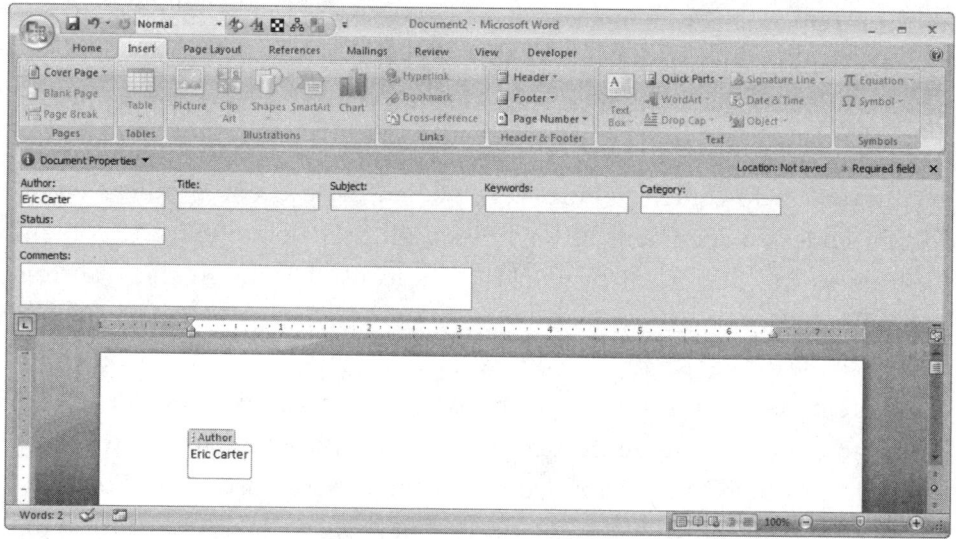

Figure 7-13: The Author property bound to a content control and displayed in the document information pane.

Listing 7-13: A VSTO Word Document Customization That Handles Content Control Related Events

```
public partial class ThisDocument
{
  private void ThisDocument_Startup(object sender,
    System.EventArgs e)
  {
  }

  private void ThisDocument_Shutdown(object sender,
    System.EventArgs e)
  {
  }

  #region VSTO Designer generated code
  private void InternalStartup()
  {
    this.ContentControlBeforeStoreUpdate +=
      new Word.DocumentEvents2_ContentControlBeforeStoreUpdateEventHandler(
        this.ThisDocument_ContentControlBeforeStoreUpdate);

    this.BuildingBlockInsert +=
      new Word.DocumentEvents2_BuildingBlockInsertEventHandler(
        this.ThisDocument_BuildingBlockInsert);

    this.ContentControlAfterAdd +=
      new Word.DocumentEvents2_ContentControlAfterAddEventHandler(
        this.ThisDocument_ContentControlAfterAdd);

    this.ContentControlOnEnter +=
      new Word.DocumentEvents2_ContentControlOnEnterEventHandler(
        this.ThisDocument_ContentControlOnEnter);

    this.Shutdown += new System.EventHandler(this.ThisDocument_Shutdown);

    this.ContentControlOnExit +=
      new Word.DocumentEvents2_ContentControlOnExitEventHandler(
        this.ThisDocument_ContentControlOnExit);

    this.ContentControlBeforeDelete +=
      new Word.DocumentEvents2_ContentControlBeforeDeleteEventHandler(
        this.ThisDocument_ContentControlBeforeDelete);

    this.Startup += new System.EventHandler(this.ThisDocument_Startup);

    this.ContentControlBeforeContentUpdate +=
      new Word.DocumentEvents2_ContentControlBeforeContentUpdateEventHandler(
        this.ThisDocument_ContentControlBeforeContentUpdate);
```

```
}
#endregion

private void ThisDocument_ContentControlAfterAdd(
  Word.ContentControl newContentControl,
  bool inUndoRedo)
{
  MessageBox.Show(String.Format(
    "ContentControl of type {0} with ID {1} added." +
    "  inUndoRedo is {2}.",
    newContentControl.Type, newContentControl.ID, inUndoRedo));
}

private void ThisDocument_ContentControlBeforeContentUpdate(
  Word.ContentControl contentControl,
  ref string content)
{
  MessageBox.Show(String.Format(
    "ContentControl of type {0} with ID {1} updated." +
    "  New content is {2}.",
    contentControl.Type, contentControl.ID, content));
}

private void ThisDocument_ContentControlBeforeDelete(
  Word.ContentControl oldContentControl,
  bool inUndoRedo)
{
  MessageBox.Show(String.Format(
    "ContentControl of type {0} with ID {1} deleted." +
    "  inUndoRedo is {2}.",
    oldContentControl.Type, oldContentControl.ID, inUndoRedo));
}

private void ThisDocument_ContentControlBeforeStoreUpdate(
  Word.ContentControl contentControl,
  ref string content)
{
  MessageBox.Show(String.Format(
    "ContentControl of type {0} with ID {1} updating " +
    "XML Store with content {2}.",
    contentControl.Type, contentControl.ID, content));
}

private void ThisDocument_ContentControlOnEnter(
  Word.ContentControl contentControl)
{
  MessageBox.Show(String.Format(
    "ContentControl of type {0} with ID {1} entered.",
    contentControl.Type, contentControl.ID));
}
```

```
private void ThisDocument_ContentControlOnExit(
  Word.ContentControl contentControl,
  ref bool cancel)
{
  MessageBox.Show(String.Format(
    "ContentControl of type {0} with ID {1} exited.",
    contentControl.Type, contentControl.ID));
}

private void ThisDocument_BuildingBlockInsert(
  Word.Range range, string name,
  string category, string blockType,
  string template)
{
  MessageBox.Show(String.Format(
    "BuildingBlock added at position {0} with name {1}, " +
    "category {2}, blockType {3}, from template {4}.",
    range.Start, name, category, blockType, template));
}
}
```

CommandBar Events

Word 2007 introduces a new user interface paradigm called the Ribbon that you can use to create buttons and menu items to invoke your custom commands. The Ribbon model is discussed in Chapter 17, "Working with the Ribbon in VSTO." Although the Ribbon can be used for many of the custom commands you may want to provide the user, there are still times you need to use the older CommandBar object model, which is discussed in more detail in Chapter 4, "Working with Excel Events." The Command-Bar object model is the only way to customize the context menu that appears when you right-click text in a Word document, for example.

As you use the CommandBar object model in Word, you will notice some differences between Excel and Word. Word, for example, can save an added toolbar or menu item in a template or a document. The default location that a new toolbar or menu item is saved to is the Normal template (normal.dotm). You can specify that the new toolbar or menu item be associated with another template or with a document by using the Application object's CustomizationContext property. The Customization-Context property takes an object that is either a Template object or a Document object. Subsequent calls to add toolbars or buttons (for example, a

CommandBarButton) will be saved in the template or document you set using the CustomizationContext property.

Listing 7-14 shows a listing similar to the Excel example in Listing 4-9, with two significant differences. First, we use the CustomizationContext property to make it so the toolbar we add will be associated with a particular document. Second, we pass true as the last parameter to the Add method when adding a CommandBar so that the command bar will be added permanently rather than temporarily. Note that in Word, you can make only a CommandBar a temporary object, even though the Add methods for other command-bar objects imply that they can be temporary objects as well.

Listing 7-14 adds a custom toolbar called My Custom Bar and a new item to the context menu that appears when you right-click text in a Word document. When you right-click text in the document, a custom command with the caption Display Message on Right Click appears in the context menu. When you run Listing 7-14, notice where the custom toolbar gets added.

As Figure 7-14 shows, Word creates an Add-Ins tab in the Ribbon and adds the controls from My Custom Bar to a group called Custom Toolbars. If you want more control over where your commands are added—if you want to display your commands in a tab other than the Add-Ins tab, for example—you need to use the Ribbon model discussed in Chapter 17, "Working with the Ribbon in VSTO."

Listing 7-14: A VSTO Word Document Customization That Uses the CommandBar Object Model

```
public partial class ThisDocument
{
  Word.Application app;
  Office.CommandBarButton btn;
  Office.CommandBarButton btnText;
  Office.CommandBarComboBox box;

  void ThisDocument_Startup(object sender, EventArgs e)
  {
    app = this.Application;

    // Store the new command bar in this document.
    app.CustomizationContext = Application.ActiveDocument;

    Office.CommandBars bars = this.CommandBars;
    Office.CommandBar bar = bars.Add("My Custom Bar",
```

```
    missing, missing, true);
  bar.Visible = true;

  btn = bar.Controls.Add(
    Office.MsoControlType.msoControlButton,
    missing, missing, missing, true) as Office.CommandBarButton;

  btn.Click += new Office.
    _CommandBarButtonEvents_ClickEventHandler(
    Btn_Click);

  btn.Caption = "Display Message";
  btn.Tag = "WordDocument1.btn";
  btn.Style = Office.MsoButtonStyle.msoButtonCaption;

  box = bar.Controls.Add(
    Office.MsoControlType.msoControlComboBox,
    missing, missing, missing, true) as
     Office.CommandBarComboBox;
  box.Tag = "WordDocument1.box";

  box.AddItem("Choice 1", 1);
  box.AddItem("Choice 2", 2);
  box.AddItem("Choice 3", 3);
  box.Change += new Office.
    _CommandBarComboBoxEvents_ChangeEventHandler(
    Box_Change);

  // Also, add a command to the text command bar
  // or the right click menu
  Office.CommandBar textBar = bars["Text"];
  btnText = textBar.Controls.Add(
    Office.MsoControlType.msoControlButton,
    missing, missing, missing, true) as Office.CommandBarButton;

  btnText.Click += new
    Office._CommandBarButtonEvents_ClickEventHandler(
      btnText_Click);

  btnText.Caption = "Display Message on Right Click";
  btnText.Tag = "WordDocument1.Text.btn";
  btnText.Style = Office.MsoButtonStyle.msoButtonCaption;
}

static void btnText_Click(Office.CommandBarButton Ctrl,
  ref bool CancelDefault)
{
  MessageBox.Show("You picked a button added to the " +
    Text context menu");
}

static void Btn_Click(Office.CommandBarButton ctrl,
  ref bool cancelDefault)
```

```
  {
    MessageBox.Show("You clicked the button.");
  }

  static void Box_Change(Office.CommandBarComboBox ctrl)
  {
    MessageBox.Show(String.Format(
      "You selected {0}.", ctrl.Text));
  }

  private void InternalStartup()
  {
    this.Startup += new EventHandler(ThisDocument_Startup);
  }
}
```

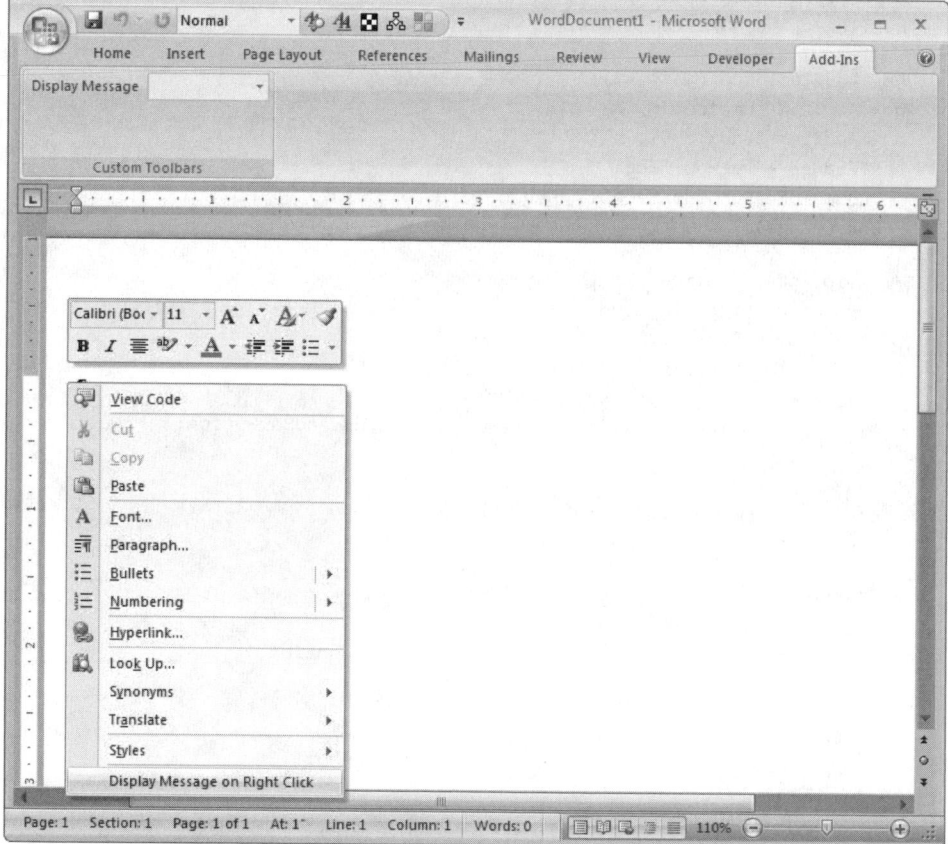

Figure 7-14: The custom toolbar created by Listing 7-14 in the Add-Ins tab and the context menu that appears when you right-click in the document.

Events in Visual Studio Tools for Office

Several events are found on VSTO objects that are not found when using the Word PIA alone. Table 7-1 lists these events. Almost all of these are events from the Word PIA that are re-raised on different objects. For example, in the Word PIA, there is no BeforeSave event on the Document. However, there is a DocumentBeforeSave event on the Application object that passes as a parameter the Document that is about to be saved. VSTO adds a BeforeSave event to the Document object for Word. The Document object's BeforeSave event is raised whenever the Application object's DocumentBeforeSave event is raised with the given Document object as a parameter.

Another case where VSTO changes events is in the naming of the Close event and the Sync event on the Document object. Both of these event names conflict with method names on Document. To avoid this conflict, VSTO renames these events to CloseEvent and SyncEvent.

VSTO adds events to some objects that have no events at all in the Word PIA. These objects include content controls, Bookmark, XMLNode, and XMLNodes objects. Table 7-1 lists the events added to these objects. You can determine what a particular event does by reading the documentation for the event from which it is re-raised.

TABLE 7-1: Events That Are Added in VSTO

Events	Raised Again From
Document Object	
ActivateEvent	Application.WindowActivate
BeforeClose	Application.DocumentBeforeClose
BeforeDoubleClick	Application.WindowBeforeDoubleClick
BeforePrint	Application.DocumentBeforePrint
BeforeRightClick	Application.WindowBeforeRightClick
BeforeSave	Application.DocumentBeforeSave

Continues

TABLE 7-1: Events That Are Added in VSTO *(Continued)*

Events	Raised Again From
Document Object	
CloseEvent	Renamed Document.Close event to prevent collisions
Deactivate	Application.WindowDeactivate
MailMergeAfterMerge	Application.MailMergeAfterMerge
MailMergeAfterRecordMerge	Application.MailMergeAfterRecordMerge
MailMergeBeforeMerge	Application.MailMergeBeforeMerge
MailMergeBeforeRecordMerge	Application.MailMergeBeforeRecordMerge
MailMergeDataSourceLoad	Application.MailMergeDataSourceLoad
MailMergeWizardSendToCustom	Application.MailMergeWizardSendToCustom
MailMergeWizardStateChange	Application.MailMergeWizardStateChange
SelectionChange	Application.WindowSelectionChange
Startup	New event raised by VSTO
Shutdown	New event raised by VSTO
SyncEvent	Renamed Document.Sync event to prevent collisions
WindowSize	Application.WindowSize
Bookmark Object	
BeforeDoubleClick	Application.WindowBeforeDoubleClick
BeforeRightClick	Application.WindowBeforeRightClick
BindingContextChanged	New event raised by VSTO for data binding
Deselected	Application.WindowSelectionChange
Selected	Application.WindowSelectionChange
SelectionChange	Application.WindowSelectionChange

TABLE 7-1: Events That Are Added in VSTO *(Continued)*

Events	Raised Again From
(from base class ContentControlBase) **BuildingBlockGalleryContentControl ComboBoxContentControl DatePickerContentControl DropDownListContentControl GroupContentControl PictureContentControl PlainTextContentControl RichTextContentControl**	
Added	Document.ContentControlAfterAdd
BindingContextChanged	New event raised by VSTO for data binding
ContentUpdating	Document.ContentControlBeforeContentUpdate
Deleting	Document.ContentControlBeforeDelete
Entering	Document.ContentControlOnEnter
Exiting	Document.ContentControlOnExit
StoreUpdating	Document.ContentControlBeforeStoreUpdate
Validated	Document.XMLAfterInsert
Validating	Document.XMLAfterInsert
XMLNode Object	
AfterInsert	Document.XMLAfterInsert
BeforeDelete	Document.XMLBeforeDelete
BindingContextChanged	New event raised by VSTO for data binding
ContextEnter	Application.XMLSelectionChange
ContextLeave	Application.XMLSelectionChange
Deselect	Application.WindowSelectionChange

Continues

TABLE 7-1:   Events That Are Added in VSTO *(Continued)*

Events	Raised Again From
XMLNode Object	
Select	Application.WindowSelectionChange
ValidationError	Application.XMLValidationError
XMLNodes Object	
AfterInsert	Document.XMLAfterInsert
BeforeDelete	Document.XMLBeforeDelete
BindingContextChanged	New event raised by VSTO for data binding
ContextEnter	Application.XMLSelectionChange
ContextLeave	Application.XMLSelectionChange
Deselect	Application.WindowSelectionChange
Select	Application.WindowSelectionChange
ValidationError	Application.XMLValidationError

Conclusion

This chapter covered the various events raised by objects in the Word object model. The chapter also examined how VSTO adds some new events to Word objects. Chapter 8, "Working with Word Objects," discusses in more detail the most important objects in the Word object model and how to use them in your code.

8

Working with Word Objects

Working with the Application Object

This chapter examines some of the major objects in the Word object model, starting with the Application object. Many of the objects in the Word object model are very large, and it is beyond the scope of this book to completely describe these objects. Instead, this discussion focuses on the most commonly used methods and properties associated with these objects.

This chapter describes these objects as defined by the primary interop assemblies for Word. You should be aware that VSTO extends some of these objects (Document, ContentControl, Bookmark, XMLNodes, and XMLNode) to add some additional functionality such as data binding support. Part III of this book, starting with Chapter 12, "The VSTO Programming Model," covers those extensions.

The Application object is the largest object in the Word object model. The Application object is also the root object in the Word object model hierarchy. You can access all the other objects in the object model by starting at Application object and accessing its properties and the properties of objects it returns. The Application object also has a number of application-level settings that prove useful when automating Word.

Controlling Word's Screen Updating Behavior

When your code is performing a set of changes to a document, you might want to set the Application object's ScreenUpdating property to `false` to prevent Word from updating the screen while your code runs. Turning off screen updating can also improve the performance of a long operation. Setting the property back to `true` refreshes the screen and allows Word to continue updating the screen.

When changing an application-level property such as ScreenUpdating, always save the value of the property before you change it and set it back to that value when you have finished. Doing so is important because your code will almost never be running by itself inside the Word process—it will usually run alongside other code loaded into the Word process.

For example, another add-in might be running a long operation on the document, and that add-in might have set the ScreenUpdating property to `false` to accelerate that operation. That add-in might change the document in some way that triggers an event handled by your code. If your event handler sets the ScreenUpdating property to `false` and then sets it back to `true` when you have finished, you have now defeated the add-in's attempt to accelerate its own long operation. If instead you save the value of ScreenUpdating before you change it, set ScreenUpdating to `false`, and then set ScreenUpdating back to its original value, your code will coexist better with other code running inside of Word.

The best way to do this is to use C#'s support for exception handling to ensure that even if an exception occurs in your code, the application-level property you are changing will be set back to its original value. You should put the code to set the application-level property back to its original value in a `finally` block because this code will run both when no exception occurs and when an exception occurs. Listing 8-1 shows an example of saving the state of the ScreenUpdating property, setting the property to `false`, and then restoring the original value of the property in a `finally` block. VSTO declares a class variable called `missing` of type `object` that is set to `System.Type.Missing`. We pass this class variable by reference to all the optional parameters. For more information on optional parameters in C#, see Chapter 1, "An Introduction to Office Programming."

Listing 8-1: A VSTO Word Document Customization That Uses the ScreenUpdating Property

```csharp
private void ThisDocument_Startup(object sender, EventArgs e)
{
  Word.Application app = this.Application;
  bool oldScreenUpdateSetting = app.ScreenUpdating;
  Word.Range range = this.Content;

  try
  {
    app.ActiveWindow.View.Zoom.Percentage = 15;
    app.ScreenUpdating = false;
    Random r = new Random();
    for (int i = 1; i < 5000; i++)
    {
      range.InsertAfter(r.NextDouble().ToString());
      if (i % 1000 == 0)
      {
        app.ScreenUpdating = true;
        app.ScreenRefresh();
        app.ScreenUpdating = false;
      }
    }
  }
  finally
  {
    app.ScreenUpdating = oldScreenUpdateSetting;
  }
}
```

In addition to the ScreenUpdating property, Word's Application object has a ScreenRefresh method. You can call this method to force a refresh of the screen—typically during an operation when you have set ScreenUpdating to `false`. For example, you might do the first few steps of an operation and then refresh the screen to show the user the new state of the document and then perform additional steps and refresh the screen again. Remember, though, that before you call ScreenRefresh you have to turn ScreenUpdating back on; then you can turn it off after you call ScreenRefresh.

Controlling the Dialogs and Alerts That Word Displays

Occasionally, the code you write will cause Word to display dialog boxes prompting the user to make a decision or alerting the user that something is about to occur. If you find this happening in a section of your code, you might want to prevent these dialog boxes from being displayed so that your code can run without requiring intervention from the user.

You can set the DisplayAlerts property to a member of the WdAlert-Level enumeration. If set to `wdAlertsNone`, this prevents Word from displaying dialog boxes and messages when your code is running and causes Word to choose the default response to any dialog boxes or messages that might display. You can also set the property to `wdAlertsMessageBox` to only let Word display message boxes and not alerts. Setting the property to `wdAlertsAll` restores Word's default behavior. Note that there are some alerts that cannot be suppressed, such as the security messages that display when a document contains macros that are not trusted.

Be sure to get the original value of this property and set the property back to its original value after your code runs. Use `try` and `finally` blocks to ensure that you set the property back to its original value even when an exception occurs.

Changing the Mouse Pointer

During a long operation, you might want to change the appearance of Word's mouse pointer to an hourglass to let users know that they are waiting for some operation to complete. Word's Application object has a System property that returns a System object. The System object has a Cursor property of type WdCursorType that enables you to change the appearance of Word's mouse pointer. You can set it to the following values: `wdCursor-IBeam`, `wdCursorNormal`, `wdCursorNorthwestArrow`, or `wdCursorWait`.

Listing 8-2 shows the use of the Cursor property. Note also the behavior of screen updating when you run Listing 8-2. Word displays updates to the current page, but when an additional page is created, a call to Screen-Refresh must be made to force Word to display the newly created pages.

Listing 8-2: A VSTO Word Document Customization That Sets the Cursor Property

```
private void ThisDocument_Startup(object sender, EventArgs e)
{
  Word.Application app = this.Application;
  Word.WdCursorType oldCursor = app.System.Cursor;
  Word.Range range = this.Range(ref missing, ref missing);

  try
  {
```

```
    app.ActiveWindow.View.Zoom.Percentage = 15;
    app.System.Cursor = Word.WdCursorType.wdCursorWait;
    Random r = new Random();
    for (int i = 1; i < 5000; i++)
    {
      range.InsertAfter(r.NextDouble().ToString());
      if (i % 100 == 0)
      {
        app.ScreenRefresh();
      }
    }
  }
  finally
  {
    app.System.Cursor = oldCursor;
  }
}
```

Displaying a Message in Word's Status Bar or Window Caption

Word lets you set a custom message in the Word status bar, which is at the lower-left corner of Word's window. StatusBar is a property that can be set to a `string` value representing the message you want to display in Word's status bar. Unlike most of the other properties in this section, you cannot save the original value of the StatusBar property and set it back after you have changed it. StatusBar is a write-only property and cannot be read.

You can control the text shown in Word's window caption using the Caption property. Caption is a property that can be set to a `string` value representing the text you want to display in Word's window caption.

Listing 8-3 shows an example of setting the StatusBar property to inform the user of the progress of a long operation. The operation has 10,000 steps, and after every 1000 steps the code appends an additional period (.) to the status bar message to indicate to the user that the operation is still in progress.

Listing 8-3: A VSTO Word Document Customization That Sets the StatusBar Property

```
private void ThisDocument_Startup(object sender, EventArgs e)
{
  Word.Application app = this.Application;
  string status = "Creating Document...";
  app.StatusBar = status;
  Word.Range range = this.Range(ref missing, ref missing);
  Word.WdCursorType oldCursor = app.System.Cursor;
```

```
try
{
  app.System.Cursor = Word.WdCursorType.wdCursorWait;
  app.ActiveWindow.View.Zoom.Percentage = 15;
  Random r = new Random();
  for (int i = 1; i < 10000; i++)
  {
    range.InsertAfter(r.NextDouble().ToString());
    if (i % 1000 == 0)
    {
      status += ".";
      app.StatusBar = status;
      app.ScreenRefresh();
    }
  }
}
finally
{
  app.StatusBar = String.Empty;
  app.System.Cursor = oldCursor;
}
}
```

Controlling the Look of Word

Word enables you to control the Word user interface through other properties, such as those listed in Table 8-1. Listing 8-4 shows code behind a
VSTO Word document that sets many of these properties.

TABLE 8-1: Properties That Control Elements of the Word User Interface

Property Name	Type	What It Does
DisplayAuto-CompleteTips	bool	Controls whether Word displays auto-complete tips for completing words, phrases, and dates as you type.
DisplayDocument-InformationPanel	bool	Controls whether Word displays the Document Information Panel (which the user can display by choosing the Office menu > Prepare > Properties).

TABLE 8-1:   Properties That Control Elements of the Word User Interface *(Continued)*

Property Name	Type	What It Does
DisplayRecentFiles	bool	Controls whether Word displays recently open files in the File menu. You can control how many files Word displays by using the RecentFiles object associated with the Application object and setting the RecentFiles object's Maximum property to a number between 0 and 50.
DisplayScreenTips	bool	Controls whether Word displays pop-up tooltips for text having comments, for footnotes and endnotes, and for hyperlinked text.
DisplayScrollBars	bool	Controls whether Word displays the horizontal and vertical scroll bars for all open documents. Note that the Window object of Word also has DisplayHorizontalScrollBar and DisplayVerticalScrollBar properties that allow you to control scrollbars on an individual document window.
Height	int	Sets the height, in points, of the main Word window when WindowState is set to wdWindowStateNormal.
Left	int	Sets the left position, in points, of the main Word window when Window-State is set to wdWindowStateNormal.
ShowWindows-InTaskbar	bool	Sets whether Word creates a window and taskbar button for each open document (true), which is also called SDI mode, or uses one window that contains all open document windows (false), which is also called MDI mode.
Top	int	Sets the top position, in points, of the main Word window when Window-State is set to wdWindowStateNormal.

Continues

TABLE 8-1: Properties That Control Elements of the Word User Interface *(Continued)*

Property Name	Type	What It Does
Visible	bool	Sets whether the Word application window is visible.
Width	int	Sets the width, in points, of the main Word window when WindowState is set to WdWindowState.wdWindowStateNormal.
WindowState	WdWindowState	Sets whether the main Word window is minimized (wdWindowStateMinimize), maximized (wdWindowStateMaximize), or normal (wdWindowStateNormal). The Width, Height, Left, and Top settings have an effect only when WindowState is set to wdWindowStateNormal.

Listing 8-4: A VSTO Word Document Customization and Helper Function That Modifies the Word User Interface

```
private void ThisDocument_Startup(object sender, EventArgs e)
{
  Word.Application app = this.Application;

  app.DisplayDocumentInformationPanel =
    GetBool("Display document properties?",
    app.DisplayDocumentInformationPanel);
  app.DisplayRecentFiles =
    GetBool("Display recent files?", app.DisplayRecentFiles);
  app.DisplayScreenTips =
    GetBool("Display screen tips?", app.DisplayScreenTips);
  app.DisplayScrollBars =
    GetBool("Display scroll bars?", app.DisplayScrollBars);
  app.ShowWindowsInTaskbar =
    GetBool("Multiple windows?", app.ShowWindowsInTaskbar);
  app.Visible =
    GetBool("Visible application window?", app.Visible);

  app.WindowState = Word.WdWindowState.wdWindowStateNormal;
  app.Width = 200;
  app.Height = 300;
```

```
  app.Top = 50;
  app.Left = 100;
}

private bool GetBool(string message, bool currentValue)
{
  return MessageBox.Show(
    String.Format("{0} (Currently set to {1})",
      message, currentValue), "Word UI Demo",
      MessageBoxButtons.YesNo) == DialogResult.Yes;
}
```

Properties That Return Active or Selected Objects

The Application object has a number of properties that return active objects—objects representing things that are active or selected within Word. Table 8-2 shows some of these properties. Listing 8-5 shows code behind a VSTO Word document that examines these properties.

TABLE 8-2: Application Properties That Return Active Objects

Property Name	Type	What It Does
ActiveDocument	Document	Returns the active Document—the document that has focus within Word. If there are no open documents, an exception is thrown.
ActivePrinter	string	Returns a string for the active printer (for example, "Epson Stylus COLOR 860 ESC/P 2 on LPT1:").
ActiveWindow	Window	Returns the active Window. If no windows are open, an exception is thrown.
NormalTemplate	Template	Returns a Template object representing the Normal template (normal.dotm).
Selection	Selection	Returns a Selection object that represents the current selection or insertion point in the document.

Listing 8-5: A VSTO Word Document Customization and Helper Function That Examines Active Objects

```csharp
private void ThisDocument_Startup(object sender, EventArgs e)
{
  Word.Application app = this.Application;
  ShowItem("ActiveDocument", app.ActiveDocument.Name);
  ShowItem("ActivePrinter", app.ActivePrinter);
  ShowItem("ActiveWindow", app.ActiveWindow.Caption);
  ShowItem("NormalTemplate", app.NormalTemplate.Name);
  ShowItem("Selection", app.Selection.Start.ToString());
}

private void ShowItem(string name, string status)
{
  MessageBox.Show(status, name);
}
```

Properties That Return Important Collections

The Application object has a number of properties that return collections that you will frequently use. Table 8-3 shows several of these properties. Listing 8-6 shows code behind a VSTO Word document that gets the count of these collections and the first item out of each collection.

TABLE 8-3: Application Properties That Return Important Collections

Property Name and Type	What It Does
CommandBars	Returns the CommandBars collection, which lets you modify or add to Word's toolbars and menus. Changes made to toolbars and menus are saved in a template or in a document; use the CustomizationContext property to set where changes are stored. CommandBars functionality is largely superceded in Word 2007 by the Ribbon UI, but there are still times when you may need to use CommandBars—to customize a context menu, for example.
Dialogs	Returns the Dialogs collection, which lets you access the built-in Word dialog boxes (of which there are more than 295). You can show a particular dialog box using this collection.

TABLE 8-3: Application Properties That Return Important Collections *(Continued)*

Property Name and Type	What It Does
Documents	Returns the Documents collection, which contains all the documents open in Word.
FontNames	Returns the FontNames collection, which contains all the fonts that are installed and available for use.
KeyBindings	Returns the KeyBindings collection, which lets you examine, modify, and add key shortcuts that are assigned to Word commands, styles, fonts, auto text entries, symbols, and Visual Basic for Applications (VBA) macros. Changes made to key bindings are saved in a template or in a document; use the CustomizationContext property to set where changes are stored.
RecentFiles	Returns the RecentFiles collection, which lets you examine and reopen any of the 50 most recently opened files.
TaskPanes	Returns the TaskPanes collection, which allows you to show or detect which of the 18 built-in task panes are visible.
Templates	Returns the Templates collection, which lets you examine the installed templates and their properties.
Windows	Returns the Windows collection, which represents the windows open in Word.

Listing 8-6: A VSTO Word Document Customization and Helper Function That Examines Collections

```
private void ThisDocument_Startup(object sender, EventArgs e)
{
  Word.Application app = this.Application;

  // Set customization context before checking CommandBars
  app.CustomizationContext = app.NormalTemplate;
  Show(String.Format("There are {0} command bars.",
    app.CommandBars.Count));
```

```csharp
Show(String.Format("CommandBar 1 is {0}.",
  app.CommandBars[1].Name));

Show(String.Format("There are {0} dialog boxes.",
  app.Dialogs.Count));

Show("Click OK to invoke the About dialog...");

app.Dialogs[Word.WdWordDialog.wdDialogHelpAbout].
  Show(ref missing);

Show(String.Format("There are {0} open documents.",
  app.Documents.Count));

object i = 1;
Word.Document doc = app.Documents.get_Item(ref i);

Show(String.Format("Document 1 is {0}.",
  doc.Name));

Show(String.Format("There are {0} fonts.",
  app.FontNames.Count));

Show(String.Format("FontName 1 is {0}.",
  app.FontNames[1]));

// Set customization context before checking KeyBindings
app.CustomizationContext = app.NormalTemplate;
Show(String.Format("There are {0} key bindings.",
  app.KeyBindings.Count));

if (app.KeyBindings.Count > 0)
{
  Show(String.Format("KeyBinding 1 is {0}.",
    app.KeyBindings[1].Command));
}

Show(String.Format("There are {0} recent files.",
  app.RecentFiles.Count));

if (app.RecentFiles.Count > 0)
{
  Show(String.Format("RecentFile 1 is {0}.",
    app.RecentFiles[1].Name));
}

Show(String.Format("There are {0} task panes.",
  app.TaskPanes.Count));
```

```
    Show("Click OK to activate the style inspector task pane.");

    app.TaskPanes[Word.WdTaskPanes.wdTaskPaneStyleInspector].
      Visible = true;

    Show(String.Format("There are {0} templates.",
      app.Templates.Count));

    Show(String.Format("Template 1 is {0}.",
      app.Templates.get_Item(ref i).FullName));

    Show(String.Format("There are {0} windows.",
      app.Windows.Count));

    Show(String.Format("Window 1 is {0}.",
      Application.Windows.get_Item(ref i).Caption));
}

private void Show(string text)
{
  MessageBox.Show(text, "Active Objects");
}
```

Accessing Items in Collections

As you might have noticed in Listing 8-6, items in a Word collection are accessed in two different ways depending on whether the index into the collection is strongly typed or weakly typed. In the case of the KeyBindings collection, the index is strongly typed as an integer. As such, you can use the index operator ([]) to get to an item in a collection. The code looks like this:

```
    Word.KeyBinding k = Application.KeyBindings[1];
```

For a collection for which the index into the collection is typed as an object passed by reference, you must use the get_Item method of the collection. The Templates collection is an example of this. It has an index of type object passed by reference. This is because you can either pass a string if you know the name of the template in the collection or you can pass an int for the index of the template in the collection. To get a Template from the Templates collection by int index, you can write this code:

```
    object index = 1;
    Word.Template t = Application.Templates.get_Item(ref index);
```

To get a Template from the Templates collection by `string` name, you can write this code:

```
object index = "Normal.dotm";
Word.Template t = Application.Templates.get_Item(ref index);
```

Note that in both cases, you must declare an `object` first and then pass a reference to the `object`. When passing parameters by reference, you must always declare an `object` variable first and then pass that declared variable by reference.

Note that if Visual Studio IntelliSense isn't displaying get_Item as a method, you can call on the collection in the pop-up IntelliSense; make sure your settings are set to show advanced members. To do this, go to the Options dialog box by choosing Tools > Options. In the tree of options, navigate to Text Editor\C#\General and uncheck the Hide Advanced Members check box, as shown in Figure 8-1.

Navigating a Document

The Browser property returns the Browser object, which gives you access to the same functionality available in the browser control that is shown directly below Word's vertical scroll bar, as shown in Figure 8-2.

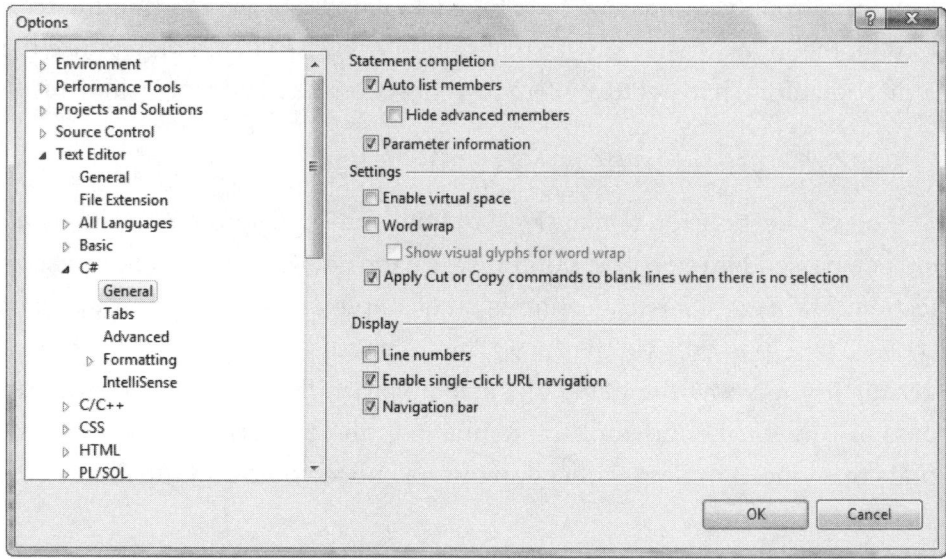

Figure 8-1: Visual Studio IntelliSense does not show the get_Item method when Hide Advanced Members is checked in the Options dialog box.

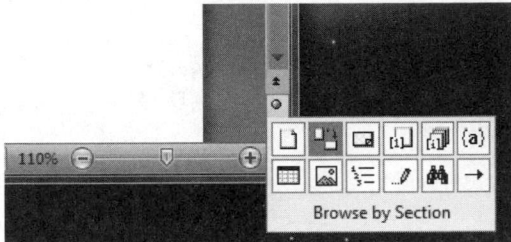

Figure 8-2: Word's browser control.

To use the Browser object, first set the Browser object's Target property to a member of the WdBrowseTarget enumeration as shown here:

- wdBrowseComment
- wdBrowseEdit
- wdBrowseEndnote
- wdBrowseField
- wdBrowseFind
- wdBrowseFootnote
- wdBrowseGoTo
- wdBrowseGraphic
- wdBrowseHeading
- wdBrowsePage
- wdBrowseSection
- wdBrowseTable

Then use the Browser object's Next and Previous methods to navigate from element to element. Listing 8-7 shows an example of this.

Listing 8-7: A VSTO Word Document Customization That Uses the Browser Object

```
private void ThisDocument_Startup(object sender, EventArgs e)
{
  // Generate some random text in the document.
  Word.Range r = Range(ref missing, ref missing);
  System.Text.StringBuilder builder = new
    System.Text.StringBuilder();
  Random rand = new Random();
```

```
for (int i = 0; i < 1000; i++)
{
  builder.Append(rand.NextDouble().ToString());
  builder.Append(System.Environment.NewLine);
}

r.Text = builder.ToString();

// Browse by page
Application.Browser.Target = Word.WdBrowseTarget.wdBrowsePage;

for (int j = 0; j < 10; j++)
{
  Application.Browser.Next();
  Application.Selection.Text =
    String.Format("<<<<<< PAGE {0} >>>>>>\n", j);
}
}
```

Note that using this approach also changes the selection in the document, which you often do not want to do. Later in this chapter, you learn about the Range object and the various ways you manipulate text with the Range object without changing the selection. The Range object's Goto, GotoNext, and GotoPrevious methods provide the same kind of navigation control that the Browser object provides, without changing the selection.

Working with Word's Options

The Options property provides access to options you might set via the Options dialog box. The Options property returns an Options object that has more than 200 properties that you can set.

Listing 8-8 shows an example that gets and then prompts the user to decide whether to change several of the properties on the Options object. The properties set are options from the Popular page of Word's Options dialog box. Listing 8-8 also shows the Popular page in the Word Options dialog box after prompting the user to change options associated with that page.

Listing 8-8: A VSTO Word Document Customization That Uses the Options Object
and Shows a Built-In Dialog

```csharp
private void ThisDocument_Startup(object sender, EventArgs e)
{
  Word.Options o = Application.Options;

  o.EnableLivePreview = DisplayAndSet("Enable Live Preview",
    o.EnableLivePreview);
  o.ShowDevTools = DisplayAndSet("Show developer tab",
    o.ShowDevTools);

  Application.Dialogs[Word.
    WdWordDialog.wdDialogToolsOptionsGeneral].
    Show(ref missing);
}

private bool DisplayAndSet(string settingName, bool settingValue)
{
  string title = "Options Demo";
  string checkState = "unchecked.";
  string action = "check";

  if (settingValue == true)
  {
    checkState = "checked.";
    action = "uncheck";
  }

  string message = String.Format(
    "{0} is {1}.\nDo you want to {2} it?",
    settingName, checkState, action);

  DialogResult r = MessageBox.Show(message,
    title, MessageBoxButtons.YesNo);

  if (r == DialogResult.Yes)
  {
    return !settingValue;
  }
  else
  {
    return settingValue;
  }
}
```

Working with the File Save Format Options

The DefaultSaveFormat property enables you to change the default format that Word saves in when the user creates a new document and then saves it. For example, setting DefaultSaveFormat to `"Text"` will cause Word to save new files in a text-only format. Setting DefaultSaveFormat to an empty string will cause Word to save in the default file format.

You can also specify that one of the installed file converters be used as the default save format. The FileConverters property returns a collection of available file converters that save in formats such as Works format. Each FileConverter object in the FileConverters collection has a ClassName property that returns a `string`. You can set the DefaultSaveFormat property to the `string` returned by the ClassName property of the FileConverter you want to use as the default save format. For example, the Works 6.0 & 7.0 FileConverter object has a ClassName property that returns `"wks632"`. Setting DefaultSaveFormat to `"wks632"` will make Works 6.0 & 7.0 the default save format.

Working with File Dialogs

Word provides several properties and methods that enable you to change the directory that the Open and Save dialog boxes default to. The Change-FileOpenDirectory method takes a `string` parameter that is the new path that you want the Open and Save dialog boxes to default to. A change made using this method only lasts until the user exits the application or Change-FileOpenDirectory is called again during the run of the application.

To permanently change the directory that the Open and Save dialog boxes default to, you can use the Options object's DefaultFilePath property. Prompt the user if you permanently change a setting like this. Users usually do not appreciate it when programs change their settings without asking their permission first.

If you need to display a customized file dialog box, you can use the get_FileDialog method, which returns a FileDialog object you can customize and show to the user. The get_FileDialog method takes a required parameter of type Office.MsoFileDialogType, which can be one of the following enumerated values: `msoFileDialogOpen`, `msoFileDialogSaveAs`, `msoFileDialogFilePicker`, or `msoFileDialogFolderPicker`.

Listing 8-9 shows an example that gets a FileDialog of type `msoFile-DialogFilePicker` and modifies it to let users select files from the desktop to copy to their documents directory. There are several things to observe in this example. First, the FileDialog object has several properties that enable you to customize the dialog box, including AllowMultiSelect, Button-Name, InitialFileName, InitialView, and Title.

Listing 8-9 also illustrates that showing the FileDialog using the Show method does not do any Word action such as opening files when the user clicks the default button. Instead, it returns an integer value that is –1 if the user clicked the default button and 0 if the user clicked the Cancel button. If the user clicks the default button and Show returns a –1, the code iterates over the FileDialog's SelectedItems collection to get the files that the user selected to copy.

Listing 8-9: A VSTO Word Document Customization That Modifies Word's File Dialog

```
private void ThisDocument_Startup(object sender, EventArgs e)
{
  Office.FileDialog f = Application.get_FileDialog(
    Office.MsoFileDialogType.msoFileDialogFilePicker);

  f.AllowMultiSelect = true;
  f.ButtonName = @"Copy to My Documents";
  f.InitialFileName = System.Environment.
    GetFolderPath(Environment.SpecialFolder.Desktop);
  f.InitialView = Office.MsoFileDialogView.msoFileDialogViewList;
  f.Title = @"Select files to copy to My Documents";
  int result = f.Show();

  if (result == -1)
  {
    foreach (string s in f.SelectedItems)
    {
      System.IO.FileInfo fileName = new System.IO.FileInfo(s);
      string myDocuments = Environment.GetFolderPath(
        Environment.SpecialFolder.MyDocuments);
      System.IO.File.Copy(fileName.FullName, myDocuments +
        @"\" + fileName.Name);
    }
  }
}
```

User Information

Word's Application object has several properties that return user information, including UserName and UserInitials. These string properties return the user information that the user entered when installing the product. The user can also edit this information by going to Word's Options dialog box and editing the fields on the Popular page.

Checking Grammar and Spelling

Word provides some application-level methods that enable you to use Word's grammar and spelling engine to check arbitrary strings. Check-Grammar is a method that takes a string and returns a bool value. It returns true if the string is deemed grammatically correct by Word's grammar checker and false if it is not. CheckSpelling is a method that that takes a string and returns true if the string is spelled correctly, false if the string is not spelled correctly.

The GetSpellingSuggestions method can take a single word that is mis-spelled and suggest possible correct spellings for the word. It takes a required string that is the word to check. It also takes a number of optional parameters. It returns a SpellingSuggestions collection that contains possible correct spellings.

Listing 8-10 shows a VSTO Word document customization that uses these application-level grammar and spell-checking functions. In Listing 8-10, optional arguments cause the code to get a little verbose. The CheckSpelling and GetSpellingSuggestions methods have multiple optional parameters, many of which are used to specify additional dictionaries to consult.

Listing 8-10: A VSTO Word Document Customization That Checks Grammar and Spelling

```
private void ThisDocument_Startup(object sender, EventArgs e)
{
  string badString = "This are grammatically incorrect.";
  string goodString = "This is grammatically correct.";
  string badString2 = "I cain't spel.";
  string goodString2 = "I can spell.";
  string singleWord = "spel";

  MessageBox.Show(String.Format(
    "{0}\nCheckGrammar returns {1}.",
    badString, Application.CheckGrammar(badString)));
```

```csharp
    MessageBox.Show(String.Format(
      "{0}\nCheckGrammar returns {1}.",
      goodString, Application.CheckGrammar(goodString)));

    MessageBox.Show(SpellingHelper(badString2));
    MessageBox.Show(SpellingHelper(goodString2));

    MessageBox.Show(String.Format(
      "Getting spelling suggestions for {0}.", singleWord));

    Word.SpellingSuggestions suggestions =
      Application.GetSpellingSuggestions(
      singleWord, ref missing, ref missing, ref missing,
      ref missing, ref missing, ref missing, ref missing,
      ref missing, ref missing, ref missing, ref missing,
      ref missing, ref missing);

    foreach (Word.SpellingSuggestion s in suggestions)
    {
      MessageBox.Show(s.Name);
    }
}

private string SpellingHelper(string phrase)
{
  bool correctSpelling = Application.CheckSpelling(
    phrase, ref missing, ref missing, ref missing,
    ref missing, ref missing, ref missing, ref missing,
    ref missing, ref missing, ref missing, ref missing,
    ref missing);
  if (correctSpelling)
    return String.Format("{0} is spelled correctly.", phrase);
  else
    return String.Format("{0} is spelled incorrectly.", phrase);
}
```

Exiting Word

The Quit method can be used to exit Word. If any unsaved documents are open, Word prompts the user to save each unsaved document. When users are prompted to save, they get a dialog box that has a Cancel button. If the user clicks Cancel, or if any code is running that is handling the Application.DocumentBeforeClose event sets the cancel parameter to true, Word does not quit.

Setting the DisplayAlerts property to wdAlertsNone will not suppress Word prompting the user to save. Fortunately, the Quit method takes three optional parameters that can control whether Word prompts the user to save. The first optional parameter, called SaveChanges, is of type object and can be passed a member of the WdSaveOptions enumeration: wdDo-NotSaveChanges, wdPromptToSaveChanges, or wdSaveChanges. The second optional parameter, called OriginalFormat, is of type object and can be passed a member of the WdOriginalFormat enumeration: wdOriginal-DocumentFormat, wdPromptUser, or wdWordDocument. This parameter controls Word's behavior when saving a changed document whose original format was not Word document format. The final optional parameter is called RouteDocument and is of type object. Passing true for this parameter routes the document to the next recipient if a routing slip is attached.

Listing 8-11 shows a VSTO application that calls Quit without saving changes. It also illustrates an issue where the Quit method and the Quit event collide on the Application object. To get the compiler to not complain and IntelliSense to work, the code casts the Application object to a Word._Application interface to let the compiler know to invoke the method and not the event.

Listing 8-11: A VSTO Word Document Customization That Calls Quit

```
private void ThisDocument_Startup(object sender, EventArgs e)
{
  Range(ref missing, ref missing).Text = "Sample text";
  object saveChanges = false;
  ((Word._Application)Application).Quit(
    ref saveChanges, ref missing, ref missing);
}
```

Working with the Dialog Object

This chapter has briefly considered the Dialogs collection returned by the Application object's Dialogs property. You have also learned about the FileDialog object. You now learn in more detail how you can use and display Word's built-in dialog boxes by using the Dialog object.

Showing the Dialog and Letting Word Execute Actions

After you have a Dialog object, typically by using the Dialog collection's index operator, you can show the dialog box in a variety of ways. The simplest way to show the dialog box associated with a Dialog object is to call the Show method, which displays the dialog box and lets Word execute any action the user takes in the dialog box. The Show method has an optional TimeOut parameter of type object that takes the number of milliseconds Word will wait before closing the dialog box automatically. If you omit the parameter, Word waits until the user closes the dialog box.

The Show method returns an int value that tells you what button the user chose to close the dialog box. If the return value is –1, the user clicked the OK button. If the return value is –2, the user clicked the Close button. If the return value is 0, the user clicked the Cancel button.

Selecting the Tab on a Dialog Box

For tabbed dialog boxes, such as the Options dialog, the Dialog object provides a DefaultTab property of type WdWordDialogTab. The DefaultTab property can be set before showing the dialog box to ensure the dialog box comes up with a particular tab selected. WdWordDialogType is an enumeration that contains values for the various tabs found in Word's built-in dialog boxes.

Showing the Dialog and Preventing Word from Executing Actions

Sometimes you will want to show a dialog box without letting Word actually execute the action associated with the dialog box. For example, you might want to show the Print dialog box but execute your own custom actions when the user clicks OK in the Print dialog box.

The Dialog object has a Display method that will show the dialog box while preventing Word from executing the action associated with the dialog box. Just as with the Show method, the Display method takes an optional TimeOut parameter of type object and returns an int value that tells you which button the user pressed to close the dialog box.

After you use the Display method to show a dialog box, you can use the Execute method to apply the action the user took in the dialog that was shown using the Display method. As an example (one that would likely annoy a Word user), you might show the Print dialog box and detect that a user clicked OK. But you might then prompt again to ask whether they are sure they want to print. If the user clicks Yes, you would call the Execute method on the dialog box to print the document, as shown in Listing 8-12.

Listing 8-12: A VSTO Word Document Customization That Uses Display and Execute to Confirm Printing

```
private void ThisDocument_Startup(object sender, EventArgs e)
{
  Range(ref missing, ref missing).InsertAfter("Test text");
  Word.Dialog d = Application.Dialogs[
    Word.WdWordDialog.wdDialogFilePrint];

  int result = d.Display(ref missing);

  if (result == -1)
  {
    DialogResult r = MessageBox.Show(
      "Are you sure you want to print?",
      "Annoying confirmation",
      MessageBoxButtons.YesNoCancel);

    if (r == DialogResult.Yes)
    {
      d.Execute();
    }
  }
}
```

Getting and Setting Fields in a Dialog

It is possible to prefill fields in a dialog box before showing it and to get fields from a dialog box after showing it. Unfortunately, it is rather difficult and inconsistent in availability and relies on some obscure functionality that originated from the original programming language for Word called Word Basic.

The Dialog object you are working with may have several late-bound properties that can be get and set. A late-bound property does not appear in the type definition for the Dialog object, and so it cannot be seen using IntelliSense. In C#, a late-bound property cannot be called directly; it must be called through reflection. To use a late-bound property, you must first determine what the late-bound property names and types are for a particular dialog box. Then you must use the .NET framework reflection APIs to get and set the property.

The available late-bound properties change depending on the type of dialog box that you got from the Dialogs collection. So when you get a wdDialogXMLOptions dialog box, it will have one set of late-bound properties, and when you get a wdDialogFilePrint dialog box, it will have a different set of late-bound properties.

Determining what the late-bound property names are for a particular dialog box involves some searching in older Word Basic help files. To get the Word Basic help files, search the Web for "wrdbasic.exe" to find an installer from Microsoft that installs Word Basic help. After you have installed the Word Basic help file, you can try to find a Word Basic function in the help file that corresponds to the dialog box you are using.

The Word Basic function is typically named as a concatenation of the menu name and command name. For example, the Word Basic function for the Print dialog box in the File menu is FilePrint. By looking in the Word Basic help file for the FilePrint method, you will find that it has 14 parameters. Table 8-4 shows some of the late-bound properties documented in the Word Basic help file for the FilePrint (and hence the Print dialog box).

For newer dialog boxes that were not around in Word 95 and are not listed in the Word Basic help file, you can try to figure out how to get to a particular dialog-box option by trial and error. For example, in the XML

TABLE 8-4: Some Late-Bound Properties Associated with the Print Dialog Box

Property Name	Type	What It Does
Range	Selected int values	If 1, prints the selection. If 2, prints the current page. If 3, prints the range of pages specified by From and To. If 4, prints the range of pages specified by Pages.
NumCopies	int	The number of copies to print.
Pages	string	The page numbers and page ranges to print, such as "1-10, 15", which would print pages 1 through 10 and page 15.

Options dialog box, which is new to Word 2003 (`WdWordDialog.wdDialog-`
`XMLOptions`), you can determine some of the properties by writing reflection code to try to invoke names that seem reasonable based on the names
of the controls in the dialog box. If the code fails, you know you guessed
the wrong property name. If the code succeeds, you have found a property name. In this way you would discover that AutomaticValidation,
IgnoreMixedContent, ShowAdvancedXMLErrors, and ShowPlaceholder-
Text are some of the properties associated with the XML Options dialog
box. At this point, however, you are really out there on your own. A search
on the Web for "ShowAdvancedXMLErrors," for example, returned no
hits—you might be the first person and the last person in the world to use
this late-bound property.

Listing 8-13 shows a VSTO Word Document Customization that pre-
populates the Print dialog box with a page range and number of copies to
print. It uses reflection to set the Range, NumCopies, and Pages properties on the Dialog object. The helper method SetPropertyHelper uses
reflection to set a late-bound property. The helper method GetProperty-
Helper uses reflection to get the value of a late-bound property. The code
in Listing 8-13 will display the Print dialog box without allowing Word to
execute any actions. The user can change values in the dialog box. The
code then shows the values of Range, NumCopies, and Pages after the dialog box has been displayed.

Listing 8-13: A VSTO Word Document Customization That Accesses Late-Bound Properties on a Dialog

```
private void ThisDocument_Startup(object sender, EventArgs e)
{
  // Create 20 pages
  Word.Range r = Range(ref missing, ref missing);
  for (int i = 1; i < 20; i++)
  {
    object pageBreak = Word.WdBreakType.wdPageBreak;
    r.InsertBreak(ref pageBreak);
  }

  Word.Dialog d = Application.Dialogs[
    Word.WdWordDialog.wdDialogFilePrint];
```

```
    // Set late-bound properties
    SetPropertyHelper(d, "Range", 4);
    SetPropertyHelper(d, "NumCopies", 2);
    SetPropertyHelper(d, "Pages", "1-10, 15");

    int result = d.Display(ref missing);

    // Get late-bound properties
    MessageBox.Show(String.Format(
      "Range is {0}.",
      GetPropertyHelper(d, "Range")));

    MessageBox.Show(String.Format(
      "NumCopies is {0}.",
      GetPropertyHelper(d, "NumCopies")));

    MessageBox.Show(String.Format(
      "Pages is {0}.",
      GetPropertyHelper(d, "Pages")));
}

private void SetPropertyHelper(object targetObject,
  string propertyName, object propertyValue)
{
  targetObject.GetType().InvokeMember(propertyName,
    System.Reflection.BindingFlags.Public |
    System.Reflection.BindingFlags.Instance |
    System.Reflection.BindingFlags.SetProperty,
    null,
    targetObject,
    new object[] { propertyValue },
    System.Globalization.CultureInfo.CurrentCulture);
}

private object GetPropertyHelper(object targetObject, string propertyName)
{
  return targetObject.GetType().InvokeMember(propertyName,
    System.Reflection.BindingFlags.Public |
    System.Reflection.BindingFlags.Instance |
    System.Reflection.BindingFlags.GetProperty,
    null,
    targetObject,
    null,
    System.Globalization.CultureInfo.CurrentCulture);
}
```

Working with Windows

The Application object has several properties that are used to control Word's windows. We have already considered several properties including Width, Height, WindowState, Top, Left, Windows, ActiveWindow, and Show-WindowsInTaskBar.

Word provides some additional methods on the Application object that prove useful for managing windows. The Application object's Activate method is used to make Word the active application when another application has focus. The Application object's Move method is used to move the active window when the WindowState is set to wdWindowStateNormal and takes a Top and Left parameter in pixels. The Application object's Resize method is used to resize the active window when the WindowState is set to wdWindowStateNormal and takes a Width and Height parameter in pixels.

Creating New Windows

The Application object's NewWindow method creates a new window for the active document and returns the newly created Window. This is the equivalent of choosing New Window from the Window menu.

You can also create a new window using the Windows collection's Add method. This method takes an optional Window parameter by reference, which tells Word which document to create a new Window for. If you omit the Window parameter, Word will create a new window for the active document.

Iterating over the Open Windows

The Windows collection returned by the Windows property of the Application object has a GetEnumerator method that allows it to be iterated over using the foreach keyword in C#, as shown in Listing 8-14.

Listing 8-14: A VSTO Word Document Customization That Iterates over the Open Windows

```
private void ThisDocument_Startup(object sender, EventArgs e)
{
  // Create 20 windows
  for (int i = 0; i < 20; i++)
  {
```

```
    Application.NewWindow();
  }

  foreach (Word.Window w in Application.Windows)
  {
    MessageBox.Show(w.Caption);
  }
}
```

Accessing a Window in the Collection

To access a Window in the Windows collection, you use a method called get_Item, which returns a Window. The get_Item method takes an Index parameter by reference that is of type object. You can pass a string representing the caption of the Window or you can pass a 1-based index into the Windows collection. You can check how many items are in a given collection by using the Count property. Listing 8-15 shows both getting a window using a 1-based index and using the caption of a window.

Listing 8-15: A VSTO Word Document Customization That Uses get_Item to Get a Window

```
private void ThisDocument_Startup(object sender, EventArgs e)
{
  Word.Application app = this.Application;

  // Create some windows
  app.NewWindow();
  app.NewWindow();
  object stringIndex = app.NewWindow().Caption;

  MessageBox.Show(String.Format(
    "There are {0} windows.",
    app.Windows.Count));

  object index = 1;
  Word.Window w = app.Windows.get_Item(ref index);
  MessageBox.Show(w.Caption);

  Word.Window w2 = app.Windows.get_Item(ref stringIndex);
  MessageBox.Show(w2.Caption);
}
```

Arranging Windows

Word has various ways of arranging windows and synchronizing those windows so that when one window scrolls, other windows scroll as well.

The Arrange method enables you to arrange a collection of windows and is the equivalent of selecting Arrange All from the Window section of the View tab. This method takes an optional `object` parameter by reference that can be passed a member of the WdArrangeStyle enumeration: `wdIcons` or `wdTiled`. Passing `wdTiled` only makes sense when you have put Word into MDI mode by setting the Application object's ShowWindowsInTaskbar to `false`. You also have to set the WindowState of each Window object to `wdWindowState-Minimize` if Arrange is to do anything when passed `wdTiled`.

The CompareSideBySideWith method enables you to synchronize the scrolling of two windows showing two different documents. This method is the equivalent of choosing View Side by Side from the View tab when you have multiple documents open in Word. The CompareSideBySide-With method takes a Document parameter that is the document you want to compare to the currently active document. To change the currently active document before you call this method, you can use the Document object's Activate method.

After you have established side-by-side mode, you can further control it by calling the ResetSideBySideWith method, which takes a Document parameter that is the document you want to reset side by side with against the currently active document. The SyncScrollingSideBySide property tells you whether you are in side-by-side mode and lets you temporarily disable the synchronization of scrolling. The BreakSideBySide method turns side-by-side mode off.

Listing 8-16 shows an example of first arranging two document windows and then establishing side-by-side mode.

Listing 8-16: A VSTO Word Document Customization That Uses the Arrange and CompareSideBySideWith Methods

```
private void ThisDocument_Startup(object sender, EventArgs e)
{
  // Create a second document
  Word.Document doc2 = Application.Documents.Add(
    ref missing, ref missing, ref missing, ref missing);
  Word.Range r1 = this.Range(ref missing, ref missing);
  Word.Range r2 = doc2.Range(ref missing, ref missing);

  // Fill both documents with random text
  Random rand = new Random();
  for (int i = 0; i < 1000; i++)
```

```
  {
    string randomNumber = rand.NextDouble().ToString();
    r1.InsertAfter(randomNumber + System.Environment.NewLine);
    r2.InsertAfter(randomNumber + System.Environment.NewLine);
  }

  // Arrange windows
  Application.Windows.Arrange(ref missing);
  MessageBox.Show("Windows are tiled.");

  // Activate this document and synchronize with doc2
  this.Activate();
  object docObject = doc2;
  Application.Windows.CompareSideBySideWith(ref docObject);
  MessageBox.Show("Windows are in side by side mode.");
}
```

Working with Templates

The Templates property on the Application object returns the Templates collection. The Templates collection provides you with access to the templates available in Word. Like most other collections in Word, you can use `foreach` to iterate over each Template in the Templates collection. You can also use the Templates collection's get_Item method to get to a particular template in the collection, passing by reference an `object` set to a `string` for the name of the template or an `int` for the 1-based index into the collection.

You can also get to a Template object by using the Application object's NormalTemplate property, which returns a Template object for normal.dotm—the global template that is always open and associated with a document when you have not specified a different template. If you have a Document object and you want to determine what template is associated with it, you can use the Document object's AttachedTemplate. When you get the value of AttachedTemplate, it returns an `object` that you can cast to a Template object. When you set the value of AttachedTemplate, you can pass either a Template object or a `string` containing the filename of the template.

The Template object's OpenAsDocument method enables you to open a template as a document and edit it. The Name property is a `string` property that returns the name of the template, such as `"Template.dotx"`. FullName is a `string` property that returns the complete filename of the template, such as "c:\my templates\Template.dotx". Path is a string property that returns the folder the template is in, such as "c:\my templates".

The Template object's Type property returns a member of the WdTemplateType enumeration that designates the type of the template. A template can be one of three types. Figure 8-3 shows the Templates and Add-Ins dialog box which illustrates two of the three types. A template can be attached to a document—in this case the template AWTemplate.dot is attached to the active document. A template attached to a document has a type of wdAttachedTemplate. The Templates collection will contain an attached template only while the document the template is attached to is opened. When the document associated with the template is closed, the Template object attached to that document will no longer be in the Templates collection (unless of course it is attached to another document that is still open).

A template can also be installed as a global template or add-in. In Figure 8-3, the template Proftemplate_61104.dot is a global add-in template. A global template has a type of wdGlobalTemplate. Templates installed in this way are often acting as a simple add-in, providing toolbars or additional menu commands to Word. A template of this type will always be in

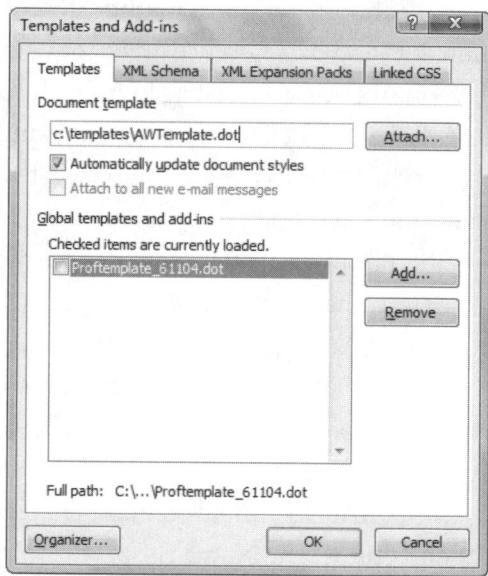

Figure 8-3: The Templates and Add-Ins dialog box
showing the attached template and global templates.

the Templates collection until it is uninstalled or removed using the Templates and Add-Ins dialog box.

The third type of template is not shown in this dialog box. The normal.dotm template is always open in Word and is of type `wdNormalTemplate`. This template is always present in the Templates collection.

The Templates collection does not have an Add method. Templates are added indirectly through actions you take with other objects. For example, setting the Document's AttachedTemplate property to change the template attached to a document adds the template to the Templates collection if it is not already there. Opening a document that has an attached template not already in the Templates collection adds the attached template to the Templates collection. Templates with type `wdAttachedTemplate` are removed from the Templates collection when all documents are closed that are using the attached template. You can also add templates of type `wdGlobalTemplate` to the Templates collection using the Add method of the AddIns collection.

Working with Documents

The Documents collection, available from the Application object's Documents property, contains a collection of Document objects currently open in Word. It also has methods used to access a Document in the collection, create a new document, open an existing document, close all the documents, and save all the documents.

Iterating over the Open Documents

The documents collection can be iterated over using the `foreach` keyword in C#. Listing 8-17 shows a simple example of iterating over the open documents in Word and printing the name of each document to the console.

Listing 8-17: Iterating over the Documents Collection Using foreach

```
foreach (Word.Document doc in Application.Documents)
{
  Console.WriteLine(doc.Name);
}
```

Accessing a Document in the Documents Collection

To access a Document in the Documents collection, you use the get_Item method, which returns a Document object. The get_Item method has an Index parameter passed by reference that is of type object. You can pass an int representing the 1-based index of the document in the collection you want to access.

Alternatively, you can pass a string representing the name of the document you want to access. The name you pass for a document is the full name of the file if it has been saved (for example, "c:\John\Doc1.docx"). If the document has not yet been saved, the name to pass is the temporary name that Word creates for a new document. This temporary name is typically something like Document1, with no file extension. Listing 8-18 shows an example of calling get_Item with a 1-based index and a string index.

Listing 8-18: A VSTO Word Document Customization That Uses get_Item to Get a Document

```csharp
private void ThisDocument_Startup(object sender, EventArgs e)
{
  // Add 5 documents
  for (int i = 0; i < 5; i++)
  {
    Application.Documents.Add(ref missing,
      ref missing, ref missing, ref missing);
  }

  // Iterate over the open documents using foreach
  foreach (Word.Document doc in Application.Documents)
  {
    MessageBox.Show(doc.Name);
  }

  // Get a document by 1-based index.
  object index = 2;
  Word.Document doc1 = Application.Documents.get_Item(ref index);
  MessageBox.Show(String.Format(
    "The document at index {0} is {1}.",
    index, doc1.FullName));

  // Get a document by full name
  object stringIndex = doc1.FullName;
  Word.Document doc2 = Application.Documents.get_Item(ref index);
  MessageBox.Show(String.Format(
    "The document at string index {0} is {1}.",
    stringIndex, doc2.FullName));
}
```

You can also use the Count property to determine the number of open documents. You should check the Count property before accessing a document by index.

Creating a New Document

To create a new document, you can use the Documents collection's Add method. The Add method returns the newly created Document object. It takes four optional by reference parameters of type `object`, as described in Table 8-5.

Opening an Existing Document

To open an existing document, use the Documents collection's Open method, which returns the opened Document object. The Open method takes one required `object` parameter to which you pass the `string` representing the filename to open. The Open method also takes 15 optional by reference parameters of type `object`, as described in Table 8-6.

TABLE 8-5: Optional Parameters for the Documents Collection's Add Method

Parameter Name	What It Does
Template	Pass as a `string` the short name of the template to be used (for example, `"mytemplate.dot"`) if the template is in the Templates collection. If the template is not in the Templates collection, pass the full filename to the template (for example, `"c:\mytemplates\template1.dot"`). If you omit this parameter, Word uses the Normal template.
NewTemplate	Pass the `bool` value `true` if the document should be opened as a template. The default is `false`.
DocumentType	Pass a member of the WdNewDocumentType enumeration: `wdNewBlankDocument`, `wdNewEmailMessage`, `wdNewFrameset`, or `wdNewWebPage`. The default is `wdNewBlankDocument`.
Visible	Pass the `bool` value `true` if the document should be opened in a visible window. The default is `true`.

TABLE 8-6: Optional Parameters for the Documents Collection's Open Method

Parameter Name	What It Does
ConfirmConversions	Pass true to display the Convert File dialog box if the filename passed to Open is not in Microsoft Word format.
ReadOnly	Pass true to open the document as read-only. If the document is already set to read-only on disk, passing false will not affect the read-only status of the document. The default is false.
AddToRecentFiles	Pass true to add the filename to the list of recently used files in the File menu. The default is true.
PasswordDocument	Pass a string representing the password for opening the document if the document is password-protected.
PasswordTemplate	Pass a string representing the password for opening the template if the template is password-protected.
Revert	If the document you are opening with the Open method is already open in Word, pass true to discard any unsaved changes in the already-open document. Pass false to activate the already-open document.
WritePasswordDocument	Pass a string representing the password for saving changes to the document if the document is password-protected.
WritePasswordTemplate	Pass a string representing the password for saving changes to the template if the template is password-protected.
Format	Pass a member of the WdOpenFormat enumeration specifying the file conversion to be used when opening the document.
Encoding	Pass a member of the Office.MsoEncoding enumeration specifying the code page or character set to be used when you open the document.
Visible	Pass true to open the document in a visible window. The default is true.
OpenConflictDocument	Pass true to open the conflict file for a document that has offline conflicts.

TABLE 8-6: Optional Parameters for the Documents Collection's Open Method *(Continued)*

Parameter Name	What It Does
OpenAndRepair	Pass true to try to repair a corrupted document.
DocumentDirection	Pass a member of the WdDocumentDirection enumeration specifying the horizontal flow of text in the opened document.
NoEncodingDialog	Pass true to prevent Word from displaying the Encoding dialog box if the text encoding of the document cannot be determined.

Listing 8-19 shows the simplest possible way to call the Open method to open a document. The code omits all the parameters by passing by reference the missing class member variable in VSTO, which is of type object and has been set to System.Type.Missing.

Listing 8-19: A VSTO Word Document Customization That Uses the Open Method to Open a Document

```
private void ThisDocument_Startup(object sender, EventArgs e)
{
  object fileName = @"c:\test\test.docx";

  Word.Document doc = Application.Documents.Open(ref fileName,
    ref missing, ref missing, ref missing,
    ref missing, ref missing, ref missing,
    ref missing, ref missing, ref missing,
    ref missing, ref missing, ref missing,
    ref missing, ref missing, ref missing);

  MessageBox.Show(String.Format(
    "Just opened {0}.", doc.Name));
}
```

Closing All Open Documents

The Close method on the Documents collection closes all the open documents in Word. It takes three optional parameters of type object by reference. The first optional parameter, called SaveChanges, is of type object and can be passed a member of the WdSaveOptions enumeration—either wdDoNotSaveChanges, wdPromptToSaveChanges, or wdSaveChanges. The second optional parameter, called `OriginalFormat`, is of type `object` and can be passed a member of the WdOriginalFormat enumeration. The second parameter controls Word's behavior when saving a changed document whose original format was not Word document format. This parameter can be passed `wdOriginalDocumentFormat`, `wdPromptUser`, or `wdWordDocument`. The final optional parameter is called `RouteDocument` and is of type `object`. Passing `true` for this parameter routes the document to the next recipient if a routing slip is attached.

It is also possible to close an individual document using the Document object's Close method, as discussed later in this chapter. You have already learned how to use the Application object's Quit method as a third way to close all open documents and quit Word. The Quit method takes the same parameters as Documents.Close and Document.Close.

Saving All Open Documents

The Save method on the Documents collection saves all the open documents in Word. It takes two optional parameters. The first optional parameter, called `NoPrompt`, is of type `object` and can be set to `true` to have Word automatically save all open documents without prompting the user. The second optional parameter, called `OriginalFormat`, is of type `object` and can be passed a member of the WdOriginalFormat enumeration. The second parameter controls Word's behavior when saving a changed document whose original format was not Word document format.

It is also possible to save an individual document using the Document object's Save or SaveAs methods, as discussed later in this chapter.

Working with a Document

The Document object represents an open document in Word. The Document object has a Name property that returns a `string` representing the name of the document (for example, `"doc1.docx"`). If the document has not yet been saved, this property returns the temporary name of the document, typically something like Document1.

Document also has a FullName property that returns a string representing the full filename of the document if the document has been saved. Once again, if the document has not been saved, this property returns the temporary name of the document, such as Document1. The FullName of the document can be passed to the get_Item method of the Documents collection to access the document by name from that collection. The Path property returns a string representing the path to the folder where the document is stored. For example, a document with FullName "c:\mydocuments\doc1.docx" returns "c:\mydocuments" for the Path property. If the document has not yet been saved, the Path returns an empty string.

The Type property is of type WdDocumentType and can be used to determine whether the document is a Word document or a Word template file. A Word document returns the enumerated value wdTypeDocument. A template returns the value wdTypeTemplate.

Preserving the Dirty State of a Document

Saved is a bool property that tells you whether a document needs to be saved. A document that has not been changed, such as a brand new document that has not been typed in yet or a document that has been opened but not edited, returns true for Saved. A document that has been changed returns false until the user or code saves the document and thereby resets the Saved property to true. A document that has been changed but not saved is often referred to as a "dirty" document.

You can also set the value of the Saved property so that a change made by your code does not dirty the document. For example, you might make a change through code to a document but you do not want to actually save the change made by your code unless the user makes some additional change to the document. This is often desirable because when users open a document and do not edit it, they are confused when they are prompted to save because code associated with the document changed the state of the document in some way. You can get the value of the Saved property, make the change to the document, and then set the value of Saved back, as shown in Listing 8-20.

Listing 8-20: A VSTO Word Document Customization That Preserves the Dirty State of the Document by Using the Saved Property

```csharp
private void ThisDocument_Startup(object sender, EventArgs e)
{
  bool oldSaved = this.Saved;

  try
  {
    Office.DocumentProperties props = this.
      CustomDocumentProperties as Office.DocumentProperties;

    Office.DocumentProperty prop = props.Add(
      "My Property", false,
      Office.MsoDocProperties.msoPropertyTypeString,
      "My Value", missing);
  }
  finally
  {
    this.Saved = oldSaved;
  }
}
```

Closing and Saving a Document

The Close method enables you to close a document. The Close method takes three optional object parameters passed by reference. The first optional parameter, called SaveChanges, is of type object and can be passed a member of the WdSaveOptions enumeration—either wdDoNotSaveChanges, wdPromptTo-SaveChanges, or wdSaveChanges. The second optional parameter, called OriginalFormat, is of type object and can be passed a member of the Wd-OriginalFormat enumeration. The second parameter controls Word's behavior when saving a changed document whose original format was not Word document format. This parameter can be passed wdOriginalDocumentFormat, wdPromptUser, or wdWordDocument. The final optional parameter is called RouteDocument and is of type object. Passing true for this parameter routes the document to the next recipient if a routing slip is attached.

The Save method saves the document and does the same thing that choosing Save from the File menu would do. If the document has already been saved, it saves the document to the location it was last saved to. If the document has not yet been saved, it brings up the Save As dialog box so that the user can select a place to save the document.

The SaveAs method takes 16 optional `object` parameters passed by reference. It gives you full control over the filename to save to as well as the file format and several other options. Table 8-7 lists the optional parameters of type `object` that are passed by reference to the SaveAs method.

TABLE 8-7: Optional Parameters for the Document Object's SaveAs Method

Parameter Name	What It Does
FileName	Pass a `string` representing the filename to use for the document. The default is the current FullName of the document.
FileFormat	Pass a member of the WdSaveFormat enumeration to specify the file format to save as.
LockComments	Pass `true` to lock the document for comments. The default is `false`.
Password	Pass the password for opening the document as a `string`.
AddToRecentFiles	Pass `true` to add the filename to the list of recently used files in the File menu. The default is `true`.
WritePassword	Pass the password for saving changes to the document as a `string`.
ReadOnlyRecommended	Pass `true` to have Word always suggest that the document be opened as read-only. The default is `false`.
EmbedTrueTypeFonts	Pass `true` to save TrueType fonts in the document. If omitted, Word will use the value of Document.EmbedTrueTypeFonts.
SaveNativePictureFormat	Pass `true` to save pictures imported from the Macintosh in their Windows version.
SaveFormsData	Pass `true` to save the data entered by the user entered in a form as a data record.

Continues

TABLE 8-7: Optional Parameters for the Document Object's SaveAs Method *(Continued)*

Parameter Name	What It Does
SaveAsAOCELetter	Pass true to save the document as an AOCE letter if the document has an attached mailer.
Encoding	Pass a member of the Office.MsoEncoding enumeration specifying the code page or character set to be used when you save the document.
InsertLineBreaks	If the document is saved in a text format (for example, you passed WdSaveFormat.wdFormatText to the FileFormat parameter), pass true to insert line breaks at the end of each line of text.
AllowSubstitutions	If the document is saved in a text format, pass true to convert some symbols with text that looks similar. Replace the symbol © with (c), for example.
LineEnding	If the document is saved in a text format, pass a member of the WdLineEndingType enumeration to specify the way Word marks line and paragraph breaks.
AddBiDiMarks	If you pass true, Word adds control characters to the file to preserve the bidirectional layout of the document.

Working with Windows Associated with a Document

A particular document can have one or more windows associated with it. Even when a document is opened with `false` passed to the `Visible` parameter of the Documents collection's Open method, it still has a window associated with it, albeit a window whose Visible property is `false`. When a document has multiple windows associated with it, you can use the Windows property to return the collection of windows associated with that document. You can determine which of the windows will have the focus when the document is active by using the ActiveWindow property. To activate a particular document and make its ActiveWindow the one with focus, use the Activate method.

Changing the Template Attached to a Document

A document always has a template associated with it. By default, the template is the Normal template (normal.dotm), also available from the Application object's NormalTemplate property. A document might be associated with some other template, usually because it was created from a particular template.

If you have a Document object and you want to determine what template is associated with it, you can use the AttachedTemplate property. When you get the value of AttachedTemplate, it returns an `object` that you can cast to a Template object. When you set the value of AttachedTemplate, you can pass either a Template object or a `string` containing the filename of the template.

Important Collections Associated with Both Document and Range

The Document and Range objects share a number of properties that return collections you will frequently use. Rather than consider these properties in both this section and the section later in this chapter on Range, they are both covered here only. Table 8-8 shows these properties associated with both Range and Document that return important collection objects.

TABLE 8-8:   Properties Associated with Both Document and Range That Return
Important Collections

Property Name and Type	What It Does
Bookmarks	Returns the Bookmarks collection. Bookmarks can be used to mark certain areas of a document and then return easily to those areas of the document. Bookmarks are discussed in more detail in the section "Working with Bookmarks" later in this chapter.
Characters	Returns the Characters collection, which enables you to work with a Document or Range at the level of an individual character. The Characters collection returns one-character-long Range objects.

Continues

TABLE 8-8:　Properties Associated with Both Document and Range That Return
Important Collections *(Continued)*

Property Name and Type	What It Does
Comments	Returns the Comments collection, which enables you to access comments made by reviewers in the Document or Range.
Endnotes	Returns the Endnotes collection, which enables you to access the endnotes associated with a Document or Range.
ContentControls	Returns the ContentControls collection, which enables you to access content controls in the Document or Range.
ContentTypeProperties	Returns the ContentTypeProperties collection, which enables you to access content type properties (if the document was created from a SharePoint content type) in the Document or Range.
Fields	Returns the Fields collection, which enables you to access the fields used in a Document or Range.
Footnotes	Returns the Footnotes collection, which enables you to access the footnotes used in a Document or Range.
Hyperlinks	Returns the Hyperlinks collection, which enables you to access hyperlinks in a Document or Range.
InlineShapes	Returns the InlineShapes collection, which enables you to access an InlineShape (an InlineShape can include a drawing, an ActiveX control, and many other types of objects enumerated in the Office.MsoShapeType enumeration) that has been inserted inline with the text in a Document or Range.
Paragraphs	Returns the Paragraphs collection, which enables you to access individual Paragraph objects associated with the Document or Range.
Revisions	Returns the Revisions collection, which enables you to access a Revision made in the Document or Range.

TABLE 8-8: Properties Associated with Both Document and Range That Return Important Collections *(Continued)*

Property Name and Type	What It Does
Sections	Returns the Sections collection, which enables you to access a Section within the Document or Range. A new Section can be added using the Break command from the Insert menu.
Sentences	Returns the Sentences collection, which enables you to work with a Document or Range at the level of an individual sentence. The Sentences collection returns a Range object for each sentence.
Tables	Returns the Tables collection, which enables you to access a Table within the Document or Range.
Words	Returns the Words collection, which enables you to work with a Document or Range at the level of an individual word. The Words collection returns a Range object for each word.

Note that the Characters, Sentences, and Words collections are special collections that return Range objects when you iterate over them. Listing 8-21 shows a VSTO Word document customization that uses these collections as well as the Paragraphs collection. It creates a document with some text in it and then a second document to output information about the first document.

Listing 8-21: A VSTO Word Document Customization That Uses the Characters, Paragraphs, Sentences, and Words Collections

```
private void ThisDocument_Startup(object sender, EventArgs e)
{
  Word.Range r = this.Range(ref missing, ref missing);
  r.Text = "Whether I shall turn out to be the hero of my own life, or whether
that station will be held by anybody else, these pages must show. To begin my
life with the beginning of my life, I record that I was born (as I have been
informed and believe) on a Friday, at twelve o'clock at night. It was remarked
that the clock began to strike, and I began to cry, simultaneously.";

  Word.Document reportDoc = this.Application.Documents.
    Add(ref missing, ref missing, ref missing, ref missing);
```

```csharp
Word.Range report = reportDoc.Range(ref missing, ref missing);

report.InsertAfter(String.Format(
  "There are {0} paragraphs.\n",
  this.Paragraphs.Count));

foreach (Word.Paragraph paragraph in this.Paragraphs)
{
  report.InsertAfter(String.Format(
    "{0}\n", paragraph.Range.Text));
}

report.InsertAfter(String.Format(
  "There are {0} sentences.\n",
  this.Sentences.Count));

foreach (Word.Range sentence in this.Sentences)
{
  report.InsertAfter(String.Format(
    "{0}\n", sentence.Text));
}

report.InsertAfter(String.Format(
  "There are {0} words.\n",
  this.Words.Count));

foreach (Word.Range word in this.Words)
{
  report.InsertAfter(String.Format(
    "{0}\n", word.Text));
}

report.InsertAfter(String.Format(
  "There are {0} characters.\n",
  this.Characters.Count));

foreach (Word.Range character in this.Characters)
{
  report.InsertAfter(String.Format(
    "{0}\n", character.Text));
}
}
```

Important Collections Associated with Document Only

Some properties return collections only associated with Document and not with Range. Table 8-9 shows several of these properties.

TABLE 8-9: Properties Associated with Document That Return Important Collections

Property Name and Type	What It Does
CommandBars	Returns the CommandBars collection. The CommandBars collection is used to add new toolbars, buttons, and menus to Word.
CustomXMLParts	Returns the CustomXMLParts collection. This collection is used to manage the custom XML parts in the document.
Shapes	Returns the Shapes collection. The Shapes collection contains Shape objects (a Shape can include a drawing, an ActiveX control, and many other types of objects enumerated in the Office.MsoShapeType enumeration) that are not inline with text but are free-floating in the document.
StoryRanges	Returns the StoryRanges collection. The StoryRanges collection provides a way to access ranges of text that are not part of the main body of the document, including headers, footers, footnotes, and so on. The StoryRanges collection's Item property is passed a member of the enumeration WdStoryType.
Versions	Returns information about the different versions of the document if the document is being checked in and out of a workspace.

Working with Document Properties

Document has a BuiltinDocumentProperties property that returns an `object` that can be cast to an Office.DocumentProperties collection representing the built-in document properties associated with the document. These are the properties that you see when you choose Properties from the File menu and click the Summary tab. These include properties such as Title, Subject, Author, and Company. Table 8-10 shows the names of all the document properties associated with a document.

Document also has a CustomDocumentProperties property that returns an `object` that can be cast to an Office.DocumentProperties collection representing any custom document properties associated with the document.

TABLE 8-10: Names of the Built-In Document Properties in Word

Application name	Language*	Number of pages
Author	Last author	Number of paragraphs
Category	Last print date	Number of slides
Comments	Last save time	Number of words
Company	Manager	Revision number
Content type*	Number of bytes	Security
Content status*	Number of characters	Subject
Creation date	Number of characters (with spaces)	Template
Document version*	Number of hidden slides	Title
Format	Number of lines	Total editing time
Hyperlink base	Number of multimedia clips	
Keywords	Number of notes	

* New in 2007

Custom properties can be created by your code and used to store name and value pairs in the document. To see the custom document properties:

1. Choose Office > Prepare > Properties to show the Document Information Panel.
2. Click the Document Properties drop-down list, and choose Advanced Properties.
3. Click the Custom tab in the Advanced Properties dialog box.

The DocumentProperties collection and DocumentProperty object are found in the Microsoft Office 12.0 Object Library (office.dll), which contains objects shared by all the Office applications. These objects are in the

Microsoft.Office.Core namespace and are typically brought into Office projects in an Office namespace as shown here:

```
using Office = Microsoft.Office.Core;
```

Listing 8-22 shows an example of iterating over the DocumentProperties collection returned by the CustomDocumentProperties and BuiltInDocumentProperties properties. We get the value of the built-in properties in a `try/catch` block because some built-in properties throw exceptions when their value is accessed.

Cast from BuiltInDocumentProperties and CustomDocumentProperties to Office.DocumentProperties Fails

Note that this code works in a VSTO document solution, but in an add-in or an automation executable, the cast from the object type that BuiltInDocumentProperties and CustomDocumentProperties to an Office.DocumentProperties property fails. To work around this issue, see the KB article http://support.microsoft.com/default.aspx?scid=303296

Listing 8-22: A VSTO Word Document Customization That Iterates over DocumentProperties Collections

```
private void ThisDocument_Startup(object sender, EventArgs e)
{
  Office.DocumentProperties cProps =
    this.CustomDocumentProperties as Office.DocumentProperties;

  Office.DocumentProperties bProps =
    this.BuiltInDocumentProperties as Office.DocumentProperties;

  Word.Document doc = this.Application.Documents.Add(
    ref missing, ref missing, ref missing, ref missing);

  Word.Range range = doc.Range(ref missing, ref missing);
  range.InsertAfter("Built-in Document Properties\n\n");

  foreach (Office.DocumentProperty bProp in bProps)
  {
```

```
  string name = bProp.Name;
  object value = null;
  try
  {
    value = bProp.Value;
  }
  catch (Exception ex)
  {
    value = ex.Message;
  }

  range.InsertAfter(String.Format(
    "{0} - {1}\n",
    name,
    value));
}

range.InsertAfter("Custom Document Properties\n\n");
foreach (Office.DocumentProperty cProp in cProps)
{
  range.InsertAfter(String.Format(
    "{0} - {1}\n",
    cProp.Name,
    cProp.Value));
}
}
```

To access a DocumentProperty in a DocumentProperties collection, you use the C# indexing syntax (`docProperties[object]`), which returns a DocumentProperty object. The indexer takes an `Index` parameter of type `object`. You can pass an `int` representing the 1-based index of the DocumentProperty in the collection you want to access. Alternatively, you can pass a `string` representing the name of the DocumentProperty you want to access. As with other collections, the Count property returns how many DocumentProperty objects are in the collection.

A DocumentProperty object has a Name property that returns a `string` containing the name of the property. It also has a Value property of type `object` that returns the value of the property. You can check what the type is of `Value` by using the Type property that returns a member of the Office.MsoDocProperties enumeration: `msoPropertyTypeBoolean`, `msoPropertyTypeDate`, `msoPropertyTypeFloat`, `msoPropertyTypeNumber`, or `msoPropertyTypeString`.

Listing 8-23 shows how a DocumentProperty is accessed.

Listing 8-23: A VSTO Word Document Customization That Accesses a DocumentProperty Using an Indexer

```
private void ThisDocument_Startup(object sender, EventArgs e)
{
  Office.DocumentProperties bProps =
    this.BuiltInDocumentProperties as Office.DocumentProperties;

  Office.DocumentProperty author = bProps["Author"];

  MessageBox.Show(String.Format(
    "Property {0} is set to {1}.",
    author.Name, author.Value));

  Office.DocumentProperty third = bProps[3];

  MessageBox.Show(String.Format(
    "Property {0} is set to {1}.",
    third.Name, third.Value));
}
```

You can add a custom DocumentProperty to a DocumentProperties collection by using the Add method. The Add method takes the parameters shown in Table 8-11.

TABLE 8-11: The DocumentProperties Collection's Add Method Parameters

Parameter Name	Type	What It Does
Name	string	Sets the name of the new property.
LinkToContent	bool	Sets whether the property is linked to the contents of the container document.
Type	optional object	Sets the data type of the property. Can be one of the following Office.MsoDocProperties enumerated values: msoPropertyTypeBoolean, msoPropertyTypeDate, msoPropertyType-Float, msoPropertyTypeNumber, or msoPropertyTypeString.
Value	optional object	Sets the value of the property if LinkToContent is false.
LinkSource	optional object	Sets the source of the linked property if LinkTo-Content is true.

Listing 8-24 shows an example of adding a custom DocumentProperty of type `msoPropertyTypeString`. Note that Word will let you set the value to a long `string`, but it will truncate it to 255 characters. Fortunately, VSTO enables developers to store larger amounts of data in a document through a feature called cached data. For more information on the cached data feature of VSTO, see Chapter 20, "Server Data Scenarios."

Listing 8-24: A VSTO Word Document Customization That Adds a Custom DocumentProperty

```
private void ThisDocument_Startup(object sender, EventArgs e)
{
  Office.DocumentProperties props =
    this.CustomDocumentProperties as Office.DocumentProperties;

  Office.DocumentProperty prop =
    props.Add("My Property", false,
    Office.MsoDocProperties.msoPropertyTypeString,
    "My Value", missing);

  MessageBox.Show(String.Format(
    "Property {0} is set to {1}.",
    prop.Name, prop.Value));
}
```

Checking Spelling and Grammar in Documents and Ranges

You can control the grammar checking in a Document or Range by using the following methods and properties. GrammarChecked is a `bool` property that returns `true` if the grammar in the document or range has been checked. If the grammar has not yet been checked, you can force a grammar check by calling the CheckGrammar method. You can control whether Word shows the grammatical errors in the document by setting the Show-GrammaticalErrors property to `true` or `false`. The GrammaticalErrors property returns a ProofreadingErrors collection, which is a collection of Range objects containing the ranges of grammatically incorrect text.

A similar set of methods and properties exist for checking spelling. SpellingChecked is a `bool` property that returns `true` if the spelling in the document or range has been checked. If the spelling has not yet been checked, you can force a spelling check by calling the CheckSpelling method. The CheckSpelling takes 12 optional `object` parameters passed by reference that you can omit unless you want to specify additional custom dictionaries to check the spelling against.

You can control whether Word shows the spelling errors in the document by setting the ShowSpellingErrors property to `true` or `false`. The SpellingErrors property returns a ProofreadingErrors collection, which is a collection of Range objects containing the ranges of incorrectly spelled text.

Listing 8-25 shows an example that uses many of these properties and methods.

Listing 8-25: A VSTO Word Document Customization That Checks Grammar and Spelling

```csharp
private void ThisDocument_Startup(object sender, EventArgs e)
{
  this.Range(ref missing, ref missing).Text =
    "This are a test of the emegency broadcastin system.";

  if (this.GrammarChecked == false)
    this.CheckGrammar();

  if (this.SpellingChecked == false)
  {
    this.CheckSpelling(ref missing, ref missing,
      ref missing, ref missing, ref missing, ref missing,
      ref missing, ref missing, ref missing, ref missing,
      ref missing, ref missing);
  }

  this.ShowGrammaticalErrors = true;
  this.ShowSpellingErrors = true;

  foreach (Word.Range range in this.GrammaticalErrors)
  {
    MessageBox.Show(String.Format(
      "Grammatical error: {0}",
      range.Text));
  }

  foreach (Word.Range range in this.SpellingErrors)
  {
    MessageBox.Show(String.Format(
      "Spelling error: {0}",
      range.Text));
  }
}
```

Printing a Document

The Document object has a PageSetup property that returns a PageSetup object that has several properties for configuring the printing of a document. The PrintOut method can be used to print a document. It has 18 optional `object` parameters passed by reference. Table 8-12 lists some of the most commonly used optional parameters for PrintOut.

Listing 8-26 shows a simple example that sets some page margin options using the PageSetup property and then calls PrintOut specifying that two copies be printed.

TABLE 8-12: Some of the Optional Parameters for PrintOut

Parameter Name	What It Does
Background	Pass `false` to prevent PrintOut from returning until the document has been printed.
Range	Pass a member of the WdPrintOutRange enumeration: `wdPrintAllDocument`, `wdPrintCurrentPage`, `wdPrint-FromTo`, `wdPrintRangeOfPages`, or `wdPrintSelection`.
OutputFileName	Pass as a `string` the full filename of the file you want to print to when PrintToFile is passed `true`.
From	Pass the starting page number to print from when Range is set to `wdPrintFromTo`.
To	Pass the ending page number to print to when Range is set to `wdPrintFromTo`.
Copies	Pass the number of copies to print.
Pages	When Range is set to `wdPrintRangeOfPages`, pass a `string` representing the page numbers and page ranges to print (for example, `"1-5, 15"`).
PageType	Pass a member of the WdPrintOutPages enumeration: `wdPrintAllPages`, `wdPrintEvenPagesOnly`, or `wdPrint-OddPagesOnly`.
PrintToFile	Pass `true` to print to a file. Used in conjunction with the OutputFileName parameter.
Collate	Pass `true` to collate.

Listing 8-26: A VSTO Word Document Customization That Uses the PrintOut Method

```csharp
private void ThisDocument_Startup(object sender, EventArgs e)
{
  this.Range(ref missing, ref missing).Text =
    "This is a test of printing.";

  // Margins are specified in points.
  PageSetup.LeftMargin = 72F;
  PageSetup.RightMargin = 72F;

  object copies = 2;
  this.PrintOut(ref missing, ref missing, ref missing, ref missing,
    ref missing, ref missing, ref missing, ref copies,
    ref missing, ref missing, ref missing, ref missing,
    ref missing, ref missing, ref missing, ref missing,
    ref missing, ref missing);
}
```

Working with Read-Only Document Protection

Read-only Document protection enables you to protect a Word document so the document can only be edited in certain ways by certain people. Read-only document protection in Word works on the principle of exclusions—you first protect the whole document as read-only, and then mark certain areas of the document as exclusions. This allows your users to edit only the parts of the document that you specify as exclusions.

Figure 8-4 shows the Protect Document task pane that is shown when you choose Restrict Formatting and Editing from the Protect Document drop-down list on the Developer tab. The Allow only this type of editing in the document check box has been checked and the drop-down set to not allow any changes. You can optionally allow users to make comments in the document, fill out forms, or make tracked changes to the document.

Given a basic protection level for the document, you can then add some exceptions by selecting the parts of the document that should be editable and checking either a Groups or Individuals check box to allow that group or individual to edit the selection. Word always provides an Everyone group, but you can add groups and individuals by clicking the More users link in the task pane. Clicking this link brings up a dialog box that lets you enter a Windows username (DOMAIN\username), Windows user group (DOMAIN\usergroup), or e-mail address.

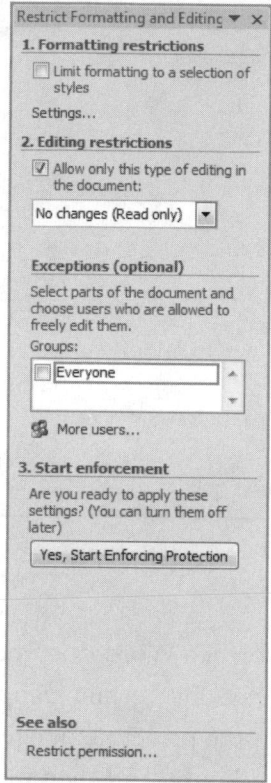

Figure 8-4: The Protect Document task pane.

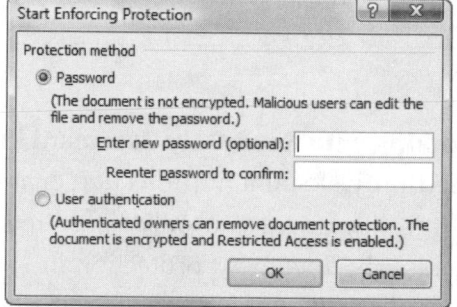

Figure 8-5: The Start Enforcing Protection dialog box.

After you have selected the parts of the document you want to be exceptions and checked the check box next to the groups or individuals you want to be able to edit those parts of the document, click the Yes, Start Enforcing Protection button to protect the document to bring up the Start Enforcing Protection dialog box, shown in Figure 8-5. Word prompts you for an optional password if you want to require a password to remove the document protection. Word can also use user authentication (Information Rights Management or IRM) to protect and encrypt the document to further protect it.

With protection enforced, Word highlights the area of the document that you are allowed to edit based on the exception set for the document. Figure 8-6 shows a document that has been protected but has the second

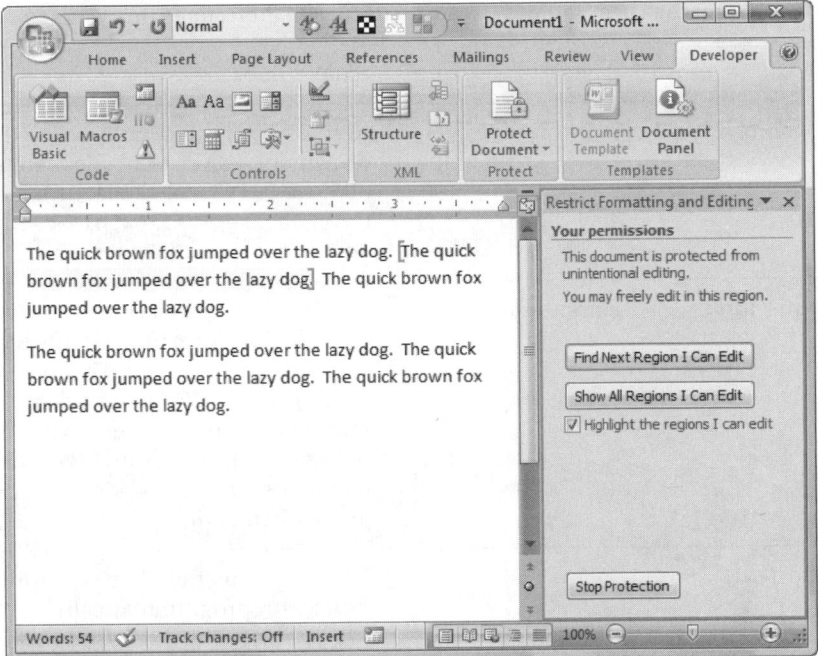

Figure 8-6: A document with protection enforced but with an exception to allow editing of the second sentence.

sentence as an editing exception for the Everyone group. Word highlights the regions that you are allowed to edit in the document and provides a task pane for navigating between regions you are allowed to edit.

Read-only document protection settings apply to code that is talking to the Word object model, too. If the user is not allowed to edit any sentence but the second sentence, code is also restricted to only being able to change the second sentence. If you run code that tries to change protected parts of the document, an exception is raised.

Word provides several properties and methods that enable you to programmatically protect the document and examine protection settings, as listed in Table 8-13.

Working with Password Protection

In addition to a password that may be associated with document protection, a Word document can have a password that must be entered to open

TABLE 8-13: Properties and Methods Used with Document Protection

Name	Type	What It Does
ProtectionType	WdProtectionType	Returns the protection type for the document: `wdAllowOnlyComments`, `wdAllowOnlyFormFields`, `wdAllow-OnlyReading`, `wdAllowOnly-Revisions`, or `wdNoProtection`.
Permission	Permission	The Permission object lets you work with IRM (Information Rights Management) permissions. This type of protection via IRM permissions is more secure than simple document protection because it involves more validation of identity and encryption of the document.
Protect(…)		The Protect method lets you apply protection programmatically.
Unprotect(…)		The Unprotect method lets you remove protection programmatically.
Range.Editors	Editors	Given a Range that is an exclusion, Range.Editors will return an Editors collection, which lets you inspect the groups and individuals allowed to edit that Range.

the document. It can also have a second password associated with it that must be entered to modify or write to the document. These passwords can be set by choosing the Tools menu in the Save dialog box and picking General Options. Figure 8-7 shows the General Options dialog box.

The Document object's HasPassword property returns true if the document has been protected with a password that must be entered to open the document. The Password property is a write-only property that can be set to a string value representing the password for the document. Word also has the notion of a password to prevent a user from saving over the original file without entering the password. If the WriteReserved property returns true, the document has been protected with a password that must

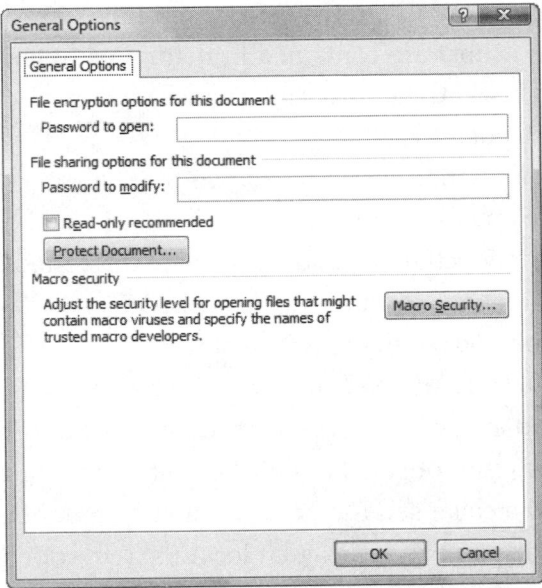

Figure 8-7: The General Options dialog box.

be entered to overwrite the original document file. The WritePassword property is a write-only property that can be set to a `string` value representing the write password for the document.

Undo and Redo

Unlike Excel, Word adds the changes you make with your code to the undo stack. You can undo and redo actions your code or a user has taken using the Document object's Undo and Redo methods. Both methods take by reference an optional `object` parameter that you can set to the number of undo steps or redo steps you want to take. The UndoClear method clears the undo stack making it so the user can neither undo nor redo any recent actions. Note that you can only undo and redo steps in order—you can't undo a particular step in the stack.

Working with the Range Object

The Range object in the Word object model is the primary way to interact with the content of the document. A Range represents a range of contiguous text and provides a way to interact with that range of text along with any additional elements that are contained in that range of text, such as tables, shapes, lists, and bookmarks. You can get and use as many Range objects as you need in your code.

Working with a Range does not change the selection in the document unless you use Range's Select method, which will make the Range you have defined into the active selection. If you are interested in working with the active selection, you can use the Selection object, which shares many properties and methods with the Range object.

A Range has a start and end that are specified in units of characters in the document and include characters that do not print, such as the carriage return between paragraphs. A Range whose start and end are the same is sometimes called a collapsed Range, and, can be thought of as the equivalent of an insertion point at a particular location in the document. Note that start and end should be used with great caution as their values are impacted by hidden text and field codes.

Word also has the concept of a "story," which is the part of the document that the Range comes from. Most commonly, you work with the main text story, which is the main body of the document. You might also want to get to other text elements in the document, such as headers, footers, comments, footnotes, and endnotes. These other text elements are different stories from the main text story.

Getting a Range

You have several ways to get a Range. We have already considered several document-level collections such as Sentences, Words, and Characters that return Range objects. The most common way to get a Range is to use the Content property on the Document object. This returns a Range for the main document content.

A second way to get a Range object is to use the Range method. The Range method takes two optional object parameters passed by reference—a Start and an End position. You can pass an int value to Start and End representing the start and end position of the Range you want to get within the document. If you omit the Start parameter, it defaults to 0, which is the first position in the document. If you omit the End parameter, it defaults to the last position in the document.

Listing 8-27 shows an example of getting a Range object using the Document object's Content property and Range method. The Range retrieved has a start index of 0 and an end index of 9. As Figure 8-8 shows, the retrieved Range includes nonprinting paragraph marks.

Listing 8-27: A VSTO Word Document Customization That Works with a Range Object

```
private void ThisDocument_Startup(object sender, EventArgs e)
{
  Word.Range r = this.Content;

  r.Text = "This\nis\na\ntest.";

  object startIndex = 0;
  object endIndex = 9;

  Word.Range r2 = this.Range(ref startIndex, ref endIndex);
  r2.Select();
  string result = r2.Text;

  MessageBox.Show(result.Length.ToString());
  MessageBox.Show(r2.Text);
}
```

Another way to get a Range is by using the Document object's Story-Ranges collection. The StoryRanges collection enables you to get a Range that is not part of the main document, such as a Range within headers, footers, or endnotes. This collection has an index operator that takes a member of the WdStoryType enumeration that specifies what StoryRange you want to access. Listing 8-28 shows some code that iterates over the StoryRanges in the document and displays the type of each StoryRange.

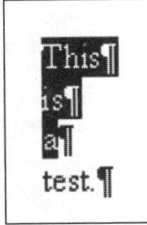

Figure 8-8: The result of running
Listing 8-27—a range of length 9,
including nonprinting paragraph

Listing 8-28: A VSTO Word Document Customization That Iterates over the StoryRanges in the Document

```
private void ThisDocument_Startup(object sender, EventArgs e)
{
  Range(ref missing, ref missing).InsertAfter("Hello world");

  Word.Range mainTextStory = this.StoryRanges[
    Word.WdStoryType.wdMainTextStory];

  foreach (Word.Range range in this.StoryRanges)
  {
    MessageBox.Show(String.Format(
      "Story range {0} has length {1}.",
      range.StoryType.ToString(), range.StoryLength));
  }
}
```

Another way to a get a Range is by getting it from the current selection. The Application object's Selection property returns the active selection in the active document as a Selection object. The Selection object has a Range property that returns a Range object that you can work with without affecting the selection (unless you change the Range in some way that forces the selection to reset such as by replacing the text in the selection). Before getting a Range from a Selection object, verify that the Selection contains a valid Range by checking the Selection object's Type property. For example, the user could have selected a shape in the document, in which case the Range would not be applicable when retrieved from Selection .Range. Listing 8-29 shows an example that checks the Selection.Type property before using Selection.Range. It also checks whether Selection is null, which is a bit of overkill for this example. This case would only arise if no documents are open.

Listing 8-29: A VSTO Word Document Customization That Gets a Range Object from a Selection Object

```
private void ThisDocument_Startup(object sender, EventArgs e)
{
  Range(ref missing, ref missing).InsertAfter("Hello world");
  Range(ref missing, ref missing).Select();

  Word.Selection s = this.Application.Selection;

  if (s != null)
```

```
  {
    if (s.Type == Word.WdSelectionType.wdSelectionNormal)
    {
      Word.Range r = s.Range;
      MessageBox.Show(r.Text);
    }
  }
}
```

Identifying a Range

A Range has several properties to help identify it. The Start and End property return the start and end character index of the Range. The Document property returns the document object the Range is associated with. The StoryType property returns a member of the WdStoryType enumeration identifying the StoryRange with which the Range is associated.

The get_Information method takes a parameter of type WdInformation and returns information as an `object` about the Range depending on the enumerated value that is passed to the method. Listing 8-30 shows an example of getting the information associated with a range. If you call get_Information on a Range with an enumerated type that is not applicable, get_Information will return –1 as a return value.

Listing 8-30: A VSTO Word Document Customization That Gets Information About a Range

```
private void ThisDocument_Startup(object sender, EventArgs e)
{
  Word.Range r = this.Range(ref missing, ref missing);

  r.Text = "This\nis\na\ntest.";

  object startIndex = 0;
  object endIndex = 9;

  Word.Range r2 = this.Range(ref startIndex, ref endIndex);
  r2.InsertAfter("\n");

  for (int i = 1; i < 27; i++)
  {
    GetInfo(r2, (Word.WdInformation)i);
  }
}

private void GetInfo(Word.Range r, Word.WdInformation info)
{
```

```
  string result = String.Format(
    "Range.Information({0}) returns {1}.\n",
    info.ToString(), r.get_Information(info));
  r.InsertAfter(result);
}
```

Changing a Range

Given a Range object, a number of properties and methods enable you to change what a Range refers to. A simple way to modify a Range object is to set the values of the Start and End properties. In addition, you can use several methods to change the Range in other ways.

The Expand method expands a Range so that it encompasses the units of the enumeration WdUnits: wdCharacter, wdWord, wdSentence, wdParagraph, wdSection, wdStory, wdCell, wdColumn, wdRow, or wdTable. The Expand method takes a range that only partially covers one of these units and expands it so that the range includes the unit specified.

For example, consider Figure 8-9. For this and subsequent figures, we have turned on Word's formatting marks (Office Menu > Word Options > Display > Show All Formatting Marks Checkbox) so that you can see clearly the spaces and any paragraph marks in the text. The original Range is shown in white text on a black background. The expanded Range after calling Expand with wdWord is shown by the larger border. The original Range only contained e qui—the last part of the word *The* and the first part of the word *quick*. Calling Expand with wdWord expands the range so that it covers complete words. The expanded Range after calling Expand contains The quick as well as the space after the word *quick*. Note that a second way to do this is to access the first element of the Words collection associated with the Range object.

Figure 8-10 shows another example where only three characters of a word are selected. Calling Expand with wdWord expands the Range so that it covers the complete word *quick* as well as the space after the word *quick*.

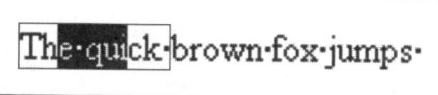

Figure 8-9: Result of calling Expand(WdUnits.wdWord) or Words(1) on a Range.

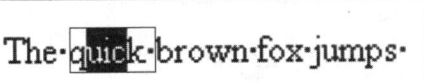

Figure 8-10: Result of calling Expand(WdUnits.wdWord) or Words(1) on a Range.

Note that calling Expand repeatedly on a Range passing wdWord does not expand the Range to cover additional words. After a Range no longer contains any partial words, calling Expand with wdWord has no effect. It also follows that a Range that does not start or end with any partial words to start with will not be changed when you call Expand and pass wdWord. This applies to the other members of the WdUnits enumeration. For example, when a Range does not contain any partial sentences, calling Expand with wdSentence has no effect.

Figure 8-11 shows an example of calling Expand passing wdSentence. The original Range contains parts of two sentences. The result of calling Expand is that two complete sentences are made part of the Range. Note that a second way to do this is to access the first element of the Sentences collection associated with the Range object.

Figure 8-12 shows another example of calling Expand passing wd-Sentence. The original Range contains just dog. Expanding the Range adds the rest of the sentence plus the spaces after the sentence.

The Expand method can change both the start and the end of a Range. The EndOf method works in a similar way to the Expand method but only changes the end of a Range. The EndOf method takes by reference two optional parameters of type object: Unit and Extend. The Unit parameter can be passed a member of the WdUnits enumeration. The Extend parameter

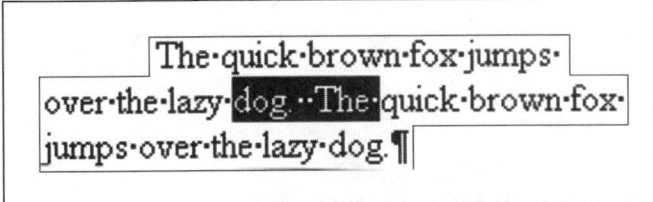

Figure 8-11: Result of calling Expand(WdUnits.wdSentence) or Sentences(1) on a Range.

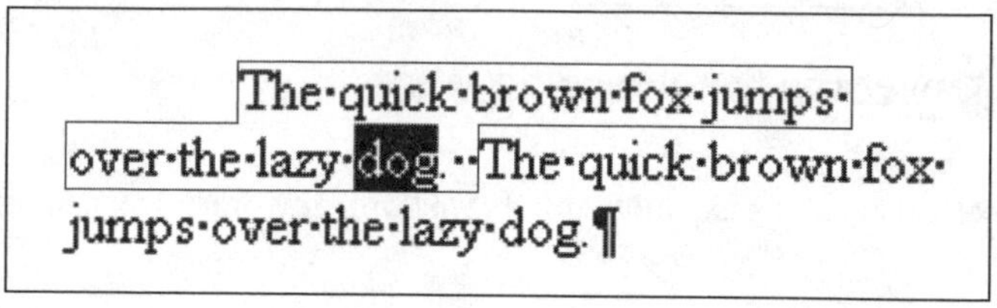

The·quick·brown·fox·jumps·
over·the·lazy·dog.··The·quick·brown·fox·
jumps·over·the·lazy·dog.¶

Figure 8-12: Result of calling Expand(WdUnits.wdSentence) or Sentences(1) on a Range.

can be passed a member of the WdMovementType enumeration: `wdMove` or `wdExtend`. If you pass `wdExtend`, the EndOf method acts like the Expand method would if it were not allowed to change the start of a Range. Figure 8-13 shows an example of calling EndOf passing `wdWord` and `wdExtend`. It expands the Range to cover the partial word at the end of the Range but does not expand to cover the partial word at the beginning of the Range.

If you pass `wdMove` for the second parameter (which is the default if you omit the parameter), EndOf returns a Range whose start and end is equal—effectively returning you an insertion point at the end of the expansion. Figure 8-14 shows a Range that initially partially covers two words. Calling EndOf on this Range and passing `wdMove` for the second parameter yields a Range whose start and end is 10—at the end of the second word.

The·quick·brown·fox·jumps·

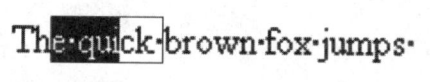

Figure 8-13: Result of calling EndOf(WdUnits.wdWord, WdMovementType.wdExtend) on a Range.

The·quick·brown·fox·jumps·

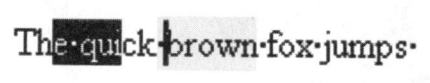

Figure 8-14: Result of calling EndOf(WdUnits.wdWord, WdMovementType.wdMove) on a Range.

The StartOf method works like the EndOf method but only changes the start of the range. The StartOf method takes by reference two optional parameters of type `object`: `Unit` and `Extend`. The `Unit` parameter can be passed a member of the WdUnits enumeration. The Extend parameter can be passed a member of the WdMovementType enumeration: `wdMove` or `wd-Extend`. If you pass `wdExtend`, the StartOf method acts like the Expand method would if it were not allowed to change the end of a range. Figure 8-15 shows an example of calling StartOf passing `wdWord` and `wdExtend`. It expands the Range to cover the partial word at the beginning of the Range but does not expand to cover the partial word at the end of the Range.

As with EndOf, the StartOf method when passed `wdMove` for the second parameter returns a Range whose start and end is equal—effectively returning you an insertion point at the beginning of the expansion. Figure 8-16 shows a Range containing a word at the end of a sentence. Calling StartOf and passing `wdSentence` and `wdMove` yields a Range where start and end are 0—effectively an insertion point at the beginning of the sentence.

Moving a Range

The Move method can be called repeatedly to move a Range by WdUnit through the document. It does not expand the Range, but instead moves

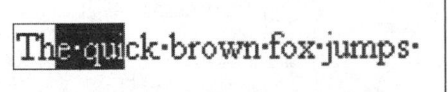

Figure 8-15: Result of calling StartOf(WdUnits.wdWord, WdMovementType.wdExtend) on a Range.

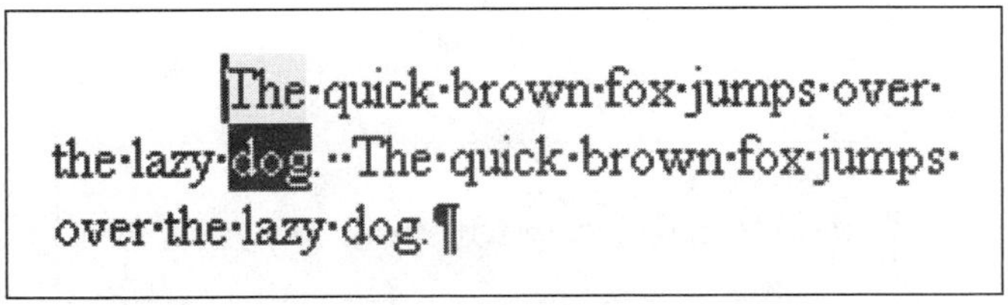

Figure 8-16: Result of calling StartOf(WdUnits.wdSentence, WdMovementType.wdMove) on a Range.

the Range, creating a Range whose start and end are equal. The Move method takes by reference optional `Unit` and `Count` parameters of type `object`. For `Unit`, you pass the member of the WdUnit enumeration that you want to move by. The default value of `Unit` is `wdCharacter`. For Count, you pass a positive or negative `int` specifying how many units you want to move forward or backward. The Move method returns the number of units by which the Range was moved or returns 0 if the Range was not moved. Figure 8-17 shows an example of calling Move passing `wdWord` and 1. Figure 8-18 shows an example of calling Move passing `wdWord` and –1. In the first case, the Range moves to the start of the next word. In the latter case, the Range moves to the beginning of the partially selected word.

The Next method works like Move when passed a positive count. Instead of modifying the Range directly, it returns a new Range that would be the result after calling Move. The Previous method works like Move when passed a negative count and also returns a new Range instead of modifying the existing Range. In the case where the Move method would have returned 0 because the Move was not possible, Next and Previous return a `null` Range.

The MoveUntil method takes a required `object` by reference parameter to which you can pass a `string` containing the characters that you want to find. It takes a second optional `object` parameter by reference to which

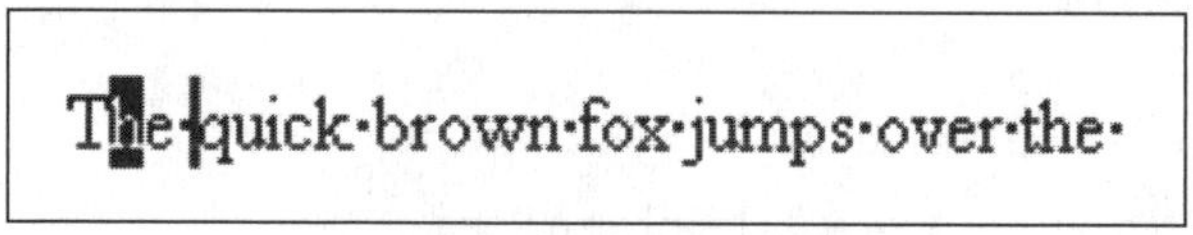

Figure 8-17: Result of calling Move(WdUnits.wdWord, 1) on a Range containing *h* from *The*.

Figure 8-18: Result of calling Move(WdUnits.wdWord, -1) on a Range containing *h* from *The*.

you can pass the number of characters after the Range to search. If Move-Until cannot find a specified character within the number of characters you pass, it will not change the Range. You can pass a negative number of characters to search the characters before the range. You can also pass to the second optional `object` parameter the constant `WdConstants.wdForward` or `WdConstants.wdBackward` to specify to search forward or backward without specifying a limit on the number of characters to search.

Figure 8-19 shows the result of calling MoveUntil passing `"abc"` as the `string` and `WdConstants.wdForward` for the second parameter. It searches forward until it finds either character *a*, *b*, or *c*. The first of those it finds is the *c* in the word *quick*. It sets the start and end of the Range to 7.

Range has a MoveStart and MoveUntilStart method that work like Move and MoveUntil but only affect the start position of the Range unless the start is moved forward to a position beyond the end, in which case Start and End are set to the same value. Similarly, Range has a MoveEnd and MoveUntilEnd method that work like Move and MoveUntil but only affect the end position of the Range.

The SetRange method takes a `Start` and `End` parameter as an `int` to set the start and end position of the Range in characters. Using the SetRange is the equivalent of setting the Start and End properties on Range.

A final property that is worth discussing when working with ranges is the Duplicate property. If you have a variable set to a Range object and you declare another Range variable and set it to the first Range object, you now have two variables that are both referring to the same range and setting properties on the one variable will affect the other. If the behavior you want is two separate ranges that can be manipulated independently from one another, set your second range variable to the Duplicate property of the first Range object.

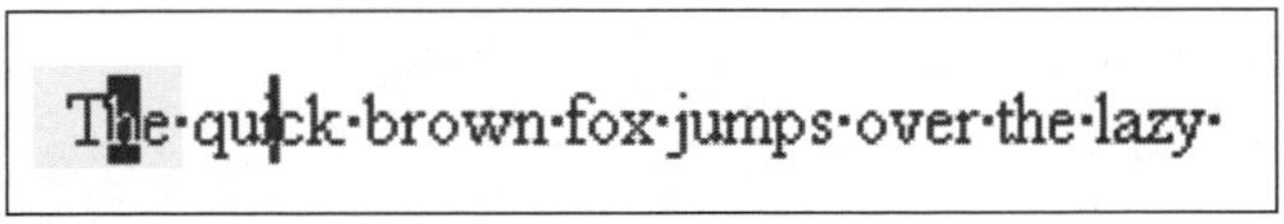

Figure 8-19: Result of calling MoveUntil("abc", WdConstants.wdForward) on a Range containing *h* from *The*.

Ranges and Stories

Given a Range, you can expand the range to include the full story associated with the Range using the WholeStory method. Some stories are split into multiple linked text elements in a document (text box stories can be linked, and header and footer stories can be linked), so calling WholeStory cannot give you each of the multiple linked text elements. For these cases, you can use the NextStoryRange property to get the next linked story of the same type.

Navigating a Range

Earlier in this chapter, you read about the Browser object, which lets you access the same functionality that is available in the browser control shown in Figure 8-2 earlier in this chapter. The Browser object enables you to easily go to the next element of a particular type in a document such as the next bookmark, comment, or field. However, the Browser object affects the selection in the document, which is often undesirable.

To go to the next element of a particular type without affecting the selection, you can use the GoTo method of the Range object. GoTo does not affect the Range object it is called on but instead returns a new Range object that represents the resulting Range after calling GoTo. The GoTo method takes by reference four optional `object` parameters. The first parameter, the `What` parameter, can be passed a member of the WdGoToItem enumeration:

- wdGoToBookmark
- wdGoToComment
- wdGoToEndnote
- wdGoToEquation
- wdGoToField
- wdGoToFootnote
- wdGoToGrammaticalError
- wdGoToGraphic
- wdGoToHeading
- wdGoToLine
- wdGoToObject

- wdGoToPage
- wdGoToPercent
- wdGoToProofreadingError
- wdGoToRevision
- wdGoToSection
- wdGoToTable

The second parameter, the Which parameter, can be passed a member of the WdGoToDirection enumeration: wdGoToAbsolute, wdGoToFirst, wdGoTo-Last, wdGoToNext, wdGoToPrevious, or wdGoToRelative. The wdGoToAbsolute value can be used to go to the n-th item of the type specified by the What parameter.

The third parameter, the Count parameter, is passed the number of the item to get and is affected by the second parameter. For example, if What is passed wdGoToLine and Count is passed 1, then depending on the Which parameter, GoTo could go to the next line after the Range (wdGoToNext) or the first line in the document (wdGoToAbsolute) or the line previous to the current Range (wdGoToPrevious).

The fourth parameter, the Name parameter, can be passed a name if the What argument specifies an element identifiable by name: wdGoToBookmark, wdGoToComment, or wdGoToField.

GoToNext and GoToPrevious are simpler versions of the GoTo method that only take the What parameter and go to the next or previous instance of the type of object specified by the What parameter.

Listing 8-31 shows an example of using the GoTo method on a Range to navigate through the pages in a document and display the first sentence on each page. We also use get_Information to get the page count and Expand to expand the collapsed Range returned by GoTo to include the first sentence on the page.

Listing 8-31: A VSTO Word Document Customization That Uses the GoTo Method

```
private void ThisDocument_Startup(object sender, EventArgs e)
{
    // Generate some random text in the document.
    Word.Range r = Range(ref missing, ref missing);
    System.Text.StringBuilder builder = new
```

```
    System.Text.StringBuilder();
Random rand = new Random();

for (int i = 0; i < 200; i++)
{
  builder.AppendLine(rand.NextDouble().ToString());
}

r.Text = builder.ToString();
int maxPage = (int)r.get_Information(
  Word.WdInformation.wdNumberOfPagesInDocument);

// GoTo to navigate the pages
for (int page = 1; page <= maxPage; page++)
{
  object what = Word.WdGoToItem.wdGoToPage;
  object which = Word.WdGoToDirection.wdGoToAbsolute;
  object count = page;
  object sentence = Word.WdUnits.wdSentence;

  Word.Range r2 = r.GoTo(ref what, ref which,
    ref count, ref missing);
  r2.Expand(ref sentence);

  MessageBox.Show(String.Format(
    "First sentence is {0} starting at position {1}.",
    r2.Text, r2.Start));
}
}
```

Collapsing a Range

We have already mentioned several times the concept of a collapsed Range—a Range whose start and end is equal. The Collapse method takes a Range and collapses it. It takes by reference an optional parameter Direction of type object. You can pass a member of the WdCollapse-Direction enumeration: wdCollapseEnd, which makes Start equal to End, or wdCollapseStart, which makes End equal to Start. If you omit the Direction parameter, the default is wdCollapseStart.

Getting Text from a Range

The Text property returns a string containing the text in the Range. The behavior of the Text property can be changed by using the TextRetrieval-Mode property, which returns a TextRetrievalMode object. Setting the

TextRetrievalMode object's IncludeFieldCodes property to true makes it so the Text property returns field codes. The default is the setting of the Field Codes check box in the View page of the Options dialog box.

Setting the TextRetrievalMode object's IncludeHiddenText property to true makes it so the Text property returns hidden text in the document. The default is the setting of the Hidden Text check box in the View page of the Options dialog box.

The TextRetrievalMode object's ViewType property can also affect what the Text property returns. The ViewType property can be set to a member of the WdViewType enumeration: wdMasterView, wdNormalView, wdOutlineView, wdPrintPreview, wdPrintView, wdReadingView, or wdWebView. When set to wdOutlineView, for example, Text only returns the text visible in outline view.

Listing 8-32 shows the creation of some text in a document that includes a field and some hidden text. The Text property is then used in several ways, showing the effect of changing TextRetrievalMode settings.

Listing 8-32: A VSTO Word Document Customization That Modifies TextRetrievalMode Settings

```
private void ThisDocument_Startup(object sender, EventArgs e)
{
  // Generate some random text in the document.
  Word.Range r = Range(ref missing, ref missing);
  r.Text = "Hello ";
  object collapseDirection =
    Word.WdCollapseDirection.wdCollapseEnd;
  object date = Word.WdFieldType.wdFieldDate;

  // Add a field
  r.Collapse(ref collapseDirection);
  r.Fields.Add(r, ref date, ref missing, ref missing);

  // Hide some text
  r.SetRange(1,2);
  r.Font.Hidden = 1;

  r = Range(ref missing, ref missing);
  r.TextRetrievalMode.IncludeFieldCodes = false;
  r.TextRetrievalMode.IncludeHiddenText = false;

  MessageBox.Show(r.Text);
  r.TextRetrievalMode.IncludeFieldCodes = true;
```

```
      MessageBox.Show(r.Text);
      r.TextRetrievalMode.IncludeHiddenText = true;
      MessageBox.Show(r.Text);
}
```

Setting the Text in a Range

Setting the Text property to a string value is the most basic way to set text in a Range. Setting the Text property replaces the text in the Range with the string value and changes the end of the Range so the start and end cover the length of the new string. If the Range is collapsed, setting the Text property does not replace any existing text, but it inserts the new string at the location of the Range and changes the end of the Range so that the start and end cover the length of the new string.

Setting the Text property only changes the characters of the Range, not the formatting. If you have one Range formatted a particular way and a second Range that you want to copy both the text of the first Range and its formatting to, you can use the FormattedText property, which takes a Range. Listing 8-33 shows an example of using the FormattedText property to take one Range that is formatted and set the text and formatting of a second Range to the first.

Listing 8-33: A VSTO Word Document Customization That Uses FormattedText to Set Text and Formatting

```
private void ThisDocument_Startup(object sender, EventArgs e)
{
  Word.Range r = Range(ref missing, ref missing);
  r.Text = "Hello Hello Happy";
  object start1 = 0;
  object end1 = 5;
  r = Range(ref start1, ref end1);
  r.Bold = 1;

  object start2 = 12;
  object end2 = 17;
  Word.Range r2 = Range(ref start2, ref end2);
  r2.FormattedText = r;
}
```

Each time you set the Text property, it replaces the existing Range and changes the end of the Range so that the start and end cover the new string. The InsertAfter method lets you add text immediately after the Range without replacing the existing Range. The InsertAfter method takes a string for the text you want to insert after the Range. InsertAfter changes the end of the Range so that the start and end cover the old Range and the string you have added after the Range.

The InsertBefore method lets you add text immediately before the Range without replacing the existing Range. The InsertBefore method takes a string for the text you want to insert before the Range. InsertBefore changes the end of the Range so that the start and end cover the old Range and the string you have added before the Range.

Inserting Nonprinting Characters and Breaks

You have several ways to insert nonprinting characters such as tabs and paragraph marks. A simple way is to use escaped string literals. In a C# string, you can specify a tab with the character sequence \t. You can specify a paragraph mark (a new line) by using either \n or \r. Listing 8-34 shows some examples of using escaped string literals to insert nonprinting characters. Figure 8-20 shows the result of running Listing 8-34 with non-printing characters showing.

Listing 8-34: A VSTO Word Document Customization That Uses Escaped String Literals and the Text Property

```
private void ThisDocument_Startup(object sender, EventArgs e)
{
  Word.Range r = Range(ref missing, ref missing);
  r.Text = "Item\tName\n";
  r.InsertAfter("111\t1/4\" pipe\n");
  r.InsertAfter("112\t1/2\" pipe\n");
  r.InsertAfter("\n\n");
  r.InsertAfter("File path: c:\\Temp\\Doc1.docx");
}
```

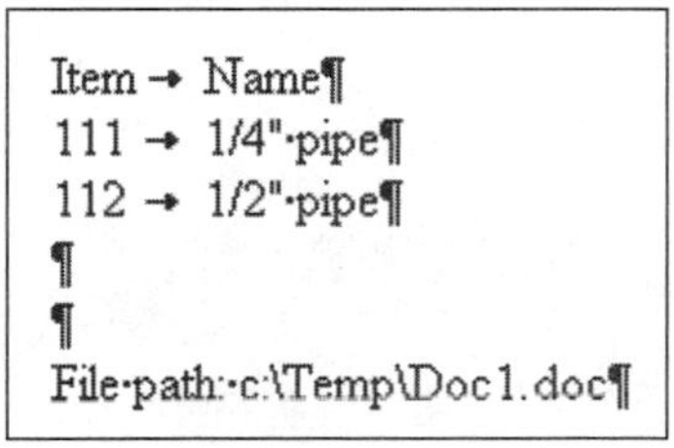

Item → Name¶
111 → 1/4"·pipe¶
112 → 1/2"·pipe¶
¶
¶
File·path:·c:\Temp\Doc1.doc¶

Figure 8-20: Result of running Listing 8-34.

It is also possible to insert paragraphs using the InsertParagraph method. The InsertParagraph method inserts a new paragraph at the start position of the Range, replacing the current Range. It changes the Range so that it covers the start position and the newly inserted paragraph mark. InsertParagraph is the equivalent of setting the Text property to \n. Insert-ParagraphBefore inserts a new paragraph at the start position of the Range and changes the end of the Range to expand it to cover the old Range and the newly inserted paragraph mark. InsertParagraphBefore is the equivalent of calling the InsertBefore method and passing \n. InsertParagraph-After is the equivalent of calling the InsertAfter method and passing \n.

Figure 8-21 shows some additional kinds of breaks that a user can insert into a document using the Breaks drop down from the Page Layout tab. These types of breaks can be inserted programmatically using Range's InsertBreak method. The InsertBreak method takes by reference an optional parameter of type `object` to which you can pass a member of the WdBreakType enumeration. The members of the WdBreakType enumeration correspond to the breaks in Figure 8-21: `wdPageBreak`, `wdColumn-`

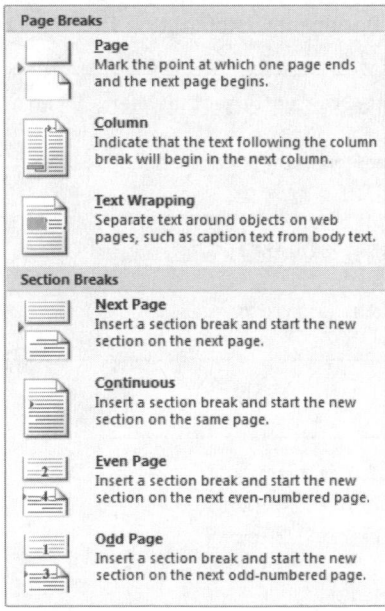

Figure 8-21: The Breaks drop-down
list from the Page Layout tab.

Break, wdTextWrappingBreak, wdSectionBreakNextPage, wdSectionBreak-Continuous, wdSectionBreakEvenPage, or wdSectionBreakOddPage. Insert-Break works like setting the Text property would—the current Range is replaced with the break, or if the Range is collapsed, the break is inserted at the position of the Range.

Working with Formatting

The Font property returns a Font object that controls font settings for the Range. Many of the properties associated with Font, such as the Bold property, that you would expect to be of type bool are instead of type int. This is because a particular Range could be all bold, partially bold, or not bold, for example. If the Range is partially bold, it returns WdConstants.wdUndefined. If the Range is not bold, it returns a 0. If the Range is all bold, it returns a –1; this is another example where the COM implementation of the Word OM peeks through because –1 corresponds to a true value in COM object models. This can cause confusion because the bool value for true in .NET when cast to an integer is 1, not –1. So when checking the value of these properties, remember to not make the mistake of comparing to 1 or the bool value of true cast to an int because this will cause your code to fail to detect the state properly. Instead, always compare to 0 or the bool value of false cast to an int.

Table 8-14 lists several of the most frequently used properties associated with the Font object.

Another way to set the formatting of a Range is to use the set_Style method. The set_Style method takes by reference an object parameter. You can pass a string representing the name of the style you want to use to format the Range.

Listing 8-35 shows some formatting of a Range using Font properties and the set_Style method. Figure 8-22 shows the document created by Listing 8-35. It is a best practice to use styles whenever you can in your Word development as it makes your code faster, easier to write and read, and documents created using styles are easier to maintain. Note also that it is a best practice to use the Word.WdBuiltinStyle enumeration to specify a style rather than a string (like "Heading 1") as the latter won't work when run in a non-English locale.

TABLE 8-14:   Frequently Used Properties Associated with the Font Object

Property Name	Type	What It Does
AllCaps	int	Set to –1 to format the font as all capital letters.
Bold	int	Set to –1 to format the font as bold.
Color	WdColor	Set to a member of the WdColor enumeration to set the color of the font.
ColorIndex	WdColorIndex	Set to a member of the WdColorIndex enumeration to set the color of the font.
Hidden	int	Set to –1 to hide the text of the Range.
Italic	int	Set to –1 to format the font as italic.
Name	string	Set to a `string` representing the name of the font.
Size	float	Set to a size in points.
SmallCaps	int	Set to –1 to format the font as small caps.
Underline	WdUnderline	Set to a member of the WdUnderline enumeration to set the underline format of the font.

Listing 8-35: A VSTO Word Document Customization That Formats a Range

```
private void ThisDocument_Startup(object sender, EventArgs e)
{
  object collapseEnd = Word.WdCollapseDirection.wdCollapseEnd;
  Word.Range r = Range(ref missing, ref missing);
  r.Text = "Item\tName\n";
  r.Font.Name = "Verdana";
  r.Font.Size = 20.0F;

  r.Collapse(ref collapseEnd);
  r.InsertAfter("111\t1/4\" pipe\n");
  r.HighlightColorIndex = Word.WdColorIndex.wdGray25;
  r.Italic = -1;
  r.Font.Size = 10.0F;
  r.Font.Name = "Times New Roman";
```

```
    r.Collapse(ref collapseEnd);
    r.InsertAfter("112\t1/2\" pipe\n");
    r.Shading.BackgroundPatternColor = Word.WdColor.wdColorBlack;
    r.Font.Color = Word.WdColor.wdColorWhite;
    r.Font.Size = 10.0F;
    r.Font.SmallCaps = -1;
    r.Font.Name = "Verdana";

    r.Collapse(ref collapseEnd);
    r.InsertAfter("This should be a heading.");
    object style = Word.WdBuiltinStyle.wdStyleHeading1;
    r.set_Style(ref style);
}
```

Figure 8-22: Result of running Listing 8-35.

Find and Replace

The Find property returns a Find object that you can use to search a Range. The Find object allows you to set options similar to the ones you find in Word's Find dialog box. The Find object's Text property can be set to the `string` you want to search for. The Find object's MatchWholeWord property can be set to `false` to allow matching of the string against a partial word in the Range. After the find options have been set up, the Find object's Execute method executes the find against the Range. Execute takes a number of optional parameters by reference—some of which correspond to properties on the Find object. So you have an option of either presetting Find properties and then calling Execute and omitting the optional parameters by passing `ref missing`, or you can skip presetting Find properties and pass optional parameters to the Execute method. In Listing 8-35, we take the former approach. Execute returns `true` if it is able to find the text specified and modifies the Range so that it covers the found text. In Listing 8-36, calling Execute modifies the Range to have a start of 20 and an end of 24.

Listing 8-36: A VSTO Word Document Customization That Uses the Find Object

```csharp
private void ThisDocument_Startup(object sender, EventArgs e)
{
  Word.Range r = Range(ref missing, ref missing);
  r.Text = "The quick brown fox jumped over the lazy dog.";

  Word.Find f = r.Find;
  f.Text = "jump";
  f.MatchWholeWord = false;

  if (f.Execute(ref missing, ref missing, ref missing,
        ref missing, ref missing, ref missing, ref missing,
        ref missing, ref missing, ref missing, ref missing,
        ref missing, ref missing, ref missing, ref missing))
  {
    MessageBox.Show(String.Format(
      "Found {0} at position {1},{2}.",
      f.Text, r.Start, r.End));
  }
}
```

It is also possible to iterate over multiple found items using the Find object's Found property instead of checking the return value of Execute each time. Listing 8-37 shows an example of iterating over every occurrence of the string "jump" in a document. This example bolds every instance of jump that it finds in the document.

Listing 8-37: A VSTO Word Document Customization That Uses the Find Object's Found Property to Iterate over Found Items

```csharp
private void ThisDocument_Startup(object sender, EventArgs e)
{
  Word.Range r = Range(ref missing, ref missing);
  r.Text = "Jumping lizards! Jump on down to Mr. Jumpkin's jumpin' trampoline store.";

  Word.Find f = r.Find;
  f.Text = "jump";
  f.MatchWholeWord = false;

  f.Execute(ref missing, ref missing, ref missing,
    ref missing, ref missing, ref missing, ref missing,
    ref missing, ref missing, ref missing, ref missing,
    ref missing, ref missing,ref missing, ref missing);

  while (f.Found)
  {
    MessageBox.Show(String.Format(
```

```
         "Found {0} at position {1},{2}.",
         f.Text, r.Start, r.End));

      r.Font.Bold = -1;

      f.Execute(ref missing, ref missing, ref missing,
         ref missing, ref missing, ref missing, ref missing,
         ref missing, ref missing, ref missing, ref missing,
         ref missing, ref missing, ref missing, ref missing);
   }
}
```

The Find object has a Replacement property that returns a Replacement object, which allows you to set options for doing a find and replace. The Replacement object's Text property lets you set the text you want to use to replace found text with. In addition, to perform a replacement, you must pass a member of the WdReplace enumeration to the `Replace` parameter of the Execute method (the eleventh optional parameter). You can pass `wdReplaceAll` to replace all found occurrences or `wdReplaceOne` to replace the first found occurrence. In Listing 8-38, we use the Replacement.Text property to set the replace string, and then call Execute passing `wdReplaceAll` to the Replace parameter.

Listing 8-38: A VSTO Word Document Customization That Performs a Replace

```
private void ThisDocument_Startup(object sender, EventArgs e)
{
  Word.Range r = Range(ref missing, ref missing);
  r.Text = "The quick brown fox jumped over the lazy dog.";

  Word.Find f = r.Find;
  f.Text = "jump";
  f.MatchWholeWord = false;
  f.Replacement.Text = "leap";

  object replace = Word.WdReplace.wdReplaceAll;
  if (f.Execute(ref missing, ref missing, ref missing,
    ref missing, ref missing, ref missing, ref missing,
    ref missing, ref missing, ref missing, ref replace,
    ref missing, ref missing, ref missing, ref missing))
  {
    MessageBox.Show(String.Format(
      "Replaced {0} at position {1},{2}.",
      f.Text, r.Start, r.End));
  }
}
```

Working with Bookmarks

Bookmarks provide you a way to name and keep track of a particular Range. The user can even edit the Range and the modified Range will still be accessible by its name unless the user completely deletes the Range.

To create and manage bookmarks, you can use Word's Bookmark command in the Insert tab. You can select some text in the document, choose Bookmark from the Insert tab, give the range of text a name, and then click the Add button to add a bookmark, as shown in Figure 8-23. Existing bookmarks can be selected and navigated to using the Go To button. They can also be removed using the Delete button.

VSTO provides some additional tools for creating bookmarks in document projects. For example, you can drag a bookmark control from the Visual Studio control toolbox to the Word document to create a bookmark. VSTO also adds any bookmarks in the document as named class member variables of the ThisDocument class. VSTO support for bookmarks is described in more detail in Chapter 12, "The VSTO Programming Model."

If you check the Show Bookmarks check box in the Advanced page of the Word Options dialog box, Word shows gray brackets around any bookmarks defined in your document. Figure 8-24 shows the brackets Word displays. Here we have created a bookmark that includes the word *brown* and the space after *brown*.

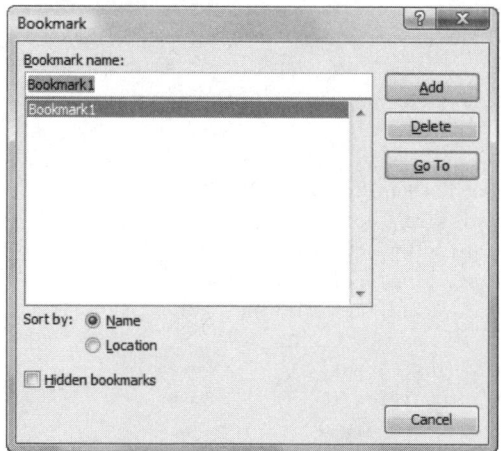

Figure 8-23: The Bookmark dialog box.

Figure 8-24: Result of checking the Show Bookmarks check box in the Advanced page of Word's Options dialog box.

To programmatically create and manage bookmarks, you can use the Document object's Bookmarks property or the Range object's Bookmarks property. Both return a Bookmarks collection; the former returns all the bookmarks defined in the document, the latter returns just the bookmarks defined within the Range you are working with. Also, the Document object's Bookmarks property returns bookmarks in alphabetical order by their name whereas the Range object's Bookmarks property returns bookmarks in the order they appear within the range. So if you want to loop through the bookmarks in the document in alphabetical order, use Document.Bookmarks, and if you want to loop through the bookmarks in the document in the order they appear use Document.Content.Bookmarks.

The Bookmarks collection's Add method adds a bookmark. It takes a required `Name` parameter to which you pass a `string` representing the name you want to use for the bookmark. The `Name` parameter must be one word. The Add method also takes by reference an optional `object` parameter to which you pass the Range you want to create a bookmark for. The method returns the newly added Bookmark object.

The Bookmarks collection's Exists method takes a `string` representing the name of a bookmark and returns a `bool` value indicating whether the bookmark exists in the document. The get_Item method allows you to get to a bookmark given its name or 1-based index in the Bookmarks collection. The get_Item method takes by reference an `object` parameter that can be set to a `string` representing the name of the bookmark or the 1-based index. Given a Bookmark object, you can get the Range it refers to by using the Bookmark object's Range property.

Listing 8-39 shows an example of working with bookmarks. It first creates several bookmarks, and then gets them again using the get_Item method.

Listing 8-39: A VSTO Word Document Customization That Works with Bookmarks

```
private void ThisDocument_Startup(object sender, EventArgs e)
{
  object collapseEnd = Word.WdCollapseDirection.wdCollapseEnd;
  Word.Range r = Range(ref missing, ref missing);
  r.Text = "The quick brown fox ";
  object range1 = r;
  this.Bookmarks.Add("FirstHalf", ref range1);

  r.Collapse(ref collapseEnd);
  r.Text = "jumped over the lazy dog.";
  object range2 = r;
  this.Bookmarks.Add("SecondHalf", ref range2);

  if (this.Bookmarks.Exists("FirstHalf") == true)
  {
    MessageBox.Show("FirstHalf exists");
  }

  object firstHalfName = "FirstHalf";
  Word.Bookmark b = this.Bookmarks.get_Item(ref firstHalfName);
  MessageBox.Show(String.Format(
    "FirstHalf starts at {0} and ends at {1}.",
    b.Range.Start, b.Range.End));
}
```

Bookmarks are easily deleted from the document. For example, setting the Text property of the Range associated with a bookmark replaces the Range and in the process deletes the bookmark associated with the Range. VSTO document projects extend Bookmark and add some additional functionality to preserve the bookmark even when you set the Text property. For more information on VSTO document project support for bookmarks and the bookmark control, see Chapter 12, "The VSTO Programming Model." Also, in Word 2007 you now have the option to use content controls which tend to be much more stable than bookmarks.

Working with Tables

As previously mentioned, both the Document and Range object have a Tables property that returns the Tables collection, which contains tables in the Document or Range. To add a Table, you can use the Tables collection's Add method, which takes a Range where you want to add the table, the number of rows and number of columns in the table, and two optional `object` parameters passed by reference that specify the auto-fit behavior of the table. The Add method returns the newly added table.

Listing 8-40 shows code that adds and populates a small table. It uses the returned Table object's Rows property to get the Rows collection. It uses the `index` operator on the Rows collection to get an individual Row object. It then uses the Row object's Cells property to get the Cells collection. It uses the `index` operator on the Cells collection to get to an individual Cell object. Finally, it uses the Cell object's Range property to get a Range corresponding to the Cell object and uses the Range object's Text property to set the value of the cell.

Listing 8-40: A VSTO Word Document Customization That Creates and Populates a Simple Table

```
private void ThisDocument_Startup(object sender, EventArgs e)
{
  Word.Range r = Range(ref missing, ref missing);
  Word.Table t = r.Tables.Add(r, 5, 5, ref missing, ref missing);

  for (int i = 1; i <= 5; i++)
  {
    for (int j = 1; j <= 5; j++)
    {
      t.Rows[i].Cells[j].Range.Text = String.Format(
        "{0}, {1}", i, j);
    }
  }
}
```

The Table object's Cell method provides an easier way of getting to a Cell. The Cell method takes an `int` row and column parameter and returns a Cell object. Listing 8-41 shows the use of the Cell method along with the use of several auto-formatting techniques as we create a simple multiplication table. The Columns object's AutoFit method is used to resize the column widths to fit the contents of the cells. The Table object's set_Style method takes an `object` by reference that is set to the name of a table style as found in the Table AutoFormat dialog box. The Table object's ApplyStyleLastRow and ApplyStyleLastColumn properties are set to `false` in Listing 8-41 to specify that no special style be applied to the last row or last column in the table.

Listing 8-41: A VSTO Word Document Customization That Creates a Multiplication Table

```csharp
private void ThisDocument_Startup(object sender, EventArgs e)
{
  Word.Range r = Range(ref missing, ref missing);
  Word.Table t = r.Tables.Add(r, 12, 12, ref missing,
    ref missing);

  for (int i = 1; i <= 12; i++)
  {
    for (int j = 1; j <= 12; j++)
    {
      Word.Cell c = t.Cell(i,j);
      if (i == 1 && j == 1)
      {
        c.Range.Text = "X";
      }
      else if (i == 1)
      {
        c.Range.Text = j.ToString();
      }
      else if (j == 1)
      {
        c.Range.Text = i.ToString();
      }
      else
      {
        int result = i * j;
        c.Range.Text = result.ToString();
      }
    }
  }

  t.Columns.AutoFit();
  object styleString = "Table Classic 2";
  t.set_Style(ref styleString);
  t.ApplyStyleLastRow = false;
  t.ApplyStyleLastColumn = false;
}
```

Working with Content Controls

As described in Chapter 7, "Working with Word Events," content controls can be inserted into a document to provide more structure and control— for example, when you have a section of the document that you want to allow the user to put a picture into or pick a value from a drop-down list. There are eight content controls available: rich text, plain text, picture, combo box, drop-down list, date picker, group, and building block gallery. These controls can be found in the Developer tab of Word's Ribbon. The developer tab isn't displayed by default in Word—to display it, choose Word Options from the Office menu, then select Show Developer tab in the Ribbon from the Popular tab of the Word Options dialog box.

Table 8-15 lists the key characteristics of the eight content control types. The Rich Text content control can contain text in multiple styles and can contain other content controls. This ability is also shared by the building block gallery and group content control. The other controls can only contain text in one style and can't contain other content controls.

TABLE 8-15: Key Characteristics of the Eight Content Control Types

Control	Key Characteristics
Rich Text	Can contain formatted text in multiple fonts and styles. It can also contain other content controls.
Plain Text	Can only contain text formatted to one font and style for the entire control. Cannot contain other content controls.
Picture	Can display pictures in any of the many formats that Word can understand. Cannot contain other content controls.
Combo Box	Can be set to arbitrary text or a value picked out of its drop-down list. Can only use one font and style for the entire control. Cannot contain other content controls.
Drop-Down List	Can only be set to a value picked out of its drop-down list. Can only use one font and style for the entire control. Cannot contain other content controls.
Date Picker	Can be set to arbitrary text or a date picked from its drop-down date picker. Can only contain text formatted to one font and style for the entire control. Cannot contain other content controls.
Building Block Gallery	Can contain formatted text in multiple fonts and styles. It can also contain other content controls. Can pick content out of a drop down that picks from existing galleries built into Word or provided out of a custom template.
Group	Can be used to group together content controls and other document content to protect it from editing or deletion.

Figure 8-25 shows a table created in Word that uses all eight content controls. To make it clear where the content controls are, we clicked on the Design Mode button in the Developer tag which turns on the display of the small titled tags around each content control. The tags show the title assigned to each content control (My Rich Text, My Plain Text, etc.). Also note in Figure 8-25 that a group content control has been used to group the document content in the left column of the table with the content controls. To create the group content control we selected the entire table and then clicked picked Group from the Group drop down in the Developer tab. If the user tries to edit the text in the left column, they will be prevented from doing so because of the use of the group content control. They will however be able to edit the content in the content controls. A group content control is an easy way to protect document content intermixed with editable content controls.

When your users are using a document like that shown in Figure 8-25, design mode will be turned off. However, one can still tell where the content controls are and what is supposed to be entered in them by using several techniques. When the user mouses over a content control area, it will be highlighted until the mouse leaves the content control area. You can also set a title to be displayed when the user clicks in the content area. Figure 8-26 shows the UI shown when a user clicks on a drop-down list content control. Note that the drop-down arrow is shown, and, in addition, a small border is displayed around the content control area. Also, a title is shown for the content control.

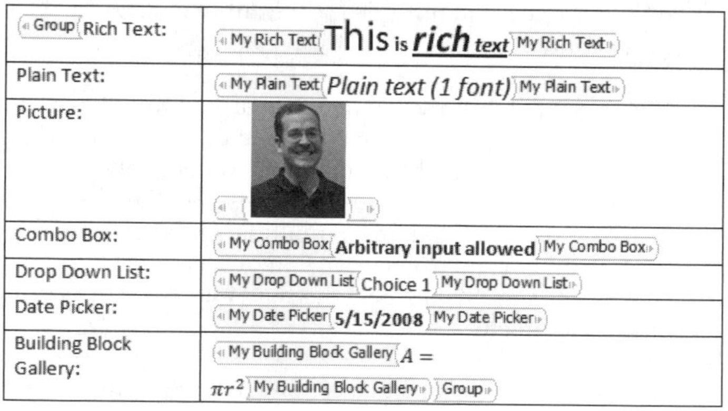

Group Rich Text:	My Rich Text This is ***rich** text* My Rich Text
Plain Text:	My Plain Text *Plain text (1 font)* My Plain Text
Picture:	
Combo Box:	My Combo Box **Arbitrary input allowed** My Combo Box
Drop Down List:	My Drop Down List Choice 1 My Drop Down List
Date Picker:	My Date Picker **5/15/2008** My Date Picker
Building Block Gallery:	My Building Block Gallery $A = \pi r^2$ My Building Block Gallery Group

Figure 8-25: An example of all eight content control types.

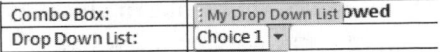

| Combo Box: | My Drop Down List owed |
| Drop Down List: | Choice 1 ▾ |

Figure 8-26: The UI shown when a user clicks a drop-down list content control.

By default the title is blank for a newly created content control. To set the title for a content control along with other key settings, click on the content control to select it, then click the Properties button in Word's developer tab. Figure 8-27 shows the Content Control Properties dialog box that is displayed for the drop-down list shown in Figure 8-26.

The General section of the Content Control Properties dialog box shows properties that are settable on all the content controls (except Group which only has one settable property—whether it can be deleted or not). These general properties include the Title that is displayed when the user clicks on the content control (by default this is blank), a Tag that can be used to identify the control programmatically, and the option to pick a document style to format the contents of the content control. Also common to all the content

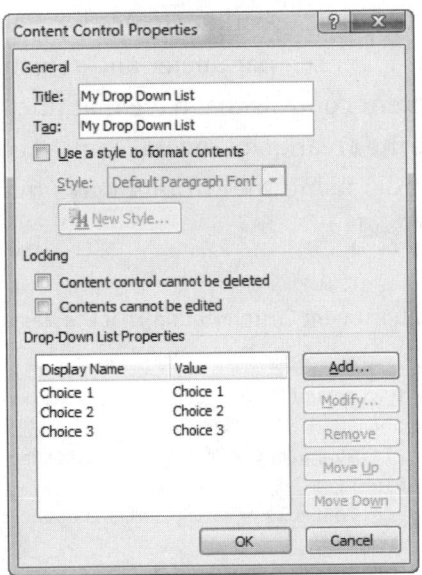

Figure 8-27: The Content Control Properties dialog box for a drop-down list.

controls are the properties in Locking which include whether the control can be deleted or edited. Finally, Figure 8-27 has an area to edit the drop-down list for the control—this is available for the combo box and drop-down list content controls.

Working with Content Controls Programmatically

The Word object model has a ContentControls property on the Document and Range object. This collection allows you add new content controls and iterate over content controls associated with the Document or Range the collection was obtained from.

You can create a new content control by using the ContentControls collection's Add method. This method takes a member of the WdContent-ControlType enumeration and an optional Range parameter by reference, which tells Word where to create the content control. If you omit the Range parameter, the content control will be added at the end of the Document or Range.

There are also several other ways to get a collection of ContentControls. The Document object's SelectContentControlsByTag takes a tag as a `string` parameter and returns a ContentControls collection with all content controls that have that tag. The Document object's SelectContentControls-ByTitle takes a title as a `string` parameter and returns a ContentControls collection with all content controls that have that title.

Listing 8-42 shows the creation of several content controls and then iterating over those controls using the various ways that a ContentControls collection can be retrieved.

Listing 8-42: A VSTO Word Document Customization That Creates and Iterates over Content Controls

```
private void ThisDocument_Startup(object sender, System.EventArgs e)
{
    Word.Range range = this.Range(ref missing, ref missing);
    range.Text = "This is a test.";
    Word.ContentControls docControls = this.ContentControls;

    object start = 5;
    object end = 7;
    range = this.Range(ref start, ref end);
```

```csharp
// Add date content control to end of document
Word.ContentControl control1 =
  docControls.Add(
  Word.WdContentControlType.wdContentControlDate,
  ref missing);
control1.Tag = "myTag";
control1.Title = "Today's Date";

// Add text content control to cover "is" range
object oRange = range;
Word.ContentControl control2 = docControls.Add(
  Word.WdContentControlType.wdContentControlText,
  ref oRange);
control2.Tag = "myTag2";
control2.Title = "Is Title";

foreach (Word.ContentControl item in docControls)
{
    MessageBox.Show(item.Title +
      " is in docControls collection");
}

Word.ContentControls rangeControls = range.ContentControls;
foreach (Word.ContentControl item in rangeControls)
{
    MessageBox.Show(item.Title +
      " is in rangeControls collection");
}

Word.ContentControls taggedControls =
  this.SelectContentControlsByTag("myTag");

foreach (Word.ContentControl item in taggedControls)
{
    MessageBox.Show(item.Title +
      " is in taggedControls collection");
}

Word.ContentControls titledControls =
  this.SelectContentControlsByTitle("Is Title");

foreach (Word.ContentControl item in titledControls)
{
    MessageBox.Show(item.Title +
      " is in titledControls collection");
}
}
```

Properties and Methods of Content Control

All eight content control types are represented by one object in the Word object model, the ContentControl object. Table 8-16 shows some of the most important properties on the ContentControl object. Note that some properties are only applicable to a particular content control type; for example, DropDownListEntries only applies to a drop-down list or combo box content control. VSTO extends the Word object model and defines eight specific types, one corresponding to each content control type. These more specific types only have properties applicable to the content control type they represent. These extensions are described in Chapter 12, "The VSTO Programming Model."

TABLE 8-16: Key Properties of the Content Control Object

Property Name	What It Does
DropDownListEntries	Returns a ContentControlListEntries collection which can be used to control what is displayed in the drop-down list for a combo box or drop-down list content control.
ID	Returns a unique identifier as a string for the content control.
LockContentControl	Set to true to prevent the content control from being deleted from the document.
Lock Contents	Set to true to prevent the contents of the content control from being edited.
MultiLine	Set to true to allow a rich text or plain text content control to span multiple lines.
ParentContentControl	Returns the parent ContentControl if the content control is nested in a parent content control.
Range	Returns a Range object for the contents of the content control.
Tag	Sets or gets the string tag value for the content control.

TABLE 8-16: Key Properties of the Content Control Object *(Continued)*

Property Name	What It Does
Temporary	If set to `true`, the content control will be removed from the document when the user edits the content control the first time. This applies only to rich text or text content controls.
Title	Sets or gets the `string` title for the content control.
Type	Gets or sets the type of the content control. Takes a member of the WdContentControlType enumeration. You can convert between content controls if they have the same characteristics as shown in Table 8-15.
XMLMapping	Configures mappings between content control and XML in the data store of the document.

Conclusion

This chapter explored some of the most important objects in the Word object model. We use many of these objects in the Word examples in subsequent chapters.

This chapter has described these objects as defined by the primary interop assemblies for Word. Be aware, however, that VSTO document-level projects extend some of these objects (Document, Bookmark, ContentControl, XML-Nodes, and XMLNode) to add some additional functionality, such as data binding support. Part III of this book, starting with Chapter 12, covers those extensions.

■ 9 ■
Programming Outlook

Ways to Customize Outlook

Outlook has an object model that consists of 158 objects. The object model has been greatly expanded in Outlook 2007 with more than 90 new objects and more than 4,000 properties and methods—more than double the size of the object model in Outlook 2003. With the expansion of the object model, there is no longer a need to use additional object models such as the Collaboration Data Objects (CDO) and Exchange Client Extensions. Therefore, this edition of the book no longer covers those additional object models.

Outlook has a larger number of events compared to the Word and Excel object models—more than 300 events. However, the large number of events is mainly due to 23 events that are duplicated on 16 Outlook objects.

The main way that you will integrate your code into Outlook is via add-ins. This model was originally designed to allow the integration of COM components written in Visual Basic 6, Visual Basic for Applications (VBA), C, or C++. However, through COM interop, a managed object can masquerade as a COM object and participate in the Outlook add-in model.

Automation Executable

As mentioned in Chapter 2, "Introduction to Office Solutions," you can start Outlook from a console application or Windows application and automate it from that external program. The problem with this approach before Outlook 2007 was that you could not add your automation executable to the exclusion list of the Outlook object model security guard.

The Outlook object model security guard prevents code from accessing sensitive parts of the Outlook object model such as the address book or the send mail functionality. Its purpose is to protect Outlook from code that might spread as an e-mail worm virus. Outlook has a mechanism to trust a particular installed add-in and let it bypass the Outlook object model guard that is discussed in Chapter 11, "Working with Outlook Objects."

Starting with Outlook 2007, automation executables can bypass the object model security guard if the machine that the automation executable is running on has antivirus software with up-to-date antivirus definitions running on it. The machine must also be running Windows XP SP2 or later and a feature called Windows Security Center must be present. Note that Windows Server SKUs do not support this feature. The antivirus software must also support registering with the Windows Security Center feature.

Add-Ins

When building add-ins for Outlook, you have two choices: You can either build a COM add-in (sometimes called a Shared add-in) or a VSTO Outlook add-in. A VSTO Outlook add-in solves many of the problems associated with COM add-in development and is the preferred model for Outlook 2007 add-in development. The only time you would want to consider building a COM add-in instead is if you need to target versions of Outlook that are older than Outlook 2003.

Outlook has a COM add-ins dialog box that lets users enable and disable add-ins. Both VSTO add-ins and COM add-ins appear in the COM Add-Ins dialog box. To access the COM Add-Ins dialog box, you must follow these steps:

1. Choose Tools > Trust Center to bring up the Trust Center dialog box.
2. Click the Add-Ins tab of the Trust Center dialog box.
3. Select COM Add-Ins from the Manage drop-down list.
4. Click the Go button next to the Manage drop-down list.

Figure 9-1 shows the COM Add-Ins dialog box.

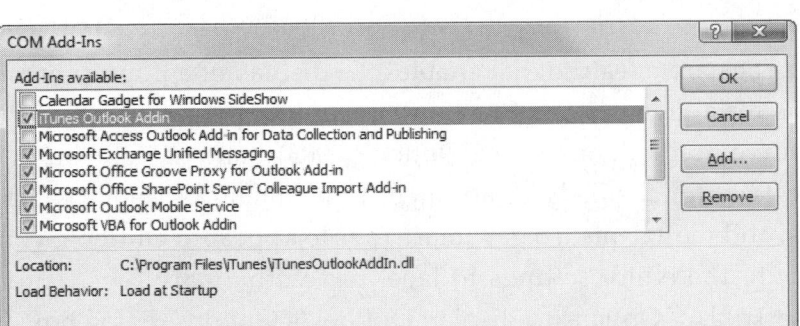

Figure 9-1: The COM Add-Ins dialog box in Outlook.

Typically, you will not have your users use this dialog box to manage COM add-ins. Instead, you will install and remove a COM add-in by manipulating registry settings with the installer you create for your COM add-in. VSTO add-ins cannot be added using the Add button in the COM Add-Ins dialog box; they must be installed by double-clicking a .vsto file or a setup.exe file associated with the VSTO add-in. The installation of VSTO add-ins is discussed in Chapter 21, "ClickOnce Deployment."

Outlook discovers the installed add-ins by reading from the registry. On Windows XP you can view the registry on your computer by going to the Windows Start menu and choosing Run. In the Run dialog box, type regedit for the program to run and then click the OK button. On Windows Vista type regedit in the search box at the bottom of the Windows Start menu. When regedit appears as a found program, right-click it and choose Run as Administrator from the context menu.

Outlook looks for VSTO and COM add-ins in the registry keys under HKEY_CURRENT_USER\Software\Microsoft\Office\Outlook\Addins. Outlook also looks for COM add-ins in the registry keys under HKEY_ LOCAL_MACHINE\ Software\Microsoft\Office\Outlook\Addins. COM add-ins registered under HKEY_LOCAL_MACHINE cannot be turned on or off by users without administrative privileges. Therefore, it is recommended that you not register your COM add-ins under HKEY_LOCAL_ MACHINE, because the add-ins can't be managed by users with non-administrator accounts.

Smart Tags

Smart Tags are a feature that enables the display of a pop-up menu with actions for a given piece of text on the screen. In Outlook 2007 Word is the only e-mail editor (unlike Outlook 2003) that enables you to create Smart Tags for the body of any item type, including contacts, appointments, and mail items. To get Smart Tags to appear in Outlook, you must configure the editor settings to label text with Smart Tags. To do this, choose Tools > Options to display Outlook's Options dialog box. On the Mail Format page, click the Editor Options button. In the Editor Options dialog box, click the Proofing tab and then click the AutoCorrect Options button. In the AutoCorrect dialog box, click the Smart Tags tab. Finally, make sure that the Label Text with Smart Tags check box is checked, as shown in Figure 9-2.

You may need to restart Outlook to get the new settings to take effect. Now, when you create a new e-mail message, you will be able to see Smart Tags in your message, as shown in Figure 9-3. These Smart Tags are the

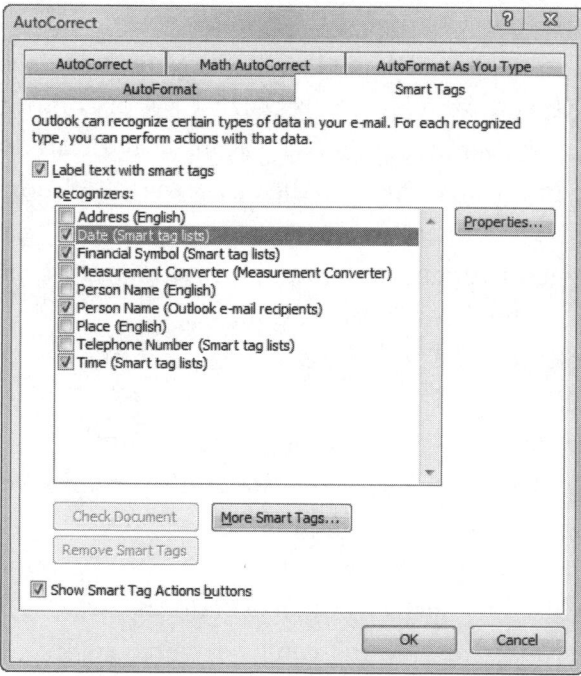

Figure 9-2: Turning on Smart Tags in Outlook 2007.

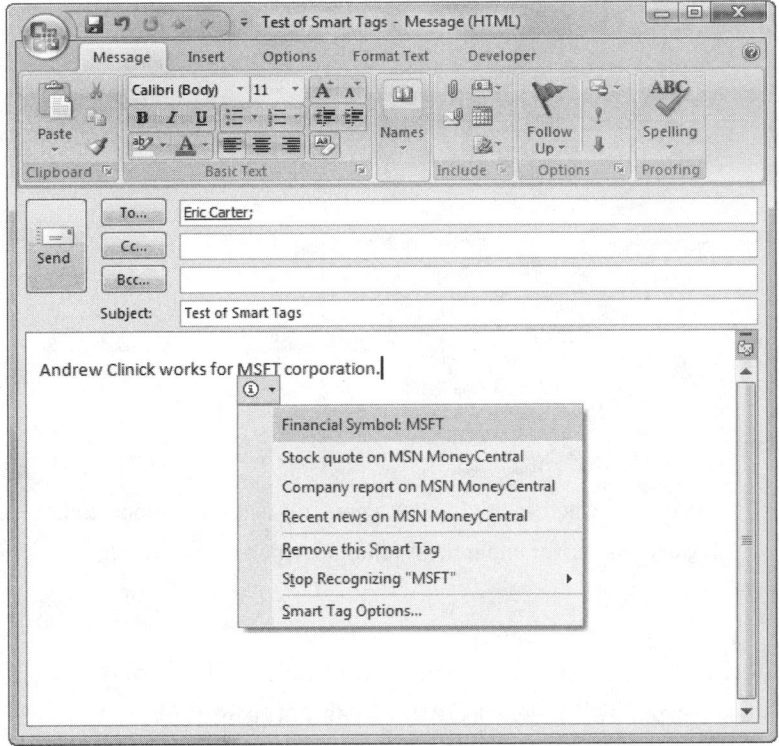

Figure 9-3: Smart Tags in an e-mail message.

same Smart Tags that are used in Word, because Word is the e-mail editor for Outlook. To make a Smart Tag available in Outlook, you must install it in Word.

When the editor is set to label text with Smart Tags, you see Smart Tags in the reading pane as well, because the Word editor is also used to display mail in the reading pane.

A second way Smart Tags are supported in Outlook is via the Persona menu. This menu appears when you right-click the name of a person in many Outlook views. Figure 9-4 shows the menu that appears when you right-click a person's name. Smart Tag actions appear in the Additional Actions submenu, as shown in Figure 9-4.

Chapter 18, "Working with Smart Tags in VSTO," describes how to create an application-level Smart Tag that could be used in mail messages and the reading pane when the editor is set to label text with Smart Tags. As we

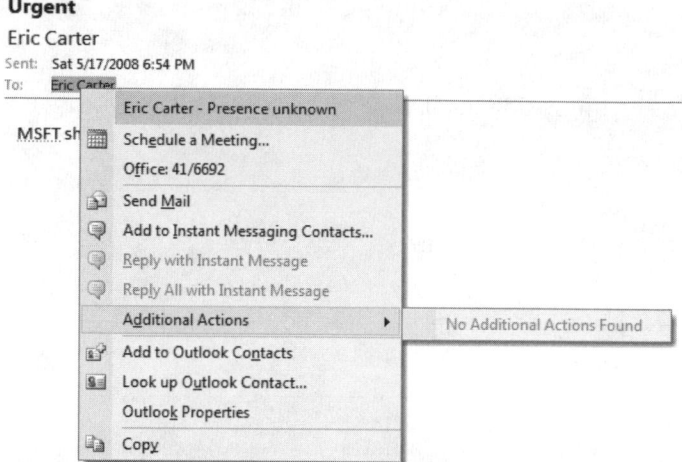

Figure 9-4: When you right-click a person's name in Outlook, Smart Tag actions appear under the Additional Actions submenu.

mentioned earlier, these Smart Tags must be installed for Word, because Word is the e-mail editor—not Outlook, as you might expect.

Custom Property Pages

An Outlook add-in can add a custom property page to the Properties dialog box for a folder or to Outlook's Options dialog box. We walk through how this is done using a VSTO Outlook add-in. First, create a VSTO Outlook add-in project in VSTO by following the instructions in Chapter 2, "Introduction to Office Solutions."

After you have created a basic VSTO Outlook add-in project, you need to add a user control project item to the project. A user control is a special kind of Windows Forms control that is useful for inserting into another window.

To add a user control to your project, click the project node in the Solution Explorer to select it; then choose Add User Control from the Project menu. You see the user control designer shown in Figure 9-5. You can resize the user control using the drag handle in the lower-right corner.

Use the controls toolbox (choose View > Toolbox if it is not already showing) to add controls to your user control surface. In Figure 9-5, we have

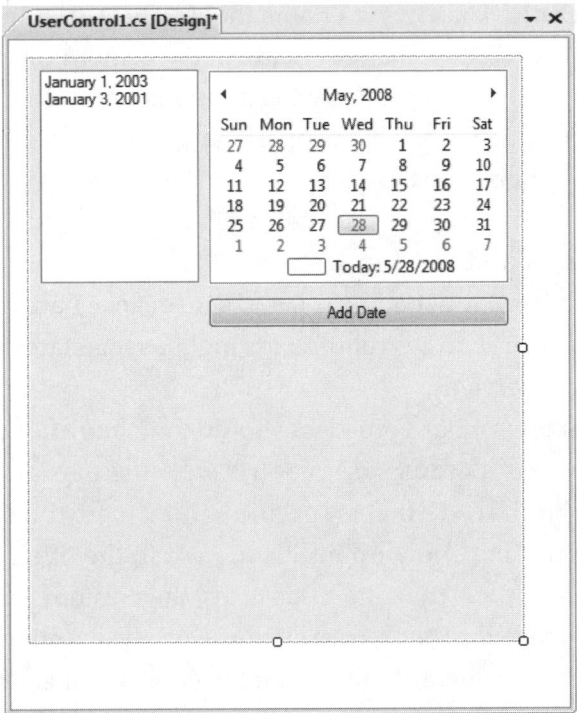

Figure 9-5: The user control designer.

added a list box, a month calendar control, and a button to the user control surface. We've also added an event handler for the button's click event that adds the date selected in the month calendar control to the list box.

To use this user control as a custom property page, we must make some modifications to the code behind it. Right-click the user control project item in the Solution Explorer and choose View Code. We first must implement an interface required by Outlook called PropertyPage. The PropertyPage interface has two methods and a property. The Apply method is called on our PropertyPage implementation when the user clicks the Apply button in the Outlook Options or Folder Properties dialog box. The GetPageInfo method gets a help filename and help context so that you can provide help for your custom property page. The Dirty property is a `bool` property that you can use to let Outlook know whether the user has changed any settings in your custom property page. When Dirty returns true, Outlook knows to enable the Apply button in the dialog box so that the user can apply changes made in the custom property page.

Second, we must add a property that Outlook will call to get the caption for the property page tab. This property must be marked with a DispId attribute that Outlook uses to identify which property will return the caption for the property page tab. The name of the property does not matter as long as it returns a string; in Listing 9-1, we name the property Page-Caption. Finally, you must add the ComVisible(true) attribute to the user control class. These changes require adding a using statement for System .Runtime.InteropServices.

Listing 9-1 shows what your class should look like after you have made these modifications. Because user controls use the partial class feature in Visual Studio, all the code that is specific to how many buttons or controls you added should not show up in this file but in the other hidden part of the partial class. Note that the code uses the System.Runtime.Interop-Services namespace for the DispID attribute on the Caption property. The code also declares a constant called captionDispID that is set to the ID Outlook expects will be associated with the Caption property.

Listing 9-1: First Version of the Modified User Control Class

```
using System;
using System.Collections.Generic;
using System.ComponentModel;
using System.Drawing;
using System.Data;
using System.Linq;
using System.Text;
using System.Windows.Forms;
using Outlook = Microsoft.Office.Interop.Outlook;
using System.Runtime.InteropServices;

namespace OutlookAddIn1
{
  [ComVisible(true)]
  public partial class UserControl1 :
    UserControl, Outlook.PropertyPage
  {
    const int captionDispID = -518;
    bool isDirty = false;

    public UserControl1()
    {
```

```
    InitializeComponent();
    this.button1.Click += new EventHandler(button1_Click);
  }

  private void button1_Click(object sender, EventArgs e)
  {
    listBox1.Items.Add(
      monthCalendar1.SelectionStart.ToLongDateString());
  }

  void Outlook.PropertyPage.Apply()
  {
    MessageBox.Show("The user clicked the Apply button.");
  }

  bool Outlook.PropertyPage.Dirty
  {
    get
    {
      return isDirty;
    }
  }

  void Outlook.PropertyPage.GetPageInfo(ref string helpFile,
    ref int helpContext)
  {

  }

  [DispId(captionDispID)]
  public string PageCaption
  {
    get
    {
      return "Test Page";
    }
  }
  }
}
}
```

With the user control created, two event handlers must be added to the add-in class. The first event handler is for the Application object's Options-PagesAdd event. This event is raised when Outlook is ready to add custom property pages to the Outlook Options dialog box, which is shown when the user chooses Options from the Tools menu. The event handler is passed a `pages` parameter of type PropertyPages that has an Add method that can be used to add a user control as a custom property page.

The second event handler is for the NameSpace object's OptionsPages-Add event. This event is raised when Outlook is ready to add custom property pages when a properties dialog box for a folder is displayed. The properties dialog box for a folder is shown when the user right-clicks a folder and chooses Properties from the context menu. The event handler is passed a `pages` parameter of type PropertyPages that has an Add method that can be used to add a user control as a custom property page. The event handler is also passed a `folder` parameter of type MAPIFolder that specifies the folder for which the properties dialog box will be shown.

Listing 9-2 shows an implementation of a VSTO ThisAddin class that handles these two events. In the event handlers for the Application object's OptionsPagesAdd event and the NameSpace object's OptionsPagesAdd event, an instance of the user control in Listing 9-1 is created and passed as the first parameter to the PropertyPages.Add method. The second property is passed an empty string because the caption for the custom property page is retrieved by Outlook calling the PageCaption property on the user control that has been attributed with a `DispID` known to Outlook.

Listing 9-2: A VSTO Outlook Add-In That Handles the OptionsPagesAdd Event on Application and Namespace

```
using System;
using System.Collections.Generic;
using System.Linq;
using System.Text;
using System.Xml.Linq;
using Outlook = Microsoft.Office.Interop.Outlook;
using Office = Microsoft.Office.Core;

namespace OutlookAddIn1
{
  public partial class ThisAddIn
  {
    Outlook.NameSpace nameSpace;

    private void ThisAddIn_Startup(object sender, EventArgs e)
    {
      Application.OptionsPagesAdd += new
        Outlook.ApplicationEvents_11_OptionsPagesAddEventHandler(
        ThisAddIn_OptionsPagesAdd);

      nameSpace = Application.Session;
      nameSpace.OptionsPagesAdd += new
```

```
      Outlook.NameSpaceEvents_OptionsPagesAddEventHandler(
      NameSpace_OptionsPagesAdd);
    }

    private void ThisAddIn_Shutdown(object sender, EventArgs e)
    {
    }

    void ThisAddIn_OptionsPagesAdd(Outlook.PropertyPages pages)
    {
      pages.Add(new UserControl1(), "");
    }

    void NameSpace_OptionsPagesAdd(Outlook.PropertyPages pages,
      Outlook.MAPIFolder folder)
    {
      pages.Add(new UserControl1(), "");
    }

    #region VSTO generated code
    private void InternalStartup()
    {
      this.Startup += new System.EventHandler(ThisAddIn_Startup);
      this.Shutdown += new System.EventHandler(ThisAddIn_Shutdown);
    }

    #endregion
  }
}
```

If you compile and run this VSTO add-in, and then restart Outlook, you get the result shown in Figure 9-6 when you show Outlook's Options dialog box and click the Test Page tab.

If you right-click a folder and choose Properties, you can also see that the custom property page is added to the folder's Properties dialog box, as shown in Figure 9-7.

If you play with these dialog boxes a bit, you will notice that the Apply button never gets enabled when you change the settings in the custom property page. Also note that the Apply method that was implemented as part of implementing the PropertyPage interface is never called. To fix this, the implementation of the user control is modified as shown in Listing 9-3 so that when we click the button in our property page that adds a date to the date list, it changes the value of the class variable isDirty to true. In addition, the code notifies Outlook that the property page state has

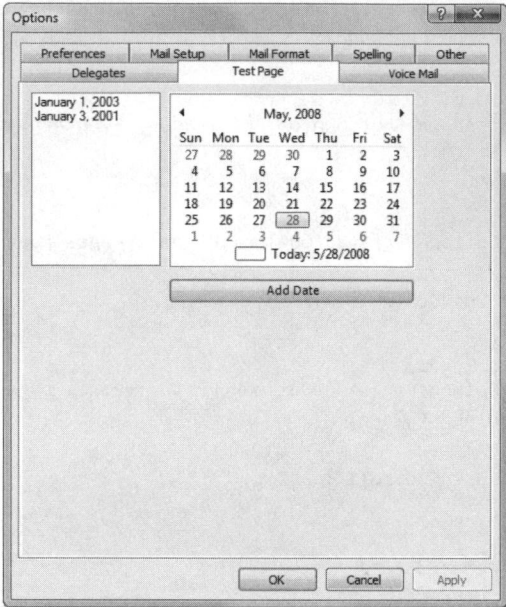

Figure 9-6: A custom property page added to Outlook's Options dialog box.

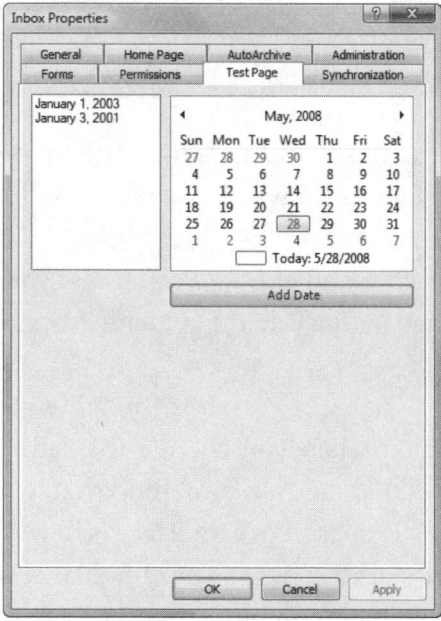

Figure 9-7: A custom property page added to a folder's Properties dialog box.

changed by connecting to Outlook's PropertyPageSite object. The code declares a propertyPageSite class member variable and sets it by calling the InitializePropertyPageSite method in the Load event handler. The Load event handler must use reflection to get the PropertyPageSite object.

With the PropertyPageSite connected, the code defines a method called SetIsDirty that changes the state of the isDirty variable and then calls Outlook's PropertyPageSite.OnStatusChange method. This notifies Outlook that it needs to call into the PropertyPage interface to get the new state of the custom property page. A complete implementation would detect any changes made to the property page that could change the dirty state and potentially detect when a change is undone and clear the dirty state back to false.

Finally, the code raises the Click event of the button on the custom property page. When the changed state changes, the code calls SetIsDirty to set the dirty state to true and notifies Outlook that the state has changed.

Listing 9-3: Second Version of a User Control Class That Handles Dirty State Properly

```csharp
using System;
using System.Collections.Generic;
using System.ComponentModel;
using System.Drawing;
using System.Data;
using System.Linq;
using System.Text;
using System.Windows.Forms;
using Outlook = Microsoft.Office.Interop.Outlook;
using System.Runtime.InteropServices;

namespace OutlookAddIn1
{
  [ComVisible(true)]
  public partial class UserControl1 :
    UserControl, Outlook.PropertyPage
  {
    const int captionDispID = -518;
    bool isDirty = false;
    private Outlook.PropertyPageSite propertyPageSite = null;

    public UserControl1()
    {
      InitializeComponent();
```

```csharp
      this.Load += new EventHandler(UserControl1_Load);
      this.button1.Click += new EventHandler(button1_Click);
   }

   void button1_Click(object sender, EventArgs e)
   {
     listBox1.Items.Add(
       monthCalendar1.SelectionStart.ToLongDateString());
     SetIsDirty(true);
   }

   void Outlook.PropertyPage.Apply()
   {
     MessageBox.Show("The user clicked the Apply button.");
   }

   bool Outlook.PropertyPage.Dirty
   {
     get
     {
       return isDirty;
     }
   }

   void Outlook.PropertyPage.GetPageInfo(ref string helpFile,
     ref int helpContext) { }

   [DispId(captionDispID)]
   public string Caption
   {
     get
     {
       return "Test Page";
     }
   }

   private void SetIsDirty(bool value)
   {
     isDirty = value;
     propertyPageSite.OnStatusChange();
   }

   void UserControl1_Load(object sender, EventArgs e)
   {
     InitializePropertyPageSite();
   }

   void InitializePropertyPageSite()
   {
```

```
    string windowsFormsStrongName =
      typeof(System.Windows.Forms.Form).Assembly.FullName;

    Type oleObjectType = Type.GetType(
      System.Reflection.Assembly.CreateQualifiedName(
      windowsFormsStrongName,
      "System.Windows.Forms.UnsafeNativeMethods")).
      GetNestedType("IOleObject");

    System.Reflection.MethodInfo getClientSiteMethodInfo =
      oleObjectType.GetMethod("GetClientSite");

    propertyPageSite = (Outlook.PropertyPageSite)
      getClientSiteMethodInfo.Invoke(this, null);
    }
  }
}
```

Now when you run the add-in and click the button in the custom property page, the dirty state is changed and Outlook's PropertyPageSite is notified. The result is that the Apply button is enabled. Clicking the Apply button invokes the test dialog box in Listing 9-3's implementation of the Apply method.

Introduction to the Outlook Object Model

Regardless of the approach you choose to integrate your code with Outlook, you will eventually need to talk to the Outlook object model to get things done. This section introduces the Outlook object model; Chapter 10, "Working with Outlook Events," and Chapter 11, "Working with Outlook Objects," describe some of the most frequently used properties, methods, and events.

The first step in starting to learn the Outlook object model is getting an idea for the basic structure of the object model hierarchy. Figure 9-8 shows some of the most critical objects in the Outlook object model and their hierarchical relationship.

The Outlook object model has the notion of an Outlook item. An Outlook item is represented in the object model as an object and can be cast to one of 18 different Outlook item types shown in Table 9-1. Some objects in the object model, such as the Folder object, contain an Items collection that

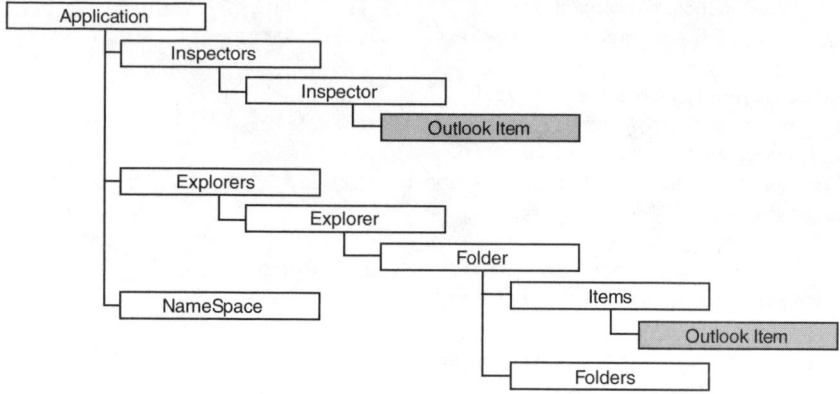

Figure 9-8: The basic hierarchy of the Outlook object model.

TABLE 9-1: Outlook Item Types

Object	Description
AppointmentItem	An appointment item, typically found in a Calendar folder.
ContactItem	A contact item, typically found in the Contacts folder.
DistListItem	A distribution list, typically found in the Contacts folder.
DocumentItem	A document that you have added to an Outlook folder by dragging and dropping it from the file system into the Outlook folder. Also corresponds to SharePoint document library items synchronized into Outlook.
JournalItem	A journal entry, typically found in the Journal folder.
MailItem	A mail message, typically found in the Inbox folder.
MeetingItem	A meeting request, typically found in the Inbox folder.
NoteItem	A note, typically found in the Notes folder.

TABLE 9-1: Outlook Item Types *(Continued)*

Object	Description
PostItem	A post in an Outlook folder.
RemoteItem	A mail message that has not yet been fully retrieved from the server but has the subject of the message, the received date and time, the sender, the size of the message, and the first 255 characters of the message body.
ReportItem	A mail delivery report, such as a report when mail delivery failed, typically found in the Inbox folder.
SharingItem*	An invitation to view or share a folder belonging to another user, typically found in the Inbox folder.
StorageItem	A hidden item in a folder that you can use to store custom data for your solution.
TaskItem	A task, typically found in the Tasks folder.
TaskRequestAcceptItem	A response to a TaskRequestItem, typically found in the Inbox folder.
TaskRequestDeclineItem	A response to a TaskRequestItem, typically found in the Inbox folder.
TaskRequestItem	A task request sent to another user, typically found in the Inbox folder.
TaskRequestUpdateItem	An update to a TaskRequestItem, typically found in the Inbox folder.

* New in 2007

can contain instances of any of the 18 Outlook item types—therefore, the folder may contain a mixture of MailItem objects, TaskRequestItem objects, and so on. When you iterate over a collection of Items, Outlook returns each item to you as an `object` that you must cast to one of the 18 Outlook item types before using it.

Another example of an Outlook object model object that is associated with multiple Outlook item types is the Inspector object. The Inspector object represents a window providing a detail view for one of the 18 different Outlook item types. It could be providing a view on a NoteItem, a MeetingItem, and so forth. Inspector has a CurrentItem property that returns the Outlook item it is displaying as an `object`. You must cast the `object` returned by CurrentItem to one of the Outlook item types in Table 9-1 before using it. Chapter 11, "Working with Outlook Objects," discusses Outlook items in more detail.

Figure 9-9 shows a more complete view of the Outlook object model. (All the objects considered Outlook items are colored gray.) Note in this diagram that the Inspector object and the Items object points to a gray circle, which represents any of the Outlook items colored gray.

Conclusion

This chapter introduced the various ways you can integrate your code into Outlook. You learned about Outlook's ability to add a custom property page to the Outlook Option's dialog box or to a folder's Properties dialog box. This chapter also introduced the basic hierarchy of the Outlook object model. Chapter 10, "Working with Outlook Events," describes the events in the Outlook object model. Chapter 11, "Working with Outlook Objects," describes the most important objects in the Outlook object model.

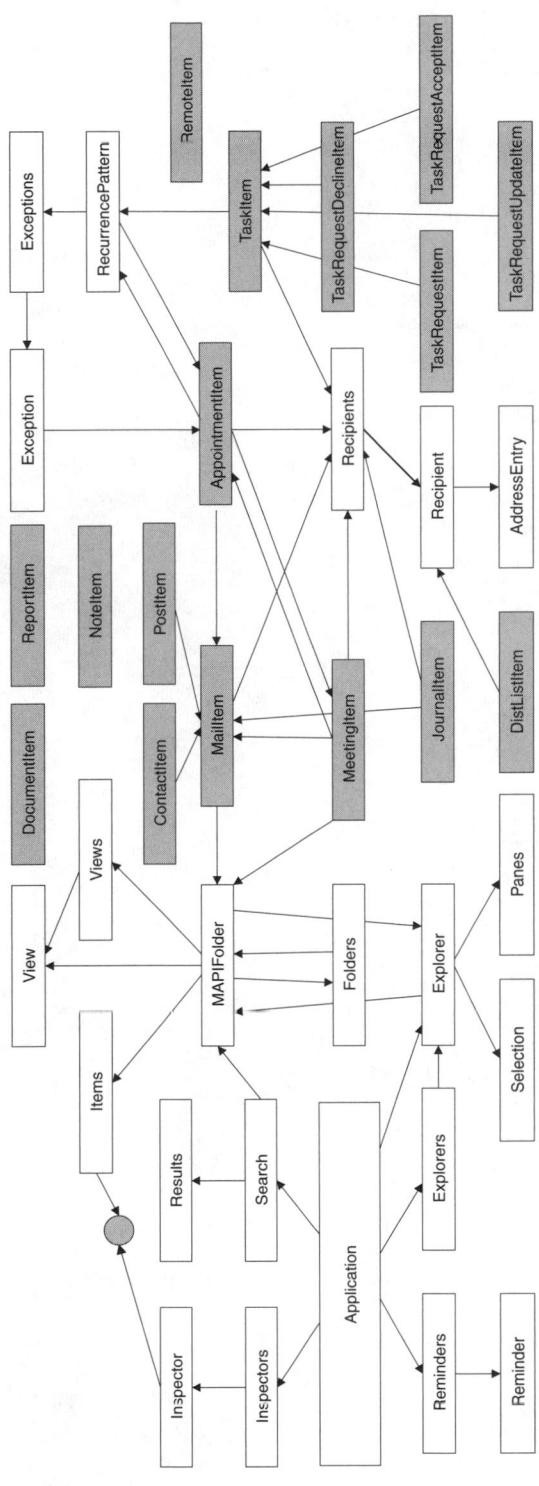

Figure 9-9: Some of the objects in the Outlook object model. Gray objects are all "Outlook items."

■ 10 ■
Working with Outlook Events

Events in the Outlook Object Model

Understanding the events in the Outlook object model is critical because this is often the primary way that your code is run. This chapter covers many of the events in the Outlook object model, when they are raised, and the type of code you might associate with these events.

Outlook associates the same set of events with all the Outlook item object types listed in Table 9-1 in Chapter 9, "Programming Outlook." In this chapter, we will refer to Item events, but there is no Item object per se in the Outlook object model. Instead, you will find the same set of Item events (defined by ItemEvents_10_Event interface) on 16 of the 17 Outlook object model objects listed in Table 9-1 (NoteItem does not implement events).

When you work with the Outlook object model, you will quickly notice multiple public interfaces, classes, and delegates associated with events. Consider the interfaces, classes, and delegates associated with Application, Explorer, Inspector, and Item:

- ApplicationEvents interface
- ApplicationEvents_Event interface
- ApplicationEvents_* delegates
- ApplicationEvents_SinkHelper class

- ApplicationEvents_10 interface
- ApplicationsEvents_10_Event interface
- ApplicationEvents_10_* delegates
- ApplicationEvents_10_SinkHelper class
- ApplicationEvents_11 interface
- **ApplicationsEvents_11_Event interface**
- **ApplicationEvents_11_* delegates**
- ApplicationEvents_11_SinkHelper class
- ExplorerEvents interface
- **ExplorerEvents_Event interface**
- **ExplorerEvents_* delegates**
- ExplorerEvents_SinkHelper class
- InspectorEvents interface
- InspectorEvents_Event interface
- InspectorEvents_* delegates
- InspectorEvents_SinkHelper class
- InspectorEvents_10 interface
- **InspectorEvents_10_Event interface**
- **InspectorEvents_10_* delegates**
- InspectorEvents_10_SinkHelper class
- ItemEvents interface
- ItemEvents_Event interface
- ItemEvents_* delegates
- ItemEvents_SinkHelper class
- ItemEvents_10 interface
- **ItemEvents_10_Event interface**
- **ItemEvents_10_* delegates**
- ItemEvents_10_SinkHelper class

The only elements from this partial list of event interfaces in Outlook that you should ever use in your code are the ones in bold text. As you can see, the pattern that emerges here is to use the event interface that has an

Event extension. For objects for which multiple event interfaces exist—such as Application (ApplicationEvents_Event, ApplicationsEvents_10_Event, and ApplicationEvents_11_Event)—use the interface that has the highest number in it (in this case, ApplicationEvents_11_Event), and use the corresponding delegates that are prefaced by ApplicationEvents_11. The *_Event interfaces in bold should only be used when you have to cast an object to its corresponding event interface because a method name and event name collide. An example of this is the Inspector object, which has both a Close method and a Close event. To disambiguate between the two, you have to cast the Inspector object to InspectorEvents_10_Event when you want to handle the Close event.

Chapter 1, "An Introduction to Office Programming," briefly explains the reason for the other items in this list. However, this explanation covers only the SinkHelper class and why there is both an *Object*Events interface and an *Object*Events_Event interface. The reason there are multiple numbered events associated with some objects goes back to the original COM implementation of the Outlook object model.

Outlook's Application, Explorer, Inspector, and Item COM objects have had their event interfaces defined over multiple versions. For example, consider the Application events. Events defined in Outlook 2000 for the Application object are on the interface named ApplicationEvents_Event. Events that were new in Outlook 2002 are on the interface named ApplicationEvents_10_Events. (Outlook 2002 was known internally at Microsoft as Outlook 10.) ApplicationEvents_10_Events also contains all the events that are in the ApplicationEvents_Event. Events that were new in Outlook 2003 and Outlook 2007 are on the interface named ApplicationEvents_11_Events. (Outlook 2003 was known internally at Microsoft as Outlook 11.) Because ApplicationEvents_11_Events contains all the events defined for Application, this is the only interface you should use for Outlook 2007 development.

Application-Level Events

This section covers events that occur at the Application level. This includes either events raised on the Application object or events that are raised on

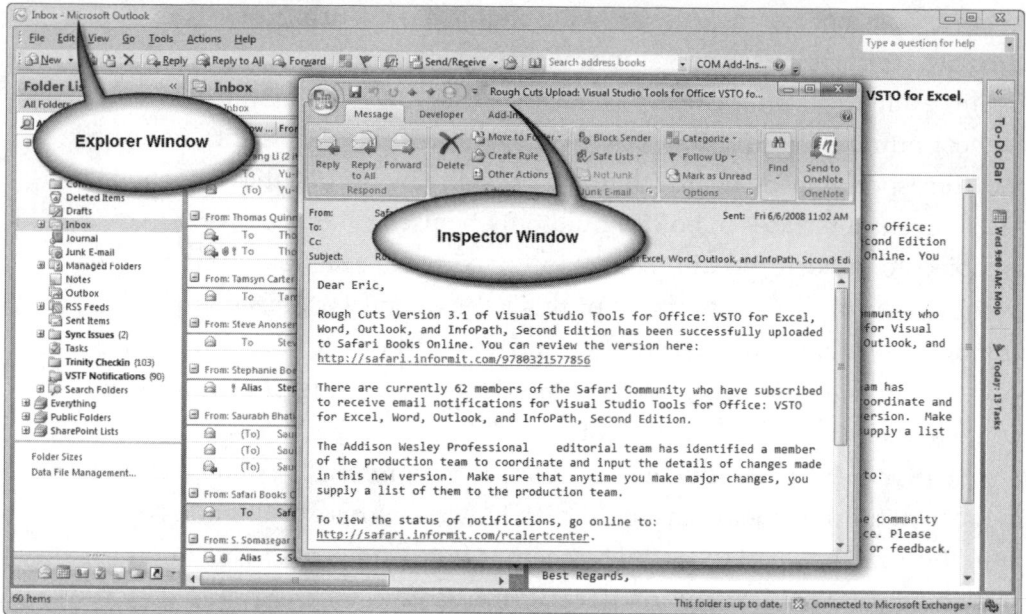

Figure 10-1: An Explorer window and an Inspector window.

the main Outlook windows. The two primary windows displayed by Outlook are represented in the Outlook object model by the Explorer object and the Inspector object. An Explorer object represents the main Outlook window in which the contents of folders display. An Inspector object represents the Outlook window that appears when you double-click an Outlook item—for example, when you double-click a mail item in your inbox. Figure 10-1 shows representative Explorer and Inspector windows.

It is possible to have zero or more Explorer and zero or more Inspector windows open at any given time. For example, if you right-click a document in the My Documents folder and choose Mail Recipient from the Send To menu, Outlook launches with only an Inspector window open. If you launch Outlook by picking it from the Start menu, it typically starts up with just the main Outlook window open, which is an Explorer window. If you right-click a folder within Outlook and choose Open in New Window, doing so creates an additional Explorer window to display that folder. Outlook can also run in a mode with neither an Explorer nor an Inspector window running—for example, when it is started by the ActiveSync application shipped by Microsoft for syncing phones and PDAs to Outlook.

Startup and Quit Events

Outlook raises several events during startup and shutdown, as does the
AddIn object, which is provided for a VSTO add-in:

- **AddIn.Startup** is raised when a VSTO add-in is loaded. This event is
  the first event raised to a VSTO Outlook add-in.
- **Application.Startup** is raised when Outlook has finished startup.
  This event is raised after all the add-ins set to load on Outlook startup
  have been loaded.
- **Application.MAPILogonComplete** is raised after Outlook has
  logged on to the mail services it is configured to connect to.
- **Application.Quit** is raised when Outlook is about to exit. This event
  is raised before add-ins have been unloaded so that an add-in can
  handle this event.

> **◼ NOTE**
>
> Quit is the name of both a method and an event on the Applica-
> tion object. Because of this collision, you will not see the Quit
> event in Visual Studio's pop-up menu of properties, events, and
> methods associated with the Application object. Furthermore, a
> warning displays at compile time when you try to handle this
> event. To get Visual Studio's pop-up menus to work and the
> warning to go away, you can cast the Application object to the
> ApplicationEvents_11_Event interface, as shown in Listing 10-1.

- **AddIn.Shutdown** is raised just before a VSTO add-in is unloaded.

The order in which the startup and shutdown events associated with a
VSTO add-in occur is shown here:

- User launches Outlook.
- AddIn.Startup event is raised in each add-in.
- Application.Startup event is raised in each add-in.
- Application.MAPILogonComplete event is raised for each add-in.
- User quits Outlook.

- Application.Quit event is raised and can be handled by each loaded add-in.
- AddIn.Shutdown is raised in each add-in; then the add-in is unloaded.

This ordering of events should suggest a couple of practices if you have multiple add-ins that depend on one another:

1. If multiple add-ins are communicating with one another, they should not assume that other add-ins are loaded during AddIn.Startup; they should wait until Application.Startup before communicating with other add-ins.
2. If multiple add-ins communicate during shutdown, they should do so when Application.Quit is raised. When AddIn.Shutdown is raised, other add-ins may already have unloaded.

Events Can Be Raised in Any Order

A note about event ordering: You shouldn't write code that relies on the same event being raised in a particular order among multiple add-ins. If you have multiple add-ins handling the Startup event, for example, there is no guarantee that your add-in will handle the Startup event before other add-ins, even if that seems to be the case on your development machine. Although an event may be raised in a particular order to multiple add-ins on your developer machine, Outlook makes no guarantees about one add-in loading or getting the same event before another add-in.

Listing 10-1 shows a VSTO add-in that handles these startup and shutdown events raised by Outlook's Application object and VSTO's AddIn object. Note that we needed to cast the Application object to the ApplicationEvents_11_Event interface to disambiguate between the Quit method and the Quit event.

Listing 10-1: A VSTO Add-In That Handles the Application Object's Quit, Startup, and MAPILogonComplete and the AddIn Object's Startup and Shutdown Events

```csharp
using System;
using System.Collections.Generic;
using System.Linq;
using System.Text;
using System.Xml.Linq;
using Outlook = Microsoft.Office.Interop.Outlook;
using Office = Microsoft.Office.Core;
using System.Windows.Forms;

namespace OutlookAddIn1
{
  public partial class ThisAddIn
  {
    private void ThisAddIn_Startup(object sender,
      System.EventArgs e)
    {
      MessageBox.Show("VSTO Startup Event");
      Application.Startup += new
        Outlook.ApplicationEvents_11_StartupEventHandler(
        Application_Startup);
      ((Outlook.ApplicationEvents_11_Event)Application).Quit +=
        new Outlook.ApplicationEvents_11_QuitEventHandler(
        Application_Quit);
      Application.MAPILogonComplete += new
        Outlook.ApplicationEvents_11_MAPILogonCompleteEventHandler(
        Application_MAPILogonComplete);
    }

    void Application_MAPILogonComplete()
    {
      MessageBox.Show("MAPILogonComplete");
    }

    void Application_Startup()
    {
      MessageBox.Show("Outlook Startup Event");
    }

    void Application_Quit()
    {
      MessageBox.Show("Outlook Quit Event");
    }

    private void ThisAddIn_Shutdown(object sender,
      System.EventArgs e)
    {
```

```
      MessageBox.Show("VSTO Shutdown Event");
    }

    #region VSTO generated code
    private void InternalStartup()
    {
      this.Startup += new System.EventHandler(ThisAddIn_Startup);
      this.Shutdown += new System.EventHandler(ThisAddIn_Shutdown);
    }
    #endregion
  }
}
```

> **▪ TIP**
>
> If you are typing the code in this chapter into multiple VSTO add-in projects, here is a tip: When you build an add-in, the add-in is built and registered in the registry at the same time. If you create a bunch of VSTO add-ins, you can quickly get to the state where many add-ins are registered on your machine. To prevent this situation, use the Clean Solution command from Visual Studio's Build menu. This command will remove the add-in from the registry so that it doesn't load the next time you launch Outlook.

Activation Events

When an Explorer or Inspector window becomes the active window (activates) or loses focus to another window (deactivates), events are raised:

- **Explorer.Activate** is raised on an Explorer object when the window it corresponds to becomes the active window.

- **Inspector.Activate** is raised on an Inspector object when the window it corresponds to becomes the active window.

- **Explorer.Deactivate** is raised on an Explorer object when the window it corresponds to loses focus to another window.

- **Inspector.Deactivate** is raised on an Inspector object when the window it corresponds to loses focus to another window.

Listing 10-2 shows a VSTO Outlook add-in that handles Activate and Deactivate events for the Explorer object.

> **▪ NOTE**
>
> Activate is the name of both a method and an event on the Explorer and Inspector object. Because of this collision, you will not see the Activate event in Visual Studio's pop-up menu of properties, events, and methods associated with the Explorer or Inspector object. Furthermore, a warning displays at compile time when you try to handle this event. To get Visual Studio's pop-up menus to work and the warning to go away, you can cast the Explorer object to the ExplorerEvents_10_ Event interface and the Inspector object to the InspectorEvents_10_ Event interface, as shown in Listing 10-2.

Listing 10-2: A VSTO Add-In That Handles the Explorer Object's Activate and Deactivate Events

```csharp
using System;
using System.Collections.Generic;
using System.Linq;
using System.Text;
using System.Xml.Linq;
using Outlook = Microsoft.Office.Interop.Outlook;
using Office = Microsoft.Office.Core;
using System.Windows.Forms;

namespace OutlookAddIn1
{
  public partial class ThisAddIn
  {
    Outlook.Explorer explorer;

    private void ThisAddIn_Startup(object sender,
      System.EventArgs e)
    {
      explorer = Application.ActiveExplorer();

      // Outlook can start up without a visible Explorer window
      if (explorer == null)
        return;

      ((Outlook.ExplorerEvents_10_Event)explorer).Activate +=
        new Outlook.ExplorerEvents_10_ActivateEventHandler(
          Explorer_Activate);

      explorer.Deactivate +=
        new Outlook.ExplorerEvents_10_DeactivateEventHandler(
          Explorer_Deactivate);
    }
```

```
void Explorer_Activate()
{
  System.Diagnostics.Debug.WriteLine(String.Format(
    "The explorer with caption {0} was activated.",
    explorer.Caption));
}

void Explorer_Deactivate()
{
  System.Diagnostics.Debug.WriteLine(String.Format(
    "The Explorer window with caption {0} was deactivated.",
    explorer.Caption));
}

#region VSTO generated code
private void InternalStartup()
{
  this.Startup += new System.EventHandler(ThisAddIn_Startup);
}
#endregion
  }
}
```

New Window Events

When a new Explorer or Inspector window is created, Outlook raises an event:

- **Explorers.NewExplorer** is raised when a new Explorer window is created. The newly created Explorer is passed as a parameter to this event.

- **Inspectors.NewInspector** is raised when a new Inspector window is created. The newly created Inspector is passed as a parameter to this event.

Window Events

When an Explorer or Inspector window is maximized, minimized, moved, or resized, events are raised by Outlook. All of these events can be canceled to prevent the change to the window from occurring:

- **Explorer.BeforeMaximize** is raised on an Explorer object when the window it corresponds to is about to be maximized. Outlook passes by reference a bool cancel parameter. The cancel parameter can be set to true by your event handler to prevent Outlook from maximizing the window.

- **Inspector.BeforeMaximize** is raised on an Inspector object when the window it corresponds to is about to be maximized. Outlook passes by reference a `bool` `cancel` parameter. The `cancel` parameter can be set to `true` by your event handler to prevent Outlook from maximizing the window.

- **Explorer.BeforeMinimize** is raised on an Explorer object when the window it corresponds to is about to be minimized. Outlook passes by reference a `bool` `cancel` parameter. The `cancel` parameter can be set to `true` by your event handler to prevent Outlook from minimizing the window.

- **Inspector.BeforeMinimize** is raised on an Inspector object when the window it corresponds to is about to be minimized. Outlook passes by reference a `bool` `cancel` parameter. The `cancel` parameter can be set to `true` by your event handler to prevent Outlook from minimizing the window.

- **Explorer.BeforeMove** is raised on an Explorer object when the window it corresponds to is about to be moved. Outlook passes by reference a `bool` `cancel` parameter. The `cancel` parameter can be set to `true` by your event handler to prevent Outlook from moving the window.

- **Inspector.BeforeMove** is raised on an Inspector object when the window it corresponds to is about to be moved. Outlook passes by reference a `bool` `cancel` parameter. The `cancel` parameter can be set to `true` by your event handler to prevent Outlook from moving the window.

- **Explorer.BeforeSize** is raised on an Explorer object when the window it corresponds to is about to be resized. Outlook passes by reference a `bool` `cancel` parameter. The `cancel` parameter can be set to `true` by your event handler to prevent Outlook from resizing the window.

- **Inspector.BeforeSize** is raised on an Inspector object when the window it corresponds to is about to be resized. Outlook passes by reference a `bool` `cancel` parameter. The `cancel` parameter can be set to `true` by your event handler to prevent Outlook from resizing the window.

- **Inspector.PageChange** is raised on an Inspector object when the active page in the form for the inspector changes. Outlook passes the name of the newly displayed page as a `string` parameter.

Close Events

When an Explorer or Inspector window is closed, Outlook raises an event:

- **Explorer.Close** is raised on an Explorer object when the window it corresponds to has been closed.

- **Inspector.Close** is raised on an Inspector object when the window it corresponds to has been closed.

⦾ NOTE

Close is the name of both a method and an event on the Explorer and Inspector object. Because of this collision, you will not see the Close event in Visual Studio's pop-up menu of properties, events, and methods associated with the Explorer or Inspector object. Furthermore, a warning displays at compile time when you try to handle this event. To get Visual Studio's pop-up menus to work and the warning to go away, you can cast the Explorer object to the ExplorerEvents_10_ Event interface and the Inspector object to the InspectorEvents_10_ Event interface, as shown in Listing 9-1.

View and Selection Change Events

As you navigate from folder to folder in an Explorer window, Outlook displays a view of the items in the folder you have selected. The user can also change the view for a particular folder by using the View menu and choosing a different view from the Current View menu in the Arrange By menu. Outlook raises events when the view changes or the selection changes:

- **Explorer.BeforeViewSwitch** is raised on an Explorer object when the user changes the view for a particular folder by using the View menu. This event is not raised when the user simply switches from folder to folder thereby changing the view (but the ViewSwitch event is). Outlook passes a `newView` parameter that is of type `object`. This parameter can be cast to a `string` value representing the name of the view about to be switched to. Outlook also passes by reference a `bool cancel` parameter. The `cancel` parameter can be set to `true` by your event handler to prevent Outlook from switching to the view the user selected.

- **Explorer.ViewSwitch** is raised on an Explorer object when the view changes either because the user changed the view using the View menu or because the user selected another folder.

- **Explorer.SelectionChange** is raised on an Explorer object when the selection in the Explorer window changes.

- **Explorer.BeforeFolderSwitch** is raised on an Explorer object before the active folder changes. Outlook passes a `newFolder` parameter of type `object`. This parameter can be cast to a Folder that represents what the new active folder will be. Outlook also passes by reference a `bool cancel` parameter. The `cancel` parameter can be set to `true` by your event handler to prevent Outlook from switching to the folder the user selected.

- **Explorer.FolderSwitch** is raised on an Explorer object when the active folder changes.

Listing 10-3 shows a VSTO Outlook add-in that handles these events.

Listing 10-3: A VSTO Add-In That Handles View and Selection Change Events

```csharp
using System;
using System.Collections.Generic;
using System.Linq;
using System.Text;
using System.Xml.Linq;
using Outlook = Microsoft.Office.Interop.Outlook;
using Office = Microsoft.Office.Core;
using System.Windows.Forms;

namespace OutlookAddIn1
{
  public partial class ThisAddIn
  {
    Outlook.Explorer explorer;

    private void ThisAddIn_Startup(object sender,
      System.EventArgs e)
    {
      explorer = Application.ActiveExplorer();

      // Outlook can start up without a visible Explorer window
      if (explorer == null)
        return;
```

```
    explorer.BeforeViewSwitch += new
      Outlook.ExplorerEvents_10_BeforeViewSwitchEventHandler(
      Explorer_BeforeViewSwitch);

    explorer.ViewSwitch += new
      Outlook.ExplorerEvents_10_ViewSwitchEventHandler(
      Explorer_ViewSwitch);

    explorer.SelectionChange += new
      Outlook.ExplorerEvents_10_SelectionChangeEventHandler(
      Explorer_SelectionChange);

    explorer.BeforeFolderSwitch += new
     Outlook.ExplorerEvents_10_BeforeFolderSwitchEventHandler(
     Explorer_BeforeFolderSwitch);

    explorer.FolderSwitch += new
      Outlook.ExplorerEvents_10_FolderSwitchEventHandler(
      Explorer_FolderSwitch);
}

void Explorer_BeforeViewSwitch(object newView,
  ref bool cancel)
{
  MessageBox.Show(String.Format(
    "About to switch to {0}.", newView));
}

void Explorer_ViewSwitch()
{
  Outlook.View view = explorer.CurrentView as Outlook.View;
  if (view != null)
  {
    MessageBox.Show(String.Format(
      "The view has been switched. Current view is now {0}.",
      view.Name));
  }
}

void Explorer_SelectionChange()
{
  MessageBox.Show(String.Format(
    "Selection changed. {0} items selected.",
    explorer.Selection.Count));
}

void Explorer_BeforeFolderSwitch(object newFolder,
  ref bool cancel)
{
```

```
Outlook. Folder folder = (Outlook.Folder)newFolder;
MessageBox.Show(String.Format(
  "The new folder will be {0}.",
  folder.Name));
}

void Explorer_FolderSwitch()
{
  MessageBox.Show("Folder switch");
}

#region VSTO generated code
private void InternalStartup()
{
  this.Startup += new System.EventHandler(ThisAddIn_Startup);
}
#endregion
  }
}
```

Folder Change Events

Given a collection of folders in Outlook, several events are raised when folders in that collection change:

- **Folders.FolderAdd** is raised on a Folders collection when a new folder is added. Outlook passes a `folder` parameter of type MAPI-Folder representing the newly added folder.

- **Folders.FolderRemove** is raised on a Folders collection when a folder is deleted.

- **Folders.FolderChange** is raised on a Folders collection when a folder is changed. Examples of changes include when the folder is renamed or when the number of items in the folder changes. Outlook passes a `folder` parameter of type MAPIFolder representing the folder that has changed.

- **Folder.BeforeFolderMove** (new in Outlook 2007) is raised on a Folder object when a folder is moved to another folder. Outlook passes a `MoveTo` parameter of type MAPIFolder representing the folder to which the current folder is moving.

> **▪ NOTE**
>
> Folder is a new object in the Outlook 2007 object model that replaces MAPIFolder, which is now deprecated. Any MAPIFolder returned in older parts of the Outlook 2007 object model can be cast to a Folder. The new Folder object adds two folder-level events for the first time to Outlook: BeforeFolderMove and BeforeItemMove. Note that Listing 10-4 contains code to cast a MAPIFolder object to a Folder object so that we can handle the new BeforeFolderMove event.

Listing 10-4 shows an add-in that handles folder change events for any subfolders under the Inbox folder. To get to a Folders collection, we first get a NameSpace object. The NameSpace object is accessed by calling the Application.Session property. The NameSpace object has a method called GetDefaultFolder that returns a MAPIFolder object to which you can pass a member of the enumeration OlDefaultFolders to get a standard Outlook folder. In Listing 10-4, we pass `olFolderInbox` to get a MAPIFolder for the Inbox. We then connect our event handlers to the Folders collection associated with the Inbox's MAPIFolder object. We also get the first child folder of the Inbox folder, cast it from a MAPIFolder to a Folder, and then handle the Folder's BeforeFolderMove event.

Listing 10-4: A VSTO Add-In That Handles Folder Change Events

```
using System;
using System.Collections.Generic;
using System.Linq;
using System.Text;
using System.Xml.Linq;
using Outlook = Microsoft.Office.Interop.Outlook;
using Office = Microsoft.Office.Core;
using System.Windows.Forms;

namespace OutlookAddIn1
{
  public partial class ThisAddIn
  {
    Outlook.Folders folders;
    Outlook.Folder folderToWatch;

    private void ThisAddIn_Startup(object sender, EventArgs e)
    {
```

```
  Outlook.NameSpace ns = Application.Session;
  Outlook.Folder folder = ns.GetDefaultFolder(
    Outlook.OlDefaultFolders.olFolderInbox) as Outlook.Folder;
  folders = folder.Folders;

  if (folders.Count > 0)
  {
    folderToWatch = folders[1] as Outlook.Folder;
    folderToWatch.BeforeFolderMove += new
      Outlook.MAPIFolderEvents_12_BeforeFolderMoveEventHandler(
      folderToWatch_BeforeFolderMove);
    MessageBox.Show(
      String.Format("Preventing {0} folder from moving.",
      folderToWatch.Name));
  }

  folders.FolderAdd += new
    Outlook.FoldersEvents_FolderAddEventHandler(
    Folders_FolderAdd);

  folders.FolderChange += new
    Outlook.FoldersEvents_FolderChangeEventHandler(
    Folders_FolderChange);

  folders.FolderRemove += new
    Outlook.FoldersEvents_FolderRemoveEventHandler(
    Folders_FolderRemove);
}

void folderToWatch_BeforeFolderMove(
  Outlook.MAPIFolder MoveTo, ref bool Cancel)
{
  MessageBox.Show(String.Format(
    "About to move {0} to {1}--cancelling",
    folderToWatch.Name, MoveTo.Name));
  Cancel = true;
}

void Folders_FolderAdd(Outlook.MAPIFolder folder)
{
  MessageBox.Show(String.Format(
    "Added {0} folder.", folder.Name));
}

void Folders_FolderChange(Outlook.MAPIFolder folder)
{
  MessageBox.Show(String.Format(
    "Changed {0} folder. ", folder.Name));
}
```

```
  void Folders_FolderRemove()
  {
    MessageBox.Show("Removed a folder.");
  }


  #region VSTO generated code
  private void InternalStartup()
  {
    this.Startup += new System.EventHandler(ThisAddIn_Startup);
  }
  #endregion
  }
}
```

Context Menu Events

Outlook raises several new events in Outlook 2007 that allow you to customize various context menus that appear when you right-click items in the Outlook UI:

- **Application.AttachmentContextMenuDisplay** is raised on the Application object before a context menu is shown for attachments that are selected. Outlook passes a `CommandBar` parameter representing the context menu about to be displayed. Outlook also passes an `Attachments` parameter of type AttachmentSelection that gives more information about the attachments that were selected.

- **Application.FolderContextMenuDisplay** is raised on the Application object before a context menu is shown for a folder. Outlook passes a `CommandBar` parameter representing the context menu about to be displayed. Outlook also passes a `Folder` parameter for the folder that was right-clicked.

- **Application.StoreContextMenuDisplay** is raised on the Application object before a context menu is shown for a store (like a PST file or an Exchange mailbox). Outlook passes a `CommandBar` parameter representing the context menu about to be displayed. Outlook also passes a `Store` parameter for the store that was right-clicked.

- **Application.ShortcutContextMenuDisplay** is raised on the Application object before a context menu is shown for a shortcut on the Outlook bar (like the Outlook Today shortcut). To see shortcuts, choose

Go > Shortcuts in Outlook. Outlook passes a `CommandBar` parameter representing the context menu about to be displayed. Outlook also passes a `Shortcut` parameter of type OutlookBarShortcut for the shortcut that was right-clicked.

- **Application.ViewContextMenuDisplay** is raised on the Application object before a context menu is shown for a view. A good place to see views used is in Contacts view; choose Go > Contacts in Outlook. Outlook passes a `CommandBar` parameter representing the context menu about to be displayed. Outlook also passes a `View` parameter for the view that was right-clicked.

- **Application.ItemContextMenuDisplay** is raised on the Application object before a context menu is shown for an Outlook item or multiple selected Outlook items. Outlook passes a `CommandBar` parameter representing the context menu about to be displayed. Outlook also passes a `Selection` parameter representing the selected Outlook items that were right-clicked.

- **Application.ContextMenuClose** is raised on the Application object after a context menu is closed. This is useful for cleaning up any objects that were created in response to the other context menu events. Outlook passes a `ContextMenu` parameter of type OlContextMenu representing the type of context menu that was closed.

Note that when handling the ContextMenuDisplay events, you should ensure that your event handler runs quickly, as your code can slow the display of the menu if it takes a long time to run.

Listing 10-5 shows a VSTO add-in that handles the various Context-MenuDisplay events and adds a menu item to the context menu using the CommandBars object model. A helper method called CommandBarHelper adds a CommandBarButton and also adds a Click event handler to the newly added CommandBarButton object. The Click event handler displays the caption of the CommandBarButton. The ContextMenuClose event is also handled to remove the Click event handler when the context menu closes.

Listing 10-5 also shows the basic pattern of handling the context menu events. First, in the ContextMenuDisplay related event, new buttons are created, the button click events are handled, and instance variables are used to hold on to parameters passed to the ContextMenuDisplay event. Then those instance variables are used when a button click event is handled. Finally, the instance variables are cleaned up, and the button click events are detached in the ContextMenuClose event.

Listing 10-5: A VSTO Add-In That Handles ContextMenuDisplay Events and ContextMenuClose

```
using System;
using System.Collections.Generic;
using System.Linq;
using System.Text;
using System.Xml.Linq;
using Outlook = Microsoft.Office.Interop.Outlook;
using Office = Microsoft.Office.Core;
using System.Windows.Forms;

namespace OutlookAddIn1
{
  public partial class ThisAddIn
  {
    Office.CommandBarButton btn;
    Outlook.Selection lastSelection = null;
    Outlook.View lastView = null;
    Outlook.OutlookBarShortcut lastShortcut = null;
    Outlook.Store lastStore = null;
    Outlook.MAPIFolder lastFolder = null;
    Outlook.AttachmentSelection lastAttachments = null;

    private void ThisAddIn_Startup(object sender, EventArgs e)
    {
      Application.AttachmentContextMenuDisplay += new Outlook.
      ApplicationEvents_11_AttachmentContextMenuDisplayEventHandler(
        Application_AttachmentContextMenuDisplay);

      Application.FolderContextMenuDisplay += new Outlook.
      ApplicationEvents_11_FolderContextMenuDisplayEventHandler(
        Application_FolderContextMenuDisplay);

      Application.StoreContextMenuDisplay += new Outlook.
      ApplicationEvents_11_StoreContextMenuDisplayEventHandler(
        Application_StoreContextMenuDisplay);

      Application.ShortcutContextMenuDisplay += new Outlook.
      ApplicationEvents_11_ShortcutContextMenuDisplayEventHandler(
        Application_ShortcutContextMenuDisplay);
```

```
  Application.ViewContextMenuDisplay += new Outlook.
  ApplicationEvents_11_ViewContextMenuDisplayEventHandler(
    Application_ViewContextMenuDisplay);

  Application.ItemContextMenuDisplay += new Outlook.
  ApplicationEvents_11_ItemContextMenuDisplayEventHandler(
    Application_ItemContextMenuDisplay);

  Application.ContextMenuClose += new Outlook.
  ApplicationEvents_11_ContextMenuCloseEventHandler(
    Application_ContextMenuClose);
}

void Application_ItemContextMenuDisplay(
  Office.CommandBar CommandBar, Outlook.Selection Selection)
{
  CommandBarHelper(CommandBar,"ItemContextMenu");
  lastSelection = Selection;
}

void Application_ViewContextMenuDisplay(
  Office.CommandBar CommandBar, Outlook.View View)
{
  CommandBarHelper(CommandBar, "ViewContextMenu");
  lastView = View;
}

void Application_ShortcutContextMenuDisplay(
  Office.CommandBar CommandBar,
  Outlook.OutlookBarShortcut Shortcut)
{
  CommandBarHelper(CommandBar, "ShortcutContextMenu");
  lastShortcut = Shortcut;
}

void Application_StoreContextMenuDisplay(
  Office.CommandBar CommandBar, Outlook.Store Store)
{
  CommandBarHelper(CommandBar, "StoreContextMenu");
  lastStore = Store;
}

void Application_FolderContextMenuDisplay(
  Office.CommandBar CommandBar, Outlook.MAPIFolder Folder)
{
  CommandBarHelper(CommandBar, "FolderContextMenu}");
  lastFolder = Folder;
}
```

```csharp
void Application_AttachmentContextMenuDisplay(
  Office.CommandBar CommandBar,
  Outlook.AttachmentSelection Attachments)
{
  CommandBarHelper(CommandBar, "AttachmentContextMenu");
  lastAttachments = Attachments;
}

void CommandBarHelper(
  Office.CommandBar CommandBar, string Message)
{
  btn = CommandBar.Controls.Add(
    Office.MsoControlType.msoControlButton,
    missing, missing, missing, true) as
    Office.CommandBarButton;
  btn.Caption = Message;
  btn.Click += new Office.
    _CommandBarButtonEvents_ClickEventHandler(btn_Click);
}

void btn_Click(
  Office.CommandBarButton Ctrl, ref bool CancelDefault)
{
  if (lastSelection != null)
  {
    MessageBox.Show(
      String.Format("ItemContextMenu for {0} items",
      lastSelection.Count));
  }
  else if (lastView != null)
  {
    MessageBox.Show(
      String.Format("ViewContextMenu for {0}", lastView.Name));
  }
  else if (lastShortcut != null)
  {
    MessageBox.Show(
      String.Format("ShortcutContextMenu for {0}",
      lastShortcut.Name));
  }
  else if (lastStore != null)
  {
    MessageBox.Show(
      String.Format("StoreContextMenu for {0}",
      lastStore.DisplayName));
  }
  else if (lastFolder != null)
  {
    MessageBox.Show(
      String.Format("FolderContextMenu for {0}", lastFolder.Name));
```

```
        }
        else if (lastAttachments != null)
        {
          MessageBox.Show(
            String.Format("AttachmentContextMenu for {0} " +
            "attachments", lastAttachments.Count));
        }
    }

    void Application_ContextMenuClose(
      Outlook.OlContextMenu ContextMenu)
    {
      // remove event handler and set btn to null
      if (btn != null)
      {
        btn.Click -= new Office.
          _CommandBarButtonEvents_ClickEventHandler(btn_Click);
        btn = null;

        lastSelection = null;
        lastView = null;
        lastShortcut = null;
        lastStore = null;
        lastFolder = null;
        lastAttachments = null;
      }
    }

    #region VSTO generated code
    private void InternalStartup()
    {
      this.Startup += new System.EventHandler(ThisAddIn_Startup);
    }
    #endregion
  }
}
```

Form Region Events

Outlook 2007 adds support for a new type of UI customization called a form region. A form region can be created to extend and modify the UI that is shown for many built-in Outlook item types: mail, contacts, appointments, and more. You can add a new tab to the pages displayed for a built-in Outlook item type or create an adjoining form region that displays at the bottom of the first page shown in an Inspector window or in the reading pane. You can also replace the first page or all pages shown for custom

Outlook types you create that derive from existing Outlook item types. Form regions are discussed in more detail in Chapter 16, "Working with Outlook Form Regions." Outlook 2007 adds a FormRegion object that has the following events:

- **FormRegion.Expanded** is raised when an adjoining form region is expanded or collapsed. Adjoining form regions have a +/- control that allows them to be collapsed and expanded by the user. Outlook passes a bool Expand parameter. If the parameter is true, the form region has been expanded; if it is false, the form region has been collapsed.
- **FormRegion.Close** is raised when a form region is closed.

Outlook Item Events

Outlook has many events that occur at the Outlook item level. We refer to Item events in this section, but there is no Item object per se in the Outlook object model. Instead, you will find Item events on each of the 17 Outlook object model objects listed in Table 9-1 in Chapter 9, "Programming Outlook."

Item Addition, Deletion, Change, and Move Events

Several events are raised when Outlook items are added, deleted, changed, or moved:

- **Items.ItemRemove** is raised when an item is deleted from the Items collection associated with a folder—for example, when an item is deleted from the collection of items in the Inbox folder. It is raised once for each item removed from the collection. Unfortunately, the item removed from the collection is not passed as a parameter to this event and is difficult to determine unless you store the previous state of the items in the folder in some way. This event is also not raised if more than 16 items are deleted at once or when the last item in a folder is deleted if the folder is in a PST file. You can work around these limitations by using the FolderChange event described in the "Folder Change Events" section earlier in this chapter. For example, you could store the number of items in the folder in a variable, and when handling the FolderChange event determine whether the number of items in the folder have decreased.

- **Items.ItemChange** is raised when an item is changed in the Items collection associated with a folder—for example, when an item is changed in the collection of Outlook items in the Inbox folder. Outlook passes the Outlook item that has changed as an `object` parameter to this event.

- **Folder.BeforeItemMove** (new in Outlook 2007) is raised when an item is moved from one folder to another. It is also raised when an item is about to be permanently deleted or moved to the deleted items folder. Outlook passes the Outlook item that is about to move to another folder as an `object` parameter to this event. It also passes a `MoveTo` parameter of type MAPIFolder for the folder to which the Outlook item is about to move. Finally, Outlook passes by reference a `bool` `Cancel` parameter. The `Cancel` parameter can be set to `true` by your event handler to prevent Outlook from moving the item to another folder.

- **Items.ItemAdd** is raised when an item is added to the Items collection associated with a folder—for example, when an item is added to the collection of Outlook items in the Inbox folder. It is raised once for each item that is added to the collection. Outlook passes the Outlook item that was added as an `object` parameter to this event. Unfortunately, this event is not raised if a large number of items are added at once. You can work around this limitation by using the FolderChange event described in the "Folder Change Events" section earlier in this chapter. For example, you could store the state of the items in the folder that you want to monitor for changes, and when handling the FolderChange event determine whether the new state of the items in the folder matches the state you have stored.

- **Item.BeforeDelete** is raised on an Outlook item when the item is deleted. However, the item must be deleted from an Inspector window—the event is not raised if you just delete the item from a folder. Outlook passes by reference a `bool` `cancel` parameter. The `cancel` parameter can be set to `true` by your event handler to prevent Outlook from deleting the item.

Listing 10-6 shows a VSTO Outlook add-in that handles these events. To get to an individual MailItem to handle the Item.BeforeDelete event, the code first gets the NameSpace object. The NameSpace object is accessed by calling the Application.Session property. The NameSpace object has a method called GetDefaultFolder that returns a MAPIFolder to which you can pass a member of the enumeration OlDefaultFolders to get a standard Outlook folder. In Listing 10-6, we pass `olFolderInbox` to get a Folder for the Inbox. We then use the Items collection associated with the Inbox's Folder to connect our event handlers to. We also use the Items collection to get to an individual MailItem for which we handle the Item.BeforeDelete event. We also use the Inbox Folder object to prevent items from being moved out of the Inbox by handling the Folder.BeforeItemMove event.

Listing 10-6: A VSTO Add-In That Handles Item Addition, Delete, Change, and Move Events

```
using System;
using System.Collections.Generic;
using System.Linq;
using System.Text;
using System.Xml.Linq;
using Outlook = Microsoft.Office.Interop.Outlook;
using Office = Microsoft.Office.Core;
using System.Windows.Forms;

namespace OutlookAddIn1
{
  public partial class ThisAddIn
  {
    Outlook.MailItem mailItem;
    Outlook.Items items;
    Outlook.Folder inbox;

    private void ThisAddIn_Startup(object sender, EventArgs e)
    {
      Outlook.NameSpace ns = Application.Session;
      inbox = ns.
        GetDefaultFolder(Outlook.OlDefaultFolders.olFolderInbox)
        as Outlook.Folder;

      foreach (object o in inbox.Items)
      {
        mailItem = o as Outlook.MailItem;
        if (mailItem != null)
        {
          break;
```

```
    }
  }

  if (mailItem == null)
  {
    MessageBox.Show("No mail item to connect to.");
  }
  else
  {
    mailItem.BeforeDelete += new
      Outlook.ItemEvents_10_BeforeDeleteEventHandler(
      MailItem_BeforeDelete);

    MessageBox.Show(String.Format(
      "Connected to the mail item with subject {0}.",
      mailItem.Subject));
  }

  items = inbox.Items;
  items.ItemRemove += new
    Outlook.ItemsEvents_ItemRemoveEventHandler(
    Items_ItemRemove);

  items.ItemChange += new
    Outlook.ItemsEvents_ItemChangeEventHandler(
    Items_ItemChange);

  items.ItemAdd += new
    Outlook.ItemsEvents_ItemAddEventHandler(
    Items_ItemAdd);

  inbox.BeforeItemMove += new
    Outlook.MAPIFolderEvents_12_BeforeItemMoveEventHandler(
    Folder_BeforeItemMove);
}

void MailItem_BeforeDelete(object item, ref bool cancel)
{
  MessageBox.Show(String.Format(
    "The mail item {0} cannot be deleted.",
    mailItem.Subject));
  cancel = true;
}

void Items_ItemRemove()
{
  MessageBox.Show("An item is about to be removed.");
}
```

```csharp
void Items_ItemChange(object item)
{
  GenerateItemMessage(item, "changed");
}

void Items_ItemAdd(object item)
{
  GenerateItemMessage(item, "added");
}

void GenerateItemMessage(object item, string operation)
{
  Outlook.MailItem mailItem = item as Outlook.MailItem;
  if (mailItem != null)
  {
    MessageBox.Show(String.Format(
      "MailItem {0} was just {1}.",
      mailItem.Subject, operation));
  }
  else
  {
    MessageBox.Show(String.Format(
      "An Outlook item was just {0}.", operation));
  }
}

void Folder_BeforeItemMove(object Item,
  Outlook.MAPIFolder MoveTo, ref bool Cancel)
{
  Outlook.MailItem mailItem = Item as Outlook.MailItem;
  if (mailItem != null)
  {
    MessageBox.Show(String.Format(
      "Preventing move {0} to folder {1}.",
      mailItem.Subject, MoveTo.Name));
    Cancel = true;
  }
}

#region VSTO generated code
private void InternalStartup()
{
  this.Startup += new System.EventHandler(ThisAddIn_Startup);
}
#endregion
  }
}
```

Copy, Paste, Cut, and Delete Events

Outlook raises several events when Outlook items are copied, cut, or pasted. These events are raised on an Explorer object. An Explorer object has a Selection property that returns the current selected items in the Explorer. Because many of the Explorer events telling you that a copy, cut, or paste is about to occur do not pass the items that are being acted upon, you must examine the Selection object to determine the items that are being acted upon:

- **Explorer.BeforeItemCopy** is raised before one or more Outlook items are copied. Outlook passes by reference a `bool cancel` parameter. The `cancel` parameter can be set to `true` by your event handler to prevent the item or items from being copied.

- **Explorer.BeforeItemCut** is raised before one or more Outlook items are cut. Outlook passes by reference a `bool cancel` parameter. The `cancel` parameter can be set to `true` by your event handler to prevent the item or items from being cut.

- **Explorer.BeforeItemPaste** is raised before one or more Outlook items are pasted. Outlook passes a `clipboardContent` parameter as an `object`. If the clipboard contains Outlook items that have been cut or copied, you can cast the `clipboardContent` parameter to a Selection object and examine what is about to be pasted. Outlook next passes a `target` parameter of type MAPIFolder. This represents the destination folder to which the item or items will be pasted. Outlook also passes by reference a `bool cancel` parameter. The `cancel` parameter can be set to `true` by your event handler to prevent the item or items from being pasted.

Listing 10-7 shows a VSTO Outlook add-in that handles these events. It uses a helper function called `GenerateItemsMessage` that iterates over the items in a Selection object and displays a dialog box with the subject of each MailItem selected.

Listing 10-7: A VSTO Add-In That Handles Copy, Cut, and Paste Events

```
using System;
using System.Collections.Generic;
using System.Linq;
using System.Text;
using System.Xml.Linq;
using Outlook = Microsoft.Office.Interop.Outlook;
using Office = Microsoft.Office.Core;
using System.Windows.Forms;

namespace OutlookAddIn1
{
  public partial class ThisAddIn
  {
    Outlook.Explorer explorer;

    private void ThisAddIn_Startup(object sender, EventArgs e)
    {
      explorer = Application.ActiveExplorer();

      explorer.BeforeItemCopy += new
        Outlook.ExplorerEvents_10_BeforeItemCopyEventHandler(
        Explorer_BeforeItemCopy);

      explorer.BeforeItemCut += new
        Outlook.ExplorerEvents_10_BeforeItemCutEventHandler(
        Explorer_BeforeItemCut);

      explorer.BeforeItemPaste += new
        Outlook.ExplorerEvents_10_BeforeItemPasteEventHandler(
        Explorer_BeforeItemPaste);
    }

    void GenerateItemsMessage(Outlook.Selection selection,
      string operation)
    {
      System.Text.StringBuilder b =
        new System.Text.StringBuilder();
      b.AppendFormat("Items to be {0}:\n\n", operation);

      foreach (object o in selection)
      {
        Outlook.MailItem mi = o as Outlook.MailItem;
        if (mi != null)
        {
          b.AppendFormat("MailItem: {0}\n", mi.Subject);
        }
        else
        {
```

```
          b.AppendLine("Other Outlook item");
        }
      }
    }
    MessageBox.Show(b.ToString());
  }

  void Explorer_BeforeItemCopy(ref bool cancel)
  {
    GenerateItemsMessage(explorer.Selection, "copied");
  }

  void Explorer_BeforeItemCut(ref bool cancel)
  {
    GenerateItemsMessage(explorer.Selection, "cut");
  }

  void Explorer_BeforeItemPaste(ref object clipboardContent,
    Outlook.MAPIFolder target, ref bool cancel)
  {
    if (clipboardContent is Outlook.Selection)
    {
      Outlook.Selection selection =
        clipboardContent as Outlook.Selection;

      GenerateItemsMessage(selection, "pasted");
    }
    else
    {
      MessageBox.Show(
        "The clipboard is not a Selection object.");
    }
  }

  #region VSTO generated code
  private void InternalStartup()
  {
    this.Startup += new System.EventHandler(ThisAddIn_Startup);
  }
  #endregion
  }
}
```

Property Change Events

A typical Outlook item has many associated properties, such as Creation-Time, Importance, LastModificationTime, and so on. All the properties associated with an Outlook item are contained by the ItemProperties collection. When any of these properties are changed, Outlook raises the

PropertyChange event. It is also possible to define additional custom properties and associate them with an Outlook item. When custom properties are changed, Outlook raises the CustomPropertyChange event:

- **Item.PropertyChange** is raised when a built-in property of an Outlook item is changed. Outlook passes a `name` parameter as a `string` that represents the name of the property that was changed.

- **Item.CustomPropertyChange** is raised when a user-defined property of an Outlook item is changed. Outlook passes a `name` parameter as a `string` that represents the name of the user-defined property that was changed.

Open, Read, Write, and Close Events

Outlook raises events when an Outlook item is opened, written to, or closed:

- **Item.Read** is raised when an Outlook item is displayed from within either an Explorer or Inspector view. This event has nothing to do with the Read or Unread status of an item, just whether it is being displayed in a view.

- **Item.Open** is raised when an Outlook item is opened in an Inspector view. Outlook passes by reference a `bool cancel` parameter. The `cancel` parameter can be set to `true` by your event handler to prevent the item from being opened.

- **Item.Write** is raised when an Outlook item is saved after being modified. Outlook passes by reference a `bool cancel` parameter. The `cancel` parameter can be set to `true` by your event handler to prevent the item or items from being written to.

- **Item.Close** is raised when an Outlook item is closed after being opened in an Inspector view. Outlook passes by reference a `bool cancel` parameter. The `cancel` parameter can be set to `true` by your event handler to prevent the item or items from being closed.

> ## ▪ NOTE
>
> Close is the name of both a method and an event on Outlook item objects. Because of this collision, you will not see the Close event in Visual Studio's pop-up menu of properties, events, and methods associated with an Outlook item. Furthermore, a warning displays at compile time when you try to handle this event. To get Visual Studio's pop-up menus to work and the warning to go away, you can cast the Explorer object to the ItemEvents_10_Event, as shown in Listing 10-8.

Listing 10-8 shows a VSTO Outlook add-in that handles these events.

Listing 10-8: A VSTO Add-In That Handles Open, Read, Write, and Close Events

```
using System;
using System.Collections.Generic;
using System.Linq;
using System.Text;
using System.Xml.Linq;
using Outlook = Microsoft.Office.Interop.Outlook;
using Office = Microsoft.Office.Core;
using System.Windows.Forms;

namespace OutlookAddIn3
{
  public partial class ThisAddIn
  {
    Outlook.MailItem mailItem;

    private void ThisAddIn_Startup(object sender, EventArgs e)
    {
      Outlook.NameSpace ns = Application.Session;
      Outlook.Folder inbox =
        ns.GetDefaultFolder(
        Outlook.OlDefaultFolders.olFolderInbox)
        as Outlook.Folder;

      foreach (object o in inbox.Items)
      {
        mailItem = o as Outlook.MailItem;
        if (mailItem != null)
        {
          break;
        }
      }
```

```csharp
    if (mailItem == null)
    {
      MessageBox.Show("No mail item to connect to.");
    }
    else
    {
      MessageBox.Show(String.Format(
        "Connected to the mail item with subject {0}.",
        mailItem.Subject));

      mailItem.Read += new
        Outlook.ItemEvents_10_ReadEventHandler(
        MailItem_Read);

      mailItem.Open += new
        Outlook.ItemEvents_10_OpenEventHandler(
        MailItem_Open);

      mailItem.Write += new
        Outlook.ItemEvents_10_WriteEventHandler(
        MailItem_Write);

      ((Outlook.ItemEvents_10_Event)mailItem).Close += new
        Outlook.ItemEvents_10_CloseEventHandler(
        MailItem_Close);
    }
}

void MailItem_Read()
{
  MessageBox.Show("Read");
}

void MailItem_Open(ref bool cancel)
{
  MessageBox.Show("Open");
}

void MailItem_Write(ref bool cancel)
{
  MessageBox.Show("Write");
}

void MailItem_Close(ref bool cancel)
{
  MessageBox.Show("Close");
}

#region VSTO generated code
private void InternalStartup()
```

```
        {
            this.Startup += new System.EventHandler(ThisAddIn_Startup);
        }
        #endregion
    }
}
```

Item Load, Unload, and BeforeAutoSave Event

Outlook 2007 introduces three new events that are useful for enforcing business logic when an Outlook item loads into memory, is autosaved, and unloads from memory. In older versions of Outlook, developers trying to enforce some business logic on an Outlook item—for example, preventing a particular property on an Outlook item from being edited—would handle the NewInspector event and then hook event handlers to the Outlook item being edited to enforce that logic. Unfortunately, an Outlook item can be edited without ever creating an Inspector window, such as when a user edits the value of a property of an Outlook item in a view with an editable cell. The ItemLoad event provides a way to hook an event to an Outlook item in a broader way than the NewInspector allowed and have business logic run even when the Outlook item is edited outside an Inspector window.

Code that you write in the ItemLoad handler is limited in what it can do to the Outlook item; only the Class and MessageClass properties can be accessed. But code that you write in the ItemLoad handler can hook up other Outlook item event handlers, and when those event handlers are invoked, the Outlook item will be fully editable.

- **Application.ItemLoad** is raised when an Outlook item is loaded into memory. Outlook passes the Outlook item being edited as an `object`. During this event, you can use only the Class or MessageClass properties of the Outlook item; the event is raised primarily to allow you to hook up Outlook item events to enforce business logic later. This event is raised for every item Outlook loads as long as the event is connected, so be aware of the performance implications, and disconnect your event handler as soon as you no longer need it.

- **Item.BeforeAutoSave** is raised before an Outlook item is autosaved. Outlook passes by reference a `bool Cancel` parameter. The `Cancel`

parameter can be set to true by your event handler to prevent the
item from being autosaved.

- **Item.Unload** is raised when an Outlook item is unloaded for memory. You can use this event to clean up any objects you created in the
  ItemLoad event or that you have used during the lifetime of the Outlook item.

Listing 10-9 uses the Application.ItemLoad event to hook up to the
Item.PropertyChange event for a mail item regardless of whether an
Inspector window is opened for the item. It uses Item.Unload to discon-
nect the event handlers when the mail item unloads from memory.

**Listing 10-9: A VSTO Add-In That Handles Application.ItemLoad, Item.Unload,
and Item.PropertyChange**

```
using System;
using System.Collections.Generic;
using System.Linq;
using System.Text;
using System.Xml.Linq;
using Outlook = Microsoft.Office.Interop.Outlook;
using Office = Microsoft.Office.Core;
using System.Windows.Forms;

namespace OutlookAddIn3
{
  public partial class ThisAddIn
  {
    Outlook.MailItem mailItem;

    private void ThisAddIn_Startup(object sender, EventArgs e)
    {
      Application.ItemLoad += new Outlook.
        ApplicationEvents_11_ItemLoadEventHandler(
        Application_ItemLoad);
    }

    void Application_ItemLoad(object Item)
    {
      if (mailItem == null)
      {
        mailItem = Item as Outlook.MailItem;
        if (mailItem != null)
        {
          mailItem.PropertyChange += new Outlook.
            ItemEvents_10_PropertyChangeEventHandler(
            mailItem_PropertyChange);
```

```
            mailItem.Unload += new Outlook.
              ItemEvents_10_UnloadEventHandler(
              mailItem_Unload);
        }
      }
    }

    void mailItem_PropertyChange(string Name)
    {
      MessageBox.Show(String.Format(
        "Don't change the property {0}", Name));
    }

    void mailItem_Unload()
    {
      if (mailItem != null)
      {
        mailItem.PropertyChange -= new Outlook.
          ItemEvents_10_PropertyChangeEventHandler(
          mailItem_PropertyChange);

        mailItem.Unload -= new Outlook.
          ItemEvents_10_UnloadEventHandler(
          mailItem_Unload);

        mailItem = null;
      }
    }

    #region VSTO generated code
    private void InternalStartup()
    {
      this.Startup += new System.EventHandler(ThisAddIn_Startup);
    }
    #endregion
  }
}
```

E-mail Events

Outlook raises several e-mail-related events when new mail is received, when an Outlook item is sent by e-mail, or when an Outlook item is forwarded or replied to:

- **Application.NewMail** is raised when new items are received in the Inbox, including mail messages, meeting requests, and task requests. This event is raised only when items are delivered to the default message store. A secondary account, such as an additional POP account delivered to its own PST, does not raise this event.

- **Application.NewMailEx** is raised when a new item is received in the Inbox, including mail messages, meeting requests, and task requests. An `entryIDs` parameter is passed as a `string`. The `entryIDs` parameter contains a single entry ID for the Outlook item that was received, because NewMailEx fires once for every new mail item. An entry ID uniquely identifies an Outlook item. This event is raised only when items are delivered to the default message store. A secondary account, like an additional POP account delivered to its own PST, does not raise this event.

- **Application.ItemSend** is raised when an Outlook item is sent—for example, when the user has an Outlook item open in an Inspector window and clicks the Send button. An `item` parameter is passed as an `object` that contains the Outlook item being sent. Outlook also passes by reference a `bool cancel` parameter. The `cancel` parameter can be set to `true` by your event handler to prevent the item from being sent.

- **Item.Send** is raised when an Outlook item is sent—for example, when the user has an Outlook item open in an Inspector window and clicks the Send button. Outlook passes by reference a `bool cancel` parameter. The `cancel` parameter can be set to `true` by your event handler to prevent the item from being sent.

- **Item.Reply** is raised when an Outlook item is replied to. A response parameter is passed as an `object` and represents the Outlook item that was created as a response to the original Outlook item. Outlook also passes by reference a `bool cancel` parameter. The `cancel` parameter can be set to `true` by your event handler to prevent the item from being replied to.

- **Item.ReplyAll** is raised when an Outlook item is replied to using the Reply All button. A response parameter is passed as an `object` and represents the Outlook item that was created as a response to the original Outlook item. Outlook also passes by reference a `bool cancel` parameter. The `cancel` parameter can be set to `true` by your event handler to prevent the item from being replied to.

- **Item.Forward** is raised when an Outlook item is forwarded. A response parameter is passed as an `object` and represents the Outlook item that was created to forward the original Outlook item. Outlook also passes by reference a `bool` `cancel` parameter. The `cancel` parameter can be set to `true` by your event handler to prevent the item from being forwarded.

Listing 10-10 shows a VSTO Outlook add-in that handles these events.

Listing 10-10: A VSTO Add-In That Handles E-mail Events

```
using System;
using System.Collections.Generic;
using System.Linq;
using System.Text;
using System.Xml.Linq;
using Outlook = Microsoft.Office.Interop.Outlook;
using Office = Microsoft.Office.Core;
using System.Windows.Forms;

namespace OutlookAddIn3
{
  public partial class ThisAddIn
  {
    Outlook.MailItem mailItem;

    private void ThisAddIn_Startup(object sender, EventArgs e)
    {
      Application.NewMail += new
        Outlook.ApplicationEvents_11_NewMailEventHandler(
        Application_NewMail);

      Application.NewMailEx += new
        Outlook.ApplicationEvents_11_NewMailExEventHandler(
        Application_NewMailEx);

      Application.ItemSend += new
        Outlook.ApplicationEvents_11_ItemSendEventHandler(
        Application_ItemSend);

      Outlook.NameSpace ns = Application.Session;
      Outlook.Folder inbox = ns.GetDefaultFolder(
        Outlook.OlDefaultFolders.olFolderInbox)
        as Outlook.Folder;

      foreach (object o in inbox.Items)
      {
```

```csharp
      mailItem = o as Outlook.MailItem;
      if (mailItem != null)
      {
        break;
      }
    }

    if (mailItem == null)
    {
      MessageBox.Show("Couldn't find a mail item.");
    }
    else
    {
      MessageBox.Show(String.Format(
        "Connected to the mail item {0}.",
        mailItem.Subject));

      ((Outlook.ItemEvents_10_Event)mailItem).Send += new
        Outlook.ItemEvents_10_SendEventHandler(
        MailItem_Send);

      ((Outlook.ItemEvents_10_Event)mailItem).Reply += new
        Outlook.ItemEvents_10_ReplyEventHandler(
        MailItem_Reply);

      ((Outlook.ItemEvents_10_Event)mailItem).ReplyAll += new
        Outlook.ItemEvents_10_ReplyAllEventHandler(
        MailItem_ReplyAll);

      ((Outlook.ItemEvents_10_Event)mailItem).Forward += new
        Outlook.ItemEvents_10_ForwardEventHandler(
        MailItem_Forward);
    }
  }

  void GenerateItemMessage(object item, string operation)
  {
    Outlook.MailItem mi = item as Outlook.MailItem;
    if (mi != null)
    {
      MessageBox.Show(String.Format(
        "MailItem {0} will be {0].",
        mi.Subject, operation));
    }
    else
    {
      MessageBox.Show(String.Format(
        "An Outlook item will be {0}.",
        operation));
    }
  }
```

```csharp
void Application_NewMail()
{
  MessageBox.Show("New mail was received");
}

void Application_NewMailEx(string entryIDCollection)
{
  MessageBox.Show(String.Format(
    "NewMailEx: {0}.",
    entryIDCollection));
}

void Application_ItemSend(object item,
  ref bool cancel)
{
  GenerateItemMessage(item, "sent");
}

void MailItem_Send(ref bool cancel)
{
  MessageBox.Show("MailItem Send");
}

void MailItem_Reply(object response,
  ref bool cancel)
{
  GenerateItemMessage(response, "generated as a reply");
}

void MailItem_ReplyAll(object response,
  ref bool cancel)
{
  GenerateItemMessage(response,
    "generated as a reply to all");
}

void MailItem_Forward(object forward, ref bool cancel)
{
  GenerateItemMessage(forward, "generated as a forward");
}

#region VSTO generated code
private void InternalStartup()
{
  this.Startup += new System.EventHandler(ThisAddIn_Startup);
}
#endregion
  }
}
```

Attachment Events

Outlook raises events when attachments are added to an Outlook item and when attachments associated with an Outlook item are read, saved, removed, and previewed:

- **Item.AttachmentAdd** is raised when an attachment is added to an Outlook item. Outlook passes an `attachment` parameter that represents the attachment that was added.

- **Item.AttachmentRead** is raised when an attachment attached to an Outlook item is opened for reading. Outlook passes an `attachment` parameter that represents the attachment that was read.

- **Item.AttachmentRemove** (new in Outlook 2007) is raised when an attachment is removed from an Outlook item. Outlook passes an `attachment` parameter that represents the attachment that was removed.

- **Item.BeforeAttachmentAdd** (new in Outlook 2007) is raised before an attachment is added to an Outlook item. Outlook passes an `attachment` parameter that represents the attachment that is about to be added. Outlook also passes by reference a `bool` `cancel` parameter. The `cancel` parameter can be set to `true` by your event handler to prevent the attachment from being added.

- **Item.BeforeAttachmentPreview** (new in Outlook 2007) that is raised before an attachment is previewed in the reading pane or an Inspector window. Outlook passes an `attachment` parameter that represents the attachment that is about to be previewed. Outlook also passes by reference a `bool` `cancel` parameter. The `cancel` parameter can be set to `true` by your event handler to prevent the attachment from being previewed.

- **Item.BeforeAttachmentRead** (new event in Outlook 2007) is raised before an attachment file is read into memory. Outlook passes an `attachment` parameter that represents the attachment that is about to be loaded into memory. Outlook also passes by reference a `bool` `cancel` parameter. The `cancel` parameter can be set to `true` by your event handler to prevent the attachment from being read into memory.

- **Item.BeforeAttachmentSave** is raised when an attachment attached to an Outlook item is about to be saved. Outlook passes an `attachment` parameter that represents the attachment that is about to be saved. Outlook also passes by reference a `bool cancel` parameter. The `cancel` parameter can be set to `true` by your event handler to prevent the attachment from being saved.

- **Item.BeforeAttachmentWriteToTempFile** (new in Outlook 2007) is raised before an attachment file is written to a temporary file. Outlook passes an `attachment` parameter that represents the attachment that is about to be written to a temporary file. Outlook also passes by reference a `bool cancel` parameter. The `cancel` parameter can be set to `true` by your event handler to prevent the attachment from being written to a temporary file.

Custom Action Events

Outlook enables you to associate custom actions with an Outlook item. A custom action is given a name and some default behavior—for example, you can create a custom action whose default behavior is to act on the original item or to create a new reply to the existing item. When the custom action is invoked from the Ribbon, the CustomAction event is raised on the associated Outlook item.

Figure 10-2 shows a custom action that has been associated with an Outlook mail item called My custom action. Outlook displays the custom action in the Action menu when an Inspector window is opened on the mail item. It also displays the custom action as a toolbar button.

Item.CustomAction is raised when a custom action associated with an Outlook item is invoked. This event is also raised for a voting button response, which is another form of custom action. Outlook passes an `action` parameter as an `object` that represents the custom action that was invoked. This parameter can be cast to an Action object. Outlook passes a `response` parameter as an `object` that represents the Outlook item created because of the custom action. Outlook also passes by reference a `bool cancel` parameter. The `cancel` parameter can be set to `true` by your event handler to prevent the custom action from being invoked.

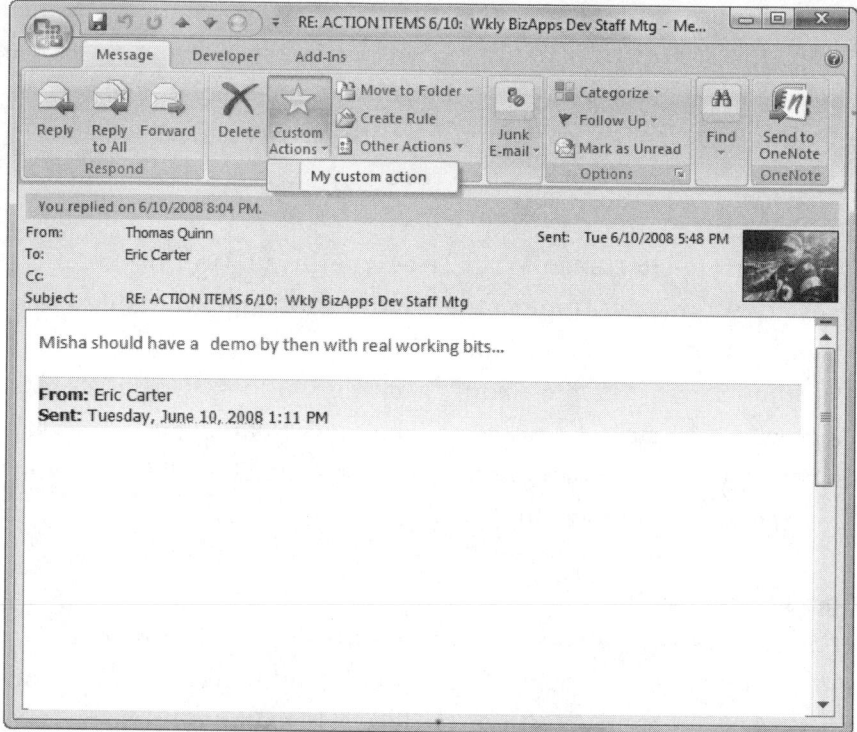

Figure 10-2: A custom action called My custom action.

Listing 10-11 shows a VSTO Outlook add-in that creates a custom action called My custom action. The CustomAction event is handled to set the subject when the custom action is invoked.

Listing 10-11: A VSTO Add-In That Creates a Custom Action and Handles a Custom Action Event

```
using System;
using System.Collections.Generic;
using System.Linq;
using System.Text;
using System.Xml.Linq;
using Outlook = Microsoft.Office.Interop.Outlook;
using Office = Microsoft.Office.Core;
using System.Windows.Forms;

namespace OutlookAddIn3
{
  public partial class ThisAddIn
```

```csharp
{
  Outlook.MailItem mailItem;

  private void ThisAddIn_Startup(object sender, EventArgs e)
  {
    Outlook.NameSpace ns = Application.Session;
    Outlook.Folder inbox = ns.GetDefaultFolder(
      Outlook.OlDefaultFolders.olFolderInbox)
      as Outlook.Folder;

    foreach (object o in inbox.Items)
    {
      mailItem = o as Outlook.MailItem;
      if (mailItem != null)
      {
        break;
      }
    }

    if (mailItem == null)
    {
      MessageBox.Show("Couldn't find a mail item.");
    }
    else
    {
      MessageBox.Show(String.Format(
        "Connected to the mail item {0}.",
        mailItem.Subject));

      mailItem.CustomAction += new
        Outlook.ItemEvents_10_CustomActionEventHandler(
        MailItem_CustomAction);

      Outlook.Action action = mailItem.Actions.Add();
      action.Name = "My custom action";
      action.ShowOn =
        Outlook.OlActionShowOn.olMenuAndToolbar;
      action.ReplyStyle =
        Outlook.OlActionReplyStyle.olLinkOriginalItem;
    }
  }

  void MailItem_CustomAction(object action,
    object response, ref bool cancel)
  {
    Outlook.Action myAction = (Outlook.Action)action;
    Outlook.MailItem mailItem = (Outlook.MailItem)response;
    if (myAction.Name == "My custom action")
    {
      mailItem.Subject = "Created by my custom action";
```

```
    }
  }

  #region VSTO generated code
  private void InternalStartup()
  {
    this.Startup += new System.EventHandler(ThisAddIn_Startup);
  }
  #endregion
  }
}
```

Other Events

Table 10-1 lists several other less commonly used events in the Outlook object model. Figure 10-3 shows the Shortcuts pane of the Outlook bar, with which several events in Table 10-1 are associated.

Figure 10-3: The Shortcuts pane showing one group (Shortcuts) and two shortcuts.

TABLE 10-1: Other Outlook Events

Events	Description
Search Events	
Application.AdvancedSearchCompleted	When the AdvancedSearch method on the Application object is invoked programmatically, this event is raised when the search is complete.
Application.AdvancedSearchStopped	When the AdvancedSearch method on the Application object is invoked programmatically, this event is raised if the search is stopped by calling Stop on the Search object returned by the AdvancedSearch method.
Synchronization Events	
SyncObject.OnError	Raised when a synchronization error occurs while synchronizing the Send\Receive group corresponding to the SyncObject.
SyncObject.Progress	Raised periodically while synchronizing the Send\Receive group corresponding to the SyncObject.
SyncObject.SyncEnd	Raised when the synchronization is complete for the Send\Receive group corresponding to the SyncObject.
SyncObject.SyncStart	Raised when the synchronization starts for the Send\Receive group corresponding to the SyncObject.
Reminder Events	
Application.Reminder	Raised before a reminder is displayed.
Reminders.BeforeReminderShow	Raised before a reminder is displayed.
ReminderCollection.ReminderAdd	Raised when a reminder is added to the ReminderCollection.
ReminderCollection.ReminderChange	Raised when a reminder is changed in the ReminderCollection.

Continues

TABLE 10-1: Other Outlook Events *(Continued)*

Events	Description
ReminderCollection.ReminderFire	Raised before a reminder in the Reminder-Collection is displayed.
ReminderCollection.ReminderRemove	Raised when a reminder is removed from the ReminderCollection.
ReminderCollection.ReminderSnooze	Raised when a reminder in the Reminder-Collection is snoozed.
Outlook Bar Shortcuts Pane Events	
OutlookBarGroups.BeforeGroupAdd	Raised before a new group is added to the Shortcuts pane in the Outlook bar.
OutlookBarGroups.BeforeGroupRemove	Raised before a group is removed from the Shortcuts pane in the Outlook bar.
OutlookBarGroups.GroupAdd	Raised when a new group is added to the Shortcuts pane in the Outlook bar.
OutlookBarPane.BeforeGroupSwitch	Raised before the user switches to a different group in the Shortcuts pane in the Outlook bar.
OutlookBarPane.BeforeNavigate	Raised when the user clicks a Shortcut in the Shortcuts pane in the Outlook bar.
OutlookBarShortcuts.BeforeShortcutAdd	Raised before a Shortcut is added to the Shortcuts pane in the Outlook bar.
OutlookBarShortcuts.BeforeShortcut-Remove	Raised before a shortcut is removed from the Shortcuts pane in the Outlook bar.
OutlookBarShortcuts.ShortcutAdd	Raised when a shortcut is added to the Shortcuts pane in the Outlook bar.

TABLE 10-1: Other Outlook Events *(Continued)*

Events	Description
Sharing Events	
Application.BeforeFolderSharingDialog*	Raised before the Sharing dialog box is shown for a folder. This event allows an add-in to cancel the default Sharing dialog box and provide a custom dialog box.
Navigation Pane Events	
NavigationPane.ModuleSwitch*	Raised when the active module in the navigation pane changes (between Mail, Tasks, Contacts, Folder List, Shortcuts, Contacts, and Calendar). The new active Navigation-Module is passed as a parameter to this event and for all modules except Folder List and Shortcuts; this can be cast to a more specialized subclass (MailModule, TaskModule, and so on).

* New in Outlook 2007

Conclusion

This chapter covered the various events raised by objects in the Outlook object model. Chapter 11, "Working with Outlook Objects," discusses in more detail the most important objects in the Outlook object model and how to use them in your code. Chapter 16, "Working with Outlook Form Regions," describes in more detail how to work with Outlook form regions.

■ 11 ■
Working with Outlook Objects

Working with the Application Object

This chapter examines some of the major objects in the Outlook object model, starting with the Application object. Many of the objects in the Outlook object model are very large, and it is beyond the scope of this book to completely describe these objects. Instead, this chapter focuses on the most commonly used methods and properties associated with these objects.

The Application object is the root object in the Outlook object model hierarchy. This means that you can access all the other objects in the object model by starting at the Application object and accessing its properties and methods as well as the properties and methods of objects it returns.

A companion object to the Application object is the NameSpace object, which is retrieved by using the Application object's Session property. Some confusion can arise because functionality that you would expect to be on the Application object is often found on the NameSpace object. For example, one way to get to the root folders that are open in Outlook is through the NameSpace object's Folders property. The Application object has no Folders property.

Methods and Properties That Return Active or Selected Objects

The Application object has a number of methods and properties that return active objects—objects representing things that are active or selected within Outlook. Table 11-1 shows some of these properties and methods.

TABLE 11-1: Application Properties and Methods That Return Active Objects

Name	Type	What It Does
ActiveExplorer()	Explorer	Returns the active Explorer object—the Explorer window that has focus within Outlook. If an Inspector window is active, this method returns the Explorer window that is frontmost in the stack of Outlook windows. If no Explorer windows are open, this method returns null.
ActiveInspector()	Inspector	Returns the active Inspector object—the Inspector window that has focus within Outlook. If an Explorer window is active, this method returns the Inspector window that is frontmost in the stack of Outlook windows. If no Inspector windows are open, this method returns null.
ActiveWindow()	object	Returns the active window as an object. If no windows are open, this method returns null. The returned object can be cast to either an Explorer or an Inspector object.
Session	NameSpace	A property that returns the NameSpace object.
GetNameSpace()	NameSpace	A method that returns the NameSpace object; takes the type of NameSpace to return as a string. The only string you can pass to GetNameSpace, however, is the string "MAPI". This method is an older way to get the NameSpace object. The newer way to access the Name-Space object that is used in this book is through the Session property.

Properties That Return Important Collections

The Application object has a number of properties that return collections that you will frequently use. Table 11-2 shows several of these properties. Listing 11-1 shows some code from a VSTO Outlook add-in that works with the active object methods and properties shown in Table 11-1 and the collections shown in Table 11-2.

TABLE 11-2: Application Properties That Return Important Collections

Property Name	What It Does
Explorers	Returns the Explorers collection, which enables you to access any open Explorer windows.
Inspectors	Returns the Inspectors collection, which enables you to access any open Inspector windows.
Reminders	Returns the Reminders collection, which enables you to access all the current reminders.

Listing 11-1: A VSTO Add-In That Works with Active Objects and Collections

```
using System;
using System.Collections.Generic;
using System.Linq;
using System.Text;
using System.Xml.Linq;
using Outlook = Microsoft.Office.Interop.Outlook;
using Office = Microsoft.Office.Core;
using System.Windows.Forms;

namespace OutlookAddIn3
{
  public partial class ThisAddIn
  {
    private void ThisAddIn_Startup(object sender, EventArgs e)
    {
      Outlook.Explorer activeExplorer =
        Application.ActiveExplorer();

      if (activeExplorer != null)
      {
```

```
    MessageBox.Show(String.Format(
      "The active explorer is {0}.",
      activeExplorer.Caption));
}

Outlook.Inspector activeInspector =
  Application.ActiveInspector();
if (activeInspector != null)
{
  MessageBox.Show(String.Format(
    "The Active Inspector is {0}.",
    activeInspector.Caption));
}

object activeWindow = Application.ActiveWindow();
if (activeWindow != null)
{
  Outlook.Explorer explorer = activeWindow
    as Outlook.Explorer;
  Outlook.Inspector inspector = activeWindow
    as Outlook.Inspector;

  if (explorer != null)
  {
    MessageBox.Show(String.Format(
      "The active window is an Explorer: {0}.",
      explorer.Caption));
  }
  else if (inspector != null)
  {
    MessageBox.Show(String.Format(
      "The active window is an Inspector: {0}.",
      inspector.Caption));
  }
}
else
{
  MessageBox.Show("No Outlook windows are open");
}

Outlook.NameSpace ns = Application.Session;
MessageBox.Show(String.Format(
  "There are {0} root folders.",
  ns.Folders.Count));

MessageBox.Show(String.Format(
  "There are {0} explorer windows.",
  Application.Explorers.Count));
```

```csharp
      foreach (Outlook.Explorer explorer in Application.Explorers)
      {
        MessageBox.Show(explorer.Caption);
      }

      MessageBox.Show(String.Format(
        "There are {0} inspector windows.",
        Application.Inspectors.Count));

      foreach (Outlook.Inspector inspector
        in Application.Inspectors)
      {
        MessageBox.Show(inspector.Caption);
      }

      MessageBox.Show(String.Format(
        "There are {0} reminders.",
        Application.Reminders.Count));

      System.Text.StringBuilder reminders =
        new System.Text.StringBuilder();

      foreach (Outlook.Reminder reminder in Application.Reminders)
      {
        reminders.AppendLine(reminder.Caption);
      }
      MessageBox.Show(reminders.ToString());
    }

    #region VSTO generated code
    private void InternalStartup()
    {
      this.Startup += new System.EventHandler(ThisAddIn_Startup);
    }
    #endregion
  }
}
```

Performing a Search and Creating a Search Folder

Outlook provides an AdvancedSearch method on the Application object that allows you to perform a search in Outlook. The AdvancedSearch method works asynchronously and raises the AdvancedSearchComplete event when the search has completed. You can also save a search you perform using the AdvancedSearch method as an Outlook Search folder. AdvancedSearch takes four parameters, as shown in Table 11-3.

TABLE 11-3: Parameters for the AdvancedSearch Method

Parameter Name	Type	Description
Scope	string	Pass the name of the folder or folders that you want to search. To search the Inbox, for example, pass the string "'Inbox'". To search the Inbox and Calendar, pass "'Inbox', 'Calendar'".
		You can pass the full name of a folder, including the path to the folder, to search a folder within a folder. The scope string "'Reference\Reviews'" searches a folder called Reviews nested in a folder called Reference in the default Outlook Store.
		You can search a folder in another PST Outlook data file that is open inside Outlook. The Scope string "'\\Archive\Backup'" searches a folder called Backup in a PST file called Archive that is open in Outlook.
Filter	optional object	Pass the filter string that specifies what you want to search for. You learn how to construct this string following this table.
SearchSubFolders	optional object	Pass true to also search any subfolders under the folders specified in Scope.
Tag	optional object	Pass a string to name the search uniquely so that when you handle the Application.AdvancedSearch-Complete event, you can distinguish between a search created by you and other searches created by other loaded add-ins. This is critical; you cannot assume that yours is the only add-in handling this event. You must carefully tag your searches with a unique string to ensure that your add-in does not act on an advanced search started by another add-in.

We now consider how to construct the filter string that was mentioned in Table 11-3. There are two basic query languages in Outlook: the DASL query language and the Jet query language. First, we consider how to build DASL queries; in "Finding an Outlook Item" later in this chapter, we explore some Jet queries.

The easiest way to build DASL queries is to use Outlook's built-in UI for constructing a DASL query string. Outlook has a Query Builder that you can turn on by setting a registry key. To turn on the Query Builder tab, follow these steps:

1. Choose Start > Run and type **regedit**, or in Windows Vista, show the Start menu and type **regedit** in the search bar at the bottom of the Start menu.

2. In the registry editor, navigate to HKEY_CURRENT_USER\Software\Microsoft\Office\12.0\Outlook.

3. Choose Edit > New > Key.

4. Type QueryBuilder for the key name.

The Query Builder shows up as a tab in the Filter dialog box. Choose View > Current View > Customize View to display the Customize View dialog box, shown in Figure 11-1.

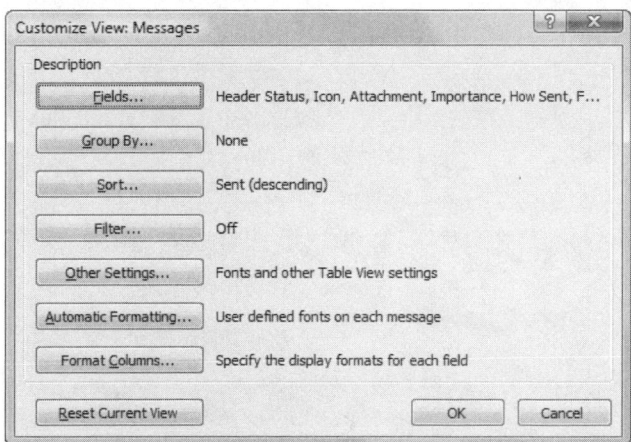

Figure 11-1: The Customize View dialog box.

Click the Filter button to display the Filter dialog box. You can use the Query Builder tab to create a custom query. In Figure 11-2, we created a simple query to show messages where the word *review* is in the subject field.

After you have edited the query to yield the results you want, click the SQL tab shown in Figure 11-3. Check the Edit these criteria directly check box. Doing so enables you to select the filter string, and copy and paste it into your code. After you have copied the filter string onto the clipboard, you can cancel out of the Filter dialog box and the Customize View dialog box.

Finally, paste the filter string into your code. You will want to use C#'s @ operator to preface the string, and you also need to expand all quotation marks to be double quotation marks. For our example, the C# code would look like this:

```
string filter = @"""urn:schemas:httpmail:subject"" " +
  "LIKE '%review%'";
```

New in Outlook 2007 is an improved Instant Search feature using Windows Desktop Search. In Listing 11-2, we determine whether Windows

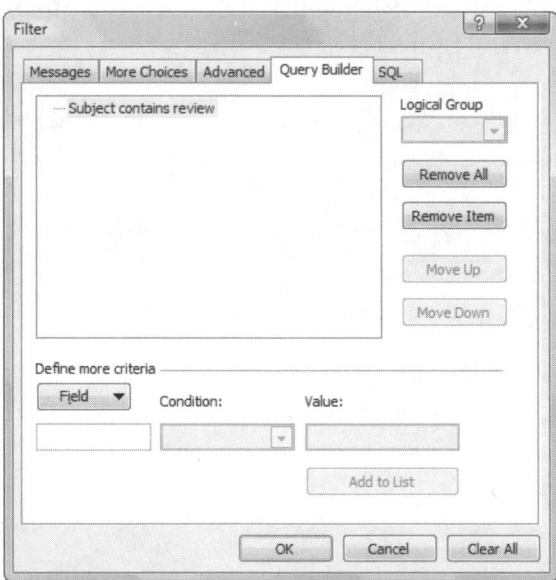

Figure 11-2: The Filter dialog box.

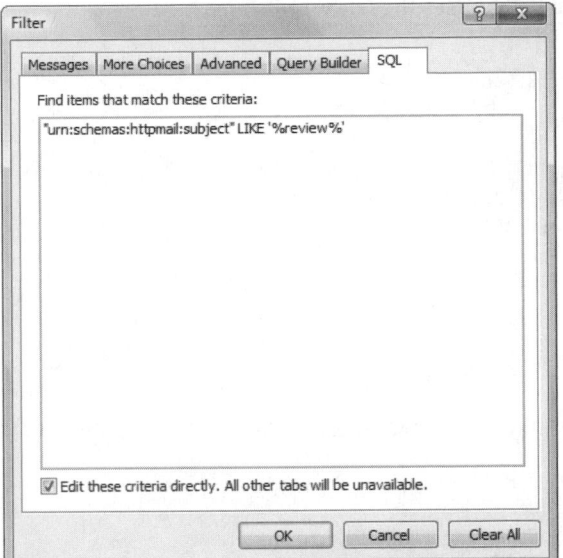

Figure 11-3: The SQL tab of the Filter dialog box displays a filter string.

Desktop Search is available by checking the Application.Session.Default-Store.IsInstantSearchEnabled property. If Windows Desktop Search is available, you can use two new keywords in a filter string for quick full-text searches: `ci_startswith` and `ci_phrasematch`. Our filter string using the `ci_phrasematch` keyword looks like this:

```
string filter = @"""urn:schemas:httpmail:subject"" " +
  "ci_startswith 'review'";
```

Listing 11-2 shows a complete example of using AdvancedSearch. Note that because the search proceeds asynchronously, we must handle the AdvancedSearchComplete event to determine when the search is finished. We also save the completed search as a search folder by calling Save on the completed Search object. Finally, we use the property IsInstantSearch-Enabled to determine whether to use the older `LIKE` keyword or the new `ci_startswith` keyword in our search. Also notice that a searchTag constant is defined; set this to your own GUID created by choosing Tools > Create GUID in Visual Studio.

Listing 11-2: A VSTO Add-In That Uses the AdvancedSearch Method

```csharp
using System;
using System.Collections.Generic;
using System.Linq;
using System.Text;
using System.Xml.Linq;
using Outlook = Microsoft.Office.Interop.Outlook;
using Office = Microsoft.Office.Core;
using System.Windows.Forms;

namespace OutlookAddIn3
{
  public partial class ThisAddIn
  {
    const string searchTag = "{59AAC219-0F9D-4ed2-AEC2-5333FA9E0EC7}";

    private void ThisAddIn_Startup(object sender, EventArgs e)
    {
      Application.AdvancedSearchComplete += new
      Outlook.ApplicationEvents_11_AdvancedSearchCompleteEventHandler(
        ThisApplication_AdvancedSearchComplete);
      Application.AdvancedSearchStopped += new
      Outlook.ApplicationEvents_11_AdvancedSearchStoppedEventHandler(
        ThisApplication_AdvancedSearchStopped);

      string scope = @"'Inbox'";
      string filter =
      @"""urn:schemas:httpmail:subject"" ";

      if (Application.Session.DefaultStore.
        IsInstantSearchEnabled == true)
      {
        filter += @"ci_phrasematch 'review'";
      }
      else
      {
        filter += @"LIKE '%review%'";
      }
      bool searchSubfolders = true;
      try
      {
        MessageBox.Show("Starting search");
        Application.AdvancedSearch(scope, filter,
          searchSubfolders, searchTag);
      }
      catch (Exception ex)
      {
        MessageBox.Show(ex.Message);
      }
    }
```

```csharp
    void ThisApplication_AdvancedSearchStopped(
      Outlook.Search searchObject)
    {
      if (searchObject.Tag == searchTag)
      {
        MessageBox.Show(String.Format(
          "Search completed. Found {0} results.",
          searchObject.Results.Count));

        // Save this search as a search folder
        searchObject.Save(searchTag);
      }
    }

    void ThisApplication_AdvancedSearchComplete(
      Outlook.Search searchObject)
    {
      if (searchObject.Tag == searchTag)
      {
        MessageBox.Show(String.Format(
          "Search was stopped. Found {0} results.",
          searchObject.Results.Count));
      }
    }

    #region VSTO generated code
    private void InternalStartup()
    {
      this.Startup += new System.EventHandler(ThisAddIn_Startup);
    }
    #endregion
  }
}
```

Copying a File into an Outlook Folder

Outlook provides a method to copy an existing document such as a spreadsheet on your desktop to an Outlook folder. The Application object's CopyFile method takes as a parameter a FilePath as a string, which is the full path to the document you want to copy into the Outlook folder. It also takes a DestFolderPath parameter, which is the name of the Outlook folder you want to copy the document to. Listing 11-3 shows an example of using CopyFile to put a spreadsheet called mydoc.xls into the Inbox and a second spreadsheet called mydoc2.xls into a folder called Reviews nested within a folder called Reference.

Listing 11-3: A VSTO Add-In Startup Handler That Uses the CopyFile Method

```
private void ThisAddIn_Startup(object sender, EventArgs e)
{
  Application.CopyFile(@"c:\mydoc.xls", "Inbox");
  Application.CopyFile(@"c:\mydoc2.xls", @"Reference\Reviews");
}
```

Quitting Outlook

The Quit method can be used to exit Outlook. If any unsaved Outlook items are opened, Outlook prompts the user to save each unsaved Outlook item. When users are prompted to save, they get a dialog box that gives them a Cancel button. If the user clicks Cancel, Outlook does not quit. There are additional cases in which the Quit method can fail to quit—when an external process created Outlook, for example, and Outlook's lifetime is being managed by the external process.

Working with the Explorers and Inspectors Collections

Listing 11-1 showed how to use C#'s foreach keyword to iterate over the Explorers and the Inspectors collections. It is also possible to get to an Explorer or Inspector using the index operator ([]) and passing an index as an object. That index can either be a 1-based index into the array of Explorers or Inspectors, or it can be a string index that is the caption of the Explorer or Inspector window in the array. Listing 11-4 illustrates using both types of indices with the Explorers and Inspectors collections.

Listing 11-4 also illustrates how to create a new Inspector and Explorer window. Both the Explorers and Inspectors collections have an Add method. The Explorers collection's Add method takes a Folder parameter of type Folder passed as object, which is the folder to display a new Explorer window for. It takes a second optional parameter of type OlFolder-DisplayMode that enables you to set the initial display used in the newly created Explorer window. The Add method returns the newly created Explorer object. To show the newly created Explorer object, you must then call the Explorer object's Display method.

The Inspectors collection's Add method takes an object parameter, which is the Outlook item to display an Inspector window for. In Listing 11-4,

> ▪▪ **NOTE**
>
> Folder is a new object in the Outlook 2007 object model, replacing MAPIFolder, which is now deprecated. Any MAPIFolder returned in older parts of the Outlook 2007 object model can be cast to a Folder. In Listing 11-4, we cast the return value of GetDefaultFolder from the deprecated MAPIFolder object to a Folder object. We also can pass a Folder to methods expecting MAPIFolder, such as the Add method of the Explorers collection.

we get an Outlook item out of the Inbox folder and create an Inspector window for it. To show the newly created Inspector object, you must then call the Inspector object's Display method, which takes an optional parameter called `Modal` of type `object` to which you can pass `true` to show the Inspector as a modal dialog box or `false` to show the Inspector as a modeless dialog box. If you omit the parameter by specifying `System.Type.Missing`, it defaults to `false`.

Listing 11-4: A VSTO Add-In That Works with Explorer and Inspector Windows

```
using System;
using System.Collections.Generic;
using System.Linq;
using System.Text;
using System.Xml.Linq;
using Outlook = Microsoft.Office.Interop.Outlook;
using Office = Microsoft.Office.Core;
using System.Windows.Forms;

namespace OutlookAddIn3
{
  public partial class ThisAddIn
  {
    private void ThisAddIn_Startup(object sender, EventArgs e)
    {
      Outlook.Folder folder = Application.Session.
        GetDefaultFolder(Outlook.OlDefaultFolders.olFolderInbox)
        as Outlook.Folder;

      // Create a new Explorer
      Outlook.Explorer newExplorer = Application.Explorers.Add(
        folder, Outlook.OlFolderDisplayMode.olFolderDisplayNormal);
```

```
      newExplorer.Display();
      string explorerIndex = newExplorer.Caption;

      // Get an Explorer by passing a string and an index
      Outlook.Explorer explorer = Application.Explorers[explorerIndex];
      MessageBox.Show(String.Format(
        "Got explorer {0}.",
        explorer.Caption));

      explorer = Application.Explorers[1];
      MessageBox.Show(String.Format(
        "Got explorer {0}.",
        explorer.Caption));

      // Create a new Inspector
      object item = folder.Items[1];
      Outlook.Inspector newInspector =
        Application.Inspectors.Add(item);
      newInspector.Display(false);
      string inspectorIndex = newInspector.Caption;

      // Get an Inspector by passing a string and an index
      Outlook.Inspector inspector =
        Application.Inspectors[inspectorIndex];
      MessageBox.Show(String.Format(
        "Got inspector {0}.",
        inspector.Caption));

      inspector = Application.Inspectors[1];
      MessageBox.Show(String.Format(
        "Got inspector {0}.",
        inspector.Caption));
    }

    #region VSTO generated code
    private void InternalStartup()
    {
      this.Startup += new System.EventHandler(ThisAddIn_Startup);
    }
    #endregion
  }
}
```

Working with the Explorer Object

The Explorer object represents an Outlook Explorer window—the main window in Outlook that displays views of folders. It is possible to open multiple Explorer windows—you can right-click a folder in one Explorer window and choose the option Open in New Window. Doing so creates a new Explorer window with the folder you selected to open in a new window as the active folder.

Working with the Selected Folder, View, and Items

The Explorer object has several methods and properties that enable you to work with the currently selected folder in the Explorer window, the view being used to display the list of items in that folder, and the currently selected items.

The CurrentFolder property returns a Folder object (you must cast from MAPIFolder) representing the folder selected in the Explorer window. An Explorer window always has a selected folder. To change the selected folder in an Explorer window, you can set the Explorer object's Current-Folder property to the Folder object you want to select. You can also determine whether a particular Folder object is currently selected by comparing it with the Explorer object's CurrentFolder object. The best way to do this comparison is to compare the FolderPath property of the CurrentFolder and the Folder you want to check.

Listing 11-5 shows some code that displays the name of the currently selected folder. It then checks to see whether the Contacts folder is selected. If it isn't selected, it selects it. Finally, it displays the name of the newly selected folder. Listing 11-5 uses the NameSpace object's GetDefaultFolder method to get a Folder object for the Contacts folder.

Listing 11-5: A VSTO Add-In That Selects the Contacts Folder

```
using System;
using System.Collections.Generic;
using System.Linq;
using System.Text;
using System.Xml.Linq;
using Outlook = Microsoft.Office.Interop.Outlook;
using Office = Microsoft.Office.Core;
using System.Windows.Forms;

namespace OutlookAddIn1
{
  public partial class ThisAddIn
  {
```

```
    private void ThisAddIn_Startup(object sender, EventArgs e)
    {
      Outlook.Explorer explorer = Application.ActiveExplorer();

      if (explorer != null)
      {
        MessageBox.Show(String.Format(
          "{0} is selected.",
          explorer.CurrentFolder.Name));

        Outlook.Folder folder =
          Application.Session.GetDefaultFolder(
          Outlook.OlDefaultFolders.olFolderContacts)
          as Outlook.Folder;

        if (explorer.CurrentFolder.FolderPath != folder.FolderPath)
        {
          explorer.CurrentFolder = folder;
        }

        MessageBox.Show(String.Format(
          "{0} is selected.",
          explorer.CurrentFolder.Name));
      }
    }

    #region VSTO generated code
    private void InternalStartup()
    {
      this.Startup += new System.EventHandler(ThisAddIn_Startup);
    }
    #endregion
  }
}
```

The CurrentView property returns a View object representing the view that is being used to display the items in the folder. A folder has a number of views that can be used to display its contents such as view by date, by conversation, by sender, and so on. It is also possible to define custom views. You can see the views that are defined for a given folder by selecting that folder in an Explorer window, then choosing View > Current View > Define Views to display the dialog box shown in Figure 11-4.

You can change the view used by an Explorer window by setting the Explorer object's CurrentView property to a View object associated with the folder. Listing 11-6 demonstrates this by selecting the Inbox folder and

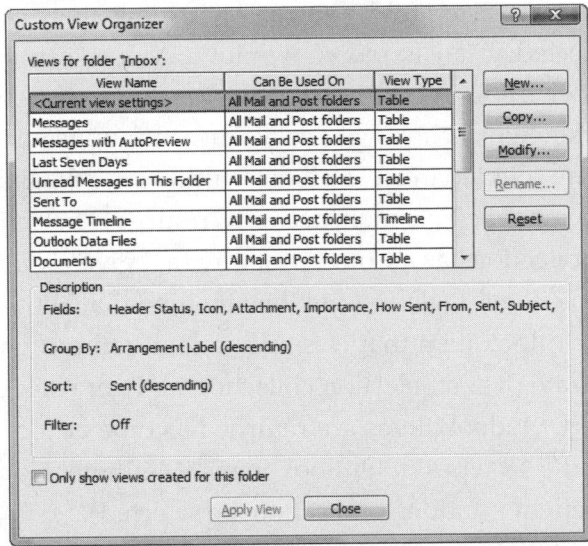

Figure 11-4: The Custom View Organizer dialog box shows views associated with a folder.

then setting the view for the Inbox folder to one of the View objects associated with the folder.

Listing 11-6: A VSTO Add-In Startup Handler That Selects the Inbox Folder and Changes the View

```
private void ThisAddIn_Startup(object sender, EventArgs e)
{
  Outlook.Explorer explorer = Application.ActiveExplorer();

  if (explorer != null)
  {
    Outlook.Folder folder = Application.Session.GetDefaultFolder(
      Outlook.OlDefaultFolders.olFolderInbox)
      as Outlook.Folder;

    explorer.CurrentFolder = folder;

    Outlook.View view = folder.Views[folder.Views.Count];
    explorer.CurrentView = view;
    MessageBox.Show(String.Format(
      "The view is now {0}.",
      view.Name));
  }
}
```

In addition to a selected folder and selected view, there can also be Outlook items selected in an Explorer window. A user can select multiple items in a folder by Shift-clicking to select a range of items or holding down the Ctrl key while clicking to select discontiguous items. To retrieve the items that are selected in an Explorer window, use the Explorer object's Selection property. The Selection property returns a Selection collection. The Selection collection has a Count property that gives you the number of selected Outlook items. It also has an Item method that allows you to get to an individual Outlook item that was selected, or you can use the foreach keyword to iterate over a Selection collection and get back Outlook items that are selected. Outlook items are returned as type object because they could be 17 of the 18 types of Outlook items (MailItem, ContactItem, and so on; a StorageItem is hidden and cannot be selected).

It is worth noting that if the user has selected a group header, the Selection collection will not contain any information about the group that is selected; neither will it contain the items that make up the group unless they were selected separately. When mail items are grouped by date, for example, if the user clicks the Today group header, no items will be returned in the Selection collection. If the user executes a command such as Delete, however, Outlook acts on all the items in the group.

In Listing 11-7, we handle the Application object's BeforeFolderSwitch event to display the items selected in a given folder before Outlook switches to a new folder. We use reflection to get the Subject property from each selected Outlook item. We know that the Subject property exists on all 18 types of Outlook items, so this is a safe property to get for any Outlook item contained in the selection. This simplifies the code so it does not have to have a cast to all 18 Outlook item types before accessing the Subject property.

Listing 11-7: A VSTO Add-In That Iterates over the Selected Outlook Items in a Folder

```
using System;
using System.Collections.Generic;
using System.Linq;
using System.Text;
using System.Xml.Linq;
using Outlook = Microsoft.Office.Interop.Outlook;
using Office = Microsoft.Office.Core;
using System.Windows.Forms;
```

```
namespace OutlookAddIn3
{
  public partial class ThisAddIn
  {
    Outlook.Explorer explorer;

    private void ThisAddIn_Startup(object sender,
      EventArgs e)
    {
      explorer = Application.ActiveExplorer();

      if (explorer != null)
      {
        explorer.BeforeFolderSwitch += new
          Outlook.ExplorerEvents_10_BeforeFolderSwitchEventHandler(
          Explorer_BeforeFolderSwitch);
      }
    }

    private object GetPropertyHelper(object targetObject,
      string propertyName)
    {
      return targetObject.GetType().InvokeMember(propertyName,
        System.Reflection.BindingFlags.Public |
        System.Reflection.BindingFlags.Instance |
        System.Reflection.BindingFlags.GetProperty,
        null,
        targetObject,
        null,
        System.Globalization.CultureInfo.CurrentCulture);
    }

    void Explorer_BeforeFolderSwitch(object newFolder,
      ref bool cancel)
    {
      Outlook.Selection selection = explorer.Selection;
      foreach (object o in selection)
      {
        string subject = (string)GetPropertyHelper(o, "Subject");
        MessageBox.Show(String.Format(
          "An Outlook Item is selected with subject {0}.",
          subject));
      }
    }

    #region VSTO generated code
    private void InternalStartup()
    {
```

```
    this.Startup += new System.EventHandler(ThisAddIn_Startup);
  }
  #endregion
 }
}
```

Working with an Explorer Window

Table 11-4 lists several properties and methods used to set and get the position of an Explorer window as well as some other commonly used properties and methods related to the management of the window.

TABLE 11-4: Explorer Properties and Methods

Name	Type	Description
Activate()		Makes the Explorer window the active window with focus.
Caption	string	Read-only property that returns a `string` value containing the caption of the Explorer window.
Close()		Closes the Explorer window.
Height	int	Gets and sets the height of the Explorer window in pixels. This property can be set only when the WindowState is set to `OlWindowState.olNormal-Window`.
Left	int	Gets and sets the left position, in pixels, of the Explorer window. This property can be set only when the WindowState is set to `OlWindowState.olNormalWindow`.
Top	int	Gets and sets the top position, in pixels, of the Explorer window. This property can be set only when the WindowState is set to `OlWindowState.olNormalWindow`.
Width	int	Gets and sets the width, in pixels, of the Explorer window. This property can be set only when the WindowState is set to `OlWindowState.olNormalWindow`.
WindowState	optional object	Gets and sets the window state of the Explorer window, using the OlWindowState enumeration. This property can be set to `olMaximized`, `olMinimized`, and `olNormalWindow`.

Adding Buttons and Menus to an Explorer Window

The CommandBars property returns a CommandBars object, which is defined in the Microsoft Office 12.0 Object Library PIA object. Outlook uses the CommandBars object model to work with buttons and menus in an Explorer window. Refer to Chapter 4, "Working with Excel Events," for more information on the CommandBars object hierarchy and examples of using the CommandBar objects. Listing 11-8 shows a VSTO add-in that creates a toolbar and a button and handles the click event for the newly added button.

Listing 11-8: A VSTO Add-In That Adds a Toolbar and Button to an Explorer Window

```csharp
using System;
using System.Collections.Generic;
using System.Linq;
using System.Text;
using System.Xml.Linq;
using Outlook = Microsoft.Office.Interop.Outlook;
using Office = Microsoft.Office.Core;
using System.Windows.Forms;

namespace OutlookAddIn3
{
  public partial class ThisAddIn
  {
    Office.CommandBarButton btn1;

    private void ThisAddIn_Startup(object sender,
      EventArgs e)
    {
      Outlook.Explorer explorer = Application.ActiveExplorer();

      if (explorer != null)
      {
        Office.CommandBar bar = explorer.CommandBars.Add(
          "My Command Bar", missing, missing, true);
        bar.Visible = true;
        bar.Position = Office.MsoBarPosition.msoBarTop;

        btn1 = (Office.CommandBarButton)bar.Controls.Add(
          Office.MsoControlType.msoControlButton, missing,
          missing, missing, true);

        btn1.Click += new
          Office._CommandBarButtonEvents_ClickEventHandler(
          Btn1_Click);
        btn1.Caption = "My Custom Button";
        btn1.Tag = "OutlookAddin1.btn1";
        btn1.Style = Office.MsoButtonStyle.msoButtonCaption;
```

```
        }
    }

    void Btn1_Click(Office.CommandBarButton ctrl,
      ref bool cancelDefault)
    {
      MessageBox.Show("You clicked my button!");
    }

    #region VSTO generated code
    private void InternalStartup()
    {
      this.Startup += new System.EventHandler(ThisAddIn_Startup);
    }
    #endregion
  }
}
```

Working with the Navigation Pane Associated with the Explorer Window

Outlook 2007 has a new object model object called NavigationPane, which gives you access to Outlook's Navigation Pane, shown in Figure 11-5. You can use Explorer's NavigationPane property to get the NavigationPane object for the Explorer window. The NavigationPane object has a read-write IsCollapsed property that can be set to true to collapse the Navigation Pane. It has a DisplayedModuleCount property that can be set to an int value representing how many of the eight Navigation Module types are shown in the NavigationPane, with large horizontal bars as opposed to small icons in the bottom-right corner. So in Figure 11-5, DisplayedModule-Count would return 4 for the Navigation Modules displayed as bars: Mail, Calendar, Contacts, and Tasks.

The NavigationPane object allows you to work with the eight Navigation Modules: Mail, Calendar, Contacts, Tasks, Journal, Notes, Folder List, and Shortcuts. The NavigationPane's CurrentModule property returns a NavigationModule object for the currently selected Navigation Module. You can also get to a NavigationModule object by using the GetNavigationModule method of the Modules collection returned by Navigation-Pane's Modules property. GetNavigationModule takes an enumerated value of type OlNavigationModuleType and returns a NavigationModule that can be cast to a specialized type for six of the Navigation Module types, as shown in Table 11-5.

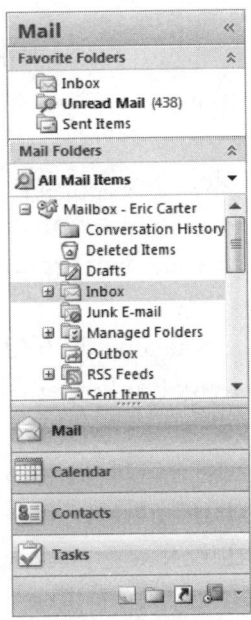

Figure 11-5: Outlook's Navigation Pane.

Table 11-5: OlNavigationModuleType Members and Corresponding Specializations of NavigationModule

OlNavigationModuleType Member	Specialized NavigationModule Type
olModuleMail	MailModule
olModuleCalendar	CalendarModule
olModuleContacts	ContactsModule
olModuleTasks	TasksModule
olModuleJournal	JournalModule
olModuleNotes	NotesModule
olModuleFolderList	No specialization; use NavigationModule
olModuleShortcuts	No specialization; use NavigationModule

You can use the NavigationModule specializations for Calendar, Contacts, Tasks, Notes, and Journal to create additional groups called Navigation Groups, which group items displayed in these Navigation Modules. A Navigation Group can be created by using the NavigationGroups property of CalendarModule, ContactsModule, TasksModule, NotesModule, and JournalModule. The NavigationGroups collection has a Create method that takes a `string` for the name of the new Navigation Group and returns a NavigationGroup object.

Given a NavigationGroup object, you can add folders to it by using the NavigationFolders property. The NavigationFolders collection has an Add method that takes a Folder object as a parameter and returns a Navigation-Folder object. Note that adding a folder to a NavigationGroup will remove it from any other NavigationGroup it may be in.

Listing 11-9 shows a VSTO add-in that works with NavigationPane, NavigationModule, a specialized NavigationModule object (TasksModule), NavigationGroups, NavigationGroup, and NavigationFolder. It sets the NavigationPane to show four modules as bars; then it adds a new folder to the user's default Tasks folder and displays that newly added folder as a Navigation Folder in a new Navigation Group created for the Tasks Navigation Module.

Listing 11-9: A VSTO Add-In That Works with the Navigation Pane

```
using System;
using System.Collections.Generic;
using System.Linq;
using System.Text;
using System.Xml.Linq;
using Outlook = Microsoft.Office.Interop.Outlook;
using Office = Microsoft.Office.Core;
using System.Windows.Forms;

namespace OutlookAddIn3
{
  public partial class ThisAddIn
  {
    private void ThisAddIn_Startup(object sender,
      EventArgs e)
    {
      Outlook.NavigationPane pane =
        Application.ActiveExplorer().NavigationPane;
```

```csharp
        pane.DisplayedModuleCount = 4;

        Outlook.NavigationModule module =
          pane.Modules.GetNavigationModule(
          Outlook.OlNavigationModuleType.olModuleTasks);

        Outlook.TasksModule tasksModule =
          module as Outlook.TasksModule;

        // Create a new tasks folder
        Outlook.Folder tasksRootFolder =
          Application.Session.GetDefaultFolder(
          Outlook.OlDefaultFolders.olFolderTasks)
          as Outlook.Folder;

        Outlook.Folder newTasksFolder =
          tasksRootFolder.Folders.Add("New Task Folder",
          Outlook.OlDefaultFolders.olFolderTasks)
          as Outlook.Folder;

        // Create a new navigation group and add
        // newly created tasks folder as a new
        // Navigation folder
        Outlook.NavigationGroup group =
          tasksModule.NavigationGroups.Create(
          "Test Navigation Group");

        group.NavigationFolders.Add(newTasksFolder);
      }

    #region VSTO generated code
    private void InternalStartup()
    {
      this.Startup += new System.EventHandler(ThisAddIn_Startup);
    }
    #endregion
  }
}
```

Associating a Web View with a Folder

It is possible to associate an HTML Web page with an Outlook folder by right-clicking a folder, choosing Properties, and then clicking the Home Page tab of the dialog box that appears. Figure 11-6 shows the Home Page tab of the Properties dialog box. You can also associate a Web page with a Folder using the Folder object's WebViewURL property. If you check the Show home page by default for this folder or set the Folder object's WebViewOn

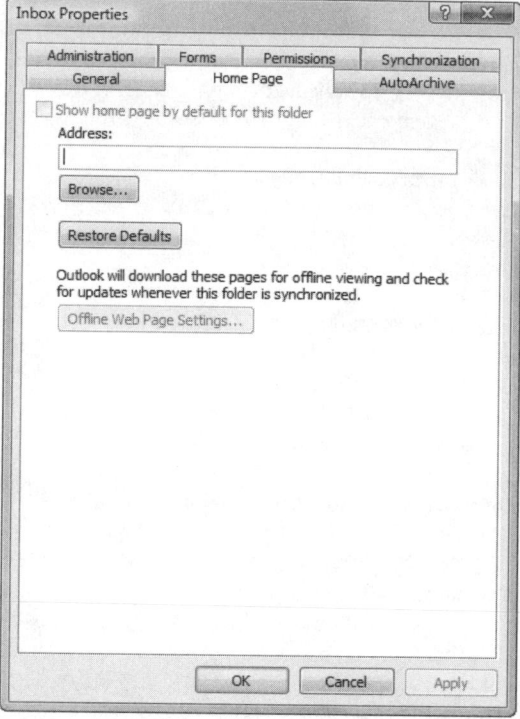

Figure 11-6: Associating an HTML page with a folder.

property to true, users are shown the Web page when they select the folder rather than an Outlook view of the items in the folder.

You can get to the HTML document object model for the Web page displayed by a folder by using the Explorer object's HTMLDocument property. This property only returns a non-null value if the selected folder is associated with a Web page. Interacting with the HTML document object model of a Web page through this property is an advanced topic and is not covered further in this book.

Setting and Clearing the Active Search for an Explorer Window

You can set and clear the active search for an Explorer window by using the Search and ClearSearch methods of the Explorer object. The Search method is passed a string to search for using AQS syntax (not Jet or DASL) and a member of the OlSearchScope enumeration—either olSearch-

ScopeCurrentFolder, which will search the currently selected folder in the Explorer window, or olSearchScopeAllFolders, which will search all Outlook folders in the currently selected module. (If the Contacts module is selected, for example, it will search all contact folders.) To clear the active search for an Explorer window, use the ClearSearch method.

Working with the Inspector Object

The Inspector window is the window in Outlook that shows detailed information for a particular Outlook item. This is the window that displays when you double-click an item in an Outlook folder. You can have multiple Inspector windows open at any given time. An Inspector window is also the only window in Outlook that has a Ribbon. We describe creating Ribbons for Outlook in Chapter 17, "Working with the Ribbon in VSTO." Inspector windows also can display form regions, which we describe in Chapter 16, "Working with Outlook Form Regions."

Working with the Outlook Item Associated with the Inspector

An Inspector window is always associated with 1 of the 18 Outlook item types listed in Table 9-1 in Chapter 9. To get to the Outlook item associated with an Inspector object, use the CurrentItem property which returns an Outlook item as an object. You can cast the returned object to 1 of the 18 Outlook item types.

Working with an Inspector Window

Table 11-6 lists several properties and methods that are used to set and get the position of an Inspector window as well as some other commonly used properties and methods related to the management of the window.

Working with an Inspector's Word Editor

The way that you typically set the body of a message without using formatting is by using the Outlook item object's Body property. All Outlook item objects support this property. To set the formatted body of a message in which the Outlook item type is MailItem, PostItem, or SharingItem, you can use the Outlook item object's HTMLBody property. For types other

TABLE 11-6: Inspector Properties and Methods

Name	Type	Description
Activate()		Makes the Inspector window the active window with focus.
Caption	string	Read-only property that returns a string value containing the caption of the Inspector window.
Close()		Closes the Inspector window.
Height	int	Gets and sets the height, in pixels, of the Inspector window. This property can be set only when the WindowState is set to OlWindowState.olNormalWindow.
Left	int	Gets and sets the left position, in pixels, of the Inspector window. This property can be set only when the WindowState is set to OlWindowState.olNormalWindow.
Top	int	Gets and sets the top position, in pixels, of the Inspector window. This property can be set only when the WindowState is set to OlWindowState.olNormalWindow.
Width	int	Gets and sets the width, in pixels, of the Inspector window. This property can be set only when the WindowState is set to OlWindowState.olNormalWindow.
WindowState	optional object	Gets and sets the window state of the Inspector window, using the OlWindowState enumeration. This property can be set to olMaximized, olMinimized, and olNormalWindow.

than MailItem, PostItem, or SharingItem, you must use the WordEditor and the Word object model if you want to format the message body (or fall back to the Body property if you don't need to do formatting).

To use the Word object model to format the message body of an Outlook item, first ensure that Word is installed. The Inspector object's EditorType property will return olEditorWord if Word is installed, and the IsWordMail property will return true. This means that Outlook has embedded the Word editor in the Inspector window and created a Word Document object to edit the Outlook item in. You can access the Word Document object by using the WordEditor property. The Inspector window must be displayed for the Outlook item you want to edit before the WordEditor object is available—so wait until the Inspector's Activate event is raised before using the WordEditor property. The WordEditor property returns an object that you can cast to Word's Document object and then use the properties and methods described in Chapter 8, "Working with Word Objects," to format the message body. Remember to add a reference in your Outlook add-in project to the Microsoft Word 12.0 Object model by choosing Project > Add Reference. Note that when you add the reference to the Microsoft Word 12.0 Object model, Visual Studio will add a second reference to Microsoft.Office.Core (office.dll) that you must remove to get the project to compile.

If you have stand-alone Outlook without Word installed on the system, WordEditor will return null, so be sure to check for this case and possibly fall back to using the Body property of the Outlook item object.

Listing 11-10 shows an example of a VSTO add-in that watches for a new Inspector window opening on a ContactItem. If a ContactItem is opened, the WordEditor is used to create a formatted Body. This example works only with a single Inspector window; to scale this to multiple Inspector windows, you would have to maintain a collection of Inspector objects as members of the class (recall the "My Button Stopped Working" issue in Chapter 1, "An Introduction to Office Programming," which requires you to keep a reference to any objects you are handling events for).

Listing 11-10: A VSTO Add-In That Uses the Word Object Model to Format the Body of a Contact

```
using System;
using System.Collections.Generic;
using System.Linq;
using System.Text;
using System.Xml.Linq;
using Outlook = Microsoft.Office.Interop.Outlook;
using Office = Microsoft.Office.Core;
using Word = Microsoft.Office.Interop.Word;
using System.Windows.Forms;

namespace OutlookAddIn3
{
```

```csharp
public partial class ThisAddIn
{
  Outlook.Inspectors inspectors;
  Outlook.Inspector inspector;

  private void ThisAddIn_Startup(object sender,
    EventArgs e)
  {
    inspectors = Application.Inspectors;
    inspectors.NewInspector += new
      Outlook.InspectorsEvents_NewInspectorEventHandler(
      Inspectors_NewInspector);
  }

  void Inspectors_NewInspector(Outlook.Inspector Inspector)
  {
    if (inspector == null)
    {
      inspector = Inspector;
      ((Outlook.InspectorEvents_10_Event)inspector).Activate +=
        new Outlook.InspectorEvents_10_ActivateEventHandler(
          Inspector_Activate);
      ((Outlook.InspectorEvents_10_Event)inspector).Close += new
        Outlook.InspectorEvents_10_CloseEventHandler(
        Inspector_Close);
    }
  }

  void Inspector_Close()
  {
    ((Outlook.InspectorEvents_10_Event)inspector).Activate -=
      new Outlook.InspectorEvents_10_ActivateEventHandler(
        Inspector_Activate);
    ((Outlook.InspectorEvents_10_Event)inspector).Close -= new
      Outlook.InspectorEvents_10_CloseEventHandler(
      Inspector_Close);
    inspector = null;
  }

  void Inspector_Activate()
  {
    Outlook.ContactItem ci =
      inspector.CurrentItem as Outlook.ContactItem;
    if (ci != null  &&
      MessageBox.Show(
      "Are you sure you want edit this contact?")
      == DialogResult.OK)
    {
      Word.Document doc = inspector.WordEditor as Word.Document;
```

```csharp
      if (doc != null)
      {
        Word.Range r = doc.Range(ref missing, ref missing);
        object collapseEnd = Word.WdCollapseDirection.wdCollapseEnd;
        r.Text = "Item\tName\n";
        r.Font.Name = "Verdana";
        r.Font.Size = 20.0F;

        r.Collapse(ref collapseEnd);
        r.InsertAfter("111\t1/4\" pipe\n");
        r.HighlightColorIndex = Word.WdColorIndex.wdGray25;
        r.Italic = -1;
        r.Font.Size = 10.0F;
        r.Font.Name = "Times New Roman";

        r.Collapse(ref collapseEnd);
        r.InsertAfter("112\t1/2\" pipe\n");
        r.Shading.BackgroundPatternColor = Word.WdColor.wdColorBlack;
        r.Font.Color = Word.WdColor.wdColorWhite;
        r.Font.Size = 10.0F;
        r.Font.SmallCaps = -1;
        r.Font.Name = "Verdana";

        r.Collapse(ref collapseEnd);
        r.InsertAfter("This should be a heading.");
        object style = "Heading 1";
        r.set_Style(ref style);
      }
      Inspector_Close();
    }
  }

  #region VSTO generated code
  private void InternalStartup()
  {
    this.Startup += new System.EventHandler(ThisAddIn_Startup);
  }
  #endregion
  }
}
```

Adding Buttons and Menus to an Inspector Window

The Inspector object's CommandBars property returns a CommandBars object, which is defined in the Microsoft Office 12.0 Object Library PIA object. Because Inspector windows in Outlook 2007 use the Ribbon, the CommandBars object is not the preferred way of adding commands to an

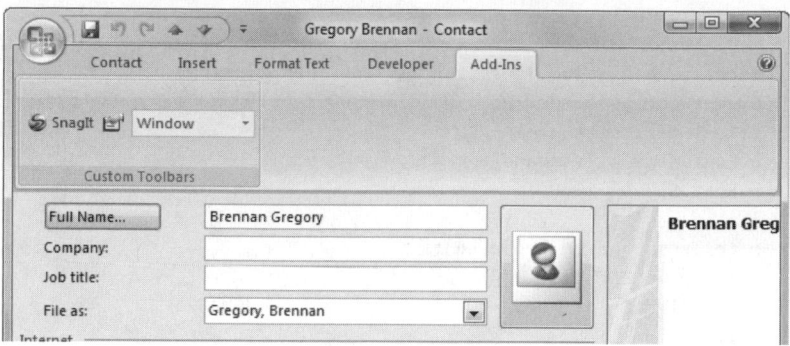

Figure 11-7: Adding commands to an Inspector window by using CommandBars results in commands being added to the Add-Ins tab in Outlook 2007.

Inspector window. If you add toolbars and menus by using the Command-Bars object model, your toolbars and commands will be added to an Add-Ins tab on the Ribbon. Figure 11-7 shows the result of adding toolbars and commands via CommandBars. For a complete discussion of how to customize the Ribbon of an Inspector window, see Chapter 17, "Working with the Ribbon in VSTO."

Working with the NameSpace Object

A companion object to the Application object is the NameSpace object, which is retrieved by using the Application object's Session property. As noted at the beginning of the chapter, some confusion can arise because functionality that you would expect to be on the Application object is actually often found on the NameSpace object. Further increasing the confusion is the Application.GetNameSpace method, which is an older way to get to a NameSpace object. This method takes a string for the type of NameSpace to return implying that you can get different types of NameSpace objects. In reality, the GetNameSpace method only accepts one string ("MAPI"). In this chapter, we use the Application object's Session property (added in Outlook 98) to get a NameSpace object rather than the older GetNameSpace method.

It is also a good idea to call the NameSpace.Logon method to ensure that the Session exists and is accessible. If Outlook is starts in an automated mode (is started by some automation executable, for example), the Session may not exist yet when the add-in is loaded, and the add-in may crash, expecting a session when one doesn't exist. The NameSpace.Logon method forces the Session to load and to be accessible.

Working with the Root Folders of the Open Outlook Stores

The NameSpace object's Folders property returns a Folders collection, allowing you to iterate over all the root folders that are open within Outlook. Each root folder is the root of what is called a Store. A root folder could correspond to an Exchange account or some other e-mail account. It could also correspond to an Outlook data file, such as a .PST file. Every folder and Outlook item under a particular root folder shares the same StoreID.

You can iterate over the Folders collection using C#'s `foreach` keyword. You can also get to a particular Folder in the Folders collection by using the index operator ([]). The index operator can be passed a `string` representing the name of the Folder in the Folders collection, or a 1-based index representing the index of the Folder within the Folders collection.

Although the Folders collection provides Add and Remove methods, these methods are not applicable to root folders because root folders represent stores that are added and removed by adding and removing e-mail accounts or adding and removing Outlook data files. The following section discusses how a Store is added and removed programmatically.

Listing 11-11 illustrates iterating over the Folders collection using `foreach`. It also shows how to get a Folder using the `index` operator on the Folders collection. Finally, it shows adding a new Folder to an existing store using the Folders collection's Add method. Note that some older methods in the object model still return a MAPIFolder object, which is deprecated. In those cases, we use the `as` keyword to cast the older MAPIFolder to a Folder.

Listing 11-11: VSTO Add-In That Iterates over the Root Folders and Adds a New Folder

```csharp
using System;
using System.Collections.Generic;
using System.Linq;
using System.Text;
using System.Xml.Linq;
using Outlook = Microsoft.Office.Interop.Outlook;
using Office = Microsoft.Office.Core;
using System.Windows.Forms;

namespace OutlookAddIn3
{
  public partial class ThisAddIn
  {
    private void ThisAddIn_Startup(object sender,
      EventArgs e)
    {
      foreach (Outlook.Folder folder in
        Application.Session.Folders)
      {
        MessageBox.Show(folder.Name);
      }

      Outlook.Folder rootFolder = Application.Session.Folders[1]
        as Outlook.Folder;
      Outlook.Folder newFolder = rootFolder.Folders.Add(
        "Test Notes Folder",
        Outlook.OlDefaultFolders.olFolderNotes)
        as Outlook.Folder;

      MessageBox.Show(String.Format(
        "A new folder {0} has been created in the store {1}.",
        newFolder.Name, rootFolder.Name));
    }

    #region VSTO generated code
    private void InternalStartup()
    {
      this.Startup += new System.EventHandler(ThisAddIn_Startup);
    }
    #endregion
  }
}
```

Another Way to Iterate over Open Outlook Stores

Outlook 2007 provides a new way to iterate over Stores. The NameSpace object has a Stores property that returns a Stores collection, allowing you to iterate over all the open Stores in Outlook. You can iterate over the Stores collection by using C#'s `foreach` keyword. You can also get to a particular Store in the Stores collection by using the index operator ([]). The index operator can be passed a `string` representing the display name of the root folder for the store or a 1-based index representing the index of the Store within the Stores collection.

The Store object is a new object in Outlook 2007 that gives additional properties and methods for working with an Outlook store. Outlook 2007 also introduces a DefaultStore property on the NameSpace object that returns a Store object representing the default store.

Adding and Removing Outlook Stores

To programmatically add a Store, you can use the NameSpace object's AddStore or AddStoreEx methods. The AddStore method takes a `Store` parameter of type `object`. You can pass a `string` representing the complete filename of the PST file to add. If the PST file you provide does not exist, Outlook creates the file for you. AddStoreEx takes the same `Store` parameter of type `object` that AddStore does. It also takes a second `Type` parameter of type OlStoreType. To this parameter, you can pass a member of the OlStoreType enumeration, which will control the format in which the PST file will be created should you pass a PST file that does not exist. The possible values you can pass are `olStoreDefault`, `olStoreUnicode`, or `olStoreANSI`.

Use the NameSpace object's RemoveStore method to programmatically remove a Store. RemoveStore removes the Store from Outlook but does not delete the actual PST file or mailbox on the server associated with the Store. RemoveStore takes a `Folder` parameter of type Folder. This parameter must be one of the root folders in the NameSpace object's Folders collection.

Managing the Master Category List

In Outlook 2007, the NameSpace object now has a Categories property that returns the master category list. You can iterate over the Categories collection by using C#'s `foreach` keyword. You can also get to a particular Category object in the Categories collection by using the index operator ([]). The index operator can be passed a `string` representing the name of the category or a 1-based index representing the index of the Category within the Categories collection. The Categories collection also provides methods to add and remove categories. The Category object, which is new in Outlook 2007, provides properties and methods to change the name, colors, and shortcut keys associated with a category.

Checking Whether Outlook Is Offline

You can determine whether Outlook is offline by getting the value of the NameSpace object's Offline property. This property returns true if Outlook is offline and not connected to a server. If the profile includes an Exchange account, you can find more details about the connection state by querying the ExchangeConnectionMode property on the NameSpace object. This property returns a member of the OlExchangeConnectionMode enumeration. Using this property, you can find out whether Outlook is disconnected from Exchange versus being offline.

Getting Standard Folders Such As the Inbox Folder

A method already used in several examples in this chapter to get standard Outlook folders such as the Inbox folder is the NameSpace object's GetDefaultFolder method. This method takes a FolderType parameter of type OlDefaultFolders and returns a MAPIFolder object that can be cast to a Folder. Table 11-7 lists the members of the OlDefaultFolders enumeration that can be passed to GetDefaultFolder and the standard Outlook folder that is returned.

Getting a Folder, Outlook Item, Store, or AddressEntry by ID

All Outlook items and folders are uniquely identified by an EntryID and a StoreID. Each Outlook item and folder within a given Store share the same StoreID. The EntryID is unique within a given Store. So the combination of an EntryID and StoreID uniquely identifies a folder or an Outlook item. When you have created a new Outlook item by using the Items collection's Add method or the Application object's CreateItem method, the newly created Outlook item will not be assigned an EntryID until you call the Save method on the newly created item.

TABLE 11-7: **Members of the OlDefaultFolders Enumeration That Can Be Passed to NameSpace Object's GetDefaultFolder Method**

OlDefaultFolders Member	GetDefaultFolder Result
olFolderCalendars	Returns the Calendar folder
olFolderConflicts	Returns the Conflicts folder
olFolderContacts	Returns the Contacts folder
olFolderDeletedItems	Returns the Deleted Items folder
olFolderDrafts	Returns the Drafts folder
olFolderInbox	Returns the Inbox folder
olFolderJournal	Returns the Journal folder
olFolderJunk	Returns the Junk E-Mail folder
olFolderLocalFailures	Returns the Local Sync Failures folder
olFolderManagedEmail	Returns the Managed E-mail folder
olFolderNotes	Returns the Notes folder
olFolderOutbox	Returns the Outbox folder
olFolderRssFeeds	Returns the RSS feeds folder
olFolderSentMail	Returns the Sent Items folder
olFolderServerFailures	Returns the Server Sync Failures folder
olFolderSyncIssues	Returns the Sync Issues folder
olFolderTasks	Returns the Tasks folder
olFolderToDo	Returns the To Do folder
olPublicFoldersAllPublicFolders	Returns the Public Folders folder

Both a Folder and the 18 Outlook item types have an EntryID property that returns the EntryID for the folder or item as a `string`. But only a Folder has a StoreID property. To determine the StoreID that corresponds to a particular Outlook item, you must get the parent Folder using the Parent property of an Outlook item and then determine the StoreID from the parent folder.

The NameSpace object's GetFolderFromID method takes an EntryID parameter as a `string` and an optional `StoreID` parameter as an `object` to which you can pass the StoreID as a `string`. If you omit the `StoreID` parameter by passing `System.Type.Missing`, Outlook assumes it should look in the default Store (the Store in which the default Inbox and Calendar are found). The GetFolderFromID method returns a MAPIFolder object identified by the EntryID and StoreID. The MAPIFolder object can be cast to a Folder.

The NameSpace object's GetItemFromID method takes an `EntryID` parameter as a `string` and an optional `StoreID` parameter as an `object` to which you can pass the StoreID as a `string`. If you omit the `StoreID` parameter by passing `System.Type.Missing`, Outlook assumes it should look in the default Store. The GetItemFromID method returns the `object` for the Outlook item identified by the EntryID and StoreID. You can then cast the returned `object` to 1 of the 18 Outlook item types listed in Table 9-1.

Stores and address entries also have a unique ID. We have already discussed how to get a StoreID from a Folder. A StoreID can also be obtained from a Store object's StoreID property. To get back a Store object given a StoreID, you can use the NameSpace object's GetStoreFromID, which takes a StoreID parameter as a `string` and returns the Store object corresponding to the StoreID. A unique ID for an AddressEntry object can be obtained from the AddressEntry object's ID property. To get back an AddressEntry object given an ID, you can use the NameSpace object's GetAddressEntryFromID, which takes an ID as a string and returns the AddressEntry object corresponding to the ID.

It is important to note that an object could have more than one EntryID that can be used to return the object. For this reason, it is important to use the NameSpace object's CompareEntryIDs to compare EntryID or StoreID values. This method will figure out whether two EntryIDs refer to the same object.

Listing 11-12 illustrates getting a folder and an Outlook item by EntryID and StoreID.

Listing 11-12: A VSTO Add-In That Uses the NameSpace Object's GetFolderFromID and GetItemFromID Methods

```
using System;
using System.Collections.Generic;
using System.Linq;
using System.Text;
using System.Xml.Linq;
using Outlook = Microsoft.Office.Interop.Outlook;
using Office = Microsoft.Office.Core;
using System.Windows.Forms;

namespace OutlookAddIn3
{
  public partial class ThisAddIn
  {
    private void ThisAddIn_Startup(object sender,
      EventArgs e)
    {
      Outlook.Folder inbox =
        Application.Session.GetDefaultFolder(
        Outlook.OlDefaultFolders.olFolderInbox)
        as Outlook.Folder;

      string inboxStoreID = inbox.StoreID;
      string inboxEntryID = inbox.EntryID;

      object outlookItem = inbox.Items[1];
      string itemStoreID = inboxStoreID;
      string itemEntryID = (string)GetPropertyHelper(
        outlookItem, "EntryID");

      Outlook.Folder theFolder =
        Application.Session.GetFolderFromID(
        inboxStoreID, inboxEntryID)
        as Outlook.Folder;

      MessageBox.Show(theFolder.Name);

      object theItem =
        Application.Session.GetItemFromID(
        itemEntryID, itemStoreID);
      MessageBox.Show((string)GetPropertyHelper(
        theItem, "Subject"));
    }
```

```
    private object GetPropertyHelper(object targetObject,
      string propertyName)
    {
      return targetObject.GetType().InvokeMember(propertyName,
        System.Reflection.BindingFlags.Public |
        System.Reflection.BindingFlags.Instance |
        System.Reflection.BindingFlags.GetProperty,
        null,
        targetObject,
        null,
        System.Globalization.CultureInfo.CurrentCulture);
    }

    #region VSTO generated code
    private void InternalStartup()
    {
      this.Startup += new System.EventHandler(ThisAddIn_Startup);
    }
    #endregion
  }
}
```

Determining the Current User and an Introduction to Recipient, AddressEntry, ContactItem, ExchangeUser, and ExchangeDistributionList

The NameSpace object's CurrentUser property returns a Recipient object representing the logged-in user. Given a Recipient object, you can use the Recipient object's Name property to get the name of the logged-in user.

You should also be aware of the relationship between a Recipient and an AddressEntry. A Recipient object can be passed to you as in the Current-User property, or you can create it by using the CreateRecipient method of the NameSpace object. The CreateRecipient method takes a string parameter, which can be the display name of the recipient as you might find it in one of your address books, the exchange alias of the recipient, or the SMTP address (person@example.com). A resolved Recipient object represents an AddressEntry object. Think of the experience of typing a name in the To field of an e-mail message. When you press Ctrl+K to force the names you've typed to be resolved, the names you typed change from Recipients to resolved AddressEntry objects and are underlined to show you that they have been resolved (or if they can't be resolved, they get a squiggly line below them as an indicator).

In a similar way, after you've created a Recipient object, there is no guarantee that it will actually resolve to a more concrete AddressEntry object. You may have picked a display name that is not unique in your address book, for example. To ensure that the recipient object maps to an actual AddressEntry object, you can call the Recipient.Resolve method. When you have a resolved Recipient object (Recipient.Resolved will return true), you can access the more concrete AddressEntry object by using the Recipient.AddressEntry property.

Given an AddressEntry object, you can get to more specific information based on the container that the AddressEntry was resolved from—specifically, a ContactItem, an ExchangeUser, or an ExchangeDistributionList. If the AddressEntry is an Exchange user, AddressEntry.GetExchangeUser() will return an ExchangeUser object, which in turn will give you access to Exchange-specific properties such as ExchangeUser.JobTitle, which shows the user's title in the address book, or methods such as Exchange-User.GetExchangeUserManager(), which returns the ExchangeUser object for the manager. If the AddressEntry is in the local Contacts folders, AddressEntry.GetContact will return the ContactItem associated with the AddressEntry. Finally, if the AddressEntry maps to an Exchange distribution list, AddressEntry.GetExchangeDistributionList() will return an ExchangeDistributionList object. This object has methods such as Get-ExchangeDistributionListMembers(), which returns an AddressEntries collection for the members of the list.

Note that some AddressEntry objects won't resolve to a ContactItem, ExchangeUser, or ExchangeDistributionList. They may be SMTP addresses that are not known by the system, for example. You can check AddressEntry's AddressEntryUserType property to get a member of the OlAddressEntryUserType enumeration to determine what kind of AddressEntry you have and determine in advance whether it is an Outlook contact item, exchange user, exchange distribution list, or some other type of AddressEntry.

Accessing Address Books and Address Entries

The NameSpace object's AddressLists property returns the AddressLists collection. The AddressLists collection is a collection containing all the available address books as AddressList objects. The AddressList object has an Addr-essEntries collection, which is a collection of AddressEntry objects.

Listing 11-13 iterates over the available address books and displays the name of each address book and the name of the first address entry in each address book. It also illustrates the relationship among AddressEntry, ContactItem, ExchangeUser, and ExchangeDistributionList.

Listing 11-13: A VSTO Add-In That Iterates over Available Address Books and Displays ContactItem, ExchangeUser, or ExchangeDistributionList Information

```
using System;
using System.Collections.Generic;
using System.Linq;
using System.Text;
using System.Xml.Linq;
using Outlook = Microsoft.Office.Interop.Outlook;
using Office = Microsoft.Office.Core;
using System.Windows.Forms;

namespace OutlookAddIn3
{
  public partial class ThisAddIn
  {
    private void ThisAddIn_Startup(object sender,
      EventArgs e)
    {
      Outlook.AddressLists lists =
        Application.Session.AddressLists;
      foreach (Outlook.AddressList list in lists)
      {
        MessageBox.Show(String.Format(
          "{0} has {1} address entries.",
          list.Name, list.AddressEntries.Count));

        if (list.AddressEntries.Count > 0)
        {
          Outlook.AddressEntry entry
            = list.AddressEntries[1];

          ProcessEntry(entry);
        }
      }
    }

    private void ProcessEntry(Outlook.AddressEntry entry)
    {
      MessageBox.Show(String.Format(
```

```csharp
        "The first address in this address book is {0}.",
        entry.Name));

    switch (entry.AddressEntryUserType)
    {
        case Outlook.OlAddressEntryUserType.
                olExchangeDistributionListAddressEntry:
            {
                Outlook.ExchangeDistributionList list =
                    entry.GetExchangeDistributionList();
                MessageBox.Show(String.Format(
                    "Distribution list with {0} recipients.",
                    list.Members.Count));
            }
            break;
        case Outlook.OlAddressEntryUserType.
                olExchangeUserAddressEntry:
            {
                Outlook.ExchangeUser user =
                    entry.GetExchangeUser();
                MessageBox.Show(String.Format(
                    "Title of user is {0}.",
                    user.JobTitle));
            }
            break;
        case Outlook.OlAddressEntryUserType.
                olOutlookContactAddressEntry:
            {
                Outlook.ContactItem item =
                    entry.GetContact();
                item.Display(false);
            }
            break;
        default:
            MessageBox.Show(String.Format(
                "Type of AddressEntry is {0}.",
                entry.AddressEntryUserType.ToString()));
            break;
    }
}

#region VSTO generated code
private void InternalStartup()
{
    this.Startup += new System.EventHandler(ThisAddIn_Startup);
}
#endregion
    }
}
```

Displaying the Outlook Select Folder Dialog Box

The NameSpace object provides a method that allows you to display Outlook's Select Folder dialog box, shown in Figure 11-8. The Select Folder dialog box provides a way for the user to select a folder as well as create a new folder. The NameSpace object's PickFolder method displays the Select Folder dialog box as a modal dialog box. The method returns the MAPI-Folder object corresponding to the folder the user selected in the dialog box. If the user cancels the dialog box, this method will return null.

Displaying the Select Names Dialog Box

The NameSpace object provides a method that allows you to display Outlook's Select Names dialog box, which is shown when a user clicks the To button in a mail message to select recipients of the mail message. The Get-SelectNamesDialog method returns a SelectNamesDialog object. You can configure the SelectNamesDialog object before showing it by using properties and methods of the object. Then you can display the dialog box modally by calling SelectNamesDialog.Display(). Finally, you can examine the Recipients collection of SelectNamesDialog to see what recipients were selected by the user.

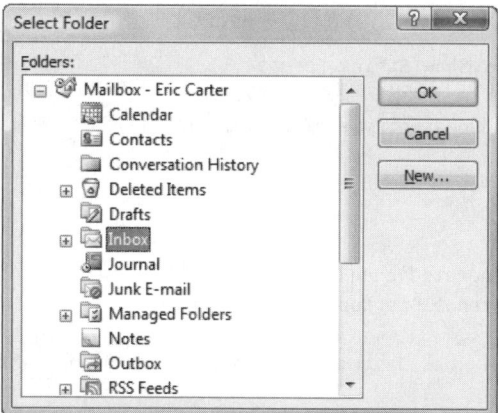

Figure 11-8: Outlook's Select Folder dialog box.

Working with the Folder Object

This chapter has already covered how to iterate over Folders collections, how to get a Folder out of a Folders collection using the index operator, how to access Outlook's default folders, how to get a Folder by EntryID and StoreID, and how to use Outlook's folder picker dialog box to get a Folder. This section now examines some additional properties and methods associated with the Folder object.

MAPIFolder and Folder

Folder is a new object in Outlook 2007 that replaces MAPIFolder, which is now deprecated. Many of the Outlook APIs still return MAPIFolder objects. You can safely cast these MAPIFolder return values to the new Folder type by using the `as` keyword as shown in many of the listings in this chapter.

Other Identifiers for a Folder

The Folder object's Name property returns the display name of a folder as a `string`. For example, the default server sync failures folder identified by `OlDefaultFolders.olFolderServerFailures` returns the string `"Server Failures"` for its Name property.

The Folder object's FolderPath property returns the full name of the folder as a `string`, including the names of the containing folders. For example, the default server sync failures folder identified by `OlDefault-Folders.olFolderServerFailures` returns the string `"\\Mailbox - Eric Carter\Sync Issues\Server Failures"` for its FolderPath property. For this example, the Server Failures folder is contained in a folder called Sync Issues in the Store called Eric Carter. Also note that Outlook uses URL-style encoding for any characters in the folder name that may have a different meaning in the folder path. A \ character in the folder name, for example, becomes %5C in the folder path.

The Folder object's Description property returns a `string` containing the description of the folder. This is a read/write property that can be set to any `string` value. The Folder object's ShowItemCount property controls whether the folder shows the unread item count, total item count, or no count when displayed in the Outlook Navigation Pane folder list. It can return or be set to a member of the OlShowItemCount enumeration: `olNo-ItemCount`, `olShowTotalItemCount`, or `olShowUnreadItemCount`. If you want to determine the number of unread items in a particular folder, use the Folder object's UnReadItemCount property, which returns an `int` value representing the unread item count.

Getting the Store for a Folder

New in Outlook 2007 is the Folder object's Store property. The Store property returns a Store object that gives more information about the Outlook store associated with a folder. A Store object has several properties and methods of note, as shown in Table 11-8.

Accessing Subfolders Contained in a Folder

A Folder may contain subfolders. The Folder object's Folders property returns a Folders collection, which contains any additional Folder objects that are subfolders of the given folder.

As described earlier, you can iterate over the subfolders contained in the Folders collection for a Folder using C#'s `foreach` keyword. You can also get to a particular Folder in the Folders collection by using the index operator ([]). The index operator can be passed a `string` representing the name of the Folder in the Folders collection, or a 1-based index representing the index of the Folder within the Folders collection.

The Folders collection's Add method enables you to add a new subfolder to the subfolders associated with a Folder. The Add method takes the name of the new folder as a `string` parameter. It also takes as an optional `object` parameter the Outlook folder type to use for the new folder. You can pass this parameter a subset of the OlDefaultFolders constants: `olFolderCalendar`, `olFolderContacts`, `olFolderDrafts`, `olFolderInbox`, `olFolderJournal`, `ol-FolderNotes`, `olPublicFoldersAllPublicFolders`, or `olFolderTasks`. If you omit this parameter by passing `System.Type.Missing`, the Outlook folder type of the newly created folder matches the folder type of the parent folder. Also note that a folder of type `olPublicFoldersAllPublicFolders` can only be added somewhere under the root public folder returned by the NameSpace object's `GetDefaultFolder(olPublicFoldersAllPublicFolders)`.

TABLE 11-8:   Key Properties and Methods Associated with the Store Object

Name	Type	What It Does
ExchangeStoreType	OlExchangeStoreType	Returns a member of the OlExchangeStoreType enumeration indicating the type of Exchange Store: `olExchangeMailbox`, `olExchangePublicFolder`, `olNotExchange`, or `olPrimaryExchangeMailbox`.
FilePath	string	Returns a `string` for the full path to the Store if the store is a .pst or .ost store. If it is neither of these, it returns an empty string.
IsCachedExchange	bool	Returns `true` if the store is a primary exchange mailbox and is using cached Exchange mode.
IsDataFileStore	bool	Returns `true` if the store is associated with a .pst or .ost store.
IsInstantSearchEnabled	bool	Returns `true` if instant search is enabled, which then allows you to use `ci_startswith` and `ci_phrasematch` in a query.
PropertyAccessor	PropertyAccessor	Returns a PropertyAccessor object, which allows you to get, set, create, and delete properties on the store.
StoreID	string	Returns a unique ID for the store.
GetRootFolder()	Folder	Returns the root Folder object for the store.

Continues

TABLE 11-8:   Key Properties and Methods Associated with the Store Object *(Continued)*

Name	Type	What It Does
GetRules()	Rules	Returns a Rules object, which then allows you to configure Rules for the store.
GetSearchFolders()	Folders	Returns a Folders collection, which contains all the search folders for the store.
GetSpecialFolder()	Folder	Takes a parameter of type OlSpecialFolders. If passed `olSpecialFolderAllTasks`, the method returns a Folder object for the All Tasks search folder. If passed `olSpecial-FolderReminders`, the method returns a Folder object for the Reminders search folder.

The Folders collection's Remove method enables you to remove a subfolder by passing the 1-based index of the folder in the Folders collection. Figuring out what the 1-based index is can be a bit of a pain—it is usually easier to just call the Delete method on the Folder object representing the subfolder you want to remove.

Listing 11-14 shows a VSTO add-in that iterates over the subfolders of the Inbox folder, and then adds a new folder using the Folders collection's Add method. It then deletes the newly added folder using the Folder object's Delete method rather than the Folders collection's Remove method.

Listing 11-14: A VSTO Add-In That Iterates over Subfolders of the Inbox Folder, Adds a New Subfolder, and Then Deletes It

```
using System;
using System.Collections.Generic;
using System.Linq;
using System.Text;
using System.Xml.Linq;
using Outlook = Microsoft.Office.Interop.Outlook;
```

```csharp
using Office = Microsoft.Office.Core;
using System.Windows.Forms;

namespace OutlookAddIn3
{
  public partial class ThisAddIn
  {
    private void ThisAddIn_Startup(object sender,
      EventArgs e)
    {
      Outlook.Folder folder =
        Application.Session.GetDefaultFolder(
        Outlook.OlDefaultFolders.olFolderInbox)
        as Outlook.Folder;

      MessageBox.Show(String.Format(
        "There are {0} subfolders in the Inbox.",
        folder.Folders.Count));

      foreach (Outlook.Folder subFolder in folder.Folders)
      {
        MessageBox.Show(String.Format(
          "Sub folder {0}.", subFolder.Name));
      }

      Outlook.Folder newSubFolder = folder.Folders.Add(
        "New Temporary Folder", missing) as Outlook.Folder;

      MessageBox.Show(
        "A new subfolder was just added under the Inbox folder");

      newSubFolder.Delete();
      MessageBox.Show("The new subfolder was just deleted.");
    }

    #region VSTO generated code
    private void InternalStartup()
    {
      this.Startup += new System.EventHandler(ThisAddIn_Startup);
    }
    #endregion
  }
}
```

Accessing Items Contained in a Folder

A Folder's main purpose in life is to contain Outlook items. When you create a new folder, you have to specify the type of folder it is. This type constrains the types of Outlook items it can contain. Figure 11-9 shows

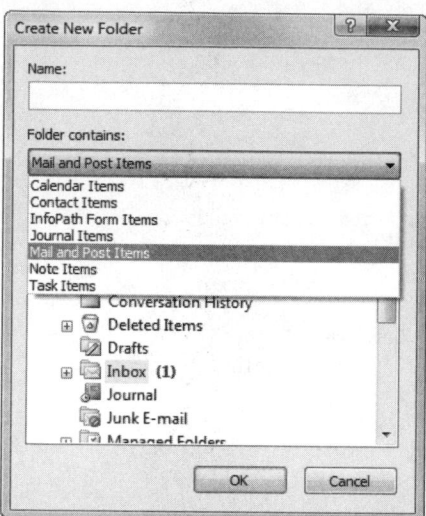

Figure 11-9: Outlook's Create New Folder dialog box.

Outlook's Create New Folder dialog box, which appears when you right-click a folder or root folder (Store) in Outlook and choose New Folder. The Create New Folder dialog box makes the user decide what kind of items the folder can contain: Calendar Items, Contact Items, Journal Items, Mail and Post Items, Note Items, or Task Items. This constraint is enforced by Outlook—if you try to drag a Mail item to a folder that was created to contain Calendar items, the item type will be changed to a Calendar item.

The Folder object's Items property returns an Items collection containing Outlook items in the folder. Each Outlook item in the folder is returned as an object. You can use the fact that folders are constrained to contain certain types of Outlook items when iterating over items in a folder. If you check the type of item that folder contains by looking at the DefaultItemType property, you can write code that only tries to cast the objects returned from the Items collection to the Outlook item types that are allowed in that folder. So for example, if you are iterating over items in a Folder whose DefaultItemType property returns olContactItem, objects returned from the Items collection can be cast to either a ContactItem or a DistListItem.

Table 11-9 shows how the member of the OlDefaultFolders enumeration you pass in when you create the folder using Folders.Add corre-

TABLE 11-9:   Relationship Among Folders.Add Folder Type (OlDefaultFolders), DefaultItemType Value, and Outlook Item Types Found in a Folder

Folder Created with OlDefaultFolders Enumeration Member	DefaultItemType Returns OlItemType Enumeration Member	Possible Outlook Item Types in Folder
olFolderCalendar	olAppointmentItem	AppointmentItem, StorageItem
olFolderContacts	olContactItem	ContactItem, DistListItem, StorageItem
olFolderJournal	olJournalItem	JournalItem, StorageItem
olFolderInbox olFolderDrafts	olMailItem	MailItem, PostItem, MeetingItem, RemoteItem, ReportItem, DocumentItem, TaskRequestAcceptItem, TaskRequestDeclineItem, TaskRequestItem, TaskRequestUpdateItem, SharingItem, StorageItem
olFolderNotes	olNoteItem	NoteItem, StorageItem
olPublicFolders-AllPublicFolders	olPostItem	PostItem, MailItem, StorageItem
olFolderTasks	olTaskItem	TaskItem, StorageItem

sponds to the returned DefaultItemType and what possible Outlook item types could be found in that folder.

Listing 11-15 shows an add-in that iterates over the top-level folders in each open Store and iterates over the items in each of those folders. It uses the DefaultItemType property to determine which kinds of items a particular folder might have in it and casts the objects returned from the Items collection to one of the expected types in the folder. Note that there is a case where the expected cast might fail. An object that is a MailItem that has restricted permissions cannot be cast to a MailItem unless the item has been opened in Outlook in an Inspector window with security permissions verified.

Listing 11-15: A VSTO Add-In That Iterates over Items in Folders and Performs Appropriate Casts

```csharp
using System;
using System.Collections.Generic;
using System.Linq;
using System.Text;
using System.Xml.Linq;
using Outlook = Microsoft.Office.Interop.Outlook;
using Office = Microsoft.Office.Core;
using System.Windows.Forms;

namespace OutlookAddIn3
{
  public partial class ThisAddIn
  {
    private void ThisAddIn_Startup(object sender,
      EventArgs e)
    {
      Outlook.Folders rootFolders =
        Application.Session.Folders;

      foreach (Outlook.Folder folder in rootFolders)
      {
        Outlook.Folders subFolders = folder.Folders;
        foreach (Outlook.Folder subfolder in subFolders)
        {
          IterateFolder(subfolder);
        }
      }
    }

    public void IterateFolder(Outlook.Folder folder)
    {
      System.Text.StringBuilder subject = new
        System.Text.StringBuilder();

      subject.AppendLine(folder.Name);
      foreach (object item in folder.Items)
      {
        subject.AppendLine(GetSubject(item,
          folder.DefaultItemType));
      }
      MessageBox.Show(subject.ToString());
    }

    public string GetSubject(object item,
      Outlook.OlItemType type)
    {
      switch (type)
      {
        case Outlook.OlItemType.olAppointmentItem:
```

```
  Outlook.AppointmentItem appointment = item
     as Outlook.AppointmentItem;
  if (appointment != null)
    return appointment.Subject;

  break;
case Outlook.OlItemType.olContactItem:
case Outlook.OlItemType.olDistributionListItem:

  Outlook.ContactItem contact = item as
     Outlook.ContactItem;
  if (contact != null)
    return contact.Subject;

  Outlook.DistListItem distlist = item as
     Outlook.DistListItem;
  if (distlist != null)
    return distlist.Subject;

  break;
case Outlook.OlItemType.olJournalItem:

  Outlook.JournalItem journal = item as
     Outlook.JournalItem;
  if (journal != null)
    return journal.Subject;

  break;
case Outlook.OlItemType.olMailItem:

  Outlook.MailItem mail = item as
     Outlook.MailItem;
  if (mail != null)
    return mail.Subject;

  Outlook.PostItem post = item as
     Outlook.PostItem;
  if (post != null)
    return post.Subject;

  Outlook.MeetingItem meeting = item as
     Outlook.MeetingItem;
  if (meeting != null)
    return meeting.Subject;

  Outlook.RemoteItem remote = item as
     Outlook.RemoteItem;
  if (remote != null)
    return remote.Subject;
```

```
    Outlook.ReportItem report = item as
      Outlook.ReportItem;
    if (report != null)
      return report.Subject;

    Outlook.DocumentItem doc = item as
      Outlook.DocumentItem;
    if (doc != null)
      return doc.Subject;

    Outlook.TaskRequestAcceptItem tra = item as
      Outlook.TaskRequestAcceptItem;
    if (tra != null)
      return tra.Subject;

    Outlook.TaskRequestDeclineItem trd = item as
      Outlook.TaskRequestDeclineItem;
    if (trd != null)
      return trd.Subject;

    Outlook.TaskRequestItem tr = item as
      Outlook.TaskRequestItem;
    if (tr != null)
      return tr.Subject;

    Outlook.TaskRequestUpdateItem tru = item as
      Outlook.TaskRequestUpdateItem;
    if (tru != null)
      return tru.Subject;

    break;
  case Outlook.OlItemType.olNoteItem:

    Outlook.NoteItem note = item as Outlook.NoteItem;
    if (note != null)
      return note.Subject;

    break;
  case Outlook.OlItemType.olPostItem:

    Outlook.PostItem post2 = item as Outlook.PostItem;
    if (post2 != null)
      return post2.Subject;

    break;
  case Outlook.OlItemType.olTaskItem:

    Outlook.TaskItem task = item as Outlook.TaskItem;
    if (task != null)
      return task.Subject;
```

```
            break;
        }

        MessageBox.Show(String.Format(
            "Couldn't cast item with subject {0} and class {1}.",
            GetPropertyHelper(item, "Subject"),
            GetPropertyHelper(item, "Class")));
        return "";
    }

    private object GetPropertyHelper(object targetObject,
        string propertyName)
    {
        return targetObject.GetType().InvokeMember(propertyName,
            System.Reflection.BindingFlags.Public |
            System.Reflection.BindingFlags.Instance |
            System.Reflection.BindingFlags.GetProperty,
            null,
            targetObject,
            null,
            System.Globalization.CultureInfo.CurrentCulture);
    }

    #region VSTO generated code
    private void InternalStartup()
    {
        this.Startup += new System.EventHandler(ThisAddIn_Startup);
    }
    #endregion
    }
}
```

Working with a Folder's View Settings

A Folder has a Views property that returns a Views collection. The Views collection contains all the available View objects for a folder that correspond to the views shown in the Custom View Organizer dialog box in Figure 11-4 earlier in this chapter. You can determine the view currently being used by the folder by accessing the Folder object's CurrentView property, which returns a View object. The CurrentView property is read-only—you cannot change the current view by setting the CurrentView property to another View object. Instead, you must access one of the View objects in the Views collection and call the View object's Apply method to make the view associated with the folder the active view.

A View can be cast to a more specialized view type in Outlook 2007. To determine the type of view you can cast to, use the ViewType property of View, which returns a member of the OlViewType enumeration. Table 11-10 shows the mapping between OlViewType enumeration members and the specialized view types in Outlook 2007.

Listing 11-16 shows add-in code that gets the name of the current view for the Inbox folder. Then the add-in uses the TableView type to make changes if the current view is a Table view. Finally, the add-in iterates over the available views for the Inbox folder and applies each view.

TABLE 11-10: Members of the OlViewType Enumeration and Corresponding Specialized View Types

OlViewType Member	Specialized View Type
olTableView	TableView
olCardView	CardView
olCalendarView	CalendarView
olIconView	IconView
olTimelineView	TimelineView
olBusinessCardView	BusinessCardView

Listing 11-16: A VSTO Add-In That Modifies the Current View and Then Iterates over Available Views for the Inbox Folder and Applies Each View

```
using System;
using System.Collections.Generic;
using System.Linq;
using System.Text;
using System.Xml.Linq;
using Outlook = Microsoft.Office.Interop.Outlook;
using Office = Microsoft.Office.Core;
using System.Windows.Forms;

namespace OutlookAddIn1
{
  public partial class ThisAddIn
```

```
{
  private void ThisAddIn_Startup(object sender,
    System.EventArgs e)
  {
    Outlook.Folder inbox =
      Application.Session.GetDefaultFolder(
      Outlook.OlDefaultFolders.olFolderInbox)
      as Outlook.Folder;

    Application.ActiveExplorer().CurrentFolder = inbox;

    MessageBox.Show(String.Format(
      "Current inbox view is {0}.",
      inbox.CurrentView.Name));

    if (inbox.CurrentView.ViewType ==
      Outlook.OlViewType.olTableView)
    {
      Outlook.TableView tview =
        inbox.CurrentView as Outlook.TableView;
      tview.AutoPreview =
        Outlook.OlAutoPreview.olAutoPreviewAll;
      tview.RowFont.Name = "Courier";
      tview.Apply();
      MessageBox.Show(
        "Changed current view");
    }

    foreach (Outlook.View view in inbox.Views)
    {
      view.Apply();
      MessageBox.Show(String.Format(
        "Current inbox view is now {0}.",
        inbox.CurrentView.Name));
    }
  }
  #region VSTO generated code
  private void InternalStartup()
  {
    this.Startup += new System.EventHandler(ThisAddIn_Startup);
  }
  #endregion
  }
}
```

Working with StorageItem Objects

Outlook 2007 introduces a new object called a StorageItem, which is stored as a hidden item in a folder. This object can be used to store add-in-specific data that you want to roam with the user and to make available online and offline through the mail account associated with the Folder.

To get or create a StorageItem object, use Folder's GetStorage method. GetStorage takes a `string` parameter that identifies the StorageItem and a member of the OlStorageIdentifierType indicating what type of identifier was passed as a `string`. Possible identifiers include `olIdentifyByEntryID`, `olIdentifyByMessageClass`, and `olIdentifyBySubject`.

If you use `olIdentifyByMessageClass`, you should use a message class that is prefaced by `IPM.Storage` and incorporates a unique identifier—your company name and add-in name, for example. So a possible message class string for a company called ACME developing an add-in called Out-Rock could use the message class `IPM.Storage.ACME.OutRock`. If you call the GetStorage method with an identifier, and no storage item is found that matches that identifier, GetStorage creates a new StorageItem with the given identifier.

If you try to get a StorageItem for a folder by using an identifier of the message class or by subject, and more than one StorageItem matches the identifier, GetStorage returns the most recently modified StorageItem that matches the identifier. You can also use the Table object to get all the StorageItem objects associated with a folder by calling Folder's GetTable method and passing `OlTableContents.olHiddenItems` as the second parameter to the method.

Given a StorageItem object, you can associate your custom data with it by adding attachments to the item, setting built-in properties of the item, or adding custom properties by using the UserProperties.Add method or the PropertyAccessor object.

Listing 11-17 shows a VSTO add-in, OutRock, that accesses a Storage-Item in the root inbox folder and adds a custom property to store the user's favorite band. To get a simple input box method, add a reference to the Microsoft.VisualBasic assembly.

Listing 11-17: A VSTO Add-In That Uses a StorageItem in the Root Inbox Folder

```
using System;
using System.Collections.Generic;
using System.Linq;
using System.Text;
using System.Xml.Linq;
```

```csharp
using Outlook = Microsoft.Office.Interop.Outlook;
using Office = Microsoft.Office.Core;
using System.Windows.Forms;

namespace OutlookAddIn1
{
  public partial class ThisAddIn
  {
    private void ThisAddIn_Startup(object sender,
      System.EventArgs e)
    {
      Outlook.Folder inbox =
        Application.Session.GetDefaultFolder(
        Outlook.OlDefaultFolders.olFolderInbox)
        as Outlook.Folder;

      Outlook.StorageItem storage =
      inbox.GetStorage("IPM.Storage.ACME.OutRock",
        Outlook.OlStorageIdentifierType.olIdentifyByMessageClass);

      Outlook.UserProperty favoriteGroup =
        storage.UserProperties["FavoriteGroup"];

      if (favoriteGroup == null)
      {
        // First time--storage was just created.
        // Add custom property
        favoriteGroup =
          storage.UserProperties.Add("FavoriteGroup",
          Outlook.OlUserPropertyType.olText,
          missing, missing);

        favoriteGroup.Value =
          Microsoft.VisualBasic.Interaction.InputBox(
          "Enter your favorite group", "Get favorite group",
          "", 0, 0);

        storage.Save();
      }
      else
      {
        MessageBox.Show(String.Format(
          "Your favorite group is {0}",
          favoriteGroup.Value));
      }
    }

    #region VSTO generated code
    private void InternalStartup()
    {
```

```
      this.Startup += new System.EventHandler(ThisAddIn_Startup);
    }
    #endregion
  }
}
```

Copying or Moving a Folder to a New Location

You can copy a folder and its dependent folders and items to a new location using the Folder object's CopyTo method. The CopyTo method takes a DestinationFolder parameter of type Folder, which will be the parent folder for the copied folder. It returns a Folder for the newly copied folder. The copy is a "deep copy" because all the items and subfolders rooted at the folder you call the CopyTo method on are copied to the new location.

You can move a folder and its dependent folders and items to a new location using the Folder's MoveTo method. The MoveTo method takes a DestinationFolder parameter of type Folder, which will be the parent folder for the moved folder. The folder is moved along with all dependent folders and items to the new location.

Displaying a Folder in an Explorer View

You can open a Folder in a new Explorer view by calling the Folder object's Display method. To use an existing Explorer view, you can set the Explorer object's CurrentFolder to the Folder you want to display in the existing Explorer view. Listing 11-16 earlier in this chapter uses this approach.

Working with the Items Collection

This chapter has already covered how to iterate over the Outlook items in a Folder by using foreach with the Items collection. This section examines some additional methods that you can use when working with the Items collection. Finally, we examine the Table object, new in Outlook 2007, which provides a much more performant way to work with multiple Outlook items.

Iterating over Outlook Items

The Items collection's SetColumns method enables you to tell Outlook to cache certain properties when you iterate over the Items collection so that access to those properties will be fast. An Outlook item has a number of properties associated with it—name value pairs that can be accessed by using an Outlook item's ItemProperties property. A typical MailItem has around 80 properties associated with it.

If you know that you are going to iterate using `foreach` over the Items collection and you are only going to be accessing the Subject and Creation-Time properties of Outlook items in that collection, you can call the Items collection's SetColumns method before iterating the collection and pass the string `"Subject, CreationTime"`. Some limitations apply to which properties can be cached (for example, properties which return objects cannot be cached)—check the documentation before using this method. After you have iterated over the collection, use the Items collection's Reset-Columns method to clear the cache of properties Outlook created.

The Items collection's Sort method enables you to apply a sort order to the Items collection before you iterate over the collection using `foreach`. The method takes a `Property` parameter as a `string`, which gives the name of the property by which to sort. You pass the name of the property enclosed in square brackets. To sort by subject you would pass `"[Subject]"`. The Sort method also takes an optional `Descending` parameter that can be passed `true` to sort descending, `false` to sort ascending. The default value if you pass `System.Type.Missing` is `false`. Some limitations apply to which properties can sorted on—check the documentation before using this method.

Listing 11-18 illustrates using the SetColumns and Sort methods. It times the operation of iterating through all the items in the Inbox and examining the Subject property without calling SetColumns. It then times the operation again but calls SetColumns first. Finally, Sort is illustrated, and the first item and last item in the sorted Items collection are accessed using the index operator. The Items collection's Count property is also used to get the index of the last item in the Items collection.

Listing 11-18: A VSTO Add-In That Uses the Items Collection's SetColumns and Sort Methods

```
using System;
using System.Collections.Generic;
using System.Linq;
using System.Text;
using System.Xml.Linq;
using Outlook = Microsoft.Office.Interop.Outlook;
```

```csharp
using Office = Microsoft.Office.Core;
using System.Windows.Forms;

namespace OutlookAddIn1
{
  public partial class ThisAddIn
  {
    private void ThisAddIn_Startup(object sender,
      System.EventArgs e)
    {
      Outlook.Folder inbox =
        Application.Session.GetDefaultFolder(
        Outlook.OlDefaultFolders.olFolderInbox)
        as Outlook.Folder;

      Outlook.Items myItems = inbox.Items;

      MessageBox.Show("Click OK to start the test.");

      System.DateTime start = System.DateTime.Now;
      foreach (object item in myItems)
      {
        string subject = (string)
          GetPropertyHelper(item, "Subject");
      }
      System.DateTime end = System.DateTime.Now;
      System.TimeSpan result1 = end.Subtract(start);

      MessageBox.Show(String.Format(
        "Not calling SetColumns took {0} ticks.",
        result1.Ticks));
      start = System.DateTime.Now;
      myItems.SetColumns("Subject");
      foreach (object item in myItems)
      {
        string subject =
          (string)GetPropertyHelper(item, "Subject");
      }
      end = System.DateTime.Now;
      System.TimeSpan result2 = end.Subtract(start);

      MessageBox.Show(String.Format(
        "With SetColumns this took {0} ticks.",
        result2.Ticks));

      myItems.ResetColumns();

      myItems.Sort("[Subject]", missing);
      object firstItem = myItems[1];
      object lastItem = myItems[myItems.Count];
```

```
      MessageBox.Show(String.Format(
        "First item is {0}.",
        (string)GetPropertyHelper(firstItem, "Subject")));
      MessageBox.Show(String.Format(
        "Last item is {0}.",
        (string)GetPropertyHelper(lastItem, "Subject")));
    }

    private object GetPropertyHelper(object targetObject,
      string propertyName)
    {
      return targetObject.GetType().InvokeMember(propertyName,
        System.Reflection.BindingFlags.Public |
        System.Reflection.BindingFlags.Instance |
        System.Reflection.BindingFlags.GetProperty,
        null,
        targetObject,
        null,
        System.Globalization.CultureInfo.CurrentCulture);
    }

    #region VSTO generated code
    private void InternalStartup()
    {
      this.Startup += new System.EventHandler(ThisAddIn_Startup);
    }
    #endregion
  }
}
```

Finding an Outlook Item

The Items collection's Find method enables you to find an Outlook item in the Items collection by querying the value of one or more properties associated with the Outlook item. The Find method takes a `string`, which contains a filter to apply to find an Outlook item. For example, you might want to find an Outlook item in the items collection with its Subject property set to `"RE: Payroll"`. We've already talked about how to create DASL queries. This section provides some examples of Jet queries. The way you would call Find using Jet syntax for the query string would look like this:

```
object foundItem = myItems.Find(@"[Subject] = ""RE: Payroll""");
```

A Jet query string has the name of the property in brackets. We use C#'s literal string syntax (@) to specify a string with quotation marks surrounding the value we are searching the Subject field for. Alternatively, you could call Find substituting apostrophes for the quotation marks used in the first example:

```
object foundItem = myItems.Find(@"[Subject] = 'RE: Payroll'");
```

If the Items collection does not contain an Outlook item whose Subject property is equal to "RE: Payroll", the Find method returns null. If there are multiple Outlook items in the Items collection whose Subject property is equal to "RE: Payroll", you can continue finding additional items by using the Items collection's FindNext method. The FindNext method finds the next Outlook item in the collection that matches the filter string passed to Find. You can continue to call FindNext until FindNext returns null indicating that no more items could be found, as shown in Listing 11-19.

Listing 11-19: A VSTO Add-In That Uses the Items Collection's Find and FindNext Methods

```
using System;
using System.Collections.Generic;
using System.Linq;
using System.Text;
using System.Xml.Linq;
using Outlook = Microsoft.Office.Interop.Outlook;
using Office = Microsoft.Office.Core;
using System.Windows.Forms;

namespace OutlookAddIn1
{
  public partial class ThisAddIn
  {
    private void ThisAddIn_Startup(object sender,
      System.EventArgs e)
    {
      Outlook.Folder inbox =
        Application.Session.GetDefaultFolder(
        Outlook.OlDefaultFolders.olFolderInbox)
        as Outlook.Folder;

      Outlook.Items myItems = inbox.Items;

      object foundItem =
        myItems.Find(@"[Subject] = ""RE:""");
      while (foundItem != null)
      {
        MessageBox.Show(String.Format(
          "Found item with EntryID {0}.",
```

```
        (string)GetPropertyHelper(
          foundItem, "EntryID")));
      foundItem = myItems.FindNext();
    }
  }

  private object GetPropertyHelper(object targetObject,
    string propertyName)
  {
    return targetObject.GetType().InvokeMember(
      propertyName,
      System.Reflection.BindingFlags.Public |
      System.Reflection.BindingFlags.Instance |
      System.Reflection.BindingFlags.GetProperty,
      null,
      targetObject,
      null,
      System.Globalization.CultureInfo.CurrentCulture);
  }

  #region VSTO generated code
  private void InternalStartup()
  {
    this.Startup += new System.EventHandler(ThisAddIn_Startup);
  }
  #endregion
  }
}
```

We have illustrated a rather simple Jet filter string that just checks to see whether a text property called Subject matches a string. It is possible to use the logical operators AND, OR, and NOT to specify multiple criteria in a Jet query. For example, the following filter strings check both the property Subject and the property CompanyName. The first finds an Outlook item where the Subject is "RE: Payroll" and the CompanyName is "Microsoft". The second finds an Outlook item where the Subject is "RE: Payroll" or the CompanyName is "Microsoft". The third finds an Outlook item where the Subject is "RE: Payroll" and the CompanyName is not "Microsoft".

```
object foundItem = myItems.Find(@"[Subject] =
  'RE: Payroll' AND [CompanyName] = 'Microsoft'");

object foundItem = myItems.Find(@"[Subject] =
  'RE: Payroll' OR [CompanyName] = 'Microsoft'");

object foundItem = myItems.Find(@"[Subject] =
  'RE: Payroll' AND NOT [CompanyName] = 'Microsoft'");
```

When searching for a property that is an integer value in a Jet query, it is not necessary to enclose the integer value you are searching for in quotes. The same is true for a property that is a boolean property. This example searches for an Outlook item whose integer property OutlookInternalVersion is equal to 116359 and whose boolean property NoAging is set to False.

```
object foundItem = myItems.Find(@"[OutlookInternalVersion] = 116359
AND [NoAging] = False";
```

Some limitations apply to which properties you can use in a filter string. For example, properties that return objects cannot be examined in a filter string. Check the documentation of the Outlook object model for more information.

If you are working with an Items collection that has a large number of Outlook items in it, consider using the Items collection's Restrict method rather than Find and FindNext. The Restrict method is used in a similar way to how SetColumns and Sort are used. You call the Restrict method on the Items collection passing the same kind of filter string you provide to the Find method. You then can use `foreach` to iterate over the Items collection, and only the Outlook items that match the filter string will be iterated over. The Restrict method can be faster than Find and FindNext if you have a large number of items in the Items collection and you only expect to find a few items. Listing 11-20 illustrates using the Restrict method.

Note that if you use a DASL-style query with the Restrict method, you must preface the query with "@SQL=". So to illustrate with our earlier DASL-style query, a Restrict DASL query would look like this:

```
@SQL="urn:schemas:httpmail:subject" ci_startswith 'review'
```

Listing 11-20: A VSTO Add-In That Uses the Items Collection's Restrict Method

```
using System;
using System.Collections.Generic;
using System.Linq;
using System.Text;
using System.Xml.Linq;
using Outlook = Microsoft.Office.Interop.Outlook;
using Office = Microsoft.Office.Core;
using System.Windows.Forms;
```

```csharp
namespace OutlookAddIn1
{
  public partial class ThisAddIn
  {
    private void ThisAddIn_Startup(object sender,
      System.EventArgs e)
    {
      Outlook.Folder inbox =
        Application.Session.GetDefaultFolder(
        Outlook.OlDefaultFolders.olFolderInbox)
        as Outlook.Folder;
      Outlook.Items myItems = inbox.Items;

      myItems = myItems.Restrict(@"[Subject] = ""RE: Payroll""");
      foreach (object foundItem in myItems)
      {
        MessageBox.Show(String.Format(
          "Found item with EntryID {0}.",
          (string)GetPropertyHelper(foundItem, "EntryID")));
      }
    }

    private object GetPropertyHelper(object targetObject,
      string propertyName)
    {
      return targetObject.GetType().InvokeMember(
        propertyName,
        System.Reflection.BindingFlags.Public |
        System.Reflection.BindingFlags.Instance |
        System.Reflection.BindingFlags.GetProperty,
        null,
        targetObject,
        null,
        System.Globalization.CultureInfo.CurrentCulture);
    }

    #region VSTO generated code
    private void InternalStartup()
    {
      this.Startup += new System.EventHandler(ThisAddIn_Startup);
    }
    #endregion
  }
}
```

Adding an Outlook Item to an Items Collection

To add a new Outlook Item to an Items collection, use the Items collection's Add method. The Add method takes an optional Type parameter of type object to

which you can pass a member of the OlItemType enumeration: `olAppoint-`
`mentItem`, `olContactItem`, `olDistributionListItem`, `olJournalItem`, `ol-`
`MailItem`, `olNoteItem`, `olPostItem`, or `olTaskItem`. If you omit the `Type`
parameter by passing `System.Type.Missing`, the type of the item is determined by the type of folder (as determined by DefaultItemType) that you are
adding the item to. You can also pass a custom message class as a string to the
Add method, such as `"IPM.Post.MyCustomClass"`. The Add method returns
an `object`, which can be cast to the Outlook item type corresponding to the
`Type` parameter that was passed in.

You must remember that you can only add an Outlook item that is com-
patible with the folder type the Items collection came from—for example,
it is not possible to add a ContactItem to an Items collection from a folder
that is designated to hold MailItems and PostItems. For more information
on the Outlook item types that can be contained by a particular folder type,
see Table 11-7 earlier in this chapter.

Listing 11-21 shows an example of using the Add method to add a Post-
Item and a MailItem to the Inbox folder. Note that using the Add method is
not sufficient to get the PostItem and MailItem added to the Inbox folder.
For the PostItem, we also have to call the Save method on the newly created Outlook item; otherwise, Outlook discards the PostItem when the
variable `postItem` that refers to it goes out of scope. We also have to call
Save on the newly created MailItem. In addition, we have to call the Move
method to move the newly created MailItem into the Inbox folder. This is
necessary because Outlook puts newly created MailItems into the Drafts
folder by default—even though we called Add on the Items collection
associated with the Inbox. Without the call to Move, the newly created
MailItem remains in the Drafts folder.

Listing 11-21: A VSTO Add-In That Adds a MailItem and a PostItem

```
using System;
using System.Collections.Generic;
using System.Linq;
using System.Text;
using System.Xml.Linq;
using Outlook = Microsoft.Office.Interop.Outlook;
using Office = Microsoft.Office.Core;
using System.Windows.Forms;
```

```
namespace OutlookAddIn1
{
  public partial class ThisAddIn
  {
    private void ThisAddIn_Startup(object sender,
      System.EventArgs e)
    {
      Outlook.MAPIFolder inbox =
        Application.Session.GetDefaultFolder(
        Outlook.OlDefaultFolders.olFolderInbox);
      Outlook.Items myItems = inbox.Items;

      Outlook.PostItem postItem = myItems.Add(
        Outlook.OlItemType.olPostItem)
        as Outlook.PostItem;
      postItem.Subject = "Test1";
      postItem.Save();

      Outlook.MailItem mailItem = myItems.Add(
        Outlook.OlItemType.olMailItem)
        as Outlook.MailItem;
      mailItem.Subject = "Test2";
      mailItem.Save();
      mailItem.Move(inbox);
    }

    #region VSTO generated code
    private void InternalStartup()
    {
      this.Startup += new System.EventHandler(ThisAddIn_Startup);
    }
    #endregion
  }
}
```

An alternate way to create an Outlook item is to use the Application object's CreateItem method. This method takes a Type parameter of type OlItemType that is passed a member of the OlItemType enumeration. It returns an object representing the newly created Outlook item. You must then save the created item and place it in the folder you want to store it in. Listing 11-22 shows code that uses CreateItem to do the same thing that Listing 11-21 does. In Listing 11-22, we must move the new MailItem and PostItem to the Inbox folder using the Move method on MailItem and PostItem.

Listing 11-22: A VSTO Add-In That Uses the Application Object's CreateItem Method to Add a MailItem and a PostItem

```csharp
using System;
using System.Collections.Generic;
using System.Linq;
using System.Text;
using System.Xml.Linq;
using Outlook = Microsoft.Office.Interop.Outlook;
using Office = Microsoft.Office.Core;
using System.Windows.Forms;

namespace OutlookAddIn1
{
  public partial class ThisAddIn
  {
    private void ThisAddIn_Startup(object sender,
      System.EventArgs e)
    {
      Outlook.Folder inbox =
        Application.Session.GetDefaultFolder(
        Outlook.OlDefaultFolders.olFolderInbox)
        as Outlook.Folder;

      Outlook.MailItem mailItem = Application.CreateItem(
        Outlook.OlItemType.olMailItem)
        as Outlook.MailItem;
      mailItem.Subject = "Test 1";
      mailItem.Save();
      mailItem.Move(inbox);

      Outlook.PostItem postItem = Application.CreateItem(
        Outlook.OlItemType.olPostItem)
        as Outlook.PostItem;
      postItem.Subject = "Test 2";
      postItem.Save();
      postItem.Move(inbox);
    }

    #region VSTO generated code
    private void InternalStartup()
    {
      this.Startup += new System.EventHandler(ThisAddIn_Startup);
    }
    #endregion
  }
}
```

Working with the Table Object

Outlook 2007 introduces a new way to work with Outlook items: the Table object. The Table object allows you to iterate over Outlook items in a more lightweight way than using the Items collection. When you're working with large numbers of Outlook items, the performance of the Table object can be up to ten times faster.

To get a Table object, use the GetTable method of the Folder object. The GetTable method takes a `Filter` parameter of type `string` that is passed either a DASL query or a Jet query. For more information on creating DASL queries, see the section "Performing a Search and Creating a Search Folder" earlier in this chapter. For more information on Jet queries, see the section "Finding an Outlook Item" earlier in this chapter.

The GetTable method also takes a `TableContents` parameter of type OlTableContents that can be passed either `olHiddenItems` to return only the hidden items in the folder (StorageItem objects) or `olUserItems` to return the nonhidden user items in the folder.

To iterate over a table, you use the Table.GetNextRow() method, which returns a Row object. While iterating over the table, check the Table.End-OfTable property, which returns `true` when you reach the end of the table.

To keep the Table object lightweight and performant, only a subset of the properties associated with the items found in the folder is returned by default as columns in the table. Table 11-11 shows the columns returned by default for different folder types. To access a column, use the Row object's Item method, and pass the column name shown in Table 11-11 as a `string`. The Item method returns the value in the column as an `object`.

You are not restricted to these default columns; you can add columns to the table for any Outlook item properties you want to examine. To add columns, use the Columns property of the Table object to return the Columns collection. Then you can use the Columns.Add method to add a column to the columns collection. The Columns.Add method takes a `string` parameter that specifies the name of the Outlook item property you want to add to the table.

TABLE 11-11:   The Default Columns Returned in a Table for Different Types of Folders

Column Index	Column Name
Columns Common to All Folders	
1	EntryID
2	Subject
3	CreationTime
4	LastModificationTime
5	MessageClass
Columns Specific to Calendar Folders	
6	Start
7	End
8	IsRecurring
Columns Specific to Contacts Folders	
6	FirstName
7	LastName
8	CompanyName
Columns Specific to Task Folders	
6	DueDate
7	PercentComplete
8	IsRecurring

Listing 11-23 shows a VSTO add-in that gets a Table object for the inbox, using a Jet query to restrict the items returned to those modified after June 1, 2008. The code also adds a column to the default set of columns retrieved (SenderEmailAddress). Then it iterates over the table by using Table.GetNextRow() and Table.EndOfTable.

Listing 11-23: A VSTO Add-In That Uses the Table Object

```csharp
using System;
using System.Collections.Generic;
using System.Linq;
using System.Text;
using System.Xml.Linq;
using Outlook = Microsoft.Office.Interop.Outlook;
using Office = Microsoft.Office.Core;
using System.Windows.Forms;

namespace OutlookAddIn1
{
  public partial class ThisAddIn
  {
    private void ThisAddIn_Startup(object sender,
      System.EventArgs e)
    {
      Outlook.Folder inbox =
        Application.Session.GetDefaultFolder(
        Outlook.OlDefaultFolders.olFolderInbox)
        as Outlook.Folder;

      Outlook.Table table =
        inbox.GetTable(@"[LastModificationTime] > '6/1/2008'",
        Outlook.OlTableContents.olUserItems);

      table.Columns.Add("SenderEmailAddress");
      System.Text.StringBuilder builder =
        new System.Text.StringBuilder();

      while (table.EndOfTable == false)
      {
        Outlook.Row row = table.GetNextRow();
        builder.Append(String.Format(
          "Found '{0}' from {1}",
          row["Subject"],
          row["SenderEmailAddress"]));
      }
      MessageBox.Show(builder.ToString());
    }

    #region VSTO generated code
    private void InternalStartup()
    {
      this.Startup += new System.EventHandler(ThisAddIn_Startup);
    }
    #endregion
  }
}
```

Properties and Methods Common to Outlook Items

This chapter has discussed the 18 Outlook item types: AppointmentItem, ContactItem, DistListItem, DocumentItem, JournalItem, MailItem, MeetingItem, NoteItem, PostItem, RemoteItem, ReportItem, SharingItem, StorageItem, TaskItem, TaskRequestAcceptItem, TaskRequestDeclineItem, TaskRequestItem, and TaskRequestUpdateItem. We group these object model types together because all of these types share many common properties and methods listed in Table 11-12. The properties and methods in this table are found on all Outlook item types. The properties and methods marked in this table with an asterisk are found on all Outlook item types except NoteItem and StorageItem. These are special cases in the Outlook item family, and they have a subset of the properties and methods that the other Outlook item types share.

We now consider several of these common properties and methods. Even though we talk about Outlook Items as if there were an OutlookItem type in the Outlook object model, there is no such type—the OutlookItem type is a conceptual way of talking about the properties and methods common to the 18 Outlook item types in the Outlook object model. So when we talk about the Save method, for example, that method is found on ContactItem, PostItem, MailItem, and all the other Outlook item types.

Given an object that you know is 1 of the 18 Outlook item types, you can either cast it to the correct Outlook item type or you can talk to the object via reflection if you are talking to a property common to all Outlook items. Some of the code listings in this section that use the GetPropertyHelper method have illustrated this point. Usually, it will be preferable to cast the object to the specific item type rather than use reflection.

Creating an Outlook Item

You have already learned the two primary ways in which you can create an Outlook item in the section "Adding an Outlook Item to an Items Collection." You can either call the Items collection's Add method or the Application object's CreateItem method. These methods take a member of the OlItemType enumeration and return an `object` that can be cast to the Outlook item type corresponding to the OlItemType enumeration, as shown in Table 11-13.

TABLE 11-12: Properties and Methods Common to All Outlook Items

Actions*	Display	NoAging*
Application	DownloadState	OutlookVersion*
Attachments*	EntryID	Parent
AutoResolvedWinner	FormDescription*	PrintOut
BillingInformation*	GetInspector	PropertyAccessor
Body	Importance*	Save
Categories	InternalVersion*	SaveAs
Class	IsConflict	Saved
Close	ItemProperties	Sensitivity*
Companies*	LastModificationTime	Session
Conflicts	Links	ShowCategoriesDialog*
ConversationIndex*	MarkForDownload	Size
ConversationTopic*	MessageClass	Subject
Copy	Mileage*	UnRead*
CreationTime	Move	UserProperties*
Delete		

* Not available on the NoteItem or StorageItem objects.

Notice that there are nine items Table 11-13, which leaves out nine Outlook item types. How do you create the other nine remaining Outlook item types? The remaining types are created by Outlook or created as a result of other actions you take with an existing Outlook item type. Table 11-14 identifies how the other Outlook item types are created.

TABLE 11-13: Correspondence Between OlItemType and Outlook Item Types

OlItemType Member	Outlook Item Type
olAppointmentItem	AppointmentItem
olContactItem	ContactItem
olDistributionListItem	DistListItem
olMailItem	MailItem
olNoteItem	NoteItem
olJournalItem	JournalItem
olPostItem	PostItem
olStorageItem	StorageItem
olTaskItem	TaskItem

TABLE 11-14: How the Other Outlook Item Types Are Created

Outlook Item Type	How Created
DocumentItem	The Items collection's Add method also accepts a member of the OlOfficeDocItemsType enumeration: olWordDocumentItem, olExcelWorkSheetItem, or olPowerPointShowItem. Calling the Items collection's Add method with any of these constants returns an object that can be cast to a DocumentItem. You can also create a DocumentItem by using the Application object's CopyFile method.
MeetingItem	Cannot be created directly; created by Outlook when AppointmentItem.MeetingStatus is set to olMeeting and sent to one or more recipients.
RemoteItem	Cannot be created directly; created by Outlook when you use a Remote Access System connection.
ReportItem	Cannot be created directly; created by the mail transport system.

TABLE 11-14: How the Other Outlook Item Types Are Created *(Continued)*

Outlook Item Type	How Created
SharingItem	Created with the NameSpace.CreateSharingItem method.
TaskRequestAcceptItem	Cannot be created directly; created by Outlook as part of the task delegation feature.
TaskRequestDeclineItem	Cannot be created directly; created by Outlook as part of the task delegation feature.
TaskRequestItem	Cannot be created directly; created by Outlook as part of the task delegation feature.
TaskRequestUpdateItem	Cannot be created directly; created by Outlook as part of the task delegation feature.

Identifying the Specific Type of an Outlook Item

You can determine the specific type of an Outlook item given to you as type object by using the as operator to cast it to the expected type, as shown in Listing 11-24. The code gets an Outlook item out of the Inbox and then uses the as operator to cast it to an Outlook MailItem. If the Outlook item is not a MailItem (for example, it might be a PostItem instead) the mailItem variable will be set to null because the as operator will be unable to cast it to a MailItem. If the casts succeeds, mailItem will be non-null and the code proceeds to display the subject of the mail message.

Listing 11-24: A VSTO Add-In That Uses the as Operator on an Outlook Item of Type object

```
private void ThisAddIn_Startup(object sender, EventArgs e)
{
  Outlook.Folder inbox = Application.Session.GetDefaultFolder(
    Outlook.OlDefaultFolders.olFolderInbox)
    as Outlook.Folder;
  object item = inbox.Items[1];

  Outlook.MailItem mailItem = item as Outlook.MailItem;
  if (mailItem != null)
    MessageBox.Show(mailItem.Subject);
}
```

You can also use the is operator to determine the specific type of an Outlook item. Listing 11-25 shows some code that uses the is operator and then the as operator to cast to either an Outlook.MailItem or an Outlook.PostItem. Using the is and as operators together is considered to be inefficient because this results in two type checks, which is more expensive than just using the as operator and checking whether the result is null, as shown in Listing 11-24.

Listing 11-25: A VSTO Add-In That Uses the is Operator on an Outlook Item of Type object

```
private void ThisAddIn_Startup(object sender, EventArgs e)
{
  Outlook.Folder inbox = Application.Session.GetDefaultFolder(
    Outlook.OlDefaultFolders.olFolderInbox)
    as Outlook.Folder;
  object item = inbox.Items[1];

  if (item is Outlook.MailItem)
  {
    Outlook.MailItem mailItem = item as Outlook.MailItem;
    MessageBox.Show(mailItem.Subject);
  }
  else if (item is Outlook.PostItem)
  {
    Outlook.PostItem postItem = item as Outlook.PostItem;
    MessageBox.Show(postItem.Subject);
  }
}
```

A final way to determine the type of an Outlook item of type object is to use reflection to invoke the Class property, which is found on every Outlook item type. The Class property returns a member of the OlObject-Class enumeration. Table 11-15 shows the correspondence between the OlObjectClass enumerated values and each Outlook item types.

Listing 11-26 shows some add-in code that uses our helper method Get-PropertyHelper to call the Class property on an Outlook item of type object. It then uses a switch statement, which for illustration purposes contains all the members of the OlObjectClass enumeration that correspond to Outlook item types. The code in Listing 11-26 would be more efficient than using the as operator if your code needs to cast to multiple specific Outlook item types given an Outlook item of type object. For

TABLE 11-15: Correspondence Between Outlook Item Type and OlObjectClass Enumerated Value

Outlook Item Type	OlObjectClass Enumeration Member
AppointmentItem	olAppointment
ContactItem	olContact
DistListItem	olDistributionList
DocumentItem	olDocument
JournalItem	olJournal
MailItem	olMail
MeetingItem	olMeetingRequest
NoteItem	olNote
PostItem	olPost
RemoteItem	olRemote
ReportItem	olReport
SharingItem	olSharing
TaskItem	olTask
TaskRequestAcceptItem	olTaskRequestAccept
TaskRequestDeclineItem	olTaskRequestDecline
TaskRequestItem	olTaskRequest
TaskRequestUpdateItem	olTaskRequestUpdate

example, the code in Listing 11-15 would be more efficient if it were rewritten to use the approach in Listing 11-26. The approach in Listing 11-26 only needs to make one reflection call to get the Class value and then one cast using the as operator to get the specific Outlook item type.

Listing 11-26: Add-In Code That Uses the Class Property to Determine the Outlook Item Type

```
using System;
using System.Collections.Generic;
using System.Linq;
using System.Text;
using System.Xml.Linq;
using Outlook = Microsoft.Office.Interop.Outlook;
using Office = Microsoft.Office.Core;
using System.Windows.Forms;

namespace OutlookAddIn1
{
  public partial class ThisAddIn
  {
    private void ThisAddIn_Startup(object sender,
      System.EventArgs e)
    {
      Outlook.Folder inbox = Application.Session.GetDefaultFolder(
        Outlook.OlDefaultFolders.olFolderInbox)
        as Outlook.Folder;
      object item = inbox.Items[1];

      Outlook.OlObjectClass objectClass =
        (Outlook.OlObjectClass)
        Enum.Parse(typeof(Outlook.OlObjectClass),
        GetPropertyHelper(item, "Class").ToString(), true);

      MessageBox.Show(String.Format(
        "Class is {0}.",
        objectClass.ToString()));

      switch (objectClass)
      {
        case Outlook.OlObjectClass.olAppointment:
          break;
        case Outlook.OlObjectClass.olContact:
          break;
        case Outlook.OlObjectClass.olDistributionList:
          break;
        case Outlook.OlObjectClass.olDocument:
          break;
        case Outlook.OlObjectClass.olJournal:
          break;
        case Outlook.OlObjectClass.olMail:
          Outlook.MailItem mail = item as Outlook.MailItem;
          if (mail != null)
          {
```

```csharp
            MessageBox.Show(String.Format(
              "Found mail item with subject {0}.",
              mail.Subject));
          }
          break;
        case Outlook.OlObjectClass.olMeetingRequest:
          break;
        case Outlook.OlObjectClass.olNote:
          break;
        case Outlook.OlObjectClass.olPost:
          Outlook.PostItem post = item as Outlook.PostItem;
          if (post != null)
          {
            MessageBox.Show(String.Format(
              "Found post item with subject {0}.",
              post.Subject));
          }
          break;
        case Outlook.OlObjectClass.olRemote:
          break;
        case Outlook.OlObjectClass.olReport:
          break;
        case Outlook.OlObjectClass.olSharing:
          break;
        case Outlook.OlObjectClass.olTask:
          break;
        case Outlook.OlObjectClass.olTaskRequest:
          break;
        case Outlook.OlObjectClass.olTaskRequestAccept:
          break;
        case Outlook.OlObjectClass.olTaskRequestDecline:
          break;
        case Outlook.OlObjectClass.olTaskRequestUpdate:
          break;
        default:
          break;
      }
    }

private object GetPropertyHelper(object targetObject,
  string propertyName)
{
  return targetObject.GetType().InvokeMember(propertyName,
    System.Reflection.BindingFlags.Public |
    System.Reflection.BindingFlags.Instance |
    System.Reflection.BindingFlags.GetProperty,
    null,
```

```
            targetObject,
            null,
            System.Globalization.CultureInfo.CurrentCulture);
    }

    #region VSTO generated code
    private void InternalStartup()
    {
        this.Startup += new System.EventHandler(ThisAddIn_Startup);
    }
    #endregion
  }
}
```

Other Properties Associated with All Outlook Items

This section covers several commonly used properties associated with all Outlook item types (with the possible exception of NoteItem). When we say properties in the context of Outlook items, some confusion can arise. Some properties are on the actual Outlook item type—for example, the Subject property is a callable property on all Outlook item object types. There are a MailItem.Subject property, PostItem.Subject, ContactItem.Subject, and so on. Sometimes a property that is on an Outlook item object type is also accessible via the OutlookItem.ItemProperties collection. If you iterate over the ItemProperties collection, you will find an ItemProperty object where ItemProperty.Name returns "Subject".

The creators of the Outlook object model exposed some of the properties in the ItemProperties collection as first-class properties on the object types themselves. So the Subject property can be accessed either by using OutlookItem.Subject or OutlookItem.ItemProperties["Subject"]. Other properties that are more obscure were not exposed as properties on the objects themselves. For example, the EnableSharedAttachments property can only be accessed via OutlookItem.ItemProperties["EnableSharedAttachments"]. You will learn more about the ItemProperties collection later in this chapter.

Table 11-16 lists several properties callable on all Outlook item object types. Properties marked with an asterisk are not available on the Note-Item or StorageItem objects.

TABLE 11-16: Properties Associated with All Outlook Items

Name	Type	What It Does
Body	string	Gets and sets the body text of the Outlook item.
Categories	string	Gets and sets the categories assigned to the Outlook item. An Outlook item assigned to the Business and Favorites category, for example, would return the string `"Business, Favorites"`.
ConversationIndex*	string	Gets an identifier for the conversation index.
ConversationTopic*	string	Gets the conversation topic of the Outlook item.
CreationTime	DateTime	Gets the DateTime when the Outlook item was created.
Importance*	OlImportance	Gets and sets the importance as a member of the OlImportance enumeration: `olImportanceHigh`, `olImportanceLow`, or `olImportanceNormal`.
LastModificationTime	DateTime	Gets the DateTime when the Outlook item was last modified.
Sensitivity*	OlSensitivity	Gets and sets the sensitivity as a member of the OlSensitivity enumeration: `olConfidential`, `olNormal`, `olPersonal`, or `olPrivate`.
Size	int	Gets the size, in bytes, of the Outlook item.
Subject	string	Gets and sets the subject of the Outlook item.
UnRead*	bool	Gets and sets whether the Outlook item has been opened by the end user.

* Not available on the NoteItem or StorageItem objects.

Copying or Moving an Outlook Item to a New Location

An Outlook item can be copied or moved from one folder to another. The Outlook item's Copy method creates a copy of the Outlook item and returns the newly created item as an object. The Outlook item's Move method moves an Outlook item from one folder to another. It takes a Dest-Fldr parameter of type MAPIFolder to which you pass the folder to which you want to move the Outlook item.

Deleting an Outlook Item

To delete an Outlook item, call the Outlook item's Delete method. Doing so causes the Outlook item to be moved to the Deleted Items folder, where it stays until the user empties the Deleted Items folder. If you do not want the item to appear in the Deleted Items folder, you must call Delete twice—the first call moves the item to the Deleted Items folder, and the second call deletes it from the Deleted Items folder, as shown in Listing 11-27.

Listing 11-27: A VSTO Add-In That Deletes an Item, and Then Permanently Deletes It by Removing It from the Deleted Items Folder

```
using System;
using System.Collections.Generic;
using System.Linq;
using System.Text;
using System.Xml.Linq;
using Outlook = Microsoft.Office.Interop.Outlook;
using Office = Microsoft.Office.Core;
using System.Windows.Forms;

namespace OutlookAddIn1
{
  public partial class ThisAddIn
  {
    private void ThisAddIn_Startup(object sender,
      System.EventArgs e)
    {
      Outlook.Folder inbox =
        Application.Session.GetDefaultFolder(
        Outlook.OlDefaultFolders.olFolderInbox)
        as Outlook.Folder;

      Outlook.PostItem postItem = inbox.Items.Add(
        Outlook.OlItemType.olPostItem) as Outlook.PostItem;
      string subject = "Test Post To Be Deleted";
```

```csharp
      postItem.Subject = subject;
      postItem.Save();

      MessageBox.Show("New post item is in inbox");
      string entryID1 = postItem.EntryID;

      postItem.Delete();
      MessageBox.Show("New post item is in deleted items");
      Outlook.Folder deletedItems =
        Application.Session.GetDefaultFolder(
        Outlook.OlDefaultFolders.olFolderDeletedItems)
        as Outlook.Folder;
      Outlook.PostItem post = deletedItems.Items.Find(
        String.Format("[Subject] = '{0}'", subject))
        as Outlook.PostItem;

      if (post != null)
      {
        string entryID2 = post.EntryID;
        if (entryID1 != entryID2)
        {
          MessageBox.Show(entryID1);
          MessageBox.Show(entryID2);
          MessageBox.Show(
            "When you delete an item its entry ID changes.");
        }
        post.Delete();
        MessageBox.Show("Removed post from deleted items folder.");
      }
    }

    #region VSTO generated code
    private void InternalStartup()
    {
      this.Startup += new System.EventHandler(ThisAddIn_Startup);
    }
    #endregion
  }
}
```

Note in Listing 11-24 that we cannot find the item we just deleted in the Deleted Items folder using the EntryID because the EntryID changes when you delete the Outlook item. Instead, we use the Subject, which is not ideal because the Subject is not guaranteed to be unique. A better approach would be to use the Move method to move the item to the Deleted Items folder (which can be retrieved by using the NameSpace object's GetDefaultFolder method passing `OIDefaultFolders.olFolderDeletedItems`). Move returns the moved item, which you can then call Delete on to do a final delete.

Displaying an Outlook Item in an Inspector View

The Outlook item's GetInspector method gives you an Inspector object to display an Outlook item. You can configure the Inspector before showing it by calling the Inspector object's Display method. The Display method takes an optional `Modal` parameter of type `object` to which you can pass `true` to show the Inspector as a modal dialog box or `false` to show it as a modeless dialog box. It is recommended that code always display Inspector windows as modeless.

If you do not need to configure the Inspector first before you display it, you can just use the Display method on an Outlook item. The Display method displays an Inspector and takes an optional `Modal` parameter of type `object` to which you can pass `true` to show the Inspector as a modal dialog box or `false` to show it as a modeless dialog box.

If an Inspector window is open for a given Outlook item, you can close the Inspector window by using the Close method on the Outlook item being displayed. The Close method takes a `SaveMode` parameter of type OlInspectorClose. You can pass a member of the OlInspectorClose enumeration to this parameter: `olDiscard` to discard changes made in the Inspector window, `olPromptForSave` to prompt the user to save if changes were made, and `olSave` to save without prompting.

Listing 11-28 creates a PostItem in the Inbox folder then calls the Display method to display an Inspector window for it. It then calls the Close method passing `OlInspectorClose.olDiscard` to close the Inspector window. Note that we have to cast the PostItem to the Outlook._PostItem interface to disambiguate between the Close method and the Close event, which collide on Outlook item objects.

Listing 11-28: A VSTO Add-In That Uses the Display and Close Method

```
using System;
using System.Collections.Generic;
using System.Linq;
using System.Text;
using System.Xml.Linq;
```

```csharp
using Outlook = Microsoft.Office.Interop.Outlook;
using Office = Microsoft.Office.Core;
using System.Windows.Forms;

namespace OutlookAddIn1
{
  public partial class ThisAddIn
  {
    private void ThisAddIn_Startup(object sender,
      System.EventArgs e)
    {
      Outlook.Folder inbox =
        Application.Session.GetDefaultFolder(
        Outlook.OlDefaultFolders.olFolderInbox)
        as Outlook.Folder;

      Outlook.PostItem postItem = inbox.Items.Add(
        Outlook.OlItemType.olPostItem) as Outlook.PostItem;
      postItem.Subject = "Test to be shown in Inspector window.";
      postItem.Save();

      postItem.Display(false);
      MessageBox.Show("Post item is shown in inspector window.");
      ((Outlook._PostItem)postItem).Close(
        Outlook.OlInspectorClose.olDiscard);
    }

    #region VSTO generated code
    private void InternalStartup()
    {
      this.Startup += new System.EventHandler(ThisAddIn_Startup);
    }
    #endregion
  }
}
```

Working with Built-In and Custom Properties Associated with an Outlook Item

The ItemProperties property returns the ItemProperties collection associated with an Outlook item. This collection contains ItemProperty objects for each property associated with the Outlook item. By property, we mean a name value pair that may or may not also have a get/set property on the Outlook item type. The ItemProperties collection can be iterated over using the foreach keyword. It also supports C#'s index operator ([]). You can pass a `string` as the index representing the name of the ItemProperty you want to access. You can also pass a 1-based index for the ItemProperty you want to access in the collection.

Listing 11-29 shows code that gets an ItemProperty object associated with a newly created PostItem using the index operator with a `string` and numeric index. Listing 11-29 also illustrates iterating over all the Item-Property objects in the ItemProperties collection using `foreach`.

Listing 11-29: A VSTO Add-In That Works with ItemProperty Objects

```
using System;
using System.Collections.Generic;
using System.Linq;
using System.Text;
using System.Xml.Linq;
using Outlook = Microsoft.Office.Interop.Outlook;
using Office = Microsoft.Office.Core;
using System.Windows.Forms;

namespace OutlookAddIn1
{
  public partial class ThisAddIn
  {
    private void ThisAddIn_Startup(object sender,
      System.EventArgs e)
    {
      Outlook.Folder inbox =
        Application.Session.GetDefaultFolder(
        Outlook.OlDefaultFolders.olFolderInbox)
        as Outlook.Folder;

      Outlook.PostItem postItem = inbox.Items.Add(
        Outlook.OlItemType.olPostItem) as Outlook.PostItem;

      MessageBox.Show(String.Format(
        "There are {0} properties associated with this post.",
        postItem.ItemProperties.Count));

      // Getting an ItemProperty with a string index
      Outlook.ItemProperty subject = postItem.
        ItemProperties["Subject"];
      MessageBox.Show(String.Format(
        "The property 'Subject' has value {0}.",
        subject.Value));

      // Getting an ItemProperty with a numeric index
      Outlook.ItemProperty firstProp = postItem.
        ItemProperties[1];
```

```
       MessageBox.Show(String.Format(
         "The first property has name {0} and value {1}.",
         firstProp.Name,
         firstProp.Value));

       // Iterating the ItemProperties collection with foreach
       System.Text.StringBuilder result = new
         System.Text.StringBuilder();

       foreach (Outlook.ItemProperty property
         in postItem.ItemProperties)
       {
         result.AppendFormat("{0} of type {1} has value {2}.\n",
           property.Name, property.Type.ToString(),
           property.Value);
       }
       MessageBox.Show(result.ToString());
     }

     #region VSTO generated code
     private void InternalStartup()
     {
       this.Startup += new System.EventHandler(ThisAddIn_Startup);
     }
     #endregion
   }
}
```

You can add your own custom properties to an Outlook item. Custom properties that you have added are accessed by using the UserProperties property. An Outlook item's UserProperties property returns a User-Properties collection that contains UserProperty objects representing custom properties you have added to an Outlook item. Just as with the ItemProperties collection, the UserProperties collection can be iterated over using the foreach keyword. A particular UserProperty in the collection can be accessed using the index operator ([]) to which you pass a string representing the name of the UserProperty or the 1-based index of the UserProperty in the collection.

To add your own custom property, use the UserProperties collection's Add method. This method takes a required Name parameter of type string to which you pass the name of the new custom property. You must also specify the type of the new property by passing a member of the OlUser-PropertyType enumeration. Common members of that enumeration you might use include olDateTime, olNumber, olText, and olYesNo. Other types are also supported—consult the Outlook object model documentation for more information. The Add method also takes two optional parameters that we omit: AddToFolderFields and DisplayFormat. Note that you can add custom properties to all Outlook item types except the NoteItem and DocumentItem types.

Listing 11-30 shows the creation of several custom properties using the UserProperties.Add method.

Listing 11-30: A VSTO Add-In That Works with Custom Properties

```
using System;
using System.Collections.Generic;
using System.Linq;
using System.Text;
using System.Xml.Linq;
using Outlook = Microsoft.Office.Interop.Outlook;
using Office = Microsoft.Office.Core;
using System.Windows.Forms;

namespace OutlookAddIn1
{
  public partial class ThisAddIn
  {
    private void ThisAddIn_Startup(object sender,
      System.EventArgs e)
    {
      Outlook.Folder inbox =
        Application.Session.GetDefaultFolder(
        Outlook.OlDefaultFolders.olFolderInbox)
        as Outlook.Folder;

      Outlook.PostItem postItem = inbox.Items.Add(
        Outlook.OlItemType.olPostItem) as Outlook.PostItem;
      postItem.Subject = "User Properties Test";
      postItem.Save();

      Outlook.UserProperties userProperties =
        postItem.UserProperties;

      Outlook.UserProperty dateProp = userProperties.Add(
        "DateProp", Outlook.OlUserPropertyType.olDateTime,
        missing, missing);
      dateProp.Value = System.DateTime.Now;

      Outlook.UserProperty numberProp = userProperties.Add(
        "NumberProp", Outlook.OlUserPropertyType.olNumber,
```

```
      missing, missing);
    numberProp.Value = 123;

    Outlook.UserProperty textProp = userProperties.Add(
      "TextProp", Outlook.OlUserPropertyType.olText,
      missing, missing);
    textProp.Value = "Hello world";

    Outlook.UserProperty boolProp = userProperties.Add(
      "BoolProp", Outlook.OlUserPropertyType.olYesNo,
      missing, missing);
    boolProp.Value = true;

    MessageBox.Show(String.Format(
      "There are now {0} UserProperties.",
      userProperties.Count));

    postItem.Save();
  }

  #region VSTO generated code
  private void InternalStartup()
  {
    this.Startup += new System.EventHandler(ThisAddIn_Startup);
  }
  #endregion
  }
}
```

PropertyAccessor: Accessing Advanced Properties

PropertyAccessor is a new object in the Outlook 2007 object model that provides a way to access properties that previously were not available through the Outlook object model. If there is a property of an Outlook item that you can't access via the ItemProperties collection or the CustomProperties collection, PropertyAccessor provides a way to access that property. Before Outlook 2007, developers had to use Extended MAPI or CDO to access properties that were not exposed through the Outlook object model.

Outlook items and many other Outlook objects have a PropertyAccessor property that returns a PropertyAccessor object. Then you can use the PropertyAccessor.GetProperty and PropertyAccessor.SetProperty methods to access properties that are not available in the ItemProperties or CustomProperties collections. An example of a property available only via PropertyAccessor is the transport header for a mail item.

Saving an Outlook Item

As you have already seen, when you create an Outlook item you have to call the Save method or the newly created item gets discarded when your variable containing the newly created item goes out of scope. You can check whether an Outlook item needs to be saved by accessing the Saved property. For example, in Listing 11-28, if we examine the Saved property right before we call postItem.Save at the end of the function, Saved would return `false` because some changes were made to the Outlook item (user properties were added) after the Save method was earlier in the function.

The code in Listing 11-28 actually works even when you omit the last call to Save. Consider what happens, however, if we omit the last call to Save. If you examine the newly created item, its Saved state is still `false` after this function runs. If you double-click the newly created item to display an Inspector view and then close the Inspector view without making any changes, Outlook prompts users to save the changes made to the item, which is confusing to users because they did not make any changes. Outlook prompts to save because it still detects that it needs to save the changes made to the user properties by the add-in code. If you exit Outlook, Outlook will save the changes to the newly created item and on the next run of Outlook, the saved state of the new item will be back to `true`.

Showing the Color Categories Dialog Box for an Outlook Item

You can show the Color Categories dialog box in Figure 11-10 by using the Outlook item's ShowCategoriesDialog method. This dialog box allows the user to select categories to associate with an Outlook item. As described earlier, the Outlook item's Categories property enables you to examine what categories an Outlook item is associated with. The Categories property returns a `string` value with each category associated with the Outlook item in a comma-delimited list.

Mail Properties and Methods

Several commonly used properties and methods are associated with items that would be found in a mail folder, such as a MailItem or a PostItem. The BodyFormat property tells you what format the body of a mail message is in. It sets or gets a member of the OlBodyFormat enumeration: `olFormatHTML`,

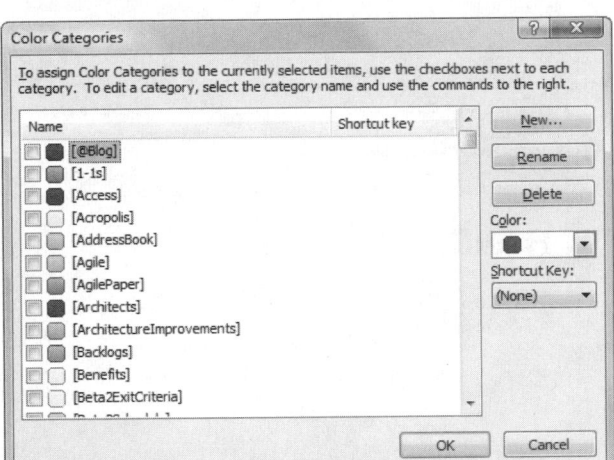

Figure 11-10: Outlook's Color Categories dialog box.

olFormatPlain, olFormatRichText, or olFormatUnspecified. When a message is set to have its BodyFormat in olFormatHTML, the HTML for the body of the message can be set or get via the HTMLBody property. This property gets and sets the string value, which is the HTML content of the message.

Listing 11-31 shows add-in code that creates a PostItem using the Body-Format and HTMLBody properties. Figure 11-11 shows the PostItem created by Listing 11-31.

Listing 11-31: A VSTO Add-In That Creates a PostItem with BodyFormat set to olFormatHTML

```
private void ThisAddIn_Startup(object sender, EventArgs e)
{
  Outlook.Folder inbox =
    Application.Session.GetDefaultFolder(
    Outlook.OlDefaultFolders.olFolderInbox)
    as Outlook.Folder;

  Outlook.PostItem postItem = inbox.Items.Add(
    Outlook.OlItemType.olPostItem) as Outlook.PostItem;
  postItem.Subject = "HTML Example";
  postItem.BodyFormat = Outlook.OlBodyFormat.olFormatHTML;
  postItem.HTMLBody =
    "<HTML><BODY><H1>Heading 1</H1><UL><LI>Item 1</LI><LI>Item 2</LI>" +
    "</UL></BODY></HTML>";
  postItem.Save();
}
```

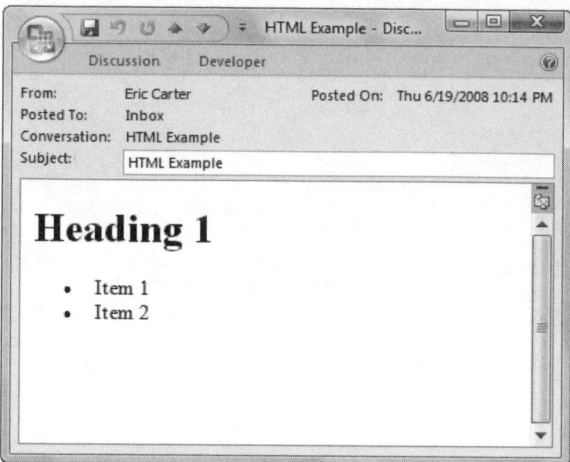

Figure 11-11: PostItem created by Listing 11-31.

The Forward method returns a new Outlook item that can be forwarded to a recipient. Given a MailItem, for example, the MailItem object's Forward method returns a new MailItem. This MailItem can then be given a recipient. Recipients of a MailItem are accessed via the Recipients property, which returns a Recipients collection. A new Recipient can be added by using the Recipients collection's Add method, which takes a `string` representing the display name of the recipient. When a recipient is added, the Outlook item can be sent in e-mail by calling the Outlook item's Send method.

Listing 11-32 illustrates working with the Forward method, the Recipients collection, and the Send method. It creates a PostItem that it then forwards as a MailItem to a recipient. Note that when calling the Forward method and the Send method, we have to cast to the _PostItem and _MailItem interfaces because Forward and Send are both method and event names.

Listing 11-32: A VSTO Add-In That Creates a PostItem and Then Forwards It as a MailItem

```
private void ThisAddIn_Startup(object sender, EventArgs e)
{
  Outlook.Folder inbox =
    Application.Session.GetDefaultFolder(
    Outlook.OlDefaultFolders.olFolderInbox)
    as Outlook.Folder;
```

```
    Outlook.PostItem postItem = inbox.Items.Add(
      Outlook.OlItemType.olPostItem) as Outlook.PostItem;
    postItem.Subject = "HTML Example";
    postItem.BodyFormat = Outlook.OlBodyFormat.olFormatHTML;
    postItem.HTMLBody =
      "<HTML><BODY><H1>Hello World</H1></BODY></HTML>";
    postItem.Save();

    // Forward the PostItem to someone
    Outlook.MailItem forwardedItem =
      ((Outlook._PostItem)postItem).Forward();
    forwardedItem.Recipients.Add("ericcarter@example.com");
    ((Outlook._MailItem)forwardedItem).Send();
}
```

An identical pattern is followed to reply or reply all to an Outlook item. The original item has its Reply or ReplyAll method called, which generates a new MailItem object. The Recipients collection of the new MailItem object is modified if needed. Finally, the new MailItem object's Send method is invoked to send the new MailItem.

Conclusion

This chapter examined some of the most important objects in the Outlook object model. The chapter covered the properties and methods common to all of the 18 Outlook item types. You also learned about new object model features in Outlook 2007, including working with the NavigationPane, Table, and StorageItem objects. Working with the Ribbon in Inspector windows is described in Chapter 17, "Working with the Ribbon in VSTO." Another new Outlook 2007 programmability feature supported by VSTO is creating custom Outlook form regions. This topic is described in Chapter 16, "Working with Outlook Form Regions."

PART III
Office Programming in VSTO

So far, you have seen how to use Visual Studio to develop managed customizations and add-ins that can run in various Office applications. Clearly, it is possible to use the power of both managed code and the rich Office object models together. But compare the development process for such solutions with, say, designing a Windows Forms-based application in Visual Studio. Developers of forms-based solutions get visual designers, powerful data binding, and a truly object-oriented programming model. These tools help professional developers manage the complexity of modern application construction.

Visual Studio Tools for Office (VSTO) takes the same approach to Word and Excel solution development. VSTO features include the following:

- Word and Excel run as designers inside Visual Studio.
- Workbooks, worksheets, and documents are represented by customizable, extensible classes in an object-oriented programming model.
- Managed controls can be hosted by worksheets and documents.
- Business process code can be logically separated from display code.

- Windows Forms data binding connects business data to controls.
- Business data can be cached in the document and manipulated as XML, enabling both offline client and server scenarios.

Part III of this book explores these features:

- Chapter 12, "The VSTO Programming Model," shows how VSTO extends the Word and Excel object models.
- Chapter 13, "Using Windows Forms and WPF in VSTO," covers adding Windows Forms controls and WPF controls to VSTO-customized documents.
- Chapter 14, "Working with Document-Level Actions Panes," shows how to add managed controls to Office's Document Actions task pane in Word and Excel.
- Chapter 15, "Working with Application-Level Custom Task Panes," shows how to add managed controls to application-level task panes in Word, Excel, Outlook, PowerPoint, and InfoPath.
- Chapter 16, "Working with Outlook Form Regions," shows how to add managed controls to Outlook's inspector views and reading pane view.
- Chapter 17, "Working with the Ribbon in VSTO," introduces the new Office 2007 Ribbon and shows how you can customize the Ribbon with your document and add-in solutions.
- Chapter 18, "Working with Smart Tags in VSTO," shows how to implement Smart Tags using managed code.
- Chapter 19, "VSTO Data Programming," and Chapter 20, "Server Data Scenarios," discuss ways to do data binding of Excel and Word controls to datasets and how to manipulate datasets associated with the document on the client and server.
- Chapter 21, "ClickOnce Deployment," shows how to deploy your customized documents and add-ins.

■ 12 ■
The VSTO Programming Model

The VSTO Programming Model for Documents

In Windows Forms programming, a form is a window that contains controls, such as buttons, combo boxes, and so on. To implement a form, you can drag and drop controls from the Visual Studio toolbox onto the form's designer. The form designer then generates a customized subclass of the Form class. Because each form is implemented by its own class, you can then further customize the form code by adding properties and methods of your own to the class. And because all the controls are added as properties on the form class, you can use IntelliSense to more rapidly program those custom methods.

VSTO's system of host items and host controls is directly analogous to Windows Forms. By *host* we mean the application—Word or Excel—which hosts the customization. Host items are like forms: programmable objects that contain user interface elements called host controls. The Workbook, Worksheet, and ChartSheet objects are host items in Excel; the Document object is the sole host item in Word. In add-in projects like Outlook, the ThisAddIn object is exposed as a host item.

As you saw back in Chapter 2, "Introduction to Office Solutions," the Visual Studio Excel and Word designers create custom classes which extend the Worksheet and Document base classes. As you place host controls such as lists, named ranges, charts, and buttons onto the worksheet they are exposed as fields on the customized subclass.

Separation of Data and View

Some people use spreadsheet software solely for its original purpose: to lay out financial data on a grid of cells that automatically recalculates sums, averages, and other formulas as they update the data. For example, you might have a simple Excel spreadsheet that calculates the total expenses for a wedding given all the costs involved. Similarly, some people use word-processing software solely for its original purpose: to automatically typeset letters, memos, essays, books, and other written material.

However, in a business setting spreadsheets and documents have evolved to have both high internal complexity and external dependencies. Unlike a wedding budget, a spreadsheet containing an expense report or a document containing an invoice is likely to be just one small part of a much larger business process. This fact has implications on the design of a programming model. Consider this VBA code that might be found in a spreadsheet that is part of a larger business process:

```
SendUpdateEmail ThisWorkbook.Sheets(1).Cells(12,15).Value2
```

Clearly, the unreadable snippet is sending an e-mail to someone, but because the Excel object model emphasizes how the *spreadsheet* represents the data, not what the *data* represent, it is hard to say exactly what this is doing. The code is not only hard to read, it is brittle; redesigning the spreadsheet layout could break the code. We could improve this code by using a named range rather than a hard-coded direct reference to a particular cell:

```
SendUpdateEmail ThisWorkbook.Names("ApproverEmail").
    RefersToRange.Value2
```

Better, but it would be even nicer if the particular range showed up in IntelliSense. VSTO builds a convenient custom object model for each worksheet, workbook, or document so that you can more easily access the named items contained therein:

```
SendUpdateEmail(ExpenseReportSheet.ApproverEmail.Value2);
```

A more readable, maintainable, and discoverable object model is a welcome addition. However, even in the preceding snippet, the VSTO programming model still does not address the more fundamental problem: We are manipulating the data via an object model that treats them as part of a spreadsheet. The spreadsheet is still the lens through which we see the data; instead of writing a program that manipulates ice cream sales records, we wrote a program that manipulates a list and a chart.

The crux of the matter is that Word and Excel are *editors*; they are for *designing documents that display data*. Therefore, their object models thoroughly conflate the data themselves with the "view," the information about how to display them. To mitigate this conflation, the VSTO programming model was designed to enable developers to logically separate view code from data code. Host items and host controls represent the "view" elements; host items and host controls can be data bound to classes that represent the business data.

Model-View-Controller

If you're familiar with design patterns, you will have already recognized this as based on the Model-View-Controller (MVC) design pattern. In the MVC pattern, as shown in Figure 12-1, the data model code represents the business data and the processes that manipulate it. The view code reads the data, listens to Change events from the data, and figures out how to display it. The controller code mediates between the view and the data code, updating the data based upon the gestures the user makes in the view (mouse clicks, key presses, and so on).

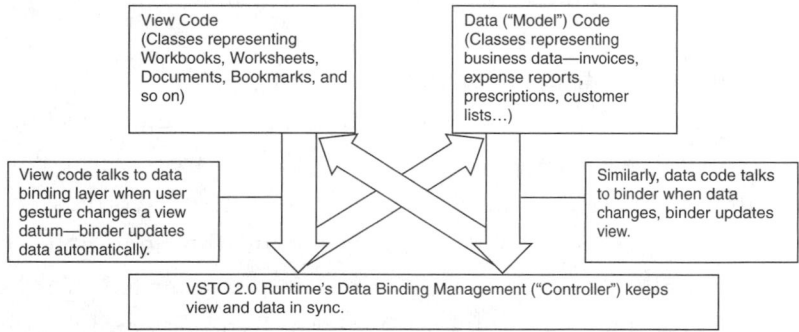

Figure 12-1: Model-View-Controller architecture.

Benefits of Separation

Logically separating the data code from the view code leads to a number of benefits when building more complex business documents on top of Word and Excel:

- Business data and rules can be encapsulated in ADO.NET datasets and reused in different applications.
- Changes to view code are less likely to unexpectedly break data code (and vice versa).
- Data code can cache local copies of database state for offline processing.
- Server-side code can manipulate cached data inside the document without starting up Word/Excel.

Now that you know some of the design philosophy behind VSTO, let's take a look at how the host items and host controls actually extend the Word and Excel object models. (The data side is covered in Chapter 19, "VSTO Data Programming," and server-side data manipulation is covered in Chapter 20, "Server Data Scenarios.")

VSTO Extensions to Word and Excel Document Objects

VSTO extends the Word and Excel object models in several ways. Although it is possible to use these features without understanding what is actually happening "behind the scenes," it is helpful to take a look back there. This section explains by what mechanisms host items and host controls extend the Word and Excel programming models. Then the discussion focuses on exactly which new features are available.

Aggregation, Inheritance, and Implementation

If you create a Word project in Visual Studio and open the Object Browser window, you will see several assemblies listed. Two are of particular interest. You already know that the Microsoft.Office.Interop.Word assembly is the primary interop assembly (PIA), containing the definitions for the interfaces that allow managed code to call the unmanaged Word object model. Similarly, the Microsoft.Office.Interop.Excel assembly is the PIA for the unmanaged Excel object model.

You can find the VSTO extensions to the Word and Excel object models in the Microsoft.Office.Tools.Word.v9.0 and Microsoft.Office.Tools.Excel.v9.0 assemblies; each contains a namespace of the same name (without the version extension).

From a VSTO Word document project, open the Object Browser and take a look at the Document host item class in the Tools namespace, as shown in Figure 12-2.

Notice that the host item class *implements* the properties, methods, and events defined by the Document interface from the PIA, and *extends* the EntryPointBindableComponentBase base class. Chapter 19, "VSTO Data Programming," gets into the details of how data-bindable components work; for now, the fact that this class implements the properties, methods, and events from the PIA interface rather than extends a base class is important. It

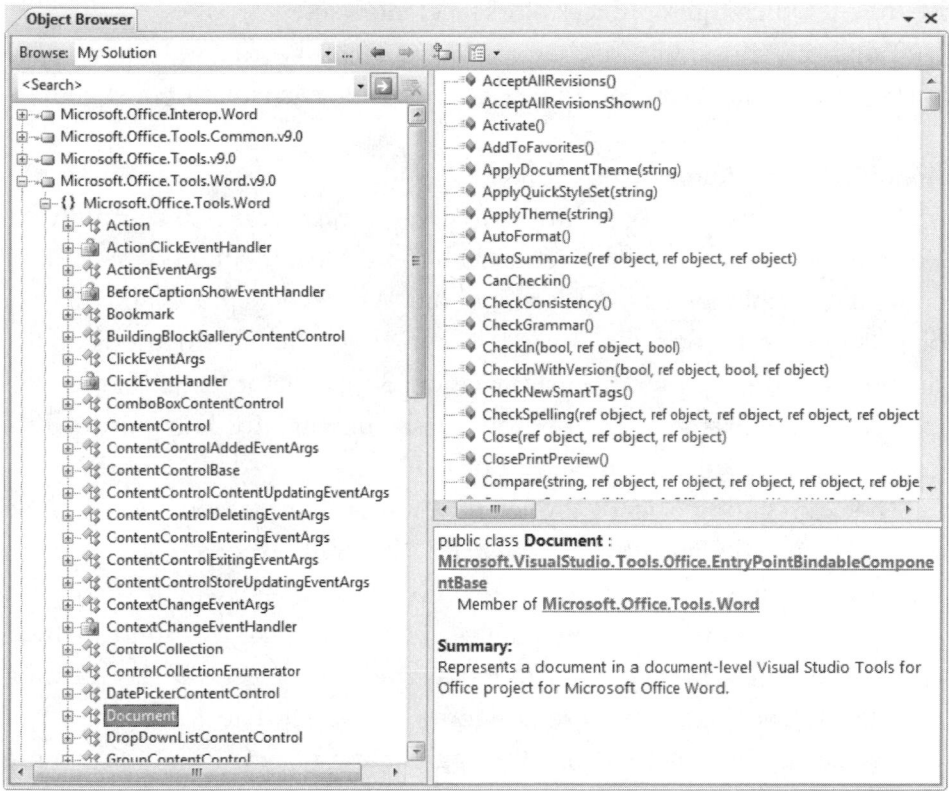

Figure 12-2: Examining the Document host item class in the Object Browser.

is important to notice that even though the Document host item class has all the methods, properties, and events of the Document interface from the PIA, the type definition does not actually say that it implements the Document *interface* itself. This is a subtle distinction that we will discuss in more detail later.

Conceptually, the difference between extending a base class and implementing the properties, methods, and events from an interface is that the former describes an "is a" relationship, whereas the latter describes a "can act like" relationship. A Microsoft.Office.Tools.Word.Document object *really is* a bindable component; it actually shares functionality—code—with its base class. But it merely *looks like* and *acts like* a Word Document object; it *is not* a Word document object as far as Word is concerned.

For example, the Sheet1 class in Excel has your event handlers and host controls. It extends the Microsoft.Office.Tools.Excel.Worksheet base class and implements the properties, methods, and events defined by the Microsoft.Office.Interop.Excel.Worksheet interface.

Table 12-1 shows the host items in VSTO 3.0 for Word and Excel and the corresponding host controls that can be added to each kind of host item.

Hooking Up the Aggregates

VSTO's host item and host control objects *aggregate* some of the underlying Word and Excel document objects (such as the Document, Bookmark, and content control objects in Word, or the Worksheet and NamedRange objects in Excel). You have already seen how you can call methods on the document object in a VSTO customization. Suppose, for instance, that you call the CheckGrammar method on the document. If this is not really a Word Document object but merely looks like one, how does it work?

The aggregating object's implementation of that method checks to see whether it has obtained the aggregated Document object already. If it has not, it makes a call into Word to obtain it (and caches away the object so that it will be available immediately when you make a second method call). After it has the reference to the aggregated object, the aggregating object calls CheckGrammar on the aggregated object. The great majority of the properties and methods on the aggregating objects do nothing more than just pass the arguments along to the PIA code, which then passes them along to the unmanaged object model.

TABLE 12-1: Host Items and Corresponding Host Controls in VSTO 3.0

Host Item	Host Controls That Can Be Added
Word Host Items and Controls (Microsoft.Office.Tools.Word)	
Document	Bookmark BuildingBlockGalleryContentControl ComboBoxContentControl ContentControl OLEControl DatePickerContentControl DropDownListContentControl GroupContentControl PictureContentControl PlainTextContentControl RichTextContentControl XMLNode* XMLNodes* Windows Forms aggregated controls (see Chapter 13)
Excel Host Items and Controls (Microsoft.Office.Tools.Excel)	
Worksheet	Chart NamedRange ListObject OLEObject XMLMappedRange* Windows Forms aggregated controls (see Chapter 13)
Workbook	None
ChartSheet	None

* Cannot be created dynamically.

Events work in the analogous way: If your code listens to an event exposed by an aggregating object, the aggregating object listens to the event on the aggregated object on your behalf. When the event is raised by the aggregated object, the aggregating object's delegate is called, which then raises the aggregating object's event and calls your event handling delegate.

All the host controls are hooked up in a similar manner as the host items. For instance, if you have a NamedRange host control member of a worksheet, the aggregating Worksheet object itself creates an aggregating NamedRange object. The first time you call a method on the host control, the aggregating class obtains the underlying "real" object from Excel and passes the call along. Table 12-1, earlier in this chapter, shows the host items and host controls supported in VSTO 3.0.

This might seem like a whole lot of rigmarole to go through just to add new functionality to the Word and Excel object models. The key benefit that this system of aggregates affords is that each host item class in each project can be customized. One spreadsheet can have an InvoiceSheet class with a CustomerNameRange property, another can have a MedicalHistory-Sheet class with a CholesterolLevelChart property, and so on.

In short, VSTO *extends* the Word and Excel object models by *aggregating* the unmanaged object models with managed objects. VSTO enables developers to further customize and extend some of those objects—those representing the workbook, worksheet, chart sheet, and document—through subclassing.

Obtaining the Aggregated Object

Much of the time, the foregoing details about how the aggregation model works are just that: implementation details. Whether the host item "is a" worksheet or merely "looks like" one seems to be an academic point. However, in some rare scenarios, it does matter.

Word's and Excel's object models were not written with the expectation that managed aggregates would implement their interfaces; when you call a method that takes a range, Excel expects that you are passing it a real range, not an aggregated range that acts like a range.

For instance, suppose you have a customized worksheet with two host controls: a NamedRange member called InvoiceTotals and a Chart object called InvoiceChart. You might want to write code something like this snippet:

```
this.InvoiceChart.SetSourceData(this.InvoiceTotals,
    Excel.XlRowCol.xlColumns);
```

This code will not compile because the SetSourceData method on the chart aggregate must be passed an object that implements the Range interface. It looks like at runtime the InvoiceChart aggregate will pass Invoice-Totals, an aggregated range, to the "real" aggregated chart. But Excel will expect that the object passed to SetSourceData *is a* range, whereas in fact it is the VSTO aggregate; it merely *looks like* an Excel range.

When just calling methods, reading or writing properties, and listening to events, the aggregate is more or less transparent; you can just use the object as though it really were the thing it is aggregating. If for any reason you need to pass the aggregate to an Excel object model method that requires the real Excel object, you can obtain the real Excel object via the InnerObject property. The previous code snippet will compile and work properly if you rewrite it to look like this:

```
this.InvoiceChart.SetSourceData(this.InvoiceTotals.InnerObject,
    Excel.XlRowCol.xlColumns);
```

Aggregation and Windows Forms Controls

If you drag and drop a Windows Forms button onto a worksheet or document, the button control is also aggregated. However, Windows Forms controls are aggregated slightly differently than the NamedRange, Bookmark, ListObject, and other controls built in to Word and Excel. There are two relevant differences between Windows Forms controls and Office's controls. First, Windows Forms controls are implemented by *extensible managed classes*, unlike the *unmanaged* Office controls, which only expose *interfaces* in their PIAs. Second, Word and Excel controls inherently know how they are situated in relation to their containing document or worksheet; non-Office controls on a worksheet do not know that they are in a worksheet.

Word and Excel overcome the second difference by aggregating an *extender* onto a control sited on a document or worksheet. Word's extender implements the properties, methods, and events of the _OLEControl interface that can be found in the Word PIA (but as with other aggregated VSTO controls, the type definition does not actually claim to implement the _OLEControl interface). It has five methods, all of which take no arguments and return no result: Activate, Copy, Cut, Delete, and Select. It also exposes floating-point read-write properties Top, Left, Height, and Width, string properties Name and AltHTML, and an Automation object. Excel's extender implements the properties, methods, and events of the _OLEObject interface that can be found in the Excel PIA.

When you drop a button onto a document or worksheet, the project system adds a new field to the host item class, but types it as Microsoft .Office.Tools.Word.Controls.Button or Microsoft.Office.Tools.Excel.Controls.Button, respectively. Because the underlying System.Windows.Forms .Button class is extensible, this time the aggregate actually is a subclass of the Windows Forms control. However, it still must aggregate the unmanaged extender interface provided by Word or Excel.

As a further convenience, the managed objects representing embedded Windows Forms controls also have read-only Right and Bottom properties aggregated onto them.

Improving C# Interoperability

The Word and Excel object models were originally designed with VBA in mind. Unfortunately, there are some language features which VBA and Visual Basic support but C# does not, such as parameterized properties. In VBA, you could do something like this:

```
Set Up = ThisWorkbook.Names.Item("MyRange").RefersToRange.End(xlUp)
```

End is a read-only property that takes an argument, but C# does not support passing arguments to property getters; arguments can only be passed to methods and indexers in C#. Therefore, the PIA exposes the property getter as a function. You could talk to the PIA like this in C#:

```
Up = ThisWorkbook.Names.Item("MyRange", System.Type.Missing,
    System.Type.Missing).RefersToRange.get_End(
    Microsoft.Office.Interop.Excel.XlDirection.xlUp);
```

Note that the PIA interface calls out that this is a "getter" function; for writable properties there would be a corresponding set_ function that took the parameters and new value as arguments.

C# does, however, support something similar to parameterized property accessors: parameterized indexers. In a VSTO project with a host item or host item control that has been extended, you can accomplish the same task like this:

```
Up = MyRange.End[Excel.XlDirection.xlUp];
```

The get_End accessor function is implemented by the aggregate, so you can still use it if you want to. However, because it is no longer necessary and there is a more elegant solution, it is not displayed in the IntelliSense drop-down.

In several places in the VSTO object model, parameterized indexers have replaced parameterized properties; you will find a list of them all along with the rest of the changes to the object model at the end of this chapter.

The Tag Field

Every host item and host control now has a field called Tag, which can be set to any value. This field is entirely for you to use as you see fit; it is neither read nor written by any code other than your customization code. It is included because it is very common for developers to have auxiliary data associated with a particular control, but no field on the control itself in which to store the data. Having the object keep track of its own auxiliary data is, in many cases, more straightforward than building an external table mapping controls onto data.

Event Model Improvements

Like VBA, VSTO encourages an event-driven programming style. In traditional VBA programming, relatively few of the objects source events, which can make writing event-driven code cumbersome. For instance, in Word, the only way to detect when the user double-clicks a bookmark using the standard VBA object model is to declare an "events" class module with a member referring to the application:

```
Public WithEvents WordApp As Word.Application
```

Then sink the event and detect whether the clicked range overlaps the bookmark:

```
Private Sub App_WindowBeforeDoubleClick(ByVal Sel As Selection, _
  Cancel As Boolean)
  If Sel.Range.InRange(ThisDocument.Bookmarks(1).Range) Then
    MsgBox "Customer Clicked"
  End If
End Sub
```

And initialize the event module:

```
Dim WordEvents As New WordEventsModule
Sub InitializeEventHandlers
  Set WordEvents.WordApp = Word.Application
End Sub
```

And then add code that calls the initialization method. In short, this process requires a fair amount of work to detect when an application-level event refers to a specific document or control. The VSTO extensions to the Word and Excel object models were designed to mitigate difficulties in some tasks, such as sinking events on specific controls. In VSTO, the bookmark object itself sources events, so you can start listening to it as you would sink any other event:

```
MyBookmark.BeforeDoubleClick +=
  new ClickEventHandler(OnDoubleClick);
```

In Chapter 2, "Introduction to Office Solutions," you saw some of the new VSTO extensions to the view object model in action. You also read about events added by VSTO in Chapter 4, "Working with Excel Events," and Chapter 7, "Working with Word Events." At the end of this chapter, we describe all the additions to the event model in detail.

Dynamic Controls in the Document

In Chapter 2, "Introduction to Office Solutions," you saw that VSTO allows developers to build customized document solutions by using Word and Excel as designers inside Visual Studio. The host item classes expose the host controls present at design time as custom properties on a class that aggregates the underlying unmanaged object.

But what about host controls not present at design time? What if you want to create new named ranges, bookmarks, buttons, or other controls at runtime? It would be nice to be able to use the new events and other extensions to the programming model on dynamically generated controls. As you will see, VSTO supports dynamically adding both host items and host controls, although the former is a little bit trickier to pull off.

Chapter 13 shows how to add Windows Forms controls dynamically to Word and Excel documents.

The Controls Collection

In a Windows Forms application, every form class has a property called Controls that refers to a collection of all the controls hosted by the form. In VSTO, each worksheet and document class contains a similarly named property; in Word, the document class contains an instance of Microsoft .Office.Tools.Word.ControlCollection; in Excel, each worksheet class contains an instance of Microsoft.Office.Tools.Excel.ControlCollection. They are quite similar; the following sections discuss their differences.

Enumerating and Searching the Collection

You can use the Controls collection to enumerate the set of aggregated controls and perform actions upon all of them. For instance, you could disable all the button controls on a sheet or document:

```
foreach (object control in this.Controls)
{
    Button button = control as Button;
    if (button != null)
        button.Enabled = false;
}
```

The Controls collection also has some of the indexing and searching methods you would expect. Both the Excel and Word flavors have methods with these signatures:

```
bool Contains(string name)
bool Contains(object control)
int IndexOf(string name)
int IndexOf(object control)
```

If the collection does not contain the searched-for control, then IndexOf returns –1. Both collections can be enumerated via the foreach loop; should you want to enumerate the collection yourself, you can call GetEnumerator. This method returns a ControlCollectionEnumerator object from the Microsoft.Office.Tools.Excel or Microsoft.Office.Tools.Word namespace, as appropriate. They are essentially identical functionally. Both classes have only three public methods:

- `object get Current`
- `bool MoveNext()`
- `void Reset()`

Current returns `null` when moved past the final element in the collection, MoveNext moves the enumerator to the next element, and Reset starts the enumerator over at the beginning of the collection.

Both collections also expose three index operators, which take a name `string`, `int index`, and `object` respectively. The indexers throw an Argument-OutOfRangeException if there is no such control in the collection.

Adding New Word and Excel Host Controls Dynamically

The worksheet and document Controls collections provide methods to dynamically create host controls. In Word, you can dynamically create aggregated bookmarks by using methods available from the Document host item's Controls property (which returns a Microsoft.Office.Tools.Word. ControlCollection). One method on ControlCollection is AddBookmark:

```
Microsoft.Office.Tools.Word.Bookmark AddBookmark(
  Microsoft.Office.Interop.Word.Range range, string name)
```

This method creates a new bookmark on the given range and aggregates it with the VSTO host control class. You can also create dynamic instances of BuildingBlockGalleryContentControl, ComboBoxContentControl, ContentControl, OLEControl, DatePickerContentControl, DropDownListContentControl, GroupContentControl, PictureContentControl, PlainTextContentControl, and RichTextContentControl. Multiple method signatures on the ControlCollection object allow you to add content controls based on existing controls or to create new ones while specifying positioning and sizing information. If you use one of the overloads that takes only a `string` name parameter, the control will be added at the current selection point.

```
Microsoft.Office.Tools.Word.Bookmark AddBookmark(
  Microsoft.Office.Interop.Word.Bookmark bookmark, string name);
```

```
Microsoft.Office.Tools.Word.Bookmark AddBookmark(
  Microsoft.Office.Interop.Word.Range range,
  string name);

Microsoft.Office.Tools.Word.BuildingBlockGalleryContentControl
  AddBuildingBlockGalleryContentControl(string name);

Microsoft.Office.Tools.Word.BuildingBlockGalleryContentControl
  AddBuildingBlockGalleryContentControl(
  Microsoft.Office.Interop.Word.ContentControl contentControl,
  string name);

Microsoft.Office.Tools.Word.BuildingBlockGalleryContentControl
  AddBuildingBlockGalleryContentControl(
  Microsoft.Office.Interop.Word.Range range, string name);

Microsoft.Office.Tools.Word.ComboBoxContentControl
  AddComboBoxContentControl(string name);

Microsoft.Office.Tools.Word.ComboBoxContentControl
  AddComboBoxContentControl(
  Microsoft.Office.Interop.Word.ContentControl contentControl,
  string name);
Microsoft.Office.Tools.Word.ComboBoxContentControl
  AddComboBoxContentControl(
  Microsoft.Office.Interop.Word.Range range, string name);

Microsoft.Office.Tools.Word.ContentControl
  AddContentControl(Microsoft.Office.Interop.Word.ContentControl
  contentControl, string name);

Microsoft.Office.Tools.Word.ContentControl
  AddContentControl(string name,
    Microsoft.Office.Interop.Word.WdContentControlType
    contentControlType);

Microsoft.Office.Tools.Word.ContentControl
  AddContentControl(Microsoft.Office.Interop.Word.Range range,
  string name, Microsoft.Office.Interop.Word.WdContentControlType
  contentControlType);

Microsoft.Office.Tools.Word.OLEControl AddControl(
  Microsoft.Office.Interop.Word.Control control,
  Microsoft.Office.Interop.Word.Range range, float width,
  float height, string name);

Microsoft.Office.Tools.Word.OLEControl AddControl(
  Microsoft.Office.Interop.Word.Control control, float left,
  float top, float width, float height, string name);
```

```
Microsoft.Office.Tools.Word.DatePickerContentControl
  AddDatePickerContentControl(string name);

Microsoft.Office.Tools.Word.DatePickerContentControl
  AddDatePickerContentControl(
  Microsoft.Office.Interop.Word.ContentControl contentControl,
  string name);

Microsoft.Office.Tools.Word.DatePickerContentControl
  AddDatePickerContentControl(
  Microsoft.Office.Interop.Word.Range range, string name);

Microsoft.Office.Tools.Word.DropDownListContentControl
  AddDropDownListContentControl(string name);

Microsoft.Office.Tools.Word.DropDownListContentControl
  AddDropDownListContentControl(
  Microsoft.Office.Interop.Word.ContentControl contentControl,
  string name);

Microsoft.Office.Tools.Word.DropDownListContentControl
  AddDropDownListContentControl(
  Microsoft.Office.Interop.Word.Range range, string name);

Microsoft.Office.Tools.Word.GroupContentControl
  AddGroupContentControl(string name);

Microsoft.Office.Tools.Word.GroupContentControl
  AddGroupContentControl(
  Microsoft.Office.Interop.Word.ContentControl contentControl,
  string name);

Microsoft.Office.Tools.Word.GroupContentControl
  AddGroupContentControl(Microsoft.Office.Interop.Word.Range range,
  string name);

Microsoft.Office.Tools.Word.PictureContentControl
  AddPictureContentControl(string name);

Microsoft.Office.Tools.Word.PictureContentControl
  AddPictureContentControl(
  Microsoft.Office.Interop.Word.ContentControl contentControl,
  string name);

Microsoft.Office.Tools.Word.PictureContentControl
  AddPictureContentControl(
  Microsoft.Office.Interop.Word.Range range, string name);

Microsoft.Office.Tools.Word.PlainTextContentControl
  AddPlainTextContentControl(string name);
```

```
Microsoft.Office.Tools.Word.PlainTextContentControl
  AddPlainTextContentControl(
  Microsoft.Office.Interop.Word.ContentControl contentControl,
  string name);

Microsoft.Office.Tools.Word.PlainTextContentControl
  AddPlainTextContentControl(
  Microsoft.Office.Interop.Word.Range range, string name);

Microsoft.Office.Tools.Word.RichTextContentControl
  AddRichTextContentControl(string name);

Microsoft.Office.Tools.Word.RichTextContentControl
  AddRichTextContentControl(
  Microsoft.Office.Interop.Word.ContentControl contentControl,
  string name);

Microsoft.Office.Tools.Word.RichTextContentControl
  AddRichTextContentControl(
  Microsoft.Office.Interop.Word.Range range, string name);
```

> **▪ NOTE**
>
> XMLNode and XMLNodes host controls cannot be created dynamically in Word. The XMLMappedRange host control cannot be created dynamically in Excel.

In Excel, you can dynamically create an aggregated Chart, Named-Range, ListObject, and OLEObject using methods off the Worksheet host item's Controls property (which returns a Microsoft.Office.Tools.Excel .ControlCollection). Of those, only Chart and OLEObject controls can be positioned at arbitrary coordinates; all the rest must be positioned with a Range object:

```
Microsoft.Office.Tools.Excel.Chart AddChart(
  Microsoft.Office.Interop.Excel.Range range, string name);

Microsoft.Office.Tools.Excel.Chart AddChart(double left,
  double top, double width, double height, string name);

Microsoft.Office.Tools.Excel.OLEObject AddControl(
  Microsoft.Office.Interop.Excel.Control control,
  Microsoft.Office.Interop.Excel.Range range, string name);
```

```
Microsoft.Office.Tools.Excel.OLEObject AddControl(
    Microsoft.Office.Interop.Excel.Control control, double left,
    double top, double width, double height, string name);

Microsoft.Office.Tools.Excel.ListObject AddListObject(
    Microsoft.Office.Interop.Excel.Range range, string name);

Microsoft.Office.Tools.Excel.NamedRange AddNamedRange(
    Microsoft.Office.Interop.Excel.Range range, string name);
```

Removing Controls

The host controls added to a worksheet or document host item class at design time are exposed as properties on the host item class. If at runtime the user were to accidentally delete one, save the document, and then reload it, the customization code would be unable to find the aggregated control. This would likely result in an exception because eventually the customization would try to listen to an event or call a method on the missing aggregated control. If the customization detects this condition, it will throw a ControlNotFoundException.

Although it is difficult to prevent end users from accidentally or deliberately deleting controls without locking the document, the Controls collection can at least try to prevent *programmatic* destruction of controls added at design time. There are four equivalent ways to remove controls from the Controls collection; all will throw a CannotRemoveControlException if you attempt to remove a control that was not added dynamically.

The four ways to remove a dynamic control are to call Delete() on the control itself, or to call Remove(object control), Remove(string name), or RemoveAt(int index) on the Controls collection itself. All four of these remove the control from the collection, remove the control from the document or worksheet, and destroy the extender object.

Most collections have a Clear() method that removes every member from the collection. Because completely clearing a Controls collection would almost always result in an exception when a design-time control was removed, this method always throws a NotSupportedException, and is hidden from IntelliSense.

Dynamic Controls Information Is Not Persisted

What happens when you add one or more dynamic controls to a document, save it, and reload it later?

Dynamically created Windows Forms controls such as buttons and check boxes do not survive being saved and then loaded. They just disappear; your customization code can create them again afresh the next time the document is loaded.

Because "host" controls such as ranges and bookmarks are themselves part of the document, they will be persisted along with the rest of the document. However, the controls do not save any information about any aggregating objects you may have created around them. When the document is reloaded, the controls will still be there, but there will be no aggregates wrapping them. You will have to re-add the controls to the Controls collection to create new aggregates for the controls. The Controls collection provides Add methods that can reconnect an aggregate to an existing control in the document without creating a new control in the document.

Advanced Topic: Class Hookup and Cookies

As you have just seen, adding new aggregated host controls onto a host item is relatively straightforward: Just call the appropriate method on the controls collection for the containing host item and the control is created, aggregated, and placed on the host item automatically.

You might wonder how the VSTO runtime, the hosting application, and the aggregating class all work together to provide working controls at runtime. To get an idea of what is happening, click the Show All Files button in the Solution Explorer and you will see that a number of normally hidden files make up the class, as shown in Figure 12-3. Look at Sheet1.Designer.cs nested under Sheet1.cs.

Look at the constructor generated for the Sheet1 class in the Sheet1 .Designer.cs file. Two strings are passed to a base constructor, the first a "cookie" and the second a "human-readable" name:

```
public Sheet1() : base("Sheet1", "Sheet1") { }
```

Recall that the aggregating object obtains the aggregated object "on demand." That is, it obtains the underlying object only when the first method or property is called that must be passed along to the underlying object. This means that the aggregating object must not require the aggregated object when the aggregating object is constructed, but it does need to

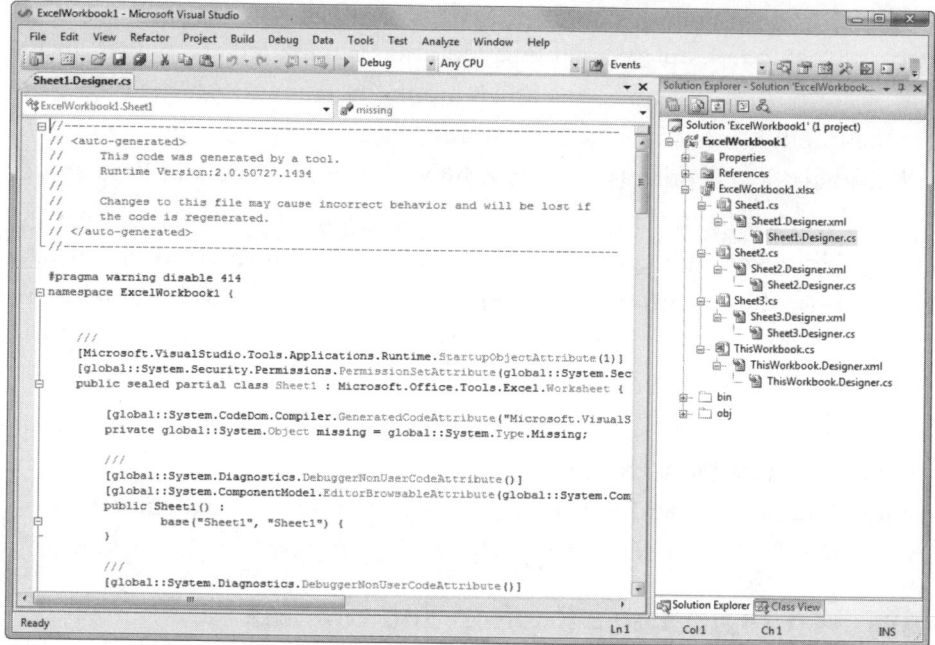

Figure 12-3: Using the Show All Files button to examine hidden code.

be able to obtain that object at any time thereafter. Somehow the aggregating object must talk to the host and obtain the unique object is aggregating.

It does so by passing a string called the "cookie," which identifies the aggregated object to the host. In the event that an error occurs when attempting to fetch the worksheet, the runtime will need to raise an error. It is possible that the cookie that uniquely identifies the aggregated object might contain control characters or be otherwise unsuitable for display. Therefore, the base constructor also takes a "human-readable" name used in the event that the host is unable to find the object to be aggregated. In this case both the cookie and the human-readable name are "Sheet1."

Let's put all this together. We need two basic things to hook up an aggregated worksheet:

1. A host-provided service that can obtain the aggregated object given a cookie

2. A unique cookie that host application can use to identify the aggregated object

How do we obtain a reference to the service that maps cookies onto unmanaged host objects? When the VSTO runtime starts up a customization, it provides the service that maps a cookie to an aggregated object by passing the appropriate interface to the base class of the host item, whether it be a Workbook, Worksheet, ChartSheet, or Document.

How do we obtain a unique cookie? This answer is different for every type of object. Let's consider Worksheet, as it is one of the more interesting examples. At design time a call is made into VBA to initialize the Code-Name property for each new worksheet that is created which provides a unique cookie for each worksheet. The VSTO design time does nothing but force VBA to initialize. It does not add a VBA project to the workbook or anything else of that nature. However, it does access the VBProject object. This is one reason why a developer using VSTO needs to trust access to the VBA project as part of the creation of the first Excel or Word VSTO project.

VSTO uses the initial name of the new Worksheet object for the human-readable name and the CodeName provided by VBA as the cookie. The cookie does not change for the lifetime of the document: Once VBA has provided VSTO with a CodeName, that CodeName never changes, even if the worksheet is renamed by the user.

When the VSTO runtime needs to get an aggregated object for each of its classes (Sheet1, Sheet2, Sheet3, ThisWorkbook) it calls into the VSTO runtime providing the lookup cookie for the object. Code that is part of the VSTO runtime talks to the host and gets back the aggregated object from the COM object model of the Office application that corresponds to the cookie.

This call to get an aggregated object happens just in time—the first time that your running code accesses a property or method of the host item that needs the aggregated object. So for example, if you never have any code that talks to any of the properties and methods of Sheet3, it will never make a call into the VSTO runtime asking for its aggregated object.

A similar "cookie-based" approach is used for host item controls like NamedRange. In this case, VBA isn't used to provide a unique name for an item—instead the Office object model already provides a way to uniquely identify a NamedRange. A NamedRange is identified by the Names collection associated with a Workbook object, so a Name from the Names collection becomes the cookie.

Later in this chapter we describe how to create worksheets dynamically at runtime in the section "Advanced Topic: Creating Worksheets Dynamically." This section should have provided you with the background to better understand that topic.

Advanced Topic: Inspecting the Generated Code

Let's take a deeper look behind the scenes at what is going on when you customize a worksheet or document. Create a new Excel C# project, create a named range, and take a look at the code for Sheet1.cs, shown in Listing 12-1.

Listing 12-1: The Developer's Customized Worksheet Class

```
namespace ExcelWorkbook1
{
    public partial class Sheet1
    {
        private void Sheet1_Startup(object sender,
          System.EventArgs e)
        {
          this.MyRange.Value2 = "Hi";
        }

        private void Sheet1_Shutdown(object sender,
         System.EventArgs e)
        {
        }

        #region VSTO Designer generated code

        /// <summary>
        /// Required method for Designer support - do not modify
        /// the contents of this method with the code editor.
        /// </summary>
        private void InternalStartup()
        {
            this.Startup +=
              new System.EventHandler(Sheet1_Startup);
            this.Shutdown +=
              new System.EventHandler(Sheet1_Shutdown);
        }

        #endregion

    }
}
```

Upon closer inspection, a few questions might come to mind. What does that `partial` mean in the class declaration? Where is the MyRange property declared and initialized? Didn't we say earlier that the customized worksheet class extends a base class? Where is the base class declaration?

It's the `partial` that is the key. C# and Visual Basic support a syntax that allows a class declaration to be split up among several files. The portion that you see before you is the home of all your developer-customized code; the automatically generated code is hidden in another portion of the class not displayed by default.

Click the Show All Files button in the Solution Explorer and you will see that a number of normally hidden files make up the class, as shown in Figure 12-3.

First, notice that behind every worksheet there is an XML file for the worksheet. If you look at the first few lines of the XML, you will see that it contains a description of the contents of the worksheet and how to represent it as a class. This "blueprint" contains information about what namespace the class should live in, what the name of the class should be, what controls are exposed on the class, how Excel identifies those controls, and so on.

Behind this language-independent representation of the class there is another C# file that contains the other half of the partial class, generated from the XML blueprint. It begins something like this:

```
namespace ExcelWorkbook1 {
[Microsoft.VisualStudio.Tools.Applications.Runtime.
  StartupObjectAttribute(1)]
[global::System.Security.Permissions.PermissionSetAttribute(
  global::System.Security.Permissions.SecurityAction.Demand,
    Name="FullTrust")]
public sealed partial class Sheet1 : Microsoft.Office.Tools.Excel.Worksheet
{
```

As you can see, here is where the base classes are specified and the member variables declared. The class also specifies that it is one of the startup classes in your customization assembly, and that code that calls members of this class must be fully trusted.

There is plenty more code in the hidden portion of the partial class, most of which is devoted to initializing controls, starting up data binding, and handling data caching; Chapter 19, "VSTO Data Programming," discusses data binding in more detail. The constructor, in particular, should look familiar:

```
[global::System.Diagnostics.DebuggerNonUserCodeAttribute()]
[global::System.ComponentModel.EditorBrowsableAttribute(
  global::System.ComponentModel.EditorBrowsableState.Never)]
public Sheet1() :
  base("Sheet1", "Sheet1")
{
}
```

This is the same code discussed in the previous section and calls the aggregate base class constructor.

If you ever want to debug through this code, ensure that Just My Code Debugging is turned off (via the Tools > Options > Debugging > General dialog box); you can then put breakpoints on any portion of the hidden code, just like any other code.

Do not attempt to edit the hidden code. Every time you make a change in the designer that would result in a new control being added, or even change a control property, the hidden half of the partial class is completely regenerated. Any changes you have made to the hidden half will be lost; this is why it is hidden by default!

The Startup and Shutdown Sequences

You have probably noticed by now that we have been putting custom initialization code in an event handler:

```
private void Sheet1_Startup(object sender, System.EventArgs e) {
  this.MyRange.Value2 = "Hello";
}
```

But exactly what happens, in what order, as the startup classes are created and initialized? Excel customizations typically have many startup classes, one for each sheet and one for the workbook itself. Which ones load first?

You already saw a clue that answers the latter question. In the hidden half of the partial class, each class declaration has an attribute:

```
[Microsoft.VisualStudio.Tools.Applications.Runtime.
    StartupObjectAttribute(1)]
```

The Workbook class has 0 for the argument, Sheet1 has 1, Sheet2 has 2, and so on. The workbook aggregate always has ordinal 0, and each worksheet is given its ordinal based on what order Excel enumerates its sheets. The startup sequence happens in four phases, and each phase is executed on each startup class in order of the given ordinal before the next phase begins.

In the first phase, each class is constructed using the constructor mentioned above. This simply constructs the classes and stores away the information that will be needed later to fetch the unmanaged aggregated objects from Excel or Word.

In the second phase, the Initialize method of each startup class is called—again, in multiclass customizations, starting with the workbook and then each worksheet by ordinal. If you look at the hidden half of the partial class, you will see the Initialize method:

```
[global::System.Diagnostics.DebuggerNonUserCodeAttribute()]
[global::System.CodeDom.Compiler.GeneratedCodeAttribute(
    "Microsoft.VisualStudio.Tools.Office.ProgrammingModel.dll",
    "9.0.0.0")]
[global::System.ComponentModel.EditorBrowsableAttribute(
    global::System.ComponentModel.EditorBrowsableState.Never)]
protected override void Initialize() {
    base.Initialize();

    Globals.Sheet1 = this;
    global::System.Windows.Forms.Application.EnableVisualStyles();
    this.InitializeCachedData();
    this.InitializeControls();
    this.InitializeComponents();
    this.InitializeData();
}
```

The attributes prevent the Initialize method from showing up in IntelliSense drop-downs and mark the method as being "not my code" for the Debug Just My Code feature. The initializer then fetches services from the host needed to initialize the view and data elements, sets up the global class (discussed in more detail later in this chapter), loads cached data, and initializes all the controls.

In the third phase, data binding code is activated. Data bindings must be activated after all the classes are initialized because a control on Sheet2 might be bound to a dataset on Sheet1.

Finally, in the fourth phase, after everything is constructed, initialized, and data bound, each startup class raises its Startup event, and the code in the developer's half of the partial class runs.

This multiphase startup sequence ensures that you can write handlers for the Startup event that can assume not just that the class itself is ready to go, but that every startup class in the customization is ready to go.

Ideally, it would be a good idea to write Startup event handlers for each class that do not depend on the order in which they are executed. If you must, however, you can always look at the startup attributes to see in what order the events will be executed.

The shutdown sequence is similar but simpler. As the host application, Word or Excel, shuts down, each host item class raises the Shutdown event. Shutdown events are raised in the same order as each phase in the startup sequence.

The Globals Class in Excel

Suppose you're writing code in the Sheet1 class that needs to set a property on a control hosted by Sheet2. You are probably going to need to obtain the instance of the *aggregated* Sheet2 class somehow. Instead of aggregating properties representing all the other sheets and the workbook aggregates onto each startup class, VSTO exposes all the sheets and the workbook as static members of the Globals class:

```
private void Sheet1_Startup(object sender, System.EventArgs e)
{
    Globals.Sheet2.MyRange.Value2 = "Hello";
}
```

Because at least the first three phases of the startup sequence have finished at this point, you know that the Globals class and Sheet2 have been initialized, although Sheet2's Startup event has probably not fired yet.

Notice that by default, controls aggregated onto the worksheet classes are given the `internal` visibility modifier. You can change the visibility modifier generated for a control by selecting the control in the designer and then selecting the Modifiers property in the Properties window. However, if you change the visibility of the control to `private`, you will be unable to access the control's field from the Globals class.

The Globals class is also constructed using partial classes, although by default there is no visible portion. Rather, each generated code file defines a portion of the Globals class. You can see this code at the bottom of the hidden file for each class. Should you for some reason want to add your own custom members to the Globals class, you can always create your own portion of the partial class.

VSTO Extensions to the Word and Excel Object Models

This section provides a detailed list of every new property, event, and method aggregated onto the Word and Excel objects by the VSTO aggregates, with the exception of the new data binding features (covered in Chapter 19, "VSTO Data Programming").

As mentioned previously, every aggregated object has a Tag property that you can use for any purpose you choose and an InnerObject property that you can use to access the aggregated object. In addition, each host control has a Delete method that removes it (if it can be added dynamically at runtime) from its document or worksheet. Because every aggregating object has these properties and methods, they are not mentioned again in the following topics.

The Word Document Class

VSTO Word projects have exactly one host item class. Every customized document class inherits from the aggregating class Microsoft.Office.Tools .Word.Document and implements the properties, methods, and events defined by the Microsoft.Office.Interop.Word.Document interface.

Document objects in VSTO source the following events shown in Table 12-2, all of which are raised by the Document object when the Application object raises the identically named event.

TABLE 12-2: New Events on VSTO's Aggregated Document Object

Event Name	Delegate	Notes
ActivateEvent	WindowEventHandler	From Application, renamed from WindowActivate
BeforeClose	CancelEventHandler	From Application
BeforeDoubleClick	ClickEventHandler	From Application
BeforePrint	CancelEventHandler	From Application
BeforeRightClick	ClickEventHandler	From Application
BeforeSave	SaveEventHandler	From Application
BuildingBlockInsert*	BuildingBlockInsertEventHandler	From Document
CloseEvent	DocumentEvents2_CloseEventHandler	From Document, renamed
ContentControlAfterAdd*	DocumentEvents2_ContentControlAfterAddEventHandler	From Document
ContentControlBeforeContentUpdate*	DocumentEvents2_ContentControlBeforeContentUpdateEventHandler	From Document
ContentControlBeforeDelete*	DocumentEvents2_ContentControlBeforeDeleteEventHandler	From Document
ContentControlBeforeStoreUpdate*	DocumentEvents2_ContentControlBeforeStoreUpdateEventHandler	From Document
ContentControlOnEnter*	DocumentEvents2_ContentControlOnEnterEventHandler	From Document
ContentControlOnExit*	DocumentEvents2_ContentControlOnExitEventHandler	From Document
Deactivate	WindowEventHandler	From Application
MailMergeAfterMerge	MailMergeAfterMergeEventHandler	From Application

* New in Word 2007 and VSTO 3.0.

TABLE 12-2: New Events on VSTO's Aggregated Document Object *(Continued)*

Event Name	Delegate	Notes
MailMergeAfter-RecordMerge	EventHandler	From Application
MailMergeBeforeMerge	EventHandler	From Application
MailMergeBefore-RecordMerge	CancelEventHandler	From Application
MailMergeData-SourceLoad	EventHandler	From Application
MailMergeWindow-SendToCustom	EventHandler	From Application
MailMergeWizard-StateChange	MailMergeWizardState-ChangeEventHandler	From Application
New	DocumentEvents2_NewEvent-Handler	From Document, delayed
Open	DocumentEvents2_OpenEvent-Handler	From Document, delayed
SelectionChange	SelectionEventHandler	From Application
Shutdown	EventHandler	Raised by VSTO
Startup	EventHandler	Raised by VSTO
SyncEvent	DocumentEvents2_SyncEvent-Handler	From Application, renamed
WindowSize	WindowEventHandler	From Application
XMLAfterInsert	DocumentEvents2_XMLAfter-InsertHandler	From Document
XMLBeforeDelete	DocumentEvents2_XMLBefore-DeleteHandler	From Document

Notice that the Sync and Close events have been renamed to avoid a naming conflict; C# does not allow a class to have an event and a method with the same name.

The Document class has OnStartup and OnShutdown methods that force the Document object to source the Startup and Shutdown events.

The New and Open events are delayed so that they are not raised until the aggregate class is fully initialized. These events would normally be raised before any user-authored code could run. If user code does not run until after the event has been raised, however, how would you add an event handling delegate to listen to the event? Therefore, the events are delayed until after the customization's event binding code can run.

The event delegate types could use some additional explanation. All the event delegate types that begin with DocumentEvents2_ are from the Word PIA. The System.EventHandler, System.ComponentModel.CancelEventHandler and System.ComponentModel.HandledEventHandler delegates are straightforward. The remaining delegate types are all defined in the Microsoft.Office.Tools .Word namespace and have signatures as follows:

```
delegate void ClickEventHandler(object sender, ClickEventArgs e);
delegate void MailMergeAfterMergeEventHandler(object sender,
  MailMergeAfterMergeEventArgs e);
delegate void MailMergeWizardStateChangeEventHandler(object sender,
  MailMergeWizardStateChangeEventArgs e);
delegate void SaveEventHandler(object sender, SaveEventArgs e);
delegate void SelectionEventHandler(object sender, SelectionEventArgs e)
delegate void WindowEventHandler(object sender, WindowEventArgs e);
```

The arguments classes of each are as follows:

- The ClickEventArgs class inherits from System.ComponentModel .CancelEventArgs and therefore has a Cancel property. It also exposes the selection that was clicked:

```
class ClickEventArgs : CancelEventArgs {
   ClickEventArgs (Interop.Word.Selection selection, bool cancel)
   Interop.Word.Selection Selection { get; }
}
```

- The MailMergeAfterMergeEventArgs class exposes the new document created:

```
class MailMergeAfterMergeEventArgs : EventArgs {
  MailMergeAfterMergeEventArgs(Interop.Word.Document newDocument)
  Interop.Word.Document NewDocument { get; }
}
```

- The MailMergeWizardStateChangeEventArgs class exposes the previous, current, and handled states:

```
class MailMergeWizardStateChangeEventArgs : EventArgs {
  MailMergeWizardStateChangeEventArgs (int fromState,
    int toState, bool handled)
  int FromState { get; }
  int ToState { get; }
  bool Handled { get; }
}
```

- The SaveEventArgs class allows the handler to instruct the event source whether the Save As dialog box should display. This is also a cancelable event:

```
class SaveEventArgs : CancelEventArgs {
  SaveEventArgs (bool showSaveAsUI, bool cancel)
  bool ShowSaveAsDialog { get; set; }
}
```

- The SelectionEventArgs class provides the selection that was changed:

```
class SelectionEventArgs : EventArgs {
  SelectionEventArgs (Interop.Word.Selection selection)
  Interop.Word.Selection Selection{ get; }
}
```

- The WindowEventArgs class provides the window that was activated, deactivated, or resized:

```
class WindowEventArgs : EventArgs {
 WindowEventArgs(Interop.Word.Window window)
  Interop.Word.Window Window { get; }
}
```

In addition to the events mentioned in this section, the Document object contains two collections provided by VSTO. First, as discussed earlier in this chapter, the Document object aggregate contains a collection of controls. Second, the Document object contains a VSTOSmartTags collection (discussed further in Chapter 18, "Working with Smart Tags in VSTO").

C# does not support parameterized properties, but two methods in the Document interface use parameterized properties. To make it easier to call these methods from C#, both properties return instances of helper classes that allow you to use parameterized indexers. They are as follows:

```
_ActiveWritingStyleType ActiveWritingStyle { get; }
_CompatibilityType Compatibility { get; }
```

> ■ NOTE
>
> The helper classes are scoped to within the customized host item's base class itself, not to the Microsoft.Office.Tools.Word namespace.

The helper classes are as follows:

```
class _ActiveWritingStyleType : System.MarshalByRefObject {
 public string this[object languageID] { get; set; }
}
class _CompatibilityType : System.MarshalByRefObject {
 public string this[Interop.Word.WdCompatibility Type] { get; set; }
}
```

This means that you can access these properties by passing the parameter to the index to fetch or set the property:

```
style = this.ActiveWritingStyle[id];
```

The derived class can be further customized to add new events, methods, and properties. As you edit the document in the Word designer, any bookmarks, Word content controls, or other host controls (such as buttons, check boxes, and so on) that you drop onto the design surface will be added as members of the document class. Similarly, any XML mappings added to the document will be added to the document class as either an

XMLNode member (if the mapping is to a single node) or an XMLNodes member (if the mapping is to a repeatable node).

The document class has one additional method provided by VSTO: RemoveCustomization, which takes no arguments and has no return value. Calling this method on the aggregated document object removes the customization information from the document, so that after it is saved and reloaded, the customization code will no longer run.

▪▪ **NOTE**

If you use the ActionsPane feature, you have to complete an additional step to clean up the ActionsPane so that it won't be loaded when the document is opened subsequently. For more information, see the section "Attaching and Detaching the Actions Pane" in Chapter 14, "Working with Document-Level Actions Panes."

Finally, the document class has a property ThisApplication which refers to the Application object and is equivalent to writing the code "this.Application" in the document class. This property exists to help migrate VSTO 2003 code that referred to a ThisApplication object. The document class also has an ActionsPane property, which is covered in detail in Chapter 14, "Working with Document-Level Actions Panes."

The Word Bookmark Host Control

Bookmark objects in the Word object model do not source any events. The aggregated host control Bookmark in VSTO sources the events shown in Table 12-3.

The delegate types and their corresponding argument classes are documented in the document class topic above.

As a convenience for both view programming and data binding, bookmark host controls also aggregate more than 150 methods and properties of the Range object that they represent. For example, these two lines of code are functionally identical:

```
columns = this.bookmark1.range.columns;
columns = this.bookmark1.columns;
```

TABLE 12-3:   New Events on VSTO's Aggregated Bookmark Object

Event Name	Delegate
BeforeDoubleClick	ClickEventHandler
BeforeRightClick	ClickEventHandler
Deselected	SelectionEventHandler
Selected	SelectionEventHandler
SelectionChange	SelectionEventHandler

The methods and properties of the Range object aggregated onto the Bookmark control are for the most part straightforward proxies that just call the method or property accessor on the aggregated range, so almost all of the methods will be functionally identical whether you call them from the Range or the Bookmark.

Three exceptions apply. First, setting the Text property on the Range object directly can sometimes result in the bookmark itself being deleted by Word. If you set the Text property by calling the new property added to the Bookmark aggregate, it ensures that the bookmark is not deleted.

Second and third, the Information and XML properties from the PIA interface are parameterized properties. Because C# does not support calling parameterized properties, the bookmark host control uses helper classes that enable you to use parameterized indexers from C#. The properties are now defined as follows:

```
_InformationType Information { get; }
_XMLType XML { get; }
```

The helper classes are scoped inside the Bookmark class itself:

```
class _InformationType : System.MarshalByRefObject {
  object this[Interop.Word.WdInformation Type] { get; }
}

class _XMLType : System.MarshalByRefObject {
  public string this[bool DataOnly] { get; }
}
```

You can then use the properties like this:

```
info = this.myBookmark.Information[WdInformation.wdCapsLock];
```

The Word XMLNode and XMLNodes Host Control Classes

When you map a schema into a Word document, element declarations that have a maxOccurs attribute in the schema equal to 1 are represented in the host item class as XMLNode objects. All others are represented as XML-Nodes objects, because there could be more than one of them.

Table 12-4 shows the events in VSTO that the XMLNode and XML-Nodes controls source.

As you can see, we have two delegate classes and therefore two event argument classes. These events are normally sourced by the Application object.

The delegates and event argument classes are all in the Microsoft .Office.Tools.Word namespace. The delegate classes are as follows:

```
delegate void NodeInsertAndDeleteEventHandler(object sender,
  NodeInsertAndDeleteEventArgs e);
delegate void ContextChangeEventHandler(object sender,
  ContextChangeEventArgs e);
```

TABLE 12-4: New Events on VSTO's Aggregated XMLNode and XMLNodes Controls

Event Name	Delegate
AfterInsert	NodeInsertAndDeleteEventHandler
BeforeDelete	NodeInsertAndDeleteEventHandler
ContextEnter	ContextChangeEventHandler
ContextLeave	ContextChangeEventHandler
Deselect	ContextChangeEventHandler
Select	ContextChangeEventHandler
ValidationError	EventHandler

- When a node is inserted or deleted, it is often interesting to know whether the change is a result of the user inserting or deleting the element directly, or whether this is part of an undo or redo operation. Nodes sometimes are inserted or deleted as part of the way Excel manages XML node controls internally when doing certain operations, and in this case, the InUndoRedo property will be true as well. This flag is therefore exposed on the event arguments class:

```
class NodeInsertAndDeleteEventArgs : EventArgs {
  NodeInsertAndDeleteEventArgs (bool inUndoRedo)
  bool InUndoRedo { get; }
}
```

- When a node is selected or deselected, the appropriate event is raised. A "context change" is a special kind of selection change in which the insertion point of the document moves from one XML node to another. Therefore, the event arguments for the ContextEnter and ContextLeave events specify the node that was until recently the home of the insertion point, and the new home.

```
class ContextChangeEventArgs : NodeSelectionEventArgs {
  ContextChangeEventArgs( Interop.Word.XMLNode oldXMLNode,
    Interop.Word.XMLNode newXMLNode, Interop.Word.Selection selection,
    int reason)
  Interop.Word.XMLNode OldXMLNode { get; }
  Interop.Word.XMLNode NewXMLNode { get; }
}
```

The XMLNode interface in the PIA has two parameterized properties, which are not supported in C#. Therefore, these properties have been redefined to return helper classes that implement parameterized indexers instead. The two methods are as follows:

```
_ValidationErrorTextType ValidationErrorText { get; }
_XMLType XML { get; }
```

Their helper classes are scoped to the XMLNode class itself. They are defined as follows:

```
class _ValidationErrorTextType : System.MarshalByRefObject {
  string this[bool Advanced] { get; }
}
```

```
class _XMLType : System.MarshalByRefObject {
  string this[bool DataOnly] { get; }
}
```

XMLNode controls also implement several convenient methods for manipulating the XML bound to the document:

```
void LoadXml(string xml)
void LoadXml(System.Xml.XmlDocument document)
void LoadXml(System.Xml.XmlElement element)
void Load(string filename)
```

All of these take the contents of the XML in the argument and insert it into the given node and its children. However, the onus is on the caller to ensure both that the XML inserted into the node corresponds to the schematized type of the node, and that any child nodes exist and are mapped into the document appropriately. These methods will neither create nor delete child nodes.

As a further convenience for both view and data programming, the XMLNode object also provides a property that aggregates the Text property of the node's range:

```
string NodeText { get; set; }
```

Chapter 14, "Working with Document-Level Actions Panes," and Chapter 19, "VSTO Data Programming," cover data binding scenarios and actions pane scenarios for XMLNode and XMLNodes objects in detail.

The Word Content Control Classes

As described in Chapter 7, "Working with Word Events," and Chapter 8, "Working with Word Objects," content controls can be inserted into a document to provide more structure and control—when you have a section of the document in which you want to allow the user to insert a picture or pick a value from a drop-down list, for example. Eight content controls are available: rich text, plain text, picture, combo box, drop-down list, date picker, building block gallery, and group. In VSTO, these controls can be dragged off the toolbox and into a Word document. Then they are added as host controls of the Word Document host item.

In the Word object model, all content control types are represented by the ContentControl class. In VSTO, eight specialized host item controls represent the eight control types, as shown in Table 12-5.

TABLE 12-5: Key Characteristics of the Eight Content Control Types and Corresponding VSTO Host Item Controls

Control	Key Characteristics	VSTO Host Item Class
Rich Text	Can contain formatted text in multiple fonts and styles. Can also contain other content controls.	RichTextContentControl
Plain Text	Can contain text formatted to only one font and style for the entire control. Cannot contain other content controls.	PlainTextContentControl
Picture	Can display pictures in any of the many formats that Word can understand. Cannot contain other content controls.	PictureContentControl
Combo Box	Can be set to arbitrary text or a value picked out of its drop-down list. Can use only one font and style for the entire control. Cannot contain other content controls.	ComboBoxContentControl
Drop-Down List	Can be set only to a value picked out of its drop-down list. Can use only one font and style for the entire control. Cannot contain other content controls.	DropDownListContentControl
Date Picker	Can be set to arbitrary text or a date picked from its drop-down date picker. Can contain text formatted to only one font and style for the entire control. Cannot contain other content controls.	DatePickerContentControl

TABLE 12-5: Key Characteristics of the Eight Content Control Types and Corresponding VSTO Host Item Controls *(Continued)*

Control	Key Characteristics	VSTO Host Item Class
Building Block Gallery	Can contain formatted text in multiple fonts and styles. Can contain other content controls. Can pick content out of a drop-down list including existing galleries built into Word or provided by a custom template.	BuildingBlockGallery-ContentControl
Group	Can be used to group content controls and other document content to protect it from editing or deletion.	GroupContentControl

Content controls in the Word object model do not source any events. The aggregated host controls representing the eight content controls source the new events shown in Table 12-6. All these specific host control classes derive from a common base class called ContentControlBase, which sources these events.

TABLE 12-6: New Events on VSTO's Aggregated Content Control Objects

Event Name	Delegate
Added	EventHandler<ContentControlAddedEventArgs>
ContentUpdating	EventHandler<ContentControlContentUpdatingEventArgs>
Deleting	EventHandler<ContentControlDeletingEventArgs>
Entering	EventHandler<ContentControlEnteringEventArgs>
Exiting	EventHandler<ContentControlExitingEventArgs>
StoreUpdating	EventHandler<ContentControlStoreUpdatingEventArgs>
Validated	EventHandler
Validating	CancelEventHandler

The arguments classes referred to in Table 12-6 are as follows:

- The ContentControlAddedEventArgs class provides information as to whether the control was added while Word was in an Undo or Redo operation. Controls sometimes are added as part of the way Word manages controls internally when doing certain operations, and in this case, the InUndoRedo property will be true as well.

```
public class ContentControlAddedEventArgs : EventArgs
{
  public ContentControlAddedEventArgs(bool inUndoRedo);
  public bool InUndoRedo { get; }
}
```

- The ContentControlContentUpdatingEventArgs class provides updated content string for the control when the control is being updated from the XML data store.

```
public class ContentControlContentUpdatingEventArgs : EventArgs
{
  public ContentControlContentUpdatingEventArgs(string content);
  public string Content { get; set; }
}
```

- The ContentControlDeletingEventArgs class provides information as to whether the control was deleted while Word was in an Undo or Redo operation. Controls sometimes are deleted as part of the way Word manages controls internally when doing certain operations, and in this case, the InUndoRedo property will be true as well.

```
public class ContentControlDeletingEventArgs : EventArgs
{
  public ContentControlDeletingEventArgs(bool inUndoRedo);
  public bool InUndoRedo { get; }
}
```

- The ContentControlContentExitingEventArgs class provides a cancel parameter to prevent the user from exiting the content control.

```
public class ContentControlContentExitingEventArgs : EventArgs
{
  public ContentControlContentExitingEventArgs(bool cancel);
  public bool Cancel { get; set; }
}
```

- The ContentControlStoreUpdatingEventArgs class provides the string that is about to be written to the XML data store when the XML data store is being updated from the content control.

```
public class ContentControlStoreUpdatingEventArgs : EventArgs
{
    public ContentControlStoreUpdatingEventArgs(string content);
    public string Content { get; set; }
}
```

The Excel Workbook Host Item Class

The aggregating workbook class raises the same 30 events as the aggregated workbook class, with the same delegate types. Aside from renaming the Activate event to ActivateEvent, so as to avoid a collision with the method of the same name, there are no changes to the events raised by the Workbook object.

The Workbook object does have two new events raised when the customization starts up and shuts down:

```
event System.EventHandler Startup;
event System.EventHandler Shutdown;
```

The aggregated Workbook object has two methods added by VSTO, OnStartup and OnShutdown, which cause the workbook to raise the Startup and Shutdown events.

As with the Word document class, the Excel workbook class gains a ThisApplication property, which refers back to the Excel Application object; an ActionsPane property, covered in Chapter 14, "Working with Document-Level Actions Panes"; and a VstoSmartTags collection, covered in Chapter 18, "Working with Smart Tags in VSTO." The Workbook object also has a method called RemoveCustomization that takes no arguments and has no return value. Calling this method on the aggregated Workbook object removes the customization information from the spreadsheet, so that after it is saved and reloaded, the customization code will no longer run.

> **▪▪ NOTE**
>
> If you use the ActionsPane feature, you have to complete an additional step to clean up the ActionsPane so that it won't be loaded when the document is opened subsequently. For more information, see the section "Attaching and Detaching the Actions Pane" in Chapter 14, "Working with Document-Level Actions Panes."

There is only one other minor change to the view programming model of the workbook class. Because C# cannot use parameterized properties, the Colors property now returns a helper class (scoped to the host item class itself) that allows you to use a parameterized index:

```
_ColorsType Colors { get; }

class _ColorsType : System.MarshalByRefObject {
  object this[object Index] { get; set; }
}
```

The Excel Worksheet Host Item Class

Much like the workbook, the aggregating worksheet class does not have any major changes to its view programming model. The aggregating worksheet class raises the same nine events as the aggregated worksheet class, with the same delegate types. Aside from renaming the Activate event to ActivateEvent, so as to avoid a collision with the method of the same name, there are no changes to the events raised by the Worksheet object.

The Worksheet object has two events raised when the customization starts up and shuts down:

```
event System.EventHandler Startup;
event System.EventHandler Shutdown;
```

The Worksheet object has two new methods, OnStartup and OnShutdown, which cause the worksheet to raise the Startup and Shutdown events. The worksheet also provides the Controls collection mentioned earlier in this chapter.

Worksheets classes can be customized by subclassing; the derived classes generated by the design have properties representing charts, named ranges, XML-mapped ranges, list objects, and other controls on each sheet.

There is only one other minor change to the view programming model of the worksheet class. Because C# cannot use parameterized properties, the Range property now returns a helper class (scoped to the worksheet class itself) that allows you to use a parameterized index:

```
_RangeType Range { get; }

class _RangeType : System.MarshalByRefObject {
   Interop.Excel.Range this[object Cell1, object Cell2] { get; }
}
```

The Excel Chart Sheet Host Item Class and Chart Host Control

Chart sheet host items and chart host controls are practically identical; the only difference between them as far as VSTO is concerned is that chart sheets are host items classes with their own designer and code-behind file. Charts, by contrast, are treated as controls embedded in a worksheet. Also, you can't add host item controls (such as a NamedRange or ListObject) to a chart sheet host item.

Both rename the Activate and Select events (to ActivateEvent and SelectEvent respectively) to avoid the name conflicts with the methods of the same name. The chart sheet host item class raises Startup and Shutdown events and has OnStartup and OnShutdown methods just as the worksheet class does.

Both the chart and the chart sheet have a parameterized HasAxis property that cannot be called from C#. The property therefore now returns an instance of a helper class that allows you to use a parameterized indexer instead:

```
_HasAxisType HasAxis { get; }

class _HasAxisType : System.MarshalByRefObject {
   object this[object Index1, object Index2] { get; set; }
}
```

The Excel NamedRange, XmlMappedRange, and ListObject Host Controls

All three of these are special kinds of Range objects. They raise the following events shown in Table 12-7.

TABLE 12-7: Events on VSTO's Aggregated NamedRange, XmlMappedRange, and ListObject Objects

Event Name	Delegate
BeforeDoubleClick	DocEvents_BeforeDoubleClickEventHandler
BeforeRightClick	DocEvents_BeforeRightClickEventHandler
Change	DocEvents_ChangeEventHandler
Deselected	DocEvents_SelectionChangeEventHandler
Selected	DocEvents_SelectionChangeEventHandler
SelectionChange	DocEvents_SelectionChangeEventHandler

All the event delegates are from the Microsoft.Office.Interop.Excel namespace in the Excel PIA.

The list object raises several more events in addition to those above, but because they all are primarily used to implement data binding functionality, we cover them in Chapter 19, "VSTO Data Programming."

There are many parameterized properties in both the NamedRange and XmlMappedRange interfaces that are not supported by C#. To make this functionality usable more easily from C#, these properties now return helper functions (scoped to the NamedRange or XmlMappedRange classes themselves) that expose parameterized indexers.

The NamedRange object has only one redefined property:

```
_EndType End { get; }
```

The _EndType helper class is defined as follows:

```
class _EndType : System.MarshalByRefObject {
  Interop.Excel.Range this[Interop.Excel XlDirection Direction]
  {
    get;
  }
}
```

The NamedRange aggregate also implements a parameterized indexer:

```
object this[object RowIndex, object ColumnIndex]
  { get; set; }
```

The following properties are redefined on both NamedRange and Xml-MappedRange aggregates:

```
_AddressLocalType AddressLocal { get; }
_AddressType Address { get; }
_CharactersType Characters { get; }
_ItemType Item { get; }
_OffsetType Offset { get; }
_ResizeType Resize { get; }
```

The corresponding helper classes are defined as follows:

```
class _AddressLocalType : System.MarshalByRefObject {
  string this[bool RowAbsolute, bool ColumnAbsolute,
    Interop.Excel.XlReferenceStyle ReferenceStyle, bool External,
    object RelativeTo] { get; }
}
class _AddressType : System.MarshalByRefObject {
  string this[bool RowAbsolute, bool ColumnAbsolute,
    Interop.Excel.XlReferenceStyle ReferenceStyle, bool External,
    object RelativeTo] { get; }
}
class _CharactersType : System.MarshalByRefObject {
  Interop.Excel.Characters this[int Start, int Length] { get; }
}
class _ItemType : System.MarshalByRefObject {
  object this[int RowIndex] { get; set; }
  object this[int RowIndex, int ColumnIndex] { get; set; }
}
class _OffsetType : System.MarshalByRefObject {
  Interop.Excel.Range this[int RowOffset, int ColumnOffset] { get; }
}
class _ResizeType : System.MarshalByRefObject {
  Interop.Excel.Range this[int RowSize, int ColumnSize] { get; }
}
```

As a convenience for both view and data programming, NamedRange host controls also expose directly all the methods of the associated Name object:

- `string RefersTo { get; set; }`
- `string RefersToLocal { get; set; }`
- `string RefersToR1C1 { get; set; }`
- `string RefersToR1C1Local { get; set; }`
- `Interop.Excel.Range RefersToRange { get; }`

If somehow the NamedRange object has been bound to a non-named range, these will throw NotSupportedException.

The NamedRange host control also has a Name property that is somewhat confusing. The property getter returns the Name object associated with this named range. If you pass a Name object to the setter, it will set the Name property, just as you would expect. If you pass a `string`, however, it will attempt to set the Name property of the underlying Name object.

The NamedRange host control also slightly changes the exception semantics of the Name property in two ways. First, in the standard Excel object model, setting the Name property of the name object of a named range to the name of another named range deletes the range, oddly enough; doing the same to a VSTO NamedRange host control raises an ArgumentException and does not delete the offending range.

Second, in the standard Excel object model, setting the Name property to an invalid string fails silently. The VSTO NamedRange host control throws an ArgumentException if the supplied name is invalid.

> **■. NOTE**
>
> The XMLMappedRange and ListObject host controls do not aggregate the methods of the Name object or change the error handling semantics of the name setter. The changes to the Name property semantics only apply to the NamedRange object.

XML mapped ranges and list object host controls in Excel are the rough equivalents of the XMLNode and XMLNodes controls in Word. The XML mapped range host control represents a mapped singleton element, and the list object host control represents a set of rows. We cover data binding scenarios in Chapter 19, "VSTO Data Programming." In this chapter, we just discuss their use as host controls.

The list object host control has a property added by VSTO called IsSelected:

```
bool IsSelected { get; }
```

This property is most useful for determining whether there is an "insert row." Excel does not display an insert row if the list object's range is not selected.

The list object host control also slightly changes the error handling semantics of these properties:

```
Interop.Excel.Range DataBodyRange { get; }
Interop.Excel.Range HeaderRowRange { get; }
Interop.Excel.Range InsertRowRange { get; }
Interop.Excel.Range TotalsRowRange { get; }
```

The only difference is that these properties now all return null rather than throwing an exception if you attempt to access the property on a list object that lacks a body, header, insert row, or totals row, respectively.

Chapter 19, "VSTO Data Programming," discusses other new properties and methods added to the list object used for data binding.

The VSTO Programming Model for Add-Ins

The VSTO programming model for add-ins is much simpler than the model for documents. In a VSTO add-in project, you have only one host item, ThisAddIn, in a file called ThisAddIn.cs. You don't have any host item controls. The ThisAddIn object has two events raised when the add-in starts up and shuts down:

```
event System.EventHandler Startup;
event System.EventHandler Shutdown;
```

The AddIn object has two methods, OnStartup and OnShutdown, that raise the Startup and Shutdown events.

The most important property of an AddIn object is the Application property, which returns an instance of the Application object for the application that the add-in is loading in: Word, Excel, Outlook, InfoPath, Power-Point, Project, or Visio. The Application property returns an instance of the Application from the corresponding Microsoft.Office.Interop namespace. In the case of Word, for example, it returns the Microsoft.Office.Interop .Word.Application object. The Application property allows you to write code in the ThisAddIn class, such as the following code in the class's Startup event handler:

```
private void ThisAddIn_Startup(object sender, System.EventArgs e)
{
  Application.Caption = "Hello"
}
```

A second key property of the AddIn object is the CustomTaskPanes collection, which is a member property of the AddIn object for applications that support application-level custom task panes (Word, Excel, Outlook, and PowerPoint). Creating application-level custom task panes is described in Chapter 15, "Working with Application-Level Custom Task Panes."

The AddIn object also provides a property called missing that you can pass to methods that have optional parameters that can be omitted. The missing property is shorthand for passing System.Type.Missing for an optional parameter. This property allows you to write code like the following in the ThisAddIn class:

```
bool spelledCorrectly = Application.CheckSpelling(
  "werd", missing, missing);
```

Like Word and Excel document projects, add-in projects have a Globals class. In the case of add-ins, this class is used primarily to get access to the ThisAddIn class from other code items and to get access to items added to the project—for example, a Ribbon or Form Region object. Any Ribbons that have been added to the project are added as static members of the Globals class. This feature is described in more detail in Chapter 17, "Working with the Ribbon in VSTO."

You can use the Globals class to give your code some added portability. Code written like the following example will run only if written in an event handler or method within the ThisAddIn class:

```
Application.Caption = "Hello World";
```

If you rewrite this code by using the Globals class, it can be moved easily from the ThisAddIn class to any other code modules or classes in the add-in project:

```
Globals.ThisAddIn.Application.Caption = "Hello World";
```

The Globals class can be found in the hidden code associated with the ThisAddIn host item. Should you want to add your own custom members to the Globals class, for some reason, you can always create your own portion of the partial class.

Using VSTO Document Features in Application-Level Add-Ins

One commonly asked-for feature in VSTO is the ability to use Word document and Excel workbook features in application-level add-in projects. Starting with Visual Studio 2008 SP1, a mechanism is available that allows you to use many of the document-level features in your application-level add-in projects.

Using this new mechanism, you can get a VSTO host item object for a document, worksheet, or workbook from a PIA object such as Microsoft .Office.Interop.Word.Document, Microsoft.Office.Interop.Excel.Worksheet, or Microsoft.Office.Interop.Excel.Workbook. When you have the VSTO host item object, you can use features such as the Controls collection to add host item controls to the document that can be data bound. You can also use features such as Smart Tags at document or workbook level.

Preparing an Add-In Project to Use Document Features

To prepare an add-in project that was created before Visual Studio 2008 SP1 to use document-level features, you must add a reference to Microsoft .Office.Tools.Excel.v9.0 if it is an Excel add-in project or Microsoft.Office .Tools.Word.v9.0 if it is a Word add-in project. This reference contains the definitions for document level types for Excel and Word, respectively.

When you've added the correct reference, make sure that your This-Addin.cs file has the following line of code added at the top of the file with the other using statements. For an Excel add-in, this using statement is required:

```
using Microsoft.Office.Tools.Excel.Extensions;
```

For a Word add-in, this using statement is required:

```
using Microsoft.Office.Tools.Word.Extensions;
```

Getting a VSTO Host Item Object for a Document, Worksheet, or Workbook

When you have the project prepared properly, you can directly obtain a VSTO host item object from the PIA object for a Document, Worksheet, and Workbook by using the method GetVstoObject. VSTO uses a new language feature called *extension methods* to extend the Microsoft.Office .Interop.Excel.Worksheet, Microsoft.Office.Interop.Excel.Workbook, and Microsoft.Office.Interop.Word.Document with a new method called GetVstoObject. GetVstoObject returns the corresponding VSTO host item object: Microsoft.Office.Tools.Excel.Worksheet, Microsoft.Office.Tools.Excel .Workbook, or Microsoft.Office.Tools.Word.Document, respectively.

To get a VSTO host item object for the Microsoft.Office.Tools.Word .Document object returned by the ActiveDocument property of Word's Application object, you would write code like the following in a Word add-in project:

```
Microsoft.Office.Tools.Word.Document vstoDocument =
    Globals.ThisAddIn.Application.ActiveDocument.GetVstoObject();
```

To get a VSTO host item object for the Microsoft.Office.Tools.Excel .Workbook object returned by the ActiveWorkbook property of Excel's Application object, you would write code like the following in an Excel VSTO add-in project:

```
Microsoft.Office.Tools.Excel.Workbook vstoWorkbook =
    Globals.ThisAddIn.Application.ActiveWorkbook.GetVstoObject();
```

To get a VSTO host item object for the Microsoft.Office.Tools.Excel .Worksheet object returned by the ActiveSheet property of Excel's Application object, you would write the following code. The code is slightly more complex because ActiveSheet returns an `object` that must be cast to a Microsoft.Office.Interop.Excel.Worksheet object before calling Get-VstoObject:

```
Microsoft.Office.Interop.Excel.Worksheet sheet =
    Globals.ThisAddIn.Application.ActiveSheet as
    Microsoft.Office.Interop.Excel.Worksheet;

Microsoft.Office.Tools.Excel.Worksheet vstoWorksheet =
    sheet.GetVstoObject();
```

Getting a VSTO Host Item Control for ListObject and Other Host Item Controls

Visual Studio 2008 SP1 also adds support to get a host item control directly for a Microsoft.Office.Interop.Excel.ListObject object by adding the Get-VstoObject method to this type via extension methods. This support means that you can write code like the following to get a Microsoft .Office.Tools.Excel.ListObject host item control object, assuming that the active worksheet has at least one list object:

```
Microsoft.Office.Interop.Excel.Worksheet sheet =
  Globals.ThisAddIn.Application.ActiveSheet as
  Microsoft.Office.Interop.Excel.Worksheet;

Microsoft.Office.Tools.Excel.ListObject vstoList =
  sheet.ListObjects[1].GetVstoObject();
```

To get to the other host item controls object, first get a VSTO host item object for a Document or Worksheet, and use the Controls collection to create host item controls dynamically, as in this example:

```
Microsoft.Office.Tools.Word.Document vstoDocument =
  Globals.ThisAddIn.Application.ActiveDocument.GetVstoObject();
Microsoft.Office.Tools.Word.PlainTextContentControl vstoTextControl =
  vstoDocument.Controls.AddPlainTextContentControl(
  vstoDocument.Range(ref missing, ref missing), "My Control");
```

Other Applications and Limitations

Given a host item for a document, worksheet, or workbook, you have a lot of VSTO document functionality available to you. You can dynamically create host item controls such as NamedRange and ListObject and data-bind to those controls as described in Chapter 19, "VSTO Data Programming." You can add Windows Forms controls or WPF controls to the document, as described in Chapter 13, "Using Windows Forms and WPF in VSTO." You can add document- or application-level Smart Tags as described in Chapter 18, "Working with Smart Tags in VSTO." Each of these chapters describes how to work with these features at add-in level and the kinds of things you need to keep in mind when using these features at add-in level.

Also, it is important to note the document-level features that are not accessible via this feature. It is not possible to create a document-level Ribbon through an application add-in, for example, or to access the document-level

ActionsPane that document-level VSTO customizations enable. Neither is it possible to work with controls that cannot be added dynamically to the Controls collection (XMLNode, XMLNodes, and XMLMappedRange).

Advanced Topic: Creating Worksheets Dynamically

One additional problem commonly encountered in the VSTO document programming model is how to attach code and data bindings to dynamically created worksheet objects. The new GetVstoObject feature, described earlier in this chapter, can also be used in document projects to dynamically create a VSTO host item for a worksheet.

Make sure that your ThisWorkbook.cs file has the following line of code added at the top of the file with the other using statements:

```
using Microsoft.Office.Tools.Excel.Extensions;
```

Then code like this can be written to obtain a VSTO host item for the dynamically created worksheet:

```
private void ThisWorkbook_Startup(object sender, System.EventArgs e)
{
  Excel.Worksheet worksheet = Sheets.Add(missing, missing, 1, missing)
    as Excel.Worksheet;
  // Force VBA to initialize
  object temp = this.VBProject;

  vstoSheet = worksheet.GetVstoObject();
}
```

The one mysterious line of code here is the call made to the VBProject property. This line of code does nothing except force VBA to initialize so that VSTO can get a valid CodeName for the VSTO host item. It does not add a VBA project to the workbook or anything else of that nature. It does access the VBProject object, however. For a solution that dynamically creates host items in Excel, you must make sure that users of your solution have the "Trust access to Visual Basic project object model" check box checked in the Macro Security settings. This check box is found in the Macro Security settings dialog which can be accessed by navigating from the Office Menu > Excel Options > Trust Center > Trust Center Settings >

Macro Settings. If the Trust Access to Visual Basic Project Object Model check box is not checked, this line of code will fail:

```
object temp = this.VBProject;
```

When you have vstoSheet as shown in the preceding code, you can use all the features of a Worksheet host item, including the Controls collection, to dynamically add host item controls. Just as dynamic host controls are not re-created when a document containing them is saved and then reloaded, dynamic host items are not re-created. You must hook up any worksheets that weren't there when the VSTO project was created each time the document is loaded.

Conclusion

VSTO brings the Word and Excel object models into the managed code world by aggregating key unmanaged objects onto managed base classes. Developers can then extend these base classes by using Word and Excel as designers in Visual Studio. This chapter discussed the programming model for both document-level and application-level projects, and described how document-level features can be used by application-level add-ins.

▛ 13 ▪
Using Windows Forms and WPF in VSTO

Introduction

Office has a user interface that has been designed to make it as easy as possible for an end user to access the functionality provided by each Office application. But the application that you are writing that is integrated with Office will have its own very specific user-interface requirements. The application you write will have user-interface needs that are not met by the default Office user interface.

In previous versions of Office, Visual Basic for Applications (VBA) provided the ability to show User Forms to meet your application user-interface requirements. You could also use custom ActiveX controls on the document surface. Visual Studio Tools for Office (VSTO) adds Windows Forms control support to Office to meet your user-interface needs. VSTO also allows you to use Windows Presentation Foundation (WPF) controls via a Windows Forms control called ElementHost.

Moving from ActiveX to Windows Forms

When we started designing VSTO, being able to build applications that extended the default Office user interface was one of our primary goals. We also wanted to ensure that developers writing managed code would not have to rely on ActiveX controls to do so—.NET developers want to use Windows Forms controls. To address these requirements, the team came up with a design to integrate Windows Forms deeply into Office. The vision was to allow you to use Windows Forms controls and forms in all the places you could use ActiveX controls and User Forms in previous versions of Office. We also wanted to make the design and coding experience similar to that of a traditional Windows Forms application.

This chapter covers how to use Windows Forms controls in your VSTO applications. You can use Windows Forms in VSTO in five basic ways:

1. You can put a Windows Forms control on the document or spreadsheet surface.

2. You can display a custom Windows Forms form as a modal or modeless dialog box.

3. You can put Windows Forms controls in the Document Actions task pane using the ActionsPane feature of VSTO for document customizations.

4. You can put Windows Forms controls in an application-level custom task pane using a VSTO add-in project.

5. You can put Windows Forms controls in an Outlook form region using a VSTO add-in project.

We cover the first two ways in this chapter. This chapter also covers how to create custom user controls that can be used to provide solutions to some of the shortcomings of the Windows Forms support in VSTO. The third way to use Windows Forms in VSTO—using controls in the Document Actions task pane—is covered in Chapter 14, "Working with Document-Level Actions Panes." The fourth way is covered in Chapter 15, "Working with Application-Level Custom Task Panes." And the fifth way is covered in Chapter 16, "Working with Outlook Form Regions."

Using WPF Controls via the ElementHost Control

In addition, anywhere where you can use Windows Forms controls, you can use WPF controls by means of the special Windows Forms control ElementHost. So WPF controls can be shown anywhere that Windows

Forms controls can be used: on the document or spreadsheet surface, in dialog boxes and form regions, and in the ActionsPane. When you use WPF controls in dialog boxes, the ActionsPane, a custom task pane, or an Outlook Form Region, the approach is relatively straightforward: You create a WPF control and add it to a Windows Forms surface by dragging and dropping an ElementHost control and then configuring the ElementHost to display the WPF control you created. When you use controls in the document, which is the primary topic of this chapter, you can add WPF controls to the document only at runtime; WPF controls cannot be dragged from the toolbox to the document in VSTO while you are designing the document. At the end of this chapter, we discuss this approach in more detail.

When to Use Controls on the Document Surface

VSTO enables developers to put Windows Forms and WPF controls on the document surface. Just because you can put a control onto the document surface does not necessarily mean it is a good idea for your particular application. When should you use a control on a document as opposed to popping up a dialog box, an intrinsic Office user-interface element such as a cell or a content control, a custom menu command or Ribbon button, a Smart Tag, or the actions pane?

Think about how you expect the document or spreadsheet to be used and how you want to extend the interface. Maybe you are going to use an Excel spreadsheet as a front end to corporate data. For example, many stockbrokers use Excel as their primary input and display mechanism when trading. In this scenario, the spreadsheet is very rarely e-mailed or printed, so changing the spreadsheet interface to meet the application requirements makes a lot of sense. Putting a Windows Forms button control on the surface of the document meets the requirement of making the spreadsheet more interactive and provides obvious actions that are available to the user of the spreadsheet. Figure 13-1 shows two Windows Forms buttons that have been placed on a spreadsheet—one that refreshes the stock quotes and the other that trades a particular stock.

Sometimes you will have data that needs to be edited with a more effective user interface than Office provides. A good example of this is date input. Excel provides a rich mechanism to display dates but does not provide

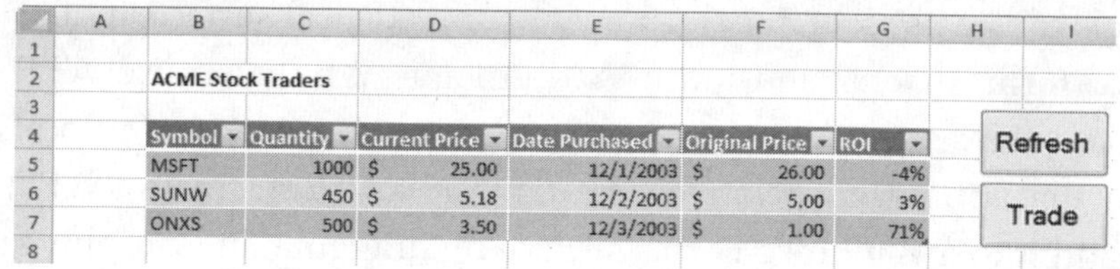

Figure 13-1:   Two Windows Forms controls on a spreadsheet.

an easy-to-use mechanism for entering dates other than basic text input. Windows Forms provides a DateTimePicker control that makes it easy for a user to enter a date. Combining the date entry interface provided by the DateTimePicker and the display capabilities of Excel result in a more effective user interface.

You could integrate the DateTimePicker into your workbook, as shown in Figure 13-2. Here we have added a DateTimePicker control for each cell containing a date. The DateTimePicker provides a combo box drop-down that shows a calendar that the user can use to pick a different date.

However, the DateTimePicker may be better used in the Document Actions task pane than on the document surface. The first problem you will encounter with a solution such as the one shown in Figure 13-2 is what you will put in the spreadsheet for the values of the cells covered by the DateTimePicker controls. It would seem reasonable that the cell covered by a particular DateTimePicker control should contain the date value

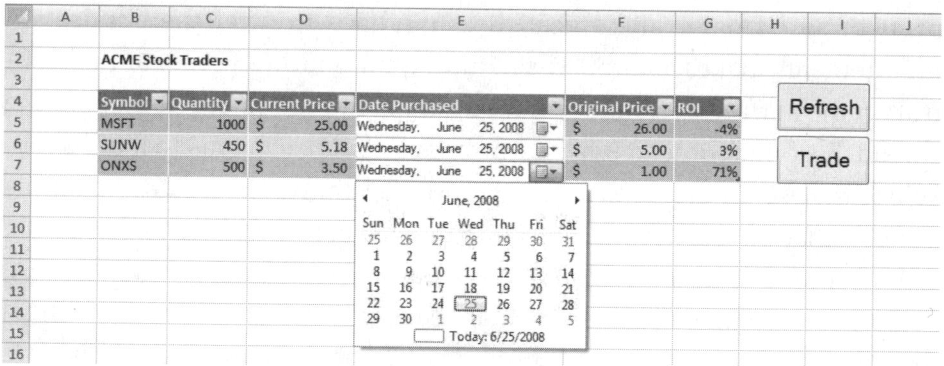

Figure 13-2: DateTimePicker controls on a spreadsheet.

being represented by the control. This way, the date value for that cell can be used in formulas and can be found when the user searches the spreadsheet with Excel's Find command.

The second problem is that if you put the DateTimePicker on the document surface, the control does not automatically save its state into the Excel workbook when the document is saved. So if in a particular session the user selects several dates and then saves the document, the next time the user opens the workbook all the DateTimePickers will reset to today's date. You will lose the date the user picked in the last session unless you write code to synchronize the DateTimePicker with the cell value covered by it on startup of the Excel workbook and whenever the DateTimePicker or underlying cell value change.

A third problem is keeping the DateTimePicker controls looking like the rest of the workbook formatting. If the user changes the font of the workbook, the controls embedded in the document will not change their font. Printing is also an issue because the control replete with its dropdown combo widget will be printed. In addition, the user will likely want to add and remove rows to the list of stocks, which means that you will have to dynamically add and remove DateTimePicker controls at runtime.

Although it is possible to work through these issues and achieve a reasonable solution, the actions pane may be an easier mechanism to use. The actions pane can show Windows Forms controls alongside the document in the Document Actions task pane rather than in the document. For example, whenever the user of your workbook has a date cell selected, the Document Actions task pane can be displayed with the DateTimePicker in it to allow the user to pick a date, as shown in Figure 13-3. Chapter 14, "Working with Document-Level Actions Panes," discusses the actions pane in more detail.

When to Use a Modal or Modeless Form

Another way to use Windows Forms in an Office application is to use a standard Windows Forms form shown as a dialog box. For example, you could handle the BeforeDoubleClick event for the worksheet and if a cell containing a date is double-clicked, you could display a custom Windows Forms form, as shown in Figure 13-4.

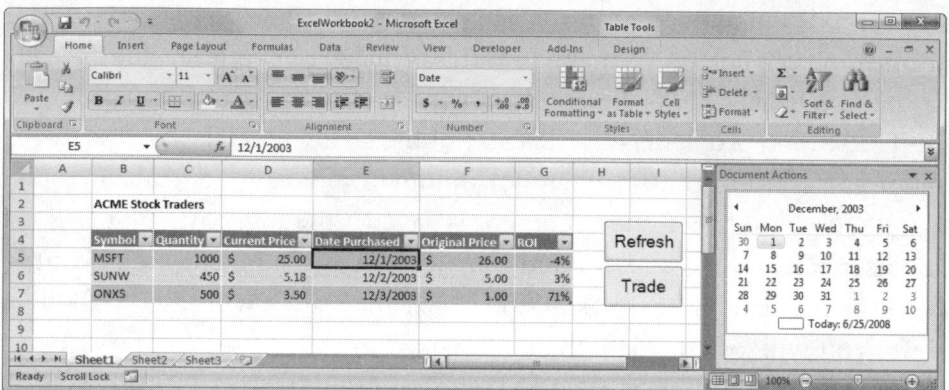

Figure 13-3: Using the DateTimePicker control in the Document Actions task pane.

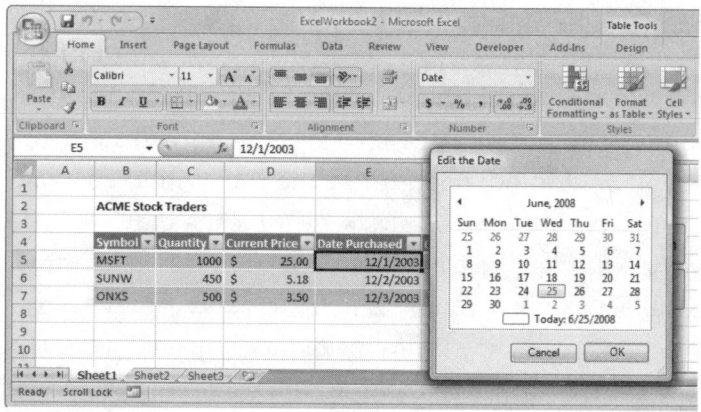

Figure 13-4: Displaying a Windows Forms dialog box when the user double-clicks a cell.

This approach is also quite useful if you want to ensure that certain information is filled in before the user starts working with a document. For example, you might want to display a wizard during the creation of a document that fills in certain portions of the document.

A choice you must make when using Windows Forms as shown in Figure 13-4 is the modality of the form. A modal form must be interacted with and dismissed by clicking the OK, Cancel, or Close button before the user can get back to editing the document. A modeless Windows Forms can float above the document and still allow the user to interact with the document even though the form has not yet been closed. When using a modeless Windows Forms dialog box, note that there are certain states an Office application can enter where your modeless dialog box cannot be activated. For example, if another modal dialog box is displayed, users must dismiss the modal dialog box before they can interact with the modeless dialog box again. Cell editing mode in Excel also affects modeless dialog boxes. If the user is editing a cell value in Excel, the user cannot activate the modeless form until the user leaves cell editing mode.

Listing 13-1 shows a VSTO Excel customization that displays a simple modeless form. The modeless form has a button that, when clicked, shows a message.

Listing 13-1: A VSTO Excel Customization That Displays a Modeless Form

```csharp
using System;
using System.Collections.Generic;
using System.Data;
using System.Linq;
using System.Text;
using System.Windows.Forms;
using System.Xml.Linq;
using Microsoft.VisualStudio.Tools.Applications.Runtime;
using Excel = Microsoft.Office.Interop.Excel;
using Office = Microsoft.Office.Core;

namespace ExcelWorkbook2
{
  public partial class Sheet1
  {
    public Button btn1;
    public Form form1;

    private void Sheet1_Startup(object sender, EventArgs e)
    {
      btn1 = new Button();
      btn1.Click += new EventHandler(btn1_Click);

      form1 = new Form();
      form1.Controls.Add(btn1);
      form1.Show();

      Globals.ThisWorkbook.BeforeClose +=
        new Excel.WorkbookEvents_BeforeCloseEventHandler(
        ThisWorkbook_BeforeClose);
    }
```

```
    void btn1_Click(object sender, EventArgs e)
    {
      MessageBox.Show("Hello from modeless form");
    }

    void ThisWorkbook_BeforeClose(ref bool Cancel)
    {
      form1.Close();
    }

    #region VSTO Designer generated code
    private void InternalStartup()
    {
      this.Startup += new System.EventHandler(this.Sheet1_Startup);
    }
    #endregion
  }
}
```

Note that using the ActionsPane feature of VSTO is often an easier way to achieve a modeless result because it provides all the benefits of a modeless form with the addition of the ability to dock within the Office window space.

Adding Windows Forms Controls to Your Document

One of the key design goals for VSTO was to keep the design experience as close to existing Windows Forms development as possible, and adding Windows Forms controls to the document is a key tenet of this goal. The great thing about adding controls to the document or spreadsheet is that you really do not have to think about it because most of the design experience is almost identical to that of creating a Windows Forms form. However, there are some differences in the experience that we examine in this section.

When you create a new project based on an Excel workbook or Word document, VSTO creates a project and automatically loads the Excel or Word document surface into Visual Studio to provide a design surface for you to drag and drop controls onto. In the C# profile, the toolbox is set to auto hide by default. It is easier to pin the toolbox to make it dock to the side of Visual Studio window because it is difficult to drag and drop from the toolbox onto Word or Excel when it is in its default auto hide mode.

Why? When the toolbox shows itself, it obscures quite a bit of the left side of the document or spreadsheet. When you drag and drop a control onto the document surface, the toolbox does not auto hide and get out of the way until the drag and drop is over.

Modes for Adding Controls

VSTO provides three modes for adding controls to the document surface:

- **Drag and drop**—This involves selecting the control from the toolbox and dragging it onto the document or worksheet. This method creates a default-sized control on the document and proves particularly useful for adding controls, such as a button, that tend to be a set size. Figure 13-5 shows this mode.

- **Drawing**—Clicking a control in the toolbox to select it and then moving your mouse pointer over the document or spreadsheet changes the cursor to the standard draw cursor. In this mode, you can click and drag a rectangle, thereby drawing the control onto the document or spreadsheet. Figure 13-6 shows this mode.

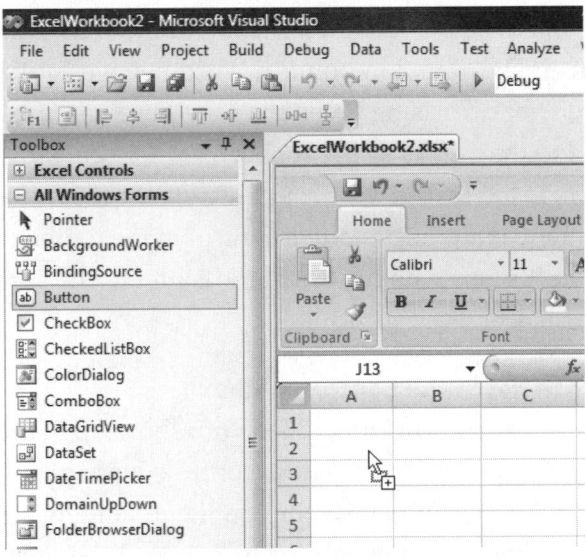

Figure 13-5: Drag and drop of a Button control from the toolbox to an Excel worksheet.

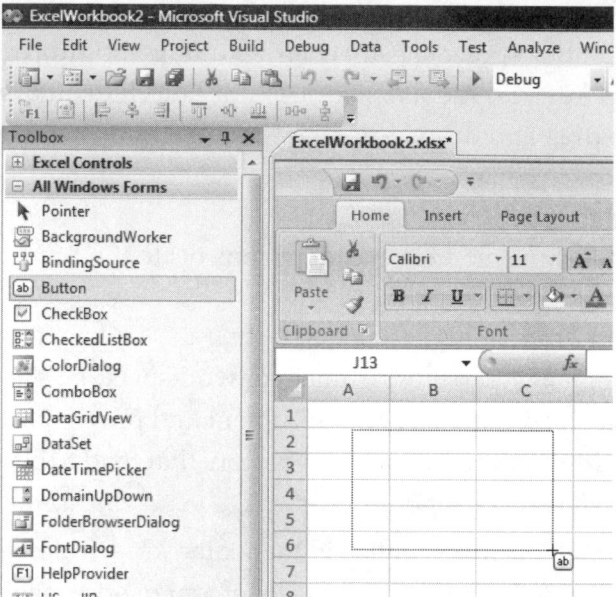

Figure 13-6: Drawing a Button control on an Excel worksheet.

- **Double-click**—Double-clicking a control in the toolbox causes a control to be added at the current insertion point in the document or spreadsheet. The insertion point in Word behaves quite differently from Excel, not surprising given the flow-based nature of a document compared to the grid of a spreadsheet. Double-clicking a control in the toolbox in a Word VSTO project inserts the control at the cursor in the document. Double-clicking a control in the toolbox in an Excel VSTO project inserts the control at the center of the spreadsheet.

Controls That Are Not in the Control Toolbox

A number of Windows Forms controls do not show up in the controls toolbox for Excel and Word projects. These controls were purposely excluded because of known issues in using them on the document surface. Some of these issues are purely design-time related in that the design-time representation of the control does not work well. This does not mean that the control cannot be used, but it might mean that the only way that you can use it on a document is by adding it programmatically at runtime or by using the control in a user control that you then add to the document.

A good example of such a control is the group box. The design-time experience of the group box does not work well in Excel or Word because the group box designer requires the container to support container drag and drop, which the Excel and Word designer does not support. You have two options to work around this limitation:

- Create the group box programmatically at runtime. This approach uses VSTO's support for adding controls at runtime that is described later in this chapter.
- Create a custom user control that contains the group box and the contained controls within the group box. After this is built, drag the user control onto the document or spreadsheet as you would any control. The advantage to this approach is that you get full-fidelity designer support in the user control designer, making it easy to lay out the controls.

Some other controls are excluded from the toolbox because of the following reasons.

- The control does not work with the VSTO control hosting architecture. For example, the DataNavigator control relies on a container model that is not supported in the VSTO control hosting architecture in order to communicate with other data components.
- The control relies heavily on being hosted in a Windows Forms form. For example, the MenuStrip control cannot be added to a document or spreadsheet, only to a form.
- The control has problems at design time. Because many controls were designed prior to the release of VSTO, some have bugs when hosted on a document or spreadsheet surface in the designer. For example, the Rich Edit control has numerous issues when running inside of Excel and Word at design time. In the interest of stability, it was removed from the controls toolbox, but you can add it to a document or spreadsheet programmatically at runtime.

Finally, as we mention earlier, the ElementHost control that allows WPF controls to be used in the document must be added programmatically at runtime, following the approach described later in this chapter in the section "Using WPF Controls in the Document."

Control Insertion Behavior in Word

A control added to Word is affected by the insertion settings set in the Word Options dialog box. A control can be inserted "in line with text," which means the control is inserted into the text flow of the document and moves as the text flow changes. It can also be inserted "in front of text," which means that the control is positioned at an absolute position in the document that does not change when the text flow changes.

The default insertion behavior in Word can be changed to be exact-position based rather than flow based by changing the Insert/Paste Pictures As setting in the Word Options dialog box from the default In line with text to Square or In front of text. After you change this setting, all controls will be positioned where you want them instead of having to be in line with the text. To change this setting, you must exit Visual Studio and launch an instance of Word (you can't do this from the instance of Word inside Visual Studio because the Office menu is not accessible). Choose Office > Word Options; click Advanced; and scroll down to the Cut, Copy, and Paste settings. Figure 13-7 shows the Insert/Paste Pictures As setting.

You can also change the way a control in Word is wrapped with the text by right-clicking the control in the designer and selecting the Format Control menu option. Doing so brings up Word's Format Object dialog box, shown in Figure 13-8. Changing the wrapping style from In line with text to Square or In Front of text provides exact positioning.

From the standpoint of the Word object model, a control whose wrapping style is set to In line with text is represented by the InlineShape object in Word's object model and found in the Document object's InlineShapes collection. A control whose wrapping style is set to Square, Tight, Behind Text, or In front of text is represented by the Shape object in Word's object model and found in the Document object's Shapes collection. Shape objects representing controls whose wrapping style is In front of text or Behind text support ZOrder, whereas the other wrapping styles do not.

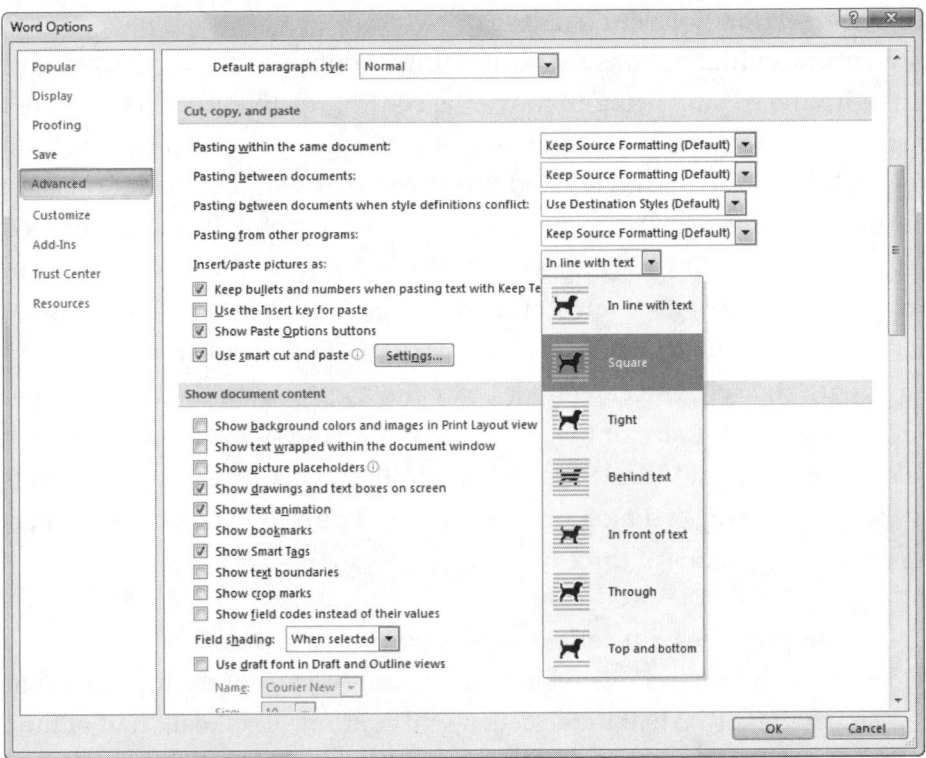

Figure 13-7: Changing the default insertion behavior in Word's Options dialog box.

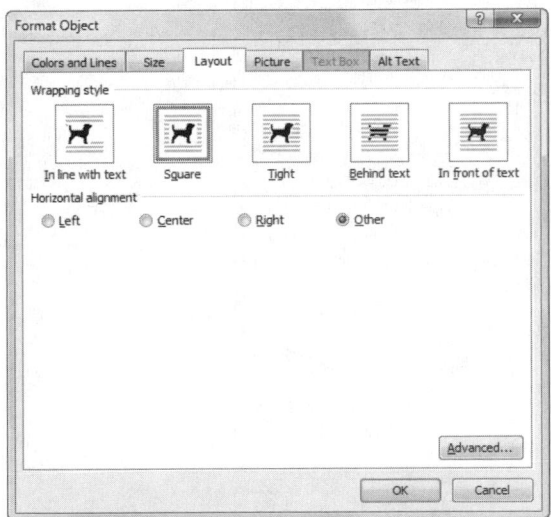

Figure 13-8: Changing the wrapping style for a control with Word's Format Object dialog box.

Control Insertion Behavior in Excel

Excel also provides options for positioning a control on the worksheet surface, with the default being to move the control relative to the cell but not to size with the cell. This setting means that when you put a control onto the worksheet surface, it is linked to the cell that you dropped it on; so if you insert or delete cells around that cell, the control will stay positioned relative to the cell it was dropped on. However, if you resize the cell you dropped, the size of the control stays the same. This is usually the behavior that you would expect when adding a control. If you want your control to resize with the cell, you can either draw the control over the cell so that it exactly matches the size of the cell (not for the faint of heart) or right-click the control inside of Visual Studio and select Format Control, which brings up the Format Object dialog box, shown in Figure 13-9. Click the Properties tab and select one of three options:

- **Move and size with cells**—This option ensures that the control resizes and repositions relative to the cell resize. For example, if your control takes up half of the cell, it will continue to take up half of the cell when the cell is resized.

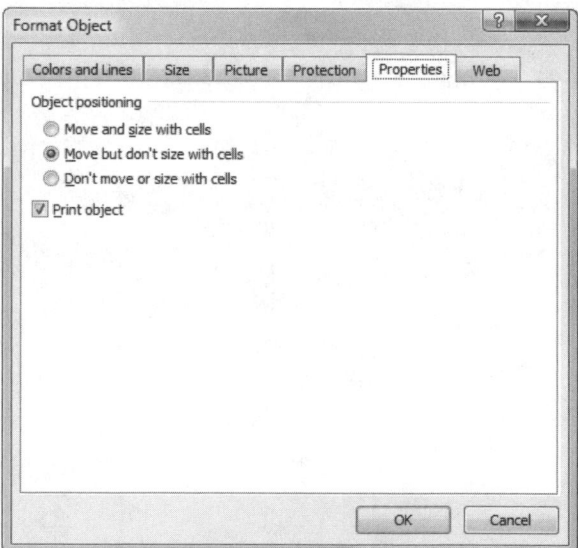

Figure 13-9: Setting object positioning options for a control in Excel.

- **Move but don't size with cells**—This is the default setting, which ensures that the control remains with the cell it was dropped on but does not resize.
- **Don't move or size with cells**—This setting provides you with exact positioning that does not change when the cell the control that was dropped on is moved or resized.

There is also a check box here that allows you to specify whether to print the object. This option can be useful if you don't want to print controls you've placed in the document.

Layout of Controls on the Document or Worksheet Surface

The Windows Forms editor in Visual Studio has some great alignment tools that make it much simpler to design professional-looking forms without having to resort to per-pixel tweaks on each control. Unfortunately, the alignment tools do not work on documents because the display surface is very different from a form. In place of these tools, a toolbar provides easy access to the alignment functionality in Word and Excel. Figure 13-10 shows the toolbar. To align controls, just select the controls you want to align, and then click the button that represents the alignment option you want.

Writing Code Behind a Control

Writing code behind a control on a document or spreadsheet is not much different from writing code behind a normal Windows Forms control. You can double-click a control and the designer will add a new event handler for the default event on the control in the partial class for the sheet or document you are working on. The only difference is where the event handler is hooked up in the code generated by the designer. In a standard Windows Forms form, the event handler is hooked up in the hidden generated code

Figure 13-10: The control positioning toolbar in VSTO.

(form1.designer.cs). In a VSTO code item, the event hookup is generated into the visible user partial class (sheet1.cs rather than sheet1.designer.cs) in the InternalStartup method.

Event handlers can also be generated by using the Events view in the Properties window. In this view, you can double-click an event handler cell to add a default named event handler for an event. Alternatively, you can enter the name of the event handler function you want to use. The event handler hookup code is generated in the same place (Internal-Startup) as if you double-clicked on the control. Listing 13-2 shows the code generated when you drop a button on a spreadsheet and then double-click the event handler cell for Click and SystemColorsChanged to generate default event handlers for these events.

Listing 13-2: Default Event Hookup and Handlers Generated by VSTO for a Button's Click and SystemColorsChanged Events

```csharp
using System;
using System.Collections.Generic;
using System.Data;
using System.Linq;
using System.Text;
using System.Windows.Forms;
using System.Xml.Linq;
using Microsoft.VisualStudio.Tools.Applications.Runtime;
using Excel = Microsoft.Office.Interop.Excel;
using Office = Microsoft.Office.Core;

namespace ExcelWorkbook1
{
  public partial class Sheet1
  {
    private void Sheet1_Startup(object sender, System.EventArgs e)
    {
    }

    private void Sheet1_Shutdown(object sender, System.EventArgs e)
    {
    }

    #region VSTO Designer generated code

    /// <summary>
    /// Required method for Designer support - do not modify
    /// the contents of this method with the code editor.
    /// </summary>
```

```csharp
private void InternalStartup()
{
  this.button1.Click +=
    new System.EventHandler(this.button1_Click);
  this.button1.SystemColorsChanged +=
    new System.EventHandler(this.button1_SystemColorsChanged);
  this.Shutdown +=
    new System.EventHandler(this.Sheet1_Shutdown);
  this.Startup +=
    new System.EventHandler(this.Sheet1_Startup);
}

#endregion

private void button1_Click(object sender, EventArgs e)
{
}

private void button1_SystemColorsChanged(object sender,
  EventArgs e)
{
}
}
}
```

Events Not Raised in Office Documents

Not all the events on a Windows Forms control are raised in an Office document. For example, the ResizeBegin and ResizeEnd events are common across all Windows Forms controls (these events are defined on the Control base class) but are never raised on controls on a document or worksheet because of the way the Windows Forms support in VSTO was designed.

The Windows Forms Control Hosting Architecture

Typically, the implementation details of a particular technology are interesting to know but not a prerequisite for using a feature. In the case of Windows Forms control hosting on an Office document, it is important to understand how the feature is implemented because you will be exposed to some implementation details as you create solutions using controls.

The Windows Forms Control Host ActiveX Control

Windows Forms control support in Office 2007 and VSTO is based on the capability of Word and Excel to host ActiveX controls on the document surface. When you add a Windows Forms control to a document, what actually is added is an ActiveX control called the Windows Forms control host. The Windows Forms control host acts as a host for each Windows Forms control added to the document. The Office application thinks that it is just hosting a basic ActiveX control because the Windows Forms control host implements all of the necessary ActiveX control interfaces.

When the customization assembly is loaded for the document or spreadsheet, the actual Windows Forms control instance is created in the same application domain and security context as the rest of the customization code. These Windows Forms control instances are then parented by a special parent Windows Forms control called the VSTOContainerControl that derives from UserControl. The VSTOContainerControl is then sited to the Windows Forms control host ActiveX control. Your control—for example, a Trade Stock button in a spreadsheet—is added as a child of the VSTOContainerControl. Figure 13-11 shows this "sandwich" architecture.

The fact that an ActiveX control is hosting the Windows Forms control on the document surface does peek through at times. One example is in the Excel design view. When you click a managed control that you have added to the Excel workbook surface, the formula bar shows that it is hosted by an embedded ActiveX control with ProgID "WinForms.Control.Host.V3," as shown in Figure 13-12.

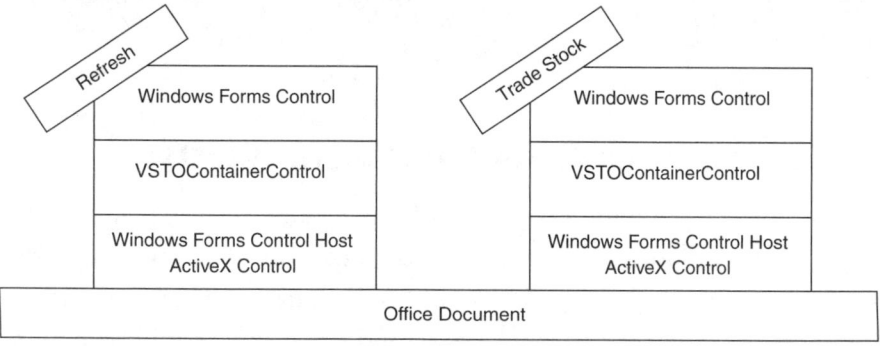

Figure 13-11: The basic hosting architecture for Windows Forms controls on the document.

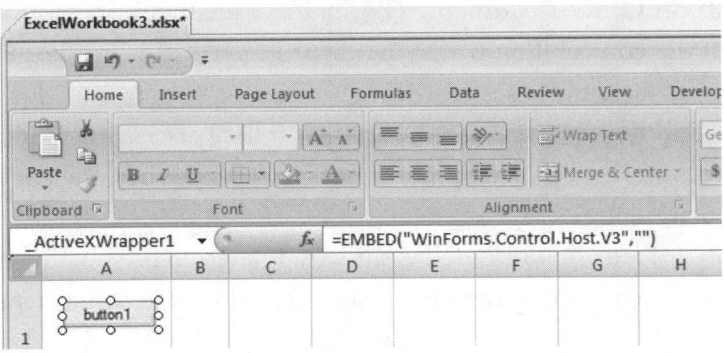

Figure 13-12: Excel shows the ProgID of the underlying ActiveX hosting control.

Why Are VSTO Controls Derived from Windows Forms Controls?

The fact that an ActiveX control is hosting the Windows Forms control dragged onto the document surface does not show up immediately in your code. VSTO adds a member variable to the ThisDocument or Sheet1 class named something like Button1 that you can code against just as you would if you were working with a traditional Windows Forms form. At first glance, the experience appears to be identical to working with a Windows Forms form, but the type of the control that you added to the document is not quite what you would expect. If you drag a button from the Windows Forms toolbox, it would be natural to expect the type of the button created on the document to be System.Windows.Forms.Button. However, when you add a button to a spreadsheet, VSTO creates a button with type Microsoft.Office.Tools.Excel.Controls.Button that derives from System .Windows.Forms.Button. When you add a button to a Word document, VSTO creates a button with type Microsoft.Office.Tools.Word .Controls.Button that derives from System.Windows.Forms.Button. Understanding why a button in VSTO derives from the standard Windows Forms button requires some further digging into the details of how Windows Forms controls are hosted in a Word or Excel document.

Windows Forms controls, be it a control in the System.Windows.Forms namespace or a custom control written by a third party or you, were originally designed to be added to a Windows Forms form and not an Office document. Luckily, much of the Windows Forms control works just fine when used in an Office document. The main special case is around the positioning of the control. If you set the Left property of a Windows Forms control hosted in a form, it sets the distance in pixels between the left edge of the control and the left edge of its container's client area. This works fine in a form or a container control but does not work well when the control is placed in a document or spreadsheet.

The reason it does not work well is directly related to the hosting architecture of controls in the document, because the control is actually hosted by the VSTOContainerControl, which is hosted by the ActiveX control. As a result, if VSTO was to expose the raw positioning properties of the control, they would be relative to the area of the VSTOContainerControl container, not the document. Setting the Left property of a control should actually move the ActiveX control within the document rather than the hosted Windows Forms control within the VSTOContainerControl.

Listing 13-3 illustrates this point. In Listing 13-3, we have a spreadsheet that we have added a Windows Forms buttons to. The button shown in Figure 13-12 is added to Sheet1 as a member variable called button1 of type Microsoft.Office.Tools.Excel.Controls.Button. We display that type in the Startup event. As mentioned earlier, Microsoft.Office.Tools.Excel .Controls.Button derives from System.Windows.Forms.Button. The Microsoft .Office.Tools.Excel.Controls.Button's override of Left sets the position of the ActiveX control hosting the Windows Forms control. The code in Listing 13-3 sets this Left to 0, which causes the control to move to the left edge of the worksheet. Casting button1 to a System.Windows.Forms.Button strips the override that VSTO adds for the Left property. Setting the Left property on button1 when cast to a System .Windows.Forms.Button sets the Left property of the control relative to the parent VSTOContainerControl. This listing when run gives the strange result in Figure 13-13, where the first call to Left moved the ActiveX control to the far-left edge of the worksheet but the subsequent calls to Left and Top on the base class System .Windows.Forms.Button moved the managed control relative to the VSTOContainerControl.

Listing 13-3: A VSTO Excel Customization That Exposes the Windows Forms Control Hosting Architecture

```csharp
using System;
using System.Collections.Generic;
using System.Data;
using System.Linq;
using System.Text;
using System.Windows.Forms;
using System.Xml.Linq;
using Microsoft.VisualStudio.Tools.Applications.Runtime;
using Excel = Microsoft.Office.Interop.Excel;
using Office = Microsoft.Office.Core;

namespace ExcelWorkbook3
{
  public partial class Sheet1
  {
    private void Sheet1_Startup(object sender, EventArgs e)
    {
      MessageBox.Show(button1.GetType().ToString());

      // Cast to a System.Windows.Forms.Button
      // to set position on underived control
      System.Windows.Forms.Button button1Base =
        button1 as System.Windows.Forms.Button;

      MessageBox.Show(button1Base.Parent.GetType().ToString());
      MessageBox.Show(button1Base.Parent.GetType().
        BaseType.ToString());

      // Moving the control on Microsoft.Office.Tools.Button
      button1.Left = 0;

      // Moving the control again on the base
      // System.Windows.Forms.Button
      button1Base.Left = 10;
      button1Base.Top = 10;
    }

    #region VSTO Designer generated code
    private void InternalStartup()
    {
      this.Startup += new System.EventHandler(this.Sheet1_Startup);
    }
    #endregion
  }
}
```

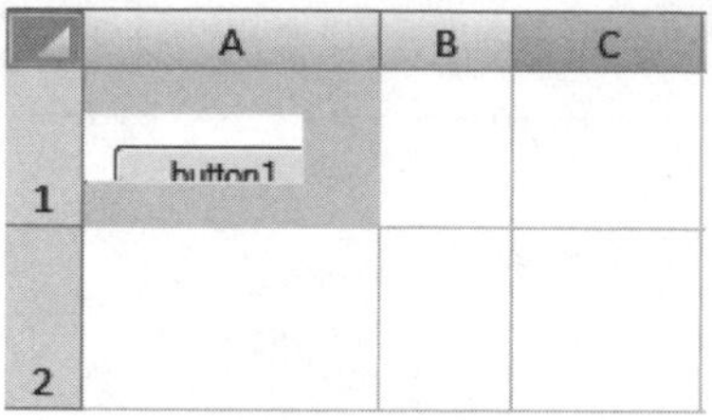

Figure 13-13: The result of running Listing 13-3. The button has been offset relative to the VSTOContainerControl in the VSTO hosting architecture.

To enable your code to set the position of the control relative to the document, VSTO creates a derived class for each control that extends the class of the original Windows Forms control and overrides the positional information with the positional information from the ActiveX control in the Office document. The object model object for Excel that provides the properties and methods to position the ActiveX control is called OLEObject, and for Word it is called OLEControl. The derived classes created for each VSTO Windows Forms control effectively merges together the original Windows Forms control class and the OLEObject object for Excel or the OLEControl object for Word.

If you create a Windows Forms control of your own or use a third-party control, when you drag and drop the control to a document or spreadsheet, VSTO automatically generates an extended class for you that merges your control with OLEObject or OLEControl. Because the ability to add custom Windows Forms controls onto a document requires the control to be extended, you can only use controls that are not sealed. The good news is that the vast majority of third-party controls are unsealed.

Security Implications of the VSTO Control Hosting Model

The security minded might be wondering about the implications of having to use an ActiveX control to host managed controls added to a document. This is something that we spent considerable time on to ensure that the ActiveX control did not provide a vulnerability to Office. The Windows Forms control host ActiveX control when initialized does not actually do anything and will not run any code until it is accessed by the customization assembly. This means that the control is safe for initialization, and the only way for it to do anything is for code with full trust (the customization) to call it. The control is marked safe for initialization to ensure that it will load in Office with the default security settings.

One strange side effect of our control hosting architecture is that Office requires Visual Basic for Applications (VBA) to be installed in order to add ActiveX controls to a document. Adding ActiveX controls to a document does not add VBA code to that document, but it does require the use of parts of the VBA engine. You therefore need to ensure that your Office installation has VBA installed to use managed controls in the document. VBA is installed by default in all versions of Office, so it is unusual for it not to be installed. VSTO also requires that the Trust access to Visual Basic Project check box be checked in the Macro security dialog box of Office on a development machine. This check box does not have to be checked on end-user machines unless you are adding dynamic worksheets at runtime as described in Chapter 12, "The VSTO Programming Model."

The macro security level in VBA can affect the loading of ActiveX controls and hence managed controls. If your user sets the VBA macro security settings to Very High (it is set to High by default), any ActiveX controls in the document will only be allowed to load in their inactive design mode state. In this state, Windows Forms controls in the document will not function properly. Luckily, the default macro security setting of High allows controls to be loaded assuming they are safe for initialization. Because all Windows Forms controls in the document are loaded by the Windows Forms control host ActiveX control, which is marked as safe for initialization, all managed controls can load in the High setting.

Limitations of the Control Hosting Model

Each Windows Forms control on the document is contained by an instance of the Windows Forms control host ActiveX control, which leads to some limitations. The most noticeable limitation that affects all controls is the lack of support for a control's TabIndex property. Tab order in a Windows Forms form is determined by the containing form or control. This is not a problem with a traditional Windows Forms form because all controls on the form are contained by one container. In VSTO, each control placed onto a document or spreadsheet is contained by its own container—by its own unique instance of the Windows Forms control host. The net result of this is that the tab index of the control is scoped to its container, and because there is a one-to-one relationship between control and container, the Tab-Index property is of little use. This can have impact on the accessibility of your application because users would expect to be able to tab between fields, but nothing happens when they press the Tab key.

Another limitation is that controls such as radio buttons really require that the control be contained within a container to make the controls mutually exclusive so that only one radio button within the container can be selected at a time. Without a common container, the radio button is not particularly useful. Adding each radio button directly onto a document or spreadsheet causes each radio button to be hosted in its own container. There is a simple way to work around this problem, however; you just create a user control that has a container (a group box, for example), and then add the radio buttons to the group box within the user control. The user control can then be added as a single control to the document.

Another limitation is that VSTO controls in the document work only when the zoom level of Word or Excel is set to 100 percent because the Windows Forms control architecture does not support scaling in such a way that the integrity of the document display can be maintained at differing zoom levels. VSTO disables the controls when the zoom level is not 100 percent, and if the user clicks the control, Office displays a message telling the user to return the zoom level to 100 percent to interact with the control. This limitation applies to WPF controls as well, because these controls are supported in VSTO by means of the Windows Forms framework hosting WPF via the ElementHost control.

Control State Is Not Saved in the Document

We considered this limitation briefly in the introduction of this chapter—the limitation that the state of a Windows Forms control is not saved in the document. To illustrate, imagine a solution that generates customer service letters in Word. One of the key pieces of information in the document is the date the customer first called customer service. To aid with entering this date, the Word document contains a DateTimePicker, as shown in Figure 13-14.

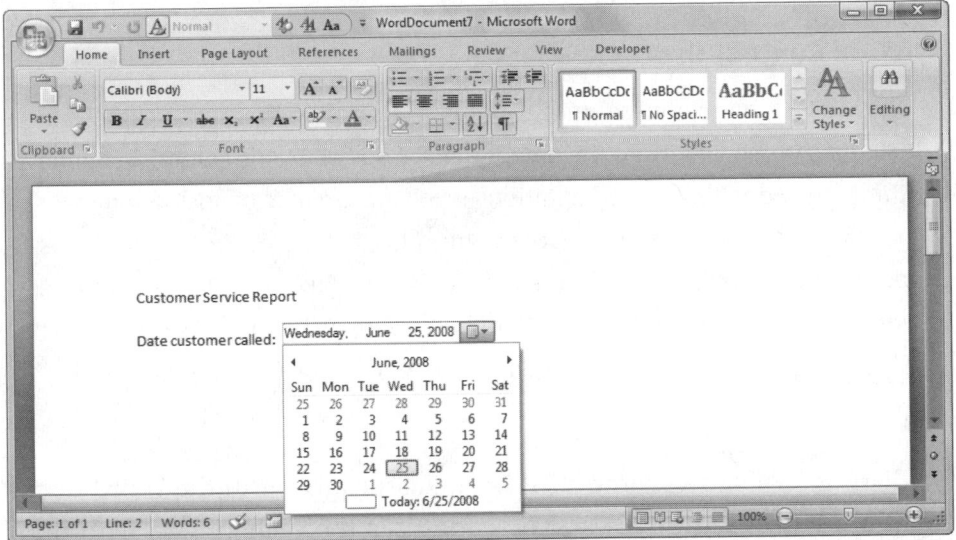

Figure 13-14: A DateTimePicker control in a Word document.

This is great functionality for your users, but where will the date that the user picks with the DateTimePicker be stored in the document? For example, consider the scenario where the user opens the document for the first time. The DateTimePicker defaults to show today's date. The user then picks a different date using the DateTimePicker and saves the document. Now we have a problem: Windows Forms controls placed in a document do not save their state into the document when the document is saved. The next time the document is opened, the DateTimePicker will just show today's date again rather than the date picked by the user the last time the document was saved.

To get the DateTimePicker to remember the date picked by the user the last time the document was saved, you have to write code to detect when the user picks a new date by handling the DateTimePicker control's Value-Changed event. You need to store the date in the document somehow so that it will be saved when the document is saved. Some options you have for storing the date that was picked include inserting some hidden text in the document, adding a custom property to the document, or using the cached data feature of VSTO to cache the date in the data island of the document. Then you have to write some code in the Startup event handler to set DateTimePicker.Value to the saved date.

Word Content Controls

New to Word 2007 are content controls, which often are better choices to use as controls in a Word document than Windows Forms controls. For one thing, they don't have the limitations involving tab index and zooming that we mention earlier in this chapter. They also have a control UI that goes away when your focus leaves the control, which makes for a more seamless integration with the document. Word has a date picker content control that would be better to use than the Windows Forms-based DateTimePicker.

Listing 13-4 shows some VSTO code associated with the Word document shown in Figure 13-14. The code uses the cached data feature of VSTO described in Chapter 20, "Server Data Scenarios," to save the date that was picked in the DateTimePicker in a public field called last-PickedDate that has been marked with the Cached attribute. The Cached attribute causes the value of lastPickedDate to be automatically saved in a data island in the document from session to session. The Startup handler puts the stored value of lastPickedDate back in the DateTimePicker each time the document is reopened. Note that to use the Cached attribute, you must include the using statement "using Microsoft.Visual-Studio.Tools.Application.Runtime;".

Listing 13-4: A VSTO Word Customization That Saves the Date That Was Picked Using the Cached Data Feature of VSTO

```
using System;
using System.Collections.Generic;
using System.Data;
using System.Linq;
using System.Text;
using System.Windows.Forms;
using System.Xml.Linq;
using Microsoft.VisualStudio.Tools.Applications.Runtime;
using Microsoft.VisualStudio.Tools.Applications.Runtime;
using Office = Microsoft.Office.Core;
using Word = Microsoft.Office.Interop.Word;

namespace WordDocument1
{
```

```csharp
public partial class ThisDocument
{
  [Cached()]
  public DateTime lastPickedDate = DateTime.MinValue;

  private void ThisDocument_Startup(object sender,
    System.EventArgs e)
  {
    if (lastPickedDate != DateTime.MinValue)
    {
      this.dateTimePicker1.Value = lastPickedDate;
    }

    this.dateTimePicker1.ValueChanged += new EventHandler(
      DateTimePicker1_ValueChanged);
  }

  void DateTimePicker1_ValueChanged(object sender, EventArgs e)
  {
    lastPickedDate = dateTimePicker1.Value;
  }

  #region VSTO Designer generated code
  private void InternalStartup()
  {
    this.Startup +=
      new System.EventHandler(ThisDocument_Startup);
  }
  #endregion

}
}
```

Why Are Controls Sometimes Slightly Blurry?

Have you noticed how sometimes a control in Word or Excel looks a little blurred when you are in the designer, but that it snaps back into focus when you run the project? This is because the Windows Forms control host ActiveX control stores a bitmap of the hosted Windows Forms control so that when Excel or Word first opens the document it can display the bitmap until the actual control is loaded. This was done because the actual control is not loaded until the customization assembly is fully loaded. If we did not do this, the control would have an attractive red x through it until the customization assembly loaded.

The reason it looks a bit out of focus is because Office anti-aliases the image when it stores it so it is not an exact copy of the original bitmap. So if you see a slightly out-of-focus control on your document, you know that your customization assembly has not loaded yet, did not load properly, or you have been up too late writing a book about Windows Forms controls on Office documents!

Properties Merged from OLEObject or OLEControl

After the control has been added to the document or spreadsheet, the experience of using the control on the design surface should be very close to that of working with a standard Windows Form control. However, there are some differences. The biggest difference appears when you click a Windows Forms control in the document and use the categorized view in the Properties window. If you compare a Windows.Forms.Controls.Button with a Microsoft.Office.Tools.Excel.Controls.Button, you will see the extra properties merged in from the OLEObject. These properties are listed in the Misc category to denote that these properties are coming from OLEObject.

Excel Control Properties That Are Added from OLEObject

The OLEObject merge done for controls in the Microsoft.Office.Tools.Excel.Controls namespace adds several properties to VSTO extended controls that are not in the base Windows.Forms controls. Table 13-1 shows the most important properties that are added for controls in Excel.

Word Control Properties Added from OLEControl

The OLEControl merge done for controls in the Microsoft.Office.Tools.Word.Controls namespace adds several properties to VSTO extended controls that are not in the base Windows.Forms controls. Table 13-2 shows the most important properties that are added for controls in Word.

TABLE 13-1: Additional Excel Control Properties

Name	Type	Access	Description
Bottom-RightCell	Excel.Range	Read-only	The Range object representing the cell that lies below the bottom-right corner of the control.
Enabled	bool	Read-write	Determines whether the control is enabled. If you set this property to `false`, the control appears grayed-out in Excel. This property enables you to control whether the control accepts input at runtime.
Height	double	Read-write	The height, in points, of the control.
Left	double	Read-write	The distance, in points, from the left edge of the control to the left edge of column A.
Placement	object	Read-write	Determines how the control will be placed. This property can be one of three values: `xlFreeFloating` (equivalent to the Do Not Move or Size with Cell setting in the Format Control dialog box), `xlMove` (equivalent to the Move but Do Not Size with Cell setting in the Format Control dialog box), or `xlMoveAndSize` (equivalent to the Move and Size with Cell setting in the Format Control dialog box).
Print-Object	bool	Read-write	Determines whether the control will print when the worksheet is printed. This option can prove to be very useful if the control you are using is something like a button that should not be part of the final printed document.

Continues

TABLE 13-1:   Additional Excel Control Properties *(Continued)*

Name	Type	Access	Description
Shadow	bool	Read-write	Determines whether Excel should provide a drop shadow for the control. When this property is set to true, Excel provides a simple black drop shadow around the control.
TopLeft-Cell	Excel.Range	Read-only	The Range object representing the cell that lies below the top-left corner of the control.
Top	double	Read-write	The distance, in points, from the top edge of the control to the top edge of row 1.
Visible	bool	Read-write	Determines whether to hide the control at runtime.
Width	double	Read-write	The width, in points, of the control.

Many of the properties for controls running in Word are dependent on the wrapping style of the control. If the control is inline with text, the Left, Bottom, Right, Top, and Width properties will throw an exception. Why? Word represents ActiveX controls as either Shapes or InlineShapes depending on how the control is positioned on the document, and the positioning properties are only available on Shapes that are controls whose wrapping style is not set to Inline with Text.

Word controls also have an InlineShape and Shape property that provide you with access to the InlineShape or Shape object in the Word object model corresponding to the control.

TABLE 13-2: Additional Word Control Properties

Name	Type	Access	Description
Bottom	float	Read-only	The distance, in points, from the top edge of the first paragraph on the page to the bottom of the control.
Height	float	Read-write	The height, in points, of the control.
Inline-Shape	InlineShape	Read	Returns the InlineShape object in the Word object model corresponding to the control; returns null if the control is not inline.
Shape	Shape	Read	Returns the Shape object in the Word object model corresponding to the control; returns null if the control is inline.
Left	float	Read-write	The distance, in points, from the left edge of the control to the left edge of the first paragraph on the page.
Name	string	Read-write	The name of the control.
Right	float	Read-only	The distance, in points, from the right edge of the control to the left edge of the first paragraph on the page.
Top	float	Read-write	The distance, in points, from the top edge of the control to the top edge of the first paragraph on the page.
Width	float	Read-write	The width, in points, of the control.

Adding Controls at Runtime

So far this chapter has described how to add controls to the document or worksheet at design time with the Visual Studio control toolbox. Often the controls needed for your application need to be added (and deleted) at runtime. For example, consider the worksheet in Figure 13-1 again. Suppose you want to provide a trade button at the end of every row that shows a stock. This would be impossible to achieve by adding buttons at design time because the number of stock rows will vary at runtime as the workbook is edited. You would need to add a button to the end of the row dynamically as stock is added at runtime.

VSTO provides a mechanism to add controls at runtime via the Controls collection present on Word's Document class and Excel's Worksheet classes. This Controls collection works a bit differently than the Controls collection in Windows Forms. In the Controls collection associated with a Windows Forms form class, you can add controls at runtime by creating an instance of the control and adding it to the form's collection of controls. You can then set positioning on the control you created:

```
System.Windows.Forms.Button btn = new
   System.Windows.Forms.Button();

form1.Controls.Add(btn);

btn.Left = 100;
```

The VSTO Controls collection cannot take this approach because although the instance of the button could be added to the collection, there would be no way for the developer to change any positional properties on it because these are not available until the ActiveX control is created and connected to the Windows Forms control. There needs to be a way to return to the developer a wrapped control that has both the original control and the OLEObject or OLEControl. The VSTO Controls collection provides two mechanisms for adding controls:

- VSTO provides a generic AddControl method that can be used with any Windows Forms control. This method takes an instance of the Windows Forms control you want to add and returns to you the

Microsoft.Office.Tools.Excel.OLEObject or Microsoft.Office.Tools .Word.OLEControl that contains the control you passed in. So the equivalent of the Windows Forms code above in VSTO is shown here. The main difference is that now you have to track two objects: the Button object and the OLEObject object, and remember to only set positioning on the OLEObject:

```
System.Windows.Forms.Button btn = new
    System.Windows.Forms.Button();

Microsoft.Office.Tools.Excel.OLEObject oleObject =
    this.Controls.Add(btn, 100, 100, 150, 100, "button1");

oleObject.Left = 100;
```

- For common Windows Forms controls, a set of helper methods on the Controls collection will return the VSTO extended control with positioning information merged in. For example, a method called AddButton is provided on Excel's Controls collection. This method returns a Microsoft.Office.Tools.Excel.Controls.Button. The code below does the same thing as the code shown earlier, except it frees you from having to track two objects:

```
Microsoft.Office.Tools.Excel.Controls.Button btn =
    this.Controls.AddButton(100, 100, 150, 100, "button1");

btn.Left = 100;
```

Listing 13-5 shows code that dynamically adds a group box to a Word document using the AddControl mechanism. It doesn't even use the returned OLEObject because it sets the position as part of the initial call to AddControl. It then goes further and adds additional RadioButton controls to that group box.

Listing 13-5: A VSTO Word Customization That Adds a Group Box to a Word Document at Runtime

```
using System;
using System.Collections.Generic;
using System.Data;
using System.Linq;
```

```csharp
using System.Text;
using System.Windows.Forms;
using System.Xml.Linq;
using Microsoft.VisualStudio.Tools.Applications.Runtime;
using Office = Microsoft.Office.Core;
using Word = Microsoft.Office.Interop.Word;

namespace WordDocument1
{
  public partial class ThisDocument
  {
    System.Windows.Forms.GroupBox myGroupBox;

    private void ThisDocument_Startup(object sender, EventArgs e)
    {
      myGroupBox = new System.Windows.Forms.GroupBox();

      // Add the group box to the controls collection on the sheet
      this.Controls.AddControl(
        myGroupBox, 100, 100, 150, 100, "groupbox");
      // Set the title of the group box
      myGroupBox.Text = "Insurance type";
      // Add the radio buttons to the groupbox
      myGroupBox.Controls.Add(new RadioButton());
      myGroupBox.Controls.Add(new RadioButton());
      // Set the text of the radio buttons
      myGroupBox.Controls[0].Text = "Life";
      myGroupBox.Controls[1].Text = "Term";
      // Arrange the radio buttons in the group box
      myGroupBox.Controls[0].Top = myGroupBox.Top + 25;
      myGroupBox.Controls[1].Top =
      myGroupBox.Controls[0].Bottom + 20;
      // iterate through each button in the controls collection
      foreach (RadioButton rb in myGroupBox.Controls)
      {
        rb.Left = myGroupBox.Left + 10;
      }
    }

    #region VSTO Designer generated code
    private void InternalStartup()
    {
      this.Startup +=
        new System.EventHandler(this.ThisDocument_Startup);
    }
    #endregion
  }
}
```

Working with the Controls Collection

The Controls collection provides a simple mechanism to add controls to your document or worksheet at runtime. Before we get into the details of the Controls collection, it is important to note that the implementation and methods exposed are different between Word and Excel. Although the behavior of the collection is the same in each application, it was necessary to have a different implementation to ensure that the collection takes advantage of the host application. For example, if you want to add a control to Excel, passing in an Excel.Range object for its position makes a lot of sense. If you want to add a control to Word, passing in a Word.Range object makes sense.

To illustrate using the collection, we start by looking at the helper methods available for all the supported Windows Forms controls that ship with the .NET Framework. The helper methods follow a common design pattern; call the method with positional arguments and an identifier and the method returns you the wrapped type for the control.

Word has two overloads for each helper method:

- A method that takes a Word Range object, a width and height for the control in points, and a `string` name for the control that uniquely identifies it within the controls collection:

```
Controls.AddButton(ActiveWindow.Selection.Range,
   100, 50, "NewButton");
```

- A method that takes a left, top, width, and height for the control in points and a `string` name for the control that uniquely identifies it within the controls collection:

```
Controls.AddMonthCalendar(10, 50, 100, 100, "NewCalendar");
```

Excel also has two overloads for each helper method:

- A method that takes an Excel range object and a `string` name for the control that uniquely identifies it within the controls collection. The control will be sized to always match the size of the range passed to the method:

```
Controls.AddButton(Range["A1", missing], "NewButton");
```

- A method that takes a left, top, width, and height for the controls in points and a `string` name for the control that uniquely identifies it within the controls collection:

```
Controls.AddMonthCalendar(10, 50, 100, 100, "NewCalendar");
```

After the control has been added to the document or worksheet, you can program against it just as you do a control added at design time. Table 13-3 shows the complete list of helper methods to add controls on the Controls collection for Excel. Word's list is the same, except that the objects come out of the Microsoft.Office.Tools.Word namespace.

TABLE 13-3: Methods on Excel's ControlCollection That Add Windows Forms Controls

Method Name	Return Type
AddButton	Microsoft.Office.Tools.Excel.Controls.Button
AddChart	Microsoft.Office.Tools.Excel.Chart
AddCheckBox	Microsoft.Office.Tools.Excel.Controls.CheckBox
AddCheckedListBox	Microsoft.Office.Tools.Excel.Controls.CheckedListBox
AddComboBox	Microsoft.Office.Tools.Excel.Controls.ComboBox
AddDataGridView	Microsoft.Office.Tools.Excel.Controls.DataGridView
AddDateTimePicker	Microsoft.Office.Tools.Excel.Controls.DateTimePicker
AddDomainUpDown	Microsoft.Office.Tools.Excel.Controls.DomainUpDown
AddHScrollBar	Microsoft.Office.Tools.Excel.Controls.HScrollBar
AddLabel	Microsoft.Office.Tools.Excel.Controls.Label
AddLinkLabel	Microsoft.Office.Tools.Excel.Controls.LinkLabel
AddListBox	Microsoft.Office.Tools.Excel.Controls.ListBox
AddListView	Microsoft.Office.Tools.Excel.Controls.ListView
AddMonthCalendar	Microsoft.Office.Tools.Excel.Controls.MonthCalendar

TABLE 13-3: Methods on Excel's ControlCollection That Add Windows Forms Controls *(Continued)*

Method Name	Return Type
AddNumericUpDown	Microsoft.Office.Tools.Excel.Controls.NumericUpDown
AddPictureBox	Microsoft.Office.Tools.Excel.Controls.PictureBox
AddProgressBar	Microsoft.Office.Tools.Excel.Controls.ProgressBar
AddPropertyGrid	Microsoft.Office.Tools.Excel.Controls.PropertyGrid
AddRadioButton	Microsoft.Office.Tools.Excel.Controls.RadioButton
AddRichTextBox	Microsoft.Office.Tools.Excel.Controls.RichTextBox
AddTextBox	Microsoft.Office.Tools.Excel.Controls.TextBox
AddTrackBar	Microsoft.Office.Tools.Excel.Controls.TrackBar
AddTreeView	Microsoft.Office.Tools.Excel.Controls.TreeView
AddVScrollBar	Microsoft.Office.Tools.Excel.Controls.VScrollBar
AddWebBrowser	Microsoft.Office.Tools.Excel.Controls.WebBrowser

AddControl

Unfortunately, helper methods are not available for every control on your machine, so there needs to be a way to add controls outside the list in Table 13-3. To do this, the Controls collection provides an AddControl method that enables you to pass in an instance of any Windows Forms control, and it will return the OLEObject (for Excel) or the OLEControl (for Word) that can be used to position the control after it is added.

```
// Declare a OLEObject variable
Microsoft.Office.Interop.Excel.OLEObject myobj;

// Add the control to the A10 cell
myobj = Controls.AddControl(new UserControl1(),
  this.Range["A10", missing], "DynamicUserControl");

// Reposition it to the top of B15
myobj.Top = (double)this.Range["B15", missing].Top;
```

A common pitfall of using AddControl is forgetting to set the positioning on the OLEObject and setting it directly on the Windows Forms control itself. If you do this, the control will change its position relative to the container rather than move its position correctly in the document. For an example of this issue, consider Listing 13-3 and Figure 13-13.

Deleting Controls at Runtime

Now that we have some controls added to the document at runtime, it is important that there be a mechanism to delete controls from the collection. VSTO provides three ways to achieve this:

- Calling the Remove method on the Controls collection and passing in the instance or name of the control that you want to remove from the collection
- Calling the RemoveAt method on the Controls collection and passing in the index of the control to be removed
- Calling the Delete method on the control itself, which will in turn delete the control

You can only delete controls that have been added at runtime. If you try to remove controls that were added at design time, you will get an exception.

Why Are Controls Added at Runtime Not Saved in the Document?

We wanted to keep the behavior of the Controls collection as close to the Windows Forms development experience so that any control added at runtime is deleted from the document when the user saves the document. For example, if you add controls to a Windows Forms application at runtime, you do not expect those controls to just appear the next time you run the application without code being written to re-create those controls. We spent many hours debating the relative merits of this approach over the alternative, which was to allow Word or Excel to save the newly added control when the document was saved. The main deciding argument for not saving the newly added control was to make it easier to write dynamic control code in the document. If we had left the control in the document when the user saved the document, it would have been very difficult to write code that could hook up controls that had been added dynamically the last time the document was open. To understand why this was difficult really involves looking into how a control is added to the document at runtime.

When a control is added to the Controls collection, the VSTO runtime adds an instance of the ActiveX control that will host the control and then sets it to host the provided control. This works fine when the document is running but quickly becomes complicated when the user saves the document. If we were to save the control into the document, all that would be stored would be the ActiveX control itself but without any instance of the Windows Forms control because it must be provided by the code at runtime. The next time the document loaded up, the ActiveX control would load but would not get an instance of the control because the code that added the instance of the Windows Forms control would run again, and it would add a new instance of the ActiveX control because it would have no link back to the saved ActiveX control. Extrapolate this situation out over a few hundred saves of a document and you quickly get a lot of "orphaned" ActiveX controls that will never be used.

The solution that was implemented in VSTO was to remove all ActiveX control instances that were added as a result of adding a control at runtime to the Controls collection. This way there will never be any "orphaned" ActiveX controls on the document, and it also makes your code simpler to write. Why is the code simpler to write? Imagine writing the code to add the buttons at the end of each row containing a stock:

```
foreach (StockRow stock in Stocks)
{
  // add stock information to row here
  this.Controls.AddButton(
    this.Range[currentrow, "12"], stock.Ticker + "btn");
}
```

If the control was persisted with the worksheet on save, the code would have to go through each control and ensure the buttons added in the last run were there, and quite possibly delete and add them again since the stock list changed. We believed it was more straightforward to just iterate through the stocks on every run of the workbook and add the buttons.

Why Are Controls in the Controls Collection Typed as Object Instead of Control?

VSTO documents and worksheets can have Windows Forms controls added to them at runtime via the Controls collection as well as host controls such as NamedRange and ListObject. Both these types of controls act like controls in the VSTO model. For example, you can click a Named-Range in VSTO and display a property window for it. You can establish data bindings to a NamedRange just as you can with a text box or any other Windows Forms control.

As a result, the VSTO model considers both NamedRange and a Windows Forms control to be a "control" associated with the worksheet or document. The Controls collection contains both host controls and Windows Forms controls. Although providing a strongly typed collection was something that we would have liked to do, there was no common type other than object that a host control and a Windows Forms control share.

Creating Controls in a Document Using an Application-Level Add-In

Starting with Visual Studio 2008 SP1, a new mechanism allows you to use many of the document-level features in your application-level add-in projects. One of the document-level features you can now use at add-in level is the feature that allows you to add Windows Forms or WPF controls to a document. Listing 13-6 shows an example add-in that adds Windows Forms controls to a document.

The code handles the WorkbookOpen and NewWorkbook events, and in these events, it calls a helper function called CreateAndConnect. This helper function gets the first worksheet in the workbook; then it uses the Worksheet's GetVstoObject extension method (added by using the Microsoft.Office.Tools.Extension statement) to get a Microsoft.Office.Tools .Excel.Worksheet object set to the vstoSheet variable. Then it uses the Controls collection off vstoSheet to create a button that is set to the vsto-Button variable. Next, an event handler is added to handle the click event. So that we don't have the "My button stopped working" problem, we must store the vstoButton object, and we do that with a Dictionary that uses Excel.Worksheet objects as the key and created buttons as the value. Later, in our handler of WorkbookBeforeClose, we clean up by looking up the closing worksheet in the dictionary, grabbing the associated button, and removing the Click event handler.

Listing 13-6: A VSTO Excel Add-in That Adds a Button to Documents at Runtime

```
using System;
using System.Collections.Generic;
using System.Linq;
using System.Text;
using System.Xml.Linq;
using Excel = Microsoft.Office.Interop.Excel;
using Office = Microsoft.Office.Core;
using Microsoft.Office.Tools.Excel;
using Microsoft.Office.Tools.Excel.Extensions;

namespace ExcelAddIn2
{
  public partial class ThisAddIn
  {
    Guid guidShapeIdentifier = new Guid(
      "{8927F9FC-4743-40d9-884E-F3B178A11E8D}");
    Dictionary<Excel.Worksheet,
      Microsoft.Office.Tools.Excel.Controls.Button>
      buttonDictionary = new Dictionary<
      Excel.Worksheet,
      Microsoft.Office.Tools.Excel.Controls.Button>();

    private void ThisAddIn_Startup(object sender,
      System.EventArgs e)
    {
      ((Excel.AppEvents_Event)this.Application).NewWorkbook +=
        new Excel.AppEvents_NewWorkbookEventHandler(
        ThisAddIn_NewWorkbook);
      ((Excel.AppEvents_Event)this.Application).WorkbookOpen +=
        new Excel.AppEvents_WorkbookOpenEventHandler(
        ThisAddIn_WorkbookOpen);
      ((Excel.AppEvents_Event)this.Application).WorkbookBeforeClose
        += new Excel.AppEvents_WorkbookBeforeCloseEventHandler(
        ThisAddIn_WorkbookBeforeClose);

      if (Application.ActiveWorkbook != null)
      {
        CreateAndConnect(Application.ActiveWorkbook);
      }
    }

    void ThisAddIn_WorkbookBeforeClose(Excel.Workbook Wb,
      ref bool Cancel)
```

```csharp
      {
        Microsoft.Office.Tools.Excel.Controls.Button vstoButton;
        Excel.Worksheet sheet = Wb.Sheets[1] as Excel.Worksheet;

        vstoButton = buttonDictionary[sheet];
        vstoButton.Click -= new EventHandler(vstoButton_Click);
        buttonDictionary.Remove(sheet);
      }

      void ThisAddIn_WorkbookOpen(Excel.Workbook Wb)
      {
        CreateAndConnect(Wb);
      }

      void ThisAddIn_NewWorkbook(Excel.Workbook Wb)
      {
        CreateAndConnect(Wb);
      }

      private void CreateAndConnect(Excel.Workbook Wb)
      {
        Excel.Worksheet sheet = Wb.Sheets[1] as Excel.Worksheet;
        Microsoft.Office.Tools.Excel.Controls.Button vstoButton;
        Microsoft.Office.Tools.Excel.Worksheet vstoSheet =
          sheet.GetVstoObject();
        Excel.Range range = sheet.Cells[1, 1] as Excel.Range;
        vstoButton = vstoSheet.Controls.AddButton(range,
          guidShapeIdentifier.ToString());
        vstoButton.Click += new EventHandler(vstoButton_Click);
        vstoButton.Text = "Click Me!";
        buttonDictionary.Add(sheet, vstoButton);
      }

      void vstoButton_Click(object sender, EventArgs e)
      {
        System.Windows.Forms.MessageBox.Show("Click from workbook" );
      }

      #region VSTO generated code
      private void InternalStartup()
      {
        this.Startup += new System.EventHandler(ThisAddIn_Startup);
      }
    }
  }
}
```

Using WPF Controls in the Document

As we mentioned earlier in this chapter, you can place WPF controls in the document by using the ElementHost control, but the ElementHost control can be added only at runtime by using Controls.AddControl.

You can add a WPF control to your Word or Excel document project by choosing Project > Add New Item in Visual Studio. From the list of available items, choose User Control (WPF). This option adds a WPF user control to your project; then you can edit this control with the WPF designer.

When you have a WPF control that you want to use, you can add it to the document dynamically. Listing 13-7 shows a VSTO Word document project that adds the WPF control called UserControl1 to the document. Here is the procedure to follow:

1. Make sure that your project has a .NET reference to WindowsForms-Integration.dll (the assembly where ElementHost is defined).
2. Create a new instance of an ElementHost control.
3. Create a new instance of the WPF control.
4. Calculate the width and height in units that Word expects by taking the Width and the Height of the WPF control in pixels and converting it to twips, using the Word Application object's PixelsToPoints method.
5. Set the Child property of the ElementHost control to the instance of the WPF control.
6. Use Controls.AddControls to add the ElementHost control to the document with the width and height previously calculated in twips.

Listing 13-7: A VSTO Word Customization That Adds a WPF Control to a Word Document at Runtime

```
using System;
using System.Collections.Generic;
using System.Data;
using System.Linq;
using System.Text;
using System.Windows.Forms;
using System.Xml.Linq;
using Microsoft.VisualStudio.Tools.Applications.Runtime;
using Office = Microsoft.Office.Core;
using Word = Microsoft.Office.Interop.Word;
```

```
namespace WordDocument7
{
  public partial class ThisDocument
  {
    System.Windows.Forms.Integration.ElementHost myElementHost;

    private void ThisDocument_Startup(object sender, EventArgs e)
    {
      myElementHost =
        new System.Windows.Forms.Integration.ElementHost();

      UserControl1 myWPFControl = new UserControl1();
      float width = Application.PixelsToPoints(
        (float)myWPFControl.Width, ref missing);
      float height = Application.PixelsToPoints(
        (float)myWPFControl.Height, ref missing);
      myElementHost.Child = myWPFControl;

      this.Controls.AddControl(
        myElementHost, 100, 100, width, height, "elementHost");
    }

    #region VSTO Designer generated code
    private void InternalStartup()
    {
      this.Startup +=
        new System.EventHandler(this.ThisDocument_Startup);
    }
    #endregion
  }
}
```

Listing 13-8 shows equivalent code for Excel. The main difference between Excel and Word is that the control width and height do not need to be converted from pixels to twips. Once again, make sure that your project has a .NET reference to WindowsFormsIntegration.dll (the assembly where ElementHost is defined).

Listing 13-8: A VSTO Excel Customization That Adds a WPF Control to an Excel Worksheet at Runtime

```
using System;
using System.Collections.Generic;
using System.Data;
using System.Linq;
using System.Text;
using System.Windows.Forms;
```

```
using System.Xml.Linq;
using Microsoft.VisualStudio.Tools.Applications.Runtime;
using Excel = Microsoft.Office.Interop.Excel;
using Office = Microsoft.Office.Core;

namespace ExcelWorkbook4
{
  public partial class Sheet1
  {
    System.Windows.Forms.Integration.ElementHost myElementHost;

    private void Sheet1_Startup(object sender, System.EventArgs e)
    {
      myElementHost =
        new System.Windows.Forms.Integration.ElementHost();

      UserControl1 myWPFControl = new UserControl1();

      double width = myWPFControl.Width;
      double height = myWPFControl.Height;
      myElementHost.Child = myWPFControl;

      this.Controls.AddControl(
        myElementHost, 100, 100, width, height, "elementHost");
    }

    #region VSTO Designer generated code
    private void InternalStartup()
    {
      this.Startup += new System.EventHandler(Sheet1_Startup);
    }
    #endregion
  }
}
```

Conclusion

The key to using Windows Forms and WPF controls in your Word or Excel solutions is to think about what user-interface options meet your requirements. VSTO provides you with considerable flexibility for extending the user interface of Word or Excel, and there is no one right answer as to which is the best way. Windows Forms and WPF controls allow you to extend the capabilities that ActiveX controls provided while leveraging the ever-growing controls ecosystem.

This chapter described how you can use Windows Forms controls to extend your Office solutions. In particular, the chapter examined how hosting controls on the document surface is a very powerful tool for developing applications. The chapter also covered the architecture of hosting controls on the document surface, and the limitations and differences in this model compared to traditional Windows Forms development. Dynamically added controls were introduced and then used to add WPF controls to the document at runtime.

Chapters 14, 15, and 16 continue the discussion of Windows Forms, WPF, and Office, specifically showing how to use Windows Forms controls and WPF controls on Office's Document Actions task pane, application-level custom task panes, and Outlook Form Regions, respectively.

14
Working with Document-Level Actions Panes

Introduction to the Document Actions Task Pane

Developing a solution that runs within an Office application provides considerable benefits because you can take advantage of the functionality that already exists in Office. However, it is sometimes hard to design a user interface that meets your needs as most of the user interface space is controlled by the Office application. Office 2003 and VSTO introduced a number of new user interface capabilities, including the ability to use Windows Forms and WPF controls on the document. (See Chapter 13, "Using Windows Forms and WPF in VSTO," for more information on this capability.)

Placing a control on the document is not always the right paradigm for the user interface of your application. For example, putting a control onto the document can often lead to issues with layout when the controls are laid out relative to a range or paragraph. If you use a button on a Word document, by default it will be in line with the text. This means that when you reformat the document, the button will move with the text. Obviously, being able to move a control with the text is something that you would want if you are developing a flow-based user interface. But this model quickly becomes difficult when developing more traditional user interfaces. Things get even more complex if you start to consider what type of behavior you want when the user prints a document. For example, do you want your Windows Forms controls to be printed with the rest of the document?

To address these user interface challenges, Office 2003 introduced the ability to put your own custom user interface into the Document Actions task pane of Word and Excel. A task pane is designed to provide a contextual user interface that is complementary to the document. For example, Word provides a task pane that displays the style of the current selection in the document, as shown in Figure 14-1. To display this task pane, press Alt+Ctrl+Shift+S.

In Office 2003, you could have only one task pane visible at a time per document. But in Office 2007, multiple task panes can be open at any given time. The drop-down menu for a task pane shown in Figure 14-2 provides commands to Move, Size, or Close the task pane. A task pane can float above the document. It can also be docked to the left, top, right, or bottom of the application window space.

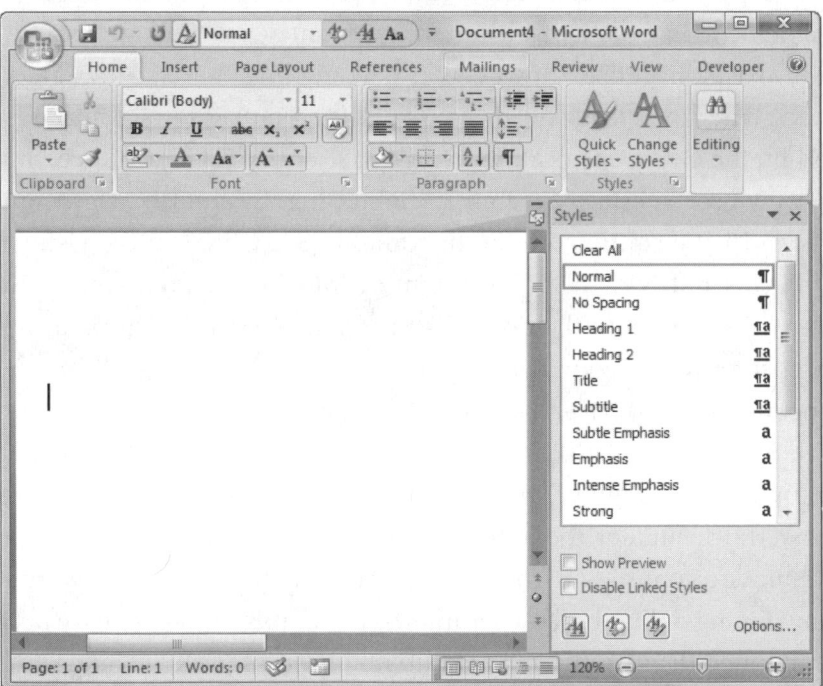

Figure 14-1: The Styles task pane in Word.

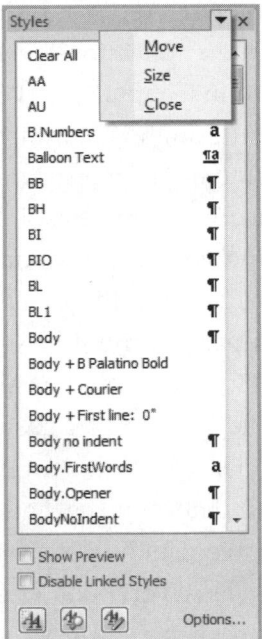

Figure 14-2: The drop-down
menu for a task pane.

The task pane that is customizable by your VSTO Word or Excel document customization is called the Document Actions task pane. In VSTO and in this book, we often refer to the Document Actions task pane as the actions pane, as kind of a contraction between the Document Actions and task pane. ActionsPane is the name of the control in the VSTO programming model that you will use to put your own content in the Document Actions task pane.

Note that the Document Actions task pane is shown for a document only when a VSTO customization associated with the document uses the ActionsPane control (or if a Smart Document solution is used, as described later in this chapter). Office allows only one Document Actions task pane to be shown per document. When you switch from document to document, the Document Actions task pane associated with the active document will be shown; if the document does not have a customization associated with it, the Document Actions task pane will be hidden.

In addition to the Document Actions task pane, Office 2007 lets application-level add-ins create application-level custom task panes. This style of task panes is described in Chapter 15, "Working with Application-Level Custom Task Panes." Although custom task panes are very similar to the Document Actions task pane in many ways, a custom task pane is not tied to any particular document, and multiple custom task panes can be created and displayed at the same time. Managing when a custom task pane is displayed is more challenging than using the Document Actions task pane. Also, custom task panes cannot be created by VSTO Word or Excel document-level customizations—only by VSTO add-ins.

Listing 14-1 shows a simple VSTO Excel customization that displays a Windows Forms button control in the Document Actions task pane. In Excel, the ActionsPane control is a member of the ThisWorkbook class. Because this code is written in Sheet1, we use the Globals object to access the This-Workbook class and from the ThisWorkbook class access the ActionsPane control. The ActionsPane control has a Controls collection that contains the controls that will be shown in the Document Actions task pane. We add to this collection of controls a Windows Forms button control we have previously created. Note that just the action of adding a control to the Controls collection causes the Document Actions task pane to be shown at startup.

Listing 14-1: A VSTO Excel Customization That Adds a Button to the Actions Pane

```csharp
using System;
using System.Collections.Generic;
using System.Data;
using System.Linq;
using System.Text;
using System.Windows.Forms;
using System.Xml.Linq;
using Microsoft.VisualStudio.Tools.Applications.Runtime;
using Excel = Microsoft.Office.Interop.Excel;
using Office = Microsoft.Office.Core;

namespace ExcelWorkbook5
{
  public partial class Sheet1
  {
    public Button myButton = new Button();

    private void Sheet1_Startup(object sender, EventArgs e)
    {
```

```
    myButton.Text = "Hello World";
    Globals.ThisWorkbook.ActionsPane.Controls.Add(myButton);
  }

  #region VSTO Designer generated code
  private void InternalStartup()
  {
    this.Startup += new EventHandler(Sheet1_Startup);
  }
  #endregion
  }
}
```

Figure 14-3 shows the result of running Listing 14-1. The Document Actions task pane is shown with a Windows Forms button displayed in the pane.

Listing 14-2 shows a similar VSTO Word customization that displays a Windows Forms Button control in the Document Actions task pane. In Word, the ActionsPane control is a member of the ThisDocument class.

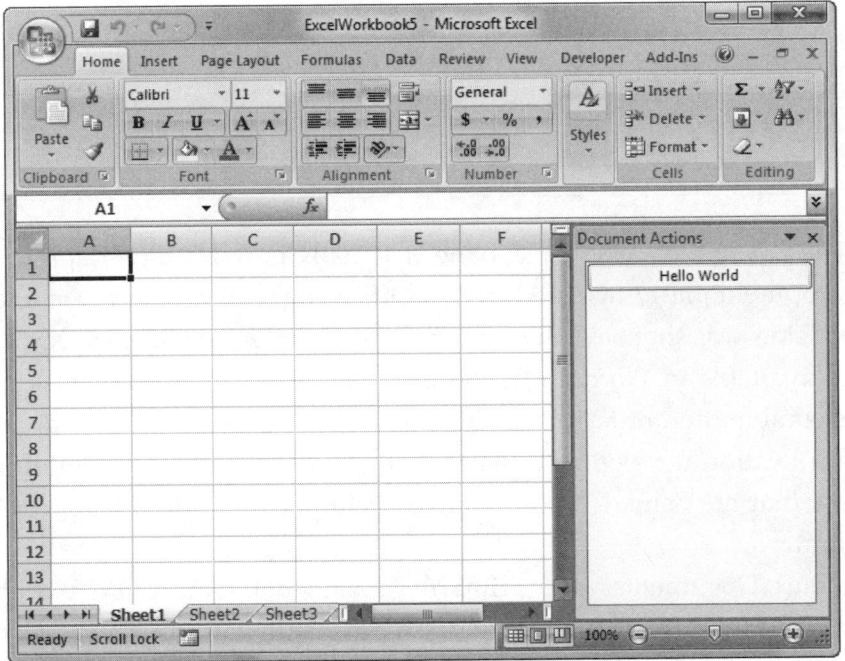

Figure 14-3: The result of running Listing 14-1.

Listing 14-2: A VSTO Word Customization That Uses the Actions Pane

```
using System;
using System.Collections.Generic;
using System.Data;
using System.Linq;
using System.Text;
using System.Windows.Forms;
using System.Xml.Linq;
using Microsoft.VisualStudio.Tools.Applications.Runtime;
using Word = Microsoft.Office.Interop.Word;
using Office = Microsoft.Office.Core;

namespace WordDocument1
{
  public partial class ThisDocument
  {
    public Button myButton = new Button();

    private void ThisDocument_Startup(object sender, EventArgs e)
    {
      myButton.Text = "Hello World";
      ActionsPane.Controls.Add(myButton);
    }

    #region VSTO Designer generated code
    private void InternalStartup()
    {
      this.Startup += new EventHandler(ThisDocument_Startup);
    }
    #endregion
  }
}
```

The Document Action task pane is actually part of a larger application development platform introduced in Office 2003 called Smart Documents. The vision was that Smart Documents would integrate the new XML features available in Word and Excel and the Document Actions task pane. This combination of XML and the Document Actions task pane provides an application development platform that makes it easier to build documents that are "smart" about their content and provide the appropriate user interface.

Smart Documents were primarily designed for the COM world. So although Smart Documents provided a powerful platform, they did not fit easily into the .NET development methodology. Why?

1. The way you create a Smart Document is to first create a component that implements the ISmartDocument interface. This interface is rather COM-centric.

2. To use a Smart Document, you must have XML schema mapped in your document. Although XML mapping provides considerable functionality to your application programming, not all documents need or want to use XML mapping.

3. The Document Actions task pane supports only a small set of built-in controls and ActiveX controls. To use a Windows Forms control, you would have to register it as an ActiveX control and then attempt to get that to work within the Document Actions task pane. This requires COM registration and COM interop.

4. The Smart Documents infrastructure requires you to create something called an XML expansion pack, which includes the following:
   - Manifest.xml—contains links to all the components within the expansion pack
   - The document to be used
   - Schema for the Smart Document
   - Configuration XML file—contains the definition of the controls to be used

VSTO provides the ActionsPane control to enable you access to all the features provided by Smart Documents with a much more .NET development experience. You do not have to implement the ISmartDocument interface or use schema mapping in the document. You do not have to register Windows Forms controls in the registry so they can act as ActiveX controls. You do not have to create an XML expansion pack. Because using the ActionsPane control is so much simpler than Smart Documents and provides all the benefits, this book does not consider building Smart Documents in the old COM way.

The ActionsPane feature of VSTO is actually implemented under the covers as a specialized Smart Document solution—when you look at a customized VSTO document and examine the attached XML expansion packs, you see that an XML expansion pack called ActionsPane is automatically attached. This schema provides the plumbing to connect

VSTO's ActionsPane control to the Smart Document platform. When you install the VSTO runtime (see Chapter 21, "ClickOnce Deployment"), the ActionsPane XML expansion pack is also installed and registered with Excel and Word, enabling the ActionsPane control to access the Document Actions task pane.

Working with the ActionsPane Control

A first step to understanding how VSTO's ActionsPane control works is delving a little into the architecture of VSTO's ActionsPane support.

The ActionsPane Architecture

The Document Actions task pane is a window provided by Office that can host ActiveX controls, as shown in Figure 14-4. VSTO places a special invisible ActiveX control in the Document Actions task pane that in turn hosts a single Windows Forms UserControl. This UserControl is represented in the VSTO programming model by the ActionsPane control—accessible in Word via Globals.ThisDocument.ActionsPane and accessible in Excel via Globals.ThisWorkbook.ActionsPane.

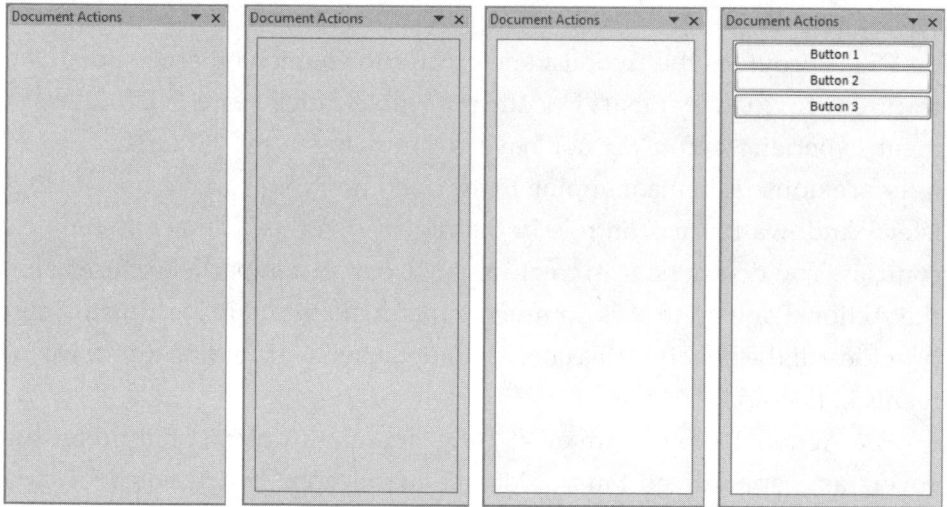

Figure 14-4: The four layers of the ActionsPane architecture. From left to right: The Document Actions task pane, the VSTO ActiveX control, the ActionsPane control, and controls parented to the ActionsPane control.

Although the Document Actions task pane can host multiple ActiveX controls, VSTO only needs to put a single ActiveX control and a single UserControl in the Document Actions task pane window because the UserControl can host multiple Windows Forms controls via its Controls collection (ActionsPane.Controls). You can add Windows Forms controls to the ActionsPane by using the ActionsPane.Controls.Add method.

The UserControl placed in the ActionsPane window is set to expand to fit the area provided by the ActionsPane window. If the area of the Document Actions task pane is not big enough to display all the controls hosted by the UserControl, it is possible to scroll the UserControl by setting the AutoScroll property of ActionsPane to true.

The ActionsPane control is a wrapper around System.Windows.Forms .UserControl with most of the properties, methods, and events of a User-Control. It also adds some properties, events, and methods specific to ActionsPane. When you understand the architecture in Figure 14-4, you will not be too surprised to know that some properties from UserControl that are exposed by ActionsPane, such as position-related properties, methods, and events, do not do anything. For example, because the position of the ActionsPane UserControl is forced to fill the space provided by the ActionsPane window, you cannot reposition the UserControl to arbitrary positions within the Document Actions task pane window.

Adding Windows Forms Controls to the Actions Pane

The basic way you add your custom UI to the actions pane is by adding Windows Forms controls to the actions pane's Controls collection. Listing 14-1, earlier, illustrates this approach. It first declares and creates an instance of a System .Windows.Forms.Button control. This control is then added to the actions pane by calling the Add method of the Controls collection associated with the actions pane and passing the button instance as a parameter to the Add method.

The actions pane is smart about arranging controls within the Actions-Pane. If multiple controls are added to the Controls collection, the actions pane can automatically stack and arrange the controls. The stacking order is controlled by the ActionsPane.StackOrder property, which is of type Microsoft.Office.Tools.StackStyle. It can be set to None for no automatic

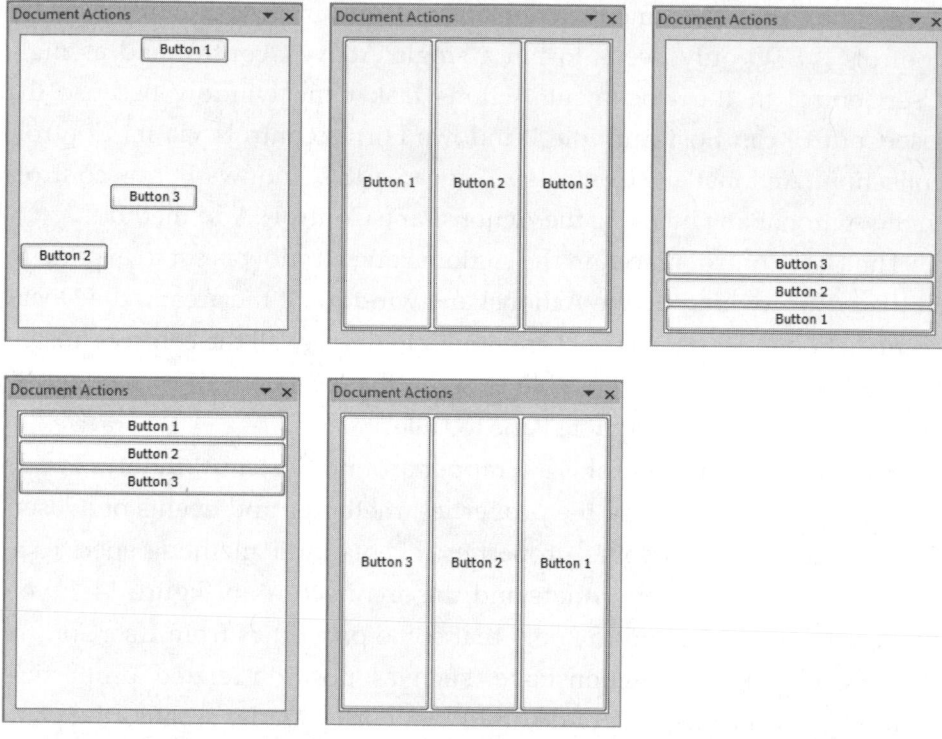

Figure 14-5: The result of changing the ActionsPane StackOrder setting. From top left: `None`, `FromLeft`, `FromBottom`, `FromTop`, and `FromRight`.

positioning or can be set to `FromTop`, `FromBottom`, `FromLeft`, or `FromRight`. Figure 14-5 shows the effect of the various StackOrder settings.

Listing 14-3 shows some code that adds and positions controls in the actions pane when StackOrder is set to either `StackStyle.FromBottom` and automatically positioned or set to `StackStyle.None` and manually positioned.

Listing 14-3: A VSTO Excel Customization That Adds and Positions Controls with Either StackStyle.None or StackStyle.FromBottom

```
using System;
using System.Collections.Generic;
using System.Data;
using System.Linq;
using System.Text;
using System.Windows.Forms;
using System.Xml.Linq;
using Microsoft.VisualStudio.Tools.Applications.Runtime;
```

```csharp
using System.Drawing;
using Excel = Microsoft.Office.Interop.Excel;
using Office = Microsoft.Office.Core;

namespace ExcelWorkbook5
{
  public partial class Sheet1
  {
    public Button button1 = new Button();
    public Button button2 = new Button();
    public Button button3 = new Button();

    private void Sheet1_Startup(object sender, EventArgs e)
    {
      button1.Text = "Button 1";
      button2.Text = "Button 2";
      button3.Text = "Button 3";

      Globals.ThisWorkbook.ActionsPane.BackColor =
        Color.Aquamarine;

      Globals.ThisWorkbook.ActionsPane.Controls.Add(button1);
      Globals.ThisWorkbook.ActionsPane.Controls.Add(button2);
      Globals.ThisWorkbook.ActionsPane.Controls.Add(button3);

      if (MessageBox.Show(
        "Do you want to auto-position the controls?",
        "StackStyle",
        MessageBoxButtons.YesNo) == DialogResult.Yes)
      {
        Globals.ThisWorkbook.ActionsPane.StackOrder =
          Microsoft.Office.Tools.StackStyle.FromBottom;
      }
      else
      {
        Globals.ThisWorkbook.ActionsPane.StackOrder =
          Microsoft.Office.Tools.StackStyle.None;
        button1.Left = 10;
        button2.Left = 20;
        button3.Left = 30;

        button1.Top = 0;
        button2.Top = 25;
        button3.Top = 50;
      }
    }

    #region VSTO Designer generated code
    private void InternalStartup()
    {
```

```
        this.Startup += new System.EventHandler(Sheet1_Startup);
    }
    #endregion
  }
}
```

Adding a Custom User Control to the Actions Pane

A more visual way of designing your application's actions pane UI is by creating a user control and adding that user control to the ActionsPane's control collection. Visual Studio provides a rich design-time experience for creating a user control. To add a user control to your application, click the project node in the Solution Explorer and choose Add User Control from Visual Studio's Project menu. Visual Studio will prompt you to give the User Control a filename such as UserControl1.cs. Then Visual Studio will display the design view shown in Figure 14-6.

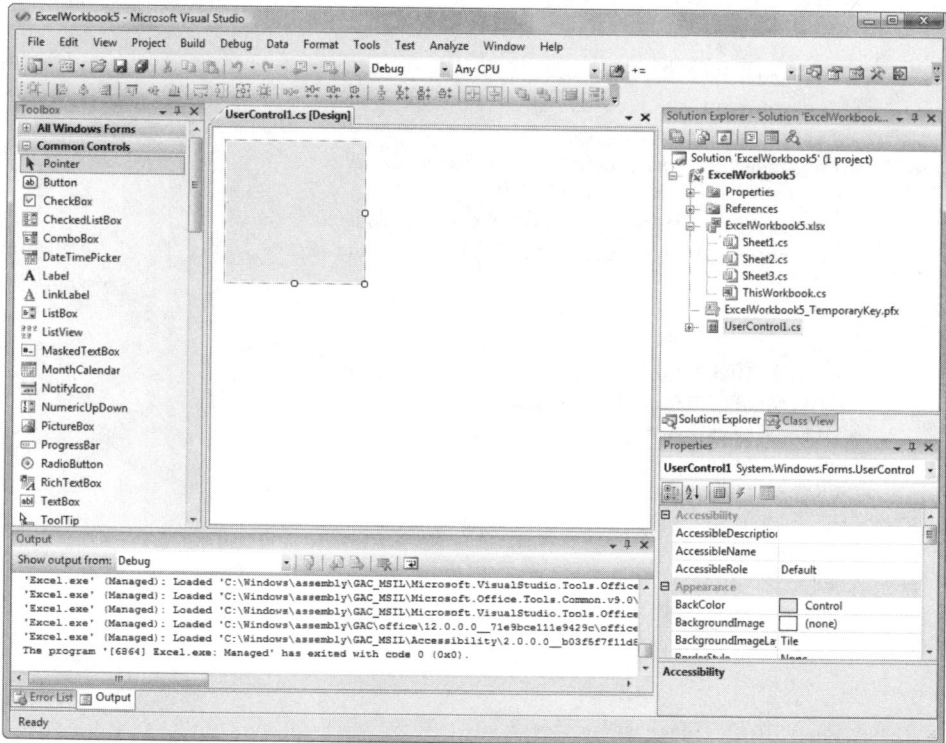

Figure 14-6: The design view for creating a custom user control.

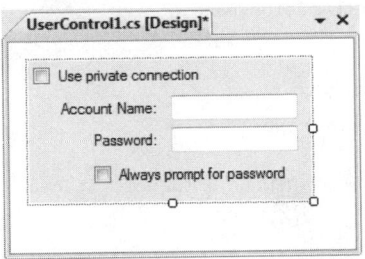

Figure 14-7: A custom user control.

The design area for the user control has a drag handle in the lower-right corner that you can drag to change the size of the user control. Controls from the toolbox can be dragged onto the user control design surface and positioned as desired. Figure 14-7 shows a completed user control that uses check boxes, text boxes, and labels.

Listing 14-4 shows a VSTO Excel customization that adds this custom user control to the Document Actions task pane. The user control created in Figure 14-7 is a class named UserControl1. Listing 14-4 creates an instance of UserControl1 and adds it to ActionPane's Controls collection using the Add method.

Listing 14-4: A VSTO Excel Customization That Adds a Custom User Control to the Task Pane

```
using System;
using System.Collections.Generic;
using System.Data;
using System.Linq;
using System.Text;
using System.Windows.Forms;
using System.Xml.Linq;
using Microsoft.VisualStudio.Tools.Applications.Runtime;
using Excel = Microsoft.Office.Interop.Excel;
using Office = Microsoft.Office.Core;

namespace ExcelWorkbook1
{
  public partial class Sheet1
  {
    public UserControl1 myUserControl = new UserControl1();

    private void Sheet1_Startup(object sender, EventArgs e)
    {
```

```
      Globals.ThisWorkbook.ActionsPane.Controls.Add(myUserControl);
    }

    #region VSTO Designer generated code
    private void InternalStartup()
    {
      this.Startup += new EventHandler(Sheet1_Startup);
    }
    #endregion
  }
}
```

Figure 14-8 shows the resulting Document Actions task pane shown when Listing 14-4 is run.

Contextually Changing the Actions Pane

A common application of the ActionsPane is providing commands in the Document Actions task pane that are appropriate to the context of the document. For example, in an order form application, the Document Actions task pane might display a button for selecting a known customer when fill-

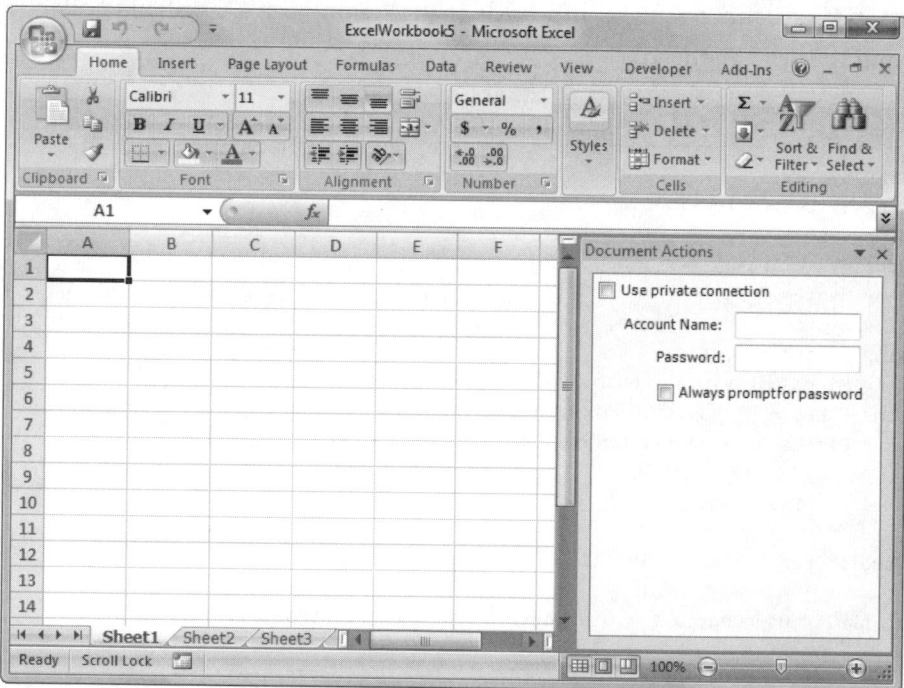

Figure 14-8: The result of running Listing 14-4.

ing out the customer information section of the document. When the user is filling out the order part of the document, the Document Actions task pane might display a button for examining available inventory.

Listing 14-5 shows a VSTO Excel customization where two named ranges have been defined. One called `orderInfo` is a range of cells where the contents of an order are placed. The other called `customerInfo` is a range of cells specifying the customer information for the customer placing the order. Listing 14-5 contextually adds and removes an `inventoryButton` when the `orderInfo` range is selected and a `customerButton` when the `customerInfo` range is selected or deselected. It does this by handling NamedRange.Selected and NamedRange.Deselected events. When the Selected event indicating the `customerInfo` range of cells is selected, Listing 14-5 adds a `customerButton` that when clicked would allow the user to pick an existing customer. Listing 14-5 removes the `customerButton` when the customerInfo.Deselected event is raised. It calls ActionsPane.Controls .Remove to remove the `customerButton` from the actions pane.

Listing 14-5 is written in a way so that if both the `customerInfo` range and the `orderInfo` range are selected at the same time, both the `customerButton` and the `inventoryButton` would be visible in the document task pane.

Listing 14-5: A VSTO Excel Customization That Changes the Actions Pane Based on the Selection

```csharp
using System;
using System.Collections.Generic;
using System.Data;
using System.Linq;
using System.Text;
using System.Windows.Forms;
using System.Xml.Linq;
using Microsoft.VisualStudio.Tools.Applications.Runtime;
using Excel = Microsoft.Office.Interop.Excel;
using Office = Microsoft.Office.Core;

namespace ExcelWorkbook1
{
  public partial class Sheet1
  {
    public Button customerButton = new Button();
    public Button inventoryButton = new Button();

    private void Sheet1_Startup(object sender, EventArgs e)
    {
```

```csharp
      customerButton.Text = "Select a customer...";
      inventoryButton.Text = "Check inventory...";

      this.orderInfo.Selected +=
        new Excel.DocEvents_SelectionChangeEventHandler(
        OrderInfo_Selected);

      this.orderInfo.Deselected +=
        new Excel.DocEvents_SelectionChangeEventHandler(
        OrderInfo_Deselected);

      this.customerInfo.Selected +=
        new Excel.DocEvents_SelectionChangeEventHandler(
        CustomerInfo_Selected);

      this.customerInfo.Deselected +=
        new Excel.DocEvents_SelectionChangeEventHandler(
        CustomerInfo_Deselected);
    }

    #region VSTO Designer generated code
    private void InternalStartup()
    {
      this.Startup += new System.EventHandler(Sheet1_Startup);
    }
    #endregion

    void OrderInfo_Selected(Excel.Range target)
    {
      Globals.ThisWorkbook.ActionsPane.Controls.Add(
        inventoryButton);
    }

    void OrderInfo_Deselected(Excel.Range target)
    {
      Globals.ThisWorkbook.ActionsPane.Controls.Remove(
        inventoryButton);
    }

    void CustomerInfo_Selected(Excel.Range target)
    {
      Globals.ThisWorkbook.ActionsPane.Controls.Add(
        customerButton);
    }

    void CustomerInfo_Deselected(Excel.Range target)
    {
      Globals.ThisWorkbook.ActionsPane.Controls.Remove(
        customerButton);
    }
  }
}
```

You can also change the contents of the Document Actions task pane as the selection changes in a Word document. One approach is to use bookmarks and change the contents of the Document Actions task pane when a particular bookmark is selected. A second approach is to use the XML mapping features of Word and VSTO's XMLNode and XMLNodes and change the contents of the Document Actions task pane when a particular XMLNode or XMLNodes is selected in the document. Finally, you'll want to consider using the new content controls in Word 2007, which raise events when a cursor in the content control leaves the control.

Detecting the Orientation of the Actions Pane

In addition to the UserControl events documented in the .NET class libraries documentation, ActionsPane adds one additional event: OrientationChanged. This event is raised when the orientation of the actions pane is changed. The actions pane can be in either a horizontal or vertical orientation. Figure 14-8 shows an actions pane in a vertical orientation. Figure 14-9 shows a horizontal orientation.

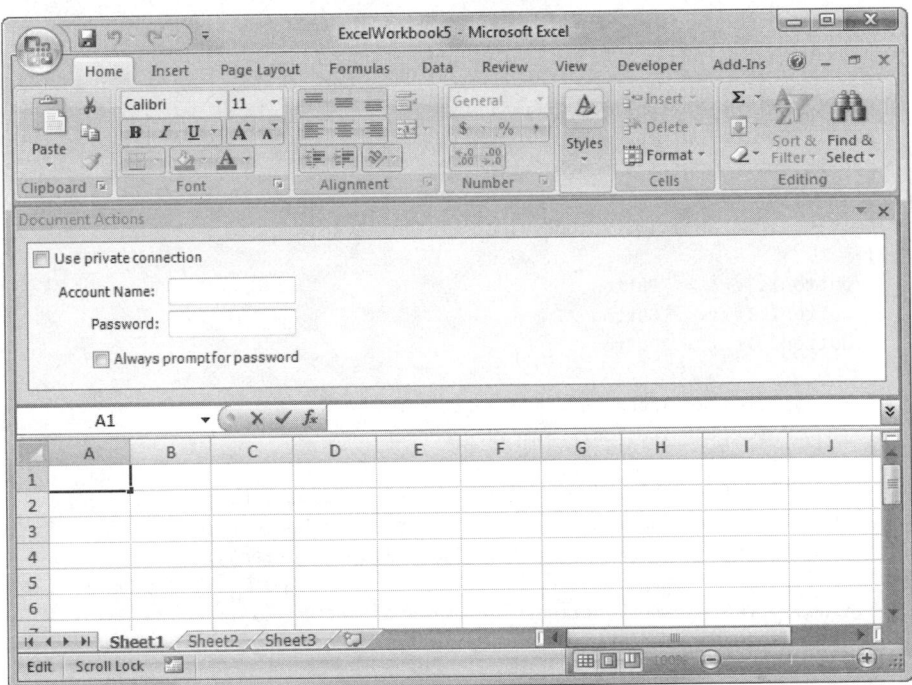

Figure 14-9: The actions pane in a horizontal orientation.

Listing 14-6 shows a VSTO Excel customization that adds several buttons to the ActionsPane's Controls collection. Listing 14-6 also handles the OrientationChanged event and displays the orientation of the ActionsPane in a dialog box. It determines the orientation of the actions pane by checking the ActionsPane.Orientation property. The Orientation property returns a member of the System.Windows.Forms.Orientation enumeration: either Orientation.Horizontal or Orientation.Vertical.

Listing 14-6: A VSTO Excel Customization That Handles the ActionsPane's OrientationChanged Event

```csharp
using System;
using System.Collections.Generic;
using System.Data;
using System.Linq;
using System.Text;
using System.Windows.Forms;
using System.Xml.Linq;
using Microsoft.VisualStudio.Tools.Applications.Runtime;
using Excel = Microsoft.Office.Interop.Excel;
using Office = Microsoft.Office.Core;

namespace ExcelWorkbook1
{
  public partial class Sheet1
  {
    public Button button1 = new Button();
    public Button button2 = new Button();
    public Button button3 = new Button();

    private void Sheet1_Startup(object sender, EventArgs e)
    {
      button1.Text = "Button 1";
      button2.Text = "Button 2";
      button3.Text = "Button 3";

      Globals.ThisWorkbook.ActionsPane.StackOrder =
        Microsoft.Office.Tools.StackStyle.FromTop;

      Globals.ThisWorkbook.ActionsPane.Controls.Add(button1);
      Globals.ThisWorkbook.ActionsPane.Controls.Add(button2);
      Globals.ThisWorkbook.ActionsPane.Controls.Add(button3);

      Globals.ThisWorkbook.ActionsPane.OrientationChanged +=
        new EventHandler(ActionsPane_OrientationChanged);
    }
```

```csharp
void ActionsPane_OrientationChanged(object sender, EventArgs e)
{
  Orientation orientation =
    Globals.ThisWorkbook.ActionsPane.Orientation;
  MessageBox.Show(String.Format(
    "Orientation is {0}.", orientation.ToString()));
}

#region VSTO Designer generated code
private void InternalStartup()
{
  this.Startup += new System.EventHandler(Sheet1_Startup);
}
#endregion
  }
}
```

Scrolling the Actions Pane

The AutoScroll property of the ActionPane gets or sets a `bool` value indicating whether the actions pane should display a scroll bar when the size of the Document Actions task pane is such that not all the controls can be shown. The default value of AutoScroll is `true`. Figure 14-10 shows a Document Actions task pane with 10 buttons added to it. Because AutoScroll is set to `true`, a scroll bar is shown when not all 10 buttons can be displayed given the size of the Document Actions task pane.

Showing and Hiding the Actions Pane

The actions pane is automatically shown when you add controls to Actions-Pane's Controls collection using the Add method. To show and hide the

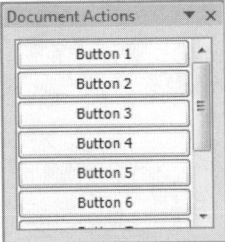

Figure 14-10: The actions pane
when AutoScroll is set to true.

actions pane programmatically, you need to use the Excel or Word object model. In Excel, set the Application.DisplayDocumentActionTaskPane property to true or false. In Word, set the property Application.Task-Panes[WdTaskPanes.wdTaskPaneDocumentActions].Visible property to true or false.

You might be tempted to call ActionsPane.Hide or set ActionsPane.Visible to false to hide the ActionsPane. These approaches do not work because you are actually hiding the UserControl shown in Figure 14-4 that is hosted by the Document Actions task pane rather than just the Document Actions task pane. You should use the object model of Excel and Word to show and hide the actions pane.

Listing 14-7 shows a VSTO Excel customization that shows and hides the actions pane on the BeforeDoubleClick event of the Worksheet by toggling the state of the Application.DisplayDocumentActionTaskPane property. Note that the DisplayDocumentActionTaskPane property is an application-level property that is only applicable when the active document has a Document Actions task pane associated with it. If the active document does not have a Document Actions task pane associated with it, accessing the DisplayDocumentActionTaskPane property will raise an exception.

Listing 14-7: A VSTO Excel Customization That Shows and Hides the Actions Pane When Handling the BeforeDoubleClick Event

```
using System;
using System.Collections.Generic;
using System.Data;
using System.Linq;
using System.Text;
using System.Windows.Forms;
using System.Xml.Linq;
using Microsoft.VisualStudio.Tools.Applications.Runtime;
using Excel = Microsoft.Office.Interop.Excel;
using Office = Microsoft.Office.Core;

namespace ExcelWorkbook1
{
  public partial class Sheet1
  {
    bool visible = true;
```

```csharp
    private void Sheet1_Startup(object sender, System.EventArgs e)
    {
      for (int i = 1; i < 11; i++)
      {
        Button myButton = new Button();
        myButton.Text = String.Format("Button {0}", i);
        Globals.ThisWorkbook.ActionsPane.Controls.Add(myButton);
      }

      this.BeforeDoubleClick +=
        new Excel.DocEvents_BeforeDoubleClickEventHandler(
        Sheet1_BeforeDoubleClick);
    }

    #region VSTO Designer generated code
    private void InternalStartup()
    {
      this.Startup += new EventHandler(Sheet1_Startup);
    }
    #endregion

    void Sheet1_BeforeDoubleClick(Excel.Range target,
      ref bool cancel)
    {
      // Toggle the visibility of the ActionsPane on double-click.
      visible = !visible;
      this.Application.DisplayDocumentActionTaskPane = visible;
    }
  }
}
```

Listing 14-8 shows a VSTO Word application that shows and hides the actions pane on the BeforeDoubleClick event of the Document by toggling the state of the Application.TaskPanes[WdTaskPanes.wdTaskPaneDocument-Actions].Visible property.

Listing 14-8: VSTO Word Customization That Shows and Hides the Actions Pane in the BeforeDoubleClick Event Handler

```csharp
using System;
using System.Collections.Generic;
using System.Data;
using System.Linq;
using System.Text;
using System.Windows.Forms;
using System.Xml.Linq;
```

```csharp
using Microsoft.VisualStudio.Tools.Applications.Runtime;
using Word = Microsoft.Office.Interop.Word;
using Office = Microsoft.Office.Core;

namespace WordDocument9
{
  public partial class ThisDocument
  {
    private void ThisDocument_Startup(object sender, EventArgs e)
    {
      for (int i = 1; i < 11; i++)
      {
        Button myButton = new Button();
        myButton.Text = String.Format("Button {0}", i);
        ActionsPane.Controls.Add(myButton);
      }

      this.BeforeDoubleClick +=
        new Microsoft.Office.Tools.Word.ClickEventHandler(
          ThisDocument_BeforeDoubleClick);
    }

    void ThisDocument_BeforeDoubleClick(object sender,
      Microsoft.Office.Tools.Word.ClickEventArgs e)
    {
      if (this.Application.TaskPanes[
        Word.WdTaskPanes.wdTaskPaneDocumentActions
        ].Visible == true)
      {
        this.Application.TaskPanes[
          Word.WdTaskPanes.wdTaskPaneDocumentActions
          ].Visible = false;
      }
      else
      {
        this.Application.TaskPanes[
          Word.WdTaskPanes.wdTaskPaneDocumentActions
          ].Visible = true;
      }
    }

    #region VSTO Designer generated code
    private void InternalStartup()
    {
      this.Startup += new EventHandler(ThisDocument_Startup);
    }
    #endregion
  }
}
```

Attaching and Detaching the Actions Pane

Sometimes you will want to go beyond just hiding the actions pane and actually detach the actions pane from the document or workbook to remove it permanently. You may want to detach the actions pane at the same time you use the RemoveCustomization method when removing a VSTO customization from a document, for example. You also may want to control whether the user of your document is allowed to detach the actions pane from the document or workbook. Recall from earlier in this chapter that the actions pane is actually a Smart Document solution, and as such it can be attached or detached from the document or workbook via Excel and Word's built-in dialog boxes for managing attached Smart Document solutions.

When the actions pane is detached from the document, this means that the Document Actions task pane will not be available for that document. To programmatically detach the actions pane from the document, call the ActionsPane.Clear method. Doing so detaches the actions pane solution from the document and hides the Document Actions pane. Calling Actions-Pane.Show reattaches the actions pane and makes it available again in the list of available task panes. Note that in Word, when you call Actions-Pane.Clear, you must follow the call with a second call to the Word object model: Document.XMLReferences["ActionsPane3"].Delete.

If you want to allow the user of your document to detach the actions pane solution by using the Templates and Add-Ins dialog box in Word, shown in Figure 14-11, or the XML Expansion Packs dialog box in Excel, shown in Figure 14-12, you must set the ActionsPane.AutoRecover property to false. By default, this property is set to true, which means that even when the user tries to detach the actions pane solution by deselecting it in these dialog boxes, VSTO will recover and automatically reattach the actions pane solution.

After an actions pane solution is attached to the document and the user saves the document, the next time the user opens the document, the actions pane will be available and can be selected at any time during the session. If your code does not add controls to the actions pane until some-time after startup, you might want to call the ActionsPane.Clear method in the Startup handler of your VSTO customization to prevent the user from showing the actions pane before your VSTO customization has added controls to the ActionsPane control.

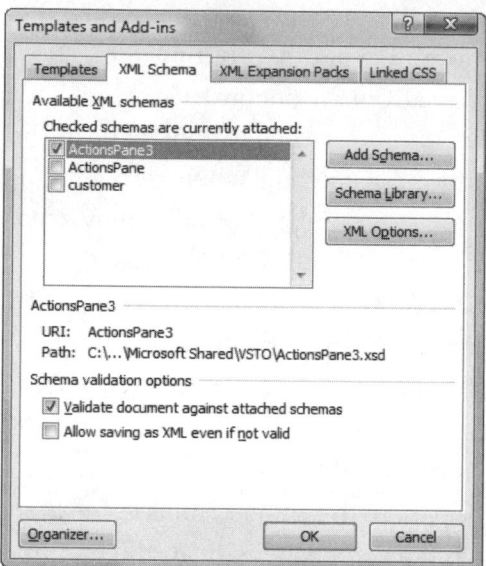

Figure 14-11: The actions pane solution attached to a Word document is visible in Word's Templates and Add-Ins dialog box and can be removed if ActionsPane.AutoRecover is not set to true.

Figure 14-12: The actions pane solution attached to an Excel workbook is visible in Excel's XML Expansion Packs dialog box and can be removed if ActionsPane.AutoRecover is not set to true.

TABLE 14-1: ActionPane Properties and Methods to Avoid

Left	Top	Width
Height	Right	Location
Margin	MaximumSize	MinimumSize
Size	TabIndex	AutoScrollMargin
AutoScrollMinSize		

Some Methods and Properties to Avoid

As mentioned earlier, the ActionsPane is a user control that has a fixed location and size that is controlled by VSTO. As such, you should avoid using a number of position-related properties and methods on the Actions-Pane control, as listed in Table 14-1.

Using WPF Controls in an Actions Pane

Starting with Visual Studio 2008, it is now easy to use WPF controls with the ActionsPane control. The simplest way to do this is to create a User-Control that uses WPF controls via the ElementHost control. To do this, follow these steps in your Word or Excel VSTO project:

1. Create a new WPF User Control by choosing Project > Add New Item.
2. In the Add New Item dialog box, click the User Control (WPF) item type; then click the Add button to create a WPF User Control called UserControl1.xaml.
3. Design your WPF UserControl1 using the visual designer.
4. Create a new Windows Forms User Control by choosing Project > Add New Item.
5. In the Add New Item dialog box, click the User Control item type; then click the Add button to create a Windows Forms User Control called UserControl2.cs and bring up the visual designer for UserControl2.

6. Build your solution by choosing Build > Build Solution.

   After you build your solution, the toolbox shown in the visual designer for UserControl2 will have a section called (if your project name was ExcelWorkbook7) ExcelWorkbook7 WPF User Controls. In that section of the toolbox, you see your WPF UserControl1.

7. Drag and drop your WPF UserControl1 onto the visual designer for UserControl2 as shown Figure 14-13.

8. Click the small triangle glyph in the top-right corner of UserControl1 to bring up a list of available tasks.

9. In that tasks list, click the Dock in Parent Container link, shown in Figure 14-13.

10. Now, in your document code (if this is a Word project), write this line:

```
Globals.ThisDocument.ActionsPane.Controls.Add(new UserControl2());
```

   In an Excel project, write this line:

```
Globals.ThisWorkbook.ActionsPane.Controls.Add(new UserControl2());
```

11. Finally, run the document project. Your WPF user control will be shown in the ActionsPane, as shown in Figure 14-14.

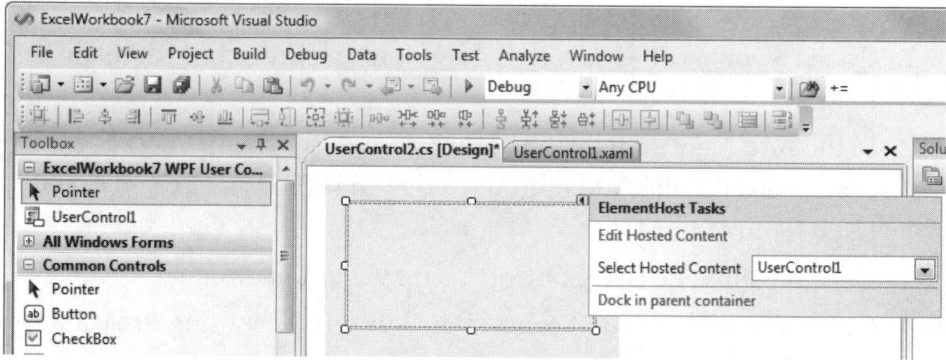

Figure 14-13: The visual designer for the Windows Forms UserControl2 after the WPF UserControl1 is dropped on the surface. Note the WPF User Controls in the toolbox and the tasks list where you can select Dock in Parent Container.

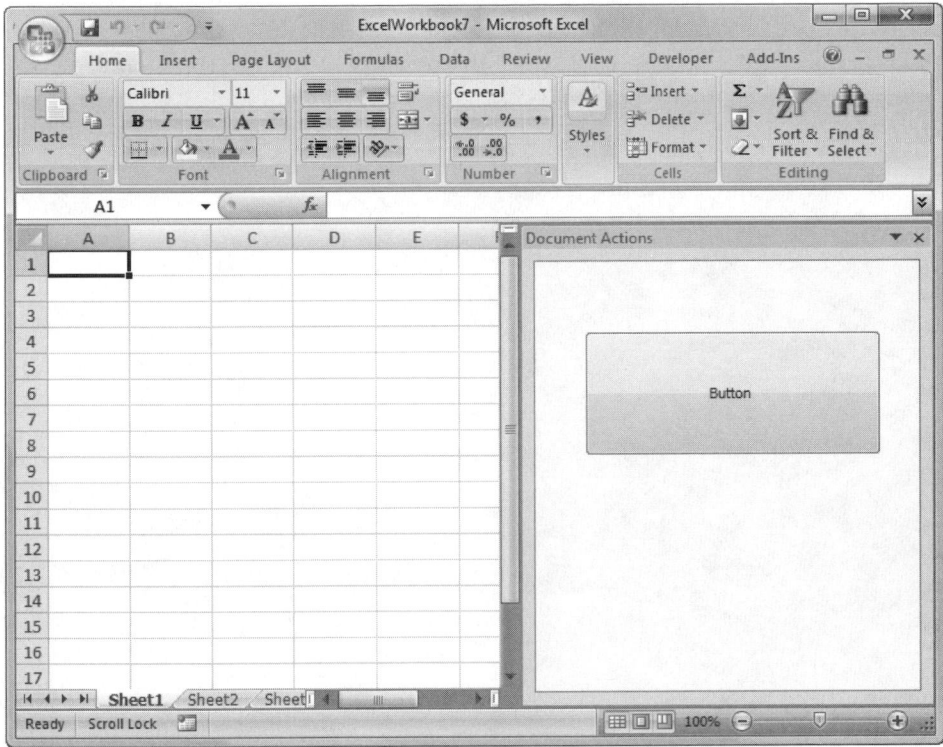

Figure 14-14: A WPF User Control shown in the Document Actions task pane.

Conclusion

The chapter described how to use the ActionsPane control in VSTO to create custom UI in your Office customization. Using the ActionsPane, you can provide a context-sensitive UI that changes when the selection in the document changes. The chapter also examined the properties, methods, and events of the ActionsPane control, and described the basic architecture of the ActionsPane. You learned how to use WPF controls in an ActionsPane.

In this chapter, we considered the ActionsPane, which can be used only in document-level customizations. If you need a task pane that isn't tied to a document and that is available at the application level, consider using the custom task pane, described in the next chapter.

■ 15 ■
Working with Application-Level Custom Task Panes

Introduction to the Application-Level Custom Task Panes

As described in Chapter 14, "Working with Document-Level Actions Panes," VSTO allows you to work with a Document Actions task pane starting with Word and Excel 2003. This feature ended up being one of the most popular features of VSTO 2.0. Developers, however, also wanted to be able to do the following:

- Create application-level task panes that weren't associated with any one document or template
- Create and show more than one task pane at a time
- Set the caption of the task pane to something other than Document Actions
- Use the task pane paradigm in other Office applications, such as PowerPoint and Outlook

To address these requests, Office 2007 introduced the ability to create application-level custom task panes. A developer can define multiple custom task panes and display several at one time, and can set the caption of the task pane. Finally, task panes are now available in five applications supported by VSTO add-ins:

- Word 2007
- Excel 2007
- PowerPoint 2007
- Outlook 2007
- InfoPath 2007

Application-level custom task panes can be used only from application-level add-ins; they cannot be used in the VSTO document projects for Word and Excel.

Listing 15-1 shows a simple VSTO Excel add-in that displays a Windows Forms button control in a custom task pane. We need several key objects to accomplish this task. For application-level task panes, we must specify a UserControl to be used as the display surface for the custom task pane, so in Listing 15-1, we create an instance of a UserControl object. Then we create a Windows Forms button control and add it to the Controls collection of the UserControl. Finally, we call the Add method on the CustomTaskPanes collection, which is a member of the ThisAddIn class. The Add method of the CustomTaskPanes collection takes the UserControl you want to show in the new custom task pane as a parameter. It also takes a `string` to set the title of the newly added task pane. The Add method returns the newly created CustomTaskPane object. Finally, we set the Visible property of the Custom-TaskPane object to `true` to show the custom task pane.

Listing 15-1: A VSTO Excel Add-In That Adds a Button to a Custom Task Pane

```
using System;
using System.Windows.Forms;
using Excel = Microsoft.Office.Interop.Excel;
using Office = Microsoft.Office.Core;

namespace ExcelAddIn4
{
  public partial class ThisAddIn
  {
    UserControl control;
    Microsoft.Office.Tools.CustomTaskPane pane;
    Button button;
```

```csharp
private void ThisAddIn_Startup(object sender,
    System.EventArgs e)
{
  control = new UserControl();
  button = new Button();
  button.Text = "Hello";
  control.Controls.Add(button);
  pane = CustomTaskPanes.Add(control, "Test Pane");
  pane.Visible = true;
}

#region VSTO generated code
private void InternalStartup()
{
  this.Startup += new System.EventHandler(ThisAddIn_Startup);
}
#endregion
  }
}
```

Figure 15-1 shows the result of running Listing 15-1. A Windows Forms button is displayed in the custom task pane.

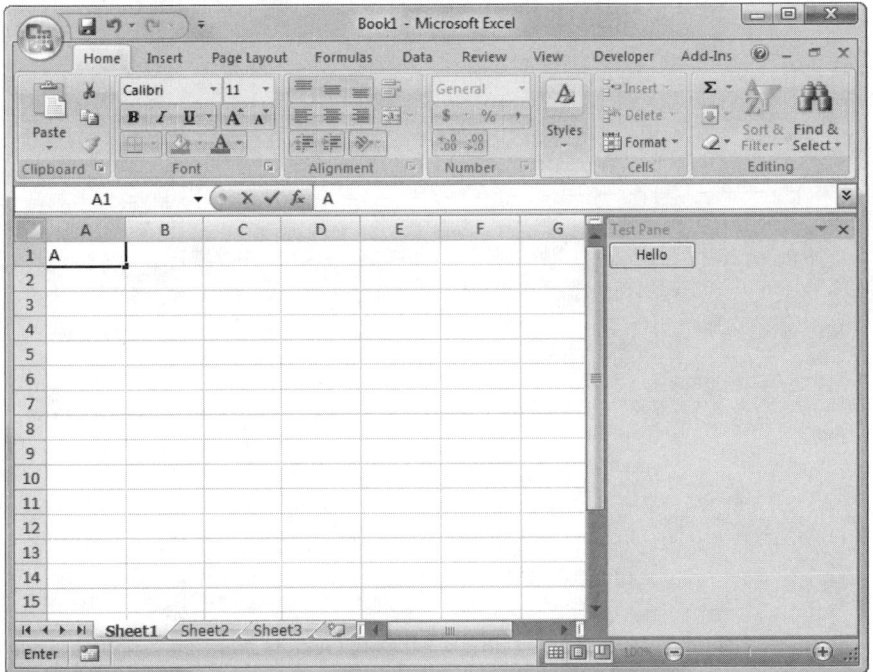

Figure 15-1: The result of running Listing 15-1.

Working with Custom Task Panes

A first step in understanding how VSTO's CustomTaskPanes collection works is delving a little into the architecture of VSTO's custom task pane support.

The CustomTaskPane Architecture

A custom task pane is a window provided by Office that can host ActiveX controls. The layers of the architecture are shown in Figure 15-2. VSTO places a special invisible ActiveX control in the Document Actions task pane that in turn hosts the UserControl that you pass to the Add method of the CustomTaskPanes collection. The UserControl you pass to the Add method can host multiple Windows Forms controls via its Controls collection (UserControl.Controls). You can add Windows Forms controls to a UserControl by using the UserControl.Controls.Add method.

The UserControl placed in a custom task pane window is set to expand to fit the area provided by the window. If the custom task pane is not big enough to display all the controls hosted by the UserControl, it is possible

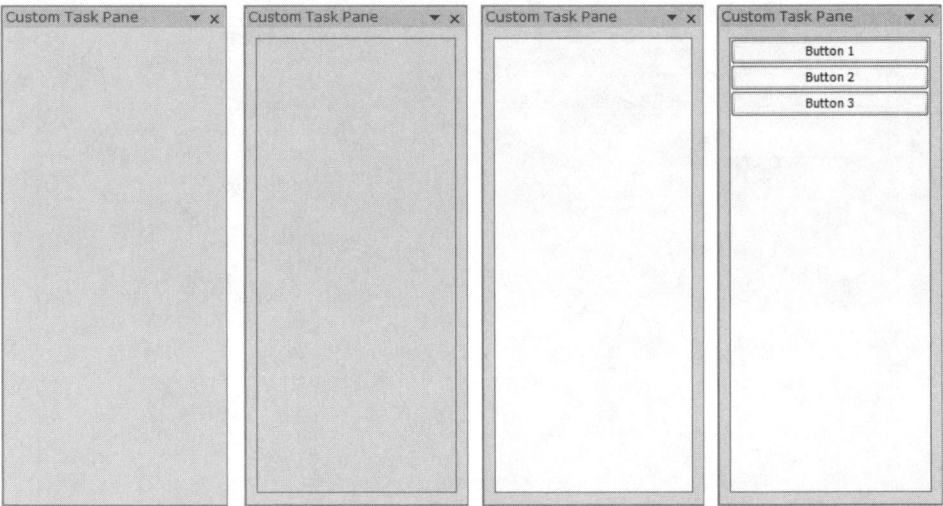

Figure 15-2: The four layers of the CustomTaskPane architecture, from left to right: the custom task pane, the VSTO ActiveX control, the UserControl, and controls parented to the UserControl.

to scroll the UserControl by setting the AutoScroll property of the User-Control to `true`.

The CustomTaskPanes Collection

The CustomTaskPanes collection provides an Add method that takes the UserControl you want to show in the new custom task pane as a parameter. It also takes a `string` to set the title of the newly added task pane. The Add method returns a CustomTaskPane object.

When a user closes a CustomTaskPane, the CustomTaskPane remains in memory until you remove it from the CustomTaskPanes collection. The CustomTaskPanes collection has a Remove and RemoveAt method that free the memory and resources used by the custom task pane. Remove takes as a parameter the CustomTaskPane object you want to remove from the CustomTaskPanes collection. RemoveAt takes an `int` parameter specifying the 0-based index for the CustomTaskPane you want to remove from the CustomTaskPanes collection.

In Listing 15-2, the VisibleChanged event of a CustomTaskPane is handled. This event is raised when the user closes a CustomTaskPane. When the CustomTaskPane is closed, the CustomTaskPanes.Remove method is called to free the memory and resources used by the custom task pane.

Listing 15-2: A VSTO Excel Add-In That Adds a Task Pane and Removes It from the CustomTaskPanes Collection When It Is Closed

```
using System;
using System.Windows.Forms;
using Excel = Microsoft.Office.Interop.Excel;
using Office = Microsoft.Office.Core;

namespace ExcelAddIn4
{
  public partial class ThisAddIn
  {
    UserControl control;
    Microsoft.Office.Tools.CustomTaskPane pane;
    Button button;

    private void ThisAddIn_Startup(object sender,
      System.EventArgs e)
    {
```

```
    control = new UserControl();
    button = new Button();
    button.Text = "Hello";
    control.Controls.Add(button);
    pane = CustomTaskPanes.Add(control, "Test Pane");
    pane.Visible = true;
    pane.VisibleChanged += new EventHandler(pane_VisibleChanged);
}

void pane_VisibleChanged(object sender, EventArgs e)
{
  if (pane.Visible == false)
  {
    CustomTaskPanes.Remove(pane);
    pane.VisibleChanged -=
       new EventHandler(pane_VisibleChanged);
    pane = null;
  }
}

#region VSTO generated code
private void InternalStartup()
{
  this.Startup += new System.EventHandler(ThisAddIn_Startup);
}
#endregion
  }
}
```

The CustomTaskPane Object

The CustomTaskPane object has two events that it can raise:

- **CustomTaskPane.DockPositionChanged** is raised when the dock position of the CustomTaskPane changes. You can check where the custom task pane is docked by using the CustomTaskPane.Dock-Position property, described in Table 15-1.

- **CustomTaskPane.VisibleChanged** is raised when the visibility of the task pane changes because it is either shown or closed. You can check whether the custom task pane is closed or open by using the CustomTaskPane.Visible property.

Table 15-1 shows the properties associated with the CustomTaskPane object.

TABLE 15-1: Properties of the CustomTaskPane Object

Name	Type	What It Does
UserControl	UserControl	Returns the UserControl that was provided to the CustomTaskPanes.Add method when the custom task pane was created. The property is read-only.
DockPosition	MsoCTP-DockPosition	Sets and gets the dock position of the custom task pane as a member of the MsoCTPDockPosition enumeration: `msoCTPDockPositionLeft`, `msoCTPDockPositionTop`, `msoCTPDockPositionRight`, `msoCTPDockPositionBottom`, or `msoCTPDockPositionFloating`.
DockPosition-Restrict	MsoCTP-DockPosition-Restrict	Sets and gets any restrictions on where the custom task pane can dock. The property can be set to `msoCTPDockPositionRestrictNone`, `msoCTPDockPositionRestrictNoChange`, `msoCTPDockPositionRestrictNoHorizontal`, or `msoCTPDockPositionRestrictNoVertical`.
Height	int	Sets and gets the height, in points, of the custom task pane. If the custom task pane is docked vertically, this property raises an exception if you try to set it.
Title	string	Gets the title of the custom task pane. The property is read-only.
Visible	bool	Sets and gets whether the custom task pane is visible.
Width	int	Sets and gets the width, in points, of the custom task pane. If the custom task pane is docked horizontally, this property raises an exception if you try to set it.
Window	object	Returns the window object associated with the custom task pane for the application. The property can be cast to a specific object in the object model corresponding to a window for the application into which the add-in loads, per Table 15-2. The property is read-only.

TABLE 15-2:   Types That the Window Object Can Be Cast to Based on the Application the CustomTaskPane Is Loaded In

Application	Type
Word	Microsoft.Office.Interop.Word.Window
Excel	Microsoft.Office.Interop.Excel.Window
PowerPoint	Microsoft.Office.Interop.PowerPoint.DocumentWindow
InfoPath	Microsoft.Office.Interop.InfoPath.WindowObject
Outlook	Microsoft.Office.Interop.Outlook.Explorer Microsoft.Office.Interop.Outlook.Inspector

Adding a Custom User Control to the Custom Task Pane

The method by which we have added controls to the custom task pane thus far has involved creating a UserControl, creating a Windows Forms control like a button, and adding the Windows Forms control to the User-Control's controls collection. A more visual way to design your custom task pane UI is to create a custom user control and add that custom user control to the CustomTaskPanes collection.

Visual Studio provides a rich design-time experience for creating a user control. To add a user control to your application, click the project node in the Solution Explorer, and choose Project > Add User Control in Visual Studio. Visual Studio will prompt you to give the User Control a filename, such as UserControl1.cs. Then Visual Studio displays the design view shown in Figure 15-3.

The design area for the user control has a handle in the bottom-right corner that you can drag to change the size of the user control. Controls from the toolbox can be dragged onto the user control design surface and positioned as desired. Figure 15-4 shows a completed user control that uses check boxes, text boxes, and labels.

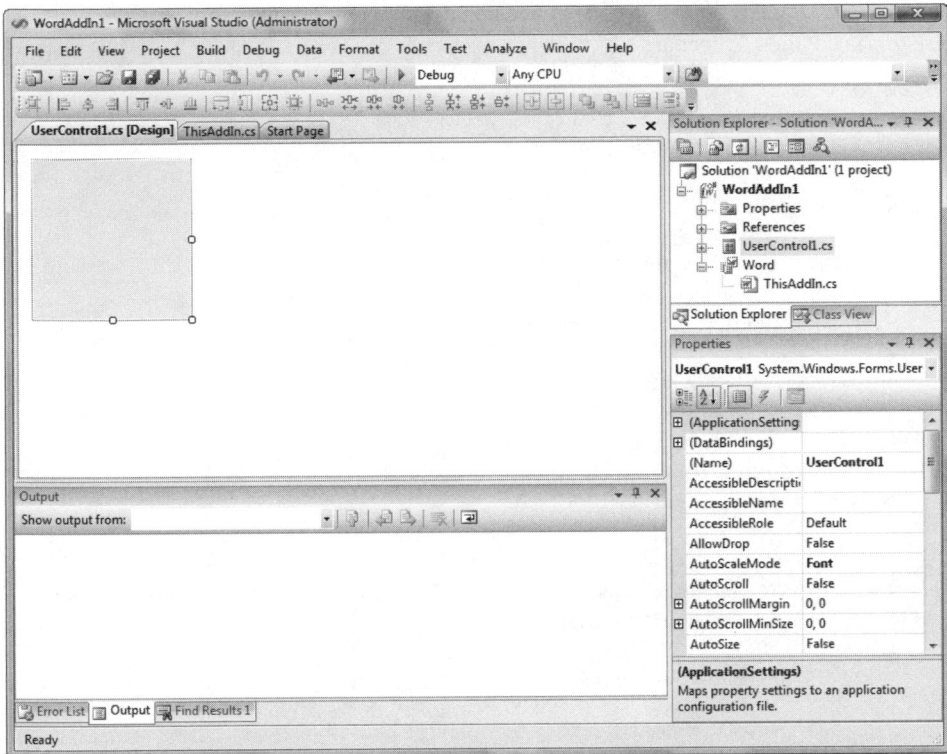

Figure 15-3: The design view for creating a custom user control.

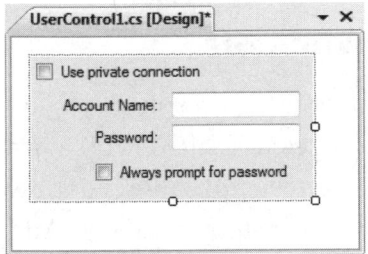

Figure 15-4: A custom user control.

Listing 15-3 shows a VSTO Word add-in that adds this custom user control as a custom task pane. The user control created in Figure 15-4 is a class named UserControl1. Listing 15-3 creates an instance of UserControl1 and adds it to the CustomTaskPanes collection using the Add method.

Listing 15-3: A VSTO Word Add-In That Adds a Custom User Control to the CustomTaskPanes Collection

```
using System;
using Word = Microsoft.Office.Interop.Word;
using Office = Microsoft.Office.Core;

namespace WordAddIn1
{
  public partial class ThisAddIn
  {
    Microsoft.Office.Tools.CustomTaskPane pane;

    private void ThisAddIn_Startup(object sender,
        System.EventArgs e)
    {
      pane = CustomTaskPanes.Add(new UserControl1(), "My Pane");
      pane.Visible = true;
    }

    #region VSTO generated code
    private void InternalStartup()
    {
      this.Startup += new System.EventHandler(ThisAddIn_Startup);
    }
    #endregion
  }
}
```

Custom Task Panes and Application Windows

The CustomTaskPanes.Add method has two overloads, one of which you already have seen. This first overload, which takes a UserControl and a string, associates a custom task pane with the active application window when this method is called. The second overload of CustomTaskPanes.Add takes a UserControl and a string as well as an object. This third object parameter can be used to specify the specific application window with which a CustomTaskPane should be associated.

Table 15-2, earlier in this chapter, shows the object types that specify the window for each Office application in which custom task panes can be created.

When working with custom task panes, you should be aware of some application-specific differences in the ways that custom task panes are associated with windows.

Custom Task Panes and Outlook-Specific Issues

Listing 15-4 shows a VSTO Outlook add-in that associates a custom task pane with Inspector windows that appear in Outlook. It handles the Inspectors.NewInspector event and associates a custom task pane with a new Inspector window by using the overload of CustomTaskPanes.Add that takes a window object; in this case, it passes Outlook's Inspector object. Listing 15-4 also handles the VisibleChanged event for each custom task pane it creates.

Listing 15-4: A VSTO Outlook Add-In That Adds a Custom Task Pane to an Outlook Inspector Window Incorrectly

```
using System;
using System.Windows.Forms;
using Microsoft.Office.Tools;
using Outlook = Microsoft.Office.Interop.Outlook;
using Office = Microsoft.Office.Core;

namespace OutlookAddIn4
{
  public partial class ThisAddIn
  {
    Outlook.Inspectors inspectors;

    private void ThisAddIn_Startup(object sender,
      System.EventArgs e)
    {
      inspectors = Application.Inspectors;
      inspectors.NewInspector += new
        Outlook.InspectorsEvents_NewInspectorEventHandler(
        inspectors_NewInspector);
    }

    void inspectors_NewInspector(Outlook.Inspector Inspector)
    {
      CustomTaskPane pane = CustomTaskPanes.Add(
        new UserControl(), System.DateTime.Now.ToLongTimeString(),
        Inspector);
      pane.Visible = true;
      pane.VisibleChanged += new EventHandler(pane_VisibleChanged);
    }

    void pane_VisibleChanged(object sender, EventArgs e)
    {
      CustomTaskPane pane = sender as CustomTaskPane;
      MessageBox.Show(pane.Title);
    }
```

```
    #region VSTO generated code
    private void InternalStartup()
    {
      this.Startup += new System.EventHandler(ThisAddIn_Startup);
    }
    #endregion
  }
}
```

If you run the add-in in Listing 15-4, you will notice some strange behavior. Double-click a mail item in your inbox and an Inspector window appears, with a custom task pane. Close the Inspector window—and the first sign of trouble arises. When you close the Inspector window, the VisibleChanged event is not raised, even though the custom task pane is not visible anymore.

Next, double-click another mail item in your inbox. Now two custom task panes are shown in the Inspector window. To make this situation even more puzzling, without closing the Inspector window that has two custom task panes displayed, double-click yet another mail item in your inbox. The second Inspector window that appears for that mail item has only one custom task pane.

The reason you got two custom task panes in one of your Inspector windows is that Outlook associates custom task panes with windows, and when possible, it recycles windows by hiding them rather than closing the windows. So the first time you closed the Inspector window, Outlook didn't destroy the window or raise the VisibleChanged event. The second time you opened an Inspector window, the first window was reused, and although the NewInspector event for the custom task pane was raised, the Inspector window is actually a reused one. When you double-click the last mail item, NewInspector is raised again, but this time the Inspector window is a new window, and only one custom task pane is shown in the window.

Furthermore, you notice that to get the VisibleChanged event to be raised for all three custom task panes created in this example, you have to exit Outlook, at which point Outlook cleans up the hidden windows and the associated custom task panes.

Listing 15-5 shows a modified approach that cleans up custom task panes properly when Inspector windows close. To do this, the Inspector.Close event must be handled for each new Inspector window. When this event is raised, the custom task pane associated with the closing Inspector window is removed from the CustomTaskPanes collection. Listing 15-5 uses a helper class called InspectorWrapper that tracks Inspector windows and their associated custom task panes.

Listing 15-5: A VSTO Outlook Add-In That Adds a Custom Task Pane to an Outlook Inspector Window Correctly

```csharp
using System;
using System.Windows.Forms;
using Microsoft.Office.Tools;
using Outlook = Microsoft.Office.Interop.Outlook;
using Office = Microsoft.Office.Core;

namespace OutlookAddIn4
{
  public class InspectorWrapper
  {
    Outlook.Inspector inspector;
    CustomTaskPane pane;

    public InspectorWrapper(Outlook.Inspector i)
    {
      inspector = i;

      pane = Globals.ThisAddIn.CustomTaskPanes.Add(
        new UserControl(), System.DateTime.Now.ToLongTimeString(),
        inspector);
      pane.Visible = true;

      ((Outlook.InspectorEvents_10_Event)inspector).Close +=
        new Outlook.InspectorEvents_10_CloseEventHandler(
        InspectorWrapper_Close);
    }

    void InspectorWrapper_Close()
    {
      Globals.ThisAddIn.CustomTaskPanes.Remove(pane);
      Globals.ThisAddIn.inspectorWrappers.Remove(this);
      ((Outlook.InspectorEvents_10_Event)inspector).Close -=
        new Outlook.InspectorEvents_10_CloseEventHandler(
        InspectorWrapper_Close);
      inspector = null;
      pane = null;
    }
  }

  public partial class ThisAddIn
  {
```

```
    Outlook.Inspectors inspectors;
    public System.Collections.Generic.List<InspectorWrapper>
       inspectorWrappers;

    private void ThisAddIn_Startup(object sender,
       System.EventArgs e)
    {
      inspectors = Application.Inspectors;
      inspectors.NewInspector += new
         Outlook.InspectorsEvents_NewInspectorEventHandler(
         inspectors_NewInspector);
    }

    void inspectors_NewInspector(Outlook.Inspector inspector)
    {
      inspectorWrappers.Add(new InspectorWrapper(inspector));
    }

    #region VSTO generated code
    private void InternalStartup()
    {
      this.Startup += new System.EventHandler(ThisAddIn_Startup);
    }
    #endregion
  }
}
```

Custom Task Panes and Word-Specific Issues

Listing 15-6 shows a VSTO Word add-in that creates a new task pane on
Word startup. This task pane gets associated with whatever document is
opened at Word startup if Word is invoked by double-clicking a document
or with a new blank document if Word is launched without a document
being specified.

Listing 15-6: A VSTO Word Add-In That Adds a Custom Task Pane at Startup

```
using System;
using System.Windows.Forms;
using Word = Microsoft.Office.Interop.Word;
using Office = Microsoft.Office.Core;

namespace WordAddIn1
{
  public partial class ThisAddIn
  {
    private void ThisAddIn_Startup(object sender,
```

```
      System.EventArgs e)
    {
      CustomTaskPanes.Add(new UserControl(),
          "Test").Visible = true;
    }

    #region VSTO generated code
    private void InternalStartup()
    {
      this.Startup += new System.EventHandler(ThisAddIn_Startup);
    }
    #endregion
  }
}
```

When you run Listing 15-6, it may seem to produce the results you want, but consider a few behaviors:

- First, in the View tab of the Ribbon, click the New Window button. A second window opens, also displaying the initial document or blank document. The second window is not associated with a custom task pane.
- Next, create a new document, leaving the initial document open. Word creates a third window to show the new document, and that window also is not associated with a custom task pane.

Listing 15-7 shows how to ensure that a custom task pane is associated with every Word window—both windows created as secondary views on the same document and windows created as views on a new document. Listing 15-7 handles the Application.WindowActivate event and checks whether it already has a custom task pane in the CustomTaskPanes collection associated with the activated window. If not, it creates a new custom task pane and associates that pane with the activated window. It also handles the VisibleChanged event to remove a custom task pane that has been closed from the CustomTaskPanes collection. One implication of the fact that you have to associate a custom task pane with every window Word shows this: You may have to do some coordination among multiple custom task pane instances that are shown for the same document to show the same information for a given document.

Listing 15-7: A VSTO Word Add-In That Adds a Custom Task Pane to Every Word Window

```csharp
using System;
using System.Windows.Forms;
using Microsoft.Office.Tools;
using Word = Microsoft.Office.Interop.Word;
using Office = Microsoft.Office.Core;

namespace WordAddIn1
{
  public partial class ThisAddIn
  {
    private void ThisAddIn_Startup(object sender,
       System.EventArgs e)
    {
      Application.WindowActivate += new
         Word.ApplicationEvents4_WindowActivateEventHandler(
         Application_WindowActivate);
    }

    void Application_WindowActivate(Word.Document Doc,
       Word.Window Wn)
    {
      foreach (CustomTaskPane item in CustomTaskPanes)
      {
        if (item.Window == Wn)
          return;
      }

      CustomTaskPane pane = CustomTaskPanes.Add(
        new UserControl(), Wn.Caption, Wn);
      pane.Visible = true;
      pane.VisibleChanged += new EventHandler(pane_VisibleChanged);
    }

    void pane_VisibleChanged(object sender, EventArgs e)
    {
      CustomTaskPane pane = sender as CustomTaskPane;
      if (pane.Visible == false)
      {
        CustomTaskPanes.Remove(pane);
        pane.VisibleChanged -=
           new EventHandler(pane_VisibleChanged);
      }
    }

    #region VSTO generated code
    private void InternalStartup()
    {
```

```
        this.Startup += new System.EventHandler(ThisAddIn_Startup);
    }
    #endregion
  }
}
```

Custom Task Panes and Excel-Specific Issues

Listing 15-8 shows a VSTO Excel add-in that creates a new task pane on Excel startup. This task pane behaves differently from what you have seen in Word and Outlook. It gets associated with Excel's main application window and stays visible when you show new windows or open new documents.

Listing 15-8: A VSTO Excel Add-In That Adds a Custom Task Pane to Excel

```
using System;
using System.Windows.Forms;
using Microsoft.Office.Tools;
using Excel = Microsoft.Office.Interop.Excel;
using Office = Microsoft.Office.Core;

namespace ExcelAddIn5
{
  public partial class ThisAddIn
  {
    Button button;

    private void ThisAddIn_Startup(object sender,
      System.EventArgs e)
    {
      button = new Button();
      button.Text = Application.ActiveWorkbook.Name;
      UserControl usercontrol = new UserControl();
      usercontrol.Controls.Add(button);
      CustomTaskPanes.Add(usercontrol, "Test").Visible = true;
      Application.WindowActivate +=
          new Excel.AppEvents_WindowActivateEventHandler(
          Application_WindowActivate);
    }

    void Application_WindowActivate(Excel.Workbook Wb,
      Excel.Window Wn)
    {
      button.Text = Wb.Name;
    }
```

```
  #region VSTO generated code
  private void InternalStartup()
  {
    this.Startup += new System.EventHandler(ThisAddIn_Startup);
  }
  #endregion
}
}
```

When you run Listing 15-8, create a new workbook, and note that the task pane is still displayed. Next, in the View tab of the Ribbon, click the New Window button. Excel opens another window to display the active workbook. The custom task pane is still visible. To really understand what is happening, click the Arrange All button in the View tab of the Ribbon. You see something like Figure 15-5. You can see clearly that the custom task pane is associated with the main Excel application window that parents all document windows.

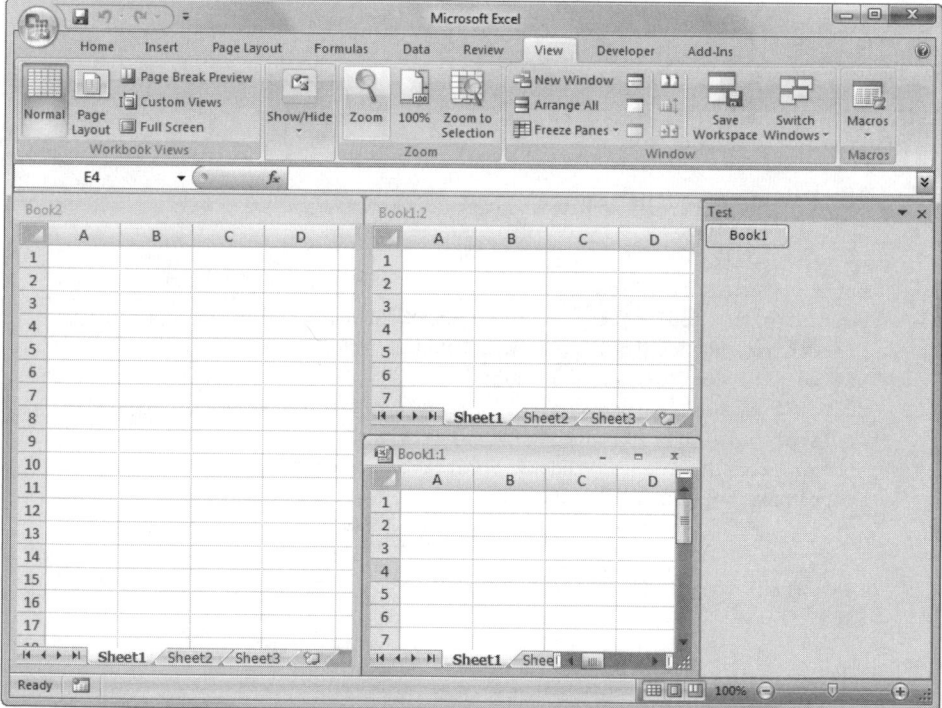

Figure 15-5: Custom task panes in Excel are associated with the application window.

One implication of the fact that Excel associates custom task panes with the main application window is that to show document-specific information, you have to track the currently active document and display information relevant to that document. Listing 15-8 does this in a small way by handling the Application.WindowActivate event and changing the button label to the name of the currently active workbook.

Using WPF Controls in a Custom Task Pane

Starting with Visual Studio 2008, it is easy to use Windows Presentation Foundation (WPF) controls with the custom task pane control. The simplest way to do this is to create a UserControl that uses WPF controls via the ElementHost control. Follow these steps in your Word, Excel, or Outlook VSTO Add-in project:

1. Create a new WPF User Control by choosing Project > Add New Item.
2. In the Add New Item dialog box, click the User Control (WPF) item type; then click the Add button to create a WPF User Control called UserControl1.xaml.
3. Design your WPF UserControl1 by using the visual designer as shown in Figure 15-6.
4. Create a new Windows Forms User Control by choosing Project > Add New Item.
5. In the Add New Item dialog box, click the User Control item type; then click the Add button to create a Windows Forms User Control called UserControl2.cs and bring up the visual designer for UserControl2.
6. Build your solution by choosing Build > Build Solution.

   After you build your solution, the toolbox shown in the visual designer for UserControl2 has a section called (if your project name was ExcelAddIn5) ExcelAddIn5 WPF User Controls. In that section of the toolbox, you see your WPF UserControl1, as shown in Figure 15-7.

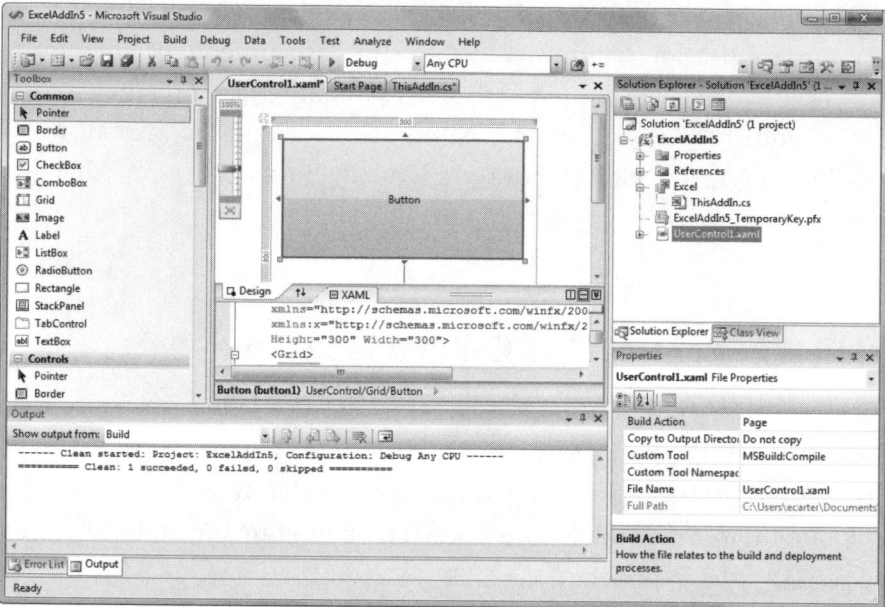

Figure 15-6: The visual designer for the WPF User Control.

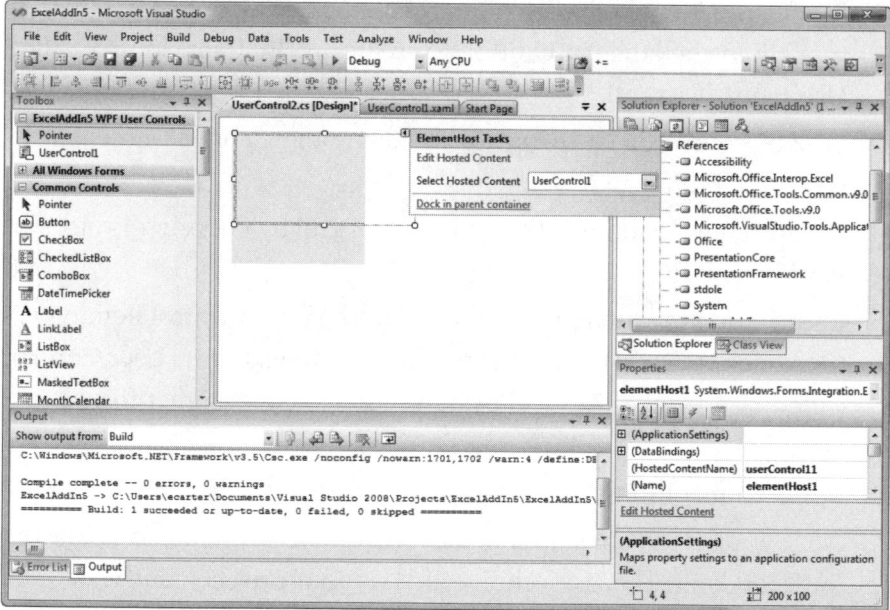

Figure 15-7: The visual designer for the Windows Forms UserControl2 after the WPF UserControl1 is dropped on the surface. Notice the WPF User Controls in the toolbox and the tasks list where you can choose Dock in Parent Container.

7. Drag and drop your WPF UserControl1 onto the visual designer for UserControl2.

8. Click the small triangle glyph in the top-right corner of UserControl1 to bring up a list of available tasks.

9. In that tasks list, click the Dock in Parent Container link, as shown in Figure 15-7.

10. Now, in your add-in code, write a line of code like this:

```
Globals.ThisAddIn.CustomTaskPanes.Add(new UserControl2(),
  "WPF").Visible = true;
```

11. Finally, run the add-in project.

    Your WPF user control appears in the custom task pane, as shown in Figure 15-8.

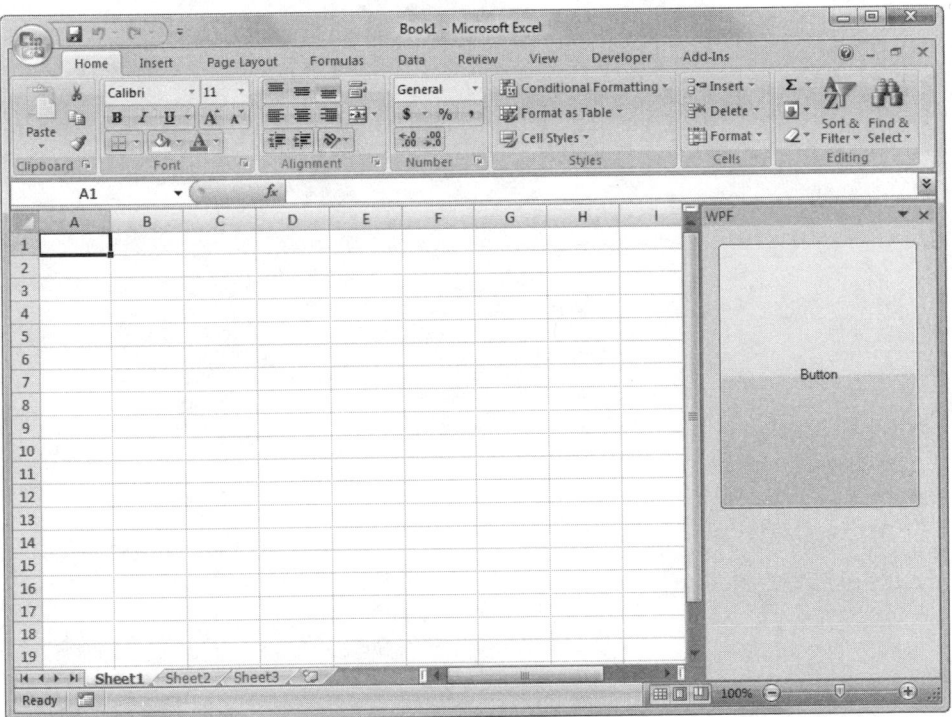

Figure 15-8: A WPF User Control shown in a custom task pane.

Conclusion

This chapter described VSTO's support for creating application-level custom task panes. We examined the properties, methods, and events unique to the CustomTaskPane control, as well as the CustomTaskPanes collection. We showed how custom task panes can behave differently with respect to application windows in the different Office applications. Finally, we showed how to use WPF controls in a custom task pane.

As you think about task panes, you should consider using a document-level task pane (ActionsPane) if you really need a pane associated with one particular document or template in Word or Excel. A document-level task pane has a simpler model than a custom task pane when it comes to application window management and may be better for certain scenarios. Finally, Chapter 17, "Working with the Ribbon in VSTO," references a technique for coordinating application-level custom task panes with the Ribbon.

Working with Outlook
Form Regions

Introduction to Form Regions

In Outlook 2007, developers have the ability to extend the Outlook UI by creating a special kind of Outlook extension called an Outlook form region. *Form regions* are used primarily to customize Inspector windows, which we introduced in Chapter 10, "Working with Outlook Events." *Inspector windows* are the Outlook windows that appear when you double-click an Outlook item—a mail item in your inbox or a task in a task list, for example. With form regions you can do things like add pages to the Inspector window, replace all the existing pages in an Inspector window with your own page, or dock some custom UI onto an existing page. You can also use a certain type of Outlook form region (an Adjoining form region) to customize the reading pane in Outlook Explorer windows.

Creating a New Form Region

To begin our exploration of Outlook form regions, let's create a simple one by using Visual Studio 2008. Start by creating a new Outlook add-in project by choosing File > New > Project. In the New Project dialog box that appears, create a new Outlook 2007 add-in, as shown in Figure 16-1.

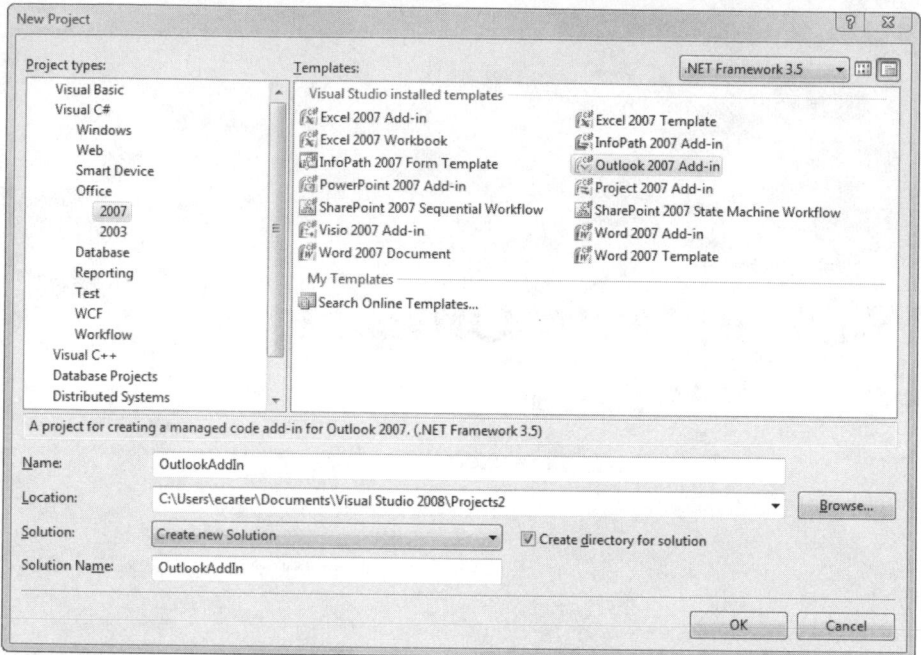

Figure 16-1: Creating a new Outlook 2007 add-in.

Now, in your new add-in project, choose Project > Add New Item. Click the Office category to filter to show just the Office-specific items. In the list of Office items, click Outlook Form Region, as shown in Figure 16-2. Name the form region—just use the default name FormRegion1. Then click the Add button.

A wizard appears, as shown in Figure 16-3. The first step in the wizard is to decide whether you want to create an Outlook form region or import a form region that was previously designed in Outlook with Outlook's built-in form designer. For this introduction, click Design a New Form Region. This option lets you use Windows Forms and keeps our editing experience within Visual Studio. Later in the chapter we show you how to use the Outlook built-in form designer, as well as discuss when you might want to use Outlook's form designer instead of Windows Forms.

After you decide whether to design a new form region with Windows Forms or to import an existing Outlook form region designed in Outlook, click the Next button to move to the second page of the wizard, shown in Figure 16-4, which allows you to pick the type of form region you want to create.

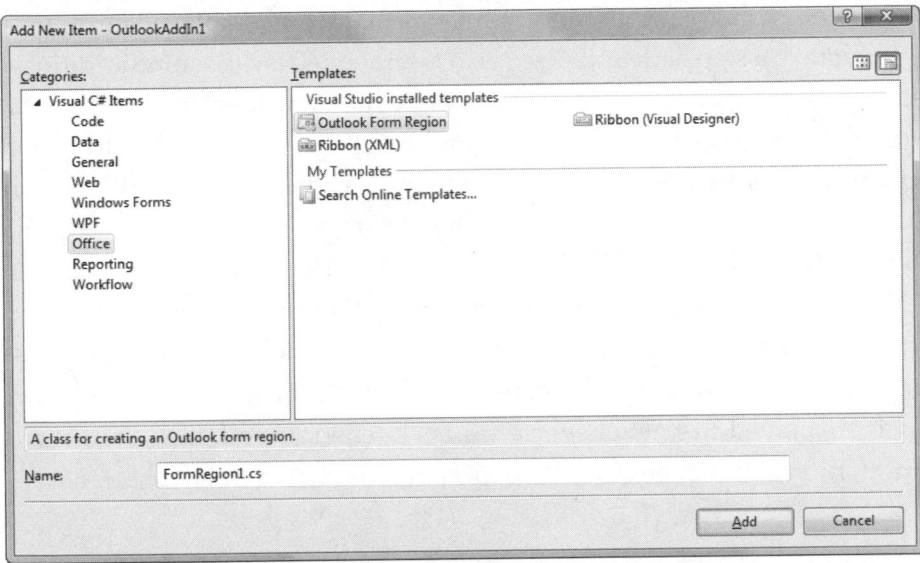

Figure 16-2: Adding an Outlook form region to an Outlook 2007 add-in project.

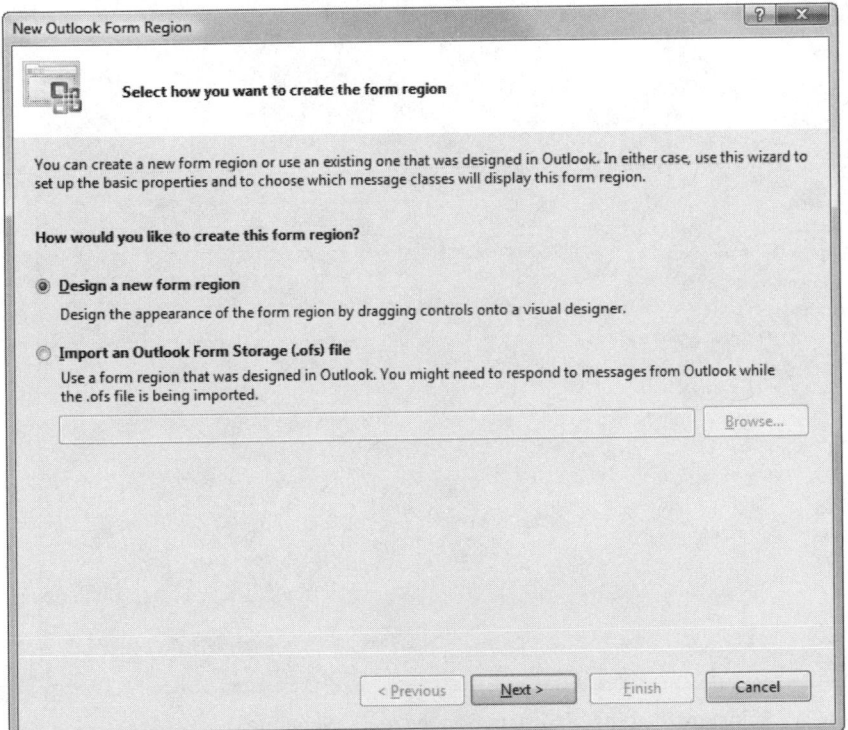

Figure 16-3: Selecting the form technology to use to create the form region.

To understand the types of form regions that are available in Figure 16-4, we must take a step back and discuss Inspector windows in some additional detail. Form regions are used primarily in Outlook Inspector windows. An Outlook Inspector window can have multiple pages associated with it, and Ribbon buttons are used to switch between the pages associated with a particular Inspector window. Consider the Inspector window that appears when you double-click an Outlook task, as shown in Figure 16-5.

Figure 16-5 has two Ribbon buttons in the Show group: Task and Details. In Figure 16-5 the Task button is selected and the Task page is displayed. The Task page is the default page for the Task Inspector window and is displayed first whenever a task is opened. If you click the Details button, the view changes to the Details page, as shown in Figure 16-6.

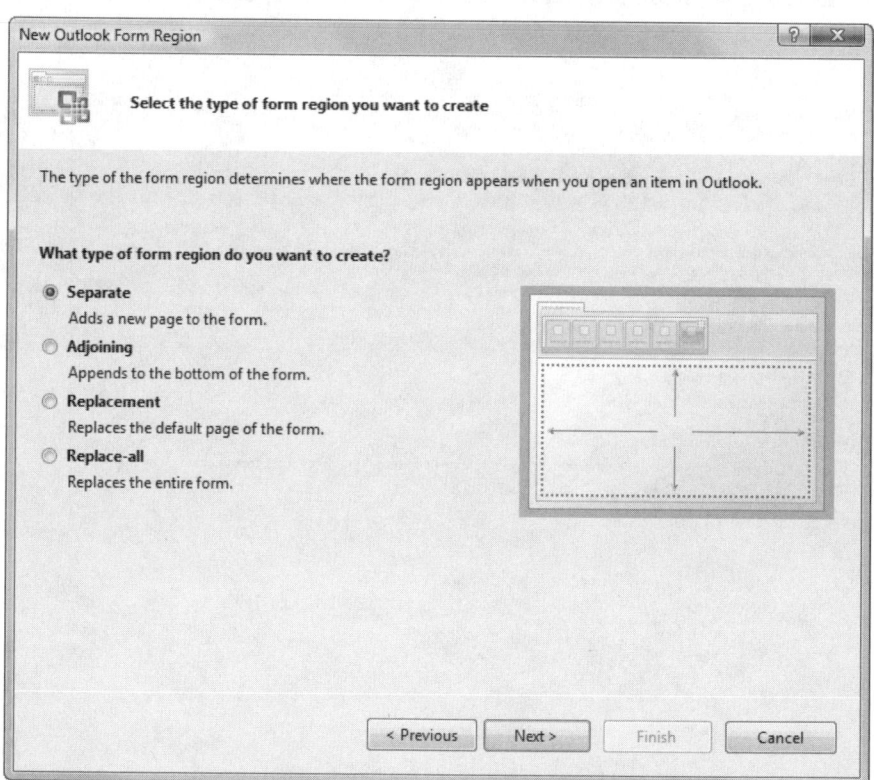

Figure 16-4: Selecting the type of form region to create: Separate.

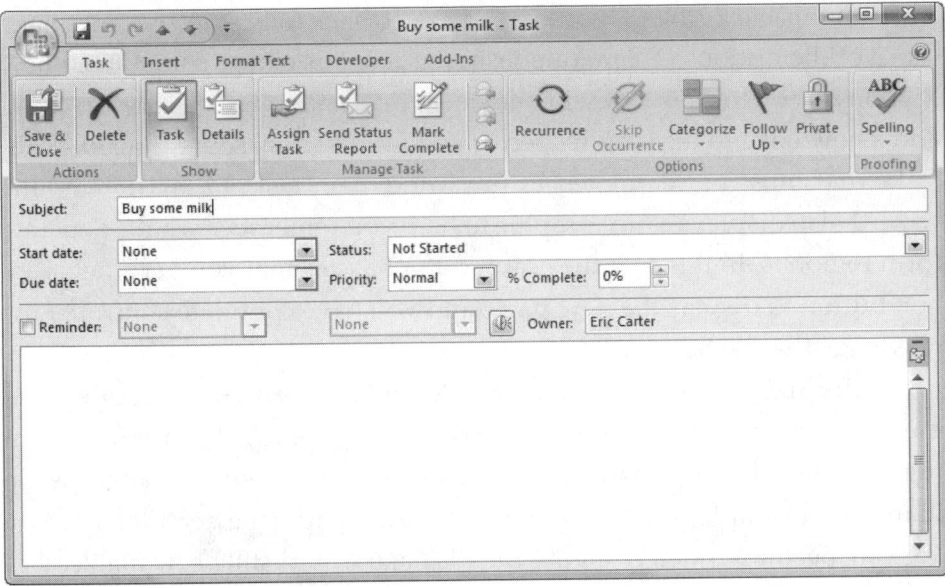

Figure 16-5: A task Inspector window with the Task page selected.

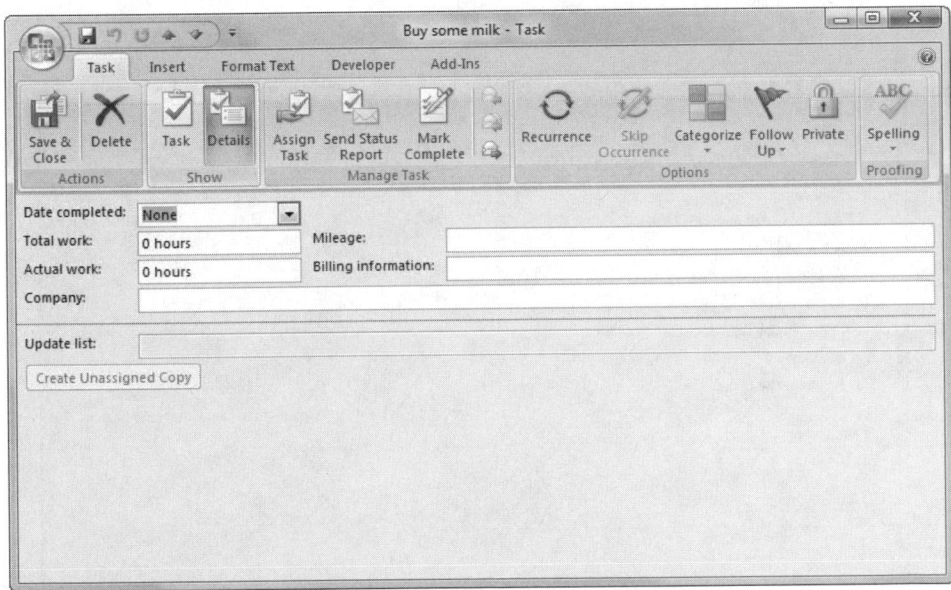

Figure 16-6: A Task Inspector window with the Details page selected.

With this background, you're ready to go back to Figure 16-4 and make sense of the options. A Separate form region adds a new page (and a new Ribbon button to activate that page) to an Inspector window. So you could add a new page to the Task Inspector window to show something like sub-tasks that must be completed to finish the main task. In Figure 16-4 the wizard also displays a nice graphic to help you remember what a Separate form region is. In this case the graphic emphasizes that you get a new Ribbon button to display the new page, and you have complete control of the new page that is shown.

Figure 16-7 shows what the wizard displays when you select Replacement instead of Separate as the type of form region. A Replacement form region allows you to replace the default page of the Inspector window. So in the task example, you could replace the Task page (the default page for a Task Inspector window), but the Details page would still be available.

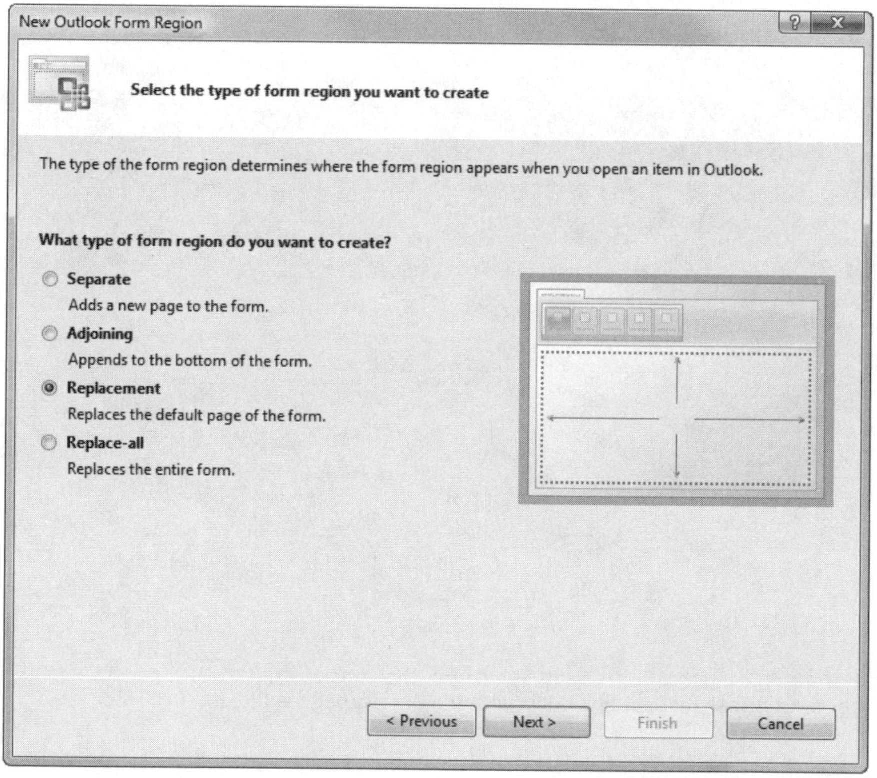

Figure 16-7: Selecting the type of form region to create: Replacement.

Figure 16-8 shows what the wizard displays when you select Replace-All as the type of form region. A Replace-All form region allows you to replace all available pages and make your page available only in the Inspector window. So in the task example, you could replace both the Task page and the Details page; your page would be the only page displayed in the Inspector window.

When you think about Replacement and Replace-All form region types, you realize that replacing the default pages for an Outlook item type is a pretty powerful capability—actually too powerful, in a way, because you could change the default page for an Outlook item type, such as a task, and implement a new default page that prevents the user from editing key data associated with that task. You may forget to provide a way to set the priority of a task in your Replacement or Replace-All form region, for example. Indeed, the creators of Outlook didn't want to give you quite that much power, enough to possibly break key functionality of Outlook.

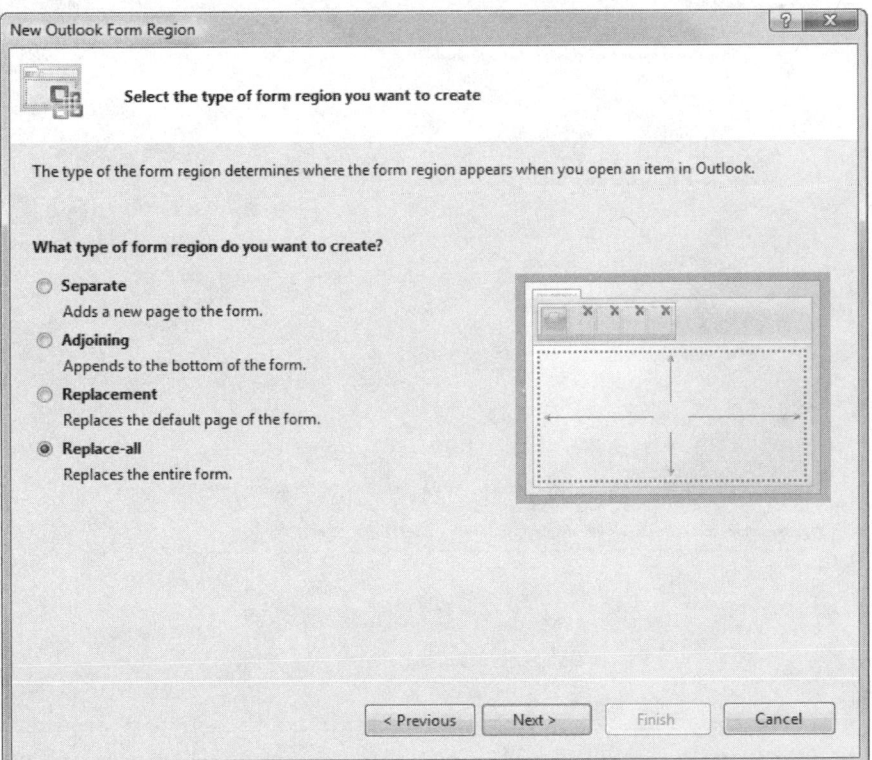

Figure 16-8: Selecting the type of form region to create: Replace-All.

To jump ahead a little, select Replacement or Replace-All as the form region type and then skip two steps ahead in the wizard by clicking the Next button twice. You see the wizard page shown in Figure 16-9, where you determine which Outlook message classes you want this form region to be associated with. When you select Replacement or Replace-All, notice that all the standard message classes (Appointment, Contact, Task, and so on) are grayed out in this dialog box. Outlook won't let you replace the default page or replace all the pages for standard message classes because you may break key features of Outlook. To use Replacement and Replace-All form region types, you must define a custom message class. A custom message class can reuse all the existing functionality of a built-in message class such as Appointment, Contact, or Task and acts as a specialized version of those built-in Outlook item objects. We discuss working with custom message

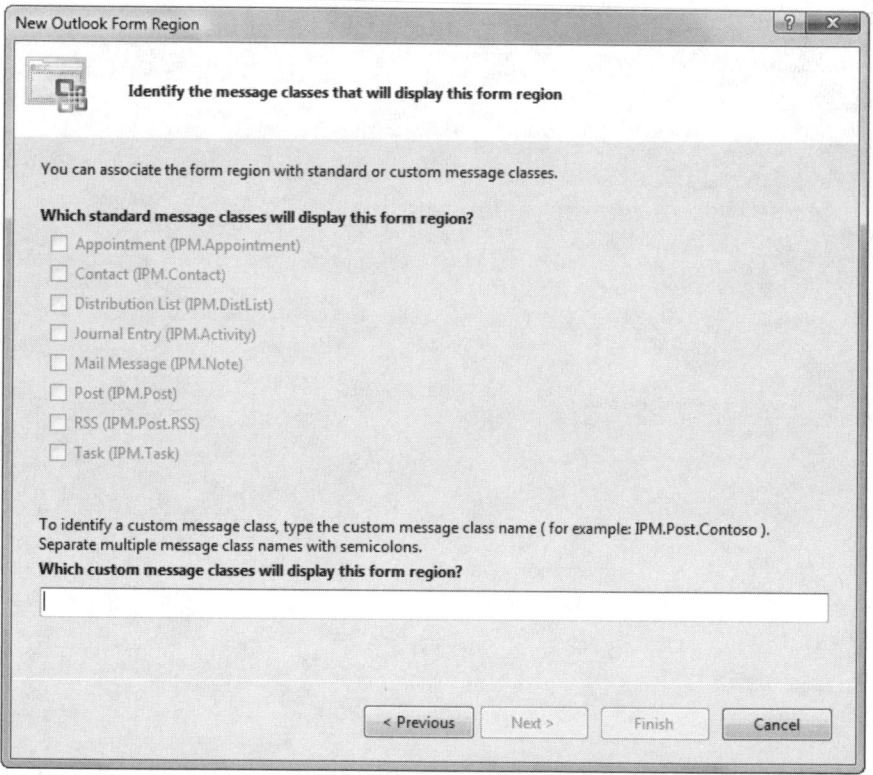

Figure 16-9: Replacement and Replace-All form regions can be associated only with custom message classes.

classes in more detail later in this chapter, in the section "Form Region Types and Custom Message Classes," because you must understand that concept to use Replacement and Replace-All form region types.

Moving back to the page in the wizard where you pick the form region type, consider the final form region type: Adjoining, shown in Figure 16-10. An Adjoining form region is appended to the bottom of the default page for an Inspector. Multiple adjoining form regions can be associated with the same message class, so potentially you can have several Adjoining form regions displayed in one Inspector window's default page. Adjoining form regions have headers that allow them to be collapsed and expanded to make more room in the default page when needed.

Another interesting application of an Adjoining form region is in an Explorer window. Specifically, an Adjoining form region can be used in the reading pane that is displayed in an Explorer window. In much the

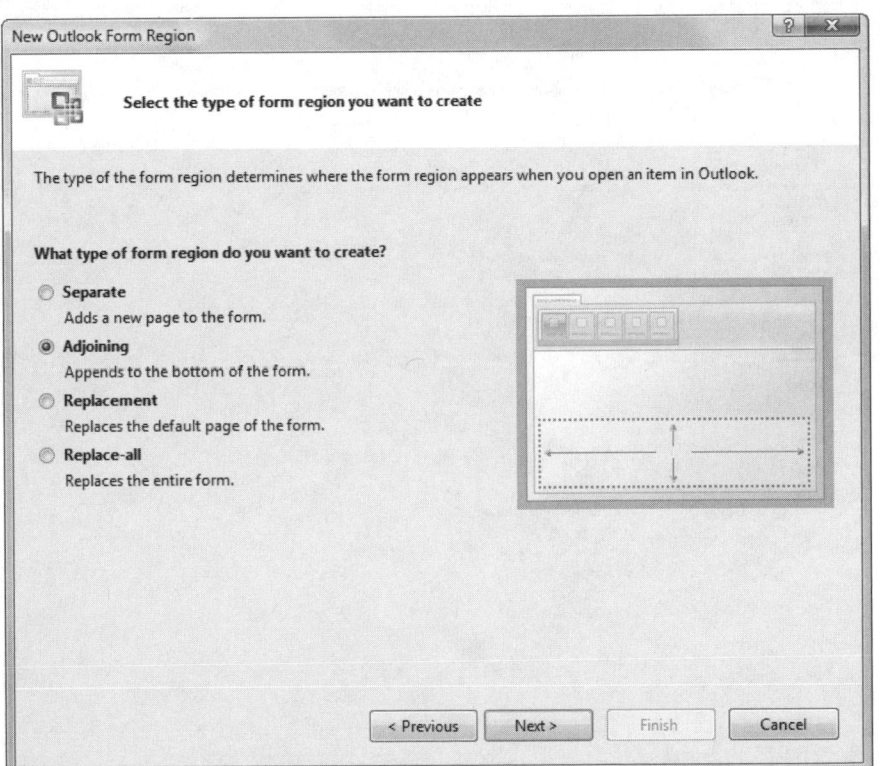

Figure 16-10: Selecting the type of form region to create: Adjoining.

same way that they are used in the default page of an Inspector window, multiple Adjoining form regions can be associated with an Outlook message class and can be displayed in the reading pane. Form regions displayed in the reading pane can also be collapsed to their headers. Replacement and Replace-All form regions can be used in the reading pane as well, although in this case they replace what is shown in the reading page and can be used only for custom message classes.

Now that you're familiar with all the form region types, select Adjoining as the form region type and click the Next button to move to the next page of the wizard, shown in Figure 16-11. In this dialog box, you set the name for the form region that will be displayed in the UI, so pick a friendly name. Title and Description are grayed out because you're creating an Adjoining form region; those options are enabled only for Replacement and Replace-All form region types.

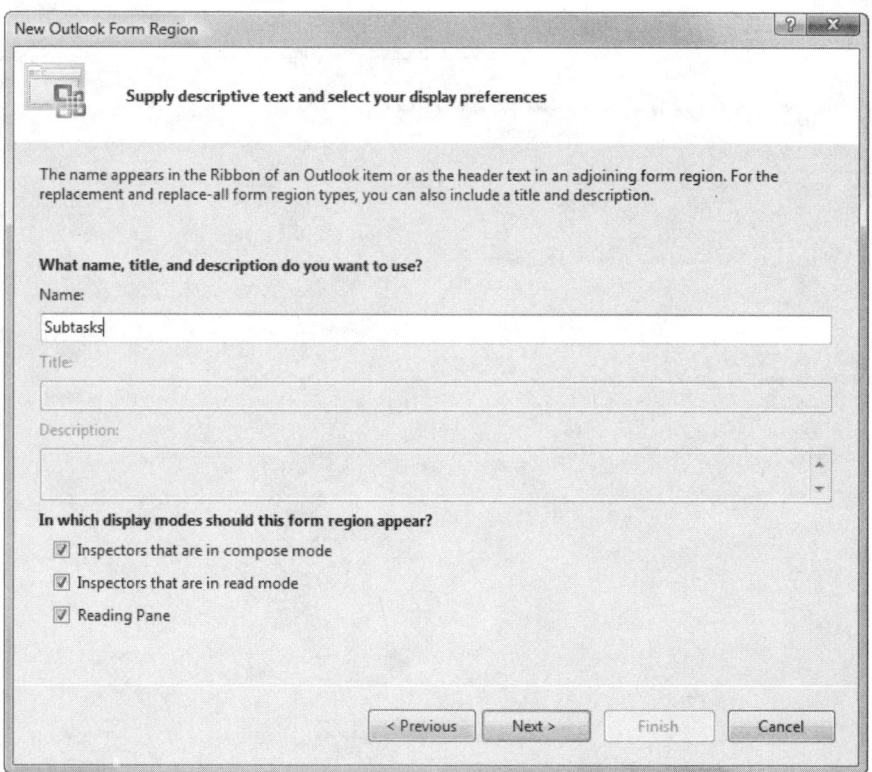

Figure 16-11: Setting descriptive text and display preferences.

This page of the wizard also has three check boxes that specify when the form region is displayed. The first check box sets whether the form region is displayed for an Inspector window that is in compose mode. An Inspector window is in compose mode when you create a new instance of the Outlook item associated with it—when you create a new task, for example. The second check box sets whether the form region is displayed for an Inspector window that is in read mode. An Inspector window is in read mode when you open an existing item—a mail message, for example. Finally, the third check box sets whether to display the form region in reading-pane view.

For this example, keep all the boxes checked and click the Next button to pick which Outlook message classes to associate the form region with, as shown in Figure 16-12. For this example, select Task. Note that you can associate the same form region with multiple built-in Outlook message

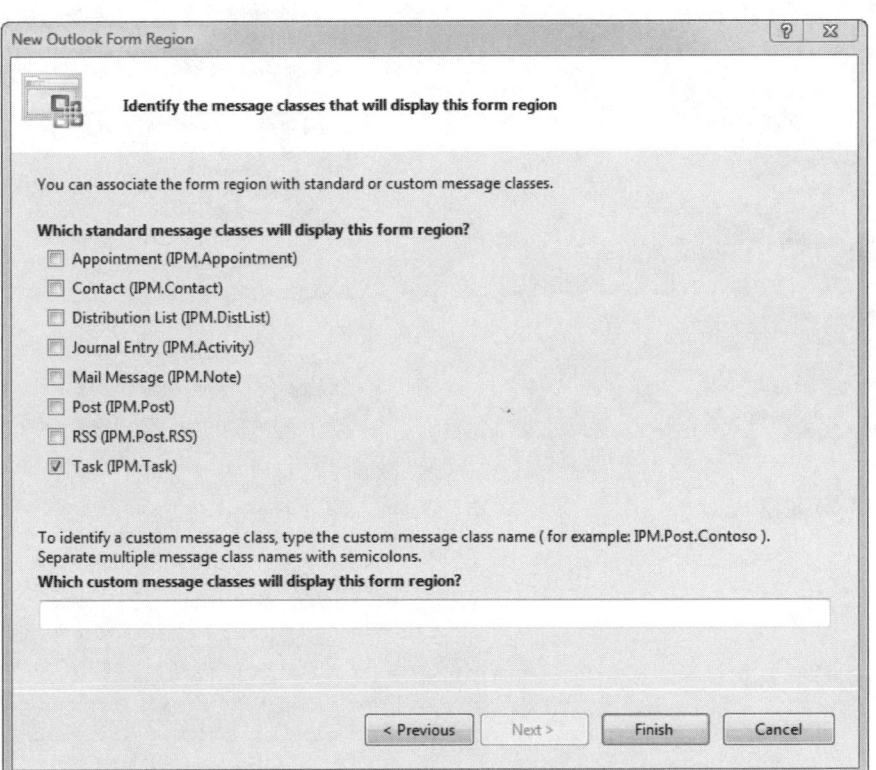

Figure 16-12: Picking which message classes will display a form region.

classes. You could have a form region that displays for both Tasks and Mail messages, for example. You can also associate a form region with custom message classes, which we discuss later in this chapter. As we describe earlier in this section, Replacement and Replace-All form region types can be associated only with custom message classes.

Associate the form region with the built-in Task type, and click the Finish button to exit the wizard. Visual Studio creates a new project item called FormRegion1.cs, as shown in Figure 16-13. It displays a visual designer in which you can drag and drop Windows Forms controls from the toolbox to construct the form region. This visual designer is much like the one you use to design user controls and task panes.

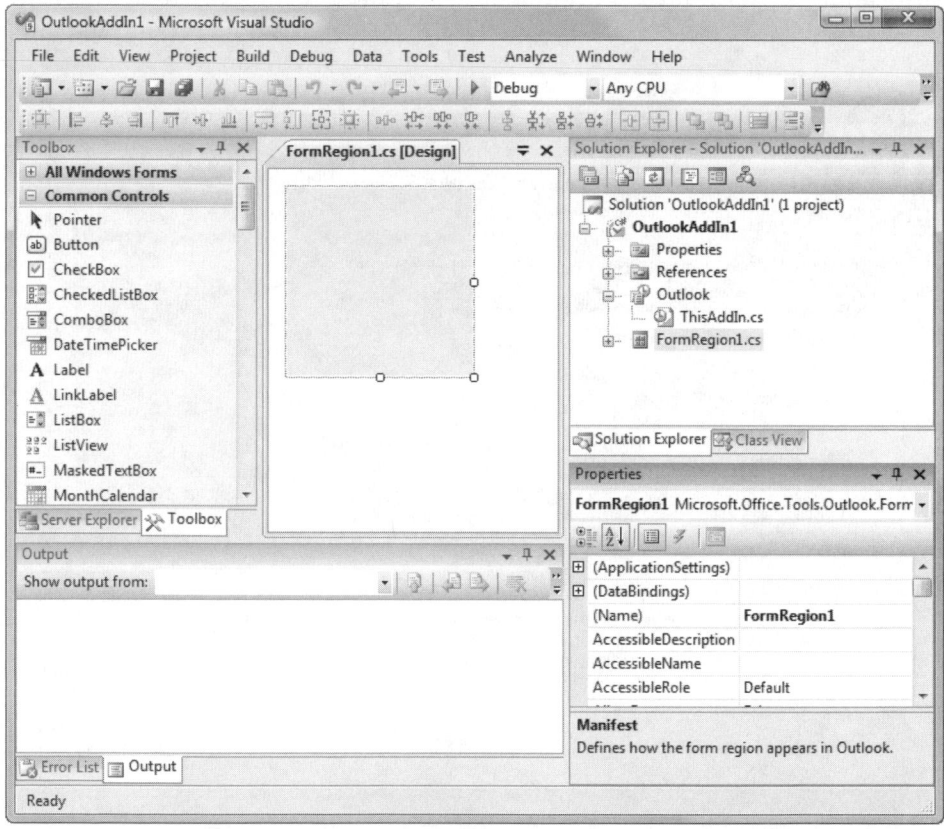

Figure 16-13: The newly created form region project item in visual design view.

Customizing a Form Region

Your goal is to add a form region in which subtasks can be associated with a task. First, drag and drop a list box control and a button to create a new task and delete an existing task. Because the user can resize the form region, use the Anchor property of the controls to anchor the list box to the top, left, bottom, and right, and anchor the buttons to the bottom and left. Figure 16-14 shows the final form region.

Before you go any further, run the add-in project and see what happens. Press F5 to build and run Outlook with the add-in project loaded. If you click a task in a task list and show reading view (by choosing View > Reading Pane > Bottom), you see that the adjoining form region is displayed docked at the bottom of reading-pane view for a task, as shown in Figure 16-15. If you double-click a task, the Adjoining form region is docked at the bottom of the default page for the Inspector window, as shown in Figure 16-16. After you've run your project, if you want to remove the form region and add-in from Outlook, choose Build > Clean.

Let's examine the adjoining form region a little more. First, notice that the Name you specified in Figure 16-11 is displayed as the caption above the Adjoining form region. To the left of the form region caption is a -/+ button that expands and collapses the form region. In Figure 16-17 you see what an Adjoining form region looks like when it is collapsed. Remember that several Adjoining form regions could be displayed in one Inspector window or reading pane; the ability to expand and collapse them is important, because it allows the end user to manage screen real estate.

Also, notice that when you resize the reading pane or the Inspector window, the form region has a default height. When the user adjusts the

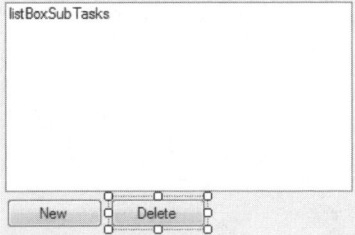

Figure 16-14: A simple form region.

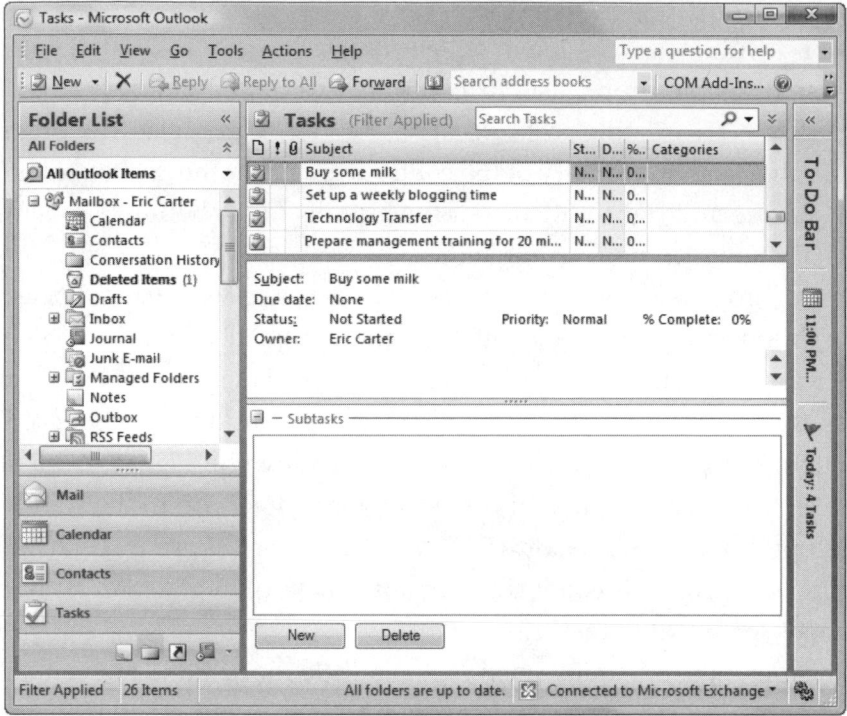

Figure 16-15: An Adjoining form region in the reading pane.

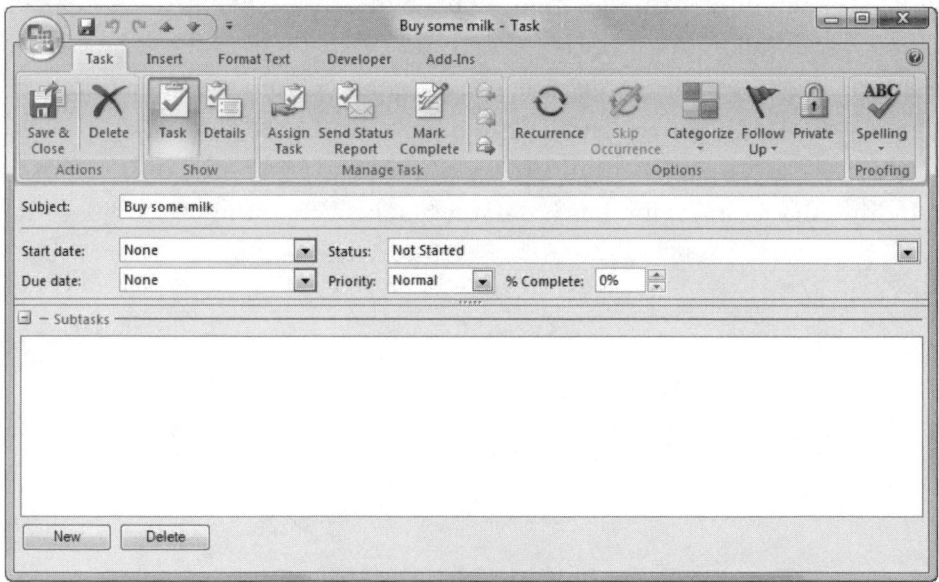

Figure 16-16: An Adjoining form region in the default page of an Inspector window.

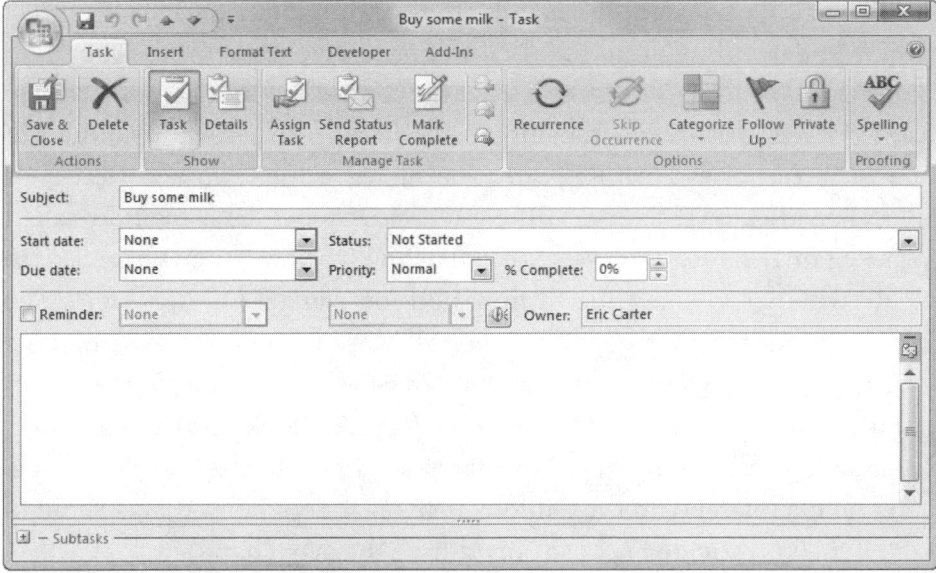

Figure 16-17: A collapsed Adjoining form region.

size of the form region, Outlook remembers the height and uses that height the next time the reading view is displayed. If you size the window small enough that the default height of the form region can't be displayed, a vertical scroll bar appears, as shown in Figure 16-18. This minimum height represents the height you set when you designed the form region. To have a smaller or larger minimum height, simply adjust the height of the visual design surface for the form region inside Visual Studio.

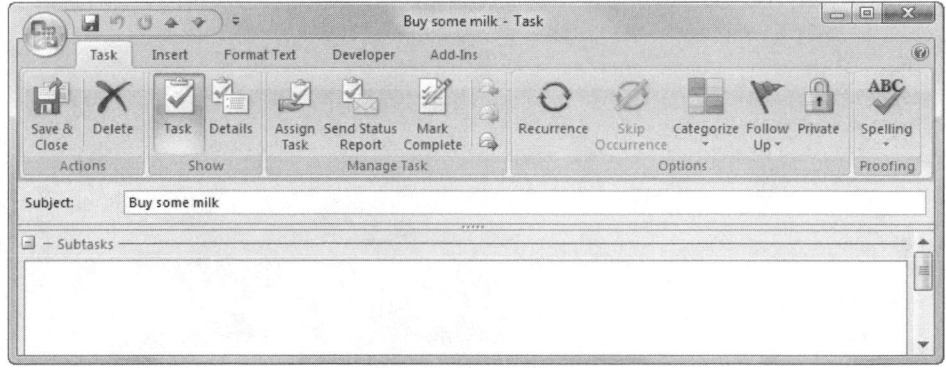

Figure 16-18: The effect of default height on the form region's vertical scroll bar.

Now exit Outlook and go back to the add-in project to put some code behind the form region. Right-click FormRegion1.cs in the Solution Explorer, and choose View Code from the context menu. The default code for a form region is shown in Listing 16-1. There are three event handlers of interest in our class FormRegion1. The first is actually in a nested class called FormRegion1Factory. This nested class provides a method called FormRegion1Factory_FormRegionInitializing where you can write code to decide whether to show the form region for a given Outlook item. The FormRegionInitializing event handler is passed a parameter e of type FormRegionInitializingEventArgs that can be used to get the Outlook item that the form region is about to be shown for (e.OutlookItem) and to cancel the showing of the form region if necessary by setting e.Cancel to true. Don't hold a reference to the Outlook item (e.OutlookItem) that is about to be shown; it is provided for use only during the event handler.

The form region class itself (FormRegion1) has a FormRegionShowing event handler that is invoked before the form region is displayed (but too late to prevent the display of the form region altogether; that is what Form-RegionInitializing is for). In the FormRegionShowing event handler, you can write code to initialize your form region. In this event handler, you can use the property this.OutlookItem to access the Outlook item associated with the form region.

When the form region is closed, the FormRegionClosed event handler is invoked. This event handler is a good place to save any changes made to the Outlook item by your form region and to do any final cleanup.

Listing 16-1: The Default Code in a New Windows Forms-Based Form Region

```
using System;
using System.Collections.Generic;
using System.Linq;
using System.Text;
using Office = Microsoft.Office.Core;
using Outlook = Microsoft.Office.Interop.Outlook;

namespace OutlookAddIn1
{
  partial class FormRegion1
  {
    #region Form Region Factory
    [Microsoft.Office.Tools.Outlook.
```

```
    FormRegionMessageClass(Microsoft.Office.Tools.Outlook.
    FormRegionMessageClassAttribute.Task)]
[Microsoft.Office.Tools.Outlook.
    FormRegionName("OutlookAddIn1.FormRegion1")]
public partial class FormRegion1Factory
{
    // Occurs before the form region is initialized.
    // To prevent the form region from appearing, set e.Cancel
    // to true. Use e.OutlookItem to get a reference to the
    // current Outlook item.
    private void FormRegion1Factory_FormRegionInitializing(
        object sender, Microsoft.Office.Tools.Outlook.
        FormRegionInitializingEventArgs e)
    {
    }
}
#endregion

// Occurs before the form region is displayed.
// Use this.OutlookItem to get a reference to the current
// Outlook item. Use this.OutlookFormRegion to get a reference
// to the form region.
private void FormRegion1_FormRegionShowing(object sender,
    System.EventArgs e)
{
}

// Occurs when the form region is closed.
// Use this.OutlookItem to get a reference to the current
// Outlook item. Use this.OutlookFormRegion to get a reference
// to the form region.
private void FormRegion1_FormRegionClosed(object sender,
    System.EventArgs e)
{
}
    }
}
```

Listing 16-2 shows a simple implementation for the subtasks form region. You don't need to write any code in FormRegionInitializing because you always want to display your form region. In FormRegionShowing, write some code to get a custom UserProperty object from the Outlook item with which the form region is associated. The custom UserProperty we will associate with the Outlook item will have the identifier "SubTasks" You'll use this custom UserProperty to store the subtasks that are edited by the form region. If the UserProperty isn't associated with the Outlook item yet, create the UserProperty for the Outlook item in FormRegionInitializing. The "SubTasks" user property contains a string value that contains subtasks delimited by a new line. You parse any subtasks that are in the string and populate the list box for the form region with the subtasks.

In FormRegionClosed, you do the reverse: Grab all the entries out of the list box and concatenate them into a string in which subtasks are separated by new lines. If the subtasks have been changed, set the "SubTasks" UserProperty's value to the new string and save the associated Outlook item.

Finally, a simple implementation for the Add button just adds the current time as a new subtask; a complete implementation would include a dialog box with an edit box in which the user could type a subtask description. The Delete button deletes the selected list item.

Listing 16-2: Form Region Code for a Simple Subtasks Form Region Based on Windows Forms

```
using System;
using System.Collections.Generic;
using System.Linq;
using System.Text;
using Office = Microsoft.Office.Core;
using Outlook = Microsoft.Office.Interop.Outlook;

namespace OutlookAddIn1
{
  partial class FormRegion1
  {
    Outlook.TaskItem task;
    Outlook.UserProperty subtasks;

    #region Form Region Factory
    [Microsoft.Office.Tools.Outlook.
      FormRegionMessageClass(Microsoft.Office.Tools.Outlook.
      FormRegionMessageClassAttribute.Task)]
    [Microsoft.Office.Tools.Outlook.
      FormRegionName("OutlookAddIn1.FormRegion1")]
    public partial class FormRegion1Factory
    {
      // Occurs before the form region is initialized.
      // To prevent the form region from appearing, set e.Cancel
      // to true. Use e.OutlookItem to get a reference to the
      // current Outlook item.
```

```
    private void FormRegion1Factory_FormRegionInitializing(
      object sender, Microsoft.Office.Tools.Outlook.
      FormRegionInitializingEventArgs e)
  {
  }
}
#endregion

// Occurs before the form region is displayed.
// Use this.OutlookItem to get a reference to the current
// Outlook item. Use this.OutlookFormRegion to get a reference
// to the form region.
private void FormRegion1_FormRegionShowing(object sender,
  System.EventArgs e)
{
  task = this.OutlookItem as Outlook.TaskItem;
  if (task != null)
  {
    // Check for custom property SubTasks
    subTasks = task.UserProperties.Find("SubTasks", true);
    if (subTasks == null)
    {
      subTasks = task.UserProperties.Add("SubTasks",
        Outlook.OlUserPropertyType.olText, false,
        Outlook.OlUserPropertyType.olText);
    }
  }

  // Convert string
  string subTasksString = subTasks.Value.ToString();
  if (!String.IsNullOrEmpty(subTasksString))
  {
    string[] delimiters = new string[1];
    delimiters[0] = System.Environment.NewLine;
    string[] tasks = subTasksString.Split(delimiters,
      StringSplitOptions.RemoveEmptyEntries);
    for (int i = 0; i < tasks.Length; i++)
    {
      listBoxSubTasks.Items.Add(tasks[i]);
    }
  }
}

// Occurs when the form region is closed.
// Use this.OutlookItem to get a reference to the current
// Outlook item. Use this.OutlookFormRegion to get a reference
// to the form region.
private void FormRegion1_FormRegionClosed(object sender,
  System.EventArgs e)
```

```csharp
    {
      if (subTasks == null || task == null)
        return;

      string oldTasks = subTasks.Value.ToString();
      StringBuilder builder = new StringBuilder();

      foreach (object o in listBoxSubTasks.Items)
      {
        string t = o as string;
        if (!String.IsNullOrEmpty(t))
        {
          builder.AppendLine(t);
        }
      }

      string newTasks = builder.ToString();

      if (!String.IsNullOrEmpty(newTasks) &&
        !String.IsNullOrEmpty(oldTasks))
      {
        if (newTasks.CompareTo(oldTasks) == 0)
          return; // no changes
      }

      subTasks.Value = newTasks;
      task.Save();
    }

    private void buttonNew_Click(object sender, EventArgs e)
    {
      // Just add current time as a subtask for simplicity
      listBoxSubTasks.Items.Add(
        System.DateTime.Now.ToShortTimeString());
    }

    private void buttonDelete_Click(object sender, EventArgs e)
    {
      if (listBoxSubTasks.SelectedItem != null)
      {
        listBoxSubTasks.Items.RemoveAt(
          listBoxSubTasks.SelectedIndex);
      }
    }
  }
}
```

When you run the form region, it displays as before, but now the Add and Delete buttons work, and you can add subtasks (set to the current time) to the current task.

Form Region Types and Custom Message Classes

Table 16-1 summarizes the behaviors and capabilities of the four types of form regions we introduced in the preceding sections. Figure 16-19 shows what the subtasks form region you created in the introduction looks like when it is changed to a Separate form region type. To make this change in Visual Studio, simply click the form region surface in the visual designer and change the FormRegionType property in the property grid. (This property can be a bit hard to find initially; it is a child property of the expandable Manifest property in the property grid.) Now when you open the Task Inspector, an additional Ribbon button appears in the Show group with the name of the separate form region—in this example, Subtasks. Subtasks is not the default page (Task is the default page), but when you click the Subtasks button, the form region page is displayed.

TABLE 16-1: Behavioral Capabilities of the Four Form Region Types

	Separate	Adjoining	Replacement	Replace-All
Inspector window behavior	Adds a new page	Appends to the bottom of the default page	Replaces the default page	Replaces all pages
Reading pane behavior	N/A	Appends to the bottom of the reading pane	Replaces the reading pane	Replaces the reading pane
Can customize standard built-in message classes	Yes	Yes	No—custom message classes only	No—custom message classes only

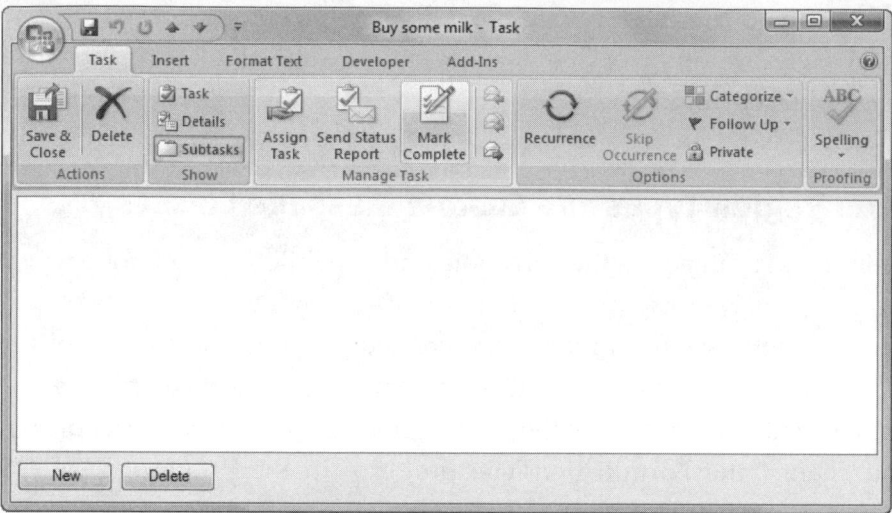

Figure 16-19: A Separate form region version of the Subtasks form region.

Built-In and Custom Message Classes

To convert the example form region to a Replacement or Replace-All form region type, you need to learn a little bit more about built-in and custom message classes. The type of all Outlook items is identified by a string value called a message class. Table 16-2 lists the message classes associated with some of the major Outlook item types.

You can define your own custom message class by defining your own message class string. The message class string must begin with a built-in message class string from Table 16-2 to ensure that you inherit the behavior associated with a built-in message class; Outlook does not support having a "baseless" message class that doesn't inherit behavior from a built-in Outlook type. Then you append your own unique identifier to the message class string to create a unique message class string. If you want to create a custom message class based on Outlook's built-in contact type that extends the contact with some information about the Facebook user ID associated with that contact, for example, your message class string might be "IPM.Contact.FacebookAware". The important thing is that your custom message class string start with a built-in message class identifier ("IPM.Contact", for example) and have some additional identifier that

TABLE 16-2: Built-In Outlook Message Classes

Outlook Item Type	Message Class String
Appointment	IPM.Appointment
Contact	IPM.Contact
Distribution List	IPM.DistList
Journal Entry	IPM.Activity
Mail Message	IPM.Note
Post	IPM.Post
RSS Post	IPM.Post.RSS
Sharing Invitation	IPM.Sharing
Task	IPM.Task

won't be picked by another add-in developer. So you might make it more unique by embedding your company name, as in "IPM.Contact.FacebookAwareAddisonWesley".

You can use these unique `string` custom message classes to create Outlook items with the Items.Add method on an Outlook Folder object. You can modify the code of the add-in you created in the introduction to edit the ThisAddIn_Startup method so that it creates an Outlook item with a custom message class based on Task, to be called "IPM.Task.MySubTaskAwareTask". Listing 16-3 shows the new ThisAddIn.cs code file.

Listing 16-3: An Outlook Add-In That Creates a New Outlook Item with a Custom Message Class Based on Task

```
using System;
using System.Collections.Generic;
using System.Linq;
using System.Text;
using System.Xml.Linq;
using Outlook = Microsoft.Office.Interop.Outlook;
using Office = Microsoft.Office.Core;
```

```
namespace OutlookAddIn1
{
  public partial class ThisAddIn
  {
    private void ThisAddIn_Startup(object sender,
      System.EventArgs e)
    {
      Outlook.Folder taskList =
        Application.Session.GetDefaultFolder(
        Outlook.OlDefaultFolders.olFolderTasks)
        as Outlook.Folder;

      Outlook.TaskItem taskItem = taskList.Items.Add(
        "IPM.Task.MySubTaskAwareTask") as Outlook.TaskItem;

      taskItem.Subject = "IPM.Task.MySubTaskAwareTask Created On "+
        System.DateTime.Now.ToLongDateString();

      taskItem.Save();
    }

    #region VSTO generated code
    private void InternalStartup()
    {
      this.Startup += new System.EventHandler(ThisAddIn_Startup);
    }
    #endregion
  }
}
```

Now that the Add-in creates a new task with a custom message class on startup, you can modify the form region to be a Replacement form region type. To do this, double-click FormRegion1.cs in the Solution Explorer to activate the form region designer. In the Properties window, pick FormRegion1 in the list of controls. Expand the Manifest section of the Properties window, and set the FormRegionType to Replacement.

Now you need to change the FormRegion1Factory so that it associates the form region with the custom message class "IPM.Task.MySubTask-AwareTask" rather than with the built-in message class for a task, "IPM.Task". To do this, you need to edit an attribute of the FormRegion-1Factory class. Looking at the FormRegion1Factory class, you see two custom attributes: FormRegionMessageClass and FormRegionName. Form-RegionMessageClass tells the factory what message class to show the form region for. Because you associated the form region with a task when you created it in the form region wizard, the FormRegionMessageClass attribute is set to display for the string specified by the constant `Microsoft.Office` `.Tools.Outlook.FormRegionMessageClassAttribute.Task`. This string is a constant string that is set to "IPM.Task". The FormRegionName attribute is set to the fully qualified name of the form region class—in this case, "OutlookAddIn1.FormRegion1". Both custom attributes are shown here:

```
#region Form Region Factory
[Microsoft.Office.Tools.Outlook.FormRegionMessageClass(
  Microsoft.Office.Tools.Outlook.
  FormRegionMessageClassAttribute.Task)]
[Microsoft.Office.Tools.Outlook.FormRegionName(
  "OutlookAddIn1.FormRegion1")]
public partial class FormRegion1Factory
{
```

Change the FormRegionMessageClass attribute to take the custom message class string "IPM.Task.MySubTaskAwareTask", as follows:

```
#region Form Region Factory
[Microsoft.Office.Tools.Outlook.FormRegionMessageClass(
  "IPM.Task.MySubTaskAwareTask")]
[Microsoft.Office.Tools.Outlook.FormRegionName(
  "OutlookAddIn1.FormRegion1")]
public partial class FormRegion1Factory
{
```

Now when you run the add-in, a new task with custom message class "IPM.Task.MySubTaskAwareTask" is created in the Startup handler for the add-in. When the new task with the custom message class is opened, an Inspector window with the default page replaced is displayed, as shown in Figure 16-20. Note in the Show group on the Ribbon, the default is now the Subtasks form region. The original default page, Task, is no longer visible in the pages that can be shown for the task.

Finally, you can go back to the add-in and use the Properties window to set the FormRegionType to Replace-All. When the add-in is run and a task with the custom message class is opened, the Inspector window has all the pages removed except for your form region, as shown in Figure 16-21.

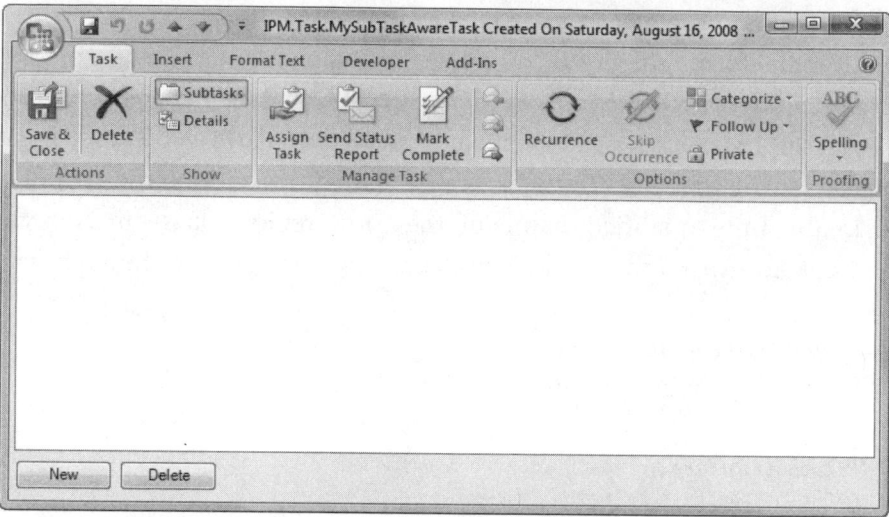

Figure 16-20: A Replacement form region version of the Subtasks form region.

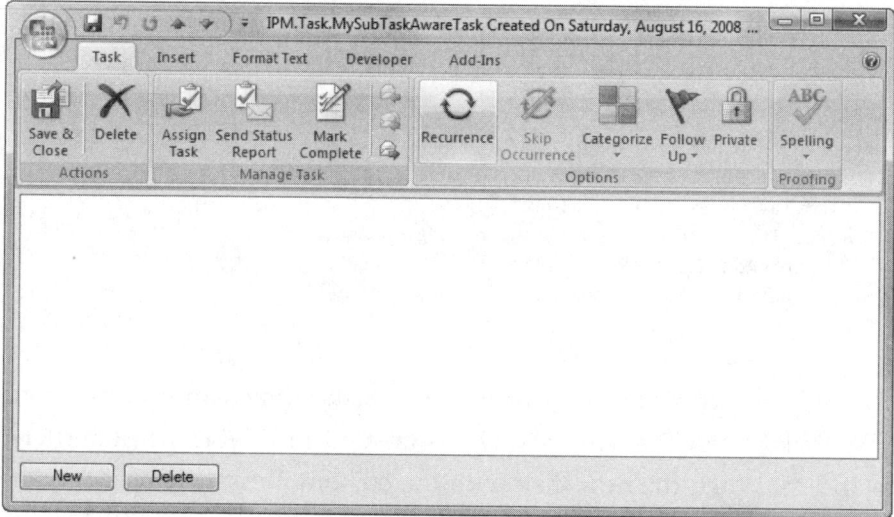

Figure 16-21: A Replace-All form region version of the Subtasks form region.

> **▪ NOTE**
>
> In Figure 16-21, the Show group on the Ribbon is no longer displayed. Because only one page is available to be displayed (your form region), there is no longer a reason to display the Show group, as no other pages can be selected.

Creating an Outlook Forms-Based Form Region

As you saw in the introduction, there are two ways to create form regions in VSTO. The first is to use the Windows Forms designers inside Visual Studio. The second is to use the Outlook Forms Designer inside Outlook. A form region designed with the Outlook Forms Designer is integrated with your .NET code through COM interop. The form region and form controls are COM objects that Visual Studio generates wrappers to communicate with.

If you use Windows Forms, you can use a forms engine that is .NET-based, which may be more familiar to you. The design-time experience for using Windows Forms is much more integrated with Visual Studio. If you use the Outlook Forms Designer, you need to design the form in Outlook and then import it into Visual Studio. If you decide that you want to change the layout or the controls on the form, you have to delete the form region in Visual Studio, go back to Outlook and redesign the form region, and then reimport it into Visual Studio via the wizard.

Although using Windows Forms is more convenient, Outlook Forms have a lot of features that Windows Forms do not. Outlook Forms, for example, have automatic data binding support to bind to properties of the Outlook items with which they are associated. Also, some Outlook Forms controls are more Outlook-like than any of the Windows Forms controls you have available to you. These controls allow you to replicate functionality available in built-in Outlook Inspector windows. Outlook Forms provide controls such as these: the Outlook Body control, which allows you to edit the item body of an Outlook item with the same editor provided for built-in Outlook editors; a Business Card control, which displays the same business-card view that is built into Outlook; and a Category control, which provides a UI for visualizing the categories with which an Outlook item is associated. So in many cases you may pick an Outlook Forms-based form region because it provides more Outlook-aware controls for you to use.

The first step in creating a form region by using Outlook Forms is launching Outlook. Next, choose Tools > Forms > Design a Form to bring up the Design Form dialog box, shown in Figure 16-22. Pick the type of built-in Outlook item type that you want to start from—for this example, Task—and then click the Open button.

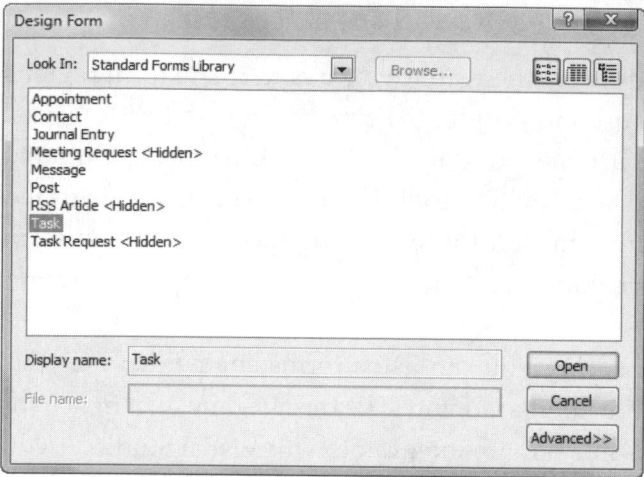

Figure 16-22: The Design Form dialog box in the Outlook Forms Designer.

Next, drop down the Design button and then the Form Region button, and choose New Form Region, as shown in Figure 16-23. (You can also use the Open Form Region command under the Form Region button if you already have a form region in an .OFS file.) A new page titled (Form Region) will appear; you can design your form region in that page.

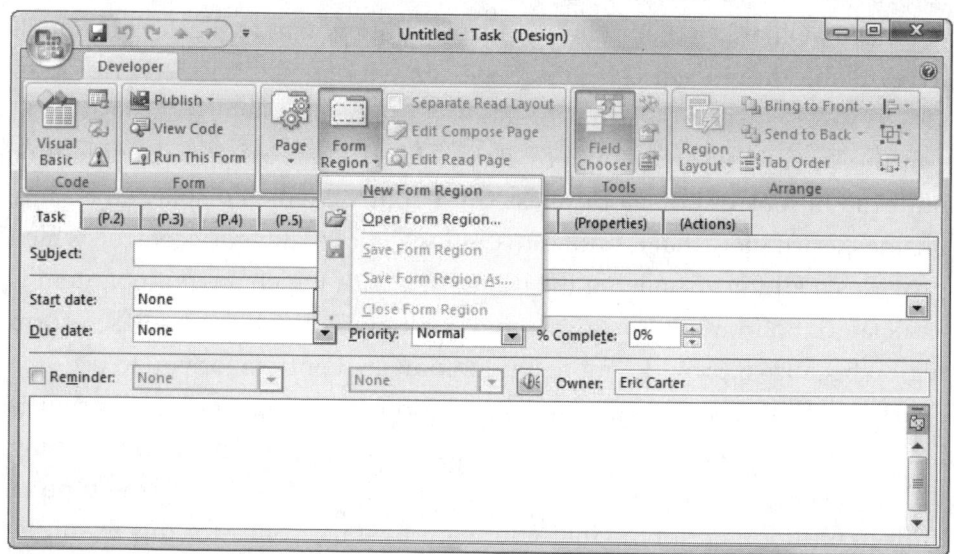

Figure 16-23: Creating a new form region in the Outlook Forms Designer.

The Tools group in the Ribbon allows you to bring up the design-time tools you will need. The Field Chooser tool lets you drag and drop fields into your form region from the Outlook item that the form region will display. These fields are automatically data bound—an advantage over Windows Forms, which require you to write additional code to bind your controls to the Outlook item associated with your form region. Also in the Tools group, the Controls Toolbox button brings up the toolbox, which displays a set of standard controls. The Advanced Properties button displays the properties window, which you can use to set properties for the selected control in the Forms Designer.

The initial set of tools in the Controls toolbox doesn't have any of the cool controls we mentioned earlier, so let's get them added to the toolbox. Right-click a blank area of the Controls toolbox, and choose Custom Controls from the context menu. The Additional Controls dialog box appears, as shown in Figure 16-24. Check all the controls in the list that start with *Microsoft Office Outlook*; then click the OK button.

Figure 16-25 shows the final design environment with all the tools visible and all the additional Outlook controls added to the Controls toolbox.

Now drag some Outlook controls to the design surface. You'll create the same form region you created in the introduction but use Outlook Forms this time. Find the OlkListBox control by hovering over the controls in the

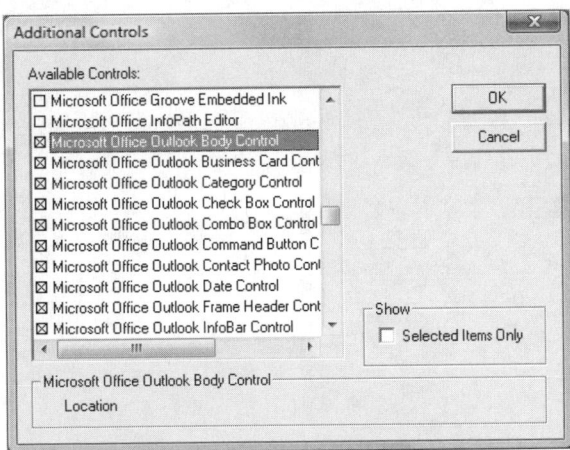

Figure 16-24: Add all the controls that start with
Microsoft Office Outlook to the Controls toolbox.

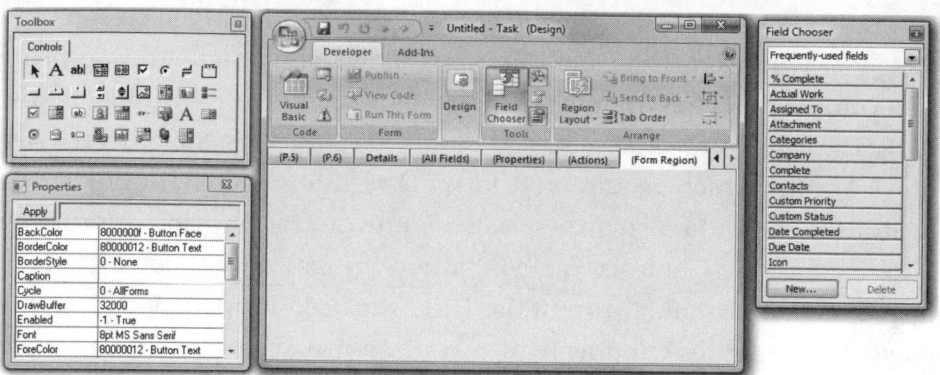

Figure 16-25: The Outlook Forms Designer with the toolbox, Properties window, and Field Chooser tool.

Controls toolbox and finding the control that shows OlkListBox in its tooltip. Drag and drop a OlkListBox, and size it to fill most of the design surface while leaving a strip at the bottom for buttons. Right-click the list-box control you added to the form, and choose Properties from the context menu to bring up the Properties dialog box, shown in Figure 16-26. Click the Layout tab, and drop down the Horizontal combo box to pick Grow/Shrink with Form. This setting allows the list box to size to fill the Inspector window.

Figure 16-26: The Properties dialog box with the Layout tab.

While the Properties dialog box is open, take some time to explore the rest of it. The Properties dialog box has a Display tab that lets you set the caption of the control, visibility, font, and color. The Layout tab lets you set size and position, as well as several useful autosizing and alignment settings. The Value tab lets you set up an automatic binding to an Outlook item property. Finally, the Validation tab lets you set up some validation rules for the control.

Next, drag two additional Outlook controls onto the design surface. Drag and drop two OlkCommandButton controls at the bottom of the Outlook Form region. The OlkCommandButton will display with a look and feel more consistent with the Outlook UI than with a CommandButton. Right-click each of the OlkCommandButton controls, and choose Properties from the context menu to display the Properties window. In the Display tab, set the caption of one button to Add and the other to Delete. Also, in the Layout tab, set the Vertical drop-down menu to Align Bottom for each of the two buttons to ensure that the buttons stay at the bottom of the form when the form is resized. The final form region should look like Figure 16-27.

With a form region designed, you need to export the form region to an Outlook form region file with a .OFS extension, which then can be imported into Visual Studio. To save the form region as an .OFS file, drop down the Design button; then drop down the Form Region button and choose Save Form Region As to bring up the Save dialog box. Save it as MyFormRegion for this example, as shown in Figure 16-28.

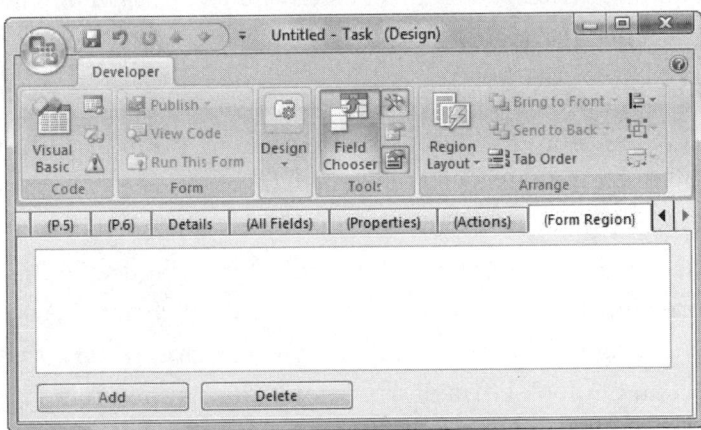

Figure 16-27: A form region designed in the Outlook Form Designer.

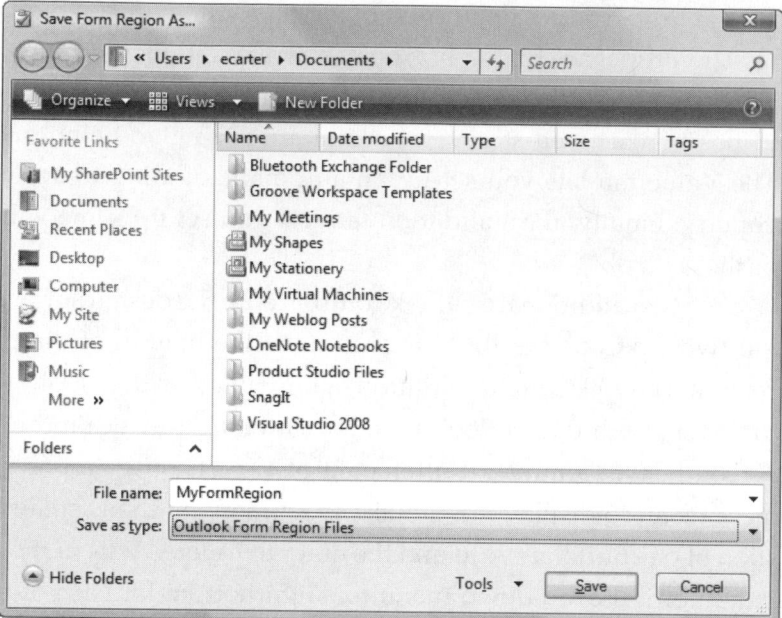

Figure 16-28: Saving the form region to an Outlook form region file (.OFS file).

TIP

At this point, we recommend that you exit Outlook before moving back to Visual Studio. The process of importing a .OFS file from Visual Studio involves Visual Studio starting up Outlook and talking to it to process the OFS file, and we've found that this process works best if you don't already have Outlook already open.

Start Visual Studio, and either create a new Outlook add-in project or open an existing Outlook add-in project. Choose Project > Add New Item. Click the Office category to show just the Office-specific items. In the list of Office items, click Outlook Form Region (refer to Figure 16-2). Name the form region—for this exercise, FormRegion2. Then click the Add button.

In the first page of the New Outlook Form Region wizard that appears, pick Import an Outlook Form Storage (.ofs) File, as shown in Figure 16-29. Click the Browse button, and locate the .OFS file that you saved earlier.

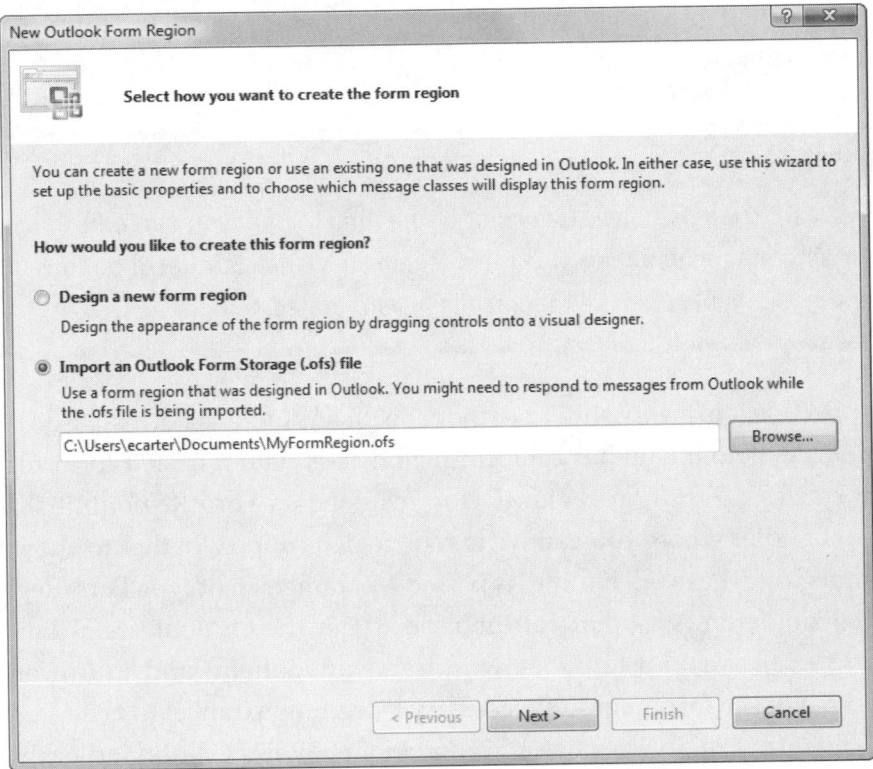

Figure 16-29: Importing an .OFS file in the New Outlook Form Region wizard.

With a .OFS file selected, click the Next button to move to the page where you set the type of the form region. For this example, select Separate as the Form Region type. Then click the Next button. On the next page, set the name you want to use for the form region—for this exercise, Subtasks—and make sure that the check boxes for Inspectors that are in compose mode and Inspectors that are in read mode are checked. Click the Next button to move to the final page. On this page, make sure that only the check box next to Task is checked; then click the Finish button. Visual Studio creates a new project item for the form region.

No visual designer is displayed within Visual Studio—just generated code. As we mention earlier in this chapter, if you want to change the form region, you have to delete the form region code item from your Visual Studio project, go back to Outlook and reopen the .ofs file, modify your form region, save it an .ofs file, exit Outlook, and then re-create the form region in Visual Studio.

> **■ TIP**
>
> If you are changing only the layout of the form region, you can edit the .ofs file without regenerating the form region in Visual Studio; just copy the modified .ofs file over the old .ofs file in your project folder.

The code looks very similar to the code for a Windows Forms-based form region. As before, you have a form region class with a nested form region factory class. The form region factory class has a FormRegionInitializing event handler where you can write code to determine whether to show the form region. The event handler is passed a parameter e of type FormRegion-InitializingEventArgs that can be used to get the Outlook item that the form region is about to be shown for (e.OutlookItem) and to cancel the showing of the form region if necessary by setting e.Cancel to true.

The form region class has a FormRegionShowing event handler that is invoked before the form region is displayed (but too late to prevent the display of the form region altogether). In this event handler, you can write code to initialize the form region and use this.OutlookItem to access the Outlook item associated with the form region.

When the form region is closed, the FormRegionClosed event handler is invoked. This event handler is a good place to save any changes made to the Outlook item by your form region and do any final cleanup.

There are also some major differences between a Windows Forms-based form region and an Outlook Forms-based form region. Because there is no design view, no property grid like the one in Windows Forms allows you to interact with key settings—especially the Manifest settings that are editable in a Windows Forms-based form region. To compensate for this deficiency in Outlook Forms-based form regions, VSTO adds a second method called InitializeManifest to the nested form region factory code, as shown in Listing 16-4. In this method, you can modify the code to change the Form region type or any of the other settings that you initially set in the Form Region wizard.

Listing 16-4: The Default Code in a New Outlook Forms-Based Form Region

```csharp
using System;
using System.Collections.Generic;
using System.Linq;
using System.Resources;
using System.Text;
using Office = Microsoft.Office.Core;
using Outlook = Microsoft.Office.Interop.Outlook;


namespace OutlookAddIn2
{
  public partial class FormRegion2
  {
    #region Form Region Factory

    [Microsoft.Office.Tools.Outlook.
      FormRegionMessageClass(Microsoft.Office.Tools.Outlook.
      FormRegionMessageClassAttribute.Task)]
    [Microsoft.Office.Tools.Outlook.
      FormRegionName("OutlookAddIn2.FormRegion2")]
    public partial class FormRegion2Factory
    {
      private void InitializeManifest()
      {
        ResourceManager resources =
          new ResourceManager(typeof(FormRegion2));
        this.Manifest.FormRegionType =
          Microsoft.Office.Tools.Outlook.FormRegionType.Separate;
        this.Manifest.Title = resources.GetString("Title");
        this.Manifest.FormRegionName =
          resources.GetString("FormRegionName");
        this.Manifest.Description =
          resources.GetString("Description");
        this.Manifest.ShowInspectorCompose = true;
        this.Manifest.ShowInspectorRead = true;
        this.Manifest.ShowReadingPane = false;


      }

      // Occurs before the form region is initialized.
      // To prevent the form region from appearing, set e.Cancel to
      // true. Use e.OutlookItem to get a reference to the current
      // Outlook item.
      private void FormRegion2Factory_FormRegionInitializing(
        object sender, Microsoft.Office.Tools.Outlook.
        FormRegionInitializingEventArgs e)
      {
      }
    }
```

```
#endregion

// Occurs before the form region is displayed.
// Use this.OutlookItem to get a reference to the current
// Outlook item. Use this.OutlookFormRegion to get a reference
// to the form region.
private void FormRegion2_FormRegionShowing(object sender,
  System.EventArgs e)
{
}

// Occurs when the form region is closed. Use this.OutlookItem
// to get a reference to the current Outlook item. Use
// this.OutlookFormRegion to get a reference to the form/
// region.
private void FormRegion2_FormRegionClosed(object sender,
  System.EventArgs e)
{
}
    }
}
```

Another obvious difference is that the form region class created when you import a .OFS file does not derive from System.Windows.Forms.User-Controls. It derives from a class in VSTO called Microsoft.Office.Tools .Outlook.ImportedFormRegion.

As you write your code in the form region class, you will find that VSTO has created member variables for all the controls you used in the .OFS file. For this example, you created a OlkListBox with a default name of OlkListBox1, an OlkCommandButton with a name of OlkCommand-Button1, and an OlkCommandButton with a name of OlkCommand-Button2. The import of the .OFS file converts the names used in the Outlook Form designer to camel case, so you have three controls named olk-ListBox1, olkCommandButton1, and olkCommandButton2.

These controls are of types that come from the Microsoft.Office .Interop.Outlook namespace. This namespace has types for many of the built-in Outlook controls. Some of the controls in the toolbox generate types that come from the Microsoft.Vbe.Interop.Forms namespace. Table 16-3 shows the names of the controls in Outlook's Controls toolbox and the .NET types associated with these controls.

TABLE 16-3: Mapping Between Outlook Controls and .NET Types

Name	Type
Microsoft Forms 2.0 CheckBox	Microsoft.Office.Interop.Outlook.OlkCheckBox
Microsoft Forms 2.0 ComboBox	Microsoft.Office.Interop.Outlook.OlkComboBox
Microsoft Forms 2.0 CommandButton	Microsoft.Office.Interop.Outlook.OlkCommandButton
Microsoft Forms 2.0 Frame	Microsoft.Vbe.Interop.Forms.UserForm
Microsoft Forms 2.0 Image	Microsoft.Vbe.Interop.Forms.Image
Microsoft Forms 2.0 Label	Microsoft.Office.Interop.Outlook.OlkLabel
Microsoft Forms 2.0 ListBox	Microsoft.Office.Interop.Outlook.OlkListBox
Microsoft Forms 2.0 MultiPage	Microsoft.Vbe.Interop.Forms.MultiPage
Microsoft Forms 2.0 OptionButton	Microsoft.Office.Interop.Outlook.OlkOptionButton
Microsoft Forms 2.0 ScrollBar	Microsoft.Vbe.Interop.Forms.ScrollBar
Microsoft Forms 2.0 SpinButton	Microsoft.Vbe.Interop.Forms.SpinButton
Microsoft Forms 2.0 TabStrip	Microsoft.Vbe.Interop.Forms.TabStrip
Microsoft Forms 2.0 TextBox	Microsoft.Office.Interop.Outlook.OlkTextBox
Microsoft Forms 2.0 ToggleButton	Microsoft.Vbe.Interop.Forms.ToggleButton

Continues

TABLE 16-3: Mapping Between Outlook Controls and .NET Types *(Continued)*

Name	Type
Microsoft Office Outlook Business Card Control	Microsoft.Office.Interop.Outlook.OlkBusinessCardControl
Microsoft Office Outlook Category Control	Microsoft.Office.Interop.Outlook.OlkCategory
Microsoft Office Outlook Check Box Control	Microsoft.Office.Interop.Outlook.OlkCheckBox
Microsoft Office Outlook Combo Box Control	Microsoft.Office.Interop.Outlook.OlkComboBox
Microsoft Office Outlook Command Button Control	Microsoft.Office.Interop.Outlook.OlkCommandButton
Microsoft Office Outlook Contact Photo Control	Microsoft.Office.Interop.Outlook.OlkContactPhoto
Microsoft Office Outlook Date Control	Microsoft.Office.Interop.Outlook.OlkDateControl
Microsoft Office Outlook Frame Header Control	Microsoft.Office.Interop.Outlook.OlkFrameHeader
Microsoft Office Outlook InfoBar Control	Microsoft.Office.Interop.Outlook.OlkInfoBar
Microsoft Office Outlook Label Control	Microsoft.Office.Interop.Outlook.OlkLabel

TABLE 16-3: Mapping Between Outlook Controls and .NET Types *(Continued)*

Name	Type
Microsoft Office Outlook List Box Control	Microsoft.Office.Interop.Outlook.OlkListBox
Microsoft Office Outlook Option Button Control	Microsoft.Office.Interop.Outlook.OlkOptionButton
Microsoft Office Outlook Page Control	Microsoft.Office.Interop.Outlook.OlkPageControl
Microsoft Office Outlook Recipient Control	Microsoft.Office.Interop.Outlook._DRecipientControl
Microsoft Office Outlook Sender Photo Control	Microsoft.Office.Interop.Outlook.OlkSenderPhoto
Microsoft Office Outlook Text Box Control	Microsoft.Office.Interop.Outlook.OlkTextBox
Microsoft Office Outlook Time Control	Microsoft.Office.Interop.Outlook.OlkTimeControl
Microsoft Office Outlook Time Zone Control	Microsoft.Office.Interop.Outlook.OlkTimeZoneControl
Microsoft Office Outlook View Control	Microsoft.Office.Interop.OutlookViewCtl.ViewCtl
Microsoft Office Outlook Body Control	Microsoft.Office.Interop.Outlook._DDocSiteControl

As you write code against Outlook controls, you will discover that you sometimes need to cast the primary Outlook control types listed in Table 16-3 to either of two different types: Microsoft.Office.Interop.Outlook.Olk-Control and Microsoft.Vbe.Interop.Forms.Control. When you cast to an OlkControl, you can set properties to configure Outlook-specific layout and binding options like those that are settable by the Properties dialog box in the Outlook Forms Designer. When you cast to a Control, you can set basic positioning properties that are common to all controls. Remember that before writing code to cast to a Microsoft.Vbe.Interop.Forms.Control, you must ensure that your project has a reference to the Microsoft Forms 2.0 Object Library.

Listing 16-5 is similar to Listing 16-2. The only difference is that it uses Outlook Forms controls, so some of the code for adding and removing items to the OlkListBox is different.

Listing 16-5: Form Region Code for a Simple Subtasks Form Region Based on Outlook Forms

```
using System;
using System.Collections.Generic;
using System.Linq;
using System.Resources;
using System.Text;
using Office = Microsoft.Office.Core;
using Outlook = Microsoft.Office.Interop.Outlook;

namespace OutlookAddIn2
{
  public partial class FormRegion2
  {
    Outlook.TaskItem task;
    Outlook.UserProperty subTasks;

    #region Form Region Factory

    [Microsoft.Office.Tools.Outlook.
      FormRegionMessageClass(Microsoft.Office.Tools.Outlook.
      FormRegionMessageClassAttribute.Task)]
    [Microsoft.Office.Tools.Outlook.FormRegionName(
      "OutlookAddIn2.FormRegion2")]
    public partial class FormRegion2Factory
    {
      private void InitializeManifest()
      {
        ResourceManager resources =
          new ResourceManager(typeof(FormRegion2));
```

```
      this.Manifest.FormRegionType = Microsoft.Office.
        Tools.Outlook.FormRegionType.Separate;
      this.Manifest.Title = resources.GetString("Title");
      this.Manifest.FormRegionName = resources.
        GetString("FormRegionName");
      this.Manifest.Description = resources.
        GetString("Description");
      this.Manifest.ShowInspectorCompose = true;
      this.Manifest.ShowInspectorRead = true;
      this.Manifest.ShowReadingPane = false;

    }


    // Occurs before the form region is initialized.
    // To prevent the form region from appearing, set e.Cancel to
    // true. Use e.OutlookItem to get a reference to the current
    // Outlook item.
    private void FormRegion2Factory_FormRegionInitializing(
      object sender, Microsoft.Office.Tools.Outlook.
      FormRegionInitializingEventArgs e)
    {
    }
}

#endregion

// Occurs before the form region is displayed.
// Use this.OutlookItem to get a reference to the current
// Outlook item. Use this.OutlookFormRegion to get a reference
// to the form region.
private void FormRegion2_FormRegionShowing(object sender,
  System.EventArgs e)
{
  this.olkCommandButton1.Click += new
    Microsoft.Office.Interop.Outlook.
    OlkCommandButtonEvents_ClickEventHandler(
    olkCommandButton1_Click);
  this.olkCommandButton2.Click += new
    Microsoft.Office.Interop.Outlook.
    OlkCommandButtonEvents_ClickEventHandler(
    olkCommandButton2_Click);

  task = this.OutlookItem as Outlook.TaskItem;
  if (task != null)
  {
    // Check for custom property SubTasks
    subTasks = task.UserProperties.Find("SubTasks", true);
    if (subTasks == null)
    {
```

```
        subTasks = task.UserProperties.Add("SubTasks",
          Outlook.OlUserPropertyType.olText, false,
          Outlook.OlUserPropertyType.olText);
      }
    }


    // Convert string
    string subTasksString = subTasks.Value.ToString();
    if (!String.IsNullOrEmpty(subTasksString))
    {
      string[] delimiters = new string[1];
      delimiters[0] = System.Environment.NewLine;
      string[] tasks = subTasksString.Split(delimiters,
        StringSplitOptions.RemoveEmptyEntries);
      for (int i = 0; i < tasks.Length; i++)
      {
        olkListBox1.AddItem(tasks[i], i);
      }
    }
  }
```

```
// Occurs when the form region is closed. Use this.OutlookItem
// to get a reference to the current Outlook item. Use
// this.OutlookFormRegion to get a reference to the form
// region.
private void FormRegion2_FormRegionClosed(object sender,
  System.EventArgs e)
{
  if (subTasks == null || task == null)
    return;

  string oldTasks = subTasks.Value.ToString();
  StringBuilder builder = new StringBuilder();

  for (int i = 0; i < olkListBox1.ListCount; i++)
  {
    string t = olkListBox1.GetItem(i);
    if (!String.IsNullOrEmpty(t))
    {
      builder.AppendLine(t);
    }
  }

  string newTasks = builder.ToString();

  if (!String.IsNullOrEmpty(newTasks) &&
    !String.IsNullOrEmpty(oldTasks))
  {
```

```
      if (newTasks.CompareTo(oldTasks) == 0)
        return; // no changes
    }

    subTasks.Value = newTasks;
    task.Save();
  }

  // New Button
  void olkCommandButton1_Click()
  {
    // Just add current time as a subtask for simplicity
    this.olkListBox1.AddItem(
      System.DateTime.Now.ToShortTimeString(),
      this.olkListBox1.ListCount);
  }

  // Delete button
  void olkCommandButton2_Click()
  {
    if (this.olkListBox1.ListIndex != -1)
    {
      olkListBox1.RemoveItem(olkListBox1.ListIndex);
    }
  }
 }
}
}
```

Outlook Form Region Programmability

In this section, we examine in more detail the Outlook form region classes that VSTO creates. As with many other VSTO project items, it uses partial classes to display user code (code edited by the developer of the add-in) and associate it with generated code (code generated by Visual Studio) to build the final Outlook form region class.

The VSTO Form Region Class

In the example from the first section of this chapter, right-clicking Form-Region1.cs and choosing View Code from the context menu shows the user code:

```
partial class FormRegion1
```

You can also see the generated code by expanding FormRegion1.cs and double-clicking the file FormRegion1.Designer.cs, which is a child of

FormRegion1.cs. Here, you see this line of code, showing that a VSTO form region class derives from Microsoft.Office.Tools.Outlook.FormRegion-Control:

```
partial class FormRegion1 :
   Microsoft.Office.Tools.Outlook.FormRegionControl
```

Then, if you look at the definition of FormRegionControl, you see that it derives from System.Windows.Forms.UserControl. A form region class is primarily a Windows Forms UserControl with extensions like the implementation of the IFormRegion interface, which is used by VSTO to start and shut down a form region:

```
public class FormRegionControl : UserControl, IFormRegion
```

When you import an .OFS file, the form region class derives from Microsoft.Office.Tools.Outlook.ImportedFormRegion.

The Form Region Factory

The form region factory is mostly an internal implementation detail of how VSTO supports Outlook form regions. You can do some advanced things with custom form region factories, such as having your form region classes in a separate assembly from the add-in or having a single factory to handle multiple form region classes. But outside these advanced scenarios, the form region factory does peek through in one significant way: It exposes the FormRegionInitializing method, which can be handled in your code to prevent a form region from being displayed for a particular Outlook item based on criteria you set. As you might expect, the Factory object creates an instance of your form region class every time an Outlook item requires a form region to be displayed. If you have an Adjacent form region that displays in the reading pane for a list of mail items, for example, each time the selection changes to a different mail item, a new instance of your form region class is created for the current mail item. The factory object is invoked first, and if the FormRegionInitializing method doesn't cancel the creation of the form region by the implementation of the method setting the Cancel property of the e parameter to true, a new instance of the form region class is created.

When you import an .OFS file, the form region factory also has a method called InitializeManifest in which you can write code to modify settings for the form region, such as the form region type. With Windows Forms-based form regions, you typically modify these form region settings in the Properties window, and no InitializeManifest method is in the form region factory.

Another key element of the form region factory class is the FormRegionMessageClass attribute, which sets the message classes—both built-in and custom—the form region will be displayed for. Listing 16-6 shows the attributes of a form region factory class associated with three built-in message classes (Appointment, Contact, and Note) and one custom message class that derives from Task (IPM.Task.Foo). VSTO provides constant strings in the Microsoft.Office.Tools.Outlook.FormRegionMessageClass-Attribute namespace for each of the built-in Outlook message classes. If you want, you can interchange the constant string. The string "IPM.Task", for example, is equivalent to the Microsoft.Office.Tools.Outlook.Form-RegionMessageClassAttribute.Task constant.

Listing 16-6: A Form Region Factory Class Associated with Three Built-In Message Classes and One Custom Message Class via FormRegionMessageClass Attributes

```
[Microsoft.Office.Tools.Outlook.FormRegionMessageClass(
  Microsoft.Office.Tools.Outlook.
  FormRegionMessageClassAttribute.Appointment)]
[Microsoft.Office.Tools.Outlook.FormRegionMessageClass(
  Microsoft.Office.Tools.Outlook.
  FormRegionMessageClassAttribute.Contact)]
[Microsoft.Office.Tools.Outlook.FormRegionMessageClass(
  Microsoft.Office.Tools.Outlook.
  FormRegionMessageClassAttribute.Note)]
[Microsoft.Office.Tools.Outlook.FormRegionMessageClass(
  "IPM.Task.Foo")]
[Microsoft.Office.Tools.Outlook.FormRegionName(
  "OutlookAddIn2.FormRegion3")]
public partial class FormRegion3Factory
```

The Manifest Object

Most of the properties that control how a VSTO form region is displayed by Outlook are found in the FormRegionManifest object returned by the Manifest property of a VSTO form region. Behind the scenes, setting properties on the FormRegionManifest object manipulates an XML manifest that describes the form region. This manifest is provided to Outlook when the add-in loads. You can modify the properties of the FormRegionManifest object via the property grid for Windows Forms-based form regions by clicking the form region surface in the designer and then using the Properties window to set properties associated with the Manifest property, as shown in Figure 16-30.

To set properties of the manifest object for a Outlook Forms-based form region, write code in the InitializeManifest method of the form region fac-

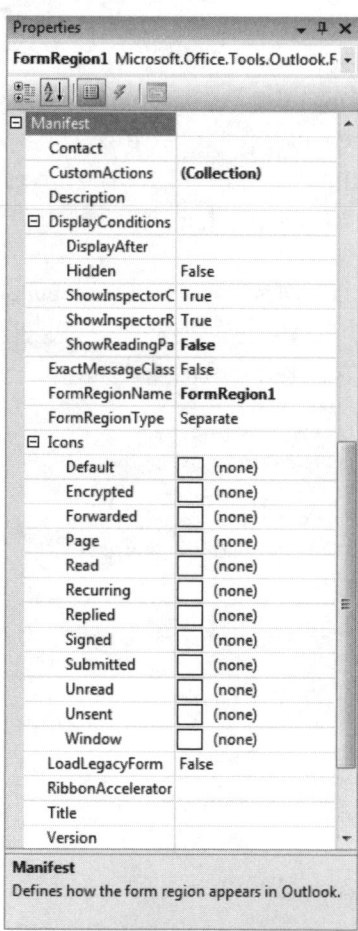

Figure 16-30: Setting properties on the manifest object for a Windows Forms-based form region.

tory. If you try to set properties on the manifest object outside these two mechanisms (the Properties window for Windows Forms and the Initialize Manifest method for Outlook Forms), chances are that Outlook will already have asked for the manifest object's settings, and your code will generate an InvalidOperationException. You can use the Locked property of the manifest object to check whether Outlook has already retrieved the settings from the manifest object. If Locked is set to true, any code you write against the manifest object will have no effect.

Table 16-4 describes the various properties of the manifest object. The table refers several times to the Choose Form dialog box, which you invoke by dropping down the New button in the Explorer window and choosing Choose Form, as shown in Figure 16-31. The dialog box shown in Figure 16-32 appears, allowing you to pick Replacement or Replace-All form regions (which are associated with custom message classes). This way, an end user can create an Outlook item with a custom message class that you defined and associated with a form region. Table 16-5 describes the icons that can be used by a form region.

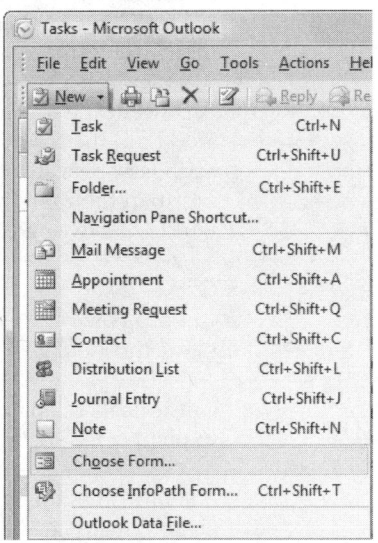

Figure 16-31: Creating a new Outlook Item
by using the Choose Form button.

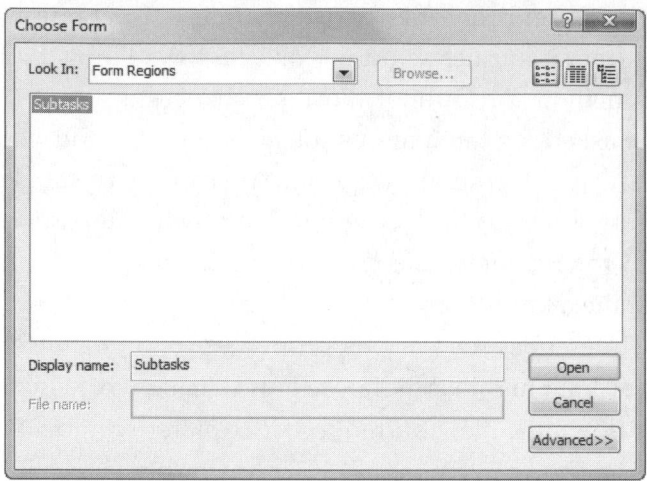

Figure 16-32: The Choose Form dialog box.

TABLE 16-4: Properties of the Manifest Object

Name	Type	What It Does
Contact	string	Gets and sets the name used in the Choose Form dialog box for Replacement and Replace-All form regions.
CustomActions	FormRegion-CustomAction-Collection	A collection with custom actions associated with the form region. The custom actions appear in a Custom Actions group in the Ribbon of the Inspector window showing the form region.
Description	string	Gets and sets the description used in the Choose Form dialog box for Replacement and Replace-All form regions.
DisplayAfter	string	Gets or sets the name of the form region to display before this form region.
ExactMessage-Class	bool	If set to true, this property prevents a custom message class derived from the message class for the form region from displaying the form region.

TABLE 16-4: Properties of the Manifest Object *(Continued)*

Name	Type	What It Does
Form-RegionName	string	Gets and sets the name used for the Ribbon button associated with this form region or the header associated with an Adjoining form region.
FormRegion-Type	FormRegion-Type	Gets and sets an enum specifying the form region type: Adjoining, Replacement, Replace-All, or Separate.
Hidden	bool	If set to true, this form region won't be displayed in the Choose Form dialog box.
Icons	FormRegion-ManifestIcons	Sets the icons used by the form region (see Table 16-5).
Locked	bool	Returns true if Outlook has already queried the manifest object for its settings. Any code you write against the manifest object after Locked is set to true has no effect.
Ribbon-Accelerator	string	Gets and sets the keyboard shortcuts for Separate, Replacement, and Replace-All form regions.
ShowInspector-Compose	bool	Gets and sets whether the form region is shown when an Inspector window is in compose mode.
ShowInspector-Read	bool	Gets and sets whether the form region is shown when an Inspector window is in read mode.
ShowReading-Pane	bool	Gets and sets whether a form region is shown for the reading pane.
Title	string	Gets and sets the name that appears in the Actions menu and the Choose Form dialog box for Replacement and Replace-All form regions.

TABLE 16-5: Icons on the Manifest Object

Name	What It Does	Applies to Form Region Types
Default	16 × 16-pixel icon that is used by default.	Replacement and Replace-All
Encrypted	16 × 16-pixel icon for encrypted items.	Replacement and Replace-All
Forwarded	16 × 16-pixel icon for forwarded items.	Replacement and Replace-All
Page	Icon used in the Ribbon of an Inspector window for the button that activates the form region. Use a PNG file for this icon.	Separate, Replacement, and Replace-All
Read	16 × 16-pixel icon for read items.	Replacement and Replace-All
Recurring	16 × 16-pixel icon for recurring items.	Replacement and Replace-All
Replied	16 × 16-pixel icon for replied-to items.	Replacement and Replace-All
Signed	16 × 16-pixel icon for digitally signed items.	Replacement and Replace-All
Submitted	16 × 16-pixel icon for items in the Outbox that are submitted for sending.	Replacement and Replace-All
Unread	16 × 16-pixel icon for unread items.	Replacement and Replace-All
Unsent	16 × 16-pixel icon for items in the Drafts folder that are not yet sent.	Replacement and Replace-All
Window	Appears in the notification area and in the Alt+Tab window for Inspector windows displaying the form region. Use a 32 × 32-pixel icon.	Replacement and Replace-All

Other Key Properties and Methods

Several other properties and methods associated with a Outlook form region class created with VSTO are worth pointing out. We've already talked about the OutlookItem property, which returns as an `object` the Outlook Item associated with the Outlook form region. You can cast the `object` returned by the OutlookItem property to the type of Outlook item you expect, based on what built-in or custom message classes your form region is associated with.

The OutlookFormRegion property returns the underlying Microsoft .Office.Interop.Outlook.FormRegion object, which represents your form region in the Outlook object model. Table 16-6 shows some of the key properties and methods on this object.

Globals Support

Whenever you create a form region in a VSTO project, it is added to the Globals object for the project. You can access the currently active form

TABLE 16-6: Key Properties and Methods on the FormRegion Object Returned by the OutlookFormRegion Property

Name	Type	What It Does
Detail	string	Gets and sets the name displayed in the header after the display name of an Adjoining form region.
Inspector	Inspector	Returns the Inspector window object associated with the form region.
IsExpanded	bool	Read-only property that returns `true` when an Adjoining form region is expanded.
Language	int	Returns the locale ID (LCID) for the current language used by Outlook.
Reflow()		Method that forces Outlook to size an Adjoining form region so that all controls are visible.
Select()		Makes the form region the active form region and forces it to be visible.

regions in three ways: You can see all the active form regions for a particular Inspector window, for a particular Explorer window, or for all open windows. You can access only form regions provided by your add-in; you can't access form regions provided by other add-ins by using the Globals object.

Listing 16-7 shows a subroutine that uses all three ways of accessing active form regions to get the count of active form regions associated with the active Explorer window, the count of active form regions associated with the active Inspector window, and the total count of all active form regions.

Listing 16-7: Three Methods of Accessing Active Form Regions: All Active, for an Explorer Window, and for an Inspector Window

```
private void ShowActiveFormRegions()
{
  Outlook.Explorer explorer =
    Globals.ThisAddIn.Application.ActiveExplorer();
  Outlook.Inspector inspector =
    Globals.ThisAddIn.Application.ActiveInspector();

  System.Windows.Forms.MessageBox.Show(
    String.Format("{0} total form regions",
    Globals.FormRegions.Count.ToString()));

  if (explorer != null)
    System.Windows.Forms.MessageBox.Show(
      String.Format("{0} for regions for the active Explorer",
      Globals.FormRegions[explorer].Count.ToString()));

  if (inspector != null)
    System.Windows.Forms.MessageBox.Show(
      String.Format("{0} for regions for the active Inspector",
      Globals.FormRegions[inspector].Count.ToString()));
}
```

Conclusion

With the new form region feature in Outlook 2007, developers have a powerful new way to customize the Outlook UI. The four types of form regions—Separate, Adjacent, Replacement, and Replace-All—provide a wide variety of UI options. In this chapter, you saw how form regions can be created to customize Inspector windows as well as the reading pane.

You also learned about custom message classes, as they are required for using the Replacement and Replace-All form region types.

VSTO supports two form technologies to create form regions with: Windows Forms and Outlook Forms. You saw how Outlook Forms can be created and imported into Visual Studio and how the controls are accessed from managed code. You also dived deeper into the programming model to discover additional ways to customize form regions.

Also in this chapter you saw a simple way in which form regions integrate with the Ribbon: They automatically add a button to switch to the form region page, for example.

In the next chapter, you see how VSTO supports creating a wider range of Ribbon customizations.

17

Working with the Ribbon in VSTO

Introduction to the Office Ribbon

One of the first things you will notice when starting to use Office 2007 is the new user interface known as the Microsoft Office Fluent user interface, and the most predominant feature of the new user interface is the Office Ribbon. The Ribbon is a replacement for traditional toolbars and menus; it is used in Word 2007, Excel 2007, Outlook 2007 (in Inspector windows but not Explorer windows), PowerPoint 2007, and Access 2007.

Let's consider the Ribbon and some related Office Fluent UI features. Figure 17-1 shows the top of the Word window. In the top-left corner is the Microsoft Office Button. This button drops down a menu of commands for working with the document—commands such as Open, Close, and Print. This menu also has a button to show the Options dialog box for the Office application—something we have used throughout this book. The menu that appears when you click the Microsoft Office Button is shown in Figure 17-2. In this case, the Print command has been selected, and commands related to printing are shown.

To the right of the Microsoft Office Button is the Quick Access toolbar, which the end user can customize to add commands. The Quick Access

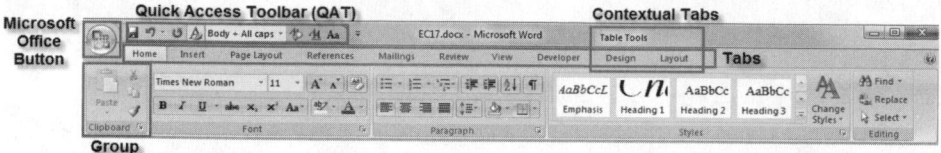

Figure 17-1: Key elements of the Office Fluent user interface: Microsoft Office Button, Quick Access toolbar, tabs, contextual tabs, and groups.

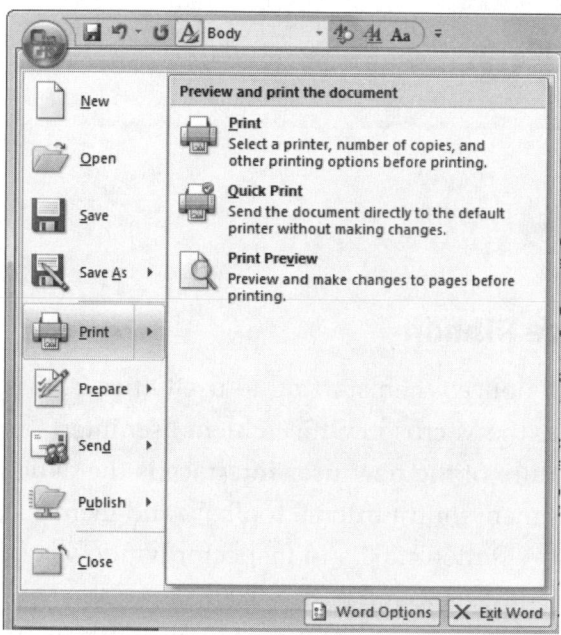

Figure 17-2: The drop-down menu that appears when you click the Microsoft Office Button.

toolbar typically is above the Ribbon, but the user can choose to show it below the Ribbon instead.

Below the Quick Access toolbar are the Ribbon tabs. All the commands in Office applications that use the Ribbon are now organized in tabs of related commands. The Home tab exists in each Office application and contains commonly used commands. The Developer tab is a tab common to all Office applications that can be shown using the Options dialog box.

The Add-Ins tab, shown only if an add-in has added a custom command, is another tab common to all Office applications; this tab is the default location for custom UI created for previous versions of Office and the recommended place for add-ins to put their commands. Also, in certain contexts, additional tabs called contextual tabs may appear. If the selection in a document is in a table, for example, the tabs Design and Layout will be added to the existing Ribbon tabs after the existing tabs.

Finally, within a tab, the commands are organized in groups of related commands by means of a Ribbon control called a Group. The Group is one of 14 controls supported by the Ribbon. Another commonly used Ribbon control is the Gallery control, shown in Figure 17-3. A Gallery control provides a set of visual options. In this case, the Gallery provides a set of options for configuring margins.

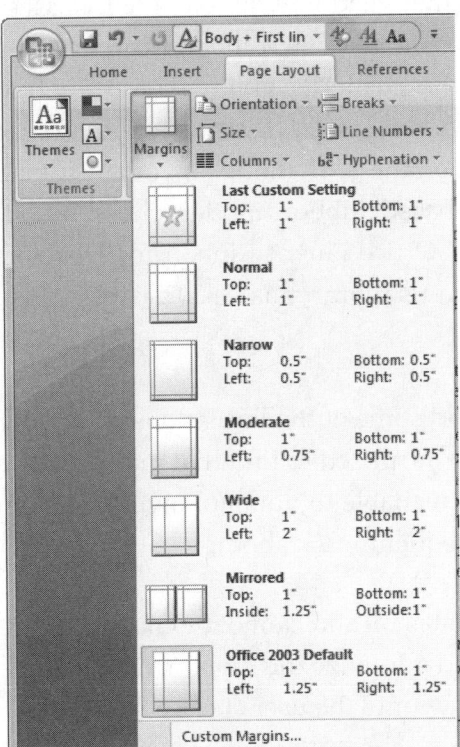

Figure 17-3: A Gallery control for configuring margins.

Introduction to Office Ribbon Programmability

If you were an early adopter of Office 2007 and experimented at all with customizing the Ribbon, you would have discovered a rather complex and difficult-to-use—but very flexible—programming model based on XML. The XML-based model relies on a system of callbacks wherein XML specifying the desired customizations to the Ribbon is provided to Office when Office starts. Office calls back on a custom interface called IRibbonExtensibility to get the initial XML-based model for the Ribbon. This process is handled for you when you use the VSTO Ribbon designer. Then Office calls on an IDispatch interface when customized Ribbon commands are invoked; once again, VSTO hides this detail from you. If you don't choose to use the visual Ribbon designer to create your Ribbon, you need to learn how to use the XML Schema for the Ribbon and how to hook up a variety of callbacks.

VSTO 2008 provides a much simpler model for customizing the Ribbon: a visual designer that generates simple .NET classes and event handlers. This book focuses on this new Ribbon programmability model and doesn't cover the XML-based model, although you will have some sense of the XML-based model when you understand VSTO's object model for the Ribbon, which is based on the XML model. If you are interested in learning more about the XML-based Ribbon model, check out the article series "Customizing the 2007 Office Fluent Ribbon for Developers" at http://msdn.microsoft.com/en-us/library/aa338202.aspx.

Ribbon Limitations

It is useful to understand some of the limitations on what you can do with the Ribbon. You may be surprised to find that many features of the Ribbon used by Office are not available to you. Following are some of the limitations that developers frequently ask about:

- The Ribbon's height is set and cannot be changed (although users can right-click a tab and minimize the Ribbon, which causes the Ribbon to move out of the way until the user clicks a tab).
- The Ribbon lays out controls in top-to-bottom, left-to-right fashion, with a maximum of three controls vertically.

- You can't put custom Windows Forms or WPF controls in the Ribbon; you can use only a fixed set of controls that are built into Office.

- You can't make the Press F1 for Help command that displays when users mouse over one of your Ribbon controls map to your own help file. Instead, Office maps this command to the help topic about how to turn off add-ins. Part of the reason is that an add-in is a "guest" in the Office model, and Office wants to always give the user the power to turn off an add-in.

- You can't create an inline gallery like the one you see in Word's Home tab for the Styles groups.

- You can't add a custom control to any of Office's built-in groups.

- You can't resize your controls dynamically when the window resizes—even though built-in Office controls do resize dynamically.

- You can't clear out all the commands in the Office menu. Some commands are always present—once again, to keep the user in control of the application.

Introduction to the Office Ribbon Controls

The Office Ribbon provides several controls in addition to the Group and Gallery controls. We consider each control separately, describing the object model and event model for each control. All the object model objects we describe in this section are located in the Microsoft.Office.Tools.Ribbon namespace contained in the Microsoft.Office.Tools.Common.v9.0.dll assembly.

All Controls

All the Ribbon controls inherit common properties from the RibbonControl object. These common properties are shown in Table 17-1.

Box Control

The Box control is used to group other Ribbon controls, either horizontally or vertically. Figure 17-4 shows two box controls. Box controls are invisible in that they don't draw a border or other UI. Figure 17-4 shows two box controls in use. The first control groups the buttons 1 through 5 horizontally; the

TABLE 17-1: Common Properties for All Ribbon Controls

Property Name	Type	What It Does
Enabled	bool	Enables or disables a control
Id	string	Returns the ID of a control
Name	string	Returns the name of a control
Tag	object	Allows you to associate custom data with a control at runtime
Visible	bool	Sets and gets whether the control is visible

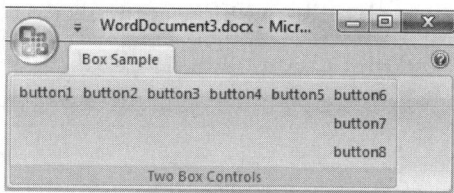

Figure 17-4: Box controls.

second control groups the buttons 6 through 8 vertically. The Box control can group Box, Button, Button Group, Check Box, Combo Box, Drop Down, Edit Box, Gallery, Label, Menu, Split Button, and Toggle Button controls.

The object model object for a Box Control is called RibbonBox. The Ribbon-Box object has an Items collection that returns a RibbonComponent-Collection object. This object can be used to iterate over the controls the Box control contains—but it cannot be used to add or remove those controls; the controls contained by the Box control are configurable only at design time. The RibbonBox object also has the BoxStyle property of type RibbonBoxStyle, which can be set to RibbonBoxStyle.Horizontal or Ribbon-BoxStyle.Vertical. This property cannot be modified at runtime.

Button Control

The Button control is likely the Ribbon control you will use most often. It can appear in several styles; Figure 17-5 shows five styles. Button 1 is a reg-

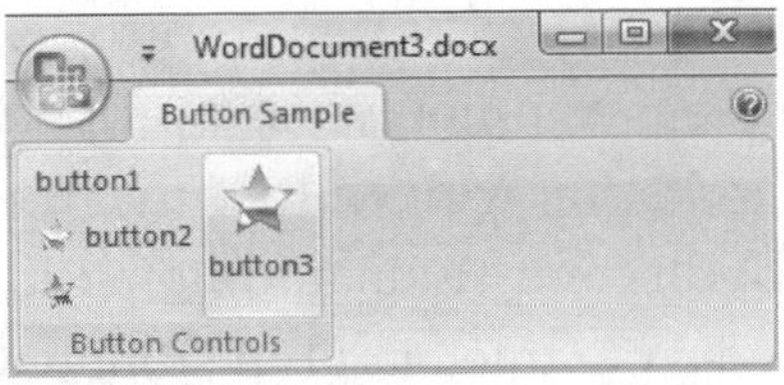

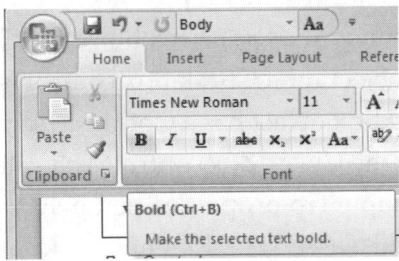

Figure 17-5: Five variations on a button.

ular-size button with only a label; Button 2 is a regular-size button with an image (16 × 16 pixels) and a label. Button 3 is a large button with an image (32 × 32 pixels) and a label. Finally, the button in the bottom-left corner of the group, showing an image only, is a regular-size button with no label.

You can have a button display a custom image that you supply or built-in Office images. For the Button control and most of the other Ribbon controls, you can provide a screen tip that appears in bold text when the user hovers over the control and a multiline super tip that can appear to provide additional information about the control. A keyboard shortcut known as a *key tip* can also be provided for the control. Figure 17-6 shows the screen tip and super tip for the Bold button in Word.

Not shown in Figure 17-6 are the key tips. Key tips are shown when you press the Alt key. Letters appear over the Ribbon, giving you the shortcut keys. If you press the Alt key in Word, for example, it would show that you have to press H to activate the Home tab. After you press H, you would see shortcut keys for individual commands in the Home tab—that you can then press 1 to select the Bold command, for example. The entire key sequence would be Alt+H+1.

Figure 17-6: The screen tip and super tip for the Bold button in Word.

The object model object for a Button Control is called RibbonButton. Table 17-2 shows the most commonly used properties for RibbonButton. As you continue in this chapter, you will see that many of these properties are found on other Ribbon controls. In addition, RibbonButton has a Click event to which is passed a parameter of type RibbonControlEventArgs.

Button Group Control

The Button Group control can arrange Button, Toggle Button, Menu, Split Button, and Gallery Controls in a horizontal orientation. It gives the grouped-together controls the look of a toolbar, even adding a subtle separator between controls and a border around the group. Figure 17-7 shows three Button Group controls. The top one contains four buttons, the middle one contains three buttons, and the bottom one contains two buttons.

The object model object for a Button Group control is called Ribbon-ButtonGroup. The RibbonButtonGroup object has an Items collection that returns a RibbonComponentCollection object. This object can be used to iterate over the controls the Button Group control contains—but it cannot be used to add or remove those controls; the controls contained in a Button Group are configurable only at design time.

The Button Group control does not support the Visible property, so you cannot hide it at runtime. To overcome this limitation, you can put a Button Group control inside a Box control and use the Box control's Visible property to make its child Button Group visible or not visible.

Check Box Control

The Check Box control allows the user to check or uncheck an option. Figure 17-8 shows a Ribbon with four Check Box controls.

The object model object for a Check Box control is called RibbonCheckBox. The RibbonCheckBox object has a Checked property of type bool that sets and gets whether the Check Box control is checked. It also has KeyTip, Label, Position, and SuperTip properties that behave the same way as the properties described in Table 17-2. RibbonCheckBox has a Click event to which is passed a parameter of type RibbonControlEventArgs.

TABLE 17-2: Most Commonly Used Properties for RibbonButton and Other Ribbon Controls

Property Name	Type	What It Does
ControlSize	Ribbon-ControlSize	Set and gets the control size as either `RibbonControlSizeLarge` or `RibbonControlSizeRegular`.
Description	string	Used when the control's ControlSize is `RibbonControlSizeLarge` and the control is contained by a Menu or Split Button control.
Image	Image	Sets and gets the image associated with the control.
ImageName	string	Used to enable a different method of loading images. If Image and OfficeImageId are not set but ImageName is, Office will raise the LoadImage event on the top-level Ribbon control. In this event, you are passed the ImageName, and you can load images in your handling of this event.
KeyTip	string	Sets a keyboard shortcut for the control. This property must be one to three uppercase characters with no spaces, tabs, or new-line characters. Key tips appear when the user presses the Alt key.
Label	string	Sets and gets the label for the control.
OfficeImageId	string	Sets and gets the ID for a built-in Office image. For more information, see the section "Using Built-In Office Images" later in this chapter.
Position	Ribbon-Position	Can be used to position the control before or after a built-in Office control. For more information, see the section "Using the Position Property" later in this chapter.
ScreenTip	string	Sets and gets the single-line tooltip text displayed when the user moves the mouse over the control. This string is shown as the name of the command when the user adds and removes commands in the Quick Access toolbar.
ShowImage	bool	Sets and gets whether an image is shown on the control. If ControlSize is `RibbonControlSizeLarge`, ShowImage is always `true`.
ShowLabel	bool	Sets and gets whether a label is shown on the control. If ControlSize is `RibbonControlSizeLarge`, ShowLabel is always `true`.
SuperTip	string	Sets and gets the multiline tooltip text displayed when the user moves the mouse over the control.

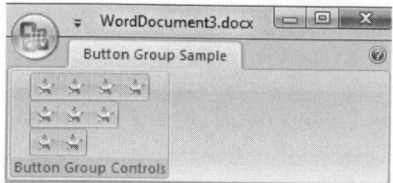

Figure 17-7: Three Button Group controls.

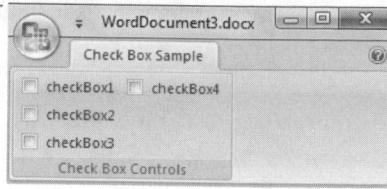

Figure 17-8: Four Check Box controls.

Combo Box Control

The Combo Box control is a combination of an edit box and a drop-down control. The edit box provides a place where the user can type a value. The drop-down control gives the user a way to fill in the edit box quickly by choosing a value from a list. The values in the list can be specified at design time or changed dynamically at runtime. As shown in Figure 17-9, a combo box can have a label and an image, and you can select whether to show the label, the image, or both. You can also control the default text shown in the edit box and the width of the edit box, but not the width of the drop-down list.

Figure 17-10 shows the drop-down list that appears when the user clicks the drop-down arrow. The drop-down list items can display a label, an image, or both. When an item is selected from the drop-down list, the text of the item is entered in the edit-box part of the Combo Box control.

The object model object for a Combo Box control is called RibbonComboBox. The RibbonComboBox object has an Items collection that returns a RibbonDropDownItemCollection. You can use this collection to add, delete, and modify RibbonDropDownItem controls at runtime. RibbonComboBox also has the properties Image, ImageName, KeyTip, Label, OfficeImageId, ScreenTip, ShowImage, ShowLabel, and SuperTip, which are described in Table 7-2 earlier in this chapter.

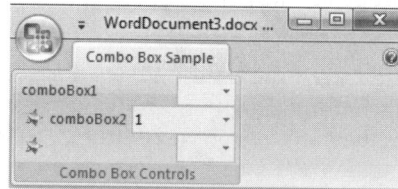

Figure 17-9: Three Combo Box controls.

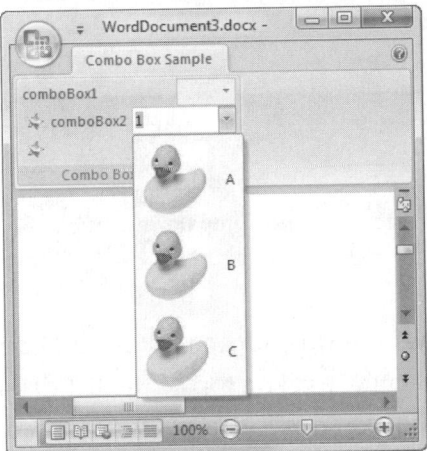

Figure 17-10: Combo Box drop-down list.

RibbonComboBox has several properties that control the edit box. The MaxLength property of type int gets and sets the maximum length of entry allowed in the edit-box part of the combo box. The Text property of type string sets and gets the text in the edit box. In addition, RibbonComboBox has a property that controls the way the drop-down list is presented. The ShowItemImage property of type bool gets and sets whether images are displayed for the RibbonDropDownItem controls in the Items collection.

RibbonComboBox has a TextChanged event that is raised when the user changes the text in the edit box and the user exits the edit box by pressing the Enter key or moving the focus somewhere else in the UI. This event is also raised when the user changes the value of the edit box by selecting a value from the drop-down list. The ItemsLoading event is raised before the drop-down list is displayed and gives the code you write a chance to modify the content of the Items collection right before it is shown.

Drop Down Control

The Drop Down control provides a drop-down list from which the user can pick a value. The Drop Down control can have a label, an image, or both. as shown in Figure 17-11. When an item is selected from the drop-down list, the text of the item is displayed in the drop-down list when the list is collapsed.

Figure 17-11: Three Drop Down controls.

Figure 17-12 shows the drop-down list for a Drop Down control with three items and three buttons. The top of the list displays the list of items. The bottom of the list displays buttons. Items and buttons can display a label, an image, or both. The Drop Down control is similar to the Gallery control, but the Gallery control allows items to be arranged in a grid rather than a list.

The object model object for a Drop Down control is called RibbonDrop-Down. The RibbonDropDown has a Buttons collection of type Ribbon-ButtonCollection, which contains RibbonButton objects. You cannot manipulate this collection at runtime to add and delete new buttons—but you can show and hide existing buttons to get a limited dynamism.

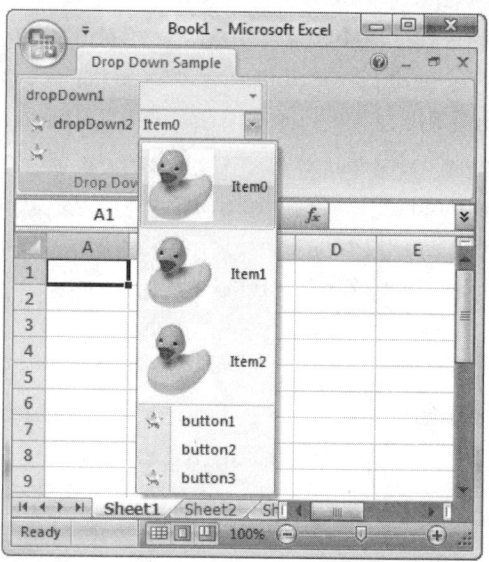

Figure 17-12: Drop-down items and buttons.

RibbonDropDown has an Items collection of type RibbonDropDown-Items that contains RibbonDropDownItem controls. This collection can be modified at runtime. In particular, an ItemsLoading event is raised before the drop-down list for the Drop Down control is displayed and gives the code you write a chance to modify the content of the Items collection right before it is shown.

RibbonDropDown has several properties for configuring the display of the Items collection. ItemImageSize is of type Size; it gets or sets the size of the images displayed in the Gallery control. SelectedItem of type Ribbon-DropDownItem gets or sets the selected item in the Items collection. Selected-ItemIndex of type `int` gets or sets the selected item in the Items collection by index. ShowItemImage of type `bool` gets or sets whether images are shown for the items in the drop-down list. ShowItemLabel of type `bool` gets or sets whether labels are shown for the items in the drop-down list.

RibbonDropDown also has Image, ImageName, KeyTip, Label, Office-ImageId, ScreenTip, ShowImage, ShowLabel, and SuperTip properties, described in Table 17-2 earlier in this chapter. RibbonDropDown also has three events: ButtonClick, which is raised with the button instance as the sender parameter when one of the buttons in the Buttons collection is clicked; SelectionChanged, which is raised when the selected RibbonDrop-DownItem in the Items collection is changed; and ItemsLoading, which is raised before the drop-down list is displayed so the content of the Items collections can be modified before the Gallery drop-down list is shown.

Edit Box Control

The Edit Box control provides a place where the user can type a value. As shown in Figure 17-13, an edit box can have a label, an image and a label, or just an image. You can also set a default value in the edit box.

The object model object for an Edit Box control is called RibbonEditBox. The RibbonEditBox control has the properties Image, ImageName, KeyTip, Label, OfficeImageId, ScreenTip, ShowImage, ShowLabel, and SuperTip, described in Table 7-2 earlier in this chapter. The MaxLength property of type `int` gets and sets the maximum length of entry allowed in the edit box. The Text property of type `string` sets and gets the text in the edit box. The SizeString property of type `string` takes a sample string that

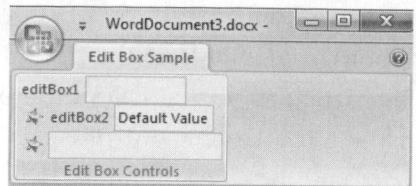

Figure 17-13: Three Edit Box controls.

is used to set the width of the edit box. RibbonEditBox also has a Text-Changed event that is raised when the user changes the text in the edit box and the user exits the edit box by pressing the Enter key or moving the focus somewhere else in the UI.

Gallery Control

The Gallery control provides a drop-down list of items displayed in a grid, along with a region at the bottom of the list for additional buttons. Figure 17-14 shows three regular-size Gallery controls displaying a label, a label and an image, and an image; it also shows one large Gallery control with a label and image. One feature that unfortunately is not supported by a Ribbon customization is the ability to show a Gallery in place, as some Office Galleries in the Ribbon do (the Styles Gallery in Figure 17-1 earlier in this chapter, for example).

Figure 17-15 shows a drop-down Gallery control. The top of the control displays the items in a grid. You can control the label and image for each item. You can also control how many rows and columns are displayed in the drop-down Gallery. If you specify fewer rows and columns than number of items to display, the drop-down gallery can display scroll bars to

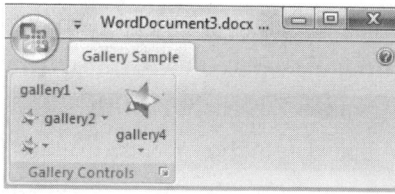

Figure 17-14: Four Gallery controls.

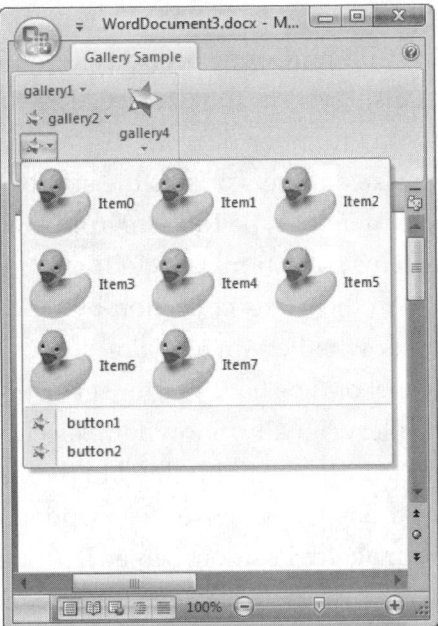

Figure 17-15: The Gallery drop-down menu with eight items and two buttons.

scroll the additional items into view. Below the Gallery items, you can display additional button controls. Figure 17-15 displays two additional buttons. The drop-down Gallery can highlight a selected item permanently, or you can turn off the highlighting of a selected item. The items in a Gallery can be specified at design time or changed dynamically at runtime.

The object model object for a Gallery control is called RibbonGallery. The RibbonGallery has a Buttons collection of type RibbonButtonCollection, which contains RibbonButton objects. You cannot manipulate this collection at runtime to add and delete new buttons—but you can show and hide existing buttons to get a limited dynamism.

RibbonGallery has an Items collection of type RibbonDropDownItems that contains RibbonDropDownItem controls. This collection can be modified at runtime. In particular, an ItemsLoading event is raised before the drop-down list for the Gallery control is displayed and gives your code a chance to modify the content of the Items collection right before it is shown.

RibbonGallery has several properties for configuring the display of the Items collection. The ColumnCount property of type int gets or sets the number of columns displayed in the Gallery. The RowCount property of type int gets or sets the number of rows displayed in the Gallery. Item-ImageSize is of type Size and gets or sets the size of the images displayed in the Gallery. SelectedItem of type RibbonDropDownItem gets or sets the selected item in the Items collection. SelectedItemIndex of type int gets or sets the selected item in the Items collection by index. ShowItemImage of type bool gets or sets whether images are shown for the items in the Gallery. ShowItemLabel of type bool gets or sets whether labels are shown for the items in the Gallery. Finally, ShowItemSelection of type bool gets or sets whether the selected item is highlighted in the Gallery.

RibbonGallery also has ControlSize, Description, Image, ImageName, KeyTip, Label, OfficeImageId, Position, ScreenTip, ShowImage, ShowLabel, and SuperTip properties, described in Table 17-2 earlier in this chapter. In addition, Ribbon Gallery has three events: ButtonClick, which is raised with the button instance as the sender parameter when one of the buttons in the Buttons collection is clicked; Click, which is raised when a Ribbon-DropDownItem in the Items collection is clicked; and ItemsLoading, which is raised before the Gallery drop-down list is displayed so the content of the Items collections can be modified before the Gallery drop-down list is shown.

Group Control

The Group control has been part of every sample we have shown so far. A Group control is a required container for most other Ribbon controls. You can't add Ribbon controls directly to a tab; you must first have a tab, and then at least one Group control, whereupon you can add Ribbon controls to the Group control. In addition to specifying a label for a Group control, you can have a Group control display an icon in the bottom-right corner called a Dialog Launcher; this icon raises an event that your code can handle to bring up a custom dialog box. Figure 17-16 shows a Group control with a Dialog Launcher icon on it. You can also specify an image and label for the Dialog Launcher for a group control, but these elements are displayed only if the user adds the Dialog Launcher to the Quick Access toolbar.

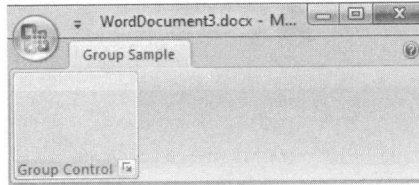

Figure 17-16: Group control with Dialog
Launcher icon.

The object model object for a Group control is called RibbonGroup. RibbonGroup has an Items collection of type RibbonComponentCollection, which returns the controls contained by the Group control. It also has a DialogLauncher property of type DialogLauncher that can be used to get and set the DialogLauncher settings for the Group control. RibbonGroup also has KeyTip, Label, and Position properties, described in Table 17-2 earlier in this chapter. It has a DialogLauncherClick event, which is raised if the RibbonGroup has a DialogLauncher associated with it and the user clicks the Dialog Launcher icon. Note that you cannot add your custom controls to an existing Office group control; you can't add a custom control to Office's built-in Font Group control, for example. This constraint is a limitation of the Ribbon.

Label Control

The Label control is used to provide a static label to some part of the Ribbon. Word, for example, uses a Label control in the Page Layout page's Paragraph group to label Indent and Spacing options. Figure 17-17 shows a simple label with the text *Sizing* that serves to label two Combo Box controls for width and height.

The object model object for a Label control is called RibbonLabel. RibbonLabel has Label, ScreenTip, ShowLabel, and SuperTip properties, described in Table 17-2 earlier in this chapter.

Menu Control

The Menu control is used to provide traditional menus that can drop down from the Ribbon. Figure 17-18 shows several variations on the Menu control.

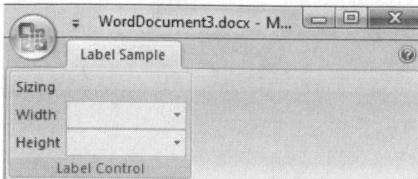

Figure 17-17: Label control with text Sizing labeling two Combo Box controls.

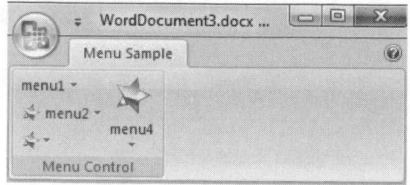

Figure 17-18: Four Menu controls.

The first control has a label but no image. The second control has a label and an image. The third control has only an image. The fourth control is large; it has a menu and an image.

Menu controls drop down a list of other controls that can include additional Menu controls (which in turn drop down more controls), Button controls, Check Box controls, Gallery controls, Separator controls, Toggle Button controls, and Split Button controls. Figure 17-19 shows a menu control that uses all these additional controls. A Menu control can control the size of child items to be regular-size or large. The items associated with a Menu control's drop-down list can be specified at design time or changed dynamically at runtime.

The object model object for a Menu control is called RibbonMenu. RibbonMenu has an Items collection of type RibbonComponentCollection, which

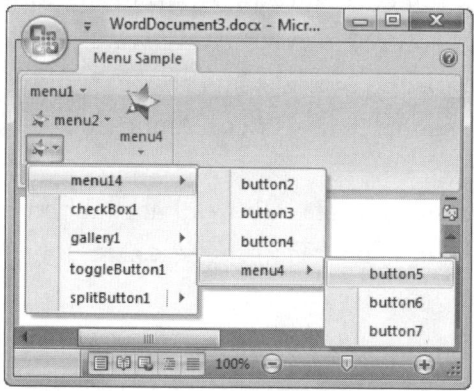

Figure 17-19: A Menu control that contains additional Menu, Button, Check Box, Gallery, Separator, Toggle Button, and Split Button controls.

contains the controls that are displayed by the Menu control. It also has an ItemsLoading event, which is raised before the menu is displayed so the Items collection can be modified before the menu is shown. The Dynamic property of type `bool` must be set to `true` to change the Items collection at runtime. The ItemSize property of type RibbonControlSize sets the size of the controls in the Items collection.

RibbonMenu has ControlSize, Description, Image, ImageName, KeyTip, Label, OfficeImageId, Position, ScreenTip, ShowImage, ShowLabel, and SuperTip properties, described in Table 17-2 earlier in this chapter. Ribbon-Menu's Title property is worth mentioning; it controls the header text shown at the top of the menu when it is dropped down.

Ribbon Control

The top-level Ribbon is also represented by an object in the object model called OfficeRibbon. OfficeRibbon has a Context property of type `object`, which can be cast to an Inspector object in Outlook; this property allows the developer to get to the Inspector associated with the Ribbon. In other applications, the Context property returns `null`. The Global property is of type `bool` and can be set to `false` to ensure that every Inspector window created in Outlook is associated with a unique Ribbon instance. The OfficeMenu property is of type RibbonOfficeMenu and returns the object representing the Office Button. The StartFromScratch property of type `bool` can be set to `true` to hide all built-in tabs and display only the tabs defined in the custom Ribbon. The Tabs property returns a RibbonComponentCollection containing all the RibbonTab objects associated with the Ribbon.

The OfficeRibbon has three events: Load, which is raised when the Ribbon is loaded; Close, which is raised when the Ribbon is closed; and Load-Image, which is raised when the Ribbon is loaded if the ImageName property is being used for any of the Ribbon controls.

Separator Control

Figure 17-20 shows two Separator controls. The first is in the Ribbon group between the three menus on the left and the menu on the right. Separator controls that appear within a Ribbon group are drawn as vertical separations. The second separator control is shown between the Gallery control

Figure 17-20: Two Separator controls: a vertical separator in a Ribbon Group and a horizontal separator in a menu.

and Toggle Button control in the drop-down menu. Separator controls that appear within a drop-down list for a Menu control are drawn as horizontal separations.

The object model object for a Separator control is called RibbonSeparator. RibbonSeparator has a Position property, described in Table 17-2 earlier in this chapter. It also has a Title property of type string that gets and sets text displayed on the Separator control when it is used in the Microsoft Office Button menu, a Menu control, or a Split Button control.

Split Button Control

The Split Button control is similar to the Menu control in that it can drop down a list of other controls that can include additional Split Button controls (which in turn drop down more controls), Button controls, Check Box controls, Gallery controls, Separator controls, Toggle Button controls, and Menu controls. Where the Split Button control differs from the Menu control is that it can be clicked directly and pushed as a button, or its drop-down list can be dropped down. It can also be configured to act like a Toggle Button control and have a toggled checked or unchecked state.

Figure 17-21 shows several Split Button controls. The top one has an image and a label. The second Split Button control is configured to act like a toggle button; it is checked, so it is drawn in a highlighted state. The third Split Button control is dropped down to show the various controls that can

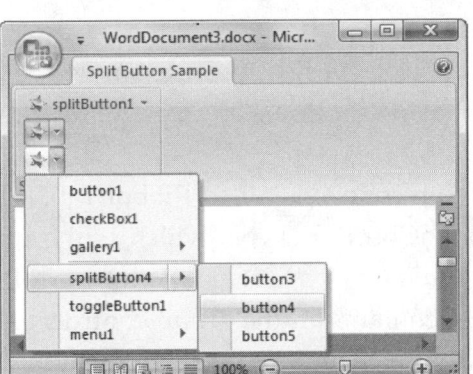

Figure 17-21: Split Button controls include one that contains additional Menu, Button, Check Box, Gallery, Separator, Toggle Button, and Split Button controls.

be added to a Split Button drop-down list. Another way in which the Split Button control differs from a Menu control is that the items it drops down *cannot* be changed dynamically at runtime.

The object model object for a Split Button control is called Ribbon-SplitButton. RibbonSplitButton has an Items collection of type Ribbon-ComponentCollection, which contains the controls that are displayed by the Split Button drop-down list. This collection cannot be modified at runtime. The ItemSize property of type RibbonControlSize controls the size of the items displayed in the drop-down list.

RibbonSplitButton has a ButtonEnabled property of type `bool` that gets and sets whether the button part of the Split Button control is enabled. The ButtonType property of type RibbonButtonType gets and sets whether the type of the button is `RibbonButtonType.Button` or `RibbonButtonType` `.ToggleButton`. If the type is `RibbonButtonType.ToggleButton`, the `bool` Checked property gets and sets whether the button is in a checked state. The Title property of type `string` gets and sets text displayed in the control that is used in the Office Button menu.

RibbonSplitButton also has Description, Image, ImageName, KeyTip, Label, OfficeImageId, Position, ScreenTip, ShowLabel, and SuperTip properties, described in Table 17-2 earlier in this chapter. The Split Button control has a Click event that is raised when the button part of the control (not the drop-down part or any controls in the drop-down list) is clicked.

Tab Control

The Tab control also has been part of every Ribbon example we have shown so far. A Tab control can have a caption and a key tip to specify a keyboard shortcut to activate the tab.

The object model object for a Tab control is called RibbonTab. It has a ControlId property of type RibbonControlIdType, which is the unique name Office uses for the tab. It also has a Groups collection of type RibbonComponentCollection that contains all the group controls created by the add-in that are associated with the tab. It does not include Office built-in group controls if the tab is a built-in Office tab. RibbonTab also has KeyTip, Label, and Position properties, described in Table 17-2 earlier in this chapter.

Toggle Button Control

A Toggle Button control is just like a regular button control except that it has a checked and unchecked state. It has several styles it can display in. Figure 17-22 shows four styles. toggleButton1 shows a regular-size button with only a label. toggleButton2 is a regular-size button with an image (16 × 16 pixels) and a label. toggleButton3 is a regular-size button with an image and no label. Finally, toggleButton4 is a large button with a label. toggleButton1, toggleButton3, and toggleButton4 are displayed in a checked state.

The object model object for a Toggle Button control is called Ribbon-ToggleButton. It has a Checked property of type bool that gets and sets whether the Toggle Button control is checked. It also has ControlSize, Description, Image, ImageName, KeyTip, Label, OfficeImageId, Position, ScreenTip, ShowImage, ShowLabel, and SuperTip properties, described in

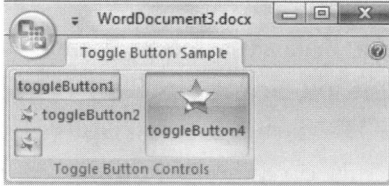

Figure 17-22: Four Toggle Button controls.

Table 17-2 earlier in this chapter. It has a Click event that is raised when the user clicks the Toggle Button control.

Office Button Control

The Office Button control can also be customized; its behavior is similar to that of a Menu control. It can drop down a list of Ribbon controls that include Split Button controls, Menu controls, Button controls, Check Box controls, Gallery controls, Separator controls, and Toggle Button controls. The items it drops down cannot be changed dynamically at runtime. Figure 17-23 shows the Office Button and the controls that can be added to it.

The object model object for the Office Button control is called RibbonOfficeMenu. It has an Items collection of type RibbonComponentCollection that contains the items in the drop-down list. This collection cannot be modified at runtime.

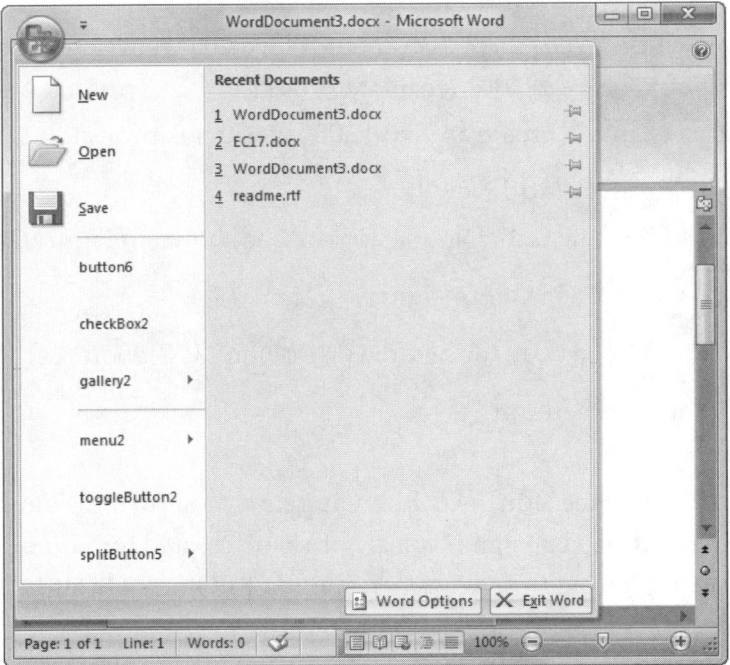

Figure 17-23: The Office Button control and controls that it can drop down: Button, Check Box, Gallery, Separator, Menu, Toggle Button, and Split Button controls.

What Applications Does VSTO Support?

VSTO supports creating document-based Ribbon customizations for Word and Excel, and application-level Ribbon customizations for Word, Excel, Outlook, and PowerPoint.

Working with the Ribbon in the Ribbon Designer

In this section, we consider the Ribbon designer in Visual Studio. The Ribbon designer shares many features with other designers you may be familiar with in Visual Studio—in particular, the Windows Forms designer. We will describe the major features of the designer and show you how to create a simple document-based Ribbon.

To create a document-based Ribbon customization, follow these steps:

1. Create a new Word 2007 document, Word 2007 template, Excel 2007 workbook, or Excel 2007 template project.

   For this example, create an Excel 2007 workbook project.

2. Choose Project > Add New Item.

   The Add New Item dialog box appears, as shown in Figure 17-24.

3. Choose Ribbon (Visual Designer).

4. Give the Ribbon class file a name (the default is Ribbon1.cs).

5. Click the Add button.

The visual designer for the Ribbon appears, as shown in Figure 17-25. By default, the Ribbon designer starts with a tab created for you by default. The default tab created for you corresponds to Office's built-in Add-Ins tab, which Office uses to add buttons and menus for any legacy add-ins that talked to the CommandBars object model. Any controls you add to the add-ins tab will appear alongside other Ribbon controls created by other add-ins.

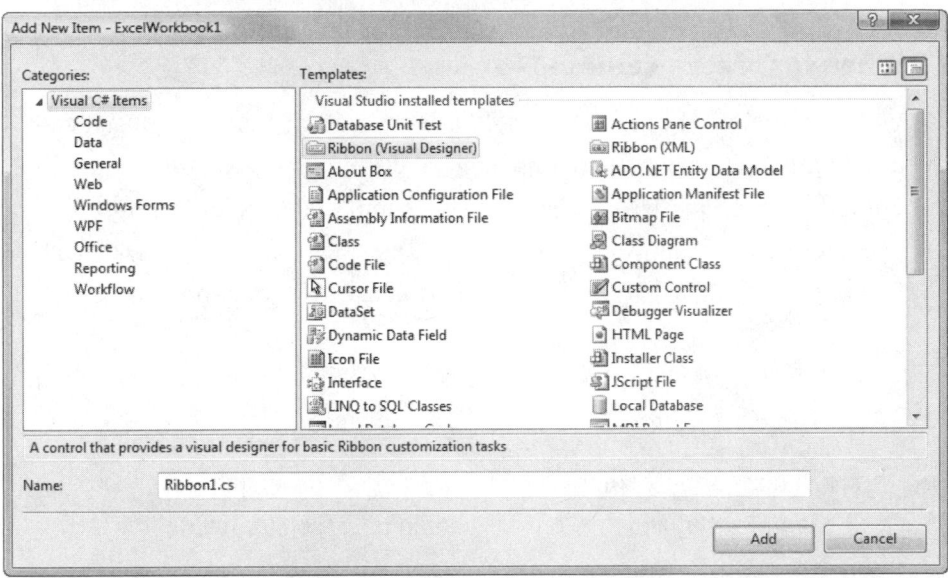

Figure 17-24: Adding a new Ribbon by using the Add New Item dialog box.

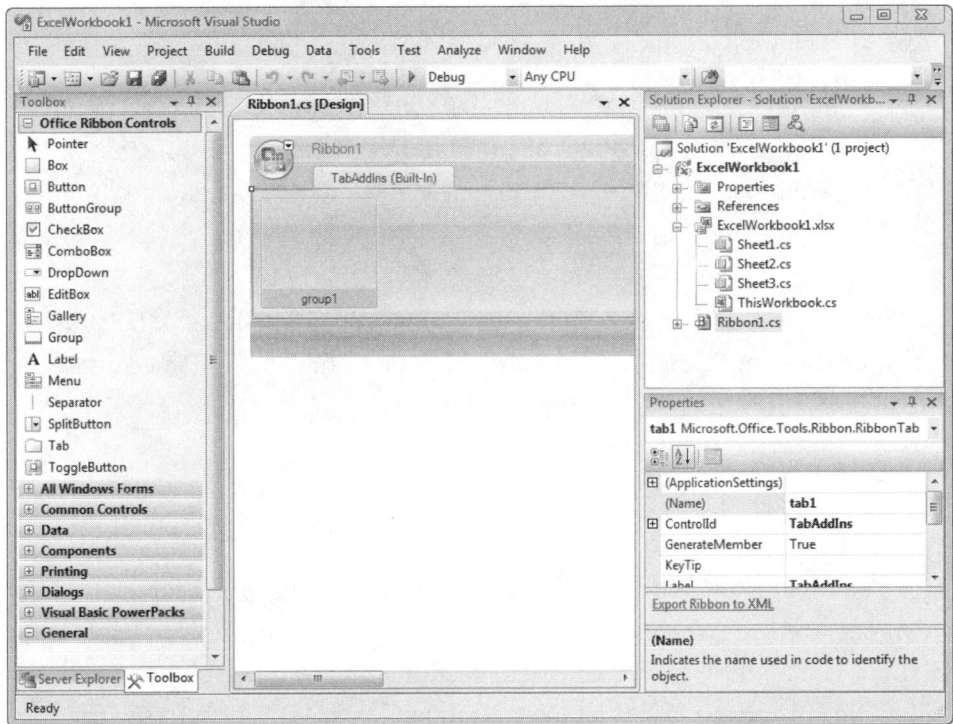

Figure 17-25: The visual designer for the Ribbon in Visual Studio.

When to Create a Custom Tab

You may wonder why the default setting for the visual designer doesn't create a brand-new tab instead. Consider what would happen if you had several add-ins loaded into an Office application, and they all created their own tabs. This situation would create an explosion of tabs that may be confusing to the user. Follow these guidelines when you think about tabs:

- Consider whether the control(s) you are providing should be added to an existing tab.

- If you are adding some functionality related to mail merge in Word, for example, perhaps the controls should be added to the Mailing tab.

- If you are adding a smaller number of controls, add them to their own Group control in the Add-Ins tab.

- If you are adding a larger number of controls, but they aren't all related, consider adding multiple Group controls in the Add-Ins tab.

- If you want to add a large number of controls, and they all are related (such as commands related to some business function or a feature you are adding), you may choose to add a custom tab that groups them together.

Consider the existing Office tabs as a guide. Most tabs have at least five groups and more than 20 controls. If you don't have that many controls, think about adding them to the Add-Ins tab instead.

The Toolbox

The Visual Studio toolbox typically is displayed in the area to the left of the designer area. If the toolbox is not displayed, choose View > Toolbox to display it. The toolbox has different sections that you can expand and collapse. Be sure to expand the Office Ribbon Controls section to see the controls you can use on the Ribbon.

The toolbox is shown in Figure 17-25 earlier in this chapter. It contains 15 controls in addition to the Pointer control, which returns you to selection mode.

You can drag and drop controls from the toolbox to the Ribbon design surface. As you drag, the cursor changes between a universal prohibited symbol (a circle with a slash through it) and an icon with a plus sign (+) to indicate where it is legal to drag and drop the control. You can double-click a control in the toolbox to add a control; this technique works only if the selected item in the Ribbon designer can contain the control you double-click. If a Tab control is selected, for example, you can add only a Group control to it. If you double-click other controls, nothing will happen. You can also click a control in the toolbox, move your mouse over the Ribbon design surface, and "draw" the control on the Ribbon by clicking and dragging in an area where you want the control to be added.

As we mention in the section "Introduction to the Office Ribbon" earlier in this chapter, you must follow several rules about what can be added where. These rules are summarized in Table 17-3. Drop regions are described in more detail in the upcoming section "Adding Child Controls to the Office Button, Split Button, and Menu Control."

Properties Window, Tasks, and Events

When you click an element such as a Tab control, the Properties window displays additional properties for the element. The Properties window typically is displayed in the bottom-right corner of the Visual Studio window. If the Properties window is not displayed, choose View > Properties Window. Figure 17-26 shows the Properties window when you click a Tab control.

■ NOTE

In addition to the properties associated with the element you clicked, some items have additional commands called *tasks*, which are displayed as blue hyperlinks at the bottom of the Properties window. In this case, a task called Export Ribbon to XML is provided, allowing you to export the Ribbon to the XML format supported by Office.

TABLE 17-3: Rules for Dragging

Drag Area	Controls That Can Be Added
Top-level Ribbon	Tab controls
Tab control	Group controls
Group control	Box, Button, Button Group, Check Box, Combo Box, Drop Down, Edit Box, Gallery, Label, Menu, Separator, Split Button, and Toggle Button controls
Button Group control	Button, Toggle Button, Menu, Split Button, and Gallery controls
Box control	Box, Button, Button Group, Check Box, Combo Box, Drop Down, Edit Box, Gallery, Label, Menu, Split Button, and Toggle Button controls
Office Button Drop Region	Button, Check Box, Gallery, Separator, Menu, Toggle Button, and Split Button controls
Menu control Drop Region	Button, Check Box, Gallery, Separator, Menu, Toggle Button, and Split Button controls
Split Button control Drop Region	Button, Check Box, Gallery, Separator, Menu, Toggle Button, and Split Button controls

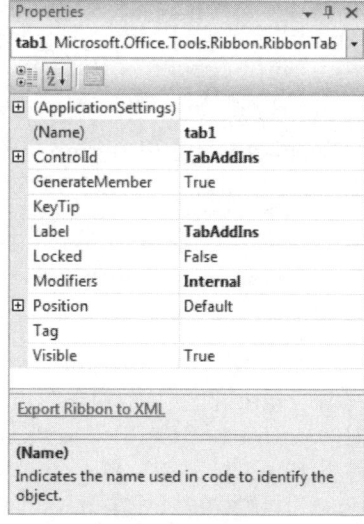

Figure 17-26: The Properties window for the Ribbon tab.

Consider also the Properties window that displays when you click a Ribbon Group control, shown in Figure 17-27. Here, we have clicked the Event button (with a lightning-bolt icon) in the Properties window to show any events associated with a Group control. For a Group control, one event can be handled: the DialogLauncherClick event. To add a handler for this event, you can type the name of a method to handle the DialogLauncher-Click event or double-click the DialogLauncherClick event text to have Visual Studio create a default handler with a default name. Two tasks are available: Add DialogBoxLauncher and Export Ribbon to XML.

An alternative way to invoke additional tasks associated with a selected control is shown in Figure 17-28. When you click a Group control, a small arrow icon appears. When you click this arrow icon, the additional tasks you can do are displayed in a pop-up menu.

Adding Child Controls to the Office Button, Split Button, and Menu Control

If you look at Figure 17-28, you also see a small down-arrow icon on the Office Button. This icon is shown for the Office Button, Split Button, and Menu control. When you click the down-arrow icon, it displays a Drop Region where you can drag in additional controls that should be shown

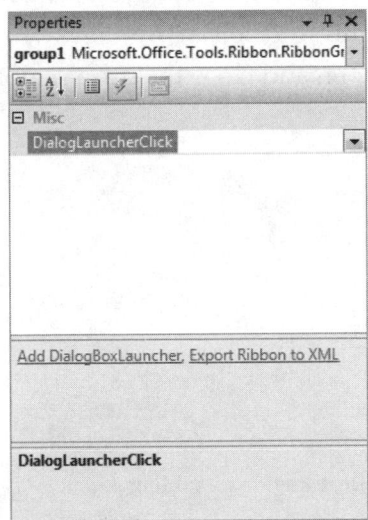

Figure 17-27: The Properties window for the Group control.

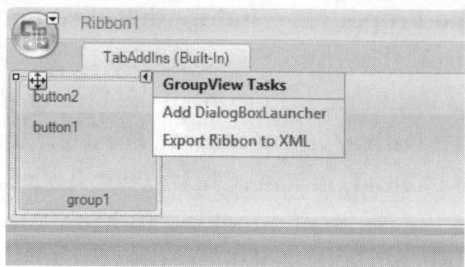

Figure 17-28: The Tasks menu for the Group control.

when the user drops down an Office Button menu, a Split Button menu, or a Menu control menu. This drop region is shown in Figure 17-29. While the drop region is displayed, the arrow icon switches from pointing down to pointing up. If you click the up-arrow icon, the drop region is hidden.

When you are working with a Menu or Split Button control that is a child of the Office Button or another Menu or Split Button control, the UI changes slightly. The small arrow icon now points to the right, as shown in Figure 17-30. When you click it to show the drop region to add child controls to the Menu or Split Button control, the small arrow icon points to the left, as shown in Figure 17-31. Clicking the left-arrow icon collapses the drop region. When you have multiple drop regions shown, a quick way to hide them all is to press the Esc key until all the drop regions are closed again. You can also press the right- and left-arrow keys when a control with a drop region is selected to open and close the drop region.

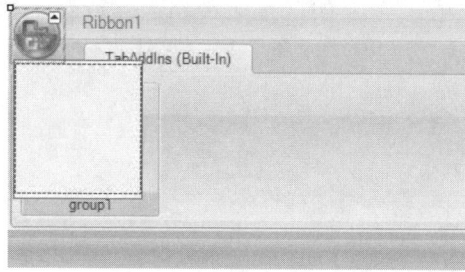

Figure 17-29: The Drop Region for adding child controls to the Office Button.

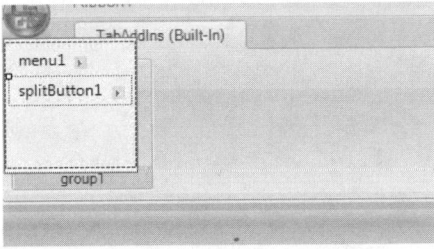

Figure 17-30: The right-arrow icon for expanding a Drop
Region when a Menu or Split Button control is a child of the
Office Button or of another Menu or Split Button control.

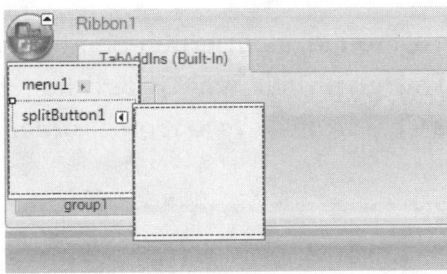

Figure 17-31: The left-arrow icon for collapsing a Drop
Region when a Menu or Split Button control is a child of the
Office Button or of another Menu or Split Button control.

Selecting Controls

In addition to using the mouse to select controls, you can use the arrow keys to switch focus among items that are contained by a common parent. Press Tab and Shift+Tab to iterate through all the available controls.

Reordering Controls

Another common task you will perform in the Ribbon designer is reorder controls. Figure 17-32 shows two UI elements that help you reorder controls. In Figure 17-32, a Group control is selected. To tell you that Group controls can be reordered, a small four-way arrow icon is displayed in the top-left corner of the Group control. In addition, in Figure 17-32 the mouse is hovering over a Button control. The mouse cursor has changed to a larger four-way arrow icon to tell you that you can reorder buttons.

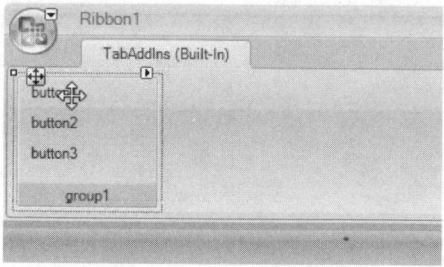

Figure 17-32: UI cues that controls can be reordered: the
four-way arrow icon displayed on a selected Group
control and the mouse icon when hovering over a button.

When you drag a control around, an insertion-point glyph appears, as
shown in Figure 17-33. This glyph tells you where the control will be
moved. You can also press Ctrl+arrow keys to reorder order items.

> **TIP**
>
> You can't drag controls between tabs, but you can use the Cut, Copy,
> and Paste commands to move controls between tabs.

Cut, Copy, and Paste

As you would expect, almost all the controls can be cut, copied, and pasted.
When you paste a control, you must have selected in the UI a container to
which that control can be added. You could copy a button contained in a

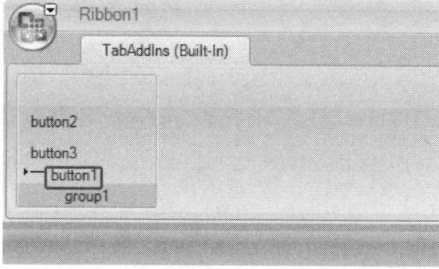

Figure 17-33: UI cues that controls can be
reordered: the insertion-point glyph.

Ribbon group, for example, expand the Office Button to show its Drop Region, click the Drop Region to select it, and then choose Paste. You could also select a Ribbon group and paste the button into that Ribbon group.

The other controls that can contain child controls are the Box and Button Group controls. If your current selection is not the top-level Ribbon, a Tab control, a Group control, a Drop Region, a Box control, or a Group control, the Paste command is disabled. The types of controls you are allowed to paste follow the rules in Table 17-3 earlier in this chapter.

WYSIAWYG

The Ribbon designer gives the appearance of being a WYSIWYG (What You See Is What You Get) designer, but it is really more of a WYSIAWYG (What You See Is Almost What You Get) designer. In many circumstances you will find that the designer gives a rough idea of what the final Ribbon will look like, but the actual final Ribbon looks different. Consider what the Ribbon designer shows you when you add three Combo Box controls to a group. The Ribbon designer view of things is shown in Figure 17-34. When you run it, you get the actual Ribbon shown in Figure 17-35. Occasionally, you have to run your Ribbon to get an exact idea of what the final Ribbon will look like.

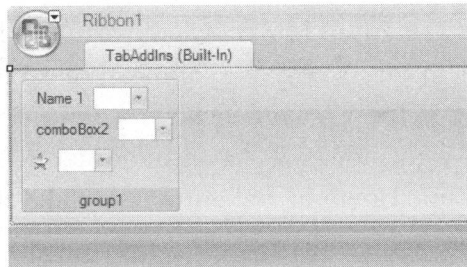

Figure 17-34: A Ribbon in the designer.

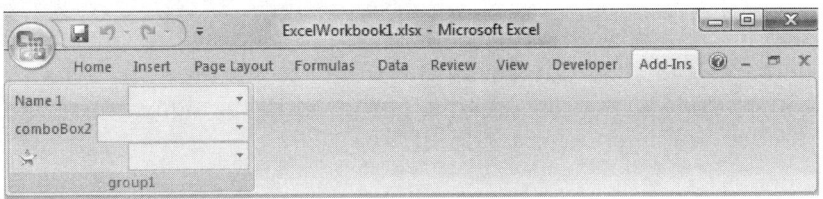

Figure 17-35: The Ribbon from Figure 17-34 at runtime.

Collection Editor

You have seen two paradigms so far for adding child controls to controls
that can have children. The first paradigm is that controls such as Box, Button Group, Group, Tab, and the top-level Ribbon can have controls
dragged, drawn, or pasted onto them. The second paradigm is that some
of the menulike controls (the Office Button, Split Button, and Menu Control) have a fly-out drop region that can be shown and hidden by using
small arrow icons that point up and down or right and left. Controls can be
dragged, drawn, or pasted into the drop region.

A third paradigm is the Collection Editor, which it is used to modify the
Items collection associated with the Combo Box, Drop Down, and Gallery
controls and the Buttons collection associated with the Gallery or Drop
Down control. This third paradigm is used when the collection is homoge-
nous—when all the elements in the collection are the same kind of control.
To see the Collection Editor in action, drag a control like the Gallery control onto a Group control. Then click the Gallery control, and view the
Properties window. The Properties window displayed for a Gallery control is shown in Figure 17-36. Two collections are associated with a Gallery
or DropDown control: the Buttons collection and the Items collection.

When you click a property containing a collection such as the Items collection, the Collection Editor dialog box appears. This editor allows you to
add and delete items in a collection. Figure 17-37 shows the result of clicking the Add button several times in this dialog box. You can select items
you have added in this dialog box in the Members list on the left side and
edit each item's properties on the right side. You can also reorder items in
the collection by clicking the up- and down-arrow buttons to the right of
the list of items you have added.

▪ NOTE

Collections that you edit using the Collection Editor are dynamic at
runtime—that is, you can change and modify the items in the collection when your application is running.

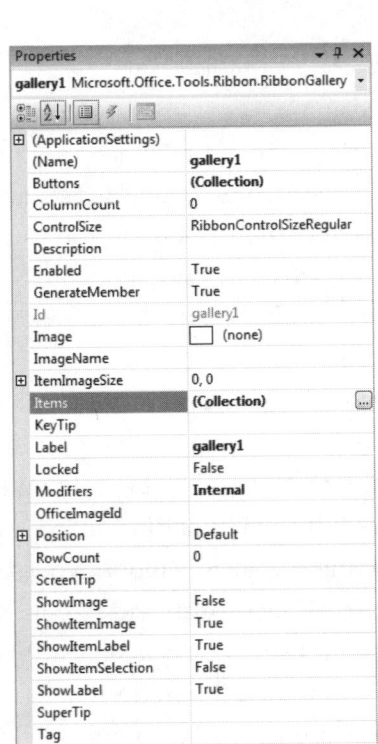

Figure 17-36: The Properties window for a Gallery control with two collections.

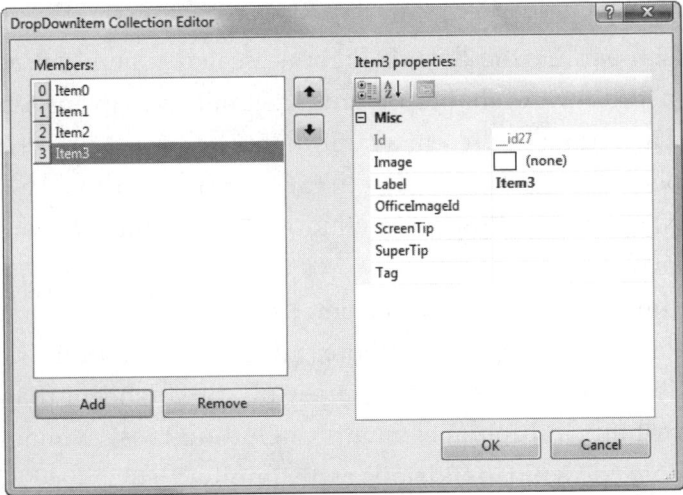

Figure 17-37: The Collection Editor.

Creating a Ribbon in an Excel Workbook Project

Now that we've introduced the Ribbon designer, we'll show you how to create a simple Ribbon and in the process use some of the concepts you've learned so far. By default, the Ribbon designer creates a tab for you and a group control. First, delete these elements and then re-create them from scratch. Click the group1 Group control to select it, and then press the Delete key (or right-click the Group control and choose Delete from the context menu).

Next, click the TabAddIns tab that is created for you, and press the Delete key (or choose Delete from the context menu that appears when you right-click the tab). The Ribbon designer is now in its minimal state; nothing else can be deleted. Click the Ribbon (anywhere but the Office Button) to select the top-level Ribbon. When you right-click the top-level Ribbon, you see a context menu that includes the commands Add Ribbon Tab and Export Ribbon to XML. You could choose Add Ribbon Tab to add a new Ribbon. Instead, drag a Tab control from the toolbox onto the Ribbon designer.

The newly added tab is called tab1. Rename it TabAddIns by clicking tab1 to select it and then using the Properties grid to change the Name property to TabAddIns. Also change the Label control in the Properties grid to TabAddIns. When you add a Tab control from the toolbox, by default it is a custom tab. To see this effect, expand the ControlId in the Properties window, and note that the ControlIdType is Custom, as shown in Figure 17-38.

As we discussed earlier, the default Ribbon created when you add a new Ribbon has a Tab control that represents the built-in Add-Ins tab. To make your newly added tab represent a built-in tab, you must first change the ControlIdType to Office by choosing Office from the drop-down list next to ControlIdType in the Properties window. Next, you must ensure that the OfficeId is set to TabAddIns.

How do you know to pick the identifier TabAddIns? Unfortunately, Visual Studio doesn't provide any help here. You must consult the documentation for Ribbon IDs—specifically, a set of spreadsheets that tell you all the IDs for built-in Ribbon elements, including tabs, available at www.microsoft.com/downloads/details.aspx?familyid=4329d9e9-4d11-46a5-898d-23e4f331e9ae&displaylang=en.

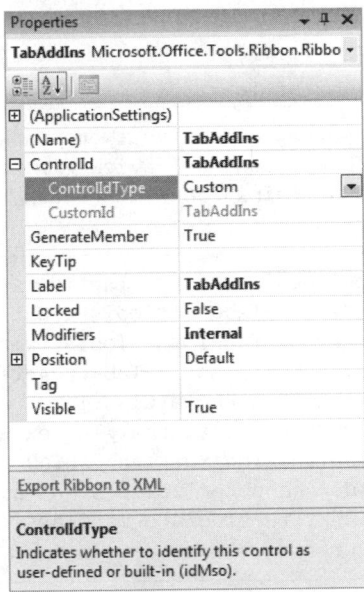

Figure 17-38: New tabs are added with ControlIdType
Custom, as shown in the Properties window.

Table 17-4 shows a list of the tab IDs for Word, Excel, and Outlook. From the name of the ID, you should be able to figure out the tab that it corresponds to. Also, Table 17-4 lists both top-level tabs and contextual tabs, which are described at the start of this chapter (refer to Figure 17-1).

Now that you have a tab that corresponds to the Add-Ins tab, add a Group control to it. To do this, you can select the Tab control and then double-click the Group control in the toolbox, click the Group control in the toolbox and drag a rectangle in the tab area, or drag and drop the Group control from the toolbox to the tab area. The Ribbon is back to the state it was in when you created it.

Next, modify the Group control slightly. Click the Group control, and set its label to Rating by using the Properties window. Also give the Group control a Dialog Launcher. To do this, click the Add DialogBoxLauncher hyperlink at the bottom of the Properties window. A little icon appears in the bottom-right corner of the Group control, and an event is raised when the user clicks this icon. You want to handle this event, but first look at the code behind the Ribbon. To view the code behind the Ribbon, right-click

TABLE 17-4: Top-Level and Contextual-Tab IDs for Word, Excel, and Outlook

Context	Tab IDs
Top-level tabs for Word	TabHome, TabInsert, TabPageLayoutWord, TabReferences, TabMailings, TabReviewWord, TabView, TabDeveloper, TabAddIns, TabOutlining, TabPrintPreview, TabBlogInsert, TabBlogPost
Contextual tabs for Word	TabSmartArtToolsDesign, TabSmartArtToolsFormat, TabChartToolsDesign, TabChartToolsLayout, TabChartToolsFormat, TabPictureToolsFormat, TabDrawingToolsFormatClassic, TabWordArtToolsFormat, TabDiagramToolsFormatClassic, TabOrganizationChartToolsFormat, TabTextBoxToolsFormat, TabTableToolsDesign, TabTableToolsLayout, TabHeaderAndFooterToolsDesign, TabEquationToolsDesign, TabPictureToolsFormatClassic, TabInkToolsPens
Top-level tabs for Excel	TabHome, TabInsert, TabPageLayoutExcel, TabFormulas, TabData, TabReview, TabView, TabDeveloper, TabAddIns, TabPrintPreview
Contextual tabs for Excel	TabSmartArtToolsDesign, TabSmartArtToolsFormat, TabChartToolsDesign, TabChartToolsLayout, TabChartToolsFormat, TabDrawingToolsFormat, TabPictureToolsFormat, TabPivotTableToolsOptions, TabPivotTableToolsDesign, TabHeaderAndFooterToolsDesign, TabTableToolsDesignExcel, TabPivotChartToolsDesign, TabPivotChartToolsLayout, TabPivotChartToolsFormat, TabPivotChartToolsAnalyze, TabInkToolsPens
Top-level tabs for Outlook	TabAppointment, TabNewMailMessage, TabDistributionList, TabContact, TabTask, TabReadMessage, TabInsert, TabFormatText, TabOptions, TabDeveloper, TabAddIns
Contextual tabs for Outlook	TabSmartArtToolsDesign, TabSmartArtToolsFormat, TabChartToolsDesign, TabChartToolsLayout, TabChartToolsFormat, TabPictureToolsFormat, TabDrawingToolsFormatClassic, TabWordArtToolsFormat, TabDiagramToolsFormatClassic, TabOrganizationChartToolsFormat, TabTextBoxToolsFormat, TabTableToolsDesign, TabTableToolsLayout, TabEquationToolsDesign, TabPictureToolsFormatClassic, TabInkToolsPens

the Ribbon designer and choose View Code from the context menu. The code shown in Listing 17-1 appears.

Listing 17-1: Default Code Behind a Ribbon

```
using System;
using System.Collections.Generic;
using System.Linq;
using System.Text;
using Microsoft.Office.Tools.Ribbon;

namespace ExcelWorkbook1
{
  public partial class Ribbon1 : OfficeRibbon
  {
    public Ribbon1()
    {
      InitializeComponent();
    }

    private void Ribbon1_Load(object sender, RibbonUIEventArgs e)
    {

    }
  }
}
```

Examining the default code, you see that your code is in a partial class. Your code in the Ribbon1.cs item is compiled together with code generated for you by Visual Studio in the file Ribbon1.Designer.cs under the Ribbon1.cs item in the Solution Explorer. The default code that is generated for you has a handler for the Ribbon's Load event. In this handler, you can put any code that you want to run when the Ribbon first loads.

Modify this code to handle the DialogBoxLauncherClick event. To do this, go back to the visual designer by double-clicking Ribbon1.cs in the Solution Explorer. Then click the Group control to select it. Click the lightning-bolt icon in the Properties window to show the events for the Group control. A single event appears there: DialogLauncherClick. Double-click the DialogLauncherClick line in the Properties window. This action creates an event handler for the Group control's DialogLauncherClick called `group1_DialogLauncherClick` and drops you into the code file for the Ribbon. Next, just add some simple code to show a dialog box when the user clicks the Dialog Launcher icon, as shown in Listing 17-2.

Listing 17-2: A Simple Handler for the Group Control's DialogLauncherClick Event

```
using System;
using System.Collections.Generic;
using System.Linq;
using System.Text;
using Microsoft.Office.Tools.Ribbon;
using System.Windows.Forms;

namespace ExcelWorkbook1
{
  public partial class Ribbon1 : OfficeRibbon
  {
    public Ribbon1()
    {
      InitializeComponent();
    }

    private void Ribbon1_Load(object sender, RibbonUIEventArgs e)
    {

    }

    private void group1_DialogLauncherClick(object sender, RibbonControlEventArgs e)
    {
      MessageBox.Show("You clicked the Dialog Launcher icon!");
    }
  }
}
```

You're going to create a set of controls that allow the user to assign a one- to five-star rating to the document. To do this, you use a Label control, a Button Group control, and five Toggle Button controls. Switch back to the visual Ribbon designer so you can add these controls to the Group control. Then drag and drop in a Label control. Set the Label control's Label property to "Rating:" by using the Properties window. Next, drag and drop a Button Group control, and drag a Toggle Button control into the Button Group control. Click the newly added Toggle Button control to select it. In the Properties window, set its image property to a graphic file. You can pick any graphic file you want, but for this example, use a star graphic. To set the image property, click the ellipsis (...) button next to the Image property in the Properties window to open the Select Resource dialog box, shown in Figure 17-39. Click the Local Resource radio button; then click the Import command button to open a dialog box where you can choose a GIF, JPG, WMF, BMP, or PNG file.

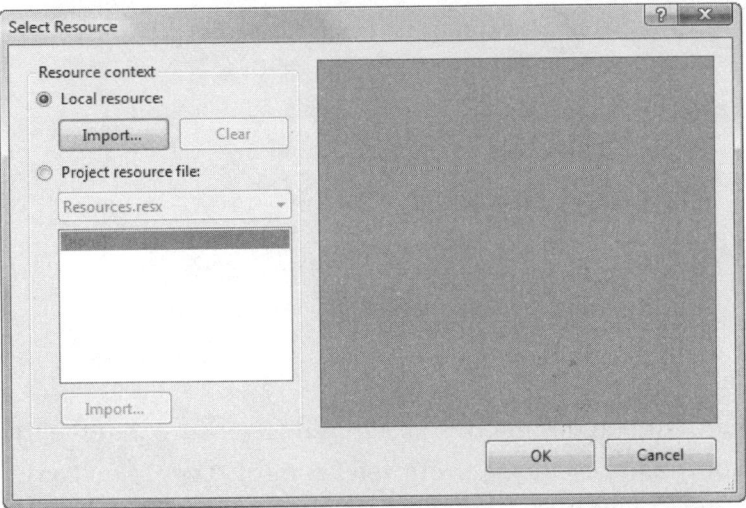

Figure 17-39: Importing an image with the Select Resource dialog box.

▪ NOTE

If you want to have transparency in your image file, you must use the transparency support provided by .PNG files or transparency support provided by .GIF files; the other file formats do not support transparency in the Ribbon.

With an image chosen for the Toggle Button control, set the ShowLabel property to `false` in the Properties Window. Now you want to create four more Toggle Button controls just like this one. To do so, click the Toggle Button control, choose Edit > Copy, select the Button Group control, and choose Edit > Paste. Repeat this procedure four times, and you should have five Toggle Button controls, as shown in Figure 17-40.

▪ TIP

Clicking the Button Group control to select it can be a little hard. You can also press Tab or Shift+Tab in the designer to move through selecting the various controls, or you can choose the control from the drop-down list at the top of the Properties window.

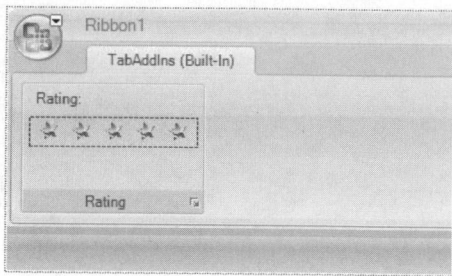

Figure 17-40: The final Ribbon design.

With the Ribbon designed, take a minute to ensure that the five Toggle Button controls are named, from left to right, toggleButton1, toggle-Button2, toggleButton3, toggleButton4, and toggleButton5. If the Toggle Button controls are in a different order, drag and drop them into the right order, as described in the "Reordering Controls" section earlier in this chapter.

Now add some more code behind the Ribbon. This code ensures that when you click a particular Toggle Button control (toggleButton4, for example), all lower-numbered toggle buttons are checked (toggleButton3, toggleButton2, and toggleButton1), and all higher-numbered toggle buttons are not checked (toggleButton5). To add the event handlers for the Toggle Button controls, you can double-click each Toggle Button control, which adds the event handler, or use the Properties window to add the event handler for each control.

You also want to store your star rating in the document as a custom document property called "StarRating". You add some code in the Ribbon load event to do this. The Globals object is used to get access to the This-Workbook object for the project. The Load event in Listing 17-3 has some interesting logic that can affect the state of the Ribbon. If the workbook doesn't already have the custom property "StarRating" associated with it, and the document is read only, you set Visible to false on the group1 control. This setting prevents the Add-Ins tab from appearing if no other add-ins are adding Group controls to that tab. If the workbook does have the custom property but is read only, you display the number of stars by using the Checked state of the Toggle Button controls, but then you disable the

Toggle Button controls so that the rating cannot be changed. Finally, when the Toggle Button controls are clicked, they call the helper method Set-Stars, which checks the appropriate button and updates the custom document property "StarRating".

Listing 17-3: A More Complete Ribbon Associated with an Excel Workbook

```csharp
using System;
using System.Collections.Generic;
using System.Linq;
using System.Text;
using Microsoft.Office.Tools.Ribbon;
using System.Windows.Forms;
using Office = Microsoft.Office.Core;

namespace ExcelWorkbook1
{
  public partial class Ribbon1 : OfficeRibbon
  {
    private Office.DocumentProperty prop = null;
    public Ribbon1()
    {
      InitializeComponent();
    }

    private void Ribbon1_Load(object sender, RibbonUIEventArgs e)
    {
      bool readOnly = Globals.ThisWorkbook.ReadOnly;

      Office.DocumentProperties props =
        Globals.ThisWorkbook.CustomDocumentProperties as Office.DocumentProperties;
      try
      {
        prop = props["StarRating"];
      }
      catch { }

      if (prop == null && readOnly == false)
      {
        // Try to add it
        try
        {
          prop = props.Add("StarRating", false,
            Office.MsoDocProperties.msoPropertyTypeNumber, 0, System.Type.Missing);
        }
        catch { }
      }
```

```csharp
    if (prop == null)
    {
      // Failed to add property, hide group control.
      this.group1.Visible = false;
      return;
    }

    SetStars(System.Convert.ToInt32(prop.Value));
    if (readOnly)
    {
      toggleButton1.Enabled = false;
      toggleButton2.Enabled = false;
      toggleButton3.Enabled = false;
      toggleButton4.Enabled = false;
      toggleButton5.Enabled = false;
    }
}

private void group1_DialogLauncherClick(object sender, RibbonControlEventArgs e)
{
  MessageBox.Show("You clicked the Dialog Launcher icon!");
}

private void SetStars(int starCount)
{
  toggleButton1.Checked = starCount >= 1;
  toggleButton2.Checked = starCount >= 2;
  toggleButton3.Checked = starCount >= 3;
  toggleButton4.Checked = starCount >= 4;
  toggleButton5.Checked = starCount >= 5;

  if (prop != null && Globals.ThisWorkbook.ReadOnly == false)
  {
    prop.Value = starCount;
  }
}

private void toggleButton1_Click(object sender, RibbonControlEventArgs e)
{
  SetStars(1);
}

private void toggleButton2_Click(object sender, RibbonControlEventArgs e)
{
  SetStars(2);
}

private void toggleButton3_Click(object sender, RibbonControlEventArgs e)
{
  SetStars(3);
}
```

```
        private void toggleButton4_Click(object sender, RibbonControlEventArgs e)
        {
          SetStars(4);
        }

        private void toggleButton5_Click(object sender, RibbonControlEventArgs e)
        {
          SetStars(5);
        }
    }
}
```

If you just paste the code in Listing 17-3 into your Ribbon1.cs code file, it won't work unless you also add the event handlers by using the Ribbon designer. Why? Remember that your class is actually a combination of the code in Ribbon1.cs and Ribbon1.Designer.cs. The event handler hookup is added in Ribbon1.Designer.cs when you double-click a Toggle Button control in the designer or use the property grid. Listing 17-4 shows the Ribbon1.Designer.cs code that is generated for this example; you can see that the event handlers are added in this code file. You typically won't edit this file, as you could break the Ribbon designer if you edited it in a way that the designer didn't understand. Also notice the partial class This-RibbonCollection in Listing 17-4, which enables you to use Globals.Ribbons .Ribbon1 to access this Ribbon from other code.

Listing 17-4: The Generated Ribbon1.Designer.cs File Associated with the Ribbon from Listing 17-3

```
namespace ExcelWorkbook1
{
  partial class Ribbon1
  {
    /// <summary>
    /// Required designer variable.
    /// </summary>
    private System.ComponentModel.IContainer components = null;

    /// <summary>
    /// Clean up any resources being used.
    /// </summary>
    /// <param name="disposing">true if managed resources should be disposed;
    /// otherwise, false.</param>
    protected override void Dispose(bool disposing)
    {
```

```
    if (disposing && (components != null))
    {
      components.Dispose();
    }
    base.Dispose(disposing);
}

#region Component Designer generated code

/// <summary>
/// Required method for Designer support; do not modify
/// the contents of this method with the code editor.
/// </summary>
private void InitializeComponent()
{
  Microsoft.Office.Tools.Ribbon.RibbonDialogLauncher ribbonDialogLauncher1 =
    new Microsoft.Office.Tools.Ribbon.RibbonDialogLauncher();
  System.ComponentModel.ComponentResourceManager resources =
    new System.ComponentModel.ComponentResourceManager(typeof(Ribbon1));
  this.TabAddIns = new Microsoft.Office.Tools.Ribbon.RibbonTab();
  this.group1 = new Microsoft.Office.Tools.Ribbon.RibbonGroup();
  this.label1 = new Microsoft.Office.Tools.Ribbon.RibbonLabel();
  this.buttonGroup1 = new Microsoft.Office.Tools.Ribbon.RibbonButtonGroup();
  this.toggleButton1 = new Microsoft.Office.Tools.Ribbon.RibbonToggleButton();
  this.toggleButton2 = new Microsoft.Office.Tools.Ribbon.RibbonToggleButton();
  this.toggleButton3 = new Microsoft.Office.Tools.Ribbon.RibbonToggleButton();
  this.toggleButton4 = new Microsoft.Office.Tools.Ribbon.RibbonToggleButton();
  this.toggleButton5 = new Microsoft.Office.Tools.Ribbon.RibbonToggleButton();
  this.TabAddIns.SuspendLayout();
  this.group1.SuspendLayout();
  this.buttonGroup1.SuspendLayout();
  this.SuspendLayout();
  //
  // TabAddIns
  //
  this.TabAddIns.ControlId.ControlIdType =
    Microsoft.Office.Tools.Ribbon.RibbonControlIdType.Office;
  this.TabAddIns.Groups.Add(this.group1);
  this.TabAddIns.Label = "TabAddIns";
  this.TabAddIns.Name = "TabAddIns";
  //
  // group1
  //
  this.group1.DialogLauncher = ribbonDialogLauncher1;
  this.group1.Items.Add(this.label1);
  this.group1.Items.Add(this.buttonGroup1);
  this.group1.Label = "Rating";
  this.group1.Name = "group1";
  this.group1.DialogLauncherClick += new
    System.EventHandler<
```

```
    Microsoft.Office.Tools.Ribbon.RibbonControlEventArgs>(
    this.group1_DialogLauncherClick);
//
// label1
//
this.label1.Label = "Rating:";
this.label1.Name = "label1";
//
// buttonGroup1
//
this.buttonGroup1.Items.Add(this.toggleButton1);
this.buttonGroup1.Items.Add(this.toggleButton2);
this.buttonGroup1.Items.Add(this.toggleButton3);
this.buttonGroup1.Items.Add(this.toggleButton4);
this.buttonGroup1.Items.Add(this.toggleButton5);
this.buttonGroup1.Name = "buttonGroup1";
//
// toggleButton1
//
this.toggleButton1.Image = ((System.Drawing.Image)
    (resources.GetObject("toggleButton1.Image")));
this.toggleButton1.Label = "toggleButton1";
this.toggleButton1.Name = "toggleButton1";
this.toggleButton1.ShowImage = true;
this.toggleButton1.ShowLabel = false;
this.toggleButton1.Click += new System.EventHandler<
    Microsoft.Office.Tools.Ribbon.RibbonControlEventArgs>(
    this.toggleButton1_Click);
//
// toggleButton2
//
this.toggleButton2.Image = ((System.Drawing.Image)
    (resources.GetObject("toggleButton2.Image")));
this.toggleButton2.Label = "toggleButton1";
this.toggleButton2.Name = "toggleButton2";
this.toggleButton2.ShowImage = true;
this.toggleButton2.ShowLabel = false;
this.toggleButton2.Click += new
    System.EventHandler<
    Microsoft.Office.Tools.Ribbon.RibbonControlEventArgs>(
    this.toggleButton2_Click);
//
// toggleButton3
//
this.toggleButton3.Image = ((System.Drawing.Image)
    (resources.GetObject("toggleButton3.Image")));
this.toggleButton3.Label = "toggleButton1";
this.toggleButton3.Name = "toggleButton3";
this.toggleButton3.ShowImage = true;
this.toggleButton3.ShowLabel = false;
```

```
        this.toggleButton3.Click += new System.EventHandler<
          Microsoft.Office.Tools.Ribbon.RibbonControlEventArgs>(
          this.toggleButton3_Click);
        //
        // toggleButton4
        //
        this.toggleButton4.Image = ((System.Drawing.Image)
          (resources.GetObject("toggleButton4.Image")));
        this.toggleButton4.Label = "toggleButton1";
        this.toggleButton4.Name = "toggleButton4";
        this.toggleButton4.ShowImage = true;
        this.toggleButton4.ShowLabel = false;
        this.toggleButton4.Click += new System.EventHandler<
          Microsoft.Office.Tools.Ribbon.RibbonControlEventArgs>(
          this.toggleButton4_Click);
        //
        // toggleButton5
        //
        this.toggleButton5.Image = ((System.Drawing.Image)
          (resources.GetObject("toggleButton5.Image")));
        this.toggleButton5.Label = "toggleButton1";
        this.toggleButton5.Name = "toggleButton5";
        this.toggleButton5.ShowImage = true;
        this.toggleButton5.ShowLabel = false;
        this.toggleButton5.Click += new System.EventHandler<
          Microsoft.Office.Tools.Ribbon.RibbonControlEventArgs>(
          this.toggleButton5_Click);
        //
        // Ribbon1
        //
        this.Name = "Ribbon1";
        this.RibbonType = "Microsoft.Excel.Workbook";
        this.Tabs.Add(this.TabAddIns);
        this.Load += new System.EventHandler<
          Microsoft.Office.Tools.Ribbon.RibbonUIEventArgs>(
          this.Ribbon1_Load);
        this.TabAddIns.ResumeLayout(false);
        this.TabAddIns.PerformLayout();
        this.group1.ResumeLayout(false);
        this.group1.PerformLayout();
        this.buttonGroup1.ResumeLayout(false);
        this.buttonGroup1.PerformLayout();
        this.ResumeLayout(false);

    }

    #endregion

    internal Microsoft.Office.Tools.Ribbon.RibbonTab TabAddIns;
    internal Microsoft.Office.Tools.Ribbon.RibbonGroup group1;
```

```
    internal Microsoft.Office.Tools.Ribbon.RibbonLabel label1;
    internal Microsoft.Office.Tools.Ribbon.RibbonButtonGroup buttonGroup1;
    internal Microsoft.Office.Tools.Ribbon.RibbonToggleButton toggleButton1;
    internal Microsoft.Office.Tools.Ribbon.RibbonToggleButton toggleButton2;
    internal Microsoft.Office.Tools.Ribbon.RibbonToggleButton toggleButton3;
    internal Microsoft.Office.Tools.Ribbon.RibbonToggleButton toggleButton4;
    internal Microsoft.Office.Tools.Ribbon.RibbonToggleButton toggleButton5;

  }

  partial class ThisRibbonCollection :
        Microsoft.Office.Tools.Ribbon.RibbonReadOnlyCollection
  {
    internal Ribbon1 Ribbon1
    {
      get { return this.GetRibbon<Ribbon1>(); }
    }
  }
}
```

Creating a Ribbon in an Outlook Add-In Project

Now consider a second example: the creation of a Ribbon in an Outlook add-in. Using the Ribbon in Outlook is slightly more complex than using the Ribbon in Word and Excel. The reason is that in Excel and Word, you create a single Ribbon for the document or for the main application window. In Outlook, you can specify a different Ribbon customization for each of the 19 types of Inspector windows that can be displayed.

For this example, you create an add-in that inserts text into the e-mail message you are composing and helps you navigate the message. Along the way, we show you several additional Ribbon features in action—specifically, how to create a new tab, how to use the Gallery and Menu controls, and how to write code that makes the content of the Gallery and Menu controls dynamic at runtime.

To get started, create a new Outlook add-in project; then choose Project > Add New Item. In the Add New Item dialog box, click Ribbon (Visual Designer) and then click the Add button. A new Ribbon is created, and the Ribbon designer is displayed. Click the Ribbon (somewhere on the top or bottom border) to select the top-level Ribbon. In the Properties window, you see a property called RibbonType, which can be set to configure which

Inspector window types the Ribbon is displayed for. You can associate a single Ribbon with one or more Inspector window types. Drop down the RibbonType list, and make sure that `Microsoft.Outlook.Mail.Compose` is checked. This setting displays the Ribbon you create in the Inspector window that you use to compose a new mail message. Figure 17-41 shows the other Inspector types with which a Ribbon can be associated in Outlook.

For this example, you want to create a new custom tab rather than use the Add-Ins tab. Remember, however, the guidance we gave earlier in this chapter about when to use the Add-Ins tab versus a new custom tab. This sample probably would not merit a new custom tab, but for this example, you will create one to illustrate the feature.

To change the default add-in tab that is created for a Ribbon to a custom tab, click the TabAddIns tab to select it. In the Properties window, expand the ControlId setting. Change ControlIdType from `Office` to `Custom`. Now the add-in will create a new custom tab. Use the Properties window to change the label of the tab to Tools.

Next, click the Group control that is created for you, and change the label in the Properties window to Tools as well. Then drag and drop a Gallery control from the toolbox onto the Group control. Use the Properties window to set the label for the Gallery control to Salutations. Next, click the Items line in the Properties window, and click the ellipsis (...) button

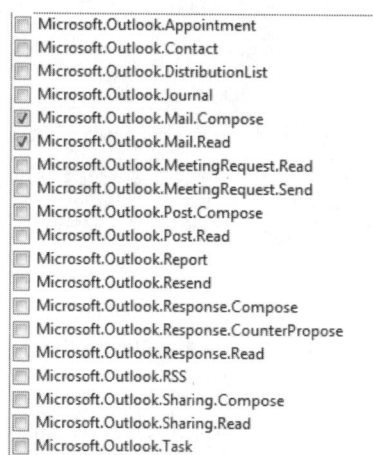

Figure 17-41: Possible values for Ribbon types corresponding to Inspector window types.

that appears to display the DropDownItem Collection Editor dialog box, in which you are going to add several members. Click the Add button six times to add six members. Now, for each member, clear the Label property so that it is empty. Next, set the tag of each item to a common salutation. You are setting the tag and leaving the label empty because you are going to generate an image dynamically for each item in the Gallery, using the text you put in the tag and the current font settings in the mail editor.

Set your six members' Tag properties to these values, respectively: "Ladies:", "Gentlemen:", "Dear Sir:", "Dear Sir or Madam:", "Dear <Name>:", and "To Whom it May Concern:". The Collection Editor dialog box should look something like Figure 17-42 when you are done editing the last item. Finally, click the OK button to complete editing the items in the Gallery.

Now you are going to edit the Buttons collection associated with the Gallery control to add a button that will pick a salutation from the Items list at random. Click the Gallery control to select it. Then click the Buttons line in the Properties window, and click the ellipsis (…) button that appears to display the Button Collection Editor dialog box. Click the Add button to add a single button. Set the Label property of the button to "Pick for me". Note while you are editing the button that its Id property is set to `button1`. You will use that fact later in your code.

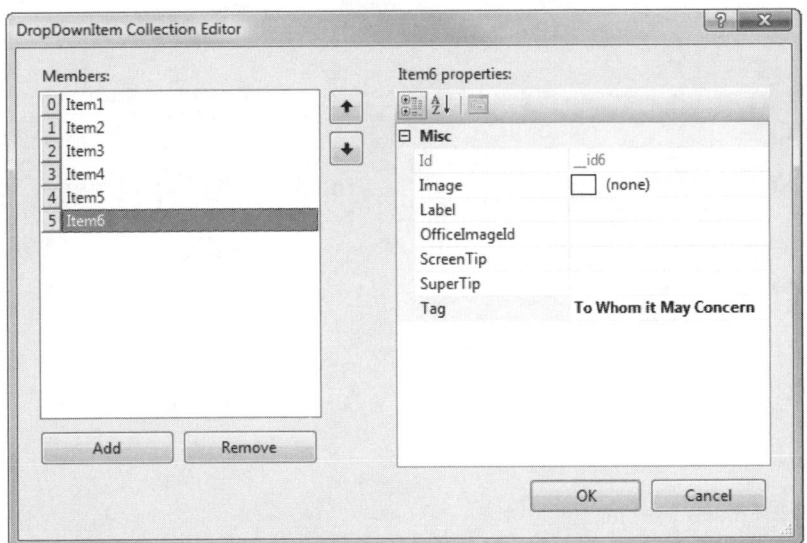

Figure 17-42: Collection Editor dialog box with salutations.

With the Gallery control configured the way you want, you can write some code behind it. Click the Gallery control again to select it. Then click the lightning-bolt icon in the Properties window to show the events for the Gallery control. Three events are displayed: ButtonClick, which is raised when a button in the Buttons collection is clicked; Click, which is raised when an item in the Items collection is clicked; and ItemsLoading, which is raised when the user drops down the Gallery control before its contents are displayed. ItemsLoading is the event that can be handled at runtime to modify the Items and Buttons lists before the Gallery control is displayed to the user.

You want to add handlers for all three events. First, write the handler for the ItemsLoading event. Double-click the ItemsLoading event in the Properties window. Visual Studio generates an event handler in the code behind the Ribbon and displays the event handler. Add a reference in your project to the Word PIA by right-clicking the References folder in the Solution Explorer and choosing Add Reference from the context menu. Click the COM tab, select the Microsoft Word 12.0 Object Library, and click the OK button to add the reference. You need this reference because you want to talk to the Word editor that's used when an Outlook e-mail is edited to see what fonts the user is currently using. You will use this font information to create images dynamically for the items in the Gallery control's Items collection.

> ■ **NOTE**
>
> Adding a reference to the Word PIA could result in two references to the Office PIA (Microsoft.Office.Core) being added. Simply delete one of the Office references from the References folder in the Solution Explorer to fix this issue.

Add these three using statements to the top of your Ribbon1.cs code file:

```
using System.Drawing;
using Outlook = Microsoft.Office.Interop.Outlook;
using Word = Microsoft.Office.Interop.Word;
```

Now consider the code in Listing 17-5, which you can add to your handler for the ItemsLoading event. First, use the Context property of the Ribbon class to get the Outlook Inspector object for the window the Ribbon is associated with. The Context property returns an `object` that can be cast to an Outlook.Inspector object if you are building an add-in for Outlook.

Next, use the WordEditor property of Outlook's Inspector object to get an instance of the Word.Document object. Then you get the current selection, which you will use to determine the font being used where the user's cursor is currently positioned. Use the Selection object's Font property to get a Font object; then use the Font object's Name and Size properties to get the Name and Size of the font in use.

Next, iterate over all the Items collection associated with the Gallery control. Each item in the Items collection is of type RibbonDropDownItem. For each item in the Items collection, you want to create a Bitmap dynamically. First, create the Bitmap object, and use the format `Drawing.Imaging.PixelFormat.Format32bppPArgb`. This format supports transparency, so use MakeTransparent in your code to make the background transparent. Then create a Graphics object on the image you created, clear the image with a `Color.White` background, and draw some lines to add a little interest to the image. Finally, call the DrawString method with the Tag for the item that you set earlier in the Collection editor for each item. You use the font name and font size that are currently being used in the Outlook mail item.

Listing 17-5: A Handler for the Gallery Control's ItemsLoading Event

```
private void gallery1_ItemsLoading(object sender, RibbonControlEventArgs e)
{
  Outlook.Inspector inspector = this.Context as Outlook.Inspector;
  Word.Document doc = inspector.WordEditor as Word.Document;
  Word.Selection selection = doc.Application.Selection;
  string font = "Sego UI";
  float fontSize = 14f;

  if (selection != null)
  {
    font = selection.Font.Name;
    fontSize = selection.Font.Size;
  }

  foreach (RibbonDropDownItem item in gallery1.Items)
  {
```

```
Bitmap image = new Bitmap(170, 50,
    System.Drawing.Imaging.PixelFormat.Format32bppPArgb);
Graphics graphics = Graphics.FromImage(image);
graphics.Clear(Color.White);
graphics.DrawLine(Pens.Blue, new PointF(0f, 2f), new PointF(0f, 50f));
graphics.DrawLine(Pens.Blue, new PointF(0f, 4f), new PointF(170f, 4f));
graphics.DrawLine(Pens.Blue, new PointF(0f, 2f), new PointF(170f, 2f));
graphics.DrawString(item.Tag.ToString(), new Font(font, fontSize),
    Brushes.Black, new PointF(0f, 12f));
image.MakeTransparent(Color.White);
item.Image = image;
    }
}
```

Figure 17-43 shows the result when you run this add-in, compose a new mail message, and then drop down the Gallery control.

Now you can handle the other two events associated with the Gallery control: Click and ButtonClick. To handle the Click event, click the Gallery control in the Ribbon designer to select it. In the Properties window, show the events by clicking the lightning-bolt icon, and double-click the Click event to add an event handler. The Click event is raised when an item in the Items collection is clicked. As shown in Listing 17-6, you use the Select-edItem property of the Gallery control to determine which RibbonDrop-

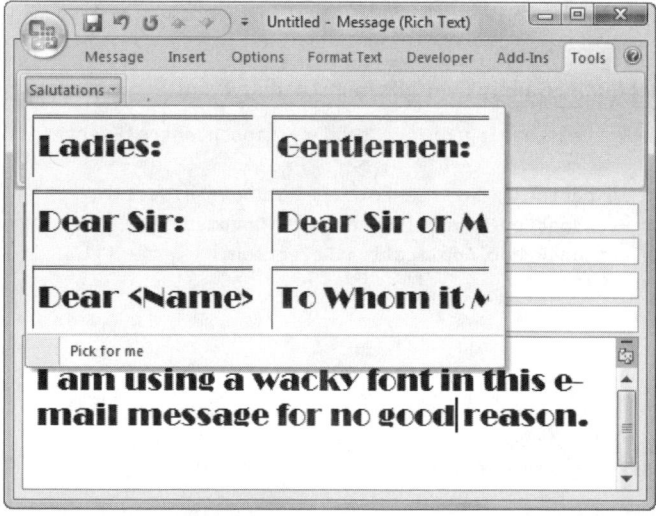

Figure 17-43: Dynamic images created for the Gallery control's Items collection.

DownItem in the Items collection was clicked. Then you call a `ClickHelper` method that we will show later and pass the Tag of the clicked-on Ribbon-DropDownItem. The Tag, as you remember, is set to the salutation text, and you'll use that text in the `ClickHelper` method to insert your salutation text into the e-mail message.

Listing 17-6: A Handler for the Click Event

```
private void gallery1_Click(object sender, RibbonControlEventArgs e)
{
  RibbonDropDownItem selectedItem = this.gallery1.SelectedItem;
  if (selectedItem != null)
  {
    ClickHelper(selectedItem.Tag.ToString());
  }
}
```

To handle the ButtonClick event, click the Gallery control in the Ribbon designer to select it. Then use the Properties window to add an event handler by clicking the lightning-bolt icon and double-clicking the ButtonClick event. The ButtonClick event is raised when a Button in the Buttons collection is clicked. As shown in Listing 17-7, you use the RibbonControlEventArgs to determine which Button in the Buttons collection is clicked. For this example, you have only one button, but if you were to add a second button to the Buttons collection, you would need to be careful to check the sender, as in Listing 17-7, to distinguish among different buttons. Then you generate a random number to pick at random one of the salutations in the Items collection and use the `ClickHelper` method to insert the salutation text into the e-mail message.

Listing 17-7: A Handler for the Gallery Control's ButtonClick Event

```
private void gallery1_ButtonClick(object sender, RibbonControlEventArgs e)
{
  if (sender == button1)
  {
    Random r = new Random();
    int randomPick = r.Next(gallery1.Items.Count);
    ClickHelper(gallery1.Items[randomPick].Tag.ToString());
  }
}
```

You've seen how to work with the Items and Buttons collections and how to change the Ribbon dynamically at runtime. Now look at one more example of changing the Ribbon dynamically. Drag and drop a Menu control onto the Group control; set the Label of the control to Paragraphs, and set the Dynamic property to true. Notice that by default, Menu controls are not dynamic, but if you set the Dynamic property to true you can change their child controls at runtime. Click the lightning-bolt icon in the Properties window and double-click the ItemsLoading event.

The handler for the ItemsLoading event is shown in Listing 17-8. The handler creates and adds a RibbonButton for each paragraph of the e-mail message. The label of each RibbonButton is set to the first 50 characters of the first sentence of the given paragraph. You use the Tag property to save the paragraph number that corresponds to the RibbonButton. Finally, you add a handler for the Click event to each created button. Also, code at the start of the handler finds any existing controls in the menu (created the last time ItemsLoading was handled), removes the Click event handlers, and then clears the Items collection associated with the menu.

> ■ **NOTE**
>
> The Items collection for the menu returns RibbonControl objects rather than a more specific type because a Menu control's Items collection can contain multiple types of controls: Menu, Button, Check Box, Gallery, Separator, Toggle Button, and Split Button.

Listing 17-8: A Handler for the Menu Control's ItemsLoading Event

```
private void menu1_ItemsLoading(object sender, RibbonControlEventArgs e)
{
  foreach (RibbonControl ctl in menu1.Items)
  {
    RibbonButton btn = ctl as RibbonButton;
    if (btn != null)
    {
      btn.Click -= new EventHandler<RibbonControlEventArgs>(btn_Click);
    }
  }
  menu1.Items.Clear();
```

```
Outlook.Inspector inspector = this.Context as Outlook.Inspector;
Word.Document doc = inspector.WordEditor as Word.Document;
Word.Range content = doc.Content;

int paragraphCount = content.Paragraphs.Count;
for (int i = 1; i <= paragraphCount; i++)
{
  if (content.Paragraphs[i].Range.Words.Count > 1)
  {
    RibbonButton btn = new RibbonButton();
    btn.Tag = i.ToString();
    string label = content.Paragraphs[i].Range.Sentences[1].Text;
    label = label.Substring(0, Math.Min(label.Length, 50));
    btn.Label = label;
    menu1.Items.Add(btn);
    btn.Click += new EventHandler<RibbonControlEventArgs>(btn_Click);
  }
 }
}
```

Also note that Listing 17-8 could be rewritten to be more efficient. It could reuse Button controls that were already created and relabel those controls rather than clear the Items collection each time, for example. For simplicity and readability, we will keep the less efficient version.

The final code for the Outlook add-in is shown in Listing 17-9. This final listing adds the `ClickHelper` method that inserts the selected salutation into the e-mail message. It also adds the event handler for the paragraph buttons that select the right paragraph. Figure 17-44 shows the final paragraph menu in action.

Listing 17-9: A Handler for the Menu Control's ItemsLoading Event

```
using System;
using System.Collections.Generic;
using System.Linq;
using System.Text;
using Microsoft.Office.Tools.Ribbon;
using System.Windows.Forms;
using System.Drawing;
using Outlook = Microsoft.Office.Interop.Outlook;
using Word = Microsoft.Office.Interop.Word;

namespace OutlookAddIn1
{
  public partial class Ribbon1 : OfficeRibbon
  {
```

```csharp
public Ribbon1()
{
  InitializeComponent();
}


private void Ribbon1_Load(object sender, RibbonUIEventArgs e)
{

}


private void gallery1_ItemsLoading(object sender, RibbonControlEventArgs e)
{
  Outlook.Inspector inspector = this.Context as Outlook.Inspector;
  Word.Document doc = inspector.WordEditor as Word.Document;
  Word.Selection selection = doc.Application.Selection;
  string font = "Sego UI";
  float fontSize = 14f;

  if (selection != null)
  {
    font = selection.Font.Name;
    fontSize = selection.Font.Size;
  }

  foreach (RibbonDropDownItem item in gallery1.Items)
  {
    Bitmap image = new Bitmap(170, 50,
      System.Drawing.Imaging.PixelFormat.Format32bppPArgb);
    Graphics graphics = Graphics.FromImage(image);
    graphics.Clear(Color.White);
    graphics.DrawLine(Pens.Blue, new PointF(0f, 2f), new PointF(0f, 50f));
    graphics.DrawLine(Pens.Blue, new PointF(0f, 4f), new PointF(170f, 4f));
    graphics.DrawLine(Pens.Blue, new PointF(0f, 2f), new PointF(170f, 2f));
    graphics.DrawString(item.Tag.ToString(), new Font(font, fontSize),
      Brushes.Black, new PointF(0f, 12f));
    image.MakeTransparent(Color.White);
    item.Image = image;
  }
}


private void gallery1_ButtonClick(object sender, RibbonControlEventArgs e)
{
  if (button1 == sender)
  {
    Random r = new Random();
    int randomPick = r.Next(gallery1.Items.Count);
    ClickHelper(gallery1.Items[randomPick].Tag.ToString());
  }
}
```

```csharp
private void ClickHelper(string text)
{
  Outlook.Inspector inspector = this.Context as Outlook.Inspector;
  Word.Document doc = inspector.WordEditor as Word.Document;
  Word.Selection selection = doc.Application.Selection;
  if (selection != null)
  {
    selection.Text = text;
  }
}

private void gallery1_Click(object sender, RibbonControlEventArgs e)
{
  RibbonDropDownItem selectedItem = this.gallery1.SelectedItem;
  if (selectedItem != null)
  {
    ClickHelper(selectedItem.Tag.ToString());
  }
}

private void menu1_ItemsLoading(object sender, RibbonControlEventArgs e)
{
  foreach (RibbonControl ctl in menu1.Items)
  {
    RibbonButton btn = ctl as RibbonButton;
    if (btn != null)
    {
      btn.Click -= new EventHandler<RibbonControlEventArgs>(btn_Click);
    }
  }
  menu1.Items.Clear();
  Outlook.Inspector inspector = this.Context as Outlook.Inspector;
  Word.Document doc = inspector.WordEditor as Word.Document;
  Word.Range content = doc.Content;

  int paragraphCount = content.Paragraphs.Count;
  for (int i = 1; i <= paragraphCount; i++)
  {
    if (content.Paragraphs[i].Range.Words.Count > 1)
    {
      RibbonButton btn = new RibbonButton();
      btn.Tag = i.ToString() ;
      string label = content.Paragraphs[i].Range.Sentences[1].Text;
      label = label.Substring(0, Math.Min(label.Length, 50));
      btn.Label = label;
      menu1.Items.Add(btn);
      btn.Click += new EventHandler<RibbonControlEventArgs>(btn_Click);
    }
  }
}
```

```
    private void btn_Click(object sender, RibbonControlEventArgs e)
    {
      RibbonButton btn = sender as RibbonButton;
      string tag = btn.Tag.ToString();
      int paragraphNumber = Convert.ToInt32(tag);
      Outlook.Inspector inspector = this.Context as Outlook.Inspector;
      Word.Document doc = inspector.WordEditor as Word.Document;
      Word.Range content = doc.Content;
      content.Paragraphs[paragraphNumber].Range.Select();
    }
  }
}
```

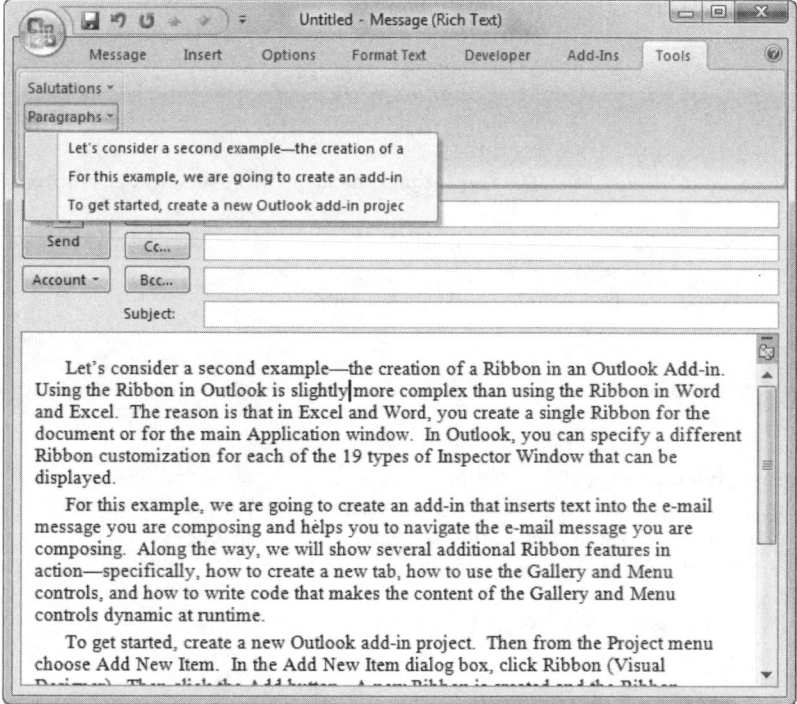

Figure 17-44: The Dynamic Paragraphs menu.

Advanced Ribbon Topics

Now that we've walked through how to create a Ribbon in VSTO, in this
section we consider several common advanced ways to customize the
Ribbon. These methods include working with multiple Ribbons in one

project, replacing the entire Office Ribbon with your custom Ribbon, dynamically adding controls to and removing controls from the Ribbon, adding custom commands to existing menus in the Office button, and delaying loading an add-in until the moment that the user invokes a Ribbon command it provides.

Multiple Ribbons in Word and Excel

You've seen that you can create multiple Ribbon project items in Outlook projects. What happens if you create multiple Ribbons in a Word or Excel document or add-in project? An add-in or document customization for Word and Excel can load only one Ribbon, so if you have multiple Ribbons, you must write some additional code to tell the Office application which of the Ribbon classes in your project to load. You might even have some logic that decides to create one Ribbon versus another based on some condition you define. But you can only pick the Ribbon to load at load time of your add-in. After you've selected a Ribbon, you can't change it until the add-in unloads and reloads at the next launch of the Office application.

Listing 17-10 shows code that can be added to the ThisDocument, ThisWorkbook, or ThisAddIn class to control which Ribbon is loaded for a project that has multiple Ribbons—in this example, Ribbon1 and Ribbon2. The code overrides the CreateRibbonObjects method, which VSTO uses to manage the Ribbon that is used by Office. We pick at random between the two Ribbons at startup.

Listing 17-10: Overriding CreateRibbonObjects in the ThisDocument, ThisWorkbook, or ThisAddIn Class

```
protected override Microsoft.Office.Tools.Ribbon.OfficeRibbon[]
  CreateRibbonObjects()
{
  Random r = new Random();
  if (r.Next(2) == 1)
  {
    return new Microsoft.Office.Tools.Ribbon.OfficeRibbon[] { new Ribbon1() };
  }
  else
  {
    return new Microsoft.Office.Tools.Ribbon.OfficeRibbon[] { new Ribbon2() };
  }
}
```

Even in Outlook the ability to create multiple Ribbon project items is limited; you can't load two Ribbons for the same RibbonType. If you create Ribbon1 and set its RibbonType to Microsoft.Outlook.Mail.Read, for example, and you create a second Ribbon called Ribbon2 and set its RibbonType to be Microsoft.Outlook.Mail.Read and Microsoft.Outlook.Mail .Compose, VSTO will display Ribbon1 when a read-only mail Inspector window is created and Ribbon2 when a compose mail Inspector window is created—but it won't display both Ribbon1 and Ribbon2 for the read-only mail Inspector window.

Replacing the Entire Ribbon

Sometimes, rather than extending the existing Ribbon, you want to throw the whole built-in Ribbon out and start from scratch. Fortunately, you have a way to do this. When you create a Ribbon in Visual Studio, click the top-level Ribbon in the designer (click the top or bottom area of the Ribbon to select the whole designer). Then, in the Properties window, you see the properties associated with the Ribbon. Set the StartFromScratch property to true. Now the Ribbon will show only the tabs you define. You can bring back any built-in tabs you want to appear by adding tabs to the Ribbon designer, setting the ControlIdType for the tab to Office, and specifying the OfficeIds listed in Table 17-4 earlier in this chapter. Also note that setting StartFromScratch to true does not clear the contents of the Office Button menu; basic commands such as New, Open, Save, Options, and Exit remain.

Dynamism and the Ribbon

You've explored several models for changing the Ribbon at runtime. First, four Ribbon controls have ItemsLoading events that let you change the content of the control's Items collection at runtime. These controls are the Menu, Gallery, Drop Down, and Combo Box controls. Remember that the Menu control's Dynamic property must be set to true for it to be dynamic at runtime.

You can also change properties of other Ribbon controls at runtime, as you saw in the Excel Rating example. In that example, you set the checked state of Toggle Button controls in the Ribbon. Although many properties can be changed at runtime, others can be modified only at design time. Table 17-5 shows these properties.

TABLE 17-5: Ribbon Control Properties That Cannot Be Changed After the Ribbon Constructor Executes

Control	Properties That Cannot Be Changed
OfficeRibbon	Global, RibbonType, StartFromScratch, Tabs
RibbonBox	BoxStyle
RibbonButton	ImageName, Position
RibbonComboBox	ImageName, MaxLength, ShowItemImage, SizeString
RibbonCheckBox	Position
RibbonDialogLauncher	ImageName
RibbonDropDown	ImageName, ShowItemImage, ShowItemLabel, SizeString, Buttons
RibbonEditBox	ImageName, MaxLength, SizeString
RibbonGallery	ColumnCount, ImageName, Position, RowCount, ShowItemImage, ShowItemLabel, ShowItem-Selection, Buttons
RibbonGroup	DialogLauncher, Position
RibbonMenu	Dynamic, ImageName, ItemSize, Position, Items (if Dynamic is set to `false`)
RibbonSeparator	Position, Title
RibbonSplitButton	ButtonType, ImageName, ItemSize, Position, Items
RibbonTab	ControlId, Groups, Position, Visible (for built-in tabs)
RibbonToggleButton	ImageName, Position

Saying that these properties cannot be changed at runtime is a bit of a simplification; the limitation is that after Office requests the Ribbon XML, they cannot be changed. So if you need to change these properties at runtime, write code in the constructor of your Ribbon object (because the constructor of your Ribbon will be invoked just before Office is handed the final Ribbon XML). You can also set these properties for controls that you create before you add them dynamically to a Menu, Gallery, Drop Down, or Combo Box control.

Finally, you can change the visibility of Ribbon controls by setting the Visible property of a control to `true` or `false`. You could use this technique to create several groups and tabs, but you might hide the ones that aren't applicable until they are needed based on the state of the application or what the user currently has selected.

Modifying the Office Button Menu

As you saw earlier, you can modify the Office Button menu by using the Ribbon designer. Clicking the down-arrow icon on the Office Button menu shows a drop region where you can drag and drop controls to be displayed in the Office Button. You can add Button, Check Box, Gallery, Separator, Menu, Toggle Button, and Split Button controls to the Office Button.

You may encounter a problem in customizing the Office Button menu: Rather than add commands to the bottom of the Office Button menu, you may want to add controls to the existing menus. You may want to add custom controls to the Save As, Print, Prepare, Send, and Publish menus, for example.

The Ribbon designer doesn't provide a simple way to accomplish this task, which is one of the limitations of the VSTO Ribbon designer that may force you down the path of using the XML programming model for Ribbon. With some additional code, however, you can continue to use the Ribbon designer and the VSTO programming model for the Ribbon, and add custom controls to these built-in menus.

To see how to do this, start by creating an Excel add-in project. Add a new Ribbon (Visual Designer) to your project. To keep things simple, delete the tab that VSTO creates for you by clicking the tab to select it and then pressing the Delete key. You are just going to customize the Office Button menu. Click the down arrow on the Office Button to show the drop region for the Office Button menu. Drag and drop five Button controls onto the drop region. Assuming that the button names are top to bottom `button1` through `button5`, set the labels for the buttons as shown in Figure 17-45. You may also want to handle the Click event for some of the buttons.

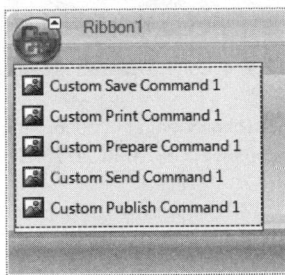

Figure 17-45: Five buttons in the Office Button menu.

Now choose Project > Add Class, name the new class CustomRibbon-Manager.cs, and edit the CustomRibbonManager class so that it looks like Listing 17-11. The most important code here is the sequence of calls to ReparentControlInOfficeMenu. For each call, the name of the control is specified, along with the ID of the built-in Office menu that the control should be a child of. You should customize this area of the code to move whichever controls you want from the Office Ribbon button to built-in submenus of the Office Ribbon button. The menu IDs were obtained from the spreadsheets with IDs for built-in Ribbon elements mentioned earlier in this chapter.

So how does this all work? As you may remember, the underlying model for the Office Ribbon is based on XML. The RibbonManager is an internal object that reads the VSTO model and translates it to an XML model. Listing 17-11 creates a custom implementation of a RibbonManager that modifies the XML model before giving it to Office. In particular, the ReparentControlInOfficeMenu method grabs the XML for the control you want to move, which is parented by the Office Ribbon button, and moves it to be a child of one of the built-in menus of the Office Ribbon Button.

Listing 17-11: CustomRibbonManager Class

```
using System;
using System.Collections.Generic;
using System.Linq;
using System.Text;
using System.Reflection;
using Microsoft.Office.Tools.Ribbon;
using System.Xml.Linq;
```

```csharp
namespace ExcelAddIn1
{
  class CustomRibbonManager : Microsoft.Office.Core.IRibbonExtensibility, IReflect
  {
    private Microsoft.Office.Tools.Ribbon.RibbonManager ribbonManager;
    const string ns = "{http://schemas.microsoft.com/office/2006/01/customui}";

    public CustomRibbonManager(
      Microsoft.Office.Tools.Ribbon.RibbonManager ribbonManager)
    {
      this.ribbonManager = ribbonManager;
    }

    string Microsoft.Office.Core.IRibbonExtensibility.GetCustomUI(string RibbonID)
    {
      // Get the default RibbonX string
      string xml = this.ribbonManager.GetCustomUI(RibbonID);

      // Parse the RibbonX and create XDocument instance
      XDocument doc = XDocument.Parse(xml);

      // Specify buttons that should move and menu ID to which they should move
      ReparentControlInOfficeMenu(doc, "button1", "FileSaveAsMenu");
      ReparentControlInOfficeMenu(doc, "button2", "FilePrintMenu");
      ReparentControlInOfficeMenu(doc, "button3", "FilePrepareMenu");
      ReparentControlInOfficeMenu(doc, "button4", "FileSendMenu");
      ReparentControlInOfficeMenu(doc, "button5", "MenuPublish");

      // return the modified XML.
      return doc.ToString();
    }

    private static void ReparentControlInOfficeMenu(
      XDocument doc, string controlId, string parentMenuId)
    {
      // Find the button1 XML element
      XElement button1 = doc.Descendants()
        .Where(x => (string)x.Attribute("id") == controlId)
        .First();

      // Remove the button1 element from the XML tree
      button1.Remove();

      // Find the officeMenu node
      XElement officeMenu = doc.Descendants()
        .Where(x => x.Name == ns + "officeMenu")
        .First();

      // See if the parentMenu node is already there.
      XElement parentMenu = officeMenu.Descendants()
```

```csharp
            .Where(x => (string)x.Attribute("idMso") == parentMenuId)
            .FirstOrDefault();

      if (parentMenu != null)
      {
        parentMenu.Add(button1);
      }
      else
      {
        officeMenu.Add(new XElement(ns + "menu",
          new XAttribute("idMso", parentMenuId), button1));
      }
    }

    FieldInfo IReflect.GetField(string name, BindingFlags bindingAttr)
    {
      return (this.ribbonManager as IReflect).GetField(name, bindingAttr);
    }

    FieldInfo[] IReflect.GetFields(BindingFlags bindingAttr)
    {
      return (this.ribbonManager as IReflect).GetFields(bindingAttr);
    }

    MemberInfo[] IReflect.GetMember(string name, BindingFlags bindingAttr)
    {
      return (this.ribbonManager as IReflect).GetMember(name, bindingAttr);
    }

    MemberInfo[] IReflect.GetMembers(BindingFlags bindingAttr)
    {
      return (this.ribbonManager as IReflect).GetMembers(bindingAttr);
    }

    MethodInfo IReflect.GetMethod(string name, BindingFlags bindingAttr)
    {
      return (this.ribbonManager as IReflect).GetMethod(name, bindingAttr);
    }

    MethodInfo IReflect.GetMethod(string name, BindingFlags bindingAttr,
      Binder binder, Type[] types, ParameterModifier[] modifiers)
    {
      return (this.ribbonManager as IReflect).GetMethod(
        name, bindingAttr, binder, types, modifiers);
    }

    MethodInfo[] IReflect.GetMethods(BindingFlags bindingAttr)
    {
      return (this.ribbonManager as IReflect).GetMethods(bindingAttr);
    }
```

```
    PropertyInfo[] IReflect.GetProperties(BindingFlags bindingAttr)
    {
        return (this.ribbonManager as IReflect).GetProperties(bindingAttr);
    }

    PropertyInfo IReflect.GetProperty(string name, BindingFlags bindingAttr,
        Binder binder, Type returnType, Type[] types, ParameterModifier[] modifiers)
    {
        return (this.ribbonManager as IReflect).GetProperty(name, bindingAttr,
            binder, returnType, types, modifiers);
    }

    PropertyInfo IReflect.GetProperty(string name, BindingFlags bindingAttr)
    {
        return (this.ribbonManager as IReflect).GetProperty(name, bindingAttr);
    }

    object IReflect.InvokeMember(string name, BindingFlags invokeAttr,
        Binder binder, object target, object[] args, ParameterModifier[] modifiers,
        System.Globalization.CultureInfo culture, string[] namedParameters)
    {
        return (this.ribbonManager as IReflect).InvokeMember(
            name, invokeAttr, binder, target, args, modifiers, culture, namedParameters);
    }

    Type IReflect.UnderlyingSystemType
    {
        get { return (this.ribbonManager as IReflect).UnderlyingSystemType; }
    }
  }
}
```

To get all this code hooked up, you must also modify your ThisAddIn,
ThisDocument, or ThisWorkbook class. For this example, because you are
creating an Excel add-in, add this code to the ThisAddIn class. First, add
these two using statements:

```
using System.Reflection;
using Microsoft.Office.Tools.Ribbon;
```

Also make sure that the ThisAddIn, ThisDocument, or ThisWorkbook
class has a customRibbonManager field declared like this:

```
private CustomRibbonManager customRibbonManager;
```

Then override the RequestService method by adding this code to your
ThisAddIn class. The code in Listing 17-12 hooks up the CustomRibbon-

Manager class and gives it an instance of the default RibbonManager class to which it delegates most of the functionality.

Listing 17-12: RequestService Override for ThisAddIn, ThisDocument, or ThisWorkbook to Use the CustomRibbonManager Class

```
protected override object RequestService(Guid serviceGuid)
{
  // Critical to call base.RequestService
  // to enable other VSTO services
  object service = base.RequestService(serviceGuid);

  Microsoft.Office.Tools.Ribbon.RibbonManager ribbonManager =
    service as Microsoft.Office.Tools.Ribbon.RibbonManager;
  if (ribbonManager != null)
  {
    if (this.customRibbonManager == null)
    {
      this.customRibbonManager = new CustomRibbonManager(ribbonManager);
    }
    service = this.customRibbonManager;
  }
  return service;
}
```

When you run this code, the controls that were parented to the Office Button menu will be parented into the submenus of the Office Button menu, as you would expect. Figure 17-46 shows the Custom Send Command 1 button in the Send menu.

Adding Commands to a Built-In Tab

As you've seen throughout this chapter, you can add custom groups to the Add-Ins tab, which is a built-in Office tab. It may not have dawned on you yet that you can use the same technique to add a custom group to one of the other built-in tabs in Office. Suppose that you want to add some Ribbon controls to the Home tab—the tab that appears first when you start Office applications.

The main restriction on adding UI to existing tabs is that you can add a new Group control only to an existing tab (and then add whatever controls you want to that new Group control). You can't add a Ribbon control to an existing Group control. You couldn't modify the built-in Font group and add a new strikethrough button to that built-in group, for example.

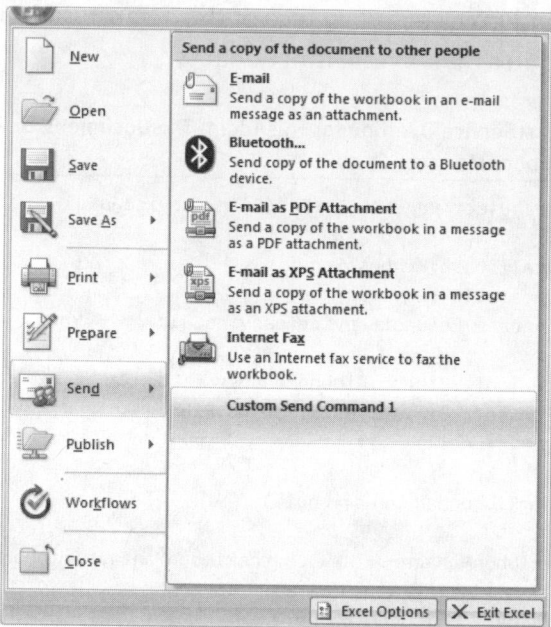

Figure 17-46: A Custom button in the Send menu.

To add a custom group to a built-in tab, simply add a new Tab in the Ribbon designer, set the ControlIdType to Office, and then set the OfficeId to the ID of a built-in tab (listed in Table 17-4 earlier in this chapter). You could use the OfficeId for the Home tab, which is TabHome. Then drag onto the tab your custom group and any other Ribbon controls you want to use within that custom group. When you run your add-in, your custom group will appear on the Home tab.

You can also set a tab in the Ribbon designer's ControlIdType to a built-in tab to hide a tab. Simply set the Visible property to false for the built-in tab you have added to the designer.

Using the Position Property

The Position property allows you to ensure that a control is positioned relative to another control. In the example in which you added a custom group to a built-in tab, the group was displayed to the right of all the existing groups on that tab. The Position property can be used to position a group relative to another built-in Office control. Position has two members:

PositionType and OfficeId. PositionType can be set to `BeforeOfficeId` or `AfterOfficeId`. OfficeId can be set to an OfficeId for the built-in Office control that you want to be positioned before or after. Remember that you can find built-in control IDs by downloading the spreadsheets mentioned in "Creating a Ribbon in an Excel Workbook Project" earlier in this chapter.

Using Built-In Office Images

For the Ribbon controls that have images, you can specify a custom image or reuse one of the built-in images that Office supplies. Controls that can use built-in Office images have an OfficeImageId property. But how do you figure out what image ID to set that property to?

Fortunately, a VSTO Ribbon IDs Power Tool helps you find IDs for built-in Office images. To download it, go to www.microsoft.com/downloads/details.aspx?FamilyId=46B6BF86-E35D-4870-B214-4D7B72B02BF9; then click the Download button to download the VSTO_PTRibbonIDs.exe file. Exit Visual Studio before running the download. When the setup is complete, relaunch Visual Studio. The Power Tool adds a new command to the Tools menu: ImageMso Window. This window, shown in Figure 17-47, has a search box where you can search for an image by name or browse all available images by clicking tabs 1 through 13. You can also pick either of two image formats: 16×16 pixels or 32×32 pixels.

To pick an image, click it. The image ID is copied to the Clipboard. Then click the control for which you want to set the OfficeImageId, and use the Properties window to paste the ID into the OfficeImageId property.

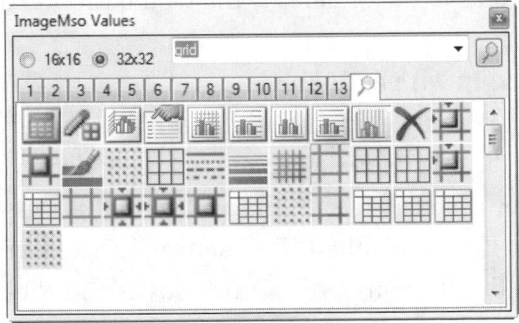

Figure 17-47: The VSTO Ribbon ID's Power Tool window.

Using Windows Forms Components

The Ribbon designer is based on the Windows Forms designer; therefore, you can drag and drop Windows Forms components (*not* controls) onto the designer and use them in your code. You could drop the Timer component onto the Ribbon designer and handle the Tick event to do periodic processing as part of your code, for example.

Coordinating Ribbons and Task Panes

Coordinating Ribbons and task panes—having a toggle button on the Ribbon that is associated with a task pane that toggles the visibility of the task pane, for example—is often difficult because of the multiple window issues described in Chapter 15, "Working with Application-Level Custom Task Panes." A VSTO Power Tool is available that helps you coordinate Ribbon and task-pane state. To download it, go to www.microsoft.com/downloads/details.aspx?FamilyId=46B6BF86-E35D-4870-B214-4D7B72B02BF9; then click the Download button to download the VSTO_PT.exe file. This file installs some sample code that you can use in the C:\Program Files\Microsoft VSTO Power Tools 1.0\UI Manager directory. You can read a document called UIManagerSampleTool created in that directory to learn how to use the classes to coordinate Ribbon and task-pane state.

Exporting a Ribbon to XML

You can export a Ribbon from the visual designer to XML by right-clicking the Ribbon designer and choosing Export Ribbon to XML from the context menu. This command creates a Ribbon.xml file and a Ribbon.cs file that follow the XML programming model for the Ribbon. After you've moved to the XML model, you can no longer use the visual Ribbon designer.

Delay Loading an Add-In with a Ribbon

An add-in can be set to delay load so that it won't load until a Ribbon control associated with the add-in raises an event. To do this, you need to set the LoadBehavior key associated with the add-in in the registry to 16 decimal when the add-in is first installed. This setting causes Office to load the add-in and retrieve the Ribbon XML. Office saves the Ribbon XML and remembers it the next time Office is launched. It also changes the Load-

Behavior key from 16 decimal to 9 decimal, which tells Office to load the add-in only when the Ribbon controls associated with the add-in are used.

Consider an add-in that adds a group with some Ribbon buttons for which the Click event is handled. On the first run, if LoadBehavior is set to 16 decimal, Office loads the add-in, gets the Ribbon XML, keeps the add-in running, and sets the LoadBehavior to 9. On the second run, the Ribbon is still loaded because Office cached the Ribbon XML. The add-in doesn't get loaded until you click a Ribbon button.

ClickOnce supports setting the LoadBehavior to 16 decimal by modifying the application manifest that is created as part of the installer. To set LoadBehavior to 16 decimal, you need to edit the application manifest after Visual Studio creates it when the add-in is published. In particular, you need to set the value of attribute "LoadBehavior" contained in the XML element <vstov3:appAddIn> to 16. Next, use the Mage tool (described in Chapter 21, "ClickOnce Deployment") to re-sign the application manifest. You also have to use Mage to regenerate the deployment manifest after the application manifest has been re-signed. The approach is similar to the approach described in the section "Setting the Friendly Name and the Description" in Chapter 21.

If you aren't using ClickOnce to deploy your add-in, you either have to write a custom installer or add some code that configures the LoadBehavior to be 16 on the first run of the add-in. Then, on the next run of the add-in, Office would cache the Ribbon XML; on the load after that, the delay-loading behavior would be activated. Code that performs this task for an Excel add-in is shown in Listing 17-13.

Listing 17-13: A Startup Event Handler That Forces an Excel Add-In to Switch to Delay Loading on First Run

```
private void ThisAddIn_Startup(object sender, System.EventArgs e)
{
  string keyPath = @"Software\Microsoft\Office\Excel\Addins\" + Assembly.GetEx-
ecutingAssembly().GetName().Name;

  RegistryKey key = Registry.CurrentUser.OpenSubKey(keyPath, true);
  if (key != null)
  {
    object value = key.GetValue("LoadBehavior");
    if (value != null)
```

```
  {
    int intValue = System.Convert.ToInt32(value);
    if (intValue == 3) // ClickOnce install value
    {
      key.SetValue("LoadBehavior", 16, RegistryValueKind.DWord);
    }
  }
 }
}
}
```

Conclusion

In this chapter we described the new Office Ribbon, the controls that are available, the object and event model for VSTO's support for Ribbon, and the visual Ribbon designer. We also considered several advanced scenarios for working with the Ribbon. In the next chapter, we consider VSTO's support for Smart Tags: a way to provide custom commands in your solution linked to text in Office documents.

18

Working with Smart Tags in VSTO

Introduction to Smart Tags

The Smart Tags feature of Word and Excel enables you to display a pop-up menu with actions for a given piece of text in a document or spreadsheet. For example, a Smart Tag could recognize stock symbols (such as the MSFT stock symbol) and display a set of actions that can be taken for that symbol. When Word finds a piece of text that a Smart Tag has recognized, it displays a red dotted line under the recognized text. If the user hovers over the text, a pop-up menu icon appears next to the cell, as shown in Figure 18-1. If the user clicks the pop-up menu icon, a menu of actions displays for the recognized piece of text, as shown in Figure 18-2. When an action is selected, Word calls back into the Smart Tag to execute the action.

When Excel recognizes a Smart Tag, it displays a little triangle in the bottom-right corner of the associated cell. If the user hovers over the cell, a pop-up menu icon appears next to the cell that the user can click to drop down a menu of actions for the recognized piece of text. Figure 18-3 shows an example menu. When an action is selected, Excel calls back into the Smart Tag to execute the action.

Figure 18-4 shows some additional detail about the drop-down menu that appears for recognized text. At the top of the drop-down menu, the name of the Smart Tag displays along with the text that was recognized. The next section of the menu shows actions that are available for the given

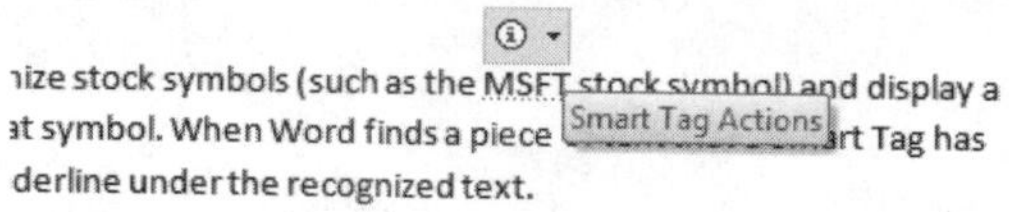

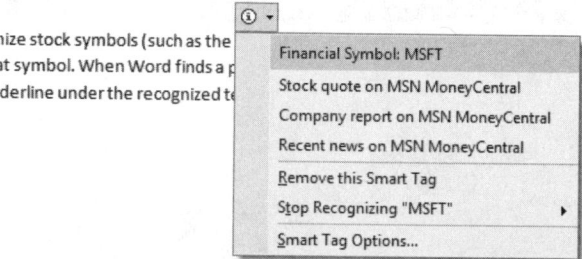

ıize stock symbols (such as the MSFT stock symbol) and display a
ıt symbol. When Word finds a piece
Smart Tag Actions
rt Tag has
derline under the recognized text.

Figure 18-1: Some recognized text in Word.

ıize stock symbols (such as the
ıt symbol. When Word finds a p
derline under the recognized te
Financial Symbol: MSFT
Stock quote on MSN MoneyCentral
Company report on MSN MoneyCentral
Recent news on MSN MoneyCentral
Remove this Smart Tag
Stop Recognizing "MSFT"
Smart Tag Options...

Figure 18-2: Dropping down the Smart Tag menu in Word.

Book1 - Microsoft Excel
Home
Insert
Page Layout
Formulas
Data
Review
View
Developer
Add-Ins
Calibri
11
General
Paste
Clipboard
Font
Alignment
Number
Styles
Insert
Delete
Format
Cells
Sort & Filter
Find & Select
Editing
D5
MSFT
Financial Symbol: MSFT
Insert refreshable stock price...
Stock quote on MSN MoneyCentral
Company report on MSN MoneyCentral
Recent news on MSN MoneyCentral
Remove this Smart Tag
Stop Recognizing "MSFT"
Smart Tag Options...
Sheet1
Sheet2
Sheet3
Ready
100%

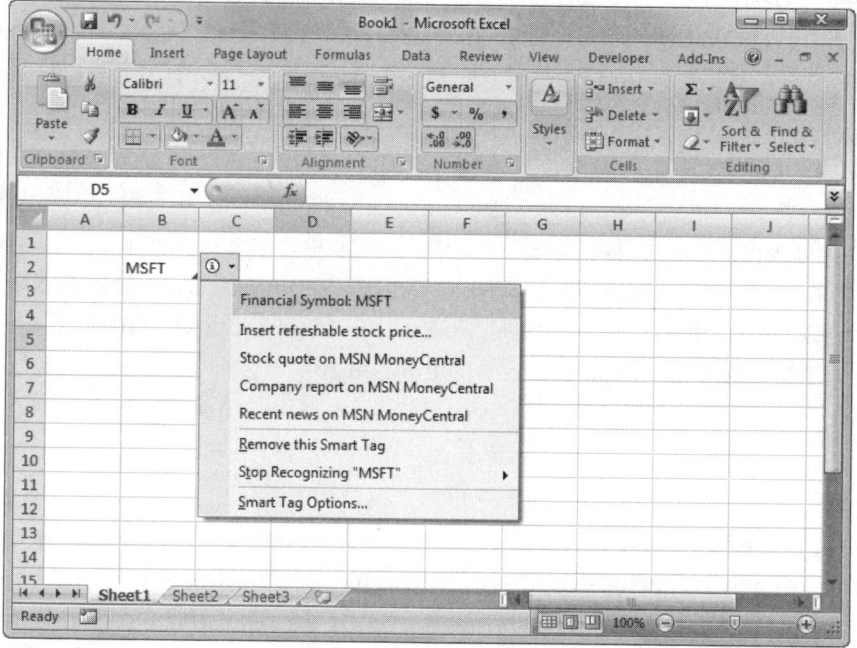

Figure 18-3: Dropping down the Smart Tag menu in Excel.

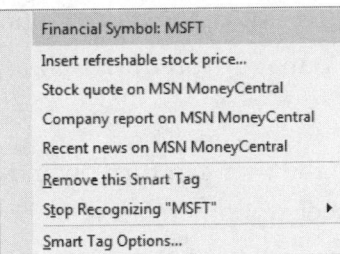

Figure 18-4: The Smart Tag menu.

Smart Tag. This particular Smart Tag, called Financial Symbol, has four actions associated with it. The bottom section of the menu provides Word- or Excel-specific options for the Smart Tag.

Configuring Smart Tags in Word and Excel

Smart Tags in Word are managed from the AutoCorrect dialog box, shown in Figure 18-5. To display the AutoCorrect dialog box, follow these steps:

1. Click the Office menu (the large circle with the Office logo on it in the top-left corner of the Word window), and choose Word Options from the bottom of the menu that drops down.

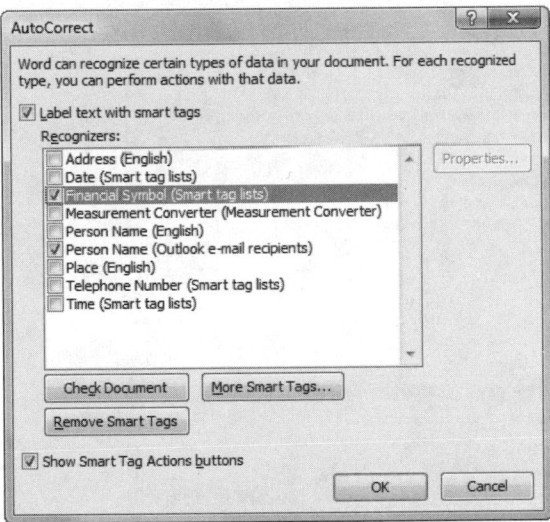

Figure 18-5: Word's Smart Tags page in the AutoCorrect dialog box.

2. Click the Add-Ins tab on the left side of the Word Options dialog box.

3. Choose Smart Tags from the Manage drop-down list, and click the Go button.

In the AutoCorrect dialog box, the user can turn on and off individual recognizers, as well as control other options relating to how Smart Tags display in the document.

Smart Tags in Excel are managed from the Smart Tags page of the Auto-Correct dialog box, shown in Figure 18-6. You can display the Smart Tags page by following these steps:

1. Click the Office menu (the large circle with the Office logo on it in the top-left corner of the Excel window), and choose Excel Options from the bottom of the menu that drops down.

2. Click the Proofing tab on the left side of the Excel Options dialog box.

3. Click the AutoCorrect Options button.

4. Click the Smart Tags page.

On the Smart Tags page of the AutoCorrect dialog box, the user can turn on and off individual recognizers, as well as control other options relating to how Smart Tags display in the workbook.

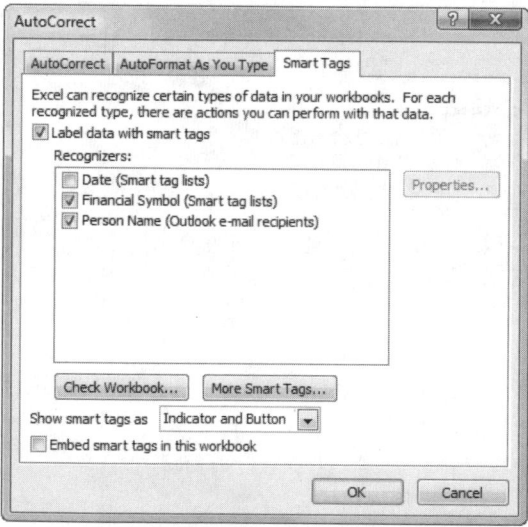

Figure 18-6: Excel's Smart Tags page in the AutoCorrect dialog box.

The Persistent Tagging Generated by Smart Tags

To understand how Smart Tags work in Office, it is helpful to have a conceptual model in your mind. Otherwise, some of the behavior you will see when working with Smart Tags will be confusing.

A Smart Tag has a recognition engine that is passed text in the document or workbook. If the Smart Tag recognizes a segment of text, it can tell Word or Excel to tag the text as being recognized. This tagging is stored and saved in the document by Word or Excel. When text is tagged, it remains tagged until the user removes the tag by choosing Smart Tag > Remove This Smart Tag. So even if a Smart Tag has stopped recognizing a particular term or is no longer active, the tagging in the document can remain.

Text that has been tagged by a Smart Tag has its tagged state saved into the document. You can see this tagging when you save into the WordProcessingML format. A document with the stock symbol MSFT has been recognized in a Word document by a Smart Tag with Smart Tag type name `customsmarttag`. This tag also can optionally store custom properties in the document when it recognizes a term. In the following example, the Smart Tag stores the properties `LongStockName` and the current `StockValue`. You can see all this in the WordProcessingML markup:

```
<st1:customsmarttag
  LongStockName="Microsoft"
  StockValue="29" w:st="on">
    <w:r><w:t>MSFT</w:t></w:r>
</st1:customsmarttag>
```

Creating Document-Level Smart Tags with VSTO

The simplest way to create a Smart Tag is to use VSTO's support for document-level Smart Tags. VSTO provides some classes that enable you to create a Smart Tag easily. First, VSTO provides a class called SmartTag in the Microsoft.Office.Tools.Word namespace and the Microsoft.Office.Tools.Excel namespace. You create an instance of this SmartTag class to define a new Smart Tag. The constructor of the SmartTag object takes two parameters: a unique identifier and the caption that will display in the Smart Tag menu. The unique identifier is constructed using a namespace URI such as "http://vsto.aw.com" and a tag type name such as "mytagtypename" separated by a number sign, resulting in "http://vsto.aw.com#mytagtypename".

The SmartTag object has several important properties and methods. The SmartTag object's Terms property returns a StringCollection to which you can add words you want to recognize. The SmartTag object's Actions property must be set to an array of Action objects representing the actions (the menu items) you want displayed for your Smart Tag. VSTO provides a class called Action in the Microsoft.Office.Tools.Word namespace and the Microsoft.Office.Tools.Excel namespace that you can instantiate. The constructor of the Action object takes one parameter: the caption that will display in the Smart Tag menu for the action. After you create an Action object for each action that you want to make available for your Smart Tag, you can set the SmartTag.Actions property to an array containing all the Action objects you want to provide. Finally, you can handle the Action.Click event for each Action to be called back by Word or Excel when the user chooses that action from the Smart Tag menu.

After you create a SmartTag object, set the SmartTag.Terms collection, create one or more Action objects, and set SmartTag.Actions, you must remember to add the newly created SmartTag to the VstoSmartTags collection on the VSTO Document object for Word and on the VSTO Workbook object for Excel.

Listing 18-1 shows a simple Word VSTO customization that illustrates these steps. First, it creates a SmartTag instance passing "http://vsto.aw.com#fish" as the identifier and "Fish Catcher" as the caption. Then it adds two terms to recognize using SmartTag.Terms: "Mackerel" and "Halibut". Note that a term cannot contain a space. A term such as "Eric Carter", for example, could not be added to the terms collection.

Two actions are created: one with the caption "&Fishing///&Catch a fish" and the other with the caption "&Fishing///&Throw it back". The ampersand (&) in these strings indicates which letter to use as an accelerator for the menu. The use of the three forward slashes tells Word to create a menu called Fishing with a child menu called Catch a fish and a second child menu called Throw it back. These actions are added to the SmartTag.Actions property by creating a new array of Actions containing both actions. Click events raised by the two actions are handled by the code.

Finally, the SmartTag instance that was created is added to the VstoSmart-Tags collection associated with the document object.

Disambiguating Action

Action is a name in both the System and Microsoft.Office.Tools.Word namespaces. So to disambiguate, we give the Microsoft.Office.Tools.Word namespace the alias VSTO and use VSTO.Action.

If the Smart Tags are not showing up, be sure to turn the Smart Tag feature on as described at the start of this chapter. Also note that Smart Tags are case sensitive, so if you type "halibut", for example, the text will not be tagged.

Ignore.xml and Stop Recognizing

One of the commands in the Smart Tag menu allows you to stop recognizing a term. When you use this command, it is added to a file called ignore.xml in the current user's AppData\Roaming\Microsoft\Smart Tags\ Exceptions folder. You can edit ignore.xml and remove the term to cause it to be recognized again.

Listing 18-1: A VSTO Word Customization That Adds a Smart Tag

```
using System;
using System.Collections.Generic;
using System.Data;
using System.Linq;
using System.Text;
using System.Windows.Forms;
using System.Xml.Linq;
using Microsoft.VisualStudio.Tools.Applications.Runtime;
using Word = Microsoft.Office.Interop.Word;
using Office = Microsoft.Office.Core;
using VSTO = Microsoft.Office.Tools.Word;
using Microsoft.Office.Tools.Word;
```

```csharp
namespace WordDocument10
{
  public partial class ThisDocument
  {
    private void ThisDocument_Startup(object sender, EventArgs e)
    {
      SmartTag mySmartTag = new SmartTag(
        "http://vsto.aw.com#fish", "Fish Catcher");
      mySmartTag.Terms.Add("Mackerel");
      mySmartTag.Terms.Add("Halibut");

      VSTO.Action myAction =
        new VSTO.Action("&Fishing///&Catch a fish...");
      VSTO.Action myAction2 =
        new VSTO.Action("&Fishing///&Throw it back...");
      mySmartTag.Actions =
        new VSTO.Action[] { myAction, myAction2 };

      myAction.Click +=
        new ActionClickEventHandler(myAction_Click);
      myAction2.Click +=
        new ActionClickEventHandler(myAction2_Click);

      this.VstoSmartTags.Add(mySmartTag);
    }

    void myAction_Click(object sender, ActionEventArgs e)
    {
      MessageBox.Show(String.Format(
        "You caught a fish at position {0}.",
        e.Range.Start));
    }

    void myAction2_Click(object sender, ActionEventArgs e)
    {
      MessageBox.Show(String.Format(
        "You threw back a fish at position {0}.",
        e.Range.Start));
    }

    #region VSTO Designer generated code
    private void InternalStartup()
    {
      this.Startup += new EventHandler(ThisDocument_Startup);
    }
    #endregion
  }
}
```

The code to add a Smart Tag in Excel is very similar and is shown in Listing 18-2. The main changes are to use the SmartTag and Action classes from the Microsoft.Office.Tools.Excel namespace and to use the Vsto-SmartTags collection off the Workbook object. Because the code in Listing 18-2 is written in Sheet1, the Workbook object is accessed by using Globals.ThisWorkbook.

If the Smart Tags are not showing up, be sure to turn on the Smart Tag feature, as described at the start of Chapter 3, "Programming Excel."

Listing 18-2: A VSTO Excel Customization That Adds a Smart Tag

```
using System;
using System.Collections.Generic;
using System.Data;
using System.Linq;
using System.Text;
using System.Windows.Forms;
using System.Xml.Linq;
using Microsoft.VisualStudio.Tools.Applications.Runtime;
using Excel = Microsoft.Office.Interop.Excel;
using Microsoft.Office.Tools.Excel;
using VSTO = Microsoft.Office.Tools.Excel;

namespace ExcelWorkbook9
{
  public partial class Sheet1
  {
    private void Sheet1_Startup(object sender, EventArgs e)
    {
      SmartTag mySmartTag = new
        SmartTag("http://vsto.aw.com#fish", "Fish Catcher");
      mySmartTag.Terms.Add("Mackerel");
      mySmartTag.Terms.Add("Halibut");

      VSTO.Action myAction = new VSTO.Action("Catch a fish...");
      VSTO.Action myAction2 = new VSTO.Action("Throw it back...");
      mySmartTag.Actions =
        new VSTO.Action[] { myAction, myAction2 };

      myAction.Click +=
        new ActionClickEventHandler(myAction_Click);
      myAction2.Click +=
        new ActionClickEventHandler(myAction2_Click);

      Globals.ThisWorkbook.VstoSmartTags.Add(mySmartTag);
    }
```

```
void myAction2_Click(object sender, ActionEventArgs e)
{
  MessageBox.Show(String.Format(
    "You threw back a fish at address {0}.",
    e.Range.get_Address(missing, missing,
    Excel.XlReferenceStyle.xlA1, missing, missing)));
}

void myAction_Click(object sender, ActionEventArgs e)
{
  MessageBox.Show(String.Format(
    "You caught a fish at address {0}.",
    e.Range.get_Address(missing, missing,
    Excel.XlReferenceStyle.xlA1, missing, missing)));
}

#region VSTO Designer generated code
private void InternalStartup()
{
  this.Startup += new EventHandler(Sheet1_Startup);
}
#endregion

    }
}
```

Action Events

In Listing 18-1 and Listing 18-2, we handled the Click event of the Action object. The code that handled the Click event used the ActionEventArgs argument e and accessed the ActionEventArgs.Range property to get a Word.Range object for Word and an Excel.Range object for Excel. The Range property allows you to access the range of text that was recognized in Word or the Excel cell that contains the recognized text.

The ActionEventArgs.Text property returns the text that was recognized. This property proves to be useful when you are matching multiple string values with a single Smart Tag class.

The ActionEventArgs.Properties property allows you to access a property bag associated with the actions pane. This property bag can be used to store additional information about the text that was recognized. We consider this topic further in the "Creating a Custom Smart Tag Class" section later in this chapter.

The Action object also raises a BeforeCaptionShow event before the caption for an Action is shown in the actions pane menu. This event is also passed an ActionEvent-Args argument e, which can be used to access information about what was recognized just as with the Click event. You can use this event to change the caption of the action before it is shown.

Listing 18-3 shows a VSTO Excel customization that handles the Click and BeforeCaptionShow events. You must add a reference to the Microsoft Smart Tags 2.0 Type Library, as shown in Figure 18-7 on page 871, to access the types associated with the property bag.

Listing 18-3: A VSTO Excel Customization That Handles the Click and BeforeCaptionShow Events and Uses the ActionEventArgs Argument

```
using System;
using System.Collections.Generic;
using System.Data;
using System.Linq;
using System.Text;
using System.Windows.Forms;
using System.Xml.Linq;
using Microsoft.VisualStudio.Tools.Applications.Runtime;
using Excel = Microsoft.Office.Interop.Excel;
using Microsoft.Office.Tools.Excel;
using VSTO = Microsoft.Office.Tools.Excel;

namespace ExcelWorkbook9
{
  public partial class Sheet1
  {
    VSTO.Action myAction;
    VSTO.Action myAction2;

    private void Sheet1_Startup(object sender, EventArgs e)
    {
      SmartTag mySmartTag = new SmartTag(
        "http://vsto.aw.com#fish", "Fish Catcher");
      mySmartTag.Terms.Add("Mackerel");
      mySmartTag.Terms.Add("Halibut");

      myAction = new VSTO.Action("Catch a fish...");
      myAction2 = new VSTO.Action("Throw it back...");
      mySmartTag.Actions =
        new VSTO.Action[] { myAction, myAction2 };

      myAction.Click +=
        new ActionClickEventHandler(myAction_Click);
```

```csharp
      myAction.BeforeCaptionShow +=
        new BeforeCaptionShowEventHandler(
        myAction_BeforeCaptionShow);

      myAction2.Click +=
        new ActionClickEventHandler(myAction2_Click);

      Globals.ThisWorkbook.VstoSmartTags.Add(mySmartTag);
    }

    void myAction_BeforeCaptionShow(object sender,
      ActionEventArgs e)
    {
      Random r = new Random();

      myAction.Caption = "Test caption " + r.NextDouble();
    }

    void myAction2_Click(object sender, ActionEventArgs e)
    {
      MessageBox.Show(String.Format(
        "You threw back a fish at address {0}.",
        e.Range.get_Address(missing, missing,
        Excel.XlReferenceStyle.xlA1, missing, missing)));

      MessageBox.Show(e.Text);
      MessageBox.Show(e.Properties.Count.ToString());
      for (int i = 0; i < e.Properties.Count; i++)
      {
        MessageBox.Show(String.Format(
          "Prop({0},(1))",
          e.Properties.get_KeyFromIndex(i),
          e.Properties.get_ValueFromIndex(i)));
      }
    }

    void myAction_Click(object sender, ActionEventArgs e)
    {
      MessageBox.Show(String.Format(
        "You caught a fish at address {0}.",
        e.Range.get_Address(missing, missing,
        Excel.XlReferenceStyle.xlA1, missing, missing)));
    }

    #region VSTO Designer generated code
    private void InternalStartup()
    {
      this.Startup += new System.EventHandler(Sheet1_Startup);
    }
    #endregion
  }
}
```

Using Varying Numbers of Terms

It is possible to vary the number of terms recognized at runtime by adding terms to and removing terms from the SmartTag.Terms collection. Listing 18-4 shows this approach. Note that instances of terms that have already been typed in the document and recognized continue to be recognized even when you remove that term from the Terms collection, but new instances of the removed term that you type are longer recognized.

Listing 18-4: A VSTO Excel Customization That Varies the Number of Terms Recognized

```csharp
using System;
using System.Collections.Generic;
using System.Data;
using System.Linq;
using System.Text;
using System.Windows.Forms;
using System.Xml.Linq;
using Microsoft.VisualStudio.Tools.Applications.Runtime;
using Excel = Microsoft.Office.Interop.Excel;
using Microsoft.Office.Tools.Excel;
using VSTO = Microsoft.Office.Tools.Excel;
using System.Text.RegularExpressions;

namespace ExcelWorkbook9
{
  public partial class Sheet1
  {
    VSTO.Action myAction;
    SmartTag mySmartTag;

    private void Sheet1_Startup(object sender, EventArgs e)
    {
      mySmartTag = new SmartTag(
        "http://vsto.aw.com#variableterms",
        "Varying Number of Terms");

      mySmartTag.Terms.Add("Hello");

      myAction = new VSTO.Action("Add a new term...");
      mySmartTag.Actions = new VSTO.Action[] { myAction };

      myAction.Click +=
        new ActionClickEventHandler(myAction_Click);

      Globals.ThisWorkbook.VstoSmartTags.Add(mySmartTag);
    }
```

```
void myAction_Click(object sender, ActionEventArgs e)
{
  Random r = new Random();
  int numberOfActionsToShow = r.Next(5);

  if (mySmartTag.Terms.Contains(
    numberOfActionsToShow.ToString()) == true)
  {
    mySmartTag.Terms.Remove(
      numberOfActionsToShow.ToString());
    MessageBox.Show(String.Format(
      "Removed the term {0}.",
      numberOfActionsToShow));
  }
  else
  {
    mySmartTag.Terms.Add(
      numberOfActionsToShow.ToString());
    MessageBox.Show(String.Format(
    "Added the term {0}.",
    numberOfActionsToShow));
  }
}

#region VSTO Designer generated code
private void InternalStartup()
{
  this.Startup += new System.EventHandler(Sheet1_Startup);
}
#endregion
  }
}
```

Using Regular Expressions

Although the Terms collection provides a way to recognize specific words, you will inevitably want to have more power in the text patterns that are recognized. The SmartTag class allows you to use regular expressions to recognize text in a Word document or Excel spreadsheet. This book does not cover how to construct a regular expression; if regular expressions are new to you, try looking at the documentation in the .NET Framework for the Regex class.

We are going to construct a regular expression that will match stock symbols in a document. A stock symbol will be defined as any three- or four-letter combination that is in all caps, such as IBM or MSFT. The regu-

lar expression we will use is shown below and will match a word (\b indicates a word boundary) composed of three to four characters (specified by
{3,4}) composed of capital letters from A to Z ([A-Z]):

```
\b[A-Z]{3,4}\b
```

This regular expression string is passed to the constructor of a Regex
object. Then the Regex object is added to the SmartTag.Expressions collection, as shown in Listing 18-5.

Listing 18-5: A VSTO Excel Customization That Adds a Smart Tag Using a Regular Expression

```csharp
using System;
using System.Collections.Generic;
using System.Data;
using System.Linq;
using System.Text;
using System.Windows.Forms;
using System.Xml.Linq;
using Microsoft.VisualStudio.Tools.Applications.Runtime;
using Excel = Microsoft.Office.Interop.Excel;
using Microsoft.Office.Tools.Excel;
using VSTO = Microsoft.Office.Tools.Excel;
using System.Text.RegularExpressions;

namespace ExcelWorkbook9
{
  public partial class Sheet1
  {
    VSTO.Action myAction;

    private void Sheet1_Startup(object sender, EventArgs e)
    {
      SmartTag mySmartTag = new SmartTag(
        "http://vsto.aw.com#stock", "Stock Trader");
      Regex myRegex = new Regex(@"\b[A-Z]{3,4}\b");

      mySmartTag.Expressions.Add(myRegex);

      myAction = new VSTO.Action("Trade this stock...");
      mySmartTag.Actions = new VSTO.Action[] { myAction };

      myAction.Click +=
        new ActionClickEventHandler(myAction_Click);

      Globals.ThisWorkbook.VstoSmartTags.Add(mySmartTag);
    }
```

```
    void myAction_Click(object sender, ActionEventArgs e)
    {
      MessageBox.Show(String.Format(
        "The stock symbol you selected is {0}", e.Text));
    }

    #region VSTO Designer generated code
    private void InternalStartup()
    {
      this.Startup += new EventHandler(Sheet1_Startup);
    }
    #endregion
  }
}
```

Another great feature when you use regular expressions is VSTO's support for named groups in a regular expression. When you create a regular expression with a named group, VSTO creates a name value pair in the property bag for each recognized term with the name and value of each named group recognized by the regular expression. You can use the ActionEventArgs object's Properties object to retrieve the value of a named group by using the group name as a key.

Using Varying Numbers of Actions

You may wonder why the SmartTag object has an Actions property that must be set to a fixed array of Actions. After all, wouldn't it be easier if you could write the code `mySmartTag.Actions.Add(myAction)`? The Actions property was designed this way to enforce the notion that the maximum number of actions for a given Smart Tag is fixed at the time you add the SmartTag object to the VstoSmartTags collection. This design is a limitation of the Office Smart Tags architecture.

A way exists to have a varying number of actions, however. The limitation still applies: The maximum number of actions is fixed at the time you first add it to the VstoSmartTags collection. But at runtime, you can set actions within the array to `null` to vary the number of available actions up to the maximum number of actions. Listing 18-6 shows this approach. The maximum number of actions is set to five by setting the initial array of actions to contain five actions. But each time an action is selected, the number of actions is changed by setting the items in the actions array to null or to an Action object.

As you test the code in Listing 18-6, you may notice a strange bit of behavior. Type a stock symbol, FOO, in a cell. The symbol gets recognized, and when you drop down the Smart Tags menu it displays five actions. When you select one of the actions, the number of actions changes to a different value (generated randomly). But if you then drop down the same Smart Tag menu, it still displays five actions. Only when you type FOO or some other stock symbol in another cell and then drop down the Smart Tag menu for that cell will the number of displayed actions in the Smart Tag menu change. The reason that you see this behavior is that after some text is recognized, Excel saves the fact that the text was recognized and saves the number of actions available. It doesn't ask the Smart Tag for an action count again unless some new text is recognized—which explains why our Smart Tag menu still displays five actions until new text is recognized by the Smart Tag and Excel requeries the Smart Tag for the number of actions it provides.

You can force a foreground recheck of all the Smart Tags in the document by calling the RecheckSmartTags method on Workbook or Document, which can work around this behavior if absolutely necessary. But the use of this method is not recommended because the whole Smart Tag system was designed to tag text in the background when there is idle time. Calling RecheckSmartTags can be slow for large documents, and in Excel it even displays a dialog box while processing.

Listing 18-6: A VSTO Excel Customization with a Varying Number of Actions

```
using System;
using System.Collections.Generic;
using System.Data;
using System.Linq;
using System.Text;
using System.Windows.Forms;
using System.Xml.Linq;
using Microsoft.VisualStudio.Tools.Applications.Runtime;
using Excel = Microsoft.Office.Interop.Excel;
using Microsoft.Office.Tools.Excel;
using VSTO = Microsoft.Office.Tools.Excel;
using System.Text.RegularExpressions;
```

```csharp
namespace ExcelWorkbook9
{
  public partial class Sheet1
  {
    VSTO.Action myAction;
    SmartTag mySmartTag;

    private void Sheet1_Startup(object sender, EventArgs e)
    {
      mySmartTag = new SmartTag(
        "http://vsto.aw.com#variableactions",
        "Varying Number of Actions");
      Regex myRegex = new Regex(@"\b[A-Z]{3,4}\b");

      mySmartTag.Expressions.Add(myRegex);

      myAction = new VSTO.Action("Change Number of Actions...");
      mySmartTag.Actions = new VSTO.Action[] { myAction, myAction,
        myAction, myAction, myAction };

      myAction.Click +=
        new ActionClickEventHandler(myAction_Click);

      Globals.ThisWorkbook.VstoSmartTags.Add(mySmartTag);
    }

    void myAction_Click(object sender, ActionEventArgs e)
    {
      Random r = new Random();
      int numberOfActionsToShow = 1 + r.Next(4);

      MessageBox.Show(String.Format(
        "Changing to have {0} actions.",
        numberOfActionsToShow));

      for (int i = 0; i < numberOfActionsToShow; i++)
      {
        mySmartTag.Actions[i] = myAction;
      }

      for (int i = numberOfActionsToShow; i < 5; i++)
      {
        mySmartTag.Actions[i] = null;
      }
    }

    #region VSTO Designer generated code
    private void InternalStartup()
    {
```

```
        this.Startup += new EventHandler(Sheet1_Startup);
    }
    #endregion
  }
}
```

Creating a Custom Smart Tag Class

When the Terms collection and the Expressions collection are not sufficient to meet your Smart Tag recognition needs, you also have the option of creating your own custom Smart Tag class that derives from the Word or Excel SmartTag class. This gives you some additional capability. First of all, you get to write your own code to process text that Word or Excel passes to your Smart Tag class to recognize. Second, you can use the ISmartTagProperties collection to associate custom Smart Tag properties in the property bag associated with each instance of recognized text.

Suppose that you are writing a Smart Tag that recognizes part numbers that are stored in a database. You know that part numbers are in a format such as PN1023, with a PN preface and four following digits. Just because that pattern is found in the text, however, does not mean that a part number is valid. The part number may have been deleted or may not exist in the database. So after finding a match for the expected part number format, you also want to make a call into the database to make sure that a row exists for the given part number. If the part number is not in the database, you do not want to tag it.

You can do this by writing your own custom Smart Tag class. Your class must derive from the Word or Excel SmartTag class in the Microsoft .Office.Tools.Word or Microsoft.Office.Tools.Excel namespaces. Your class must have a constructor that calls into the base class constructor passing the Smart Tag type name and the caption for the Smart Tag. The custom class must also override the Recognize method of the base class shown here:

```
protected override void Recognize(string text,
  Microsoft.Office.Interop.SmartTag.ISmartTagRecognizerSite site,
    Microsoft.Office.Interop.SmartTag.ISmartTagTokenList tokenList)
  {
  }
```

The Recognize method passes the text to recognize as a string, an ISmartTagRecognizerSite object that your code will use if it associates custom Smart Tag properties with an instance of recognized text, and a token-List parameter. Your implementation of Recognize could find the basic part number format, and if a match is found it can look up the part number in a database to verify that it is a valid part number. If it is a valid part number, your implementation of Recognize must call into the base class's PersistTag method to specify the index within the text where the part number occurred, the length of the part number, and (optionally) custom Smart Tag properties to associate with the text that will be tagged.

Custom Smart Tag properties are useful when you need to cache additional information that was determined at recognize time that might be used later when an action associated with a tag is executed. In our example, we talked to a database to get the row out of the database corresponding to the part number. Perhaps one of the actions available will be to display the price of the part. Because we have accessed the database row for the part, we already have the price. Rather than have to look up the price again in the database when the action displaying the price is invoked, you could choose to create custom Smart Tag properties and add the price as a custom property to the recognized text. A custom Smart Tag properties collection of type ISmartTagProperties can be created by calling the GetNewPropertyBag method on the ISmartTagRecognizerSite object passed into the Recognize method. To get the definition of ISmartTagProperties and ISmartTag-RecognizerSite, you must add a reference to your project to the Microsoft Smart Tags 2.0 Type Library, as shown in Figure 18-7.

The code in Listing 18-7 illustrates these ideas by defining a custom Smart Tag class that recognizes part numbers of the format PN1023 and uses ISmartTagRecognizerSite, ISmartTagProperties, and the PersistTag method to associate the custom property "Price" with a part number that has been recognized. Our class CustomSmartTag derives from the SmartTag class in the Microsoft.Office.Tools.Word namespace because this custom Smart Tag will be used with Word. It implements a simple constructor that calls into the base constructor passing an identifier and caption. An action is created and added to the Smart Tag that will display the part cost already stored in the tagged text. It does this by accessing the ISmartTag-

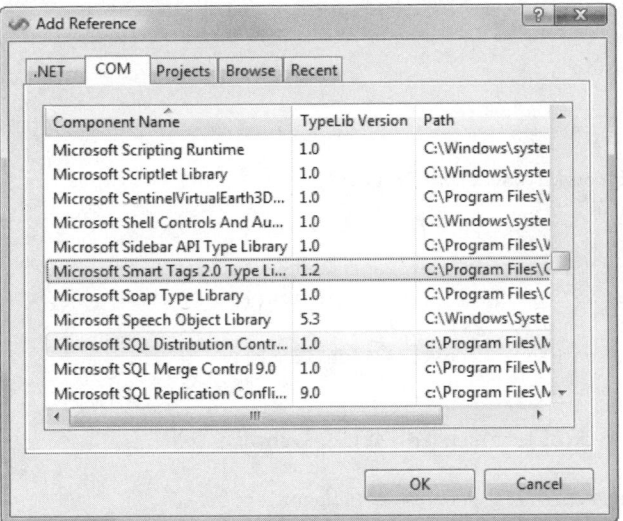

Figure 18-7: A reference to the Microsoft Smart Tags 2.0 Type Library is required to use the ISmartTagProperties and ISmartTagRecognizerSite interfaces in your code.

Properties associated with the tagged text, using the Properties property of the ActionEventArgs argument passed to the Action.Click event.

We override the Recognize method to write custom logic that looks for the part number and calls IsValidPart to find out whether the part number is in the database and then get the price for the part, if available. The implementation of IsValidPart does not actually connect to a database for this sample; instead, it requires a part number to be greater than 1000. To simulate getting a price from a database, it generates a random price that will be saved in the document when the text is tagged. You can easily imagine this function being rewritten to query a database instead.

Listing 18-7: A Custom Smart Tag Class for Word

```
using System;
using System.Text;
using Microsoft.Office.Tools.Word;
using VSTO = Microsoft.Office.Tools.Word;
using System.Windows.Forms;
using SmartTag = Microsoft.Office.Interop.SmartTag;

namespace WordDocument11
{
```

```
internal class CustomSmartTag : VSTO.SmartTag
{
  VSTO.Action customAction;

  internal CustomSmartTag()
    : base(
    "http://www.aw-bc.com/VSTO#customsmarttag",
    "Custom Smart Tag")
  {
    customAction = new VSTO.Action("Get Part Cost...");
    base.Actions = new VSTO.Action[] { customAction };
    customAction.Click +=
      new ActionClickEventHandler(customAction_Click);
  }

  void customAction_Click(object sender, ActionEventArgs e)
  {
    SmartTag.ISmartTagProperties props = e.Properties;
    for (int i = 0; i < props.Count; i++)
    {
      MessageBox.Show(String.Format(
        "{0} : {1}", props.get_KeyFromIndex(i),
        props.get_ValueFromIndex(i)));
    }
  }

  protected override void Recognize(string text,
    SmartTag.ISmartTagRecognizerSite site,
    SmartTag.ISmartTagTokenList tokenList)
  {
    string textToFind = "PN";

    int startIndex = 0;
    int index = 0;

    while ((index = text.IndexOf(
      textToFind, startIndex)) >= 0)
    {
      if (index + 6 < text.Length)
      {
        string partNumber = text.Substring(index, 6);
        string price = "";
        if (IsValidPart(partNumber, out price))
        {
          SmartTag.ISmartTagProperties props =
            site.GetNewPropertyBag();
          props.Write("Price", price);
          base.PersistTag(index, 6, props);
        }
      }
```

```
        startIndex = index + textToFind.Length;
      }
    }

    private bool IsValidPart(string partNumber, out string price)
    {
      int numericPartNumber = 0;
      try
      {
        numericPartNumber = System.Convert.ToInt32(
          partNumber.Substring(2, 4));
      }
      catch { };

      // Only part numbers greater than 1000 are valid
      if (numericPartNumber > 1000)
      {
        Random rnd = new Random();
        price = rnd.Next(100).ToString();
        return true;
      }

      price = "N/A";
      return false;
    }
  }

  public partial class ThisDocument
  {
    private void ThisDocument_Startup(object sender, EventArgs e)
    {
      this.VstoSmartTags.Add(new CustomSmartTag());
    }

    #region VSTO Designer generated code
    private void InternalStartup()
    {
      this.Startup += new EventHandler(ThisDocument_Startup);
    }
    #endregion
  }
}
```

Using Smart Tag Properties Wisely

You must consider some other issues when using Smart Tag properties. These properties are serialized into the document, and the recognizer is not given a chance to re-recognize text that has already been recognized.

For example, you might type in the part number on May 1, and the Recognize method runs. Then you save the document, and the price is saved with the document. When you reopen the document on May 31 and click the Smart Tag menu to select the Get Part Cost action, the action will go to the Smart Tag property created on May 1 and display the May 1 price. Therefore, if the prices of parts change frequently, the part price stored as a custom property may be out of date when the action is invoked at some time later than when the Recognize method was called.

Also, remember that any Smart Tag properties you put in the document for recognized text will be visible in the saved document file format. So be sure not to put Smart Tag properties in the document containing sensitive information. You could have a document full of part numbers that you send to a competitor, for example. If the custom Smart Tag in Listing 18-7 has recognized all the part numbers in the document before you save the document and send it to the competitor, the prices of all those parts will also be embedded in the document with each tagged part number. You can turn off the saving of Smart Tag information to the document by unchecking the Embed Smart Tags option in the advanced tab of the Word Options dialog box or by unchecking Embed Smart Tags in this workbook in the Smart Tags page of Excel's AutoCorrect dialog box. But you pay a performance penalty: When the document reopens it will take some time for all the Smart Tags to be recognized again during idle time.

Creating Application-Level Smart Tags

VSTO's document-level Smart Tags are great when you want to recognize a term in a particular document or a class of document created from a template. What are your options when you want to recognize a term in all open documents?

Starting with VSTO 3.0 SP1, you can create a VSTO add-in that can access the VstoSmartTags collection. This add-in allows you to use VSTO Smart Tags at add-in level. To use VSTO Smart Tags in an add-in, first make sure that you have SP1 of VSTO 3.0 and Visual Studio 2008 installed. Also note that end users of your solution must have SP1 of the VSTO 3.0 runtime installed.

Next, create a new Word or Excel add-in in Visual Studio 2008 SP1. New add-in projects created with Visual Studio 2008 SP1 have a VstoSmartTags collection as a member of the ThisAddIn class.

Listing 18-8 shows a VSTO Word add-in that recognizes the terms "Mackerel" and "Halibut" in all Word documents by using the new VstoSmartTags collection available to VSTO Word and Excel add-ins. We will also describe later in this section how to retrofit an existing add-in project to add application-level Smart Tag support.

Listing 18-8: Creating Smart Tags in an Application-Level VSTO Word Add-In

```
using System;
using Word = Microsoft.Office.Interop.Word;
using Office = Microsoft.Office.Core;
using Microsoft.Office.Tools.Word;
using VSTO = Microsoft.Office.Tools.Word;
using Microsoft.Office.Tools.Word.Extensions;
using System.Windows.Forms;

namespace WordAddIn3
{
  public partial class ThisAddIn
  {
    SmartTag mySmartTag;
    VSTO.Action myAction;
    VSTO.Action myAction2;

    private void ThisAddIn_Startup(object sender, System.EventArgs e)
    {
      mySmartTag = new SmartTag(
        "http://vsto.aw.com#fish", "Fish Catcher");
      mySmartTag.Terms.Add("Mackerel");
      mySmartTag.Terms.Add("Halibut");

      myAction =
        new VSTO.Action("&Fishing///&Catch a fish...");
      myAction2 =
        new VSTO.Action("&Fishing///&Throw it back...");
      mySmartTag.Actions =
        new VSTO.Action[] { myAction, myAction2 };

      myAction.Click += new
        ActionClickEventHandler(myAction_Click);
      myAction2.Click += new
        ActionClickEventHandler(myAction2_Click);
```

```
      VstoSmartTags.Add(mySmartTag);
    }

    void myAction2_Click(object sender, ActionEventArgs e)
    {
      MessageBox.Show(String.Format(
        "You threw back a fish at position {0}.",
        e.Range.Start));
    }

    void myAction_Click(object sender, ActionEventArgs e)
    {
      MessageBox.Show(String.Format(
        "You caught a fish at position {0}.",
        e.Range.Start));
    }

    #region VSTO generated code
    private void InternalStartup()
    {
      this.Startup += new System.EventHandler(ThisAddIn_Startup);
    }
    #endregion
  }
}
```

Listing 18-9 shows an alternative approach that can provide more flexibility if you want to have an application-level add-in that associates different Smart Tags with different documents. This alternative approach accesses the VstoSmartTags collection associated with each document. This approach is instructive because it will help you understand the new GetVstoObject method that gives you access to document-level features at add-in level.

To use document-level features in an add-in, first make sure that you have SP1 of VSTO 3.0 and Visual Studio 2008 installed. Also note that end users of your solution must have SP1 of the VSTO 3.0 runtime installed.

Next, create a new add-in in Visual Studio 2008 SP1, or if you have an existing add-in, add the line "using Microsoft.Office.Tools.Word.Extensions" for a Word add-in and "using Microsoft.Office.Tools.Excel.Extensions" for an Excel add-in. To access the VstoSmartTags collection associated with a Word document or Excel workbook, use the GetVstoObject extension method that is available off of a Microsoft.Office.Interop.Word.Document object or Microsoft.Office.Interop.Excel.Workbook object.

The code below shows a VSTO Word add-in that recognizes the terms "Mackerel" and "Halibut" in all open Word documents. In ThisAdd-In_Startup, we iterate over any open documents and call our AttachSmartTag method. The AttachSmartTag method initializes a single SmartTag object that is held in the class variable mySmartTag and two Action objects: myAction and myAction2. These three objects can be used with multiple documents. Finally, the line of code below adds the mySmartTag object to the VstoSmartTags collection associated with the Word document object doc passed to AttachSmartTag:

```
doc.GetVstoObject().VstoSmartTags.Add(mySmartTag);
```

The GetVstoObject extension method returns the Microsoft.Office .Tools.Word.Document object corresponding to the Microsoft.Office.Interop .Word.Document object. Then the VstoSmartTags property is used to get a VstoSmartTags collection, and the Add method of the collection is called to add the Smart Tag.

After the ThisAddIn_Startup method iterates over currently open documents to attach Smart Tags, the add-in handles the DocumentOpen and NewDocument events so that when new documents are created or documents are opened, a Smart Tag is added to the VstoSmartTags collection associated with these documents as well.

Listing 18-9: An Alternative Approach to Creating Smart Tags in an Application-Level VSTO Word Add-In

```
using System;
using Word = Microsoft.Office.Interop.Word;
using Office = Microsoft.Office.Core;
using Microsoft.Office.Tools.Word;
using VSTO = Microsoft.Office.Tools.Word;
using Microsoft.Office.Tools.Word.Extensions;
using System.Windows.Forms;

namespace WordAddIn2
{
  public partial class ThisAddIn
  {
    SmartTag mySmartTag;
    VSTO.Action myAction;
    VSTO.Action myAction2;
```

```csharp
private void ThisAddIn_Startup(object sender,
  System.EventArgs e)
{
  foreach (Word.Document doc in Application.Documents)
  {
    AttachSmartTag(doc);
  }

  this.Application.DocumentOpen += new
    Word.ApplicationEvents4_DocumentOpenEventHandler(
    Application_DocumentOpen);
  ((Word.ApplicationEvents4_Event)Application).NewDocument +=
    new Word.ApplicationEvents4_NewDocumentEventHandler(
    Application_NewDocument);
}

void Application_NewDocument(Word.Document doc)
{
  AttachSmartTag(doc);
}

void Application_DocumentOpen(Word.Document doc)
{
  AttachSmartTag(doc);
}

void AttachSmartTag(Word.Document doc)
{
  if (mySmartTag == null)
  {
    mySmartTag = new SmartTag(
      "http://vsto.aw.com#fish", "Fish Catcher");
    mySmartTag.Terms.Add("Mackerel");
    mySmartTag.Terms.Add("Halibut");

    myAction =
      new VSTO.Action("&Fishing///&Catch a fish...");
    myAction2 =
      new VSTO.Action("&Fishing///&Throw it back...");
    mySmartTag.Actions =
      new VSTO.Action[] { myAction, myAction2 };

    myAction.Click += new
      ActionClickEventHandler(myAction_Click);
    myAction2.Click += new
      ActionClickEventHandler(myAction2_Click);
  }
  doc.GetVstoObject().VstoSmartTags.Add(mySmartTag);
}
```

```
    void myAction2_Click(object sender, ActionEventArgs e)
    {
      MessageBox.Show(String.Format(
        "You threw back a fish at position {0}.",
        e.Range.Start));
    }

    void myAction_Click(object sender, ActionEventArgs e)
    {
      MessageBox.Show(String.Format(
        "You caught a fish at position {0}.",
        e.Range.Start));
    }

    #region VSTO generated code
    private void InternalStartup()
    {
      this.Startup += new System.EventHandler(ThisAddIn_Startup);
    }
    #endregion
  }
}
```

All the same techniques discussed for document-level VSTO Smart Tags can be used with application-level Smart Tags created with the methods shown in Listing 18-8 and Listing 18-9. You can use document-level Smart Tag features including using multiple and varying numbers of terms, using regular expressions, using varying numbers of actions, and creating custom Smart Tag classes.

You may wonder what happens if your add-in isn't loaded. Any documents that had terms that were recognized in sessions where your add-in was loaded will have saved into the file format the recognized terms (if embed Smart Tags is enabled). When these document reopen, Office detects whether your add-in is loaded. If the add-in is loaded, and code like the code in Listing 18-9's AttachSmartTag method has run, the Smart Tags will just continue to work. If the add-in doesn't load or doesn't run code like the code in AttachSmartTag, Office strips the Smart Tagged text out of the document on open, and no tag appears.

Conclusion

This chapter examined VSTO's support for document-level Smart Tags. VSTO provides a simple way to get started by using terms and actions. VSTO also supports more powerful techniques, including support for regular expressions and support for multiple actions, as well as the ability to create your own custom Smart Tag classes.

This chapter also covered how to build an application-level Smart Tag by using Visual Studio 2008 SP1's support for the VstoSmartTags collection off the ThisAddIn object, as well as accessing the document-level VstoSmartTags collection from an add-in by using the GetVstoObject method.

19

VSTO Data Programming

A FULL TREATMENT OF Microsoft's ADO.NET data programming model could easily fill an entire book of its own. Therefore, this chapter starts with an example of how to use the VSTO designer to create a data-bound customized spreadsheet without writing a single line of code. After that, the chapter examines some ADO.NET features and then delves into the Word- and Excel-specific programming model.

To understand ADO.NET in all its complexity, read Shawn Wildermuth's *Pragmatic ADO.NET* (Addison-Wesley, 2002) and the data binding chapters of *Windows Forms Programming in C#* (Addison-Wesley, 2003) by Chris Sells.

Several developer scenarios in Office development leverage data binding. If you use data binding with Windows Forms controls in an Actions-Pane, custom task pane, Outlook form region, or dialog box, data binding works just like it does in any Windows Forms application. This chapter discusses in particular how to use ADO.NET data binding against built-in types in Excel and Word documents such as an Excel list object or range and a Word content control. We first consider how to do this in document-level projects; at the end of the chapter we consider how to use data binding from an application-level add-in that operates against any open document.

This chapter also describes caching datasets and the values of other .NET objects in a Word or an Excel document—a feature that can be used only in document-level projects and that is not supported in application-level add-ins.

Creating a Data-Bound Customized Spreadsheet with VSTO

Creating a no-frills data-bound customized document using the VSTO designer requires no coding but a whole lot of mouse clicking. What we are going to do is first tell Visual Studio about a data source—in this case, the Northwind sample database that comes with Office—and then drag and drop some data-bound controls onto the spreadsheet.

Defining a Data Source

Let's start up Visual Studio and create a new Excel Workbook project. From Visual Studio's Data menu, choose Show Data Sources to display the Data Sources pane. Click the Add New Data Source link in the Data Sources tool window to start the Data Source Configuration Wizard, as shown in Figure 19-1.

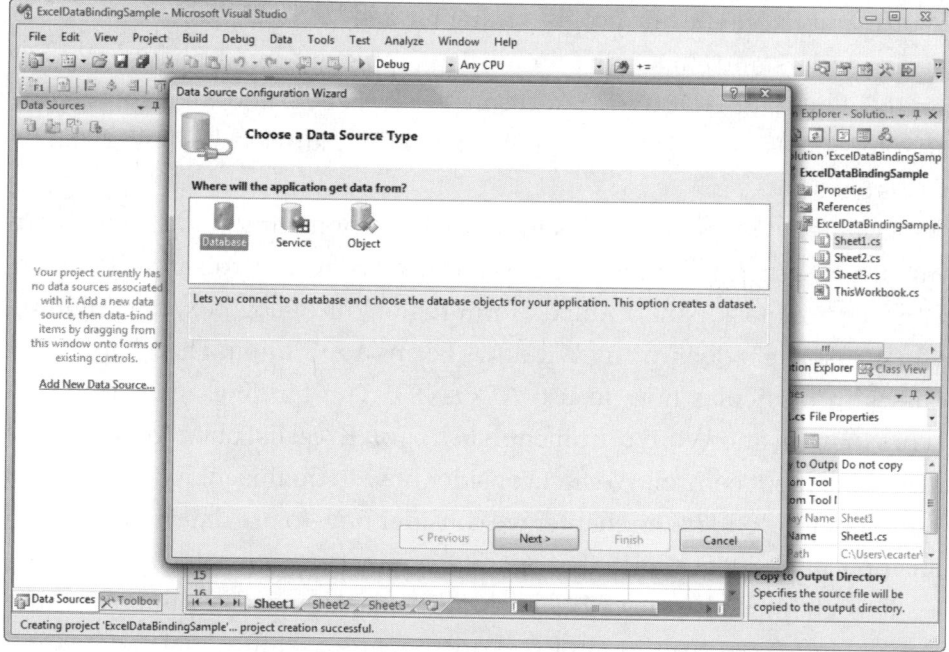

Figure 19-1: Starting the Data Source Configuration Wizard.

Choose Database and click Next. Click New Connection. A second wizard will appear as shown in Figure 19-2.

Choose Microsoft Access Database File and click Continue to go on to the Connection dialog box, shown in Figure 19-3. The Northwind database can be downloaded from http://www.microsoft.com/downloads/details.aspx ?familyid=C6661372-8DBE-422B-8676-C632D66C529C&displaylang=en. No security is enforced on this database file, so the default username Admin and a blank password are fine.

> **▪▫ NOTE**
>
> In a real-world application with a secured database, it would be a very bad idea to have a blank administrator password. See the section "Data Sources and Security Best Practices" later in this chapter for more information.

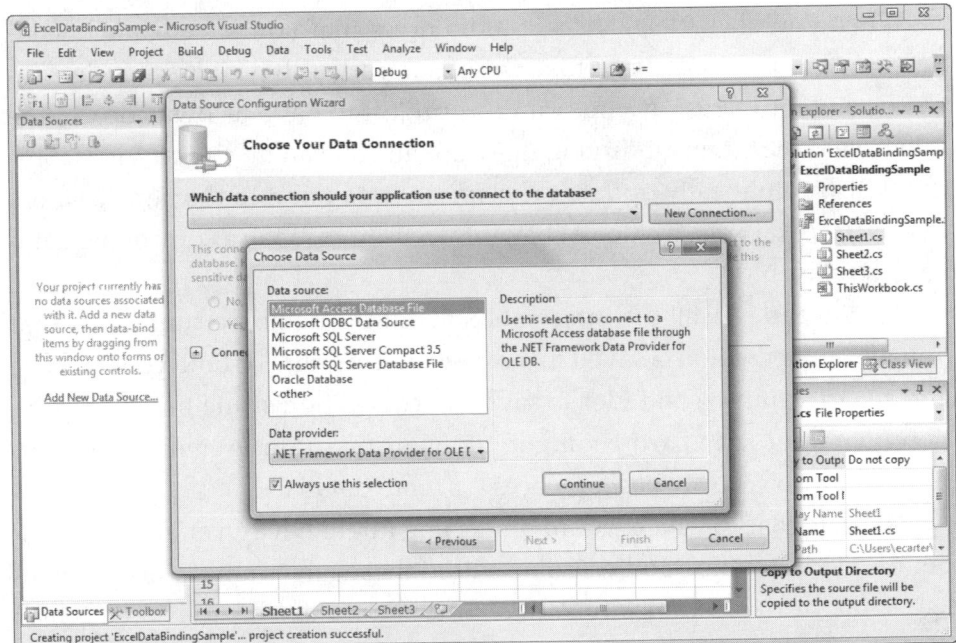

Figure 19-2: Choose Data Source dialog box.

Figure 19-3:　Creating the database connection.

Click Next to continue the Connection Wizard and continue with the Data Source Wizard, shown in Figure 19-4.

When you click Next, Visual Studio notes that you are creating a connection to a local database file that is not part of the current project, as shown in Figure 19-5. If you want this project to have its own copy of the database rather than modifying the original, you can do so and Visual Studio will automatically update the connection to point to the new location. In this first example, we do not have any reason to make a copy of the database, so click No.

As you can see, all the information about the database connection that you have just created is saved in a connection string. For both convenience and security, it is a good idea to save that connection string in a configuration file rather than hard-coding it into your program. Again, see the section below on security best practices for more details.

The database to which we are connecting might have an enormous number of queries, tables, and columns within those tables and so on. To manage some of this complexity, Visual Studio enables you to choose which portions of the database will display in Visual Studio. Let's select the entire

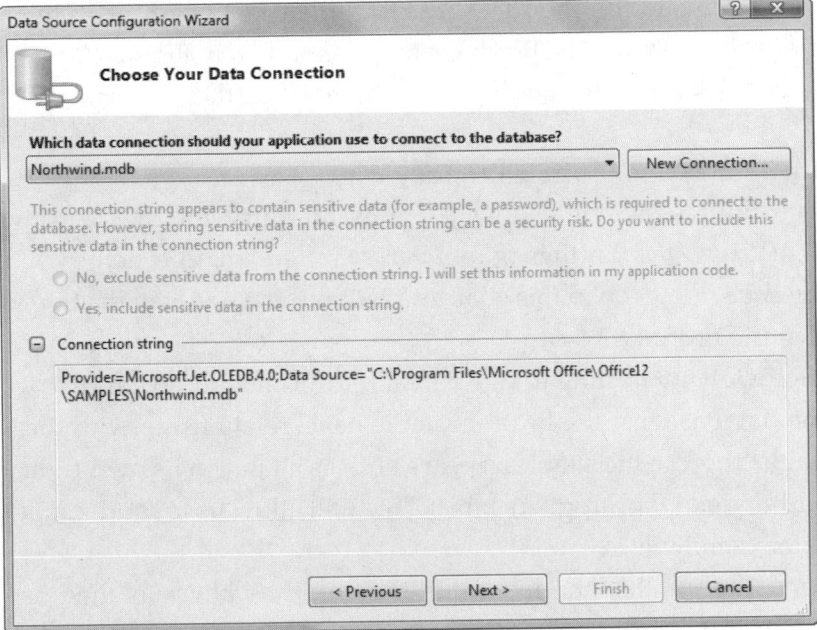

Figure 19-4: Viewing the connection string.

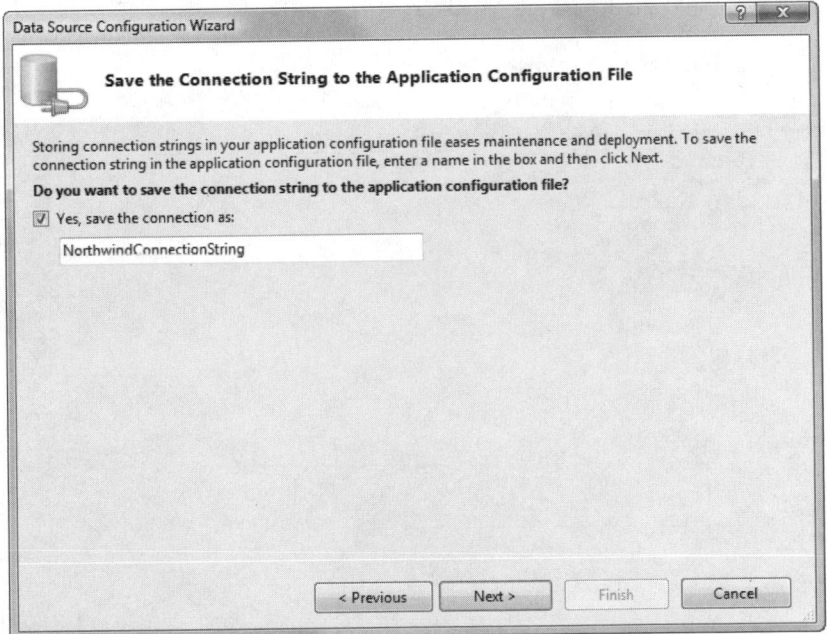

Figure 19-5: Save the connection string in the application configuration file.

Suppliers table and the ProductName, SupplierID, QuantityPerUnit, and UnitPrice columns from the Products table, as shown in Figure 19-6.

Finally, click Finish to exit the Data Source Wizard.

Creating Data-Bound Controls the Easy Way

The Data Sources window now contains an entry for the Northwind-DataSet. (Why *dataset* rather than *database*? We explain exactly what we mean by *dataset* later on in this chapter.) Expand the nodes in the tree view, as shown in Figure 19-7.

Notice a few interesting things here. First, Visual Studio has discovered from the database that the Products table has a relationship with the Suppliers table; the Products table appears both as a table in its own right, and as a child node of the Suppliers table. This will allow us to more easily create master-detail views.

Second, notice that the icons for the columns have "named range" icons, indicating that if you drag and drop the icon onto the worksheet, you will get a data-bound named range to this column. The default for a

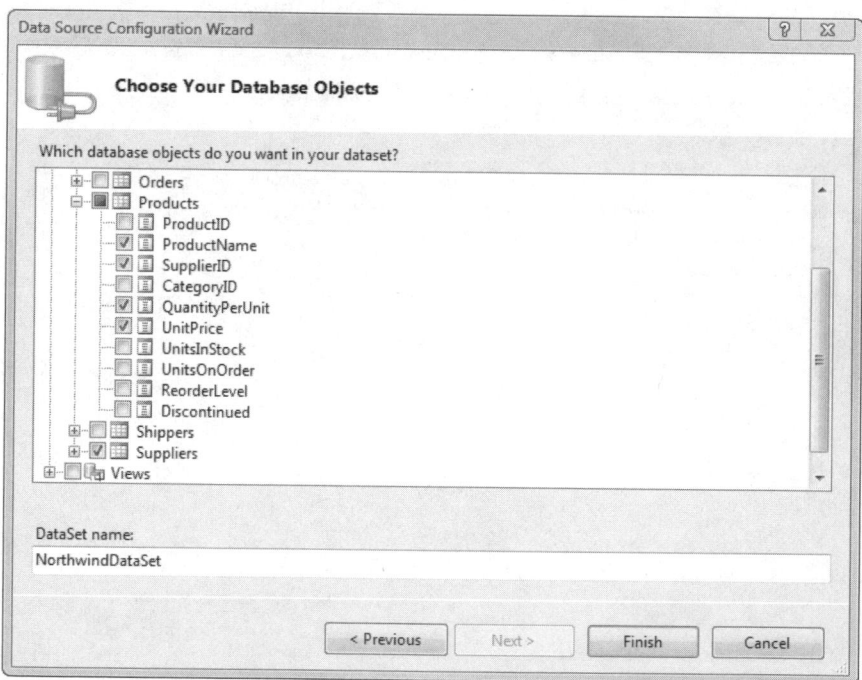

Figure 19-6: Choose your tables.

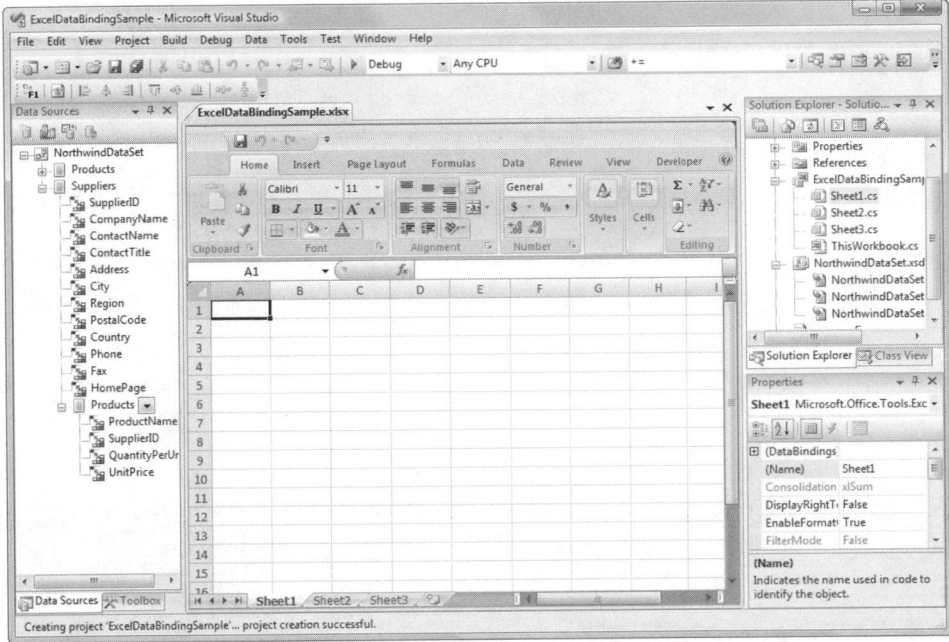

Figure 19-7: The Data Sources pane contains the dataset tree view.

column is a named range, and the default for an entire table is a list object, but you can choose other controls by clicking the item and selecting a drop-down. Suppose we want to have a combo box bound to the CompanyName, for instance. You can choose ComboBox from the drop-down list as the control to use for CompanyName, as shown in Figure 19-8.

Drag the CompanyName as a combo box, the ContactName as a named range, and the entire Products table as a list object. Use the Products table that is the child of the Suppliers table in the Data Sources tree view to get a nice master-detail view, as shown in Figure 19-9.

Two Controls Created

When you drag a column as something other than a named range, two controls are created: a label control with the name of the column and the control you picked for the column. You can delete the label control without affecting the data binding of the second control.

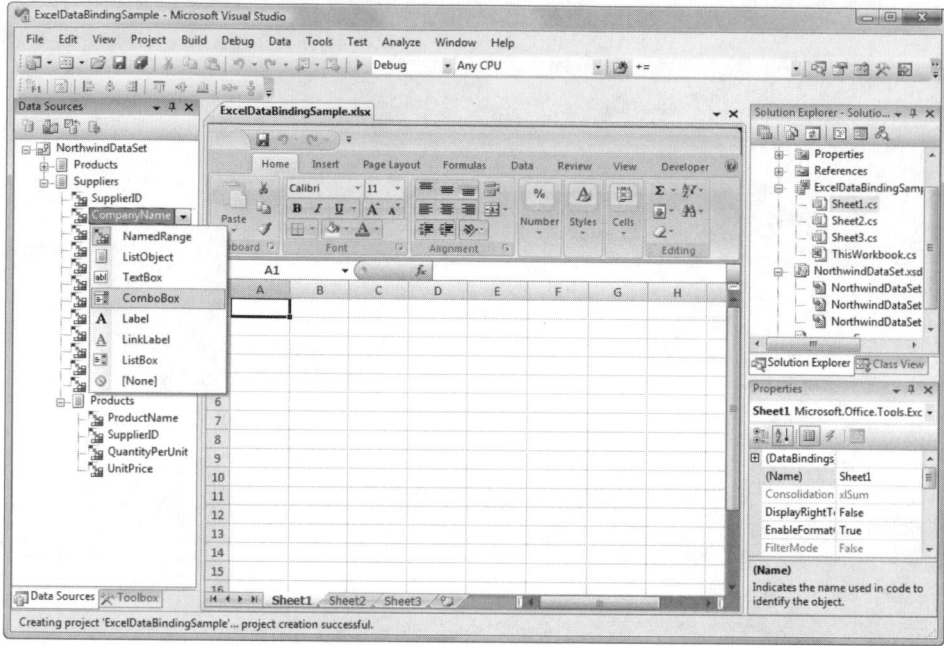

Figure 19-8: Choosing the control type.

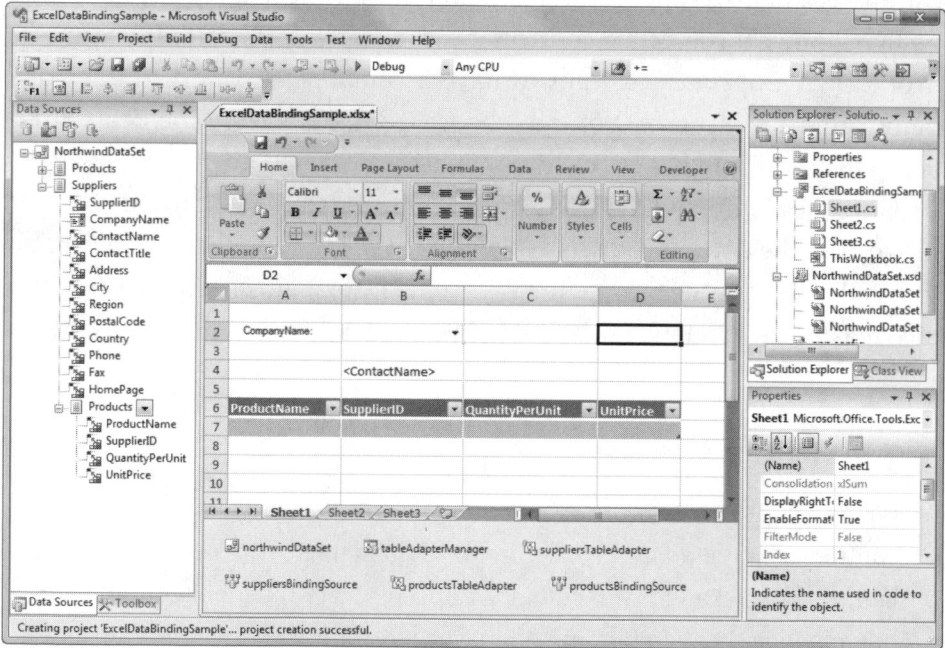

Figure 19-9: Creating the data-bound view.

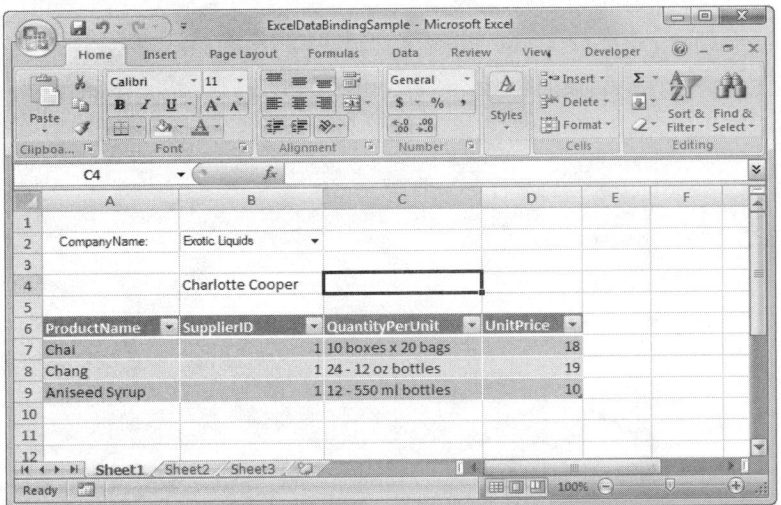

Figure 19-10: A data-bound master-detail spreadsheet.

A whole lot of stuff has magically appeared in the component tray below the Excel designer: a dataset, a table adapter manager, two binding sources, and two table adapters. We get into the details of what these components are for later in this chapter. For now, compile and run the application. Without writing a single line of code, we have gotten a data-bound master-detail view on an Excel spreadsheet. As you select different items from the combo box, the named range and list object automatically update themselves, as shown in Figure 19-10.

Creating a Data-Bound Customized Word Document with VSTO

We can create a similar data-bound document in Word using bookmarks rather than named ranges and a data grid rather than an Excel List object. Create a new Word document project and again add the Northwind database as a data source to the Data Sources pane. Visual Studio should remember the connection string from last time, so you will not need to configure it again.

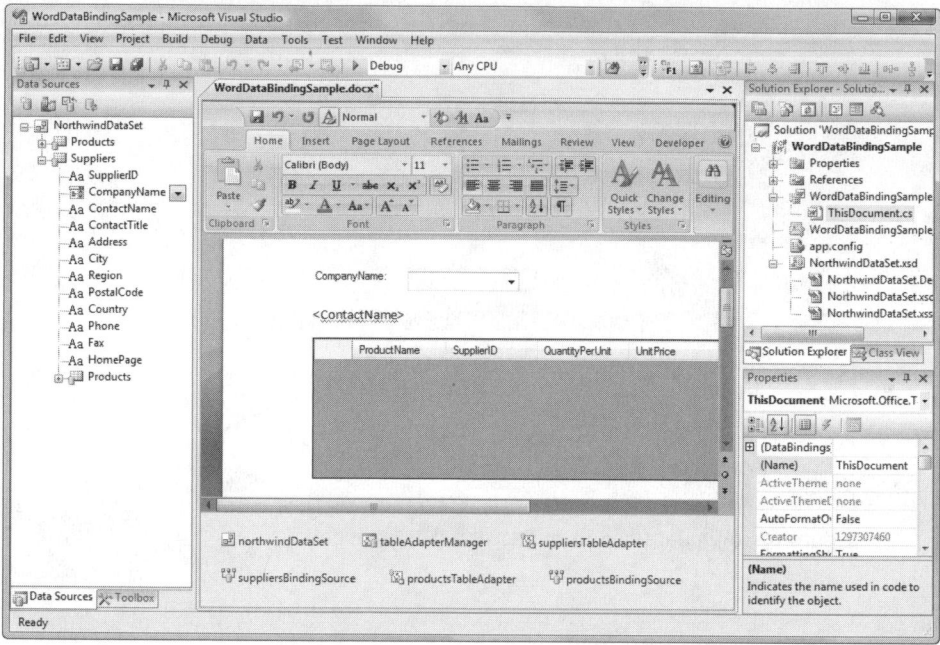

Figure 19-11: A data-bound master-detail Word document in the designer.

In the last step of the Data Source Wizard, select the entire Suppliers table and the ProductName, SupplierID, QuantityPerUnit, and UnitPrice columns in the Products table. Finally, click Finish to exit the Data Source Wizard.

As before, in the Data Sources window (shown in Figure 19-7), choose ComboBox from the column drop-down list in the CompanyName column. Note that in Word, the default control used for columns is the plain text content control (a built-in Word control) and the default control used for tables is the Windows Forms DataGridView control.

Drag the CompanyName as a combo box, the ContactName as a plain text content control, and the entire Products table as a DataGridView control. Use the Products table that is the child of the Suppliers table in the Data Sources tree view to get a nice master-detail view as shown in Figure 19-11.

When we build and run the customized Word document, again we have a master-detail view of a data table running in Word without writing a single line of code, as shown in Figure 19-12.

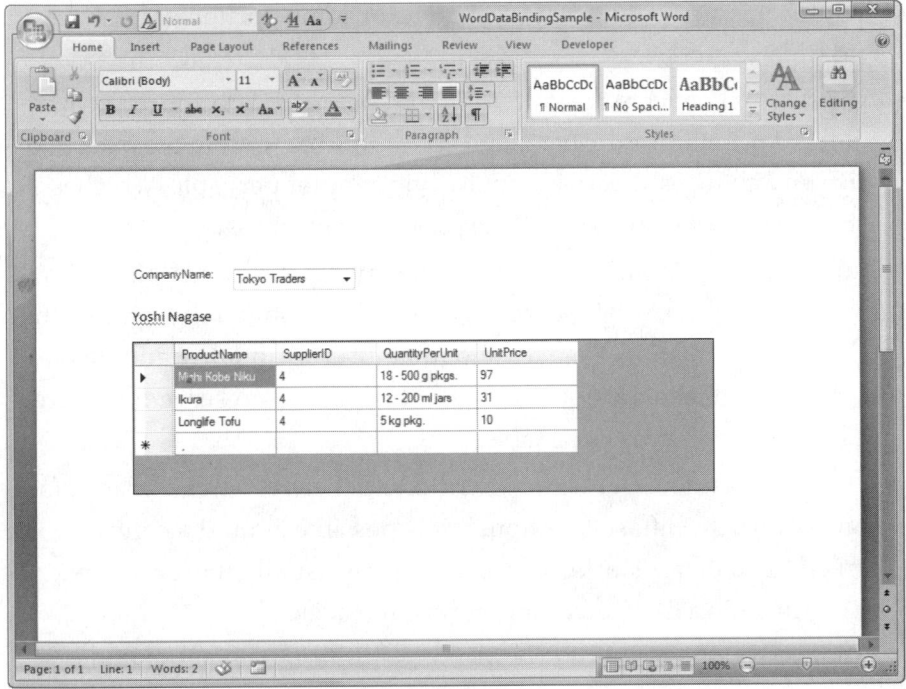

Figure 19-12: The master-detail view at runtime.

> **■ NOTE**
>
> You may expect to be able to use a combo box content control rather than a Windows Forms combo box in this exercise. Unfortunately, the combo box content control doesn't bind to lists of data as the Windows Forms combo box does in this release of VSTO.

Datasets, Adapters, and Sources

Now that we have seen a couple no-coding-required examples, let's take a peek under the hood and see how data binding actually works. Several players make data binding work, many of which can be seen on the component tray or design surface:

- A **back-end data source**, such as an Access database, a remote SQL Server database, a Web service, or some other data storage and retrieval system, is where the data ultimately lives.

- A **dataset** is a disconnected local cache of some portion of the back-end data source.

- An **adapter** connects the dataset to the back-end data source, to both fill the dataset from the back-end source and to update the back end with any changes. There is usually one adapter per table, which is why we saw two adapters in the preceding example.

- A **table adapter manager** manages the saving of related data tables. If two tables are related by a foreign-key relationship, for example, the table adapter manager makes sure that inserts, updates, and deletes to the related tables are sent in the right order to preserve the referential integrity of the related tables.

- A **binding source** acts as the intermediary between the user interface control and the dataset. Although it is possible to bind a control directly to a dataset, as discussed later, it is usually more convenient to go through a dedicated binding source object.

- A **data-bindable control** provides a user interface element that enables the user to read or write the data.

The back-end data source is represented in a VSTO project by the connection string passed to the adapter; everything else is represented by a member of the customized host item (the worksheet or document) class. Let's take a look at these different components in more detail.

Data Sources and Security Best Practices

As you probably noticed in the Connection Wizard, all the information required to connect to the back-end data source is stored in a "connection string" generated by the wizard. It typically looks something like this:

```
Server=MyDataServer; Database=Customers; Integrated Security=true;
```

That is, it says where the database is located, what it is called, and how the user should be authenticated. All this is potentially sensitive information! Use caution when embedding connection strings into your programs; remember, even without the source code it is very easy to figure out which strings are embedded in a managed application. This particularly applies to connection strings where, instead of using Windows NT integrated security, you simply embed `UserID=eric;Password=BigSecret123` directly.

Furthermore, hard-coded embedded strings in your source code make it hard for developers, testers, end users, and database administrators to update your application should the database connection information change over time. As discussed previously, Visual Studio gives you the option of embedding the connection string in the configuration file. The automatically generated configuration file in the previous example looks something like Listing 19-1.

Listing 19-1: A Typical Database Connection String in a Configuration File

```xml
<?xml version="1.0" encoding="utf-8" ?>
<configuration>
  <configSections>
  </configSections>
  <connectionStrings>
    <add name="ExcelDataBindingSample.Properties.Settings.
      NorthwindConnectionString"
      connectionString="Provider=Microsoft.Jet.OLEDB.4.0;
        Data Source=&quot;C:\Program Files\Microsoft Office\
        Office12\SAMPLES\Northwind.mdb&quot;"
      providerName="System.Data.OleDb" />
  </connectionStrings>
</configuration>
```

It is also a good idea to use the "principle of least privilege." This is one of the fundamental principles of secure design: Grant exactly as much privilege as you need to get the job done, no more, no less. For example, if your user needs to be able to read from the database but not write to it, do not specify a connection string that gives the user administrator rights to the database. Instead, choose a connection string that specifies a username and password with read-only access. That way, if the username and password are ever compromised, at least the attacker does not get administrator access out of it.

Better still, do not use stored user IDs and passwords at all; some databases use integrated Windows authentication, so the logged-on user can seamlessly use his already authenticated credentials. Or, if your database system requires a username and password, make the user type them in rather than storing them. As you'll see later when we discuss adapters, you can manually change the connection string used by the adapter before it fills the dataset. That way you could ask the user to type in his user ID and password and then generate a new connection string from that information.

Datasets

The cornerstone of the VSTO data model, and of ADO.NET in general, is the dataset. We should motivate the existence of datasets by describing the old way of doing data access. Back in the twentieth century, you typically communicated with a database via "ADO Classic" something like this:

1. Create and open a connection to a database.
2. Create and execute a database command (such as `SELECT partnumber FROM invoices WHERE price > 100`).
3. Enumerate the resulting record set.
4. Close the connection.

This approach worked fairly well, but it has several drawbacks. The principle drawbacks are consequences of the fact that this model requires a live connection to a database. If there are going to be many live connections, the server needs to be scalable and robust, which can be expensive. Therefore, to minimize load upon the server, we want connections to be short-lived. But because the connection is open while the user is enumerating the record set, the connection is typically open for quite some time—as long as the user is working with the data.

Furthermore, even if the server-side expense of keeping connections open is unimportant, this model does not work well in a world where you want to be able to work with your data even if you temporarily lack network connectivity.

A Disconnected Strategy

Database connections are both expensive and necessary and therefore must be managed carefully. In a typical ADO application, much developer effort is expended writing code to ensure that the connection is open for as little time as possible while still meeting the needs of the application's users. ADO.NET addresses the problems of ADO by going straight to the root; if we cannot make connections inexpensive, we can at least make them less necessary. ADO.NET is therefore fundamentally a *disconnected* strategy. A typical ADO.NET scenario goes something like this:

1. Create a DataAdapter to manage the connection to a specific database or other data source.

2. Set properties on the adapter that tell it what query to execute against the database.

3. Create a dataset to be filled.

4. Invoke a method on the adapter to take care of the details of opening a connection, executing the query, saving the results in the dataset, and closing the connection as soon as possible.

5. Work with the data in the now-disconnected dataset.

6. When you have finished working with the data, invoke a method on the adapter to re-open the connection to the database and update it with any changes.

And indeed, as you will see later when we discuss adapters, VSTO does exactly this on your behalf.

Because the dataset acts much like the original database, the connection need be open only as long as it takes to fill the dataset. After the data has been copied to the dataset, you can query and manipulate the dataset for as long as you want without worrying that you are consuming a valuable database connection.

Furthermore, there is no reason why the data used to fill the dataset have to come from a connected database; you could fill the dataset from an XML file, or write a program to add tables and rows to build one "from scratch." Datasets have no knowledge of where the data they contain came from; if you need it, all that knowledge is encapsulated in the adapter.

Typed and Untyped Datasets

In the Solution Explorer of the Word or Excel projects we created earlier, you will find a NorthwindDataSet.xsd file containing the database schema. This is an XML document that describes the tables, columns, and relationships that make up the dataset. One of the child nodes in the Solution Explorer tree view is NorthwindDataSet.Designer.cs. This file contains the automatically generated code for the dataset and table adapters.

> **▪▪ NOTE**
>
> The foregoing is not to say that old-fashioned connected data access is impossible in ADO.NET, or even discouraged; the DataReader class allows for traditional always-connected access to a database. However, neither Windows Forms controls nor VSTO host items/host controls can use DataReaders for data binding, so we speak of them no more in this book.

The first line of the declaration is interesting:

```
public partial class NorthwindDataSet : System.Data.DataSet {
```

The generated class is partial so that if you need to add your own extensions to it, you can do so in a separate file; it is a bad idea to edit automatically generated files. More importantly, this dataset extends the System .Data.DataSet class. A System.Data.DataSet consists of a collection of data tables. As you would expect, data tables consist of a collection of data columns and data rows. Each class exposes various collections as properties that allow you to navigate through the dataset.

System.Data.DataSet is not an abstract class; you can create instances and fill them from *any* back-end data source. But that would be an *untyped* dataset; the NorthwindDataSet is a *typed* dataset. Untyped datasets give you great flexibility but are so general that they are somewhat harder to use.

For example, if you were to fill an untyped dataset with data from the Northwind database file, you could access a particular datum with an expression such as this:

```
name = myDataSet.Tables["Products"].Rows[1]["ProductName"];
```

But that flexibility comes at a cost: You can accidentally pass in a bad table name, a bad column name, or make a bad assumption about the type of the data stored in a column. Because none of the structure of the tables or types of the columns is known at compile time, the compiler is unable to verify that the code will run without throwing exceptions. Also, the Intelli-

Sense engine is unable to provide any hints about the dataset's structure while you are developing the code.

Typed datasets mitigate these problems. A typed dataset is a class that extends the dataset base class; it has all the flexible, untyped features of a regular untyped dataset, but also has compile-time strongly typed properties that expose the tables by name. A typed dataset also defines typed data table and data row subclasses, too.

As you can see from the NorthwindDataSet.Designer.cs file, the typed dataset has public properties that enable you to write much more straightforward code, such as this:

```
name = myDataSet.Products[1].ProductName;
```

Typed datasets extend untyped datasets in many ways; some of the most important are as follows:

- Tables are exposed as read-only properties typed as instances of typed data tables.
- Tables have read-only properties for each column.
- Tables have an indexer that returns a typed data row.
- Event delegates for row change events pass typed change event arguments. Each row type has a row-changing, row-changed, row-deleting, and row-deleted event. (You might be wondering where the row-adding and row-added events are. The changing/changed events pass a DataRowAction enumerated type to indicate whether the row in question was newly created.)
- Tables provide methods for adding and removing typed data rows.
- Rows provide getters, setters, and nullity testers for each column.

In short, it is almost always a good idea to use a typed dataset. Weakly typed code is harder to read, harder to reason about, and harder to maintain.

Adapters

Take a look at the Startup event handler in either the Word or Excel examples above. Visual Studio has automatically generated the code in Listing 19-2 on your behalf.

Listing 19-2: Autogenerated Table-Filling Code

```
public partial class ThisDocument
{
  private void ThisDocument_Startup(
    object sender, System.EventArgs e)
  {
    // TODO: Delete this line of code to remove the default
    // AutoFill for 'northwindDataSet.Products'.
    if (this.NeedsFill("northwindDataSet"))
    {
      this.productsTableAdapter.Fill(
        this.northwindDataSet.Products);
    }
    // TODO: Delete this line of code to remove the default
    // AutoFill for 'northwindDataSet.Suppliers'.
    if (this.NeedsFill("northwindDataSet"))
    {
      this.suppliersTableAdapter.Fill(
        this.northwindDataSet.Suppliers);
    }
  }
}
```

We discuss what exactly NeedsFill is for in more detail when we discuss data caching later in this chapter and in Chapter 20, "Server Data Scenarios." But for now, this should look fairly straightforward: If the two tables need to be filled from the back-end data source, the adapters fill the appropriate tables.

There are a number of reasons why you might want to not automatically fill the data tables in the Startup event, which is why the comment points out that you can remove the autogenerated code. For example, as mentioned earlier, you might want to require that the user enter a database password before attempting to fill the dataset. You can generate a new connection string and then set the adapter's Connection.ConnectionString property.

Or perhaps you want to give the user the option of whether to connect to the back end. If the user is on an expensive or slow connection, the user might want to skip downloading a large chunk of data. For any number of reasons, you might not want to connect right away or use the default connection string, so Visual Studio allows you to modify this startup code.

Visual Studio generates strongly typed custom adapters at the same time as it generates the typed dataset. If you read through the generated adapter code in NorthwindDataSet.Designers.cs, you will see that the generated adapter has been hard-coded to connect to the database specified by the connection string in the configuration file. The bulk of the generated adapter code consists of the query code to handle reading from the back-end data store into the typed dataset, and then taking any changes in the dataset and updating or deleting the appropriate rows in the store.

The adapter takes care of all the details of opening the connection, executing the query, copying the data into the dataset, and closing the connection. At this point, we have a local copy of the data, which we can use to our heart's content without worrying about taxing the server further.

Also, a generated TableAdapterManager object is new in Visual Studio 2005. This object can update all the tables associated with the dataset. In addition, it is smart about updating, inserting, and deleting in the right order when foreign-key relationships exist among the various tables associated with the dataset. In previous versions of Visual Studio, the developer had to write complex code to update multiple related tables. Now TableAdapterManager can manage related tables for you.

When you are done editing the local copy of the data in the dataset, you can use the adapter to update the database with the changes by calling the Update method of the adapter. The adapter will then take care of making the additions, changes, and deletions to the back-end database. Or, if you have multiple tables that are related by foreign-key constraints, you can call the UpdateAll method of the generated TableAdapterManager to update all the tables associated with the dataset.

▪ NOTE

By default, the adapter assumes that you want "optimistic concurrency." That is, other users will be able to update the database unless you are currently in the process of updating the database. Other concurrency models are possible but beyond the scope of this text. If you want either "pessimistic concurrency" (that is, the database remains locked during the whole time that you have the offline dataset) or "destructive concurrency" (that is, the database is never locked even when multiple people are writing at once), consult a reference on ADO.NET to see how to configure your adapter appropriately.

Using Binding Sources as Proxies

Why does Visual Studio bind the controls to a BindingSource "proxy" object, rather than binding controls directly to the data table?

The reason is because the control can bind to the proxy even if the data in the table is not currently available. For instance, perhaps the data table is going to be derived from a call to a Web service, which will not happen until long after the initialization is complete, or until the user types in his password or presses a button to start the database connection.

The proxy object is created when the customization starts up and controls can be bound to it even if there is no "real" data available. When the real data is available, the binding source updates the controls. It is essentially just a thin "shim" that makes it easier to set up bindings before the data is all available.

As you saw in the examples, multiple controls can share the same binding source and therefore have the same "currency." That is, when one control is updated, every other control linked to the same binding source is also updated automatically. Controls on different worksheets or even on the actions pane can share binding sources and thereby share currency. You will learn about currency management in more detail later in this chapter.

Data-Bindable Controls

The last piece of the data binding puzzle is the host control or Windows Forms control on the spreadsheet or document that actually displays the bound data. There are two flavors of data-bindable controls: "simple" and "complex." Controls that can bind a single datum to a particular property are "simple-data-bindable." Controls that can bind multiple rows and/or columns are "complex-data-bindable."

In the preceding examples, the list object in Excel and the combo box and data grid Windows Forms controls are complex-data-bindable; the list object and data grid display multiple rows and columns from a table, and the combo box displays multiple rows from a single column. The bookmark and named range controls by contrast are simple-data-bindable; only a single datum is bound to the Value property of the named range.

All the Windows Forms controls support simple-data-binding, as do almost all of the Word and Excel host items and host controls. (There is one exception: Word XMLNodes host control is neither simple- nor complex-data-bindable.) Of the host items and host controls, only Excel's list object is complex-data-bindable.

The behind-the-scenes mechanisms by which controls implement data binding and manage currency are fairly complex; we cover them in more detail toward the end of this chapter. But first, now that we have gotten a little context as to what all these parts are and how they relate, let's take a look at a somewhat more labor-intensive way to do data binding in Excel. This time we are going to actually write a few lines of code.

Another Technique for Creating Data-Bound Documents

Unlike our previous example, in this case we do not define ahead of time where the back-end data store is located; you have to write a few lines of code to obtain the data.

Create a new Excel project, and click the Developer tab in the Excel Ribbon. Then click the Source button to show Excel's XML Source task pane. (If the Developer tab isn't visible in the Ribbon, you need to exit Visual Studio, launch Excel, choose Office > Excel Options, and click the Show Developer tab in the Ribbon check box. Then exit Excel and restart Visual Studio.) As you can see in the XML Source task pane, no XML schemas are mapped into this document. Create a new .XSD XML schema file, using Notepad or Visual Studio, and type the schema shown in Listing 19-3. Then click the XML Maps button in Excel and add the .XSD XML schema file.

Listing 19-3: A Schema for a Two-Table Dataset

```xml
<?xml version="1.0"?>
<xs:schema
  id="OrderDataSet"
  targetNamespace="http://myschemas/Order.xsd"
  xmlns="http://myschemas/Order.xsd"
  xmlns:xs="http://www.w3.org/2001/XMLSchema">
  <xs:element name="Order">
    <xs:complexType>
      <xs:sequence>
```

```
        <xs:element name="Customer" type="xs:string"
    minOccurs="0" maxOccurs="1" />
        <xs:element name="Book" minOccurs="0" maxOccurs="unbounded">
          <xs:complexType>
            <xs:sequence>
              <xs:element name="Title" type="xs:string" minOccurs="0" />
              <xs:element name="ISBN" type="xs:string" minOccurs="0" />
              <xs:element name="Price" type="xs:double" minOccurs="0" />
            </xs:sequence>
          </xs:complexType>
        </xs:element>
      </xs:sequence>
    </xs:complexType>
  </xs:element>
</xs:schema>
```

This is a dataset schema that defines an Order as consisting of a single
Customer and any number of Books, where each book has a Title, ISBN,
and Price. In a database, this would be organized as two related tables, as
you will see. When you add the schema file in the XML Source task pane,
Visual Studio detects the new XML map and creates a dataset in the project
for it—in this case, a dataset called OrderDataSet.xsd.

The structure of the XML schema appears in the XML Source pane, and
you can drag and drop elements of the schema onto the spreadsheet. Try
dragging the Customer node onto a cell. The single datum creates a named
range host control called OrderCustomCell. If you then drag over the Book
node, you get a List object called Table2. However, Visual Studio knows
nothing about what the source of the data will be, so it does not generate
any adapters.

Next, let's bind the OrderCustomerCell named range. Expand the Data-
Bindings tree view in the properties window. Data-bind the value of
OrderCustomerCell by setting the Value under DataBindings to the Cus-
tomer column under Other Data Sources > Project Data Sources > Order-
DataSet > Order > Customer, as shown in Figure 19-13.

Visual Studio automatically adds two components to the component
tray when you bind the OrderCustomerCell. First, it adds an orderDataSet,
which is an instance of the typed dataset defined by the Order schema. Second, it adds an orderBindingSource component, which is associated with
the orderDataSet's Order table. Finally, the OrderCustomerCell named
range is bound to orderBindingSource's Customer column.

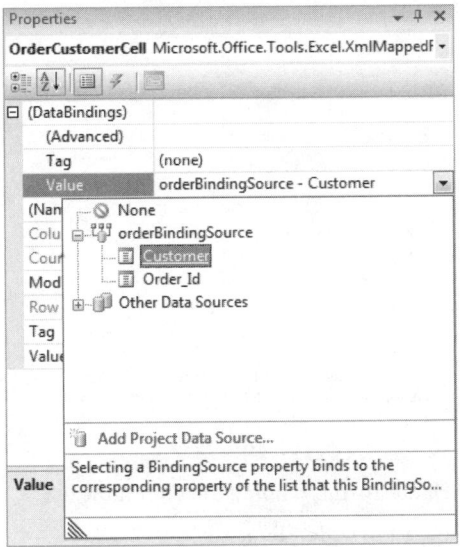

Figure 19-13: Binding the OrderCustomerCell's
Value property to Customer.

Next, click the list object you created by dragging the Book node onto the worksheet. Rename it bookTable, using the properties window. In the properties window, set the DataSource of the list object to the Order_Book table under the orderBindingSource, as shown in Figure 19-14. Note that in this case, the Order_Book table contains the books associated with a particular order rather than all books from all orders. To represent this binding, Visual Studio creates a second binding source called orderBook-BindingSource, which is bound to orderBindingSource's Order_Book data member. Finally, bookTable is bound to the newly created orderBook-BindingSource.

If you compile and run the customization, not much will happen; the data binding sources are hooked up, but the dataset contains no actual data.

We have gotten almost everything we need; the only thing left is to put some data in the typed dataset instance we have added. Typically, we would fill the dataset by creating an adapter to talk to some external database; for this example, we just fill the typed dataset manually, using the code in Listing 19-4. (You could also fill it by loading XML out of a file or

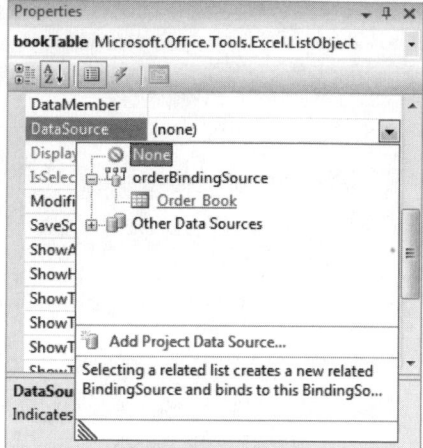

Figure 19-14: Binding the bookTable list object to Order_Book.

downloading XML from a Web service.) Listing 19-4 also defines a sheet double-click event handler. When you double-click the worksheet, it toggles between the two orders that were created.

Listing 19-4: Filling a Typed Dataset from Scratch

```
using System;
using System.Data;
using Microsoft.VisualStudio.Tools.Applications.Runtime;
using Excel = Microsoft.Office.Interop.Excel;
using Office = Microsoft.Office.Core;

namespace ExcelXmlDataBindingSample
{
  public partial class Sheet1
  {
    private void Sheet1_Startup(object sender, System.EventArgs e)
    {
      // An order has a customer column
      this.orderDataSet.Order.AddOrderRow("Vlad the Impaler");
      // A book has a title, ISBN and price, and is associated with
      // a particular order.
      this.orderDataSet.Book.AddBookRow("Blood For Dracula",
        "0-123-45678-9", 34.95, this.orderDataSet.Order[0]);
      this.orderDataSet.Book.AddBookRow("Fang Attack!",
        "9-876-54321-0", 14.44, this.orderDataSet.Order[0]);
```

```
    // An order has a customer column
    this.orderDataSet.Order.AddOrderRow("John the Gardener");
    // A book has a title, ISBN and price, and is associated with
    // a particular order.
    this.orderDataSet.Book.AddBookRow("Northwest Plants",
      "3-323-44444-9", 34.95, this.orderDataSet.Order[1]);
    this.orderDataSet.Book.AddBookRow("Famous Weeds",
      "3-999-55555-0", 14.44, this.orderDataSet.Order[1]);

    this.BeforeDoubleClick +=
      new Excel.DocEvents_BeforeDoubleClickEventHandler(
      Sheet1_BeforeDoubleClick);
  }

  void Sheet1_BeforeDoubleClick(Excel.Range Target,
    ref bool Cancel)
  {
    if (this.orderBindingSource.Position == 0)
      this.orderBindingSource.MoveLast();
    else
      this.orderBindingSource.MoveFirst();
  }

  #region VSTO Designer generated code
  private void InternalStartup()
  {
    this.Startup += new System.EventHandler(Sheet1_Startup);
  }
  #endregion

  }
}
```

Now build and execute the customized spreadsheet, and see a result similar to Figure 19-15. You'll see that when the Startup event runs and creates the new row in the book table, the data binding layer automatically updates the list object. When you double-click the spreadsheet, you move back and forth between the two orders. Furthermore, data binding to list objects goes both ways; updating the data in the host control propagates the changes back to the data table.

Complex and Simple Data Binding

What you have just seen included an example of "complex" data binding: the binding of Order_Book to the bookTable list object. Complex data

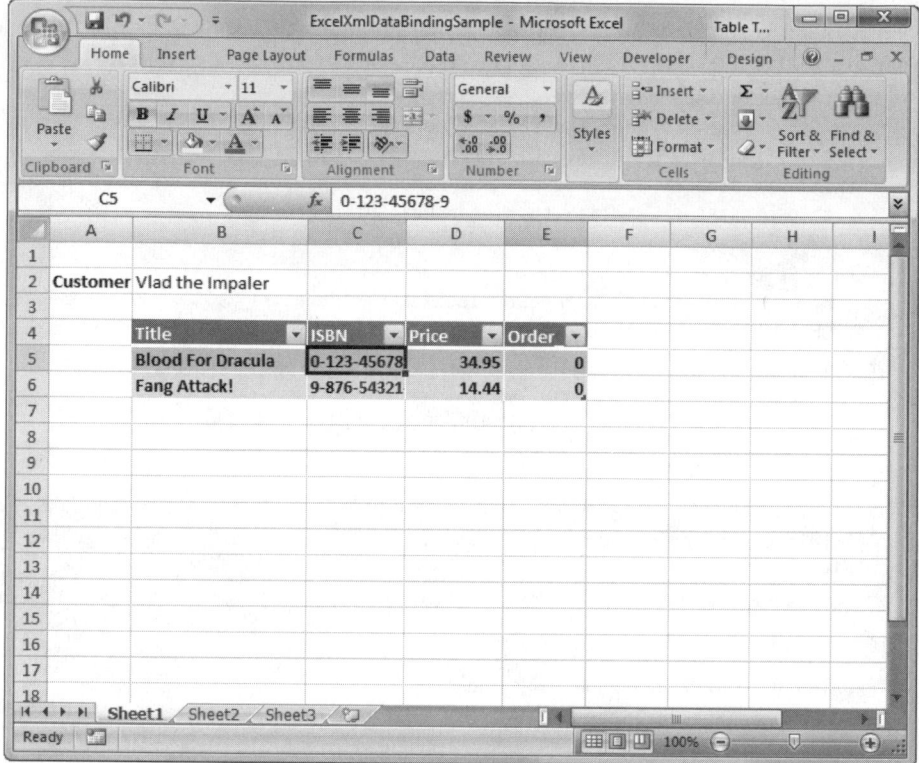

Figure 19-15: The List object is bound to the data table.

binding is so named not because it is particularly difficult, but because many data are bound at once to a relatively complicated host control. Controls must be specially written to support complex data binding; the list object control is one such control.

You also saw an example of "simple" data binding: the binding of OrderCustomerCell to orderBindingSource's Customer field. Simple data binding binds a single datum to a single property of a host control. To be more specific, the Value property of OrderCustomerCell is bound to the Customer field in the dataset via the orderBindingSource component. When we run the code, the value from the dataset is automatically copied into the host control, and when the dataset is changed or when we double-click to move the binding source, the host control is kept up to date. However, it does not work the other way; unlike the case with bookTable, changing the value in the OrderCustomerCell does not automatically propagate that change back to the dataset. Why not?

Click the OrderCustomerCell again, and expand the DataBindings tree control. Click the Advanced button. You see the dialog box shown in Figure 19-16. You can see that OrderCustomerCell's Value property is bound to the Customer field via orderBindingSource. In the Data Source Update Mode drop-down list in the top-right corner of the dialog box are three choices: Never, OnPropertyChanged, and OnValidation. The second choice certainly seems like a sensible choice; when a property on the control changes, update the data source to keep it in sync.

Unfortunately, that does not work with Excel host controls. Why? Because you can create a binding to any old property of a host control, but we cannot change the fact that the aggregated Range objects do not source any "some property just changed" event that the binding manager can listen to. Windows Forms Controls do source such an event, but Word and Excel host controls do not.

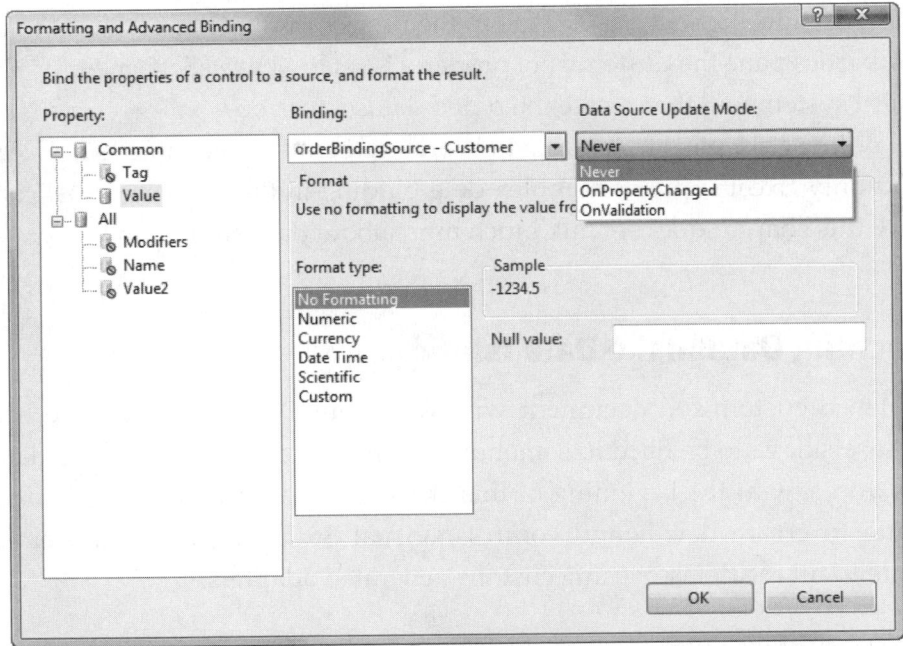

Figure 19-16: The Formatting and Advanced Binding dialog box for OrderCustomerCell.

This means that we need to tell the binding manager explicitly that the data source needs to be updated, instead of relying on the control informing its binding manager for you. Fortunately, this is simply done. Double-click the mapped range in the designer to automatically create a Change event handler, and then fill it in with the line of code which forces the binding to update the source:

```
private void OrderCustomerCell_Change(Excel.Range Target)
{
  this.OrderCustomerCell.DataBindings["Value"].WriteValue();
}
```

Now all changes made to the dataset will be propagated into the mapped range, and vice versa.

Data Binding in Word Documents

Word also supports creating XML mapped documents. However, unlike the Excel designer, the Word designer does not automatically create typed datasets from mapped schemas. If you want to create a typed dataset from a schema mapped into Word, you have to add it to the project system yourself. Just add the schema XSD file to the project, and then ensure that in its Properties pane the Custom Tool property is set to MSDataSetGenerator; the build system will then create the typed dataset for you.

Because simple data binding in Word is essentially the same as in Excel, and only Excel supports complex data binding in the list object host control, this chapter does not talk much more about data binding in Word.

Caching Data in the Data Island

When a customized document with data-bound controls starts up, the datasets have to be filled in somehow before the controls display the data. As you saw at the beginning of this chapter, if you use the Data Sources pane to create data-bound controls, Visual Studio automatically emits code to fill the datasets using custom-generated adapters:

```
private void ThisDocument_Startup(object sender, System.EventArgs e){
  if (this.NeedsFill("northwindDataSet"))
    this.productsTableAdapter.Fill(this.northwindDataSet.Products);
```

But under what circumstances would the dataset ever *not* need to be filled at startup? Consider, for example, a spreadsheet with a dataset containing a single table. One worksheet has a single datum bound to a named range. If you save that spreadsheet, only that one datum is going to be saved; all the other information in the dataset is just a structure in memory at runtime that will be lost when the workbook is closed. The data is potentially going to have to be fetched anew every time the worksheet host control starts up.

One of the key benefits of Word and Excel documents is that they are useful even on machines that are not connected to networks. (Working on a spreadsheet or document on a laptop on an airplane is the canonical scenario.) It would be unfortunate indeed if a data-bound customized document required your users to always be connected.

Fortunately, VSTO solves this problem. Click the icon for the typed dataset in the component tray, and then look at the Properties pane for this component. A CacheInDocument property defaults to `false`. If you set it to `true`, when you save the document the VSTO runtime will turn the dataset into XML and store the XML in a "data island" inside the document.

The next time the document starts up, the VSTO runtime detects that the data island contains a cached dataset and fills in the dataset from the cache. The call to NeedsFill in the Startup event will then return `false`, and the startup code will not attempt to fill in the data from the adapter. Essentially, the NeedsFill method returns `false` if the object was loaded from the cache automatically, `true` otherwise. Your code can fill the dataset on the first run of the document or whenever the document is first opened with a connection available for the database. Your code can write back changes to the database when a connection is available. In between connection availability, the dataset can be serialized into the cache associated with the document.

Caching Your Own Data Types

You can cache almost any kind of data in the XML data island, not just datasets. To be cacheable by the VSTO runtime, you must meet the following criteria:

- The data must be stored in a *public* member variable or property of a host item (a customized worksheet, workbook, chart sheet, or document class).

- If stored in a property, the property must have no parameters and be both readable and writable.

- The *runtime type* of the data must be either dataset (or a subclass), data table (or a subclass), or any type serializable by the System.Xml.Serialization.XmlSerializer object.

To tell Visual Studio that you would like to cache a member variable, just add the Cached attribute to its declaration. Make sure you check whether the member was already filled in from the cache; the first time the document is run there will be no data in the cache, so you have to fill in the data somehow. For example, you could use the code in Listing 19-5.

Listing 19-5: Autogenerated Table-Filling Code

```
public partial class ThisDocument
{
  [Cached]
  public string CustomerName;

  private void ThisDocument_Startup(object sender,
    System.EventArgs e)
  {
    if (this.NeedsFill("CustomerName"))
      this.CustomerName = "Unknown Customer";
  }
}
```

Dynamically Adding and Removing Cached Members from the Data Island

Cached data can be large; what if you decide that at some point you want to stop caching a particular dataset in the data island? Or, conversely, what if you do not want to automatically fill in a dataset and store it in the cache on the first run of the document, but rather want to start caching a member based on some other criterion? It would be unfortunate if the only way to tell VSTO to cache a member in the data island was to tag it with the Cached attribute at design time.

Therefore, all customized view item classes generated by a VSTO project expose four handy functions that you can call to query and manipulate the caching semantics, as follows:

- `bool NeedsFill(string memberName)`
- `bool IsCached(string memberName)`
- `void StartCaching(string memberName)`
- `void StopCaching(string memberName)`

NeedsFill we have already seen; if the named member was initialized from the data island by the VSTO runtime when the customization started up, this returns `false`. Otherwise, it returns `true`.

IsCached might seem like it is just the opposite of NeedsFill, but it is not. NeedsFill tells you whether the item in question was loaded out of the data island; IsCached tells you whether the item will be saved to the data island when the user saves the document.

StartCaching and StopCaching dynamically add and remove members from the set of members that will be saved to the data island. It is illegal to call StartCaching on a member already in the cache or StopCaching on a member not in the cache; use IsCached to double-check if you need to. The same rules that apply to cached members added to the cache by the `Cached` attribute apply to dynamically added members; only call StartCaching on public fields or public readable/writable properties.

> ### ◾ NOTE
>
> If a cached member is set to `null` at the time that the document is saved, the VSTO runtime assumes that you intended to call StopCaching on the member and it will be removed from the data island.

Advanced Topic: Using ICachedType

Suppose you have a large cached dataset that you loaded out of the data island when the customization started up. Serializing a dataset into XML can be a time- and memory-consuming process; so if there have been no changes to the dataset when the document is saved, the VSTO runtime is pretty smart about skipping the serialization.

This is also important if the user closes Word or Excel without saving the document. The host application needs to know whether to create the

"Do you want to save changes?" dialog box. If the dataset is clean, there are no changes to save and the dialog box should not be created.

How can VSTO tell whether a custom class added to the cached members is dirty? The VSTO runtime can track the Change events on a dataset or data table to tell whether they are dirty, but in general, any other types simply have to be written out every time. To prevent the "Do you want to save?" dialog box, the VSTO runtime must pessimistically serialize the object and compare it to the state that it loaded; this is again potentially time-consuming.

If you require more finely grained control over the caching process for a particular member, you can implement the ICachedType interface. This interface enables you to not only hint to the VSTO runtime whether the item needs to be re-serialized, it also allows you to dynamically abort a save or load, and receive notification when the save or load is done. Listing 19-6 shows its members.

Listing 19-6: The ICachedType Interface

```
namespace Microsoft.VisualStudio.Tools.Applications.Runtime
{
  public interface ICachedType
  {
    bool IsDirty { get; }
    bool BeforeLoad();
    void AfterLoad();
    bool BeforeSave();
    void AfterSave();
  }
}
```

If you implement this interface on a particular class and then add a member containing an instance to the class, the VSTO runtime will do the following:

- Call your BeforeLoad method when the item is loaded out of the cache. If you return `false`, the load will be aborted.
- Call your AfterLoad method when the XMLSerializer is done loading your object. (If you are tracking the dirty state of the object, this would be a good time to set it to clean.)

- Call IsDirty before saving the document; if the object has no changes since it was last loaded or saved, return `false` to avoid unnecessary expensive serializations.

- Call BeforeSave before saving the member to the data island. If for some reason you determine that the object is not in a state that can be saved, you can return `false` and the object will be removed from the cache.

- Call AfterSave when the XMLSerializer is done saving the document to the data island. (Again, this would be a good time to note that the object is clean.)

Manipulating the Serialized XML Directly

Chapter 20, "Server Data Scenarios," discusses how to view and edit the contents of the data island, start and stop caching members, and so on, without actually starting Word or Excel.

Advanced ADO.NET Data Binding: Looking Behind the Scenes

The preceding section gave some of the flavor of ADO.NET data binding; we should more carefully describe what is happening behind the scenes here. After all, you might want to write your own code to set up data binding rather than relying on the code generated for you by the designer.

The first thing we need to do is describe what objects work together to bind data to controls. In the Excel data binding example, many objects are involved. There are the two controls (the list object and the XML mapped range), the dataset, and the two data tables.

Each control implements IBindableComponent, so each control has a DataBindings property that returns an instance of ControlBindings-Collection. This object maintains a collection of Binding objects, one for each simple data binding. The collection is indexed by the name of the property, which has been simple-data-bound.

Each Binding object contains all the information necessary to describe the binding: what member of what data source is bound to what property of what control, how the data is to be formatted, and so on.

One important member of the Binding object is the BindingManager-Base property. The binding manager is the object that actually does the work of the data binding: listening to changes in the data source and bound controls, and ensuring that they stay synchronized.

The binding manager for data tables and other "list" data sources keeps track of the "currency" of the data source. If you bind a list to a control that displays a single datum, the control will display the current item as determined by the currency manager. (Because we'll almost always be talking about binding to list data sources, we use *binding manager* and *currency manager* interchangeably throughout.)

Most of the time, each binding source has exactly one currency manager associated with it; two controls bound to the same binding source share a currency manager and therefore share currency. In the event that you want to have two controls bound to a single binding source but with different currency, each control needs to have its own "binding context." A binding context is a collection that keeps track of pairs of binding sources and binding managers; within each context, every binding source has a unique binding manager, but two contexts can associate different managers with the same source, thereby keeping two or more currencies in one binding source.

In typical scenarios, there is only one binding context, so this point is largely moot. Even when you have only one, the binding context does have one use. When complex data binding, the binding context exposed by a list object lets you obtain the currency manager for the binding source.

Binding-Related Extensions to Host Items and Host Controls

All data-bindable host items and host controls allow you to bind any single datum to any writable property. These objects implement IBindableComponent, which defines two properties:

- `BindingContext BindingContext { get; set; }`
- `ControlBindingsCollection DataBindings { get; }`

Typically, you will have only one binding context; should you need to have two controls bound to the same list data source but with different currency for each, you can create new binding contexts and assign them to the controls as you want. Each host item and host control will raise a BindingContextChanged event if you do.

The ControlBindingsCollection object has many methods for adding and removing binding objects; there is one binding for each bound property on the control. It also has a read-only indexer that maps the name of a property to its binding object.

Extensions to the List Object Host Control in Excel

The list object aggregate in Excel has a large number of new properties, methods, and events added on to support complex data binding. We described the view extensions earlier; now that we have covered how data binding works, we can discuss the data model extensions.

New Data-Related List Object Host Control Properties and Methods

The two most important properties on the ListObject host control determine what data source is actually complex-data-bound to the control:

```
object DataSource { get; set; }
string DataMember { get; set; }
```

The reason that the list object divides this information up into two properties is because some data sources contain multiple lists, called "members." For example, you could set the DataSource property to a dataset and the DataMember property to the name of a data table contained by the dataset.

The properties can be set in any order, and binding will not commence until both are set to sensible values. However, it is usually easier to use one of the SetDataBinding methods to set both properties at once:

```
void SetDataBinding(object dataSource)
void SetDataBinding(object dataSource, string dataMember)
void SetDataBinding(object dataSource, string dataMember,
  params string[] mappedColumns)
```

Notice that in the last overload, you can specify which columns in the data table are to be bound. Doing so proves quite handy if you have a large, complicated table that you want to display only a portion of, or if you want to change the order in which the columns display.

In some cases, the data source needs no further qualification by a data member, so you can leave it blank. For instance, in the preceding example, the designer automatically generates code that creates a BindingSource proxy object, which needs no further qualification. The generated code looks something like the code in Listing 19-7.

Listing 19-7: Setting Up the Binding Source

```
this.OrderBookBindingSource = new System.Windows.Forms.BindingSource();
this.OrderBookBindingSource.DataMember = "Book";
this.OrderBookBindingSource.DataSource = this.orderDataSet1;
this.BookList.SetDataBinding(this.OrderBookBindingSource, "",
  "Title", "ISBN", "Price");
```

Because the binding source knows what table to proxy, the list object needs no further qualification.

> **■ NOTE**
>
> Unlike the DataGrid control, the list object does not allow you to set the bound columns using a column chooser in the list object's Properties pane. However, if you have a data-bound list object in the designer, you can simply delete columns at design time; Visual Studio will update the automatically generated code so that the deleted column is no longer bound when the code runs.

The information about which columns and tables are bound to which list objects is persisted in the document; you do not need to explicitly rebind the list objects every time the customization starts up. Should you want to ensure that all the persisted information about the data bindings is cleared from the document, you can call the ResetPersistedBindingInformation method:

```
void ResetPersistedBindingInformation()
```

The data source of the list object must implement either IList or IList-Source. Should you pass an invalid object when trying to set the data source, the list object will throw a SetDataBindingFailedException (as described later in this chapter).

You can check whether the data source and data members have been set properly and the list object is presently complex-data-bound by checking the IsBinding property:

```
bool IsBinding { get; }
```

Complex-data-bound list objects keep the currency—the currently "selected" row in the currency manager for the data source—in sync with the currently selected row in the host. You can set or get the currency of the data source's binding manager with this property:

```
int SelectedIndex { get; set; }
```

Note that the selected index is one-based, not zero-based; –1 indicates that no row is selected. When the selected index changes, the list object raises the SelectedIndexChanged event. It raises IndexOutOfRangeException should you attempt to set an invalid index.

If the AutoSelectRows property is set to true, the view's selection is updated whenever the currency changes:

```
bool AutoSelectRows { get; set; }
```

Three other properties directly affect the appearance of data-bound list objects:

```
XlRangeAutoFormat DataBoundFormat { get; set; }
FormatSettings DataBoundFormatSettings { get; set; }
bool AutoSetDataBoundColumnHeaders { get; set; }
```

The DataBoundFormat property determines whether Excel does automatic reformatting of the list object cells when the data change. You have several dozen formats to choose from; the default is xlRangeAutoFormat-None. If you want no formatting at all, choose xlRangeAutoFormatNone. You can also pick and choose which aspects of the formatting you want applied by setting the bit flags in the DataBoundFormatSettings property. (By default, all the flags are turned on.)

```
enum FormatSettings
{
    Number      = 0x00000001,
    Font        = 0x00000010,
    Alignment   = 0x00000100,
    Border      = 0x00001000,
    Pattern     = 0x00010000,
    Width       = 0x00100000
}
```

The AutoSetDataBoundColumnHeaders property indicates whether the list object data binding should automatically create a header row in the list object that contains the column names. It is set to `false` by default.

Data-Related List Object Events

There are several new data-related events on ListObject, listed in Table 19-1.

The DataSource and DataMember properties on the list object aggregate determine to what data source the list object is complex-data-bound. The DataSourceChanged and DataMemberChanged events are raised when the corresponding properties are changed.

TABLE 19-1: New Events Associated with ListObject

Event Name	Delegate Type
DataSourceChanged	EventHandler
DataMemberChanged	EventHandler
SelectedIndexChanged	EventHandler
DataBindingFailure	EventHandler
BeforeAddDataBoundRow	BeforeAddDataBoundRowEventHandler
ErrorAddDataBoundRow	ErrorAddDataBoundRowEventHandler
OriginalDataRestored	OriginalDataRestoredEventHandler

The SelectedIndexChanged event is primarily a "view" event; when the user clicks a different row, the event is raised. However, note that changing the selected row also changes the currency of the binding manager. This can be used to implement master-detail event binding.

If for any reason an edit to the list object fails—for instance, if the data binding layer attempts unsuccessfully to add a row or column to the list, or if a value typed into the list object cannot be copied back into the bound data source—the DataBindingFailure event is raised.

The BeforeAddDataBoundRow event has two primary uses. Listing 19-8 shows its delegate.

Listing 19-8: The BeforeAddDataBoundRow Event Types

```
delegate void BeforeAddDataBoundRowEventHandler(object sender,
  BeforeAddDataBoundRowEventArgs e);
class BeforeAddDataBoundRowEventArgs : EventArgs
{
  object Item { get; }
  bool Cancel { get; set; }
}
```

The item passed to the event handler is the row that is about to be added. The event can be used to either programmatically edit the row just before it is actually added, or to do data validation and cancel the addition should the data be somehow invalid.

After the BeforeAddDataBoundRow event is handled, the list object attempts to commit the new row into the data source. If that operation throws an exception for any reason, the list object deletes the offending row. Before it does so, however, it gives you one chance to fix the problem by raising the ErrorAddDataBoundRow event. Listing 19-9 shows its delegate.

Listing 19-9: The ErrorAddDataBoundRow Event Types

```
delegate void ErrorAddDataBoundRowEventHandler(object sender,
  ErrorAddDataBoundRowEventArgs e);
class ErrorAddDataBoundRowEventArgs : EventArgs
{
  object Item { get; }
  Exception InnerException { get; }
  bool Retry { get; set; }
}
```

The exception is copied into the event arguments; the handler can then analyze the exception, attempt to patch up the row, and retry the commit operation. Should it fail a second time, the row is deleted. The exception thrown in this case may be the new SetDataBindingFailedException, which is documented below.

A data source may have a fixed number of rows or a fixed number of columns. A data source can also contain read-only data or read-only column names. Therefore, attempting to edit cells, add rows, remove rows, add columns, or remove columns can all fail. In these cases, the list object disallows the change and restores the original shape. When it does so, it raises the OriginalDataRestored event. Listing 19-10 shows its delegate.

Listing 19-10: The OriginalDataRestored Event Types

```
delegate void OriginalDataRestoredEventHandler(object sender,
  OriginalDataRestoredEventArgs args)

class OriginalDataRestoredEventArgs : EventArgs
{
  ChangeType ChangeType { get; }
  ChangeReason ChangeReason { get; }
}
enum ChangeType
{
  RangeValueRestored,
  ColumnAdded,
  ColumnRemoved,
  RowAdded,
  RowRemoved,
  ColumnHeaderRestored
}

public enum ChangeReason
{
  ReadOnlyDataSource,
  FixedLengthDataSource,
  FixedNumberOfColumnsInDataBoundList,
  ErrorInCommit,
  Other,
  DataBoundColumnHeaderIsAutoSet
}
```

Data-Related Exception

Data binding can fail under many scenarios; the SetDataBindingFailed-Exception is thrown in three of them:

- If the data source of the list object is not a list data source
- If the data source of the list object has no data-bound columns
- If the list object cannot be resized when the data change

The exception class has these public methods and a Reason property shown in Listing 19-11.

Listing 19-11: The SetDataBindingFailedException Types

```
[Serializable] class SetDataBindingFailedException : Exception
{
  SetDataBindingFailedException()
  SetDataBindingFailedException(string message)
  SetDataBindingFailedException(string message,
    Exception innerException)
  void GetObjectData(SerializationInfo info, StreamingContext context)
  FailureReason Reason { get; }
}

enum FailureReason
{
    CouldNotResizeListObject,
    InvalidDataSource,
    NoDataBoundColumnsSpecified
}
```

Using Data Binding and Dynamic Controls from an Application-Level Add-In

Starting with Visual Studio 2008 SP1, it is possible to use data binding features from an application-level add-in. Listing 19-12 illustrates how this feature can be used to add data bound controls to a document—even though that document doesn't have a VSTO document customization run with it. The add-in creates a custom task pane with two buttons: one to add controls to an existing document and one to randomize the data in a data table to which we bind those controls so you can see that data binding is working. The add-in dynamically creates a named range and a list object, and binds them to a data table. As you would expect, by using the dynamic controls feature, the add-in easily adds a data-bindable NamedRange and ListObject object to the document and data-binds them. This code is found primarily in the CreateControlsAndDatabind method.

The tricky part is when the user saves that document and reopens it; we need to reconnect the controls and reestablish the data binding. To do this, Listing 19-12 handles the WorkbookOpen event so that it can check when a document is opened if it already contains our named range and list object. We've given both unique identifiers: a GUID for the list object and a unique string to identify the name. So if the objects were created and saved in the document by our add-in at a previous time, we iterate the Names collection looking for the identifier for the named range and the List-Objects collection looking for the identifier for the list object. If we find them, we use the dynamic controls feature again to reconnect to the existing objects and reestablish data binding. This code is found primarily in the CheckForExistingControlsAndDatabind method.

One other thing to note: We hook up a double-click event to both controls. We use the technique of creating a Dictionary object that maps worksheets to our created list object and named range control; that way, we can hold on to the dynamically created controls and won't have the "my button stopped working" problem that we discuss in Chapter 1, "An Introduction to Office Programming."

Listing 19-12: Data Binding and Dynamic Controls in an Application-Level Add-In

```
using System;
using System.Collections.Generic;
using System.Linq;
using System.Text;
using System.Xml.Linq;
using Excel = Microsoft.Office.Interop.Excel;
using Office = Microsoft.Office.Core;
using Microsoft.Office.Tools.Excel;
using Microsoft.Office.Tools.Excel.Extensions;

namespace ExcelAddIn3
{
  public partial class ThisAddIn
```

```
{
  System.Guid guidListObject = new System.Guid(
    "{1755AE13-D66E-4c4f-A677-C7BA98513DEF}");
  const string idRange = "giuewroiafhdjkzvkdfdoiquewr";
  System.Windows.Forms.Button buttonAddControls;
  System.Windows.Forms.Button buttonRandomizeData;
  System.Windows.Forms.UserControl userControl;
  Microsoft.Office.Tools.CustomTaskPane taskPane;
  System.Data.DataTable dataTable;

  Dictionary<Excel.Worksheet, ListObject>
    listObjectDictionary = new
    Dictionary<Excel.Worksheet, ListObject>();

  Dictionary<Excel.Worksheet, NamedRange>
   rangeDictionary = new
   Dictionary<Excel.Worksheet, NamedRange>();


  private void ThisAddIn_Startup(object sender,
    System.EventArgs e)
  {
    InitDataTable();

    ((Excel.AppEvents_Event)this.Application).WorkbookOpen +=
      new Excel.AppEvents_WorkbookOpenEventHandler(
        ThisAddIn_WorkbookOpen);
    ((Excel.AppEvents_Event)this.Application).WorkbookBeforeClose
      += new Excel.AppEvents_WorkbookBeforeCloseEventHandler(
        ThisAddIn_WorkbookBeforeClose);

    foreach (Excel.Workbook wb in Application.Workbooks)
    {
      CheckForExistingControlsAndDatabind(wb);
    }

    CreateCustomTaskPane();
  }

  private void CreateCustomTaskPane()
  {
    userControl = new System.Windows.Forms.UserControl();
    buttonAddControls = new System.Windows.Forms.Button();
    buttonAddControls.Text = "Add controls and databind";
    userControl.Controls.Add(buttonAddControls);

    buttonRandomizeData = new System.Windows.Forms.Button();
    buttonRandomizeData.Text = "Randomize Data";
    userControl.Controls.Add(buttonRandomizeData);
    buttonRandomizeData.Top = buttonAddControls.Height + 5;
```

```csharp
    taskPane = CustomTaskPanes.Add(userControl,
      "Control Create and Data Bind");
    buttonAddControls.Click += new
      EventHandler(buttonAddControls_Click);
    buttonRandomizeData.Click += new
      EventHandler(buttonRandomizeData_Click);
    taskPane.Visible = true;
}

void buttonRandomizeData_Click(object sender, EventArgs e)
{
  RandomizeTable(false);
}

void buttonAddControls_Click(object sender, EventArgs e)
{
  if (Application.ActiveWorkbook != null)
  {
    CreateControlsAndDatabind(Application.ActiveWorkbook);
  }
}

private void CreateControlsAndDatabind(Excel.Workbook workbook)
{
  if (CheckForExistingControlsAndDatabind(
    Application.ActiveWorkbook))
    return;

  Excel.Worksheet sheet = workbook.Sheets[1] as
    Excel.Worksheet;
  Microsoft.Office.Tools.Excel.Worksheet vstoSheet =
    sheet.GetVstoObject();
  Excel.Range namedRangeRange = sheet.get_Range("A1", "A1");
  NamedRange vstoRange;

  ListObject vstoListObject = null;
  Excel.Range listObjectRange = sheet.get_Range("A3", "D24");

  vstoListObject = vstoSheet.Controls.AddListObject(
    listObjectRange, guidListObject.ToString());
  ConnectListObject(sheet, vstoListObject);

  vstoRange = vstoSheet.Controls.AddNamedRange(
    namedRangeRange, idRange);
  ConnectNamedRange(sheet, vstoRange);
}

private bool CheckForExistingControlsAndDatabind(
  Excel.Workbook workbook)
{
```

```csharp
Excel.ListObject listObject = null;
Excel.Range range = null;
Excel.Worksheet sheet = workbook.Sheets[1] as
  Excel.Worksheet;
Microsoft.Office.Tools.Excel.Worksheet vstoSheet =
  sheet.GetVstoObject();

// Have we already hooked these up?
// If so they'll be in the dictionary
if (listObjectDictionary.ContainsKey(sheet) ||
  rangeDictionary.ContainsKey(sheet))
  return true;


foreach (Excel.ListObject l in sheet.ListObjects)
{
  if (l.Name.CompareTo(guidListObject.ToString()) == 0)
  {
    listObject = l;
    break;
  }
}

foreach (Excel.Name n in workbook.Names)
{
  if (n.Name.CompareTo(idRange) == 0)
  {
    range = n.RefersToRange;
    break;
  }
}

if (listObject == null || range == null)
  return false;

if (listObject != null)
{
  ListObject vstoListObject =
    vstoSheet.Controls.AddListObject(
    listObject);

  ConnectListObject(sheet, vstoListObject);
}

if (range != null)
{
  NamedRange vstoRange = vstoSheet.Controls.AddNamedRange(
    range, idRange);
  ConnectNamedRange(sheet, vstoRange);
}
```

```csharp
      return true;
    }

    private void ConnectNamedRange(Excel.Worksheet sheet,
      NamedRange vstoRange)
    {
      vstoRange.BeforeDoubleClick +=
        new Excel.DocEvents_BeforeDoubleClickEventHandler(
          vstoRange_BeforeDoubleClick);

      rangeDictionary.Add(sheet, vstoRange);
      vstoRange.DataBindings.Add("Value2", dataTable,
        dataTable.Columns[0].ColumnName);
    }

    private void ConnectListObject(Excel.Worksheet sheet,
      ListObject vstoListObject)
    {
      vstoListObject.BeforeDoubleClick +=
        new Excel.DocEvents_BeforeDoubleClickEventHandler(
        vstoListObject_BeforeDoubleClick);

      listObjectDictionary.Add(sheet, vstoListObject);
      vstoListObject.DataSource = dataTable;
    }

    private void InitDataTable()
    {
      dataTable = new System.Data.DataTable();
      RandomizeTable(true);
    }

    private void RandomizeTable(bool first)
    {
      dataTable.BeginLoadData();
      Random r = new Random();

      if (first == true)
      {
        for (int i = 0; i < 4; i++)
          dataTable.Columns.Add("Col " + i.ToString());

        for (int i = 0; i < 20; i++)
          dataTable.Rows.Add(r.NextDouble(), r.NextDouble(),
          r.NextDouble(), r.NextDouble());
      }
      else
      {
```

```csharp
    for (int i = 0; i < 20; i++)
      dataTable.Rows[i].ItemArray = new object[]
      {r.NextDouble(), r.NextDouble(),
       r.NextDouble(), r.NextDouble()};

  }

  dataTable.EndLoadData();
  dataTable.AcceptChanges();
}

void vstoRange_BeforeDoubleClick(Excel.Range Target,
  ref bool Cancel)
{
  System.Windows.Forms.MessageBox.Show(
    "Range code is hooked up!");
}

void vstoListObject_BeforeDoubleClick(
  Excel.Range Target, ref bool Cancel)
{
  System.Windows.Forms.MessageBox.Show(
    "ListObject code is hooked up!");
}

void ThisAddIn_WorkbookBeforeClose(Excel.Workbook Wb,
  ref bool Cancel)
{
  Excel.Worksheet sheet = Wb.Sheets[1] as Excel.Worksheet;
  if (listObjectDictionary.ContainsKey(sheet))
  {
    listObjectDictionary[sheet].BeforeDoubleClick -=
      new Excel.DocEvents_BeforeDoubleClickEventHandler(
      vstoListObject_BeforeDoubleClick);
    listObjectDictionary.Remove(sheet);
  }

  if (rangeDictionary.ContainsKey(sheet))
  {
    rangeDictionary[sheet].BeforeDoubleClick -=
      new Excel.DocEvents_BeforeDoubleClickEventHandler(
      vstoRange_BeforeDoubleClick);
    rangeDictionary.Remove(sheet);
  }
}

void ThisAddIn_WorkbookOpen(Excel.Workbook Wb)
{
  CheckForExistingControlsAndDatabind(
    Application.ActiveWorkbook);
}
```

```
    #region VSTO generated code
    private void InternalStartup()
    {
      this.Startup += new System.EventHandler(ThisAddIn_Startup);
    }
    #endregion
  }
}
```

Conclusion

Using data binding effectively requires many objects to work well together: controls, datasets, data tables, binding sources, binding contexts, binding managers, and so on. This chapter, and indeed this book, by no means describes all the data binding tools at your disposal. Fortunately, the designer generates many of the objects that you need and wires them up to one another sensibly. Still, having an understanding of what is happening behind the scenes helps considerably when designing data-driven applications.

The next chapter covers some more techniques for building data-driven applications—in particular, how to programmatically manipulate the data island without starting Word or Excel.

■ 20 ■
Server Data Scenarios

Populating a Document with Data on the Server

Consider the following portion of an all-too-common server scenario. An authenticated user, perhaps a salesperson, requests an Excel spreadsheet from a server. The spreadsheet is an expense report, and the server is an ASP, ASP.NET, or SharePoint server. The server code looks up some information about the user from a database, Active Directory, or Web service. For example, perhaps the server has a list of recent corporate credit card activity that it will prepopulate into the expense list. The server starts up Excel but keeps it "invisible" because there is no interactive user on the server. It then uses the Excel object model to insert the data into the appropriate cells, saves the result, and serves up the resulting file to the user.

This is a very suboptimal document life cycle for two reasons. First, it is completely unsupported and strongly recommended against by Microsoft. Word and Excel were designed to be run interactively on client machines with perhaps a few instances of each running at the same time. They were not designed to be scalable and robust in the face of thousands of Web server hits creating many instances on "headless" servers that allow no graphical user interfaces.

Second, this process thoroughly conflates the "view" with the data. The server needs to know exactly how the document is laid out visually so that it can insert and remove the right fields in the right places. A simple change in the document format can necessitate many tricky changes in the server code.

But automatically serving up documents full of a user's data is such a compelling scenario that many organizations have ignored Microsoft's guidelines and build solutions around server-side manipulation of Word and Excel documents. Those solutions tend to have serious scalability and robustness problems.

What can we do to mitigate these two problems?

Data-Bound VSTO Documents

As discussed in Chapter 19, "VSTO Data Programming," one way to solve this problem is to move the processing onto the client. Just serve up a blank document that detects whether there is no cached data in its data island and fills its datasets from the database server if there is none. When the client is ready to send the data back to the database, it connects again and updates the database. No special document customization has to happen on the server at all, and the database server is doing exactly what it was designed to do.

This solution has a major drawback, however: It requires that every user have access to the database. From a security perspective, it might be smarter to only give the document server access to the database, thereby decreasing the "attack surface" exposed to malicious hackers. What we really want to do is have the document ready to go with the user data in it from the moment they obtain the document, but without having to start up Word or Excel on the server.

XML File Formats

Avoiding the necessity of starting up a client application on the server is key. Consider the first half of the scenario above: The server takes an existing on-disk document and uses Excel to produce a modified version of the document. Excel is just a means to an end; if you know what changes need to be made to the bits of the document and how to manipulate the file format, you have no need to start up the client application.

The Word and Excel binary file formats are "opaque," but Word and Excel now support persisting documents in a much more transparent XML format. It is not too hard to write a program that manipulates the XML document without ever starting up Word or Excel.

But we have not addressed the second problem that we identified earlier. Now we are not just manipulating the view, we are manipulating the *persisted state* of the view to insert or extract data. It would be much cleaner if we could simply get at the data island.

We need a way to solve these additional problems; we need a solution that works on binary non-human-readable files, works with VSTO-customized documents, and cleanly separates view from data.

Accessing the Data Island

Chapter 19, "VSTO Data Programming," shows how to cache the state of public host item class members that contain data in a "data island" so that they could be persisted into the document as XML, independent of their user-interface representation. The VSTO runtime library comes with a class, ServerDocument, which can read and write the data island directly; it does not need to start up Word or Excel on the server. The ServerDocument object can read and write Word and Excel documents in binary or XML format.

Let's re-create the above document life cycle using the data island. Then we describe the advanced features of the ServerDocument object model in more detail.

Using ServerDocument and ASP.NET

Many pieces must be put together here, but each one is fairly straightforward. Here is what we are going to do:

1. Create an ASP.NET Web site.
2. Create a simple VSTO customized expense report spreadsheet that has a cached dataset that is data bound to a list object and a cached string assigned to a named range in the Startup handler.
3. Publish the expense report template to the Web site.
4. Create an .aspx page that populates the data island (the cached dataset) before the document is served up.
5. As an added bonus, we adapt that page and turn into a custom file type handler.

In Visual Studio, select File > New > Web Site and create a new ASP.NET site. Suppose for the sake of this example that the server is http://accounting, and the Web site is http://accounting/expenses.

We come back to this Web site project later. For now, close it down and create a VSTO Excel spreadsheet project. Let's start by putting together a simple customization with one named range and one list object control bound to an untyped dataset. We will make the user's name and the expense dataset cached, so that the server can put the data in the data island when the document is served up. Figure 20-1 shows the spreadsheet with a named range and a list object. You can also see in Figure 20-1 the code behind Sheet1. The code defines a `string` called `EmpName` that is cached as well as a DataSet called `Expenses` that is cached. In the Startup

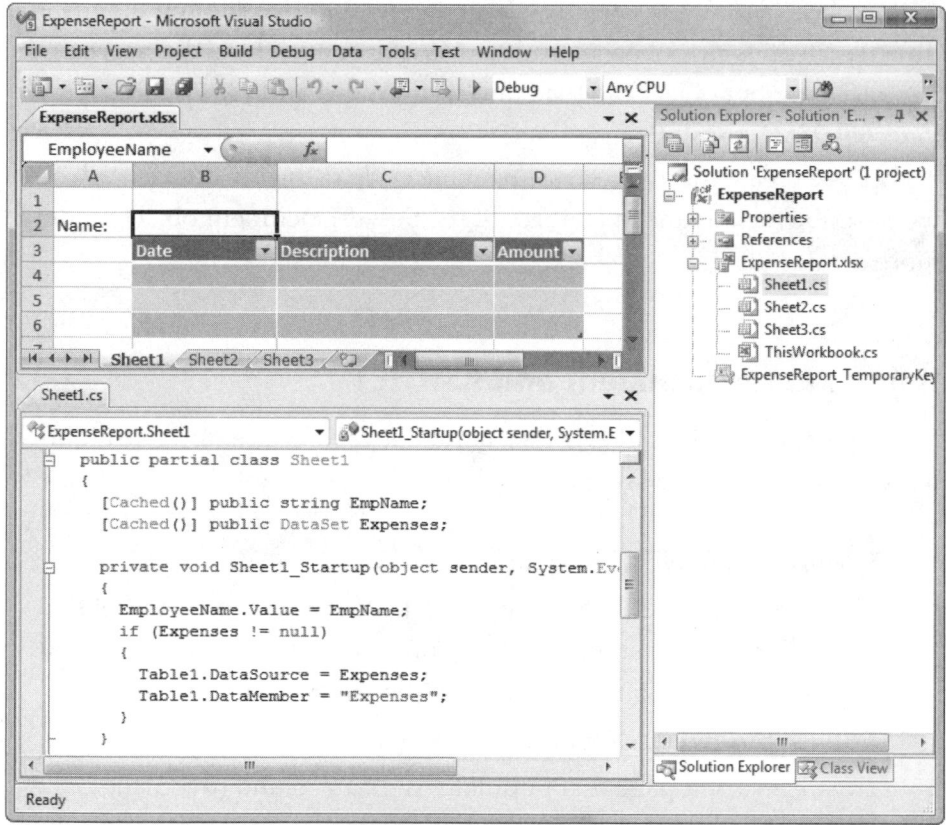

Figure 20-1: A simple expense report worksheet with two cached class members: EmpName and Expenses.

handler for Sheet1, the code sets the Value property of the NamedRange called `EmployeeName` to the cached value `EmpName`. It also data binds the `Expenses` dataset to the ListObject called `Table1`.

Choose Build > Publish; then use the Publishing Wizard to build the spreadsheet and put it up on http://accounting/expenses. Doing so sets up the document so that it points to the customization on the Web server rather than the local machine. (Chapter 21, "ClickOnce Deployment," covers deployment scenarios in more detail.)

For the customization to run on the client machine, you need to make http://accounting/expenses a trusted location, because the VSTO Excel spreadsheet will be loaded from a location that isn't in the default list of Office trusted locations. Chapter 21, "ClickOnce Deployment," covers the whys and wherefores of trusted locations in detail; for now, just trust that you need to add this location as trusted. On the client machine, launch Excel and follow these steps:

1. Choose Office > Excel Options to bring up the Excel Options dialog box.

2. In the dialog box, click the Trust Center tab.

3. Click the Trust Center Settings button to bring up the Trust Center dialog box.

4. In the dialog box, click the Trusted Locations tab.

5. Make sure that the Allow Trusted Locations on My Network check box is checked.

6. Click the Add New Location button to bring up the Microsoft Office Trusted Location dialog box.

7. In the dialog box, type `http://accounting/expenses` in the Path text box.

8. Check the Subfolders of This Location Are Also Trusted check box.

9. Click OK to close the Microsoft Office Trusted Location dialog box.

10. Click OK to close the Trust Center dialog box.

11. Click OK to close the Excel Options dialog box.

We have not set up the handler on the server yet, but do a quick sanity check on the client to make sure that the document can be downloaded and the customization run on the client machine. There will not be any data in it yet; let's take care of that next.

Setting Up the Server

Use Visual Studio to open the expenses Web site created earlier, and you will see that the deployed files for this customized spreadsheet have shown up. Now all we need to do is write a server-side page that loads the blank document into memory and fills in its data island before sending it out over the wire to the client. Right-click the Web site and choose Add New Item. Add a new .aspx Web form.

We need to add a reference to Microsoft.VisualStudio.Tools.Applications .ServerDocument.v9.0.DLL to get at the ServerDocument class, as shown in Listing 20-1. After we do that, the code is fairly straightforward right up until the point where we set the serialized state. We discuss how that works in more detail later in this chapter.

Listing 20-1: An ASPX Web Form That Edits the Data Island on the Server

```
<%@ Page Language="C#" Debug="true" AutoEventWireup="true" %>
<%@ Import Namespace="System.Configuration" %>
<%@ Import Namespace="System.Web.Configuration" %>
<%@ Import Namespace="System.Data"%>
<%@ Import Namespace="System.Data.Common"%>
<%@ Import Namespace="System.Data.OleDb"%>
<%@ Import Namespace="System.IO"%>
<%@ Import Namespace= "Microsoft.VisualStudio.Tools.Applications"%>

<script runat=server>

const int Forbidden = 403;

protected void Page_Load(object sender, EventArgs e)
{
  // If the user is not authenticated, we do not want
  // to give the user any expense report at all.
  if (!User.Identity.IsAuthenticated)
  {
    Response.StatusCode = Forbidden;
    Response.End();
    return;
  }

  // If we do have a username, fetch the user's personal data from
  // the database (or Web service or other data source).
```

```
DataSet dataset = new DataSet();
DataTable datatable = dataset.Tables.Add("Expenses");
OleDbDataAdapter adapter = new OleDbDataAdapter();

// Authenticated usernames are hard to malform. If there is a
// chance that a string could be provided by a hostile caller,
// do not use string concatenation without vetting the string
// carefully. Better still, avoid SQL injection attacks entirely
// by using stored procedures.

adapter.SelectCommand = new OleDbCommand(
  "SELECT [Date], Description, Cost " +
  "FROM Expenses WHERE EmployeeName = \"" +
  User.Identity.Name + "\"");

// It's a good idea to store connection strings in the web.config
// file, both for security - they can be encrypted in web.config -
// and for convenience - you can update the config file when the
// database server changes.

string connectionString = ConfigurationManager.
  ConnectionStrings["expenses"]. ConnectionString;
adapter.SelectCommand.Connection =
  new OleDbConnection(connectionString);
adapter.Fill(datatable);

// We do not want to modify the file on disk; instead, we'll read
// it into memory and add the user's information to the in-memory
// document before we serve it.

FileStream file = new FileStream(
  @"C:\INETPUB\WWWROOT\EXPENSES\ExpenseReport.XLSX",
  FileMode.Open, FileAccess.Read);
byte[] template;
try {
  template = new byte[file.Length];
  file.Read(template, 0, (int)file.Length);
}
finally {
  file.Close();
}

// Finally, we'll create a ServerDocument object to manipulate
// the in-memory copy. Because it has only a raw array of bytes
// to work with, it needs to be told whether it is looking at an
// .XLS, .XLSB, .XLSX, .XLSM, .XLT, .XLTB, .XLTX, .XLTM,
// .DOC, .DOCX, .DOCM, .DOT, .DOTX, or .DOTM

ServerDocument sd = new ServerDocument(template, ".XLSX");
try {
```

```
  sd.CachedData.HostItems["ExpenseReport.Sheet1"].
    CachedData["EmpName"].SerializeDataInstance(User.Identity.Name);
  sd.CachedData.HostItems["ExpenseReport.Sheet1"].
    CachedData["Expenses"].SerializeDataInstance(dataset);
  sd.Save();

  // "template" still has the original bytes. Get the new bytes.
  template = sd.Document;
}
finally {
  sd.Close();
}
Response.ClearContent();
Response.ClearHeaders();
Response.ContentType =
  "application/vnd.openxmlformats-officedocument.spreadsheetml.sheet";
Response.OutputStream.Write(template, 0, template.Length);
Response.Flush();
Response.Close();
}
</script>
<html></html>
```

An Alternative Approach: Create a Custom Handler

It seems a little odd to go to an .aspx page to download a spreadsheet or document. An alternative approach to solving the problem of customizing documents on the server is to intercept requests for particular file extensions and customize the response before it goes out to the client.

This time, instead of creating a new .aspx Web form, create a new.ashx generic handler (see Figure 20-2).

The code shown in Listing 20-2 is essentially identical; the only difference is that because a handler is not an instance of a Web page, we do not have any of the standard page objects such as Response, Request, User, and so on. Fortunately, the context of the page request is encapsulated in a special "context" object that is passed to the handler.

Listing 20-2: Creating a Custom Handler That Edits the Data Island

```
<%@ WebHandler Language="C#" Class="XLSXHandler" %>

using System;
using System.Configuration;
using System.Data;
using System.Data.Common;
```

```csharp
using System.Data.OleDb;
using System.IO;
using System.Web;
using Microsoft.VisualStudio.Tools.Applications;

public class XLSXHandler : IHttpHandler {
  const int Forbidden = 403;
  public void ProcessRequest (HttpContext context) {

    if (!context.User.Identity.IsAuthenticated)
    {
      context.Response.StatusCode = Forbidden;
      context.Response.End();
      return;
    }

    DataSet dataset = new DataSet();
    DataTable datatable = dataset.Tables.Add("Expenses");
    OleDbDataAdapter adapter = new OleDbDataAdapter();

    adapter.SelectCommand = new OleDbCommand("SELECT [Date], " +
      "Description, Cost FROM Expenses WHERE EmployeeName = \"" +
      context.User.Identity.Name + "\"");

    string connectionString = ConfigurationManager.
      ConnectionStrings["expenses"]. ConnectionString;
    adapter.SelectCommand.Connection =
      new OleDbConnection(connectionString);
    adapter.Fill(datatable);

    FileStream file = new FileStream(
        @"C:\INETPUB\WWWROOT\EXPENSES\ExpenseReport.XLSX",
        FileMode.Open, FileAccess.Read);
    byte[] template;
    try
    {
      template = new byte[file.Length];
      file.Read(template, 0, (int)file.Length);
    }
    finally
    {
      file.Close();
    }

    ServerDocument sd = new ServerDocument(template, ".XLSX");
    try
    {
      sd.CachedData.HostItems["ExpenseReport.Sheet1"].
        CachedData["EmpName"].SerializeDataInstance(
        context.User.Identity.Name);
```

```csharp
        sd.CachedData.HostItems["ExpenseReport.Sheet1"].
          CachedData["Expenses"].SerializeDataInstance(dataset);
        sd.Save();

        // "template" still has the original bytes. Get the new
        // bytes.
        template = sd.Document;
      }
      finally
      {
        sd.Close();
      }

      context.Response.ContentType =
      "application/vnd.openxmlformats-officedocument.spreadsheetml.sheet"
;

      context.Response.OutputStream.Write(template, 0,
        template.Length);
  }
  public bool IsReusable
  {
    get { return false; }
  }
}
```

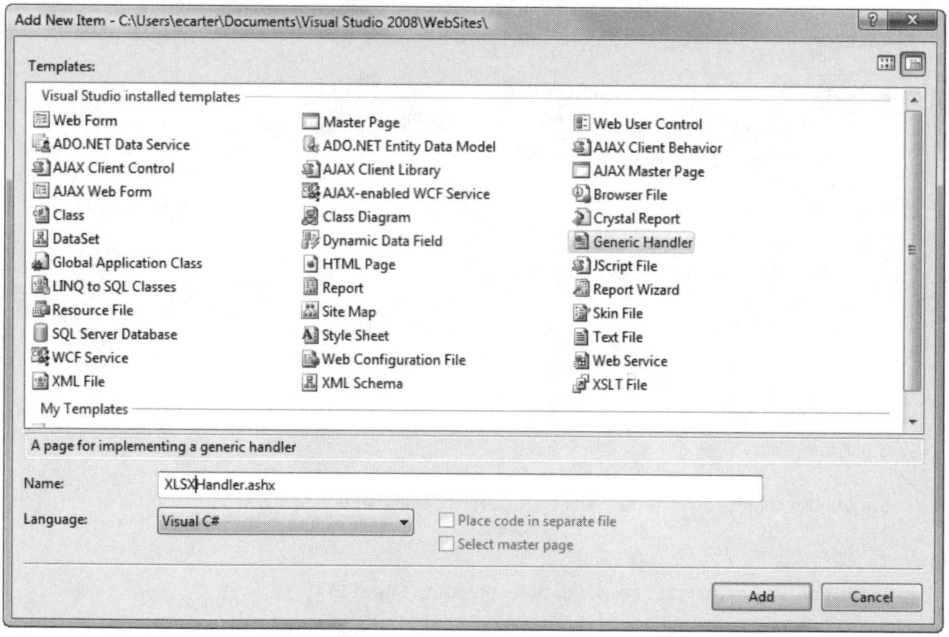

Figure 20-2: Creating a custom handler item.

Finally, to turn this on, add the information about the class and assembly name for the handler to your Web.config file in the application's virtual root. If you want to debug the server-side code, you can modify debugging information in the configuration file, as shown in Listing 20-3.

Listing 20-3: A Web Configuration File to Turn on the Handler

```
<configuration>
  <system.web>
    <httpHandlers>
      <add verb="GET" path="ExpenseReport.xlsx"
        type="XLSXHandler, XLSXHandler"/>
    </httpHandlers>
    <compilation debug="true"/>
  </system.web>
</configuration>
```

Now when the client hits the server, the handler will intercept the request, load the requested file into memory, contact the database, create the appropriate dataset, and serialize the dataset into the data island in the expense report—all without starting Excel.

A Handy Client-Side ServerDocument Utility

The ServerDocument object was aptly named. It was primarily designed for exactly the scenario we have just explored: writing information into a document on a server. However, it can do a lot more, from reading the data back out of a document to adding customizations to documents. We start by describing the data-manipulating tools in ServerDocument and then show how ServerDocument can be used to add customizations to documents.

Let's take a look at another illustrative use of the ServerDocument object, and then we give a more complete explanation of all its data properties and methods. Listing 20-4 shows is a handy C# console application that dumps out the "cached data manifest" and serialized cached data in a document. When you create the console application, remember to add a reference to Microsoft.VisualStudio.Tools.Applications.ServerDocument.v9.0 for Server-Document and also a reference to Microsoft.VisualStudio.Tools.Applications .Runtime.v9.0 for the CannotLoadManifestException definition.

Listing 20-4: Creating a Cache Viewer with ServerDocument

```csharp
using System;
using System.IO;
using Microsoft.VisualStudio.Tools.Applications;
using Microsoft.VisualStudio.Tools.Applications.Runtime;

namespace VSTOViewer
{
  public class MainClass
  {
    public static void Main(string[] args)
    {
      if (args.Length != 1)
      {
        Console.WriteLine("Usage:");
        Console.WriteLine("    CacheViewer.exe myfile.doc");
        return;
      }

      string filename = args[0];
      ServerDocument doc = null;

      try
      {
        doc = new ServerDocument(filename);
        Console.WriteLine("\nCached Data Manifest");
        Console.WriteLine(doc.CachedData.ToXml());

        foreach (CachedDataHostItem view in
          doc.CachedData.HostItems)
        {
          foreach (CachedDataItem item in view.CachedData)
          {
            if (item.Xml != null && item.Xml.Length != 0)
            {
              Console.WriteLine("\nCached Data: " + view.Id + "." +
                item.Id + " xml\n");
              Console.WriteLine(item.Xml);
            }
            if (item.Schema != null && item.Schema.Length != 0)
            {
              Console.WriteLine("\nCached Data: " + view.Id + "." +
                item.Id + " xsd\n");
              Console.WriteLine(item.Schema);
            }
          }
        }
      }
```

```
      catch (CannotLoadManifestException ex)
      {
        Console.WriteLine("Not a customized document:" + filename);
        Console.WriteLine(ex.Message);
      }
      catch (FileNotFoundException)
      {
        Console.WriteLine("File not found:" + filename);
      }
      catch (Exception ex)
      {
        Console.WriteLine("Unexpected Exception:" + filename);
        Console.WriteLine(ex.ToString());
      }
      finally
      {
        if (doc != null)
          doc.Close();
      }
    }
  }
}
```

After you compile this into a console application, you can run the console application on the command line and pass the name of the document you want to view. The document must have a saved VSTO data island in it for anything interesting to happen.

Now that you have an idea of how the ServerDocument object model is used, we can talk about it in more detail.

The ServerDocument Object Model

The ServerDocument object model enables you to read and write all the deployment information and cached data stored inside a customized document. This section goes through all of the "data" properties and methods in this object model, describing what they do, their purpose, and why they look the way they do. Later in this chapter we describe the "deployment" portions of the object model.

> **■■ NOTE**
>
> Before we begin, note that the ServerDocument object model is what we like to call an "enough rope" object model. Because this object model enables you to modify all the information about the customization, it is quite possible to create documents with inconsistent cached data or nonsensical deployment information. The VSTO runtime engine does attempt to detect malformed customization information and throw the appropriate exceptions; but still, exercise caution when using this object model.

ServerDocument Class Constructors

The ServerDocument class has four constructors, but two of them are mere "syntactic sugars" for these two:

```
ServerDocument(byte[] bytes, string fileType)
ServerDocument(string documentPath, System.IO.FileAccess access)
```

These correspond to the two primary ServerDocument scenarios: Either you want to read/edit a document in memory or on disk. Note that these two scenarios cannot be mixed; if you start off by opening a file on disk, you cannot treat it as an array of bytes in memory and vice versa.

The in-memory version of the constructor takes a string that indicates the type of the file. Because all you are giving it is the bytes of the file, as opposed to the name of the file, the constructor does not know whether this is an .XLS, .XLT, XLSX, .XLTX, XLSB, XLTB, .DOC, .DOT, .DOCX, .DOTX, or .XML file. Pass in one of those strings to indicate what kind of document this is. The byte array passed in must be an image of a customized document. The ServerDocument object model does not support in-memory manipulation of not-yet-customized documents. The on-disk version takes the document path, from which it can deduce the file type.

The file access parameter can be `FileAccess.Read` or `FileAccess.ReadWrite`. If it is "read-only," attempts to change the document will fail. (Opening an uncustomized document on the client in read-only mode is not a very good idea; the attempt to customize the document will fail.)

The other "in-memory" constructor is provided for convenience; it simply reads the entire stream into a byte array for you:

```
ServerDocument(System.IO.Stream stream, string fileType)
```

Finally, the remaining "on-disk" constructor acts just like the two-argument constructor above with the file access defaulting to ReadWrite:

```
ServerDocument(string documentPath)
```

Saving and Closing Documents

The ServerDocument object has two important methods and one property used to shut down a document:

```
void Save()
byte[] Document { get; }
void Close()
```

If you opened the ServerDocument object with an on-disk document, the Save method writes the changes you have made to the application manifest, cached data manifest, or data island to disk. If you opened the document using a byte array or stream, the changes are saved into a memory buffer that you can access with the Document property. Note that reading the Document property if the file was opened on disk results in an error.

It is a good programming practice to explicitly close the ServerDocument object when you have finished with it. Large byte arrays and file locks are both potentially expensive resources that will not be reclaimed by the operating system until the object is closed (or, equivalently, disposed by either the garbage collector or an explicit call to IDisposable.Dispose).

Server-side users of ServerDocument are cautioned to be particularly careful when opening on-disk documents for read-write access. It is a bad idea to have multiple writers (or a single writer and one or more readers) trying to access the same file at the same time. The ServerDocument class will do its best in this situation; it will make "shadow copy" backups of the file so that readers can continue to read the file without interference while writers write. However, making shadow copies of large files can prove time-consuming.

If you do find yourself in this situation, consider doing what we did in the first example in this chapter: Read the file into memory, and edit it in memory rather than on disk. As long as the on-disk version is only read, it will never need to be shadow-copied and runs no risk of multiple writers overwriting each other's changes.

Static Helper Methods

Developers typically want to perform a few common scenarios with the ServerDocument object model; the class exposes some handy static helper methods so that you do not have to write the boring "boilerplate" code. All of these scenarios work only with "on-disk" files, not with "in-memory" files. The following static methods are associated with ServerDocument:

```
static void AddCustomization(
   string documentPath,
   System.Uri deploymentManifestUrl)
static void RemoveCustomization(string documentPath)
static bool IsCustomized(string documentPath)
static bool IsCacheEnabled(string documentPath)
static int GetCustomizationVersion(string documentPath)
```

AddCustomization

AddCustomization takes an uncustomized Word document or Excel workbook and adds a VSTO customization to it. It requires the document to customize and an already created deployment manifest (and related application manifest and dlls). The easiest way to get a deployment manifest to attach is to create an Excel or Word solution in Visual Studio, publish it, and then reuse the generated deployment manifest (and associated application manifests) to attach to uncustomized documents. Figure 20-3 shows the dialog box that appears when you choose to publish an Excel workbook solution by choosing Build > Publish. In this case, after creating an Excel workbook solution, we published it to C:\MyApplication.

Listing 20-5 shows a simple console application that takes two command-line parameters. The first parameter specifies the name of the uncustomized Excel workbook to attach a VSTO customization to. Valid Excel file types that can be passed include those with the XLS, XLSX, XLSB, XLSM, XLT, XLTX, XLTB, and XLTM extensions. The second command-line parameter is the path to the deployment manifest (the .VSTO file found in the root

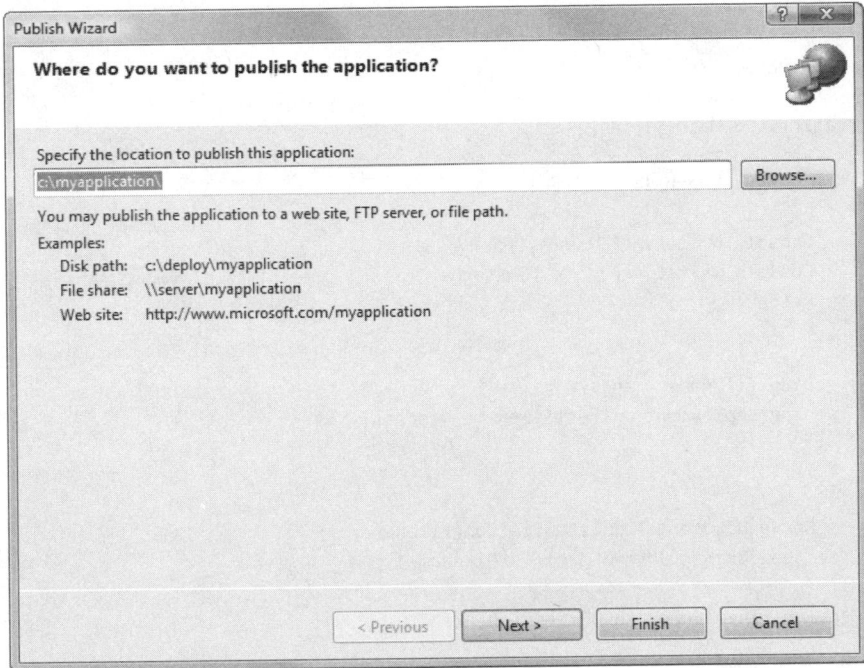

Figure 20-3: Publishing an Excel solution to a local path.

directory where we published the customization). So the console application in Listing 20-5 would be invoked as follows, given that the original name of the Excel workbook solution we created in Visual Studio was `Excel-Workbook1` and an uncustomized Excel file called `uncustomizeddoc.xlsx` is in the `c:\docs` folder:

```
Vstoattacher.exe c:\docs\uncustomizeddoc.xlsx
   c:\MyApplication\ExcelWorkbook1.vsto
```

As in the previous console application, you must add a reference to the Microsoft.VisualStudio.Tools.Applications.ServerDocument.v9.0 and Microsoft.VisualStudio.Tools.Applications.Runtime.v9.0 assemblies.

Listing 20-5: A Console Application to Attach a VSTO Customization with ServerDocument

```
using System;
using System.IO;
using Microsoft.VisualStudio.Tools.Applications;
using Microsoft.VisualStudio.Tools.Applications.Runtime;
```

```csharp
namespace VSTOAttacher
{
  class Program
  {
    static void Main(string[] args)
    {
      if (args.Length != 2)
      {
        Console.WriteLine("Usage:");
        Console.WriteLine("   VSTOAttacher.exe [document] [deployment manifest]");
        return;
      }

      string filename = args[0];
      string deploymentManifestFilename = args[1];

      try
      {
        ServerDocument.AddCustomization(filename,
          new Uri(deploymentManifestFilename));
      }
      catch (InvalidManifestException ex)
      {
        Console.WriteLine("Not a valid deployment manifest:" +
          deploymentManifestFilename);
        Console.WriteLine(ex.Message);
      }
      catch (UnknownCustomizationFileException ex)
      {
        Console.WriteLine("Not a supported file extension:" +
          filename);
        Console.WriteLine(ex.Message);
      }
      catch (DocumentNotCustomizedException ex)
      {
        Console.WriteLine("Document was corrupt or insufficient permissions:" +
          filename);
        Console.WriteLine(ex.Message);
      }
      catch (FileNotFoundException)
      {
        Console.WriteLine("File not found:" + filename);
      }
      catch (Exception ex)
      {
        Console.WriteLine("Unexpected Exception:" + filename);
        Console.WriteLine(ex.ToString());
      }
    }
  }
}
```

RemoveCustomization

RemoveCustomization removes all customization information from a document, including *all* the cached data in the data island. Calling RemoveCustomization on an uncustomized document results in an invalid operation exception.

IsCustomized and IsCacheEnabled

IsCustomized and IsCacheEnabled are similar but subtly different because of the following scenario. Suppose you have a customized document that contains cached data in the data island, and you use the ServerDocument object model to remove all information about what document/worksheet classes need to be started up. In this scenario, the document will not run any customization code when it starts up, and therefore there is no way for the document to access the data island at runtime. Essentially, the document has become an uncustomized document with no code behind it, but all the data is still sitting in the data island. The VSTO designers anticipated that someone might want to remove information about the code while keeping the data island intact for later extraction via the ServerDocument object model.

IsCustomized returns true if the document is customized *and* will attempt to run code when it starts up. IsCacheEnabled returns true if the document is customized at all, and therefore has a data island, *regardless* of whether the customization information says what classes to start up when the document is loaded. (Note that IsCacheEnabled says nothing about whether the data island actually contains any data, just whether the document supports caching.)

GetCustomizationVersion

GetCustomizationVersion returns the version of VSTO that was used to customize a document. It takes as a parameter the full path to the document that is customized. It returns 0 if the document is not customized, 1 if it was customized with Visual Studio 2003 Tools for Office, 2 if it was customized with Visual Studio 2005 Tools for Office Second Edition, and 3 if it was customized by VSTO 3.0 (Visual Studio 2008).

Cached Data Objects, Methods, and Properties

As you saw in our handy utility previously, a customized document's data island contains a small XML document called the cached data manifest, which describes the classes and properties in the cache (or, if the document is being run for the first time, the properties that need to be filled). The cached data is organized hierarchically; the manifest consists of a collection of view class elements, each of which contains a collection of items corresponding to cached members of the class. For example, here is a cached data manifest that has one cached member of one view class (Sheet1). The cached data member contains a `string` variable called `EmpName`:

```
<cdm:cachedDataManifest cdm:revision="1"
  xmlns:cdm="http://schemas.microsoft.com
  /2004/VisualStudio/Tools/Applications/CachedDataManifest.xsd">
  <cdm:view cdm:viewId="ExcelWorkbook2.Sheet1">
    <cdm:dataInstance cdm:dataId="EmpName" cdm:dataType="" />
  </cdm:view>
</cdm:cachedDataManifest>
```

Having a collection of collections is somewhat more complex than just having a collection of cached items. The cached data manifest was designed this way to avoid the ambiguity of having two host item classes (such as Sheet1 and Sheet2) each with a cached property named the same thing. Because each item is fully qualified by its class, there is no possibility of name collisions.

The actual serialized data is stored in the data island, not in the cached data manifest. However, in the object model it is more convenient to associate each data instance in the cached data manifest with its serialized state.

The Cached Data Object Model

To get at the cached data manifest and any serialized data in the data island, the place to start is the CachedData property of the ServerDocument class. The CachedData object returns the CachedDataHostItemCollection, which contains a CachedDataHostItem for each host item in your customized document. A CachedDataHostItem is a collection of CachedDataItem objects that correspond to each class member variable that has been marked with the `Cached` attribute. Figure 20-4 shows an object model diagram for the objects returned for the example in Figure 20-1.

To get to the CachedData object, use the ServerDocument object's CachedData property:

```
public CachedData CachedData { get; }
```

There are no constructors for any of the types we will be discussing. The CachedData class has four handy helper methods (Clear, FromXml, ToXml, and ClearData) and a collection of CachedDataHostItem:

```
void Clear()
void FromXml(string cachedDataManifest)
string ToXml()
void ClearData()
CachedDataHostItemCollection HostItems { get; }
```

Like the application manifest, the Clear method throws away all information in the cached data manifest, the FromXml method clears the manifest and repopulates it from the XML state, and the ToXml method serializes the manifest as an XML string.

The ClearData method throws away all information in the data island, but leaves all the entries in the cached data manifest. When the document is started up in the client, all the corresponding members will be marked as needing to be filled.

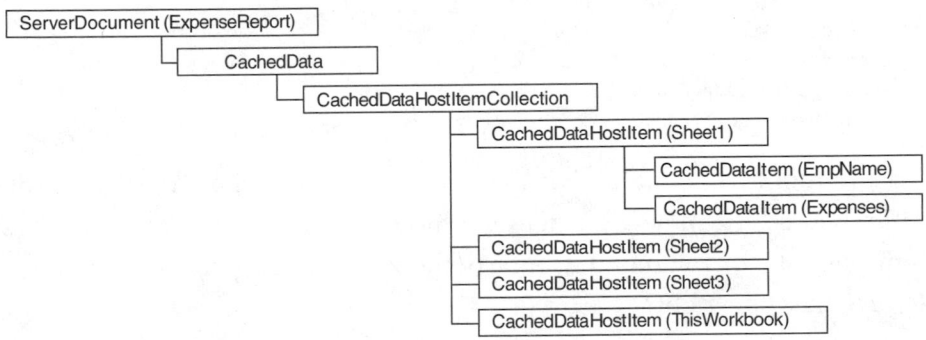

Figure 20-4: The cached data object model for the example in Figure 20-1.

The CachedDataHostItem Collection

The HostItems collection is a straightforward extension of CollectionBase that provides a simple strongly typed collection of CachedDataHostItem objects. (It is called "host items" because these always correspond to items provided by the hosting application, such as Sheet1, Sheet2, or ThisDocument.)

```
CachedDataHostItem Add(string id)
bool Contains(string id)
int IndexOf(CachedDataHostItem item)
void Remove(CachedDataHostItem item)
void Remove(string id)
CachedDataHostItem this[string id] {get;}
CachedDataHostItem this[int index] {get;}
void CopyTo(CachedDataHostItem[] items, int index)
void Insert(int index, CachedDataHostItem value)
```

The `id` argument corresponds to the namespace-qualified name of the host item class. Be careful when creating new items to ensure that the class identifier is fully qualified.

The CachedDataHostItem Object

Each CachedDataHostItem object corresponds to a host item in your document and is a collection of CachedDataItem objects that correspond to cached members of the customized host item class:

```
CachedDataItem Add(string dataId, string dataType)
bool Contains(string dataId)
void Remove(CachedDataItem data)
int IndexOf(CachedDataItem data)
void Remove(string dataId)
CachedDataItem this[int index] {get;}
CachedDataItem this[string dataId] {get;}
void CopyTo(CachedDataItem[] items, int index)
void Insert(int index, CachedDataItem item)
```

You might wonder why it is that you must specify the type of the property when adding a new element via the Add method. If you have a host item class like this, surely the name of the class and property is sufficient to deduce the type, right?

```
class Sheet1 {
  [Cached] public NorthwindDataSet myData;
```

In this case, it would be sufficient to deduce the compile-time type, but it would not be if the compile-time type were `object`. When the document is run in the client and the cached members are deserialized and populated, the deserialization code in the VSTO runtime needs to know whether the runtime type of the member is a dataset, datatable, or other serializable type.

The CachedDataItem Object

The identifier of a CachedDataItem is the name of the property or field on the host item class that was marked with the `Cached` attribute. The CachedDataItem itself exposes the type and identifier properties:

```
string DataType { get; set; }
string Id { get; set; }
```

CachedDataItem also has two other interesting properties and a helper method:

```
string Xml { get; set; }
string Schema { get; set; }
void SerializeDataInstance(object value)
```

Setting the Xml and Schema properties correctly can be slightly tricky; the SerializeDataInstance method takes an `object` and sets the Xml and Schema properties for you. However, if you do not have an instance of the object on the server and want to manipulate just the serialized XML strings, you must understand the rules for how to set these properties correctly.

The first thing to note is that the Schema property is ignored if the DataType is not a DataTable or DataSet (or subclass thereof). If you are serializing out another type via XML serialization, there is no schema, so just leave it blank. On the other hand, if you are writing out a DataSet or DataTable, you must specify the schema.

Second, the data island may contain DataSets and DataTables in either in regular "raw" XML form or in "diffgram" form. The regular format that you are probably used to seeing XML-serialized DataSets in looks something like this:

```
<DataSet1 xmlns="http://www.foocorp.org/schemas/customers.xsd">
  <dbo_Customers>
    <Name>Maria Anders</Name>
    <Address>Obere Str. 57</Address>
```

```
  </dbo_Customers>
  <dbo_Customers>
    <Name>Ana Trujillo</Name>
    <Address>Avda. de la Constitución 2222</Address>
  </dbo_Customers>
```

And so on. A similar DataSet in diffgram form looks different:

```
<diffgr:diffgram>
  <NorthwindDataSet
    xmlns="http://www.foocorp.org/schemas/NorthwindDataSet.xsd">
    <Customers diffgr:id="Customers1" msdata:rowOrder="0">
    <CustomerID>ALFKI</CustomerID>
    <CompanyName>Alfreds Futterkiste</CompanyName>
    <ContactName>Maria Anders</ContactName>
```

You can store cached DataSets and DataTables by setting the Xml property to either format. By default the VSTO runtime saves them in diffgram format. Why? Because the diffgram format not only captures the current state of the DataSet or DataTable, but also records how the object has changed because it was filled in by the data adapter. That means that when the object's data is poured back into the database, the adapter can update only the rows that have changed instead of having to update all of them.

Be Careful

One final caution about using the ServerDocument object model to manipulate the cache: The cache should be "all or nothing." Either the cached data manifest should have *no* data items with serialized XML, or they should *all* have XML. The VSTO runtime does not currently support scenarios where some cached data items need to be filled and others do not. If when the client runtime starts up it detects that the cache is filled inconsistently, it will assume that the data island is corrupted and start fresh, refilling everything. If you need to remove some cached data from a document, remove the entire data item from the host item collection; do not just set the XML property to an empty string.

Conclusion

The ServerDocument object model was primarily designed to enable server-side code to edit the contents of the data island before serving up a document, but it does much more. You can use it to read or write the data island, and to add customization assemblies to uncustomized documents.

The ServerDocument object model provides fine-grained control over the information stored in a document and assumes that you know what you're doing. Be very careful, and test your scenarios thoroughly when using the ServerDocument object model.

■ 21 ■
ClickOnce Deployment

Introduction

So you've built the ultimate Office application, and you're ready to show it to the world. Now how do you deploy it? In previous versions of VSTO, deployment was fairly difficult and required an understanding of the rather complex .NET security policy. Fortunately, in Visual Studio 2008, deployment has been greatly simplified and is built on *ClickOnce*—the technology used to deploy Windows Forms applications. .NET security policy is no longer used to decide whether to run an add-in; instead, a simple inclusion list is used. Also, running a customization associated with a document when you go offline is much more robust in VSTO 2008 because customizations are stored in the ClickOnce cache instead of the Internet Explorer cache used by VSTO 2005.

This chapter first considers the prerequisites for running a VSTO solution on an end user's machine. Most of these prerequisites can be installed automatically by the installer created for you by ClickOnce. We also discuss how to deploy add-ins and how to deploy document solutions. Installing a document solution is slightly more complex because you need to worry about where the document comes from as well as where the customization comes from. After we cover the basics, we consider ClickOnce security in more detail. Finally, we cover some advanced deployment scenarios.

Creating a Custom Windows Installer Setup

You can still use Visual Studio setup projects or your favorite third-party setup authoring tools to create a custom Windows Installer setup. This topic is beyond the scope of this book, however. For more information on creating a custom Windows Installer setup, you should read a white paper that was written by the VSTO team. Part I of the paper is at http://msdn.microsoft.com/en-us/library/cc563937.aspx, and Part II is at http://msdn.microsoft.com/en-us/library/cc616991.aspx.

Prerequisites

Several prerequisites must be installed on the user's machine to enable a VSTO solution to run successfully. Many of these prerequisites can be installed by the ClickOnce installer, but at least one must be installed before the ClickOnce installer can run—namely, Office 2007.

Office 2007

Although this requirement is somewhat obvious, the end user must have Office 2007 installed before installing a VSTO customization. In VSTO 2005, document customizations would work only in Office 2003 Professional or the stand-alone versions of Word 2003 and Excel 2003. Fortunately, in VSTO 2008, this limitation is removed, and an add-in or document customization will work with any SKU of Office 2007.

Windows Installer 3.1

The Windows Installer 3.1 component is a prerequisite for ClickOnce applications. This prerequisite is automatically included as a prerequisite in your ClickOnce installer, as you see in "Deploying Add-Ins" later in this chapter. If the Windows Installer 3.1 is not installed, it will install and then require a reboot before the setup can continue.

.NET Framework 3.5 SP1 or .NET Framework Client Profile

The end user must also have .NET 3.5 or later installed. The ClickOnce installer for a VSTO solution can install .NET for the end user. A new option with VSTO 2008 SP1 is to specify the Client-Only Framework subset (aka the .NET Framework Client Profile), which has a smaller footprint than .NET 3.5 as it includes only common components used in client-side programming and omits components used primarily in server-side programming. The .NET Framework is automatically included as a prerequisite in your Click-Once installer, as you see in "Deploying Add-Ins" later in this chapter.

Microsoft Office 2007 Primary Interop Assemblies

When Office is installed, if possible the .NET Programmability Support option should be installed as well; this option will install the Office 2007 primary interop assemblies (PIAs). When you set up Office, check the Choose Advanced Customization of Applications check box in the first step of the Office 2007 Setup Wizard. In the tree control that appears in the next screen of the wizard, you see a .NET Programmability Support node below each application for which PIAs are available, as shown in Figure 21-1. Click each of these .NET Programmability Support nodes, and make sure that you set them to Run from My Computer. Also, below the Office Tools node in the tree, you may want to turn on Microsoft Forms 2.0 .NET Program-mability Support if you plan to use Outlook form regions that are imported from OFS files and Smart Tag .NET Programmability Support if you plan to write a more complex Smart Tag. A second method of getting the Office 2007 PIAs is to do a complete install of Office 2007; all the .NET programmability support will be turned on for you automatically.

Unfortunately, although you can be sure that Office 2007 is installed on a machine, it is always possible that .NET Programmability Support—and, hence, the Office 2007 PIAs—are not installed. One common way this might happen is if you install Office 2007 before .NET is installed. If .NET is not installed on the machine when Office 2007 is installed, the PIAs can-not be installed, even if you try to install .NET Programmability Support.

Fortunately, starting with VSTO 2008 SP1, the Office 2007 PIAs are included automatically as a prerequisite in your ClickOnce installer.

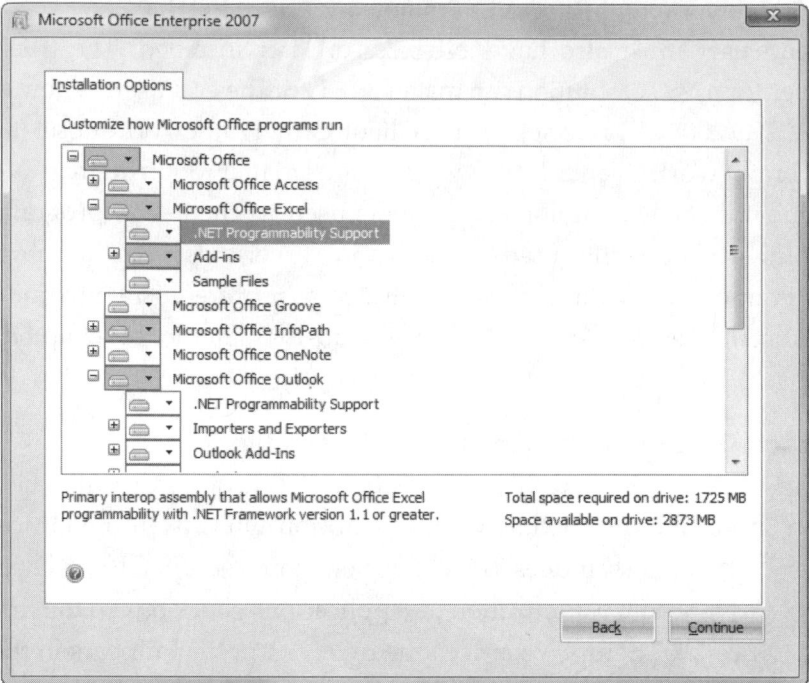

Figure 21-1: Configuring the installation options for Office setup to install .NET programmability support.

Visual Studio Tools for the Office System 3.0 Runtime

The final prerequisite is the VSTO runtime, which is responsible for loading and security-checking VSTO solutions in Office. It also provides services to your solution while it is running. The VSTO runtime supports the cached data feature at runtime, for example. The VSTO runtime also installs the libraries used for the Microsoft.VisualStudio.Tools namespace. The VSTO runtime is included automatically as a prerequisite in your ClickOnce installer.

Deploying Add-Ins

To get started with ClickOnce deployment, deploy a VSTO add-in solution. Start by creating a VSTO add-in—a Word add-in, for this example. In ThisAddIn_Startup in the ThisAddIn.cs file, add some code like Listing 21-1 to display the version of the add-in.

Listing 21-1: A Simple ThisAddIn.cs File That Shows Version Information

```
private void ThisAddIn_Startup(object sender,
  System.EventArgs e)
{
  System.Windows.Forms.MessageBox.Show("Version 1.0.0.0");
}
```

Right-click the Project node and choose Properties from the context menu to show the properties for the project. Click the Publish tab to open the Publish Properties page, which is shown in Figure 21-2.

Publish Location

The first section in the Publish Properties page, Publish Location, has two text boxes: Publishing Folder Location and Installation Folder URL. The Publishing Folder Location is the path where you want Visual Studio to copy the setup files for your VSTO solution when you choose Project > Publish or click the Publish Now button at the bottom of the Publish Properties

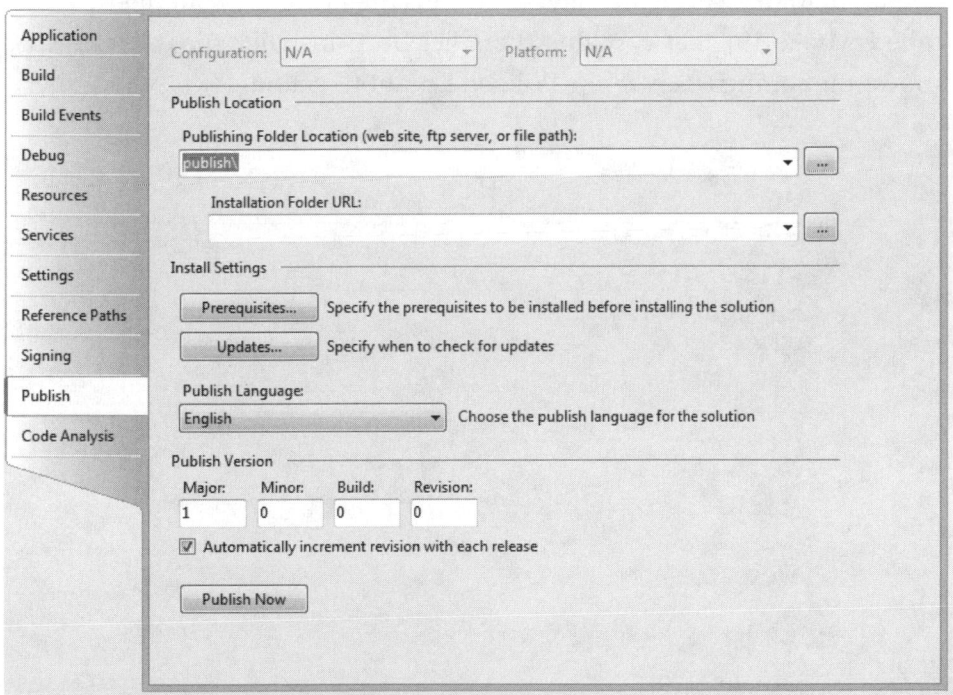

Figure 21-2: The Publish Properties page.

page. The Installation Folder URL is the URL or UNC (Universal Naming Convention) path from which the end user will install the VSTO solution.

The Publish Location section has these two options because you may need to stage the deployment of your installer. You may set Publishing Folder Location to c:\temp\MyAddIn as the location where you want Visual Studio to build your ClickOnce installer, for example, but then you might hand your installer files off to IT, and you know that IT will eventually put it on a file share with the UNC path of \\server\installers\MyAddIn\.

You also need two options for even simpler scenarios. Suppose that you want to publish the files to your local Web server via a local path like c:\inetpub\MyAddIn; users will access your installer via a URL like www.cooladdins.com/MyAddIn. In this case, you would set Publishing Folder Location to c:\inetpub\MyAddIn and Installation Folder URL to http://www.cooladdins.com/MyAddIn.

For this example, publish to a folder called c:\ClickOnceTemp\MyAddIn and set Installation Folder URL to a UNC path of \\ecarter-t61p\installers\MyAddIn. This UNC path refers to the server ecarter-t61p, with a shared folder called installers. The installers folder contains a folder called MyAddIn that contains the ClickOnce installer files. Figure 21-3 shows the settings used in the Publish Location section.

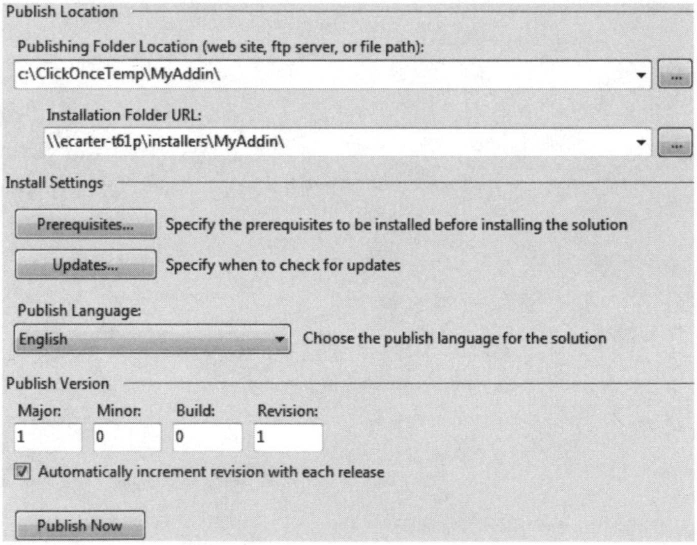

Figure 21-3: The Publish Location settings.

Install Settings

Before you click the Publish Now button, look at the other sections of the Publish Properties page. First, the Install Settings section has Prerequisites and Updates buttons as well as a Publish Language drop-down menu. When you click the Prerequisites button, you see the dialog box shown in Figure 21-4.

By default in Visual Studio 2008 SP1, the following prerequisites are checked:

- Windows Installer 3.1
- .NET Framework 3.5 SP1
- Microsoft Office 2007 Primary Interop Assemblies
- Visual Studio Tools for the Office System 3.0 Runtime Service Pack 1

With these prerequisites checked, Visual Studio will build a setup.exe that can install these prerequisites. To support the installation of the PIAs,

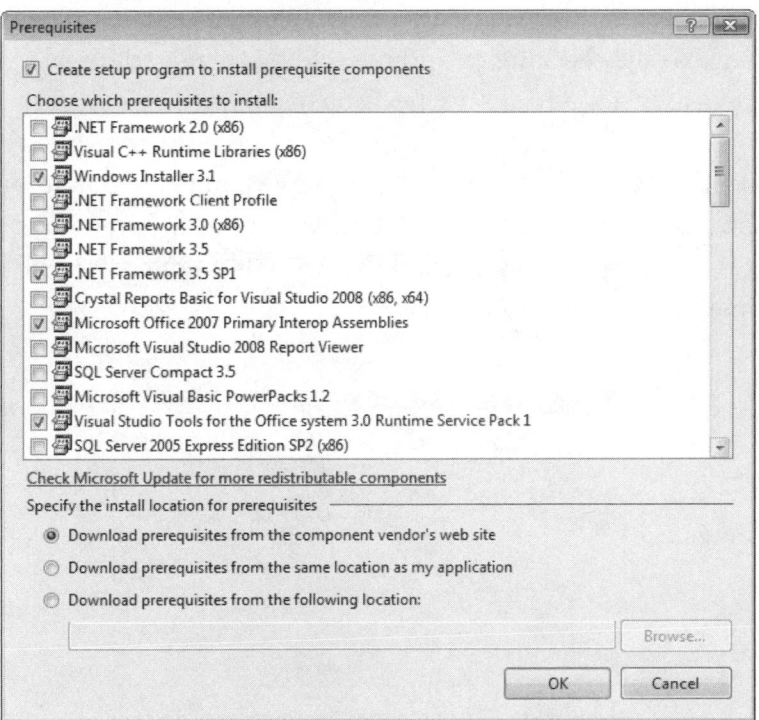

Figure 21-4: The Prerequisites dialog box.

Visual Studio copies some additional files alongside setup.exe in a folder called Office2007PIARedist.

The Updates button displays the Customization Updates dialog box, shown in Figure 21-5. The default is to check for an update every seven days. Updates are checked when an add-in or customization is loaded. You can also specify to check for updates every time a customization is loaded or never check for updates. The Check at Interval setting can be adjusted as well and can use units of hours, days, or weeks.

The VSTO team set the default for update checking to every seven days. The main reason why this default was chosen, rather than checking every time the customization runs, is that checking for an update can cause performance issues. Suppose that you have seven Outlook add-ins, each from a different company. If all seven add-ins check for updates every time they are run, every time you start Outlook multiple Web sites or UNC shares will have to be accessed to see whether updates are available. These accesses could significantly slow Outlook startup, depending on network speed. If, instead, each developer uses the default, each add-in is set to check for updates seven days after it is installed (and every seven days thereafter). So the checking of updates will be staggered (unless you happen always to install add-ins on the same day of the week).

Unfortunately, this default setting can be confusing when you are learning about ClickOnce, because you may republish your solution and expect an add-in to update, but it won't update until seven days pass. To prevent confusion, for this example set update frequency to be checked every time the customization runs.

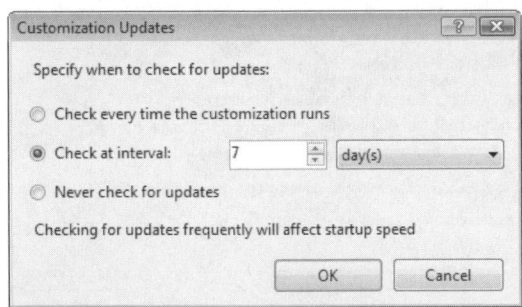

Figure 21-5: The Customization Updates dialog box.

Another issue to consider is that updates are checked only when the add-in starts up. If an end user has an Outlook add-in loaded but does not shut down Outlook and instead leaves it running for many days or weeks at a time, even when an update is available, the user won't get the update unless he exits and then restarts Outlook.

The Publish Language drop-down menu is where you choose the language used by the prerequisite installers that the setup.exe program runs.

Publish Version

The final section of the Publish Properties page is Publish Version, which contains settings for the version number of the published solution. This version number can be different from the version number used by the primary executing assembly of your solution. This version number pertains to the deployment manifest, which we discuss later in this chapter. Click-Once uses this version number to determine whether an update is available. A check box titled Automatically Increment Revision with Each Release automatically increases the revision number after you click the Publish Now button or choose Build > Publish. So the first time you publish, the version number would be 1.0.0.0, and the second time you publish, the version number would be 1.0.0.1.

Also in the Publish Version section is the Publish Now button. Click that button to publish your add-in.

Publishing

When you click the Publish Now button or choose Build > Publish, your VSTO project is built and your solution is published. In the Output window you can see the result of publishing. Your add-in WordAddIn1 has been successfully published to a directory called C:\ClickOnceTemp\ MyAddIn:

```
========== Build: 1 succeeded or up-to-date, 0 failed, 0 skipped ==========
Building WordAddIn1...
Connecting to 'C:\ClickOnceTemp\MyAddIn\'...
Publishing files...
Publish success.
```

Now explore the files created in the root publishing folder c:\ClickOnce-Temp\MyAddIn. The tree structure and files generated are shown in Figure 21-6.

Visual Studio creates two important files in the root publishing folder. The .vsto file is called the VSTO deployment manifest. A user can double-click the VSTO deployment manifest to install the add-in, but only if pre-requisites are already present on the machine—in particular, Office 2007, Windows Installer 3.1, Office 2007 PIAs, .NET Framework 3.5 SP1, and the VSTO 3.0 Runtime SP1.

If all the prerequisites are not yet installed, the user must use the setup.exe application created in the root publishing folder. The setup.exe application installs the prerequisites that were configured in the Prerequisites dialog box and then installs the add-in.

Also in the root publishing folder is an Application Files folder, which in turn contains a folder titled WordAddIn1_1_0_0_0. This folder contains all the files needed to install one version of the add-in. This folder is given the name of the add-in (WordAddIn1) with the version appended (_1_0_0_0). Over time, as you create updates to your add-in, additional folders will be created in the Application Files folder—one for each version you have published. So after the add-in has been published three times, assuming that you checked the Automatically Increment Revision with Each Release check box in the Publish Properties page, you have the folders WordAddIn1_1_0_0_0, WordAddIn1_1_0_0_1, and WordAddIn1_1_0_0_2 in the Application Files folder.

Inside the WordAddIn1_1_0_0_0 folder is a VSTO deployment manifest file for the 1.0.0.0 version of the add-in. This file is a duplicate of the

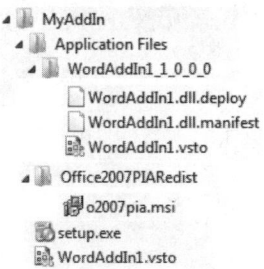

Figure 21-6: The tree structure and files generated by a ClickOnce publish.

deployment manifest in the root publishing folder. Each time you publish a new version of your add-in, the deployment manifest in the root publishing folder is replaced by the deployment manifest specific to the latest published version. You can also roll back to an earlier version by copying a deployment manifest from an earlier version folder to the root publishing folder. Suppose that you've published three times, and you have the folders WordAddIn1_1_0_0_0, WordAddIn1_1_0_0_1, and WordAddIn1_1_0_0_2. The deployment manifest file (WordAddIn1.vsto) in the root publishing folder will match the deployment manifest in the folder WordAddIn1_1_0_0_2. To roll back to the 1.0.0.1 version of the add-in, you can simply copy the deployment manifest file in the folder WordAddIn1_1_0_0_1 to the root publish folder and overwrite the 1.0.0.2 deployment manifest that is there.

What Can I Delete?

If you are sure that you will never roll back to an older version, you can safely delete the folder containing that version's files. In the example in this section, if you are sure that you will never need to roll back to the version in the folder WordAddIn1_1_0_0_1, you can delete that folder with no effect on later versions. Just don't delete the current version folder (WordAddIn1_1_0_0_2, in the example).

Also inside the WordAddIn1_1_0_0_0 folder are other files needed to install the add-in. The WordAddIn1.dll.deploy file is the assembly built by the add-in project with a .deploy extension tacked on. The WordAddIn1.dll.manifest file, called the application manifest, describes the assemblies loaded by the VSTO solution.

Post Publishing

In this example, you still have a post-publishing step to complete. Remember that you have a publishing folder called c:\ClickOnceTemp\MyAddIn and a separate installation folder URL called \\ecarter-t61p\installers\ MyAddIn. For this example, you have two separate folders: a temporary folder where you build the install and the final folder where IT puts the final installer. So all the files in the MyAddIn folder (including all child folders) must be copied to the server location \\ecarter-t61p\installers\ MyAddIn. This also means that users will run the setup application \\ecarter-t61p\installers\MyAddIn\setup.exe if they don't have the prerequisites and \\ecarter-t61p\installers\MyAddIn\WordAddIn1.vsto if they do have the prerequisites.

Another post-publishing step you will often want to do is pass your solution off to another entity to sign it with a publisher certificate. We describe this process in "ClickOnce Security" later in this chapter.

Installing

Now that your installer files have been copied out to a network share, any users who have read access to that share can run the setup.exe to install the solution with prerequisites (if they have administrator privileges), and if they already have the prerequisites installed, they can just launch the WordAddIn1.vsto file to install the solution without administrator privileges.

Consider the install experience for users who have none of the prerequisites (except Office 2007, which must be installed before setup.exe is run). First, if they try to double-click the WordAddIn1.vsto file, they get no result except a "Windows cannot open this file" error message, because to get a result when you double-click a deployment manifest, the VSTO runtime must be installed.

For this example, you've set up a separate Windows XP machine for the user of your add-in on the same network as your ecarter-t61p server machine. That Windows XP machine can access the setup.exe file via the shared folder path \\ecarter-t61p\installers\MyAddIn\setup.exe. When the user double-clicks setup.exe, the installer first checks to see whether any of the prerequisites are missing. For each prerequisite that is missing, the installer prompts the user to accept the associated EULA (End User License Agreement), as shown in Figures 21-7, 21-8, and 21-9. The Office 2007 PIAs don't have a EULA, but the user is still prompted to install them, as shown in Figure 21-10. If the user cancels any of these dialog boxes, the setup exits without installing the VSTO customization.

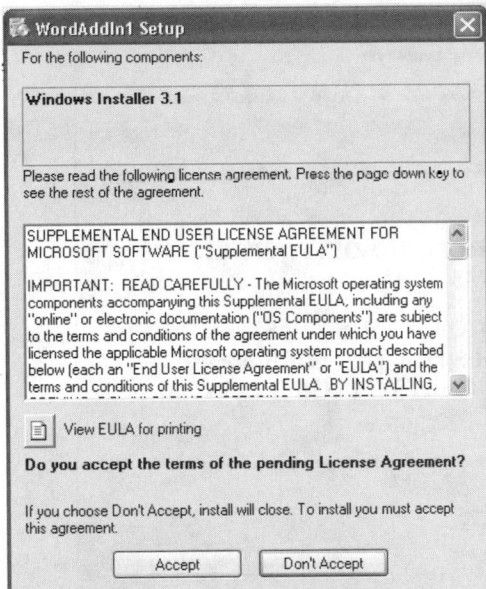

Figure 21-7: The EULA dialog box for the Windows Installer 3.1 prerequisite.

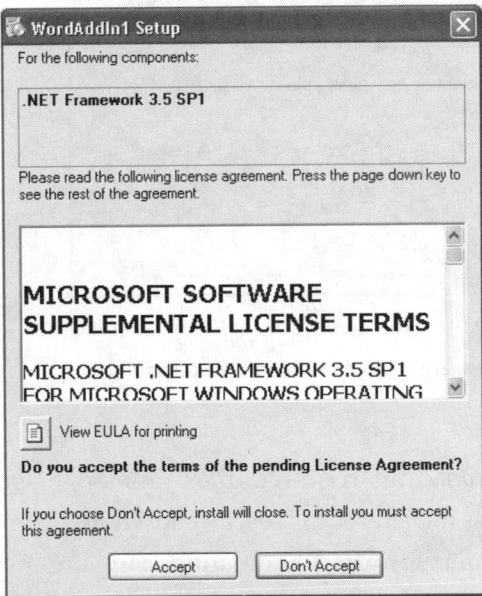

Figure 21-8: The EULA dialog box for the .NET Framework 3.5 SP1 prerequisite.

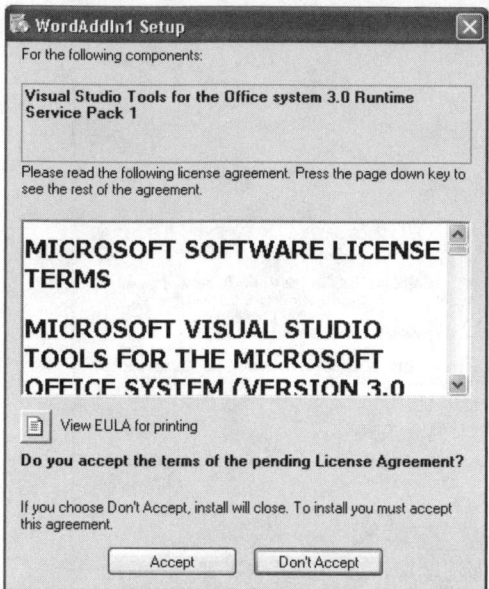

Figure 21-9: The EULA dialog box for the Visual Studio Tools
for the Office System 3.0 Runtime Service Pack 1 prerequisite.

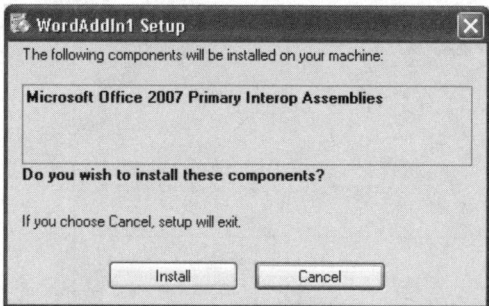

Figure 21-10: The dialog box for the Microsoft Office
2007 Primary Interop Assemblies prerequisite.

Next, a "Downloading required files" message is shown while the
installer downloads the prerequisites, as shown in Figure 21-11.

After the prerequisites are downloaded, they are installed. A progress
dialog box appears, showing the user which prerequisite is currently being
installed and the progress of installation. Figure 21-12 shows the progress
dialog box for the Windows Installer 3.1 prerequisite.

Figure 21-11: "Downloading required files" message.

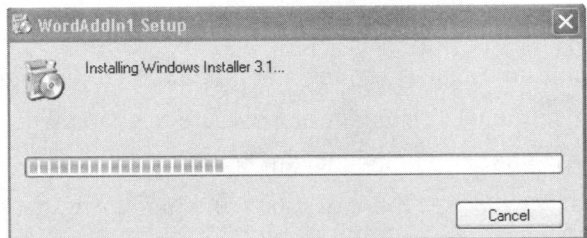

Figure 21-12: Installing Windows Installer 3.1 progress
dialog box.

If You Install on the Same Machine You Build On

You should consider a couple of gotchas if you try to install on the same
machine that you build on. Whenever you build a VSTO project on your
developer machine (and publishing invokes a build as part of the process), the add-in or document solution gets "registered" on your
machine. We use the word *registered* because it isn't a full ClickOnce
install. The customization does not get installed in the ClickOnce cache,
for example; instead, Visual Studio registers the customization in the
bin\debug directory of your VSTO projects. If you then try to run the
installer for a solution that has already been registered, you can get into a
confusing state in which the solution is both installed and registered.

There are two times you need to consider this issue. The first is when
you have been developing the solution in Visual Studio (which uses the
register approach) and you now want to test the installer of your solution

on the same machine. To avert having your solution be both registered and installed at the same time, choose Build › Clean Solution for the solution you want to install. This command unregisters the solution. Then run the installer you built. The solution is now installed.

The second time to consider this issue is if you have tested the installer by installing it on your development machine and you now want to continue developing that solution in Visual Studio. To do this, you need to uninstall the solution first—remember that a solution can't be installed and registered at the same time, and when you rebuild the solution in Visual Studio it will try to register it again. Before switching back to develop that solution in Visual Studio, be sure to go to the Add or Remove Programs dialog box and uninstall your solution.

A second gotcha that you can run into when trying to install on the same machine you build on is that when working with Excel document solutions, you must ensure that the visual Excel document designer for the solution is closed before you run an installer for that solution. If the visual designer for the Excel document is open inside Visual Studio, the install of the same document outside Visual Studio will fail silently.

In the case of the Windows Installer 3.1 prerequisite, a reboot is required before the setup can continue. So if this prerequisite is installed, the dialog box shown in Figure 21-13 appears.

After the user reboots—either by clicking Yes in this dialog box or by clicking No and then rebooting manually—the setup continues when the machine restarts, resuming the installation of the next prerequisite, as

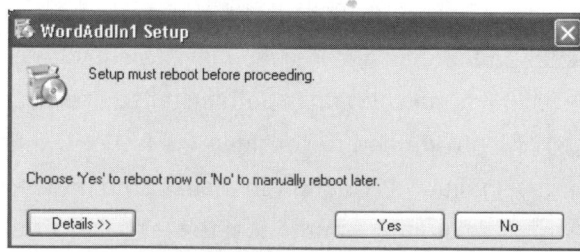

Figure 21-13: "Setup must reboot before proceeding" message.

shown in Figure 21-14. Progress dialog boxes also appear for the Visual Studio Tools for the Office System 3.0 Runtime Service Pack 1 and the Microsoft Office 2007 Primary Interop Assemblies.

When all the prerequisites are installed, the actual downloading and installation of the VSTO customization starts. First, a dialog box appears while the deployment manifest is retrieved from the network, as shown in Figure 21-15.

Next, the setup does a series of security checks to determine whether to install the customization. We describe security in the "ClickOnce Security" section later in this chapter. For now, it is sufficient to know that the deployment manifest was not signed with a trusted certificate, so installation cannot continue without prompting the user. Also, the certificate you are using is the test certificate automatically created in your VSTO project, rather than a publisher certificate issued from a company like VeriSign. Because the deployment manifest is coming from the intranet, prompting the user is allowed for both test and publisher certificates, and the dialog box shown in Figure 21-16 opens. If the deployment manifest was coming

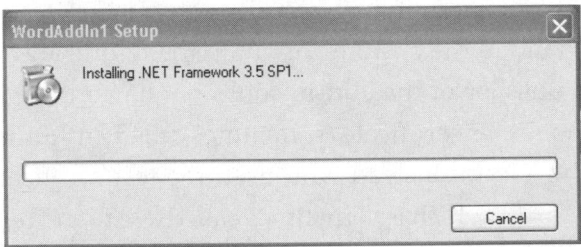

Figure 21-14: Installing .NET Framework 3.5 SP1 dialog box.

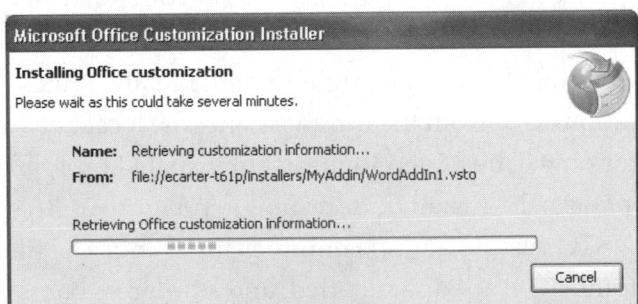

Figure 21-15: "Retrieving Office customization information" message.

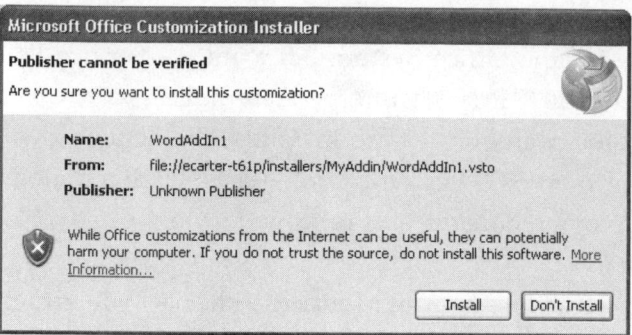

Figure 21-16: The "Are you sure you want to install this customization?" prompt.

from the Internet, the defaults do not allow for an install prompt for a test certificate, and the install would fail. If a real publisher certificate were used, a deployment manifest coming from the Internet would result in an install prompt.

The dialog box shown in Figure 21-16 contains a More Information link. When the user clicks this link, she sees the dialog box shown in Figure 21-17. This dialog box contains additional security information to help the user decide whether to install the customization. In the figure, for example, you can see that the publisher of the add-in could not be verified, because you didn't use a real publisher certificate (sometimes called an Authenticode certificate) to sign the add-in. Instead, you used the test certificate generated automatically by VSTO, which is sometimes called a *self-cert*. Test certificates cannot be verified, as publisher certificates can. We discuss certificates in more detail in "ClickOnce Security" later in this chapter.

The dialog box shown in Figure 21-17 also warns that the add-in will have full access to the computer. (VSTO customizations run in full trust and can do anything the user has right to do.) Finally, it tells the user that the customization came from the intranet zone (the local network) and that the customization will be added to the list of installed programs.

If the user clicks the Install button shown in Figure 21-16 earlier in this chapter, the VSTO customization continues installing. The files associated with the customization are downloaded, and a progress bar is displayed as

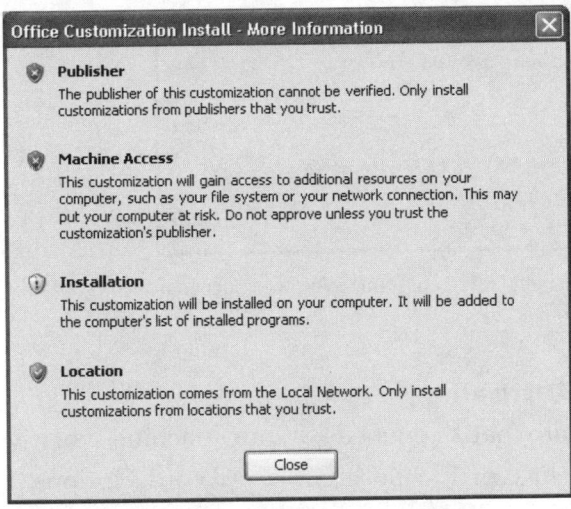

Figure 21-17: The More Information dialog box.

they are downloaded, as shown in Figure 21-18. This example adds a 21.44 MB resource file to the add-in to force this dialog box to appear; most add-ins are small and don't require a lot of download time. This dialog box won't appear if the download time is short.

When the add-in is installed, the dialog box shown in Figure 21-19 is displayed, indicating success. If you launch Word, the add-in will be loaded. A dialog box displaying the text *1.0.0.0* will appear. Click OK to dismiss this dialog box.

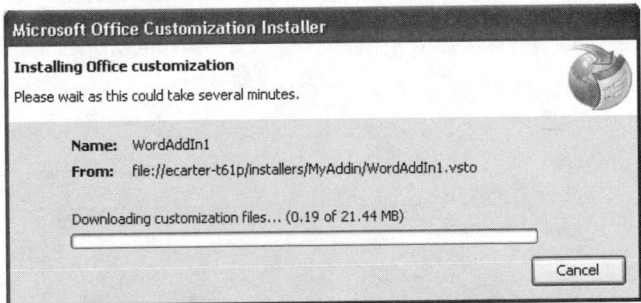

Figure 21-18: Downloading customization files.

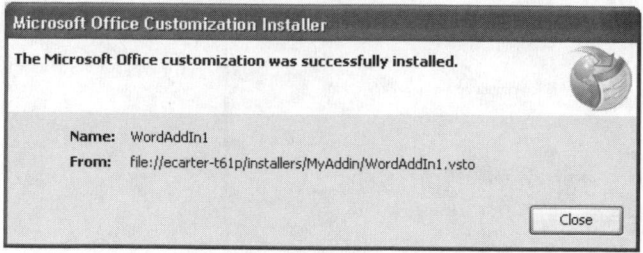

Figure 21-19: The Microsoft Office customization was successfully installed.

Installation: The Aftermath

Now take a look at what happened to your machine when you installed this add-in. First, in Word, choose Office > Word Options. In the Word Options dialog box, click the Add-Ins tab. Notice that the add-in you installed—WordAddIn1—is listed as an installed add-in, as shown in Figure 21-20. If you click the WordAddIn1 line, you see additional detail,

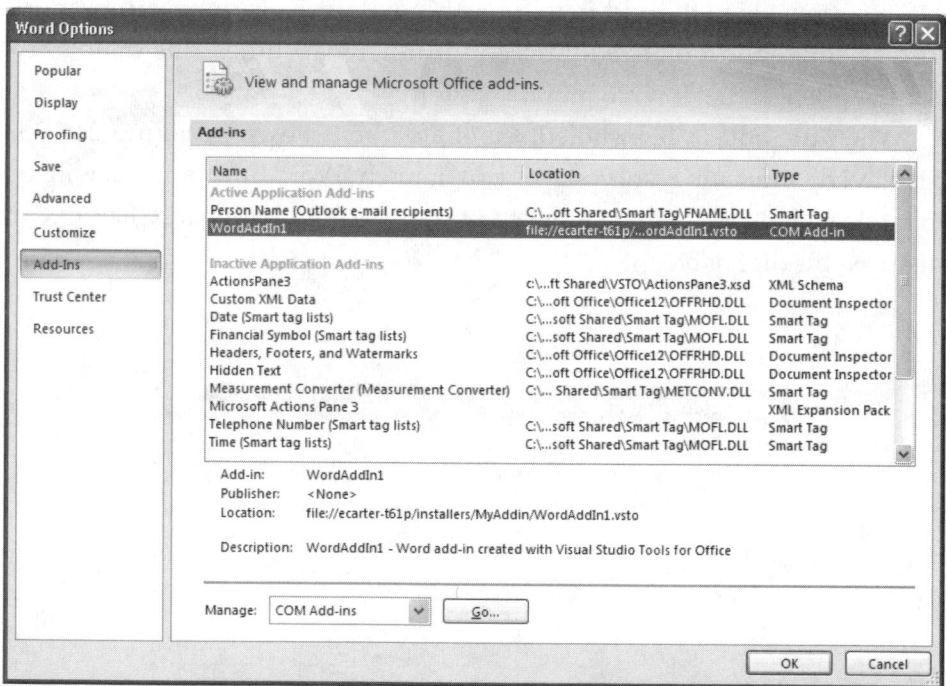

Figure 21-20: Information for WordAddIn1 shown in the Add-Ins tab of the Word Options dialog box.

including the location of the add-in, which is the path to the deployment manifest for the add-in. In the "Advanced Topic: Editing Manifests Using Mage" section later in this chapter we show you how to change the add-in name (WordAddIn1) known as the Friendly Name and the Description ("WordAddIn1 – Word add-in created with Visual Studio Tools for Office") to something else. The Publisher line cannot be changed; it is a property that Office currently does not recognize for VSTO add-ins.

Word discovers what add-ins to load by reading the registry. If you run regedit.exe to launch the Registry Editor, you can examine the values that the ClickOnce installer put in the registry for the add-in, as shown in Figure 21-21. The installer creates a key in HKEY_CURRENT_USER\Software\ Microsoft\Office\Word\Addins called WordAddIn1. Within that key, you can see the values Description, FriendlyName, LoadBehavior, and Manifest. Description, FriendlyName, and Manifest were displayed by Word's Add-Ins Page. Manifest points to the location of the deployment manifest; this setting matches the Installation Folder URL setting you specified in the Publish Location section of the Publish Properties page.

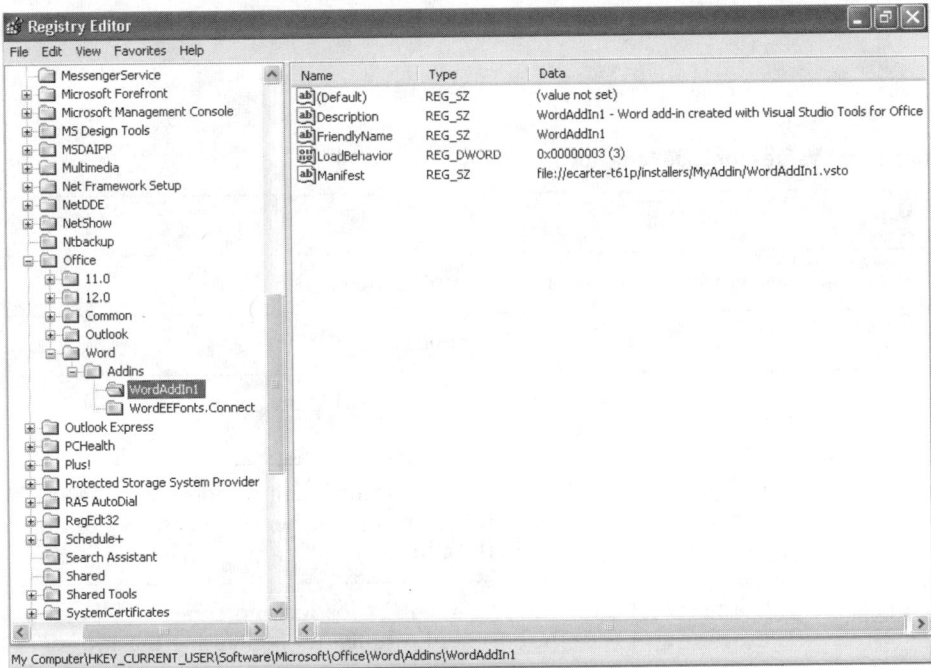

Figure 21-21: Registry settings for WordAddIn1.

LoadBehavior is a DWORD value that describes the load behavior of the add-in. The value to which LoadBehavior can be set can be bitwise or one of the values in Table 21-1. Typically, this value should be set to 3 to load and connect the add-in at startup. If LoadBehavior is set to 2, the add-in is loaded but never connected, which effectively amounts to the add-in's being disabled. The values 16 and 8 are used for load-on-demand scenarios, which we describe in Chapter 17, "Working with the Ribbon in VSTO."

Another place affected by your ClickOnce install is the Add or Remove Programs dialog box. Go to the Control Panel, and in Vista, click the Uninstall a Program link. In Windows XP, go to the Control Panel and choose Add or Remove Programs. In Windows XP, you see the dialog box shown in Figure 21-22. Note that the add-in you installed (WordAddIn1) is in the list of currently installed programs. You can remove the add-in by clicking the Remove button. Also in this dialog box, you see all the prerequisites that got installed: Microsoft .NET Framework components, the Microsoft Office 2007 Primary Interop Assemblies, the Visual Studio Tools for the Office System 3.0 Runtime, and Windows Installer 3.1. When you uninstall an add-in, the prerequisites stay installed. The user has to uninstall the prerequisites manually.

TABLE 21-1: Values for LoadBehavior

Value	Description
0	Disconnected. The add-in is not loaded.
1	Connected. The add-in is loaded.
2	Load at startup. The add-in will be loaded and connected when the host application starts.
8	Load on demand. The add-in will be loaded and connected when the host application requires it (for example, when a user clicks a button that uses functionality in the add-in).
16	Connect first time. The add-in will be loaded and connected the first time the user runs the host application after registering the add-in.

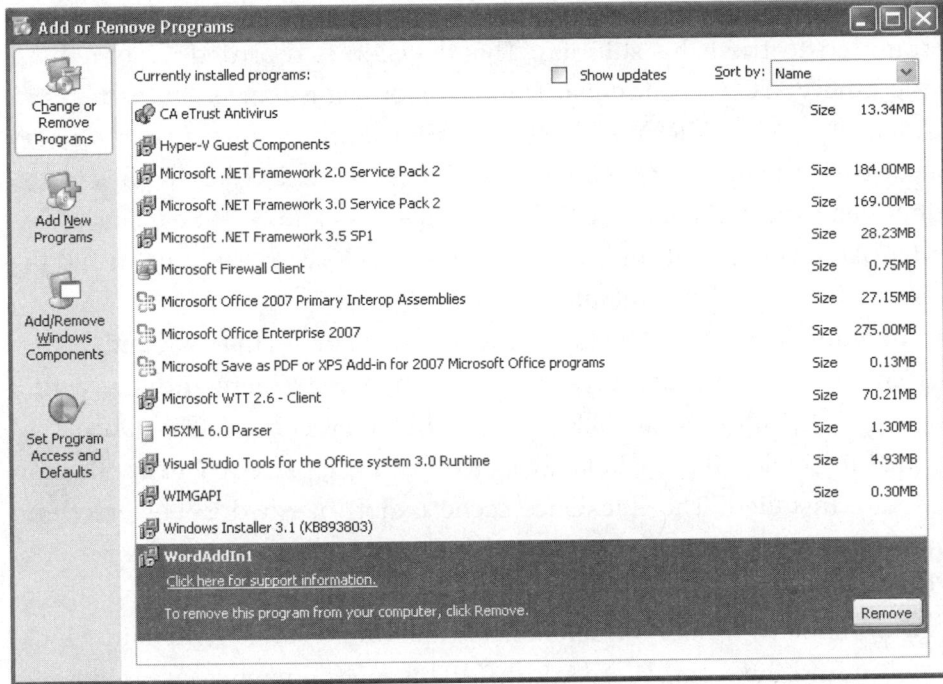

Figure 21-22: Add-in listed among currently installed programs.

If you click the Click Here for Support Information link associated with WordAddIn1, you see the dialog box shown in Figure 21-23. This dialog box displays the publisher, the version, and a link to click for product updates. In the "Advanced Topic: Editing Manifests Using Mage" section later in this chapter, we show you how to modify this information.

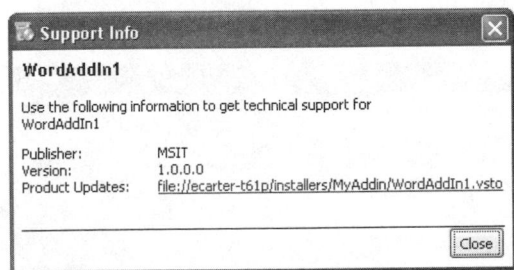

Figure 21-23: Support Info dialog box.

Office also has to track the fact that the user chose Yes when he was prompted to trust this solution. This decision is recorded in something called the VSTO inclusion list. The inclusion list is located in the registry under the key HKEY_CURRENT_USER\Software\Microsoft\VSTO\ Security\Inclusion. For each solution that is trusted, a key with a GUID identifier is created under the Inclusion key—also known as an inclusion list entry. An inclusion list entry includes the PublicKey for the solution and the URL to the deployment manifest for the solution. We consider the inclusion list in more detail in the "Inclusion List" section later in this chapter.

You have one more mystery to solve here: Where did the actual WordAddIn1.DLL get installed? What directory is it in? ClickOnce uses something called the ClickOnce cache, which is a place where application files are installed. The ClickOnce cache is not intended to be something that you browse or worry about. ClickOnce manages the cache for you. The cache is in a set of hidden directories under the Local Settings directory of the current user's Document and Settings folder. With a little luck, you can find the actual WordAddIn1.dll by spelunking in those folders, as shown in Figure 21-24. At times you may deploy with your VSTO customization some local data files that you need to access and modify at runtime. To access these files, you use classes in the System.Deployment namespace to determine their runtime location. The property DataDirectory of the System.Deployment.ApplicationDeployment class gives you the location of the local data directory for the VSTO application.

Updating

Now that the add-in has been installed, you can update the add-in. For this example, change the Word add-in to display *1.0.0.1*, as shown in Listing 21-2.

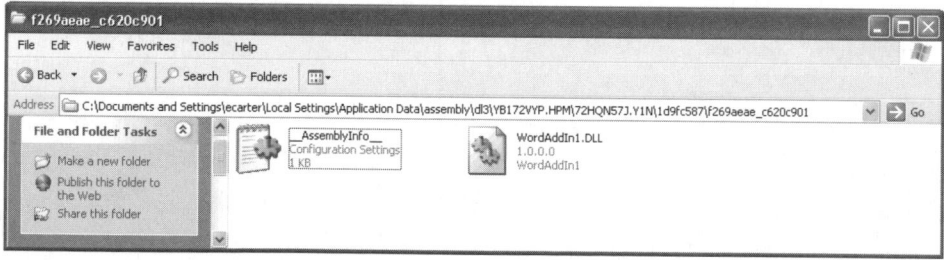

Figure 21-24: The WordAddIn1.dll in the ClickOnce cache.

Listing 21-2: Changing ThisAddIn.cs Version Information

```
private void ThisAddIn_Startup(object sender,
  System.EventArgs e)
{
  System.Windows.Forms.MessageBox.Show("1.0.0.1");
}
```

Now, to republish, right-click the project node in the Solution Explorer, and choose Properties from the context menu (or choose Project > WordAddIn1 Properties). This command brings up the Properties window for the project. Make sure that the Publish tab is selected. If you checked the Automatically Increment Revision with Each Release check box, the Publish Version should already be set to 1.0.0.1. If it is still 1.0.0.0, be sure to update the revision number to 1. Then click the Publish Now button.

As before, this procedure builds the solution and publishes all files needed by the ClickOnce installer to the publishing folder location—in this example, c:\ClickOnceTemp\MyAddIn. Now the directory looks like Figure 21-25. A new folder has been created in ApplicationFiles called WordAddIn1_1_0_0_1 for the new version. The files in that folder represent version 1.0.0.1 of the add-in. The deployment manifest WordAddIn1.vsto in the root Publish Folder now matches the deployment manifest in the WordAddIn1_1_0_0_1 folder.

Remember that you specified a different publishing folder location from the installation folder URL, so the files in the MyAddIn folder

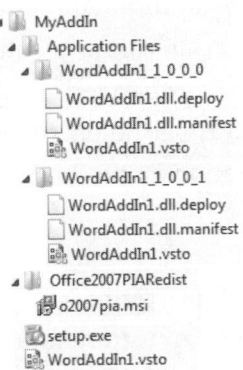

Figure 21-25: The tree structure and files after the second ClickOnce publish.

(including all child folders) must be copied to the server location \\ecarter-t61p\installers\MyAddIn. Alternatively, you could just copy the root WordAddIn1.vsto file in the c:\ClickOnceTemp\MyAddIn directory and the WordAddIn1_1_0_0_1 folder from the Application Files folder to the corresponding publishing folder location.

Now go back to the Windows XP machine where you installed version 1.0.0.0 of the add-in. If that machine still has Word running, remember that you must exit and then restart Word to reload the add-in before the update can be detected. Also, if you didn't use the Customization Updates dialog box to set the update-checking frequency to every time the customization runs (refer to Figure 21-5 earlier in this chapter), even restarting Word won't update the add-in until the time set in that dialog box has elapsed.

Setting the update frequency to an undesired value is a chicken-and-egg-type problem. Suppose that the frequency of updates was seven days in version 1.0.0.0, and you change it to check every time the solution runs for version 1.0.0.1. This is all well and good, but existing users are not going to see the change in update behavior (moving to "every time") until their version 1.0.0.0 checks for updates after seven days elapse.

Assuming that your update frequency is set to check every time the solution runs, when Word launches it checks for updates and displays the progress dialog box shown in Figure 21-26. After finding and installing the update—no prompts must be responded to during update—the add-in is updated, and *1.0.0.1* appears in a dialog box.

If the update takes a long time, the user has the option to click the Cancel button in the dialog box shown in Figure 21-26. In Visual Studio 2008, this would cause the add-in to be disabled and not run until you reinstall it by double-clicking the deployment manifest again or running setup.exe again. For Visual Studio 2008 SP1, this behavior was changed. When the user clicks Cancel, the old version loads. The next time the user loads the customization, VSTO tries to update the customization again.

Variations on the Deploying Add-ins Theme

In this section, we consider some other scenarios that you may use when deploying add-ins. In the example, you deployed to an intranet file share, but you could also deploy to an intranet Web server, as shown in "Deploy-

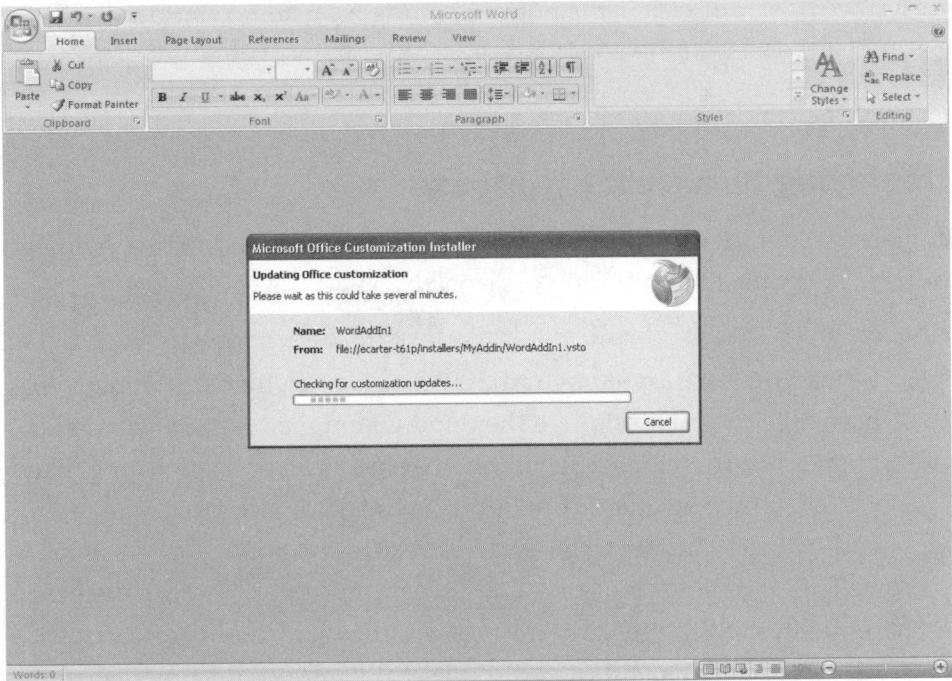

Figure 21-26: Checking for updates when Word starts.

ing Document Solutions" later in this chapter. You could also deploy to an Internet web server, but for that method work, you must have a publisher certificate to sign your add-in. The default ClickOnce security settings require a publisher signature to be used to install the deployment manifest before it prompts a user to install an add-in from the Internet zone. For more information on prompt settings, see the "ClickOnce Security" section later in this chapter.

You could also deploy your add-in via a CD or USB key. When you deploy an add-in this way, ClickOnce does not support updates, so you must pick a local path on your machine as the publishing folder location and leave the Installation Folder URL text box blank. Then you can copy the files from your root publishing folder location to a USB key or CD.

Finally, you may decide not to use ClickOnce directly and instead deploy your add-in via a custom MSI-based installer. Although that topic is not covered in this book, we provide a link to a white paper that describes this approach in the note "Creating a Custom Windows Installer Setup" at the start of this chapter.

Deploying Document Solutions

In general, deploying a document solution is very similar to deploying an add-in. A couple of key differences exist, however:

- When you have a document that is customized, the document itself has embedded in it a link to the deployment manifest. So when you open for the first time a document that has a customization associated with it, Office automatically detects a linked deployment manifest and starts the install of the associated customization.

  This situation has a couple of caveats, however. First, all the prerequisites have to be installed before Office can automatically open the deployment manifest and successfully install a document customization. Second, ClickOnce security rules continue to apply, so if the deployment manifest is in the Internet zone and signed with a test certificate, the customization won't install.

- The location from which the document is being opened is considered before a VSTO customization is allowed to install and run. So a document that is opened directly from an e-mail message attachment, for example, is considered to be coming from an untrusted location, and the VSTO customization associated with the document will not be allowed to install or run. A document that is being opened from a **network** location that is not in Office's Trusted Location list, which we describe in this section, also is not allowed to install or run.

Publishing a Document Solution to a Web Server

In this section, you create an Excel workbook customization and then publish it. First, create an Excel Workbook project in Visual Studio. In the Sheet1_Startup event handler, write some code to show a message box displaying *Version 1.0.0.0,* as shown in Listing 21-3.

Listing 21-3: Displaying Version Message Box in Sheet1_Startup

```
private void Sheet1_Startup(object sender,
  System.EventArgs e)
{
  MessageBox.Show("Version 1.0.0.0");
}
```

For this example, we show you how to publish to a Web server that is running Vista and Internet Information Server 7 (IIS 7). We show Visual Studio's support for publishing to IIS 7 when Visual Studio and IIS 7 are running on the same machine. If you don't have IIS 7 enabled on Vista, you can enable it by using the Turn Windows Features On or Off option in the Control Panel, shown in Figure 21-27. In addition to checking Internet Information Services, which preselects a set of default features, you must turn on several specific additional features if you want Visual Studio to manage the configuration of the Web site for you. Specifically, you must select three options: IIS Metabase and IIS 6 Configuration Compatibility, ASP.NET, and Windows Authentication. Also, to use the Visual Studio and IIS 7 integration, you must run Visual Studio as Administrator in Vista. If you are not currently running Visual Studio as Administrator, exit Visual Studio; then restart Visual Studio as Administrator by right-clicking the Visual Studio icon in the Vista Start menu and choosing Run As Administrator from the context menu.

With IIS configured and Visual Studio running with Administrator privileges, display the project properties by right-clicking the project node in the Solution Explorer and choosing Properties from the context menu. Click the Publish tab, and click the ellipsis (…) button next to the Publishing Folder Location text box. This button brings up the Publishing Location dialog box. Click the Local IIS button to bring up the Local Internet Information Server dialog box, shown in Figure 21-28, which shows the Web sites on your local machine.

You are going to create a new virtual directory to publish your workbook to. Select Default Web Site, as shown in Figure 21-28. Then click the Create New Virtual Directory button (the folder icon in the top-right corner of the Publishing Location dialog box). This button brings up the New

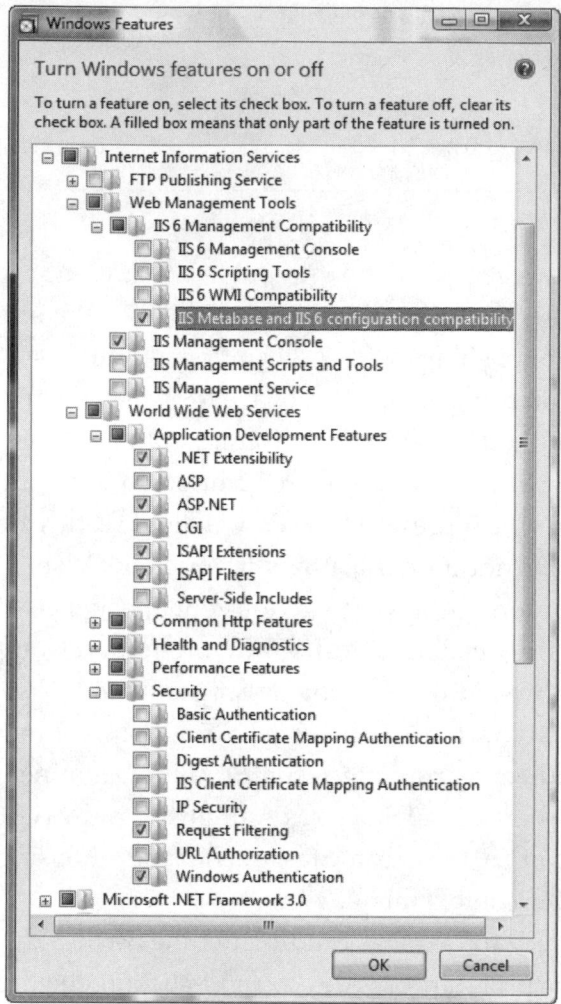

Figure 21-27: Configuring IIS 7 in Vista to work with Visual Studio.

Virtual Directory dialog box, shown in Figure 21-29. In the Alias Name text box, type a name for the new virtual directory; for this example, use MyWorkbook. Also, you must specify a folder for the virtual directory; for this example, use the path c:\inetpub\wwwroot\MyWorkbook. Then click the OK button. Finally, with the new virtual directory selected in the Publishing Location dialog box, click the Open button to select it.

This procedure sets Publishing Folder Location to http://localhost/My-Workbook/ and Installation Folder URL to http://localhost/MyWorkbook.

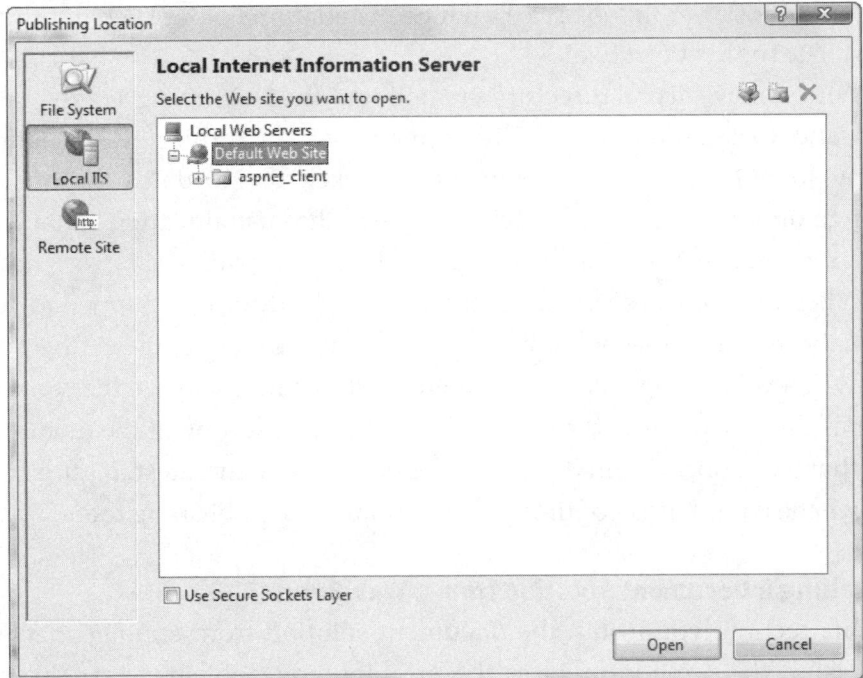

Figure 21-28: Publishing to the default Web site by using the Publishing Location dialog box.

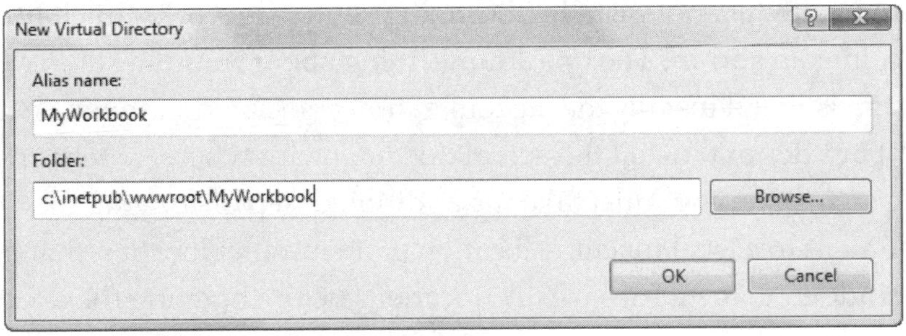

Figure 21-29: The New Virtual Directory dialog box.

Unfortunately, this result isn't exactly what you want. If a second machine is going to install this workbook customization by contacting your Web server, giving the Installation Folder URL the server name localhost will just cause that second machine to try to contact itself. So change the Installation Folder URL setting so that it uses the name of your server rather

than localhost. For this exercise, change Installation Folder URL to http://
ecarter-t61p/MyWorkbook.

With a new virtual directory created and the Publishing Folder Location and Installation Folder URL options set correctly, you are almost
ready to publish. As with your add-in, click the Updates button and
change update checking to check every time the customization runs. Then
click the Publish Now button to publish the customization.

When the publish succeeds, you can check the directory mapped to your
virtual directory to see what happened—for this example, the c:\inetpub\
wwwroot\MyWorkbook directory. In this directory, you see the same set
of files that are published for an add-in, with the addition of the document
file that has embedded in it a link to the deployment manifest. Figure 21-30
shows the complete set of files you will find in the publishing folder.

Installing a Document Solution from a Web Server

In this section, you install the document solution from another machine
that is on the same intranet as the machine you published on. The first
question to consider is what approach to use to install the solution, as you
have three possibilities:

- The first approach is to run the setup.exe file, which is required if the
  prerequisites are not installed. Running setup.exe works much like
  installing an add-in. The one strange thing about running setup.exe
  though is that it installs the customization associated with the document but doesn't install the actual document anywhere. After running setup.exe, you must take the additional step of copying the
  document to a local machine location or an intranet location that has
  been added to the Office trusted locations before opening the document directly.

- The second approach is to launch the .vsto deployment manifest. This
  approach is preferred for add-ins for which the prerequisites are
  already installed, but for document solutions, the third approach is best.

- The third approach, which also requires prerequisites to be installed,
  is to open the document directly, as the document has an embedded
  link to the deployment manifest. Opening the document triggers the
  install of the customization.

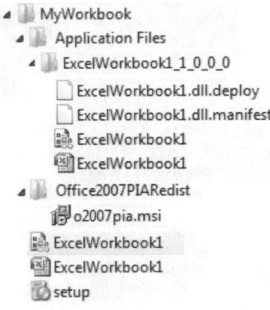

▲ 📁 MyWorkbook
　▲ 📁 Application Files
　　▲ 📁 ExcelWorkbook1_1_0_0_0
　　　　📄 ExcelWorkbook1.dll.deploy
　　　　📄 ExcelWorkbook1.dll.manifest
　　　　📊 ExcelWorkbook1
　　　　📗 ExcelWorkbook1
　▲ 📁 Office2007PIARedist
　　　📦 o2007pia.msi
　📊 ExcelWorkbook1
　📗 ExcelWorkbook1
　🔧 setup

Figure 21-30: The files published for a document customization.

So you may think that you could just open the URL http://ecarter-t61p/MyWorkbook/ExcelWorkbook1.xlsx, and the customization would install and run. If you navigate to that URL in Internet Explorer, you get a dialog box prompting you to open or save the workbook, as shown in Figure 21-31.

If you choose Open, Excel starts up, the workbook opens, and an error message is displayed ("The customization assembly could not be found or could not be loaded"). When you click the Details button to see what the problem is, as shown in Figure 21-32, the additional error message says, "Customization does not have the permissions required to create an application domain. . . . Customized functionality in this program will not work

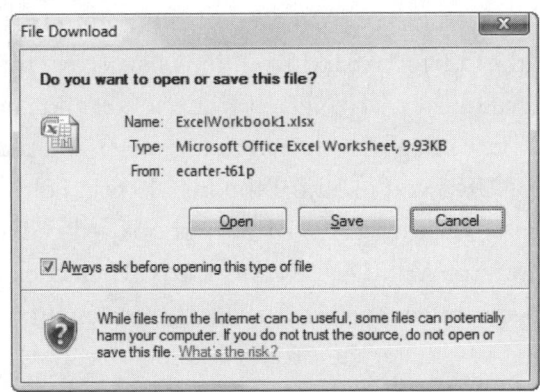

Figure 21-31: The dialog box displayed by Internet Explorer when you click a document link.

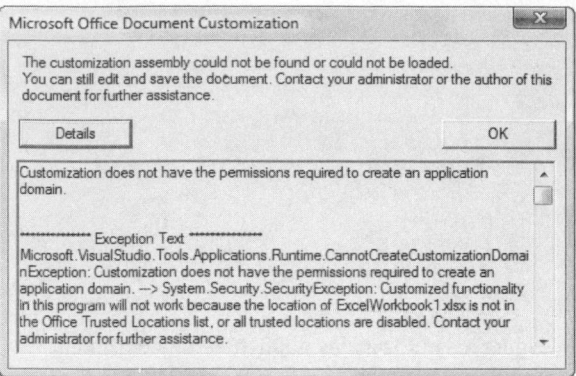

Figure 21-32: The customization assembly could not be loaded.

because the location of ExcelWorkbook1.xlsx is not in the Office Trusted Locations list."

Documents that are customized by VSTO which are opened from an intranet location must have that intranet location added to the Office Trusted Locations list to be allowed to run. Note that documents that are customized by VSTO which are opened from a local machine location like a local hard disk do *not* need to be added to the Office Trusted Locations list. To edit the Office Trusted Locations list in Excel, choose Office > Excel Options, click the Trust Center tab of the Excel Options dialog box, click the Trust Center Settings button, and then click the Trusted Locations tab. Figure 21-33 shows this tab.

To open your Excel workbook directly from an intranet URL, you must add that URL to the Office Trusted Locations list. To do this, first check the Allow Trusted Locations on My Network check box and click the Add New Location button. The dialog box shown in Figure 21-34 opens. In this dialog box, type the same URL you used for the Installation Folder URL setting in Visual Studio: http://ecarter-t61p/MyWorkbook. Also check the Subfolders of This Location Are Also Trusted check box. Then click the OK button.

Now when you open the URL http://ecarter-t61p/MyWorkbook/ ExceWorkbook1.xlsx, you get the prompt dialog box shown in Figure 21-35. The reason you get prompted is discussed in more detail in "ClickOnce

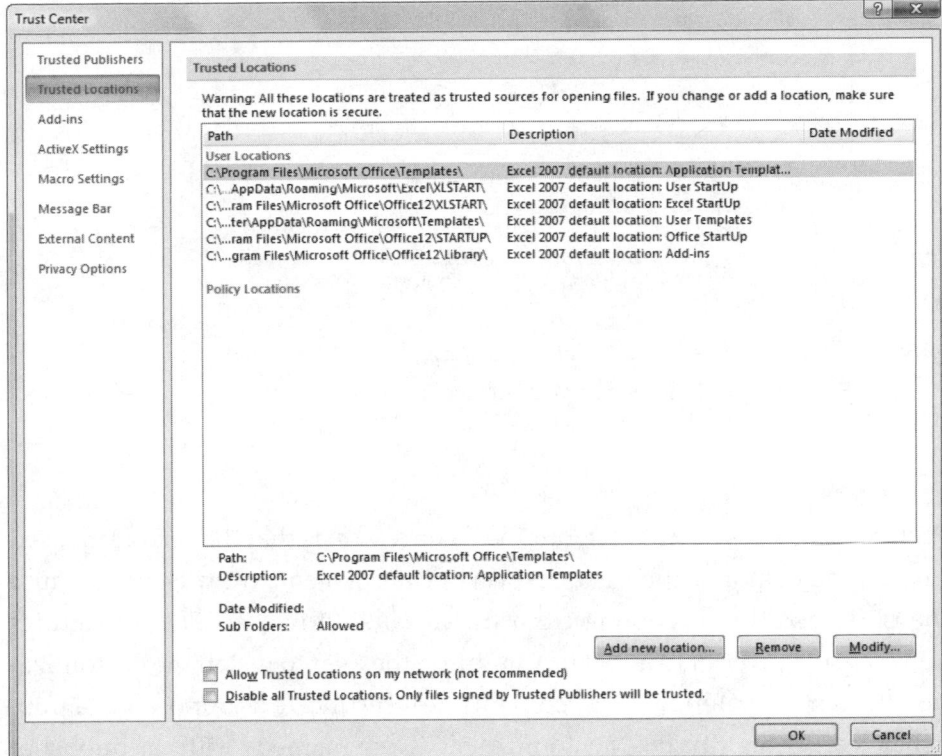

Figure 21-33: Trusted Locations tab.

Figure 21-34: Adding a trusted location.

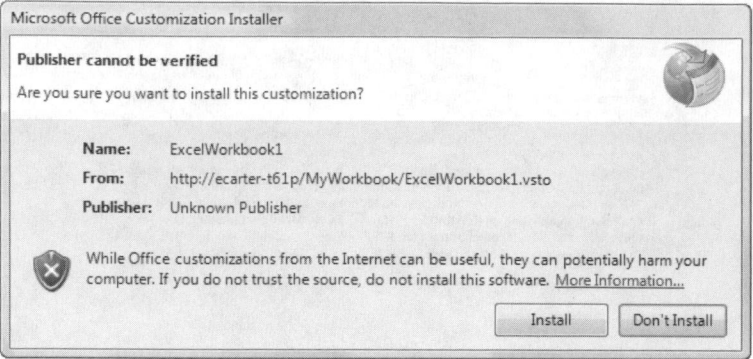

Figure 21-35: Trust prompt for a document customization.

Security" later in this chapter, but the basic reason is that the certificate used to sign the customization is a test certificate, which isn't trusted. Because the customization is coming from the intranet, however, default settings allow a trust prompt to appear, prompting the user to install the customization even if the solution is signed with a test certificate as opposed to a publisher certificate. If the customization were signed with a publisher certificate that was already added to the list of trusted certificates, no prompt would occur; the customization would just install and run.

▪▪ NOTE

If you have a problem at this stage getting the prompt dialog box in Figure 21-35, you may have a problem with MIME types. For more information, see "Deploying to a Web Site Other Than IIS 7" later in this chapter.

If you respond to the dialog box shown in Figure 21-35 by clicking the Install button, the customization installs (a progress dialog box appears while the customization is downloaded); then the document opens and the customization runs. No "successful install" dialog box is displayed, like the one in Figure 21-19 earlier in this chapter, because the fact that the document opened without an error dialog box is confirmation that the customization installed. When the document opens, the code you put in Sheet1_Startup runs, and a dialog box displaying the message *Version 1.0.0.0* is displayed.

Document Installation Aftermath

In this section, you look at what happened to your machine when you installed the customization for this document. First, because the user was prompted to trust the customization and chose to trust it, an entry was added to the inclusion list described earlier in this chapter. The inclusion list is also considered in more detail in the "Inclusion List" section later in this chapter.

Second, the assembly associated with the customization was installed in the ClickOnce cache. As discussed in "Installation: The Aftermath" earlier in this chapter, the ClickOnce cache is not intended to be something that you worry about; the location of the files is obfuscated, although you can work with any local files that were deployed with your customization by using the property DataDirectory of the System.Deployment.ApplicationDeployment class.

Finally, if you go to the Add or Remove Programs dialog box in Windows XP, or Programs and Features in Windows Vista, and click the Uninstall a Program link, you see that the ExcelWorkbook1 customization has been added to the list of installed programs, as shown in Figure 21-36. Later in this chapter we show you how to customize what is displayed here, including adding a support link.

What does it mean when you uninstall ExcelWorkbook1 from the installed programs? You uninstall the ExcelWorkbook1 customization

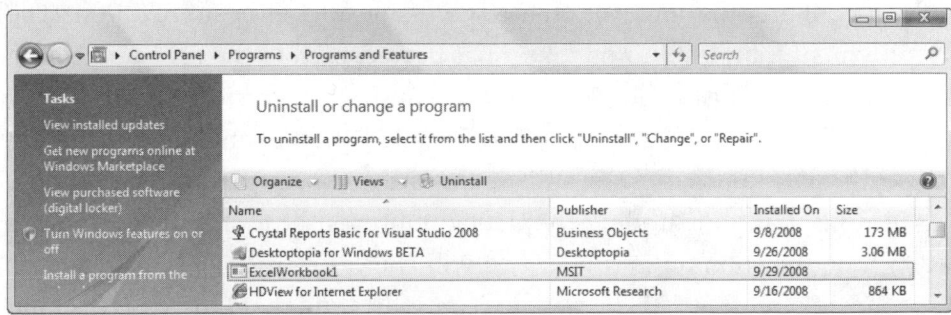

Figure 21-36: Excel Workbook1 added to programs and features.

from the ClickOnce cache and remove it from the list of installed programs. You don't remove any of the documents that may be on the machine that use the customization. In fact, as soon as the user opens one of those documents, Office will try to reinstall the customization, because the document still has an embedded link to the deployment manifest. We discuss later in this chapter how you can use ServerDocument to remove or modify the embedded link in documents.

It is also worth noting what is *not* installed when you install a document solution. Unlike the case with add-ins, no registry keys have to be added to the registry (except for the inclusion list) to tell Office that the document is customized; all the customization information is obtainable by the link embedded in the document. Second, as we have already noted, the setup doesn't really try to install the document itself anywhere; it is left to the user to manage where the document is copied to or run from. Finally, the setup does not edit the Office Trusted Locations list directly; this operation is left to users and administrators to manage if the document will reside in an intranet location.

Updating a Document Solution from a Web Server

Now create an update. Go back to Visual Studio, and edit the code in Sheet1_Startup so that it displays *Version 1.0.0.1* instead. Then go to the Publish Properties page of the Project properties. Assuming that the Automatically Increment Revision with Each Release check box is checked, the revision number should be 1. Click the Publish Now button. If you navigate to c:\inetpub\wwwroot\MyWorkbook, you find a second folder in the Application Files directory, called ExcelWorkbook1_1_0_0_1. This folder contains the files for the new version of the customization. The deployment manifest in this folder has been copied to the root publishing folder to overwrite the old deployment manifest for version 1.0.0.0.

Switch back to the machine you installed the document solution on, close the workbook if it is still open, and then reopen the workbook. Assuming that your update-frequency option is set to check for updates each time the solution is run, Office will check for updates. A dialog box like the one in Figure 21-26 may appear, indicating that Office is checking for updates; this dialog box appears only if the check for updates takes longer than a few seconds. Then, if an update is found, it is downloaded, and if the download takes long enough, the dialog box shown in Figure 21-37 opens. In this example, a large file is embedded in the assembly associated with the workbook to force this dialog box to appear; often, updates are quick enough that neither dialog box appears. If the user cancels the update, the old version of the document customization will load and the document will be updated the next time Office checks for updates.

One important thing to note about updates is that they update only the customization associated with the document; they don't update the document itself. You need to be very careful about updates and make sure that you don't create an update that would break in older versions of your document. Suppose that in the first release of your workbook customization, you had a named range called Range1 in the workbook and code in

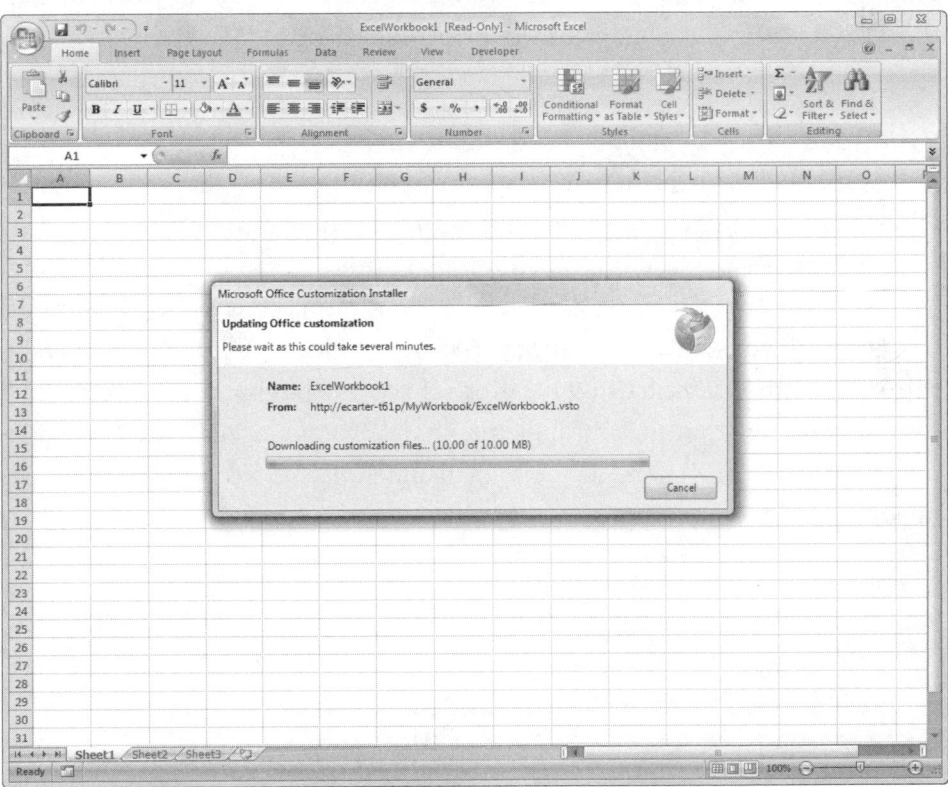

Figure 21-37: Updating Office Customization dialog box.

Sheet1_Startup that set the value of Range1. Then, in the second version of your workbook customization, you edited the workbook to create a second named range called Range2 and edited the code in Sheet1_Startup to set the value of Range2. The problem is that your users who have the old version of the workbook have only a named range called Range1. When they get the update, the workbook won't be updated (so no new named range called Range2 will be added to their workbook), but the code associated with the older workbook will be updated, and when the new Sheet1_Startup runs and tries to set the value of Range2, it will fail.

You can employ some strategies to update old workbooks programmatically. Because you know that your second version needs a second range called Range2, you could rewrite Sheet1_Startup so that it first ensures that a named range called Range2 is created in the workbook, if it doesn't exist yet. You can also use dynamically added view controls and managed controls rather than add new statically created view controls, as these controls won't be hooked up if the older document is used.

Variations on the Deploying Documents Theme

In this section, we consider some other possible scenarios that you may use when deploying document customizations. In this example, you deployed to an intranet Web server. You could also deploy to an intranet file share, as described in "Deploying Add-Ins" earlier in this chapter. The main difference with add-in deployment to an intranet file share is that you have to think about the Office trusted locations if you are having users open a document directly from the intranet file share. If your users copy the document from the file share to their local machine, no additional steps are needed.

> **■ NOTE**
>
> Office trusted locations can be rolled out by your enterprise with group policy, so you may want to use this approach when publishing to intranet sites.

In this example, you deployed to an intranet Web server, but you could also deploy to an Internet web server. To get that method to work, you would need to have a publisher certificate to sign your document customization with, as the ClickOnce security settings require an publisher signature before a user is prompted to install a customization from the internet zone. Also, Office trusted location rules do not allow you to trust a document that is opened directly from an Internet location, so you would have to copy the document from the Internet location to an Office trusted location on the intranet or the user's local machine to get the customization to run.

You could also deploy your document customization via a CD or USB key. When you deploy a customization this way, ClickOnce does not support updates. So you must pick a local path on your machine as the publishing folder location and leave the Installation Folder URL text box blank. Then you can copy the files out of your root publishing folder location to a USB key or CD.

Another scenario that is of interest is deploying your customized document to a SharePoint server. We describe strategies for deploying documents to SharePoint in "Deploying to SharePoint" later in this chapter.

Finally, you may decide not to use ClickOnce directly and instead deploy your customization via a custom MSI-based installer. Although this topic is not covered in this book, we provide a link to a white paper that describes this approach in the note "Creating a Custom Window Installer Setup" at the start of this chapter.

ClickOnce Security

In this section we consider ClickOnce security in more detail. First, we look at some key concepts of ClickOnce security that you need to understand. Then we examine the checks that Office goes through to determine whether to allow a customization to be installed and run.

Certificates

A VSTO deployment manifest must be signed by a certificate. As we have explained, two types of certificates can be used. The first kind of certificate is called a test certificate or a self-cert. When you create a VSTO add-in or document solution, a test certificate is created for your project automatically. As shown in Figure 21-38, the certificate has the same name as the project with _TemporaryKey.pfx appended.

The test certificate that VSTO creates for you is configured to sign the deployment manifest each time you publish. To see how this is configured, right-click the Project node in the Solution Explorer and choose Properties from the context menu. Click Signing to display the Signing page, shown in Figure 21-39. The Sign the ClickOnce Manifests check box is checked. In VSTO, ClickOnce manifests must always be signed; only Windows Forms applications support an option to have unsigned manifests.

The Signing page shows information about the test certificate that was created for you. If you want to use a different certificate, click the Select from Store or Select from File button to select it. You can also create a new test certificate by clicking the Create Test Certificate button. One reason you may need to create a new test certificate is when an existing certificate expires in an old project. The test certificate created for you by VSTO expires one year after it is created, so if you have a project that you have kept around for more than a year since creation, you need a new test certificate to continue building the project.

If you click the More Details button, you see something like Figure 21-40. This window shows additional information about the certificate. As you can see, the Issued To and Issued By fields are the same—hence, the name self-cert.

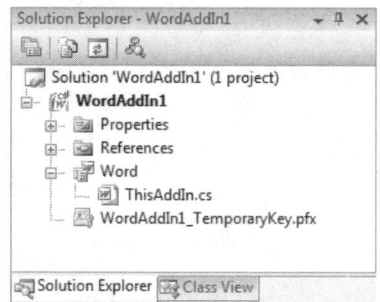

Figure 21-38: The test certificate created
in your project automatically by VSTO.

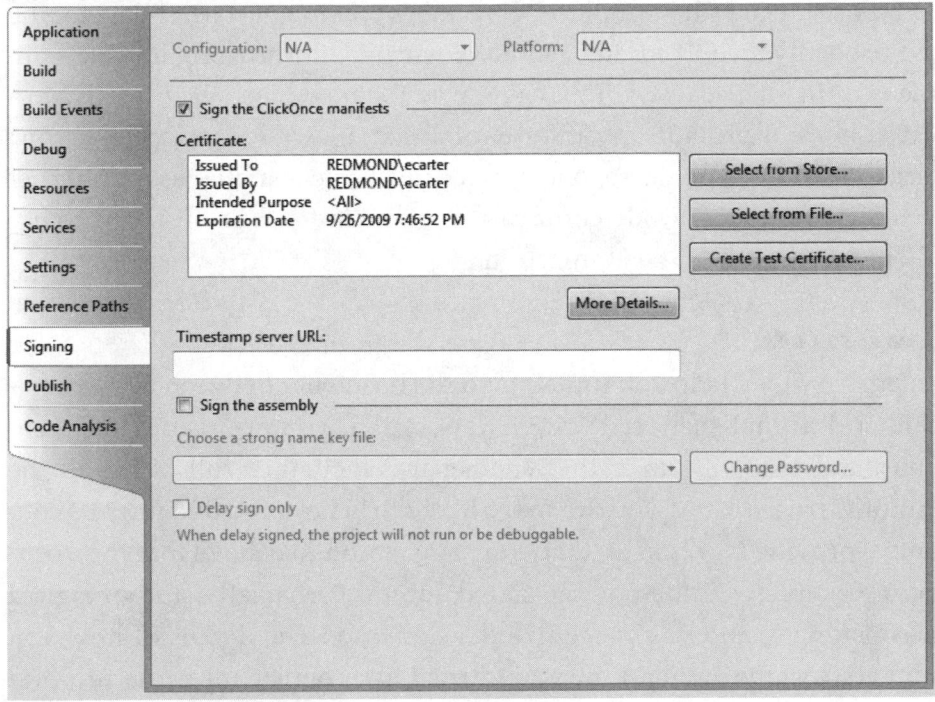

Figure 21-39: The Signing page.

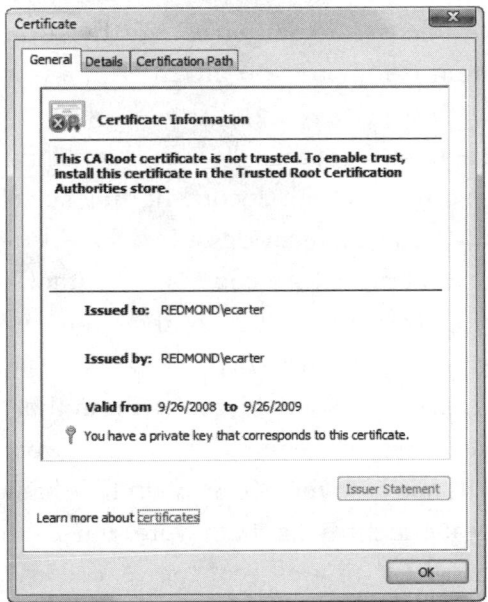

Figure 21-40: Certificate information.

Test certificates have a place; they allow you to get started developing and probably are OK for intranet deployments. But trusting a test certificate is difficult, because you have no way to know whether it is trustworthy. It doesn't provide any information that allows you to make a trust decision. That's why the second type of certificate—known as a publisher certificate or authenticode certificate—is the kind you really want to use when signing a VSTO customization.

License to Code

An analogy may help you understand the difference between a test certificate and a publisher certificate. Suppose that you are reading a document, and you want to know whether it is factual or full of lies. If the author is trustworthy, you are more likely to believe the document's contents—provided, of course, that you have reason to believe that the document was in fact written by the stated author. Perhaps the author signed the document, and you recognize the signature. The details of how you came to trust the author, how you learned to recognize the signature, and so on are left up to you.

Now suppose that you have the signed document, and you trust the author, but you do not know what the author's signature looks like. Therefore, you cannot tell whether this document is actually trustworthy; anyone could have signed it. This situation is the one you are in with a test certificate.

But if you also have a notarized statement from the editor-in-chief of the Encarta encyclopedia attesting to the accuracy of the document, that statement may be enough. The notarized, dated statement describes the document in question, identifies the author, and provides a copy of the author's signature for comparison. You do recognize the signature of the editor-in-chief and trust her to put her imprimatur only on trustworthy authors.

That's what a publisher certificate is like: It not only identifies the author, but also names a trusted authority who attests to the identity and trustworthiness of the author. It indicates details such as who everyone in the chain of trust is and when the various certificates identifying them were signed.

We use certificate-based evidence all the time in real life. A driver's license identifies the bearer by providing a description (name, age, height, weight, eye color, hair color), a photograph, and a signature. It also attests that the individual thereby identified has passed a driving test. To be useful as evidence, the description must match the bearer, and it must actually have been issued by the department of motor vehicles. Furthermore, it is valid only for a certain period, so out-of-date licenses become invalid.

Various organizations that need to determine the trustworthiness of individuals about whom they know nothing use certificate-based evidence in their policies. If you are trying to get into a bar, any state-issued evidence that indicates your age probably is good enough. If you are trying to rent a car, odds are pretty good that you will need a driver's license, as further evidence that you passed a driving test at some point. But either way, organizations are leveraging their trust of one entity—the state—to obtain evidence about the identity and trustworthiness of an unknown individual.

Publisher certificates are essentially licenses to write code, not to drive. A publisher certificate identifies a particular author and also identifies the certifying authority (CA), which vouches for the identity and trustworthiness of the author.

Trusting the CA to make decisions for you, of course, once more trades convenience for risk. The CA may choose poorly or fail to exercise due diligence in vetting its authors. Also, you may not agree with the criteria that the CA uses to decide who is trustworthy. In such cases, do not trust the CA! You would not rent a car to a driver who presented a driver's license from Bob's Discount Driver's License Emporium, so trust only certifying authorities that you believe give certificates to trustworthy people.

Code-signing certificates, like drivers' licenses, expire after a certain date, and, like driver's licenses, they can be revoked by the CA due to bad behavior. Certifying authorities publish lists of revoked certificates; individuals can configure their computers to download recent changes to the revocation lists automatically so that they are less likely to be fooled by untrustworthy individuals who managed to obtain a certificate.

Obtaining a Publisher Certificate
Suppose you decide that your customizations should be signed by a publisher certificate. Where you get your publisher certificate depends on how

your customers' policies are likely to be configured. Obtaining a certificate from a CA that your customers do not trust makes it unlikely that the administrators will actually grant full trust to your customization assembly. If you plan on distributing a customization widely to the public, you might consider getting a code-signing certificate from a widely trusted CA, such as VeriSign, GlobalSign, or thawte.

On the other hand, if you are creating a customization to be rolled out inside an enterprise, you can be your own CA by installing Microsoft Certificate Server and issuing your own code-signing certificates to your signing authority. After you have a code-signing certificate from your CA, you can use the certmgr.exe utility to manage your certificates. Then you can use the Select from Store or Select From File button in the Signing page of the project properties to use the publisher certificate.

Signing a Deployment Manifest with a Publisher Certificate

Most likely, you will not have direct access to a publisher certificate or will not have permission to sign by using your organization's publisher certificate. In this case, you should still use your test certificate to do the initial signing, but someone else with access to your organization's publisher certificate will have to resign the deployment manifest. Signing can be done by that someone else with a tool called Mage. Mage is part of the .NET SDK, and the easiest way to run it on your machine is to launch the Visual Studio 2008 Command Prompt (located in the Tools folder inside the Microsoft Visual Studio 2008 folder created in the Start menu). From the command prompt, you can type **mage.exe** to run the Mage command-line tool. Alternatively, you can launch a UI-based tool by typing **mageui.exe**. Although both a command-line tool called mage.exe and the graphical tool called mageui.exe are available, for the purpose of this discussion, we refer to the tool just as Mage.

Before you use Mage to sign the deploy manifest, open the deploy manifest in a text editor like Notepad; look for the block of text that starts with <publisheridentity and ends with "/>; and remove it (in other words, remove the publisheridentity element from the XML). You need to do this to work around a bug in mageui.exe.

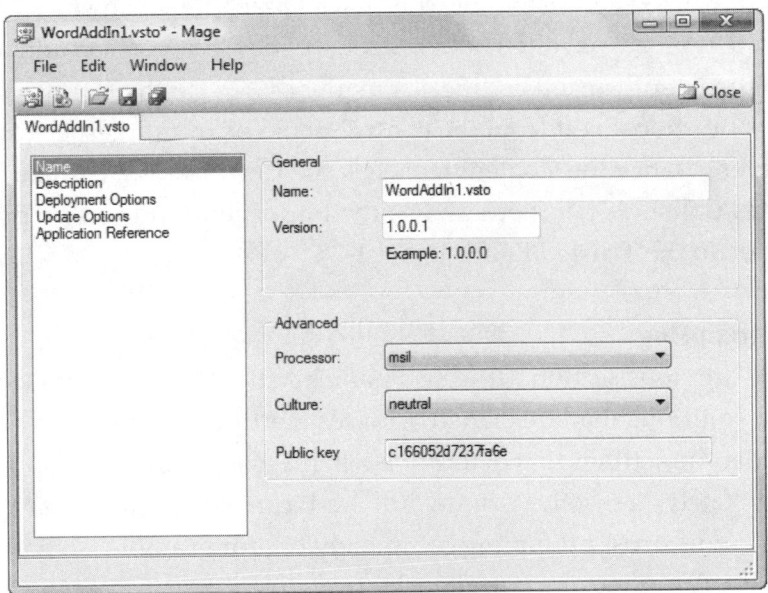

Then launch Mage, and open the deploy manifest you want to sign by choosing File > Open. The default filter for Mage's Open dialog box does not show .vsto files, so drop down the filter combo box and choose All Files *.* as the filter. Browse to the .vsto file you want to sign, select it, and click the Open button. The .VSTO file you will want to sign is the one in the latest version-specific folder (such as Application Files\SomeVSTO-Solution_1_0_0_1). Mage will then display the XML-based manifest in a friendly editable view, as shown in Figure 21-41.

Mage gives you some options for editing the manifest. As you will see in "Advanced Topic: Editing Manifests Using Mage" later in this chapter, you can use Mage to change things like the name of the product and publisher. For now, you are interested in signing. Mage signs the manifest when you save it. To set the certificate that is used to sign the manifest, choose File > Preferences. In the Preferences dialog box, check the Sign on Save and Use Default Signing Certificate check boxes, as shown in Figure 21-42. Then click the ellipsis (…) button to browse to the .pfx file for your certificate. When you save the manifest by clicking the Save button, the manifest will be

Figure 21-41: Opening a VSTO manifest in Mage.

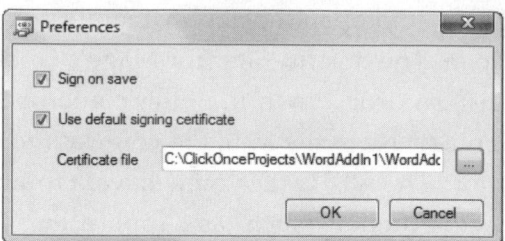

Figure 21-42: Setting up Sign on Save in the Preferences dialog box of Mage.

signed with the certificate you specified. After you save, be sure to copy that .VSTO file back to the root publishing folder (the parent directory of the Application Files folder).

Trusting a Publisher Certificate

Now that you are signing with a real publisher certificate, your user will get a better trust prompt, displaying information that the publisher can be verified. But it would be even better if your users didn't see the trust prompt at all. To arrange that, you must add your publisher certificate to the list of trusted certificates on your user's machine. In an enterprise, this certificate typically is rolled out via group policy, but you can add a certificate to the list of trusted certificates manually. To do this, launch Internet Options by choosing it from the control panel or from Internet Explorer's Tools menu. Click the Content tab; click the Certificates tab; then click the Trusted Publishers tab. You can use the Import button to add a publisher certificate to the Trusted Publishers list.

Trust Prompting

Lest the previous section made you panicky about how easy it is for users to trust solutions that are signed with test certificates, you'll be happy to know that the settings that determine when a trust prompt is displayed are actually fairly restrictive by default and can be customized. You can choose to turn trust prompting completely off, for example.

Trust prompting is controlled by zone. The five zones are Internet, Untrusted Sites, My Computer, Local Intranet, and Trusted Sites. You can see which sites are included in these groups by checking the Security tab of the Internet Options dialog box. My Computer is not listed there but includes any local drives on your computer.

The default settings for trust prompting are shown in Table 21-2. The Zone and Setting column headers in Table 21-2 correspond to string sub-keys and values that can be set in the registry. For any zone, you can change the registry settings to disallow trust prompting, allow trust prompting only when the solution is signed by a publisher certificate, or allow trust prompting for publisher or test certificates.

To modify the inclusion list settings, you must create registry keys. Launch regedit, and navigate to the following registry key or create it if it doesn't already exist. Typically, the key will not be there; you must create it to customize the behavior of prompting.

```
\HKEY_LOCAL_MACHINE\SOFTWARE\MICROSOFT\.NETFramework\
   Security\TrustManager\PromptingLevel
```

Under that key, ensure that you find string value subkeys named Internet, UntrustedSites, MyComputer, LocalIntranet, and TrustedSites. Set the string values of these keys to AuthenticodeRequired, Disabled, Enabled, Enabled, and Enabled. The resulting registry is shown in Figure 21-43.

Now you have the registry keys created to control the behavior of prompting. If you want to turn off prompting altogether, just set all the values of the String Value subkeys to Disabled. If you want prompting, but only for publisher certificates, change any Enabled values to Authenticode-Required.

TABLE 21-2: Default Inclusion List Settings

Zone	Setting
Internet	Authenticode (prompt only for a publisher certificate; don't prompt for a test certificate)
UntrustedSites	Disabled (never prompt)
MyComputer	Enabled (prompt for any kind of certificate)
LocalIntranet	Enabled (prompt for any kind of certificate)
TrustedSites	Enabled (prompt for any kind of certificate)

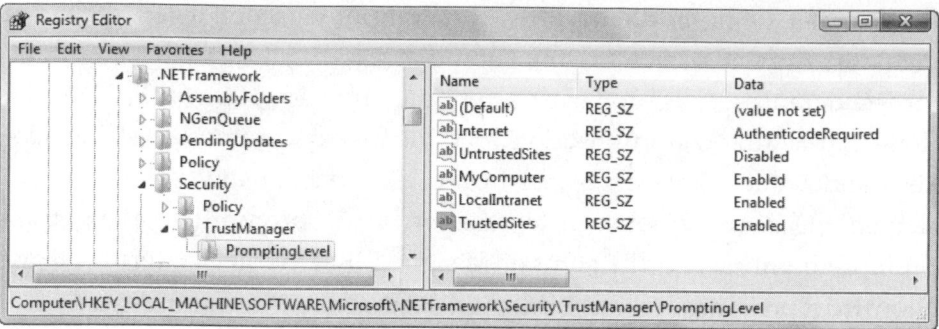

Figure 21-43: Prompting level settings in the registry.

Office Trusted Locations

We discussed the Office Trusted Locations list in some detail in "Deploying Document Solutions" earlier in this chapter. The user can edit this list by choosing Office > [current application] Options, clicking the Trust Center page, clicking the Trust Center Settings button, and then clicking the Trusted Locations page. The Trusted Locations page is shown in Figure 21-33 earlier in this chapter.

To add intranet locations to the Office Trusted Locations list, you must check the check box Allow Trusted Locations on My Network. The Add New Location button is used to add new locations to the list. You can specify an http:// path only if it points to a server that supports Web Distributed Authoring and Versioning (WebDAV) or FrontPage Server Extensions Remote Procedure Call (FPRPC). An http:// path to a SharePoint document library would meet these requirements. When a new location is added, also be sure to check the Subfolders of This Location Are Also Trusted check box if you plan to add more deployments to this location.

Office trusted locations can also be modified by group policy, which is probably the best approach to use if you are distributing Office solutions in an enterprise.

Inclusion List

When a user makes a trust decision due to a prompt, that trust decision must be recorded. It is recorded in the registry under the key HKEY_CURRENT_USER\Software\Microsoft\VSTO\Security\Inclusion. For each solution that is trusted, a key with a GUID identifier is created under the Inclusion key—also known as an inclusion list entry. An inclusion list entry includes the PublicKey for the solution and the URL to the deployment manifest for the solution. The PublicKey corresponds to the RSAKeyValue element in the VSTO deployment manifest file.

The inclusion list can be edited programmatically by using the AddInEntrySecurity class in the Microsoft.VisualStudio.Tools.Office.Runtime .Security namespace. This class is contained in the Microsoft.VisualStudio .Tools.Office.Runtime.v9.0 assembly. For more information on editing the inclusion list programmatically, see http://msdn.microsoft.com/en-us/ library/bb398239.aspx.

Security Checks

Now that you have a background in certificates, trusted locations, inclusion lists, and trust prompting, you're ready to put it all together and walk through the specific security checks that are made when a solution is installed or run. Eight checks are evaluated in the order listed in the following sections.

Check 1: Is the Document on the Local Machine or in a Trusted Location?

This step applies only to document solutions. Office requires that the document associated with a VSTO customization be opened from the local machine or a trusted location. In the previous section, we walked through how to add a trusted intranet location to the list of trusted locations for Excel. If the document is not on the local machine or a trusted location, the document will open, but an error dialog box will appear, indicating that the customization could not be loaded.

Check 2: Is the Deployment Manifest Requesting Full Trust?

As anyone who has ever been infected by a Word or Excel macro virus knows, the code behind a customized document does not always do what you want, and you do not always know what it does. Fortunately, that scenario is exactly what code-access security systems were invented to handle. A problem exists with code-access security in Office customizations, however: You have no way to partially trust any code that accesses the Office object models. Trust is all or nothing for Office development.

The Internet Explorer object model was specifically designed from Day One so that code running inside the Web browser was in a "sandbox." Code can run, but it is heavily restricted. The browser's objects inherently cannot do dangerous things such as write an arbitrary file or change your registry settings. Code is partially trusted: trusted enough to run but not trusted enough to do anything particularly dangerous. The Office object models, by contrast, are inherently powerful. They manipulate potentially sensitive data loaded from and saved to arbitrary files. These object models were designed to be called only by fully trusted code. Therefore, the deployment manifest for a VSTO customization must request full trust to run at all.

Check 3: Is the Deployment Manifest Signed with a Certificate in the Untrusted Publishers List?

If the deployment manifest has been signed with a certificate that has been added to the untrusted publishers list, the solution will not install or run. To see the untrusted publisher list on your machine, launch Internet Options from the Control Panel or from Internet Explorer's Tools menu. Click the Content tab. Then click the Certificates button to bring up the Certificates dialog box. Finally, click the Untrusted Publishers tab, shown in Figure 21-44. This list contains certificates that have been compromised or are fraudulent and that are specifically blocked.

Check 4: Is the Certificate in the Trusted Publishers List?

If the deployment manifest has been signed with a certificate that has been added to the trusted publishers list, the solution will automatically install and run without prompting the user for permission. To see the trusted publisher list on your machine, click the Trusted Publishers tab in the Certificates dialog box shown in Figure 21-44.

Check 5: Is the Deployment Manifest Coming from Internet Explorer's Restricted Zone?

If the deployment manifest is coming from a location that has been added to Internet Explorer's restricted zone, the solution will not install or run. To see the locations in the restricted zone, launch the Internet Options dialog

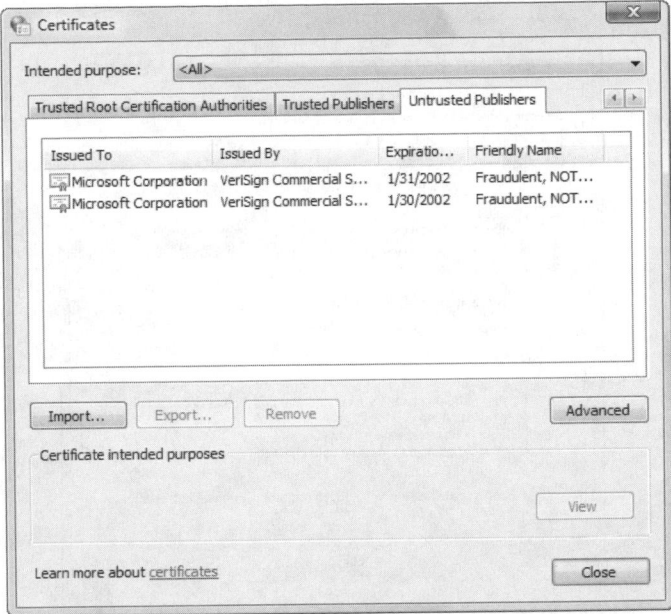

Figure 21-44: Untrusted publishers in the Certificates dialog box.

box; click the Security tab; click the Restricted sites icon; and click the Sites button, shown in Figure 21-45. If you click the Sites button, you can add and remove sites from the Restricted Sites zone, as shown in Figure 21-46.

Check 6: Is Trust Prompting Permitted?

Next, the trust prompting settings described in "Trust Prompting" earlier in this chapter are checked to see whether a trust prompt can be displayed and whether inclusion lists can be used. The defaults for these settings are described earlier in this chapter. If trust prompting is not permitted, the solution will not install or run.

Check 7: Is the Solution Already in the Inclusion List?

Next, the security system checks the public key and location of the deployment manifest and compares this information with the inclusion list. If the public key and deployment manifest location are already in an entry in the inclusion list, the solution is installed and run. The entry may be in the inclusion list if this solution has been installed previously and the user clicked

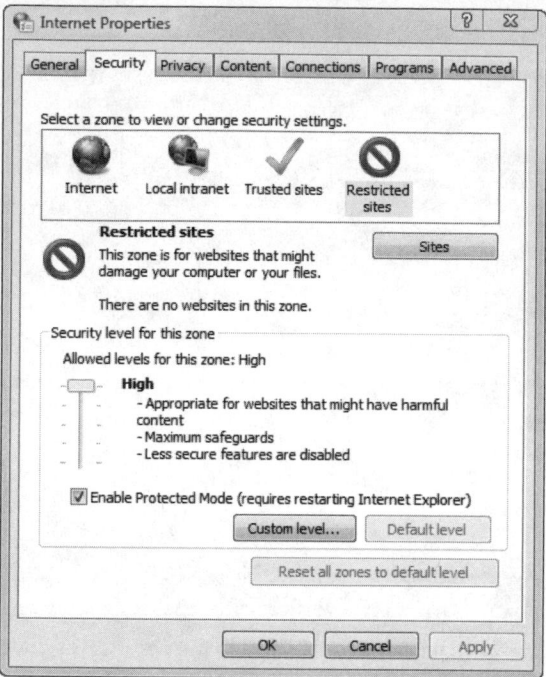

Figure 21-45: The Restricted Sites zone in the
Internet Options dialog box.

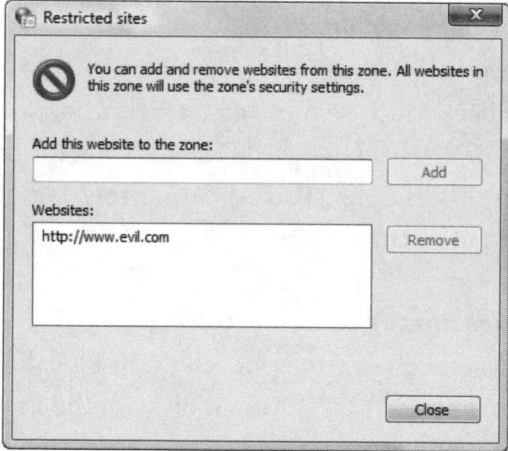

Figure 21-46: Editing restricted sites.

Install for a trust prompt, or if a custom program or installer modified the inclusion list before launching the ClickOnce install. The inclusion list is described in the section "Inclusion List" earlier in this chapter.

Check 8: When the Trust Prompt Is Shown, Does the User Click Install?

If you've gotten this far, you have had no reasons yet to trust the solution, but you also didn't get any No answers that prohibited you from showing a trust prompt. So if you get this far, a trust prompt is displayed, and the user gets to make a trust decision. If the user clicks Yes, an entry is added to the inclusion list, and the solution is installed and run.

Other Deployment Scenarios

In this section we consider several additional deployment scenarios that you may want to support, including deploying to a Web site that isn't backed by IIS 7, deploying to a CD or USB key, deploying to a SharePoint site, and creating custom Windows Installer setups.

Deploying to a Web Site Other Than IIS 7

We covered deploying to a Web site in "Deploying Document Solutions" earlier in this chapter. We should mention one additional gotcha: If you want your users to install from a .VSTO file on a Web site, you must make sure that a MIME type for the .VSTO extension is configured for the Web server. In the latest versions of IIS and Visual Studio 2008 SP1, the MIME type is already set up properly, but earlier versions of IIS may not have the proper MIME handler for the .VSTO file. To configure the server properly, the .VSTO extension should be associated with the MIME type "application/x-ms-vsto".

Deploying to a CD or USB Key

You can create a deployment to go on a CD or USB key, but you cannot have live updates. You could deploy from a CD or USB key, for example, but you cannot have the installed application check an online deployment manifest like http://mycompany.com/addin/myaddin.vsto. To deploy to a CD or USB key, simply set the publishing folder to a local directory on your development machine—something like c:\ClickOnceTemp\MyAddIn. Then make sure that the Installation Folder URL text box is left blank. After you publish to the publishing folder, copy all the files in the publishing folder to your USB key or CD.

Deploying to SharePoint

You have no way to deploy a VSTO solution—that is, all the files and folders that get created in your root publishing folder—to a SharePoint library. The best way to get around this limitation is to publish to an intranet location that is available to your users and then upload the document in the root publishing folder to the SharePoint document library. The users of the SharePoint document library will have to have read access to the intranet location, whether that be a share or a Web server. They also will have to add the path to the SharePoint document library to the Office Trusted Locations list.

If you use a VSTO customized document as a content type template for a document library, you have to add the path to the content type as an Office trusted location as well, because the user will first open the template and then save to the document library.

Custom Windows Installer Setups

You can create custom Windows Installer setups to install your VSTO add-in or document solution. This topic is beyond the scope of this book, however. For more information on creating a custom setup, see the white paper provided by the VSTO team. Part I of the white paper is at http://msdn .microsoft.com/en-us/library/cc563937.aspx, and Part II is at http://msdn .microsoft.com/en-us/library/cc616991.aspx.

Advanced Topic: Editing Manifests Using Mage

As we mentioned earlier in this chapter, at times you have to use the Mage tool to work with the ClickOnce manifest—to re-sign a deploy manifest with a publisher key, for example. Also, some advanced tasks such as setting the product name, publisher name, and support URL for an install can be accomplished only with the Mage tool.

Setting the Product Name, Publisher Name, and Support URL with Mage

Before using the Mage tool, you need to have published your solution. You will be opening the .VSTO file that was published from the latest version-specific folder in the Application Files folder in the root publishing folder. So if your solution is called SomeVSTOSolution, you are on your second version (1.0.0.1), and the root publishing folder is c:\temp, you will be opening the file c:\temp\Application Files\SomeVSTOSolution_1_0_0_1\ SomeVSTOSolution.vsto. After you've edited the manifest and re-signed it, you copy the new .vsto file back to the root publishing folder (c:\temp) and overwrite the old SomeVSTOSolution.vsto file.

To run Mage, launch the Visual Studio 2008 command prompt (located in the Tools folder inside the Microsoft Visual Studio 2008 folder created in the Start menu). At the command prompt, you can type **mageui.exe** to run the UI tool. In Mage, choose File > Open. The default filter for Mage's Open dialog box does not show .vsto files, so drop down the filter combo box and choose All Files *.* as the filter. Then browse to the .vsto file you want to edit, click it, and click the Open button. The .VSTO file you will want to sign is the one in the latest version-specific folder (such as Application Files\SomeVSTOSolution_1_0_0_1).

After you open the .VSTO deployment manifest, click the Description entry in the list box on the left side of the Mage window. You see Publisher, Product, and Support text boxes, as shown in Figure 21-47. The Publisher setting shown in Figure 21-47 is not to be confused with the publisher certificate. In the ClickOnce setup dialog boxes, information about the publisher is determined by looking at the publisher certificate or test certificate, not from the Publisher setting you see in Figure 21-47. Where Publisher and Product Name *do* appear is in the Add or Remove Programs dialog box.

The support URL is used in the trust prompt dialog box that appears when the user is prompted to install a customization, as shown in Figure 21-48. When the support URL is set, the name of the solution becomes a hyperlink; if the user clicks that link, the support URL launches. Figure 21-48 also illustrates the point that Publisher in this dialog box refers to the certificate used. Because you signed with a test certificate in this example, the publisher is Unknown Publisher, even though you edited the Publisher setting in the deployment manifest.

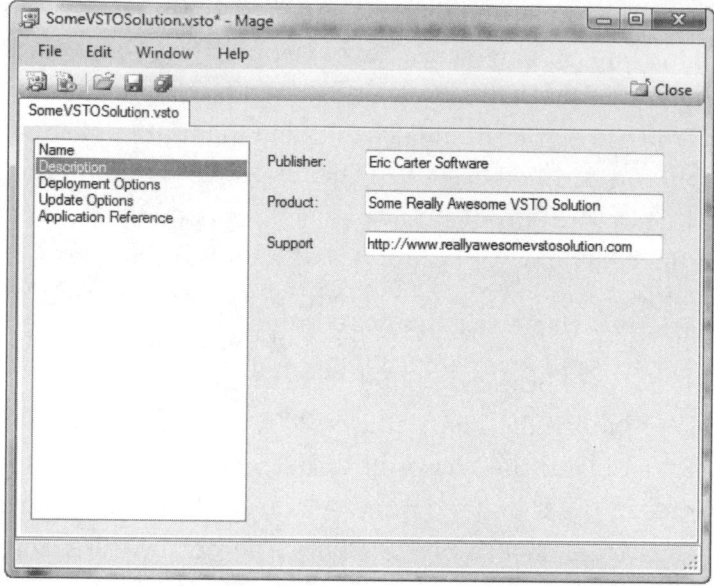

Figure 21-47: Using Mage to edit the publisher, product, and support URL.

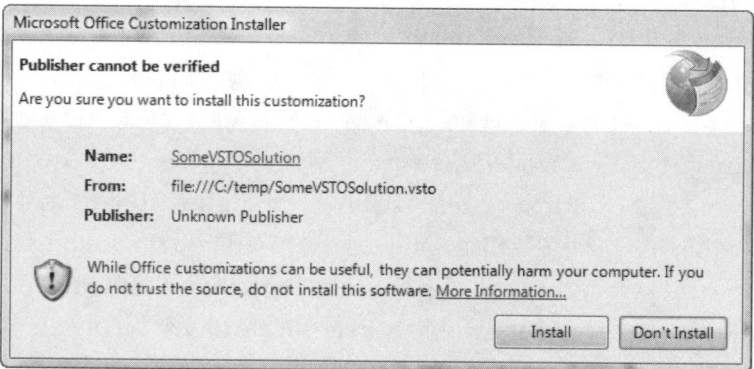

Figure 21-48: With the support URL set, the name of the solution is hyperlinked to the support URL.

Mage needs to sign the manifest when you save it, otherwise your modified deployment manifest won't work. To set the certificate that is used to sign the manifest, choose File > Preferences. In the Preferences dialog box, check the Sign on Save and Use Default Signing Certificate check boxes. Then click the ellipsis (...) button to browse to the .pfx file for your certificate. If you just want to use the test certificate created for you by

VSTO, browse to the same folder where your solution project is, and use the file with the .pfx file extension—in this example, SomeVSTOSolution_ TemporaryKey.pfx. When you save the manifest by clicking the Save button, the manifest is signed with the certificate you specified. After you save, be sure to copy that .VSTO file back to the root publishing folder (the parent directory of the Application Files folder).

Setting the Friendly Name and the Description

Two other properties in the manifest that you may want to change are the friendly name and description of the add-in. The friendly name is used in the trust prompt dialog box shown in Figure 21-48 and is also used in Office add-in management dialog boxes. The description is displayed in the Office add-in management dialog boxes.

To set the friendly name and description, you must edit both the deployment manifest and a second manifest called the application manifest. The application manifest is stored in the version-specific folder and has the extension .dll.manifest. For this example, you will open the application manifest file c:\temp\Application Files\SomeVSTOSolution_1_0_ 0_1\SomeVSTOSolution.dll.manifest.

The complete operation is a three-step process:

1. Open the application manifest (.dll.manifest) file, using a text editor like Notepad, and set the friendlyName and description elements inside the file to the desired values.

2. Open the modified application manifest file with Mage, and save it to re-sign it.

3. Open the deployment manifest (.VSTO) file in the root application folder, update the application references settings, and then save the file to re-sign it as well.

Start by opening the application manifest file in the version-specific folder with Notepad. The .dll.manifest file you want to edit is the one in the latest version-specific folder (such as Application Files\SomeVSTO-Solution_1_0_0_1). Inside the application manifest file, find the XML element <vstov3:friendlyName>. Inside this element is the current friendly name. Edit the contents of this element to have a new friendly name. Right next to the friendly-name element is the description element: <vstov3:description>. Edit the contents of this element with the description you want to use; then save the application manifest file.

Next, launch Mage and choose File > Open. The default filter for Mage's Open dialog box does not show .dll.manifest files, so drop down the filter combo box and choose All Files *.* as the filter. Then browse to the .dll.manifest file you just edited in Notepad, click it, and click the Open button. After you've opened the application manifest, make sure that Mage is set to use the certificate you want to use to sign the manifest. To do this, choose File > Preferences. In the Preferences dialog box, check the Sign on Save and Use Default Signing Certificate check boxes. Then click the ellipsis (…) button to browse to the .pfx file for your certificate. If you just want to use the test certificate created for you by VSTO, browse to the same folder where your solution project is, and use the file with the .pfx file extension—for this example, SomeVSTOSolution_TemporaryKey.pfx. Save the manifest by clicking the Save button, and the manifest is signed with the certificate you specified.

Now that the application manifest has a new friendly name and description and has been signed, you need to use Mage to open the deployment manifest .VSTO file in the root publishing folder and update the reference from the deployment manifest to the newly updated application manifest. Open the deployment manifest, and click the Application References element in the list box on the left side of the Mage window. Click the Select Manifest button, browse to the application manifest you just edited and signed, and then save the deployment manifest. This procedure updates and re-signs the deployment manifest to point to the updated application manifest file.

After you save, be sure to copy the updated .VSTO file back to the version-specific folder to which it corresponds, in case you need to roll back in the future.

Delay Signing

If you are delay signing your VSTO customization binaries and then doing a real sign prior to release, you must follow similar steps to those outlined in the previous section "Setting the Friendly Name and the Description." After you have generated fully signed binaries, overwrite your delay signed binaries in your version-specific folder with the fully signed binaries. Then follow steps 2 and 3 in the previous section to re-sign the application manifest file and re-sign the deployment manifest file.

Conclusion

In this chapter, we considered ClickOnce setup support, which is new in VSTO 2008. ClickOnce allows you to build installers easily for VSTO add-in projects and VSTO document projects. You can distribute your setups via the intranet, via a CD or USB key, and via the Internet. The setup.exe application created by VSTO for your project can install all the prerequisites needed for the solution to work (except for Office 2007).

We also looked at security for VSTO solutions and discussed certificates, trust prompting, trusted document locations, and inclusion lists. Finally, we considered some advanced deployment scenarios, including deploying to SharePoint and working with additional files that are part of your ClickOnce deployment.

This chapter brings us to the end of the journey of describing the power of using VSTO 2008 and Office 2007 to create exciting solutions for your customers. We are continuing to improve VSTO, and we're excited about what future versions of Office and VSTO will bring to the Office developer community.

Participate in the discussion by visiting the .NET4Office blog at http://blogs.msdn.com/eric_carter. Here, you will find new postings on the latest developments in the VSTO and Office developer community, as well as a way to contact the authors to provide your feedback on the book and everything Office and VSTO.

We hope that you have as much fun using VSTO as we had helping create it.

Bibliography

Data Programming

Homer, Alex, Dave Sussman, and Mark Fussell. *A First Look at ADO.NET and System.Xml v. 2.0.* Boston: Addison-Wesley, 2004.

Wildermuth, Shawn. *Pragmatic ADO.NET.* Boston: Addison-Wesley, 2003.

Windows Forms and WPF Programming

Nathan, Adam. *Windows Presentation Foundation Unleashed.* Indianapolis: Sams Publishing, 2007.

Sells, Chris. *Windows Forms Programming in C#.* Boston: Addison-Wesley, 2004.

Sells, Chris, and Justin Gehtland. *Windows Forms Programming in Visual Basic .NET.* Boston: Addison-Wesley, 2004.

Infrastructure

Box, Don, Aaron Skonnard, and John Lam. *Essential XML: Beyond Markup.* Boston: Addison-Wesley, 2000.

Hejlsberg, Anders, Scott Wiltamuth, and Peter Golde. *The C# Programming Language.* Boston: Addison-Wesley, 2004.

Nathan, Adam. *.NET and COM: The Complete Interoperability Guide.* Indianapolis: Sams Publishing, 2002.

Office Programming

Byrne, Randy, and Ryan Gregg. *Programming Applications for Microsoft Outlook 2007.* Redmond, WA: Microsoft Press, 2007.

Mosher, Sue. *Microsoft Outlook Programming.* Burlington, MA: Digital Press, 2003.

Whitechapel, Andrew. *Microsoft .NET Development for Microsoft Office.* Redmond, WA: Microsoft Press, 2005.

Security

Howard, Michael, and David LeBlanc. *Writing Secure Code.* 2nd ed. Redmond, WA: Microsoft Press, 2003.

LaMacchia, Brian, Sebastian Lange, Matthew Lyons, Rudi Martin, and Kevin T. Price. *.NET Framework Security.* Boston: Addison-Wesley, 2002.

Lippert, Eric. *Visual Basic .NET Code Security Handbook.* Birmingham, UK: Wrox Press, 2003.

Index

Microsoft .NET Development Series

.NET Framework Standard Library Annotated Reference
Volume 1: Base Class Library and Extended Numerics Library

Brad Abrams

978-0-321-15489-7

.NET Framework Standard Library Annotated Reference
Volume 2: Networking Library, Reflection Library and XML Library

Brad Abrams
Tamara Abrams

978-0-321-19445-9

Essential Windows Presentation Foundation

Chris Anderson

978-0-321-37447-9

A Developer's Guide to SQL Server 2005

Bob Beauchemin
Dan Sullivan

978-0-321-38218-4

Advanced ASP.NET AJAX Server Controls
For .NET Framework 3.5

Adam Calderon
Joel Rumerman

978-0-321-51444-8

Visual Studio Tools for Office
Using C# with Excel, Word, Outlook, and InfoPath

Eric Carter
Eric Lippert

978-0-321-33488-6

Visual Studio Tools for Office
Using Visual Basic 2005 with Excel, Word, Outlook, and InfoPath

Eric Carter
Eric Lippert

978-0-321-41175-4

Domain-Specific Development
with Visual Studio DSL Tools

Steve Cook
Gareth Jones
Stuart Kent
Alan Cameron Wills

978-0-321-39820-8

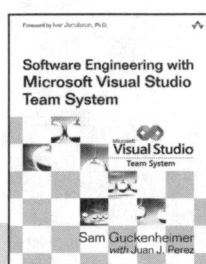

Software Engineering with Microsoft Visual Studio Team System

Sam Guckenheimer
with Juan J. Perez

978-0-321-27872-2

The C# Programming Language
Third Edition

Anders Hejlsberg
Mads Torgersen
Scott Wiltamuth
Peter Golde

978-0-321-56299-9

ASP.NET 2.0 Illustrated

Alex Homer
Dave Sussman

978-0-321-41834-0

The .NET Developer's Guide to Directory Services Programming

Joe Kaplan
Ryan Dunn

978-0-321-35017-6

Smart Client Deployment with ClickOnce
Deploying Windows Forms Applications with ClickOnce

Brian Noyes

978-0-321-19769-6

Essential ASP.NET 2.0

Fritz Onion
with Keith Brown

978-0-321-23770-5

Essential Windows Communication Foundation
For .NET Framework 3.5

Steve Resnick
Richard Crane
Chris Bowen

978-0-321-44006-8

.NET Internationalization
The Developer's Guide to Building Global Windows and Web Applications

Guy Smith-Ferrier

978-0-321-34138-9

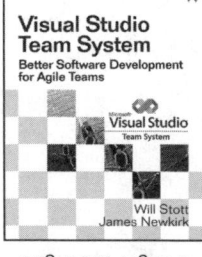

Visual Studio Team System
Better Software Development for Agile Teams

Will Stott
James Newkirk

978-0-321-41850-0

978-0-201-73411-9

978-0-321-22835-2

978-0-321-54561-9

978-0-321-43482-1

978-0-321-33421-3

978-0-321-53392-0

978-0-321-15493-4

978-0-321-24673-8

978-0-321-26892-1

978-0-321-41059-7

978-0-321-30363-9

978-0-321-26796-2

978-0-321-39983-0

978-0-321-16951-8

978-0-321-17403-1

978-0-321-17404-8

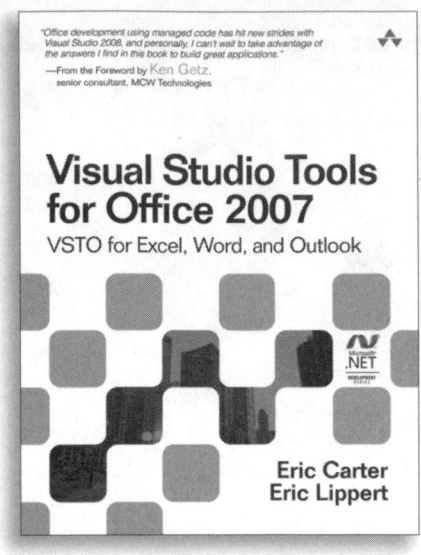

FREE Online Edition

Your purchase of **Visual Studio Tools for Office 2007** includes access to a free online edition for 45 days through the Safari Books Online subscription service. Nearly every Addison-Wesley Professional book is available online through Safari Books Online, along with more than 5,000 other technical books and videos from publishers such as, Cisco Press, Exam Cram, IBM Press, O'Reilly, Prentice Hall, Que, and Sams.

SAFARI BOOKS ONLINE allows you to search for a specific answer, cut and paste code, download chapters, and stay current with emerging technologies.

Activate your FREE Online Edition at www.informit.com/safarifree

> **STEP 1:** Enter the coupon code: UBHJIXA.

> **STEP 2:** New Safari users, complete the brief registration form.
> Safari subscribers, just log in.